Canadian **HUMAN RESOURCE** Management

A STRATEGIC APPROACH

Ninth Edition

Hermann Schwind

Professor Emeritus

Saint Mary's University

Hari Das

Saint Mary's University

Terry Wagar

Saint Mary's University

McGraw-Hill Ryerson

Connect. Learn. Succeed.

Canadian Human Resource Management: A Strategic Approach
Ninth Edition

ISBN-13: 978-0-07096738-0
ISBN-10: 0-07-096738-5

1 2 3 4 5 6 7 8 9 10 WCD 1 9 8 7 6 5 4 3 2 1 0

Vice President, Editor-in-Chief: Joanna Cotton
Senior Sponsoring Editor: Kim Brewster
Marketing Manager: Cathie Lefebvre
Developmental Editor: Lori McLellan
Senior Editorial Associate: Christine Lomas
Photo/Permissions Researcher: Tracy Leonard
Supervising Editor: Graeme Powell
Copy Editor: Wendy Yano
Proofreader: Tara Tovell
Production Coordinator: Sharon Stefanowicz
Cover Design: Michelle Losier
Interior Design: Michelle Losier
Page Layout: S R NOVA Pvt Ltd, Bangalore, India
Printer: Worldcolor Dubuque (U.S.)
Cover Images: STAN HONDA/AFP/Getty Images

Library and Archives Canada Cataloguing in Publication

Schwind, Hermann Franz, 1935-
    Canadian human resource management : a strategic approach/Hermann Schwind, Hari Das, Terry Wagar.—9th Canadian ed.

Includes index.
    First and 2nd ed. published under the title: Canadian personnel management and human resources. 3rd ed.: Canadian human resources management/William B. Werther ... [et al.]. 4th ed.: Canadian human resource management/Hermann F. Schwind ... [et al.].
    ISBN 978-0-07-095176-1

    1. Personnel management—Textbooks. 2. Personnel management—Canada—Textbooks. I. Das, Hari, 1948- II. Wagar, Terry H. III. Title.

HF5549.C35 2009   658.3   C2009-905403-5

About the Authors

DR. HERMANN F. SCHWIND

Dr. Schwind is Professor Emeritus (Human Resource Management) at Saint Mary's University in Halifax. He received his Ph.D. from the University of British Columbia, BBA and MBA degrees from the University of Washington, and mechanical and industrial engineering degrees from German institutions. He has 15 years of industrial experience and has taught as Visiting Professor at the University of Ottawa, in Japan at Sophia University in Tokyo, and at the Institute for International Studies and Training in Fujinomiya, a Japanese management training centre.

Dr. Schwind was a founding member and Vice-President of the British Columbia Society for Training and Development, President of the Halifax and District Personnel Association (1984/86; now the Human Resource Association of Nova Scotia), and President of the Administrative Science Association of Canada (1989). In addition to co-authoring the present text on Canadian human resource management, Dr. Schwind has published and presented over 80 articles and papers and contributed chapters to 7 books. He also worked as a human resource consultant for 25 years.

DR. HARI DAS

Hari Das, B.Com, PGDM (IIMC), M.Sc, AICWA, Ph.D, received his doctorate from the University of British Columbia. He teaches graduate and doctoral level courses in business with particular focus on human resource management, performance management, research methodology, and international management. He has served as the Director of the MBA Program and Chair of the Department of Management and has received a teaching excellence award and a nomination for best professor. He has written five books and over 100 articles and papers in areas such as organizational control, performance management, disaster management, cross-cultural management, ethics, power and influence, and organizational training. His latest book is *Recruitment, Selection and Deployment of Human Resources: A Canadian Perspective* (Toronto: Pearson Education, 2007) an advanced-level university text on the topic of attracting and managing human capital has already been adopted in several reputed graduate and undergraduate programs in this country. He is the author of *Organizational Theory with Canadian Applications* (Toronto: Gage Publications, 1990), the first Canadian work on designing and changing organizations. His co-authored work, *Canadian Human Resource Management: A Strategic Approach* (Toronto: McGraw-Hill Ryerson, 2007) is now in its 9th edition and is the market leader in its field, having sold over 170,000 copies until last year. His work, *Strategic Organization Design: For Canadian Firms in a Global Economy* (Toronto: Prentice-Hall, 1998) examines the challenge of preparing Canadian firms to face global economy, while *Performance Management* (Toronto: Pearson Education, 2003) focuses on the importance of strategy-performance management system linkage to achieve excellence.

Dr. Das has served as a consultant to a number of organizations in Canada and abroad and has led workshops on a variety of topics such as MBO, human resource audit, international management and business ethics. He was a member of the team that identified certification (and ethical) standards for HR Professionals in Nova Scotia. In addition to being a member of the Academy of Management and the Administrative Sciences Association of Canada, Dr. Das, who is listed in *Canadian Who's Who in Business*, has served as an academic reviewer for journals and granting agencies including SSHRC and Shastri Indo-Canadian Institute and as an external examiner for a number of doctoral programs. Currently, he is working on a couple of research projects related to business ethics. He can be reached at tpharidas@yahoo.ca.

DR. TERRY H. WAGAR

Terry H. Wagar is a Professor of Human Resource Management/Industrial Relations at Saint Mary's University in Halifax. He was a Research Associate at the National Institute of Labour Studies, Flinders University of South Australia and has also taught at the University of South Australia, Wilfrid Laurier University, and the University of Western Australia. Dr. Wagar's degrees include an MBA from the University of Toronto, a Master of Industrial Relations from Queen's University, an

LLB from the University of Ottawa Law School, and a Ph.D. in labour relations, human resource management and statistics/research methods from Virginia Tech.

During the 2002–2003 academic year, he was a Visiting Professor at the Gatton College of Business and Economics, University of Kentucky. In 2002 and 2004, he was a Visiting Scholar at the University of Waikato Management School in Hamilton, New Zealand. During the 2008–09 school year, Dr. Wagar was on sabbatical—he spent Fall 2008 as a Visiting Professor at Queen's University, and from January to July 2009, he was a Visiting Professor/Research Fellow at the University of Western Australia.

In 2006, Dr. Wagar received the International Personnel Management Association (Canada) President's Award. The President's Award is IPMA-Canada's highest award and is presented to an individual who has made an outstanding contribution to the practice of human resource management in Canada. Other awards include the Excellence in Education Award from the U.S. Labor and Employment Relations Association (LERA), the Distinguished Teacher Award from the Association of Atlantic Universities (Award for Excellence in Teaching), and the Leaders in Management Education Award (sponsored by National Post, PricewaterhouseCoopers, and Bell Nexxia). His research has been published in Canada, the United States, Europe, Asia, Australia and New Zealand.

Letter to Students

Dear Student,

This book was written with you, our customer, in mind. We have tried to make it readable and, wherever possible, we have included practical "how-to-do" steps.

Each chapter includes many common elements, such as learning objectives, terms for review, and case studies. We hope the following guide will help you make maximum use of the textbook so that you will be successful with your studies in human resource management.

At the beginning of each chapter, we offer a quote from an expert on the subject matter to give you an insight into the concepts or issues discussed. Following the opening quote, you will find the chapter objectives. These will give you an overview of the chapter content.

Within each chapter, you will find a "Spotlight on HRM" box. These timely articles from journals and magazines in the field illustrate a manager's or consultant's point of view on HRM or offer a sharing of practical HRM experiences relevant to the chapter.

Each chapter also contains an "Ethics Box", where an ethics issue relevant to the chapter content is raised. It is ideally suited for class discussion.

Photos of real job situations offer insights into work environments the book is discussing. Cartoons add some humor to the otherwise quite serious content.

We highlight important terms and concepts with boldface and italic type in the text. All terms appearing in boldface are also defined in the margin and referenced in the Terms for Review section at the end of each chapter and in the Subject Index, highlighted in a secondary colour. Wherever appropriate, we also provide World Wide Web addresses, where you will find additional information to research the topic under discussion. In addition, students interested in earning the Certified Human Resource Professional (CHRP) designation find topics relevant for exams marked with an RPC (Required Professional Capability) symbol and the specific number of the seven Body of Knowledge domains (see inside cover).

An end-of-chapter summary offers you an abbreviated version of the chapter content for review. A self-test allows you to check whether you are able to apply the concepts discussed. The Terms for Review, where all important terms (and buzzwords) are listed, is an excellent tool for conducting another self-test. Similarly, the Review and Discussion Questions will help you test your understanding of the most critical topics in the chapter.

For a higher level of self-testing, the Critical Thinking Questions help you to discover whether you are able to see the broader relationships and interactions of the concepts discussed.

The Web Research assignments offer you the opportunity to make use of a computer and the Internet to search for additional information. As a self-test, it assesses your ability to conduct on-line research.

The Incident is a short case that usually does not require extensive analytical work, unlike the more comprehensive case studies later in the chapter, which test your thorough understanding of concepts and their impact on an organization.

Exercises are usually conducted under the supervision of your instructor; however, they can also be used as part of a group exercise, away from the classroom.

The References provide you with the sources for the information given in the chapter. They can also be used as a starting point for more detailed research.

If you have any feedback regarding the readability of the textbook or suggestions on how we could improve the next edition, please contact us via the e-mail addresses given below.

Good luck with your studies!

hermann.schwind@smu.ca
hari.das@smu.ca
terry.wagar@smu.ca

Brief Table of Contents

Table of Contents

PART THREE   Attracting Human Resources   143

Chapter 5

Recruitment 173

Chapter 6

Selection 211

PART SIX   Maintaining High Performance   389

Chapter 11

Managing Employee Relations   390

Chapter 12

Diversity Management   424

PART SEVEN   Strategy Evaluation   529

Chapter 15

Human Resource Auditing   530

Preface

We believe that human resource departments will play a critical role in determining the success of Canadian organizations in the twenty-first century.

—The Authors

Teachers and students ultimately determine the value of any university textbook. *Canadian Human Resource Management: A Strategic Approach* is no exception. Its eighth edition passed the test of the marketplace by earning adoptions and re-adoptions in more than sixty colleges and universities in Canada and becoming the best-selling human resource management text in this country. The book's thrust on presenting key concepts, issues, and practices of this exciting field without being encyclopedic, its practical focus, and its emphasis on readability have endeared it to hundreds of instructors and thousands of students in Canada. Equally gratifying, a large number of students retained this book for their professional libraries after course completion, suggesting that they found real value in the book.

BALANCED COVERAGE

We attribute the book's popularity to its balanced coverage of both theory and practice, and of traditional materials and emerging concerns. Regardless of their orientation, readers will sense our belief that people are the ultimate resource for any employer. How well an organization obtains, maintains, and retains its human resources determines its success or failure. And the success or failure of our organizations shapes the well-being of every individual on this planet. If the events of the last decade are any indication, the human race is entering a totally new phase in its evolution. The breakup of protectionist trade barriers and ideological walls that separate countries of the world may mean that the manager of the 21st century has to operate in a more complex and dynamic global setting that is also much more interdependent. Training in human resource management (HRM) will become even more critical in this new setting.

The ninth edition of *Canadian Human Resource Management* builds on the strengths of the eighth edition. The book is divided into seven parts.

- **Part 1: The Strategic Human Resource Management Model** introduces the strategic model that will be used as a guide through all chapters.
- **Part 2: Planning Human Resources** describes the two pre-hiring processes, analyzing the jobs in question and planning for future staff needs. New job options have to be integrated into the organization as part of the planning process.
- **Part 3: Attracting Human Resources** covers the legal aspects of any hiring decision and discusses recruitment and selection processes.
- **Part 4: Placing, Development, and Evaluation of Human Resources** discusses the importance of preparing employees for new challenges through training and development and providing timely performance feedback.
- **Part 5: Motivating and Rewarding Human Resources** reviews the many ways a human resource department can contribute to a more effective organization through a fair and equitable compensation system and proficient benefits administration. Creating a motivating environment is another responsibility of the HR manager.
- **Part 6: Maintenance of High Performance Levels** brings up the issues related to managing a diverse work force, something Canadian managers have to become familiar with. Workplace safety is of concern to every manager and this concern has to be conveyed to all employees through an effective communication system. Good interpersonal relations require appropriate and fair discipline procedures. This part also discusses in detail the union-management framework, union organizing, collective bargaining, and collective agreement administration.
- **Part 7: Strategy Evaluation**, the final part, reveals how human resource departments should evaluate their own effectiveness.

UPDATED IN THE NINTH EDITION

The chapters in the new edition have been streamlined and organized for easier reading and retention of material by students. The focus of the text continues to be the strategic contribution of HR function in organizations, but an explicit recognition of the relationship between HR strategies, tactics and systems has been incorporated into the model and throughout the text material. Within this format, both present and emerging concerns of a significant nature are highlighted. Key terms are bolded and an extensive glossary of HR terms is included at the end of the text. This edition has a very thorough coverage of Canadian human rights legislation and an in-depth discussion of the Canadian Charter of Rights and Freedoms. A number of recent trends and potentially promising HRM strategies have been incorporated into appropriate chapters of the new edition. HRM has recently played a more important role in the overall strategy of companies. This trend is strongly reflected in the new edition. All chapters now include a discussion of how the topic dealt with in the chapter should be mirrored in the HRM strategy and how this strategy fits into the overall strategy of the organization. This edition also discusses the national Certified Human Resource Professional (CHRP) designation requirements and the competencies identified by the task force on this matter. All HR associations are referenced and all relevant Web links are included.

All chapters have been updated. Information on legislative changes, especially in the area of employment equity (women, sexual orientation, the disabled, and First Nations People), statistics, and demographics, is the latest available. Diversity management, discussed in Chapter Twelve, has become an important topic. Canada's immigration policy now brings into the country mostly immigrants from Asia, people with very different cultural values and behaviours, and Canadian managers must learn to cope with these new challenges. Similarly, growing international trade dictates that Canadians may be required to go abroad to manage subsidiaries or to work in joint ventures. A thorough pre-departure training is a must. New work options provide organizations not only with opportunities to be more effective but also offer employees more flexible work opportunities, better suited to their needs. The text provides over one hundred examples and anecdotes of Canadian and global firms- private and public, local and national and large and small.

Some reviewers suggested that more emphasis be placed on the "how to" discussions. This suggestion has been followed in almost all chapters and, whenever possible, a step-by-step approach has been used. It should be mentioned that human resource auditing is still a concept that is practiced only by progressive organizations (Chapter Fifteen).

KEY FEATURES

In addition to new features, important key features from previous editions have been retained.

Running Cases: This is the only Canadian HR text to have two cases anchored to material in every single chapter. Maple Leaf Shoes Ltd. symbolizes traditional HR practices—mostly responding to problems in a reactive fashion. In contrast, Canadian Pacific and International Bank symbolizes the progressive, proactive, and strategic role of HR in today's organizations. By comparing the practices of the two firms, the student should be able to learn how HR can make a significant contribution to organizational success and growth.

> **CASE STUDY**   CPIB   Canadian Pacific and International Bank
>
> *Redefining Jobs for the Future**
>
> Canadian Pacific and International Bank (CPIB) is a premier Canadian financial institution with assets of over $150 billion and operations across Canada and internationally. Today, its 25,000-plus employees provide personal, commercial, corporate, and investment banking services to individuals and businesses in 33 countries. More details of the bank are given at the end of Chapter 1.
>
> CPIB, through its strategic initiatives, was successful in building long-term value for its shareholders while providing regular returns on their investments. A vital component of its recent strategy is growth through acquisition of smaller banks and other financial institutions in this country and internationally. The passage of the bill relating to bank mergers in June 2000 in Parliament accelerated this process for CPIB.
>
> Last month, the bank acquired Central Canadian Trust Company (CCTC), a trust company located in Ontario employing over 3,000 employees. While the trust company was a very successful player in the financial industry in Ontario and Quebec, CPIB management felt that the human resource practices in the firm were inferior to those of the bank.
>
> Initially, the identity of CCTC will be maintained; however, over the next year or so, all branches will be converted into CPIB branches. This means that, with immediate effect, CCTC staff must be trained to offer the highest quality of customer service that CPIB customers have come to expect. Compared to CPIB, CCTC is also far behind in electronic and telephone banking. CPIB expects all its managers to be able to offer extensive counselling (including in areas such as portfolio management, margin trading, and the establishment of
>
> **Case written by Professor Hari Das of the Department of Management, Saint Mary's University. All rights reserved by the author. © 2002.*

SPOTLIGHT ON HRM
The Many Uses of a Job Description

Excerpt from an article by Mary Massa, June 2005

It's not just for screening candidates anymore. Today, business owners are finding numerous ways to put an employee's job description to work for them.

Who knew that a good job description could be such a versatile management tool? Though it still remains a hiring tool in the most traditional sense—a written description identifying a job by title, essential functions and requirements—a well-crafted description also spells out the knowledge, abilities and skills required to perform a job successfully. These additional descriptions are extremely helpful when it comes to employee training and career development.

employee performance "above and beyond" the job description in order to receive recognition and rewards.

- Discipline. Use the job description to illustrate that an employee isn't adequately performing job functions.

- Return-to-work programs. A job description is also useful to prepare for light or modified duty options to allow for a smoother transition from a workers' compensation injury or leave.

- Essential job function analysis. Written job descriptions have become increasingly important for employ-

Spotlights: Each chapter provides a "Spotlight on HRM" focusing on an emerging practice, issue or HR opportunity. Some Spotlights from previous editions have been retained at the request of reviewers; the new ones reflect current trends and practices.

Ethics Box: A significant feature is the "Spotlight on Ethics" box, in which an ethics issue relevant to the chapter content is discussed.

Web Research: To assist students to make optimal use of the Internet for more information on HR topics, extensive listings of HR related websites are provided in the margins throughout the text. To facilitate class discussion, a web research question has been added at the end of every chapter.

In-Margin Glossary: Important terms and concepts are highlighted with boldface and italic type in the text. Allowing students to find critical definitions at a glance, all terms appearing in boldface are also defined in the margin and referenced in the Terms for Review section at the end of each chapter and in the Subject Index, highlighted in a secondary colour. If you prefer to reference a full list of glossary terms, please go to our online learning centre at www.mcgrawhill-connect.ca to download the complete glossary.

stages of an interview
Key phases in an employment interview: interviewer preparation, creation of rapport, information exchange, termination, and evaluation.

Market Yourself Video
Résumé hosting company
www.marketyourselfsmarter.com

The Interview Process

The five stages of a typical employment interview are listed in Figure 6-19. These **stages of an interview** are interviewer preparation, creation of rapport, information exchange, termination, and evaluation. Regardless of the type of interview used, each of these steps must occur for a successful interview to result. They are discussed briefly to illustrate how the actual interview process develops.

Stage 1: Interviewer Preparation

Obviously, before the interview begins, the interviewer needs to prepare. This preparation requires that specific questions be developed by the interviewer. It is the answers to these questions that the interviewer will use in deciding the applicant's suitability. At the same time, the interviewer must consider what questions the applicant is likely to ask. Since the interview is used to persuade top applicants to accept subsequent job offers, the interviewer needs to be able to explain job duties, performance standards, pay, benefits, and other areas of interest. A list of typical questions asked by recruiters and other interviewers appears in Figure 6-20. Note that several of these questions, while popular, are of questionable predictive power in assessing the future work performance of the applicant. Further, under the law, questions relating to gender, family status, race, etc., are prohibited. As can be seen from the list, these questions are intended to give the interviewer some insight into the applicant's interests, attitudes, and background. The same figure provides modified versions of the same questions that provide greater insights into an applicant's strengths and attitudes. Specific or technical questions are added to the list according to the type of job opening. Note that in all instances, the questions should not be discriminatory.

Another action the interviewer should undertake before the interview is to review the application form. Research shows that the quality of the interviewer's decision is significantly better when the application form is present.[91] With or without the application form, interviewers seem to take about the same length of time to reach a conclusion—from 4 to 10 minutes.[92] The longer the interview is scheduled to last and the better the quality of the applicants, the longer it takes the interviewers to reach a decision.

With the average cost of hiring new employees often exceeding $5,000 for managerial and professional employees, the interviewer's preparation should be aimed at making the interview process efficient and comfortable for the applicant. Often the interviewer is one of the first representatives of the company with whom the applicant has an opportunity to talk. A strong and lasting impression of the company is likely to be formed at this stage. If the interviewer does not show courtesy to the applicant, that impression is certain to be negative. If the applicant is a promising candidate for the job, he or she likely has other job prospects.

Given the importance of interviewer preparation and skills in determining the overall effectiveness of the interview (as a selection tool), several organizations have begun to train their managers in interview techniques. Large companies often train their interviewers in matters such as human rights legislation and techniques to get more information from job candidates.[94] However, such training

---

⊙ SELF-ASSESSMENT EXERCISE

Understanding Benefits

Benefits tend to be neglected when it comes to considerations of labour costs, but with the average benefit package in Canada now being close to 35 percent of payroll, HR managers are well advised to pay special attention to the management of benefits. Test yourself on your expertise.

1. If the current trend continues, soon benefits will make up over one-half of most firms' payroll. T F
2. Vacations, along with holidays and rest breaks to reduce fatigue and enhance productivity, are part of employees' objectives. T F

5. Vesting gives workers the right to pension benefits even if they leave the company. T F
6. Meal breaks, rest breaks, wash-up time, sick leave, holidays, and vacations make up the costliest major category of benefits. T F
7. Cafeteria benefits allow employees free meals. T F
8. Benefits play a major role in retaining employees. T F
9. Benefits cannot be taxed. T F

Self-Assessment Exercises: A self assessment is offered to the student at the end of each chapter.

At the end of each part, a role-play team exercise gives students the opportunity to test their communication skills by enacting situations common in the HRM field.

⊙ ROLE-PLAY 5: Flexible Benefits

Time required: 40–50 minutes

Objectives of the Role-Play

1. To help the students understand the pros and cons of flexible benefits.
2. To enhance their skills to listen and respond to employee concerns.
3. To help them prepare for their role as human resource managers.

Prior Preparation

1. Study Chapter 10 of the text.
2. Read descriptions of Maple Leaf Shoes Ltd. at the end of Chapters 1 and 2.

Guidelines for Conducting the Role-Play

In this role-play, an employee, Megan Litkoff, is meeting with Jane Reynolds to inquire into the possibility of a flexible work hours and benefit plan.

1. Two students, one for the role of Jane Reynolds and the other for Megan Litkoff, should be identified.

FIGURE 6-7 — Testing Methods Used in Canadian Firms

27%
43%
30%

- Aptitude tests
- Personality tests
- Other tests

Learning and Pedagogical Devices: Also retained from previous editions are the following features:

Figures: Charts and diagrams are included to illustrate relevant ideas and concepts.

Terms for Review: All important terms and buzzwords are included. It is an excellent tool for self-testing.

Chapter Objectives: This useful tool enables students to gauge their progress and understanding while working through each chapter.

Source: Chart adapted and prepared by the authors on the basis of data on 133 Canadian firms reported by Sean Way and James Thacker in "Selection Practices: Where Are Canadian Organizations?" *HR Professional*, Vol. 16, No. 5, October/November, 1999, p. 34.

End-of-Chapter summaries: The authors provide an abbreviated version of the main ideas, theories, and strategies of each chapter.

Review and Discussion Questions: Review and Discussion Questions test students' understanding of the chapter material and suggest topics for class or group discussions.

Critical Thinking Questions: These questions challenge students to expand on what they have just learned, discussing broader relationships and interactions of the concepts in the chapter.

○ SUMMARY

Human resource planning requires considerable time, staff, and financial resources. The return on this investment may not justify the expenditure for small firms. Increasingly, however, large organizations use human resource planning as a means of achieving greater effectiveness. Human resource planning is an attempt by companies to estimate their future needs and supplies of human resources. Through an understanding of the factors that influence the demand for workers, planners can forecast specific short-term and long-term needs.

Given some anticipated level of demand, planners try to estimate the availability of present workers to meet that demand. Such estimates begin with an audit of present employees. Possible replacements are then identified. Internal shortages are resolved by seeking new employees in the external labour markets. Surpluses are reduced by normal attrition, leaves of absence, layoffs, or terminations.

Both external and internal staffing strategies can be used to meet human resource needs. More recently, a variety of alternate work arrangements have also been emerging to better meet the needs of the workforce and the employers. Finally, the usefulness of a human resource information system and human resource accounting was also outlined in this chapter.

Chapters 5 and 6 elaborate on the external staffing strategy, more specifically those relating to employee recruitment and selection. Material in later chapters will examine various issues involved in the management of human resources, with a focus on internal strategies. But before that, it is important to study the impact of governmental policies on a firm's human resource policies and practices. This will be attempted in the next chapter.

○ TERMS FOR REVIEW

attrition **p. 110**	human resource information	replacement charts **p. 104**
Canadian Occupational Projection	system **p. 124**	replacement summaries **p. 104**
System (COPS) **p. 109**	indexation **p. 98**	shorter workweek **p. 120**

○ ETHICS QUESTION

You are a plant manager, and one of your supervisors is a good friend of yours, the friendship going back to your high school years. His normally average performance has been deteriorating over the last two years, mainly because of his sick wife, a situation that causes him to miss many working days. He also has five children. You know that money is a big issue for him, and if you give him above-average performance ratings he would receive significant bonuses.

Discuss the ethical issues involved.

○ WEB RESEARCH EXERCISE

Help Tips for Performance Appraisal

http://iso9k1.home.att.net/pa/performance_appraisal.html#how
Dexter Hansen describes how traditional performance appraisals can hurt quality and teamwork. What suggestions do you have to avoid this outcome?

360-Degree Performance Appraisal

www.mansis.com/page1237.htm
http://performance-appraisals.org/appraisal-library/360_Degree_Feedback
What are the strengths and weaknesses of a 360-degree performance appraisal? Would you be comfortable using it if you were a manager? Why or why not?

○ INCIDENT 8–1

The Malfunctioning Regional Human Resource Department

For one month, the corporate human resource department of Universal Insurance Ltd. had two specialists review the operations of their regional human resource department in Vancouver. The review of the regional office centred on the department's human resource information base. A brief summary of their findings listed the following observations:

- Each employee's performance appraisal showed little change from the previous year. Poor performers rated poor year in and year out.
- Nearly 70 percent of the appraisals were not initialled by the employee even though company policy required employees to do so after they had discussed their review with the rater.
- Of those employees who initialled the evaluations, several commented that the work standards were irrelevant and unfair.
- A survey of past employees conducted by corporate office specialists revealed that 35 percent of them believed performance feedback was too infrequent.

- Another 30 percent complained about the lack of advancement opportunities because most openings were filled from outside, and no one ever told these workers they were unpromotable.

The corporate and regional human resource directors were dismayed by the findings. Each thought the problems facing the regional office were different.

1. What do you think is the major problem with the performance appraisal process in the regional office?
2. What problems do you think exist with the regional office's (a) job analysis information, (b) human resource planning, (c) training and development, and (d) career planning?

○ EXERCISE 8–1

Developing a Performance Appraisal System

Time: 1 hour. Form groups of five to six. Assume that your group is the Faculty Evaluation Committee assigned the task to assess the performance of the course instructor.

1. Define at least three performance criteria for the instructor.
2. How would you measure them so that the results would be useful for a tenure and promotion decision?

3. Which type of instrument or method do you suggest? Why?
4. Who should be the appraisers?
5. Time permitting, compare the results in your group with those of another group.

Ethics Questions: These questions provide thought-provoking scenarios to the student and ask them what decisions they would make.

Incident: The short case tests students' understanding of concepts and their impact on the organization.

Exercises: These offer students the opportunity to apply strategies to specific situations and arrive at their own conclusions or discuss with the instructor and fellow students.

Suggested Readings: The authors offer research articles and books on related topics for students or instructors who wish to pursue chapter topics further.

Subject Index: All chapter topics are indexed by subject. Glossary terms and page references are included in a secondary colour.

Reference Notes: Specific cases and other source references are gathered at the end of the text for more detailed research purposes.

The most comprehensive glossary in the HR field– over 600 items– completes the book, allowing students to find definitions of most HR terms and concepts.

Full Colour: This edition uses a four-colour print, which is designed to make the text visually attractive and stimulating to read. Over 70 colour photographs have been added to illustrate concepts and to make the text more student-friendly.

STUDENT SUPPLEMENTS

Connect™ (www.mcgrawhillconnect.ca): Developed in partnership with Youthography, a Canadian youth research company, and hundreds of students from across Canada, McGraw-Hill Connect™, embraces diverse study behaviours and preferences to maximize active learning and engagement.

With McGraw-Hill Connect™, students complete pre- and post-diagnostic assessments that identify knowledge gaps and point them to concepts they need to learn. McGraw-Hill Connect™ provides students the option to work through recommended learning exercises and create their own personalized study plan using multiple sources of content, including a searchable e-book, multiple-choice and true/false quizzes, chapter-by-chapter learning objectives, interactivities, personal notes, videos, and more. Using the copy, paste, highlight, and sticky note features, students collect, organize, and customize their study plan content to optimize learning outcomes.

McGraw-Hill Connect™—helping instructors and students Connect, Learn, Succeed! Authored by Linda Eligh, University of Western Ontario

Canadian Human Resource Management: A Strategic Approach, Ninth Edition offers a complete, integrated supplements package for instructors to address all of your needs.

INSTRUCTOR SUPPLEMENTS

Connect™ (www.mcgrawhillconnect.ca): McGraw-Hill Connect™ assessment activities don't stop with students! There is material for instructors to leverage as well, including a personalized teaching plan where instructors can choose from a variety of quizzes to use in class, assign as homework, or add to exams. They can edit existing questions and add new ones; track individual student performance—by question, assignment, or in relation to the class overall—with detailed grade reports; integrate grade reports easily with Learning Management Systems such as WebCT and Blackboard; and much more. Instructors can also browse and search teaching resources and text-specific supplements and organize them into customizable categories. All your teaching resources are now located in one convenient place.

McGraw-Hill Connect™—helping instructors and students Connect, Learn, Succeed!

Connect also offers instructors downloadable supplements, including an Instructor's Manual, Microsoft® PowerPoint® slides, streaming video cases, as well as access to the Integrator and PageOut, the McGraw-Hill Ryerson Web site development centre. Also included on Connect is a sample of the Group-Video Resource Manual. This online matrix and accompanying manual is available to adopters and contains everything an instructor needs to successfully integrate McGraw-Hill technology and additional group activities into the classroom.

Instructor's Manual: Prepared by the text authors, this contains a short topic outline of the chapter and a listing of learning objectives and key terms, a resource checklist with supplements that correspond to each chapter, a detailed lecture outline including marginal notes recommending where to use supplementary cases, lecture enhancers, and critical thinking exercises.

Computerized Test Bank: Prepared by Michele Way, Conestoga College, the computerized version allows instructors to add and edit questions, save and reload multiple test versions, select questions based on type, difficulty, or key word and use password protection. True/False questions test three levels of learning: (1) knowledge of key terms, (2) understanding of concepts and principles, and (3) application of principles.

Microsoft® PowerPoint® Presentations: Prepared by Sandra Steen, University of Regina, the slideshows for each chapter are based around the learning objectives and include many of the figures and tables from the textbook, as well as some additional slides that support and expand the text discussions. Slides can be modified by instructors with PowerPoint®.

Videos for all Chapters: Complementary videos from CBC programs and customized business segments from the McGraw-Hill Management Library are available on DVD and also can be accessed on the password-protected area of Connect.

Manager's Hot Seat Videos: In today's workplace, managers are confronted daily with issues such as ethics, diversity, working in teams, and the virtual workplace. The Manager's Hot Seat is an online resource that allows students to watch as 15 real managers apply their years of experience to confront these issues. These videos are available as a complementary instructor supplement or for bundling with student textbooks.

The Integrator: Keyed to the chapters and learning objectives of *Canadian Human Resource Management: A Strategic Approach*, Ninth Edition, the Integrator is prepared by John Hardisty, Sheridan Institute of Technology and Advanced Learning. This tool ties together all of the elements in your resource package, guiding you to where you will find corresponding coverage in each of the related support package components—be it the Instructor's Manual, Computerized Test Bank, PowerPoint® slides, or videos. Link to the Integrator via Connect at www.mcgrawhillconnect.ca.

Create Online: McGraw-Hill's Create Online gives you access to the most abundant resource at your fingertips—literally. With a few mouse clicks, you can create customized learning tools simply and affordably. McGraw-Hill Ryerson has included many of our market-leading textbooks within Create Online for e-book and print customization as well as many licensed readings and cases.

MANAGEMENT ASSET GALLERY

McGraw-Hill Ryerson, in conjunction with McGraw-Hill/Irwin Management, is excited to now provide a one-stop-shop for our wealth of assets making it super quick and easy for instructors to locate specific materials to enhance their course. The Asset Gallery includes our non text-specific management resources (Self-Assessments, Test Your Knowledge exercises, Videos and information, additional group & individual exercises) along with supporting PowerPoint® and Instructor materials.

WEBCT AND BLACKBOARD

In addition, content cartridges are available for these course management systems. These platforms provide instructors with user-friendly, flexible teaching tools. Please contact your local McGraw-Hill Ryerson *i*Learning Sales Specialist for details.

eINSTRUCTION'S CLASSROOM PERFORMANCE SYSTEM (CPS)

CPS is a student response system using wireless connectivity. It gives instructors and students immediate feedback from the entire class. The response pads are remotes that are easy to use and engage students.

- **CPS** helps you increase **student preparation, interactivity, and active learning** so you can receive immediate feedback and know what students understand.
- **CPS** allows you to administer quizzes and tests, and provide immediate grading.
- With **CPS** you can create lecture questions that can be multiple-choice, true/false, and subjective. You can even create questions on the fly as well as conduct group activities.
- Not only does **CPS** allow you to **evaluate classroom attendance, activity, and grading** for your course as a whole, but CPSOnline allows you to provide students with an immediate study guide. All results and scores can easily be imported into Excel and can be used with various classroom management systems.

CPS-ready content is available for use with *Canadian Human Resource Management: A Strategic Approach*, Ninth Edition. Please contact your *i*Learning Sales Specialist for more information on how you can integrate CPS into your classroom.

SUPERIOR SERVICE

Service takes on a whole new meaning with McGraw-Hill Ryerson and *Canadian Human Resource Management: A Strategic Approach*. Rather than just bringing you the textbook, we have consistently raised the bar in terms of innovation and educational research—both in the study of business and in education in general. These investments in learning and the educational community have helped us understand the needs of students and educators across the country and allow us to foster the growth of truly innovative, integrated learning.

iLearning Sales Specialist: Your Integrated Learning Sales Specialist is a McGraw-Hill Ryerson representative who has the experience, product knowledge, training, and support to help you assess and integrate any of the above-noted products, technology, and services into your course for optimum teaching and learning performance. Whether it's how to use our test bank software, helping your students improve their grades, or how to put your entire course online, your *i*Learning Sales Specialist is there to help. Contact your local *i*Learning Sales Specialist today to learn how to maximize all McGraw-Hill Ryerson resources!

iLearning Services Program: McGraw-Hill Ryerson offers a unique *i*Services package designed for Canadian faculty. Our mission is to equip providers of higher education with superior tools and resources required for excellence in teaching. For additional information, visit www.mcgrawhill.ca/highereducation/iservices/.

Acknowledgements

The writing of a textbook requires the cooperation and support of many people. *Canadian Human Resource Management* is no exception. We are deeply indebted to the following persons for their time, expertise, and guidance in reviewing and commenting on the ninth edition:

Cathy Fitzgerald, Okanagan College
Doug Fletcher, Kwantlen University College
Jennifer Percival, University of Ontario Institute of Technology
Stan Arnold, Humber College
Maureen Nummelin, Conestoga College
Sarah Holding, Vancouver Island University
Gordon Barnard, Durham College
Lisa Guglielmi, Seneca College of Applied Arts and Technology
John Hardisty, Sheridan College Institute of Technology and Advanced Learning
Steve McKenna, York University
Morris Mendelson, University of New Brunswick
Sean MacDonald, University of Manitoba
Colleen Marshall, Confederation College
Julie Bulmash, George Brown College
Nita Chhinzer, University of Guelph
Chantal Westgate, McGill University
Jerome Collins, St. Clair College
Aaron Schat, McMaster University
Laura Jean Taplin, Humber College
Jacqueline Power, University of Windsor
Linda Eligh, University of Western Ontario

We are also thankful to the many students, instructors, researchers, and practitioners who have used and commented on our last edition. Ultimately, it is the users of this book who can tell us about what we did right in the past and what we should do in the future. We hope the readers will find this ninth edition even more useful in teaching and learning about human resource management.

A very special thank you goes to the editorial staff of McGraw-Hill Ryerson, Kim Brewster, Senior Sponsoring Editor; Lori McLellan, Developmental Editor; Graeme Powell, Supervising Editor; Sharon Stefanowicz, Production Coordinator; Wendy Yano, Copy Editor; Tara Tovell, Proofreader. With their special expertise, they have guided us toward a better product.

And finally, we would like to express our deeply felt thanks to those who assisted us in many tangible and intangible ways: Ruth, Mallika, and Leslie.

Hermann F. Schwind
Hari Das
Terry H. Wagar

PART 1

The Strategic Human Resource Management Model

A human resource department helps organizations and their employees attain their goals. But it faces many challenges along the way. This chapter explores some of these challenges and outlines a strategic human resource management model upon which the rest of this book builds.

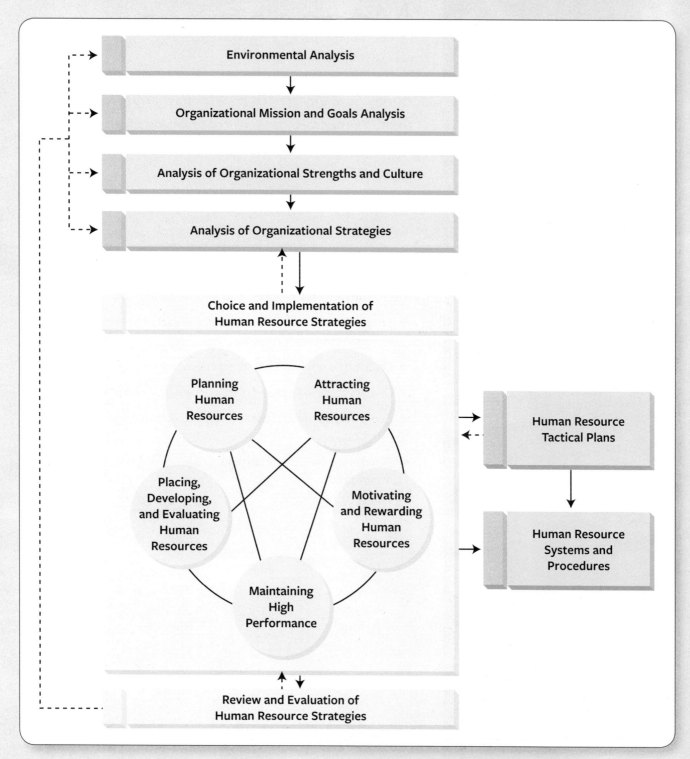

Strategic Importance of Human Resource Management

The successful 21st-century organization will not take the loyalty of talented people for granted. It will constantly try to recruit and keep them... The mutual commitment of an employer and an employee will be one of the most important factors for a 21st-century organization.

Subhir Chowdhury[1]

CHAPTER OBJECTIVES

After studying this chapter, you should be able to:

➡ *List* challenges facing Canadian organizations in the context of managing their workforce.

➡ *Discuss* the objectives of human resource management.

➡ *Discuss* steps in strategic management of human resources.

➡ *Explain* how human resource departments are organized and function.

➡ *Discuss* the role of human resource professionals in today's organization.

CHAPTER 1

Name the greatest accomplishment of the last century. Landing on the moon? Computers? Biogenic engineering? Cloning of life forms?[2] And what awaits us in the new millennium? Routine travel to distant planets? Human longevity unimaginable in the past? Working and shopping without ever stepping out of our homes? Growing our own food in our kitchen? Flying to any destination of our choice in automatically piloted flying cars? Living in undersea settlements? The possibilities are immense. Indeed, our future achievements may be limited only by our imagination. All major achievements and technological advances share a common feature: organizations.

Canada is the world's largest producer of newsprint, nickel, and asbestos, thanks to the efforts of several organizations in those industries. Canadian cities such as Vancouver, Toronto, and Montreal are rated as some of the best cities in the world on various criteria including health care, education, and crime rates. The Canadian Broadcasting Corporation, which owns and operates several radio and television stations, brings you the news, music, and entertainment. In each case, it is organizations that have marshalled the resources needed to achieve these results.

Even on a more day-to-day basis, organizations play a central role in our lives. The water we drink, the food we eat, the clothes we wear, and the vehicles we drive are products of organizations. When future historians view our era, they may see organizations as one of our greatest accomplishments. It is nothing but a marvel to have tens of thousands of people with highly individualized backgrounds, skills, and interests coordinated in various enterprises to pursue common institutionalized goals.[3]

People are the common element in all social organizations. They create the objectives, the innovations, and the accomplishments for which organizations are praised. When looked at from the perspective of the organization, people are resources. They are not inanimate resources, such as land and capital; instead, they are *human* resources. Without them, organizations would not exist. The following incident shows how important human resources can be:

TransCanada Minerals was a small company that owned several nickel and zinc leases. In exchange for several million dollars, it sold all its mineral claims. Total balance-sheet assets consisted of some office furniture, miscellaneous prospecting equipment of little value, and nearly $15 million on deposit with the Royal Bank of Canada. While the president of the company looked for investments in the brewing industry, one of the firm's few remaining geologists discovered a large deposit of zinc. Within a short period the company's stock doubled.

Although TransCanada Minerals' balance sheet did not list the human "assets," these resources were at work. Before the zinc discovery, a casual observer would have considered the $15-million deposit as the company's most important asset; afterward, the mineral claim would have been considered the major asset. However, a keen observer would note that neither the bank account nor the mineral claim could be of great value without capable people to manage them.

More and more top managers are beginning to recognize that organizational success depends upon careful attention to human resources. Some of the best-managed and most successful Canadian organizations are those that effectively make employees meet organizational challenges creatively:

In high-tech organizations, it is critical to motivate the engineers to come out with creative designs and systems; in research organizations, fostering creativity and free flow of ideas among researchers may be the key to success; in some manufacturing organizations, cost control spells success; while in retail and service industries, the difference between growth and extinction is marked by the quality of service. In all instances, it is the employees who decide a firm's future.

This means that the human resource practices are intricately intertwined with the organization's strategies to meet its various challenges. Below we look at the key challenges facing Canadian organizations in general and their implications for managing the workforce.

CHALLENGES FACING CANADIAN ORGANIZATIONS

Canadian organizations face a number of challenges today. Some of the more important ones are listed in Figure 1-1. These challenges may be economic (e.g., recession), technological (e.g., computerization), political (e.g., new government policies), social (e.g., concern for our environment), demographic (e.g., changing composition of our workforce), legal (e.g., changes in minimum wage

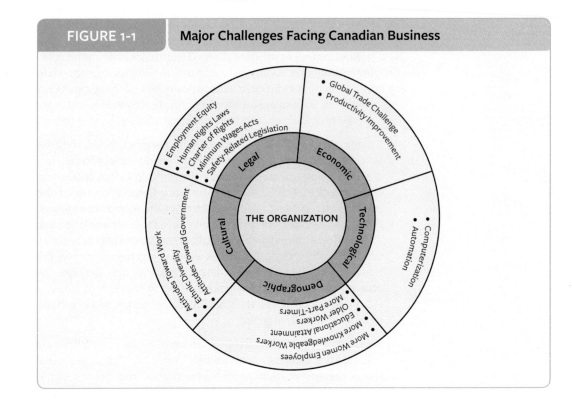

FIGURE 1-1   **Major Challenges Facing Canadian Business**

laws), cultural (e.g., ethnic diversity), or otherwise in nature. For discussion purposes, the major challenges facing a Canadian organization (especially those affecting human resource management) can be grouped under five heads: *economic, technological, demographic, cultural, and legal.* The first four challenges will be discussed in this chapter. The critical importance of legal compliance for the human resource function warrants a more elaborate review of the subject matter. Hence, this topic is detailed in Chapter 4.

Economic Challenges

economic challenges
Economic factors facing Canadian business today, including global trade challenges and the challenge to increase one's own competitiveness and productivity levels.

Today, Canadian business faces three critical **economic challenges**: *surviving a recessionary cycle, facing the global trade challenge, and meeting the challenge of productivity improvement.* Although these are interrelated challenges, for the purpose of discussion, they are considered separately below.

Surviving a Recessionary Cycle

Capitalist economies go through boom and bust business cycles. The Canadian economy is no exception to this. In today's globally connected world, misfortunes originating in one economy are soon passed on to the others. As this text goes to the printer, the Canadian economy is in the grip of a major recession unlike any seen in the last 20 years or so. By the end of March 2009, the recession had eliminated 357,000 jobs in Canada. In the month of March alone, the Canadian job market lost 61,300 jobs—all full-time—and pushed the unemployment rate up to 8 percent, the highest in seven years. The job cuts hit all parts of the country, and a wide array of industries, from manufacturing and construction to finance, real estate, and insurance. The number of unemployed people has soared a whopping 32.1 percent in 2008–09 alone (resulting in a national unemployment rate of about 8 percent of total workforce). Meanwhile, Canada's non-inflation adjusted gross domestic product plummeted by 14.9 percent for the first quarter of 2009. By September 2009, however, the trend changed, offering hope that the country may have passed the worst and is now on the way to a less uncertain time.

Human resource managers face special challenges during a recessionary period. They often have to carry out the unpleasant task of planning, communicating, and implementing employee layoff. Often, wage concessions have to be sought from labour for the sheer survival of the firm (as is currently happening in General Motors and Chrysler). The workforce morale, by and large, is low during a recessionary period; supplementary employee counselling may become necessary. At times, the entire organization may assume a crisis management posture, in turn creating new challenges to the HR manager in policy formulation, communication, and implementation.

Job insecurity associated with recession causes erosion of employee trust in management. A survey of 5,114 employees indicated that nearly one-half of the respondents did not trust their employers. The workers felt that the managers do not care about them. The way managers make decisions does little to foster trust. Most of the time, layoff and financial decisions affecting the workers are done behind closed doors with little openness or transparency.[4]

Facing the Global Trade Challenge

International trade has always been critical to Canada's prosperity and growth. Canada ranks high among exporting nations: on a per capita basis, we export much more than either the United States or Japan. The combination of a relatively small population and a large natural resource base gives Canada a trade advantage internationally.

> In 2009, approximately 40 percent of Canada's gross domestic product came out of exports, up from 27 percent over a decade ago. Canada is the biggest trader in the Group of Seven industrialized nations. Approximately 79 percent of our exports go to the United States; 2.8 percent to UK, and a little over 2 percent to China.[5]

More than ever before, Canadian jobs and economic prosperity depend upon our international trade. To capture the growing market opportunities abroad, Canadian organizations are opening new plants and expanding activities in foreign countries that are closer to their customers or where labour is cheaper. While the United States continues to be our largest trading partner, Canada today exports to varying locations.

While our ability to compete in the international market place has been generally strong, in the last three years there has been an erosion in our overall competitiveness. Thus, in 2005, Canada was the fifth most competitive nation in the world; however, we have fallen today to eighth. We are, however, still ahead of several of our trading partners including Japan, China, India, and Mexico (see Figure 1-2). More recently, Canada has also become an important global player in high-tech and nontraditional exports. Our bio-tech, transportation, banking, and engineering industries have been increasingly making inroads into several foreign markets. Consider these examples:

> When the global financial meltdown occurred in 2008, Canadian banks, by and large, were relatively unaffected by the international crisis. Indeed, today, some of the Canadian banks (e.g., Royal Bank) are among the largest international banks. Similarly, several Canadian firms have major involvement in countries such as India, Thailand, and Chile, whether it is related to environmental and pollution control projects, construction and infrastructure, electronics designs, or banking.

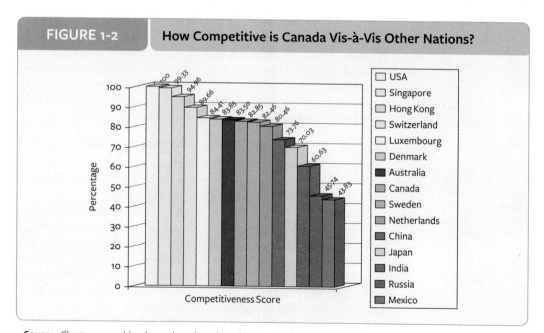

| FIGURE 1-2 | How Competitive is Canada Vis-à-Vis Other Nations? |

Source: Chart prepared by the authors based on data reported in *The World Competitiveness Year Book, 2008*, IMO, www02.imd.ch/documents, retrieved April 2009.

Canada's highly skilled, multicultural workforce has given the country a competitive advantage in dealing with other countries and cultures, anticipating their needs and concerns, and proactively responding to them. However, the international marketplace is ever changing and new challenges are constantly emerging. The emergence of several low-cost trading nations (which have vast resources of highly skilled, cheap labour) such as Thailand, China, and India has caused us to lose our market shares in traditional strongholds such as pulp and paper, cotton yarn, and steel manufacturing. Unless we are able to add value to our products or reduce the costs of production, many firms may be unable to survive in the new marketplace.

> For example, the North American Free Trade Agreement (NAFTA) meant considerable initial pain to the Canadian economy causing as many as 8,000 Canadian factories to shut down in the early 1990s.[6] At the same time, multinational firms are increasingly locating their new plants in countries such as Mexico, India, and China because of low-cost labour, further eroding our ability to create new jobs.

Further, our largest trading partner, the United States, has been improving its productivity at a faster pace than our own. This factor is discussed in the next section. This, combined with other social and economic policies, has created new challenges for Canadian employers.

> For example, because of several factors including significant differences in salaries, personal taxes, and other rewards, Canada has been losing some of its most talented employees to the United States and other countries.

This means that to attract and involve highly skilled, innovative employees, progressive human resource practices have to be adopted. HR issues now dominate corporate strategic priorities raising expectations from HR departments:

> A survey of 200 CEOs and other top executives in the United States, United Kingdom, France, Spain, Germany, and Australia indicates that four of the five top strategic priorities most commonly identified by business executives are HR related (ranks in parentheses): attracting and retaining skilled staff (1); improving workforce performance (3); changing leadership and management behaviours (4); and changing organizational culture and employee attitudes (5). The other priority, rated second overall, was increasing customer service—while a marketing priority, still closely linked to HR activities such as training, compensation, and performance management. Only 13 percent of the respondents, however, reported satisfaction with the way their HR departments achieved these priorities, thus underscoring the major strides HR has to make to fulfill organizational expectations.[7]

In summary, the arrival of the global village requires major changes in the way we manage our employees. The emergence of open borders has presented newer opportunities to Canadian firms and professionals. However, along with this, considerable brain drain (especially to the U.S.) has also occurred. In recent times, there has been incidence of "poaching" of Canadian nurses, doctors, and high-tech personnel by American employers. While the recession has decelerated or even reversed these trends in some sectors, progressive human resource practices and new government policies may be critical to meet these challenges.[8] The challenge of productivity improvement is so critical today that it deserves separate discussion below.

Meeting the Challenge of Productivity Improvement

productivity
The ratio of a firm's outputs (goods and services) divided by its inputs (people, capital, materials, energy).

Productivity refers to the ratio of an organization's outputs (goods and services) to its inputs (people, capital, materials, and energy), as seen in Figure 1-3. Productivity increases as an organization finds new ways to use fewer resources to produce its output.

In a business environment, productivity improvement is essential for long-run success. Through gains in productivity, managers can reduce costs, save scarce resources, and enhance profits. In turn, improved profits allow an organization to provide better pay, benefits, and working conditions. The result can be a higher quality of work life for employees, who are more likely to be motivated toward further improvements in productivity. Human resource managers contribute to improved productivity directly by finding better, more efficient ways to meet their objectives and indirectly by improving the quality of work life for employees.

How do we measure productivity? The index that relates all *inputs* (e.g., capital, raw materials, labour, etc.) to *outputs* (shown in Figure 1-3), while theoretically meaningful, may not help

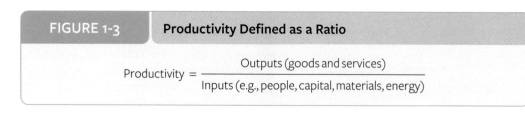

FIGURE 1-3 | Productivity Defined as a Ratio

$$\text{Productivity} = \frac{\text{Outputs (goods and services)}}{\text{Inputs (e.g., people, capital, materials, energy)}}$$

decision makers to identify potential areas of improvement. For practical use, productivity measures of each of the major components of production may be more useful. For example, one can think of labour productivity, productivity of machinery, and so on. Employee productivity can be measured using output per worker or output per work hour, while productivity of equipment and machinery may be measured by sales or production per dollar of investment in equipment, and so on.

A major challenge facing Canadian managers is productivity improvement while maintaining a high quality of work life for the employees. Cost pressures are not new to most organizations. What is new, however, is the strength and relative permanence of these competitive pressures:

> The competitors of a Canadian manufacturer of computer software typically live not next door, but abroad. They may be operating in some remote part of the world such as a small town in South Korea, Singapore, India, or Mexico. Often, Canadian organizations must compete for investment capital not with other Canadian or U.S. organizations, but with a firm in Hungary, the Czech Republic, Chile, or China.

What is most worrisome today is the gap in the productivity levels of Canada and its biggest trade partner, the United States.[9] Over the last decade, U.S. productivity has been consistently outpacing that of this country. A recent report estimates that if the gap in overall productivity growth between the United States and Canada were to persist, this factor alone would reduce Canadian living standards from 61 percent of U.S. levels in 1999 to 52 percent in 2010.[10] In recent years, Canadian managers and policy makers have recognized the urgency of improving Canadian productivity. As a consequence, the Canadian economy has undergone a dramatic transformation—we have learned to produce more outputs with fewer workers.

Workplace innovation and redesign of jobs to achieve high productivity levels are two popular means used to attain these objectives.[11] However, Canada's continuing gap in productivity growth when compared to the U.S.—its biggest trading partner—raises some concerns.[12]

> Canada is steadily losing its ability to innovate and create wealth compared with other rich countries, according to a study by Massachusetts Institute of Technology. In this study, which ranked the 16 leading members of the Organization for Economic Cooperation and Development, Canada had slipped to ninth spot from sixth over the past decade. What is even more troublesome is the study's forecast that unless Canada changes its course soon, the country will lose more ground early in this millennium (the report projects that Canada's rank is likely to remain at the tenth position in the immediate future).[13]
>
> Results of a study by the Science, Technology, and Innovation Council released in 2009 tracking Canada's performance by an array of measures including federal and business spending on research and development, the number of citizens with advanced degrees, venture capital investment, and basic literacy among workforce gave the country a mediocre grade compared to other nations.[14]

If Canada is to improve—even maintain—its competitiveness, innovation on two fronts, namely people management and technology, are a must.

> While the U.S. and Japan combined accounted for over 60 percent of all world patents, Canada's share was approximately a mere 2 percent—a "D" grade in innovation according to the Conference Board of Canada.[15]

Since a large percentage of Canadian production is currently geared for highly competitive export markets, updating technology to increase our productivity levels becomes a high-priority task facing managers in this country. While Canada has improved its overall global competitiveness in the past, we still have scope for improvement. Indeed, our high standard of living may depend on our ability to maintain and improve our world competitiveness.

> Improvements in technology and automation have helped the British Columbia lumber industry to increase its production by 25 percent in the past decade with 6,000 fewer workers. In the pulp and paper industry, the production has increased by a quarter in the past decade; however, we have 9 percent fewer jobs now (having lost 12,000 jobs in the change process).[16]

These are not jobs lost temporarily to adjust to a business cycle or to make short-term adjustments to competition—the new ways of working mean that these positions are lost forever. Productivity improvement has also left a painful scar on Canadian society; by the late 1990s, more than 350,000 manufacturing jobs (many of them blue-collar) had disappeared—never to return.[17] The global economic recession in 2008–09 has further worsened this picture. For example, by the end of March 2009, the recession had eliminated an additional 357,000 jobs in Canada.

One strategy that is getting increasingly popular to cut costs (thus indirectly raising the productivity figures) is **outsourcing**. Outsourcing enables organizations to reduce the number of workers on permanent payroll and to contract out tasks to outside agencies as and when needs arise, thus reducing the total wage bill. A past study by Hewitt Associates involving 500 CFOs of companies with $1 billion or more in revenues revealed that nearly 90 percent did outsource some services, while 41 percent outsourced some or all of their HR functions.[18]

outsourcing
Contracting tasks to outside agencies or persons.

> The most commonly outsourced function is legal work, followed by transportation and information systems management. Kodak, which in the past employed 1,400 persons in its data processing and information system sections, began outsourcing its information system needs. Air Canada began outsourcing the maintenance of its Boeing 747s a decade ago.[19] Other common outsourcing areas include printing, payroll, security, and accounting.

Outsourcing has major implications for the human resource manager. Reduced employee morale caused by job insecurity is a major issue. During contract negotiations with unions, this may pose a major hurdle for the human resource manager. Further, to meet employee goals, a human resource department may have to initiate retraining for displaced workers (to take up other jobs) or help them find jobs elsewhere (referred to as **outplacement**).

outplacement
Assisting employees to find jobs with other employers.

In summary, the current emphasis on productivity improvement has necessitated a renewed emphasis on strategic thinking and creative responses. It also involves using new technology to improve productivity and create value. This will be discussed in the next section.

Technological Challenges

Technology influences organizations and the way people work. Often it can affect an entire industry, as the following example illustrates:

> The technology of cars and airplanes modified the transportation industry—often to the detriment of railway companies. Automobile and aviation companies grew and created demand for more employees and training. The career opportunities for employees improved substantially. On the other hand, in railway companies, reduced revenues and limited growth opportunities reduced the advancement opportunities for employees. Today, the economic recession and altered customer preferences for fuel efficient cars have resulted in major auto manufacturers such as GM and Chrysler Canada being forced to lay off workers. HR departments in these companies have to reduce the workforce and cut the overall labour costs.

In the foreseeable future, technological innovations may cause fundamental shifts in our lifestyles, how and where we work, and what we do. Generally, two major technological changes have revolutionized Canadian businesses: computerization and automation. Each of these is discussed below.

Computerization

computerization
A major technological change allowing the processing of vast amounts of data at great speeds, enabling organizations to improve efficiency, responsiveness, and flexibility in operations.

In recent years, Canada has witnessed the rapid growth of **computerization** and access to high-speed information transmission systems affecting almost all walks of life. An unprecedented degree of computerization has changed the way we work, play, study, and even entertain ourselves, while access to the information highway has affected the way several organizations conduct their business:

Canada has one of the highest rates of Internet usage in the world. Currently, over half of Canadian households have at least one person with regular access to the Internet. Furthermore, Canadians are heavy users, with around 90 percent of users using email at least weekly. The Canadian Internet access market continues to grow strongly with over 64 percent of Canadians having regular Internet access. There were around 5 million residential broadband subscribers in early 2004.

Canada is also seen as a world leader in ecommerce. The government has actively encouraged initiatives, including the development of digital and broadband networks, to develop high-speed access throughout the country suitable for wireless and Internet applications.[20]

Today's computerized technology facilitates alternate ways of designing and performing tasks. Key developments in this area are briefly outlined below:

Processing Large Volumes of Information on a Timely Basis. Part of the appeal of computers is that they make it possible to process and provide large amounts of data to managers:

A manager of a Canadian company with multinational operations can compare the performance, pay, absenteeism, and safety records of its hourly and salaried workforce in Canada and its foreign plant by the touch of a computer keyboard. The same manager can transfer large data files to Australia or southern Africa in seconds. Often, decisions that took weeks in the past can now be made in hours or even minutes.

Another advantage of computers is that they make information available with great speed. Soon after events occur, the computer can list them in summary fashion—giving the information the important property of timeliness. Given the turbulence in today's business environments, this is a very useful attribute as it enables managers to take timely corrective actions.

Flexible Work Design and Telecommuting. Computers bring considerable flexibility into when and where the work is carried out. In several instances, computers permit employees to work without ever leaving their homes. Workers communicate with other employees through telephone, facsimile (fax) machines, and computerized information systems. Such **telecommuting** has been found to cut employee stress and boost worker productivity in several instances, while also reducing the costs of operations.[21]

AT&T in the United States in a project that introduced telecommuting in selected departments, found that in 80 percent of the cases, the change led to improved worker productivity. Two-thirds of the supervisors also indicated that it increased the overall efficiency of their departments.[22]

Not all jobs lend themselves to at-home work; but with the advances in computer technology, virtually any job—or any part of a job—that involves work that is independent of other people and special equipment may, one day, be performed away from the workplace. Currently, jobs such as word processing, copy-editing, routine accounting, and data entry are increasingly carried out by telecommuters. The major obstacle to telecommuting appears to be "conservative management with industrial revolution mind-sets"[23] who fear that they might lose control over employees who are not physically near them. Several Canadian organizations, such as Bell Canada and Royal Bank, have developed policies on telecommuting. Lack of concrete policies and procedures can lead to communication and performance-related problems; so does the inadequate training of managers who are entrusted with the responsibility of supervising telecommuters. Managing from a distance is simply different from managing in person. It is also a smart strategy to do a pilot program when implementing telecommuting so that early bugs can be removed before implementing it in full scale.[24]

Information Sharing and Knowledge Management. Finally, computers also enable organizations to manage their operations innovatively, often reducing costs or capitalizing on new opportunities.

McCarthy Tetrault, Canada's biggest law firm, saw technology as an area of opportunity and began recruiting lawyers with high-tech expertise. This in turn enabled the firm to take advantage of the opportunities in intellectual capital management.[25]

Many organizations today have intranets or private information networks that are accessible to all or selected organizational members, thus increasing the speed of decision making and the speed of response to customers, employees, and other stakeholders.

More effective *knowledge management*—the process of capturing organizational knowledge and making it available for sharing and building new knowledge—has been another outcome of

telecommuting
Paid labour performed at the employee's home, full-time or part-time, with assistance of PCs, modems, fax machines, etc.

computerized information systems. Intranets and integrated information systems help store and access information speedily and accurately. Modern tools such as collaborative technologies and database applications help facilitate this. Another trend, namely the use of eportfolios—a collection of digital artifacts and reflections saved on electronic media—captures what an employee learns during various training programs (or over a time period) and evidence of performance improvement. When the annual performance interview is conducted, an eportfolio can identify the on-the-job competencies of an employee. The aggregation of the skill sets and competencies of all employees help the organization manage its human capital more effectively.[26]

The exact effects of computerization on organizations will vary (depending on size, management practices, culture, and so on). In general, computerization results in a faster, multiway of communication, nontraditional marketing strategies, improved quality control, and more online inventory control. This in turn requires newer human resource practices in the areas of hiring, compensation, training, performance evaluation, and employee relations. For example, the new competencies needed on the part of employees in a highly computerized firm makes it necessary to continually upgrade employee skills.

The second generation of Web development that facilitates collaboration on World Wide Web (popularly referred to as "Web 2.0") has led to the development of a host of new services today including social networking sites, video-sharing sites, wikis, blogs, and other interactive opportunities. Increasingly, the Internet has become a platform for communication and interaction, which has profound impact on human resource management activities. The fact that users can own and control data as well as add value to the applications they use has resulted in rapid use of the technology for a variety of purposes.

> In firms with geographically dispersed units, area offices can input and control own information which, in a matter of seconds, the head office can integrate to generate guidelines for strategic and policy planning. A number of firms have begun to check applicant background by systematically vetting social networking sites. Today, many employers opt for electronic screening of applicants who are later video-interviewed in an effort to reduce hiring costs while electronic surveys enable the HR department to take timely corrective actions in response to employee demands.

In the not-too-far future, the third-generation Web (or "Web 3.0" as it is called) is expected to emerge with potential for natural language processing, machine-based learning and reasoning, and intelligent applications that are open to everyone. Open-source software and open data make vastly new applications possible with profound implications for the way we communicate with and manage individuals.

The advancing computer and Internet technology has arrived at a cost—namely, reduced individual privacy. Closed-circuit videos and computer-based performance monitoring are common today; electronic spying has become a significant threat to the privacy and dignity of the individual. The issue of privacy is dealt with in Chapter 3 of this text.

Automation

automation
The automatically controlled operation of a process, system, or equipment by mechanical or electronic devices.

Automation is the other major technological change that has affected Canadian organizations and their human resource management practices:

> Before the introduction of automatic banking machines, human resource departments of major Canadian banks used to recruit large numbers of semiskilled clerks. Not anymore—computers have eliminated several of these routine jobs; further, automation means that highly skilled programmers who can process data and program computers are needed. The recruiting and training programs in these banks had to be changed dramatically to meet the needs of new technology.

Why do organizations automate various activities?

The first reason is the push for *speed*. Competition from other countries has made it imperative that we improve our manufacturing practices if we want to stay competitive.

> For instance, capital equipment items that on average take six to twelve months to make in Canada take six to twelve weeks to make in Japan. The desire to control labour cost and increase productivity continues to drive automation.

A second reason for automation is to provide better service to the customer, to *increase predictability* in operations, and to *achieve higher standards* of quality in production. Machines do not go on strike, nor do they ask for raises.

Automation also allows *flexibility* in operations. In several automated production facilities, even small production batches become economically viable since the time, cost, and effort involved in changing setups are minimal. The ability to produce small batches in turn enables a firm to focus on the needs of different customers and market segments and speed up delivery schedules.

Automation is not the sole answer to a firm's productivity problems. Experienced human resource managers recognize this fact. Automation, to be beneficial, should permit elegant meshing of existing and new technologies. Further, the lack of availability of capital for buying expensive robots puts such purchases beyond the reach of most small and medium-sized organizations. Negative union attitudes toward mechanization is another barrier to the introduction of robots in the workplace. Automation may result in a smaller workforce together with fewer opportunities for socialization on the job. Lastly, to use expensive robots effectively (during an automation), more and more factories may find it necessary to work two or three shifts a day.

Despite these issues, it is a reasonable prediction that in the future most hazardous and boring jobs will be taken over by robots.

> Dangerous jobs—such as working with toxic chemicals and paints—will be changed by substituting robots for people. Likewise, highly repetitive assembly tasks will continue to be taken over by robots in the future.

In summary, human resource managers today must be conversant with the emerging technologies and their implications for organizational strategies, processes, and employee behaviours. New procedures for employee recruitment, training, communication, appraisal, and compensation may have to be designed to meet the challenges posed by computerization and automation while negotiations with the unions may prove more challenging for at least some organizations.

Demographic Challenges

demographic changes
Changes in the demographics of the labour force (e.g., education levels, age levels, participation rates) that occur slowly and are usually known in advance.

The demographics of the labour force describe the composition of the workforce: the education levels, the age levels, the percentage of the population participating in the workforce, and other population characteristics.

While **demographic changes** occur slowly and can be predicted in most instances, they still exert considerable influence on organizational decisions. A close look at the labour market indicates several trends.

Robots are increasingly being used in Canadian factories. What are the pros and cons of using robots in today's factories to perform tasks that were previously handled by humans?

© Vladimir Pcholkin/Taxi/Getty Images

Trend 1: The Increasing Number of Women in the Workforce

As of March 2009, Canada's labour force consisted of almost 18.3 million people aged 15 years or older, up from 14.2 million in 1991. The number of women in the labour force grew at twice the pace of men until 2006 (see Figure 1-4).[27] Beginning in 2008, the recessionary economic climate reduced the participation rates for both sexes. It is interesting to note that compared to several other industrialized nations, the participation rate of Canadian women is high. More women have also left traditional, nonprofessional occupations (such as clerical and sales) and now work in management, law, engineering, and medical fields. The fact that women accounted for 70 percent of the total employment growth in Canada in the last two decades has underscored issues of child care, work–family balance, dual-career families, and employment equity.[28] Partly due to factors such as these, more women than men tend to work part-time (see Figure 1-5).

Trend 2: Shift Toward Knowledge Workers

Currently, there is a shift from employment in primary and extractive industries (such as mining and fishing) to service, technical, and professional jobs. The relative employment in various industries in March 2009 is shown in Figure 1-6. Service industries such as education, health care, tourism, trade, and public administration make significant contributions to our national wealth today—all services combined currently account for more than 75 percent of the gross domestic product (GDP).[29] Highly skilled occupations accounted for one-half of the total labour force growth over 1991–2008.

Nearly 75 percent of the total labour force is employed in service-producing industries, 24.3 percent of total labour force being in education, health, professional, and technical jobs. Today, people in highly skilled occupations normally requiring a university education account for 16 percent of the total labour force.[30] Other services such as finance, insurance, real estate, hospitality, etc. account for over 25 percent of total labour force in this country. Many of these services also require specialized training.

Today's workforce can be divided into two main categories: information and non-information workers. Information workers can be further divided into two groups: **data workers** and **knowledge workers.** Data occupations involve the manipulation of symbolic information, whereas knowledge occupations involve the development of ideas or expert opinions. Thus, data workers (e.g., most clerical occupations) use, transmit, or manipulate knowledge, while knowledge workers such as scientists, engineers, management consultants, and so on, produce it.[31] The non-information category is composed of persons working in the manufacturing and service sectors (e.g., machine operators and assemblers, security guards, and babysitters).

Knowledge workers have been the fastest-growing type of workers in the Canadian labour force over the last quarter century or so.[32] While total employment grew at an average rate of 2.1 percent per year in the past two decades, the employment of knowledge workers grew at a rate of 5.2 percent

data workers
Members of occupations (e.g., most clerical occupations) that use, transmit, or manipulate symbolic information created by knowledge workers.

knowledge workers
Members of occupations generating, processing, analyzing, or synthesizing ideas and information (like scientists and management consultants).

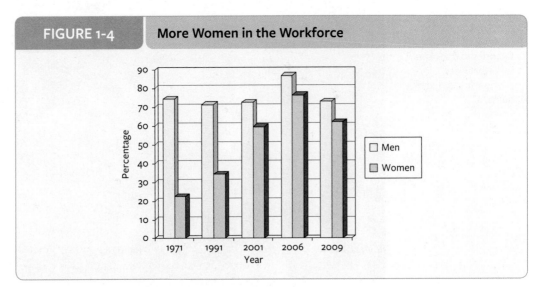

FIGURE 1-4   More Women in the Workforce

Source: Chart prepared by the authors based on the data reported in Statistics Canada, CANSIM II, Tables 282-0088, 282-0089 on March 10, 2006 and 282-0002, Modified, October 11, 2002; available from http://www41.statcan.gc.ca/2006/2621/ceb2621_003-eng.htm; accessed August 31, 2009.

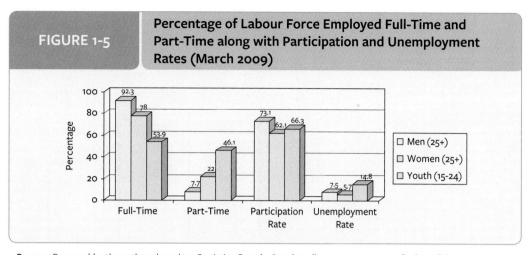

FIGURE 1-5 **Percentage of Labour Force Employed Full-Time and Part-Time along with Participation and Unemployment Rates (March 2009)**

Source: Prepared by the authors based on Statistics Canada data. http://www40.statcan.gc.ca/l01/cst01/labor23a-eng.htm?sdi=participation%20rate%20sex and www.statcan.gc.ca/subjects-sujets/labour-travail/lfs-epa/t090409a2-eng.htm; accessed August 31, 2009.

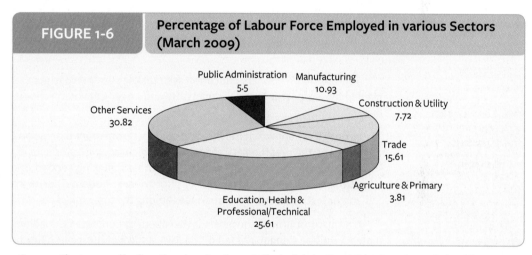

FIGURE 1-6 **Percentage of Labour Force Employed in various Sectors (March 2009)**

Sources: Chart prepared by the authors based on figures in "Latest Release From Labour Force Survey," *The Daily*, Statistics Canada, March 10, 2006; also from CANSIM Tables 282-0088 and 282-0089 of Statistics Canada. http://www40.statcan.gc.ca/l01/cst01/labor23a-eng.htm?sdi=participation%20rate%20sex; accessed April 8, 2009.

per year. This is twice the pace of service workers, the second-fastest-growing group of workers over that period.

Despite the recent down turn in the high-tech and computer sectors, information workers continue to constitute a near majority in the workforce. The proportion of the labour force employed in blue-collar and unskilled jobs simultaneously reflects a decrease.

In the foreseeable future, the demand for knowledge workers is likely to grow faster than ever before.[33] The ability of organizations to find, keep, and continually retrain these workers might spell success in the coming years.

Trend 3: Educational Attainment of Workers

As mentioned above, today's Canadian economy needs highly skilled, well-educated workers. A look at the **educational attainment** of Canadian workers, however, presents an intriguing picture. On the one hand, the educational attainment of Canadians has increased dramatically over the past several years and is expected to maintain its upward trend (see Figure 1-7).

Over 19 percent of Canadian men and 17 percent of women aged 25 or above hold a university degree or better (the corresponding figure a decade ago was less than 10 percent).[34]

Human Resources and Skills Development Canada
www.hrsdc.gc.ca

educational attainment
The highest educational level attained by an individual worker, employee group, or population.

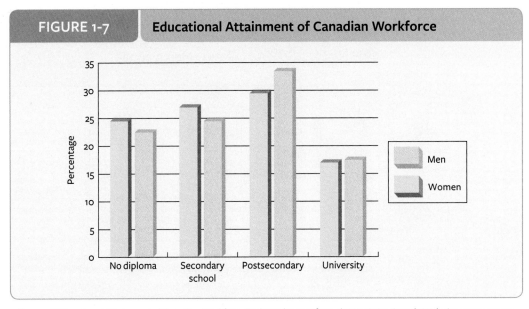

| FIGURE 1-7 | Educational Attainment of Canadian Workforce |

Source: "Educational Attainment of Canadian Workforce," adapted in part from the Statistics Canada Web site, www.statcan. ca/english/Pgdb/labor62.htm; Human Resources Development Canada, "Education Attained of Canadian Workforce: Based on *Quarterly Labour Marketing and Income Review*," reproduced with the permission of the Minister of Public Works and Government Services Canada, 2003.

Primary and secondary education systems play a key role in generating the new supply of skills needed by our post-industrial society. By and large, Canadian schools appear to be ready for this task.

In one study, approximately 30,000 students from more than 1,000 Canadian schools were compared on their mathematical and scientific literacy with students in 31 other countries. Canadian students performed well compared to others, ranking second in reading, fifth in science, and sixth in mathematics. In a majority of provinces, students' performance in reading, science, and mathematics placed these provinces among the top-ranked countries.[35]

The disturbing news, however, is that about 22 percent of Canadians aged 16 or over (or approximately 5 million Canadians) fall in the lowest level of literacy.[36] They have difficulty understanding printed materials and most likely experience problems reading any written words. Another 24 to 26 percent of Canadians fall in the second-lowest level of literacy and can deal only with material that is simple and clearly laid out, and where tasks involved are not overly complex. Not only do such low literacy rates reduce the overall productivity levels in our industries, but they may also be a major contributor to safety violations and accidents.

About 9 percent of women and 15 percent of men drop out of school before they graduate.[37] It is estimated that currently more than 8 million Canadians lack a basic school certificate or diploma.[38] What is worse, our education system still frequently produces persons who do not have basic literary and numerical skills.

Faced with this disheartening prospect, the Corporate Council on Education identified a set of "employability skills" consisting of basic academic skills (e.g., communication, thinking, learning), personal management skills (e.g., positive attitudes and behaviours, ability to accept responsibility, adaptability to new challenges), and teamwork skills (e.g., ability to work with others, ability to lead a team). These skills were considered to be the foundation skills for employability in the future.[39] Some of the more progressive employers have recognized workplace literacy as a serious issue and have taken proactive action to minimize its adverse consequences.

Durabelt Inc., a company based in Prince Edward Island that manufactures conveyor belts for vegetable harvesters, was nominated for a national award for excellence in workplace literacy. The "Duraschool project," which has been in operation since 1997, converts the lunchroom and offices into classrooms for two evenings each week where several employees and family members routinely gather to update their math, reading, and writing skills.[40]

FIGURE 1-8	Population Projections for Canada			
Year	9–14	15–64	65+	Average Age
2001	18.8%	68.6%	12.7%	37.6 years
2006	17.1%	69.5%	13.3%	39.5 years
2011	15.7%	69.8%	14.5%	41.0 years
2021	15.0%	66.2%	18.8%	42.5 years

Source: "Population Projections for Canada," adapted from the Statistics Canada Web site, www.statcan.ca/english/Pgdb/demo23a.htm, www.statcan.ca/english/Pgdb/demo23b.htm, and www.statcan.ca/english/Pgdb/demo23c.htm, and from the Statistics Canada CANSIM database at http://cansim2.statcan.ca, Table 051-0001.

Trend 4: Employment of Older Workers

old age crisis
Refers to the social (health care) and organizational (new workplace ergonomics) challenges caused by aging of population.

One of the impending issues for human resource managers is what *Maclean's* termed our **old age crisis**.[41] In 1996, about 28 percent of the population (or almost 7.6 million Canadians) were more than 50 years old. Beginning in 2010, the proportion of the population in the age group 65 and over will expand rapidly, reinforced by a low birth rate and longer life expectancy. By 2011, the age group comprising those age 65 and over will form over 18 percent of the population (see Figure 1-8). The average age of the Canadian population has been steadily increasing.

> The province with the highest proportion of the labour force aged 55 and over was Saskatchewan, where this age group represented 15 percent of the total, compared to 11.8 percent for Canada as a whole. Saskatchewan's labour force had the highest average age for all provinces, at 39.8 years.[42]

Information on Canadian Demographic Trends
www.statcan.gc.ca

The exact consequences of this trend for the human resource management function are hard to predict. An increasingly hectic scramble for jobs (especially the traditional sectors) may be one consequence. This is because the fear of post-retirement poverty (fuelled by uncertainty about government-sponsored pension plans and the recent volatility in the stock market which eroded the savings of many Canadians) may motivate employees to hold on to their current jobs. This may create unprecedented bottlenecks in professional and unionized industries.

> Several of the skilled trades in the construction sector have a relatively large share of older workers, which may lead to shortages in the coming years. The average age, at about 43, is relatively high among contractors and supervisors in the construction sector. Nearly 18 percent of bricklayers are aged 55 or more; so are 14.3 percent of plumbers. The average age of electricians has grown more rapidly than most other skilled professions; at the same time, the number of younger workers in this occupation has fallen off dramatically. As a result, the ratio of younger to older electricians plunged from 6.3 in 1991 to 2.8 in 2001.[43]

Pressures for expanded retirement benefits, variable work schedules, coordination of government benefits (e.g., Canada/Quebec Pension Plan benefits) with company benefits, and retraining programs are just a few of the challenges that await human resource specialists in the future.

> One major challenge facing Canadian organizations is retaining older, more experienced and skilled employees whose expertise is in demand in the labour market. The past view of people as expendable cogs who are responsible for managing their own careers has encouraged employees to leave their employers as soon as a better opportunity emerges elsewhere. To retain older workers, employers have to show respect and appreciation, facilitate career growth within the organization, offer flexible work and opportunities to telecommute, and recognize their skills and experience.[44]

The abolition of mandatory retirement in several provinces has also brought in new challenges as well as opportunities. An aging population affects many human resource functions, especially recruitment and selection, job design, training, appraisal, and compensation and benefits administration.

> The availability of retirees provides an opportunity to employers who are looking for experienced, part-time workers. The reduction in the supply of young workers (a staple source of recruits by

many fast food restaurants and grocery chains) may be compensated by the availability of older workers willing to work part-time. Experienced and highly motivated retirees may be a welcome source of recruits for employers and nonprofit/voluntary agencies searching for persons who can accept supervisory responsibilities.

Trend 5: More Part-Time, Contract, and Contingent Workers

The structure of employment in Canada has also changed in recent years. There are more **part-time workers** now than ever before. Indeed, the growth rate of part-time employment has been higher than in the case of full-time jobs during the last decade.

> Part-time and contingent workers account today for about a quarter of the entire labour force. For men, the percentage is 12.6 percent while 36.1 percent of all women employees are part-timers.[45] In the near future, part-time and contingent workers are expected to account for over 25 percent of the workforce.[46] This is particularly likely if the recessionary trends persist, since most employers attempt to control labour costs by hiring part-time workers.

The increasing proportion of part-time workers has raised new concerns about pay inequity and has provided momentum to the "equal pay for work of equal value" concept. Part-timers (typically, women aged 25 or older in lower-paying sales or service jobs) are far less likely to reap the benefits of increased demand and pay for highly skilled jobs.[47]

There is also an increasing trend to use **contract (or contingent) workers** in the workplace. By using contingent workers, organizations can benefit from the services of trained personnel without increasing their payroll costs in a permanent fashion.

> The use of contractors is not restricted to lower-level, clerical, or secretarial jobs; today, many lawyers, accountants, bankers, executives, and even scientists provide freelance services. Information systems, finance, and engineering were functions that were most likely to be contracted out.

Contract workers are of two major types: *Freelancers* are employees who work for the employer through independent contract arrangements. *Leased employees*, in contrast, are typically former company employees who are members of a leasing firm and work for the previous employer on an as-needed basis. Contractors have often been found to be more productive and efficient than in-house employees because freelancers do not spend a lot of time complying with company bureaucracy and attending meetings. They can also provide an outsider's fresh perspective on things. However, the contractor's loyalty to the firm may be limited, especially if the contractor is working for several different clients concurrently.

Cultural Challenges

As cultural values change, human resource departments discover new challenges. While several **cultural challenges** face Canadian managers, three more important ones are discussed below: work-related attitudes, ethnic diversity, and attitudes toward government and those in power.

Work-Related Attitudes

The increasing entry of women and educated young persons into the labour force has resulted in some changes in employee expectations. The old cultural value that "men work and women stay at home" underwent radical modification during the last two decades.

> This shift carries implications for human resource managers. For example, child care facilities provided by the employer will become a more common demand confronting human resource departments. Sick days—paid days off for illness—have become "personal leave days," and "maternity leave" has been renamed "parental leave" to reflect the reality of working men leaving the workforce to take care of their young children.

Due to changing **attitudes toward work** and leisure, human resource departments have been confronted with requests for longer vacations, more holidays, and varied workweeks. Supervisors increasingly turn to human resource professionals for help with employee motivation. Generation X (also sometimes called the Nexus generation) employees, who are born between 1966 and 1980, are considered to be different from the baby boomers (the previous generation). While Generation X-ers are not averse to hard work, they place a premium on work–life balance and like to be active participants in decision making.[48] They are likely to show disdain for a "command and rule" culture and are unlikely to have more loyalty to their profession and competency building than to their employers.

---

part-time workers
Persons working fewer than required hours for categorization as full-time workers and who are ineligible for many supplementary benefits offered by employers.

contract (or contingent) workers
Freelancers (self-employed, temporary, or leased employees) who are not part of regular workforce and are paid on a project completion basis.

cultural challenges
Challenges facing a firm's decision makers because of cultural differences among employees or changes in core cultural or social values occurring at the larger societal level.

attitudes toward work
Variety of work-related assumptions and values including the role of work in a person's life and the role of women and diverse groups in organizations.

Some writers claim that Gen X-ers think of work as a job while boomers view it as a career. X-ers are unfazed by power and authority; boomers are impressed and attracted by it. X-ers mistrust most business practices; boomers instituted many of them. X-ers are self-reliant; boomers are team-oriented.[49]

The newest generation in the labour market, *Generation Y*, is qualitatively different from either of the above groups:

Generation Y-ers—those people who are entering the workforce today for the first time—may not respond well to traditional management practices. While it is risky to over-generalize about any group, significant numbers of Gen Y-ers seek continuous learning, ongoing feedback, teamwork, up-to-date technology, security, respect, and work–life balance. Their biggest fear is boredom. Some consider these new entrants to the workplace to hold unrealistically high expectations of themselves and others, often resulting in the setting of unrealistic targets and resultant frustration.[50]

There is also a greater demand today for more ethical conduct of business. The unethical practices of several large companies including Bre-X, Enron, and WorldCom underscored the social costs of unethical and fraudulent business practices. Businesses, especially big corporations, have been accused of acting totally out of self-interest and furthering the interest of a few members of the top management. In recent years, a variety of unethical practices have been reported including creative accounting, insider trading, securities fraud, excessive payments made to top management not reflective of their contributions, and bribery and kickbacks. Indeed, greed and short-term orientation accompanied by creative accounting played no small role in the stock market meltdown and the acceleration of personal bankruptcies in 2008.

A recent survey of Canadian firms indicated that 57 percent of respondents had been victims of fraudulent activities such as secret commissions, inflated expense reports, and personal use of company property. The most important ethical issues confronting Canadian firms today would seem to relate to avoiding conflicts of interest and maintaining honest governance, employee and client privacy, environmental protection, and security of information.[51]

This has resulted in many Canadian firms instituting code of ethics for their employees. Over 70 percent of the responding firms in a survey[52] had also instituted a program to promote ethical values and practices. Needless to say, the human resource department will be a key player in this important activity.

SPOTLIGHT ON ETHICS

What Is a "Right" Behaviour?

Ethics are moral principles that guide human behaviours and are often based on a society's cultural values, norms, customs, and beliefs, which means that different cultures and even individuals within the same society have widely varying standards of behaviour. How are we to differentiate "right" from "wrong" or "good" from "bad"? There are no simple answers. Many adopt one of the following postures in dealing with such ambiguous situations:

1. **Universalist approach:** Persons who embrace this view assert that some moral standards are universally applicable. In other words, regardless of society or place, a bad act (such as killing or stealing) is bad. There are no exceptions to moral "rights" and "wrongs."

2. **Situational approach:** What is good or bad depends essentially on the situation or culture surrounding the actor. While telling the truth is desirable, there may be situations in which lying is acceptable or even necessary, or other cultures may not value truth to the same extent. Similarly, while killing is bad, there may be situations in which this act is justified. It all depends on the situation. While high morals are to be followed, an individual may have to make exceptions when outcomes justify them.

3. **Subjectivist approach:** In this approach, the individual decision maker facing a situation determines what is right and wrong after considering all aspects of the situation. Moral decisions are based on personal values and preferences. Needless to say, the standards imposed by individuals are vastly different depending on their upbringing, current circumstances, values, and beliefs.

Another useful model to understand and guide ethical behaviour is offered by Lawrence Kohlberg. Kohlberg, an American psychologist, posits six stages that form an invariant and universal sequence in individual development; thus, everyone is supposed to go through the same stages in the same sequence. It is, however, possible for a person to be "stuck" at one of the following stages and not proceed to the next level. The six stages of moral development identified by Kohlberg[53] are:

STAGE 1: OBEDIENCE AND PUNISHMENT STAGE: The only reason for a person to perform the "right" act at this stage is obedience to others who have the power to punish.

STAGE 2: RECIPROCITY STAGE: Here, the individual enters into reciprocal agreements with others so that he or she receives the greatest good or reward. The focus is on achieving one's own objectives and on self-interest; for this, the individual concerned is willing to take actions that others want him or her to take.

STAGE 3: INTERPERSONAL CONFORMITY STAGE: What is "right" is determined by expectations of others who are close to the individual. Close relatives, friends, and other "reference groups" help the individual identify the "right" action in any setting.

STAGE 4: LAW AND ORDER STAGE: Doing one's duty and obeying society's rules is considered the "right" behaviour at this stage.

STAGE 5: THE SOCIAL CONTRACT STAGE: Here, the individual goes beyond the minimal standards established by laws and rules. "The greatest good of the greatest number" in the society is the maxim that guides the individual's behaviour at this stage.

STAGE 6: UNIVERSAL ETHICAL PRINCIPLES STAGE: At this stage, the individual is guided by high moral principles. People are to be treated as ends in themselves, not just as means to one's ends or even to the ends of a whole group or society. People are considered as inherently valuable and to be treated in the "right" way. Very few individuals reach this level.

The field of human resource management is full of situations that involve hard choices between good and bad, right and wrong, desirable and undesirable. Indeed, 52 percent of the 462 American HR professionals surveyed in the 2003 Business Ethics Survey[54] reported feeling at least some pressure to compromise their organization's ethical standards. The reasons most often cited for engaging in unethical behaviours were a need to follow the boss's orders (49 percent of the respondents), pressure to meet overly aggressive business objectives (48 percent), and helping the organization to survive (40 percent). Also mentioned frequently was pressure to be a "team player."

The Spotlight on Ethics feature in this book will introduce you to one or more ethical challenges associated with the topic discussed in each chapter. Once you have identified your responses, compare your answer to those of your friends or family members. Find out why each person chose differently. Try to categorize the responses under the three categories and six stages of moral development listed above. Which approach seems to be used by most of your friends and acquaintances? At what stage of moral development are you and your friends? Why? What are the implications for yourself and your employer? What prevents you and your friends from moving to the next stage?

Instructions: Consider the following situation. Make a note of your answer on a separate sheet and compare it with those of your friends and acquaintances.

After graduation, you joined the human resource department of a highly respected multinational apparel firm with operations in 14 countries, including five developing nations. Because of the tight labour market, you went through over 20 job interviews before you landed this job. You consider yourself extremely fortunate to have secured this job, since your employer is a very large firm offering considerable prospects for promotion and career development. Even if you don't stay with this firm for many years, the very fact that you worked here for a few years could open several other doors. This is your eighth month with your employer.

Recently, you were sent to a developing country, which supplies over 20 percent of your firm's products sold in that region. You were looking forward to this trip to provide you with some essential international experience in HR. However, what you saw in the country appalled you. You now wish you had never taken that trip. The "factory" where the garments were tailored turned out to be a shack hardly 1.5 metres tall, with a 74-square-metre area where over a dozen adults and 20 children—ages 8 to 14—sat on the floor and worked for over 16 hours each day, often earning less than $0.50 a day in wages. Many slept on the floor when they did not work; others looked haggard and hungry. You know that your company makes a tidy 80 percent profit from each garment bought from this supplier.

You are unsure about the course of action to take. On the one hand, you feel that you should not profit from the toil of the poor and helpless; however, as a junior member of the management team, what action can you possibly take without alienating your senior colleagues and hurting your own chances for career progress? Also, is it really your responsibility to improve the working conditions of a group of workers living in that country?

Ethnic Diversity

The coexistence of anglophones and francophones along with dozens of other national, racial, and ethnic groups, each with its unique cultural and social background, makes Canadian society a **cultural mosaic**.[55] "Business immigrants" have often acted as engines of economic growth in this country, while immigrants from nontraditional sources such as Hong Kong, Vietnam, India, Sri Lanka, and the Philippines have added to the cultural diversity and richness of this country. Indeed, in recent years, the entire face of the Canadian population has undergone a major change.

> Today, less than half of Canada's immigrants originate from European countries. Instead, many of our immigrants come from Asia, Africa, and South America.

Unlike the American notion of the "melting pot," Canada has encouraged each ethnic minority to maintain its unique cultural heritage to form part of the Canadian cultural mosaic. Canada is no longer a two-language nation; millions of Canadians have neither English nor French as their language of origin.

Today, almost 5 million Canadians are referred to as *allophones*, which literally means "other speaking." For example, today, more Canadians speak Chinese than Italian and can claim it as the most common nonofficial language.[56]

For the practising manager, this cultural diversity simultaneously brings additional opportunities and challenges, some of which will be discussed in Chapter 12. Often, it is the human resource department's responsibility to maximize the beneficial outcomes and minimize the challenges posed by a diverse workforce.

Attitudes Toward Governments

Historically, Canadians have always been far more positive than Americans toward government participation in economic activities (even in the earliest days of Confederation, private and public capital was combined to create the Canadian Pacific Railway). In the past, issues such as government-funded health care and education were of higher importance to Canadians than to Americans.[57]

cultural mosaic
Canadian ideal of encouraging each ethnic, racial, and social group to maintain its own cultural heritage, forming a national mosaic of different cultures.

Information on American and Canadian Workforce
http://digitalcommons.ilr.cornell.edu/

Canada's workplaces become more and more diverse as each visible minority is encouraged to maintain his or her unique cultural heritage. What potential conflicts can develop because of this "encouragement"?

© Michael Blann/Stone/Getty Images

attitudes toward government
Basic assumptions about the role of government in business and society, including the desirability of a welfare state with a key interventionist role for the government.

However, in recent years, **attitudes toward government** have slowly shifted for many Canadians. "The notion that governments have the ability and wisdom to steer the economy is being dispelled. The growing view is that the government is just an economic facilitator that provides the appropriate infrastructure for prosperity."[58] This sentiment has already been reflected in basic attitudinal shifts in how the government and the public view unemployment insurance, family allowances, welfare payments, and the overall focus of regional development plans.

In the past, the Canadian national character was called a "conservative syndrome,"[59] to reflect Canadians' tendency to be guided by tradition and focus on maintenance of order and predictability. Canadians were said to be a hybrid product of several nationalities and ethnic groups "not quite as American as the Americans, not quite as British as the British … and not quite as French as the French."[60] However, more recently, Canada's national self-image has changed somewhat (as evidenced by the Charter of Rights and Freedoms, aggressive entry into foreign markets, and reduced dependence on governmental programs).

As a result, individuality and a kind of do-it-yourself attitude seem to be supplanting faith in government in the minds of many.

In summary, a fundamental shift is under way in how and where the world's work gets done, with potentially serious consequences for Canada. Today's "global village" requires major changes in the way managers—especially human resource managers—think and operate. The Canadian firms that will succeed in the future will be the ones that can survive amid fierce global competition and successfully meet challenges posed by incessant and rapid changes in technology, changing social expectations, and the emergence of a diverse workforce. How critical human resource management is to organizations facing these new realities is discussed in the following pages.

OBJECTIVES OF HUMAN RESOURCE MANAGEMENT

Human resource management aims to improve the productive contribution of individuals while simultaneously attempting to attain other societal and individual employee objectives. The field of human resource management thus focuses on what managers—especially human resource specialists—do and what they should do.

Improving the contribution of human resources is so ambitious and important that all but the smallest firms create specialized human resource departments to enhance the contributions of people.[61] It is ambitious because human resource departments do not control many of the factors that shape the employee's contribution, such as capital, materials, and technology. The department decides neither strategy nor the supervisor's treatment of employees, although it strongly influences both. Nevertheless, the role of human resource management is critical to the success—indeed, even the very survival—of the organization. Without a motivated and skilled workforce, and devoid of gains in employee productivity, organizations eventually stagnate and fail.

While the role of human resource departments (HRDs) shows considerable variation across organizations, almost all HRDs carry out several common activities, including the following:

- assist the organization to attract the right quality and number of employees;
- orient new employees to the organization and place them in their job positions;
- develop, disseminate, and use job descriptions, performance standards, and evaluation criteria;
- help establish adequate compensation systems and administer them in an efficient and timely manner;
- foster a safe, healthy, and productive work environment;
- ensure compliance with all legal requirements insofar as they relate to management of workforce;
- help maintain a harmonious working relationship with employees and unions where present;
- foster a work environment that facilitates high employee performance; and
- establish disciplinary and counselling procedures.

To guide its many activities, a human resource department must have objectives. Objectives are benchmarks against which actions are evaluated. These must be formulated after a detailed analysis of the organization and its environments. Human resource management in most organizations attempts to achieve three key objectives—*organizational, societal,* and *employee.*

Organizational Objectives

The major aim of the human resource department is to contribute to organizational effectiveness. Human resource management is not an end in itself; it is a means of helping the organization to achieve its primary **organizational objectives**. It should help an organization to identify the right quality, type, and number of employees. The importance of this function is illustrated by the following example where a change in employee selection procedure contributed to improved organizational effectiveness:

> The Atlantic Brewery always sought the best workers it could find. "Best" meant, among other things, the brightest and most reliable individuals. Usually, the company recruited students from surrounding schools and universities. With one job, however, this strategy created problems. The job required the worker to stand in the bottling plant eight hours a day inspecting beer bottles for damage. The work floor was damp, noisy, and full of fumes coming from the beer tanks. Employees usually quit within four months. Bright, ambitious persons found this simple, repetitive job boring. A possible solution was to assign this job to individuals with lower ambitions and career expectations, or to rotate the job assignment among several people in shorter shifts.

It should be emphasized that the contribution of a human resource department should be kept at a level appropriate to the organization's needs. Resources are wasted when the human resource department is more or less sophisticated than the organization demands. The department's level of service must be appropriate for the organization it serves. Cost–benefit analyses and systematic program reviews are vital to achieve this goal. This text provides sample measures for evaluating several HR activities such as recruitment, selection, training, and orientation in the following chapters.

Societal Objectives

Human resource management should be responsive to the needs and challenges of society while minimizing the negative impact of such demands upon the organization. The failure of organizations to use their resources for **societal objectives** may result in restrictions being imposed on the organizations. In effect, society may pass laws that limit human resource decisions.

> For example, employees of many organizations are environmentally conscious. They demand that their employer recycle and reduce waste wherever possible. Everything from paper clips to large cardboard cartons or metal containers is routinely recycled in many organizations today. In some instances, employees' concern for their environment surpasses their concern for other tangible rewards.
>
> Being a good corporate citizen may also add to the bottom line of the organization. A Vancouver based HR consulting firm recently reported that encouraging workers to telecommute not only responds to our environmental concern to reduce greenhouse gases, but can also reduce costs for the employer. For example, 265 virtual workers can avoid 2.5 million kilometres of travel and 728 tons of carbon dioxide emissions each year. The employees are also likely to be more engaged in their work since this helps them to balance their work and family responsibilities better.[62]

Human resource strategies in such organizations will need to reflect society's ecological concerns.

Employee Objectives

Human resource strategies should assist employees in achieving their personal goals, at least insofar as these goals enhance the individual's contributions to the organization. If **employee objectives** are ignored, then worker performance may decline, or employees may even leave the organization.

The above three objectives are beacons that guide the strategies and day-to-day activities of human resource departments. However, not every human resource decision meets these objectives every time or in equal degree. Trade-offs do occur. The relative importance of the three objectives in any single situation is decided after a careful analysis of all relevant variables involved in the particular situation. But these objectives serve as a check on decisions. The more these objectives are met by the human resource department's actions, the better will be its contribution to the organization, its people, and the larger society.

organizational objectives
An organization's short- and long-term goals that the HR department aims to achieve.

societal objectives
Societal priorities (e.g., lower pollution levels) that HR department targets while setting own objectives and strategies.

employee objectives
Goals set by HR department to assist employees to achieve personal goals that will enhance their contribution to the organization.

⭕ STRATEGIC HUMAN RESOURCE MANAGEMENT

A strategy is similar to a game plan. In its earlier military sense, a strategy involved the planning and directing of battles or campaigns on a broad scale. In an organizational setting, it involves large-scale, future-oriented, integrated plans to achieve organizational objectives and respond to uncertain and competitive environments facing the organization.

Strategies are typically formulated at three levels: *corporate,* involving the entire organization; *business,* involving a major activity, business, or division in a large multibusiness organization; and *functional,* involving managers of different activities, services (e.g., finance, marketing), or geographical areas. Depending on organizational conditions, strategies may be developed at any or all of these three levels.

Strategies can vary significantly.

Thus, one organization's strategy may be to be a low-cost producer of a product, while another in the same industry may aim to produce a high-quality, higher-priced product that aims to satisfy a particular customer market. A firm may invest considerable resources in research and development to come out with new products, while another may decide to focus on aggressive marketing of existing products.

strategic human resource management *is systematically linked to the strategic needs of an organization and aims to provide it with an effective workforce while meeting the needs of its members and other constituents in the society.* In contrast to strategies, human resource departments also employ varying tactics periodically. Tactics are methods, procedures, or systems employed by human resource professionals to achieve specific strategies.

It is important that human resource strategies and tactics are mutually consistent. Even the best-laid strategies may fail if they are not accompanied by sound programs or procedures.

For example, a strategy of attracting and maintaining a technically qualified and innovative workforce is unlikely to be successful unless accompanied by sound hiring and training and development procedures.

Further, a human resource strategy should almost always reflect the larger organizational mission and strategy. When the human resource strategy and tactics accurately reflect organizational priorities, the results can be very positive:

The experience of Camco Inc., the country's largest appliance manufacturer, illustrates the importance of sound human resource management in raising employee productivity and organizational profits. After eight years of operation, Camco management decided to break its organizational chain of command and listen to its workers. The organization's structure became "flat" when every worker was encouraged to talk to everyone else. The results went beyond the most optimistic expectations. Employees made several recommendations that at first seemed not workable, but because of the commitment of employees, they became realities. For example, in the production of glass microwave shelves, the employees made a suggestion that was originally considered to be impractical, but when implemented it saved Camco $25,000 annually. Productivity improvement in just one year after the change was 25 percent, and absenteeism was reduced by 30 percent.[63]

Steps in Strategic Human Resource Management

Human resource management as a specialist function evolved from very small beginnings. (See Appendix A at the end of this chapter for the growth of human resource functions over time.) What began as the role of helping employees to deal with their personal problems, such as housing and medical issues, grew over a period of time and is now an integral part of the strategic position that an organization assumes—inseparable from key organizational goals, product-market plans, technology and innovation, and last but not least, an organization's strategy to respond to governmental and other pressures. Figure 1-9 outlines the strategic human resource management model that is used in this book.

To be effective, a human resource management strategy should be formulated after considering an organization's environment, mission and objectives, strategies, and internal strengths and weaknesses, including its culture. Typically, the strategy formulation and implementation process consists of the six steps outlined below.

---

strategic human resource management
Integrating human resource management strategies and systems to achieve overall mission, strategies, and success of the firm while meeting needs of employees and other stakeholders.

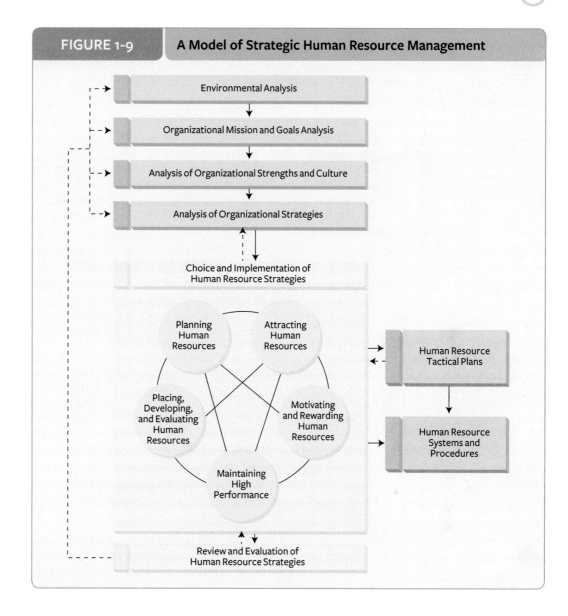

| FIGURE 1-9 | A Model of Strategic Human Resource Management |

Step 1: Environmental Analysis

Through careful and continuous monitoring of economic, social, and labour market trends and noting changes in governmental policies, legislation, and public policy statements, a human resource manager will be able to identify environmental threats and opportunities that in turn help formulate new action guidelines:

> A large electric utility, sensing society's increasing concern about air pollution, decided to reduce coal burning and shift to hydro power. This in turn necessitated replacement of its plant and equipment as well as making major changes in its human resource strategy. Not only were new skills required, but the changeover from existing procedures and systems (e.g., compensation, appraisal, training) also had to be smooth and cause as little disruption to the work as possible. A strategy based on considerable in-house and external training was drawn up and implemented. By the time the utility switched to hydro power, it had the necessary supply of skilled labour.

Step 2: Organizational Mission and Goals Analysis

An organizational analysis, involving a close look at the organization's overall mission and goals, is a second integral aspect of identifying human resource strategies. Even similar organizations often pursue different goals; however, some goals such as profitability (or revenue surplus), organizational growth, employee satisfaction, efficiency, adaptiveness to environmental changes, and so on are common across most Canadian organizations.

mission statement
Statement outlining the purpose, long-term objectives, and activities the organization will pursue and the course for the future.

The way in which an organization defines its mission also significantly influences human resource strategies. A **mission statement** specifies what activities the organization intends to pursue and what course is charted for the future. It is a concise statement of "who we are, what we do, and where we are headed" and gives an organization its own special identity, character, and path of development.

For example, two similar electronic manufacturers may have varying missions. One may define the mission as "to become a successful organization in the entertainment business," while the other may define it as "to occupy a technological leadership position in the industry." The associated strategies are likely to show significant differences. Apart from manufacturing electronic goods used for home entertainment, the former firm may acquire video and film production firms and get into the music industry (e.g., produce compact discs), while the focus of the second firm may be more committed to developing innovative electronic products through research and development.

Step 3: Analysis of Organizational Strengths and Culture

Human resource strategies should be formed only after a careful look at the strengths and weaknesses of the organization concerned and its culture. In the same way, organizational strategies that cannot be built on existing human resource capabilities should be avoided (unless it is possible to remove these deficiencies immediately, either through training or selection of employees). Consider this example:

Calgary Electronics, which employs twelve salespeople and seven service and repair personnel, was concerned about the growing competition in the electronics equipment market. Historically, the firm had sold and repaired all makes of electronic and electrical equipment (ranging from blenders to large-screen TV and complex security alarm systems). To meet the competition, the firm initially decided to implement an aggressive advertising and personal selling strategy. However, a detailed investigation into the company's past performance indicated that the strength of the firm lay in its prompt and cheap repair service. A review of the employee skills and training also indicated that several of the salespeople lacked any formal training in selling. On the basis of the results of the internal analysis, Calgary Electronics decided to focus on repairs and after-sales service in its advertising campaigns.

organization character
The product of all of an organization's features—people, objectives, technology, size, age, unions, policies, successes, and failures.

Every organization is unique. Similarities between organizations can be found among their parts, but each whole organization has a unique character. **Organization character** is the product of all of an organization's features: its employees, its objectives, its technology, its size, its age, its unions, its policies, its successes, and its failures. Organization character reflects the past and shapes the future.[64] Human resource specialists should be clearly familiar with and adjust to the character of the organization. For example, it is sometimes overlooked that objectives can be achieved in several acceptable ways. This idea, called *equifinality*, means there are usually many paths to any given objective. The key to success is choosing the path that best fits the organization's character:

Human resource manager Aaron Chu feared that his request to hire a training assistant would be turned down. So instead of asking for funds to hire someone, Aaron expressed concern that poor supervisory skills were contributing to employee complaints and some resignations. He observed at the weekly management meeting that unskilled replacements might lead to rising labour costs. Knowing that top management was concerned that the company remain a low-cost producer, Aaron was not surprised when the plant manager suggested hiring "someone to do training around here." Aaron received a budget increase for training. By adjusting to the organization's character, he achieved his objective.

The understanding of organization character is so critical for the success of an HR manager that this will be discussed in greater depth later in this chapter.

Step 4: Analysis of Organizational Strategies

Even organizations with similar goals show remarkable differences in their strategies to achieve those goals. There are at least three major generic strategies that a firm may pursue: cost leadership, differentiation, or focus.[65]

cost leadership strategy
Strategy to gain competitive advantage through lower costs of operations and lower prices for products.

differentiation strategy
Strategy to gain competitive advantage by creating a distinct product or offering a unique service.

focus strategy
Strategy to gain a competitive advantage by focusing on the needs of a specific segment of the total market.

Firms that pursue a **cost leadership strategy** aim to gain a competitive advantage through lower costs. They aggressively seek efficiencies in production and use tight controls (especially in managing costs) to gain an advantage over their competitors.

The Bic Pen Company is a good example of a firm that attempts to compete successfully by producing pens as cheaply as possible. Similar cost leadership strategy is seen in the case of Timex (watches) and Federal Express (overnight package delivery).

Product **differentiation strategy** focuses on creating a distinctive or even unique product that is unsurpassed in quality, innovative design, or other features. This may be accomplished through product design, unique technology, or even through carefully planned advertising and promotion. Firms that use this strategy may even be able to charge higher-than-average prices for their products.

Nikon (cameras) and Calvin Klein (fashion apparel) are firms that employ a differentiation strategy.

Under the **focus strategy**, a firm concentrates on a segment of the market and attempts to satisfy it with a low-priced or a highly distinctive product. Within this specific market or target customer group, a focused firm may compete on the basis of either differentiation or cost leadership. The target market in this instance is usually set apart either by geography or by specialized needs.

An automobile manufacturer sells its station wagons only in North America since Americans and Canadians seem to like station wagons more than people in other countries do. The same firm sells its smaller and fuel-efficient economy car in less developed countries because consumers there have lower disposable income.

Depending on the overall strategy employed by the firm, the human resource strategies will show substantial variation. (See Figure 1-10 for some variations in organizational priorities under the three strategies.)

Step 5: Choice and Implementation of Human Resource Strategies

Given the firm's objectives, strategies, and constraints, the human resource manager should examine each strategic option for its viability. Unsuitable strategic options must be dropped from consideration. The ones that appear viable should be scrutinized in detail for their advantages and weaknesses before being accepted for implementation. Some of the questions to ask at this time include the following:

- Are our assumptions realistic?
- Do we really have the skills and resources to make this strategy viable?

FIGURE 1-10	Variations in HR Priorities and Practices Under Different Competitive Strategies[66]		
	Cost Leadership	Focus	Differentiation
Desired employee behaviours	Predictable, repetitive	Predictable, repetitive	Creative, innovative
Skill application by employees	Narrow	Moderate	Broad
Employee flexibility to change emphasized	Low	Moderate	High
Concern for quantity of production	High	Moderate	Moderate
Emphasis on training	Lower	Higher	Higher
Focus of employee performance appraisal procedures	Control	Mostly control; some development	Employee development

- Is this strategy consistent internally? Do the various elements of the strategy "hang together"?
- What are the risks? Can we afford them?
- What new actions must be taken to make the strategy viable?

Strategic choice and implementation involves identifying, securing, organizing, and directing the use of resources both within and outside the organization. Consider the following example:

> Maple Leaf Grocers Ltd., which operated grocery stores in six residential districts in a large metropolitan city, had followed a strategy of high volume, low margin, limited selection, and limited service in the past. Recently, a new grocery chain, Trans Canada Superstores, made a major breakthrough in several other cities by operating large warehouse-style stores with rock-bottom prices. The typical "superstore" was about three times as large as a Maple Leaf store, and offered little service, but had considerably more variety of produce at prices that were 10 to 15 percent lower. The superstore was planning to start a new unit close to where one of the Maple Leaf stores was situated. Unable to match the competitor's low prices and wider selection, and not inclined to move to a new, more spacious location, the management at Maple Leaf decided to follow a new strategy based on superior customer service and "a family atmosphere." This required all cashiers and store personnel (including the store manager) to receive additional training in listening to and serving customers. Greater emphasis was placed on each employee knowing about all major products in at least three different store departments; special assistance was provided to the elderly and single parents who shopped there (the shop also allocated a portion of its floor space for a mini playpen). Store management and staff were actively encouraged to participate in community activities and to donate to neighbourhood parties and sports activities. When the superstore began operations in the area about a year later, Maple Leaf Grocers was able to retain over 80 percent of its customers.

As the above example shows, the human resource strategy must reflect every change in the organizational strategy and support it. Simply stating that "we are strategic in our focus" does not, in fact, result in a contribution to organizational strategy.

> A 2008 survey of 700 HR professionals found that 66 percent of the respondents felt that many HR professionals who think they are strategic are simply not so in their actions. Only 4 percent of the respondents felt that HR professionals are, on the whole, strategic and recognized for their strategic thinking by relevant others. However, 73 percent of the respondents believe that the word "strategic" is overused in HR.[67]

Articles on HR Activities
www.hrmguide.net

Mere use of the term "strategic" without clear actions that support it simply reduces the credibility of the HR profession and its members. In formulating strategies, the human resource department must continuously focus on the following five major groups of activities:

1. Planning Human Resources. A *job analysis* enables the human resource manager to collect important information about various jobs, including required job behaviours and performance standards. *Human resource planning* enables the determination of demand and supply of various types of human resources within the firm. The results of job analysis and human resource planning shape the overall human resource strategies in the short run and facilitate employment and training planning.

2. Attracting Human Resources. In recruiting and selecting workers, a human resource manager should *meet all legal requirements* (e.g., equal employment opportunity laws, affirmative action policies). *Recruitment* is the process of finding and attracting capable job applicants and results in a pool of high-quality candidates. The selection process is a series of specific steps used to decide which recruits should be hired, and aims to match job requirements with an applicant's capabilities.

3. Placing, Developing, and Evaluating Human Resources. Once hired, new employees need to be oriented to the organization's policies and procedures and placed in their new job positions. Since new workers seldom fit the organization's needs exactly, they must be *trained* to perform effectively. They must also be prepared for future responsibilities through systematic career planning.

Performance appraisals give employees feedback on their performance and can help the human resource department identify future training needs. This activity also indicates how well human resource activities have been carried out since poor performance might often mean that selection or training activities need to be redesigned.

> For example, in the past, the management of Montreal-headquartered Aeroplan, a loyalty marketing company with about 1,200 employees, found that its performance appraisal system was lacking in providing accurate and timely information on the capabilities of its employees. With professional assistance, the firm introduced a new performance management system that helped it not only to assess employee performance but also to make managerial succession plans and other decisions related to career management. The new system provided relevant information to the employees to help them grow and develop new competencies.[68]

4. Motivating Employees. When employees perform acceptably, they must receive *compensation*. Some of the *employee benefits* are required (for example, Canada/Quebec Pension Plan), while several others are voluntary (for example, dental plans). Since *employee motivation* is also partially determined by internal work procedures, climate, and schedules, these must be continually modified to maximize performance.

> It has often been observed that people leave their bosses, not their organizations. Many a time, an employee may quit because the boss does not inspire, make good decisions, possess relevant knowledge, or treat fairly and with respect. Recognizing this fact, many progressive HR departments have initiated actions to identify problems before they cause an employee to leave the firm. An example here is the BMO Financial, which fosters a culture to address problem managers. One tool used is the employee opinion survey with its specific questions on managers. The other is the employee call centre, which allows employees to convey their problems anonymously. A few times a year, a representative of the HR department conducts an "employee relations visit" to investigate a potential problem and find solutions.[69]

5. Maintaining High Performance. The human resource strategy should ensure that the productive contribution from every member is at the maximum possible level. Most effective organizations have well-established *employee relations* practices, including good communication between managers and employees, standardized disciplinary procedures, and counselling systems. In today's work setting, internal work procedures and organizational policies must be continuously monitored to ensure that they meet the needs of a *diverse workforce* and ensure safety to every individual. In many organizations, employees may decide to join together and form self-help groups called unions. When this occurs, management is confronted with a new situation: *union–management relations*. To respond to the collective demands by employees, human resource specialists may have to negotiate a collective agreement and administer it. Poor union–management relations also result in work stoppages.

> Canada's record in work stoppages is by no means flattering. In the recent past, Canada lost over 4 million person-days due to strikes and lockouts. Most of Canada's largest telecoms, Bell, Telus, MTS, and Aliant, have been involved in work stoppages; so have Canada Post, the CBC, Videotron, and Bell's subsidiary, Entourage. Other significant stoppages occurred in the supermarket sector, in meat packing, and in paper and wood products industries.[70]

Strategic choice and implementation involves an examination of the entire management philosophy, the formal and informal organizational structures, and the climate of the organization. It should also pay close attention to the organization's history, culture, and overall character.

Identifying the HR strategy of an organization is often a complex task. It is not unusual to see the same organization adopting somewhat different employment practices for different employee groups or in different regions.[71] Although in any given organization, there tends to be a *dominant* HR strategy, multiple bundles of HR practices are likely to develop to cater to the unique needs of organizations in a subgroup or industry.[72] Recent research studies[73] have identified four archetypical HR strategies: commitment, compliance, paternalistic, and collaborative.

commitment strategy
An organizational strategy that attempts to forge a commonality of interest between the organization (often symbolized by the management) and its employees.

Commitment Strategy. A **commitment strategy** *attempts to forge a commonality of interest between the organization (often represented by the management) and the employees.* To develop that commonality of interest, there is heavy emphasis on employee training and development, internal staffing and career development and compensation levels formulated on the basis of internal equity norms rather than market rates.[74]

compliance strategy
An organizational strategy whose focus is on achieving labour efficiencies through control over labour costs, use of a temporary or contingent workforce and maximum control over processes and using it as a key competitive weapon.

paternalistic strategy
An organizational strategy in which some minimal degree of training and competency-building through training, job rotation, etc. is done with the objective of achieving flexibility of staffing and task assignments and maintaining workforce stability.

collaborative strategy
An organizational strategy that relies on highly skilled contract labour to supply the needed specialized by hiring them on an "as-needed" basis or retaining them on an "on-call" basis.

Compliance Strategy. In a **compliance strategy**, *focus is on achieving labour efficiencies through control over labour costs, use of a temporary or contingent workforce, and maximum control over processes and using it as a key competitive weapon.* Jobs are designed to be simple to ensure a constant and stable supply of employees and reduce training costs. To ensure uninterrupted production and eliminate all uncertainties, employees are expected to behave in a prescribed manner.

Paternalistic Strategy. In a **paternalistic strategy**, *some minimal degree of training and competency building through training, job rotation, etc. is done with the objective of achieving flexibility of staffing and task assignments and maintaining workforce stability.* Management typically provides to labour some employment guarantees as well as a system of internal staffing, normally based on seniority.[75]

Collaborative Strategy. An organization using a **collaborative strategy** *relies on highly skilled contract labour to supply the needed specialized staff by hiring them on an "as-needed" basis or retaining them on an "on-call" basis.* These highly skilled and specialized "crafts" people[76] are, most often, solely evaluated on the basis of their performance outcomes. Often, this is a strategy of choice by "virtual organizations."[77]

As already noted, no single organization may neatly or fully fall into any one of the above categories; further, the same organization may employ multiple strategies at different stages of its life cycle or when dealing with different labour markets. HR strategies will show variation depending on the organization's size and overall strategy, the nature of its environments, and the type of technology in use.

To be effective, a strategy should also have clearly defined action plans with target achievement dates (see Figure 1-11). Otherwise, it will simply end up being an exercise on paper.

Step 6: Review and Evaluation of Human Resource Strategies

Human resource strategies, however effective they prove to be, must be examined periodically. An organization's contextual factors, such as technology, environments, government policies, and so on, change continuously; so do several of its internal factors, such as membership characteristics, role definitions, and internal procedures. All these changes necessitate periodic strategy evaluation to ensure their continued appropriateness.

For example, a study by Statistics Canada reported that attempts at innovative HR have actually increased labour turnover in Canadian manufacturing operations. The study examined how six specific alternative work practices—problem-solving teams, self-managed teams, flexible job design, profit sharing, merit pay, and formal training on team work—affect turnover. While the professionals have always argued that innovative practices cause lower turnover, this particular study did not support the claim.[78]

Since 2005, Hewlett-Packard has carried out formal research to identify links between employee experience and the firm's operational performance. The company grouped employees based on their function, recognizing that certain functions have more direct impact on operational outcomes. Results from the study indicate that "effective collaboration" combined with "empowerment to make decisions" tend to be related to customer attitudes.[79]

Results of program evaluation such as the above produce valuable *feedback*, which is information that helps evaluate success or failure. Such information, in turn, helps the firm to fine tune its practices or even abandon some actions that do not seem to have performance potential. Alternatively, in the case of successful projects, additional resources can be allocated to them to reap full benefits. Consider the situation faced by Natalie Marchand, human resources manager at Municipal General Hospital:

A predicted shortage of medical technologists caused Natalie to start an in-house development program to prepare six lab assistants to become licensed medical technologists. After 15 months, they finished the program and passed the provincial certification test. Since the program was a success and the shortage had grown worse, eight more lab assistants were recruited for the second program.

The objective here was to achieve the organizational objective of finding qualified medical technologists. The strategy employed by the human resource manager was an in-house development program. When all six technologists passed the provincial certification test, those results provided feedback that the strategy was a success.

FIGURE 1-11	Metro Hospital's Strategic Approach to Human Resource Management

Background Information

Metro Hospital, a large hospital in a major Canadian city, currently faces an 18 percent turnover among its nursing staff. In fact, the turnover among nurses has been on the increase in the last two years. Kim Cameron, the hospital's newly appointed human resource manager, would like to reverse this trend and bring down the turnover rate to under 5 percent in the near future. As a first step, she looked through all available company records to find out more about the background of nurses who left the organization. She interviewed 14 nurses who had left the hospital recently and another 10 nurses who are currently employed in the hospital. Here are some of Cameron's findings:

- Forty percent of the nurses who left the hospital commented that their supervisors did not "treat them well"; only about 25 percent of the nurses who are currently with the hospital made the same comment.

- Six of the nurses who left and five of the present staff complained that the heating and air conditioning systems in the hospital do not work well so that it is very hot inside the hospital in the summer months and too cold in the winter.

- Fifty-five percent of those she talked to said that the fringe benefits in the hospital were not as good as elsewhere, while the salary level was found to be similar to that available elsewhere.

- Research of hospital records indicated that only about 10 percent of the nursing supervisors had undergone any type of supervisory leadership skills training in the past.

Kim Cameron's Objective

After her initial research, Kim Cameron identified the following as one of her major objectives for the immediate future: "To reduce the turnover among nursing staff from the present 18 percent to 4 percent by July 1, 2010, by incurring costs not exceeding $—— (at current dollars)."

Kim Cameron's Overall Strategy

To achieve the above goal, Kim Cameron realized that it was critical that the overall job satisfaction of nurses (especially their satisfaction with supervisors, working conditions, and rewards) be monitored and improved (if necessary). She set out the following action plans for the immediate future for herself and others in her department.

Kim Cameron's Action Plans

Action Number	Action Description	Person Responsible for Action	Date by Which Action to Be Completed	Budget Allocated
1.	Conduct an attitude survey among all nurses; collect information on their attitudes toward their job, supervisor, pay, benefits, working conditions, and colleagues	Asst. HRM	31-3-2009	$5,000
2.	Identify steps for improving morale among nurses	Self (in consultation with others)	30-5-2009	——
3.	Ask physical plant to check condition of A/C and heating systems	Self	25-1-2009	——
4.	Complete training program for 50 percent of nursing supervisors	Training manager	15-2-2010	$9,000
5.	(Depending on the survey findings, other actions that have to be initiated will be listed here.)			
6.				

Proactive Human Resource Management Strategies

Strategic human resource management often enables an organization to anticipate a problem and respond to it before it can cause serious damage to the organization. For example, reconsider Natalie Marchand's situation when she learned of the impending shortage of technologists:

Natalie Marchand: My department budget must be increased by $20,000 so we can train more technologists.

Anna Newman: Hold on! The municipality has put a freeze on the hospital budget for six months and as director of administrative services my hands are tied. Why not wait until we can show the Municipal Council complaints from the doctors? Then the shortage will be real and we can get the board to react to it now.

Natalie Marchand: But then we will probably have to spend $25,000 for training. We will probably have to pay another $30,000 for overtime to the technologists we now have while we train new ones. Besides, with all that overtime, error rates will jump and so will lawsuits for faulty lab work. All I need is $20,000, but I need it now.

Anna was suggesting that Natalie's department wait until an actual problem occurred and then react. Natalie wanted to take action in anticipation of the problem without waiting for the feedback of doctors' complaints or lawsuits. Anna's approach to this human resource challenge was **reactive**, while Natalie's was **proactive**.

Reactive human resource management occurs when decision makers respond to human resource problems. Proactive human resource management occurs when human resource problems are anticipated and corrective action begins before the problem exists. For example:

A large electronics firm uses contract labour to staff its human resource needs during periods of peak business activity. During peak demand, some of the workers it uses will be contracted from a temporary help agency. Not only can the agency provide extra staff more quickly, but these agency workers also do not become the firm's employees. The result is that the human resource department is able to meet the staffing needs of its divisions while providing high levels of employment security to its own employees.

The policy of using contract labour is another example of how proactive strategies can better meet the needs of organizations. In the example of the electronics firm, the human resource department did not wait for the economy to go up or down and then react. Rather, it developed strategies that allowed the organization to adjust smoothly to changes caused by technology, the economy, and other factors beyond its control.

reactive
A management approach wherein decision makers respond to problems rather than anticipate them.

proactive
A management approach wherein decision makers anticipate problems and likely challenges and take action before a problem occurs.

THE ORGANIZATION OF HUMAN RESOURCE MANAGEMENT

The responsibility for human resource management (HRM) activities rests with each manager. If a manager does not accept this responsibility, then human resource activities may be done only partially or not at all. When a manager finds that HRM work seriously disrupts other responsibilities, this work may be reassigned. The assignment might be to a worker or a specialized department that handles human resource matters. This process of getting others to share the work is called delegation. But delegation requires the manager to assign duties, grant authority, and create a sense of responsibility; if these three elements are not explained clearly to the delegate, delegation often fails. And even though others may have been asked to handle human resource activities, the manager still remains responsible. Delegation does not reduce a manager's responsibility; it only allows the sharing of that responsibility with others.

For example, many managers ask a senior worker to train new employees. However, if the senior worker errs and the new employee makes a costly mistake, the manager will appropriately be held responsible by superiors.

A separate department usually emerges only when human resource activities would otherwise become a burden to other departments in the organization—that is, when the expected benefits of a human resource department usually exceed its costs. Until then, managers handle human resource activities themselves or delegate them to subordinates. When a human resource department emerges,

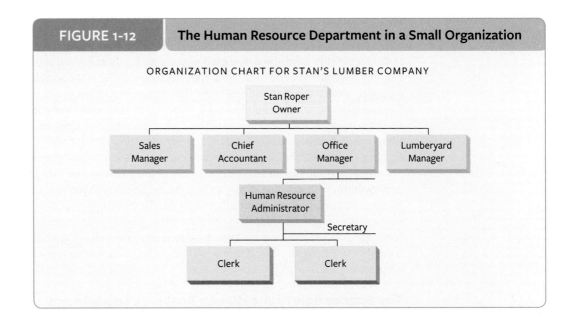

FIGURE 1-12 **The Human Resource Department in a Small Organization**

ORGANIZATION CHART FOR STAN'S LUMBER COMPANY

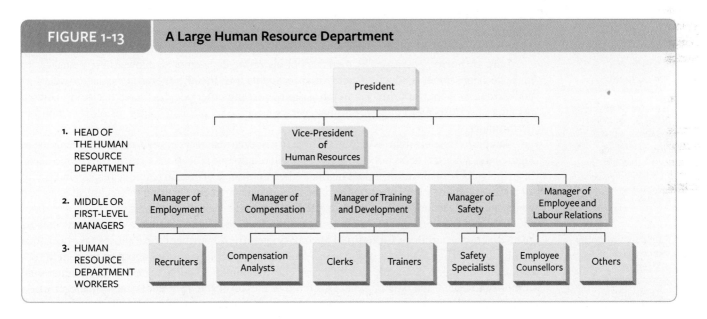

FIGURE 1-13 **A Large Human Resource Department**

1. HEAD OF THE HUMAN RESOURCE DEPARTMENT

2. MIDDLE OR FIRST-LEVEL MANAGERS

3. HUMAN RESOURCE DEPARTMENT WORKERS

Competencies Needed by Human Resource Professionals
www.tbs-sct.gc.ca/tal/comp-eng.asp

it is typically small and reports to some middle-level manager. Figure 1-12 illustrates a common placement of a human resource department at the time it is first formed. The activities of such a department are usually limited to maintaining employee records and helping managers find new recruits. Whether the department performs other activities depends upon the needs of other managers in the firm.

As demands on the department grow, it increases in importance and complexity. Figure 1-13 demonstrates the increased importance by showing the head of human resources reporting directly to the chief operating officer, who is the company president in this figure. The greater importance of the head of human resources may be signified by a change in title to vice-president. In practice, increased complexity also results as the organization grows and new demands are placed on the department, or jobs in the department become more specialized. As the department expands and specializes, it may become organized into highly specialized subdepartments.

The size of the human resource department varies widely, depending largely on the size of the organization being supported. One study reported a high ratio of workers to human resource employees of 277 to 1. The low ratio in that study was 29:1.[80] Another study reported an average of 36 human resource professionals per 1,000 employees for a ratio of 28:1.[81] By and large, a ratio of 1:100 (i.e., 1 human resource staff to 100 employees) may be adequate in most settings.

Departmental Components

The subdepartments of a large human resource department approximately correspond with the activities already mentioned. For each major activity, a subdepartment may be established to provide the specialized service, as shown in Figure 1-13. The employment department assists other managers with recruiting and selection. The compensation manager establishes fair pay systems. The training and development manager provides guidance and programs for those managers who want to improve their human resources. Other activity managers contribute their expertise and usually report directly to the head of human resources. This specialization allows members of the department to become extremely knowledgeable in a limited number of activities.

Activities not shown in Figure 1-13 are shared among the different sections. For example, employment, training, and development managers may share in human resource planning and placement. Performance appraisals are used to determine pay, and so the compensation division may assist managers in appraising performance. Required services fall to the benefits and safety sections. Control activities (communications and counselling) are divided among all subdepartments, with employee and labour relations doing much of the work. Employee and labour relations sections also provide the official union–management coordination.

The Service Role of the Human Resource Department

Human resource departments are service departments. They exist to assist employees, managers, and the organization. Their managers do not have the authority to order other managers in other departments to accept their ideas. Instead, the department has only **staff authority**, which is the authority to advise, not direct, managers in other departments.

Line authority, possessed by managers of operating departments, allows these managers to make decisions about production, performance, and people. It is the operating managers who normally are responsible for promotions, job assignments, and other people-related decisions. Human resource specialists merely advise line managers, who alone are ultimately responsible for employee performance.

Sample job responsibilities of line and human resource managers in key areas are summarized in Figure 1-14. While the list is not exhaustive and will require modifications to meet the unique needs of an individual organization, it does highlight the importance of human resource responsibilities of all managers. In most organizations, human resource departments provide the technical expertise while line managers use this expertise to effectively manage their subordinates.

In highly technical or extremely routine situations, the human resource department may be given functional authority. **Functional authority** gives the department the right to make decisions usually made by line managers or top management. For example, decisions about fringe benefits are technically complex, so the top manager may give the human resource department the functional authority to decide the type of benefits offered to employees. If each department manager made separate decisions about benefits, there might be excessive costs and inequities. To provide control, uniformity, and the use of expertise, functional authority allows human resource specialists to make crucial decisions effectively.

The size of the department affects the type of service provided to employees, managers, and the organization. In small departments, the human resource manager handles many of the day-to-day activities related to the organization's human resource needs. Other managers bring their problems directly to the head of human resources, and these meetings constantly remind the human resource manager of the contribution expected.

When the human resource function grows larger, more problems are handled by subordinates. Not only do human resource managers have less contact with lower-level managers, but others in the department become increasingly specialized. At this point, human resource managers and their subordinates may lose sight of the overall contributions expected of them or the limits on their authority. Experts sometimes become more interested in perfecting their specialty than in asking how they may serve others. While improving their expertise, they may fail to uncover new ways of serving the organization and its employees. Consider what happened at a fast-growing maker of minicomputers:

> For the past five years, Imaxum Computers Ltd. had grown at an average rate of 25 percent a year. To keep up with this growth, the HR department manager, Earl Bates, used budget increases to hire new recruits. His strategy meant that the human resource department was well prepared to

staff authority
Authority to advise, but not to direct, others.

line authority
Authority to make decisions about production, performance, and people.

functional authority
Authority that allows staff experts to make decisions and take actions normally reserved for line managers.

FIGURE 1-14	Sample Job Responsibilities of Line and Human Resource Managers	
Sample Activity	**Line Manager**	**Human Resource Manager**
Human resource planning	Provide details of all job positions and associated skills needed to human resource manager. Identify training needs of employees and communicate to the human resource department.	All activities associated with human resource planning. More specifically: • Translate organization needs into forecast of people required (both type and number). • Forecast potential supply of qualified workers from internal and external sources. • Plan strategies to match supply with demand.
Job analysis	Provide all necessary data to conduct job analysis. Identify performance standards and communicate to human resource department. Collaborate with the human resource manager in preparation of job description and specifications.	Conduct job analysis. Prepare job description and specification in collaboration with the line manager.
Recruitment and selection	Provide details of performance standards and job success and skill factors. Interview job applicants. Integrate the information collected by HR department and make a final decision on hires.	Ensure compliance with human rights laws and organization's policy on employment equity. Plan and actual conduct of all activities related to hiring, interviewing, and communication with job applicants.
Development and evaluation	Provide on-the-job training. Provide orientation to the job and coworkers. Implement job enrichment and enlargement programs. Offer timely and valid appraisal of subordinates and communication to the human resource department. Promote and transfer employees using agreed-upon criteria. Coach subordinates.	Facilitate accurate and timely appraisal. Provide orientation to the organization and its policies. Arrange for technical and management development programs. Offer organizational development activities. Develop valid appraisal programs in collaboration with line managers. Keep accurate records of each employee's skills, past training, and work accomplishments and make these available to line managers. Offer career counselling to employees.
Compensation and safety	Decide on pay raises to employees on the basis of merit or other agreed-upon criteria. Provide technical safety training. Enforce all safety regulations. Ensure fair treatment of employees. Provide all necessary data for accurate job evaluation.	Oversee compensation policy and administration. Provide safety training and ensure compliance with safety rules. Provide job evaluation. Offer retirement counselling. Oversee benefit planning and administration.
Employee and labour relations	Ensure noise-free communication to employees. Discipline and discharge from own unit after due warnings. Implement motivational strategies. Implement organizational change. Coach employees. Provide conflict resolution. Promote teamwork.	Conduct employee surveys to assess satisfaction with organizational policies and initiate corrective actions. Provide outplacement service. Offer career counselling. Establish grievance handling procedures. Negotiate with unions. Initiate organizational change efforts.

find new employees. But the recruiting specialists paid little attention to other human resource problems. In one month, three of the company's best computer design engineers quit to go to work for a competitor. Before they left, they were interviewed. They complained that they saw desirable job openings being filled by people recruited from outside the organization. No design engineer had been promoted to supervisor in three years. So each of these engineers found jobs where the promotion possibilities looked better.

When Earl reminded these engineers that they lacked experience or training as supervisors, one of them commented that the company should have provided such training. As a result, when the HR department received its next budget increase, Earl hired a specialist in employee training and development.

The human resource manager and the recruiting specialists at Imaxum Computers overlooked the variety of activities that their department is supposed to perform. And they failed to identify the services that the organization needs from the human resource department. They also did not recognize the connection between different human resource management activities.

To be effective, human resource specialists must determine the areas of concern of different levels of management and different departments of the organization. Otherwise, their advisory authority will be less effective and more likely ignored.

Human Resource Function and the Organization Character

Every organization has a unique history and way of doing business. As already pointed out, organization character refers to the sum of an organization's history, culture, philosophy, and unique ways of doing things. To be effective, a human resource manager must recognize the organizational character and the constraints imposed by it on its own function. Three factors that are related to an organization's character are particularly noteworthy here: technology, managerial philosophy, and strategic posturing.

Technology

The technology employed by different firms shows considerable variation. In organizations such as a large steel factory or lumber mill, the production processes are fairly routine. In several such organizations, improving predictability of operations assumes great importance. This often requires human resource managers to focus more on predictability of employee performance (e.g., by providing explicit job descriptions, job-specific training, and focusing on performance monitoring). In contrast, in firms with nonroutine production processes (such as advertising firms and software developers), flexible human resource practices that foster creativity, innovation, and entrepreneurship may add more value.

Managerial Philosophy

Often, several key managerial decisions and values are a "given" for the human resource manager. In some organizations, the top management may follow an autocratic decision-making style and foster a strong organizational hierarchy. In contrast, other organizations consciously make an effort to create an egalitarian, participative, and entrepreneurial work climate. HR practices such as seniority- and rank-based pay and top-down communication channels are likely to work best in the former situation while results-oriented (and competency-based) pay and up-and-down communication channels are likely to work best in the latter instance.

The managerial philosophy also influences the type of organization structure and the HR department's role within the firm. For instance, in a highly formal bureaucracy that is structured along functional lines (e.g., marketing, finance, production, etc.), HR's role is often to preserve the existing division of work through clear job descriptions, hiring of specialists for each division, and introducing training systems that foster functional expertise. In contrast, in organizations that have flexible structures, socialization of employees to create an organizationwide perspective, creation of broad job classes, etc. may assume greater importance. Finally, an **organizational culture** or the core beliefs and assumptions that are widely shared by all organizational members, shape work-related and other attitudes and significantly influence overall job commitment and performance. Clearly, human resource management has a role in shaping this; however, even here, the culture has to be consistent with the overall mission and strategy of the organization concerned.

organizational culture
The core beliefs and assumptions that are widely shared by all organizational members.

Organization's Strategic Posturing

In the preceding pages, we looked at the impact of strategic differences on the role of human resource function. Organizations differ on other strategic dimensions as well. For example, some organizations are *defenders*[82]—or conservative business units that prefer to maintain a secure position in relatively stable product or service areas instead of attempting to expand into uncharted territories. In contrast, some other organizations are *prospectors* that emphasize growth, entrepreneurship, and an eagerness to be the first players in a new market or selling a new product, even if some of these efforts fail. Human resource managers in a defender organization are more likely to be asked to support control systems, emphasize reliability and predictability in operations, and foster employee policies that encourage long-term employee attachment to the firm. In contrast, human resource managers in prospector organizations are more likely to be asked to foster a flexible, decentralized organizational structure, emphasize creativity and adaptability, and support systems that reward risk taking and performance.

Before concluding this section, it should be emphasized that human resource management is the management of people. Thus, human resource management should be carried out professionally—in fact, humanely! The importance and dignity of human beings should not be ignored for the sake of expediency. Only through careful attention to the needs of employees do organizations grow and prosper.

○ TODAY'S HUMAN RESOURCE MANAGEMENT PROFESSIONAL

In the last decade or so, there has been an enormous increase in the number of human resource managers. In 1971, there were only 4,055 human resource managers in this country; in 1999, the corresponding number was estimated to be over 43,000.[83] However, the status of human resource professionals within organizations historically has not been high. In a national survey of chief human resources officers, it was found that only 60 percent of respondents report directly to the chief executive officers and only 62 percent were members of their organization's executive committee.[84]

Thus, despite its enormous growth, human resource management has been slow to evolve into a full-fledged profession. Until recently in many Canadian provinces, there were no minimum qualifications for practising as a human resource professional. Since the actual capability of practising human resource experts varies widely, it became increasingly evident that professionalism of the human resource management field was needed. To meet these ever-increasing challenges, human resource managers were expected to possess a number of competencies, including the following:[85]

- **Business Mastery.** HR professionals must know the business of their organization thoroughly and recognize and incorporate financial and economic realities into their analyses and decisions. They should understand and foster customer orientation and be familiar with external realities and challenges facing the organization and the larger industry.

- **Mastery of Human Resource Management Tools.** As professionals, they should be familiar with state-of-the-art tools in areas such as staffing, training, compensation planning, performance appraisal and planning, employee relations and communication, and organizational change interventions. Along with CHRP designation, an MBA or Master's degree with specialization in HR is considered a very attractive background for HR professionals who are looking to climb the executive ranks.[86]

- **Change Mastery.** Not only should HR professionals possess an abundance of problem-solving, critical thinking, negotiation, and interpersonal skills, they should also be well versed in using these to bring about changes in the organization and its various subsystems. Strong communication skills combined with strong networking skills facilitate HR managers' attempts to influence others;[87] reputation as a team player is a necessary prerequisite in most settings for successful change initiatives.

- **Personal Credibility.** The HR professional should project an image of a trustworthy, ethical, socially responsive, courageous leader who can build relationships and inspire others to work for larger causes.

**Human Resources
Professionals Association**
www.hrpa.ca

To achieve this goal, accreditation and/or certification of the HR professional was considered as an imperative. In the past, provinces had held widely varying accreditation requirements.

Canadian Council of Human Resource Associations
www.cchra.ca

For example, in Ontario, the certification, in the past, was based on a candidate successfully completing specific academic requirements, passing a comprehensive examination, and having three years' managerial experience. In British Columbia, a greater number of years of work experience was typically expected, especially for candidates with lower levels of formal education.[88] This disparity had encouraged a move toward a set of uniform national standards for HR practitioners. The Canadian Council of Human Resource Associations (CCHRA) is a collaborative effort of Human Resource Associations across Canada that currently represents the interests of all HR practitioners in this country.

Based on extensive national and regional consultations with employers, human resource professionals and researchers, CCHRA has identified a set of "required professional capabilities" (RPCs) in key HR areas such as compensation, staffing, and employee relations apart from possessing skills in fundamental business areas, such as accounting (see Figure 1-15). While these standards are continually being reviewed and updated, Figure 1-15 provides a summary of the requirements for the **Certified Human Resources Professionals** (**CHRP**) designation.

For human resource staff in the civil service and government organizations, the accreditation body is the Canadian Public Personnel Management Association, which is based in Ottawa.

Certification alone does not make human resource management a profession or improve its status in the eyes of organizations. One approach to improving the human resource manager's status within the organization may be to strengthen the position's contribution to the enhancement of organizational performance and effectiveness. This is already beginning to take place. The higher status given to human resource experts in want ads and organizational charts indicates that the importance of human resource management activity is being recognized.

The typical business of tomorrow may bear little resemblance to that of 30 or 40 years ago. "It will be knowledge based, an organization composed largely of specialists who direct and discipline their own performance through organized feedback from colleagues, customers and headquarters."[89] The typical organization will be information based, and the intellectual capital (that is, the knowledge and expertise possessed by the employees) will spell success or failure. Already, jobs today demand a level of expertise unimagined 30 years ago. For managers, the challenge of managing intellectual capital lies in the fact that today's knowledge workers must be managed differently than in the past. New HR strategies, systems, and procedures are a must to succeed in this context. Continuous upgrading of his or her own skills and fostering an attitude of continuous learning may separate the superior HR manager from the mediocre one in the future.

Certified Human Resources Professionals (CHRP)
Human resource practitioner, formally accredited to practise, who reflects a threshold professional level of practice.

International Personnel Management Association for Human Resources
www.ipma-hr.org

⊙ THE FRAMEWORK USED IN THIS BOOK

This textbook is divided into seven parts.

Part 1: The Strategic Human Resource Management Model offers a strategic model of managing human resources in Chapter 1. The key objectives of the human resource function are outlined here along with the steps for implementing a strategic HR approach in practice.

Part 2: Planning Human Resources is contained in two chapters. Chapter 2 deals with the important topic of job analysis—detailing the various methods of collecting data about jobs, the steps involved in writing job descriptions and job specifications and setting performance standards. Chapter 3 discusses the various factors that need to be considered when planning the supply and demand for human resources in organizations.

Part 3: Attracting Human Resources deals with the various steps in acquiring human resources. Chapter 4 details key provisions of human rights legislation and the Canadian Constitution along with their implications for hiring employees. Chapters 5 (Recruitment) and 6 (Selection) deal with the various tools, options, and strategies open to the human resource manager in attracting and selecting qualified applicants for the job.

Part 4: Placing, Developing, and Evaluating Human Resources deals with all key activities involved in orienting, training, developing, and evaluating employees. Chapter 7 outlines the key steps involved in the orientation and training of employees; it also focuses on the development of employees to take on greater responsibilities in the future, including career counselling to staff. Chapter 8 deals with various appraisal techniques that help an organization to monitor and improve employee performance.

FIGURE 1-15	How to Obtain a Certified Human Resources Professional (CHRP) Designation*

In order to obtain the CHRP designation, candidates must successfully complete a series of steps. As of January 1, 2011, CHRP Candidates—those who have passed the National Knowledge Exam® (NKE)—will require a minimum of a Bachelor's degree from an accredited college or university in order to register for the National Professional Practice Assessment® (NPPA) and qualify for the CHRP designation.

Step One: Application for Association Membership

If you are not currently a member of a provincial CHRP designation granting HR association, you must apply for membership in the province or territory in which you reside. If there is no association where you reside, you may choose to join an association closest to your residence. In the case that you currently live outside Canada, you can attain membership in the provincial HR association of your choice. Your provincial HR association will provide details regarding various membership categories and fees. Once your membership application is approved, an information package, which includes material on CHRP certification, CHRP candidacy, and the CCHRA's National Code of Ethics will be forwarded to you.

Step Two: Pass the National Knowledge Exam

The National Knowledge Exam® (NKE) is a nationally regulated academic exam that tests your academic knowledge of the Required Professional Capabilities® (RPCs) HR's body of knowledge. Consisting of 150 multiple-choice questions, candidates choose the best of four possible answers. A minimum grade of 70 percent is required to pass. Upon successful completion of the exam, you will be recognized as a CHRP candidate. Prior to writing the NKE, you must first meet the prerequisites set by your provincial HR association.

The percentages against the various topics indicate relative emphasis in the exam.

Functional Dimensions	Weight
Professional Practice	24.0%
Organizational Effectiveness	8.3%
Staffing	19.8%
Employee & Labour Relations	10.4%
Total Compensation	10.4%
Organizational Learning, Training & Development	18.8%
Occupational Health, Safety & Wellness	8.3%
Total	100.0%

Step Three: Pass the National Professional Practice Assessment

(NOTE: At the time this book is going to print, HRPA is considering removing the NPPA and substituting it with a mandatory three years' work experience in HR area. The decision has not yet been finalized.)

The National Professional Practice Assessment® (NPPA) is a nationally recognized exam that tests your judgment of situations related to the RPCs, the HR profession's body of knowledge. CHRP candidates are tested on their ability to apply theory and knowledge to situations typically encountered by HR professionals. For each of the 45 scenarios based on real-life situations encountered by HR professionals, the candidate must select the most appropriate and the least appropriate of four possible solutions. Candidates should have at least three to five years of practical experience in human resources management prior to writing the exam. They must attain a minimum of 70 percent on the exam to pass. In order to obtain certification, the NPPA must be written within five years of passing the NKE.

The NPPA is quite different from the National Knowledge Exams in both format and focus. Although the NPPA questions are based on the same functional dimensions as RPCs, they are more experience-based. The chart below indicates the relative weight given to each functional dimension.

Functional Dimensions	Weight
Professional Practice	19.8%
Organizational Effectiveness	15.4%
Staffing	12.1%
Employee & Labour Relations	16.5%
Total Compensation	16.5%
Organizational Learning, Training & Development	8.8%
Occupational Health, Safety & Wellness	10.9%
Total	100.0%

The National Professional Practice Assessment is offered in the spring and fall of each year.

* Please note that these are the CHRP requirements as of April 9, 2009. There are impending changes to the requirements.

Source: "How to Obtain a CHRP Designation," www.cchra.ca/Web/certification/content.aspx?f=29788#Step1; accessed April 9, 2009. Used with permission of CCHRA.

SPOTLIGHT ON HRM
Will the 21st Century Belong to Canada?

The ingredients are all there, but human capital is the key.

Today it is recognized that natural, financial and technical resources no longer provide a sufficient basis for improving productivity at a rate equal to or better than other developed countries. These traditional foundations for productivity improvement are widely available globally through international trade and electronic commerce. In addition, we now understand that more money and technology do not by themselves increase productivity. It is the ability of people to effectively use these resources, through their knowledge and skills, that creates value and enhances results. [The] ... capability of people is seen as key to sustaining continuous improvement in productivity. This improvement depends on our ability to keep enhancing the knowledge and skills of people, using their knowledge and skills, and creating and disseminating new knowledge.

The challenge is that the productive capacity of people does not improve quickly. Developing expertise in any field takes years of development and experience. In addition, it takes time to adapt the organizational and cultural context in order to apply an individual's capability to the fullest. An added complexity is that people don't work in isolation—group or team dynamics are powerful forces impacting both behaviour and productivity in the workplace. In short, how well we develop and manage people is critical to sustaining significant improvements in productivity.

Productivity Depends on Investment

Increasing productivity must be viewed as a long-term investment in developing and using human capital. Investments need to take a wide range of forms with sustained effort over significant periods of time. They require continuing efforts by government, individuals and organizations. The most obvious form of investment is through education and training. To continue to improve productivity and living standards, Canada needs a well-educated workforce that is knowledgeable and skilled to fill jobs in the growing occupations.

Formal education programs need to focus on providing a liberal science education that prepares people entering the workforce for the 21st century. Employment rates and salaries are higher in the business, science, and technology fields, yet enrolment in these educational areas remains stagnant.

Training Is Everyone's Responsibility

As a society, we need to promote furthering the minimum education of everyone. Completing a quality secondary education must be the minimum education for every person in this country. ...

Organizations must also invest in the continuing development and specialized training of their employees. Organization-funded training must be seen as a long-term rather than a variable operating cost that is cut or reduced during poor economic times.

Individuals must also invest in improving their capabilities. We live in an age where continual change is the norm and life-long learning is no longer a vague concept or jargon from training professionals. ...

To sustain increasing levels of productivity, Canada must invest heavily in the research and developing of new knowledge in a broad range of disciplines.

Investment in developing new knowledge is really an investment in Canada's people and their future well-being. This not only keeps Canada's best and brightest at home, it also keeps the innovation and subsequent jobs within Canada.

To survive, all organizations invest in innovation, particularly around their products, services and core operating processes. Most organizations are also increasingly investing in new technology, especially information technology. Far fewer organizations have recognized the need for significant investment in the development of the human resource management systems, processes and capabilities. ...

In summary, to maintain our standard of living relative to other countries, Canada must reverse the current trend by making substantial, sustained investments in developing its human resources. Improving our standard of living in the 21st century will require world class human resource management capability.

Source: © *Canadian HR Reporter,* December 29, 1997, pp. 18–19, by permission of Carswell, Toronto, ON, 1-800-387-5164. Web site: www.hrreporter.com.

Part 5: Motivating Human Resources discusses the critical tasks of motivating and rewarding employees. Chapter 9 deals with direct compensation, including methods of evaluating the worth of each job and the incentive schemes currently available. Chapter 10 discusses how careful planning enables an organization to make the most out of its benefits package. It also deals with various work options and other arrangements that have implications for employee motivation.

Part 6: Maintaining High Performance focuses on the various human resource actions to ensure high performance. Chapter 11 details the methods of improving communication and enforcing discipline when employees violate organizational policies. Chapter 12 deals with the special challenges of managing a diverse workforce. Chapter 13 discusses two types of security offered by modern human resource departments: financial and physical. Chapter 14 discusses strategies for dealing with unions and outlines the human resource manager's role during negotiations with unions.

Part 7: Strategy Evaluation deals with the various approaches to assess the effectiveness of human resource strategy. The final chapter in this book discusses how a human resource department's contribution—and the effectiveness of its strategy—can be evaluated. Indices that measure an organization's success in human resource management are listed along with strategies for collecting data in each case.

SUMMARY

The central challenge for organizations today is to survive and prosper in a very turbulent world. To do this, most organizations find it necessary to maintain high productivity and effectiveness levels and have a global focus. Strategic management of organizations is suggested as one method for coping with this environmental turbulence. **Human resource management** *aims to improve the productive contribution of individuals while simultaneously attempting to attain other societal and individual employee objectives.* The field of human resource management thus focuses on what managers—especially human resource specialists—do and what they should do. While the role of human resource departments (HRDs) shows considerable variation across organizations, almost all HRDs carry out several common activities. These include

- assisting the organization to attract the right quality and number of employees;
- orienting new employees to the organization and place them in their job positions;
- developing, disseminating, and using job descriptions, performance standards, and evaluation criteria;
- helping to establish adequate compensation systems and administer them in an efficient and timely manner;
- fostering a safe, healthy, and productive work environment;
- ensuring compliance with all legal requirements insofar as they relate to management of workforce;
- helping to maintain a harmonious working relationship with employees and unions where present;
- fostering a work environment that facilitates high employee performance; and
- establishing disciplinary and counselling procedures.

Human resource departments in most organizations have three major objectives: to contribute to organizational effectiveness, to be responsive to larger societal concerns, and to meet the personal needs of the organization's employees. It was pointed out that human resource management is the responsibility of every manager. The human resource department provides a service to other departments in the organization. In the final analysis, however, the performance and well-being of each worker is the dual responsibility of that worker's immediate supervisor and the human resource department.

Strategic human resource management *is systematically linked to the strategic needs of an organization and aims to provide it with an effective workforce while meeting the needs of its members and other constituents in the society.* In contrast to strategies, human resource departments also employ varying tactics periodically. Tactics are methods, procedures, or systems employed by human resource professionals to achieve specific strategies. It is important that human resource strategies and tactics are mutually consistent. Even the best-laid strategies may fail if they are not accompanied by sound programs or procedures.

Strategic human resource management necessitates an exhaustive evaluation of an organization's internal and external environments. Factors that should be reviewed before formulating human resource strategies were discussed. These include economic, technological, demographic, and cultural challenges. Continuous evaluation of strategy and proactive management were pointed out as critical to ensure the successful management of human resources.

The profession of human resource management has undergone rapid changes in recent years as well. In some provinces, an accreditation process now exists that ensures that all human resource professionals possess minimum standards of expertise. While this will certainly elevate the status of the profession in the long term, the status of the function within an organization is likely to be determined by its contribution to the organization's overall success. Strategic management of human resources may be one key to this success.

⊙ TERMS FOR REVIEW

attitudes toward government **p. 20**
attitudes toward work **p. 16**
automation **p. 10**
Certified Human Resources
     Professionals (CHRP) **p. 36**
collaborative strategy **p. 28**
commitment strategy **p. 27**
compliance strategy **p. 28**
computerization **p. 8**
contract (or contingent)
     workers **p. 16**
cost leadership strategy **p. 25**
cultural mosaic **p. 19**
cultural challenges **p. 16**

data workers **p. 12**
demographic changes **p. 11**
differentiation strategy **p. 25**
economic challenges **p. 4**
educational attainment **p. 13**
employee objectives **p. 21**
focus strategy **p. 25**
functional authority **p. 32**
knowledge workers **p. 12**
line authority **p. 32**
mission statement **p. 24**
old age crisis **p. 15**
organization character **p. 24**
outplacement **p. 8**

outsourcing **p. 8**
organizational culture **p. 34**
organizational objectives **p. 21**
part-time workers **p. 16**
paternalistic strategy **p. 28**
proactive **p. 30**
productivity **p. 6**
reactive **p. 30**
societal objectives **p. 21**
staff authority **p. 32**
strategic human resource
     management **p. 22**
telecommuting **p. 9**

⊙ SELF-ASSESSMENT EXERCISE

How Knowledgeable Are You about Human Resource Management?

A successful human resource manager should possess knowledge in a number of areas, including job design, human resource planning, recruitment, selection and training of employees, and employee relations. The following self-test helps you assess your present knowledge level in some of these areas. Read each statement and indicate whether the statement is true or false.

1. A human resource manager should take corrective actions only after a problem has been crystallized and well understood.   **T   F**

2. When assigning jobs to employees, I should ensure that there is no significant variation in job challenges from one employee to the next.   **T   F**

3. Two experienced workers and three trainees can complete a project in 10 days; three experienced workers and two trainees can do the same project in 8 days. If I hire two experienced workers and one trainee, they should be able to complete the project in $11\frac{1}{2}$ days.   **T   F**

4. When designing a job application form, I should make sure to ask for the social insurance number of the applicant in order to complete the employee file.   **T   F**

5. When I visit campuses to recruit graduates, I should focus on the quality of education they received in the school rather than whether they meet specific job requirements.   **T   F**

6. When hiring an administrative assistant, the best way to assess the candidate's skills is by requiring the person to undergo a word processing or other performance test.   **T   F**

7. The best way to teach a person a new accounting program is to give a short lecture on the subject matter.   **T   F**

8. Measuring the students' learning before they begin this course and again at the end of the course may be a better indicator of this course's effectiveness rather than asking the students about their satisfaction level about what they learned in this course.   **T   F**

9. Today, in Canada, women and men get paid equally in all occupations.   **T   F**

10. If a person has to choose between two jobs that are alike in all respects, except that one job pays $45,000 in straight salary and the second one pays $35,000 in salary and $10,000 in benefits, the individual is better off accepting the second job.   **T   F**

SCORING

For statements 1, 2, 3, 4, 5, 7, and 9, if you answered false, you get one point each. For questions 6, 8, and 10, if you answered true, you get one point each. Add up your scores.

Scores of 8–10: Wow! You already know several important HR concepts. You can build on these by carefully studying the text chapters and actively participating in class discussions. You will also be a valuable source of information to others. So, participate actively in and outside the classroom!

Scores Less Than 8: As you read the various chapters in this text, you will find the rationale behind the above statements. (The question numbers correspond to the chapter in this book in which this material is discussed.) Human resource management is an exciting profession—it also means that several assumptions that are popularly considered to be true are not. Keep reading!

◆ REVIEW AND DISCUSSION QUESTIONS

1. What are the goals of a human resource department? Choose an organization that you are familiar with and indicate which of these goals will be more important in this organization and discuss why.

2. Draw a diagram of a human resource department in a firm that employs over 5,000 persons and name the likely components of such a department. Which of these functions are likely to be eliminated in a small firm employing 50 persons?

3. Identify and briefly describe three major external challenges (choosing one each from economic, technological, and demographic categories) facing human resource managers in Canada, and their implications.

4. Outline the three major strategies pursued by Canadian businesses. What implications do they have for the human resource function within the firms? Illustrate your answer with suitable examples.

5. What are four trends (or attributes) in the Canadian labour market that have implications for a human resource manager? Explain your answer, citing which of the human resource functions will be affected and how.

◆ CRITICAL THINKING QUESTIONS

1. Suppose your employer is planning a chain of high-quality restaurants to sell food products that it already produces. Outline which areas of human resource management will be affected.

2. If a bank is planning to open a new branch in a distant city, with what inputs will the human resource department be concerned? What activities will the department need to undertake in the transition to a fully staffed and operating branch? What type of feedback do you think the department should seek after the branch has been operating for six months?

3. Find two recent news items and explain how these developments might affect the demands made on the human resource department of an organization.

4. If the birthrate during the early 2000s was to double from the low rates of earlier decades, what are its implications in the years 2020 and 2030 for (a) grocery stores, (b) fast-food restaurants, (c) the Canadian Armed Forces, (d) large metropolitan universities?

5. Assume you were hired as the human resource manager in a firm that historically has given low importance to the function. Most of the human resource management systems and procedures in the firm are outdated. Historically, this function was given a low-status, "record-keeping" role within the firm. Armed with sophisticated HR training, you recently entered the firm and want to upgrade the HR systems and status of the department. In other words, you want to make the management recognize the true importance of sound HR practices for strategic success. What actions will you take in the short and long term to achieve your goal? Be specific in your action plans and illustrate your steps where relevant.

◆ ETHICS QUESTION

After graduation, you were hired as a management trainee in the human resource department of a large organization with widely held stock. Your boss, the human resource manager, is away on holidays and asked you to make all decisions in her absence, including the hiring of an assistant in your department. A senior manager in the company recently indicated to you how much he would like the position to be given to Bob, his nephew who had applied for the position. When you looked through the records, you found that while Bob meets the basic requirements, there were at least two other better candidates—a male far superior than Bob and a female. (Your firm had recently indicated a commitment to employment equity initiatives.) You realize that the senior manager has considerable influence in the company and may even be able to influence your career progress within the firm.

◆ WEB RESEARCH EXERCISE

Select three jobs: one knowledge-based, one manufacturing, and one in the service sector. Based on your search of Web sites of Human Resource and Social Development Canada, Statistics Canada, and other relevant Web sources, what patterns in employment and job vacancies do you see? What are the implications for large human resource departments in these industries?

➡ INCIDENT 1-1

Human Resource Decision Making at Calgary Importers Ltd.

Calgary Importers Ltd. (CIL) is a large importer of linens, china, and crystal from a number of Asian, European and South American countries. While nearly 55 percent of linens are imported from China, nearly 70 percent of crystals and diamond items originate in India. Most of the china comes from European and South American countries. Several other handicrafts and household products are imported from other East European countries and Japan. Different geographical offices of CIL specialize in different products; for example, the Toronto and Vancouver offices primarily deal with suppliers in India (specializing in different industry groups), while the Calgary office conduct all negotiations with South America. CIL's offices in Montreal and Halifax primarily deal with their European counterparts. Over time, management practices, including HR activities, in various CIL offices have begun to show considerable differences, posing problems for the senior managers. Recently, the following conversation took place between the vice-president of human resources and the vice-president of distribution.

Rob Whittier: You may not agree with me, but if we are going to have consistency in our human resource policies, then key decisions about those policies must be centralized in the human resource department. Otherwise, branch managers will continue to make their own decisions, focusing on different aspects. Besides, the department has the experts. If you needed financial advice, you would not ask your doctor; you would go to a banker or other financial expert. When it comes to deciding compensation packages or hiring new employees, those decisions should be left to experts in salary administration or selection. To ask a branch manager or supervisor to make those decisions deprives our firm of all of the expertise we have in the department.

Henri DeLahn: I have never questioned your department's expertise. Sure, the people in human resources are more knowledgeable than the line managers. But if we want those managers to be responsible for the performance of their branches, then we must not deprive them of their authority to make human resource decisions. Those operating managers must be able to decide whom to hire and whom to reward with raises. If they cannot make those decisions, then their effectiveness as managers will suffer.

1. If you were the president of Calgary Importers Ltd. and were asked to resolve this dispute, whose argument would you agree with? Why?
2. Can you suggest a compromise that would allow line managers to make these decisions consistently?

➡ INCIDENT 1-2

Canadian Bio-Medical Instruments Ltd.

Canadian Bio-Medical Instruments Ltd., founded 10 years ago, manufactures a variety of bio-medical instruments used by physicians and surgeons both in their clinics and in hospitals. The high quality of its products led to quick market success, especially for products such as artificial heart valves, operating-room pumps, and respiratory modules. The company, which had sales of less than $900,000 in the first year, today enjoys an annual turnover of $150 million. However, the industry is competitive and the research development and promotional budgets of some of the key players in the industry are several times that of the firm.

Given the successful track record for its existing products and the competitiveness of the North American market, the management of the firm believed that gaining new market shares in Europe was easier than expanding against well-entrenched domestic producers. Preliminary market studies supported management's thinking.

A decision was made to open a small sales office in Europe, probably in Frankfurt, Germany, given the nonstop flight facilities that currently exist from Toronto, where the firm's head office is located. Three employees were sent to Germany to identify possible office sites and to learn about European testing procedures and what documentation would be legally required to prove the safety and effectiveness of the company's medical instruments. All three employees were fluent in German. If the reports on Germany are favourable, the firm expects to have about 20 employees working in Europe within the next year.

1. Assume you are the vice-president in charge of human resources. What additional information would you want these three employees to find out?
2. What human resource issues or policies are you likely to confront in the foreseeable future?

CASE STUDY   🍁   Maple Leaf Shoes Ltd.

A Strategic Management Exercise*

Maple Leaf Shoes Ltd. is a medium-sized manufacturer of leather and vinyl shoes located near Wilmington, Ontario. It began operations in 1969 and currently employs about 400 people in its Ontario plant and 380 others in offices and warehouses across Canada and internationally.

History

Maple Leaf was the brainchild of Mario Mansini, an Italian immigrant who left his native country to begin a new life in Canada in the late 1950s. After a couple of unsuccessful ventures (a stage show and a sailboat business), Mansini hit upon the idea of starting a shoe factory. "As long as people walk, they need shoes," he is said to have told the bank, which asked for a financial guarantee, given his past failures. Though not well educated (he dropped out of Grade 8), Mansini was an extrovert and a flamboyant man who could impress and inspire others around him. In the end, his personality and optimism swayed the bank manager to extend a small loan for the new venture.

With the bank loan and financial assistance from some friends and relatives, Mansini built a small plant near Wilmington— two floors of shoes and about a dozen temporary sheds where employees lived and slept. In 1969, the firm formally opened for business.

What began as a small operation quickly grew into a regional and national operation. Despite his lack of education, Mansini was an astute businessman and he was also able to successfully recruit skilled workers. The folklore is that many of his erstwhile artist friends worked for practically no wages in his factory during the day and played music and rehearsed plays in the evenings. He had very close friendships with his employees, and many were willing to pitch in whenever he needed help. The firm quickly developed a reputation for quality footwear, especially shoes used for outdoor and sports purposes. Apart from a couple of major footwear firms in the United States, competition was virtually absent and the firm thrived.

Mansini worked long hours to make Maple Leaf a success. He was a loyal citizen (the firm's original name was Quality Footware; Mansini changed it to Maple Leaf Shoes). He also employed a paternalistic management style. He knew most workers by name and always took the time to inquire about their welfare. No one but Maple Leaf workers lived in the area where the factory was located. Over time, the location where Maple Leaf operated became unofficially known as "Leaf Town," although the closest town was Wilmington. For most workers, their houses were close enough to work to enable them to walk home for lunch. There was a Maple Leaf Grocery Store, Maple Leaf Recreation Hall, Maple Leaf teams, Maple Leaf Drug Store and Dispensary, and Maple Leaf Club for the higher echelon of the workforce. There was even a Leaf Cinema and Leaf Pub. Virtually everything was available in Leaf Town; residents only had to travel to nearby Wilmington for schools and medical assistance.

Consistent with his management style, Mansini had few organized procedures or systems in place. He noted: "If you lose touch with your men, you lose them. Systems come and go; people are more important." There were few formal procedures— each event was looked at for its unique features and responded to accordingly. Mansini often worked 15 to 18 hours— he was involved in most decisions including hiring of personnel, product planning, financing strategy, shoe design, and handling employee grievances. During his time, efforts were made by local and international unions to organize the workers; however, they were unsuccessful (in the most recent attempt, the union was able to get less than 10 percent of the workers to sign up).

But Mansini's first love was music and arts. So, when a national conglomerate approached him with an offer to purchase a controlling share of Maple Leaf in the mid-1980s, he was only too willing to sell it. "I don't have any children to take over the firm," he said. (He died a bachelor soon after the sale of the company; a part of his estate was donated to Leaf Art Guild and Sports Team and the remainder was divided among his relatives and the Canadian Cancer Society.) "In any case, how long can a man spend his life looking at what is under the feet rather than what is above?" he mused.

Since the Takeover

The group that took over the firm modernized the manufacturing operations and attempted to extend its operations both nationally and internationally. During these efforts, it found that many of the company's past practices were archaic and inefficient. There was an attempt to improve efficiency and gross margin. New equipment was installed and several routine activities were automated or otherwise mechanized to reduce costs. While attempts were also made to update management practices, the firm was slow in this regard. Unfortunately, there was also above-average turnover in the top management team in the company in the initial years. Robert Clark, who was hired as the CEO of the firm, has now been with the firm for eight years and holds a significant share of the company stock apart from holding options.

While Maple Leaf Shoes makes shoes of all kinds, descriptions, and sizes today, it specializes in the manufacture of women's and youth athletic shoes. The company's designers were successful in producing a product that was both stylish and yet comfortable to wear and durable. The firm's shoes, marketed under the brand names of *Fluffy Puppy*, *Cariboo*, and *Madonna*, were very popular among ladies in the 19–40 age group.

*Case prepared by Professor Hari Das of the Department of Management, Saint Mary's University, Halifax, Canada. All rights retained by the author. Das © 2002.

Its *Young Athlete* brand, aimed at boys and girls in the 9–14 age group, was a market leader in the children's sports shoes market in British Columbia. Historically, the shoes produced by the firm were cheaper than those of its competitors. This price advantage was a critical aspect of the company's marketing strategy in the past.

Emerging Challenges

Recently, the company has faced a number of issues that require immediate attention by its management. *First*, the cost of production at Maple Leaf Shoes has been rising slowly but steadily. Labour costs currently account for over 45 percent of manufacturing costs and have been increasing rapidly. The productivity levels of the employees have not shown any increase in the preceding three years. If the present trend continues, the firm is likely to lose its price advantage over its competitors. Already, for two out of six popular brands sold by Maple Leaf Shoes, the prices for the firm's products are equal to or higher than its competition. This has stalled the firm's growth and profitability. Some financial details of the firm are shown in Table 1. Figure 1 shows the firm's stock price during the preceding five years. The market reaction to the firm's potential has not been very positive, as indicated by the overall decline of its share price from a high of $25 about five years ago. The market meltdown in 2002 further worsened this picture, pulling the share price down to about $11, from which it has not yet recovered to any significant extent.

Second, over 60 percent of the company's staff are unionized. There are indications that remaining nonmanagerial staff are also about to be unionized. Management believes that this will reduce the already limited autonomy it possesses in hiring, terminating, and managing employees.

Third, in the recent past, competition in the shoe industry has been intense. Over the years, trade barriers across countries have disappeared, which has meant that cheaper, high-quality shoes made in countries such as Korea, Taiwan, Singapore, India, and Mexico pose serious competition to the firm within and outside Canadian markets. Despite this, Maple Leaf Shoes has been able to perform fairly well in the export markets. Currently, over 15 percent of its production is exported—mainly to western parts of the United States and Europe (the corresponding figure five years back was a tiny 2 percent). While the company increased its U.S. sales after the Canada–U.S. Free Trade Agreement, it is somewhat apprehensive about the future. Robert Clark, president of Maple Leaf Shoes, commented:

> The market has changed dramatically in the last five years. The Asians and the Chinese are fast conquering the world footwear market. How can we compete with the Malaysians, Thais, and the Indians, who pay a fraction of the wages we pay here? In China, from where most of the shoes sold in North America originate, the labour is cheap and employment standards are low. And mind you, those Asian workers are good. It will be a totally new game now with a new set of rules. ... We simply would not

be able to compete with them on labour costs ... but what we have on our side is technology. We will constantly need to think of new products and newer strategies if we are to survive.

The firm's past strategy of responding to these challenges has been to automate its manufacturing functions and to downsize. It has also sold off some of its non-performing assets and facilities and contracted out some of the services in a bid to cut costs. This strategy, while it has resulted in some improvements in the financial picture, has also brought with it negative union reaction and a decline in employee morale.

Maple Leaf recently signed an agreement with the producers of *Bumpy Bears*, a popular TV series aimed at young children. Under this agreement, the firm will have exclusive rights to reproduce the various animal characters seen in the show on its foot wear. *Ticky* the black bear, *Rumpy* the arctic bear, and *Moosy* the white bear are beloved characters in the show. This is expected to increase the sales of children's shoes; however, the embossing technology is expensive and may require initial heavy capital investments and additional training for some members of the workforce.

Finally, the need for managerial training is felt now more than ever. The firm expects its activities to grow; however, given market conditions, it is not keen on expanding the size of its managerial cadre significantly. Instead, it would like to provide managerial and team-management skills to more of its employees and empower them to make decisions.

In a recent interview, Robert Clark identified a number of issues that require immediate attention:

1. Contracts with two of the four unions in the company will expire in another eight months. The remaining two unions will not start their contract negotiations for another 18 months; however, what happens in the negotiations with these two unions could have a significant impact on all future contract negotiations. One of the unions with which negotiations are to begin soon, the Leather Workers' Association, recently elected a leader who is rumoured to be militant and highly focused on results. A strike in the immediate future could paralyze the firm, and it is doubtful whether the firm would recover from its debilitating results for quite some time.

2. Recently, two complaints of sex discrimination were filed by women employees. One complaint was settled internally in consultation with the concerned union, while the other had to go before the provincial Human Rights Commission. The decision of the commission was in favour of the employee who had filed the grievance.

3. The management of Maple Leaf Shoes believes that growth through expanded activities is critical now, especially given the competitive challenge. Growth is possible only by expanding its operations within and outside Canada. The management would like to expand its operations to Atlantic Canada and Quebec in the next three years—a new plant in Quebec is being considered

TABLE 1	Recent Financial Information on Maple Leaf Shoes Ltd.			
	Current Year	**Last Year**	**Year Before**	**3-Year Growth Rate**
Total revenue ($000)	1,512,904	1,461,604	1,488,840	1.45%
Earnings before interest and tax ($000)	65,645	65,772	59,200	8.06%
Profit/loss ($000)	26,258	29,597	29,008	–10.53%
Earnings per share	1.33	1.47	1.35	–7.85%
Dividends per share	0.30	0.33	0.35	
Total assets ($000)	617,814	622,469	660,241	
Number of employees	783	843	897	

for entry into that market because the product styling must be somewhat modified to meet the demands of the French market. It is felt that the same plant can produce footwear that can be exported to France and other parts of Europe. Currently, Maple Leaf shoes are sold (although in small numbers) in Belgium and Luxembourg. These markets were developed almost accidentally: a few years back, a cousin of Robert Clark, the president, took samples of *Young Athlete* shoes for display in his sports equipment shops in Belgium and Luxembourg; the shoes became popular locally. Maple Leaf Shoes also sells its shoes through a home-building and hardware store in England. However, about 80 percent of its foreign sales are in Oregon and California, where the shoes are displayed and sold through fashion boutiques.

4. Production levels in Maple Leaf Shoes have been continuously increasing; however, management has fought hard not to increase its workforce. The company currently uses a large number of part-time and contract workers for various services. While this strategy has resulted in some reduction in costs, it has also been accompanied by negative reactions from workers, supervisors, and unions.

This is expected to be a major issue during the next bargaining session.

5. As far as possible, the company attempts to fill managerial positions through internal promotions and transfers; however, this has meant that management training is more critical today than ever before.

6. In an effort to take advantage of cheap labour abroad, the firm, in the recent past, has attempted to enter into joint venture partnerships with firms in Indonesia, Mexico, and India. However, this has also resulted in exposing the firm to additional risks characteristic of international operations. While its negotiations with the Mexican and Indian partners have been proceeding according to schedule, its experience in Indonesia was less than satisfactory. The firm's Indonesian partner fell victim to the "Asian crisis" of 1997–98, when the Indonesian currency, the rupiah, fell by more than 33 percent in a matter of days. Its partner was on the verge of declaring insolvency. Maple Leaf is currently looking for another Indonesian partner.

Added to the above is the void created by the resignation of John McAllister, the personnel manager who left the firm to

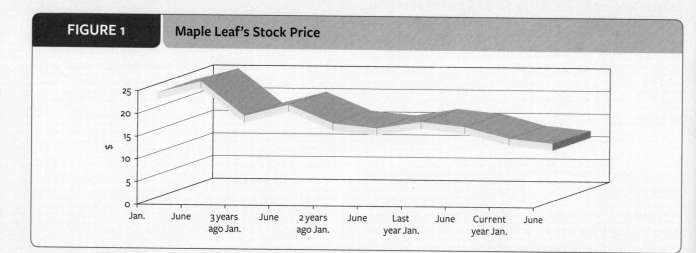

FIGURE 1 Maple Leaf's Stock Price

take up a similar position in the west. Currently, the position of personnel manager in the firm is vacant. Pat Lim, general manager (marketing), is currently in charge of the human resource function, although all routine decisions and procedures are handled by Jane Reynolds, special assistant to the personnel manager. (Indeed, because of increased national and international marketing activities, Lim is often away from the office.) Robert Clark recently decided to rename the function as "human resource manager" to reflect the increasing importance of the activity. The management recognizes that a number of human resource procedures and systems within the firm are antiquated and must be replaced; however, cost pressures and day-to-day priorities have prevented the firm from systematizing various HR functions such as hiring, orientation, training, appraisal, and compensation. The firm hopes to hire a new human resource manager (HRM, as the position is now called) in the near future, who will bring about the needed changes.

McAllister was with the company for only about three years. While he was credited with having "run a tight ship," several of his colleagues complained about his dominating and centralized leadership style. One of the managers went as far as saying that "*Maple Leaf Shoes would not have been unionized this fast and to this extent but for John.*" McAllister's predecessor, Tim Donovan, was not a popular personnel manager either. Donovan, who resigned his position after a mere ten-month stay at Maple Leaf Shoes, did not have positive things to say about the company and its management. On the eve of his departure, he is reported to have confided in an associate: "*The management system here is primitive. It's as if you are surrounded by forces of darkness. Of course, I could stay here and fight it out—maybe I would win in the end. But then I'm not masochistic!*"

Discussion Questions

1. What are some changes within Maple Leaf Shoes and in its environment that have caused a shift in its strategy? List the challenges facing the company using the classification provided in your text.

2. Assume that you are hired as a consultant to help the firm hire a new human resource manager. What immediate and long-term job responsibilities will you identify for the new job incumbent?

3. Identify three sample objectives of the human resource department at Maple Leaf Shoes and list associated strategy and action plans to be implemented by the department.

➡ CASE STUDY CPIB Canadian Pacific and International Bank*

Canadian Pacific and International Bank (CPIB) is one of Canada's premier financial institutions, with assets of over $150 billion. CPIB, which began as a "western" bank in the early 1950s with its head office in Vancouver, British Columbia, spread its operations all over Canada and the United States by the mid-1960s. Originally called Pacific and Western Bank, the bank changed its name about 15 years ago to reflect its international character. Today, more than 25,000 employees provide personal, commercial, corporate, and investment banking services to individuals and businesses in 33 countries. Some recent financial and employee statistics for CPIB are shown in Figure 1.

CPIB, through its strategic initiatives, was successful in building long-term value for its shareholders while providing regular return on their investments. The market price of CPIB's share increased by over 40 percent in the preceding two years, bringing the bank's total market capitalization to nearly $18 billion, up from $10 billion just a few years back. In the current year, the share price has remained more or less static largely due to investor preferences for Internet stocks over "conservative" bank stocks.

Globally, CPIB serves more than 6 million customers in three key areas: personal and commercial banking, wealth management, and wholesale and corporate banking—marketed under the name CPIB Securities (see Figure 2).

Personal and Commercial Banking: Through its 673 retail outlets, CPIB offers a wide variety of products and services.

In addition, *CP Anytime*, CPIB's electronic banking service, offers customers access to retail products, services, and accounts via telephone banking. The 1781 automated banking machines that form the Purple Touch network, CP Web Banking, and CP Day-Night Investor provide service around the clock. In a recent independent survey, the bank was cited as number two in four out of seven dimensions of customer service, including friendliness and customer responsiveness. The bank aims to further enhance customer service levels and flexibility (e.g., a single-number dial or a single Web site to meet all retailing and investment needs of small-volume customers). Through such efforts, it aims to build market share in small and medium-sized businesses.

Wealth Management: CPIB's wealth management business includes its discount brokerage and mutual fund operations. CPIB Investment is one of Canada's leading discount brokerages, currently with over 1 million customer accounts in the United States and Canada and a growing clientele in Australia, the United Kingdom, and Japan. Although smaller than TD Canada Trust's TD Waterhouse Group or Royal Bank's Action Direct, CPIB is attempting to make fast inroads into this highly competitive but lucrative sector of banking. Historically, CPIB had charged lower commissions ($25 for most transactions compared to $29 charged by TD Waterhouse and Action Direct). In the near future, the firm plans to increase its market penetration ratio. Currently, CPIB manages nearly $24 billion in mutual funds, pension funds, trusts, and endowments. In the

*Case written by Professor Hari Das of the Department of Management, Saint Mary's University, Halifax, Canada. All rights retained by the author © 2002.

near future, the bank wants to reorganize and integrate wealth management activities to improve customer service and sales support for all products.

CPIB Securities: CPIB offers a full range of services to its clients in all key areas of finance and specialized solutions for corporate and government clients. Included here are investment

FIGURE 1	Summary of Financial and Employee Statistics			
	This Year	**Last Year**	**Year Before**	**3-Year Growth**
Total revenue ($000)	13,442,571	11,309,142	8,979,429	20.02%
Earnings before interest and tax ($000)	3,980,571	2,806,286	2,435,143	26.16%
Profit/loss ($000)	2,555,143	960,857	932,571	48.12%
Earnings per share	4.20	1.55	1.52	49.17%
Total assets ($000)	183,786,000	155,855,140	140,444,570	18.18%
Dividends per share	0.62	0.57	0.48	
Return on equity	27.39	12.77	14.05	
Employees	25,059	26,594	24,500	

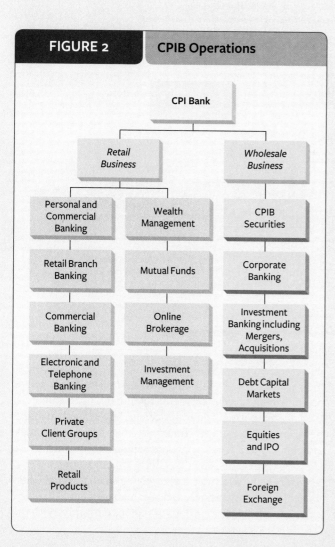

FIGURE 2 — CPIB Operations

banking (which includes merchant banking, corporate banking, and syndications), foreign exchange, loans, debt capital markets (including initial public offerings and underwritings), mergers and acquisitions, and derivatives. In a recent ranking by a business magazine of North American firms offering integrated corporate services, CPIB was rated eighth in North America. The bank's priorities continue to be developing stronger client relationships, expanding industry specialty groups, and achieving maximum operating efficiency.

Organization of the Bank

Since CPIB is an extremely large organization with operations in over 30 countries, the overall structure of the bank is very complex and not easily depicted. It also varies somewhat from one country to another to better respond to the local realities and challenges.

The chair and chief executive officer of the bank is Michael Bennett, who is also chair of the board of directors to which he is accountable. The 18-member board (17 men, 1 woman) represents a cross-section of top leaders in manufacturing and service industries and academic and professional institutions in Canada. The board has several committees entrusted with special tasks. Examples: *audit and risk management committee*, which, among other duties, reviews the audited financial statements and approves policies related to risk and liquidity management and internal control; *management resources committee*, which reviews and approves senior office appointments and executive compensation plans; and *corporate governance committee*, which, among other activities, deliberates on the board composition and functioning. CPIB's hybrid organizational structure attempts to maximize the advantages of

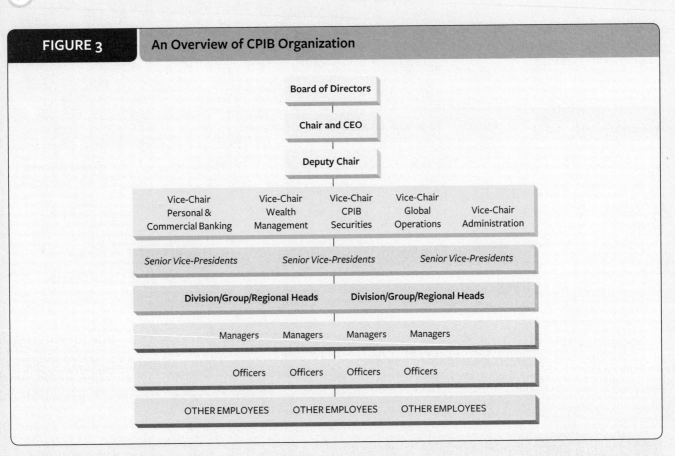

FIGURE 3   **An Overview of CPIB Organization**

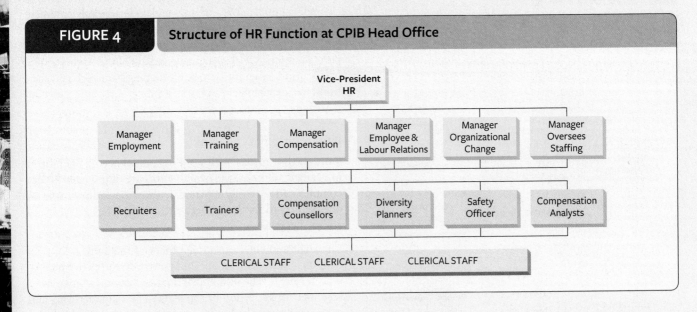

FIGURE 4   **Structure of HR Function at CPIB Head Office**

functional, product-based, and geographic structures (see Figure 3). The bank has a 472-page manual that describes in detail the position descriptions and required competencies of various managerial positions.

The chair, assisted by a deputy chair and five vice-chairs, approves all critical decisions affecting the bank's future. Three of the vice-chairs are in charge of personal and commercial banking, wealth management, and CPIB Securities; the fourth is in charge of global operations and the last

one in charge of overall administration. The seven senior vice-presidents are in charge of retail banking, commercial banking, mutual funds and brokerage, investment management, corporate and investment banking, human resources, and global operations. Below the senior vice-presidents are heads of various divisions including human resources, economic analysis, securities and foreign exchange, retail banking, real estate operations, and risk management. There are 36 heads of divisions or groups or regions currently. With the bank's expansion into electronic banking and foreign markets, more group heads and even vice-presidents may have to be hired in the near future. The three foreign division heads are located outside Canada: Asian Division in Singapore, European Division in London, and Middle East and African Division in Istanbul.

For ease of administration and to better respond to customer requirements, the domestic banking is divided into five regions (head offices in parentheses): Atlantic (Halifax), Quebec (Montreal), Ontario (Toronto), Prairie (Winnipeg), and Pacific (Vancouver). The corporate head office is also located in Vancouver. Several other functions are centralized at the head office to reap economies of scale and facilitate communication. Example: CP Economics Division that monitors Canadian and world economic trends and prepares routine and special reports for use by the bank in its various investment and client divisions. Some of the other functions (e.g., CP Ombudsperson) are located at the head office but with strong regional presence and frequent meetings with staff at various regions and branches to better respond to their queries and proactively deal with emerging issues or likely problems.

Corporate Strategies

CPIB, which is known for its ability to capitalize on opportunities, was one of the first Canadian banks to enter Asian and Latin American markets, introduce automated tellers throughout Canada, begin a Web-based brokerage, and offer integrated wealth management and financial counselling services. Its extensive online delivery of wealth management and banking services has made CPIB a key player in the development of ecommerce and places it in the top dozen financial services firms in the world as measured by the number of online customer accounts. In a bid to dominate the market, CPIB recently acquired Maple Leaf Trust, a large trust firm with its head office in Toronto. CPIB is currently concluding negotiations for the acquisition of International Investors Inc., a large stock exchange brokerage firm located in New York. When completed (it is expected that the deal will be finalized in less than two months), the new investment arm of CPIB, namely Canadian and International Investors, will be among the top dozen financial services firms in the world. Reflecting its strategy of investing in the future of financial services, CPIB is progressing in the new millennium as a leader in online delivery.

CPIB has always prided itself on its record of enhancing shareholder value. Its consistently high net incomes (in some years, reflecting record growth for the entire banking industry in this country) and its focus on running a lean operation have resulted in considerable increase in shareholder value over the years. To finance its newer acquisitions, the firm plans to make initial public offerings (IPOs) soon. Already, a number of large investors and brokerage firms have expressed considerable interest in the IPOs.

CPIB has a solid reputation as a good corporate citizen, having increased its charitable donations by 9.2 percent to

$7.3 million last year. Two years ago, the bank created the slogan "Bank for Your Community" and began contributing 1 percent of pre-tax domestic income to improve the community. Its donations have focused primarily on children's health and education, university scholarships (its Canadian University Scholarship is a coveted award), and donations for art and sports events (over 100 children attend minor league sports or the Canadian Conservatory of Music each year). The bank is a major sponsor of Save the Children Network, a network of hospitals serving over a million children across Canada. In the future, the bank wants to expand its community service to include foreign countries as well.

Immediate Challenges

CPIB recognizes that it has no time to rest on its laurels. To maintain and improve its competitive position, it must innovate and grow. Big competitors such as Royal Bank, TD Canada Trust, Canadian Imperial Bank of Commerce, Bank of Nova Scotia, and Bank of Montreal have been making fast inroads into electronic banking and foreign markets while smaller banks and credit unions, because of their small volumes, are able to provide more personal service compared to the large banks. Standardization and automation brought in considerable predictability and efficiency in operations, but it was also fraught with the risk of impersonal service and bureaucratic red tape. How to improve efficiency and predictability while offering personal and custom service? How to reap the advantages of smaller organizations such as flexibility without losing the economies of scale? There seem to be no simple answers.

More recently, a large number of "virtual banks" have appeared on the scene. These banks pay 4 to 5 percent interest even on small balances irrespective of the type of accounts (most Canadian banks do not pay any significant interest on chequing accounts). Because of the absence of any overhead costs, these virtual banks have been able to offer premium interest rates on other types of accounts as well as offer loans at cheaper rates. How can the bank compete with the virtual banks without losing the advantages of traditional banking and sacrificing the security and reputation?

Some have predicted that future societies may be "money-free"—in an Internet age, where most commodities can be virtually traded (including air miles, bonus points issued by gas stations, Canadian Tire coupons, and gift certificates), there is no reason why people should continue to use only currency notes or bank cheques as media of transaction.[90] If this scenario occurs, what will be the fate of traditional banks? No one quite knows.

While computerization and Internet trading have brought substantial benefits, they have also exposed banks and their systems to hackers and computer viruses that paralyze trading and, in some instances, wipe out a bank's entire computer memory. For instance, in early 2000, the "Love Bug" infected more than 2 million computer files around the world—over 90 percent of the sites being in North America—causing damage exceeding US$1 billion.[91] In the future, when banks increase their reliance on computerized trading, the risk element is only likely to grow.

In recent years, "shareholder democracy" has been gaining momentum. Organizations such as the Association for the Protection of Quebec Savers and Investors (APQSI) have been demanding a greater voice in bank decisions. In a recent Bank of Montreal shareholders' meeting,[92] APQSI proposed a course of action that was accepted by majority shareholders—even when the bank management recommended voting against it. The banks have been the focus of activist efforts because they are all widely held national institutions with a great deal of power. In the near future, there may be greater accountability of directors and senior bank executives to shareholders who are asking tough questions on all aspects of their operations. How can the bank respond to shareholder concerns without losing managerial authority and decision-making power? That is the question many bank managers ask themselves today.

Canada's banks operate in a highly regulated environment. Among the various restrictions they face is the complicated approval process needed for any merger. (In 1999, when Royal Bank and Bank of Montreal wanted to merge, the necessary approval was not granted.) In early 2001, the federal government was drafting legislation that could impose an even more complicated approval process on any merger among the big banks.[93] When the legislation is complete, any banking merger would require extensive public hearings on practically every aspect of the deal—a factor causing considerable frustration for Canadian banks, which find that their global status is coming down (the U.S. and Japanese banks have considerable resources and opportunity for cross-ownership of banks). In Royal Bank CEO John Cleghorn's words, "We are in a highly competitive game and we are hamstrung in our ability to deal with it."[94] Canadian bankers have also been complaining about intrusive consumer regulations that risk putting them at a disadvantage in relation to their U.S. competitors. The existing and proposed regulations will restrict the banks from using their customer databases to sell products to a targeted audience, including selling insurance through the branches. This is especially worrisome since large credit card companies have no similar restrictions imposed on them in this regard. "I worry a bit about the propensity to put consumer-type safeguards on banks only," Peter Godsoe, chairman of Bank of Nova Scotia, pointed out. "I think it has some dangers in it because database marketers can sit in the United States and sell the databases and all sorts of products."[95]

As an international organization, the bank is susceptible to all political and economic uncertainties in foreign countries. In the recent past, there was a significant slowdown in several Asian economies, resulting in, at times, massive losses to all major banks including CPIB. There were also instances where foreign governments suddenly changed their investment policies, prohibiting repatriation of capital and profits.[96] How can the bank expand without overexposing itself to risk? Clearly, there are no easy answers.

Human Resource Function

While its financial goals have been the driving force behind CPIB's externally focused strategies, management always recognized that it could not have achieved any of these results but for its highly competent and motivated employees—whether they are senior executives or clerks in remote branches. From its inception, the bank was committed to progressive human resource management practices in all its operations. It was one of the first banks to institute standardized selection and performance appraisal procedures, a well-designed human resource planning system, a detailed counselling system for employees, and financial assistance for university education for its employees. While occasional layoffs and staff reduction have been inevitable to cut costs, this has been done as humanely as possible. Mary Keddy, senior vice-president—human resources, an MBA from Saint Mary's specializing in human resources with an outstanding performance record in the steel industry, joined the firm six years ago. Since her arrival, she has tried to introduce state-of-the-art techniques and systems to the management of human resources. Compared to other banks, the staff turnover rate in CPIB is 2 percent lower. Past employee surveys have indicated that staff morale is high and rising. In Keddy's words,

> I know it is a cliché to say that "human resources are our most important assets." Many organizations proclaim this as their policy, but then it is business as usual. Honestly, I do believe in the maxim and what is fortunate for me, CPIB also believes in it. My predecessor, John Galsworthy, was a progressive human resource manager. He was one of those visionaries—he realized the potential of humans and was determined to tap that to the fullest extent. What is more, he genuinely cared for the employees. I am told that he knew several tellers in distant branches by their first names. Even a year before his retirement from the bank, he was found to spend long hours—often 12 to 13 hours—in his office to refine our HR practices. Fitting into his shoes, naturally, was a daunting task initially. But he also left a good system to build on. And that is what I have been doing: building on our strengths.

Keddy's views on the importance of human resources are echoed by several senior executives, including the CEO. At a time when several Canadian banks had their HR function represented only at the divisional or group level, CPIB raised its status to a vice-president level. In the foreseeable future, especially if the present expansion and merger plans proceed according to plans, HR may be elevated to vice-chair level, adding organizational change to the function.

Most of the specialized HR functions are located at the Vancouver head office. The regional offices do have their own HR managers and staff, but all major policy decisions are made at the head office—of course, after extensive consultations with all concerned (see Figure 4).

According to Keddy, some areas that HR is currently investigating are as follows:

> While the bank has been a progressive employer, the number of female senior managers in its ranks continues to be low. At the junior levels of management, the ratio between male and female managers is currently 65:35; however, as one goes up the hierarchy, the ratio changes drastically in favour of the males. Of the eight vice-presidents, only one is a woman; of the remaining senior managers, less than 5 percent are women. While the bank has been aware of the situation and would like to correct it, it has not been easy. There is also a larger turnover among female managers, making the task even more difficult. An examination of the employee records does not show any significant differences between males and females either in terms of educational qualifications or prior work experience. Also, at lower levels, in many branches, female employees seem to score higher on tenure and overall productivity. The situation, thus, is somewhat perplexing.
>
> In many large cities such as Toronto and Vancouver, the percentage of visible minorities in the general population and labour market has been significant—often totalling 40 percent of the workforce. CPIB has also a number of clerks and lower-level staff who belong to this group. However, even at the supervisory and junior managerial level, the percentage of minorities has been insignificant (often less than one-tenth of 1 percent). The bank would like to encourage more minorities and people with physical disabilities to reach middle-level and senior managerial levels.

After the merger with Investors, all duplication in services needs to be eliminated, which is likely to result in some job losses. How can the bank minimize job losses and employee anxiety? Keddy is currently heading a human resource steering committee that is looking into this matter and deliberating on staff reductions. She also wants to regularize communication flow to the employees on the matter to minimize rumours. The new employees from Investors also need to be socialized into CPIB's culture.

In recent months, Keddy and some of her senior colleagues have been seriously debating an ethical issue. Several manufacturers in developing economies employ young children (often aged seven or eight years) at very low wages (sometimes as low as less than a dollar per day) for long hours (12 hours and more in some cases) to produce cheap products such as soccer balls and volleyballs, jeans, and shoes. These manufacturers are important customers of the bank—often accounting for 25 percent or more of its loans in some regions.

Keddy believes that the bank has a moral responsibility to do what is ethically right, but is not sure how it can influence the events in other countries.

Finally, how to reduce labour costs while minimizing the adverse impact on employee morale and customer satisfaction? Automation and computerization can reduce labour costs significantly, but could also result in layoffs, lower employee morale, and longer waiting lines for customers in some cases. What is the optimal tradeoff between efficiency and morale?

Immediate Goals

For the next year, the bank has the following financial objectives:

Efficiency ratio: This ratio (also called "productivity" ratio) measures non-interest expenses as a percentage of revenue; the lower the percentage, the greater the efficiency. The bank aims to maintain an efficiency ratio of 58 percent (the six other major Canadian banks have productivity ratios ranging from 63 to 68 percent) compared to 61.6 percent last year and 63.8 percent two years ago.

Earnings on share: The bank aims to generate growth in earnings per common share from the present $4.20 to $4.62, or a 10 percent increase.

Return on equity: The bank wants to maintain its earning premium over risk-free Government of Canada Bonds, which currently translates into a return on equity (on cash basis) of about 17 percent. The bank wants to improve its overall return by 1 percentage point.

Provision for credit losses: Most Canadian banks average 0.37 percent (some banks with as high a rate as 0.5 percent) of net average loans as provision for credit losses. CPIB would like to keep it at 0.40 percent. CPIB had found that the bank's previous year's credit losses were far higher than normal because of the meltdown of the high-tech and telecom sectors and the general downturn of the U.S. and foreign economies in 2001–2002. The bank had also made significant loans to firms operating in Argentina, Japan, and Brazil—all of which had considerable loan defaults in the immediate past.

Market ratings for debt: The bank's credit ratings from Moody's and Standard Poor are strong at AA3 and AAMinus respectively. The bank would like to improve these.

Discussion Questions

1. What are some major challenges facing CPIB?

2. What are the specific implications for the human resource function?

3. What suggestions do you have for the current challenges faced by the HR function?

PART ENDING VIDEOS

"Under the Radar"

Source: *Venture*, show number 925, October 31, 2004, running time 9:52.

Go to **www.mcgrawhillconnect.ca** to access the videos.

ROLE-PLAY 1: Importance of HR Management Activities

Time required: 40–50 minutes

Objectives of the Role-Play

1. To sensitize the student to differences in perceptions of the importance of HR activities in organizations.
2. To enhance their negotiating skills as future HR managers during budget negotiations.
3. To enhance their communication skills in conveying HR priorities.

Prior Preparation

1. Study Chapter 1 of the text.
2. Read the descriptions of Maple Leaf Shoes Ltd. at the ends of Chapters 1 and 2 in the text.

Guidelines for Conducting the Role-Play

The role-play enacts a meeting between Jane Reynolds, Special Assistant to the Human Resource Manager, with Tim MacDonald, General Manager of Finance. Ms. Reynolds is requesting an increase in the budget for training and HR system improvement. Ms. Reynolds and Mr. MacDonald hold differing views on the role of HR management in the company.

1. Two students, one for the role of Jane Reynolds and the other for Tim MacDonald, should be identified.
2. Students should read their own role description in the Instructor Resource Manual along with the company details given at the ends of Chapters 1 and 2.
3. The instructor should signal the beginning and the end of the meeting. The meeting will last a maximum length of 30 minutes. It may be ended earlier.
4. The remainder of the class time is used for discussion of the behaviours observed during the role-play and outcomes.
5. Observers should be asked to make notes against the questions listed below and discuss their findings at the end of the role-play.
6. Instructor should sum up by highlighting the differing HR strategies and their implications for organizational practices and outcomes.

Instructions for Observers

As you observe the meeting between Jane Reynolds and Tim MacDonald, make notes against each of the questions below. Pay particular attention to the behaviours and verbal and nonverbal expressions of each person.

1. Are there differences in the assumptions of the two parties about the role and importance of HR? How?
2. How did Jane begin the meeting?
3. Was there open communication between the two?
4. Did Jane get what she wanted?
5. Is there anything Jane could have done to change Tim's attitude? What?
6. Would you have done anything differently? If so, what?

● APPENDIX A

Origins of Human Resource Management

The origins of human resource management are unknown. Probably the first cave dwellers struggled with problems of utilizing human resources. Even the Bible records selection and training problems faced by Moses. Moses was confronted with one of the earliest recorded personnel challenges when Jethro, his father-in-law, advised: "And thou shalt teach them ordinances and laws, and shalt shew them the way wherein they must walk, and the work they must do. Moreover, thou shalt provide out of all the people able men ... to be rulers" (Exod. 18: 20–21).

During the thousands of years between Moses and the Industrial Revolution, there were few large organizations. Except for religious orders (the Roman Catholic Church, for example) or governments (particularly the military), small groups did most of the work. Whether on the farm, in small shops, or in the home, the primary work unit was the family. There was little need for formal study of human resource management.

The Industrial Revolution changed the nature of work. Mechanical power and economies of scale required large numbers of people to work together. Large textile mills, foundries, and mines sprung up in England and then in North America. Collectively, people were still an important resource, but the Industrial Revolution meant greater mechanization and unpleasant working conditions for many workers.

By the late 1800s, a few employers reacted to the human problems caused by industrialization and created the post of welfare secretary. Welfare secretaries existed to meet worker needs and to prevent workers from forming unions. Social secretaries, as they were sometimes called, helped employees with personal problems such as education, housing, and medical needs. These early forerunners of human resource specialists sought to improve working conditions for workers. The emergence of welfare secretaries prior to 1900 demonstrates that the personnel activities in large organizations had already become more extensive than some top operating managers alone could handle. Thus, social secretaries marked the birth of specialized human resource management, as distinct from the day-to-day supervision of personnel by operating managers.

Scientific Management and Human Needs

The next noteworthy development was scientific management. The scientific management proponents showed the world that the systematic, scientific study of work could lead to improved efficiency. Their arguments for specialization and improved training furthered the need for HR management. The first decades of the twentieth century saw primitive "personnel departments" replace welfare secretaries. These new departments contributed to organizational effectiveness by maintaining wages at proper levels, screening job applicants, and handling grievances. They also assumed the welfare secretary's role of improving working conditions, dealing with unions, and meeting other employee needs.

By the First World War, personnel departments were becoming common among very large industrial employers. But these early departments were not important parts of the organizations they served. They were record depositories with advisory authority only. At that time, production, finance, and marketing problems overshadowed the role of personnel management. The importance of personnel departments grew slowly as their contribution and responsibilities increased.

From the end of the First World War until the Great Depression of the 1930s, personnel departments assumed growing roles in handling compensation, testing, unions, and employee needs. More and more attention was paid to employee needs. The importance of individual needs became even more pronounced as a result of the research studies in the United States at Western Electric's Hawthorne plant during this period. These studies showed that the efficiency goals of scientific management had to be balanced by considerations of human needs. These observations eventually had a profound impact on personnel management. But the Depression and the Second World War diverted attention to more urgent matters of organizational and national survival.

Modern Influences

The Depression of the 1930s led citizens to lose faith in the ability of business to meet society's needs. They turned to government. Government intervened to give workers minimum wages and the right to join labour unions. In 1940, Canada started an unemployment insurance program to help alleviate financial problems during the transition from one job to another. In general, the government's emphasis was on improving employee security and working conditions.

This drafting of legislation during the 1930s helped to shape the present role of personnel departments by adding legal obligations. Organizations now had to consider societal objectives and the need for legal compliance, which elevated the importance of personnel departments. In practice, personnel departments were made responsible for discouraging unionization among employees. But with newfound legal protection, unions grew dramatically. These organizing successes startled many organizations into rethinking their use of paternalism, their "management knows best" approach to employee welfare. Personnel departments began replacing a paternalistic approach with more proactive approaches that considered employee desires. When workers did organize, responsibility for dealing with unions also fell to the personnel department, sometimes renamed the industrial relations department to reflect these new duties.

Personnel departments continued to increase in importance during the 1940s and 1950s. The recruiting and training demands of the Second World War added to the credibility of the personnel departments that successfully met these challenges. After the war, personnel departments grew in importance as they contended with unions and an expanding need for professionals such as engineers and accountants. The increasing attention given to behavioural findings led to concern for improved human relations. These findings helped underscore the importance of sound personnel management practices.

In the 1960s and 1970s, the central influence on personnel was again legislation. Several laws were passed that affected the working conditions, wage levels, safety, and health and other benefits of employees. These acts began to provide personnel department managers with a still larger voice—a voice that began to equal that of production, finance, and marketing executives in major corporations.

Human resource management—as the personnel function is known today—did not emerge until recently. It is only very recently that human resource specialists have started to exert great influence on organizational strategy or have been chosen as chief executives. But today, in many organizations, there is a genuine recognition that human resources spell the difference between strategic success and organizational decline. The emphasis placed on strategic human resource management and formal certification of HR specialists are evidence of this growing role of human resource management.

PART 2

Planning Human Resources

This part introduces you to the important task of planning for human resources. Chapter 2 discusses the various approaches to conducting a job analysis. Steps to create valid job descriptions, specifications, and performance standards are outlined in this chapter. Chapter 3 discusses the various factors that need to be considered when forecasting the demand for and supply of human resources. It also outlines several popular techniques for making such forecasts. Together, these two chapters help you to identify the type, number, and degree of sophistication of human resources needed by your firm.

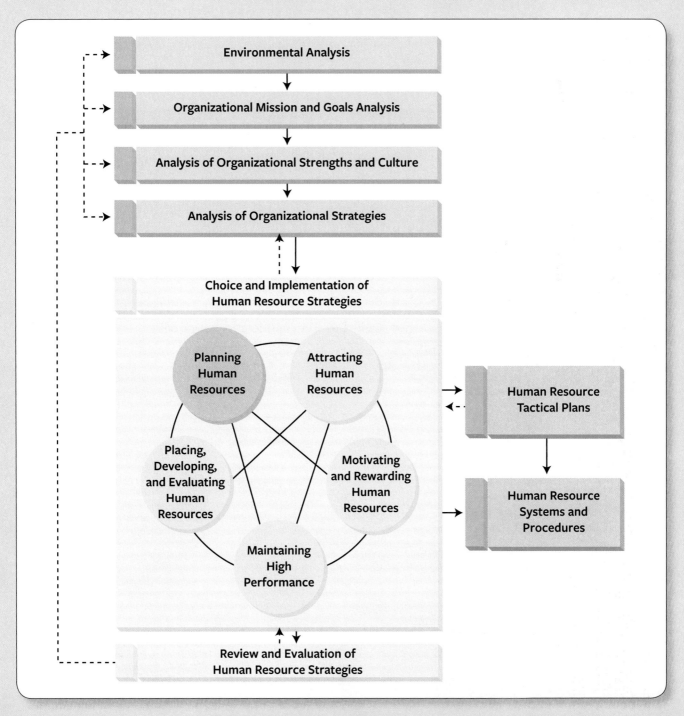

Job Analysis and Design*

The data generated by job analyses have significant use in nearly every phase of human resource administration: designing jobs and reward systems; staffing and training; performance control and more. Few other processes executed by organizations have the potential for being such a powerful aid to management decision making.

Philip C. Grant[1]

CHAPTER OBJECTIVES

After studying this chapter, you should be able to:

➡ *Describe* the uses of job analysis information for human resource managers.

➡ *Discuss* the various steps in conducting job analysis and methods of job data collection.

➡ *Describe* the contents of a job description and a job specification.

➡ *Discuss* the various approaches to setting performance standards.

➡ *Outline* the key considerations in job design.

*It has been suggested to reverse the sequence of Chapters 2 and 3—that is, to discuss human resource planning before job analysis. However, we feel that job analyses come first. Without them no human resource planning is possible.

CHAPTER 2

I n this part of the book, we will explain why making the right selection decision is, in all probability, the most crucial decision a manager ever has to make. A failure in this attempt will haunt the organization for a long time, given the difficulties in dismissing employees who are not performing to expectations.

To be proactive in this decision-making process, a human resource department needs accurate information about a variety of aspects of the job in question. This chapter explains how human resource specialists discover the actual characteristics that presently exist in each job.

Knowledge about jobs and their requirements must be collected through **job analysis**. This knowledge is vital to the effective functioning of an HR department, as exemplified in the following dialogue:

Service Manager: Before we had a human resource department, we took care of people matters pretty well. Now there is too much paperwork on each job. I wonder if it's a help or a hindrance.

HR Manager: I can empathize. Before the department was set up, you probably had complete authority for people matters. Right?

Service Manager: I sure did! And I did it without the paperwork.

HR Manager: Sure you did. You know every job in your department, in and out. You had all the information you needed stored in your experiences.

Service Manager: That's my point. If I got along without all this make-work, why can't you?

HR Manager: Why? Because you deal with those jobs every day. You've probably done most of them yourself. But my department is also responsible for jobs in sales, production, warehouse, supervision, and others. Without the documentation describing these jobs, we would have no idea of their requirements. And without knowing these requirements, how could we plan our recruitment programs, make effective hiring decisions, determine training needs, assess job performance, decide on fair compensation, and develop career paths? Do you see now how essential this paperwork is?

Service Manager: Gosh, no ... I hadn't thought of all that. Am I glad that I don't have that burden hanging on me! I guess you earn your pay.

Jobs are at the core of every organization's productivity. If they are not well designed and done right, productivity suffers, profits fall, and the organization is less able to meet the demands of society, customers, employees, and other stakeholders. The importance of well-designed jobs is perhaps best illustrated by an example:

A small construction company, consisting of the owner, two administrators, and fourteen bricklayers and carpenters, experienced rapid growth, but the performance per staff member declined. A consultant found that the company had no job descriptions, causing uncertainty in employees about job responsibilities and performance expectations. Job analyses clarified everybody's role in the organization and established performance standards based on industry data. Job performance and quality improved significantly, as did job satisfaction, resulting in lower turnover.

For a human resource department to be effective, its members must have a clear understanding of the jobs found throughout the organization. Without this information base, the human resource department would be less able to redesign jobs, recruit new employees, train present employees, determine appropriate compensation, and perform many other human resource functions.

A **job** consists of a group of related activities and duties. A job may be held by a single employee or several persons. The collection of tasks and responsibilities performed by an individual employee is called a **position**.

In a department with one supervisor, three clerks, and twelve service personnel, there are sixteen positions, but only three jobs.

With hundreds—or even thousands—of jobs, it is nearly impossible for the human resource professionals in large companies to know the details of every job. It is, however, unnecessary to collect information on identical jobs separately. Consider this example:

One insurance company has 90 clerical employees who process incoming premium payments. Each job is the same. Therefore, job analysis requires only a random sample of these positions. Data collection on a few of these jobs generates an accurate information base for all 90 positions.

job analysis
Systematic study of a job to discover its specifications, skill requirements, and so on, for wage-setting, recruitment, training, or job-simplification purposes.

Job-Analysis.Net
www.job-analysis.net

job
Group of related activities and duties.

position
Collection of tasks and responsibilities performed by an individual.

Large organizations store information on various jobs using a *human resource information system* (*HRIS*). A sophisticated HRIS permits easy retrieval of relevant job details; it also provides a variety of information about the job, jobholders, and past performance standards. Further details about designing an HRIS are in the next chapter. Smaller companies may not require a complex HRIS system, but even they will benefit from a proper job analysis as the example of the small construction company above demonstrated.

Figure 2-1 lists major human resource actions that rely on job analysis information. For example, without job analysis information, human resource specialists will find it difficult to evaluate how environmental challenges or specific job requirements affect employees' quality of work life. To match job applicants to openings, human resource specialists must understand what each job requires. Similarly, compensation analysts cannot be expected to determine a fair salary without detailed knowledge of each job. Human resource departments formalize the collection, evaluation, and organization of this information.

This chapter describes the information sought by job analysts and the techniques to collect it. The chapter also describes how the data are converted into a useful human resource information system.

⟶ STEPS IN THE JOB ANALYSIS PROCESS

Job analysis has three phases: preparation, collection of job information, and use of job information for improving organizational effectiveness (see Figure 2-2). Each phase consists of several actions discussed below.

FIGURE 2-1	Major Human Resource Management Activities That Rely on Job Analysis Information

1. Careful study of jobs to improve employee productivity levels.
2. Elimination of unnecessary job requirements that can cause discrimination in employment.
3. Matching of job applicants to job requirements.
4. Planning of future human resource requirements.
5. Determination of employee training needs.
6. Fair and equitable compensation of employees.
7. Efforts to improve quality of work life.
8. Identification of realistic and challenging performance standards.
9. Redesign of jobs to improve performance and/or employee morale.
10. Fair and accurate appraisal of employee performance.

FIGURE 2-2	The Job Analysis

Phase 1			Phase 2			Phase 3
Preparation for Job Analysis			Collection of Job Analysis Information			Use of Job Analysis Information
Step 1	Step 2	Step 3	Step 4	Step 5	Step 6	
Familiarize with the organization and the jobs	Determine uses of job analysis	Identify jobs to be analyzed	Determine sources of job data	Data collection instrument design	Choice of method for data collection	• Job description • Job specification • Job performance standards • Job redesign • Designing HRIS • Changing HR systems (e.g., compensation) • Organization change (e.g., redesigning workflow in plant)

HR-Guide
www.hr-guide.com/data/
Gooo.htm

Phase 1: Preparation for Job Analysis

Three key activities are performed in this phase:

Step 1: Familiarization with the Organization and Its Jobs

Before studying jobs, it is important to have an awareness of an organization's objectives, strategies, structure, inputs (people, materials, and procedures), and desired outcomes. Job analysis procedures are influenced by the organization character, discussed in Chapter 1. In unionized organizations, job analysis steps also have to meet the various provisions of the collective agreement between the management and the union (more details about this relationship are discussed in Chapter 14). Job analysts may also study industry and government reports about the jobs to be analyzed. In all instances, the intent is to collect relevant and accurate information about jobs and factors determining job success.

Step 2: Determine Uses of Job Analysis Information

As shown in Figure 2-1, job analysis plays a critical role for many HR functions. While the most common uses are in the selection process, training, and designing performance appraisal and compensation systems,[2] job analysis may also be done to eliminate discrimination against specific employee groups or assist in job redesign. In some cases, job analysis aids other objectives such as identifying nontraditional career paths for employees, as the following example shows:

> One job analysis study[3] found that the skills, knowledge, and abilities essential for performance in secretarial and clerical positions are very similar to those needed in entry-level management positions. If female or minority employees are concentrated in secretarial or clerical positions, this information can be used to move them into managerial positions. Such employees can also use this information to make the best use of their work experience and training and develop career paths.

The details collected during a job analysis are influenced by the objectives of the study; hence, it is critical to define the objectives early on.

Step 3: Identify Jobs to Be Analyzed

While almost all job positions might benefit from an in-depth analysis, resource and time constraints often preclude organizations from conducting job analyses. Likely targets of job analysis are jobs that are critical to the success of an organization; jobs that are difficult to learn or perform (to determine the extent of training); jobs in which the firm continuously hires new employees (identification of

Discriminatory practices for firefighters are prohibited as long as a person is able to do the job. Women usually are able to carry less weight than men. Should that be taken into account during hiring?

clear job requirements assumes great importance); or jobs that exclude members of the protected classes described in Chapter 4. Jobs should also be analyzed if new technology or altered work environments affect how the job is performed. If inappropriate job requirements are used, the organization may even be in violation of laws as the following example illustrates:

> In the past, the Vancouver Fire Department required that all successful job applicants be at least 175 centimetres (five feet, nine inches) tall. After one of the applicants complained, the Human Rights Board looked into the Department's selection practices and could not find any correlation between the height of a firefighter and injuries or productivity of the employees. The Department was found to be in violation of the *Human Rights Act*.[4]

In general, senior management and all key supervisors of the firm should be consulted before selecting jobs for in-depth analysis, as the jobs selected for analysis can affect the strategic success and overall human resource policies (e.g., hiring, training) of the firm. The type, number, and geographical dispersion of the jobs selected for analysis also influence the choice of data collection method.

Phase 2: Collection of Job Analysis Information

This phase contains three interrelated activities: determining the source of job data, data collection instrument design, and choosing the method of collection.

Step 4: Determine Sources of Job Data

Although the most direct source of information about a job is the job incumbent, various other sources—both human and nonhuman—may be used for this purpose. Figure 2-3 lists alternative sources of job information.

Occasionally, materials published in professional journals and magazines provide information about how jobs are performed in other organizations and settings. This information can be valuable when establishing performance standards and benchmarks for quality. Other publications, such as the *National Occupational Classification* (NOC) in Canada (discussed in greater detail later in this chapter) and the U.S. Department of Labor's *Handbook for Analyzing Jobs*, provide information on various jobs.

The Internet has become a valuable source for information about various jobs and occupational groups. Web sites of several professional associations and private consulting firms offer a wealth of material relevant to job analysis and job descriptions.

The job incumbents, their supervisors, and colleagues provide the most valid information about the way jobs are performed. However, other parties can also provide important information about jobs:

> In the case of a salesperson, contacting past customers provides additional insights about job behaviours. In the case of college or university faculty, students may be able to provide important information on in-class behaviours related to effective job performance.

FIGURE 2-3	Sources of Job Data	
Nonhuman Sources		**Human Sources**
Existing job descriptions and specifications		Job incumbents
Equipment design blueprints		Supervisors
Equipment maintenance manuals and records		Job experts
Training and safety manuals		Work colleagues
Organization charts and other company records		Subordinates
National Occupational Classification		Customers
Videos/films supplied by appliance/machine manufacturers		
Professional journals/magazines/publications		
Internet research		

Step 5: Data Collection Instrument Design

job analysis schedules
Checklists that seek to collect information about jobs in a uniform manner.

To study jobs, analysts most often develop questionnaires that are called checklists or **job analysis schedules**. These questionnaires seek to collect job information uniformly. They uncover the duties, responsibilities, human abilities, and performance standards of the jobs investigated.

The questionnaires are particularly important when collecting information from human sources. Even in the case of nonhuman sources, the quality and comparability of information collected can be enhanced by the use of common checklists. It is important to use the same questionnaire on similar jobs. Analysts want differences in job information to reflect differences in the jobs, not differences in the questions asked. Uniformity is especially hard to maintain in large organizations; where analysts study similar jobs in different departments, only a uniform questionnaire results in usable data.

Figure 2-4 shows an abbreviated sample form for conducting job analyses that can be modified to suit the needs of specific situations. Most standardized forms, however, attempt to measure the following items:

- **Status and identification.** *Status* refers to whether the job is exempt from overtime laws. Other *identification* information includes job title, division, and title of supervisor(s), and sometimes a unique job identification number. Without these entries, users of job analysis data may rely on outdated information or apply the information retrieved to the wrong job. Because most jobs change over time, outdated information may misdirect other human resource activities:

  At Maple Leaf Department Stores, new job analysis information for the job of billing clerk had not been collected for two years. The outdated information indicated that bookkeeping experience was the major skill needed by clerks. However, in the last two years, the store's entire billing system had been computerized, thereby making bookkeeping skills unimportant; instead, billing clerks now needed keying skills to process billing information into the computer.

- **Duties and responsibilities.** A job analysis explains the purpose of the job, what the job accomplishes, and how the job is performed. A summary provides a quick overview. The specific duties and responsibilities are listed to give more detailed insight into the position. Questions on responsibility are expanded significantly when the checklist is applied to management jobs. Additional questions map areas of responsibility for decision making, controlling, organizing, planning, and other management functions.

Job/Content Analysis Tool
www.ceismc.gatech.edu/MM_Tools/JCAT.html

- **Human characteristics and working conditions.** Besides information about the job, analysts need to uncover the particular skills, abilities, training, education, experience, and other characteristics that jobholders need. This information is invaluable when filling job openings or advising workers about new job assignments. Information about the job environment improves understanding of the job. Working conditions may explain the need for particular skills, training, knowledge, or even a particular job design. Likewise, jobs must be free from recognizable health and safety hazards. Knowledge of hazards allows the human resource department to redesign the job or protect workers through training and safety equipment.

- **Performance standards.** The job analysis questionnaire also seeks information about job standards, which are used to evaluate performance. This information is collected on jobs with objective standards of performance. When standards are not readily apparent, job analysts may ask supervisors or industrial engineers to develop reasonable standards of performance.

Various standardized forms are currently available for job analysis (two of the more popular ones are Functional Job Analysis and Position Analysis Questionnaire):

- **Functional job analysis (FJA).** The FJA classifies tasks using three functional scales related to data, people, and things.[5] Each functional scale ranks behaviours according to complexity. For example, the lowest level in the people scale is "taking instruction," while the highest is "mentoring others." Similarly, "comparing data" is the simplest of the behaviours in dealing with data ("synthesizing" is the most complex). The job analyst, when studying a job, indicates the level at which the employee is operating for each of the three categories. For example, the job might involve "50 percent copying." This is done for each of the three functional scales, resulting in a quantitatively evaluated job.

O*NET Consortium
www.onetcenter.org/overview.html

- **Occupational Information Network (O*NET).** For many decades, the U.S. Department of Labor used a *Dictionary of Occupational Titles* (DOT) to classify jobs and job skills, but changing

FIGURE 2-4	Job Analysis Questionnaire

Maple Leaf Department Stores
Job Analysis Questionnaire
(Form 18-JAQ)

A. Job Analysis Status
1. Job analysis form revised on _____
2. Previous revisions on _____
3. Date of job analysis for specified job _____
4. Previous analysis on _____
5. Job analysis is conducted by _____
6. Verified by _____

B. Job Identification
1. Job title _____
2. Other titles _____
3. Division(s) _____
4. Department(s) _____
5. Title of supervisor(s) _____

C. Job Summary
Briefly describe purpose of job, what is done, and how.
_____

D. Duties
1. The primary duties of this job are best classified as:
   Managerial _____   Technical _____
   Professional _____   Clerical _____
2. List **major** duties and the proportion of time each involves:
   a. _____   _____ %
   b. _____   _____ %
   c. _____   _____ %
3. List other duties and the proportion of time each involves:
   a. _____   _____ %
   b. _____   _____ %
   c. _____   _____ %
4. What constitutes successful performance of these duties? _____
5. How much training is needed for normal performance of these duties? _____

E. Responsibility
1. What are the responsibilities involved in this job and how great are these responsibilities?

Extent of Responsibility	Minor	Major
Responsibility for:		
a. Equipment operation	_____	_____
b. Use of tools	_____	_____
c. Materials usage	_____	_____
d. Protection of equipment	_____	_____
e. Protection of tools	_____	_____
f. Protection of materials	_____	_____
g. Personal safety	_____	_____
h. Safety of others	_____	_____
i. Others' work performance	_____	_____
j. Other (Specify _____)	_____	_____

FIGURE 2-4	Job Analysis Questionnaire (continued)

F. Human Characteristics

1. What physical attributes are necessary to perform the job? _____
2. Of the following characteristics, which ones are needed and how important are they?

Characteristic	Unneeded	Helpful	Essential
1. Vision	_____	_____	_____
2. Hearing	_____	_____	_____
3. Talking	_____	_____	_____
4. Sense of smell	_____	_____	_____
5. Sense of touch	_____	_____	_____
6. Sense of taste	_____	_____	_____
7. Eye–hand coordination	_____	_____	_____
8. Overall coordination	_____	_____	_____
9. Strength	_____	_____	_____
10. Height	_____	_____	_____
11. Health	_____	_____	_____
12. Initiative	_____	_____	_____
13. Ingenuity	_____	_____	_____
14. Judgment	_____	_____	_____
15. Attention	_____	_____	_____
16. Reading	_____	_____	_____
17. Arithmetic	_____	_____	_____
18. Writing	_____	_____	_____
19. Education (Level)	_____	_____	_____
20. Other (Specify)	_____	_____	_____

3. Experience for this job:

_____ a. Unimportant

_____ b. Includes _____ (months) as (job title)

4. Can training be substituted for experience?

_____ Yes   How: _____

_____ No   Why: _____

G. Working Conditions

1. Describe the physical conditions under which this job is performed.
2. Are there unusual psychological demands connected with this job?
3. Describe any unusual conditions under which the job is performed.

H. Health or Safety Features

1. Describe fully any health or safety hazards associated with this job.
2. Is any safety training or equipment required?

I. Performance Standards

1. How is the performance of this job measured?
2. What identifiable factors contribute most to the successful performance this job?

J. Miscellaneous Comments

Are there any aspects of this job that should be especially noted? _____

_____

_____

_____

_____	_____
Job Analyst's Signature	Date Completed

technology required a different approach. The new O*NET lists only 1000 occupations, compared to 12 000 used by DOT.[6]

- **Fleishman Job Analysis System (F-JAS).** The F-JAS is a well-researched job analysis method, based on a list of 52 cognitive, psychomotor, physical, and sensory abilities.[7] The actual scales use a seven-point anchor indicating the different levels of abilities. The scale is used mainly in the U.S. market.

- **Position Analysis Questionnaire (PAQ).** The PAQ,[8] designed to apply to all types of jobs, offers an even more quantitative and finely tuned description of jobs than the F-JAS. Using a five-point scale, it aims to determine the degree to which 194 different task elements are involved in performing a particular job (the five-point scale measures a continuum of "nominal or very infrequent" at the lowest level to "very substantial" at the highest). The PAQ allows grouping of job elements in a logical and quantitative manner and the number of job elements covered under various categories are large (e.g., there are 36 different elements that measure "relationships with other people"). This, in turn, is claimed to make job comparison easy. Past research, however, has indicated PAQ to be more useful for lower-level jobs.[9]

- **Critical Incident Method (CIM).** Duties and responsibilities are important aspects of a job analysis, and the CIM is ideally suited for this purpose because it focuses on critical job behaviours. If a job analyst wants to develop a job description for an instructor using the CIM approach, a job incumbent will be asked to give examples of behaviours required to do the job effectively and the way and means to do it. An instructor may explain:

  I have to teach undergraduate classes, using handouts and teaching aids, such as a blackboard or overhead projector. Of course, I have to prepare the lectures beforehand. For that I have to collect material from books, journals, or the Internet. I also give exams, using question banks.

  The job analyst will translate this description into specific job responsibilities:

  - Prepares lectures from library material or Internet.
  - Presents lectures, using a blackboard or overhead projector.
  - Conducts examinations based on a data bank.

  For job analysis purposes, about 10 statements will suffice.

Step 6: Choice of Method for Data Collection

There is no one best way to collect job analysis information. Analysts must evaluate the tradeoffs between time, cost, and accuracy associated with each method.[10] Once they decide which tradeoffs are most important, they use interviews, questionnaires, employee logs, observations, or some combination of these techniques.

Interviews. Face-to-face **interviews** are an effective way to collect job information. The analyst has the questionnaire as a guide, but can add other questions where needed. Although the process is slow and expensive, it allows the interviewer to explain unclear questions and probe into uncertain answers. Typically, both jobholders and supervisors are interviewed. The analyst usually talks with a limited number of workers first and then interviews supervisors to verify the information. This pattern ensures a high level of accuracy. The validity of the information received depends on the representativeness of the sample of the respondents and the types of questions used. Some guidelines for conducting interviews are as follows:

1. Interviews should be conducted with the job incumbents, as well as with all others who may be expected to be knowledgeable about the job's duties and responsibilities.

2. The interviewer should establish rapport with the interviewee before getting into the main theme. The interviewee should be briefed about the objectives of the interview and offered all relevant information to reduce defensiveness.

3. A structured checklist of questions very similar to Figure 2-4 should be used. In any case, the checklist should collect information on a variety of matters, including
   - major purpose and outcomes of the job and the recipients of its outcomes;
   - major duties and percentage of time spent on each;
   - major responsibilities, including the type of equipments and processes used;
   - education, skills, competencies, and experience levels needed;

Sample Job Analysis Data Collection Form
www.worksupport.com/ Topics/downloads/ chap4-tab2sample.PDF

interview
Approach to collecting job- and performance-related information by a face-to-face meeting with jobholder, typically using a standardized questionnaire.

- current performance standards and improvements needed; and
- physical demands, working conditions, and safety and health issues.

4. In those instances in which the respondent does not perform routine duties, the job incumbent should be asked to list all duties, their relative importance to the overall success of the job, and the frequency of their occurrence.
5. The information collected should be reviewed and verified by both the interviewee and the immediate supervisor.

Mailed Questionnaires. A fast and less costly option is to survey employees using a **mailed questionnaire**. This can be done using email, internal (or interoffice) mail, Canada Post, or fax. This approach allows many jobs to be studied at once and at little cost. However, there is less accuracy because of the likelihood of misunderstood questions, incomplete responses, and unreturned questionnaires. Supervisors can also be given questionnaires to verify employee responses.

Employee Log. An **employee log** or diary is a third option. Workers periodically summarize their tasks and activities in the log. If entries are made over the entire job cycle, the diary can prove quite accurate.

Logs are not a popular technique. They are time-consuming for jobholders and human resource specialists, which makes them costly. Managers and workers often see them as a nuisance and resist their introduction. Moreover, after the novelty wears off, accuracy tends to decline as entries become less frequent.

Observation. Another approach is direct **observation**. It is slow, costly, and potentially less accurate than other methods. Accuracy may be low because the analysts may miss irregularly occurring activities. But observation is the preferred method in some situations. When analysts question data from other techniques, observation may confirm or remove doubts. The existence of language barriers with foreign-language-speaking workers may also necessitate the observation approach.

Combinations. Since each method has its shortcomings, analysts often use a **combination** of two or more techniques concurrently:

> A lumber company had six facilities scattered across Canada and the United States. To interview a few workers and supervisors at each facility was considered prohibitively expensive; to rely only on questionnaire data was thought to be too inaccurate. Therefore, the human resource department interviewed selected employees at the home office and sent questionnaires to other facilities.

Past research studies indicate that different job analysis methods better suit varying human resource management purposes.[11] Figure 2-5 provides a scheme for using job analysis information. It should be noted that the figure highlights only the relative strength of each method for each purpose. For example, information collected through observation is most useful for selection and appraisal of employees. Key considerations in the choice of job analysis method should include method–purpose fit, practical feasibility, cost, and reliability of the data collected for making valid decisions. Job analysis information enables an organization to take the proactive actions discussed.

mailed questionnaires Standardized questionnaires used to survey employees to collect information about jobs, working conditions, and other performance-related information.

employee log Approach to collecting job- and performance-related information by asking the jobholder to summarize tasks, activities, and challenges in a diary format.

observation An approach to collecting job- and performance-related information by direct observation of jobholder by a specialist.

combination Concurrent use of two or more job analysis techniques (e.g., interviews and observation).

FIGURE 2-5	Different Job Analysis Methods Best Suit Different HR Goals				
Method of Data Collection	Job Description and Design	Selection	Training	Compensation	Counselling
Interviews	*	*	*	*	*
Questionnaires	*	*	*	*	
Employee log	*		*		*
Observation	*	*	*		

Source: Based on several past writings, including E.L. Levine, R.A. Ash, and N. Bennett, "Explorative Comparative Study of Four Job Analysis Methods," *Journal of Applied Psychology*, Vol. 65, 1980, pp. 524–35; and E.L. Levine, R.A. Ash, H. Hall, and F. Sistrunk, "Evaluation of Job Analysis Methods by Experienced Job Analysts," *Academy of Management Journal*, Vol. 26, No. 2, 1983, pp. 339–48.

Writing Job Descriptions
http://hrmanagement.gc.ca/
gol/hrmanagement/site.nsf/
en/hr11538.html

Phase 3: Use of Job Analysis Information

The information collected about various jobs is put into such usable forms as job descriptions, job specifications, and job standards. Together, these applications of job analysis information provide a minimum human resource information system and data necessary for formulating various HR strategies. The remainder of this chapter discusses these applications.

→ JOB DESCRIPTION

job description
A recognized list of functions, tasks, accountabilities, working conditions, and competencies for a particular occupation or job.

A **job description** is a written statement that explains the duties, working conditions, and other aspects of a specified job.

Contents of a Typical Job Description

Within a firm, all the job descriptions follow the same style, although between organizations, form and content may vary. One approach is to write a narrative description that covers the job in a few paragraphs. Another typical style breaks the description down into several subparts, as shown in Figure 2-6.

FIGURE 2-6   **A Job Description**

Maple Leaf Department Stores
Job Description

Job Title: _____   Job Code: _____

Date: _____   Author: _____

Job Location: _____   Job Grade: _____

Report To: _____   Status: _____

Job Summary: Interacts with customers on a daily basis, promptly responding to all inquiries in a courteous and efficient manner. Encourages the sale of company products at every opportunity and applies exemplary customer relation skills that promote a superior company image. Provides information to customers about product features and substitutes when asked.

Responsibilities: Responds to customer inquiries on product features, prices, services, and delivery terms.

Takes customer orders for products and communicates these accurately to supply and servicing personnel in the company.

Accepts returns of merchandise by customers and gives them credit for the same.

Displays and stocks merchandise on shelves.

Appropriately prices items based on instructions received from the supervisor.

Prepares necessary documents and transmits/files copies to relevant offices within the company.

Responds to other miscellaneous inquiries especially those related to warranties, delivery terms, servicing frequencies (in the case of equiment).

Undertakes other tasks assigned by the supervisor.

Operates cash register and balances accounts at the end of the shift.

Working Conditions: Works in a well-ventilated office. Must be able to work shifts.

The above information is correct as approved by:

(Signed) _____   (Signed) _____

    Customer Service Representative   Customer Service Supervisor

This figure shows a job description that parallels the job analysis checklist that originally generated the data (see Figure 2-4).

The key parts of a job description are as follows: job identity, job summary, job duties, and working conditions. Most job descriptions also identify the author, the work supervisor, and the date on which it was prepared.

Job Identity

The section on **job identity** typically includes job title, job location, job code, job grade, and its status (whether or not exempted from overtime laws). **Job codes** use numbers, letters, or both to provide a quick summary of the job. These codes are useful for comparing jobs. Figures 2-7, 2-8, and 2-9 explain the coding used in the **National Occupational Classification** (**NOC**). The two major attributes of jobs that were used as classification criteria in developing the NOC were *skill level* (amount and type of education and training) and *skill type* (type of work performed). Other factors, such as industry and occupational mobility, were also taken into consideration.[12]

- **Skill level.** Four skill level categories are identified in the NOC, describing the educational and training requirements of occupations (see Figure 2-7).

- **Skill type.** Skill type is defined generally as the type of work performed. Ten broad occupational categories (0 to 9) are identified in the NOC. Figure 2-8 describes these in detail.

An even more refined job classification for certain jobs, particularly useful for applied science and engineering disciplines, is provided by the Canadian Technology Human Resources Board.

Job Summary and Duties

Following the job identification section (in Figure 2-6), the next part of the description is the job summary. It summarizes the job in a few sentences, telling what the job is, how it is done, and why.

job identity
Key part of a job description, including job title, location, and status.

job code
A code that uses numbers, letters, or both to provide a quick summary of the job and its content.

National Occupational Classification (NOC)
An occupational classification created by the federal government, using skill level and skill types of jobs.

FIGURE 2-7	NOC Skill Level Criteria	
	Education/Training	**Other**
Skill Level A	University degree (Bachelor's, Master's, or postgraduate)	
Skill Level B	Two to three years of post-secondary education at college, institute of technology, or CEGEP *or* Two to four years of apprenticeship training *or* Three to four years of secondary school and more than two years of on-the-job training, training courses, or specific work experience	Occupations with supervisory responsibilities are assigned to Skill Level B. Occupations with significant health and safety responsibilities (e.g., firefighters, police officers, and registered nursing assistants) are assigned to Skill Level B.
Skill Level C	One to four years of secondary school education. Up to two years of on-the-job training, training courses, or specific work experience	
Skill Level D	Up to two years of secondary school and short work demonstration or on-the-job training	

Source: Human Resources Development Canada, National Occupation Classification. Reproduced with permission of the Minister of Public Works and Government Services Canada, 2003.

FIGURE 2-8	NOC Skill Type Categories

When the first digit is ... the Skill Type Category is

1	Business, Finance, and Administrative Occupations
2	Natural and Applied Sciences and Related Occupations
3	Health Occupations
4	Occupations in Social Science, Education, Government Service, and Religion
5	Occupations in Art, Culture, Recreation, and Sport
6	Sales and Service Occupations
7	Trades, Transport and Equipment Operators, and Related Occupations
8	Occupations Unique to Primary Industry
9	Occupations Unique to Processing, Manufacturing, and Utilities

When the second digit is ... the Skill Level Category is

1	Skill Level A (Professional Occupations)
2 or 3	Skill Level B (Technical, Paraprofessional, and Skilled Occupations)
4 or 5	Skill Level C (Intermediate Occupations)
6	Skill Level D (Labouring and Elemental Occupations)

Important Note: This applies to all occupations except management occupations. For management, the first digit is "o" and the second digit represents the skill type categories, from 1 to 9, as above.

Source: Human Resources Development Canada, National Occupation Classification. Reproduced with permission of the Minister of Public Works and Government Services Canada, 2003.

Canadian Technology Human Resources Board (CTHRB)
www.cthrb.ca

working conditions
Facts about the situation in which the worker acts. Includes physical environment, hours, hazards, travel requirements, and so on, associated with a job.

Most authorities recommend that job summaries specify the primary actions involved. Then, in a simple, action-oriented style, the job description lists the job's responsibilities, or duties.

This section is important to human resource specialists. A well-developed job description helps an organization to define clearly the required duties and responsibilities associated with a position.[13] In essence, this section explains what the job requires. The effectiveness of other human resource actions depends upon this understanding, because each major duty is described in terms of the actions expected.*

Working Conditions

A job description also explains **working conditions**, which may go beyond descriptions of the physical environment. Hours of work, safety and health hazards, travel requirements, and other features of the job expand the meaning of this section.

Approvals

Because job descriptions affect most human resource decisions, their accuracy should be reviewed by selected jobholders and their supervisors. Then supervisors are asked to approve the description. This approval serves as a further test of the job description and a further check on the collection of job analysis information.

*One of this book's authors once consulted with a hospital in Halifax that had serious human resource problems: high turnover, absenteeism, low job satisfaction, low morale, etc. Employees who were interviewed complained of lack of objectives, clear responsibilities, performance feedback, and recognition, among other things. It turned out that the job descriptions used at the hospital were at least five years old, had never been updated, and, worst of all, had not even been used.

FIGURE 2-9	Examples of NOC Unit Groups

NOC Coding System. A two-digit code is assigned at the major group level. A third digit is added at the minor group level, and a fourth digit is added at the unit group level. For example:

- Major Group 31—Professional Occupations in Health
- Minor Group 314—Professional Occupations in Therapy and Assessment
- Unit Group 3142—Physiotherapists

Using the above coding system, the following codes are identified:

0211	Engineering Managers
0212	Architecture and Science Managers
0721	Facility Operation Managers
0722	Maintenance Managers
2231	Civil Engineering Technologists and Technicians
2234	Construction Estimators
3223	Dental Technicians
3412	Dental Laboratory Bench Workers
4164	Social Policy Researchers, Consultants, and Program Officers
4165	Health Policy Researchers, Consultants, and Program Officers
4214	Early Childhood Educators and Assistants
6443	Amusement Attraction Operators and Other Amusement Occupations
6671	Attendants in Recreation and Sport
7265	Welders
9515	Welding, Brazing, and Soldering Machine Operators

JOB SPECIFICATIONS

job specification
A written statement that explains what a job demands of jobholders and the human skills and factors required.

A **job specification** lists knowledge, skills, abilities, and other characteristics (KSAOs) necessary to do a job. These requirements include experience, training, education, and physical and mental demands.

Because the job description and the job specification both focus on the job, they are often combined. Whether part of a job description or a separate document, job specifications include the information illustrated in Figure 2-10. The data to compile specifications also come from the job analysis checklist.

A job specification should include specific tools, actions, experiences, education, and training (i.e., the individual requirements of the job). For example, it should describe "physical effort" in terms of the special actions demanded by the job. "Lifts 40-kilogram bags" is better and more specific than "Lifts heavy weights." Clear behaviour statements give a better picture than vague generalities.[14] Specifications of mental effort help human resource experts to determine the intellectual abilities needed to perform the job. Figure 2-10 contains several examples of the kind of information about physical and mental efforts needed by customer service representatives working for a department store.

Do the working conditions make any unusual demands on jobholders? The working conditions found in job descriptions may be translated by job specifications into demands faced by workers. Figure 2-11 provides examples for the job of hospital orderly. It shows that a simple statement of working conditions found in the job description can have significant implications for jobholders. For example, compare points 2 and 3 under the job description column with points 2 and 3 under job specifications.

FIGURE 2-10	A Job Specification Sheet

Maple Leaf Department Stores
Job Specification

Job Title: _____   Job Code: _____

Date: _____   Author: _____

Job Location: _____   Job Grade: _____

Report To: _____   Status: _____

Skill Factors

Education: Ten years of general education or equivalent.

Experience: Prior selling experience in a consumer-goods industry is desirable.

Communication: Strong interpersonal skills a must.

                        Ability to empathize with customer needs when communicating.

                        Knowledge of French highly desirable.

                        Should have strong oral communication skills.

Effort Factors

Physical Demands: Normally limited to those associated with clerical jobs although
                          long periods of standing may be required in some instances.

                          Should be able to lift products weighing 10 kilograms or less.

                          Finger dexterity to operate a computer keyboard and cash register
                          is essential.

Mental Demands: Ability to respond to customer inquiries regarding prices, service terms,
                          etc. a must. This requires good short-term memory.

                          Ability to learn and remember product codes of popular items.

Working Conditions: Works in a well-ventilated office.

                          May have to work outdoors in the case of lawn/gardening-related
                          equipment.

The above information is correct as approved by:

(Signed) _____   (Signed) _____

Customer Service Representative   Customer Service Supervisor

FIGURE 2-11	Translation of Working Conditions for Job Description to Job Specification

Calgary General Hospital
Hospital Orderly

Job Description Statement of Working Conditions	Job Specifications Interpretation of Working Conditions
1. Works in physically comfortable surroundings.	1. (Omitted. This item on the job description makes no demands on jobholders.)
2. Deals with physically ill and diseased patients.	2. Exposed to unpleasant situations and communicable diseases.
3. Deals with mentally ill patients.	3. May be exposed to verbal and physical abuse.

The job specifications for these hydro workers should clearly state that working outdoors under extreme conditions is a regular part of the job. What consequences could there be if that was not the case?

CP/Fred Chartrand.

When preparing specifications, it is critical not to include needless job requirements, as the following example illustrates:

> In one instance, an employer required a high-school diploma for nearly all jobs within the company except those in the labour pool. When the need for a diploma was challenged, the employer could not show that it was absolutely necessary to perform many of the jobs for which it was officially required, and although this requirement was applied equally to all applicants, it had an unequal impact on applicants from minority groups. As a result, many persons belonging to such groups were offered labour-pool jobs only.

Further, needless job requirements exclude potentially qualified individuals from consideration, which may reduce the effectiveness not only of hiring, but also of other human resource activities.

More recently, competency-based job descriptions and specifications have become increasingly popular. A **competency** is a knowledge, skill, ability, or characteristic associated with high performance on a job; examples are problem solving, analytical thinking, and leadership.[15] Others have defined the concept as an *attribute bundle*, consisting of task competencies; results competencies; and knowledge, skills, behaviours, and attitude competencies.[16] Whatever the precise definition, the objective in most cases is to identify characteristics associated with superior job performance.

Competencies are identified after a careful analysis of the work of high performers. This may be done through observation, listings of critical behaviours or incidents at work, interviews, employee logs, or otherwise. Some organizations have used competencies as the foundation for job design, new performance management systems, selection and career pathing, compensation, training and development, and, in a few cases, a highly integrated human resource management system called *competency-based management*.

> A survey of 219 Canadian organizations by the Conference Board of Canada found that 45 percent of the responding firms used a competency framework for training and development activities. A large number of the respondents had also used it for hiring, compensation, and performance management. According to 85 percent of the respondents, the adoption of a competency framework had enabled their training programs to become more strategic, while facilitating decision

competency
A knowledge, skill, ability, or characteristic associated with superior job performance.

competency model (competency framework)
A list of competencies required in a particular job.

Sample Competency Model
www.workitect.com/pdf/
Competencies
Competitiveness.pdf

making. This was because a competency framework allowed employees to quickly identify the success factors in their organizational and personal work.[17]

A **competency model** (or **competency framework**) describes a group of competencies required in a particular job, usually 10 to 15, often bundled in clusters. Competency models can be developed for individuals, specific jobs, teams, work units, or the total organization. For example, applied to HR functions they would be useful for planning, selection, orientation and training, career development, performance appraisal, and succession planning.

Individuals can use a competency model as a guide in their own career path. It would require a valid assessment of their own competencies and a comparison with required competencies of a specific job. It would identify areas in need of further development.

JOB PERFORMANCE STANDARDS

job performance standards
The work performance expected from an employee on a particular job.

Job analysis has a third application, **job performance standards**. These standards serve two functions. First, they become objectives or targets for employee efforts. The challenge or pride of meeting objectives may serve to motivate employees. Once standards are met, workers may feel accomplishment and achievement. This outcome contributes to employee satisfaction.

Second, standards are criteria against which job success is measured. They are indispensable to managers or human resource specialists who attempt to control work performance. Without standards, no control system can evaluate job performance.

All control systems have four featurets: standards, measures, correction, and feedback. The relationship among these four factors is illustrated in Figure 2-12. Job performance standards are developed from job analysis information, and then actual employee performance is measured. When measured performance strays from the job standard, corrective action is taken. The corrective action, in turn, may result in changes in either the standards (if they were inappropriate) or actual job performance:

> In the Calgary Trust Company, current standards dictated that each loan supervisor review 350 mortgage-loan applications per month. Yet the actual output averaged 290. When more recent job information was collected, analysts discovered that since the standards had been first set, several new duties had been added for each supervisor. Corrective action resulted in new job designs, revised job descriptions, and more realistic standards.

When the standards are wrong, as in the trust company example, they alert managers and human resource specialists to problems that need correction. The example also underscores the need for keeping job analysis information current.

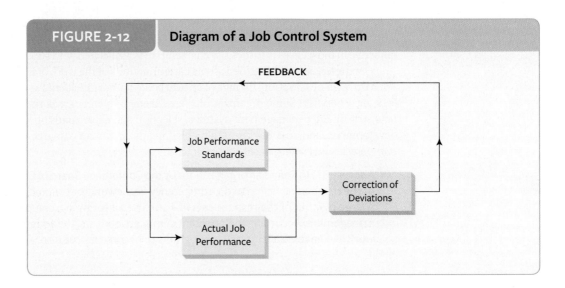

| FIGURE 2-12 | Diagram of a Job Control System |

SPOTLIGHT ON HRM
The Many Uses of a Job Description

Excerpt from an article by Mary Massa, June 2005

It's not just for screening candidates anymore. Today, business owners are finding numerous ways to put an employee's job description to work for them.

Who knew that a good job description could be such a versatile management tool? Though it still remains a hiring tool in the most traditional sense—a written description identifying a job by title, essential functions and requirements—a well-crafted description also spells out the knowledge, abilities and skills required to perform a job successfully. These additional descriptions are extremely helpful when it comes to employee training and career development.

A business owner can use a good job description not only as a valuable aid in the job-recruiting process, but also as an outline for reporting relationships and working conditions. A well-crafted job description can also be used for:

- Performance management.   Set measurable performance goals based on duties in the job description, and then coach employees to meet these goals as needed.

- Training and employee development.   Use employee job descriptions, along with descriptions of possible job promotions, as incentives for employees to pursue classes, seminars and other career development activities.

- Compensation.   Job descriptions can be helpful in developing a standardized compensation program with minimums and maximums for each position.

- Recognition and rewards.   Use the descriptions as a baseline for performance, and as a tool to encourage employee performance "above and beyond" the job description in order to receive recognition and rewards.

- Discipline.   Use the job description to illustrate that an employee isn't adequately performing job functions.

- Return-to-work programs.   A job description is also useful to prepare for light or modified duty options to allow for a smoother transition from a workers' compensation injury or leave.

- Essential job function analysis.   Written job descriptions have become increasingly important for employees with disabilities. A well-developed job description can provide details on the "essential functions" of a job. This is very helpful when an employee requests a reasonable accommodation. The job description can contain prerequisites for positions such as educational requirements, employment experience, physical requirements, supervisory responsibilities and certificates or licenses needed. Well-developed, accurate job descriptions may also prove useful in providing a defence against charges of employment discrimination beyond the recruiting process.

When it comes to job description, flexibility is the key. It may be wise to create more generic job descriptions that emphasize expectations and accountabilities, rather than specific tasks, thereby encouraging employees to focus on results rather than job duties. A more wide-ranging job description is also easier to maintain—it doesn't require modification with every minor change in duties.

Source: http://www.entrepreneur.com/humanresources/hiring/article78506.html

Job standards are obtained either from job analysis information or from alternative sources. For example, industry standards may be used as benchmarks for performance in certain jobs (especially service functions such as human resource management function).[18] Job analysis information is usually sufficient for jobs that have the following features:

- Performance is quantified.
- Performance is easily measurable.
- Performance standards are understood by workers and supervisors.
- Performance requires little interpretation.

Jobs with short work cycles often exhibit these features. An example is an assembly-line job. For these jobs, questions on the job analysis checklist may generate specific, quantitative answers. When confirmed by supervisors, this information becomes the job performance standard. In the case of some service jobs, quantifiable "outputs" may not be readily available; but even here, performance can be appraised by looking at the behaviours of the jobholders. More details of behaviourally oriented performance appraisals will be discussed in Chapter 8.

SPOTLIGHT ON ETHICS
Job Design: Happy Workers or Higher Profits?

A small manufacturer of snowboards and skateboards faces a dilemma. His 15 employees work in loose production teams on cutting, layering, edging, pressing, drilling, painting, drying, mounting, and printing the boards. Job satisfaction is high and there is almost no turnover. But because of competition, the company had little profits for the last two years and he wants to change that. His choice is to ask his employees to accept a significant pay cut, switch to an assembly-line system, or, the most profitable solution, install an automated machine, which would require only 3 workers, making the remaining 12 redundant. All of his employees are married and have children and have been with him for 15 and more years. He feels a strong obligation toward them, but is convinced that a workflow change is necessary.

Of what nature are his obligations toward his employees? What is the optimal solution for a) His employees? b) His company? c) Himself?

JOB DESIGN

Worldwide competition, complex technology, and increasing worker expectations have necessitated redesign of many jobs. Computerization, which barely existed 50 years ago, has brought about a revolution that has changed millions of jobs. While some jobs have grown more challenging, others are increasingly being automated or eliminated altogether. And yet, despite this vast increase in automation and computerization, human resources have become more, not less, important in today's organizations:

> For example, the cost of human error in a nuclear plant* or in flying a supersonic jet can be enormous. Whether it is the high-speed computers or the traditional auto assembly plant now run by robots, the contribution of human beings continues to be critical. Indeed, new technologies may be dangerous or unforgiving when operated by uncommitted or poorly skilled persons.

job design
Identification of job duties, characteristics, competencies, and sequences taking into consideration technology, workforce, organization character, and environment.

How well people perform is shaped, at least in part, by the characteristics designed into their jobs.[19] Not only is productivity affected, but quality of work life is also tied to **job design**. Jobs are the central link between employees and the organization. Poorly designed jobs not only lead to low productivity, but they can cause employee turnover, absenteeism, complaints, sabotage, unionization, resignations, and other problems. One insurance firm's experience of redesigning jobs is noteworthy in this context:

> At the General Life and Home Insurance Company, each clerk had narrowly defined responsibilities. Each clerk performed a specific function and moved the "paperwork" on to someone else. The result was that no one was responsible for handling an application for a policy conversion. In fact, no single department had responsibility because activities were spread over three departments. In a job redesign effort, clerks were grouped into teams of five to seven employees, and each team was trained to do the functions of all three departments. Members learned new skills, job satisfaction went up, and pay improved as each team member now had greater skills and responsibilities.

In this case, the company had to consider the various environmental, organizational, and employee-related factors before redesigning the jobs. Typically, job redesign results in some tradeoffs. Under the new structure in General Life and Home Insurance Company, each clerk needed to have knowledge of several activities. Therefore, more training for these clerks was necessary. And, as the clerks become more qualified, the company will need to pay them higher salaries.

Figure 2-13 illustrates four critical elements that deserve consideration when designing jobs: organizational, ergonomic, employee, and environmental considerations. Each is discussed below.

---

*A good example is the meltdown in the reactor of the Chernobyl nuclear power station in April 1986 in Ukraine, caused by a faulty test execution. The explosion released 100 times more radiation than the atomic bomb explosions in Hiroshima and Nagasaki. The long-term impact to the health of over seven million people is still not clear. The contamination stretched to Norway and Germany.

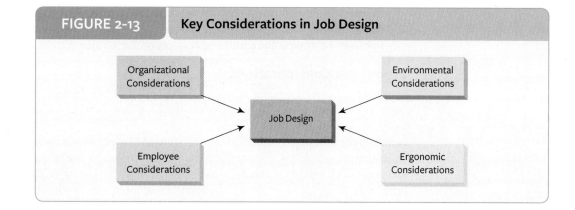

FIGURE 2-13   Key Considerations in Job Design

Organizational Considerations

Simply put, each job should contribute to the overall organizational objectives effectively and efficiently. The overall organizational mission is accomplished through a series of interrelated tasks or activities. If the organization is to remain successful and grow, these tasks and activities should be performed in a timely, effective, and efficient manner. This involves focus on two interrelated concepts: efficiency and work flow.

Efficiency

efficiency
Achieving maximal output with minimal input.

Concern for high task **efficiency** or achieving maximum output with minimum expenditure of time, effort, or other resources was first underscored by *scientific management* around the turn of the century. *Industrial engineering*, which evolved from this movement, focuses on analyzing work methods and establishing optimal time standards by finding the best ways to do jobs.[20] As discussed earlier, time standards are established by recording the time needed (typically using a stopwatch or, more recently, video monitors) to complete each element in a work cycle. These industrial engineers study work cycles to determine which, if any, job elements can be combined, modified, or eliminated to reduce the overall time needed to perform the task. *Task specialization* was suggested as a key strategy to improve efficiency. According to these engineers, when workers are limited to a few repetitive tasks, output is usually higher, because specialized jobs lead to *short job cycles*. The automotive industry is a good example of such industrial engineering practices:[21]

> For example, an assembly-line worker may pick up a headlight, plug it in, twist the adjustment screws, and pick up the next headlight within 30 seconds. Completing these tasks in 30 seconds means this worker's job cycle takes half a minute. The job cycle begins when the next headlight is picked up.

Headlight installation is a specialized job, so specialized that training takes only a few minutes. The short job cycle means that the assembler gains much experience in a short time. Said another way, short job cycles require small investments in training and allow the worker to learn the job quickly. Training costs remain low because the worker needs to master only one job.

The above approach stresses efficiency in effort, time, labour costs, training, and employee learning time. Today, this technique is still widely used in assembly operations. It is especially effective when dealing with poorly educated workers or workers who have little industrial experience. But the efficient design of jobs also considers such organizational elements as work flow, ergonomics, and work practices.

Work Flow

work flow
The sequence of and balance between jobs in an organization needed to produce the firm's goods or services.

The **work flow** in an organization is strongly influenced by the nature of the product or service. The product or service usually suggests the sequence of, and balance between, jobs if the work is to be done efficiently. For example, the frame of a car must be built before the fenders and doors can be added. Once the sequence of jobs is determined, the balance between jobs is established:

> Suppose it takes one person 30 seconds to install each headlight. In two minutes, an assembler can put on four headlights. If, however, it takes four minutes to install the necessary headlight receptacles, the job designer must balance these two interrelated jobs by assigning two people

to install the receptacles. Otherwise, a production bottleneck results. Therefore, the work flow demands two receptacle installers for each headlight installer: one worker specializes on the right-side receptacle and another specializes on the left side.

Ergonomic Considerations

ergonomics
The study of relationships between physical attributes of workers and their work environment to reduce physical and mental strain and increase productivity and quality of work life.

Optimal productivity requires that the physical relationship between the worker and the work be considered in designing jobs. Derived from the Greek words *ergo* meaning "work" and *nomos* meaning "laws," **ergonomics** in a general sense means the "laws of work" and focuses on how human beings physically interface with their work.[22] The study of ergonomics is multidisciplinary, using principles drawn from biology (especially anatomy and physiology), the behavioural sciences (psychology and sociology), and physics and engineering. Although the nature of job tasks may not vary when ergonomic factors are considered, the locations of tools, switches, and the work product itself are evaluated and placed in a position for ease of use. In other words, ergonomics focuses on fitting the task to the worker in many instances rather than simply forcing employees to adapt to the task.[23]

On an automobile assembly line, for example, a car frame may actually be elevated at a work station so that the worker does not become fatigued from stooping. Similarly, the location of dashboard instruments in a car is ergonomically engineered to make driving easier.

Attention to details of work settings can lead to significant improvements in efficiency and productivity, as exemplified by the case of Saturn Corporation:

Saturn uses state-of-the art manufacturing and job design techniques—including industrial engineering, ergonomics, and behavioural considerations. Cars pass through the assembly line on

If an employee has to remain in a seated position for many hours, an ergonomically correct seat and a suitably placed monitor are essential. What are other benefits of ergonomic considerations?

**Environmental Science
Engineering**
www.esemag.com/0596/
canadian.html

hydraulic lifts that allow employees to raise or lower the cars to suit their own height. Employees are allowed to ride the platform and take up to six minutes to finish their tasks correctly (traditional assembly lines allot less than one minute). Industrial engineers videotape employee actions and simplify operations to minimize motion. In one instance, employees saved one-third of the steps walking to and from cars, thereby conserving energy.[24]

Ergonomic considerations are also important to maintain safety at the workplace. Ignoring a proper fit between work station and worker can be catastrophic.[25]

Workplace accidents cost Canadian firms about $31 billion annually. A significant percentage of these accidents stem from poor workplace or task design.[26]

Ergonomics will become more important in the future as the Canadian workforce ages:

By 2015, the 45-to-54-year-old segment of the Canadian population will grow by 155 percent (compared to the size of this population segment during the mid-1990s). Those of pre-retirement age (55 to 64 years) will grow by 194 percent. Because aging results in a decrease in several hand functions (e.g., grip strength, precision), lowered muscular strength, and reduced vision and hearing, the need for ergonomics-based work improvements to reduce physical demands will be higher than ever before. Items such as mechanical assists for lifting (e.g., tilters, vacuum lifts) and for assembly (e.g., screw-guns, adjustable tables) will be essential. Such improvements will also be needed for lighting arrangements and size of character displays in terminals to respond to older workers' diminished visual capabilities.[27]

Employee Considerations

Jobs cannot be designed by using only those elements that aid efficiency. To do so overlooks the human needs of the people who are to perform the work. Instead, job designers draw heavily on behavioural research to provide a work environment that helps satisfy individual needs. In general, jobs have to be designed not only to maximize productivity, but also to help the employees achieve better work–life balance.

Research studies indicate that employee productivity can be up to 20 percent higher in organizations that implement work–life balance programs.[28]

This section briefly describes the Job Characteristic Model, which discusses the importance of high autonomy, variety, task identity, feedback, and task significance in a job design context.[29] According to this model, these five characteristics result in three psychological states: meaningfulness, responsibility, and knowledge of outcomes. Employees who find themselves in jobs that provide these experiences tend to have higher motivation, job satisfaction, and productivity.

Autonomy

autonomy
In a job context, independence—having control over one's work and one's response to the work environment.

Autonomy refers to the concept of assuming responsibility for what one does. It is the freedom to control one's response to the environment. While employee personality influences the relationship between autonomy and specific task performance,[30] in most instances, jobs that give workers the authority to make decisions tend to increase employees' sense of recognition, self-esteem, job satisfaction, and performance. The absence of autonomy, on the other hand, can cause employee apathy or poor performance:

A common problem in many production operations is that employees develop an indifferent attitude because they believe they have no control over their jobs. On the bottling line of a small brewery, however, teams of workers were allowed to speed up or slow down the rate of the bottling line as long as they met daily production goals. Although total output per shift did not change, there were fewer cases of capping machines jamming or breaking down for other reasons. When asked about this unexpected development, the supervisor concluded, "Employees pride themselves on meeting the shift quota. So they are more careful to check for defective bottle caps before they load the machine."

Variety

variety
An attribute of jobs wherein the worker has the opportunity to use different skills and abilities, or perform different activities.

A lack of **variety** may cause boredom. Boredom in turn leads to fatigue, and fatigue causes errors. By injecting variety into jobs, human resource specialists can reduce fatigue-caused errors.

> Being able to control the speed of the bottling line in the brewery example added variety to the pace of work and probably reduced both boredom and fatigue.

Past research studies have found that variety in work may be related to effective performance and can be a major contributor to employee satisfaction.

Task Identity

task identity
The feeling of responsibility of pride that results from doing an entire piece of work, not just a small part of it.

One problem with some jobs is that they lack any **task identity**. Workers cannot point to some complete piece of work. They have little sense of responsibility and may lack pride in the results. After completing their job, they may have little sense of accomplishment. When tasks are grouped so that employees feel they are making an identifiable contribution, job satisfaction may be increased significantly.

> In the earlier General Life and Home Insurance Company example, we saw that productivity and satisfaction increased when employees became responsible for an identifiable and sensible group of tasks.

Feedback

feedback
Information that helps evaluate the success or failure of an action or system.

When jobs do not give the workers any **feedback** on how well they are doing, there is little guidance or motivation to perform better.

> For example, by letting employees know how they are doing relative to the daily production quota, the brewery gives workers feedback that allows them to adjust their efforts. Providing feedback leads to improved motivation.

Task Significance

task significance
Knowing that the work one does is important to others in the organization or to outsiders.

Closely related to the above dimensions is **task significance**. Doing an identifiable piece of work makes the job more satisfying for employees. Task significance, knowing that the work is important to others within the organization or outside it, makes the job even more meaningful for incumbents. Their personal sense of self-importance is enhanced because they know that others depend on what they do. Pride, commitment, motivation, satisfaction, and better performance are likely to result.

> A good example was the Porsche car company. Mechanics, who assembled complete engines, punched their names into the engine block, a cause of extreme pride, but also useful for feedback purposes. Rationalization eliminated this procedure, resulting in lower satisfaction, lower quality, and higher turnover.

Job Specialization

As workers become more educated and affluent, routine jobs that are very specialized, such as assembly-line positions, hold less and less appeal for many people. These jobs seldom offer opportunities for accomplishment, recognition, psychological growth, or other sources of satisfaction. To increase the quality of work life for those who hold such jobs, human resource departments often use a combination of *job rotation*, *job enlargement*, and *job enrichment*.

Job Rotation

job rotation
Moving employees from one job to another to allow them more variety and to learn new skills.

Job rotation moves employees from job to job. Jobs are not actually changed; only the workers are rotated. Rotation breaks the monotony of highly specialized work by calling on different skills and abilities. The organization benefits because workers become competent in several jobs rather than one. Knowing a variety of jobs improves self-image, provides personal growth, and makes the worker more valuable to the organization.

> Job rotation was introduced by the Volvo car company in 1973 to reduce the monotony of the assembly line. Work teams exchanged jobs during the day. Job satisfaction increased and turnover decreased.

A caution about the use of job rotation: it does not improve the jobs, as the relationships between tasks, activities, and objectives remain unchanged. It may even delay the use of more effective techniques while adding to training costs. Implementation should occur only after other techniques have been considered.

Job Enlargement

job enlargement
Adding more tasks to a job to increase the job cycle and draw on a wider range of employee skills.

Job enlargement expands the number of related tasks in the job. It adds similar duties to provide greater variety. Enlargement reduces monotony by expanding the job cycle and drawing on a wider range of employee skills.

> IBM reported that job enlargement led to higher wages and more inspection equipment, but improved quality and worker satisfaction offset these costs. Maytag Company claimed that production quality was improved, labour costs declined, worker satisfaction and overall efficiency were increased, and management production schedules became more flexible.[31]

Job Enrichment

job enrichment
Adding more responsibilities and autonomy to a job, giving the worker greater powers to plan, do, and evaluate job performance.

Job enrichment adds new sources of needs satisfaction to jobs. It increases responsibility, autonomy, and control. Adding these elements to jobs is sometimes called *vertical loading.* (*Horizontal loading* occurs when the job is expanded by simply adding related tasks, as with job enlargement.) Enrichment views jobs as consisting of three elements—*plan, do,* and *control*. Job enlargement (or horizontal loading) adds more things to do, whereas enrichment (vertical loading) attempts to add more *planning* and *control* responsibilities. This, coupled with rethinking the job itself, often leads to increased motivation and other improvements:

> Since 1999, every year Statistics Canada has sampled information from over 6,000 Canadian workplaces about workforce characteristics and job organization, with specific questions regarding decision making, quality circles, teams, suggestion programs, feedback, and self-directed work. Two researchers used the data to determine whether enriched jobs result in higher motivation and job satisfaction. The study included feedback from 43,917 employees. The results strongly support the hypothesis that enriched jobs increase motivation and satisfaction.[32]

Job enrichment, however, is not a cure-all—if it were, this book could end here! Job enrichment techniques are merely tools, and they are not applicable universally. When the diagnosis indicates that jobs are unchallenging and limit employee motivation and satisfaction, human resource departments may find job enrichment to be the most appropriate strategy.

Employee Involvement and Work Teams

More recently, other approaches, such as employee involvement groups (also known as *quality circles*), employee teams, and other approaches, have been introduced to increase employee involvement at the workplace. Work itself is increasingly being organized around teams and processes rather than activities or functions. Over 40 percent of the respondents in a national survey by the Conference Board of Canada reported use of teams in their workplaces.[33] Self-managed and autonomous work teams have become a normal part of several organizations. These and other employee involvement approaches are discussed in detail in Chapter 11. The intent of all such approaches, however, is to provide more autonomy, feedback, and task significance to workers.

> At Compaq Computers (which has now merged with Hewlett-Packard), nearly a quarter of its employees work in teams. A cross-section of other organizations, including CIBC, Xerox Canada, and Vancouver City Savings, demonstrated that employee teams result in better quality, lower turnover and absenteeism, and a sense of accomplishment for their workforce.[34]

As in the case of job enrichment, employee involvement and teams may not be appropriate for all organizations or all situations. The complexity of the task involved, the prevalence of the shift system, and the skill levels of employees involved may moderate the applicability of such systems in a particular situation.[35] The introduction of team management, if not accompanied by changes in other systems (e.g., performance appraisal, compensation), may cause frustration. To be successful, top management has to be truly committed to the notion of employee empowerment—that is, granting employees the power to initiate change and take charge of what they do.

Use of Job Families in HR Decisions

job families
Groups of different jobs that are closely related by similar duties, responsibilities, skills, or job elements.

Often, in the context of job design, the human resource manager looks at **job families** rather than single jobs. Job families are groups of jobs that are closely related by similar duties, responsibilities, skills, or job elements. The jobs of clerk, word processor, clerk-typist, and secretary constitute a job family, for example.

Job families can be constructed in several ways. One way is by careful study of existing job analysis information. Matching the data in job descriptions can identify jobs with similar requirements. A second method is to use the codes in the *National Occupational Classification* discussed earlier in this chapter. Similarities in the job codes indicate similarities in the jobs. A third approach is to use the *Position Analysis Questionnaire*, also discussed earlier in this chapter, and statistically analyze information on tasks and worker traits to identify clusters of similar jobs.

Job families allow human resource managers to plan job rotation programs and make employee transfer decisions. The compensation levels of jobs that form a family should also be comparable; this means that equitable compensation strategies cannot be formed without considering the entire job family. In some instances, it may also be economical to use similar recruitment methods and sources to hire individuals who belong to the same job family.

Environmental Considerations

environmental considerations
The influence of the external environment on job design. Includes employee ability, availability, and social expectations.

The environments within which the firm and job exist also need to be considered when redesigning jobs. As with most human resource activities, job designers cannot ignore **environmental considerations**—the influence of the external environment, which affects workforce availability, values, and practices.

Workforce Availability

Efficiency considerations must be balanced against the abilities and availability of the people who will actually do the work. An extreme example underlines this point:

> Governments of less developed countries often think they can "buy" progress. To be "up to date," they seek the most advanced equipment they can find. Leaders of one country ordered a computerized oil refinery, necessitating a level of technology that exceeded the abilities of the country's available workforce. As a result, these government leaders have now hired Europeans to operate the refinery.

In less developed nations, the major risk is jobs that are too complex. But in industrialized nations with highly educated workers, jobs that are too simple can produce equally disturbing problems.

> For example, even when unemployment rates are high, many simple and overly specialized jobs are sometimes hard to fill, as longstanding newspaper want ads for janitors attest.

Social Expectations

social expectations
The larger society's expectations from employees regarding job challenge, working conditions, and quality of work life.

The acceptability of a job's design is also influenced by **social expectations**. For example, working conditions that would have been acceptable to some early Canadian immigrants are no longer acceptable to our present generation.

> When rail lines were being laid across Canada, many persons were willing to work long hours of hard labour. They had fled countries where jobs were unavailable, which made a job—any job—acceptable to them. Today, industrial workers are much better educated and have higher expectations about the quality of work life.

Even where work flow might suggest a particular job design, the job must meet the expectations of workers. Failure to consider these expectations can create dissatisfaction, poor motivation, and low quality of work life.

Work Practices

work practices
The set ways of performing work in an organization.

Work practices are set ways of performing work. These methods may arise from tradition or from the collective wishes of employees. Either way, the human resource department's flexibility to design jobs is limited, especially when such practices are part of a union–management relationship. Failure to consider work practices can have undesired outcomes:

General Motors decided to increase productivity at one of its American plants by eliminating some jobs and adding new tasks to others. These design changes caused workers to stage a strike for several weeks because traditional practices at the plant had required a slower rate of production and less work by the employees. The additional demands on their jobs by management were seen as an attempt by the company to disregard past work practices.

JOB ANALYSIS IN TOMORROW'S "JOBLESS" WORLD

Global competition, fast technological obsolescence, changing worker profile, and rapid increases in knowledge requirements for various jobs have made accurate and timely job descriptions difficult. Indeed, some writers have gone so far as to say that jobs as we see them today may not exist in the future.[36] Today's global village has resulted in "boundary-less" and "de-jobbed" organizations, in which traditional boundaries between a firm, its suppliers, customers, and even competitors have disappeared and "jobs" as we knew them in the past have begun to disappear.[37] Many employees are no longer responsible for producing specific outcomes; rather, they are members of teams entrusted with many responsibilities. In tomorrow's world, a firm may be valued by its ideas rather than its assets or products.[38]

How do organizations that operate in such fast-changing environments conduct valid job analyses? How can the task and person requirements identified today be relevant for an unknown tomorrow?

Of course, there are no simple solutions. A few attempts have been made to meet the newfound challenges. One strategy has been to adopt a future-oriented style when describing job activities and specifications. Rather than asking what the current job incumbent does, the focus is on what the job incumbent must do to effectively carry out and further organizational strategies and the new competencies required of the jobholder. Thus, present and future requirements, rather than past actions, guide job descriptions and the hiring and training of employees.

Another strategy utilizes the competency approach discussed earlier in the chapter. The focus is on the tasks and competencies needed to match an organization's strategy, structure, and culture. Rather than simply looking at the purely functional skills of the job, this approach focuses on the many competencies (e.g., decision making, conflict resolution, adaptiveness skills) required. Figure 2-14 shows an example in an engineering firm. Each of the six competencies is measured

FIGURE 2-14	An Example of Competency Matrix in an Engineering Firm

Engineer: $T = 6; P = 4; C_1 = 3; C_2 = 5; O = 3; L = 2$

Manager: $T = 3; P = 6; C_1 = 5; C_2 = 5; O = 6; L = 6$

Levels

High	7	7	7	7	7	7
	6	6	6	6	6	6
	5	5	5	5	5	5
	4	4	4	4	4	4
	3	3	3	3	3	3
	2	2	2	2	2	2
Low	1	1	1	1	1	1
Competency:	Technical Expertise (T)	Problem Solving (P)	Creativity (C1)	Communication Skills (C2)	Organizational Ability (O)	Leadership (L)

at seven levels (Level 1 being the lowest, Level 7 the highest). Employees may be expected to possess all competencies, though to varying degrees. An engineer may be required to possess high technical expertise and medium problem-solving abilities, while a manager may have to possess more sophisticated higher problem-solving skills and lower levels of technical expertise; both are expected to have adequate communication abilities. Use of a competency matrix shifts the focus from performing specific duties to developing broader skills needed. It also empowers employees to assume new responsibilities. Such a system must be supported by an effective training and development strategy and a competency-based compensation system. These will be discussed in later chapters.

Further, job analysis will continue to be relevant for legal compliance and defensibility in the event of a court action.[39] Traditional sources of information (such as job incumbents, supervisors) may, however, need to be supplemented by data emerging from customers, peers, and technical experts to incorporate the ever-changing job demands.

⟹ SUMMARY

Job analysis information provides the foundations of an organization's human resource information system. Analysts seek to gain a general understanding of the organization and the work it performs. Then they design job analysis questionnaires to collect specific data about jobs, jobholder characteristics, and job performance standards. Job analysis information can be collected through interviews, mailed questionnaires, employee logs, direct observation, or some combination of these techniques. Once collected, the data are converted into such useful applications as job descriptions, job specifications, and job standards.

Job analysis information is important because it tells human resource specialists what duties and responsibilities are associated with each job. This information is then used when these specialists undertake other human resource management activities such as job design, recruiting, and selection. Jobs are the link between organizations and their human resources. The combined accomplishment of every job allows the organization to meet its objectives. Similarly, jobs represent not only a source of income to workers but also a means of fulfilling their needs. For the organization and its employees to receive these mutual benefits, jobs must provide also a high quality of work life. This means that when designing jobs, organizational priorities (e.g., efficiency) alone should not play the decisive role. The needs of employees as well as environmental realities also play critical roles in job design efforts. This is especially true with the emergence of a "de-jobbed" and "boundary-less" work world where employees are expected to take initiative and solve problems creatively.

⟹ TERMS FOR REVIEW

autonomy **p. 77**
combination **p. 65**
competency **p. 71**
competency model (competency
    framework) **p. 72**
efficiency **p. 75**
employee log **p. 65**
environmental considerations **p. 80**
ergonomics **p. 76**
feedback **p. 78**
interview **p. 64**
job **p. 57**

job analysis **p. 57**
job analysis schedules **p. 61**
job code **p. 67**
job description **p. 66**
job design **p. 74**
job enlargement **p. 79**
job enrichment **p. 79**
job families **p. 80**
job identity **p. 67**
job performance standards **p. 72**
job rotation **p. 78**
job specification **p. 69**

mailed questionnaires **p. 65**
National Occupational Classification
    (NOC) **p. 67**
observation **p. 65**
position **p. 57**
social expectations **p. 80**
task identity **p. 78**
task significance **p. 78**
variety **p. 78**
work flow **p. 75**
work practices **p. 80**
working conditions **p. 68**

⊙ SELF-ASSESSMENT EXERCISE

How Enjoyable Was That Work or Project?

Consider a job that you held in the past. If you have no work experience, consider a course project or other effort where you had to work for a reward. Please respond to the following questions frankly:

Statement About Your Work/Project	Strongly Disagree	Disagree	Agree	Strongly Agree
1. I felt that I had control over the quality and performance of my job.				
2. I was not allowed to plan the optimal pace at which I could work.				
3. The work/project involved various activities.				
4. It was the same routine every day; I did the same things day after day.				
5. At the end of a day, I could see a finished job or part of the project.				
6. There were many days when I had little sense of accomplishment.				
7. My boss/supervisor always told me whether I did the work well or poorly.				
8. I got little feedback from anyone about how well I performed during the course of the project.				
9. The work I did (or the project I completed) was an important one.				
10. Often I felt that it made little difference how I did on this job/project.				

SCORING

For the odd-numbered statements, assign a score of 1, 2, 3, or 4 for Strongly Disagree, Disagree, Agree, and Strongly Agree, respectively. For the even-numbered statements, reverse the scoring—that is, Strongly Disagree gets a score of 4 and Strongly Agree gets a score of 1. Add up your scores for all 10 statements.

Your score should lie somewhere in between 10 and 40. If you received a score of 32 or higher, you had an enjoyable experience with your past work or assignment—at least most of the time. If you scored less than 20, it is unlikely that you had much fun doing the job or project.

While this is not a validated instrument, statements 1 and 2 above indicate the overall autonomy you had in doing the project; 3 and 4 measure the dimension of variety; 5 and 6 reflect task identity; 7 and 8 measure feedback; and 9 and 10 measure task significance. On each dimension, your scores can range anywhere from 2 to 8. It is possible for you to get a high score on one dimension and a low score on another, although an "enriched" project would have had high scores on all dimensions.

⊙ REVIEW AND DISCUSSION QUESTIONS

1. Suppose you work for an organization that does not conduct job analysis. What arguments will you make to introduce it? What method(s) of collecting job analysis information will you recommend and why?

2. Define job descriptions and job specifications, illustrating how the two are related, yet different.

3. Why are clear job specifications important? What are the costs of imprecise specifications?

4. How can performance standards be set for production jobs when job analysis information is insufficient? How would you set standards of performance for a research scientist if you were chief scientist?

5. What factors need to be considered when redesigning jobs? Of these, which is (are) most important?

⊙ CRITICAL THINKING QUESTIONS

1. Suppose you were assigned to write the job descriptions for a shirt factory in British Columbia employing mostly Chinese immigrants who spoke little English. What methods would you use to collect job analysis data?

2. You work in the human resource department of a large brewery in Atlantic Canada. You are in the process of writing job descriptions for all managerial and supervisory staff. One manager who is in the production division of the brewery refuses to complete a job analysis questionnaire.

   (a) What reasons would you use to persuade that individual to complete it?

   (b) If, after your best efforts at persuasion failed, you still wanted job analysis information on the manager's job, how would you get it?

3. Suppose that you have been assigned to design the job of ticket clerk for a regional airline in Ontario. How would you handle the following tradeoffs?

   (a) Would you recommend highly specialized job designs to minimize training or very broad job designs with all clerks cross-trained to handle multiple tasks? Why?

   (b) Would you change your answer if you knew that employees tended to quit the job of ticket clerk within the first six months? Why or why not?

4. Assume that you are told to evaluate a group of jobs in a boat-building business. After studying each job for a considerable amount of time, you identify the following activities associated with each job. What job redesign techniques would you recommend for these jobs, if any?

   (a) **Sailmaker:** Cuts and sews materials with very little variety in the type of work from day to day. Job is highly skilled and takes years to learn.

   (b) **Sander:** Sands rough wood and fibreglass edges almost continuously. Little skill is required in this job.

   (c) **Sales representative:** Talks to customers, answers phone inquiries, suggests customized additions to special-order boats.

   (d) **Boat preparer:** Cleans up completed boats, waxes fittings, and generally makes the boat ready for customer delivery. Few skills are required for this job.

5. What are the key performance dimensions of the instructor who is teaching this course? How will you go about setting performance standards for the individual? Establish performance standards and associated time-bound, specific objectives in any two areas of your choice.

⊙ ETHICS QUESTION

Your firm, an importer of a large number of consumer goods including garments, sent you to a developing country to negotiate a deal with a local exporter. Under the proposed contract, your firm will invest 25 percent of the capital necessary to open a new garment tailoring plant, with the exporter investing the balance. During your week-long stay in the country, you realize that child labour is fairly common in this country, although a number of local employers categorically refuse to employ anyone under 18 years of age in their plants. During

discussions with the local plant manager, you understand that he plans to use 12-to-15-year-old children in the factory, and the children will have performance standards at levels equal to or higher than a typical adult Canadian worker in the same industry. You know that a couple of other foreign firms are currently interested in reaching a deal with this exporter because he has a reputation for reliability and quality. This is your first visit to this country.

What action, if any, will you take?

● WEB RESEARCH EXERCISE

Select any job position (e.g., a financial accountant) of your choice. Consider various recruiters on the Web. (Chapter 5, on recruitment, provides some Web site addresses for you to begin your search.) Are there any differences in the job specifications listed by different recruiters? Are any patterns visible across industry groups?

● INCIDENT 2-1

Hillary Home Appliances Corporation

Hillary Home Appliances and Furnishings Corporation (HHAC) is a medium-sized manufacturer of home appliances. Historically, the firm has followed a low-cost strategy to successfully operate in a highly competitive industry. Recently, increasing global competition has made it necessary for the firm to revise its strategy in favour of improved customer service. The organization had paid virtually no attention to the human resource function; its human resource department (called "personnel and staffing department") focused primarily on compensation administration and staffing. Now, however, the top management of the firm is convinced of the need for strategic use of its human resources. An indication of this new thrust is the hiring of Leslie Wong, who has a reputation as a results-oriented HR manager (in two previous organizations), and the renaming of the department to "Human Resources." However, progressive HR practices have been slow to find acceptance at lower levels. In a recent meeting with two work supervisors, Jeff Gidoe and Mike Tarson, Leslie Wong, the newly hired human resource manager, faced these arguments:

Jeff Gidoe: I agree that good employee relations are important. But I simply cannot afford to let the HR staff interrupt our daily work with job analysis. Already, with the arrival of two new competitors, we have lost most of our cost advantage. Spending time on activities such as this further reduces our production and increases our costs.

Mike Tarson: Your plan to invite ideas from employees for product improvement is good; however, I should warn you that many of the workers in my section are school dropouts. They simply cannot accept responsibility. They care only for the wages they get and are constantly looking at the clock for quitting time.

Jeff Gidoe: At least a few of my employees will object to the time spent on job analysis. As you know, we have a production bonus plan in this plant. Every minute they spend on activities such as this costs them money. Already, several of them feel that the production standards are too high.

Mike Tarson: Your new idea of employee involvement teams is also likely to create problems. Already, they waste a fair bit of time each day jesting and horseplaying. If you put them into groups, things will only get worse, not better.

Leslie Wong: I value your comments. As supervisors, you know your employees best. I recognize that you are experts in your production areas. However, I can tell you this: the facts you have provided have simply reconfirmed the need for job analysis. Even more, it tells me that HR has a key role to play in this firm. I'll tell you why.

1. What prompted the HR manager to make the above statement?

2. If you were the HR manager, what arguments would you provide to convince the two supervisors of the desirability of job analysis and employee involvement teams?

● EXERCISE 2-1

A Good Work Environment

Think of some work-related situation that you have found enjoyable. Think of the job and identify the features that made it more enjoyable than other jobs that you have held. The job need not have been a formal, full-time job. It may simply have been some temporary job or even some chore you have had to perform. Make a list of those characteristics of the job that made it so enjoyable.

1. In reviewing your answers with others, do you find any similarities between your list and the lists of others who did different jobs?

2. Do these characteristics indicate what job features provide a good work situation?

⊙ EXERCISE 2-2

Strength and Weaknesses of Job Descriptions*

Step 1. Students should bring several job descriptions to class.

Step 2. Create teams of three. Discuss the job descriptions. Do they adequately reflect the responsibilities and KSAOs that the employee will need to perform? Compare the job descriptions to the information in your text. What are the weaknesses and strengths of the job descriptions? What specific changes would make the job descriptions more measurable?*

⊙ CASE STUDY 🍁 Maple Leaf Shoes Ltd.

An Exercise in Job Analysis*

Maple Leaf Shoes Ltd. is a medium-sized manufacturer of leather and vinyl shoes located near Wilmington, Ontario. It began operations in 1969 and currently employs about 400 persons in its Ontario plant and some 380 more in offices and warehouses throughout Canada and internationally. In recent months, the company has experienced a number of challenges and problems (see the Case Study in Chapter 1 for further background). Added to these problems was the departure of John McAllister, the company's human resource manager. McAllister had been with the company for a little over three years and was reputed to have "run a tight ship."

Robert Clark, president and a major shareholder of Maple Leaf Shoes, decided to reevaluate the role of the company's human resource manager before hiring a new person. Tim Lance, a graduate of the University of Manitoba and now the chief executive and owner of Productivity Systems, a management consulting operation located in Saskatoon, was hired to "look into the present and future role of Maple Leaf's human resource department and suggest appropriate action plans to improve its contribution to the organization and help the company meet its future challenges."

Views of the Senior Managers

Lance began his assignment by interviewing the senior managers of Maple Leaf Shoes. He made a short checklist of questions to prepare for his interview with the managers (see Figure 1). He was, however, determined not to restrict his interview to these questions. By keeping an informal and free-flowing format, he felt that he could gain a better understanding of the structure, processes, and culture of the organization. His intent, therefore, was to use these questions as a springboard for letting the interviewee speak out and pursue any point that he or she may consider relevant. Lance was able to meet two of the five "key" managers in the company, plus the president. Figure 2 shows an approximate chain of command in the company. At the time Lance conducted his study, André Cardin, manager of Design & Research, was away on holidays. Lance was also unable to have an interview with the production manager, Bob Smith, because he was away on trips to Montreal and Winnipeg investigating the potential of expanding the company's operations to those cities. Lance felt that the half-hour interview with Robert Clark (interrupted by three or four phone calls "on urgent matters that unexpectedly arose") was totally inadequate for his purpose. However, Clark was due to leave town the next day, and Lance could not wait until Clark's return to proceed with his study.

After going through his notes, Lance realized that the human resource function was viewed very differently by the three people with whom he spoke. Clark had told him:

> I believe that we need a mover and shaker here. McAllister was all right, but he did not have the time or inclination to have a good system in place. He made most of the human resource decisions himself. I'm not saying that they weren't the correct decisions for those occasions; but he wasn't a popular man with either the employees or several managers. And as you know, this is one job where you need a lot of rapport with people at all levels.

Excerpts from Lance's interview with Clark follow:

> I believe that the new person should be able to work with the people. In fact, not simply working with the people, but leading them. He or she should be able to look beyond today's needs ... into the technological and other challenges that face this company and our managers in the new millennium. ...

> The future of Maple Leaf Shoes? I have mixed feelings on this. On the one hand, shoes are something that everyone needs—every day, every week, and throughout their lives. Also, most persons don't mind buying an extra pair if the price is right. But there's the catch. It's a pretty competitive market and what we do here and how well we do it depends quite a bit on how good our competitors are. To succeed, we need to have a clear market segment, control our costs, and meet our customers' needs. Two of our brands, which were leaders in the western Canada shoe market, are facing intense competition from products manufactured in China, Indonesia, and Korea. ... The currency crisis in Asia

*Exercise suggestion: C. Fitzgerald, Okanagan College, Kelowna, B.C.

*Case written by Professor Hari Das of the Department of Management, Saint Mary's University. All rights reserved by the author. © 2002.

FIGURE 1	Checklist Prepared by Lance for Interviewing the Senior Managers

- What do you expect from the human resource department in this company?
- What is your evaluation of the human resource department's contributions in the past?
- What activities should the human resource department of this company carry out?
- Which of these are done now? How well are you satisfied with the performance of the department in those fields?
- Overall, are you happy with the human resource staff? Why?
- What are the major challenges facing Maple Leaf Shoes in the next five years?
- What are the unique needs of your department?
- What new services or information should the human resource department provide you?

FIGURE 2	An Approximate Chain of Command in Maple Leaf Shoes Ltd.

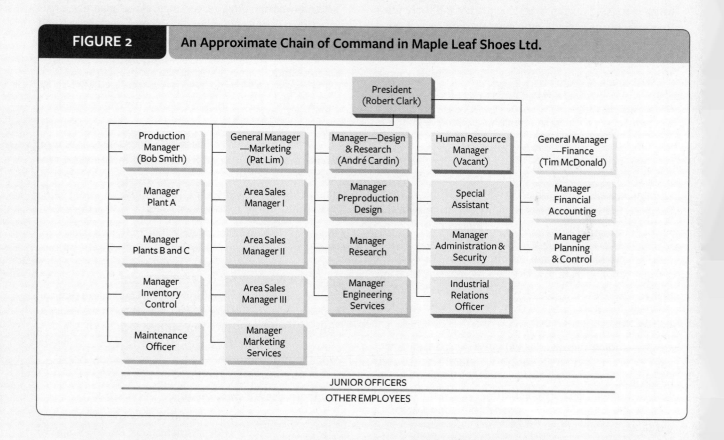

(especially in Korea and Indonesia) can both hurt and help us. On the one hand, the prices of the imported shoes are getting lower by the day, thus cutting into our markets. The other side is that Western investments in these countries may slow down—at least in the short run. This means that we have breathing room to cope with this onslaught. ... So, all in all ... who knows?

The most immediate problem? I should say we have two pressing issues: first, we must upgrade our production processes if we are to improve our efficiency and competitiveness. I personally believe that we have more employees than we need. If we could automate many of the production processes, we could improve the efficiency and reduce costs. But that is easier said than done. We have strong unions, and firing someone is going to be awfully hard in the future. At the same time, the reality is that no customer is going to pay 15 or 20 percent extra for our shoes if we cannot give a damn good reason for that. With the free trade worldwide, the market is flooded with Asian and South American products. We simply cannot compete with the Chinese and the Mexicans on the labour costs. ... Our survival may very well depend on technological upgrading and improving worker productivity.

A second and related issue is dealing with unions. We have four major unions and I would term two of them as militant. Actually, our workers are pretty good—many of them have been with us for several years now—it's the union leadership that's causing much of the problem. The new human resource manager hired must be tough with the unions, yet caring and understanding. In the last three or four years, union–management relations have gone from bad to worse. We have to turn a new leaf now or else all of us will sink.

The responses to Lance's questions from the other two senior managers at Maple Leaf Shoes were varied. Excerpts from his interview with Tim McDonald, general manager, finance, are provided below:

I don't think human resource management is the most critical activity in the management of a shoe company. True, we have to pay the employees adequately and there must be a system for keeping employee records. But, beyond that, I don't think that the human resource department has anything major to offer that has a significant impact on an organization's working. What we really should focus on now is how to control our costs and come out with a sound marketing program. We especially need a good advertising campaign; we need to hire competent sales staff and upgrade the skills of the present sales force. ...

The human resource department here hasn't done much, if you ask me. They haven't had any input into job design or organizational planning. Part of the problem stems from the fact that there has been little continuity in that department. A typical manager in the human resource department stays for about three years before he moves out. Neither McAllister nor his predecessor stayed in the company for five years. Tony Rezkov, the manager in charge of administration and security, is new; so are several of the other junior officers and staff in the department. ... I do believe there is a problem there. ...

Oh, don't get me wrong. The human resource department staff are very friendly and cooperative. McAllister had a few rough edges, but overall he was someone whom I grew to like. He was one of those tough guys—straight out of an old John Wayne movie. He made fast decisions and was sort of a troubleshooter here. ...

The big challenge? Global competition, of course. We'd better be prepared to meet the Koreans, the Chinese, and the Mexicans. Unless we maintain our competitiveness, we are just not going to survive. It's as simple as that. ...

Of course, global free trade also brings with it a great opportunity. NAFTA gave us access to a market now that is several times the size of our local market. Freer trade in Asia and Eastern Europe will do the same. ... But can we make use of this opportunity? That's the big question.

Pat Lim, general manager, marketing (and who was currently overseeing the human resource function until a new HR manager is appointed), had a somewhat different vision of the role of the human resource department:

It's probably one of the most important functions in this company. In my university days, I was taught that human resources are the single most important asset of any organization. After working for nearly 25 years in the management area, I've grown to realize how true that statement is. In my mind, people make all the difference. You can have all the resources you want, but in the absence of good employees, all those resources are worthless. The human resource department is the backbone of our employee relations. ...

What do I expect from the human resource department? Quite a lot, I should say. I believe that the department can play a leadership and developmental role. Until now, it has played a somewhat low-key, record-keeping, staff role. It's time the department became involved seriously in employee planning, job redesign, career planning, organizational design, and other development activities. Gone are the days when it could simply play a support role. Look at all the successful companies in this country and the United States, especially those that are listed in books such as *In Search of Excellence*. It's the people and people management that differentiate them from the common crop. ...

The new human resource manager should be an expert—an expert on systems and people. We need new ideas here, and with a growing workforce we need more formal procedures and systems, whether it's orientation or performance appraisal. Right now, many of the human resource activities are done on an ad hoc basis.

Above all, I believe that the new human resource manager needs to bring a new philosophy to deal with the unions. In the past several months, there has been an increasing degree of hostility between the unions and management. I'm not blaming anyone for this. But I do believe that we, as part of the management team, have the responsibility to solve some of these problems. It's up to us to take the initiative to improve the situation. Isn't that the essence of good management?

View from the Human Resource Department

As part of the study, Lance met with the three key staff members in the human resources department: Jane Reynolds, special assistant to the human resource manager; Tony Rezkov, manager of administration and security; and Joseph McDonald, the industrial relations officer (no relation to Tim McDonald). Rezkov, being new on the job, was unable to tell Lance much about his position or the human resource function. In Lance's opinion, his two meetings (lasting approximately an hour each) with Jane Reynolds were more productive.

Lance studied the various comments made by Reynolds:

The possibilities here are simply enormous. With a little determination and the right type of resources, we can make this one of the best human resource departments in this country. To be really effective, I believe that human resource management must be well integrated with the strategic and operational planning in a firm. That has not occurred here yet. ...

When I joined this company two years ago, it didn't have any system—at least, not anything that is worth mentioning. My job since I arrived has been to introduce new procedures and decision support systems. For example, recently, we started a formal orientation program for all plant workers. We are also in the process of developing two performance appraisal instruments—one for the plant employees and the other for administrative staff. We are beginning to provide absenteeism and turnover data to various department and section managers. But I want to emphasize that these are just the beginning. With the right support, we can do wonders here. ...

Why do I sound pessimistic? Well, look at our department's staff strength compared to human resource departments in similar-sized organizations in this part of the country. We probably employ less than 50 percent of the number you would see elsewhere. As a cost-cutting strategy, when we downsized the organization, we lost two positions in our department. We also do not have the computer hardware or software support and the necessary number of PCs to do an adequate job. ...

Sure, despite everything, we could have still done better if we had the will to do it. I will be totally frank with you. You will keep my observations confidential, won't you? Not that I mind too much if someone comes to know about it. It's as if we are a poor cousin here. Being in human resources is just not considered to be important or very useful. We're looked upon by many others as an unnecessary appendage.

Lance found that Joseph McDonald ("Call me Joe, everyone does"), the industrial relations officer, was the toughest to handle. McDonald was very friendly and supportive, but did not give a direct or coherent answer to any of Lance's questions. Lance felt that McDonald was one of those people who talked to you for hours at a time nonstop without giving any useful information. Lance realized that he got only two points of information out of his 45-minute meeting with McDonald. First, one of the unions in the company was very militant and might go on strike when its contract expired in the next few months; and second, McDonald's son was planning to go to medical school—Lance knew the former fact already and didn't care to know about the latter.

In less than 10 days, Lance was scheduled to meet Robert Clark to give a summary of his findings and recommendations. Already, Lance had received a call from his office in Saskatoon informing him that one of his consultants had been injured in an automobile accident and would not be returning to work for the next several weeks. This meant that Lance had to return to his office soon to complete that project himself. Given the time constraints, Lance was wondering how he should proceed from here.

Discussion Questions

1. What is your evaluation of Lance's approach to the project?

2. What would you do if you were in Lance's position right now?

CASE STUDY CPIB   Canadian Pacific and International Bank

Redefining Jobs for the Future*

Canadian Pacific and International Bank (CPIB) is a premier Canadian financial institution with assets of over $150 billion and operations across Canada and internationally. Today, its 25,000-plus employees provide personal, commercial, corporate, and investment banking services to individuals and businesses in 33 countries. More details of the bank are given at the end of Chapter 1.

CPIB, through its strategic initiatives, was successful in building long-term value for its shareholders while providing regular returns on their investments. A vital component of its recent strategy is growth through acquisition of smaller banks and other financial institutions in this country and internationally. The passage of the bill relating to bank mergers in June 2000 in Parliament accelerated this process for CPIB.

Last month, the bank acquired Central Canadian Trust Company (CCTC), a trust company located in Ontario employing over 3,000 employees. While the trust company was a very successful player in the financial industry in Ontario and Quebec, CPIB management felt that the human resource practices in the firm were inferior to those of the bank.

Initially, the identity of CCTC will be maintained; however, over the next year or so, all branches will be converted into CPIB branches. This means that, with immediate effect, CCTC staff must be trained to offer the highest quality of customer service that CPIB customers have come to expect. Compared to CPIB, CCTC is also far behind in electronic and telephone banking. CPIB expects all its managers to be able to offer extensive counselling (including in areas such as portfolio management, margin trading, and the establishment of

*Case written by Professor Hari Das of the Department of Management, Saint Mary's University. All rights reserved by the author. © 2002.

Internet banking accounts) to their customers; in contrast, CCTC being a trust company, historically had underplayed this role and concentrated on pension fund management and loan/mortgage services. CPIB also has a culture of transferring its employees to help them gain international experience whereas CCTC is primarily a regional institution where staff transfers are less common.

During the pre-acquisition survey, Mary Keddy, senior vice-president of human resources at CPIB, observed that CCTC did not have any regular job analysis procedure built into its HR systems. Since CPIB was contemplating the installation of a bank-wide electronic job data system (called the "Job Bank") in the next six months, Keddy decided to use the present opportunity to test the new system. Given the relatively small number of employees involved in CCTC (compared to CPIB), it was easier to fix all the "bugs" there before implementing it in its entirety in CPIB.

Under the proposed system, through their personal computers and other consoles, all managers will be able to store and retrieve human resource data from the company's mainframe computer. This means that when managers or human resource specialists needed a job description, they could simply obtain one from the computer.

After computerizing all human resource information in CCTC, HR staff began to notice that job descriptions, job specifications, and job standards were constantly being changed by jobholders. It seemed that whenever a manager or worker reviewed a job description or job specification that seemed outdated, he or she would "write in" a correction on the computer's memory. Thus, although in the beginning human resource specialists were pleased that workers were showing an interest by updating the computerized job analysis information, they eventually became worried because workers with the same job titles had different views of their jobs. Changes would come from almost anyone, and there was no consistency in style or content.

The HR staff at CPIB were bewildered. On the one hand, they did not want to introduce too many restrictions on employees updating their job descriptions; this was also contrary to the "open" culture that existed in CPIB. On the other hand, if not controlled, the problem could get out of hand, especially when implemented within such a large and diverse multilingual workforce.

Discussion Questions

1. Assume you are invited as a consultant by CPIB. What procedures would you introduce that would ensure that the restudied job information was correct?

2. Given the ability of most managers to "communicate" directly with the computer, can CPIB use this to its advantage in collecting job analysis information? Explain.

3. What additional skills and competencies would you focus on while planning a training program for CCTC staff? How should CPIB establish performance and skill standards for CCTC staff?

Human Resource Planning

Human resource planning is ... designed to translate strategic objectives into targeted quantitative and qualitative skill requirements, identify the human resource strategies and objectives necessary to fulfill those requirements ... and ... to assess progress.

Abdul Rahman bin Idris and Derek Eldridge[1]

CHAPTER OBJECTIVES

After studying this chapter, you should be able to:

➡ *Explain* the importance of human resource plans for strategic success.

➡ *Discuss* methods for estimating an organization's demand for human resources.

➡ *Explain* the various methods of estimating a firm's supply of human resources.

➡ *Identify* solutions to shortages or surpluses of human resources.

➡ *Discuss* key work options and arrangements.

➡ *Discuss* the major contents of a human resources information system (HRIS).

CHAPTER 3

Perhaps, more than any other human resource activity, planning allows the human resource department to be proactive. This, in turn, improves the department's contribution to the organization's objectives. Through human resource planning, management prepares to have the right people at the right places at the right times to fulfill both organizational and individual objectives. Human resource planning can make or break an organization—particularly over the long term, since without planning an organization may find itself with a plant or an office without the employees to run it productively. The plans themselves may range from simple projections based on past trends to sophisticated computer models. However, it is important that some form of planning exists. Consider this dialogue:

Sy Wolfe: All I ever seem to do is "put out fires." Every day different department heads tell me they need new employees. Well, we are a service department, so we rush around and try to find someone. And I thought being a city human resource manager would be a snap.

Jean-Marie Gasse: Why don't you do like we do in the police department and develop plans?

Sy Wolfe: Plans? How am I supposed to know who is going to quit?

Jean-Marie Gasse: You don't need to know exactly. Try estimating job vacancies. No one tells us when crimes or accidents are going to happen. We try to anticipate the need for traffic and crime squads for each shift based on past experience.

Sy Wolfe: Hey! Now that looks like a good idea. I could look at the various departments in our office and compare the employee turnover rates. I could then project these for next year. Thanks for the idea. I'll buy your coffee for that.

RELATIONSHIP OF HUMAN RESOURCE PLANNING TO STRATEGIC PLANNING

Human resource planning systematically forecasts an organization's future demand for and supply of employees and matches supply with demand. By estimating the number and types of employees that will be needed, the human resource department contributes to the success of an organization's strategic plan in a number of ways, as detailed in the following sections.

Proper Staffing is Critical for Strategic Success

An organization's strategic plan, involves, among other things, decisions such as an organization's primary mission, new business acquisitions, divestiture of current business units, or new ways of doing business. If an organization is not properly staffed with the right numbers and types of people, strategic success is endangered.[2]

For example, the decision of high-technology firms such as IBM, Bombardier, BCE, and others to develop new products or enter new markets often depends on the availability of qualified technical and support staff. Without an adequate number of competent persons, market opportunities can be lost to competitors.

Different Strategies Require Varying Human Resource Plans

An organization's growth or expansion strategy is usually accompanied by aggressive hiring, training, and/or promotions of employees. In contrast, a retrenchment or cost reduction strategy often necessitates layoff and early retirement of surplus employees. As seen in Chapter 1, a shift from a cost leadership to a focus or differentiation strategy requires changes in the number and skill levels of employees.

Human Resource Planning Facilitates Proactive Responses

Human resource planning—or *employment planning*, as it is also called—by facilitating better recruitment, selection, and training strategies not only helps companies meet their legal obligations but also allows them to face challenges proactively.

An anticipated change in the demographic composition of the labour market can help an organization to take proactive corrective actions. Thus, several organizations that in the past depended on young school students for their temporary workforce now target the growing pool of seniors in their recruitment efforts.

Human Resource Planning Society
www.hrps.org

Successful Tactical Plans Require Appropriate Human Resource Plans

A firm's strategic plan is often executed through a number of short-range, tactical (or operational) plans that focus on current operations. Purchasing a new personal computing system to improve efficiency, recalling a defective product, and managing inventory more effectively are some examples of tactical planning. Whatever the plan, it is made and carried out by people, which necessitates the proper staffing of organization, as this example illustrates:

> A combination of a unique baking formula and good customer service has made Country Farm Do-Nuts extremely successful throughout Saskatchewan. Since the firm began operations nearly 20 years ago, it has grown rapidly, now operating 14 stores across the province. The firm has currently embarked on an aggressive market development strategy, initially expanding to Alberta and B.C. by buying six existing doughnut shops in Vancouver, Calgary, and Edmonton. This means that the existing employees of these newly acquired doughnut shops have to be retrained in baking and customer service to retain the firm's strengths in product quality and customer service.

Figure 3-1 shows the relationship between strategic plans of an organization and its human resource plans. As can be seen, the overall organizational strategy defines the human resource objectives that are accomplished through the implementation of appropriate human resource plans. Successful organizations—both large and small, and public as well as private—recognize the importance of "intellectual" or "human" capital. An effective human resource plan is a critical tool to take advantage of this valuable asset.

> In one large electronics firm, strategic business planning begins with "top down" revenue and profit targets established by the company's policy committee. Then, executives of the different business areas develop the strategies and sales volumes needed to achieve these goals. From here, various divisions create functional strategies for development, manufacturing, marketing, and service. Line managers are responsible for folding the functional plans into divisional ones. The human resource department's role is to review all divisional plans before they are sent to the top management. Although line managers have wide latitude in addressing human resource issues, human resource concerns are injected into the business plans by proactive human resource specialists who work closely with divisional managers. These managers are encouraged to involve human resource staff in decision making because the business plans will be reviewed for human resource considerations before they are finalized. Through their involvement in the strategic business planning process, the human resource planners in this firm are better able to develop their corporate and functional human resource plans.

Human resource planning is about more than head counting and matching supply with demand. It involves the creation of an HR vision for the future, including answering questions such as, what should our employees look like? What competencies should they possess? How should we groom our employees for emerging challenges and opportunities? This, in turn, necessitates an integrated strategy of hiring, training, employee development, and redeployment in several instances. Several large organizations develop three- and five-year strategic plans followed by shorter, tactical plans. Through such planning, these organizations are better able to develop their corporate and functional plans and integrate these with their human resource plans as well. This also ensures a better fit between short-term and long-term plans in such organizations. It should be noted that organization strategies and tactics and human resource plans mutually influence each other (this fact is recognized by the dotted arrows in Figure 3-1).

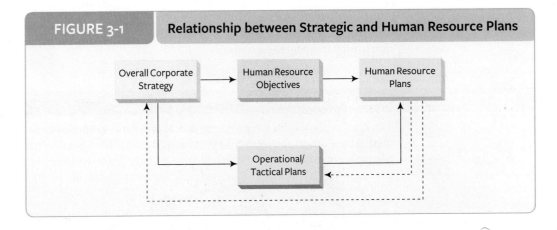

FIGURE 3-1   **Relationship between Strategic and Human Resource Plans**

Employment planning is more common in large organizations because it allows them to do the following:

- improve the utilization of human resources;
- match human resource–related activities and future organization objectives efficiently;
- achieve economies in hiring new workers;
- expand the human resource management information base to assist other human resource activities and other organizational units;
- make major demands on local labour markets successfully; and
- coordinate different human resource management programs such as employment equity plans and hiring needs.

Large Canadian employers such as Onex (237,000 employees), George Weston (155,400 employees), Magna International (70,700), and Royal Bank (65,045) pay considerable attention to employment planning since even a 1 percent increase or decrease in the total workforce can result in significantly different labour costs.

A small organization can expect similar advantages, but the gains in effectiveness are often considerably fewer because its situation is less complex. In fact, the benefits of human resource planning for small firms may not justify the time and costs. Consider the different situations faced by a small- and large-city government:

Rural City employs 20 workers and is growing at a rate of 10 percent a year. Metropolis has 8,000 employees, and Sy Wolfe estimates it is growing by 5 percent annually. That means 400 new employees every year plus replacement for those who leave. If it costs $400 to find and hire a typical employee, Rural City will spend $800 to hire two more workers. Metropolis will spend $160,000 just to add new employees. If employment planning saves 25 percent, Rural City's manager cannot justify detailed planning efforts for $200. But for $40,000, Metropolis can afford a specialist and still save thousands of dollars after planning expenses are deducted.

Knowledge of human resource planning, thus, is useful to human resource specialists in both small and large organizations. It shows small employers the human resource considerations they will face should they expand rapidly. (For example, if Rural City attracted several large factories to its area, expansion of city services would depend partly on the city's human resource planning.) Large organizations can benefit from knowledge of employment planning because it reveals ways to make the human resource function more effective.

Figure 3-2 provides an overview of the material that will be discussed in this chapter. The figure identifies the major causes of human resource demand, which are external, organizational, and workforce factors. These causes of demand are forecast by experts, trend data, or other methods to determine the short- and long-range demand for human resources. This demand is fulfilled either internally by present employees or externally by newcomers. The internal supply is shown in replacement charts, which are based on audits of the organization's human resources. Sources of external candidates are identified by analysis of the labour market. The results include both short- and long-range human resource plans. Strategies must be formulated to match supply and demand for human resources.

Each component in the figure will be discussed below. The discussion begins with a look at factors causing human resource demand, followed by strategies to estimate demand and supply and match current and future supply with demand. The discussion is followed by the more innovative work arrangements that are seen today. The chapter ends with a brief a look at the human resource information system (HRIS) and human resource accounting (HRA)—vital links in effective utilization of human resource capabilities.

THE DEMAND FOR HUMAN RESOURCES

An organization's future demand for people is central to employment planning. Most firms try to predict their future employment needs (at least informally), but they may not estimate their sources of supply. For example, one study found that employers are two times more likely to estimate demand than supply. The challenges that determine this demand and the methods of forecasting it merit brief review.

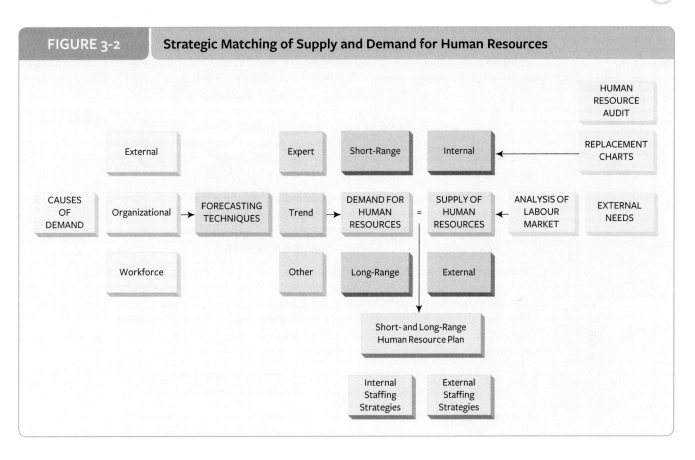

FIGURE 3-2 | **Strategic Matching of Supply and Demand for Human Resources**

Causes of Demand

Although countless challenges influence the demand for human resources, changes in the environment, the organization, and the workforce are usually involved. These factors are common to both short-range and long-range employment plans. The causes of these changes are summarized in Figure 3–3. Some of these causes are within the organization's control, and others are not.

External Challenges

Economic Developments. Developments in the organization's environment are difficult for human resource specialists to predict in the short run and sometimes impossible to estimate in the long run. Reconsider the example of the small-city government. City planners seldom know of major factory relocations until shortly before construction begins. Other economic developments have a noticeable effect, but are difficult to estimate.

> Examples include inflation, unemployment, and interest rates. For example, the economic downturn that began in mid-2008 brought about rapid decline in GDP, high unemployment, and decline in interest rates.

FIGURE 3-3 | **Causes of Demand for Human Resources in the Future**

External	Organizational	Workforce
• Economic developments	• Strategic plans	• Retirement
• Social-political-legal challenges	• Budgets	• Resignations
• Technological changes	• Sales and production forecasts	• Terminations
• Competitors	• New ventures	• Deaths
	• Organization and job designs	• Leaves of absence

Statistics Canada
www.statcan.gc.ca

Social-Political-Legal Changes. Changes occurring in social, political, and legal spheres are easier to predict, but their implications are seldom clear. As the demographics change, so do employee attitudes toward work and their employers (see "Spotlight on HRM" on page 128 for the emerging attitudes of the young workers). The impact on human resource planning of the *Canadian Human Rights Act,* passed more than 20 years ago, is still somewhat unclear. Major judicial verdicts, changes in employment laws such as minimum wages, federal and provincial government regulations, and so on all have great implications for the human resource planner. Although many large firms have established employment equity programs, the results of a change from the notion of "equal pay for equal work" to that of "equal pay for work of equal value" (see Chapter 4) will have profound implications.

> In the recent past, an independent committee recommended to the Department of Justice in Nova Scotia to make it mandatory for law firms in the province to hire a certain percentage (some members recommending 20 percent) of lawyers from visible minorities in the future with profound implications for law firms operating in the province.[3]

Technological Changes. Technological changes, which are normally difficult to predict, can affect both demand for and supply of human resources.[4] Many thought the computer would mean mass unemployment, for example. While it is true that computerization has eliminated certain types of jobs, the computer industry today employs hundreds of thousands of people and is a high-growth industry. Very often, technological changes tend to reduce employment in one department while increasing it in another, making planning arduous.

> The rapid computerization and automation[5] of many work activities may necessitate new skills on the part of employees, which may be hard to accurately predict.

Competitors. Competitors affect an organization's demand for human resources, though not in any uniform manner. Employment in some of the traditional sectors (such as the steel industry) barely grows because of foreign competition and a push for productivity improvement. But in the high-tech and electronics industries, competition causes lower prices, larger markets, and additional employment.

Organizational Decisions

Major organizational decisions affect the demand for human resources. Five of these are discussed below.

strategic plan
Involves identification of a firm's mission and objectives and plans for achieving those objectives.

Strategic Plan. The organization's **strategic plan** commits the firm to long-range objectives such as growth rates and new products, markets, or services. These objectives determine the numbers and types of employees needed in the future. Obviously, a fast-growing firm has more beginning-level vacancies. The number of higher-level openings also depends on how well the human resource department assists employees to develop their capabilities. If workers are not encouraged to expand their capabilities, they may not be ready to fill future vacancies.

The firm's strategic plan has a decisive influence on human resource plans. In Chapter 1, three alternate competitive strategies (focus, cost leadership, and differentiation) were identified. A firm making a fundamental change in its strategy should recognize the implications for its HR systems and priorities.

> An electronics manufacturer employing a cost leadership strategy may thus have to encourage high task specialization, resulting in lower production costs, while another firm operating in the same field using a differentiation strategy may find it necessary to encourage broad, innovative skill application on the part of the employees.

Budgets. Budget increases or cuts are the most significant short-run influence on human resource needs.

Sales and Production Forecasts. The sales and production forecasts are less exact than budgets, but may provide even quicker notice of short-run changes in human resource demand:

> The human resource manager for a nationwide chain of furniture outlets observed a sharp decline in sales, brought on by a recession. The manager quickly discarded the short-run human resource plan and imposed an employment freeze on all outlets' hiring plans.

New Ventures. New ventures mean new human resource demands. When begun internally, the lead time may allow planners to develop short-run and long-run employment plans. But new ventures begun by acquisitions and mergers cause an immediate revision of human resource demands. A reorganization, especially after a merger or an acquisition, can radically alter human resource needs. Several positions or jobs may have to be eliminated to avoid duplication, while new integrating roles may have to be created for smooth operating of merged units.

> Metro Electronics (which employed over 2,000 people) merged with Bargain Hunters, another large electronics firm, to form the giant Bargain Electronics employing nearly 7,600 people. It has plans to open 14 new sales outlets in the next year and will need to hire store managers, sales people, and maintenance technicians. However, because of the merger, there were significant economies of scale, making several positions in purchasing, administration, and accounting redundant. Instead of discharging the excess employees, the company attempted to retrain and transfer qualified employees to new positions. The result? The company did not have to spend as much resources on recruiting and selecting new personnel. It also boosted the morale of the employees since it showed them that the employer cared for their welfare.

Organizational and Job Design. Changes in the structure have major implications for human resource needs.

> Gennum Corporation, a Canadian high-tech company that designs and manufactures silicon integrated circuits changed from its existing function-based structure (employing specialist functional departments like marketing and production) to a product-based structure. Under the new structure, there would be separate divisions for video products and for hearing instrument products. This decision created new positions as well as the need to generate new employee competencies—especially at supervisory and managerial levels—resulting in changes in HR functions such as hiring and training.[6]

Automation, computerization, and job redesign also necessitate major revisions in human resource need estimates. The impact of automation and computerization on HR was detailed in Chapter 1.

Workforce Factors

The demand for human resources is modified by employee actions. Retirements, resignations, terminations, deaths, and leaves of absence all increase the need for human resources.

> While the recent recession has meant gloomy stories of layoffs and high unemployment, it has hidden an increasing danger to our economic welfare—namely, an impending shortage of skilled tradespeople. A paper published by the Atlantic Institute of Market Studies (AIMS) points out that only a sustained recession of some 20 years will be able to avoid an acute shortage of skilled trade workers. The research study, which modelled the effects of demographic shifts until 2026, found that Canada, like most industrialized nations, would face significant labour shortages in the years to come unless this is counterbalanced by significant improvement in productivity or increase in labour participation either by the domestic workforce or by immigrant workers.[7]

In the organizational context, when large numbers of employees are involved, past experience usually serves as a reasonably accurate guide. However, reliance on past experience means that human resource specialists must be sensitive to changes elsewhere:

> In the past, Jim Stitz kept a close track of employees nearing retirement so that his human resource plan remained accurate. With the abolition of a mandatory retirement age in the province, Jim could no longer use his past experience as a guide to predicting when older workers would retire. Given the recessionary economic times facing the country, many workers opted to work beyond normal retirement age. Alternatively, a few who had achieved financial security had indicated their plans to take early retirement. To improve the accuracy of his predictions, Jim decided to conduct an employee survey and find out more about each employee's retirement plans.

Forecasting Human Resource Needs

forecasts
Estimates of future resource needs and changes.

Human resource **forecasts** are attempts to predict an organization's future demand for employees. As Figure 3-4 shows, forecasting techniques range from the informal to the sophisticated. Even the most sophisticated methods are not perfectly accurate; instead, they are best viewed as approximations.

FIGURE 3-4	Forecasting Techniques for Estimating Future Human Resource Needs		
Expert		**Trend**	**Other**
• Informal and instant decisions		• Extrapolation	• Budget and planning analysis
• Formal expert survey		• Indexation	• New-venture analysis
• Delphi technique		• Statistical analysis	• Computer models

Most firms make only casual estimates about the immediate future. As they gain experience with forecasting human resource needs, they may use more sophisticated techniques (especially if they can afford specialized staff). Each of the forecasting methods in Figure 3-4 is explained below.

Expert Forecasts

Expert forecasts rely on those who are knowledgeable to estimate future human resource needs. At the first level of complexity, the manager may simply be convinced that the workload justifies another employee:

> **Manager:** How come the credit card balance statements haven't gone out yet?
>
> **Billing clerk:** I know they should have, but we're short-handed. The new computer system has some bugs that haven't been fixed yet. Right now, the two computer systems are not mutually compatible. We've been working overtime on this; but nothing helps.
>
> **Manager:** Yes, I talked to Janet about it. It seems it will take at least another four months for the new system to be fully operational. Meanwhile, I'll ask the HR department to get us a temporary employee. The salary will be more than recovered by the cost of overtime and lost interest in unpaid accounts.

The example above illustrates an informal and instant forecast. But it is not part of a systematic planning effort. A better method is for planners to survey managers, who are the experts, about their department's future employment needs. The centralization of this information permits formal plans that identify the organization's future demand.

The survey may be an informal poll, a written questionnaire, or a focused discussion using the **nominal group technique** (NGT). The NGT presents a group of managers with a problem statement, such as, "What will cause our staffing needs to change over the next year?" Then each of the 5 to 15 participants writes down as many answers as he or she can imagine. After about 5 to 10 minutes, these ideas are shared in round-table fashion until all written ideas and any new ones they stimulated have been recorded. The group's ideas are then discussed and ranked by having each member of the group vote for the three to five most important ones.[8]

If the experts cannot be brought together, sophistication can be added to the survey approach with the **Delphi technique**. This technique solicits estimates from a group of experts, usually managers. Then human resource department planners act as intermediaries, summarizing the various responses and reporting the findings to the experts. The experts are surveyed again after they get this feedback. Summaries and surveys are repeated until the experts' opinions begin to agree on future developments. (Usually four or five surveys are enough.) For example, the human resource department may survey all production supervisors and managers until an agreement is reached on the number of replacements needed during the next year.

Trend Projection Forecasts

Perhaps the quickest forecasting technique is to project past trends. The two simplest methods are extrapolation and indexation. **Extrapolation** involves extending past rates of change into the future. For example, if an average of 20 production workers were hired each month for the past two years, extrapolation indicates that 240 production workers will probably be added during the upcoming year.

Indexation is a method of estimating future employment needs by matching employment growth with a selected index. A common example is the ratio of production employees to sales. For example, planners may discover that for each million-dollar increase in sales, the production department

---

nominal group technique
A focused, group discussion where members write down their ideas and share them. All new thoughts on a topic are recorded and ranked for importance.

Delphi technique
The soliciting of predictions about specified future events from a panel of experts, using repeated surveys until convergence in opinions occurs.

extrapolation
Extending past rates of change into the future.

indexation
A method of estimating future employment needs by matching employment growth with a selected index, such as the ratio of production employees to sales.

By analyzing the staffing needs of existing oil rigs, planners of a new rig can forecast their human resource needs until changes in technology occur. How can planners react to shortages of skilled staff?

PhotoLink/Getty Images.

requires 10 new assemblers. Figure 3-5 shows an example of the indexation method in the case of a direct marketing firm. The relevant business factor here is sales figures in dollars. An overall index productivity for all relevant sales personnel is computed. This ratio, with appropriate modifications, enables the firm to estimate its demand for personnel for the next period. It should, however, be noted that the growth or decline rate in the labour force may be different during growth and downsizing periods (typically, the growth of the management tier happens at a somewhat faster pace than its compression). When using indexation, this factor must be recognized.

Extrapolation and indexation are crude, short-run approximations because they assume that the causes of demand—external, organizational, and workforce factors—remain constant, which is seldom the case. They are very inaccurate for long-range human resource projections. The more sophisticated statistical analyses make allowances for changes in the underlying causes of demand.

Other Forecasting Methods

There are several other ways planners can estimate the future demand for human resources.

Budget and Planning Analysis. Organizations that need human resource planning generally have detailed budgets and long-range plans.

> A study of department budgets reveals the financial authorizations for more employees. These data plus extrapolations of workforce changes (resignations, terminations, and the like) can provide short-run estimates of human resource needs. Long-term estimates can be made from each department or division's long-range plans.

New-Venture Analysis. When new ventures complicate employment planning, planners can use *new-venture analysis*. New-venture analysis requires planners to estimate human resource needs by comparison with firms that already perform similar operations.

> For example, an integrated steel company that owns steel plants and iron ore mines decides to explore iron ore at a new site. The management can estimate its employment needs in the new mine by looking at employment levels of other iron ore mines and making necessary adjustments for productivity improvements.

Computer-Based Simulation Models. The most sophisticated forecasting approaches involve computers. *Computer models* are a series of mathematical formulas that simultaneously use extrapolation, indexation, survey results, and estimates of workforce changes to compute future human

FIGURE 3-5	An Illustration of the Indexation Method

Plastics, Mugs, and Housewares (PMH), a direct marketer of household plastics products with its head office in Calgary, began operations in 1994. PMH, which began as a very small firm operating in Calgary, soon grew rapidly and employed 530 persons in 2009. The firm hopes to have even higher growth rates in the next two years. The dollar sales value and the staff strength for the last seven years (for which company information is readily available) are shown below. The firm forecasts it will have a 20 percent increase in sales in 2010 and another 15 percent (over 2010 figures) in year 2011. Because of technological improvements and improved training, the sales productivity is expected to show a 15 percent improvement in 2010. (No substantial improvement is expected for the year after.) PMH is currently attempting to forecast its human resource needs for 2010 and 2011.

One possible approach here is as follows:

Year	Number of Employees	Dollar Sales (000s)	Sales Productivity Index (dollar sales divided by number of employees)
2003	300	150	0.5000
2004	310	160	0.5161
2005	400	210	0.5250
2006	430	222	0.5163
2007	430	228	0.5302
2008	520	273	0.5250
2009	530	280	0.5283

Sales targets for the next two years are:

| 2010 | ? | 336 | 0.6075 |
| 2011 | ? | 386.4 | 0.6075 |

Since the target sales are expected to rise by 20 percent in 2010 and 15 percent in 2011, the figures for the two years will be: 336 in 2010 (280 × 1.2) and 386.4 (336 × 1.15). The labour productivity is expected to increase by 15 percent in 2010 (or reach 0.6075). The human resource needs for the next two years will, hence, be:

2010 = 336   divided by 0.6075 = 553.09, and

2011 = 386.4   divided by 0.6075 = 636.05

This means that the firm will need to hire approximately 23 (or 553 – 530) persons for 2010 and 83 persons (636 – 553) a year later. Of course, the exact numbers can be arrived at only after a detailed look at the various types of job positions within the organization, their interdependencies, and differences in productivity levels across job positions. These figures also do not include hiring needed to replace employees who retire or otherwise leave the organization.

resource needs. They simulate and forecast changes in demand for human resources caused by various internal and external factors discussed earlier. Over time, actual changes in human resource demand are used to refine the computer's formulas.

Across firms, human resource forecasting shows wide variations in its complexity (see Figure 3-6). At the lowest level, it is portrayed in informal discussions and instant decisions. Computerized forecasting systems with online predictive capabilities reflect the highest level of complexity. Naturally, the more sophisticated techniques are found among large organizations that have had years of experience in human resource planning. Small firms, or those just beginning to forecast human resource needs, are more likely to employ a Level 1 approach and progress to other levels as planners seek greater accuracy.

FIGURE 3-6	Increasing Levels of Complexity in Human Resource Planning

Low	Complexity		High
Level 1	Level 2	Level 3	Level 4
Highly informal and subjective. Managers discuss goals and numbers of people needed in the short term. No long-term orientation.	Annual planning for human resources is present. There is a general recognition of potential human resource challenges.	Computers are increasingly used to systematically track demand and supply of human resources. Records of continuous employee turnover and absenteeism are used to predict future scenarios.	Existence of a sophisticated human resource information system permits modelling and simulation of talent needs, flows, and costs to project needs and take corrective action.

staffing table
A list of anticipated employment openings for each type of job.

Listing Human Resource Requirements

Forecasts translate the causes of demand into short-range and long-range statements of need. The resulting long-range plans are, of necessity, general statements of probable needs. Specific numbers are either omitted or estimated.

Short-term plans are more specific and may be reported as a **staffing table**, as in Figure 3-7. A staffing table lists the future employment needs for each type of job. The listing may be a specific number or an approximate range of needs, depending on the accuracy of the underlying forecast. Staffing tables (also called *manning* tables) are neither complete nor wholly accurate. They are only approximations. But these estimates allow human resource specialists to match short-run demand and supply. They help operating departments run more smoothly and can enhance the image of the human resource department:

> **Sy Wolfe:** You know, your suggestion worked! My employment projections helped me to start looking for people even before vacancies emerged.

> **Jean-Marie Gasse:** The advantage of doing it this way is that it reduces the disruptions managers experience while waiting for replacements to be found, assigned, and taught their jobs.

> **Sy Wolfe:** Yes. And their usual gripes about how long it takes the human resource department to fill jobs have diminished greatly. I owe you one!

With specific estimates of future human resource needs, personnel specialists can become more proactive and systematic. For example, a review of Figure 3-7 shows that the city's human resource department must hire 32 police academy recruits every three months. This knowledge allows recruiters in the human resource department to plan their recruiting campaign so that it peaks about six weeks before the beginning of the next police academy class. The advanced planning allows the department to screen applicants and notify them at least three weeks before the class begins. For those still in school or otherwise unable to be ready that quickly, recruiters can inform them when the following class begins. If the human resource department waited for the police department to notify them, notification might come too late to allow a systematic recruiting and screening process. Staffing tables enable recruiters to be proactive and to better plan their activities.

THE SUPPLY OF HUMAN RESOURCES

Once the human resource department makes projections about future human resource demands, the next major concern is filling projected openings. There are two sources of supply: internal and external. The internal supply consists of present employees who can be promoted, transferred, or demoted to meet anticipated needs.

FIGURE 3-7   **A Partial Staffing Table for a City Government**

Metropolis City Government Staffing Table

Date Compiled: _____

Budget Code Number	Job Title (as found on job description)	Using Department(s)	Total	Anticipated Openings by Month of the Year											
				1	2	3	4	5	6	7	8	9	10	11	12
100-32	Police Recruit	Police	128	32			32			32			32		
100-33	Police Dispatcher	Police	3	2					1						
100-84	Meter Reader	Police	24	2	2	2	2	2	2	2	2	2	2	2	2
100-85	Traffic Supervisor	Police	5	2			1			1			1		
100-86	Team Supervisor — Police (Sergeant)	Police	5	2			1			1			1		
100-97	Duty Supervisor — Police (Staff Sergeant)	Police	2	1					1						
100-99	Shift Officer— Police (Inspector)	Police	1	1											
200-01	Car Washer	Motor Pool	4	1			1			1			1		
200-12	Mechanic's Assistant	Motor Pool	3				1			1			1		
200-13	Mechanic III	Motor Pool	2	1									1		
200-14	Mechanic II	Motor Pool	1					1							
200-15	Mechanic I (Working Supervisor)	Motor Pool	1	1											
300-01	Clerk IV	Administration	27	10			5			6			6		

For example, Jean-Marie Gasse (in the previous dialogue) works in the police department of Metropolis, but is applying for a transfer into the human resource department. She is part of the internal supply of human resources to the city government. The external supply consists of people in the labour market who do not work for the city. These include employees of other organizations and those who are unemployed.

Internal Supply Estimates

Estimating the internal supply involves more than merely counting the number of employees in an organization. Planners audit the present workforce to learn about the capabilities of present workers. This information allows planners to estimate tentatively which openings can be filled by present employees. These tentative assignments usually are recorded on a replacement chart. Considering present employees for future job openings is important if workers are to have lifelong careers with their employer rather than just dead-end jobs. The patterns of employee transition among jobs, hence, must be carefully assessed and taken into consideration. Audits, replacement charts, and employee transition matrices (more popularly called **Markov analysis**) also are important additions to the personnel department's information base. With greater knowledge of employees, the department can more effectively plan recruiting, training, and career-planning activities. A human resource department can also help meet its employment equity goals by identifying internal minority candidates for job openings.

Internal supply estimates are made using human resource audits and transition matrices employing Markov analysis. These are explained more fully below.

Markov analysis
Forecast of a firm's future human resource supplies, using transitional probability matrices reflecting historical or expected movements of employees across jobs.

Human Resource Audits

Human resource audits summarize the employee's skills and abilities and generate skills and management inventories that, in turn, facilitate the preparation of a replacement chart and replacement summaries. Chapter 15 of this text details the HR audit process. Below is a brief discussion of skills inventories in the context of human resource planning.

Skills Inventories. An inventory catalogues each comprehensive understanding of the capabilities found in the organization's workforce. When referring to nonmanagers, the audits result in **skills inventories.**

An example of a skills inventory is found in Figure 3-8. It is divided into four parts. Part I can be completed by the human resource department from employee records. It identifies the employee's

skills inventories
Summaries of each nonmanagerial worker's skills and abilities.

FIGURE 3-8	Skills Inventory Form for Metropolis City Government

Part I (To be completed by human resource department)
1. Name _____
2. Employee Number _____
3. Job Title _____
4. Experience _____ years
5. Age _____
6. Years with City _____
7. Other Jobs Held:

        With City: Title _____ From _____ to _____
                      Title _____ From _____ to _____
        Elsewhere: Title _____ From _____ to _____
                      Title _____ From _____ to _____

Part II (To be completed by employee)
8. *Special Skills.* List below any skills you possess, even if they are not used in your present job. Include types and names of machines or tools with which you are experienced.

        Skills _____
      Machines _____
         Tools _____

9. *Duties.* Briefly describe your present duties. _____
_____

10. *Responsibilities.* Briefly describe your responsibilities for:

      City Equipment: _____
           City Funds: _____
     Employee Safety: _____
  Employee Supervision: _____

11. *Education.* Briefly describe your education and training background:

	Years Completed	Year of Graduation	Degree and Major
High School:	_____	_____	_____
University:	_____	_____	_____
Job Training:	_____	_____	_____
Special Courses:	_____	_____	_____

Part III (To be completed by human resource department with supervisory inputs)
12. Overall Evaluation of Performance _____
13. Overall Readiness for Promotion _____

        To What Job(s): _____
          Comments: _____

14. Current Deficiencies:
_____

15. Supervisor's Signature _____ Date: _____

Part IV (To be completed by human resource department representative)
16. Are the two most recent performance evaluations attached? _____ Yes _____ No
17. Prepared by _____ Date: _____

job title, experience, age, and previous jobs. Part II seeks information about skills, duties, responsibilities, and education of the worker. From these questions, planners learn about the mix of employee abilities. The human resource department may collect these data by phone or in face-to-face interviews. Or the questions may be sent to the employee through the company mail.

The employee's potential is briefly summarized by the immediate supervisor in Part III. Performance, readiness for promotion, and any deficiencies are noted here. The supervisor's signature helps ensure that the form's accuracy is reviewed by someone who knows the employee better than the human resource specialists. Part IV is added as a final check for completeness and for the addition of recent employee evaluations, which give more insight into past performance.

To be useful, inventories of human resources must be updated periodically. Updating every two years is sufficient for most organizations if employees are encouraged to report major changes to the human resource department when they occur. Major changes include new skills, degree completions, changed job duties, and the like. Failure to update skills inventories can lead to present employees being overlooked for job openings within the organization.

Management Inventories.   Audits of managers are called **management inventories**. As in the case of skills inventories, these are comprehensive reports of available management capabilities in the organization. Like skills inventories, management inventories should be updated periodically, since they also are used for key human resource–related decisions. In fact, some employers use the same form for managers and nonmanagers. When the forms differ, the management inventory requests information about management activities. Common topics include

- number of employees supervised
- types of employees supervised
- total budget managed
- management training received
- duties of subordinates
- previous management duties

Replacement Charts.   **Replacement charts** are a visual representation of who will replace whom in the event of a job opening. The information for constructing the chart comes from the human resource audit. Figure 3-9 illustrates a typical replacement chart. It shows the replacement status of only a few jobs in the administration of a large city.

Although different firms may seek to summarize different information in their replacement charts, the figure indicates the minimum information usually included. The chart, which is much like an organization chart, depicts the various jobs in the organization and shows the status of likely candidates. Replacement status consists of two variables: *present performance* and *promotability*. Present performance is determined largely from supervisory evaluations. Opinions of other managers, peers, and subordinates may contribute to the appraisal of present performance. Future promotability is based primarily on present performance and the estimates by immediate superiors of future success in a new job. The human resource department may contribute to these estimates through the use of psychological tests, interviews, and other methods of assessment. Replacement charts often show the candidates' ages.

Human resource and management decision makers find that these charts provide a quick reference. Their shortcoming is that they contain little information.[9] This is addressed through the preparation of replacement summaries.

Replacement Summaries.   To supplement the chart—and, increasingly, to supplant it—human resource specialists develop **replacement summaries**. Replacement summaries list likely replacements and their relative strengths and weaknesses for each job. As Figure 3-10 shows, the summaries provide considerably more data than the replacement chart. This additional information allows decision makers to make more informed decisions.

Most companies that are sophisticated enough to engage in detailed human resource planning computerize their human resource records, including job analysis information and human resource inventories. Then, through a simple computer program, planners can compile replacement summaries each time a job opening occurs. These summaries also show which positions lack human resource backups:

Canada Grocers Ltd., which has a chain of grocery stores in five Canadian provinces, has computerized its search for fast trackers in the organization. Every six months, the organization's

management inventories
Comprehensive reports of available management capabilities in the organization.

replacement charts
Visual representations of who will replace whom when a job opening occurs.

replacement summaries
Lists of likely replacements for each job and their relative strengths and weaknesses.

FIGURE 3-9 · A Partial Replacement Chart for a Municipal Government

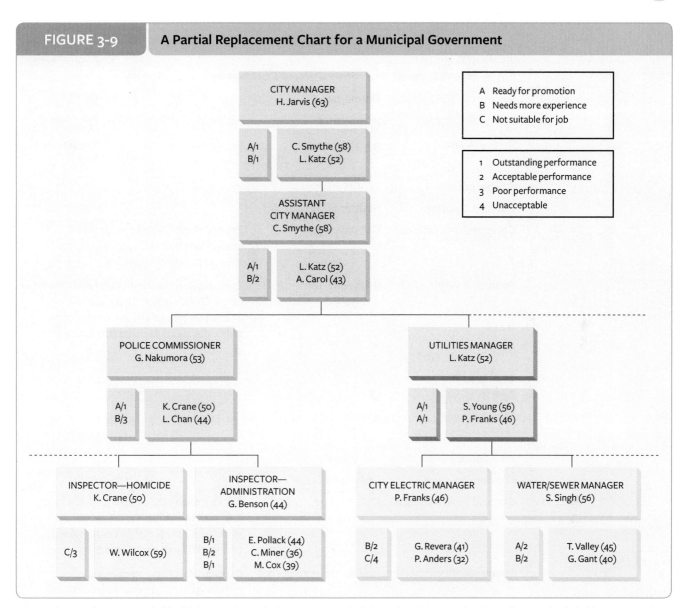

As mandatory retirement gets abolished, it becomes increasingly unnecessary to include age in replacement chart. It may, however, be *desirable* to gather retirement intentions to facilitate long-term planning.

managers submit performance appraisals to the human resource department indicating the promotability of their subordinates. By consolidating these reports on a computer, the company has been able to identify the "outstanding" workers. A separate program helps produce career-development plans, pinpointing weaknesses and suggesting solutions—university courses, in-house training, or a different job assignment.

In the long run, the human resource department can encourage employees to upgrade their capabilities and prepare for future vacancies. In the short run, an opening without a suitable replacement requires that someone be hired from the external labour market.

Whether replacement charts or summaries are used, this information is normally kept confidential. Confidentiality not only guards the privacy of employees but also prevents dissatisfaction among those who are not immediately promotable.

Transition Matrices and Markov Analysis

Markov analysis is a fairly simple method of predicting the internal supply of human resources in the future. This is particularly useful in organizations where employees move from one job (or rank) to another on a regular basis. It is particularly useful in organizations where jobs or human resource movements do not fluctuate rapidly due to external (e.g., technological) or internal (e.g., strategic) change.

FIGURE 3-10	A Replacement Summary for the Position of City Manager

Replacement Summary for the Position of City Manager

Present Office Holder	Harold Jarvis	Age	63
Probable Opening	In two years	Reason	Retirement
Salary Grade	99 ($86,000)	Experience	8 years

Candidate 1	Clyde Smythe		
Current Position	Assistant City Manager		
Current Performance	Outstanding	**Explanation** Clyde's performance evaluations by the City Manager are always the highest possible.	
Promotability	Ready now for promotion	**Explanation** During an extended illness of the City Manager, Clyde assumed all duties successfully, including major policy decisions and negotiations with city unions.	
Training Needs	None		
Age	58		
Experience	4 years		
Candidate 2	Larry Katz		
Current Position	Utilities Manager		
Current Performance	Outstanding	**Explanation** Larry's performance has kept costs of utilities to citizens 10 to 15 percent below that of comparable city utilities through careful planning.	
Promotability	Needs more experience	**Explanation** Larry's experience is limited to utilities management. Although successful, he needs more broad administrative experience in other areas. (He is ready for promotion to Assistant City Manager at this time.)	
Training Needs	Training in budget preparation and public relations would be desirable before promotion to City Manager.		
Age	52		
Experience	5 years		

transition matrices
Describe the probabilities of how quickly a job position turns over and what an incumbent employee may do over a forecast period of time, such as stay in the current position, move to another position within the firm, or accept another job in another organization.

Markov analysis reflects the patterns in these human resource movements using **transition matrices**. A transition probability matrix describes the probabilities of an incumbent staying in his or her present job for the forecast time period (usually one year), moving to another job position in the organization, or leaving the organization. When this matrix is multiplied by the number of employees in each job at the beginning of a year, the forecaster is easily able to identify the number of persons who will remain in the job at the end of the year.

FIGURE 3-11	An Example of Markov Analysis

(a) Transition Probability Matrix

Year Beginning	Year End				
	Job A	**Job B**	**Job C**	**Job D**	**Exit**
Job A	0.80	0.10	0.05	0.00	0.05
Job B	0.10	0.70	0.00	0.10	0.10
Job C	0.00	0.00	0.90	0.05	0.05
Job D	0.00	0.00	0.00	0.90	0.10

(b) Expected Movements of Employees

	Initial Staffing Level	Job A	Job B	Job C	Job D	Exit
Job A	200	160	20	10	0	10
Job B	70	7	49	0	7	7
Job C	60	0	0	54	3	3
Job D	100	0	0	0	90	10
Predicted End-of-the-Year Staffing Level		167	69	64	100	30

Figure 3-11 shows a sample transition matrix. The table shows that 80 percent (or 0.8) of the incumbents in Job A remain in their present position at the end of the year, 10 percent (or 0.1) move to Job B, 5 percent (or 0.05) more to Job C, none to Job D, and 5 percent (or 0.05) leave the organization (through resignations or otherwise). When these probabilities are multiplied by the number of persons in Job A at the beginning of the year (namely, 200), we see that 160 of them remain in their present position, 20 of them move to Job B, 10 of them move to Job C, and the remaining 10 leave the organization. When similar calculations are performed for all the jobs (in the case of this firm, for Jobs A, B, C, and D), we are able to predict the approximate number of employees who will remain in each job position.

Many firms use the previous year's transition rates for predicting next year's movements. However, if the previous year was atypical, the predictions may be erroneous.[10] Markov analysis is popular because of the ease of its use. However, it is only as good as the transition probabilities used. The probabilities are not very reliable if there are only a few incumbents in each job. Generally, Markov analysis works best if there are at least 50 employees in each job position.[11] This makes it more appropriate only for medium-sized and large organizations.

Markov analysis can also be used speculatively to assess the impact of possible changes in transition analysis. Thus, "what if" analyses can be undertaken to understand the impact of possible future scenarios (e.g., "What if the quit rate for Job A doubles from its present 6 percent per year?"). This makes it a useful tool for human resource forecasting, especially in the context of strategic planning.

In the past, a leading lumber firm used a sophisticated Markov-type model to plan its human resources. The model analyzed the flow of human resources from the supply point (whether internal or external) to the point of demand (requirements for specific jobs). The model also allowed the company's planners to identify transition rates (rates at which staff moved from one level to the next in the hierarchy) and to use them as constraints in balancing supply and demand for human resources. For instance, under the assumptions of varying transition rates, the company could forecast the workforce supply and demand for different levels and different time periods. The Markov-type model enabled the policy makers of the company to analyze the impact of different policies on human resource supply and demand.[12]

Most Markov models are closed systems. They do not interact with the environment or show dynamics that occur in their environment. Today's sophisticated computers permit the incorporation of these interactions with environments through complex modelling techniques. *Holonic modelling* is a technique that can be used today even by non-mathematical managers to portray interactions with environments and reflect the impact of strategic decisions on supply of human resources at different organizational levels.[13] The benefits associated with holonic modelling include improved formulation ability, greater flexibility, and greater insights to the decision maker.

External Supply Estimates

Not every future opening can be met with present employees. Some jobs lack replacements to fill an opening when it occurs. Other jobs are entry-level positions; that is, they are beginning jobs that are filled by people who do not presently work for the organization. When there are no replacements or when the opening is for an entry-level job, there is a need for external supplies of human resources.

When estimating external supplies, three major factors must be examined: trends in the labour market, community attitudes, and demographic trends. These are briefly outlined below.

Labour Market Analysis

labour market analysis
The study of a firm's labour market to evaluate the present or future availability of different types of workers.

The human resource department's success in finding new employees depends on an accurate **labour market analysis**. Even when unemployment rates are high, many needed skills are difficult to find:

> According to Statistics Canada, in March 2009 the overall unemployment rate in Canada was 8 percent. However, in many occupations such as physicians, surgeons, and radiologists the demand far exceeded supply in several regions in the country.[14]

In the short run, the national unemployment rate serves as an approximate measure of how difficult it is to acquire new employees. Human resource specialists realize that this rate varies for different groups, as well as from province to province and city to city:

> In March 2009, there were some wide variations in Canadian labour markets. For example, Saskatchewan had an unemployment rate of only 4.7 percent while Prince Edward Island and Newfoundland and Labrador had unemployment rates of 11.5 percent and 14.7 percent respectively.[15]

Regardless of the unemployment rate, external needs may be met by attracting employees who work for others. In the long run, local developments and demographic trends have the most significant impact on labour markets. Local developments include community growth rates and attitudes.

> For example, many farm towns find their population declining. When they attempt to attract new business, employers fear that a declining population may mean future shortages in the local labour market. So the new businesses often locate elsewhere.

The lack of jobs results in still more people leaving the local labour market. This is particularly so in the case of minorities and other disadvantaged groups of society.

During a recessionary period, the job prospects of minorities and new immigrants are more adversely affected. One estimate shows that immigrants lose their jobs at more than three times the rate of Canadian born workers. In the Toronto region, almost 50 percent of residents are born outside Canada, which means that what happens to their jobs can have a profound impact on the overall economy.[16]

Conversely, growing cities are attractive to employers because they promise even larger labour markets in the future.

While people move across labour markets, language and cultural barriers may often act as deterrents. Sometimes, migrants from other areas may receive a hostile welcome in the local labour market as happened in Saint John, N.B., in September 2009:

> When contract workers from Alberta were brought in to Saint John to build a new storage tank for a N.B. energy project, the local residents were furious at what they viewed as carpetbaggers taking scarce jobs. Protesters massed repeatedly outside the hotel where the migrant workers stayed despite a police injunction that they keep their distance from the new arrivals.[17]

Community Attitudes

Community attitudes also affect the nature of the labour market. Anti-business or nongrowth attitudes may cause present employers to move elsewhere. The loss of jobs forces middle-class workers to relocate, and the shrinking workforce discourages new businesses from becoming established.

Workopolis job site
www.workopolis.com

Demographic Trends

Demographic trends are another long-term development that affects the availability of external supply. Fortunately for planners, these trends are known years in advance of their impact:

> The low birthrates of the 1930s and early 1940s were followed by a baby boom during the late 1940s and 1950s. When the post–Second World War babies started to go to university in the 1960s, the low birthrates of the 1930s led to a shortage of university teachers. These demographic trends were already in motion by 1950. Long-range human resource planning, which was sensitive to demographic developments, could have predicted the shortage soon enough for proactive universities to take corrective action.

Canadian Occupational Projection System (COPS)

Provides up to 10-year projection of Canadian economy and human resource needs.

The **Canadian Occupational Projection System** (**COPS**) was designed by Human Resources Development Canada (since renamed as Human Resources and Skills Development or HRSD). The COPS provides a highly detailed projection of the Canadian economy up to 10 years in the future.[18] While there are several COPS models, the most popular is the COPS Demand Model, which estimates industry employment by simulating through a macroeconomic model[19] and checking through a consultative process.[20] The final labour market projection is a synthesis of the consensus among major private sector forecasters, the judgment of the Occupational Projections and Macroeconomic Studies Unit of HRSD, and the judgment of COPS partners in HRSD's regional offices. COPS projects expected imbalances (between supply and demand of human resources) by occupation and type of education.

> For example, according to HRSD, occupations such as computer system design and professional and health services are likely to show continuing demand patterns, while employment requirements in fishing and forestry are expected to decline.[21]

The *COPS Macroeconomic Projections*, which provide long-range demographic and labour market supply forecasts, are supplied at both national and provincial levels.[22] This is done at a high level of industry detail for each province, including major indicators for each province.

Job Futures[23] is a group of products available from Service Canada that identifies trends in the world of work. It outlines job outlooks by occupation as well as by field of study, and estimates the prospect of finding jobs in a specific occupation or field. Job Futures provides Canadians with the latest information available about work—information that is important for anyone in the process of making decisions or advising others in the area of career planning.

> For example, Job Futures forecasts that the chance of finding work as an occupational therapist, registered nurse, radiation technologist, or dental assistant is "good" (the scale used is "limited," "fair," and "good"). Further, concern about corporate fraud may create opportunities in forensic accounting.[24]

For the human resource manager as well as the job seeker, such information is invaluable.

The Economic Council of Canada has developed another model useful for the human resource planner in predicting the Canadian economy: CANDIDE—Canadian Disaggregated Interdepartmental Econometric Model. It uses over 1,500 regression equations to forecast unemployment, real domestic product, and so on. Human resource planners forecasting occupational composition in Canada may also find the *Microelectronics Simulation Model* useful. This model incorporates the impact of technological change on the occupational composition in this country.

National human resource plans assume that the skill needs of a country can be validly assessed for a 5- or 10-year period in order to take timely and effective corrective actions (such as retraining). In practice, many countries have found this to be a daunting task.[25] Indeed, Canada is one of the few (if not the first) Western industrialized countries to adopt industrial human resource planning.

> In a cross-country comparison of national human resource forecasting methods, Canada's tools and methods rated well. The study, which looked at forecasting methods in the United States, the U.K., Germany, Netherlands, Sweden, and Canada, found that Canada's system was strong in many areas relative to other countries. Our strengths lay in our ability to analytically assess skill shortages through such tools as occupational forecasting models and sector studies. Our most serious shortcoming lay in our lack of processing of the administrative data that is collected as part of our normal operations. The Netherlands' system was found to be the best equipped overall.[26]

Statistics Canada also publishes reports on labour force conditions on a monthly, quarterly, annual, and occasional basis. Information available on total labour force projections includes geographic, demographic, and occupational variables; labour income; census data; and population projections by sex and province over various years. Data such as these have implications for many businesses:

> Fast food restaurants depend on 16- to 24-year-olds for many jobs. By 2016, there will be a decline of 495,500 in this age category. At the same time, the trend toward eating more meals away from home will cause an increased demand for restaurant employees.

STRATEGIES TO MATCH SUPPLY AND DEMAND FOR HUMAN RESOURCES

Typically, human resource planners face two decision situations: they find that the available supply of human resources is either less or greater than their future needs. It is only the rare fortunate planner who finds that the supply and demand are equal. Each of the above two situations requires somewhat different corrective actions, which are discussed below.

Strategies in the Wake of Oversupply of Human Resources

When the internal supply of workers exceeds the firm's demand, a human resource surplus exists. This is handled in a variety of ways, discussed below.

Hiring Freeze

Most employers initially respond to a surplus with a hiring freeze. This freeze stops the human resource department from filling openings with external applicants. Instead, present employees are reassigned. Voluntary departures, called **attrition**, slowly reduce the surplus. Attrition is the normal separation of employees from an organization as a result of *resignation*, *retirement*, or *death*. It is initiated by the individual worker and not by the company. In most organizations, the key component of attrition is resignation, which is a voluntary separation. Although attrition is a slow way to reduce the employment base in an organization, it presents the fewest problems. Voluntary departures simply create a vacancy that is not filled, and the staffing level declines without anyone being forced out of a job:

attrition
Loss of employees due to their voluntary departures from the firm through resignation, retirement, or death.

> Faced with a surplus of employees and a slow-growing economy, a major department store resorted to a hiring freeze. On average, its attrition rate was 5 percent; within 18 months, it had reduced its staff level from 30,000 to about 27,750.

Early and Phased Retirement Offers

A special form of attrition is *early retirement*. It is one form of separation that the human resource department can actively control. It is used to reduce staffing levels and to create internal job openings. Early retirement plans are designed to encourage long-service workers to retire before the normal retirement age in the organization (say, 65 years). Since employees who retire before age 65 will draw benefits longer, their monthly retirement benefits may be reduced proportionately.

Some companies are allowing older employees to reduce their work activity and gradually *phase into* retirement without loss or reduction of pension benefits. The most typical pattern in **phased retirement** is to allow gradually shortened workweeks, a preferred schedule among older workers according to some surveys.[27] Most companies in the survey required that an employee first work a minimum of five years in the firm and be at least 55 years old in order to participate in a phased retirement program, and over half allowed employees to later change their minds. An example of phased retirement is provided by McGill University:

phased retirement
Gradual phase into retirement with loss or reduction of pension benefits.

> McGill University in Montreal offers its faculty members a pre-retirement package that allows a faculty member to choose to teach only half of his or her normal teaching load for 65 percent of

---

Pros and Cons of Phased Retirement

Pros	Cons
More time for retiree to develop other interests	Loss of income before retirement
Chance to "try out" retirement	Not compatible with some pension benefit packages
Loss of key personnel is cushioned	

the salary. This assumes that the faculty member will still carry on with his or her normal administrative work (e.g., attending department and other committee meetings and being available for student counselling, and so on).[28]

In the past, the Quebec government adopted legislation to facilitate phased retirement and early retirement.[29]

Job Sharing

Reducing the number of total work hours through **job sharing** is yet another option. Job sharing, also called *job splitting*, involves dividing duties of a single position between two or more employees. From the employer's perspective, this eliminates the need to lay off one employee completely. But the employees also benefit by having more free time at their disposal.

> "It makes good business sense for us to offer work sharing," says Norma Tombari, manager of the Royal Bank of Canada's work and family program. "We get to recruit and keep good employees, and our customers benefit because employees who feel the company is supporting them provide better service." The program is particularly popular with the women employees of the bank. Women constitute a large percentage of RBC's workforce.[30]

Work sharing programs are also used to avoid layoffs. A major initiative is the federal work sharing program administered by Human Resources and Skills Development Canada. It allows employees to voluntarily reduce their hours to spread available work around.[31]

The major advantage claimed for job sharing is increased productivity from workers who are not fatigued. Problems arise from the increased paperwork and administrative burden associated with two employees doing the job of one. Another problem is that of benefits. Human resource specialists are forced to decide whether job sharers should be given benefits equal with other employees or benefits that are scaled down in proportion to the employee's hours.[32]

Use of Part-Time Workers

Eliminating full-time positions and replacing them with part-time positions, thus reducing the total work hours and labour costs, is another strategy used in several settings.

> Since part-timers earn only a fraction of the salary earned by full-time workers, employers find it economical to use part-time employees.[33] A past study found that among 87 Canadian companies only 20 percent paid benefits to their part-time employees.[34]

Very often, part-time employees are paid no benefits. The significantly increased benefit costs, especially health care and pensions, provide a great incentive for employers to make more use of regular *part-time work*, defined as "less than full-time work by employees on a company's regular payroll."[35] Employers that do pay benefits tend to be in the public sector, such as health care facilities and municipal governments. Another advantage of part-time work is that it increases flexibility so that employers can match the workforce with peak demands. Part-time employment is also popular for a few other reasons, such as the following:

- the growing number of women in the labour force, with a preference for part-time positions
- the higher demand in the service industries, which employ more than 40 percent of all part-timers[36]
- the need for cost-cutting[37]

job sharing
A plan whereby available work is spread among all workers in a group to reduce the extent of layoffs when production requirements cause a substantial decline in available work.

Pros and Cons of Job Sharing

Pros	Cons
Individuals maintain work experience while devoting time to raising children, caring for elders, upgrading education	Salary and benefits lower than full-time job
	Advancement possibilities limited
	Higher administration costs
Reduced absenteeism for personal appointments	
Potentially higher productivity	
Training for two necessary	

Pros and Cons of Part-Time Work

Pros	Cons
Individuals can maintain work experience while devoting time to raising children, elder care, upgrading education	Salary and benefits lower than full-time job
	Fewer skills, less experience, and less training
Reduced absenteeism for personal appointments	Employees less loyal, more difficult to keep
May reduce staffing costs	

Part-time work has public costs. Part-time workers have limited entitlement to government-run employment insurance and disability benefits, resulting in potentially serious financial problems should they be unable to work. Without disability benefits they have no income and may end up on the welfare rolls.[38] In some settings, converting full-time to part-time work may be fraught with legal challenges as well.

Part-time work should not be confused with job sharing. Employees sharing jobs share a full-time job equally, including responsibilities and even the benefits. Part-time employees may be assigned any range of job responsibility, frequently without being paid benefits, or with prorated benefits. Some part-timers are hired on an on-call or intermittent basis.

Some employers have recognized the hidden costs of using a part-time workforce and begun to move in the opposite direction. Consider Loblaws's example:

> In early 2009, Canada's largest grocery chain, Loblaws, was planning to convert about 10 percent of its part-time workforce to create 10,000 full-time jobs. The organization felt that this move would benefit not only the organization by improving employee morale and loyalty but also the local economy overall. The management felt that the additional costs incurred by the company in creating the full-time jobs would be more than offset by the improvement in customer service, reduction in labour turnover, and improvement in overall productivity.[39]

Internal Transfers

Organizations with progressive human resource policies attempt to find new internal jobs for surplus and displaced employees:

> A financial services company with over 10,800 employees found itself forced to reduce staff in some areas to meet the twin pressures of increased competition and a recessionary economy. Rather than simply letting the employees go, the firm retrained the employees to take up new positions in areas where the firm was expanding. In the first two months since the program began, 75 percent of the over 130 displaced employees were retained by the firm in other positions. In almost every case, those employees not retained by the firm had had unsatisfactory performance records or had maintained a very narrow job focus or location requirements.[40]

Layoffs

Layoffs, the temporary withdrawal of employment to workers, are also used in cases of a short-run surplus. Layoffs are the separation of employees from the organization for economic or business reasons. The separation may last only a few weeks if its purpose is to adjust inventory levels or to allow the factory to retool for a new product. When caused by a business cycle, the layoffs may last many months or even years. However, if the layoff is the result of restructuring or rescaling of an industry, the "temporary" layoffs may be permanent.

As unpleasant as layoffs are for both workers and management, they may be required when attrition is insufficient to reduce employment to acceptable levels. In some organizations, each employee who is laid off may receive a supplemental employment benefit over and above government EI benefits. However, during severe economic downturns, the employer's ability to provide these benefits may be seriously jeopardized.

While the terms of collective agreement dictate layoff procedures in unionized settings, non-union employers may have to consider other factors or be exposed to constructive dismissal claims.

For example, in Ontario, the province's Employment Standards Act permits a temporary layoff of an employee without pay for up to 13 weeks in a consecutive 20-week period. If the unpaid layoff exceeds that period, it will no longer be deemed "temporary" and the employer will become liable for reasonable notice and severance pay, if applicable.[41]

When the layoffs are expected to be of a short duration—as when an automobile plant temporarily closes to change its tooling for a new model—layoffs may not follow the normal pattern of forcing the most recently hired employees to accept unemployment. Rather than following seniority, some contracts have "juniority" clauses. Juniority provisions require that layoffs be offered first to senior workers. If the senior worker wants to accept the layoff, that person collects employment insurance and the other organizational benefits and the juniors keep their jobs. Senior workers are likely to accept layoffs of short duration because they receive almost the same take-home pay without working. When the layoff is of an unknown duration, the seniors usually decline to exercise their juniority rights and fewer senior employees are put on layoff.

Of course, employees may be separated by termination of the employment relationship.

Leave Without Pay

One way to temporarily reduce the number of employees on the payroll is to give them an opportunity to take a leave of absence without pay either to attend college or university or to pursue other personal interests. Employees who are offered this leave are usually those who are financially able to leave the organization for a little while and whose jobs may be eliminated in the future. Thus, this strategy might help some employees to prepare for oncoming changes.

Loaning or Flexforce

Some innovative companies have come up with a new way to use their employees for the mutual benefit of employee and employer. Seasonal companies, like soft-drink bottlers or ice cream manufacturers, experience a slowdown when their products are in lower demand. Rather than laying off employees, these companies have found it useful to "loan" their employees to companies who tend to hire temporary workers during certain times of the year. Typically, higher-paid employees are loaned for other organizations, special projects with government, to civic bodies, or for work at charitable organizations. Typically, the firm pays these employees a reduced salary and the difference is made up by the agency.

While not yet popular in Canada, two U.S. companies pioneered the sharing or *Flexforce* idea.

Brooks Beverage Management Inc. (BBMI), a soft-drink bottler based in the city of Holland, Michigan, tried to find ways to avoid laying off its permanent staff during the annual production slowdown in September and October. Its partner was Haworth Inc., a neighboring furniture manufacturer. Haworth was a fast-growing company and had a difficult time recruiting enough qualified workers. After some intense negotiations, both companies came to a satisfying solution for both sides.

Haworth had its own cyclical trend: Corporate America buys more office furniture at the end of the year, creating a peak demand that lasts through the beginning of the next year. Both companies tended to staff for the low periods and then supplement for the high-demand periods. With the involvement of employees, the agreement called for the transfer, on a loan basis, of 31 employees from BBMI to Haworth, to cover the peak production period. The BBMI employees were put into assembly-line positions, requiring a minimum of training. In March, when production at Haworth slowed down and production at BBMI increased, the BBMI employees returned to their previous jobs. Both sides were very happy with this novel idea.[42]

Termination

Termination is a broad term that encompasses the permanent separation from the organization for any reason. Usually this term implies that the employee was fired as a form of discipline. When employees are discharged for business or economic reasons, it is commonly, although not always, called a layoff. Sometimes, however, the employer needs to separate some employees for business reasons and has no plans to rehire them. Rather than being laid off, those workers are simply terminated. In these cases, the employees may receive severance pay and outplacement assistance.

Severance pay is money—often equal to one or more week's salary—that is given to employees who are being permanently separated. Many organizations give severance pay only for involuntary separations and only to employees who have been performing satisfactorily. For example, if a factory

Pros and Cons of Employee Sharing	
Pros	**Cons**
Keeping jobs permanent	Extra training required
No need for layoffs during economic downturns	
Lower compensation expenses	
Task variety	

is going to close and move operations to another province, employees who are terminated may be given an extra week's salary for each year they have worked for the organization. Some organizations have developed innovative severance pay policies to achieve their human resource objectives, as the following example illustrates:

> Herman Miller Inc., a major manufacturer of office furniture employing over 7,000 persons in 40 countries, instituted a novel approach to severance pay, called a "silver parachute." Unlike the "golden parachutes" offered only to senior executives at firms likely to be targets of a takeover, the "silver parachutes" extend to all employees who have been with the company for two or more years. "The parachute would be activated in the event of a hostile takeover, and the rip cord would be pulled if a worker's job were eliminated, salary reduced, or working conditions or benefits altered." Those employees with between three and five years' tenure with the company would receive one full year's compensation. Longer-service employees receive 2.5 times their previous 12 months' salary. Besides assuring employees of severance pay should they lose their job in a hostile takeover, this benefit makes the company a less attractive takeover target.[43]

Outplacement

outplacement
Assisting employees to find jobs with other employers.

The blow of discharge may be softened through formal **outplacement** procedures, which help present employees find new jobs with other firms. These efforts may include the provision of office space, secretarial services, photocopying machines, long-distance phone calls, counselling, instructions on how to look for work, and even invitations to competitors to meet with employees. Not only do such efforts help the former employee, but they also give evidence to the remaining employees of management's commitment to their welfare.

Strategies to Overcome Shortage of Employees

If the internal supply of human resources cannot fulfill the organization's needs, a human resource *shortage* exists. In the short and long runs, somewhat different strategies are employed. Planners have very few options in the short run, while a long-term shortage can be handled through carefully crafted human resource strategies.

Overtime

A popular strategy is to ask existing employees to work beyond the organization's normal working hours. Indeed, even during a non-shortage situation, regular overtime has become a fact of life in many firms that do not want to incur additional fixed expenses of hiring permanent employees.

> In many organizations, employees—especially supervisory and managerial staff—are expected to work overtime, most of it unpaid. The culture of the organization requires the employee to put in the extra effort without expecting any reward. This is particularly so in nonunionized settings.

Higher employee fatigue, stress levels, accident and wastage rates, and so on, are some of the unwanted consequences of using overtime on a recurring basis. Recognizing this fact, some of the progressive employers have gone against the mainstream—namely reducing the number of work hours—and ended up improving their productivity levels and competitiveness in the labour market. One U.S. manufacturer's experience is noteworthy:

> Metro Plastics Technologies Inc. in Columbus, Indiana, could not fill eight vacancies in its plant as the unemployment rate in the area hovered between 1 and 3 percent. To get a recruiting advantage,

SPOTLIGHT ON ETHICS
Cutting Costs

Like other human resource management activities, HR planners often face ethical challenges. Consider the following two situations and respond to them. Once you have written down your answers, please compare them with those of your team- or classmates. Are there differences in your approaches? What facts and arguments seem to justify one action over the other?

Facing fierce price-based competition, your firm employing over 470 persons, has been trying to reduce costs in a variety of ways.

1. One action currently being considered is to move Production Unit 1 from its present location in an interior Canadian town to a developing country. Your manufacturing unit is the sole employer in that town and currently employs 128 persons. Most of the employees are semi-skilled and would find it hard to find employment elsewhere immediately. You know that in the case of many employees, they are the sole breadwinner for their families. Your firm located in this town because of a variety of tax advantages and subsidies the province offered to you for the first two years of your operations. Under those terms, your firm was expected to operate for a minimum period of four years. This is your sixth year in the province.

2. Your firm is also considering converting a number of your full-time employees in the head office and Production Unit 2 to a part-time workforce (You may assume that this is legal in the province where you are employed). Approximately 200 persons will be affected by this plan. This can generate significant savings for your firm, since a number of benefits currently offered to full time employees need not be offered any more to the part-timers. You realize that a number of your employees depend on the company benefits to take care of their children and the elderly in the family.

it adopted an innovative "30-hour work week for 40-hour pay" strategy under which an employee had to put in only 30 hours a week instead of the traditional 40 hours. A single newspaper ad brought hundreds of qualified applicants to the firm and the firm was able to fill the vacancies immediately. The benefits did not stop there. Within two years, customer returns had fallen by 72 percent and many internal costs had dropped dramatically. The same results have been reported in a number of other plants, in a variety of industries.[44]

Part-Time Workers

As already pointed out above, an increasingly popular strategy for meeting human resource needs is to use part-time employees. Part-time employees are an attractive option to the employer since it adds flexibility in scheduling. Traditionally, part-timers have been employed by service businesses such as restaurants and retail stores that experience considerable fluctuation in demand during peak and off-peak times. However, more recently, many firms, after a downsizing or restructuring, employ part-timers to provide services that had previously been offered by full timers.

> For example, in the past, United Parcel Service created 25-hour-per-week part-time jobs for shipping clerks and supervisors who sort packages at its distribution centres. Until the change, full-time staff carried out the same jobs.

Employment of part-timers reduces overall payroll costs since part-timers are, typically, not eligible for several of the expensive benefits offered to the full-time workforce. However, there are variations across provinces and human resource managers should carefully check the legal requirements before introducing new policies. For example, Saskatchewan has extended a number of benefits to part-time workers under specific conditions:

> In Saskatchewan, a full-time employee is anyone who works 30 hours or more per week. All businesses with 10 or more full-time equivalent employees must provide benefits to eligible part-time employees. To qualify, part-time employees must have been employed for 26 consecutive weeks and have worked 390 hours in those 26 weeks. To maintain eligibility, the employee should work for at least 780 hours in a calendar year. Eligible benefits include dental plans, group life, accidental death or dismemberment plans, and prescription drug plans.[45]

116   PART 2   Planning Human Resources

Part-time or contract workers are often hired for special jobs. What are the societal costs and benefits of large numbers of part-time workers?

CP/Simon Wilson.

Temporary Employment Agencies

Temporary employees, or "temps" as they are called, are provided by a number of private agencies. Temps work for a temporary employment agency and are assigned to different employers that contact the agency for the temporary filling of positions. This is particularly suitable for the supply–demand imbalance caused by short-term leaves of absence of permanent employees. Such employment can also be used to increase output when there is a sudden spurt in demand for the firm's products or services and some of the activities performed by "core" employees can be contracted out to someone else. Temps usually receive lower salaries or wages than core workers and are not eligible for several health, insurance, and retirement benefits.

> Traditionally, temps have been popular in clerical and secretarial jobs; however, more recently, even highly skilled scientific and professional jobs have been contracted out to temporary workers.

From a management perspective, temporary agency hires provide considerable staffing flexibility during periods when companies are experiencing either a staffing shortage (e.g., during holiday seasons or unexpected high turnover), or a seasonal market demand for special services (e.g., income-tax filing assistance). Problems with the temporary agency staffing arrangement are high costs and uneven quality of work.[46]

Internal Temporary Pools

An internal temporary pool consists of persons who are on call as needed. The company manages the pool internally. Because of the relatively higher costs of temporary agency hires mentioned above, many human resource managers rely more on internal temporary pools, consisting typically of people between jobs, retirees, homemakers returning to the workforce, former employees, and students. Such pools tend to be small and to consist mainly of individuals who perform clerical and administrative work. Retirees are perceived to be a good source of internal temporary pools, because they tend to know the requirements of the company and there seems to be a preference for coming back for a short period of time.

> A major Canadian university's homepage indicates that the temporary pool is the most common entry point to employment at the university.

Employee Leasing

More recently, a new type of organization has emerged and is already booming: the professional employer organization (PEO), now an almost billion-dollar industry. A PEO is a new type of

---

Pros and Cons of Employee Leasing

Pros	Cons
Staffing flexibility	Potential loss of trade secrets
Fast availability of professionals	Lack of employee commitment to the organization
No recruitment, hiring, benefits, or training costs	Expensive, at least in the short term
No long-term commitments	Dual authority relationship

---

employee leasing
The practice of outsourcing job functions, such as payroll, to organizations specializing in the field

employee leasing company, providing a wide range of outsourced services, from payroll and taxes to hiring and discipline, depending on a client's needs. While it may resemble a temporary employment agency, its scope is far broader. Clients tend to be small and mid-size employers with fewer than 100 employees, who cannot afford to hire top-flight HR or other experts.

> "If you run a restaurant, chances are you're good at that, not at payroll," says Carl Kleimann, Senior Vice President of 1st Odyssey Group, a Houston PEO that manages 12,000 employees. "The growth of our industry is coming from businesses that are tired of the headaches of dealing with government regulations. They fear they didn't complete something correctly. They don't understand or don't want to hassle with wage and hour laws and employment laws. Fear of lawsuits is another concern."[47]

Transfers

transfer
Movement of an employee from one job to another that is relatively equal in pay, responsibility, and organizational level.

A typical internal action used is the **transfer** of employees within the organization. Transfers occur when an employee is moved from one job to another that is relatively equal in pay, responsibility, and/or organizational level. Besides improving the utilization of their human resources, organizations can also make transfers beneficial to jobholders. The broadening experience of a transfer may provide an employee with new skills that make him or her a better candidate for future promotions. Transfers may even improve an individual's motivation and satisfaction, especially when a person finds little challenge in the old job. The new position, although not a promotion, may offer new technical and interpersonal challenges. In turn, these challenges may prove to be a growth opportunity for the transferee. Even when the challenges are minimal, the transfer at least offers some variety, which may enhance feelings of job satisfaction.

It should be noted that transfers result in the creation of a vacancy in another part of the same organization. Further, as Pinder and Das[48] observed, there may be hidden costs associated with transfers, such as the psychological stress and social uprooting of the transferee and his or her family. In the case of two-career families (where both spouses pursue careers), it may be difficult to persuade an employee to move to a place where his or her spouse cannot attain career progress.

Contract Workers

Contract workers (also sometimes called *consultants* and *freelancers*) are employees who have a direct contractual working relationship with the firm employing them. Many professionals with specialized skills are hired as contract workers.

> Universities use adjunct and part-time instructors; hospitals use emergency-room physicians on a contract basis; publishers use editors on a project basis; several civil engineering and construction firms use architects and other skilled persons on a contract basis. Underlying all these arrangements is the objective of meeting human resource needs without incurring permanent payroll costs to the firm.

Employers tend to make use of this type of staffing very selectively, especially for skills not available in the organization. In many cases, former executives, who either left voluntarily or were "invited to leave," or employees who were laid off, took early retirement, or left the company to start their own businesses are hired back as consultants.[49] These arrangements are often closely linked to particular tasks—for example, a market analysis, overseeing or arranging a merger, assisting a small business to get off the ground, and so on.[50]

Contractors in professional or technical areas, for example, often like the autonomy and the financial advantages of being self-employed. Many such contractors can command higher compensation than they would as employees. Contract workers are likely to be more productive and efficient since they are not constrained by the firm's routines and policies except in a broad sense. They do not have to attend meetings or go through channels to get approvals or the right information.

However, contracting work is not without problems. It should be remembered that contractors are not part of the organization and may not feel loyalty to any one client. Their focus is also likely to be on getting the present job done rather than what is good for the organization in the long term. Contracting out can also be exploitative.

> For example, some "self-employed" women, hired to do routine clerical work for one employer, are given daily quotas to meet and are paid on a piece-rate basis. In effect, they perform as employees, but receive less compensation because they have no benefit protection.[51]

Sometimes questions arise about whether the individual is, in fact, an employee or a contractor. In doubtful cases, Canada Revenue Agency (CRA) can be asked to make a ruling. To establish an employee's status, CRA reviews certain activities that generally indicate whether individuals are employees:

- Did they have a set number of working hours each day?
- Did they have to account for their time?
- Were they given specific job instructions?
- Were they members of the company's benefit plans?
- Did they have use of the company's computer equipment and office supplies?
- Did the company supply them with offices?
- Were they given specific titles and business cards on the company's letterhead?

To summarize, to be considered independent contractors, workers must agree to do specific jobs with no commitment for numbers of hours. They also must work on their own without supervision. They have to bill the employer directly and receive cheques for the completed work. They must keep their own financial books and records of accounting. In addition, they must not receive any company benefits. Independent contractors operate from their own offices with their own equipment; they should go to employers only for meetings. They also must provide services to more than one organization. CRA has developed four tests (see Figure 3-12) to check the authenticity of contract status.

FIGURE 3-12	CRA's Tests for Contract Labour

Canada Revenue Agency developed four tests, which assist human resource managers in deciding whether a person working for the organization should be considered to be an employee or an independent contractor:

1. **Control Test.** This test determines whether the employee is restricted under a "master–servant" relationship. Usually, an employer has more control over an employee than over an independent contractor. For example, in a master–servant relationship, the "master" can not only order what is to be done, but also how and when. Independent contractors are usually free to choose how their services are to be performed.

2. **Ownership of Tools Test.** What tools or materials are needed for the work to be done? Who owns them? If the business owns them, it looks more like an employer–employee relationship.

3. **Risk of Loss and Chance of Profit Test.** Who bears the financial risk that will provide an opportunity for profit? Who controls the pricing of the work done? If there is little financial risk, then again it looks more like a dependency relationship.

4. **Integration Test.** This test answers the question of whether the work performed by an employee under an employment contract is done as an integral part of the business. If a worker were under contract for services, his or her work would be classified as only "necessary" to the business, and not an integral part of the company. The more "critical" the work is for the business, the less likely it is done by an independent contractor.[52]

Promotions

A promotion occurs when an employee is moved from one job to another that is higher in pay, responsibility, and/or organizational level. It is one of the more pleasant events that happens to an employee. Generally, a promotion is a recognition of a person's past performance and future promise. Promotions usually are based on merit and/or seniority. Merit-based promotions occur when an employee is promoted because of superior performance in the present job. However, promotion as a "reward" for past efforts and successes may raise two major problems. One problem is whether decision makers can objectively distinguish the strong performers from the weak ones. When merit-based promotions are being used, it is important that the decision reflect the individual's performance and not the biases of the decision maker.[53]

> An example would be when the best performer is a member of a protected class and the decision maker is prejudiced.

The decision maker should not allow personal prejudices to affect promotions. Decisions that are swayed by personal feelings are more common when job performance is not measured objectively. When promotion decisions result from personal biases, the organization ends up with a less competent person in a higher, more important position. The resulting resentment among those not promoted is likely to harm their motivation and satisfaction.

A second problem with merit-based promotions is put forth in the Peter Principle.[54] It states that, in a hierarchy, people tend to rise to their level of incompetence. Although not universally true, the "principle" suggests that good performance in one job is no guarantee of good performance in another.

> If one of the new engineers hired at a telephone company consistently made major cost-saving design changes, that would be an example of superior performance. However, suppose the engineer were promoted to supervisor. The skills needed to be an effective supervisor are very different from those needed to be a top engineer. As a result of such a promotion, the firm might gain an ineffective supervisor and lose a superior engineer.

In some situations, the most senior employee receives the promotion. "Senior" in this case means the employee who has the longest service with the employer. The advantage of this approach is that it is objective. All one needs to do is compare the seniority records of the candidates to determine who should be promoted.

Part of the rationale for this approach is to eliminate biased promotions and to require management to develop its senior employees since they will eventually be promoted. Seniority-based promotions usually are limited to hourly employees.

> For example, a promotion from Mechanic Second Class to Mechanic First Class may occur automatically by seniority whenever an opening for mechanic first class occurs. Labour organizations often seek this type of promotion to prevent employers from discriminating among union members.

Most human resource experts express concern about the competency of those promoted solely because of seniority since not all workers are equally capable. Sometimes the person who is the best mechanic, for example, is not the most senior one. Under seniority-based promotions, the best person is denied the job unless the individual happens to be the most senior worker as well.

Full-Time Employees

For several positions where internal transfer or promotion may not be feasible, hiring full-time employees is the only alternative. As mentioned already, many organizations are averse to this strategy since it incurs additional fixed costs. Hiring full-time staff also requires a more detailed look at their competencies in terms of the organization's long-term strategies. The steps involved in hiring employees are discussed in Chapters 5 and 6.

Today, a variety of alternate work arrangements have found favour with employers and employees. These not only provide greater freedom to employees in choosing their work hours, but also help employers to reduce employment and operating costs in a variety of ways. Some of the emerging work options are discussed in the next section.

HRM Guide
www.hrmguide.net

⟳ EMERGING WORK OPTIONS AND ARRANGEMENTS

work options
Various and flexible alternatives to the traditional workplace or the traditional 40-hour work week.

shorter workweek
Employee scheduling variations that allow full-time employees to complete a week's work in less than the traditional five days.

Alternative arrangements in staffing, or **work options**, as they are some times called, can provide management with greater flexibility as well as reduce costs. They can also meet employees' needs for flexibility and help them better balance work–family demands. The 40-hour workweek was designed for a workforce consisting largely of men with stay-at-home wives. Today, however, almost half of Canada's workforce is female, and 40 percent of full-time workers have a spouse who also works full-time. As a result, men and women both are finding flexible work options an attractive and, in some cases, absolutely necessary option. For society as a whole, often the emerging work arrangements can reduce economic and social costs. The more popular work options are detailed below.

Shorter or Compressed Workweeks

A **shorter workweek** (also referred to as *compressed workweek*) compresses 40 hours of work into fewer than five full days. Some plans even shorten the workweek to fewer than 40 hours. The most popular version has been 40 hours of work compressed into four days.

> Fire departments and staff at some hospitals use a three-day, 36-hour schedule.

> Another option is the "weekender," where employees work 12-hour shifts on Saturdays and Sundays, but are paid 40 hours instead of the 24 hours actually worked.

> Management and the union of the 3M Canada plant in London, Ontario, agreed upon this arrangement.

The advantages include less time wasted due to startup, washup, breaks, and cleanup. In addition, absenteeism and turnover tend to be lower and employee morale higher, and it seems to stimulate employee motivation and productivity. The disadvantages are that customers may be inconvenienced, there could be some scheduling problems, and the long hours could be boring and monotonous.[55] The longer working day may also result in more fatigue, which could pose a safety risk. Another potential drawback is that some employers must pay overtime to nonmanagerial employees who have to work more than eight hours in a given day due to overlapping work requirements with those employees who are on a different schedule. Some provinces allow averaging of hours, while others do not. This means that in some instances, overtime pay might be required. Despite these drawbacks, some companies report success with the shorter workweek:

> A Canadian bank in a small town operates from 9:30 a.m. to 8:30 p.m. Monday to Friday, and 9:30 a.m. to 5:30 p.m. Saturday. Instead of staggering workers' hours, the manager worked out a scheme for a compressed workweek. There are two teams at each branch, a Monday–Wednesday team and a Thursday–Saturday team. Each team works three days a week, 12.5 hours per day. The altered arrangement resulted in greater accuracy on the part of employees.

> Some employers also use the shorter workweek as a means of avoiding layoffs.

> In the past, British Columbia's InterFor, one of Canada's largest sawmills, minimized layoffs from a major restructuring by changing shift arrangements.[56]

Flextime

flextime
A scheduling innovation that abolishes rigid starting and ending times for each day's work.

A recent survey by the Conference Board of Canada showed that 93 percent of responding companies have introduced flexible time schedules.[57] **Flextime** abolishes rigid starting and ending times for the workday. Instead, employees are allowed to report to work at any time during a range of hours. The

---

Pros and Cons of the Compressed Workweek Approach

Pros	Cons
More flexibility in balancing work and family	Physically and mentally draining
One extra day off at full-time income	Extra child care may be needed
Commuting outside rush hours	

Pros and Cons of Flextime

Pros	Cons
Flexibility to schedule errands, take care of family illness	More difficult to coordinate group activities
Avoid rush hour traffic	Staff supervision may be more difficult
May assist in child care requirements	Potential customer dissatisfaction
Reduced absenteeism because of family commitments	

---

day is usually divided into two periods, core time and flexible time. During the core time, the employee must be on the job, while during the flexible time the employee has the choice as to when to complete the required time.

> For example, starting time may be from 7 a.m. to 9 a.m., with all employees expected to work during the core hours of 9 a.m. to 3 p.m. The workday usually remains unchanged at eight hours. Therefore, the end of the workday is also variable.

Flextime is best suited for customer-independent units. However, there are several variations in the flextime approach which make it feasible in a number of settings:

- *flexitour*, where employees choose their working time and have to stick to it for a period of time (e.g., a week or a month);
- *gliding time*, permitting flexible starting and quitting time;
- *variable day*, or flexible workdays (e.g., 12 hours one day and 4 hours the next);
- *maniflex*, with flexible workday, but core time on certain days (e.g., Monday and Friday);
- **flexiplace**, allowing flexibility in working time and place (e.g., office and home);[58]
- *annualized hours*, where employer and employee agree on an annual total number of hours, worked in variable quantities over the year;[59]
- *zero-hour contracts*, often made between agencies for temporary workers and their employees, practically an "on call" arrangement;[60] and
- *time accounts*, a formalized way of the well-known method of taking time off to compensate for extra time worked.[61]

The following example indicates how one of these options work:

> Ontario Hydro has used a flextime arrangement for many years. Staff may start any time before 9 a.m. and leave any time after 3 p.m. as long as they work a full day. They also may adjust the length of their lunch hour. The schedule allows employees to avoid the worst of Toronto's traffic with an early start.

flexiplace
A flexible work arrangement in which employees are allowed or encouraged to work at home or in a satellite office closer to home.

The outcome of a flextime program, however, is contingent upon the nature of the firm's operations. For example, the major disadvantage of flextime is the difficulty in meeting minimum staffing needs early and late in the day. Assembly-line and customer service operations find this problem to be especially significant. But in many operations, users have reported noteworthy successes.[62] In some instances, managers may also feel obliged to be present at work as long as any subordinate is present. Some employees may misuse the system by coming late and leaving early, especially in those instances where time clocks are not used.

Telecommuting

telecommuting
Paid labour performed at the employee's home.

More recently, **telecommuting** is becoming increasingly popular.[63] Working at home suits the work habits and lifestyles of some personalities, particularly those self-disciplined self-starters who can work with a high degree of autonomy. Aiding in this trend are the decreasing costs of personal computers, modems, photocopiers, and fax machines. Some organizations also set up *telework centres*, or a suite of offices or a building that has been designed for employees to use instead of their regular office location.[64] These sites may be away from the normal operating premises, thus allowing employees to choose convenient locations for performing work.

Pros and Cons of Telecommuting

Pros	Cons
Less commuting time	Isolation of employees from supervisors and coworkers
Better integration of work and family life	Lack of visibility (overlooked for promotion decision making)
Freedom to work independently and at own pace	Supervision more difficult
Less overhead cost for employers	Distractions at home (TV, kids, tradespeople)

In a survey by the Conference Board of Canada over 50 percent of the respondents reported using some form of telecommuting. Similar results were reported in another study involving over 5,000 Canadians.[65]

Telecommuting is ideal for employees who do independent jobs, such as insurance claim officers, catalogue sales agents, computer software writers, telephone solicitors, and so on. The "information highway" will probably increase the number of people working in the "electronic cottage industry." However, not everybody is positive about this new approach. Unions especially raise some objections. They fear that this trend will lead to new forms of exploitation.[66]

Telecommuting seems to have positive results on the bottom line for employers.

Productivity increases ranging from 15 to 35 percent and reduced absenteeism are some of the benefits of telecommuting as reported by organizations employing it. The cost of setting up a telecommuting employee is also lower than office expenses. Pacific Bell pays $1,700 per employee, far less than the cost of a work station. Another major retailer found that it could set up employees for half the cost of an office.[67] In the past, Royal Bank managers estimated that the bank's flexible work arrangements added $170 million to its bottom line because of higher employee efficiency and higher ability to meet deadlines.[68]

Telecommuting has found favour with several employees:

Toronto Virtual Assistant Judith Mathison is into her sixth year of telework: "I started telework about six years ago and have done it both full- and part-time. I enjoy the control over my time that it gives me and I accomplish a great deal more. I have teenagers at home and the only time I get my computers from them is when they're at school. Works for me!"[69]

In Greater Vancouver, veteran Royal Bank of Canada employee Jan McNeill works at home while her four-year-old daughter plays nearby with a Dictaphone and calculator.

In Ottawa, federal public servant Pierre Rondeau researches trademarks from a battery of home computers, and figures he saves $300 to $350 a month by not going into the office.[70]

As Joyce Everhart, managing editor of *Public Works Online*, comments: "Telecommuting, or teleworking, is a business solution that is here to stay."[71] However, telecommuting is not for everyone or every organization (see the box "Pros and Cons of Telecommuting"). Sometimes employers use this option to convert full-time employees into independent contractors to strip them of various benefits and overtime pay. In some instances, telecommuting may also have an adverse impact on families, especially dual-career families, who might find that work at home cuts into their leisure and time with family.

The Virtual Organization

virtual organization
An operational domain of any organization whose workforce includes a significant portion of remote workers.

Is it possible to have a company with 2,700 employees in 84 offices around the world and no formal headquarters—a **virtual organization**? The answer is yes!

Golder Associates, a Calgary company specializing in engineering and environmental consulting, is one of the Canadian companies with employees spread around the globe. Communication is electronic most of the time, via email and conference calls, with only four annual face-to-face

Pros and Cons of the Virtual Organization

Pros	Cons
Working independently and at own pace	Communication tends to be more difficult
No commuting	Supervision difficult
Avoidance of rush hours	Isolation of employees from supervisor and colleagues
Lower overhead costs	Lack of role clarity

meetings for strategic decisions. It seems to work very well for the company, which has had annual growth of more than 10 percent since its creation in 1960 and was ranked the twentieth best company in Canada to work for by Report on Business magazine.[72]

"Having people all over the world ensures a better range of perspectives," says Steve Thompson, president of Golder Associates Inc. "The bad part is that it puts extra stress on communication, coordination, and decision making. Where we get into trouble is when the management teams around the world get disconnected from the needs and wants of our people," he says. But then "the phones start ringing and the emails start flying, and they get your attention very quickly."[73]

A good example of a virtual manufacturing organization is Proctor & Gamble's (PG) Reflect.com, a Web-based cosmetic company, where there are no products until customers design them.

Reflect.com makes available over 50,000 formulas created by PG, not just the traditional 20. Customers describe their hair colour, eye colour, skin condition, and their favourite look, then a highly automated laboratory mixes the appropriate ingredients and sends out the personalized products, with the customer's name on each product. Reflect.com has over 500,000 users per month.[74]

Just-in-Time Employees

The latest development in the area of flexible staffing seems to be the *just-in-time* employee, a term coined by *Business Week* in its special issue on the 21st Century Corporation.[75] *Business Week* describes a human capital exchange (HCE) model, which works much like NASDAQ and the New York Stock Exchange, with the value of employees—free agents—determined by the open market: "lawyers down $2, engineers up a buck." According to Christopher Meyer, director of the Center for Business Innovation, these free agents "are much more likely to get what they are worth—they will participate in the downside and the upside."

Arrangements such as the above not only enhance organizational flexibility and efficiency and help reduce costs, but also enable human resource departments to better respond to employee needs. Many successful organizations supplement such strategies with sophisticated human resource information systems (HRISs) to keep track of changing employee competencies and profiles and link these to human resource strategy. The more enlightened human resource departments periodically assess the value of their human resources. Human resource accounting (HRA) provides these organizations with valuable information about one of the most (if not the most) important ingredients of organizational success—namely human resources. Given their importance, HRIS and HRA are discussed separately below.

HUMAN RESOURCE INFORMATION SYSTEMS

A **human resource information system** (HRIS) is a system used to collect, record, store, analyze, and retrieve data concerning an organization's human resources. All good human resource decisions require timely and accurate information. A good HRIS is, hence, critical for the effective functioning of the HR department and the larger organization. The larger the organization and the more dynamic an organization's environments, the greater the need for a sophisticated HRIS. Consider Chevron:

human resource information system
Gathers, analyzes, summarizes, and reports important data for formulating and implementing strategies by HR specialists and line managers.

> Chevron Corporation, a large, international oil company with several thousands of employees working in over 50 countries, in the past initiated a sophisticated information system called "CHRIS" (Chevron Human Resource Information System). CHRIS can provide all necessary information on the firm's human resources to the managers of this conglomerate (containing 13 distinct companies) widely separated geographically.[76]

An HRIS can be as large or as small as is necessary.[77] The information contained in an HRIS varies from one organization to the next. Figure 3-13 lists some key elements seen in HRISs of several large organizations. The following provides another example:

> A major investment firm has a computerized human resources inventory that enables a manager to find out all relevant information on the firm's employees using a series of questions that require only a "yes" or "no" decision. For example, to find an appropriate person for a higher position, the manager uses this inventory by specifying the requirements, such as education, years of experience, number of languages in which the job incumbent should be fluent, and so on. The computer will automatically identify appropriate candidates and flash their brief résumés on the screen.

When designing a HRIS, the organization must pay careful attention to several factors. Some of these are discussed below.

Relational Versus Nonrelational Systems

Sophisticated HRI systems use relational databases. That is to say, information about an employee needs to be entered only once into the system to make it available for all HR purposes.

> For instance, if an employee has completed a new university program, in an advanced HRIS it will need to be entered into the files only once; this information will appear in all appropriate tables (or computer screens and files). The computer program behind the HRIS will know how to use this new information for all relevant decisions affecting this employee—for example, compensation, skills listing, performance competencies, benefits, and so on.

FIGURE 3-13 | **Information Typically Contained in an HRIS in a Large Organization**

- Wage and salary data (pay structure, raises received by employees, wage histories of employees)
- Benefits (types, choices, used/accumulated by employees, choices by employee group)
- Staff profile (minorities, women, people with physical disabilities, managerial versus nonmanagerial)
- Grievances (types, frequency, decisions by adjudicator)
- Training and development (types, dates offered, training records of employees, training needs of personnel, training costs)
- Health and safety (accidents, costs, tolerance limits for various dangerous substances)
- Succession plans (skills, specialties, work experience, performance record, promotion capabilities of employees)
- Job families (jobs, number, training needs, salary)
- Employee information (all relevant data including those for tax and pension plan purposes)
- Organizational data (structure, levels, reporting pattern, major policies)
- Demographics (staff profiles including education, age, etc.)
- Environmental and census data (population trends, economic indices)
- Productivity data

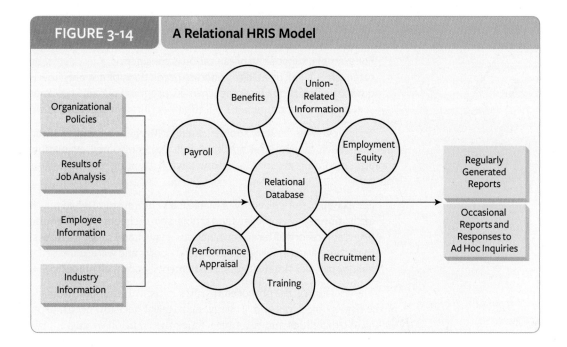

FIGURE 3-14   **A Relational HRIS Model**

In the older, nonrelational systems, information on employee name, age, home address, job title, pay rate, and so on will have to be separately entered into the payroll file, the benefits file, performance appraisal records, and several other places. Any change in employee information will have to be updated separately in each file. The probability of an error in inputting information was very high in the nonrelational systems. Probability of delays and inconsistencies in information updating was also higher in the nonrelational systems. Figure 3-14 shows how a relational database would help an organization in its strategic and operational plans.

Referential Integrity

Some relational databases have built-in systems to prevent errors and catch inconsistencies. This feature, called *referential integrity*, ensures that an organization's policies are operationalized or implemented consistently throughout the organization.

> For example, in a sophisticated HRIS, a new employee cannot be hired until a vacancy has been approved or established (through retirement or departure). There are also built-in checks against out-of-range values (e.g., employees whose age is shown as below 15 or above 70) and automatic red flags for violation of laws (e.g., when wage rate is shown as less than $3.00).

Breadth and Size of HRIS

Based on the organization's needs, a decision must be made on the type, size, and breadth of coverage of HRIS. Will the HRIS reside on a microcomputer? Several computers? Mainframe computer? If the organization is not too large, the entire system could be maintained on one computer or a few networked computers. On the other hand, if the organization is very large and operating in several countries, several networked computers that continuously transmit data to each other may be essential. Often, the firm may begin with a simple HRIS and expand to cover several areas and meet various HR and organizational needs, as illustrated by the experience of FedEx:

> FedEx, which has a very sophisticated HRIS, began its system with only basic employee records consisting of 10 screens of data. In a few years, it had grown into a multifunction system with over 600 different screens. More than 25,000 paperless transactions are processed each day, covering transfers, promotions, merit raises, and internal job placements of its more than 90,000 employees.[78]

Type of Outputs

All HRISs produce some regular reports, such as employee records, salary and benefit details, retirement benefits, and so on. However, as a firm's HRIS increases in sophistication, it goes beyond these regular reports and is able to produce special reports, answer questions interactively, and play an important role in decision support.

For example, suppose an organization is considering a new dental benefit program. In a sophisticated HRIS, it will be able to generate predictions of not only how many employees are likely to qualify for and probably accept the new program, but also how much it will cost the firm over a specific period of time, how it will affect recruitment success and employee turnover, and so on.

Today, even moderately sophisticated HRISs have a number of modules that perform specific functions such as applicant tracking, recruitment source evaluation and costing, performance appraisal recording, compensation and payroll, training records maintenance, and human resource forecasts.

For example, the University of Manitoba's HRIS system, when fully implemented, will enable the institution to pay employees and scholarship recipients, enroll and de-enroll employees in benefit plans, and record all hires, terminations, leaves, and salary increases, applying all the appropriate rules that pertain. It will provide timely reports and will automatically calculate service, statutory holiday pay, sick time, vacation entitlements, and much more.[79]

The decision on the proposed HRIS's sophistication should be made only after a careful analysis of the firm's objectives and strategy, managerial decision needs, organizational size, and current technical capabilities and resources. Since the addition or upgrading of an HRIS requires careful analysis and planning (and is usually expensive, complex, and time-consuming), the desired outcomes from the HRIS should be clearly identified before proceeding with system installation. Figure 3-15 shows the more popular applications of HRIS in organizations.

FIGURE 3-15	Selected HRIS Outcomes in Organizations

- Absenteeism figures for employees, job categories, and departments
- Applicant tracking
- Benefits utilization categorized by employee and employee groups; cost summaries and projections of benefits programs
- Employee records and employment histories
- Employment equity–related reports, especially concentration and underutilization patterns across jobs and job families
- Health and safety records
- Human resource plans
- Job descriptions, specifications, and standards
- Job evaluation information
- Job postings
- Safety and health figures and trends
- Payroll
- Pension and retirement plans
- Skills inventories
- Short- and long-term disability records
- Succession plans
- Performance records
- Time and attendance
- Turnover indices
- Union contract details

Developing Internal Software Versus Buying

Another decision is whether to develop the software using internal experts or to buy and use off-the-shelf software. This, of course, is related to type and size of HRIS planned by the firm. Building an HRIS within an organization requires a great deal of time, expertise, and money. Custom purchased software is quicker than building from scratch, but still requires extensive in-house documentation and substantial development time. In the early days of HRISs, it was necessary to extensively modify or customize off-the-shelf software to meet a firm's requirements. However, this is no longer the case. In the recent past, many programs have become commercially available. Except in the case of a few large organizations with very unique HR needs, it is seldom necessary or cost effective today to design your own system from scratch. Purchased systems also have the advantage of regular updates.

Access to HRIS Information

Who should have access to the information contained in HRIS? Needless to say, HR staff and key managers should have access to all information that enables them to make informed decisions; however, this should be weighed against the need for confidentiality and the need to respect employees' privacy. Most HRISs collect and retain only the employee information needed for business or legal reasons, and establish controls for internal use and external release of this information. Sensitive information—such as security and medical reports, investigative and grievance files, insurance and benefit records, information related to performance and disciplinary actions, and so on—should be tightly protected and offered to persons only on a need-to-know basis.

The decision about who should have the right to change input data is also critical. On the one hand, restricting data entry to a few persons can improve consistency and prevent errors; on the other hand, it can also result in delays. The system should also have built-in checks against errors and system malfunction, yet be easily accessible by all concerned.

> At FedEx, managers and employees do much of their own data entry. For instance, managers wanted to reduce the time it took to get a new employee on the payroll; now they can do it themselves in a few minutes rather than submitting a form to the HR department and waiting several days. All employees can also access the system to enter their change of address or other personal particulars.[80]

Security

Closely related to the above is the issue of security of HRIS data.

> In a survey of more than 1,320 Chief Information Officers and senior systems professionals, more than 80 percent of respondents said employees posed the greatest danger to the unauthorized disclosure of confidential information. Next on the list were computer terrorists, feared by about another 80 percent. Nearly 8 out of 10 firms surveyed reported financial losses in the immediate past due to breaches of security.[81]

As one manager noted, "The difficulty in this day and age for management is that employees are not looking at long-term employment. So, if they've been downsized or not handled well or harassed the attitude is 'I'm going to fix my employer. I'll take the data with me or I'll destroy it.'" An employee who suspects he or she might be let go from the organization puts a virus in the computer system set to go off in six months. If not let go at that time, the employee will eliminate it. But if the employee is terminated two months after planting the virus, and four months later the virus completely wipes out the database, there are no obvious suspects.[82]

It is not only evil-intentioned workers who pose a threat to valuable information, but also those who do not protect their passwords or who download virus-infected games or other files off the Internet. Sometimes even simple passage of time can corrupt disks on which important data are stored.

In recent years, several organizations, especially large ones, have used internal Web sites—referred to as **intranets**—for a variety of purposes including dissemination of corporate policy information to employees and the general public, informing current employees and potential recruits about personnel benefits and employee services, and conveying information related to marketing. Indeed, the growth of intranets in the recent past has been incredible.[83]

intranet
An organization-specific internal computer network.

Disney placed its corporate HRIS on the Disney Corporate Web to provide support and share information among departments. The site has become an important communications tool for corporate HRIS. It includes status information on corporate and business unit projects, a calendar of HR-related events, links to other Disney Web sites, companywide meeting notes and downloadable PowerPoint presentations and HR-related tables.[84]

Intranets are the logical extension of HRIS. There will be enterprisewide business management systems of which information pertaining to human resources will be only one component. Such an Integrated Information System (IIS) may cross all boundaries—often going even beyond the organizational database.[85] Future organizations may also be able to outsource several components of HRIS and obtain information needed directly via the Internet and corporate intranet.[86]

Currently, there are a number of software packages and enterprise-level programs that help plan and foster human capital effectively.

A popular software is PeopleSoft, used for human capital management. This Web-based employee and manager self-service program can be used for most tasks related to human capital management including time management, payroll administration, e-recruiting, and performance management. SAP, another organization-wide electronic architecture claims to offer integrated solutions for all aspects of human resource management and helped Carl Zeiss Group, a global provider of optical and opto-electronic products to reduce time-to-market for new integration projects.[87]

Information on PeopleSoft Software
www.2020software.com/
products/PeopleSoft_
Enterprise_Human_
Capital_Management.asp

Information on SAP
www.sap.com/platform/soa/
brochures/index.epx

HUMAN RESOURCE ACCOUNTING

More recently, some progressive organizations have attempted to quantify the overall value of their organizations through **human resource accounting** (HRA). HRA is the process of identifying, measuring, accounting, and forecasting the value of human resources in order to facilitate effective management of an organization.[88] HRA attempts to put a dollar figure on the human assets of an organization using cost or value models:[89] The cost models attempt to place a dollar value on human assets based on some kind of cost calculation—acquisition, replacement, or opportunity costs. The value-based models, on the other hand, attempt to evaluate human resources on the basis of their economic value to the organization. HRA can be a blessing to salary administrators, trainers, human resource planners, and union–management negotiators if it provides them with the kind of objective and reliable information they have long needed to plan these functions.

human resource accounting
A process to measure the present cost and value of human resources as well as their future worth to the organization.

SPOTLIGHT ON HRM

Dude, Where's My Job?

It was only 18 months ago that the *Wall Street Journal* ran an article outlining the lavish demands of a new generation of workers, known collectively as Gen Y, Millennials, or Net Gen. At the time, the thinking was that this group—aged 30 and under—had employers over a barrel. For one thing, there were relatively few of them, and employers, facing an imminent wave of boomer retirements, would be competing for the best of this young cohort. Also, since this is the Internet generation, they were believed to possess magical and mysterious tech skills that would prove invaluable in the workplace of the future.

Emboldened by these dual advantages, Millennials set their expectations high. Not only did they want fun, fulfilling work, with flexible hours, good salaries, and ample vacation, they wanted to be celebrated, too. Literally, feted. Savvy employers had taken to embracing measures like prize packages for a job well done, "public displays of appreciation," and, in the case of one manufacturer in Texas, retaining a "celebration assistant" in charge of helium balloons and confetti. This was smart business, according to 30-year-old Jason Ryan Dorsey, a self-appointed Gen Y expert—who consults with companies like Kraft and Four Seasons Hotels and Resorts about the peculiarities and preferences of his generation. "Marking milestones is major," he told *Forbes* magazine. "No birthday should go uncelebrated, and the first day on the job should be unforgettable." Which is great, except for one thing: what happens when the most entitled generation in history slams into the worst job market in 30 years?

At the turn of 2009, in the midst of massive layoffs and hiring freezes, not to mention cut-rate Christmas parties where punch just wasn't in the budget, these demands seem cringe-worthy—even more so than they did before. If ever there was a sign that the era of the sellers' employment market is over, it came last month when Google—the Santa Claus of corporate perk-giving—instituted a hiring freeze and, among other things, cancelled its New York office's decidedly Millennial-friendly tradition of afternoon tea. Almost as soon as they began for this cohort, it would appear its halcyon days are over.

In November alone, 71,000 Canadians lost their jobs—27 percent of the newly unemployed are people aged 24 and under—and economists predict this is only a bellwether of worse to come. Suddenly, many of those retiring boomers can't afford to retire. Making matters worse, Millennials are saddled with more debt than any previous generation (an average of $5,631 per year in student debt alone, not to mention the load sitting on their credit cards, and what they're doling out in car payments). This recession is not what they signed up for.

"They were absolutely told that 'You're part of a blessed generation and you are going to be in control of your own destiny,'" says Winnipeg native Steven Rothberg, owner of CollegeRecruiter.com, a company that recruits college graduates mostly in the U.S. "The spring 2008 grads have had to do some major adjusting. They graduated with the expectation that it was going to be a sellers' market, that they were going to have multiple offers, step into an upper management role and have significant strategic impact on a Fortune 500 company, and that's just not the reality." Until last year, he said, university and college students in their senior year, even the mediocre ones, could expect job offers as early as Oct. 1 of their final year. Now, employers are waiting until the spring to make hiring decisions, waiting to see how the economy shakes out, and leaving more students graduating into uncertainty.

There will be schadenfreude from those who see Millennial entitlement as a moral failing. "I hear people say this a lot," says Dorsey of his boomer executive clients. "They say, 'Your generation just needs one good recession and then they'll appreciate their jobs.'" But this is too simplistic an assessment of why "kids today" are the way they are. They're not genetically lazy or spoiled, any more than children of the Depression are inherently thrifty. Whatever overblown expectations this generation has are the product of decades of conditioning, and not only by overzealous boomer parents. Well-intentioned attempts to make this generation feel good about itself have, in fact, left them poorly prepared to weather a tough economic storm.

Consider that this is the first cohort to come of age in a time of institutionalized self-esteem. Beginning in the seventies, programs designed to boost children's self-esteem were installed in schools and at home, in the form of books and TV shows like *Mister Rogers' Neighborhood*. Throughout the eighties, according to the research of Jean Twenge, a professor of psychology at San Diego State University, the number of studies published on the benefits of self-esteem programs doubled, and in the nineties, it doubled again. Then came the elimination of competition, harsh red marking pens, and the arrival of books with titles like *Celebrate Yourself: Six Steps to Building Your Self-Esteem*. "Generation Me's expectations are highly optimistic," Twenge wrote in her 2006 book on the narcissistic tendencies of this group. "They expect to go to college, to make lots of money, and perhaps even to be famous." Unfortunately, there's a fine line between optimism and confidence, and irrational entitlement.

But it wasn't just indulgent teachers and coddling parents that formed this generation's world view. The self-esteem revolution happened to dovetail with a consumer shift toward an ever-greater focus on the individual. Marketers trained their sights on young people more intently than ever before, piggybacking on the self-esteem movement to offer youth heaps of affirmation in the form of a countless array of products—just for them! They realized that parents, flush with credit and disposable income, were inordinately concerned with their kids' opinions, even when it came to grown-up purchasing decisions (from cars to family vacations). Tweens spend about $2.9 billion a year and influence purchases worth another $20 billion. From the age of eight, Millennials saw themselves reflected everywhere: in ads for tween shampoos, designer fashions, and fragrances. By the time they got to university, credit card companies were handing out application forms along with student orientation packages. The message, as always: if you want it, you should have it.

It only makes sense that the environment in which they were raised would inform what they expected from a job—namely, flexibility, authority, instant respect and continuous affirmation. (This is a generation, after all, in which seven out of ten rank themselves "above average" in academic ability.) "They're not going to put up with the 'paying your dues' and being in the mailroom for the first three years," says Rothberg. "In their mind it's, 'I graduated. I've always succeeded. I've always got a trophy for everything I've done. All of my friends and everyone I know is above average, so when I go into a place of work, I'm either going to set that place on fire or they're not good enough for me and I'm out of there.'"

But there is a surprising upside to this attitude that may wind up benefiting both the young workers and the companies that employ them. Ironically, the Millennials' addiction to affirmation may also turn out to be their saving grace. "What is interesting about this generation," says Max Valiquette, president of Toronto-based youth marketing firm Youthography, "is that a lot of the carrots and perks they're asking for have nothing to do with money, and almost everything to do with how they work." Very few of them have had hard experience scrimping to make rent. (In fact, in 2006, 44 percent of Canadian adults ages 20 to 29 were living with mom and dad). Instead, Dorsey says, the incentives they crave involve self-determination, being recognized for good work, and regular feedback—things that cost no money at all. In other words, to some degree employers may be able to substitute applause for hard currency and still keep young employees perfectly happy, a potential boon in a cash-strapped economy.

For those young workers fortunate enough to find or keep work in the midst of the storm, life is about to provide some eye-opening lessons, and the same might be said for the companies trying to balance their need for young ambitious workers with their immediate need to keep costs down. "Smart companies are going to see this as an unparalleled opportunity to build Gen Y loyalty," says Dorsey. "I always mention the birthday thing because it's so simple, but Gen Y really does believe that the most important holiday of the year is their birthday because it's the one they don't have to share." If this turns out to be true, expect to be eating a lot of cake in 2009.

Source: Lianne George, "Dude, Where's My Job?" *MacLean's* January 19, 2009, pages 48–49. Originally appearing in *The Ego Boom: Why the World Really Does Revolve Around You.* Key Porter, 2009.

◉ SUMMARY

Human resource planning requires considerable time, staff, and financial resources. The return on this investment may not justify the expenditure for small firms. Increasingly, however, large organizations use human resource planning as a means of achieving greater effectiveness. Human resource planning is an attempt by companies to estimate their future needs and supplies of human resources. Through an understanding of the factors that influence the demand for workers, planners can forecast specific short-term and long-term needs.

Given some anticipated level of demand, planners try to estimate the availability of present workers to meet that demand. Such estimates begin with an audit of present employees. Possible replacements are then identified. Internal shortages are resolved by seeking new employees in the external labour markets. Surpluses are reduced by normal attrition, leaves of absence, layoffs, or terminations.

Both external and internal staffing strategies can be used to meet human resource needs. More recently, a variety of alternate work arrangements have also been emerging to better meet the needs of the workforce and the employers. Finally, the usefulness of a human resource information system and human resource accounting was also outlined in this chapter.

Chapters 5 and 6 elaborate on the external staffing strategy, more specifically those relating to employee recruitment and selection. Material in later chapters will examine various issues involved in the management of human resources, with a focus on internal strategies. But before that, it is important to study the impact of governmental policies on a firm's human resource policies and practices. This will be attempted in the next chapter.

◉ TERMS FOR REVIEW

attrition **p. 110**
Canadian Occupational Projection
    System (COPS) **p. 109**
Delphi technique **p. 98**
employee leasing **p. 117**
extrapolation **p. 98**
flexiplace **p. 121**
flextime **p. 120**
forecasts **p. 97**
human resource
    accounting **p. 128**

human resource information
    system **p. 124**
indexation **p. 98**
intranet **p. 127**
job sharing **p. 111**
labour market analysis **p. 108**
management inventories **p. 104**
Markov analysis **p. 102**
nominal group technique **p. 98**
outplacement **p. 114**
phased retirement **p. 110**

replacement charts **p. 104**
replacement summaries **p. 104**
shorter workweek **p. 120**
skills inventories **p. 103**
staffing table **p. 101**
strategic plan **p. 96**
telecommuting **p. 121**
transfer **p. 117**
transition matrices **p. 106**
virtual organization **p. 122**
work options **p. 120**

⊙ SELF-ASSESSMENT EXERCISE

How Do External Supplies Affect Your Chosen Career?

Consider the job you plan to search for after graduation. (If you are already working and do not plan to leave your present job, you can look at the job rank [or grade] you want to have in five years after graduation.). This self-test involves looking at the external labour market and forming conclusions about how it affects your career. If you are not familiar with the labour market conditions, you may have to conduct an Internet search to identify answers to the following questions. You can start with Statistics Canada (http://www.statcan.gc.ca/start-debut-eng.html) and Human Resource and Skills Development Canada (http://www.hrsdc.gc.ca/eng/home.shtml) Web sites, but need not restrict your search to these. Once you have done this, please respond to the following statements.

Statement	Strongly Agree	Agree	Undecided	Disagree	Strongly Disagree
1. The way the job is done is significantly affected by technological changes.					
2. The growth rate in the number of jobs in this profession/job category is more than rate of employment growth rate.					
3. The career/job position I aspire to is likely to be found attractive by persons in all age and social groups.					
4. Because of demographic changes, there are fewer persons like me likely to be applying for a job/career such as the one I am aspiring to.					
5. The job position I have in mind is a glamorous or high-paying one.					
6. Most persons in my age or socio-economic group are unlikely to apply for the job position that I have in mind.					
7. The job I have in mind is likely to be found attractive by even individuals who live thousands of kilometres away.					
8. The location or the nature of the job may make it unattractive to persons who live in other provinces.					
9. Currently the unemployment rate in this job category is over 6 percent.					
10. There is hardly any unemployment in this job category, especially if a person is prepared to relocate.					

SCORING

For statements 1, 3, 5, 7 and 9, assign a score of 5, 4, 3, 2 and 1 for Strongly Agree, Agree, Undecided, Disagree, and Strongly Disagree respectively. For statements 2, 4, 6, 8 and 10, assign a score of 1, 2, 3, 4 and 5 for Strongly Agree, Agree, Undecided, Disagree, and Strongly Disagree. Add up the scores for all 10 statements.

INTERPRETATION

The total score may lie anywhere between 10 and 50. If the score is 33 or higher, you are aspiring for a job position that is very much in demand and likely to be found attractive by a large number of persons. This means that you have to equip yourself with additional competencies or unique skills to be attractive to employers. Even if the total score is lower, changes in economy or technology may change the picture considerably any time in the future!

⮕ REVIEW AND DISCUSSION QUESTIONS

1. What are the key steps in human resource planning in organizations? Which of your actions, if any, would be different if you were planning human resources for a smaller firm (that employs fewer than 50 persons in all) instead of a larger firm (which has 500 employees)?

2. What are staffing tables and replacement charts? Of what use are they to a human resource manager?

3. Discuss any three techniques for estimating the demand for human resources. Provide examples where relevant.

4. What are some popular approaches to match the supply and demand of human resources. Briefly discuss two approaches (each) for situations when demand exceeds and is less than supply of human resources, highlighting their advantages and limitations.

5. "Alternate work arrangements are useful approaches for both the employer and the employee." Discuss.

6. What are some factors you have to consider when you are about to implement a human resource information system?

⮕ CRITICAL THINKING QUESTIONS

1. Suppose human resource planners estimated that due to several technological innovations your firm will need 25 percent fewer employees in three years. What actions would you take today?

2. Suppose you managed a restaurant in a winter resort area. During the summer it was profitable to keep the business open, but you needed only one-half the cooks, table servers, and bartenders. What actions would you take in April when the peak tourist season ended?

3. If your company locates its research and development offices in downtown Windsor, Ontario, the city is willing to forgo city property taxes on the building for 10 years. The city is willing to make this concession to help reduce its high unemployment rate. Calgary, Alberta, your company's other choice, has a low unemployment rate and is not offering any tax breaks. Based on just these considerations, which city would you recommend and why?

4. Assume you are the human resource manager in a Canadian university employing approximately 300 faculty members. Since these faculty members constitute a "valuable" resource of your organization, you decide to install an accounting procedure for changes in the value of this asset. How will you go about it? What problems do you anticipate in the process?

5. For a high-tech organization where the job specifications and customer needs continually change, which of the forecasting techniques discussed in the text are likely to be relevant? Why?

6. Some fire departments and hospital staff are using the 3-day, 36-hour schedule. Do you see any negative aspects to this schedule?

7. Assume you work for a firm that employs 30 managerial and 70 clerical/sales employees. As a cost-cutting strategy, your firm is forced to terminate the services of 10 percent of your managers and 5 percent of your clerical staff. What specific actions will you take to help the departing employees?

⮕ ETHICS QUESTION

Two months ago, you joined Canada Construction and Design Incorporated, an engineering firm that designs and builds large residential and office complexes, as its human resource manager. Of the 320 employees in the firm, 84 are engineers with various specializations. You find that engineers work routinely for 60–70 hours a week, often taking their work home or coming to the office even on the weekends or in the late evenings. Under the firm's job classification, the engineers are considered to be managerial or supervisory and hence not eligible for any overtime benefits. You also recognize that the culture of the organization expects people, especially managerial and supervisory staff, to put in extra effort. While there is no formal rule requiring overtime, it is clear that "nonperforming" engineers do not receive promotions or even merit increases. You are concerned about the impact of the current setup on the long-term mental health and family welfare of the engineers, yet don't know whether you should "make waves" so soon after your arrival in the firm. However, you feel that it is morally wrong to make an individual work without giving any rewards.

What actions, if any, will you take? Why?

◗ WEB RESEARCH EXERCISE

Visit the Web sites of agencies such as Statistics Canada and Human Resources and Skills Development and identify trends in employment and occupational demand patterns for the following positions in one western and one Atlantic province: electricians, fishers, nurses, and blue-collar workers in the paper and pulp industry. What patterns do you see? What are the implications for students about to graduate from high schools this year? For employers? Compare your findings and present your summary findings to the class.

◗ INCIDENT 3-1

Eastern University's Human Resource Needs

For years, Eastern University operated at a deficit. This loss was made up from the provincial budget, since Eastern was provincially supported. Because of government cutbacks, the deficits had continued to increase, forcing the university to raise its tuition fees every year. The university's total budget in 2009 was approximately $140 million.

Several members of the provincial cabinet heard that university enrollments were to decline from 2005 to 2020. A decline in enrollment would lead to overstaffing and even larger deficits. The president of the university hired Bill Barker to develop a long-range human resource plan for the university. An excerpt from his report stated:

> The declining birthrates of this country in the past will cause a decline in university-age students at least to the year 2020. Despite the world economic recession, our regional economy here has been fairly strong and unemployment relatively low. This means that a large number of high-school graduates do not come to us for higher studies. If the university is to avoid soaring deficits, it must institute an employment freeze now. Furthermore, a committee should be formed to develop new curricula that appeal to those segments of the workforce that are going to experience growth between now and 2020.

Zach Taylor, president of Eastern University Faculty Union, argued:

> An employment freeze would cut the university off from hiring new faculty members who have the latest training in new areas. Besides, our enrollments have grown by 2 to 4 percent every year in the recent past. I see no reason to doubt that trend will continue. Even if our past birthrates are low, there are other creative options to this university rather than opting for an employment freeze.

1. Assuming you are a member of the provincial cabinet, would you recommend that the university implement an employment freeze or not?

2. If Bill Barker had used national birthrate information, what other population information could the president of the faculty union use to support his argument that the university will probably keep growing?

3. Are there any strategies you would recommend that would allow the university to hire newly trained faculty and avoid serious budget deficits in the next few years if enrollments do drop?

◗ INCIDENT 3-2

Human Resource Consultants

In 2010, Human Resource Consultants of Hamilton, Ontario, employed 10 consultants (including 2 trainees), 5 secretaries, 2 clerical assistants, an office manager-cum-accountant, and a marketing representative. Consulting work and secretarial work are both expected to increase by 20 percent in 2011. However, a new computer system, which will be operational by

January 1, 2011, will do the equivalent of 80 hours of secretarial work per week and 40 hours of clerical work per week (but will require maintenance of 40 hours per week). As of January 1, 2011, a number of employees are leaving the firm. Bill, a 64-year-old consultant, is planning to retire; John, a Queen's MBA and first-year consultant trainee, has accepted a position with CUSO; Clara, the senior secretary (and supervisor of the

secretarial/clerical staff), has agreed to join Ontario Consultants and is taking two other secretaries with her; and Herman, the office manager/accountant, is planning to move to western Canada.

1. Determine the human resource needs at Human Resource Consultants for 2011.

➡ CASE STUDY 🍁 Maple Leaf Shoes Ltd.

A Human Resource Planning Exercise*

Maple Leaf Shoes Ltd. is a medium-sized manufacturer of leather and vinyl shoes located near Wilmington, Ontario. It began operations in 1969 and currently employs about 400 persons in its Ontario plant and some 380 more in offices and warehouses throughout Canada and internationally. More information on the firm and its operations is provided at the end of Chapter 1.

The cost of production at Maple Leaf Shoes has been rising slowly but steadily. Labour costs currently account for over 53 percent of manufacturing costs and have been increasing rapidly. The productivity levels of the employees have not shown any significant increase in recent years. Concerned with the situation, Maple Leaf Shoes' management has been attempting to introduce more sophisticated technology in its various plants. More capital-intensive, automated production processes are being considered by the management as part of the solution to the productivity challenge facing the firm.

The company is now in the midst of a strategic reorientation. As part of the exercise, Robert Clark, the president, has asked Jane Reynolds, Special Assistant in the Human Resources Division in the firm, to prepare a human resources forecast for the company.

Reynolds examined the company records that were likely to help her in her task. To her dismay, she found that very few plans or systematic procedures existed that will assist her in human resource planning. She decided to begin her analysis with the division in charge of shoes for children and youths (commonly—and half humorously—referred to as the "juvenile division" in the company). It currently employed fewer than 150 persons in total and seemed to have the most complete records related to employee hiring, transfers, exits, and training. But even here, production and labour statistics for several years were incomplete or inaccurate.

Her survey of company records resulted in the information given below. Reynolds also met with key managers in the firm (including Clark) several times to find out more about their

goals and action plans for the immediate future. Her findings are also summarized below.

1. All of the juvenile division's manufacturing operations were located in Ontario. Reynolds considered that there were four distinct manufacturing stages: cutting, shaping, assembling, and finishing. (Of course, each of these stages contained several tasks; for example, "shaping" involved several subtasks such as bending the leather, vinyl, or plastic; making lace holes; attaching reinforcers, padding, and so on.) Reynolds also found that the operations progressively became more complex, from "cutting" to "finishing." Workers were normally hired as cutters and then progressively moved up to do shaping, assembling, and then finishing as they gained experience.

2. Cutting and shaping were more repetitive and boring, while assembling and finishing required greater attention and expertise and therefore were more challenging. Despite this, a few workers who were doing assembling chose to do shaping since the latter almost always fetched them more overtime work (and significantly higher earnings). No one doing final finishing had so far asked for reassignment to shaping or cutting. Employee movements during 2009–2010 among the four operations are shown in Table 1.

3. The firm's labour productivity has not shown any significant improvement in the recent past. This has also been true of the juvenile division. Table 2 shows the production and staffing records of the entire division.

4. Through the introduction of computer-integrated technology and automated work systems, the firm expects to increase the division's productivity level by 25 percent in 2012 over its 2011 record. Much of this will be achieved by automating much of the cutting operations. It is expected that automation will reduce the need for 33 percent of cutters. The productivity of other operations (namely, shaping, assembling, and finishing) is also expected to increase, but at lower levels than in the case of cutting. The productivity improvement in these operations is expected to be equal. Workers who lose their jobs as a result of automation and computerization will receive severance pay.

---

*Case written by Professor Hari Das of the Department of Management, Saint Mary's University, Halifax. All rights retained by the author. Das © 2003. Revised © 2009.

TABLE 1	Movements of Workers Across the Four Operations (2009–2010)					
From:			**To:**			
	Cutting	**Shaping**	**Assembling**	**Finishing**	**Exits**	**Total**
Cutting	21	3	1	0	1	26
Shaping	0	32	4	2	2	40
Assembling	0	2	26	5	0	33
Finishing	0	0	0	37	0	37
Total at the end (after accounting for exits)						133

TABLE 2	Production and Workforce Statistics in the Juvenile Division	
Year	**Production (000s of pairs)**	**Number of Employees**
1978	50	65
—	—	—
1989	75	91
—	—	—
2002	90	110
2003	92	120
2004	93	122
2005	98	125
2006	102	127
2007	110	140
2008	109	140
2009	106	136
2010	105	133
2011*	93	125

(*Projected figures based on first eight months' production)

5. Compared to other divisions, the juvenile division has an aging workforce. (On average, 3 to 8 percent of the division's workforce retire each year.) For calculation purposes, Reynolds is planning to use a flat 5 percent retirement figure. Table 1 figures do not include exits through retirement.

6. There are 10 persons in sales and order processing associated with the juvenile division products. Another 15 clerical staff are involved in a variety of related activities (such as billing, product movement, and so on) in the division. There are four managerial persons in the division.

7. As a cost-cutting measure, two of the above managerial positions will be eliminated in the next year. Because of the computerized billing initiated recently, the productivity of the clerical staff is expected to increase by 50 percent, making some of the clerical positions redundant. Where possible, the displaced workers will be transferred to other divisions or trained to do other activities in the firm.

8. The firm plans to open two new sales outlets in the next year. It is estimated that each outlet will require one supervisor and two sales assistants initially.

9. The percentage of women workers in the four operations were as follows: cutting, 72 percent; shaping, 70 percent; assembling, 63 percent; and finishing, 61 percent. Women account for 68 percent of the sales assistants and 55 percent of the clerical staff. No woman occupies a managerial position in the juvenile division.

10. A number of women in the past have requested job sharing and flextime work arrangements. The firm currently has no provision for nontraditional work arrangements.

11. Estimated production (based on projected market demand for shoes) for 2012 is 98,000 pairs of shoes. As is the case with several shoe manufacturers in this country (and the U.S.), footwear production has declined each year due to international competition.

Discussion Questions

1. Prepare a human resources plan for the juvenile division for 2012.

2. What other suggestions and comments would you make to the management if you were in Reynolds' position?

CASE STUDY   CPIB   Canadian Pacific and International Bank

*Planning Human Resources at HBI**

Canadian Pacific and International Bank (CPIB) is a premier Canadian financial institution with assets over $150 billion and operations across Canada and in 33 countries. Today, its over 25,000 employees provide personal, commercial, corporate, and investment banking services to individuals and businesses around the world. More details of the bank are given at the end of Chapter 1.

CPIB, through its strategic initiatives, was successful in building long-term value for its shareholders while providing regular return on their investments. A vital component of its recent strategy is growth through acquisition of smaller banks and other financial institutions in this country and internationally.

Recently, the bank acquired Hudson Bay Investors (HBI), a medium-sized investment banking firm located in Central Canada with 38 branches operating in 5 Canadian provinces. For now, CPIB intends to maintain the separate identity of HBI; however, the internal systems and procedures of the firm will be rationalized to bring them in line with those at CPIB. In the long term, HBI branches are likely to be replaced by CPIB branches.

HBI's major sources of income are trade processing and brokerage commissions, revenues from mutual funds sales, securitization and underwriting fees, fund transfer fees, portfolio and estate management fees, and custody and safe-keeping fees. Like most other investment and asset management firms, HBI uses the services of not only in-house financial advisors and counsellors but also hundreds of independent financial advisors in other dealer firms actively distributing HBI's products and services. In recent years, this strategy has been particularly important to reduce salary and overhead expenses. Hiring outside advisors on a commission basis not only reduces fixed salary expenses but also reduces investments in overheads such as office space, electricity, and computer systems. In future years, this strategy is likely to be used even further to maintain a lean operation.

Compared to CPIB, HBI is somewhat behind in electronic services. This is expected to change in the next two years. CPIB expects all HBI advisors to be able to offer extensive counselling (including in areas such as portfolio management, margin trading, and setting up of Internet banking accounts) to their customers using multiple tools including the Internet. CPIB plans to install counselling booths in various locations where customers can sit in front of a TV monitor and receive assistance from advisors located thousands of kilometres away and print out recommendations at the end of the session.

During the pre-acquisition survey, Mary Keddy, senior vice-president of human resources, observed that HBI's human resources practices were somewhat inferior compared to those of CPIB. She is determined to improve this situation. CPIB has a culture of transferring its employees to provide them with cross-cultural and international experience, while HBI has been primarily a regional institution where staff transfers are less common.

Organizational Structure

Currently, HBI's 155 managers and officers are organized functionally (see Figure 1) into three major divisions: operations, marketing, and administration. Each of the three divisions is headed by a vice-president. Human resources, public relations, legal and liaison work, and transportation were grouped under administration. The 43 regional and branch offices of HBI fell under operations, while the vice-president in charge of marketing controlled all marketing initiatives including advertising and new product development. While the branch managers reported to VP Operations, they had extensive communication lines with members of marketing and administration departments. While HBI had clear reporting relationships within each function, it always encouraged the free flow of communication and continuous evolvement of jobs.

Recently, HBI has been considering a possible shift to a modified product structure, under which a product manager would be responsible for the success or failure of one or more products/services rather than that of a region, branch, or function. CPIB encouraged this proposal, given its own corporate philosophy of delegation and employee empowerment. Steve Johnson, VP (Marketing) indicated the scope of the responsibilities of a manager under the proposed system:

> I am sure HBI can significantly benefit from a product-type of organization structure. Most of the large consumer products companies, General Foods, Kellogg, and Procter & Gamble to mention just three, are built on the product manager idea. There is no reason why financial institutions cannot also follow this pattern. In fact, CPIB itself is a good example of a bank whose structure is focused on products and customers. The product manager will be held responsible for the product planning and for constant monitoring of the products' success. Here at HBI we don't believe in lines and arrows to show relationships among people. If problems at the branch are holding up sales of specific types of investments, we expect the sales staff to go to the branch or call the branch manager to iron out the

* Case written by Professor Hari Das of Department of Management, Saint Mary's University, Halifax. All rights retained by the author. Das © 2003. Revised © 2009.

FIGURE 1 — The Three Divisions at HBI

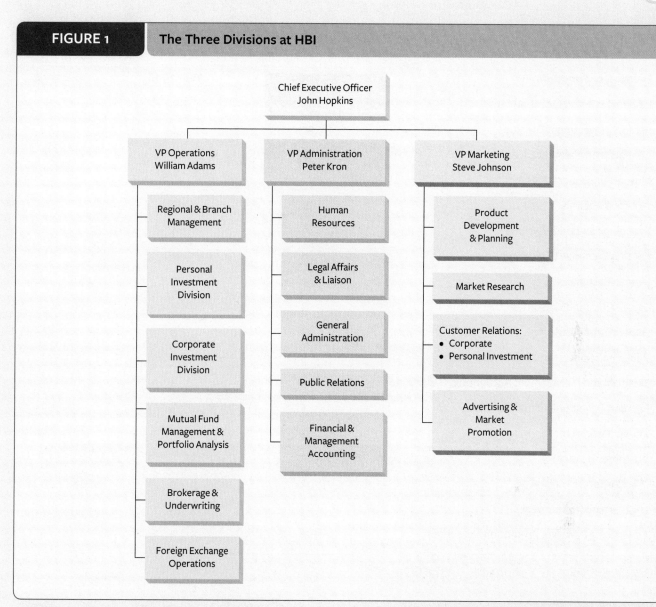

problems. That is already the way we work here. What we are trying to do is to make it more systematic so that our reward system recognizes responsibility and individual achievement.

Details on the number of managerial employees in HBI are given in Figure 2.

Compared to other investment firms of its size, HBI has done remarkably well. Its earnings for the recent past and future projection are shown in Figure 3.

HBI was in the midst of planning a major expansion of its activities when CPIB acquired the firm. Some of the details are given below:

1. By 2011, HBI plans to expand its operations to two more provinces and open 20 more branches. This will involve the creation of two new regional offices as well.

2. As Figure 3 indicates, the mutual funds and underwriting activities are expected to grow rapidly in the next two years. During 2008, when both the U.S. and Canada faced bearish stock markets, the mutual fund industry contracted. However, HBI's own mutual fund operations showed considerable resiliency during that period because of aggressive marketing, focus on unconventional segments (e.g., bio-tech and eco-friendly firms, high growth firms in Asia and Latin America). With the recovery of the U.S. and Canadian economy, mutual funds are expected to show even greater growth in the near future. Meanwhile, the funds focus on the still relatively healthy BRIC, Chinese, and Indian markets.

By and large, the number of managers and analysts involved in mutual fund operations has shown a steady

FIGURE 2	HBI Managers and Officers Classified by Function or Activity		
Division or Function	2009	Year 2008	2004
Regional & Branch Management	43	30	19
Personal Investment Division	35	23	16
Corporate Investment Division	8	4	2
Mutual Fund Operations &			
Portfolio Analysis	19	13	6
Brokerage and Underwriting	6	4	2
Foreign Exchange Operations	8	6	2
Human Resources	4	3	2
Legal Affairs and Liaison	3	3	2
General Administration	7	3	3
Public Relations	3	2	1
Financial and Management Accounting	5	3	2
Product Development and Planning	4	3	2
Market Research	3	2	1
Customer relations			
• Corporate	2	1	1
• Personal Investment	3	2	1
Advertising & Market Promotion	2	2	1

Note: The numbers do not include vice-presidents and president of the firm.

relationship with volume of business (although not engraved in stone, HBI generally expects each manager to do at least $1.5 million business). Past experience indicates that the number of analysts needed is one half of that of managers. Improved efficiency and computerization is expected to help a manager to handle $2 million worth of business in the immediate future. CPIB wants to take advantage of the recessionary period to attract high calibre employees and improve its overall global presence.

3. To take advantage of the aging Canadian population, HBI is planning to give special focus on estate planning. It is expected that the number of customers of HBI aged 60 and over who will require estate planning services will increase by 20 percent in the next five years. To meet the needs of growth, the firm estimates that it will need to hire three new middle-level managers and seven junior officers.

4. By the end of next year, HBI will complete its reorganization into a product structure. Under the new structure, the firm will have two major divisions: *Corporate Clients* and *Personal Investments*. The corporate clients will consist of three major subdivisions: Large Clients, Small Businesses, and Brokerage & Foreign Exchange Operations. The Personal Investments division will have two subdivisions: Gold Service (aimed at high-income clients who are more likely to demand estate management and other associated services) and Personal Service (which will look after the needs of small and medium individual investors). For ease of operation, each of the two major division will have its own associated accounting, HR, administration, and marketing services, with these functions centrally coordinated at the vice-president level. The reorganization is expected to result in a 10 percent reduction in most services, except product development and human resource management, in which the change

FIGURE 3	HBI's Earnings (Estimated in Millions of Dollars)			
Earnings	**2011**	**2009**	**2008**	**2004**
Personal investment counselling & estate management	73	49	33	21
Mutual funds operations	54	36	19	9
Interest on loans & advances	9	8	4	2
Corporate underwriting, brokerage & investment management	16	12	8	4
Gains on marketable securities	12	8	4	2
Foreign exchange and clearing operations	6	4	3	1
Other investment and dividends	18	12	6	2
Expenses				
General administrative expenses	27	18	12	8
Commission, fees, salaries	23	15	10	5
Interest expenses	7	5	3	1
Depreciation and amortization	12	10	8	5

(**Note:** Only major headings are shown here.)

will necessitate a 10 percent increase in staff size including managerial staff.

Many of the managers realized that the promise of continued rapid growth of the company would mean changes in the structure and processes of the company. As one manager in the operations division pointed out:

Growth for HBI means something quite different from what it is for most other firms. For a conglomerate, growth may often mean new acquisitions or new diversified units that will be operating independently. For a company like HBI, however, it means entering new product-market situations and finding new ways of delivering our services. The competition in the industry is fierce, to put it mildly. But, if you have a reputation for the quality of your service, there is a growing market out there for you to grab. The proposed product structure may be a good idea to take advantage of this opportunity; however, it will also necessitate massive changes in our present style of operating.

Human Resource Policies

HBI has a policy of promoting qualified personnel from within the company before seeking outside candidates. The policy further implies consideration of the best-qualified people from all departments within HBI, rather than simply promoting only from within the department in which the opening occurs (unless the skill needed is very specific or legal requirements prevent someone without specific qualifications to be considered for the position, as in the case of legal or brokerage positions). Typically, the human resource department provides assistance in locating qualified candidates and takes pride in its "managerial inventory" used for this purpose. This inventory consists of names, certain characteristics (e.g., age, education), and skills of the managers working for HBI. Figure 4 shows relevant portions of the managerial inventory in the company. Currently, this inventory only lists senior officers of the firm, although plans are under way to include all supervisory and managerial personnel in the inventory in the near future. The company uses the services of an assessment centre located in Toronto. Periodically, managers were sent to this centre where, for periods ranging from two to four days, they were given tests and interviews. During their stay, participants also took part in management games, group discussions, in-basket exercises, and other role-plays. These managers were later rated by the centre for their leadership potential. Frequent performance or client ratings (in the case of advisors and brokers) are also carried out to improve quality of service provided by HBI. This information is also used in designing training programs for staff.

FIGURE 4		Managerial Inventory for Senior Officers (Excluding CEO) at HBI Ltd.*						
Manager	Division	Current Performance Level (1 = Lowest 5 = Highest)	Gender (M = male F = female)	Education	Age	Current Management Level (1 = Lowest 5 = Highest)	Assessment Centre Rating of Leadership Skill	Time in Present Job in Months
W.C. Adams	Opers.	5	M	CFA	58	6	10	90
S.R. Allen	Admn.	4	F	CGA	56	5	9	62
P.T. Anderson	Opers.	5	M	MA, CFA	63	6	8	92
R. Bensoff	Admn.	5	M	HS	58	6	7	105
R.K. Bloom	Opers.	4	M	BSc, CFA	37	5	7	26
T.P. Buyer	Opers.	4	M	MBA CMA	39	5	9	16
N.T. Cayon	Opers.	4	M	CFA CMA	38	3	4	17
E.S. Conway	Opers.	3	M	CA	39	4	7	36
R.T. Dickoff	Admn.	5	F	MBA, CHRP	47	6	8	60
P. Frost	Mktg.	5	M	HS	48	5	7	30
W.K. Goodwin	Mktg.	4	F	MBA	48	5	7	50
K.N. Griggs	Admn.	4	M	MBA, LL.B	49	5	7	16
P. Hack	Mktg.	5	M	Bcomm	40	6	8	42
K. Heneman	Opers.	4	M	MS	44	6	8	43
S. Hickory	Opers.	5	M	Bsc LL.B	64	6	10	108
P. Jackson	Opers.	3	M	HS	47	5	5	60
S.P. Johnson	Mktg.	5	M	BA	51	6	9	64
S. Kiefel	Mktg.	4	M	HS	61	5	7	59
P.Q. Kimble	Opers.	5	F	Bsc CFA CMA	31	4	9	11
T. Knoll	Opers.	5	M	Msc	29	4	7	19
P. Kron	Admn.	5	M	HS	61	6	8	31
E.F. Pederson	Opers.	4	M	Bcomm CFA	47	5	6	19
N.T. Potler	Opers.	5	M	BTech	31	5	7	20
A. Ranallo	Admn.	4	M	BA LL.B	39	5	5	29
H.C. Reeves	Opers.	5	M	BSc	60	6	8	63
T. Reitman	Mktg.	4	F	Bcomm MBA	39	5	9	39
J. Sorenson	Admn.	5	M	Bcomm	32	6	7	11
H. Walden	Admn.	4	M	HS	59	5	8	69

BA=Bachelor of Arts, BComm = Bachelor of Commerce, BSc = Bachelor of Science, CA = Chartered Accountant, CFA=Certified Financial Advisor, CMA = Certified Management Accountant, HS = High School, LL.B = Bachelor degree in Law, MBA = Master of Business Administration, MSc = Master of Science.

*This inventory lists top and senior middle-level managers in the firm. The firm is in the process of preparing a more exhaustive inventory that includes all managerial and supervisory personnel. Almost everyone listed has undergone corporate-sponsored training programs in specific subject areas.

The salaries offered by HBI are competitive compared to industry standards. Despite this, the firm had problems in attracting qualified managers. This is likely to become even worse in terms of attracting software managers and financial counsellors in the foreseeable future. The mandatory retirement age at HBI is 65. The company is committed to the development of its employees and in the past has sent many of its employees for training to local universities and colleges, apart from refunding tuition paid by its employees for training program done elsewhere.

Discussion Questions

1. Prepare a staffing forecast for 2011 for HBI. Your forecast should show (among other things) the total number of managers needed, the number needed in each function and division, and the plans for filling vacancies through transfers or new hires as well as redundancies caused by restructuring or productivity improvement.

2. What challenges face the HR manager in the firm?

3. What improvements, if any, would you recommend to its HR policies and practices?

➡ PART ENDING VIDEOS

"High Anxiety"

Source: *Venture*, show number 918, March 14, 2004, running time 7:41.

Go to **www.mcgrawhillconnect.ca** to access the videos.

➡ ROLE-PLAY 2: PREPARING FOR JOB ANALYSIS

Time required: 40–50 minutes

Objectives of the Role-Play

1. To help students understand the steps in preparing for job analysis

2. To enhance their skills in negotiating with line managers

3. To help them prepare for the staff role of HR manager and enhance their ability to influence line managers through persuasion

Prior Preparation

1. Study Chapter 2 of the text.

2. Read descriptions of Maple Leaf Shoes Ltd. at the ends of Chapters 1 and 2.

Guidelines for Conducting the Role-Play

The role-play enacts an interview between Jane Reynolds and Steve Smith, Supervisor of the Cutting Division of Maple Leaf Shoes Ltd. Ms. Reynolds has been seeking cooperation from Mr. Smith for job analysis of workers in his section. He has been delaying and ignoring her request, citing extreme work pressures. She is about to meet with him one last time to try to persuade him.

1. Two students, one for the role of Jane Reynolds and the other for Steve Smith, should be identified.

2. Students should read their own role description below, along with the company details given at the ends of Chapters 1 and 2.

3. The instructor should signal the beginning and the end of the meeting. The interview will last about 25 minutes.

4. The remainder of the class time is used for discussion of the behaviours during the role-play and the outcomes.

5. Observers should be asked to make notes against the questions listed below and discuss their findings at the end of the role-play.

6. Instructor should sum up by highlighting the importance of job analysis and the staff role of human resource managers.

Instructions for Observers

As you observe the meeting between Jane Reynolds and Steve Smith, make notes related to each of the questions below.

1. How did Jane begin the meeting? Would it have been better to begin it in some other manner?

2. What was Smith's response? Were his arguments sound?

3. Was there open communication between the two?

4. Did Jane respond to his objections well?

5. Did the two parties come up with a satisfactory solution? Were there other solutions they could have looked at?

6. What did you learn from this exercise?

PART 3

Attracting Human Resources

A company hires employees to meet its objectives. First, it has to identify the target groups and find the ways and means to get the necessary information to them, taking into account the requirements of human rights legislation regarding discrimination. Then it has to select those candidates who best meet its needs.

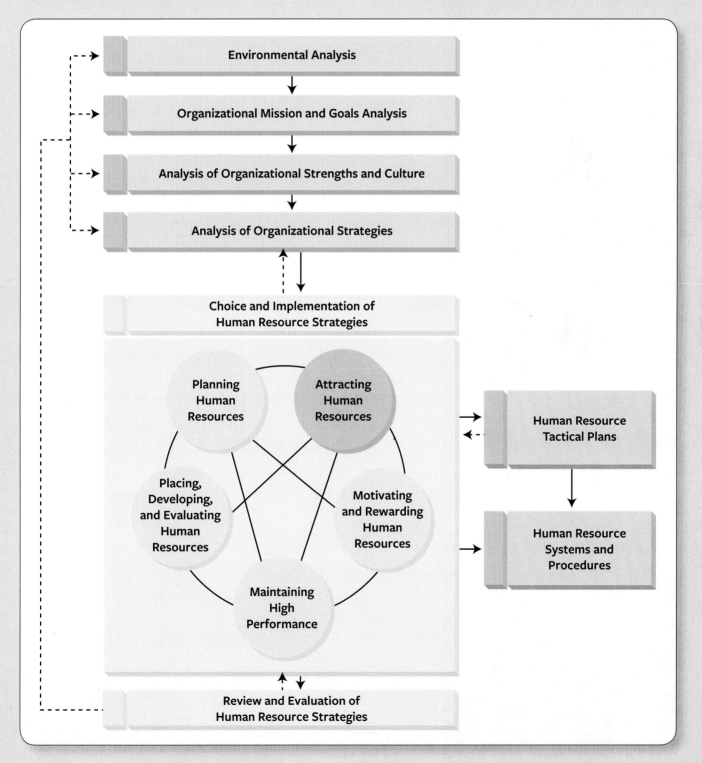

Meeting Legal Requirements

All human beings are born free and equal in dignity and rights.

Article 1, Universal Declaration of Human Rights, December 1948, United Nations (http://www.ohchr.org/EN/UDHR/Pages/introduction.aspx)

All individuals should have an equal opportunity to make for themselves the lives that they are able and wish to have, consistent with their duties and obligations as members of society, without being hindered in or prevented from doing so by discriminatory practices based on race, national or ethnic origin, colour, religion, age, sex, sexual orientation, marital status, family status, disability or conviction for an offence for which a pardon has been granted.

Section 2, *Canadian Human Rights Act*

CHAPTER OBJECTIVES

After studying this chapter, you should be able to:

➡ *Explain* the impact of government on human resource management.

➡ *Identify* the jurisdictions of Canadian human rights legislation.

➡ *List* the major provisions of the *Canadian Human Rights Act*.

➡ *Explain* the effect of human rights legislation on the role of human resource specialists.

➡ *Define* harassment and explain what is meant by the term sexual harassment.

➡ *Outline* an employment equity program.

CHAPTER 4

GOVERNMENT IMPACT

Government of Canada
Information on all
matters related to human
rights and Charter issues
http://canada.gc.ca

Canadian Human
Rights Commission
Information specific to
the *Human Rights Act*
www.chrc-ccdp.ca

regulations
Legally enforceable
rules developed by
governmental agencies
to ensure compliance
with laws that the
agency administers.

Few challenges encountered by human resource departments are as overwhelming as those presented by government. Government—through the enforcement of laws—has a direct and immediate impact on the human resource function. The federal and provincial laws that regulate the employee–employer relationship challenge the methods human resource departments use. Some laws, such as the *Canada Labour Safety Code* of 1968, make major demands on human resource departments. The impact of these laws has helped elevate the importance of human resource decisions.

Many aspects of human resource management are affected by human rights legislation. To human resource specialists, government involvement requires compliance and proactive efforts to minimize the organizational consequences. At appropriate points throughout this book, employee-related laws are explained to illustrate the challenges modern human resource departments encounter and the actions they must take.

To avoid flooding the courts with complaints and the prosecution of relatively minor infractions, federal and provincial governments often create special regulatory bodies, such as commissions and boards, to enforce compliance with the law and to aid in its interpretation. Examples are the various human rights commissions and labour relations boards, which evaluate complaints and develop legally binding rules, called **regulations**. Human resource specialists become involved because legislation and regulations affect the employment relationship. The involvement creates three important responsibilities. First, human resource experts must stay abreast of the laws, interpretation of the laws by regulatory bodies, and court rulings. Otherwise, they will soon find their knowledge outdated and useless to the organization. Second, they must develop and administer programs that ensure company compliance. Failure to do so may lead to the loss of government contracts, poor public relations, and suits by regulatory bodies or affected individuals. Third, they must pursue their traditional roles of obtaining, maintaining, and retaining an optimal workforce. No organization benefits from compliance with government constraints at the expense of a well-qualified workforce.

THE CHARTER OF RIGHTS AND FREEDOMS

Canadian Charter of
Rights and Freedoms
Federal law enacted
in 1982, guaranteeing
individuals equal rights
before the law.

Communications
Policy, Treasury Board
of Canada Secretariat
Information and
documents relating to
government issues
www.tbs-sct.gc.ca/pol/
doc-eng.aspx?id=12316

An example of government legislation that has profound implications for employers is the *Constitution Act* of 1982, which contains the **Canadian Charter of Rights and Freedoms**.[1] The Charter provides some fundamental rights to every Canadian. These are as follows:

- freedom of conscience and religion;
- freedom of thought, belief, opinion, and expression, including freedom of the press and other media of communication;
- freedom of peaceful assembly; and
- freedom of association.

The Charter provides protection to every Canadian in the following specific areas:[2]

- fundamental freedoms;
- democratic rights;
- the right to live and seek employment anywhere in Canada;
- legal rights: the right to life, liberty, and personal security;
- equality rights for all individuals;
- officially recognized languages of Canada;
- minority language education rights;
- Canada's multicultural heritage; and
- Aboriginal peoples' rights.

The Canadian Charter of Rights and Freedoms is probably the most far-reaching legal challenge for human resource managers. When it came into effect in 1982, it created high expectations among the collective bargaining partners—unions and management. Both parties hoped that the Charter would strengthen their positions vis-à-vis each other. A review of the application of the Charter to human resource and industrial relations issues in the intervening years reveals that the impact has been modest so far. One reason is that it takes considerable time for cases to reach the Supreme Court, the ultimate interpreter of the Charter. In the following sections, we examine the effects the Charter has had on human resource management and industrial relations in Canada.

Content and Applicability of the Charter

Section 1 of the Charter guarantees rights and freedoms "subject only to such reasonable limits prescribed by law as can be demonstrably justified in a free and democratic society." Of course, such adjectives as "reasonable" and "demonstrably justified" will lead to different interpretations by different judges. This is one of the reasons why many cases are winding their way through the judicial system up to the Supreme Court, just to get a final opinion. Every time a court invokes one of the rights or freedoms, it must determine if the infringement is justified.

Section 2 of the Charter guarantees freedom of association, a very important aspect in industrial relations, especially for unions. A key question in this context is whether the freedom to associate carries with it the right to bargain collectively and the right to strike, the main reasons for the existence of unions. As will be shown, these rights cannot be taken for granted anymore.

Section 15—the equality rights part—came into effect on April 17, 1985, having been delayed for two years in its enactment to allow the federal government and the provinces to create or change laws to ensure compliance with the Charter. It states in its first paragraph:

> Every individual is equal before the law and under the law and has the right to the equal protection and benefit of the law without discrimination and, in particular, without discrimination based on race, national or ethnic origin, colour, religion, sex, age, or mental or physical disability.

This section of the Charter was expected to—and has—caused a flood of litigation that will take many years to resolve.

The Charter of Rights and Freedoms applies only to individuals dealing with federal and provincial governments and agencies under their jurisdiction, but its impact is far-reaching, since potentially every law can be challenged. Courts have the delicate task of balancing individual and collective rights.

Areas of Application

Some of the more prominent issues that have been before the courts relate to the use of closed-shop union security provisions, whereby workers must be members of a union in order to be hired; the imposition of first collective agreements designed to help weak unions; the use of union shop arrangements, whereby workers must become union members within specified time periods after they are hired; the right to picket; the right to strike; the right to bargain collectively; employment equity programs; and mandatory retirement. Some of the latest issues relate to sexual orientation and benefits to same-sex partners.

The Right to Bargain Collectively and to Strike

On April 9, 1987, the Supreme Court of Canada rendered a long-awaited judgment on the impact of the Charter on federal and provincial collective bargaining laws. The three cases in question arose from challenges of the federal public sector laws imposing compulsory arbitration for the right to strike, back-to-work legislation, and wage-restraint legislation.

In a 4–2 split decision, the Supreme Court held that Section 2 of the Charter does not include the right to bargain collectively and to strike. The judgment was a real blow to Canadian unions, as workers have taken these rights for granted. The court affirmed that Section 2 protects the freedom to work for the establishment of an association, to belong to an association, to maintain it, and to participate in its lawful activities without penalty or reprisal. However, it also held that the rights to bargain collectively and to strike are not fundamental freedoms, but are statutory rights created and regulated by the legislature. Under this ruling, governments can curtail the collective bargaining process by limiting salary increases, legislating strikers back to work, and imposing compulsory arbitration.

The Right to Picket

In another decision, the Supreme Court ruled that the right to picket is not protected under the Charter because it applies only to situations involving government action. It follows that this right is not available to employees in the private sector, where the vast majority of workers are employed. Employers can ask for injunctions to restrict the number of pickets or any other reasonable limitation of picketing activity.

From the rulings of the Supreme Court, it can be seen that the effect of the Charter of Rights and Freedoms on human resource management and industrial relations so far has been significant to a certain degree, but not drastic. It appears that the court takes a conservative approach in interpreting the Charter in regard to union activities, meaning that it appears to associate more with employers' interests and the public's interests rather than with unions' and workers' interests. As one law professor put it:

> Anglo-Canadian courts have been dealing with issues of individual and collective labour law for at least 200 years. During that entire period, the courts virtually never, not on any given occasion, created a right which might be asserted by or on behalf of working people. Nor have they since the enactment of the Charter. Nor, I conclude, is it likely that they ever will.[3]

The Right to Work

In two decisions, the Supreme Court of Canada has upheld Section 15(c) of the *Canadian Human Rights Act*, which excludes mandatory retirement at the normal age from its prohibition on age discrimination. The court concluded that the objectives of mandatory retirement were of sufficient significance to justify the limitation of a constitutional right to equality if a province chose to impose one, with the limitation that this discriminatory practice be reasonable and justifiable.

> In 1985, Professor Olive Dickason, who taught history at the University of Alberta, was asked to retire at the age of 65. Dr. Dickason claimed that mandatory retirement at age 65 violated her constitutional rights. The Supreme Court, which rendered its decision in September 1992, ruled that mandatory retirement at age 65 is permissible.

At the provincial level, mandatory retirement is discriminatory under the human rights legislation. However, it is considered that there is no discrimination when there are bona fide and reasonable requirements for an employment or occupation.

⊙ HUMAN RIGHTS LEGISLATION

1, 2, & 4

Canadian Human Rights Act
www.efc.ca/pages/
law/canada/canada.H-6.
head.html

Canadian Human Rights Commission Discriminatory practices
www.chrc-ccdp.
ca/discrimination/
discrimination-en.asp

3

While the Charter of Rights and Freedoms guarantees equality before the law for every Canadian, the *Human Rights Act* seeks to provide equal employment opportunities without regard to people's race, national or ethnic origin, colour, religion, age, sex, sexual orientation, marital status, family status, disability, or conviction for an offence for which a pardon has been granted. Common sense dictates such a policy, but the human rights legislation requires every employer to ensure that equal opportunities are, in fact, reality and that there is no discrimination either intentional or unintentional. No other laws rival the impact human rights legislation has on human resource management.[4]

Scope

Usually, employment-related laws and regulations are limited in scope; their impact on the human resource management process is confined to a single human resource activity. For example, minimum-wage laws specify the lowest amount an employer can pay for each hour worked; in spite of their importance, these laws affect only the compensation management function. Other human resource activities—selection, training, and labour relations—are largely unaffected.

Human rights legislation, however, is an exception. Its role is not limited to a single human resource activity. Instead, human rights legislation affects nearly every human resource function: human resource planning, recruiting, selection, training, compensation, and labour relations.

Overview

Human rights legislation is a family of federal and provincial acts that have as a common objective the provision of equal employment opportunity for members of protected groups. Figure 4-1 summarizes these two layers of employment laws. Discrimination between workers on the basis of their effort, performance, or other work-related criteria remains both permissible and advisable:

> Shelly Rossie complained to her provincial Human Rights Commission and charged her former employer with discrimination. When questioned, she insisted to the commission that the real

FIGURE 4-1	Types, Sources, Objectives, and Jurisdiction of Canadian Human Rights Legislation	
Type	**Source**	**Objectives and Jurisdiction**
Federal Law	Passed by Parliament and enforced by federal Human Rights Commission	To ensure equal employment opportunities with employers under federal jurisdiction
Provincial Law	Enacted by provincial governments and enforced by provincial human rights commissions	To ensure equal employment opportunities with employers under provincial jurisdiction

reason for her discharge as a welder was that the company discriminated against women in traditionally male jobs. Shelly's case was dismissed when the company showed the Commission records of her excessive absenteeism and poor productivity. (Undoubtedly, the company's case was strengthened when, later, a woman was hired to replace Shelly.)

Human rights legislation does permit employers to reward outstanding performers and penalize insufficient productivity. Its only requirement is that the basis for rewards and punishments be work-related, not based on a person's race, sex, age, or other prohibited criteria.

The following discussion focuses on federal human rights legislation, because **provincial human rights laws** tend to differ only slightly, mainly in terminology (e.g., some provinces use "national origin," others use "ethnic origin"). The examples used in the discussion of federal legislation are also quite typical of provincial situations. By and large, provincial laws mirror the federal law. The major exceptions are pay equity and employment equity.

provincial human rights laws
All provinces and two territories have their own human rights laws and human rights commissions, with discrimination criteria, regulations, and procedures.

The *Canadian Human Rights Act*

The *Canadian Human Rights Act* was passed by Parliament on July 14, 1977, and took effect in March 1978. The act proclaims:

> The purpose of this Act is to extend the laws in Canada to give effect, within the purview of matters coming within the legislative authority of Parliament, to the principle that all individuals should have an opportunity equal with other individuals to make for themselves the lives that they are able and wish to have and to have their needs accommodated, consistent with their duties and obligations as members of society, without being hindered in or prevented from doing so by discriminatory practices based on race, national or ethnic origin, colour, religion, age, sex, sexual orientation, marital status, family status, disability or conviction for an offence for which a pardon has been granted.[5]

Canadian Human Rights Act
A federal law prohibiting discrimination.

The act applies to all federal government departments and agencies, Crown corporations, and business and industry under federal jurisdiction—such as banks, airlines, railways, and interprovincial communication (radio and TV) companies—in their dealings with the public and in their employment policies.

In areas not under federal jurisdiction, protection is given by provincial human rights laws. Each of Canada's provinces and territories—with the exception of Nunavut, which is still under federal jurisdiction—has its own antidiscrimination laws, which are broadly similar to the federal law. Figure 4-2 compares federal and individual provincial human rights legislation as to different grounds of discrimination prohibited.

Discrimination Defined

Webster's New World Dictionary of the American Language defines discrimination as: "a showing of partiality or prejudice in treatment; specific action or policies directed against the welfare of minority groups."

Former Iraq hostage James Loney says that a Catholic youth camp, where he was on staff, was ordered to close down because he is gay. Should sexual orientation play a role in staffing decisions in religious organizations?

CP/Bernard Weil.

FIGURE 4-2	Prohibited Grounds of Discrimination in Canada*	
Prohibited Ground	**Jurisdiction**	**Comments**
Race or Colour		
Employment	All jurisdictions	
Provision of Service	All jurisdictions	
Religion		
Employment	All jurisdictions	Yukon's act reads "religion or creed, or religious belief, religious association or religious activity."
Provision of Service	All jurisdictions	Yukon's act reads "religion or creed, or religious belief, religious association or religious activity."
Physical or Mental Disability		
Employment	All jurisdictions	Quebec uses the phrase "handicap or use of any means to palliate a handicap."
Provision of Service	All jurisdictions	Quebec uses the phrase "handicap or use of any means to palliate a handicap."
Dependence on Alcohol or Drugs		
Employment	All except Yukon and Northwest Territories	Policy to accept complaints in British Columbia, Alberta, Saskatchewan, Manitoba, Ontario, New Brunswick, and Prince Edward Island; included in "handicap" ground in Quebec; previous dependence only in New Brunswick and Nova Scotia.

FIGURE 4-2	Prohibited Grounds of Discrimination in Canada* (continued)	
Prohibited Ground	**Jurisdiction**	**Comments**
Provision of Service	All except Yukon, Northwest Territories, and Quebec	Previous dependence only in New Brunswick and Nova Scotia; included in "handicap" ground in Quebec.
Age		
Employment	All jurisdictions	British Columbia: 19–65; Alberta: 18+; Saskatchewan: 18–64; Ontario: 18–65; Newfoundland: 19–65; Quebec: except as provided for by law.
Provision of Service	All except British Columbia, Alberta, and Newfoundland	For tenancy only in British Columbia; Saskatchewan does not include accommodation; in Ontario, applies to those 18 years and older, although 16- and 17-year-olds who have left the care of parents or guardians are protected regarding accommodation; in Quebec, except as provided for by law.
Sex (includes pregnancy and childbirth)		
Employment	All jurisdictions	British Columbia includes breast-feeding; Alberta uses the term "gender"; Manitoba includes gender-determined characteristics; Ontario recognizes the protection of transgendered persons and accepts complaints related to "gender identity"; Ontario accepts complaints related to female genital mutilation; in Quebec, pregnancy as such is considered a ground of discrimination.
Provision of Service	All jurisdictions	Alberta uses the term "gender"; Manitoba includes gender-determined characteristics; Ontario recognizes the protection of transgendered persons and accepts complaints related to "gender identity"; Ontario accepts complaints related to female genital mutilation; in Quebec, pregnancy as such is considered a ground of discrimination.
Marital Status		
Employment	All jurisdictions	Quebec uses the term "civil status."
Provision of Service	All jurisdictions	Quebec uses the term "civil status."
Family Status		
Employment	All except New Brunswick and Newfoundland	Saskatchewan defines as being in a parent–child relationship; Quebec uses the term "civil status."
Provision of Service	All except New Brunswick and Newfoundland	Saskatchewan defines as being in a parent–child relationship; Quebec uses the term "civil status."
Sexual Orientation		
Employment	All jurisdictions	The Supreme Court of Canada read sexual orientation into the *Alberta Human Rights, Citizenship and Multiculturalism Act* in 1998.
Provision of Service	All jurisdictions	The Supreme Court of Canada read sexual orientation into the *Alberta Human Rights, Citizenship and Multiculturalism Act* in 1998.

FIGURE 4-2	Prohibited Grounds of Discrimination in Canada* (continued)	
Prohibited Ground	**Jurisdiction**	**Comments**
National or Ethnic Origin (including linguistic background)		
Employment	All except British Columbia and Alberta	Saskatchewan and Northwest Territories use the term "nationality"; Ontario's Code includes both "ethnic origin" and "citizenship."
Provision of Service	All except British Columbia and Alberta	Saskatchewan and Northwest Territories use the term "nationality"; Ontario's Code includes both "ethnic origin" and "citizenship."
Ancestry or Place of Origin		
Employment	Yukon, British Columbia, Alberta, Saskatchewan, Manitoba, Northwest Territories, Ontario, and New Brunswick	
Provision of Service	Yukon, British Columbia, Alberta, Saskatchewan, Manitoba, Northwest Territories, Ontario, and New Brunswick	
Language		
Employment	Yukon, Ontario, and Quebec	Ontario accepts complaints on the grounds of ancestry, ethnic origin, place of origin, and race; New Brunswick will accept language-related complaints filed on the basis of ancestry, although it is not an enumerated ground.
Provision of Service	Yukon, Ontario, and Quebec	Ontario accepts complaints on the grounds of ancestry, ethnic origin, place of origin and race; New Brunswick will accept language-related complaints filed on the basis of ancestry, although it is not an enumerated ground.
Social Condition or Origin		
Employment	Quebec, Northwest Territories, New Brunswick, and Newfoundland	
Provision of Service	Quebec, Northwest Territories, New Brunswick, and Newfoundland	
Source of Income		
Employment	Alberta, Saskatchewan, Manitoba, Quebec, Prince Edward Island, and Nova Scotia	Defined as "receipt of public assistance" in Saskatchewan; included under social condition in Quebec.
Provision of Service	British Columbia, Alberta, Saskatchewan, Manitoba, Ontario, Prince Edward Island, and Nova Scotia	Applies to tenancy only (not public services or facilities) in British Columbia; defined as "receipt of social assistance" in Saskatchewan; Ontario bans discrimination in accommodation on the grounds of receipt of public assistance; included under social condition in Quebec; applies to occupancy or accommodation only in Nova Scotia.

FIGURE 4-2	Prohibited Grounds of Discrimination in Canada* (continued)	
Prohibited Ground	**Jurisdiction**	**Comments**
Assignment, Attachment, or Seizure of Pay		
Employment	Newfoundland	Included under social condition in Quebec.
Provision of Service	Newfoundland	Included under social condition in Quebec.
Based on Association		
Employment	Yukon, Manitoba, Ontario, New Brunswick, Nova Scotia, Northwest Territories, and Prince Edward Island	Northwest Territories has prohibition on basis of "political association."
Provision of Service	Yukon, Manitoba, Ontario, New Brunswick, Nova Scotia, Northwest Territories, and Prince Edward Island	Northwest Territories has prohibition on basis of "political association."
Political Belief		
Employment	Yukon, British Columbia, Manitoba, Quebec, Nova Scotia, Prince Edward Island, New Brunswick, and Newfoundland	Newfoundland has prohibition on basis of "political opinion."
Provision of Service	Yukon, Manitoba, Quebec, Nova Scotia, Prince Edward Island, New Brunswick, and Newfoundland	Yukon includes political activity and political association; Newfoundland has prohibition on basis of "political opinion."
Record of Criminal Conviction		
Employment	Yukon and Quebec	Yukon's act reads "criminal charges or criminal record."
Provision of Service	Yukon, British Columbia, Quebec, and Prince Edward Island	Yukon's act reads "criminal charges or criminal record."
Pardoned Conviction		
Employment	Federal, Yukon, and Northwest Territories	
Provision of Service	Federal, Yukon, and Northwest Territories	

*This document provides comparative information on the grounds of discrimination covered by federal, provincial, and territorial human rights legislation in Canada. In some instances, prohibited grounds for employment differ from those for the provision of services.

Source: Canadian Human Rights Commission, "Prohibited Grounds of Discrimination in Canada," March 2006, Publications, CHRC site, www.chrc-ccdp.ca/publications/prohibitedgrounds-en.asp, accessed August 1, 2006. Produced by the Canadian Human Rights Commission in cooperation with provincial and territorial human rights commissions as a service to the public. This chart is for quick reference only; for interpretation or further details, contact the appropriate human rights commission.

Discrimination is not defined in the Charter of Rights and Freedoms, nor in any federal or provincial human rights legislation with the exception of Quebec. Section 10 of the Quebec Charter states:

> Every person has a right to full and equal recognition and exercise of his human rights and freedoms without distinction, exclusion, or preference based on race, colour, sex, sexual orientation, civil status, religion, political convictions, language, ethnic or national origin, social condition, or the fact that he is a handicapped person, or that he uses any means to palliate his handicap. Discrimination exists where such a distinction, exclusion, or preference has the effect of nullifying or impairing such a right.

Direct Versus Indirect (Systemic) Discrimination

Normally, intentional direct discrimination on grounds specified in the human rights legislation is illegal. However, under certain circumstances intentional direct discrimination is acceptable. A fashion store catering to women will be allowed to advertise for female models, and schools controlled by religious groups are permitted to limit their hiring to members of the specific faith. This legal discrimination is called **bona fide occupational qualification** (BFOQ).

Indirect, unintentional, or **systemic discrimination** takes place if there is no intention to discriminate, but the system, arrangements, or policies allow it to happen. Such employment practices may appear to be neutral and may be implemented impartially, but they exclude specific groups of people for reasons that are not job-related or required for safe or efficient business operations. As a chief commissioner of the Ontario Human Rights Commission put it:

> The traditional flight of stairs leading into a building was not put there specifically to keep people with mobility impairments out. There's nothing intentional about it; it simply was the way that buildings were designed. But it operates as a very real and substantial and inappropriate barrier to access and entry by people with mobility impairment. That's systemic discrimination.[6]

Examples include

- minimum height and weight requirements for employment with police forces, which make it more difficult for women and Canadians of Asian origin to be hired;
- minimum scores on employment tests, which discriminate against distinct groups (e.g., the use of culturally biased intelligence tests, which tend to screen out a disproportionate number of minorities);
- internal hiring policies, word-of-mouth hiring, or the requirement to submit a photograph with the application form;
- limited accessibility of buildings and facilities, which often makes it impossible for persons with disabilities to be employed with organizations using such places;
- psychological inability of people to deal with persons with disabilities;
- unavailability of alternative formats or forms of tools (e.g., publications in Braille for the blind or telephone devices for the deaf);
- job evaluation systems that tend to undervalue jobs traditionally held by women (e.g., give more points to compensable factors that favour men, such as physical strength, and fewer points to such factors as dexterity);
- promotion criteria that favour factors such as seniority and experience in traditionally male-dominated organizations in which women have not had the chance to acquire either;
- organizational culture in which minority groups feel unwelcome and uneasy, resulting in a disproportionate turnover rate for such groups; and
- lack of explicit anti-harassment guidelines, which allows an atmosphere of abuse to develop in the workplace.

Indirect or systemic discrimination is more difficult to detect and to fight, because often it is hidden and requires a special effort to deal with effectively. The **Canadian Human Rights Commission (CHRC)** has taken specific steps to define and detect the causes and sources of indirect or systemic discrimination. It initiated a number of surveys to assess the accessibility of federal government offices, and the availability of facilities, tools, and services for persons with disabilities. The commission believes that the Charter of Rights and Freedoms gives it the legal basis to combat such discrimination.[7]

Race and Colour

It is sometimes difficult to see which of these two characteristics is the actual basis of discrimination; often both are involved. The discrimination can be intentional or unintentional, subtle or very open, as two examples will show:

> The Western Guard Party of Toronto was operating a tape-recorded message that could be heard by telephone. The message proclaimed the supremacy of the white race and attacked Jews for being determined to destroy the white race by means of communism. The party refused to withdraw or change the message. The Human Rights Commission therefore held a tribunal, which found the messages to be discriminatory and ordered the respondents to refrain from using this subject matter in any future messages.

bona fide occupational qualification (BFOQ)
A justified business reason for discriminating against a member of a protected class.

systemic discrimination
Any company policy, practice, or action that is not openly or intentionally discriminatory, but has an indirect discriminatory impact or effect.

Bona fide occupational qualification (BFOQ) Explanation and examples
www.chrc-ccdp.ca/discrimination/occupational-en.asp?highlight=1

Canadian Human Rights Commission (CHRC)
Supervises the implementation and adjudication of the *Canadian Human Rights Act.*

A bank in a small town advertised a position specifying that the applicant should have a pleasing appearance and requested that a recent photograph be submitted. The bank personnel were all Caucasian. A black community leader filed a discrimination complaint, which was settled when the bank agreed to include human rights training in its courses on interviewing, human resource selection, and counselling.

Of course, not all cases end in favour of the complainant.

Daljit Dhanjal, a Sikh, was employed in the engineering branch of Air Canada. He claimed that he was harassed and subjected to racial slurs by his supervisor, who at one point hit him. Shortly after this latter incident, he was offered an early retirement package. Mr. Dhanjal contended that he was forced to accept this offer because of the atmosphere of discrimination prevailing in this workplace. A human rights tribunal found the complaint to be unsubstantiated: Mr. Dhanjal was not a victim of racial harassment, race, or religion. The tribunal accepted the employer's evidence that Mr. Dhanjal was a poor employee who had trouble getting along with his fellow workers.

There is an interesting side issue in this case. In the tribunal's words, "the poor performance reviews received by the complainant [were] due to the fact that Mr. Dhanjal refused to accept the overbearing and authoritarian management style of his supervisor and that he interpreted this management style subjectively as colonialist and racist behaviour toward him while, in fact, the supervisor was behaving in the same manner toward all of his subordinates." In other words, the supervisor did not discriminate in his abusive behaviour.[8]

National or Ethnic Origins

It is also illegal for human resource decisions to be influenced by the national or ethnic origins of applicants or of their forebears. Hence, the discrimination process can be either direct or indirect. The refusal to hire or promote people because of their national or ethnic origins is a direct and obvious violation:

A Canadian citizen originally from Haiti was refused entrance into the Armed Forces because he was not eligible for security clearance until he had lived in Canada for at least 10 years. He had been in this country for 6 years and was unusually highly qualified in every other respect. During investigations of his complaint, the Armed Forces agreed to invoke a rule already in place that allowed for the 10-year residency requirement to be waived for exceptional candidates. He was cleared and offered enrollment as an officer cadet.

An example of an indirect (systemic) violation based on ethnic origin can be briefly summarized. In one case (which will be detailed later), the hiring requirements for a certain job specified that the candidate had to be 173 centimetres tall (five foot eight). But reflection reveals that such a standard disproportionately discriminates against Asian Canadians, who tend to be shorter than descendants of immigrants from European countries. Because of this, although the height rule may not intend to discriminate, the result is discriminatory.

Religion

A person's religious beliefs and practices should not affect employment decisions. An employer must accommodate an employee's religious practices, unless those practices present undue hardship to the employer:

A Muslim employee of a communications company lost his job over the question of having time off each week to attend prayers at his mosque. After conciliation, a settlement was reached, which did not impose undue hardships on the employer and by which the employee was allowed to take one-and-a-half hours per week of leave without pay. He was reinstated with retroactive pay and benefits.

If an employer does not make a reasonable attempt to accommodate workers' religious practices, he or she can be found guilty of violating the *Human Rights Act*.

duty to accommodate
Requirement that an employer must accommodate the employee to the point of "undue hardship."

The terms "undue hardship" and **duty to accommodate** have been extended in another important decision by the Supreme Court of Canada in a ruling against Central Alberta Dairy Pool (1990). The complainant worked at a milk-processing plant. After becoming a member of the Worldwide Church of God, he requested unpaid leave for a particular Monday in order to observe a holy day of his church. The request was refused, because Mondays were especially busy days at the plant. When the employee did not report for work, he was fired.

A Supreme Court judgment forced the RCMP to accommodate its Sikh officers' religious requirement to wear a turban at all times. Should Jewish men be accommodated to wear a yarmulke?

CP/Paul Henry.

The court ruled that Dairy Pool had discriminated on the basis of religion. Although the company had not done so directly, it had an adverse effect on the complainant due to his religion. It is of importance to note that the court stated that the employer must meet the "duty to accommodate" up to the point of "undue hardship."

The court did not define "undue hardship." However, it stated that relevant considerations would include financial cost, disruption of a collective agreement, problems of morale of other employees, and interchangeability of workforce and facilities. It found that Dairy Pool could cope with employee absences on Mondays because of illnesses. Therefore, it could also accommodate a single instance for absence due to religious reasons, particularly if the employee had tried to accommodate the employer.[9]

Age

The use of age as an employment criterion has also received considerable attention in the past. Many employers consider that the laying down of minimum or maximum ages for certain jobs is justified, although evidence is rarely available that age is an accurate indication of one's ability to perform a given type of work:

> The General Pilotage Regulations require that a pilot be removed from the eligibility list after reaching the age of 50. A special human rights tribunal found that such a regulation was invalid and ordered that pilots affected by this rule be restored to their former positions. An appeal court set aside the tribunal's decision on the basis that the removal of the pilots from the eligibility list because of age was not a discriminatory practice. The Canadian Human Rights Commission appealed to the Supreme Court of Canada, but the appeal was denied.

As mentioned earlier, the law makes an exception when it comes to retirement age. It is not considered a discriminatory practice if a person's employment is terminated because that person has reached the normal age of retirement for employees working in similar positions.

Sex

The *Human Rights Act* also prevents discrimination on the basis of an individual's sex (often erroneously referred to as *gender*, which is a grammatical term; the act specifically uses the term *sex*). Not only is it illegal to recruit, hire, and promote employees because of their sex, it is unlawful to have separate policies for men and women. For example, it is discriminatory to reserve some jobs for men only or women only. It is even illegal to apply similar standards to men and women when such standards arbitrarily discriminate more against one sex than against the other. When standards discriminate

SPOTLIGHT ON ETHICS
The Hiring Dilemma

The manager of an accounting department has to hire the replacement for a retiring accountant. Over 20 applicants have applied and 3 were put onto the short list. One of the shortlisted candidates is a 60-year-old CA, more experienced than the other two, who also have a CA certificate. The manager knows that the department will change accounting practices in the near future (no date has been set yet) and introduce new accounting software, which will require extensive retraining of current staff. If he hires the more experienced candidate, he will be faced with the question of whether it is justified to invest a considerable amount in retraining a person who will retire soon after. But if he hires one of the younger candidates, he might face an age discrimination charge. What should he do?

against one sex (or race, national or ethnic origin, religion, age, or marital status), the burden is on the employer to prove that the standards are necessary:

> A woman complained that she had been refused an interview for a job as a bus driver because she was under the minimum height requirement of 173 centimetres (five foot eight). She claimed that this requirement discriminated against women. After conciliation, the case was settled with the company, discontinuing the practice of requiring applicants to be 173 centimetres tall for drivers' jobs. Two women under that height have since been hired. As part of the settlement, the company agreed that the Commission would monitor the company's driver application records for one year. The complainant was paid $3,500 for lost wages and general damages.

Although the standard did not discriminate against women per se, the arbitrary height requirement tended to exclude most female applicants. To keep the height rule, since it discriminates against women, the employer must show that it is necessary given the nature of the job. If this cannot be shown, the employer can be compelled to drop the requirement.

A recent and far-reaching Supreme Court decision relating to sex discrimination concerns the earlier mentioned bona fide occupational qualification (BFOQ). The case involved a woman who had been employed by the Province of British Columbia in an elite firefighting unit for more than two years.

> In 1994, Ms. Meiorin failed one of several new fitness tests, a 2.5 kilometre run to be completed in 11 minutes, and lost her employment. A subsequent grievance launched by her union was appealed to the Supreme Court. The Court decided in favour of Ms. Meiorin, agreeing with an earlier arbitrator's ruling that the government had failed to justify the test as a BFOQ by providing credible evidence that her inability to meet the standard created a safety risk.[10]

The court established three new criteria to assess the appropriateness of a BFOQ:

1. Is the standard rationally connected to the performance of the job?
2. Was the standard established in an honest belief that it was necessary to accomplish the purpose identified in stage one?
3. Is the standard reasonably necessary to accomplish its purpose?

The new and stricter rules will make it more difficult for human resource managers to establish and defend BFOQs.

Sexual Orientation

As stated in the 1999 Canadian Human Rights Commission's annual report, that year may come to be regarded as a watershed year for gay and lesbian Canadians. The issue of discrimination against same-sex relationships was effectively addressed by the Supreme Court of Canada when it decided that same-sex couples must be treated the same way as heterosexual couples. Polls show that the majority of Canadians not only favour legislation to eliminate discrimination against lesbians and gay men, but also increasingly approve of measures to protect and support their families.

Same-sex marriage legislation
http://canadaonline.about.com/library/weekly/aa021300b.htm

It began in 1996, when a human rights tribunal ordered the federal government to extend medical and dental benefits to the same-sex partners of its employees. The same year, the government amended the *Human Rights Act* to add sexual orientation as a prohibited ground of discrimination. Since then, several Supreme Court decisions have forced provinces to amend their benefit and tax laws to include same-sex couples into their considerations.

In 2000, Parliament passed legislation treating same-sex partners the same as legally married and common-law couples for all purposes of federal law, but left the traditional definition of marriage as between a man and a woman. Only in June 2005 did Parliament also change the definition of marriage to include same-sex couples.[11]

Marital Status

The idea of what constitutes a family has undergone considerable changes in Canadian society in recent years. Nontraditional families, such as those resulting from common-law marriages, or single-parent families, are now far more numerous than in the past. But there is still a strong feeling that the traditional family is a unique institution deserving special consideration.

The *Human Rights Act* spells out quite clearly that any discrimination based on marital status is illegal:

> A woman was denied a job with the CBC because her husband was already employed by the corporation at the same station. After a complaint and hearing, the CBC changed its employment practices, which formerly discriminated on the basis of marital status, and placed the woman in a position in the same station in which her husband was employed.

Family Status

In a widely cited case regarding family status, the Canadian Human Rights Commission initiated action against the Canada Employment and Immigration Commission (CEIC).

Ms. Ina Lang alleged that the CEIC denied her application for funding under the Challenge 86 program because she wished to hire her daughter to help in her family child care business. A tribunal held that the CEIC had discriminated against Ms. Lang on the basis of her family status when it denied her the funding she sought, and awarded her $1,000 for hurt feelings. The CEIC appealed the decision to the Federal Court of Appeal, but the court upheld the decision.

Marital and family status are often linked, as in the case of Diane Richer's complaint against the Canadian Armed Forces:

> Ms. Richer alleged that the CAF discriminated against her on the basis of marital and family status when she was refused admittance as a guest to the Junior Ranks Mess because she was married to an officer. The complaint was settled when the CAF agreed to admit such visitors into messes regardless of the rank of their military spouses. Ms. Richer received $500 for hurt feelings and a letter of apology.

That *nepotism* is a form of discrimination based on family status is something a Canadian airline found out. It had a policy of hiring the children of its employees for summer jobs. The CHRC ruled that this amounted to discrimination. A federal court rejected an appeal.

Disability

No person should be denied employment solely for the reason of his or her being disabled. Of course, there are exceptions. A blind person cannot be a truck driver, or a deaf person a telephone operator. However, the principle of **reasonable accommodation** has been established. It means that an employer can be expected to take reasonable measures to make available a suitable job to a person with a physical handicap if it does not impose undue hardships on the organization:

reasonable accommodation
Voluntary adjustments to work or workplace that allow employees with special needs to perform their job effectively.

> A man was refused a technician's job because he failed a hearing test. However, he had been tested without his hearing aid; he asserted that he could perform the job using a hearing device. Medical advisors for the company claimed that the job required perfectly normal hearing. After conciliation, the company agreed that with a hearing aid the man would be able to do the job. The complaint was settled with the complainant being hired as a technician and paid damages of $750.

Many organizations have established rigid physical standards for certain jobs without being able to show that these standards are truly relevant to the requirements of the job. Some complainants have been refused jobs when their disability might be a problem in a speculative situation; for example, the firm might argue that a deaf person would be unable to hear a fire alarm. Other complainants have been disqualified for jobs not because they are physically handicapped now, but because they may become so in the future:

> A machinist who had suffered an injury to his leg was refused a position on the hypothesis that at some time in the future he might develop complications that might affect his ability to work, which might in turn lead to a finding against the employer for compensation. After an investigation by the Canadian Human Rights Commission, the company had to agree that its assumptions were highly speculative. In the settlement, the complainant was paid the additional wages, approximately $2,000, that he would have earned if he had not been denied the position, as well as compensation in respect of his feelings and self-respect.

Canadian Human Rights Commission
Issues relating to disability
www.chrc-ccdp.ca/discrimination/physical_mental-en.asp

Being drug-dependent can also be interpreted as a disability. In 1991, the Toronto-Dominion Bank introduced a mandatory drug test for new and returning employees. A federal court ruled that this policy was discriminatory, reversing an earlier human rights tribunal's decision. Although the policy in question appeared to be applied in a neutral manner, the court confirmed that it clearly affected the protected group of drug-dependent persons and therefore constituted "adverse impact" discrimination.[12]

Another case also has interesting consequences for human resource managers. In *Fortin v. CP Rail*, a federal court ruled that a company's obligation to accommodate an alcoholic employee may be quite far-reaching and is not influenced by that employee's misconduct.

> Louis Fortin, a 30-year employee of CP Rail, was caught taking office funds, making unauthorized use of company expenses, and misappropriating company money for his own use. While the Canadian Human Rights Commission rejected his complaint of unfair dismissal based on his disability, a Federal Court found that the medical evidence indicated that the employee's conduct was recognizable as the behaviour of an alcoholic.[13]

Acquired immune deficiency syndrome (AIDS) continues to draw the attention of the Canadian Human Rights Commission. The Commission holds that discrimination on grounds of HIV infection or AIDS, whether diagnosed or suspected, is a violation of the *Human Rights Act*. The Commission recommends that employers develop and publicize corporate AIDS policies to provide information and offer reassurance: "Discrimination and AIDS both thrive on ignorance and concealment. Education not only removes unnecessary fears, it may encourage both fairness and compassion."[14]

In its 2001 annual report, the Canadian Human Rights Commission suggests a new approach to dealing with barriers to the hiring of disabled persons. As an example, the chief commissioner points to new legislation in Ontario, the *Ontarians with Disabilities Act*, 2001. This act allows for the establishment of barrier-free standards on accessibility matters such as building access and public transportation. It requires architects to consider during the planning process for a building the regulations of the act. It is the first example in Canada of a standards-based barrier removal legislation.[15]

Pardoned Convicts

The *Canadian Human Rights Act* prohibits discrimination against a convicted person if a pardon has been issued for the offence. Pardon may be granted by a parole board after five years following release, parole, or the completion of a sentence:

> A person convicted and paroled on a drug offence applied for a job with a government agency dealing with drug abuse. He was denied employment because of his conviction. Subsequently, the National Parole Board granted his request for a full pardon. The government agency maintained, however, that, pardoned or not, he remained a security risk and that being without a criminal record was a BFOQ of a correctional service's staff. He appealed to the Canadian Human Rights Commission, and after the Commission's investigation, the government agency decided that a criminal record would not, in fact, inhibit the applicant's ability to meet the requirements of the job, and, satisfied that he was suitable, offered him the position.[16]

The Canadian Human Rights Commission has also been approached by several persons who claim to have been refused employment on the basis of their arrest record, even when the arrest did not lead to a conviction. These persons are without legal protection, because the *Human Rights Act* does not address this type of discrimination. For the human resource manager, this does not mean that all applicants can be asked for their arrest record. It must still be shown that it is relevant to the job. For this reason, the Commission has advised employers under federal jurisdiction that applicants should not be asked, "Have you ever been convicted of an offence?" It is recommended—if such information is legitimately needed for employment purposes—that the question be phrased: "Have you ever been convicted of an offence for which you have not received a pardon?"

It should be noted, however, that British Columbia, Quebec, and Yukon include records of criminal conviction in their list of prohibited discrimination criteria.

Harassment

The *Human Rights Act* contains the following prohibition against harassment:

It is a discriminatory practice,

a) in the provision of goods, services, facilities or accommodation customarily available to the general public,

b) in the provision of commercial premises or residential accommodation, or

c) in matters related to employment to harass an individual on a prohibited ground of discrimination.

Such behaviour may be verbal, physical, deliberate, unsolicited, or unwelcome; it may be one incident or a series of incidents. Protection against harassment extends to incidents occurring at or away from the workplace, during or outside normal working hours, provided such incidents are employment-related.

Harassment may include

- verbal abuse or threats;
- unwelcome remarks, jokes, innuendo, or taunting about a person's body, attire, age, marital status, ethnic or national origin, religion, and so on;
- displaying of pornographic, racist, or other offensive or derogatory pictures;
- practical jokes that cause awkwardness or embarrassment;
- unwelcome invitations or requests, whether indirect or explicit, or intimidation;
- leering or other gestures;
- condescension or paternalism that undermines self-respect;
- unnecessary physical contact such as touching, patting, pinching, or punching; and
- physical assault.

It will be assumed that harassing behaviour has taken place if a "reasonable person ought to have known that such behaviour was unwelcome."[17]

Sexual harassment has become an important topic in human resource management, evidenced by the increased number of complaints lodged. A Canadian Human Rights Tribunal identified three characteristics of sexual harassment:

1. the encounters must be unsolicited by the complainant, unwelcome to the complainant, and expressly or implicitly known by the respondent to be unwelcome;

2. the conduct must either continue despite the complainant's protests or, if the conduct stops, the complainant's protests must have led to negative employment consequences; and

3. the complainant's cooperation must be due to employment-related threats or promises.

The most consequential case undoubtedly was that of *Robichaud v. Department of National Defence*, because it made its way up to the Supreme Court. The court ruled that the employer shared the responsibility for the actions of one of its supervisors who had sexually harassed Ms. Robichaud. It added that "only an employer can remedy undesirable effects [of discrimination]; only an employer can provide the most important remedy—a healthy work environment." The DND was ordered to pay Ms. Robichaud $5,000 for pain and suffering, to issue a written apology, and to post the written apology in all DND facilities.

Women are not the only employees who may be subjected to sexual harassment:

R.R., a deck-hand on a tugboat owned by Sea-West Holdings Ltd., was sexually harassed by the tug's skipper. He complained to the owner of Sea-West, but nothing was done. He was eventually fired. A tribunal held that the sexual harassment had created a poisoned work situation in which the individual is given a work environment which is intimidating, hostile, and offensive. The tribunal also felt that there is a duty upon the owner so informed (of harassment) to put an immediate stop to such practices. R.R. was awarded $2,000 for hurt feelings and $1,760 for lost wages.

Canadian Human Rights Commission Harassment issues
www.chrc-ccdp.ca/discrimination/harassment-en.asp

Sample of sexual harassment policy and procedures (from Saint Mary's University)
www.smu.ca/administration/hr/documents/Harassment_policy.pdf

harassment
Occurs when a member of an organization treats an employee in a disparate manner because of that person's sex, race, religion, age, or other protective classification.

sexual harassment
Unsolicited or unwelcome sex- or gender-based conduct that has adverse employment consequences for the complainant.

SPOTLIGHT ON HRM

When a Manager Is Accused of Sexual Harassment

How you first respond to a complaint of sexual harassment filed against you is extremely critical. Knowing what to do and what not to do can have a big impact on the results of the investigation that follows.

Employers have an obligation to conduct an inquiry into the allegations when a complaint of sexual harassment has been lodged.

Although every case is different and the nature and extent of the investigation will depend on the circumstances, here are a few suggestions on how you should react if a complaint is filed against you:

Avoid any emotional reaction when first confronted with the complaint. It is not unusual for an accused person to become defensive, angry, threatening, or incoherent after being advised of a complaint. Restrain yourself from any overt behaviour that can later be categorized one way or the other. Try to keep the first meeting brief so you can leave to collect your thoughts and seek appropriate advice.

Never provide any response when first advised of the complaint. It will be hard to stay rational when you are first told about the complaint. You are at a disadvantage at this point; therefore, avoid any knee-jerk response that you may regret later.

It is important to understand the nature of the complaint. As an accused, you are entitled to know every allegation that has been made by both the complainant and any witnesses. Ask to be provided with a copy of the written complaint and any statement by witnesses.

If the complaint has not been recorded in writing, ask that the employer go back to the complainant and obtain a signed copy. This also applies to witnesses. The reason is that you want to confine the complaint and avoid any subsequent changes. And ask what the complainant is seeking by filing it.

Does the employer have a sexual or workplace harassment policy? Whether the conduct that you are accused of will be characterized as sexual harassment may depend on the definition in the company policy. It should outline how the investigation will be conducted and what types of corrective action could be taken by the employer if you are found guilty.

Retain an employment lawyer who has experience in sexual harassment cases. You are entitled to retain a lawyer, usually at your cost. An experienced counsel will provide you with a clear understanding of the law of sexual harassment

and will assist you throughout the investigation. Your lawyer may not be permitted to accompany you during your interview with investigators. Still, you should press your employer for the right to have counsel present.

You have a right to respond to all allegations made against you. This will normally occur during your interview with investigators and it is usually done orally. However, circumstances may require that you provide a written response along with your oral interview. Be prepared to explain the context in which any behaviour occurred and to provide the names of any witnesses that you want the investigators to talk to.

You should avoid being uncooperative or engaging in any retaliatory behaviour. There could be serious consequences for you if you engage in this type of conduct. Cooperation does not mean waiving any of your rights, but you should always be respectful of the process and be honest in your approach.

Avoid any conduct that could be characterized as interfering with the investigation. This usually means trying to contact the complainant or any of the witnesses. Do not engage in any kind of retaliation against either of these parties.

For example, changing the terms of employment or threatening to discipline or terminate the complainant or any witnesses could qualify as retaliation. Threatening to sue the complainant for defamation during the course of the investigation may also be considered a form of retaliation. Such conduct will usually be treated as a violation of company policy.

Avoid making denials where the truth is required. You may be surprised to know that just because you deny something occurred and there are no witnesses does not mean you can't be found guilty of sexual harassment. In many cases there are no witnesses and investigators must make a decision on the basis of conflicting evidence and credibility.

If there is no reasonable explanation for your conduct, be honest in your response and acknowledge any shortcomings in your behaviour. Misleading or lying to investigators can only make things worse for you. When a complaint of sexual harassment is filed against you, it is a very serious matter. It could result in discipline or even termination and, in most cases, would undermine your relationship with your co-workers and your reputation. The manner in which you respond may well determine your fate.

Source: Courtesy of Malcolm MacKillop.

Employer Retaliation

It is a criminal act to retaliate in any way against those who exercise their righ' *Human Rights Act.* Those who file charges, testify, or otherwise participate ir action are protected by law. If a supervisor tries to get even with an employee who filed she violates the act.

Enforcement

The responsibility for the enforcement of the *Human Rights Act* lies in the hands of a specially created Canadian Human Rights Commission (CHRC). It consists of a chief commissioner, a deputy chief commissioner, and from three to six other members who are appointed by the governor-in-council. The chief commissioner and his or her deputy are full-time members. Full-time members are appointed for a term of not more than seven years, and part-time members for a term of not more than three years.

CHRC deals with complaints it receives concerning discriminatory practices covered by the act. It may also act on its own when it perceives a possible infraction. CHRC may issue guidelines interpreting the act. If warranted, the Commission can ask the president of the Human Rights Tribunal Panel to appoint a tribunal, which may order cessation of the discriminatory practice, the adoption of measures to ensure that it will not recur, and possibly compensation for the party discriminated against.

Any individual or group with reasonable grounds to believe they have been discriminated against may file a complaint. The Commission may refuse to accept the complaint if it is submitted by someone other than the person who allegedly has been discriminated against, unless the alleged victim permits investigation of the claim. It may also refuse to deal with complaints if other procedures seem more appropriate, if the complaint seems trivial or made in bad faith, or if too much time (one year) has elapsed since the alleged discrimination took place. As mentioned above, CHRC may itself initiate a complaint if it has reasonable grounds to assume a party is discriminating.

After a complaint has been accepted, an investigator is appointed to gather facts about the case. He or she submits a report recommending a finding of either substantiation or nonsubstantiation of the allegation. If the allegation is substantiated, a settlement may be arranged in the course of the investigation, or the Commission may, after adoption of the report, appoint a conciliator.

Should the parties involved be unable to reach a conciliation agreement, a Human Rights Tribunal Panel consisting of up to three members—most consist of one—may be appointed to investigate the complaint. Figure 4-3 describes the discretion of the tribunal in settling a complaint. Should the tribunal find that the discriminatory practice was maintained purposely or recklessly, or that the victim's feelings or self-respect have suffered as a result of the practice, it may order the person or organization responsible to compensate the victim appropriately.

A person who obstructs an investigation or a tribunal, or fails to comply with the terms of a settlement, or reduces wages in order to eliminate a discriminatory practice, can be found guilty of an offence punishable by a fine and/or jail sentence. If the guilty party is an employer or an employee organization, the fine may be up to $50,000. For individuals, the penalty may be up to $5,000.[18] As mentioned previously, provinces have their own rules regarding human rights violations.

FIGURE 4-3   Remedies for Violations

A Canadian Human Rights Tribunal can order a violator to:

- Stop the discriminatory practice.
- Restore the rights, opportunities, and privileges denied the victim.
- Compensate the victim for wages lost and any expenses incurred as a result of the discriminatory practice.
- Compensate the victim for any additional cost of obtaining alternative goods, services, facilities, or accommodation as a result of the discriminatory practice.
- Develop and implement employment equity programs to equalize opportunity for certain groups that have suffered from discriminatory practices in the past.

Provincial Human Rights Laws and Human Rights Commissions

Most provinces and two territories (Northwest Territories and Yukon) have their own human rights laws and commissions, with similar discrimination criteria, regulations, and procedures. British Columbia abolished its commission in 2003, but retained its Human Rights Tribunal. The new territory of Nunavut has no commission, but does have a *Fair Practices Act* that addresses human rights issues.

If a person feels discriminated against, he or she will contact a provincial human rights officer, who will investigate the complaint and attempt to reach a settlement that will satisfy all parties. Experience has shown that the majority of cases are settled at this stage. Should there be no agreement, the case will be presented to the provincial human rights commission. The members of that commission study the evidence and then submit a report to the minister in charge of administration of the *Human Rights Act*. The minister may appoint a Board of Inquiry, which has powers similar to those of a tribunal at the federal level. Noncompliance with the course of action prescribed by the Board may result in prosecution in a provincial court of law. Individuals can be fined between $500 and $1,000, and organizations or groups between $1,000 and $10,000, depending on the province. If an issue at hand has nationwide implications, any provincial court decision may ultimately be appealed to the Supreme Court of Canada.

Employment Equity

The Abella Commission on Equality in Employment (chaired by Judge Rosalie Abella) was appointed in 1983 to inquire into the most effective, efficient, and equitable methods of promoting employment opportunities for four designated groups: women, persons with a disability, Aboriginal people, and members of a visible minority. The Commission recommended that all organizations set mandatory equality programs and urged the provincial and federal governments to pass equity legislation—a recommendation that has since been implemented by the federal and all provincial governments. The commission also recommended to use the term *employment equity* in Canada to distinguish it from the U.S. term, *affirmative action*, because, in the opinion of the commission, the latter carried too many negative associations.*

Canadian Human Rights Commission Employment equity issues
www.chrc-ccdp.ca/employment_equity/default-en.asp

Employment Equity Act
Federal law to remove employment barriers and to promote equality.

As a result of the Abella Commission's report, the federal government proclaimed the *Employment Equity Act* in August 1987. Its intent is to remove employment barriers and promote equality of the four designated group members. The act requires employers with 100 and more employees under federal jurisdiction to develop annual plans setting out goals and timetables and to maintain these plans for three years. The act requires further that each employer submit annual reports describing the progress in attaining the goals set out in the abovementioned plans. The Canada Employment and Immigration Commission forwards employer reports to the Human Rights Commission. Employers who do not comply may be investigated by the Human Rights Commission and, if necessary, prosecuted under the *Human Rights Act*.

The *Employment Equity Act* was amended in 1996. It now contains two specific provisions regarding "reasonable accommodation." Section 5 provides that:

> "Every employer shall implement employment equity" by, among other measures, "making such reasonable accommodations as will ensure that persons in a designated group" achieve a degree of representation commensurate with their representation in the Canadian workforce and their availability to meet reasonable occupational requirements.

The four designated groups are women, Aboriginal people, persons with a disability, and members of a visible minority. (This is in contrast to human rights legislation, which requires equal treatment of *all* groups.)

Section 10 of the act specifies that an employer shall prepare an "employment equity plan" that provides for "reasonable accommodation ... to correct ... under-representation." Some examples of reasonable accommodation are

- providing a sign-language interpreter for a job interview with a deaf applicant;
- providing telephone or computer equipment to accommodate persons who are hard of hearing or blind;
- constructing a barrier-free work site for wheelchair-bound employees;

---

*The major difference between Canadian employment equity and U.S. affirmative action programs is that the former are based on the principle of equitable access in all employment systems, while the latter are based on the principle of righting past wrongs.

- allowing religious minorities to alter their work schedules to accommodate religious obligations; and
- altering dress or grooming codes to allow Aboriginal people to wear braids.

The amended act also established the Canadian Human Rights Commission as the monitoring agency that would carry out compliance audits for federally regulated public- and private-sector employers.

Functional Impact

Virtually every human resource function is affected by employment equity plans:

- *Human resource plans* must reflect the organization's employment equity goals.
- *Job descriptions* must not contain unneeded requirements that exclude members of protected classes.
- *Recruiting* must ensure that all types of applicants are sought without discriminating.
- *Selection* of applicants must use screening devices that are job-relevant and nondiscriminatory.
- *Training and developmental* opportunities must be made available for all workers, without discrimination.
- *Performance appraisal* must be free of biases that discriminate.
- *Compensation programs* must be based on skills, performance, and/or seniority and cannot discriminate against jobholders in other respects.

Even when human resource specialists know that their intent is not to discriminate, they must carefully review the results of these human resource functions to ensure that the results are not discriminatory. Otherwise, lawsuits may arise and the current employment equity plan may need to be revised or scrapped.

Employment Equity Programs

The *Employment Equity Act* gives the Canadian Human Rights Commission great latitude in pursuing the enforcement of the act. One way for the commission to comply with the intent of the act to improve equal employment opportunities for special groups is for it to encourage **employment equity programs**.

employment equity programs
Developed by employers to undo past employment discrimination or to ensure equal employment opportunity in the future. Called affirmative action programs in the United States.

Section 15(1) of the act specifies special programs as a legitimate mechanism for improving the opportunities of a group through the elimination, reduction, or prevention of discrimination:

> It is not a discriminatory practice for a person to adopt or carry out a special program, plan, or arrangement designed to prevent disadvantages that are likely to be suffered by, or to eliminate or reduce disadvantages that are suffered by, any group or individuals when those disadvantages would be or are based on or related to the race, national or ethnic origin, colour, religion, age, sex, marital status, or physical handicap of members of that group, by improving opportunities respecting goods, services, facilities, accommodation, or employment in relation to that group.

Such programs are developed by employers to remedy past discrimination or to prevent discrimination in the future. For the organization, such a program usually involves a self-evaluation of its hiring, promotion, and compensation policies. If discrepancies are found, it would be good human resource practice to check the criteria used for different decisions, adjust them if necessary, and make sure that they are consistently applied.

Employment equity programs exist for several reasons. From a practical standpoint, employers seldom benefit by excluding people who belong to a particular group. To exclude an entire class of workers, such as women or visible minorities, limits the labour pool available to the human resource department. Open discrimination can also lead to negative public relations, boycotts by consumers, and government intervention. To ensure that such discrimination does not occur, employers often develop equity programs voluntarily.

It should be noted that mandated equity programs take place mainly at the federal level—that is, in organizations and industries under federal jurisdiction. At the provincial level, such programs are implemented almost exclusively on a voluntary basis, when organizations recognize an advantage in it. For example, at Saint Mary's University in Halifax, an employee equity program, approved by the Nova Scotia Human Rights Commission, was implemented to balance a perceived employment inequity between male and female faculty.

FIGURE 4-4	Major Steps in Employment Equity Programs

1. Exhibit strong employer commitment.
2. Appoint a high-ranking director.
3. Publicize commitment internally and externally.
4. Survey the workforce for underutilization and concentration.
5. Develop goals and timetables.
6. Design remedial, active, and preventive programs.
7. Establish control systems and reporting procedures.

Regardless of the reasons or goals of such programs, human resource departments should adhere to the guidelines discussed below and summarized in Figure 4-4.

- **Exhibit commitment.** No matter how favourably the human resource department is viewed by others in the organization, the president of the company should support the program in writing. Anything less than total support from top officials raises questions about the sincerity of the organization's commitment in the eyes of government agencies, courts, and employees. To exhibit this commitment forcefully, company officials may make raises, bonuses, and promotions dependent upon each manager's compliance.
- **Appoint a director.** Some member of the organization should be responsible for equity issues. Commonly, the vice-president of human resources is appointed director, although day-to-day implementation may be delegated to a compliance specialist in the human resource department.
- **Publicize commitment.** An employment equity program is ineffective unless publicized externally and internally. Outside the company, sources of potential recruits must be made aware of the new policy. School guidance counsellors, employment agencies, and officers of Canada Employment Centres are likely candidates for notification. Organizations should include the phrase "An equal opportunity employer" on company stationery and in classified ads to further publicize its policy. Internally, the practice should be conveyed, in strong enough terms, to everyone involved in the hiring process. Otherwise, top management may pursue one policy and lower levels another.
- **Survey the workforce.** The human resource department needs to know how the composition of the employer's workforce compares with the composition of the workforce in the labour market. For example, if the employer's mix of male and female employees differs significantly from the labour market from which the employer attracts workers, it is possible that discrimination has occurred. When a survey of the employer's workforce indicates such differences, the employer may find examples of underutilization or concentration. **Underutilization** exists when a company or department has a smaller proportion of protected class members than is found in the labour market. For example, when a company has no female managers even though the labour market is 37 percent female, underutilization exists. **Concentration** is just the opposite, occurring when protected class members are concentrated in a few departments, out of proportion with their presence in the labour market.
- **Develop goals and timetables.** When, through surveys, underutilization and concentration are found (possibly as consequences of past discrimination), human resource specialists should set up goals and timetables to eliminate them.
- **Design specific programs.** To reach goals, human resource specialists must design remedial, active, and preventive programs. *Remedial programs* correct problems that already exist. *Active programs* imply that management goes beyond instructing supervisors about new hiring policies and waiting for things to happen. It means going to high schools in areas dominated by minorities, approaching community leaders in such areas for assistance, inviting residents to attend information sessions, and advertising in newspapers or other media outlets accessible to minorities and special target groups:

> The Law School at Dalhousie University in Halifax developed an Indigenous Black and Mi'kmaq Program to train more black and Mi'kmaq lawyers. It appointed a director and

underutilization
A condition that exists when a department or employer has a lesser proportion of members of a protected class than are found in the employer's labour market.

concentration
A condition that exists when a department or employer has a greater proportion of members of a protected class than are found in the employer's labour market.

began a publication campaign aimed at these groups by advertising in local newspapers and association publications. The program director visits high schools and universities and holds information sessions at reserves and community centres. An advisory board made up of law school representatives, community leaders, and the two student groups assists in identifying ways to reach the target groups. The program has graduated over 90 lawyers from these minority groups so far.[19]

Preventive programs are more proactive. They involve an assessment of human resource management policies and practices. Policies that discriminate (such as height rules) or practices that continue past discrimination (such as hiring exclusively from employee referrals) must be eliminated.

- **Establish controls.** An employment equity program is likely to fail unless controls are established. Human resource specialists and line managers must perceive their rewards as depending upon the success of the program. To evaluate that success, monthly, quarterly, and yearly benchmarks should be reported directly to the director of the program and to the president or another senior official.

Contract Compliance Policy

In addition to companies or agencies under federal jurisdiction, the federal government requires compliance with the *Employment Equity Act* from any company doing business with the federal government. Companies with 100 or more employees bidding on contracts for goods and services of $200,000 or more are subject to the employment equity criteria listed in the act. Under this policy, companies are required to certify in writing at the tendering stage of a contract their commitment to implement employment equity. Employers will be subject to random reviews to ensure their compliance with the act.

Pay Equity

In 2005, according to Statistics Canada, women earned, on average, 85 cents for every $1 earned by men. There are many reasons for this pay gap, including differences in work experience, education, major field of study, occupation and industry of employment, as well as reasons that are still not understood. Pay equity legislation attempts to remedy these inequities. At the federal level, the *Canadian Human Rights Act* prohibits discrimination based on sex; it is therefore illegal to pay women less than men if their jobs are of equal value, a principle known as "equal pay for work of equal value," which is discussed in more detail in Chapter 9. Provinces, with the exception of Alberta, British Columbia, and Saskatchewan, have their own pay equity laws, but they differ in coverage. Quebec and Ontario have laws covering the public and private sector, while other provinces and the Yukon restrict the application to the public sector. Northwest Territories has its *Fair Practices Act*, which deals with pay equity issues.

That the "equal pay for work of equal value" concept can be very costly was shown in the case of 390 federal library science employees—mostly women—who earned less than historical researchers—mostly men—though the library science work was claimed to be of equal value. The settlement, requiring individual salary increases of up to $2,500 a year, cost the federal government $2.4 million.

On October 19, 1999, the longest and largest pay equity case was resolved when Mr. Justice John Evans upheld a Human Rights Tribunal's ruling that the federal government owed about 230 000 (mostly female) workers 13 years of back pay. The final settlement cost the Treasury Board over $3.5 billion. The federal government decided not to appeal this decision.

In the private sector, the largest case involves Bell Canada and about 20,000 employees, mostly women. The Supreme Court of Canada decided not to hear an appeal by Bell Canada against a judgment by a Human Rights Tribunal that it paid female-dominated jobs between $1.50 and $5 per hour less than male-dominated jobs of equal value. The Supreme Court held that it was up to the tribunal to decide on a settlement for Bell employees. On May 15, 2006, Bell Canada announced that it had reached an agreement with the Communications, Energy and Paperworkers Union of Canada (CEP) on pay equity that will benefit as many as 4765 current and former Bell employees. The settlement is valued at approximately $100 million.

The implication for human resource people is that they must make very sure their wage and salary system does not subtly discriminate on the basis of sex.

Canadian Human Rights Commission
Pay equity
www.chrc-ccdp.ca/
DisputeResolution_
ReglementDifferends/
payequity_paritesalariale-
en.asp

Statistics Canada
The feminization of work
www.statcan.ca/english/kits/
pdf/social/feminization.pdf

Reverse Discrimination

The use of employment equity programs can lead to charges of reverse discrimination against employers. The charges usually arise when an employer seeks to hire or promote a member of a protected group over an equally (or better) qualified candidate who is not a member of a protected group. For example, if an employer has an employment equity program that gives preference to women over men when promotions occur, a qualified male may sue the employer and claim that he was discriminated against because of his sex.

Charges of reverse discrimination may put human resource departments in a difficult position. On the one hand, the human resource manager is responsible for eliminating concentration and underutilization. On the other hand, to give preference to members of a protected class (such as women) raises questions about whether the human resource department is being fair:

> In a landmark decision in 1984, the Canadian Human Rights Commission imposed a mandatory employment equity program on CN. The company was ordered to hire women for one in four nontraditional or blue-collar jobs in its St. Lawrence region until women held 13 percent of such jobs. CN appealed the decision to the Supreme Court of Canada, which let stand the order for quotas. This ruling is important, as it allows employment equity programs as acceptable measures, even if they result in potential reverse discrimination.

Although preferential treatment will always raise questions of fairness, the *Human Rights Act* declares employment equity programs nondiscriminatory if they fulfill the spirit of the law.

Principle of natural justice
http://en.wikipedia.org/wiki/
Natural_justice

The Principle of Natural Justice

Many people in an organization have the power of making decisions that can greatly affect the life or career of organization members. To ensure that a decision-making process is fair, the principle of **natural justice** has been accepted internationally—for example, as nonlegal guidelines for arbitrators or mediators, but also by courts in their legal judgment process. The rules of natural justice are minimum standards of fairness and are implied obligations for decision makers. Some of the rules are as follows:

natural justice
Minimum standards
of fair decision making
imposed on persons
or bodies acting in a
judicial capacity.

- the right to a fair hearing;
- the right to a bias-free proceeding (e.g., a person adjudicating a dispute should have no personal interest in the outcome of the proceedings);
- the right to present the opposing argument;
- the right of legal representation;
- the right of timely notice of a hearing; and
- the right to a timely process (according to the principle, "Justice delayed is justice denied").

Court decisions have decreed that natural justice rules supersede organizational policies and regulations. This means that human resource managers have to make sure that organizational procedures follow the above rules.

Other Legal Challenges

This chapter has dealt mainly with legal discrimination and harassment issues. Of course, there are many other potential legal challenges, not all of which can be detailed here. The following are some of these relevant issues, most of which will be discussed in later chapters:

Department of Justice
Canada Labour Code
www.hrsdc.gc.ca/eng/lp/lo/
fll/part3/index-fll.shtml

- The *Canada Labour Code.* The *Industrial Disputes Investigation Act* of 1907 was modified and reenacted in 1971 as the *Canada Labour Code.* It regulates union certification, the right to organize, union prosecution, and mediation and arbitration procedures, all of which are discussed in more detail in Chapter 14. Provincial equivalents to the code are the *Employment* (or *Labour*) *Standards Acts.*
- **Dismissal.** According to common law, every employee has a contract with his or her employer, even if there is nothing in writing. An employee or employer can terminate an employment relationship by giving reasonable notice. An immediate dismissal is possible if an employee is compensated through appropriate severance pay. See Chapter 13.
- **Hours of work and overtime regulations.** The *Canada Labour Code* sets the standard workday at eight hours and the standard workweek at 40 hours, and overtime pay at one-and-a-half times the regular pay.

- **Minimum wages.** These are set by provincial and federal boards and discussed in Chapter 9.
- **Occupational health and safety.** The *Canada Labour Code* also regulates occupational health and safety issues, discussed in Chapter 12.
- **Weekly rest day.** The *Canada Labour Code* specifies that employees must be given at least one full day of rest during the week, preferably on Sunday.
- **Workplace Hazardous Material Information System (WHMIS).** WHMIS regulates the handling of dangerous material, discussed in Chapter 12.

These are some of the federal laws that have an impact on human resource managers. Most of them have their provincial equivalent. It is ultimately the human resource manager who is responsible for knowing and enforcing the law.

Strategic Implications of Legal Challenges

If there is one basic rule in human resource management, it is "Obey the law." The human resource manager must make sure all policies and rules take legal aspects into account (e.g., hiring and termination procedures, pay equity regulations, health and safety rules, and the handling of dangerous products). Given the current priority accorded employment equity, human resource managers also have to ensure that all long-range strategic plans that have an impact on staff and staffing follow employment equity requirements. Not doing so can be costly, as some of the examples given in this chapter have shown.

It is also desirable for a corporation to be perceived by the public as being a "good corporate citizen." One of the objectives of an organization is to project external equity, which determines its attractiveness as perceived by job applicants (discussed in Chapters 5, 6, and 9).

Following legal requirements also has implications for training. Managers and supervisors have to be familiar with the laws as they apply to human resource management. Sexual harassment is an issue that has cost business and government organizations large amounts of money in fines, court costs, and compensation to the victims. Unjust dismissal is another prominent issue. More and more employees dismissed for unsatisfactory performance or other reasons have challenged their dismissal, and management has had to prove that the decision was valid.

Finally, if a company plans to do business with the federal government, it had better make sure that all the requirements of the *Employment Equity Act* are fulfilled. This chapter has underlined the fact that the legal aspects of human resource management play a significant role in strategic planning and decision making.

SUMMARY

Government is a significant variable that strongly shapes the role of human resource management. It influences human resources through laws governing the employment relationship. The application of the Charter of Rights and Freedoms was awaited with high expectations from both labour and management. However, its impact on the human resource management field has been modest so far. Decisions of the Supreme Court of Canada affirmed the right to associate, but found that the right to bargain collectively and to strike is not a fundamental one, but rather is subject to government regulations. The Charter does not apply to picketing, which means that employers can ask for injunctions to restrict the number of pickets. The court upheld the right of governments to impose mandatory retirement, subject to limitations that are reasonable and justifiable.

The two sources of equal employment laws are the federal and provincial human rights statutes. The *Canadian Human Rights Act* of 1978 applies to federal government departments and agencies, Crown corporations, and businesses and industries under federal jurisdiction, such as banks, airlines, and railway companies. Areas not under federal jurisdiction are protected by provincial human rights laws. Each of Canada's provinces and territories has its own antidiscrimination laws that are broadly similar to the federal law.

To eliminate past discrimination and ensure future compliance, many organizations have developed employment equity programs. The programs identify areas of past and present discrimination, develop affirmative goals, and design remedial, active, and preventive programs.

To actively promote the employment of women, Aboriginal people, persons with a disability, members of a visible minority, the federal government introduced the *Employment Equity Act*, which requires employers with 100 employees or more under federal jurisdiction to develop plans and timetables for the employment of these groups. It also requires annual reports that have to be submitted to the Canadian Employment and Immigration Commission. Also, a new policy requires employers with 100 employees or more, and bidding for government contracts worth $200,000 or more, to comply with the above-mentioned guidelines.

TERMS FOR REVIEW

SELF-ASSESSMENT EXERCISE

How Knowledgeable Are You About Human Resource Legal Issues?

1. The Charter of Rights and Freedoms guarantees the right to bargain collectively to every employee.   **T   F**

2. The Bank of Nova Scotia falls under the jurisdiction of federal *Human Rights Act*.   **T   F**

3. Minimum height requirements are considered systemic discrimination.   **T   F**

4. The "duty to accommodate" means that an employer has to accommodate employees even if it involves "undue hardship."   **T   F**

5. Discrimination based on age is prohibited.   **T   F**

6. It is illegal to ask a candidate whether he or she has been convicted of a crime, unless it is job-related.   **T   F**

7. Drug dependency can be interpreted as a disability.   **T   F**

8. If a supervisor harasses an employee, the employer can be held liable.   **T   F**

9. Employment equity laws are designed especially to assist women in finding jobs.   **T   F**

10. Pay equity laws cover the public and private sector.   **T   F**

SCORING

If you answered statements 1, 4, 5, 9, 10 as False you get one point each. All other statements are True, resulting again in one point each.

Scores of 8–10: Very good! Congratulations on a job well done.

Scores 5–7: You made it, but barely. It would be advisable for you to go over the chapter text again.

Scores of less than 5: Are you sure you read the chapter?

REVIEW AND DISCUSSION QUESTIONS

1. Suppose that during your first job interview after graduation you are asked, "Why should a company have an employment equity program?" How would you respond?

2. List the major prohibitions of the *Canadian Human Rights Act*.

3. Since a human resource department is not a legal department, what role does it play in the area of equal employment law?

4. Suppose that you are told that your first duty as a human resource specialist is to construct an employment equity program. What would you do? What types of information would you seek?

5. What conditions would have to be met before you could bring suit against an employer who discriminated against you because of your sex?

6. A job applicant for a teller's job tells you that he has been convicted of cash theft, which he committed on his previous job, but that he had received a full pardon. The applicant appears to be the most qualified, but you are afraid that he may steal again. Is there a legal way to deny him the job?

7. Under the Charter of Rights and Freedoms, the Supreme Court of Canada has made a number of important decisions pertaining to union rights. What impact do these decisions have on management and unions?

8. A job candidate answers "yes" to the question of whether she is a smoker. She is well qualified, but you decide not to hire her. Does she have legal recourse?

CRITICAL THINKING QUESTIONS

1. If you are a supervisor in a bank and an employee demands to be allowed to miss work on Fridays for religious reasons, what would you do? Under what circumstances would you have to let the employee have time off? Under what circumstances could you prohibit it?

2. You have a job opening for a warehouse helper, a position that requires sometimes heavy lifting, up to 50 kilograms. A woman applies for the job and claims that she is able to do the work. She looks rather petite, and you are afraid that she may hurt herself. When you deny her the job, she threatens to complain to the Human Rights Commission. What do you do?

3. You are the human resource manager in a hospital. A nurse informs you, in confidence, that he has been diagnosed HIV-positive. Are you required to take action? What legal options do you have in dealing with this case?

4. Do you think more groups will receive special legislation to protect them from discrimination? Which groups might get additional protection?

ETHICS QUESTION

Reverse discrimination has, so far, not been a salient issue in Canada, especially since human rights legislation allows employers to use employment equity programs "to correct past wrongs"—that is, hire more protected groups, such as women, members of a visible minority, and Aboriginal people, ideally to more accurately reflect the distribution of protected groups in the community in the makeup of the organization's staff. Despite the legality of employment equity programs, the question has been raised as to whether it is ethical to choose a less qualified candidate over a better qualified one. Shouldn't the "best" candidate get the job? Please comment.

WEB RESEARCH EXERCISE

1. Government of Canada **http://canada.gc.ca**

   (a) Find the Canadian Human Rights Commission's view on the national AIDS policy and action taken. Give a summary.

   (b) How many agencies and government services that relate to human resources in a broad sense are you able to identify?

2. Canadian Human Rights Commission **www.chrc-ccdp.ca**

   (a) Find and summarize three cases decided last year in favour of employers and three cases decided in favour of employees.

   (b) What are the implications of the latest case decisions on gay rights for human resource managers?

3. Ontario Network for Human Rights **www.geocities. com/CapitolHill/6174**

   (a) Find a case that offers an example of a discrimination situation. Can you generalize from this case to other organizations?

   (b) Find an article on racism in companies and give a summary. What action would management have to take to combat racism in its organization?

4. Canadian Public Health Association **www.cpha.ca**

   (a) Go to the HIV/AIDS Information Centre and give a summary of the resources available to organizations to inform about AIDS.

5. Pay Equity Commission of Ontario **www.payequity.gov. on.ca/index_pec.html**

   (a) How is progress in the pay equity process monitored?

INCIDENT 4-1

Metropolitan Hospital's Employment Equity Needs

A large metropolitan hospital in Ontario recently developed an employment equity program. Under the program, the hospital agreed to promote two women into supervisory ranks for each man promoted. This practice was to continue until 40 to 45 percent of all supervisory jobs in the hospital were held by women.

The need for the first supervisory promotion occurred in the medical records department. The manager of medical records was one of the few female managers in the hospital. Nevertheless, she argued that Roy Biggs should become a medical records supervisor, as he was best qualified. Roy had two years of medical school and was a graduate of a medical records program at the local community college. The assistant director of hospital operations agreed that Roy should get the promotion. The equal employment compliance specialist in the human resource department argued that Kate VanDam should get the promotion, because of the employment equity program and because she had more seniority and experience in the department than Roy. The records manager, the assistant administrator, and the compliance specialist decided that the human resource manager should make the final decision.

1. What weight would you give to (a) Kate's seniority and experience, (b) Roy's superior training, (c) the recommendation of the records manager, and (d) the new Employment Equity Program?

2. What are the implications for the equity program if Roy gets the job? What are the implications for the employees presently taking job-related courses if Kate gets the promotion?

3. What decision would you make if you were the human resource manager?

⬤ EXERCISE 4-1

Carver Jewellery Company

Carver Jewellery Company Ltd. has the following workforce composition:

Job Classes	Male	Female	White	Black	Asian	Native Peoples
Executive	9	1	10	0	0	0
Management	71	9	79	0	1	0
Salaried/commission	43	31	74	0	0	0
Hourly paid	24	164	168	10	8	2

An analysis of the local labour force from which Carver draws its employees is as follows:

Male	Female	White	Black	Asian	Native Peoples
53%	47%	84%	8%	3%	5%

On the basis of this information:

1. Identify which job classes at Carver exhibit underutilization.

2. Identify which job classes at Carver exhibit concentration.

⬤ CASE STUDY   🍁   Maple Leaf Shoes Ltd.

Legal Challenges

Maple Leaf Shoes Ltd. is a medium-sized manufacturer of leather and vinyl shoes located in Wilmington, Ontario. It was started in 1969 and currently employs about 400 persons in its Wilmington plant and some 380 more in offices and warehouses throughout Canada and internationally. More information on the firm and its operations is provided at the end of Chapter 1.

Eva White was the operator of a leather-cutting machine. When Eva heard the bell ring, indicating the end of the

workday, she shut down her cutting machine and headed toward the women's locker room. It had been a long day and standing for eight hours on the machine didn't do her back any good. When she approached her locker, she saw that Rosetta Maurizio, who used the locker next to hers, was already there, changing into her street clothing. Eva and Rosetta had been hired together 10 months earlier. They had not known each other before, and, although they worked in different parts of the building, they kept each other company in the cafeteria during their lunch breaks. As her name indicated, Rosetta was of Italian descent. She had immigrated to Canada from Italy with her parents several years before, but her Italian accent was still quite noticeable.

Eva made some remarks about the hot day, when she noticed that Rosetta had red eyes, as if she had been crying. She asked Rosetta whether she had problems and whether she could be of any help. Rosetta seemed to be reluctant to talk, but when she finally responded she sounded quite agitated. The following dialogue developed:

Rosetta: As you know, I am one of the 2 women in the finishing section working with about 20 guys. They seem to enjoy making fun of me. It starts in the morning when I arrive. They call me risotto, which means "rice with gravy" in Italian, and give me some mock Italian greetings. They sometimes ask me whether I had a good time with my Italian boyfriend the night before and what we had done together. They also tell each other their own experiences with their girlfriends, each one bragging more than the other, but always so that I can hear it. I think they do it intentionally to embarrass me. I tend to blush and that seems to amuse them. When they tell a dirty joke, they ask me whether I understood it or whether I could tell one myself. Some of them have centrefolds pinned to the wall behind their machines. Today, one guy asked me whether I prefer Italian men over Canadian men; when I told him to let me alone and to mind his own business, he said that Italians are just braggarts, only good with their mouths. I was so angry that I had to go to the washroom to hide my tears. I am thinking of quitting this job; it is just getting too much.

Eva: Have you talked to Al, the supervisor, about that?

Rosetta: I don't want to talk to him about this. He's very friendly with the guys, and when they tell jokes when he's around, he laughs with them, which seems to encourage them. But they never tell him the types of jokes they tell me. I mentioned to him that I would like to find another job in the company. When he asked why, I told him that I had trouble breathing the vapour of the polish in the air. He said that he would find out whether there were other jobs open, but that was over a month ago. I do not dare to bring it up again.

Eva: You have to talk to him. Don't let it go on, otherwise you will suffer too much.

Rosetta: But when I complain to him and he talks to the guys, they will probably make it worse for me. No, I'd rather not.

Eva: Should I talk to him?

Rosetta: No, no, please don't. I will think about it.

Next morning, when they met in the changeroom again, Eva encouraged Rosetta once more to talk to her supervisor. She even offered to come with her if she wanted some support. Rosetta promised to do something, but declined Eva's offer.

In the evening, Eva noticed that Rosetta's locker was empty. The next day she asked the personnel department about what had happened to Rosetta and was told that Rosetta had quit, citing family reasons.

Eva was upset. She felt that Rosetta had been treated unfairly and that she should not be forced to quit her job because some coworkers had made her life miserable.

She decided to do something. She asked her own supervisor for a break and went over to the finishing workroom to talk to Al.

Al was sitting in his office when Eva walked in. He looked surprised when he saw her. He knew that she worked in the company, but had never talked to her. He offered her a seat and asked what he could do for her, and added quickly that if she was looking for a job in his division he had one opening, due to a recent vacancy.

Eva: That's not the reason I want to talk to you, although it is related to that vacant job. What happened to Rosetta?

He seemed to be taken aback by her aggressive tone, but kept his cool and answered: "Rosetta quit. She didn't like the job anymore."

Eva: Was that all she said?

Al: Well, she said that she didn't like to work in a place that made her feel uncomfortable. She mentioned that the guys in the finishing room were telling dirty jokes she didn't like and that they made fun of her. Well, I told her that I have been supervisor for 10 years in this division, and that I never heard an outright dirty joke, just some good old-fashioned fun jokes, nothing to be shocked by. I think she was just too sensitive. The guys just want to have a good time. The job is boring and they need something to distract them. They are not mean guys.

Eva: But there was more to this than just telling jokes. Rosetta told me that the guys also made fun of her Italian background.

Al: I think it's ridiculous to make that an issue. We have Ukrainians, Germans, British, Chinese, Indians, and some others. There has never been a problem. And as far as making fun of her, we all make fun of each other, but that's good-natured. I think she takes herself too seriously. My philosophy is that we have to be able to laugh at ourselves now and then. Life is tough enough.

Eva: But she did feel uncomfortable. She even cried because of what she went through. Don't you think that you have to accept some responsibility for that? I think that she has been treated unfairly and that you should have made an attempt to help her.

Al: I resent being called unfair. I think that I'm a very fair supervisor. We have the lowest number of grievances in our division, so I think that such a complaint is totally unjustified. She left of her own will, and I will not run after her.

Eva, angrily: Well, I don't think that you have heard the last of that.

Eva left, determined to take some action on behalf of Rosetta and her other female coworkers.

Discussion Questions

1. Is there a case of sexual harassment in this situation or is it only fun?

2. If you were Eva, what would—and could—you do? What are the options? What is the probability of success of each option?

3. What are Al's responsibilities in this instance? Did he carry them out well? Why or why not?

⊙ CASE STUDY   CPIB   Canadian Pacific and International Bank

Mary Keddy, senior vice-president of human resources, had a problem on her hands, literally, in form of a letter from the Canadian Human Rights Commission. In 2000, the Commission had audited the bank, and this letter was its report. While the Commission lauded the bank's employment equity program for women as exemplary, the audit report pointed out that the bank was deficient in its objectives in employing Aboriginal people and persons with a disability. Ideally, the makeup of an organization's employee base reflects the makeup of the community at large, but Mary had to admit that the employee makeup of the CPIB did not even come close to the Canadian population mix. While Aboriginal people made up 10.3 percent of Canada's citizens, according to the 1996 Census, CPIB's employee mix showed only a 3.2 percent representation. Persons with a disability made up 6.5 percent of the population; CPIB's mix, however, had only 0.7 percent. The report asked specifically to establish an employment equity program with the objective of reaching 50 percent of the benchmark consensus data within two years, and a 90 percent compliance after five years.

Mary felt somewhat frustrated. In previous years, the bank had been criticized for its apparent "glass ceiling," and Mary had concentrated her efforts on correcting this problem and had been very successful at resolving it, regrettably at the expense of the objectives to increase the representation of Aboriginal people and persons with a disability. Now this had to be the new priority. She knew that it was quite a challenge, especially with the hiring of Aboriginal people. In every hiring advertisement, the bank encouraged Aboriginal people and persons with a disability to apply, but very few actually did, particularly Aboriginal people. She wondered what the bank had to do to solve this problem. She had to come up with more effective measures, that was obvious, but with what? The turnover rate was another issue. While persons with a disability had the lowest turnover of all groups, Aboriginal people had triple the turnover rate of the average CPIB employee. What was the explanation for that, Mary wondered?

Discussion Questions

You are a human resource consultant. What advice will you give Mary? What measures should the bank take to increase (a) the applications of Aboriginal people and persons with a disability, (b) the actual hiring of such candidates, and (c) their survival in the organization?

Recruitment

In this ever-changing, global, technologically demanding business environment, sourcing and retaining talent becomes the competitive battleground. Just as sports teams recruit aggressively for best athletes, business organizations in the future will compete aggressively for the best talent ... Successful firms will be those most adept at attracting, developing and retaining individuals with the skills, perspective and experience sufficient to drive a global business.

Dave Ulrich[1]

CHAPTER OBJECTIVES

After studying this chapter, you should be able to:

➡ *Explain* the strategic importance of the recruitment function.

➡ *Discuss* the constraints facing a typical recruiter.

➡ *Identify* the appropriate recruiting methods for different types of jobs.

➡ *List* the critical elements in a job application form.

➡ *List* key measures for evaluating the effectiveness of the recruitment function.

CHAPTER 5

Finding new employees for the organization is a continuing challenge for most human resource departments. Sometimes the need for new workers is known well in advance because of detailed human resource plans. At other times, the human resource department is faced with urgent requests for replacements that must be filled as quickly as possible. In either case, finding qualified applicants is a key activity:

> Shirley Dodd was a junior mechanical engineer for Ontario Electronics when she quit to work for a competitor. Her resignation created a problem for the head of the mechanical engineering department, Sid Benson. As he expressed it, "She was doing an important job of developing the mechanical tolerances for our new electronic scale. It was all theoretical work, but it was going to save three months' worth of product development time. We must have a bright junior engineer to complete her work. I hope someone can be recruited."

recruitment
The process of finding and attracting capable applicants to apply for employment.

selection
The identification of candidates from a pool of recruits who best meet job requirements, using tools such as application blanks, tests, and interviews.

Recruitment is the process of finding and attracting capable individuals to apply for employment. The process begins when new recruits are sought and ends when their applications are submitted. The result is a pool of job seekers. **Selection** involves the identification of candidates from this pool of applicants who best meet job requirements using tools such as application blanks, tests, and interviews. The selection process begins with a review of the applicant pool and ends with job offer to the successful candidate(s).

Responsibility for recruitment usually belongs to the human resource department. This responsibility is important because the quality of an organization's human resources depends on the quality of its recruits. Since large organizations recruit almost continuously, their human resource departments use specialists for the activity. These specialists are called *recruiters.*

As Figure 5-1 illustrates, recruitment can be done only after the identification of job openings through human resource planning or requests by managers. As mentioned in Chapter 3, advance knowledge of job openings allows the recruiter to be proactive.

After identifying openings, the recruiter learns what each job requires by reviewing job analysis information, particularly the job descriptions and specifications. This information tells the recruiter the characteristics of both the jobs and the future job incumbents. When the job analysis information appears outdated or superficial, recruiters can learn more about a job's requirements from the

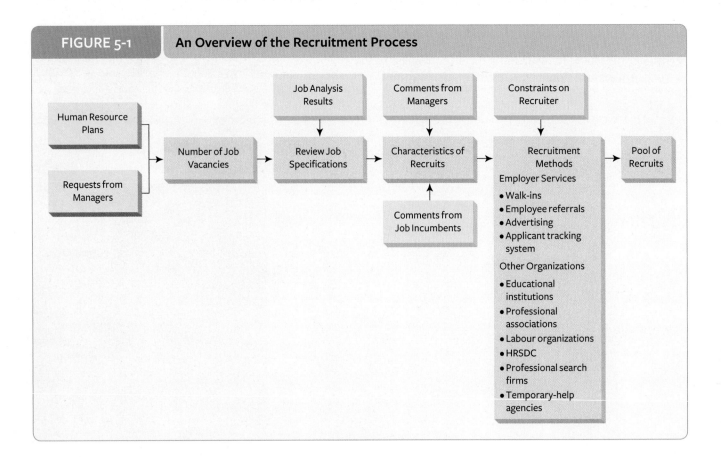

FIGURE 5-1   **An Overview of the Recruitment Process**

requesting manager. The job's requirements influence the recruiter's methods of finding satisfactory applicants.

Almost all recruiters face a variety of constraints. Some of these constraints may be imposed by the employer, while others may be environmental, such as a shortage of highly skilled employees in the local labour market.

Typically, most recruiters use more than one recruitment method to find suitable candidates for vacant job positions. Recruitment methods include school, college, and university campus visits; recruitment advertisements; contacts with professional and labour associations; and use of government agencies such as Human Resources and Skills Development Canada. Sometimes, to attract high-quality applicants, a recruiter may have to use unconventional procedures, as the following example shows:

> A large insurance firm routinely had to fill approximately 1,000 full-time, part-time, and temporary jobs in its head office each year. While many of the jobs were temporary or part-time, they required specific skills on the part of potential job incumbents. To attract high-quality recruits, the human resource director encouraged the recruiters to "sell" the company to graduates of local schools, community colleges, and training agencies for minorities and the physically challenged. In addition, she also joined forces with other local groups to lobby for increased governmental aid to local schools to enhance business education. Further, the human resource director extensively used the company's in-house training program to train marginally qualified applicants and make them competent to handle various responsibilities.

Recruitment involves far more than just getting people to apply for jobs, and success in recruitment is not simply measured by the number of applications received. The right type of applicants is far more important than the number of applicants. Many successful organizations have recognized the strategic importance of recruitment and made it an integral part of their overall human resource management strategy. The following section discusses the strategic importance of the recruitment function.

STRATEGIC IMPORTANCE OF RECRUITMENT FUNCTION

In the recent past, recruitment has gained considerable attention among practitioners as well as in the media. A variety of factors, including an aging population, which results in a large number of retirements, stiff competition for talents, and rising compensation and aspiration levels of new entrants, has been found to make the task of recruiting very challenging—a challenge that is likely to become even greater in the next decade when many baby boomers retire.[2] Front-line positions are the easiest to fill, while executives, skilled trades, and high-tech jobs are the toughest to recruit for. Even in the current recessionary settings, some jobs such as physicians, nurses, and radiologists continue to be hard to fill in several parts of Canada.

Today, recruitment of human resources has a significant impact on the organization and its strategic success. The more important HR and organizational activities affected by recruitment are examined below.

Gaining Competitive Advantage from Human Capital

Successful firms recognize that today, more than ever before, human capital spells the difference between success and failure. Despite the existence of state-of-the-art human resource systems and procedures, poorly qualified and motivated recruits often prove extremely costly to firms. In contrast, in today's global knowledge economy, the presence of highly skilled and motivated workers can be a real **competitive advantage**.

competitive advantage
A competitive advantage exists when the firm is able to deliver the same value and benefits as competitors but at a lower cost (cost advantage), or deliver more benefits or unique value that exceed those of competing products (differentiation advantage).

> Experience working in a foreign country is considered a major asset by many employers. As one executive recruiter noted, "an international assignment on your CV gives you an edge over competitors because it shows breadth of experience and adaptability."[3] In one survey[4] of 6,000 employees, 75 percent of the respondents considered foreign work credentials "essential" or "extremely useful." However, managers with foreign country experience are also hard to come by. Only about 37 percent of 2,700 executives surveyed stated that they would consider taking an overseas assignment. This makes people with foreign work experience extremely valuable, which in turn makes recruiting them difficult.

Further, if applicants lack the necessary skills and/or aptitudes, considerable additional resources may have to be invested into selection, training and development, employee communication systems, and employee relations practices. A small pool of recruits also poses a major challenge to the selection procedure (which will be discussed in the next chapter).

Reaping the Benefits of Diversity Management

Today, many Canadian firms recognize the vitality and competitive advantage that often accompanies a diverse workforce (see Chapter 14 for a discussion on leveraging diversity). Further, as discussed in Chapter 4, if the firm's workforce does not reflect the larger labour market composition, the firm may be asked to pursue an employment equity program to correct imbalances. Progressive employers monitor their environments continuously and adjust their recruitment strategies to deal with the emerging trends in a proactive manner:

> Maple Leaf Electronics, a software manufacturer, has 50 computer programmers on its payroll, of which 45 are men. Recently, the Statistics Canada figures on the local labour market indicated that, in the larger labour market, about 35 percent of the programmers were women. The company's human resource manager realized that the current 10 percent utilization rate of women was far below the societal figure and decided to actively seek out women when recruiting.

Hiring from a larger, diverse pool of candidates offers a greater choice of job applicants to the firm. A diverse workforce also offers greater flexibility and additional capabilities in some instances. It reflects an organization's commitment to broader social goals and projects a better image of the firm to clients and other constituents.

Focusing on Employee Development

When recruiting (especially for middle- and upper-level jobs), a firm has a choice: it can either develop and promote internal candidates or hire from outside. The strategic choice of internal versus external recruitment has profound implications for an organization.

The advantage of hiring skilled employees from outside is that they already possess the necessary skills to begin work immediately and little training may be needed. However, this must be weighed against the fact that current employees, especially in smaller organizations, know a lot more about the organization, its strategy, and its culture. This means that in the latter instance employees do not have to go through the learning process. A conscious effort to train and develop employees to assume higher job positions in the future also acts as a strong motivator for many employees. The amount of money it might take to attract high-calibre employees from outside is usually higher.

Figure 5-2 lists some of the advantages and weaknesses of each strategy. Needless to say, the specific strategy chosen by the firm has major implications for recruitment and salary costs, employee morale, and organizational innovation and change.

NCR Corporation
www.ncr.com

Investing Resources into Recruitment

The decision about the total recruitment budget affects the quality of recruits and the overall effectiveness of recruitment activity. It is important to note that the costs of recruitment are not simply the hiring costs (such as the costs of advertisement, recruiter's travel, and so on). Often the costs of a bad hire may not be translatable into monetary terms as there is no accurate way of measuring the number of lost customers or resources due to delays and inefficient handling of a situation.[5] Further, inappropriate recruits often leave the organization, causing significant additional costs to hire and train replacements. Often such costs are not apparent. However, some organizations, such as NCR Corporation, have recognized the importance of the recruitment function and have found innovative ways to recruit qualified persons and reduce recruitment costs:

> NCR Corporation, which produces point-of-sale terminals, automated teller machines, cheque-processing systems, barcode scanners, and one of the largest providers of IT maintenance support services, operates in a highly turbulent industry. It maintains its competitive edge by hiring employees at the entry level, retaining them, and promoting from within. In the past, its recruitment program, "Project 6K," used standardized procedures to recruit the best university students for entry-level positions. Universities and colleges are rated on a four-point scale ("1" being the best). In the number 1 category, students with a GPA of 3.2 or higher will be contacted; at a school rated in the number 4 category, only students with a GPA of 3.4 or better would be considered

FIGURE 5-2	Internal versus External Recruiting

Internal Recruiting

Advantages

- Employee is familiar with the organization and its culture
- Lower recruitment costs.
- Employee is "known" to the firm; this improves the organization's ability to predict the person's success in the new job.
- Improves workforce morale and motivation.

Weaknesses

- Internal rivalry and competition for higher positions; can reduce interpersonal and interdepartmental cooperation.
- No "new blood" is brought into the system, which can prevent creative solutions from emerging.
- Poor morale (leading to possible turnover) of employees who were not promoted.

External Recruiting

Advantages

- Organization is able to acquire skills or knowledge that may not be currently available within.
- Newer ideas and novel ways of solving problems may emerge.

Weaknesses

- Newcomers may not fit in with the organization and into its present culture.
- Newcomers take a longer time to learn about the organization's culture, policies, and practices.
- Usually, hiring from the outside is more expensive.
- Lowered morale and motivation levels of current employees who don't see any career growth possibilities within the firm.

by the recruiter. The company believes that such a focused recruitment effort helps it to secure high-quality recruits while minimizing the recruitment costs. The company actively seeks a competitive advantage through its employees by hiring top people and creating a work climate where they are highly productive.

Key issues in the context of evaluating the effectiveness of the recruitment function and its contribution to organizational success will be discussed in a later section in this chapter. But first, it is important to recognize the several constraints a recruiter faces.

CONSTRAINTS ON RECRUITMENT

A successful recruiter must be sensitive to the constraints on the recruitment process. These limits arise from the organization, the recruiter, and the external environment. Although the emphasis may vary from situation to situation, the following list includes the most common constraints:

- organizational policies
- human resource plans
- diversity management
- recruiter habits
- environmental conditions
- job requirements
- costs
- inducements

organizational policies
Internal policies that affect recruitment, such as "promote-from-within" policies.

Organizational Policies

Organizational policies can constrain the recruiter. Policies seek to achieve uniformity, economies, public relations benefits, and other objectives unrelated to recruiting. Four policies that have implications for recruitment are highlighted below.

1. Promote-from-Within Policies

As already pointed out, promote-from-within policies are formulated to give present employees the first opportunity for job openings and facilitate their career growth. These policies are widespread. Promoting from within aids employee morale, attracts recruits looking for jobs with a future, and helps retain present employees. Although these policies reduce the flow of new people and ideas into different levels of the organization, the alternative is to pass over employees in favour of outsiders.

> Sid Benson, head of mechanical engineering at Ontario Electronics, requested that the human resource department find two new junior engineers. Charles Shaw, a recruiter, reviewed the job's requirements and discovered that applicants should have a basic understanding of mechanical engineering concepts. No experience was required. Charles decided to seek applicants from among the graduating class of a small engineer-oriented university in the area. Two technicians in the firm who were studying engineering at night school were disheartened to hear about the external search. They expressed their unhappiness to the HR manager. Charles was then instructed to search for internal talents before going outside.

Bypassing current employees can lead to employee dissatisfaction and turnover. On the other hand, promoting a positive organizational culture encourages people to join and stay with a firm.[6] Employees are likely to be loyal to their employer only if they believe the organization values them:

> A survey of Canadian workers found that almost three-quarters of all respondents intended to stay with their organization for "several years." However, the same survey found that there is an underlying mood of ambivalence in the workforce. Less than 50 percent were willing to recommend their organizations as one of the best places to work. Almost 30 percent would leave for a pay hike of 10 percent or less.[7]

The "employee goal" discussed in Chapter 1 also necessitates the human resource manager to recognize and foster employee aspirations at the workplace.

2. Compensation Policies

A common constraint faced by recruiters is pay policies. Organizations with human resource departments usually establish pay ranges for different jobs. Recruiters seldom have the authority to exceed stated pay ranges:

> If Charles Shaw in Ontario Electronics decides to recruit externally, the pay range will influence the job seeker's desire to become a serious applicant. For example, when the market rate for junior engineers is $3,500 to $3,800 per month, satisfactory applicants will be few if Charles can offer only $3,000 to $3,200 per month.

3. Employment Status Policies

Some companies have policies restricting the hiring of part-time and temporary employees. Although there is growing interest in hiring these types of workers, several unionized settings have limitations against hiring part-time, temporary, and contract workers, which can cause recruiters to reject all but those seeking full-time work. Likewise, policies against hiring employees who "moonlight" by having second jobs also inhibit recruiters. Prohibitions against holding extra jobs are intended to ensure a rested workforce.

4. International Hiring Policies

Policies in some countries, including Canada, may also require foreign job openings to be staffed with local citizens. The use of foreign nationals, however, does reduce relocation expenses, lessen the likelihood of nationalization, and if top jobs are held by local citizens, minimize charges of economic exploitation. Moreover, unlike relocated employees, foreign nationals are more apt to be involved in the local community and understand local customs and business practices.

Human Resource Plans

The **human resource plan** is another factor recruiters consider. Through skills inventories and promotion ladders, the plan outlines which jobs should be filled by recruiting and which ones should be filled internally. The plan helps recruiters because it summarizes future recruiting needs. This foresight can lead to economies in recruiting:

> At Ontario Electronics, Charles Shaw checked the human resource plan before recruiting junior mechanical engineers. The plan indicated a projected need for three junior electrical engineers and one more mechanical engineer (in addition to the two current vacancies) during the next four months. The two internal candidates were hired for two of the junior positions. For the other positions, there were no internal candidates available. Charles decided to recruit electrical engineering candidates at the same time when he was looking for the remaining junior mechanical engineer. If advertisements were to be placed in the university newspaper, there would be no additional cost for seeking both types of engineers. Travel costs, advertising costs, and the time devoted to a second recruiting trip would be saved.

human resource plan
A firm's overall plan to fill existing and future vacancies, including decisions on whether to fill internally or to recruit from outside.

Diversity Management Programs

Where **diversity management** and employment equity programs exist, recruitment must also take these programs into account.

> Ontario Electronics never pursued policies that intentionally discriminated against any group. But over the years, its sources of engineering recruits had been mostly white males who attended the small local university. In the recent past, the firm had initiated a voluntary diversity management program that focused on bringing more women and minorities into its technical and managerial cadres. To fulfill the intent of the diversity management program, Charles decided to recruit engineering technicians at a large metropolitan university, where female recruits were more likely to be found.

As we saw in Chapter 4, employers cannot discriminate against people with physical disabilities unless the disability would prevent the person from doing the job after reasonable accommodation by the employer. Proactive employers such as Pizza Hut use innovative recruitment programs to tap the skills of a diverse workforce:

> Realizing that there are thousands of physically challenged individuals who seek work, Pizza Hut actively started to recruit entry-level personnel among this group, even among those with mental disabilities.[8]

diversity management
Recognizing differences among employees belonging to heterogeneous groups and creating a work environment in which members of diverse groups feel comfortable.

Recruiter Habits

A recruiter's past success can lead to habits. Admittedly, habits can eliminate time-consuming deliberations that reach the same answers. However, **recruiter habits** may also perpetuate past mistakes or obscure more effective alternatives. So although recruiters need positive and negative feedback, they must guard against self-imposed constraints.

> Consider again the recruitment of the junior engineer at Ontario Electronics. Suppose that the engineering department expresses satisfaction with recruits from the nearby university. Such positive feedback encourages recruiters to make a habit of using this source for beginning engineers. Since all these engineers have a similar curriculum, they may also share strengths and weaknesses. As a result, the engineering department may suffer because of the educational uniformity of new recruits.

recruiter habits
The propensity of a recruiter to rely on methods, systems, or behaviours that led to past recruitment success.

Environmental Conditions

External conditions strongly influence recruitment.

> Faced with a labour market that had a severe shortage of experienced drivers, Coastal Pacific Xpress Inc., a Surrey, B.C.–based long-haul trucking firm, increased the pay of its owner-operators by 45 percent in four months to attract more recruits.[9]

Changes in the labour market and the challenges mentioned in Chapter 2 affect recruiting. The unemployment rate, the pace of the economy, spot shortages in specific skills, projections of the labour force by Statistics Canada, labour laws, and the recruiting activities of other employers—all of these factors affect the recruiter's efforts.

> A significant number of baby boomers are planning to retire in the next decade, which may mean an acute shortage of employees in a variety of occupations. Over the next 10 years, permanent retirements from the labour market are expected to climb from 250,000 in 2001 to 430,000 by 2014, while the retirement rate out of total employment, which is currently at 1.7 percent, will rise to 2.4 percent. By 2014, 75 percent of job openings are expected to be accounted for by retirements.[10]

Although these factors are considered in human resource planning, the economic environment can change quickly after the plan is finalized. To be sure that the plan's economic assumptions remain valid, recruiters can check three fast-changing measures.

**Statistics Canada
Employment by industry**
www40.statcan.ca/l01/
cst01/labr67a.htm

www.cic.gc.ca/english/work/
special-tech.asp

www12.statcan.ca/english/
census01/Products/
Analytic/companion/paid/
subprovs.cfm

1. Leading Economic Indicators

Statistics Canada routinely publishes the direction of the leading indicators. The economic indices suggest the future course of the national economy. If these indices signal a sudden downturn in the economy, recruiting plans may have to be modified. Other agencies such as Human Resources and Skills Development Canada, Industry Canada, the World Bank, and the International Monetary Fund also publish information that is of great interest to national and international organizations.

2. Predicted Versus Actual Sales

Since human resource plans are partially based upon the firm's predicted sales, variations between actual and predicted sales may indicate that these plans also are inaccurate. Thus, recruiting efforts may need to be changed accordingly.

3. Employment Statistics

Statistics Canada routinely reports various employment statistics. Periodically, it produces reports on the state of employment in different industry sectors.

Employers can also monitor competition for specific job groups by looking at the want ads in major newspapers. For clerical and production workers, who are usually recruited on a local basis, the human resource department may want to create its own want ads index to monitor local changes in want ads.

Organizations worldwide are likely to face a spiralling employee attrition rate over the next decade or so.

> A survey of more than one million workers in 50 countries indicated that one third of the global workforce will change employers in two years. Sixty-four percent of employees who reported being uncertain or not committed to staying with their employer actually left the company within five years.[11]

Tighter competition for applicants may require more vigorous recruiting. When business conditions decline, an opposite approach is called for, as the following example illustrates:

> As a major recreation centre was opening in Quebec, the leading economic indicators dropped. Although the human resource plan called for recruiting 100 workers a week for the first month, the employment manager set a revised target of 75. Lower recruiting and employment levels helped establish a profitable operation even though first-year admissions fell below the projections used in the human resource plan.

Job Requirements

Of course, the requirements of each job are a constraint. Highly specialized workers, for example, are more difficult to find than unskilled ones. Recruiters learn of a job's demands from the requesting manager's comments and job analysis information. Job analysis information is especially useful because it reveals the important characteristics of the job and applicants. Knowledge of a job's requirements allows the recruiter to choose the best way to find recruits, given the constraints under which the recruiter must operate.

"Find the best and most experienced applicant you can" is often a constraint that is imposed on recruiters as though it were a job requirement. At first, this demand seems reasonable: all managers want to have the best and most experienced people working for them. But several potential problems exist with this innocent-sounding request. One problem in seeking out the "best and most experienced" applicant is cost. People with greater experience usually command higher salaries than less experienced people. If a high level of experience is not truly necessary, the recruit may become bored soon after being hired. Moreover, if the human resource department cannot show that a high degree of experience is needed, then experience may be an artificial requirement that discriminates against some applicants. Another point about experience is worth remembering: for some people in some jobs, 10 years of experience is another way of saying 1 year of experience repeated 10 times. Someone with 10 years of experience may not be any better qualified than an applicant with only 1 year.

Costs

costs
Expenses related to attracting recruits.

Like all other members of an organization, recruiters must also operate within budgets. The **costs** of identifying and attracting recruits are an ever-present limitation:

> Manitoba Engineering Company Ltd. found that the average cost of recruiting engineers in the company was more than $3,300 per hire. To hire senior engineers and managers, the cost was even higher. To fill a $70,000-a-year position, the company often had to pay $5,000 to $6,000 to search firms. To monitor and control costs, the human resource manager of the company was asked to assess the effectiveness of the company's recruitment programs and costs of recruitment under alternative recruitment methods.

Careful human resource planning and forethought by recruiters can minimize these expenses. For example, recruiting for several job openings simultaneously may reduce the cost per recruit. Of course, a better solution would be to take action to reduce employee turnover, thus minimizing the need for recruiting. Proactive human resource management actions go far in achieving this objective.

Inducements

inducements
Monetary, nonmonetary, or even intangible incentives used by a firm to attract recruits.

The recruiter is very much like a marketer—he or she is selling the company as a potential place of work to all eligible recruits. As with any marketing effort, **inducements** may be necessary to stimulate a potential recruit's interest. The growing global marketplace means that workers are also mobile, and attracting them may require unconventional incentives or inducements:

> KFC in Japan developed a unique strategy for attracting qualified employees by offering them a trip to Hawaii. This enabled the company to meet local competition and competition from other international organizations for Japanese workers effectively.[12]

Not all inducements are monetary or even tangible.

> A department of an Atlantic Canadian university takes all its potential faculty recruits to the scenic areas for a day's car tour in an effort to "sell" the location (and through that the institution). Faced with severe constraints on the compensation package it can offer, the department decided to use its "intangible" assets to assist in its recruitment and selection process.

Flextime, high quality of life, etc., can be potential selling points for a firm; in some instances, certain items (such as flextime) can also be a constraint if all major employers are using them. In such an instance, a firm needs to meet the prevailing standards. Inducements may be a response to overcoming other limitations faced by the recruiter:

> The fast food industry, which employs a large percentage of young workers, typically experiences high employee turnover. To reduce turnover and thereby its recruiting costs, one fast food chain introduced an educational assistance program. Under the program, an employee could accrue up to $2,000 worth of tuition credits over a two-year period. Result? Turnover among participants in the program is a mere 22 percent compared to a 97 percent turnover of those who were not part of the plan. It significantly reduced the firm's recruitment efforts and costs.

More recently, several employers have been using nontraditional benefits to attract and retain their employees:

> Some of the benefits offered today include fitness centre subsidies, reimbursement of professional membership fees and course fees, on-site vaccination programs, employee mental health insurance, retiree health care benefits, financial planning assistance, and on-site parking.[13]

The key in all cases is to understand the needs and motivations of the target recruits and offer a set of inducements that appeal to them. Not all inducements have to be monetary.

RBC Financial Group finds that its focus on workplace diversity has paid rich dividends when recruiting employees. It found that when job candidates come in for interviews at RBC, they often ask about the bank's diversity initiatives and whether resource groups exist. The fact that the bank has four resource groups is a big drawing factor when recruiting. The bank's Reach focuses on people with disabilities; Royal Eagles focuses on the needs of the Aboriginals; Pride is for lesbian, gay, bi-sexual, and transgendered people; and Mosaic helps members of visible minorities and new Canadians to integrate into the workforce and the larger community.[14]

RECRUITMENT METHODS

Traditionally, recruiters and applicants have contacted each other using a few popular methods. In the past, applying directly (by sending a résumé) to the employer was the most popular job search method in this country. However, today, applicants tend to use several methods in their search for employment. Research evidence also indicates that persons with higher educational qualifications tend to use more methods to find a job than those with lower educational levels.[15]

Walk-ins and Write-ins

walk-ins/write-ins
Job seekers who arrive at or write to the human resource department in search of a job without prior referrals and not in response to a specific ad.

Walk-ins are job seekers who arrive at the human resource department in search of a job. **Write-ins** are those who send a written inquiry. With the emergence of the Internet, it is common for applicants today to record the information at the Web sites of employers. Indeed, today, a significant percentage of human resource managers prefer to receive résumés via email because of the ease of storage and retrieval.[16] Whatever the format used, in most cases, the applicant is asked to complete an application form describing his or her training, experience, interests, and skills. Suitable applications are kept in an active file until an appropriate opening occurs or until the application is too old to be considered valid—usually six months. Larger firms relate information collected like this into their overall human resource information systems. Using scanners, recruiters can store résumés on databases for fast, easy access using a few key words:

Organizations such as MCI Telecommunications and Disneyland Resorts use computer scanning to take advantage of the large number of applications they receive (apart from Internet queries). When résumés arrive at either MCI or Disneyland Resorts, clerks scan the résumés into a computer database. Later, recruiters can search the database for candidates with specific qualifications. When the hiring manager needs to fill a position, he or she tells the recruiter the job requirements and applicant profile. The recruiter then searches the database using key words. The computer displays the number of résumés that meet the required criteria. If the number is too large or too small, the recruiter can change the required qualifications (for example, if a search for candidates who have had 10 years of work experience yields only 5 résumés, the recruiter can change the search criterion to 7 years of experience). Once the program finds a manageable number of applicants, the recruiter can view the résumés or résumé summaries online and eliminate any that are not appropriate. Then, the recruiter can print selected résumés.[17]

Employee Referrals

employee referrals
Recommendations by present employees to the recruiter about possible job applications for a position.

Present employees may refer job seekers to the human resource department. **Employee referrals** have several unique advantages. First, employees with hard-to-find job skills may know others who do the same work.

Faced with an acute shortage of software programmers and information technologists in some geographical areas in the recent past, several high-tech firms requested that their present employees recommend professional colleagues and classmates for job openings in the firm. Several employers, such as McDonald's, have paid a referral bonus to employees who recommend qualified candidates.[18]

Second, new recruits already know something about the organization from those employees who referred them. Thus, referred applicants may be more strongly attracted to the organization than are walk-ins. Third, employees tend to refer friends whom they identified through personal networking. These persons are likely to have similar work habits and work attitudes. Even if work values are different, these candidates may have a strong desire to work hard so that they do not let down the person who recommended them.

Employee referrals are an excellent and legal recruitment technique. However, recruiters must be careful that this method does not intentionally or unintentionally discriminate. The major problem with this recruiting method is that it tends to maintain the racial, religious, sex, and other features of the employer's workforce. Such results can be viewed as discriminatory.

The Canadian Forces have organized recruitment campaigns designed to attract more women to military careers. Should there be limitations as to choice—for example, wanting to be a submariner?

CP/Andrew Vaughan.

Advertising

Advertising is another effective method of seeking recruits. Since it can reach a wider audience than employee referrals or unsolicited walk-ins, many recruiters use it as a key part of their efforts.

Want ads describe the job and the benefits, identify the employer, and tell those who are interested how to apply. They are the most familiar form of employment advertising. For highly specialized recruits, ads may be placed in professional journals or out-of-town newspapers located in areas with high concentrations of the desired skills.

For example, recruiters in finance often advertise in Vancouver, Toronto, Montreal, and Halifax newspapers because these cities are major banking centres.

Want ads have some severe drawbacks. They may lead to thousands of job seekers for one popular job opening. Often the ideal recruits are already employed and not reading want ads. Finally, secretly advertising for a recruit to replace a current employee cannot easily be done with traditional want ads.

These problems are avoided with **blind ads**. A blind ad is a want ad that does not identify the employer. Interested applicants are told to send their résumé to a box number at the post office or to the newspaper.

The **résumé** (or *curriculum vitae*), which is a brief summary of the applicant's background, is then forwarded to the employer. These ads allow the opening to remain confidential, prevent countless telephone inquiries, and avoid the public relations problem of disappointed recruits.

want ads
Advertisements in a newspaper, magazine, etc. that solicit job applicants for a position.

blind ads
Want ads that do not identify the employer.

résumé
A brief listing of an applicant's work experience, education, personal data, and other information relevant to the job.

Often, a résumé is the first piece of information about a job candidate that an employer will see. In the case of organizations that do not have formal job application forms, it is the only information that an employer will have. In the case of unsolicited applications, it is the information source that a recruiter will use in deciding whether the applicant is worthy of further consideration. This makes the résumé a vital part of a job search for any person. Some dos and don'ts in the context of preparing a résumé are listed in Figure 5-3.

FIGURE 5-3	Some Dos and Don'ts in Preparing a Résumé

You need to prepare both a print and an electronic version of your résumé. Most of the comments below apply to both versions, although some of the stylistic matters are more important for the print version.

- *Presentation style:* To distinguish your résumé from the dozens, if not hundreds, of résumés that a recruiter gets, it must look sharp and dynamic. Your résumé should use modern-looking and easily readable fonts, such as Bookman, Helvetica, Times Roman, Courier, or Arial, printed on conservatively coloured paper, such as white, ivory, or light grey. A little creativity, such as using light ivory paper with a darker ivory border, can help your résumé stand out from others. Do not use a point size smaller than 10, and do not overuse boldface or italic. A high-quality 20-bond-weight paper that has some cotton content normally creates a better first impression on the reader than the typical duplicating or printer paper.

- *Content:* There should be a natural logical progression in your résumé. Rather than listing all job responsibilities you held in the past, your résumé should focus on the relevant ones for each job position you are applying for. You should not provide job descriptions; rather, you should focus on your on-the-job accomplishments and the contributions you made to your past employers. Thus, stating that *"this position was responsible for the marketing and distribution of toys"* is unlikely to convey much to a prospective employer; however, stating that you *"planned and executed marketing of Toy XYZ in Winnipeg, thus increasing the overall market share of the product by 2 percent"* is likely to impress a future employer, especially if accompanied by other relevant details of the project. Generalizations are rarely impressive. *"I had significant managerial responsibilities"* does not tell the reader anything about your real responsibilities. However, *"I managed a team of five that was in charge of total quality of process K; during the time I was in charge, the number of complaints about product quality went down by 12 percent compared to the previous period"* tells the reader more about the nature and extent of your responsibility. Specific numbers, percentages, ratios, and so on are preferred over broad adjectives or adverbs.

- *Goals and focus:* Your résumé should indicate to the reader your career goals and how those are consistent with your past experience, skills, and competencies, as well as with the recruiter's objectives. At times, an applicant may be making a switch in his or her career; however, even in this case, the applicant should indicate how the competencies acquired in the previous jobs will help him or her to do well in the new job. A stated objective such as "Seeking a challenging management position directing fundraising in a high growth nonprofit organization" tells more to the reader than one that reads, "Seeking a responsible position in an organization where I can contribute to the growth of the firm."

- *Spelling, grammar, and syntax:* The résumé is the first indicator of your competence and concern for quality to your future employer. This means that even a single spelling mistake or grammatical or syntactical error will result in the premature death of your application. Proofread your résumé several times and ask other people to review it.

- *Language:* The language you use in your résumé should be appropriate for the job and the type of firm to which you are applying. In general, use simple, easy-to-understand words. However, technical words may be acceptable for specific jobs (e.g., "TQM" for a quality control job position; but even here, using the phrase "total quality management" with "TQM" in parentheses for its first usage ensures that there is no confusion in the mind of the reader). The language that is appropriate for a senior management level job in a multinational firm will be inappropriate if you are sending your résumé to a small, owner-operated bakery shop in your neighbourhood.

FIGURE 5-3	Some Dos and Don'ts in Preparing a Résumé (continued)

- *Use of specific words:* For electronic résumés, which are typically processed through the use of software, it is important that your application contain key words relevant for the job position. Thus, for a senior marketing position, words such as "pricing," "market research," "sales management," "distribution," and "customer service" are important, and should appear in the past work experience or competency profile part of your résumé. In addition to your résumé, you should also include a brief but professional-looking and informative cover letter. The cover letter should reflect your interest in the job and briefly outline why you are a candidate worthy of consideration. The cover letter should be original, and it should be addressed to a specific recruiter (not *To Whom It May Concern*). Your cover letter should not "oversell"; rather, it should result in the reader wanting to know more about you and look into your attached résumé.

As far as possible, recruitment advertisements should be written from the viewpoint of the applicant and his or her motivations rather than exclusively from the point of view of the company. Since the cost of most classified advertising is determined by the size of the advertisement, short blurbs are the norm. These ads usually describe the job duties, outline minimum job qualifications, and tell interested readers how to apply. Figure 5-4 provides an example of an ad that provides relevant job information and at the same time "sells" the company to potential applicants.

FIGURE 5-4	Sample Want Ad

Why work for one of the best banks in the country, when you can work for one of the best in the world?

Recipient of BCAMA
Marketer of the Year Award

HSBC is the leading international bank in Canada with over 150 offices across the country. We're part of the HSBC Group, one of the world's largest financial services companies with over 6,000 offices in 81 countries and territories. Providing our employees with the best possible work environment has ranked us among the country's top 35 companies to work for (The Globe and Mail, Feb. 2000). If you're looking for a career in a dynamic environment and feel that your qualifications meet the requirements below, we'd like to hear from you.

SENIOR MANAGER
ADVERTISING AND PROMOTIONS
(VANCOUVER)

This exciting opportunity will appeal to a strong marketing professional who is ready to develop advertising and communication strategies that support marketing objectives. This position will see you manage, plan, execute and track expenditures of advertising and promotions programs while ensuring that all materials produced support the brand positioning and corporate image. In addition, you will assist in managing marketing communications activities and integrate marketing plans to ensure consistency of global brand image and positioning.

You possess a degree in Marketing and a minimum of 7 years of experience in advertising or product/brand management. You have a history of developing successful marketing strategies and programs, including direct-response marketing, direct mail, advertising research and creative development. As a result, you have a sound knowledge of advertising and promotions practices, and are able to set priorities and build relationships with internal and external clients. Proficiency with PCs and excellent management, organization and presentation skills will reinforce your success.

If you see this opportunity as an exciting path to a financial career with a promising future and room for growth, send your resume, in confidence to: Laura Suter, Manager, Human Resources, HSBC Bank Canada, 3rd Floor, 885 West Georgia Street, Vancouver, B.C., V6E 3E9. HSBC recognizes the value of diversity in our workforce and encourages all qualified applicants to apply. We appreciate all qualified responses and advise that follow-up phone calls are not necessary as all applicants will be acknowledged.

HSBC

YOUR WORLD OF FINANCIAL SERVICES   *Issued by HSBC Bank Canada*   **www.hsbc.ca**

Traditional recruitment advertisements may be insufficient, particularly when recruiting people with hard-to-find skills or when labour markets are tight. Want ads must contain not only information about the job but also information presented in a way that effectively portrays a message about the job, the work environments, management style, organizational climate, and future growth potential. This can't be done if the ad contains information that explains only what responsibilities the job includes, who can be qualified, where it is located, and how and when to apply. Figure 5-5 lists some of the information contained in good want ads along with other desirable attributes.

Advertisements for recruits through other media—billboards, television, and radio, for example—are seldom used because the results rarely justify the expense. However, these approaches may be useful when unemployment is low and the target recruits are not likely reading want ads.

FIGURE 5-5	Attributes of Good Want Ads

Good want ads, in general, seem to have several common characteristics, such as the following:

1. They address the audience and use a language that the applicant finds comfortable.

2. They use short sentences and familiar words that are action-oriented.

3. They contain all relevant information about the job and the firm. Some major items here are:
   - job title
   - working conditions
   - a clear description of the job
   - training offered
   - organizational and work culture
   - major skills, competencies, and educational requirements
   - career and personal development possibilities
   - location of the job
   - salary, benefits, and other incentives
   - travel and other requirements
   - company selling points

4. They sequence the content logically and in an engaging manner.

5. They respect provisions of human rights and other laws and the dignity of the readers.

6. They do not use sexist, racist, or otherwise unacceptable language. Even the use of adjectives that are normally associated with males or whites may be unacceptable to other groups (e.g., use of adjectives such as "assertive," "dominant," "aggressive," etc., usually connote male sex roles; while terms such as "compassionate," "gentle," and "sympathetic" signify female sex roles[19]).

7. They stand out from other advertisements with good copy layout, visual balance, visual tension, and colour contrast.

8. Their size and presentation should be cost-effective compared with other recruitment methods and considering size and location of target audience.

9. They should make a favourable projection of corporate image and activities without boasting or making unsupported claims.

Because most readers will be travelling in an automobile, the amount of information that can be conveyed on a billboard is limited. Another limitation of this approach is that it generally requires considerable lead time to prepare a sign. In deciding whether to use a billboard, the recruiter should consider the type of job to be advertised. If it is a job for which the firm is continuously recruiting, it may be worthwhile to have a billboard in visible locations.[20]

Transit advertising involves placing posters in buses, commuter trains, and subway stations. By and large these are only used by employers who have difficulty filling positions using traditional methods.

In the past, one major U.S. airline placed ads along mass transit routes in immigrant neighbourhoods and significantly enhanced its recruitment success rate.[21]

Transit job advertising is relatively inexpensive. If it is placed in a specific geographic location (such as a particular bus stop), it allows an organization to target its advertising to a specific demographic or even ethnic group. If placed in a bus or train, a job advertisement can be seen by thousands of persons each week (or even day). In order to make it easy to respond, the organization should attach coupons that can be torn off, completed, and mailed.

Whatever media are used, the layout, design, and copy of an advertisement should reflect the image and character of the company and departments that are being represented.[22] This includes dimensions such as the size of the organization, the degree of decentralization seen in the firm, the degree of dynamism and progressive policies typical of the unit, and so on. This in turn means that an ad should emphasize the nature of the organization and the benefits of the package that it offers to attract the applications of qualified people, but at the same time be specific enough to screen out the wrong persons.

SPOTLIGHT ON ETHICS
FACING RECRUITMENT DILEMMAS

Like many other HR activities, recruitment often raises ethical dilemmas and questions. Consider the following situations. Do you believe that there are ethical issues here? Rate each item on a five-point scale with these anchors:

1. Very unethical
2. Somewhat unethical
3. Can't decide
4. Somewhat ethical
5. Very ethical

What values, beliefs, or other arguments justify your conclusion? Please list them on a separate sheet of paper along with your ratings, using the above scale.

1. Because of a sudden spurt in demand for your products caused by the temporary closure of a competing plant, you need an additional manager. Your plant is located in a somewhat remote place devoid of many urban conveniences. You know that this is only a temporary position, but if you publicize it as such, you are unlikely to attract any competent candidates. In your advertisements and during the job interviews, you decide not to make any statements about the short-term nature of the position. You will not make any false statements, but also will not divulge that the position is going to be available for only about six months.

2. Of late, your firm, a designer clothing firm, has not been very successful in coming out with many innovative designs. If you do not make a breakthrough in the immediate future, the possibility exists that your firm may go under. You meet the chief designer of your competitor and offer an $8,000 raise to him in an effort to attract him to your firm and turn around your fortunes.

3. Your firm has been attempting to introduce diversity at your workplace. You have had a fair degree of success until now, except with members of one ethnic community who your HR department finds to be "troublemakers." Employees who belong to this community are found to be emotionally upset even over minor matters and are very vocal in their complaints. You find that a lot of productive time is wasted in managing conflicts and settling disputes. During a recent conversation with a professional colleague in another firm, you mentioned this matter. He confirmed similar experiences in his organization. He also told you that whenever he gets applications from members of this community (who can be identified from their names), he tends to pass them into the inactive file without serious consideration. He suggested that you follow the same practice until the situation improves.

4. Your firm, a successful software programmer with a 25 percent market share of a specific product, badly needs to know more about a competitor's patented program. While you do not intend to infringe their patents, a good knowledge of the intricacies of their program and future product plans can help you get a head start in the next phase of development and capture some of their market share. You offer a very attractive salary and a share of profits emerging from the new product to the star programmer with your competitor. You are hopeful that when she joins your firm, she will be able to tell you secrets of your competitor's success and future plans.

Human Resources and Skills Development Canada
www.hrsdc.gc.ca

> **Human Resources and Skills Development Canada** Federal agency that provides programs and services for employers and present and potential employees.

Human Resources and Skills Development Canada

Human Resources and Skills Development Canada (HRSDC) works to improve the standard of living and the quality of life of all Canadians by promoting a highly skilled and mobile workforce as well as an efficient and inclusive labour market. It offers a variety of programs and services for both employers and prospective employees, including the following:

- **Income Security and Social Development.** This branch is the focal point for social policy and programs designed to ensure that children, families, seniors, persons with disabilities, homeless persons, and others who are facing social challenges have the support, knowledge, and information they need to maintain their well-being and facilitate their participation in the labour force and the larger society.
- **Learning.** This branch helps Canadians attend higher education institutions by providing advice, loans, and other assistance to students, by encouraging individuals and organizations to save for a child's post-secondary education, and by assisting children from low-income families through grants.
- **Skills Employment**. This branch provides programs and initiatives that promote skills development, labour market participation and inclusiveness, as well as ensuring labour market efficiency. Specifically, these programs seek to address the employment and skills needs of those facing employment barriers, and contribute to life-long learning and building a skilled inclusive labour force. Other programs that support an efficient labour market include the labour market integration of recent immigrants, the entry of temporary foreign workers, the mobility of workers across Canada, and the dissemination of labour market information. This branch is also responsible for programs that provide temporary income support to eligible unemployed workers.

More specifically, in the human resource management context, HRSDC has three complementary objectives:

1. To help Canadians prepare for, find, and keep work by assisting employers and job applicants in their search.

2. To assist workers in this country in their efforts to provide financial security for themselves and their families.

3. To promote a fair, safe, healthy, stable, cooperative, and productive work environment for Canadians.

HRSDC attempts to achieve these objectives through a variety of programs. Service Canada was created in 2005 to improve the delivery of government programs and services to Canadians, by making access to them faster, easier, and more convenient. Service Canada offers single-window access to a wide range of Government of Canada programs and services for citizens (including several of those from HRSDC) through more than 600 points of service located across the country, call centres, and the Internet. Programs and activities such as a job bank, electronic labour exchange, and income security are available today.

The Job Bank

Human Resource Development Canada Electronic Labour Exchange
http://gateway.cotr.bc.ca/
Canada/ElectLabEx.asp

The Job Bank provides a comprehensive database of thousands of jobs and work opportunities available across Canada. When an employer has a job opening, the human resource department voluntarily notifies HRSDC of the job and its requirements, which are then posted at the Web site. Here prospective employees can scan the job openings and discuss any vacancy with one of the counsellors available. When an applicant expresses interest in some particular job, counsellors interview that person. Over 40,000 employers use the services to advertise full-time, part-time, and summer job opportunities.[23]

Electronic Labour Exchange

The Electronic Labour Exchange (ELE) is a computer-based recruitment tool that can match employer profiles with job seeker profiles. It relies on standard occupation checklists, with categories such as education, experience, and skills. The ELE uses information entered in the profile to automatically match job seekers to employers who are looking for candidates with the suitable skills for the job.

Work Destinations
www.workdestinations.org/
home.jsp?lang=en

Work Destinations Web Site

The bilingual Work Destinations Web site is a comprehensive source of information on regulated trades and professions in Canada. It contains information on entry requirements in both official languages and is the only site designed primarily for professional or tradespeople moving within Canada. It also provides information for persons considering immigration to Canada about job prospects in specific professions.

This site is particularly useful for people who desire to

- start work in a regulated trade or profession;
- move and work in a regulated occupation in another province or territory; or
- immigrate and work in a regulated trade or profession in Canada.

Job Search Tools

Job Search Tools
http://www.jobsetc.ca/
toolbox/job_search/
jobSearch.do?lang=e

A variety of job search tools and information is available from HRSDC, including information on matching your own interests and job, various occupations, and the labour market. It covers everything from résumé writing to interview techniques and from potential employment opportunities to starting your own business.

Services for Business

Services for Business
www.hrsdc.gc.ca/en/
gateways/business/menu.
shtml#hrm

A variety of services, including labour market information, workplace issues and supports, employment trends, and various occupations and careers, are provided at virtually no cost to anyone who needs them. Many of the job vacancies posted in the Job Bank are still for white-collar, blue-collar, or technical employees rather than managerial and professional persons.

Private Employment Agencies

Private employment agencies—which now exist in every major metropolitan area—arose to help employers find capable applicants. Placement firms take an employer's request for recruits and then solicit job seekers, usually through advertising or from walk-ins. Candidates are matched with employer requests and then told to report to the employer's human resource department. The matching process conducted by private agencies varies widely.

Some placement services carefully screen applicants for their client. Others simply provide a stream of applicants and let the client's human resource department do most of the screening. Some of the private employment firms match their strategies to the emerging environmental trends, as the following illustration shows:

> A metropolitan placement agency marketed its services on the basis of skill, dedication, and ready availability of its temporary workers. When faced with a shortage of school students who worked part-time, the agency began looking at other population segments. One group met all the three requirements of the agency—the recently retired and about-to-retire persons were skilled, dedicated, and prepared to accept temporary assignments. In a short while, the firm began to rely solely on this group for all its temporary staff needs.

Use of a private employment agency may be necessary when the employer needs only a few persons and on a temporary or irregular basis. Also, when the employer has a critical need to fill a position quickly, this method can be very useful. In times of tight labour markets, it may be necessary to attract individuals who are already employed on a part-time basis. Private employment agencies can achieve this more cost-effectively, especially if the employer has limited experience in the local labour market.

In many provinces, it is either illegal for private employment agencies to charge applicants a fee for placement, or the fees charged are regulated. Most fees are paid by the agencies' clients—that is, the prospective employers. The fees commonly equal either 10 percent of the first year's salary or one month's wages, but the amount may vary with the volume of business provided by the client and the type of employee sought.

Professional Search Firms

professional search firms
Agencies that, for a fee, recruit specialized personnel by telephone and, at times, recruit from a computer.

Professional search firms are much more specialized than placement agencies. Search firms usually recruit only specific types of human resources for a fee paid by the employer. For example, some search firms specialize in executive talent, while others use their expertise to find technical and scientific personnel. Perhaps the most significant difference between search firms and placement agencies is their approach. Placement agencies hope to attract applicants through advertising, but search firms actively seek out recruits from among the employees of other companies. Although they may advertise, the telephone is their primary tool for locating and attracting prospective recruits:

> B.C. Radar Company needed a quality control manager for its assembly line. After several weeks of unsuccessful recruiting efforts, the human resource manager hired a search firm. The search firm reviewed the in-house phone directories of competing firms and telephoned the assistant quality control manager at one of B.C. Radar's competitors. The phone call was used to encourage this assistant manager to apply for the position at B.C. Radar.

This brief example illustrates several important points. First, search firms have an in-depth experience that most human resource departments lack. Second, search firms are often willing to undertake actions that an employer would not, such as calling a competitor. Third, it can be seen that some human resource professionals would consider search firms unethical because these firms engage in "stealing" or "raiding" among their clients' competitors. This last example shows why search firms are sometimes called "headhunters."[24]

In the past few years, the number of executive recruiting firms in Canada has been growing rapidly. While most of them are located in large metropolitan cities such as Toronto, Montreal, or Vancouver, an increasing number of these firms are making an appearance in smaller cities and towns.

Many human resource departments view executive search firms as a regular part of their operations. As one writer wrote, "The enlightened human resource executive ... views executive search as corporate management does its accounting firm, law firm or other consultants."[25] Retainer search firms—those that work on fee-paid assignments—are more popular among HR managers than contingency search firms—those that receive a fee only if an employer hires the candidate suggested by the search firm. The latter are considered to be more aggressive and, given their reward structure, at times tempted to fill a position at any cost—even if the fit between the job and applicant is less than optimal.[26]

What is the reason for the growing popularity of executive search firms? According to one writer, the use of a search firm leads to more objectivity, less cost per recruit, and an overall higher success rate in recruiting the right quality personnel.[27]

> In one survey of 107 Canadian organizations, over 75 percent of the responding human resource departments indicated that executive search firms could reach applicants who were unreachable through other means. However, the same survey found that a majority of respondents felt search firms were more appropriate for larger firms. Over 60 percent also indicated that their own recruiters and departments had a better understanding of the firm's employment needs than search firms.[28]

When choosing a search firm, care must be taken to test the "fit" between the firm and the client organization. Some of the search firms, especially the smaller ones, are often highly specialized and may not be able to meet the general needs of a client. Checking the recruiting record of the firm and its reputation is, consequently, very important. The larger firms can be quite expensive, often charging 30 percent of the candidate's gross starting salary as fees (not inclusive of other expenses).[29] Some of the factors that should be considered in evaluating a recruiting firm include the size of the firm, staff qualifications, ability to meet time requirements, financial soundness of the firm, proven validity of the testing/selection instruments and practices, and provision of measurable results from previous contracts (track record and acceptable references).

Educational Institutions

educational institutions High schools, technical schools, community colleges, and universities where applicants for job positions are sought.

For entry-level openings, **educational institutions** are another common source of recruits. Counsellors and teachers often provide recruiters with leads to desirable candidates in high schools. Many universities, community colleges, and technical schools offer their current students and alumni placement assistance. This assistance helps employers and graduates to meet and discuss employment opportunities and the applicant's interest.

> Campus recruitment is a very competitive activity. This is especially so for employers in the mining sector because so few students are graduating from mining engineering programs in Canada. A typical chemical engineering class will have several hundred students, but the mining engineering

Employers are required to reasonably accommodate the physically challenged. What if the accommodation requires the installation of an elevator for $100,000 in a branch of a national bank?

© Digital Vision/Getty Images.

program at Dalhousie University in Halifax had just 10 and the program at Queen's University in Kingston had only 30 in 2008. Graduates in mining engineering consequently have been able to pick and choose employers. The average job-offer acceptance rate across all industries was 82 percent, but it was just 59 percent for job offers in the mining industry.[30]

Past research studies indicate that students desire campus recruiters to be well informed, honest, and skilled. The title and age of the recruiter may also be important factors in creating a favourable impression on recruits.[31] Some other characteristics of successful campus recruiters are shown in Figure 5-6. However, not many recruiters are successful in getting the best talents during their campus visits. Wasted staff time to interview unqualified applicants, difficulties with assessing applicants who possess no relevant experience, and applicants who provide standardized answers to interview questions can all lead to the selection of wrong candidates. A focus on the actual job duties and performance requirements can significantly overcome these problems.[32]

Increasingly, several organizations find that summer internships significantly facilitate college and university recruitment efforts.

These summer internships are more popular in large companies such as Procter & Gamble and Aetna Life Insurance; however, even smaller organizations find that hiring students to complete summer projects helps them to identify qualified, motivated, and informed recruits.

Students can be evaluated on the basis of their success in completing their special projects in summer months. These interns are also exposed to the organization so that they have a clear idea of

FIGURE 5-6	A Profile of an Ideal Recruiter

- Hires for specific positions rather than looking for future recruits without any clear idea about job vacancies.
- Possesses considerable knowledge about the firm and the job position.
- Discusses strengths and limitations of the firms knowledgeably.
- Never exaggerates or oversells the employers.
- Studies the student's résumé carefully before the interview and asks specific questions.
- Validly assesses the student's awareness of and interest in the job and the company.
- Asks thought-provoking questions to measure the student's knowledge on relevant job matters.
- Expresses interest in the student as an individual.
- Is upbeat about the company and his or her own role in the firm.
- Displays good interpersonal skills and appears polite and sincere.
- Follows up promptly with feedback and evaluation.
- Is professional and ethical in demeanour.

Source: Based partially on and expanded from John E. Steele, "A Profile of the Ideal Recruit," *Personnel Journal*, February 1997, pp. 58–59.

what to expect from the firm when they later join as full-time employees. Such "informed" recruits are less likely to leave the firm soon after they are hired.

In recent years, cooperative education has become increasingly popular in Canada. Under the "co-op education" program, students alternate study and work terms. Their work terms expose them to the realities of the work world. This also provides an excellent opportunity for the employer to assess the potential employee's ability and attitudes without incurring any significant costs.[33] Universities that provide business administration programs aimed at senior- and middle-level managers (such as executive MBA programs) are also a valuable source for recruiting managers.

Professional Associations

Recruiters find that professional associations also can be a source of job seekers. Many associations conduct placement activities to help new and experienced professionals get jobs; some have publications that accept classified advertisements. Professionals who belong to the appropriate associations are considered more likely to remain informed of the latest developments in their field, and so this channel of recruitment may lead to higher-quality applicants. Another advantage of this source of applicants is that it helps recruiters zero in on specific specialties, particularly in hard-to-fill technical areas.

Labour Organizations

When recruiters want people with trade skills, local labour organizations have rosters of those people who are looking for employment. The local union of plumbers, for example, keeps a list of plumbers who are seeking jobs. In the construction industry, many contractors often hire on a per-project basis. A union hiring hall is a convenient channel for attracting large numbers of pretrained recruits for new projects.

Armed Forces

Trained personnel leave the armed forces every day. Some veterans, such as those who have been trained as mechanics, welders, or pilots, have hard-to-find skills. Human resource departments that need skills similar to those found in the military often find nearby military installations a valuable source of recruits.

Many of the technicians who maintain commercial jet airliners were first trained in the military, for example.

Canadian Labour Congress Information and links
www.canadianlabour.ca

Temporary-Help Agencies

Most large cities have **temporary-help agencies** that can respond quickly to an employer's need for help. These agencies do not provide recruits. Instead, they are a source of supplemental workers. The temporary help actually work for the agency and are "on loan" to the requesting employer. For temporary jobs—during vacations, peak seasons, illnesses, and so on—these agencies can be a better alternative than recruiting new workers for short periods of employment. Besides handling the recruiting and bookkeeping tasks caused by new employees, these agencies can often provide clerical and secretarial talent on short notice—sometimes within less than a day. And when the temporary shortage is over, there is no need to lay off surplus workers, because "temporaries" work for the agency, not the company.[34] Occasionally, temporary help are recruited to become permanent employees.

Homepage of a popular temp agency
www.manpower.ca

Departing Employees

An often overlooked source of recruits is among departing employees. These workers might gladly stay if they could rearrange their schedules or change the number of hours worked. Family responsibilities, health conditions, or other circumstances may lead a worker to quit when a transfer to a part-time job could retain valuable skills and training. Even if part-time work is not a solution, a temporary leave of absence may satisfy the employee and some future recruiting need of the employer.

> An employee who leaves a company to pursue another job or venture and is later rehired is known as a "boomerang employee." As competition for top talent has intensified, the number of boomerang employees has grown vastly. A company such as Ernst & Young LLP, a Toronto-based accounting firm, actively cultivates a continuing connection with its past employees. Former employees have access to Web casts sponsored by E&Y that discuss developments in the accounting field. A newsletter is sent a couple of times a year and several social events are held for former staff. When people leave the firm, they are even given a password to access the Web site, which includes a directory of current and former employees, details of what former employees are doing, and a place to post résumés. Encouraging former employees to reconsider E&Y is definitely one of the objectives of such efforts, according to a director of E&Y.[35]

A **buy-back** occurs when an employee resigns to take another job and the original employer outbids the new job offer. The following dialogue provides an example:

Employee: I quit. I got a new job as a system analyst at International Plastics.

Manager: You're too valuable for us just to let you walk out the door. How much is International offering?

Employee: They're offering me $10,000 a year more!

Manager: Stay and I'll recommend a $6,000 raise.

Employee: No. I'm going.

Manager: How about $7,500?

Employee: Well, okay.

Even when the authority to enter into a bidding war exists, the manager may discover that other workers expect similar raises. Many HR practitioners are averse to this approach because of its ethical implications. Employees may also reject a buy-back attempt because of the ethical issue raised by not reporting to a job that has already been accepted.

Open House

A relatively new technique of recruiting involves holding an open house. People in the adjacent community are invited to see the company facilities, have refreshments, and maybe view a film about the company. This method has proven successful for recruiting clerical workers when people with office skills are in tight supply.

Job Fairs

Attending job fairs can pay rich dividends to recruiters who are looking for specialized talents or a number of personnel. Over years, budgetary constraints and the emergence of Internet recruitment have resulted in a decline in the popularity of job fairs. However, even today, there are examples of striking successes:

> The job fair organized by the University of Waterloo, Wilfrid Laurier University, Conestoga College, and University of Guelph has tripled in size of attendees since it was first organized in 1994. In the recent past, the event attracted some 200 companies and 2,500 to 3,000 students, making it the largest job fair in Canada. Over 10,000 visitors were estimated to have attended the event.[36]

Some job fairs are scheduled one year in advance; hence, employers should plan well ahead. More recently, it has also become popular to give out "swags," such as pens, notepads, magnets, and key chains to visitors to promote the organization.[37]

The Internet

The Internet is increasingly becoming one of the most important tools to match jobs with candidates—whether one is a recruiting firm or a job applicant. There are four major reasons for this. *First*, the Internet is accessible all the time—without the limitations of a public library, an employment office, or even a newspaper ad. This means that a person can access it 24 hours a day, 7 days a week, without even leaving the house. *Second*, it broadens the recruitment area significantly. The Internet offers a cost-effective distribution of information to over 100 countries and millions of users. *Third*, by specifying the exact qualifications and job skills needed, the time needed to weed out unsuitable job candidates is minimized. Indeed, the applicants themselves may, on the basis of information supplied, decide not to apply for unsuitable positions. This also adds to the recruiting process the important attribute of timeliness. *Fourth*, it is relatively inexpensive. Compared to the commissions to be paid to an executive search firm or the travel expenses of a campus recruiter, the cost of putting an ad on the Internet is minimal, making it an attractive alternative for many organizations.

> One company reported savings of $70,000 a day in recruitment costs by switching to the Internet as the main recruitment tool.[38]

internet recruiting
Job recruitment using the Internet.

No wonder then that there has been great interest in **Internet recruiting** in recent months (see "Spotlight on HRM" on page 195).

> The Internet has such a significant impact on recruitment that about 50 percent of all resumes today are submitted electronically.[39] More than 10 percent of U.S. companies are already hiring a majority of their employees from the Web.[40] Monster.com's job seeker accounts have risen from 5.2 million in 1999 to 12.5 million in 2001. The number of job openings listed on Yahoo!'s careers site has doubled in one year to 800,000.[41] Workopolis, an online career resource with job postings from across Canada, is now offering employers a creative new way to sell themselves to potential recruits—namely Workopolis TV, featuring career advice and employers talking about what makes their companies great places to work as they highlight available positions.[42]

According to a poll conducted by the Society for Human Resource Management, 88 percent of HR professionals use Internet postings to find the right candidates, and 96 percent of job seekers access online Web sites.[43] The emergence of new softwares permits the recruiter to store, classify, and share résumés and other information in digital format, thus increasing the speed and overall value of information.[44] Virtual job fairs and Web 2.0 applications such as video games to test applicant aptitudes are becoming increasingly popular today. Despite such impressive statistics, much of the recruiting on the Internet to date has focused on technical and information technology-related jobs and has been used by firms operating in that industry or other large organizations. A large majority of Canadians, especially those who are less educated or do not have broadband service access, cannot take full advantage of the Internet,[45] thus limiting its recruitment effectiveness.

However, this is expected to change considerably in the near future as job seekers and employers recognize the power of this medium. Further, since the Internet opens up recruiting to a global audience, great care has to be taken when designing want ads and choosing hiring procedures.

> Although many countries use English as their major language for business, there are vast differences in English usage across countries. For example, several words and expressions used in North America are alien to people in Hong Kong, Australia, or India, although many applicants in those countries are fluent in English. Many symbols and graphics also have vastly different meanings in different

countries. For example, a thumbs-up gesture meant to signal a positive thought would be obscene in Sicily.[46] Job applicants in Holland and France expect that employers will ask them about personal details such as gender, age, and marital status, although such questions are illegal in Canada.

SPOTLIGHT ON HRM
Recruiting on the Net

Recruiting on the Internet is one of the hottest topics in human resource management currently; however, its effectiveness is dependent on the care and planning behind the strategy. Recruiting is often among the first functions developed on a corporate Web page.[47] This means that the message and tone you convey on the Web page can affect not only your recruitment effectiveness but also the general public image of the company. Some organizations have experienced a remarkable increase in the number of applications they receive when recruiting on the Internet. (Good Guys, an electronics chain in the United States, increased the number of applications it received from 14 000 to 32 000 in one year by recruiting on the Internet.) Some of the suggestions for improving a firm's recruitment success on the Internet are as follows:

1. Make your postings attractive: In the past, print media costs and space constraints have forced recruiters to use brief job descriptions. Online job postings can be longer and more informative, can be visually more exciting, and can be interactive. Because the Web site has to compete for attention from surfers, it is important that the Web site be attention-grabbing, be easy to surf, and have self-contained information.

2. Publish your Web address on everything: Make sure that your Web address (URL) is included in your traditional want ads in the newspapers, marketing information, public relations notices, and all other corporate communication devices.

3. Continue to look for unconventional recruitment outlets: Even when you announce job openings in less conventional locations (e.g., a minority language newspaper), include your URL in your message.[48]

4. When publishing material for college, university, or trade school markets, always include your URL: This group, of all population segments, accesses the Internet most often. Research evidence indicates that Internet surfers are younger, well educated, technologically oriented, and male.

5. Register your site: Make sure that you register your site with all popular search engines, such as Yahoo, AltaVista, MSN, and Google.

6. Use specialized recruitment Web sites: Today, a plethora of recruitment sites specialize in different kinds of personnel. By advertising on specialized Web sites,

you are likely to target specific markets. Examples include the following:

For teachers: www.recruitingteachers.org

For fire and police personnel: www.ifpra.com

For engineers: www.engineeringjobs.org

For information technology personnel: www.jobserve.com

For jobs in sports and recreation field: www.canadiansport.com/jobs

For accounting jobs: www.acctjob.ca

Careers in oil and gas industry: www.careersinoilandgas.com

For working from home: www.hea-employment.com

For hospitality careers: www.hcareers.ca

7. Target the Web sites in the province or territory where the job is: The Department of Human Resources and Skills Development (HRSDC) can give you a breakdown of applicants in each province for a specific job. There are also specialized Web sites for each province (e.g., for Government of B.C. recruitment: www.postings.gov.bc.ca).

8. When national recruitment efforts fail, consider attracting foreign nationals: Once again, there are many choices in terms of recruitment Web sites, including the following:

For New Zealand: www.iconrec.co.nz

For the U.K.: www.topjobs.co.uk

For E-countries: www.ecountries.com

9. Post the recruitment ad in Internet newsgroups: They are free (at least most of them are). Because the newsgroups continuously update materials, you will need to periodically reinsert your ad. This also gives you an opportunity to revise your ad. Some examples of popular newsgroups are "can.jobs," "ont.jobs," and "tor.jobs." Some of the other interesting Web sites (most of them originating in the U.S.) are:[49]

CareerBuilder.com: www.careerbuilder.com

Career Magazine: www.careermag.com

MonsterTrak: www.jobtrak.com

Irrespective of where the ad is listed, it should contain all key words likely to be used by a firm's recruits when accessing the information using search engines.[50]

10. Take advantage of special Internet advertisement offers: Advertise your openings with popular online newspapers and magazines as their Web sites are well surfed.

11. List your ad with all major Web-based job banks (including HRSDC's): Use the various career sites to send applicants to you.[51] Included here are the following:

www.workopolis.com

www.monster.ca

www.recruitersonline.com

www.brassring.ca

12. Remove the ad as soon as the position is filled: If the recruitment is for a one-time position, the advertisement should be removed as soon as the position is no longer available. The site should also indicate the period of time during which applications are kept active.

13. Choose software carefully: Software that scans the résumés should be keyed for pertinent, jobrelevant words. A periodic review of the "screened out" applications indicates whether the software is deleting applications from protected employment groups systematically. Such validation studies can help to avoid potential legal challenges.

Nontraditional Recruitment Methods

Several other approaches, not very popular in the past, are becoming increasingly so. These are briefly discussed below.

Applicant Tracking Systems

Advances in computer technology and information transmission have made it possible to use newer methods in recruiting employees. Several employers and placement agencies now rely on videos and disks to convey information about job positions to potential recruits. In high-tech professions, email is also sometimes used to reach recruits. Some organizations have installed **applicant tracking systems** (ATS) to identify ideal candidates for each vacant job position. Under this system, the recruiter keeps a large file (or is electronically connected to other master files) of potential candidates, which not only broadens the recruitment pool but also enables a good match between the job requirements and applicant skills.[52]

> When a manager submits a requisition for an opening, the recruiter simply matches the key requirements of the job with applicant characteristics. Thus, job requirements such as "needs significant selling experience" and "should know French" can immediately be matched with applicant characteristics. Such computerized systems not only lead to a better match between jobs and candidates, but also significantly reduce recruitment time and costs.[53]

applicant tracking system
Databases of potential candidates that enable a good match between job requirements and applicant characteristics and also enlarge the recruitment pool.

Contingent/Contract/Leased Workers

A very large segment of our labour market is composed of **contract workers**. They include the self-employed, temporary or leased employees (those who work for an agency that has trained them and supplies these employees on a need basis), and independent contractors.[54] **Contingent workers** are useful when the work is of limited duration, so the firm can avoid fixed salary commitments. **Employee leasing** is a term used to reflect the hiring of employees for longer periods of time. One reason for the popularity of leased workers is cost. The employer pays a flat fee for the employees (and is not responsible for benefits). Contract and self-employed workers, often, are compensated on the basis of task completion and hence need less supervision. Often, they also require lower training costs. making this an attractive proposition.

> More organizations employ contract workers now than ever before. In many organizations, the proportion of the staff who were on contract is 7 to 10 percent. Information systems personnel were most likely to be on contract. Administration, finance, engineering, legal, and technical positions also use contract staff to an extent.[55]

contingent/contract workers
Freelancers (self-employed, temporary, or leased employees) who are not part of the regular workforce and are paid on a project completion basis.

employee leasing
The practice of hiring previously trained employees for extended periods of time, generally longer time frames than temporary workers.

It should be noted that contract and leased employees may not always be committed to the goals and philosophy of the organization. Because the contingent employees are not part of an organization's regular workforce, they do not benefit from the statutory protections offered by various provincial employment laws. The contracting firm is also not responsible for remitting

Canada Pension Plan premiums or withholding income tax. However, determining whether an individual is an independent contractor or an employee is not as easy as it appears. Courts and arbitrators have been increasingly monitoring contractual agreements to ensure that the employer is not using the independent contractor relationship to avoid its statutory and common law obligations.[56] Accordingly, it is important for the contracting parties to know where they stand in order to understand their rights and obligations. (For a more detailed discussion of this issue, see Chapter 12.)

Alumni Associations

alumni associations
Associations of alumni of schools, colleges, or other training facilities.

Another source for experienced employees are **alumni associations** of schools, colleges, and institutes.[57] These are particularly useful for hiring technical and managerial staff.

Partnerships with Social Agencies

Faced with acute competition for valuable human resources, employers are forming partnerships with social agencies and community associations to help them with their recruiting.

> As a group, people with disabilities make up some 13 percent of the working age population and offer a major source for highly qualified employees for a variety of jobs. In a study involving 75 employers, a significant percentage of respondents were eager to hire qualified job seekers from this group, but were facing challenges in moving forward on this front. Many did not know how to communicate their hiring needs to members of the disabled community. However, in Nova Scotia, Alberta, and B.C., employers have formed partnerships with a small number of organizations to convey their messages on a timely basis. For example, the Dartmouth Work Activity Society in Nova Scotia and EmployAbilities in Edmonton have been successful in placing the disabled in a number of organizations. Employers also benefit because such targeted efforts result in speedier recruiting.[58]

> Similarly, South India Cultural Association of the Maritimes, a cultural association in which the second author of this book is a founding member, receives periodical inquiries from employers in the public and non-profit sectors for possible recruits. Such targeted recruiting efforts, apart from increasing the pool of recruits, also benefit the organization by increasing the diversity of its workforce.

Direct Mail Solicitations

direct mail recruiting
Recruitment targeted at specified population segments or regions using a variety of means.

Drawing upon marketing strategies, some firms have attempted **direct mail recruiting** with some success. This enables an organization to target a specific segment of the population or a geographical area (using postal codes).

> Some firms use door hangers, bargain shopper price lists, welcome wagons, and point-of-sale messages as their recruiting media as well.[59]

Recruitment Abroad

More recently, several Canadian employers are looking abroad to secure skilled, hard-to-find employees.

> Many high-tech and software companies today look at India as a major source of highly skilled programmers. Some of the software manufacturers have gone as far as locating their operations in Indian cities such as Bangalore and Hyderabad, while others have formed partnerships with Indian firms that periodically send their own staff to North America on a contract basis.

In the recent past, Canada has been recruiting a large number of skilled workers from other countries. Figure 5-7 shows the origins of 58,860 skilled workers who entered the country. With an aging domestic workforce and a predicted shortage of technical and highly skilled employees, foreign nationals may become an important source of our workforce.

Foreign workers, especially those from developing countries, may be less expensive in some instances (at least initially). Relocation expenses may have to be paid in some instances, which can significantly add to the total cost. Firms hiring from abroad will need to train new recruits to adapt to local and organizational culture. The process of getting employment visas may also be time-consuming in some instances.

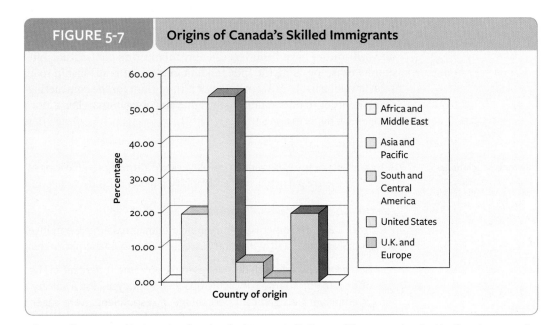

Source: Chart prepared by the authors based on the data reported in *Facts and Figures 2001: Immigration Overview.*, page 96, published by Citizenship and Immigration Canada, Catalogue No. MP43-333/2002E, 2002.

Many Canadian high-tech companies are taking advantage of India's low labour costs and highly skilled programmers, thus displacing local workers. Should there be a law against exporting jobs?

© FINDLAY KEMBER/AFP/Getty Images.

JOB APPLICATION FORMS

The job application form collects information about recruits in a uniform manner, and hence is an important part of all recruitment efforts. Even when recruits volunteer detailed information about themselves, applications are often required so that the information gathered is comparable. Each human resource department generally designs its own form. Nevertheless, certain common features exist. Figure 5-8 provides a typical example of an application form and its major divisions.

FIGURE 5-8	A Typical Application Form

Kanata Electronics, Inc.
"An Equal-Opportunity Employer"
Application for Employment

Personal Data

1. Name _____

2. Address _____ 3. Phone number _____

Employment Status

4. Type of employment sought _____ Full-time _____ Part-time
   _____ Permanent _____ Temporary

5. Job or position sought _____

6. Date of availability, if hired _____

7. Are you willing to accept other employment if the position you seek is unavailable?
   _____ Yes _____ No

8. Approximate wages/salary desired $ _____ per month

Education and Skills

9. Circle the highest grade or years completed.
   9 10 11 12 13   1 2 3 4   1 2 3 4
   High School   University   Graduate School

10. Please provide the following information about your education.
    (Include only vocational schools and colleges.)

    a. School name _____ Degree(s) or diploma _____
       School address _____
       Date of admission _____ Date of completion _____

    b. School name _____ Degree(s) or diploma _____
       School address _____
       Date of admission _____ Date of completion _____

11. Please describe your work skills. (Include machines, tools, equipment, and other abilities you possess.)

Work History

Beginning with your most recent or current employer, please provide the following information about each employer. (If additional space is needed, please use an additional sheet.)

12. a. Employer _____ Dates of employment _____
       Employer's address _____
       Job title _____ Supervisor's name _____
       Job duties _____
       Starting pay _____ Ending pay _____

    b. Employer _____ Dates of employment _____
       Employer's address _____
       Job title _____ Supervisor's name _____
       Job duties _____
       Starting pay _____ Ending pay _____

Memberships, Awards, and Hobbies

13. What are your hobbies? _____

14. List civic/professional/social organizations to which you have belonged.
    _____

15. List any awards you have received. _____

FIGURE 5-8	A Typical Application Form (continued)

References

In the space provided, list three references who are not members of your family.

16. a. Name_____   Address_____
       Name_____   Address_____
       Name_____   Address_____

17. Please feel free to add any other information you think should be considered in evaluating your application.
    By my signature on this application, I:

    a. Authorize the verification of the above information and any other necessary inquiries that may be needed to determine my suitability for employment.

    b. Affirm that the above information is true to the best of my knowledge.

Applicant's Signature _____   Date _____

Name and Address

Most application forms begin with a request for personal data. Name, address, and telephone number are nearly universal. But requests for some personal data, such as place of birth, marital status, number of dependants, sex, race, religion, or national origin, may lead to charges of discrimination. Since it is illegal to discriminate against applicants, an unsuccessful applicant may conclude that rejection was motivated by discrimination when discriminatory questions are asked. The human resource department must be able to show that these questions are job-related if it asks them.

When applications solicit information about health, height, weight, disabilities that relate to the job, major illnesses, and claims for injuries, potential legal problems exist. Discriminating against people with disabilities is prohibited under the *Canadian Human Rights Act*. The burden of proof that such questions are job-related falls on the employer.

Employment Status

Some questions on the application form concern the applicant's employment objective and availability. Included here are questions about the position sought, willingness to accept other positions, date available for work, salary or wages desired, and acceptability of part-time and full-time work schedules. This information helps a recruiter match the applicant's objective and the organization's needs. Broad or uncertain responses can prevent the application from being considered. An example follows:

> **Inexperienced recruiter:** Under "position sought," this applicant put "any available job." Also, under "wages desired" the applicant wrote "minimum wage or better." What should I do with this application?

> **Employment manager:** You are not a career counsellor. You are a recruiter. Put that application in the inactive file and forget about it.

Education and Skills

The education and skills section of the application form is designed to uncover the job seeker's abilities. An understanding of the applicant's personality may be gained from this section too. Traditionally, education has been a major criterion in evaluating job seekers. Educational attainment does imply certain abilities and is therefore a common request on virtually all applications. Questions about specific skills are also used to judge prospective employees. More than any other part of the application form, the skills section reveals the suitability of a candidate for a particular job.

Work History

Job seekers must frequently list their past jobs. From this information, a recruiter can tell whether the applicant is one who hops from job to job or is likely to be a long-service employee. A quick review of the stated job title, duties, responsibilities, and ending pay also shows whether the candidate is a potentially capable applicant. If this information does not coincide with what an experienced recruiter expects to see, the candidate may have exaggerated job title, duties, responsibilities, or pay.

Memberships, Awards, and Hobbies

Recruits are more than potential workers. They are also representatives of the employer in the community. For managerial and professional positions, off-the-job activities may make one candidate preferable over another. Memberships in civic, social, and professional organizations indicate the recruit's concern about community and career. Awards show recognition for noteworthy achievements. Hobbies may reinforce important job skills and indicate outlets for stress and frustrations, or opportunities for further service to the company:

> When handed a pile of completed applications for manager of the car- and truck-leasing department, Frank Simmons (the human resource manager for a Toronto Ford dealership) sorted the completed applications into two piles. When asked what criteria were being used to sort the applications, he said, "I'm looking for golfers. Many of our largest car and truck accounts are sold on Saturday afternoons at the golf course."

Some applications request information on military experience. Such information is particularly useful for jobs in which the applicant has to function in a structured environment. Questions usually include date of discharge, area of service, rank at discharge, and type of discharge.

References

Besides the traditional references from friends or previous employers, applications may ask for other "reference-like" information. Questions may explore the job seeker's criminal record, credit history, friends and relatives who work for the employer, or previous employment with the organization. Criminal record, credit history, and whether the applicant has friends or relatives who work for the company may be important considerations if the job involves sensitive information, cash, or other valuables. Job-relatedness must be substantiated if these criteria disproportionately discriminate against some protected group. Previous employment with the organization means there are records of the applicant's performance.

Signature Line

Candidates are usually required to sign and date their applications. Adjacent to the signature line, a blanket authorization commonly appears. This authorization allows the employer to check references; verify medical, criminal, or financial records; and undertake any other necessary investigations. Another common provision of the signature line is a statement that the applicant affirms the information in the application to be true and accurate as far as is known. Although many people give this clause little thought, falsification of an application form is grounds for discharge in most organizations:

> Jim LaVera lied about his age to get into the police officers' training program. As he neared retirement age, Jim was notified that he would have to retire in six months, instead of 30 months as he had planned. When Jim protested, the lie he made years before came to the surface. Jim was given the option of being terminated or taking early retirement at substantially reduced benefits.

When the application is completed and signed, the recruitment process is finished. Its unanswered questions and implications continue to affect human resource management, as the Jim LaVera example illustrates. In fact, the end of the recruitment process marks the beginning of the selection process, discussed in the next chapter.

EVALUATING THE RECRUITMENT FUNCTION

Like most other important functions, the recruiting activity in an organization should also be sub-jected to periodic evaluation. Sweeping changes continue to reshape the workplace; this means that today, more than ever, knowledgeable employees constitute a key component of a firm's competitive strategy.[60] Typically, the recruitment process is expensive. Unless efforts are made to identify and control these costs, the potential benefits from the activity may end up being lower than the costs. Like all other corporate HR functions, recruiters will not be able to justify their own efforts unless these contribute to "bottom line" financial performance.[61] Recruitment costs can run as high as 50 percent of the yearly salary for professionals and managers; what is even more important, recruitment can reflect a firm's overall human resource strategy.[62] This means that the effectiveness of the recruiting function should be evaluated on an ongoing basis. Several indices have been suggested in the past. The more popular ones are discussed below.

Cost per Hire

The dollar cost per person recruited is one possible measure of the effectiveness of the recruiting function. The costs should include not only the direct costs (e.g., recruiters' salaries, costs of adver-tisement, consultants' fees, and so on), but also apportioned costs and overheads (e.g., time of oper-ating personnel, stationery, rent). However, often cost data are either not collected at all or are not interpreted so as to facilitate the evaluation of recruiting. Cost data collected from previous recruit-ing activities could serve as useful benchmarks for comparison.

Quality of Hires and Cost

A major criticism of using a simple dollar cost per hire as a measure of effectiveness is that it ignores the quality of the people hired. The performance, absenteeism, and motivation levels of employees recruited from one source (or using one media) may differ from those of other sources.

> Recruits selected through advertisements in professional journals and professional conventions may have qualitatively superior performance compared to those who were selected through campus recruitment efforts.

The number and quality of résumés received gives an indication of the overall effectiveness of a recruitment method or source.

Offers–Applicants Ratio

A somewhat better index is the ratio between the number of job offers extended and the total number of applicants calculated for each recruitment method or media. Even if a recruiting source brings in better-quality résumés, this may not be translated finally to job offers; an offers–applicants ratio gives a better picture of the overall quality of the applicant pool. The ratio of number of offers accepted to total number of job offers extended to applicants gives an indication of the overall effectiveness of the recruiting. Caution is, however, in order. The acceptance of a job offer is dependent on a number of extraneous variables, including the labour market situation, the compensation package offered by the organization and its competitors, and the firm's location. However, when used judiciously, this measure can point up weaknesses such as lack of professionalism and long delays in the recruiting process that could encourage a prospective employee to go elsewhere. This is particularly true for good candidates, who may receive multiple job offers from employers.

Time Lapsed per Hire

The number of days, weeks, or months taken to fill a position provides yet another measure of the effectiveness of the recruitment system. Clearly, a firm that takes a week to fill a position when the industry average is 10 days or two weeks is, in comparison, more efficient. Once again, several exter-nal and uncontrollable factors (including the nature of the job, labour market conditions, and loca-tion) affect the time for recruiting; consequently, this index should be used in conjunction with other information.

FIGURE 5-9	Popular Measures Used for Evaluating Effectiveness of Recruitment Function

1. Total number of applications received
2. Time required to get applications
3. Time elapsed before filling positions
4. Costs per hire
5. Ratio of offers extended to number of applicants
6. Ratio of offers accepted to number of offers extended
7. Ratio of number of qualified applicants to total number of applicants
8. Performance rating of hires
9. Turnover of hires

Figure 5-9 shows some of the more popular measures used to evaluate the recruiting function. Naturally, many of these measures are influenced by a firm's selection, training, and compensation systems. Indeed, an evaluation system that explicitly considers various factors related to the selection process and that contains job performance information (including tenure and value of job to the organization) may be very useful in several organizational settings. The next chapter will look at the various steps involved in the selection of personnel from the pool of applicants identified during recruiting.

SUMMARY

Recruitment is the process of finding and attracting capable applicants for employment. This responsibility normally is associated with specialists in the human resource department called recruiters. Before recruiters can solicit applicants, they should be aware of the constraints under which they operate. Of particular importance are such limitations as organizational policies, human resource plans, employment equity plans, recruiter habits, environmental conditions, and the requirements of the job.

At the recruiter's disposal are a variety of methods to find and attract job seekers. Employer sources include walk-ins, write-ins, employee referrals, and direct solicitations through want ads and other forms of advertisement. Applicants can be found through referrals from Human Resources and Skills Development Canada offices, private placement agencies, or search firms. Of course, recruits can be found through a variety of institutions, such as educational, professional, and labour organizations; the military; and government training programs. Some firms have reported success in converting temporary employees into permanent ones, on a full- or part-time basis, and in inducing departing employees to remain. An open house may bring people into the facility and prompt them to submit applications.

The end of the recruiting process is a completed application form from ready, willing, and able candidates. Application forms seek a variety of answers from recruits, including personal, employment, educational, and work history information. Questions may be asked about hobbies, memberships, awards, and personal interests. References are usually solicited on the application form as well.

Like all other human resource functions, the recruitment activity also needs to be evaluated for its degree of effectiveness and efficiency. This is to ensure that the recruitment function achieves both organizational and individual objectives. A number of indices for evaluating the recruitment activity were suggested in this chapter. Bear in mind that all of these indices are affected by a firm's selection, training, compensation, and general human resource–related policies. With a pool of recruits and the information contained in completed application forms, the human resource department is now ready to assist line managers in the process of selecting new employees.

⊙ TERMS FOR REVIEW

alumni associations **p. 197**
applicant tracking system **p. 196**
blind ads **p. 183**
buy-back **p. 193**
competitive advantage **p. 175**
contingent/contract workers **p. 196**
costs **p. 181**
direct mail recruiting **p. 197**
diversity management **p. 179**
educational institutions **p. 190**

employee leasing **p. 196**
employee referrals **p. 182**
human resource plan **p. 179**
Human Resources and Skills
     Development Canada **p. 188**
inducements **p. 181**
internet recruiting **p. 194**
organizational policies **p. 178**
professional search firms **p. 189**
recruiter habits **p. 179**

recruitment **p. 174**
résumé **p. 183**
selection **p. 174**
temporary help agencies **p. 193**
walk-ins/write-ins **p. 182**
want ads **p. 183**

⊙ SELF-ASSESSMENT EXERCISE

How Do You Recruit Employers?

Just as organizations have to recruit potential employees, most individuals also need to scan their environments for potential employers. Take this simple self-test to see how you go about collecting information about your future employers. Answer all questions on a five-point scale of strongly agree (SA), agree (A), undecided (U), disagree (D) and strongly disagree (SD).

Statement	Strongly Agree	Agree	Undecided	Disagree	Strongly Disagree
1. I have a clear idea of the type of job I want and the general competencies it requires.					
2. Looking at newspaper want ads is a waste of time; most jobs are filled even before they are advertised anyway.					
3. I frequently look at want ads in newspapers circulating in the region I am interested in.					
4. I rarely (if ever) look at the annual reports of the firms where I would like to work in the future.					
5. I tell all my friends and acquaintances who work in the industry or profession that I am looking for a job in that field.					
6. I do not have a clear idea of the region or the industry where I want to work.					
7. I regularly surf the Internet to find out more about possible job openings in the industry or occupation I am interested in.					
8. I don't watch TV news or read newspapers.					
9. I keep in touch with my school and college friends, and network with them on social or professional events.					
10. In general, I never talk to others about their experiences in job hunting.					

SCORING

For the odd-numbered statements, give yourself a score of 5, 4, 3, 2, and 1 for SA, A, U, D, and SD, respectively. For the even-numbered statements, give a score of 1, 2, 3, 4, and 5 for SA, A, U, D, and SD, respectively. Add up all scores.

Your total score can lie anywhere from 10 to 50 in this exercise. If your score is 40 or above, you are doing a good job of keeping yourself abreast of the events in the job market. If you got a lower score, you may want to do some of the things indicated above. Getting the right job takes a lot of effort and time, and you have to begin efforts in that direction today!

⊙ REVIEW AND DISCUSSION QUESTIONS

1. What background information should a recruiter have before beginning to recruit job seekers?

2. Give three examples of how organizational policies affect the recruitment process. Explain how these influence a recruiter's actions.

3. Under what circumstances would a blind ad be a useful recruiting technique?

4. "If a job application form omits important questions, needed information about recruits will not be available. But if a needless question is asked, the information can be ignored by the recruiter without any other complications." Do you agree or disagree with this statement? Why?

5. Suppose your employer asks you, the human resource manager, to justify the relatively large recruiting budget that you have been historically assigned. What arguments would you provide? What indices or measures will you provide to show that your recruitment is cost effective?

⊙ CRITICAL THINKING QUESTIONS

1. After months of insufficient recognition (and two years without a raise), you accept an offer from another firm that involves a $2000-a-year raise. When you tell your boss that you are resigning, you are told how crucial you are to the business and are offered a raise of $2500 per year. What do you do? Why? What problems might exist if you accept the buy-back?

2. Suppose you are a manager who has just accepted the resignation of a crucial employee. After you send your request for a replacement to the human resource department, how could you help the recruiter do a more effective job?

3. If at your company the regular university recruiter became ill and you were assigned to recruit at six universities in two weeks, what information would you need before leaving on the trip?

4. In small businesses, managers usually handle their own recruiting. What methods would you use in the following situations? Why?

    (a) The regular janitor is going on vacation for three weeks.

    (b) Your office assistant who manages all appointments and handles all filing in your office has the flu and won't be in office for two days.

    (c) Two more salespeople are needed: one for local customers and one to open a sales office in Victoria, British Columbia.

    (d) Your only chemist is retiring and must be replaced with a highly skilled person.

    (e) Your only computer programmer/analyst plans to go next week on a three week leave to India to visit his sick mother. If his mother's health turns for the worse, he may be delayed by another week or two.

5. You are the human resource manager in a large auto-assembly unit employing 2,000 semiskilled and skilled employees. Each year, you recruit dozens of full-time and part-time workers. Recently, the vice-president (Finance) pointed out that recruitment costs in your firm are increasing steadily. She was proposing a freeze in the recruitment budget. What kind of information will you provide in an effort to change her mind on the matter?

⊙ ETHICS QUESTION

Darrow Thomas worked as a professional placement specialist for L.A. and D. Inc., an executive search firm. For the last three months, Darrow had not been very successful in finding high-level executives to fill the openings of L.A. and D.'s clients. Not only did his poor record affect his commissions, but the office manager at L.A. and D. was not very pleased with Darrow's performance. Since Darrow desperately needed to make a placement, he resolved that he would do everything he could to fill the new opening he had received that morning.

The opening was for a director of research and development at a major food processor. Darrow began by unsuccessfully reviewing the in-house telephone directories of most of the large companies in this industry. Finally, he stumbled across the directory of a small food processor in the west. In the directory he found a listing for Suzanne Derby, assistant director of product development. He called her, and the following conversation took place:

Suzanne: Hello. P.D. Department, Suzanne Derby speaking.

Darrow: Hello. My name is Darrow Thomas, and I am with L.A. and D. One of my clients has an opening for a director of research and development at a well-known food processor. In discussions with people in the industry, your name was recommended as a likely candidate. I was ...

Suzanne: Who recommended that you call me?

Darrow: I'm awfully sorry, but we treat references and candidates with the utmost confidentiality. I cannot reveal that name. But rest assured, he thought you were ready for a more challenging job.

Suzanne: What company is it? What does the job involve?

Darrow: Again, confidentiality requires that the company name go unmentioned for now. Before we go any further, would you mind answering a few questions? Once I feel confident you are the right candidate, I can reveal my client.

Suzanne: Well, okay.

Darrow: Good. How many people do you supervise?

Suzanne: Three professionals, seven technicians, and two clerks.

Darrow: Approximately how large a budget are you responsible for?

Suzanne: Oh, it's about half a million dollars a year.

Darrow: What degree do you hold, and how many years have you been assistant director?

Suzanne: My undergraduate degree and Master's are in nutrition science. After I graduated in 1985, I came to work here as an applications researcher. In 1993, I was promoted to chief applications researcher. In 1996, I was appointed assistant director of product development.

Darrow: Good career progress, two degrees, and managerial experience. Your background sounds great! This is a little personal, but would you tell me your salary?

Suzanne: I make $79,500 a year.

Darrow: Oh, that is disappointing. The opening I have to fill is for $96,000. That would be such a substantial jump that my client would probably assume your past experience and responsibility are too limited to be considered.

Suzanne: What do you mean?

Darrow: Well, the ideal candidate would be making about $90,000 a year. That figure would indicate a higher level of responsibility than your lower salary. We could get around that problem.

Suzanne: How?

Darrow: On the data sheet I have filled out I could put down that you are making, oh, say $88,000. That sure would increase my client's interest. Besides, then they would know a salary of $96,000 was needed to attract you.

Suzanne: Wow! But when they checked on my salary history, they'd know that $88,000 was an inflated figure.

Darrow: No, they wouldn't. They wouldn't check. And even if they did, companies never reveal the salary information of past employees. Besides, my client is anxious to fill the job. I'll tell you what, let me send them the data sheet; I'm sure they'll be interested. Then we can talk about more of this. Okay?

Suzanne: Well, if you think it would mean a raise to $96,000, and they really need someone with my background, I guess I'd be interested.

1. Although "headhunters" do not necessarily engage in the practice of "inflating" an applicant's wage, it does happen occasionally. What would you do in Suzanne's place? Would you allow your name to be used?

2. Since most "headhunters" receive a commission that is a percentage of the successful applicant's starting salary, what safeguards would you suggest to prevent "headhunters" from inflating salaries?

3. If Suzanne goes along with Darrow's inflated salary figure and she is hired, what problems may she face?

WEB RESEARCH EXERCISE

Choose any two Internet recruiting sites. Select advertisements for two different job positions in each site (i.e., four in all). Compare their features and strengths. Do you expect different types of recruits to respond to these advertisements and sites? Why? Which of the four advertisements that you chose is the best? Which is the worst? Why? What suggestions do you have to enhance the effectiveness of poor ads? Report your findings to the class.

⭘ INCIDENT 5-1

Ontario Electronics Expansion

Ontario Electronics developed a revolutionary method of storing data electronically. The head of research and development, Guy Swensen, estimated that Ontario Electronics could become a supplier to every computer manufacturer in the world. The future success of the company seemed to hang on securing the broadest possible patents to cover the still-secret process.

The human resource director, Carol Kane, recommended that Swensen become a project leader in charge of developing and filing the necessary patent information. Swensen and Kane developed a list of specialists who would be needed to rush the patent applications through the final stages of development and the patent application process. Most of the needed skills were found among Ontario Electronics' present employees. However, after a preliminary review of skills inventories and staffing levels, a list of priority recruits was developed. It required the following:

- An experienced patent lawyer with a strong background in electronics technology.

- A patent lawyer who was familiar with the ins and outs of the patent process and the patent office in Hull, Quebec.
- Twelve engineers. Three had to be senior engineers with experience in the latest computer technology and design. Four had to be senior engineers with experience in photographic etching reduction. Five junior engineers were also requested in the belief that they could handle the routine computations for the senior engineers.
- An office manager, ten keyboard operators, and four secretaries to transcribe the engineering notebooks and prepare the patent applications.

Swensen wanted these 29 people recruited as promptly as possible.

1. Assuming you are given the responsibility of recruiting these needed employees, what channels would you use to find and attract each type of recruit sought?
2. What other actions should the human resource department take now that there is the possibility of very rapid expansion?

⭘ CASE STUDY   🍁   Maple Leaf Shoes Ltd.

*A Case Study in Recruitment**

Robert Clark was a worried man.

He looked at the letter from Sam Polanyi, president of the Leather Workers' Union's local unit in Maple Leaf Shoes again. Polanyi had warned him of "dire consequences" if the firm did not proceed slowly on automation in its local plant. The union had urged its members to adopt a "work slow" tactic beginning next month. Worried by the decline and demise of giant organizations such as General Motors, Chrysler, and Nortel, Maple Leaf's workforce was strongly against any impending automation that can further reduce the workforce number at a time when the unemployment rates in various parts of Canada were at historical highs. In three months' time, the contract negotiations with the same union had to be concluded. Automation and the newly proposed workweek would surely be important bargaining items.

But what option did the firm have now? The competition from China, Korea, Indonesia, and Malaysia was devastating. Just in the last six months, the firm had lost two major retail suppliers in the United States, which had pointed out that Maple Leaf's shoes were too high-priced for its customers. Meanwhile, there were industry rumours that a major Indian footwear firm is planning to enter the North American market. When that materializes, Maple Leaf Shoes will likely face even

greater competition at home. India has had a long history of producing quality footwear and can also take advantage of its cheap labour and emerging high-tech industries in producing high fashion, cheap dress shoes, and high-endurance "cross-trainer" footwear.

The recent warning from the local Human Rights Commission (HRC) did not help matters either. Apparently two female employees, who were denied promotion in the past, had complained to the Commission. They had argued that the promotion criteria employed by the firm for supervisory positions worked against women. When the HRC looked at the complaint, it did not consider their cases to be strong enough to proceed further. However, it had warned the company about the concentration of women in low-paid jobs and lack of clear job specifications for supervisory positions. The Commission had urged immediate remedial actions, including an in-depth look at supervisory competencies and job specifications. The firm was expected to come out with a remedial plan in the next 12 months.

To top it all, neither Pat Lim nor Jane Reynolds was there in Wilmington to help him. John McAllister, the firm's previous human resource manager, had resigned to take up a similar position in Western Canada. Maple Leaf Shoes had not hired

* Case prepared by Professor Hari Das of Department of Management, Saint Mary's University, Halifax. All rights reserved by the author Das©2002. Revised 2009.

a new manager in his place. Until now, Pat Lim, General Manager (Marketing) was overall in charge of the human resource function, although most of the routine decisions were made by Jane Reynolds, who in the past had served as special assistant to John McAllister. But recently Reynolds was admitted to a local hospital for a surgical procedure. Clark has now been informed that Reynolds will not be returning for some time.

Given all the pressures, Clark decided to immediately fill the human resource manager's position. Clark retrieved the want ad the company had used when hiring John McAllister. He made some minor changes to it and decided to place it in local newspapers as soon as possible. A copy of the final advertisement that Clark prepared is shown in Exhibit 1.

It was after making arrangements for the newspaper ad that Clark remembered his childhood friend, Joy Flemming, who ran a temporary help agency in Toronto. Clark and Flemming were schoolmates and had kept in touch with each other over the years. Flemming had built up a successful agency that supplied clerical and office staff on a temporary basis. While Clark knew that Flemming's agency primarily supplied clerical workers (and some technical/supervisory personnel), he was convinced that Flemming's years of experience in the local industry would have exposed her to successful human resource professionals elsewhere. He decided to hire Joy to also conduct a search.

Joy was certain to ask him what kind of a person he was looking for. In Clark's mind, he needed a tough individual—someone like John McAllister who could stand up to the unions and take charge. Clark personally disliked handling employee-related matters; he would like to hire someone who would consult him on major issues but who was capable of making decisions on his or her own. There was no formal job description for the HR manager's position in Maple Leaf Shoes, although a consultant was currently working on writing a detailed job description. However, Clark did not value such a document. He was a great believer that these documents meant little except adding to the paperwork. A good person was what he needed now—a well-rounded, tough, experienced person like John who would run a tight ship.

Oh, how much he missed John, Clark reflected sadly.

Discussion Questions

1. What is your evaluation of the recruitment strategy used by Maple Leaf Shoes?

2. Evaluate the recruitment advertisement.

3. Design a new recruitment advertisement for the position of the human resource manager.

4. Design an application form to be used for hiring a human resource manager in the firm.

EXHIBIT 1

Maple Leaf Shoes Limited
requires
A HUMAN RESOURCE MANAGER

Maple Leaf Shoes Limited, the maker of Fluffy Puppy, Cariboo, Madonna, and other brands of high-quality footwear, which currently employs over 650 persons, requires a Human Resource Manager for its head office in Wilmington, Ontario. We are a fast-growing company with plans to expand operations to several provinces and countries in the near future. Currently, we export to the United States and a number of European countries.

As the Human Resource Manager, you will be responsible for overseeing all human resource functions for this large, expanding organization. You will be directly reporting to the President and be part of the top management team.

We are looking for an aggressive, results-oriented individual who can meet the organization's challenges and facilitate our growth plans in the 21st century. This is a senior position and the typical recruit for this position will have at least 15 years' experience in a senior management capacity. The salary and benefits will be commensurate with qualifications and experience.

We are an Equal Employment Opportunity Employer and welcome applications from qualified women and minority candidates.

Apply in confidence to:

Office of the President

Maple Leaf Shoes Limited

1, Crown Royal Lane, Maple Leaf Town

Wilmington, Ontario.

We help you put your best foot forward!

CASE STUDY CPIB Canadian Pacific and International Bank

Evaluating Recruitment Function*

Canadian Pacific and International Bank (CPIB) had achieved significant expansion in its operations in the recent past and is currently a major global financial institution (see end of Chapter 1 for more details on the bank). One key component of its growth strategy was the acquisition of other financial institutions. While in most instances CPIB has been able to achieve a seamless merger of operations, there were times when the systems and culture of the newly acquired organization were at variance with CPIB's. This had necessitated routine internal audits of all major systems in newly acquired institutions.

Mary Keddy, vice-president of human resources, is currently looking through the results of an audit of the recruitment function in Ontario Financial Planners (OFP), an investment firm CPIB had acquired in the past. Table 1 shows a summary of relevant data for two major groups of employees: investment managers and analysts, and sales staff for the last two years. The other categories of staff (such as administrative and clerical) remained more or less stable across time. Several other activities in the firm were also contracted out to agencies or carried out by part-time employees. Other details of the workforce are given below.

OFP, which was begun by two brothers as a family business unit, had over time grown rapidly because of its professional approach to conducting business and friendly client relations. To ensure maximum predictability in employee behaviours, historically the firm had focused on employing family members, friends, and others referred by them. Over a period, however, this practice was replaced by several other recruiting methods. The firm also attempted to have representation from minority groups and women in all its job categories, although this has not always been successful. Financial planning industry has, by and far, always been a white-male-dominated profession—over 75 percent of the investment and financial planners in the industry were white males. The senior and middle-level managers were also mostly white males, Asian Canadians being one of the more successful minorities to reach the position of portfolio or fund managers. The only exception to this general trend was commission-based sales jobs where women were making fast inroads, often reaching nearly one half of total workforce in that category.

Getting well-qualified and competent financial planners was a challenging task since demand for proven analysts and managers was great until the stock market crash of 2008. During the global financial crash, banks were particularly affected.

While CPIB had relatively minor investments in the risky portfolios that fatally affected several American and European banks, even CPIB's mutual funds division faced a significant and adverse decline in demand, necessitating reconfiguration of its workforce. This meant that the attrition of qualified persons was high, often reaching upwards of 20 percent for many firms. Hiring qualified analysts and investment managers was also fraught with considerable difficulties since the wrong hire could cause considerable damage to the company's reputation and customers' trust at a time when investment confidence was already at a low.

The average age of investment analysts and managers in OFP was in the low to mid-forties. Hardly anyone had retired in that job category in the past year. In the sales category, the average age was slightly higher. One person had retired in the last year.

The figures in Table 1 reflect historical costs. The following recruitment methods are found to be more expensive currently, requiring upward adjustment.

Campus recruiting:	increase by 15%
Advertisements:	increase by 10%
Internet recruiting:	increase by 5%

While common selection criteria were employed in hiring employees irrespective of the recruitment methods they came through, OFP's experience was that recruits from different sources required different levels of on-the-job training before they could be placed into job positions. The average cost of a day's training was approximately $700, which accounted for all costs including time lost. The firm's records show the following training statistics for various recruits:

Unsolicited applicants:	3 days
Recruits from HRSDC, Internet, advertisements:	2 days
Campus recruits, applicants referred by current employees:	1 day

Discussion Questions

1. Make your recommendation on the best recruitment method(s) for each type of workforce.

2. What other conclusions can you arrive at when looking at the figures provided in the case?

* Case prepared by Professor Hari Das of Saint Mary's University, Halifax. All rights retained by the author. Das © 2003. Revised 2009.

TABLE 1	Recruiting Method Used During the Last Year

Recruiting Method Used During the Past Year

	Investment Managers and Analysts	Sales Staff
Gender:		
Males	85%	60%
Females	15%	40%
Age:		
Less than 30 years	60%	30%
30–45 years	20%	45%
46–65 years	20%	25%
Education:		
High school or less	10%	60%
University degree or higher	90%	40%

Recruiting Method Used During the Past Two Years

	Unsolicited Applications	HRSDC	Campus Recruitment	Advertise-ments	Internet Recruitment	Referrals from Employees
Total Number of Applications						
Investment managers	50	70	60	200	250	30
Sales staff	40	60	40	300	100	10
Number of Candidates Who Were Offered Jobs						
Investment managers	1	7	9	12	13	9
Sales staff	2	3	2	30	10	2
Number of Candidates Who Accepted Job Offers						
Investment managers	1	3	6	6	10	6
Sales staff	1	2	2	21	4	1
Cost per Recruit in Dollars (includes all overheads)						
Investment managers	45	36	66	60	16	26
Sales staff	42	30	63	48	17	23
Number of New Hires Who Left the Firm Within Two Years						
Investment managers	0	1	1	3	6	1
Sales staff	1	1	0	2	1	1

Selection

The notion of trying to find "good employees" is not very helpful—organizations need to be as specific as possible about the precise attributes they are seeking ... the skills and abilities hired need to be carefully considered and consistent with particular job requirements and the organization's approach to its market. Simply hiring the "best and the brightest" may not make sense in all circumstances.

Jeffrey Pfeffer[1]

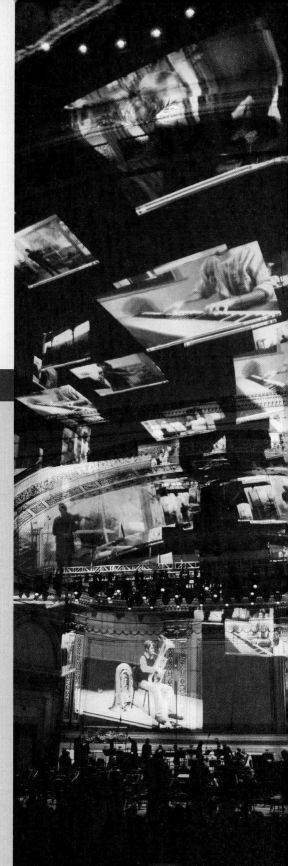

CHAPTER OBJECTIVES

After studying this chapter, you should be able to:

➡ *Explain* the strategic significance of the selection function.

➡ *Describe* the various steps in the selection process.

➡ *Discuss* the types and usefulness of application blanks in selecting employees.

➡ *Explain* the role of employment tests in the selection process.

➡ *Discuss* the major approaches to test validation.

➡ *Outline* the various steps in conducting an employment interview.

CHAPTER 6

Once a pool of suitable applicants is created through recruiting, the process of selecting applicants begins. This process involves a series of steps that adds time and complexity to the hiring decision. Consider the hiring process at Merrill Lynch:

Merrill Lynch, a global investment company owned by Bank of America, with operations in over 43 countries pays considerable attention to the selection function. Applicants for the position of account executive in the past had to complete an application, take a written test, and undergo an interview. In addition to this, the firm's account-executive simulation exercise tested how applicants perform under stressful conditions similar to those that a real stockbroker faces. The test works by telling each applicant that he or she is replacing a stockbroker who has gone to another office. The stockbroker left the client book, which describes the accounts of each client. In addition, the applicants are given a variety of unanswered memos, letters, and telephone messages that they must sort through and decide how to treat. In the background, recorded sounds of a brokerage office are played to add an air of confusing noises, shouts, telephone rings, and other unexpected distractions. During the three hours, fictitious clients call and other messages and reports are dropped on the applicant's "desk."[2]

The simulation exercise is only one part of Merrill Lynch's selection process. Other steps precede and follow it. In the past, all aspiring recruits were encouraged to take a self-test available at the Merrill Lynch Web site. Only those who could truthfully answer "yes" to at least 15 of the 17 questions in the quiz were considered to "have what it takes to become a Merrill Lynch Financial Consultant" and encouraged to proceed. More recently, Merrill Lynch has updated its Web site to provide very specific job information to different categories of applicants—undergraduate and graduate students, full-time positions, and summer internship assignees.[3]

Although most employers do not use such elaborate screening devices, all but the smallest employers put applicants through a variety of steps called the **selection process**. The selection process is a series of specific steps used to decide which recruits should be hired. The process begins when recruits apply for employment and ends with the hiring decision. The steps in between match the employment needs of the applicant and the organization. When these steps are not understood, selection seems like a stressful time and a bureaucratic process rather than the important function it is.

Merrill Lynch Financial Management Company
www.ml.com

selection process
A series of specific steps used by an employer to decide which recruits should be hired.

STRATEGIC SIGNIFICANCE OF THE SELECTION FUNCTION

In many human resource departments, recruiting and selection are combined and called the *employment function*. In very small firms, the owner-manager typically does the hiring.[4] In large human resource departments, the employment function is the responsibility of the employment manager. In smaller departments, human resource managers handle these duties. Whatever the title, in most firms, employment is associated closely with the human resource department.

A proper selection process is integral to the strategic success of firms. Below, we discuss the more critical dimensions of an organization's strategy that are affected by this function.

Successful Execution of an Organization's Strategy Depends on the Calibre of Its Employees

An organization's overall effectiveness and success depends on the quality and calibre of the employees it hires. Poor selection practices also result in the HR department not meeting the three objectives specified in Chapter 1. In turn, an organization's mission and overall strategy affects the selection process and places major constraints on the human resource manager when selecting employees. This is because the skills and qualifications of the new hires need to closely match the organization's culture and strategic requirements, as the following example of Apple Computer illustrates:

In the past, Apple Computer Inc. wanted to hire a line manager to take over a business unit in which the person would, in addition to daily administrative duties, also "sell" new ideas and strategies to the firm's top management. The manager had to be very comfortable dealing with ambiguity because no aspect of the job was totally defined. Indeed, the new hire was expected to take charge and define the job and then sell to others why this approach was better. The company interviewed a woman candidate whose past experience and qualifications (as detailed in her résumé) would have indicated hiring on the spot. However, during the interview it became clear that the applicant wanted a well-defined, predictable task. This led to a closer look at the applicant's past job.

When past job duties were examined, it became clear that they had focused mostly on the implementation of ideas mapped out by someone else. Clearly, this was not the type of individual that Apple wanted.[5]

It should be noted that selection practices not only affect the strategic success of the organization but also often shape internal and external realities of the organization. When most employees do not perform at their best, not only do organizations suffer but a country's fortunes may be adversely affected, as suggested by one writer who linked Britain's lack-lustre performance in the marketplace to employee attitudes:

> A past study of approximately 1,000 human resource directors in Britain indicated that more than 60 percent of the staff are so poorly engaged that most employers would not rehire them. Nearly a quarter of the survey respondents did not believe that their workforce gave their organizations a competitive edge.[6]

An Organization's Selection Decisions Must Reflect Job Requirements

As we saw in Chapter 2, the results of job analysis help an organization to identify job duties, specifications, and performance standards. A mismatch between these and the selection criteria will not only result in poor hires but will also expose the organization to possible lawsuits from job applicants who believe that they have been discriminated against.

> Gian Singha, an immigrant from India who was fluent in four languages including English, held postgraduate degrees including a Ph.D. from Germany in environmental science, and was a co-author of two books and numerous research papers, applied for a mid-level position as a regulatory officer with the Mackenzie Valley Land and Water Board. He scored among the highest of the 12 applicants the board chose to interview. Yet, to his shock a few days later, he was told that his application had been rejected because he was overqualified. The Board felt that he would become bored with the job's routine nature and quit prematurely. Mr. Singha complained to the Canadian Human Rights Tribunal, and in a groundbreaking decision, the Tribunal ruled that the Board's action discriminated against Mr. Singha and visible minority immigrants in general. Mr. Singha was awarded damages and, more significantly, it ordered the Board to cease using any hiring policies that would automatically disqualify visible minority immigrants on the grounds that they are overqualified.[7]

As discussed in Chapter 1, rejecting applicants, especially those with foreign qualifications, on the grounds that they are "overqualified" has been a major barrier against immigrants and has resulted in systemic discrimination against them. Today, the employer is required to show that the tools used for selecting employees are reliable and valid (and not simply "feelings" as in the above case where the Board members used unsupported assumptions to reject a qualified applicant). This means that performance-based job descriptions[8] and valid selection tools are necessary in the context of selection. Mere "myths" are not valid arguments for continuing to use an irrelevant predictor such as educational qualification. Figure 6-1 lists some of the popular myths in the context of hiring.

FIGURE 6-1	Sample Myths in the Context of Hiring
Myth	**Reality Emerging from Research Findings**
Conscientiousness is a better predictor of employee performance than intelligence.	Several research studies indicate that intelligence is as or more important than conscientiousness.
Integrity tests don't work.	While it is true that many people attempt to make themselves appear more ethical than they really are, a well-developed and validated integrity test can be a good predictor of a person's likely future behaviour.
Integrity tests have adverse effects on racial minorities.	Racial and ethnic differences on integrity test scores are, typically, insignificant. Well-developed and scientifically administered tests normally do not result in discrimination against specific racial groups.

Source: Abridged, Adapted and summarized from Sara L. Rynes, Kenneth G. Brown, and Amy E. Colbert (2002). "Seven Common Misconceptions about Human Resource Practices: Research Findings versus Practitioner Beliefs." *Academy of Management Executive*, Vol. 16, No. 3.

Selection Strategy Must Be Well Integrated with Organizational Priorities

As seen in Chapter 1, organizations differ in their strategic posture. Organizational characteristics—including such factors as product lines, market share, and culture—vary widely and are dynamic in nature. As a firm grows, different priorities start to emerge:

> A startup business typically has a few product lines and places heavy emphasis on entrepreneurship. In contrast, a multinational organization with operations in several different countries and cultures worries about achieving control over operations while providing adequate autonomy to local operations. An aging or declining organization needs to emphasize renewal if it is to survive. The type of employees sought are also somewhat different in each instance. An infant organization may attempt to hire entrepreneurial managers, while a mature organization needs managers who can continually search for economies of scale and implement efficient systems. In contrast, a declining organization may seek managers who can cut costs, generate revenues, rebuild the organization, and turn it around.

The specific needs of an organization are determined by a variety of factors (and not merely by its stage in the life cycle); however, an organization's stage in the life cycle provides a starting point in linking an organization's overall needs and its selection strategy.

Selection Strategy Must Recognize Organizational Constraints

All organizations have finite resources. This means that the systems employed for the selection of human resources should be cost-effective. The selection process is not an end; it is a means through which the organization achieves its objectives. Most organizations impose some limits, such as budgets and policies, that may hinder the selection process. Without budget limitations, selection procedures could be refined. But without limits, employment expenses could be so high that organizational effectiveness would suffer.

The firm's policies may expand existing challenges or simply add more constraints. Policies against discrimination reinforce external prohibitions, for example. Internal decrees may exceed legal demands from outside. For example, policies to hire ex-convicts further societal objectives (discussed in Chapter 1), but are not legally required. Such internal policies add still another challenge for employment specialists.

Selection Strategy Must Adapt to Labour Market Realities

It is important to have a large, qualified pool of recruits from which to select applicants. But some jobs are so hard to fill that there are few applicants per opening.

> For example, Canada currently has a shortage of doctors in some specialities. Thus, hospital looking for specialists will face an unfavourable selection ratio. This will be even more acutely felt by hospitals in smaller towns and rural districts.

selection ratio
The ratio of the number of applicants hired to the total number of applicants.

A **selection ratio** is the relationship between the number of applicants hired and the total number of applicants available. A selection ratio such as 1:25 (compared to a selection ratio of 1:2) means there are a large number of applicants from which to select. In many instances a selection ratio such as 1:3 or 1:5 also means a low quality of recruits. The ratio is computed as follows:

$$\frac{\text{Number of applicants hired}}{\text{Total number of applicants}} = \text{Selection ratio}$$

> Wes Klugh, an employment manager for a chain of motels, faced an adverse selection ratio for the third-shift desk clerk's job. Although it paid 50 cents an hour more than the day or evening clerk jobs, few people applied for it. Wes decided to redesign the job by enriching it. The job was expanded to include responsibility for completing the daily financial report and other bookkeeping tasks. The additional duties justified the substantial raise and new title—night auditor. The result was more applicants.

The number of applicants for a position is also partially dependent on a firm's salary and benefit package compared to others in the industry. Industry information can be secured from Statistics Canada, Human Resources and Skills Development Canada, or other associations.

SPOTLIGHT ON ETHICS
Selection Practices Must Be Ethical

An organization's selection strategy should be ethical. Since employment specialists strongly influence the hiring decision, that decision is shaped by their ethics. Consider the following situations and rate them as ethical or unethical. If unethical, what actions will you take to achieve the goals while at the same time maintaining high ethical standards?

Compare your answers with those of your friends. Do you see any differences? What accounts for the differences?

You are the human resource manager in a medium-sized firm and report to the director of human resources. Your boss gives you a lot of discretion in decision making and, in general, you are very happy with your job. However, more recently, the following three events have caused you some concern:

1. You are told to find "some positions" in the company for some of the executives' children for the coming summer months. You feel that disobeying the order may affect your career. However, you wonder whether hiring some of them would be an admission that you selected people on criteria other than merit.

2. An executive search firm, which your firm had hired in the past year to do a routine job search, has given you an expensive watch as a Christmas gift. Even a casual glance shows you that the watch was worth over $750. You wonder whether accepting it puts you under a moral obligation to the firm and taints your future decisions when hiring search firms. While you had no problems with the service provided by the firm, the firm by no means is the best service provider in the industry or region, nor the cheapest.

3. John McIntosh, your neighbour for 20 years now, indicated to you that his niece has applied for a position in your firm and it will be nice if "you can look into it." John has been a very kind neighbour and has been of immense help to your family, which had to stay back in Canada while you were away on an international assignment last year. You looked at his niece's background. While she meets the minimum requirements, there are a number of candidates who are far better than her. What is worse, some of the other candidates are known to a number of employees who will wonder why they were not hired.

Figure 6-2 summarizes the key factors that influence and are affected by a firm's selection strategy. As can be seen, selection affects virtually all major human resource functions within the organization. It should be noted that an organization's policies on other matters (e.g., compensation levels, training) have an impact on selection strategy at least in the long term. This fact is indicated by the dotted arrow in Figure 6-2.

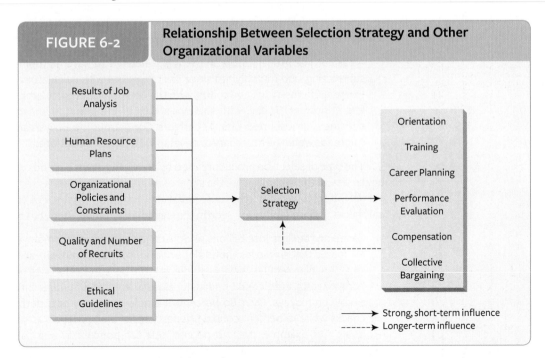

FIGURE 6-2   Relationship Between Selection Strategy and Other Organizational Variables

This chapter introduces you to various tools at the disposal of human resource managers in formulating an effective selection strategy. The next section begins the discussion by outlining major steps in the selection of human resources.

STEPS IN THE SELECTION OF HUMAN RESOURCES

The selection process is a series of steps through which applicants pass. Sometimes the process can be made simple and effective; however, simplicity should not be achieved at the cost of lower effectiveness. Consider this:

> At a large bank, the selection process was simplified and computerized in order to match present employees with internal openings. The specific tasks required of various jobs were programmed into the computer along with the specific abilities of employees. Whenever clerical or routine job openings emerged, employee profiles were computer-matched with task requirements. Those employees with the highest match for a given opening are then considered for the job.

A major shortcoming of the above computerized approach is that the matching process largely ignores other factors such as attitudes, personality, and the like. To ensure that both task and nontask factors are considered, human resource departments commonly use a more involved sequence of steps, as shown in Figure 6-3. Note that these steps reflect considerable variation from one organization to the next.

> For instance, some employers find it useful to introduce a realistic job preview at an earlier stage to save the time and expense of administering tests and interviews for applicants who are unlikely to fit the position.

An applicant may also be rejected at any step in the process.

> For example, for internal applicants, there is seldom a need to verify references from outsiders, or do a medical evaluation. But with external applicants, the steps in Figure 6-3 are common. In most organizations, a medical evaluation, if done at all, is carried out only after a hiring decision is made. In such cases, the job offer is conditional on the applicant satisfactorily completing the medical evaluation.

Also, it should be noted that in small organizations the hiring decision is based on a single interview by the owner or manager concerned. Further, depending on the unique constraints facing an organization, some of the stages may be combined or their sequence altered.

Whatever the exact steps employed and their sequence, an organization's selection system should be integrally related to the job descriptions and specifications. The job specifications should form the basis of all selection decisions. Continuous job analysis should also ensure that these specifications reflect changes in tasks, technology, and job demands.

> A cashier in a grocery store in the 1960s needed to have mathematical skills (such as adding, subtracting, and multiplying) since cash registers with calculators were relatively uncommon. However, in the 1970s and 1980s, with the abundance of calculators, this skill became relatively less important. Today, with the availability of electronic scanners, mathematical skills have become even less important for cashiers. Continuous job analysis and monitoring of technological trends would be necessary to develop valid job specifications.

The type of selection procedure used by an organization depends on a variety of factors including the size of the organization, the stage of its growth (e.g., new versus established for some time), and the jobs involved. There are also variations across industries. For example, use of honesty tests and checks for bondability are seen in the Canadian retail industry, but not in the education sector.

> Canadian retailers lose billions of dollars each year due to employee and customer thefts. It is estimated that employee thefts alone cost employers $3 million each day. To overcome the problem, Canadian retailers have been doing more personal reference checks, paper-and-pencil and honesty tests, credit and bondability assessments, and multiple interviews to screen out undesirable employees. Over 80 percent of employers verify past performance through reference checks while 10 percent conduct honesty tests. Multiple tools are often used to check honesty levels (for example, over 20 percent test for bondability and past criminal behaviours, and 17 percent verify past educational attainment).[9]

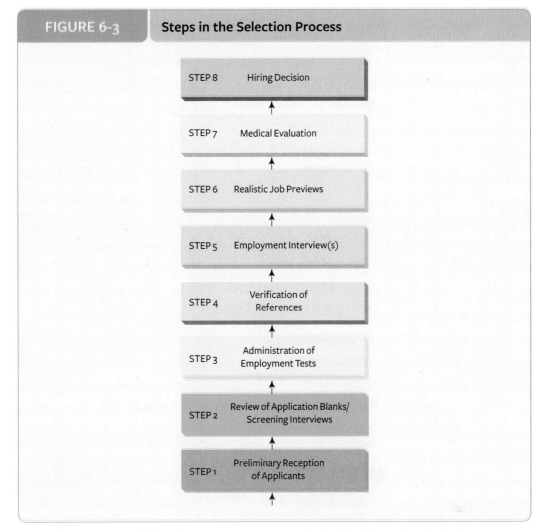

FIGURE 6-3 | **Steps in the Selection Process**

STEP 8 — Hiring Decision

STEP 7 — Medical Evaluation

STEP 6 — Realistic Job Previews

STEP 5 — Employment Interview(s)

STEP 4 — Verification of References

STEP 3 — Administration of Employment Tests

STEP 2 — Review of Application Blanks/ Screening Interviews

STEP 1 — Preliminary Reception of Applicants

Note: The above sequence is likely to show some variation across organizations. Not all firms go through all the above steps or in the above sequence. In general, an applicant who disqualifies on a step does not advance to the next step.

Past surveys of employers indicate that letters of reference and weighted application blanks are most popular for the selection of white-collar professional workers while biographical information blanks are more frequently used for white-collar nonprofessional jobs.[10] Personality tests are popular for selecting middle-management employees, and aptitude tests are most common for white-collar nonprofessional jobs. Nearly 50 percent of employers use at least one paper-and-pencil test. A summary of the selection practices in Canadian organizations is shown in Figure 6-4. Figure 6-5 shows the major predictors used by the same organizations in selecting persons for different positions.

Step 1: Preliminary Reception of Applicants

Job applicants may make initial contact either in person, in writing, or by email. Sometimes applicants may "walk in," inquiring about possible job vacancies—often, the receptionist provides them with basic information on jobs available, pay rates, and hours of work. When the applicant is a "walk-in," a preliminary interview—typically with a representative of the human resource department or the store manager in the case of a very small firm—is often granted as a courtesy. This "courtesy interview," as it is sometimes called, is unlikely to be as rigorous as otherwise, but it does attempt to screen out obvious "misfits" (e.g., someone who is not willing to travel but is interested in a salesperson's job with the firm requiring considerable travel). Such courtesy interviews are also an important part of good public relations by the firm, as information conveyed during these meetings and the professionalism displayed by the HR manager during this early encounter may have lasting implications for its future recruitment and marketing success. Candidates applying in writing are often sent a polite letter of acknowledgment. If the applicant looks promising (either on the basis of the initial

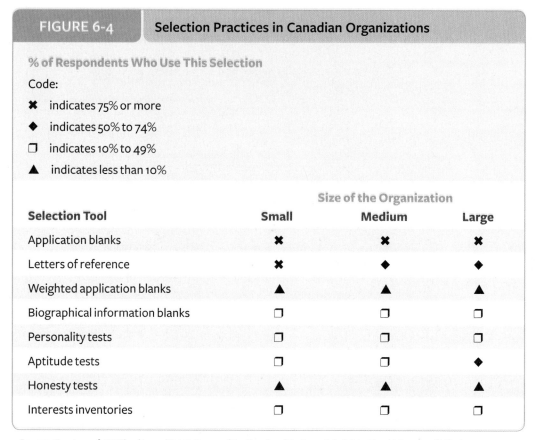

FIGURE 6-4	Selection Practices in Canadian Organizations

% of Respondents Who Use This Selection

Code:

✖ indicates 75% or more

◆ indicates 50% to 74%

❐ indicates 10% to 49%

▲ indicates less than 10%

	Size of the Organization		
Selection Tool	**Small**	**Medium**	**Large**
Application blanks	✖	✖	✖
Letters of reference	✖	◆	◆
Weighted application blanks	▲	▲	▲
Biographical information blanks	❐	❐	❐
Personality tests	❐	❐	❐
Aptitude tests	❐	❐	◆
Honesty tests	▲	▲	▲
Interests inventories	❐	❐	❐

Source: Courtesy of J.W. Thacker and R.J. Cattaneo of the Faculty of Business Administration, University of Windsor.

FIGURE 6-5	Major Predictors Used in Selecting Employees for Different Positions

Code:

✖ indicates 75% or more

◆ indicates 50% to 74%

❐ indicates 10% to 49%

▲ indicates less than 10%

	% of Respondents Using This Selection Tool for This Class of Employees			
	Managerial	**Professional**	**White Collar**	**Blue Collar**
Letters of reference	✖	✖	✖	❐
Weighted application blanks	◆	✖	✖	◆
Biographical blanks	◆	✖	✖	◆
Tests (personality)	◆	◆	◆	❐
Assessment centre reports	◆	❐	❐	▲

Source: Adapted from a working paper by J.W. Thacker and R.J. Cattaneo of the Faculty of Business Administration, University of Windsor.

letter or the courtesy interview), he or she is typically asked to complete a formal application form. With the increasing use of the Internet for providing general information about the company and responding to preliminary inquiries from applicants, this particular step in selection has disappeared in several organizations, especially larger ones.

Step 2: Review of Application Blanks/Screening Interviews

application blank
A job application form.

Undoubtedly, one of the most popular selection tools is an **application blank**. Most Canadian organizations require a job applicant to complete an application form, especially for lower-level jobs. However, an application form, if not carefully developed, can serve little purpose and may even be illegal.

> An Ontario security firm that required applicants to fill out a form asking for information regarding place of birth, eye and hair colour, and complexion was found to be discriminatory.[11]

Application forms, hence, should be developed with great care.[12] A good application form can provide valuable information on a number of job-relevant dimensions (see Figure 6-6). A typical job application form was presented in Chapter 5.

One might suspect that some aspects of a person's background (e.g., years of education, previous experience in similar positions) would have a greater relationship to job success than some other factors (e.g., number of part-time jobs held while in school). A **weighted application blank** (WAB) technique provides a means of identifying which of these aspects reliably distinguish groups of satisfactory and unsatisfactory job incumbents.[13] Weights are assigned in accordance with the predictive power of each item so that a total "success score" can be calculated for each job applicant. A cut-off score can be established that, when used in selection, will eliminate the maximum number of potentially unsuccessful candidates. WABs have been found to be particularly valuable for job positions that require long and expensive training, where a large number of applicants apply for a few positions, and where employee turnover or attrition is abnormally high.[14]

weighted application blank (WAB)
A job application form in which various items are given differential weights to reflect their relationship to criterion measure.

biographical information blank (BIB)
A type of application blank that uses a multiple-choice format to measure a job candidate's education, experiences, opinions, attitudes, and interests.

In some instances, **biographical information blanks** (BIBs) have been developed. The BIB is similar to the WAB and is a self-report instrument. However, it is exclusively in a multiple-choice format and typically includes items that are not usually covered in a WAB. Thus, questions pertaining to a job candidate's early life experiences, hobbies, opinions, attitudes, and interests are common in a BIB. Although primary emphasis is on past behaviours as a predictor of future behaviour, BIBs frequently also look at present behaviours and attitudes.

Properly developed WABs and BIBs have been found to be useful in several occupations, including life insurance agents, sales clerks, engineers, research scientists, and architects. A review of 58 studies that used biographical information as a predictor of job success showed that over various occupations, the average validity was 0.35.[15] A subsequent analysis of 44 such studies showed the average validity to be 0.37.[16]

Given this, carefully designed application blanks (especially in WAB and BIB format) seem to hold considerable potential as a selection tool.

FIGURE 6-6	Usefulness of Application Forms

A well-designed application form, among other things, will
- collect specific information about the applicant's past work experience in similar and related jobs;
- collect information on the applicant's educational background summarizing key competencies and job relevant skills;
- collect information on the applicant's special training or unique skills/competencies;
- help identify gaps and unaccounted-for time in the record;
- help summarize the overall direction and consistency in the applicant's career progression;
- provide insights into the applicant's motivation, indicating whether the energies are all focused in one direction or diffused in several directions;
- avoid illegal, unethical, and personally intrusive questions;
- assess the applicant's overall leadership qualities and outside interests;
- reveal potential problem areas such as language deficiency, inability to travel, and ethical concerns (e.g., if the applicant is currently working for a competitor in a sensitive area); and
- indicate how the applicant may introduce innovative practices on the job.

Biographical information blanks often contain questions relating to a candidate's early life experiences, e.g., hobbies and interests. How are these related to the job at hand? Are these questions legal?

© David Young-Wolff/Getty Images

Today, more progressive employers have applicant tracking systems that store key information from each applicant and retrieve them as job vacancies emerge (see Chapter 5 for details). It is expected that in the near future, interactive résumé-building will become the norm for several employers.[17]

Many firms today are developing Web applications that build a résumé for the applicant by asking a series of questions. Applicants must answer the questions to get through the application, and in so doing supply the information the firm needs to decide whether to interview the applicant.

Whatever the type of application form used, information given in an application form or résumé may contain elements of embellishment and even outright fabrication. Indeed, in recent years, *résumé fraud* (as it is called) has become a major concern of recruiters.

A newly hired Chief Administrative Officer of the City of Waterloo was fired because he had not disclosed critical information about his problems on the previous job. In a survey of 300 executive recruiters, it was found that "reasons for leaving prior jobs" was the item which was fabricated most, closely followed by "results and accomplishments on past jobs." Past salary, job responsibilities, education, dates of employment, and job titles were other major items where the candidates provided false information.[18]

This means that application forms and résumés have to be carefully analyzed for inconsistencies and checked against information coming from other sources such as references or background checks. In the case of several jobs, key KSAs (knowledge, skills, and attitudes) are also assessed through standardized and validated tests. The following section discusses the use of employment tests to assess the key competencies required for a job.

Online Hiring Firm
Hire.com
www.hire.com

employment tests
Devices that assess the probable match between applicants and job requirements.

Step 3: Administration of Employment Tests

Employment tests are useful for obtaining relatively objective information, which can be compared with that pertaining to other applicants and present workers. **Employment tests** are devices that assess the match between applicants and job requirements. Some are paper-and-pencil tests; others are exercises that simulate work conditions. A math test for a bookkeeper is an example of a paper-and-pencil test, and a manual-dexterity test for an assembly worker is an example of a simulation exercise. Manual dexterity tests are used more frequently for jobs that pay an hourly wage than for salaried positions because hourly jobs usually call for a limited number of skills or activities that can be tested easily. Management and professional jobs are often too complex to be tested fairly and economically in this manner.

In general, paper-and-pencil tests are popular for selecting white-collar and managerial positions in Canada, but not for blue-collar jobs. Personality tests are popular for selecting managers. The use of personality and aptitude tests becomes more popular as the firm size increases. In contrast, honesty tests are not very popular. One past study found that they were restricted mostly to small firms (see Figure 6-4).[19] Figure 6-7 summarizes the findings of one study that looked at the selection tools used in 133 Canadian firms.

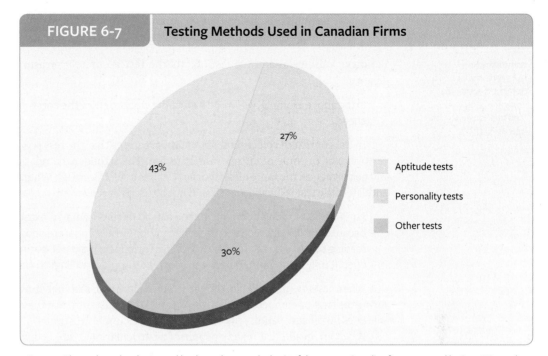

FIGURE 6-7   **Testing Methods Used in Canadian Firms**

- 43%
- 27%
- 30%

Legend:
- Aptitude tests
- Personality tests
- Other tests

Source: Chart adapted and prepared by the authors on the basis of data on 133 Canadian firms reported by Sean Way and James Thacker in "Selection Practices: Where Are Canadian Organizations?" *HR Professional*, Vol. 16, No. 5, October/November, 1999, p. 34.

The use of tests should be guided by their reliability and validity. These are discussed in some detail below.

Reliability and Validity of Selection Tests

Testing became popular on a large scale during the First World War, when intelligence tests were given to army recruits. During the following 60 years, tests were developed for a wide range of employment uses, but many of these tests were assumed to be valid without sufficient proof.

For a test to be useful, it must meet the twin criteria of reliability and validity.

Reliability.   **Reliability** means that the test yields consistent results.

> For example, a test of manual dexterity for assembly workers should give a similar score each time the same person takes the test. If the results vary widely with each retest because good scores depend on luck, the test is not reliable.

Reliability of a test may become low for a variety of reasons, including the following:

- The test questions may be hard to understand or ambiguous, thus resulting in different test takers reading different meanings into the same question or sentence. It is also possible that the same person may interpret a question differently on different occasions because of poor test construction.
- The test questions may be so hard or boring that the examinee loses all interest and begins to respond almost randomly or erratically.
- Some external factor (e.g., noise, smell), event (e.g., war), or personal characteristic (e.g., being ill at the time of test taking) may result in random errors.
- There could be changes in the examinee, especially if a long test is being used. The examinee may get tired or bored, making responses to later questions unreliable.

Being aware of the above factors help the test maker to avoid them and improve reliability. However, high reliability alone does not ensure that a test is in fact valid or useful.

> Consider a clock that gains 5 minutes each day. On the first day, we can arrive at the correct time by deducting 5 minutes from the time shown in the clock. If the clock is not corrected, on the second day, it will be 10 minutes ahead of the true time. Since the clock is gaining exactly 5 minutes each day, the time is predictable. However, the clock is still not an accurate device and hence of

reliability
A selection device's ability to yield consistent results over repeated measures. Also, internal consistency of a device or measure.

limited usefulness in the long run (for example, without knowing the number of days the clock ran uncorrected, we will not be able to predict the correct time).

Validity. **Validity** asks the question: "Is the test accurately measuring what it is purported to measure?"

In the above example, we would expect the clock to show the correct time each day, not 5 minutes ahead.

In the context of selection tests, validity requires that the test scores significantly relate to job performance or some other relevant criterion. The stronger the relationship between test results and performance, the more effective the test is as a selection tool. When scores and performance are unrelated, the test is invalid and should not be used for selection:

> An Ontario trucking company once gave all its applicants an extensive reading test. However, because the drivers received their instructions orally and were shown on a map where to go, the reading test had no relationship to job performance; it did not distinguish good drivers from bad ones. It only distinguished between those who could read English well and those who could not.

When tests are not reliable, they are also, in almost all instances, invalid, since they are not measuring the trait or competency with any degree of consistency. But the mere fact that the test is reliable does not ensure validity (as our earlier clock example illustrates).

When an invalid test rejects people of a particular race, sex, religion, or national origin, it violates the *Canadian Human Rights Act* or related provincial legislation. However, test validity as it is related to discrimination has not received a great deal of attention in Canada. Given that many of the tests we use were developed in the United States, one wonders whether they are particularly valid, since they were developed for a different group of workers. Too often, tests fail to predict job performance.[20] A Toronto-based industrial psychologist has estimated that "only 3 percent of firms use properly validated selection tests."[21] If this estimate is correct, then an increased scrutiny of testing and its relationship to discrimination may well be a future trend in the human resource area.

To assure that its tests are valid, human resource departments should conduct *validation studies*. These studies compare test results with performance of traits needed to perform the job. Figure 6-8 summarizes the most common approaches to validation.

Empirical approaches rely on **predictive** or **concurrent validity**. Both methods attempt to relate test scores to some criterion, usually performance. The main difference between the two approaches lies in the sample used (see Figure 6-8 for details). The higher the correlation between test scores and the criterion, the more effective the test is. Empirical approaches are generally preferred because they are less subjective than rational methods.

Rational approaches include content and construct validity (see Figure 6-8). **Content validity** is established by ensuring that the test includes an adequate and representative sample of items from the domain of interest.

> For example, to be content valid, a quiz on "staffing" should contain an adequate and representative sample of all key human resource management concepts relevant to recruitment, selection, and deployment of human resources, as these are normally considered to be the relevant dimensions of "staffing." If the quiz contains only questions pertaining to recruitment, then it has not included items from the other two dimensions of the domain of interest.

Construct validity is the hardest to establish in practice. Evidence for construct validity is established over time through a variety of approaches, including comparing the results of the test with the results in other similar tests.

> For example, if the test is supposed to be assessing intelligence, then the scores on this test should be positively correlated with scores on other established and validated tests of intelligence.

Sometimes, construct validity is also established by looking at how the test scores relate to score on tests that measure different constructs.

> For example, to assess the construct validity of a new test on employee morale, the researcher may compare the scores on the test with the employee's scores on an established test for job alienation. Since morale is theoretically conceptualized to be opposite to alienation, we would expect the scores on the two tests to show negative correlation if the new test has any construct validity.

validity
A key attribute of a selection device that indicates its accuracy and relationship to job-relevant criteria.

predictive validity
An empirical approach to validation that correlates predictor and criterion scores.

concurrent validity
An empirical approach to validation that measures the predictor and criterion scores concurrently.

content validity
A rational approach to validation that examines the extent to which the selection device includes elements of the job domain.

construct validity
A rational approach to validation that seeks to establish a relationship to a construct, attribute, or quality related to job performance.

FIGURE 6-8	An Explanation of Common Approaches to Test Validation

Empirical Approaches

Empirical approaches to test validation attempt to relate test scores with a job-related criterion, usually performance. If the test actually measures a job-related criterion, the test and the criterion exhibit a positive correlation between 0 and 1.0. The higher the correlation, the better the match.

- *Predictive validity* is determined by giving a test to a group of applicants. After these applicants have been hired and have mastered the job reasonably well, their performance is measured. This measurement and the test score are then correlated.

- *Concurrent validity* allows the human resource department to test present employees and correlate these scores with measures of their performance. This approach does not require the delay between hiring and mastery of the job.

Rational Approaches

When the number of subjects is too low to have a reasonable sample of people to test, rational approaches are used. These approaches are considered inferior to empirical techniques, but are acceptable validation strategies when empirical approaches are not feasible.

- *Content validity* is assumed to exist when the test contains an adequate and representative sample of items from the domain of the construct that it is attempting to measure. For example, a vocabulary test should contain a representative sample of words contained in an unabridged dictionary. If all the words in a test contain only words beginning with M or Q, or if they are all four-letter words containing the letter "e," the test is not content-valid.

- *Construct validity* is established by showing that the test measures the construct and only the construct under consideration. For example, an intelligence test should measure intelligence, not simply a person's reading ability or memory. Establishing construct validity is the hardest, since it can be done only over time by comparing the outcomes of the test with the outcomes of other tests and measures. For instance, the construct validity of a test on job stress may be established by comparing the scores on the test with other measures of stress or predicted outcomes of stress. Needless to say, such a relationship is established over time and by using theoretical arguments.

These techniques are used when empirical validity is not feasible because the small number of subjects does not permit a reasonable sample upon which to conduct the validation study.

Regardless of which approach is used, testing experts advise separate validation studies for different subgroups, such as women and minorities. The use of such separate studies ensures **differential validity**. Without differential validity, a test may be valid for a large group (white male applicants), but not for subgroups of minorities or women. Yet even when tests have been validated, the type of validation used is still important. Faulty procedures, no matter how well intentioned, cannot be relied on to prove a test's validity. An example of this point follows:

differential validity
Test validation process aimed at discovering the validity of a test for various subgroups, e.g., females and members of visible minorities.

> The Albemarle Paper Company, a U.S. firm, gave several black workers a battery of tests that had not been validated. The workers sued Albemarle, so the company then implemented a validation study. But the study had several weaknesses, and the court ruled the tests invalid and discriminatory.
>
> The problems for Albemarle:
>
> - It used the tests that had been validated for advanced jobs, not the entry-level positions to which tests were being applied. Such validation does not prove that tests are valid for entry-level jobs. Tests must be validated on those jobs to which tests are being applied.
> - It validated the test on one group (white workers) and then applied the test to another group (black workers). Tests must be validated for all the groups to whom the test applies.[22]

It is also important to test for systemic differences in reliability and validity for different employee groups (on the basis of their gender, race, or other criteria).[23] Otherwise, the test may, over time, result in systemic discrimination against specific, protected groups.

Available evidence on validation of various selection tests by Canadian organizations portrays a disappointing picture. In a survey of 202 Canadians, 73 percent of the reporting organizations indicated they did not validate any of their selection methods, including interviews. Indeed, many respondents did not even know the meaning of various types of validity or how to validate using the various methods (see Figure 6-9). This means that many Canadian organizations are not using as effective a selection process as they could or should.

Types of Tests (3)
American Psychological Association
Information on testing
www.apa.org/science/
testing.html

Personality Tests
www.2h.com/
personality-tests.html

Variety of Tests
www.queendom.com/tests/

Types of Tests

There is a wide variety of employment tests. But each type of test has only limited usefulness. The exact purpose of a test, its design, the directions for its administration, and its applications are recorded in the test manual, which should be reviewed before a test is used. The manual also reports the test's reliability and the results of validation efforts by the test designer. Today, many tests have been validated on large populations. But human resource specialists should conduct their own studies to make sure a particular test is valid for its planned use. The HR specialist should be also aware of the confounding effects of situational variables on a job applicant's performance in a specific test.

For example, test-taking anxiety levels may vary across applicant groups. Some past studies indicate that females exhibit higher levels of emotionality and worry than do males.[24]

Each type of test has a different purpose. Figure 6-10 lists examples and a brief explanation of popular employment-related tests.

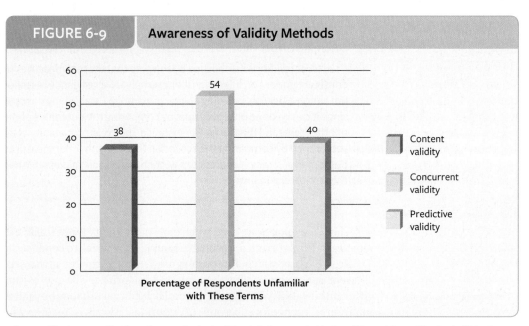

FIGURE 6-9	Awareness of Validity Methods

Source: Chart prepared by the authors on the basis of the statistics reported by Sean Way and James Thacker in "Selection Practices: Where Are Canadian Organizations?" *HR Professional*, October/November, 1999, p. 35.

FIGURE 6-10	Popular Employment-Related Tests

	Psychological Tests
Name	**Application (Subjects)**
Minnesota Multiphasic Personality Inventory	Measures personality or temperament (executives, nuclear power security)
California Psychological Inventory	Measures personality or temperament (executives, managers, supervisors)
Guilford-Zimmerman Temperament Survey	Measures personality or temperament (sales personnel)

FIGURE 6-10	Popular Employment-Related Tests (continued)

Psychological Tests

Name	Application (Subjects)
Watson-Glaser Critical Thinking Appraisal	Measures logic and reasoning ability (executives, managers, supervisors)
Owens Creativity Test	Measures creativity and judgment ability (engineers)

Knowledge Tests

How to Supervise?	Measures knowledge of supervisory practices (managers and supervisors)
Leadership Opinion Questionnaire	Measures knowledge of leadership practices (managers and supervisors)
General Aptitude Test Battery	Measures verbal, spatial, numeric, and other aptitudes and dexterity (job seekers at unemployment offices)

Performance Tests

Stromberg Dexterity Test	Measures physical coordination (shop workers)
Revised Minnesota Paper Form Board Test	Measures spatial visualization (draftsmen and draftswomen)
Minnesota Clerical Test	Measures ability to work with numbers and names (clerks)
Job Simulation Tests, Assessment Centres	Measures a sample of "on the job" demands (managers, professionals, supervisory, and nonsupervisory employees)

Integrity Tests

Lie Detector	Honesty and truthfulness (police, retail store workers)
Honesty Test	Measures attitudes about theft and related subjects (retail workers, securities employees, banks)

Attitude Tests

Work Opinion Questionnaire	Measures attitudes about work and values (entry-level, low-income workers)

Medical Tests

Drug Tests	Measures the presence of illegal or performance affecting drugs (athletes, government employees, equipment operators)
Genetic Screening	Identifies genetic predispositions to specific medical problems
Medical Screening	Measures and monitors exposure to hazardous substances (miners, factory workers, researchers), as well as applicant's ability to perform the job at required level

Source: Adapted from Hari Das and Nathan Kling, "Verbal Ability and Composition Test," Faculty of Commerce, Saint Mary's University, Halifax, 1981.

Personality Tests. These tests measure personality or temperament. If not well designed and adequately tested for their psychometric properties, these tests can prove to be unreliable. Indeed, several off-the-shelf tests not rigorously developed and tested using different segments of the population have low reliabilities. Validity suffers because the exact relationship between personality and performance is unknown and even nonexistent in several instances. However, well-developed and validated tests can be a powerful tool to predict the future behaviours of applicants.

Some personality dimensions such as conscientiousness (e.g., achievement-oriented, organized), openness to experience (e.g., imaginative, intellectually curious), and agreeableness (e.g., cooperative, eagerness to help) have shown some promise as predictors of job performance.[25] For example, the CEOs of several large and successful firms such as Southwest Airlines, Heinz, and Rubbermaid have been reported to often work 80 to 90 hours a week in the past.[26] Conscientiousness seems to be a particularly useful predictor of performance in a number of instances.

For example, measures of conscientiousness have shown to be inversely related to absenteeism.[27] "Big Five Personality Factors," such as neuroticism, extraversion, openness to experience, agreeableness, and conscientiousness, have been found to have some relationship with performance, but, even here, the average correlation has been modest (typically, 0.20 to 0.30).[28] Some measures of personality and cognitive abilities may, thus, be a useful part of a HR manager's arsenal of selection tools.[29]

knowledge tests
Tests that measure a person's information or knowledge.

Knowledge Tests. Knowledge tests are more reliable than personality tests because they determine information or knowledge.

Arithmetic tests for an accountant, knowledge of tax laws for a tax specialist, and a weather test for a pilot are examples of knowledge tests.

Human resource specialists must be able to demonstrate that the knowledge is needed to perform the job. The Ontario trucking company example is a case wherein the tested knowledge (reading at an advanced level) was not needed. Figure 6-11 shows an example of a knowledge test where verbal ability is being assessed.

performance tests
Test that measure ability of job applicants to perform specific components of the job for which they are to be hired.

Performance Tests. Performance tests measure the ability of applicants to do some parts of the work for which they are to be hired.

A keying test for keyboard operators or a driving test for cab or truck drivers are obvious examples of performance tests.

Validity is often assumed when the test includes a representative sample of the work the applicant is to do when hired. However, if the test discriminates against some minority group, the human resources department's assumption must be supported by detailed validation studies.

assessment centre (AC)
A standardized form of employee appraisal that relies on several types of evaluation and multiple assessors. Assessment centres are typically used not only to assess present skills but future potential.

Assessment Centres. A popular procedure used for identifying managerial potential is the **assessment centre (AC).**[30] Currently, ACs are popular at Alcan, Nortel, and Steinberg Ltd., to mention a few organizations in the private sector. Assessment centres are increasing in popularity in several municipal, provincial, and federal government units as well.

FIGURE 6-11	A Segment of a Verbal Ability Test

Directions: Each of the following questions consists of a word printed in italics followed by four words or phrases, lettered (a) through (d). Choose the word that is most nearly *identical* in meaning to the word in italics.

1. *affect:* (a) to insult (b) to move, stir, or have influence upon (c) to imitate or pretend (d) the impression or result produced
2. *inane:* (a) humorous (b) careless (c) dejected (d) silly
3. *soporific:* (a) soapy (b) sleep-inducing (c) unsophisticated (d) saturated
4. *latent:* (a) backward (b) dormant (c) extreme (d) obvious

Source: Adapted from Hari Das and Nathan Kling, Verbal Ability and Composition Test, Faculty of Commerce, Saint Mary's University, Halifax, 1981.

Assessment centres use several methods of assessment, including paper-and-pencil tests, job simulations, in-basket exercises, projective tests, interviews, personality inventories, and/or leaderless group discussions. Typically, the tests are used to measure intellectual ability, work orientation, and career orientation. Leaderless group discussions, role-playing, and in-basket exercises measure an applicant's administrative skill. However, assessment centres do more than simply test applicants. Through the use of multiple assessment techniques and multiple assessors (or panel judges), ACs are able to predict a candidate's future job behaviour and managerial potential. The assessment process itself may vary in length from a few hours to several days, depending on an organization's needs and objectives. A typical AC evaluation for a first-level supervisory job lasts one to two days. In recent years, the AC technique has become increasingly popular for nonsupervisory and skilled labour as well.

> A major automobile manufacturer uses an 18-hour assessment centre procedure for all its production staff.

Research studies evaluating the validity of the assessment centre technique have reported positive conclusions, by and large, indicating a median 0.40 correlation coefficient between AC ratings and such criteria as career progress, salary advances, supervisor ratings, and evaluations of potential progress. This has led to a phenomenal growth in the number of organizations using the AC technique. Currently, over 20,000 organizations on this continent are estimated to use the AC technique; and more are doing so each year. More details on AC procedures will be given in Chapter 9.

computer-interactive performance tests
Performance tests using computer simulations that can measure skills, comprehension, spatial visualization, judgment, etc.

Computer-Interactive Tests. A more recent development is the use of **computer-interactive performance tests**. The advent of microprocessors and minicomputers has opened up new possibilities for measuring perceptual-motor skills (e.g., reaction time, control precision), perceptual speed, and spatial visualization. Computers can also measure human capabilities not measurable by printed tests:

> For instance, through simulation, an applicant's abilities such as time sharing, ability to concentrate, ability to work under different time pressures, and so on, can be measured using computer-interactive performance tests. In one life insurance company, fact-based scenarios are presented to job applicants on the computer. The candidates' reactions to the scenarios, both mental (e.g., comprehension, coding, calculation) and motor (e.g., keying speed, accuracy) are assessed as the job candidate processes "claims" presented on the computer screen.[31]

The computer can also be used to capture the complex and dynamic dimensions of managerial work. By utilizing video, it is possible to show movement and depict richer and more detailed behavioural incidents. By presenting a more detailed and accurate portrayal of the situation, the fidelity with which judgment is measured is presumably increased.

> A program called AccuVision shows the job applicant actual job situations likely to be encountered on the job on videotape. In turn, the applicant selects a behavioural option in response to that situation. The response is entered in the computer and scored according to predetermined criteria.[32]

Watching a video-based test also exposes the candidate to the types of activities encountered on the job, which in turn provide a realistic job preview (discussed later in this chapter). Finally, video-based tests can be administered to groups of candidates at the same time, thus reducing the costs. Available research evidence seems to indicate high reliability for such interactive tests.[33]

Relying on the old adage that "behaviour predicts behaviour," developers of these interactive tests assume that behaviour in situations similar to those encountered on the job will provide a good indication of the actual behaviour on the job.[34] An example of an interactive test is shown in Figure 6-12.

integrity tests
Employment tests that measure an applicant's honesty and trustworthiness.

Integrity Tests. **Integrity tests**, which measure an applicant's honesty and trustworthiness, are of great interest to employers for two reasons: first, if the candidate is not honest in filling out the job application form and in his or her answers during the job interview, much of the information collected to assess the applicant's suitability for the position is useless; second, all employers desire employees whom they can trust.

> One U.S. study places the amount of workplace theft at $40 billion annually in that country.[35] Over 6 percent of job applicants may be involved in thefts in previous jobs; many others commit felonies or minor crimes. It is estimated that crime increases retail prices by approximately 15 percent. While comparable Canadian data are not available, statistics such as these have prompted several employers to use tests and other devices to measure the integrity of job applicants.

FIGURE 6-12	An Example of a Computer-Interactive Test

You are the human resource manager in our firm. At 8 a.m. when you walk into your office, you find the following email messages on your computer:

Sharon (your colleague): Can we start our meeting at 10? It should take two hours to get the Job Evaluation briefing sharpened up. As planned, we should be able to do the presentation in 90 minutes leaving 30 minutes for questions.

Chan (a manager): Can we meet for, say, one hour—no, make that one and a half hours—today? It is urgent. I am free any time between 9:30 and 12 and after 3 p.m.

Andre (your boss): Can you interview a job candidate this morning? She is in town only this morning; so you will have to meet her between 9 and 10:30 a.m. She looks really good for the position we advertised. So I would not want to miss this opportunity.

Jim (your secretary): Just to let you know that the Job Evaluation briefing to the staff is now moved up. It is going to be at 1 p.m. and not at 2 p.m. The message came in only as I was leaving the office at 6 p.m. Didn't want to call you at home and inform.

What is the earliest time you can meet with Chan?
a. 9:30   **b.** 3*   **c.** 4:30   **d.** 12:30   **e.** not possible today

*Correct answer.

---

graphic response tests
Tests that attempt to measure an applicant's honesty by measuring body responses.

polygraph
Machine that attempts to measure a person's honesty by assessing body reactions. Often called a lie detector.

A number of methods have been developed to help employers assess the integrity level of new hires. All methods are controversial. The various methods currently in vogue include graphic response tests, paper-and-pencil tests, credit report checks, and voice stress analyzers. The first two, which are also the more popular methods, will be discussed here.

Graphic response tests seek information about applicants in ways that cannot be distorted easily. The **polygraph** (or lie detector) is a popular approach. It measures physiological changes as a person responds to questions. When a person tells a lie, the conscience usually causes involuntary physiological reactions that are detected by the polygraph. At $30 to $60 per test, it is more economical than a detailed background check on applicants. In addition to ethical and public relations considerations, there are serious questions about the ability of most lie detector operators to administer and interpret the results validly.[36] Despite this, Canadian companies continue to use them. In the United States, a large percentage of retail firms are reported to use polygraph and other forms of integrity tests.

In Ontario, the use of lie detector tests for the purpose of employment is prohibited under the *Employment Standards Act*. Employers desiring to use this test should check its legality in other provinces.[37]

paper-and-pencil integrity tests
Measures of honesty that rely on written responses rather than observations.

Employers have turned to **paper-and-pencil integrity tests** because of their ease of use and inexpensiveness (typically available at less than $20 per administration). Unlike the use of polygraphs, there is also less organized opposition to these tests. Most paper-and-pencil integrity tests (also called "honesty tests") fall into one of two categories: overt tests that ask direct questions about past thefts or attitudes toward dishonest behaviours, or covert measures of the same.

Stanton Survey, an honesty test developed by Pinkerton Services Group, was tested for its validity using 4,665 applicants. Fifty percent of the applicants were given the Stanton Survey, the other 50 percent were not. Of the applicants, 37 percent of those not tested were later dismissed for theft while only 22.6 percent of those tested with Stanton Survey were dismissed for the same reason. The number of policy violators in the untested group was 10.4 percent compared to 1.5 percent in the tested group. The average loss from the untested group was approximately $208 higher compared to the tested group.[38]

When confronted by direct questions, many individuals are not likely to openly admit theft. Personality-oriented integrity tests, on the other hand, do not ask direct questions about theft or other dishonest behaviours, but measure the reliability and social conformity of employees and make inferences about their honesty from these scores. A review of a dozen paper-and-pencil integrity tests found potential validity for some of the tests.[39] Other comprehensive analyses of honesty and integrity tests also reveal that they have some degree of validity in predicting a wide range of disruptive behaviours such as theft, disciplinary problems, and absenteeism.[40]

> For example, the London House Personnel Selection Inventory (PSI) significantly predicted employees who were caught stealing. The PSI, which resulted from over 15 years of research by psychologists, criminologists, and legal experts, is reported to have a reliability of over 0.9 and convergent validity with polygraph scores, anonymous admissions of theft by the applicants, and results of quasi-experiments using the same respondents.[41]

Graphic response and honesty tests present human resource specialists with an inherent dilemma. On the one hand, these methods offer some additional screening tools to better ensure an optimal workforce. On the other hand, such tests are subject to errors. When they are inaccurate, needless discrimination results. Similarly, when tests discriminate against members of a protected class disproportionately, human rights violations may occur. In the United States, in some jurisdictions, for example, carriers of the HIV virus are protected by new laws or ordinances or by coverage under laws intended to protect people with disabilities.

In Canada, a clear national policy on this issue has been slow to emerge, so that each province has its own policies and standards on these tests. Also, to many applicants and employees, these tests are an invasion of their privacy.

attitude tests
Tests that seek to learn the attitudes of job applicants and employees about job-related subjects.

Attitude tests. **Attitude tests** are being used in some circumstances to learn about the attitudes of applicants and employees on a variety of job-related subjects. As polygraph tests draw criticisms about their accuracy and appropriateness, attitude tests are being used to assess attitudes about honesty and, presumably, on-the-job behaviours.[42] For example, a paper-and-pencil test on honesty has been developed to measure cheating, deceiving, and stealing.[43] Attitude tests also reveal employee attitudes and values about work. The Work Opinion Questionnaire, for example, has been effectively used in predicting job performance of entry-level, low-income workers.[44]

Besides specific cautions associated with individual tests, human resource specialists should realize that testing is not always feasible. Even when tests can be developed or bought, their cost may not be justified for jobs that have low selection ratios or that are seldom filled. Examples include technical, professional, and managerial jobs. Even when feasible, the use of tests must be flexible. They need not always be the first or last step in the selection process. Instead, human resource experts use tests during the selection process at the point they deem appropriate. Consider the comments of an experienced human resource manager of a large chain of grocery stores:

> Many human resource managers in other industries use testing only after other steps in the selection process. In the grocery business you must test first. Why waste time interviewing a grocery clerk who doesn't know that three for 88 cents is 30 cents apiece? Besides, when we take applications on Tuesdays, we may have 300 of them. Interviews would take 75 hours a week, and my staff consists of a clerk and myself. But through testing, we can test the entire group in an hour. Then we interview only those who score well.

Lastly, employment tests are only one of several techniques used in the selection process because they are limited to factors that can be tested and validated easily. Other items, not measurable through testing, may be equally important.

Step 4: Verification of References

What type of person is the applicant? Is the applicant a good, reliable worker? To answer these questions, employment specialists use references. Many professionals have a very skeptical attitude toward references. *Personal references*—those that attest to the applicant's sound character—are usually provided by friends or family. Their objectivity and candor are certainly questionable. When a reference is in writing, the author usually emphasizes only positive points. Thus, personal references are not commonly used (see Figure 6-13).

employment references
Evaluations of an employee's past work performance and job-relevant behaviours provided by past employers.

Employment references differ from personal references because they discuss the applicant's work history. Many human resource specialists doubt the usefulness of these references because former supervisors or teachers may not be completely candid, especially with negative information. Further, many managers do not seek the right information or ask the right questions while checking references.

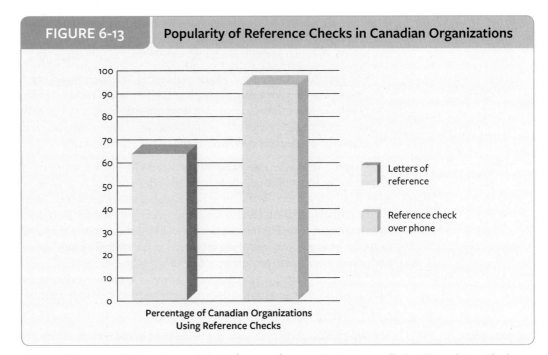

FIGURE 6-13   **Popularity of Reference Checks in Canadian Organizations**

Letters of reference

Reference check over phone

Percentage of Canadian Organizations Using Reference Checks

Source: Chart prepared by the authors on the basis of a survey of 202 organizations reported by Sean Way and James Thacker in "Selection Practices: Where Are Canadian Organizations?" *HR Professional,* October/November, 1999, p. 35.

A recent survey showed that 84 percent of companies have had to fire people for reasons that could have been discovered by proper reference checks. More than 93 percent of the respondents said they had found exaggerations on résumés and 86 percent had found outright misrepresentations.[45]

Often, many employment references are little more than confirmation of prior employment. Many employers are concerned about the risk of possible legal action by past employees who were not given positive references. In some cases, employers provide only basic information to protect themselves (e.g., simply stating that a person worked for them in the past in a certain capacity during specific dates). This lack of candour has caused some human resource specialists to omit this step entirely from the selection process. Other specialists have substituted telephone inquiries for written references. Besides getting a faster response, often at lower cost, telephone inquiries have the advantage of directness: voice inflections or hesitation over blunt questions may tip off the interviewer to underlying problems. In practice, however, only a small proportion of all reference checks seek negative information. Most reference checks are used to verify application information and gather additional data:

John Adams impressed his interviewers a few minutes after the interview began. The position was that of a store manager in a large building supplies chain. His ready wit, ability to think on the spot, and keen mind appealed to the interviewers. Equally attractive was what his previous employers had to say about him. One of the references called him a "young dynamo" because of his drive and enthusiasm; another commented on John's ability to "come out with totally creative ideas" and his "methodical approach to problems." Adams, who was hired for the position by the firm, did perform true to these statements for the first three months. It was by sheer accident that one day a colleague noted a shortfall in the cash register. On investigation, it was found that Adams had been systematically stealing money from his employer. Even worse, he had a history of embezzling accounts with his three previous employers. One of the previous employers admitted being aware of a couple of incidents when Adams had received kickbacks from vendors. None of the references, however, made any mention of these facts in their letters.[46]

reference letters
Written evaluations of a person's job-relevant skills, past experience, and work-relevant attitudes.

Lack of candour in **reference letters** may be due to a variety of reasons, including fear of legal reprisal, legal requirements (as in the United States) to show reference letters to an applicant, desire

FIGURE 6-14	How to Get the Truth Out of References

Use the phone: Most references are more likely to be honest over the phone or in person than in a formal letter.

Seek information on job-related behaviour: Ask for details on job behaviours, such as tardiness and absenteeism, rather than on personality traits, such as ambition and intelligence, which are hard to evaluate reliably.

Ask direct questions: Questions such as "Would you rehire this employee now?" or "How is this person's behaviour in a group setting?" would result in more honest answers than when a person is asked to write a paragraph on the strengths and weaknesses of the employee.

Combine references with other predictors: Reference letters are no substitute for application blanks, tests, and interviews.

Use credible sources only: Former work supervisors are, typically, the most useful reference sources. Letters from acquaintances and friends are usually worthless for predicting future job success.

Note frequency of job changes: A person who has not stayed in any organization for more than a few months may be either an extremely successful employee or a problem employee. Persons who have been moving laterally across organizations without any apparent change in job challenge, rewards, or working conditions should be carefully watched.

Watch out for phrases with hidden meanings: Most references do not blatantly lie; they simply don't tell the whole truth. A person who is described as "deeply committed to family and friends" may be someone who will not work beyond five o'clock; an "individualist" may be a person who cannot work with others.

Source: Adapted and summarized from Hari Das and Mallika Das, "But He Had Excellent References: Refining the Reference Letter," *The Human Resource*, June/July 1988, pp. 15–16.

to get rid of an employee, and reluctance to pass judgment on a fellow human being. Given this state of affairs, an employer can get to the truth about a potential employee's character and work performance in a number of ways.

Some of the possible strategies are shown in Figure 6-14. In all cases, the references should be combined with information from other predictors such as biographical data, tests, and interviews. Questions such as "What are your general impressions about the applicant's suitability for this position?" or "Does the applicant have initiative, integrity, a positive attitude, and willingness to learn?" should be avoided since they are too subjective and susceptible to personal bias. They also do not provide quantifiable information or measurable results.[47]

More recently, several firms have begun to include a background investigation as part of their selection process. Some applicants exaggerate their skills, education, and/or past work experience. While virtually every qualification listed in an application form or résumé can be verified, the cost of doing it may be prohibitive, especially for smaller employers. Some large organizations today use the services of specialized agencies to conduct background checks:

It is reported that Pinkerton Security and Investigation Services screens more than one million job applicants each year.[48]

Another emerging trend is the use of social networking Web sites such as Facebook to learn more about the applicant's interests and behaviours:

Several recruiters check applicants' backgrounds through search results on Google and other search engines. They can also access social networking sites such as Facebook to learn more about an applicant's position on morality, drugs, sex, and various social phenomena as well as gather personal profiles that indicate age, gender, race, ethnicity, political affiliation, etc. While it is illegal to use any of the latter in making a hiring decision, hiring decisions based on behaviours and self-stated opinions and other posted material may not be considered discriminatory.[49]

Whatever the approach, employers should be aware of their legal obligations when collecting and using employee information and abide by them. The federal *Information Protection and Electronic Document Act* (PIPEDA) applies to the collection, use, retention, and disclosure of "personal information" about employees in federally regulated organizations. In Alberta and British Columbia, there is a similar *Personal Information Protection Act* (PIPA). Broadly speaking, "personal information" has been interpreted to include all opinions, evaluations, comments, social status, and disciplinary actions. Only that part of personal information that is "reasonably required" in order to establish, manage, or terminate employment relationship should be collected or disseminated to avoid possible legal challenges.[50]

Step 5: Employment Interview(s)

The immediate supervisor is ultimately responsible for newly hired workers. Since that responsibility is ever-present, supervisors should have input into the final hiring decision. The supervisor is often better able to evaluate the applicant's technical abilities than is the human resource department. Likewise, the immediate supervisor can often answer the interviewee's specific job-related questions with greater precision. As a result, one study reported that in more than three-quarters of the organizations surveyed, the supervisor had the authority to make the final hiring decision.

When supervisors make the final decision, the role of the human resource department is to provide the supervisor with the best applicants available. From these two or three applicants, the supervisor decides whom to hire. Some organizations leave the final hiring decision to the human resource department, especially when applicants are hired into a training program instead of for a specific job. If supervisors constantly reject particular groups of applicants, such as minorities or women, the human resource department may be given final hiring authority to avoid future charges of discrimination.

In larger organizations, it is also common for the applicant to be interviewed by several persons (especially for supervisory and managerial positions). The immediate work supervisor will still have considerable influence on the final decision; however, the "satisfactory" candidate also will have to satisfy larger organizational requirements and fit well with the culture of the organization.

Regardless of who has the final hiring authority, the personal commitment of supervisors is generally higher when they participate in the selection process. Their participation is best obtained through the supervisory interview. Through a variety of structured and nonstructured questions, the supervisor attempts to assess the technical competency, potential, and overall suitability of the applicant. The supervisory interview also allows the recruit to have technical, work-related questions answered. Often, the supervisory interview is supplemented with a realistic job preview that better enables the employee to comprehend the job before being hired and stay on the job longer.

Employment references discuss the applicant's work history. Some employers refuse to answer questions relating to former employees on the phone. Are there ways to overcome this?

Eric Audras/Photoalto/PictureQuest.

When the supervisor recommends hiring an individual, he or she has made a psychological commitment to assist the new employee. If the candidate turns out to be unsatisfactory, the supervisor is then more likely to accept some of the responsibility for failure.

Since interviewing is a critical step in the selection process, this will be discussed in some detail at a later section in this chapter.

Step 6: Realistic Job Previews

realistic job preview (RJP)
Involves showing the candidate the type of work, equipment, and working conditions involved in the job before the hiring decision is final.

Often, the supervisory interview is supplemented with a realistic job preview. A **realistic job preview (RJP)** allows the potential employee to understand the job setting before the hiring decision is made—often by showing him or her the type of work, equipment, and working conditions involved.

Unmet expectations about a job probably contribute to initial job dissatisfaction. The realistic job preview attempts to prevent job dissatisfaction by giving the newcomer an insight into the job. Recently hired employees who have had a realistic job preview are less likely to be shocked by the job or the job setting on the first day they report to work.[51] Two writers concluded the following:

> The RJP functions very much like a medical vaccination. ... The typical medical vaccination injects one with a small, weakened dose of germs, so that one's body can develop a natural resistance to that disease. The RJP functions similarly by presenting job candidates with a small dose of "organizational reality." And, like the medical vaccination, the RJP is probably much less effective after a person has already entered a new organization.[52]

Past experience has shown that in 9 out of 10 cases, employee turnover was higher when job previews were not used.

> In one organization, a film was used to "warn" potential employees about the unpleasant aspects of a job. The job was that of a telephone operator. The film made it clear that the work was repetitive and closely supervised and sometimes required dealing with rude or unpleasant customers. Use of realistic job preview (RJP) was found to be related to decreased turnover rates, but RJP had no effect on job performance.

The adverse effect of RJP may be more candidates refusing to accept job offers when the working conditions do not appear appealing. Many RJPs may also focus unduly on extrinsic and job-context factors rather than on job content (or intrinsic) factors. Also, RJPs are no substitute for continuous monitoring of working conditions and in-depth job analysis. Informing job applicants about unpleasant working conditions may increase the probability that they will remain on the job once hired; however, they are unlikely to be any more satisfied with the job than those who were not told and did not leave. This means that only a conscious and continuous effort at improving "irritants" at the workplace is the real, long-term solution.

Step 7: Medical Evaluation

medical evaluation
Assessment of physical and/or mental health of an applicant through self reports and/or medical examination by a preferred physician.

The selection process may include a **medical evaluation**. Normally, the evaluation is a health checklist that asks the applicant to indicate health and accident information. The questionnaire is sometimes supplemented with a physical examination by a company nurse or physician. The medical evaluation may

- entitle the employer to lower health or life insurance rates for company-paid insurance;
- be required by provincial or local health officials—particularly in food-handling operations where communicable diseases are a danger; and/or
- be useful to evaluate whether the applicant can handle the physical or mental stress of a job.

Many employers have done away with this step because of the costs involved. Also, if an applicant is rejected, charges of discrimination under the *Canadian Human Rights Act* or related provincial legislation may be brought. A congenital health condition may be considered a disability, and failure to hire may be seen as discrimination against the qualified applicant. If the employer wants a medical evaluation, it may be scheduled *after* the hiring decision. Medical examinations are usually conducted only if the job requires a clearly determined level of physical effort or other abilities (e.g., ability to climb poles). Even here, an applicant can be rejected only if reasonable accommodations cannot be made to allow the person to perform the job.

> For example, imposing a height restriction for telephone installers on the grounds that short persons cannot get ladders from the truck would be deemed discriminatory. Provision of stools for workers to stand on while removing the ladders permit even short persons to perform the job.

The expertise with which the medical evidence was interpreted will also determine the strength of the employer's case in the event of a legal action by a rejected job applicant. Consider this example:

> Tony Kearsley applied for a position as a firefighter with the city of St. Catherines. He was accepted, conditional upon passing a medial examination. During the medical examination, it was discovered that he had atrial fibrillation. The medical practitioner, a general practitioner, refused to pass him, claiming that it increased the risk of a stroke by 1 to 5 percent a year. In addition, the medical examiner felt that Mr. Kearsley's condition might result in the heart not being able to pump sufficient blood to his organs during the extreme rigours of firefighting. Other experts whom the complainant consulted had advised him that it was a benign condition that would not impact on his ability to do the job. During the proceedings, the Ontario Human Rights Commission called in a medical expert in the area of atrial fibrillation, who testified that the increase in probability of a stroke for someone of Kearsley's age was inconsequential and possibly 0.2 percent per year. The expert also testified that there was no increased risk of heart failure in some one like Kearsley who was otherwise in good health. The Board asked the City to hire Kearsley within 75 days and pay him damages for the salary he lost until that date.[53]

In summary, to avoid possible allegations of discrimination, medical examinations should be conducted only when they are absolutely necessary. Guidelines for conducting medical examinations provided by Ontario Human Rights Commission include the following:[54]

- Where medical testing is appropriate, the employer should notify job applicants of this requirement at the time an offer of employment is made.
- There should be an objective, rational justification for the test. There should be an objective basis to believe that the degree, nature, scope, and probability of risk caused by the medical condition will adversely affect the safety of coworkers or the public.
- Medical testing should be conducted by qualified professionals and the results analyzed in a competent laboratory.
- Procedures should be instituted for the physician to review the test results with the employee concerned.
- All health assessment information should remain exclusively with the examining physician and separate from the employee's personnel file.

drug tests
Tests that include whether a job applicant uses marijuana, cocaine, or other drugs.

One noteworthy exception to the trend of fewer medical evaluations are **drug tests**. Since the use of drugs such as marijuana and cocaine by employees on the job as well as outside the workplace has been on the increase, a growing number of employers in Canada have begun to include drug testing as part of the selection process.

> In the United States, the U.S. Department of Labor estimates that drug use in the workplace costs employers $75 to $100 billion annually in lost time, accidents, health care, and workers' compensation costs. Sixty-five percent of all accidents on the job are directly related to drugs or alcohol.[55]

In the United States, more than two-thirds of large employers test job applicants for drugs. The drug tests continue even after hire—on a periodic or random basis and of all persons involved in accidents or suspected of drug use.

> Concern about employee drug use has spurred IBM, American Airlines, and many other organizations to require all job applicants to pass a urinalysis test for marijuana and cocaine. Typically, drug screening is done either before or immediately after the hiring decision. These organizations seek to avoid the economic and legal risks associated with drug users.

Increases in mortality rates, accidents, theft, and poor performance affect the employer's economic performance. Moreover, if the drug user's performance carries negative consequences for customers or fellow employees, lawsuits are likely. Through the analysis of urine or blood samples, laboratories are able to screen for the presence of drugs. While professional and amateur intercollegiate athletes have been tested for many years to assure the absence of steroids and stimulants, their popularity in work organizations has been more recent.

> Workplace substance abuse is estimated to cost Canadian employers $2.6 billion annually.[56] Although drug abuse among workers in Canada is still quite moderate when compared to the state of affairs in the United States, it warrants serious attention in major centres such as Toronto,

In some jobs, even 'one drink' may be too risky and lead to major work place accidents. Should organizations abolish any alcohol usage during work hours?

S. Pearce/PhotoLink/Getty Images.

Vancouver, and Montreal. TD Canada Trust (formerly Toronto-Dominion Bank), Imperial Oil Limited, and the Federal Transport Department are among organizations that use drug testing in Canada.

A large majority (86 percent) of CEOs of Canadian organizations who responded to a survey considered substance abuse as a serious or a very serious problem. A similar survey in the United States resulted in a figure of US$26 billion annually in higher health care costs and lost productivity.[57] Given these figures, it is not surprising that some companies are advocating the use of drug tests.

CN Rail introduced this measure in the mid-1980s as a screening test for its blue-collar workers.[58] Toronto-Dominion Bank and Imperial Oil followed suit in the private sector, as did the Winnipeg police force and the transportation industry (under federal jurisdiction) in the public sector.[59]

Executives of Toronto-Dominion Bank argued that drug users are more likely to associate with criminal elements and are therefore more susceptible to criminal influence that might lead to blackmail and perhaps theft.

TD Bank's policies required all new and returning employees to undergo urinalysis within 48 hours of accepting an offer of employment. TD's aim was to address the potential impact of drugs on the health and work performance of the employees and preserve the safety of funds and employees. If habitual substance abusers refused to participate in rehabilitation services (funded by the bank or under government health plans) or those services were of no avail, the abuser faced dismissal. The same fate awaited casual users if they tested positive on three or more occasions and persisted in drug use. The bank paid full wages and benefits to employees in rehabilitation programs.[60]

The Canadian Civil Liberties Association called for an outright ban on employee drug tests, saying no person should "be required to share urine with a stranger" as a condition of employment.[61] It pointed out that there was no evidence to suggest that Canadian society has a serious drug problem or such a problem among those with full- or part-time employment. Nor "are drug tests totally reliable indicators of safe performance in the here-and-now—at best they show only that an employee may have used a particular drug at some point in the past, perhaps several weeks before."[62] The Association launched a complaint against the mandatory drug test imposed by TD Canada Trust but lost it.[63] However, the court did find the mandatory urinalysis intrusive. In 1998, the Federal Court of Appeal in a two-to-one decision found the bank's anti-drug program discriminatory. Justice F. Joseph Macdonald held that the bank's policy resulted in indirect discrimination against drug-dependent employees. While the bank's rule of three positive tests leading to dismissal applied to both new and returning employees, "the rule directly impacts more negatively on a protected class of individuals under the *Canadian Human Rights Act*—drug-dependent users."[64]

This means that, today, an employer must delicately balance the individual rights of the employee against risk of liability and lack of safety at the workplace. Drug and alcohol testing without any demonstrable relationship to job performance has been found to be a violation of employee rights. This means that all the cautions listed in the context of **psychological tests** and general medical tests also apply to drug tests. A relationship or rational connection between the drug or alcohol testing and job performance is an important component of any lawful drug or alcohol testing policy.[65]

psychological tests
Tests that measure a person's personality or temperament.

In *Chiasson v. Kellogg Brown & Root (Canada) Co.*, a construction company terminated a new employee who failed a mandatory pre-employment drug test. The Alberta Court of Appeal upheld the employer's policy on the belief that such testing legitimately perceives that employees who are drug users are a safety risk in an already dangerous workplace. The court also pointed out that the effects of marijuana can linger for several days.[66]

Because most drug tests do not yield accurate data on current impairment or usage level and may be unreliable, even the pursuit of a productive, safe workplace may not justify universal, mandatory drug testing. If the testing policy is a bona fide occupational requirement of the job, particularly in a safety sensitive job position, an employer might have better luck defending it as policy.[67]

More recently, simple tests that measure impairment of manual dexterity and hand–eye coordination have been developed with considerable promise for identifying impaired employees.[68] Hopefully, the arrival of more such tests would help firms achieve their objectives while maintaining employee dignity and privacy.

As technology has improved, genetic and other forms of testing have become technically and financially feasible. Genetic screening may alert employers to those with higher chances of developing specific diseases. Likewise, medical monitoring of diseases such as Acquired Immune Deficiency Syndrome (AIDS) or the buildup of toxic chemicals such as lead or mercury poisoning among workers may alert employers to high-risk employees or shortcomings in health standards at the workplace. Note that employers in Ontario are prohibited from subjecting job applicants to any medical tests for the HI virus that is associated with AIDS.

Step 8: Hiring Decision

Whether made by the supervisor or the human resource department, the final hiring decision marks the end of the selection process. When a single predictor such as a job interview is used (as is the case in a number of smaller organizations), the decision is simple: whoever had the best interview performance is typically selected. However, when multiple predictors such as tests, interviews, and reference checks are used, the decision process becomes more complex. A brief discussion on the decision process is attempted in the following section.

Tradeoffs Among Predictors

Alternate approaches to combine the scores on different predictors exist. Three popular approaches are the subjective approach, multiple cutoff approach, and compensatory approach.

Subjective Approach. In the **subjective approach**, also referred to as the clinical approach, the decision maker looks at the scores received by the various applicants on predictors and subjectively evaluates all of the information and comes to an overall judgment.

subjective approach
In a subjective approach, the decision maker looks at the scores received by the various applicants on predictors and subjectively evaluates all of the information and comes to an overall judgment.

Ontario Electronics had three finalists for a marketing position who received the following scores in a sales aptitude test and in the job interview, both scored out of a maximum of 100 points.

Candidate A: Sales Aptitude Test = 80, Interview = 50

Candidate B: Sales Aptitude Test = 40, Interview = 80

Candidate C: Sales Aptitude Test = 70, Interview = 70

The decision maker who looks at the above data may choose Candidate A if he believes that Sales Aptitude scores of the individual are the most critical in predicting future performance.[69]

It should be noted that another decision maker who looks at the same data may come to a different conclusion, especially if the person believes that interview performance is more important than aptitude. In that instance, Candidate B would be chosen. Similarly, a decision maker who believes that both are equally important and that a high score on one dimension does not compensate for a low score on another may come out with a totally different conclusion—namely, Candidate C. It is precisely the judgmental nature of the decision that causes confusion and potential problems. Decisions are based on gut feelings and may be hard to justify in the event of human rights complaints. Despite this, in many small, owner-managed firms, judgmental combining of predictors continues to be used.

multiple cutoff approach
In a multiple cutoff approach, scores are set for each predictor and each applicant is evaluated on a pass–fail basis.

Multiple Cutoff Approach.   In a **multiple cutoff approach**, cutoff scores are set for each predictor and each applicant evaluated on a pass–fail basis. Applicants are rejected if any one of their predictor scores fall below a set minimum score.

In the example of Ontario Electronics, if the employer has set a cutoff score of 60 for the test and 60 for interview scores, only Candidate C would qualify.

It is easy for managers to understand this approach.[70] Hence, the acceptance level for this approach may be high. However, under this method, the deficiency in one predictor cannot be compensated by superior performance on another. In the absence of strong evidence supporting such an assumption, the organization may reject a number of applicants who may be actually qualified to do the job.[71] This can, in turn, result in poor public relations and possible legal challenges.

compensatory approach
In a compensatory approach, a higher score on a predictor may compensate a low score on another.

Compensatory Approach.   In a **compensatory approach**, a higher score on a predictor may compensate a low score on another. Predictors are assumed to be additive and to compensate for one another (in our above example, performing well on the test compensates for a relatively poorer performance on the interview).[72] When using a number of predictors and large number of applicants, it is virtually impossible to do a compensatory model without the use of computers (or at least a calculator). Statistical regression analysis is typically used to calculate the total score for each applicant. The applicant with the highest total score will be selected for the position.

Regression equations can also be designed for related jobs using the same predictors but with different weights or using altogether different predictors. However, proper use of these equations requires some knowledge of statistical methods and assumptions behind various types of analyses—something that may be beyond the capabilities of many decision makers. For this reason, many managers continue to prefer nonstatistical and subjective approaches, although statistical approaches have consistently shown to be more reliable and valid than clinical strategy.[73]

During selection, some organizations employ a sequential elimination process called the *multiple hurdles approach*, where an applicant has to pass a predictor satisfactorily before he or she can proceed to the next predictor.

In the Ontario Electronics example, under the multiple hurdles approach, only those who achieve a satisfactory score in the sales aptitude test will be interviewed. Thus, if the organization has set up a minimum test score of 60 as satisfactory, then only Candidates A and C will be interviewed.

The multiple hurdles approach is particularly relevant to organizations that put newly hired employees through long and expensive training programs.[74] It is also helpful when some of the predictors used are expensive (e.g., an expensive assessment centre evaluation, inviting job applicants from abroad).[75] In such instances, by keeping these predictors in the later half of the selection process, the firm is able to screen out candidates who are unlikely to meet organizational needs and thereby save considerable resources. However, the underlying assumption here (as in the case of the multiple cutoff model) is that a high score on one predictor does not compensate for a low score on another predictor. However, unlike in the case of other models, in the multiple cutoff, as soon as an applicant receives a lower than desired score on a predictor, he or she shall be removed from further consideration and will not proceed to the next stage.

Selection for Self-Managed Teams

In traditional organizations, the selection function is the joint responsibility of the manager(s) and the HR department. However, today, with the emergence of empowered, self-managing teams, the responsibility for hiring may be delegated to the teams.

> In the past, Ford Motor Company's Windsor engine plant extensively used teams in their operations. The employees, mostly working in teams, were empowered to take responsibility for the day-to-day functioning of several activities. The team members and leader were entrusted with some or all of the management responsibilities that were once the duties of the first line supervisor.

When such conditions exist, the selection process also has to undergo changes to reflect the new reality.[76] Employees will now have a more active role in the hiring of their coworkers. In those instances where the supervisor's position (a nonunion position) has been abolished and a team leader (a union member) is put in charge, the selection of workers may cease to remain a management prerogative and may be done by union members.

When workers are empowered to hire their coworkers, multiple views and varied experiences are incorporated into the selection process, thus enhancing the overall validity.[77] Employees are also likely to hire others whom they can "count on," thus increasing the probability that the new hire will be a productive worker. However, in close-knit teams with a strong culture, there may be a tendency to hire "people like us," thus reducing diversity of views and backgrounds and perpetuating the existing culture.

After Selection

Once the person is selected, the successful candidate has to be contacted immediately. Having a good employment contract is a must in most instances. When drawing up the employment contract, particular attention should be paid to the following areas:[78]

- **Specify probationary period if applicable.** A common misunderstanding is that all new employees are automatically subject to a probationary period, which is not the case.
- **Specify start date and terms of employment clearly.** In today's competitive labour market, employees move frequently from one job to another. If the employment contract does not specify the start date, under certain circumstances the employers may find themselves competing for the employee's service with a previous employer (especially if the required notice was not given by the employee).
- **Specify reasonable restrictive covenants.** Confidentiality of information and noncompete clauses should be specific, reasonable, and explicit.
- **Ensure that termination procedures are legally enforceable.** Ensure that termination procedures, if specified in the contract, meet the provincial minimum employment standards.

More information on employment contracts
www.employmentlawtoday.com
www.gowlings.com/resources/

Dispositioning of Applicants

Throughout the selection process, there will be applicants whom the organization no longer wish to pursue. The organization's decision should be communicated to them at the earliest possible opportunity. From a public relations standpoint, other applicants should be notified that they were not selected. However, the increased use of electronic technology in the recruitment function has resulted in large volumes of job seekers applying for positions, making such a policy impractical. Several employers advise their applicants that only successful ones will be contacted. While this relieves the employer of the responsibility to contact all applicants it still may not be advisable from a public relations' point of view. It is also important to pay careful attention to the wording of the rejection letter. The wording should be positive, and the reason offered for rejection should not be offensive or reduce the self-esteem of the applicant.

Employment specialists may also want to consider rejected applicants for other openings, since these applicants have already expressed an interest in the firm and may have gone through various stages of the selection process. Informing the applicants of such an action enhances public goodwill. Even if no openings are immediately available, applications of candidates with potential but who were not hired should be kept on file for future openings. Retaining these applications can also be useful if the employer is charged with employment discrimination.

The job applications of those hired should be carefully preserved as well. This not only enables the human resource department to update its HR information system (HRIS), but also helps to learn about the source of its applicants, and their age, sex, race, or other work-related characteristics. Information on sex, race, and age of employees helps the human resource department assess the extent of underutilization and concentration (referred to in Chapter 4) and to take necessary corrective action proactively.

If some recruits prove unsatisfactory after they are hired, human resource specialists may be able to reconstruct the selection process beginning with the application. In their reconstruction, they may uncover invalid tests, improperly conducted interviews, or other flaws in the selection process.

The newly hired employee should be treated with respect and consideration. An employer does not get a second chance to make a good first impression with a new hire. The new hire's supervisor or coworker should call the person a few days before the start date. Sending a welcome note to the entire family may be appropriate in some instances, especially if the employee's family is moving from another location. The time and place the new hire should report on arrival should be clearly communicated.[79] Some of the unwritten rules (such as dress code) should also be communicated so that the new hire does not arrive formally dressed on casual Friday, for example. A detailed orientation should follow on arrival. More on orientation and job placement will be discussed in the next chapter.

EMPLOYMENT INTERVIEW

employment interview
A formal, in-depth, face-to-face, or more recently, a phone or video conference between an employer and a job applicant to assess the appropriateness of the applicant for the job under consideration.

The **employment interview** is a formal, in-depth conversation conducted to evaluate the applicant's acceptability. The interviewer seeks to answer two broad questions: Can the applicant do the job? How does the applicant compare with others who are applying for the job?

Employment interviews, or *in-depth interviews* as they are also known, are the most widely used selection technique. Their popularity stems from their flexibility. They can be adapted to unskilled, skilled managerial, and staff employees. They also allow a two-way exchange of information: interviewers learn about the applicant and the applicant learns about the employer.

Interviews do have shortcomings. The most noticeable flaw is their varying reliability and validity. Some early studies reported an average validity coefficient (i.e., the correlation between the interview assessment of candidates and their actual performance) of 0.10, or virtually nil.[80] More recently, validity coefficients of 0.24 or above have been reported—still not high enough to allow a supervisor to make accurate predictions as far as job performance is concerned. Why then are they still so widely used? There are several reasons:

- An interview allows a personal impression. Besides assessing a candidate's ability to perform well on the job, an interviewer also wants to make sure that there is a match between the person's personality and the team with which he or she has to work. An interview provides an opportunity to do this.
- An interview offers the firm an opportunity to sell a job to a candidate. In high-demand areas such as engineering, electronics, and business administration, "selling" the company to top candidates assumes great importance. Typically, the employment policies, compensation, flexible work arrangements, career opportunities, and overall quality of work life are highlighted in an effort to convince top applicants to choose the firm.
- An interview offers the organization an opportunity to answer the candidate's questions regarding the job, career opportunities, and company policies.
- An interview is an effective public relations tool. Interviewees are potential consumers, clients, or voters; their perception of fair treatment could have important consequences.

High reliability means that the interpretation of the interview results should not vary from interviewer to interviewer. In reality, it is common for different interviewers to form different opinions. Reliability is improved when identical questions are asked, especially if interviewers are trained to record responses systematically. Validity is questionable because few human resource departments conduct validation studies on their interview results. However, proactive human resource departments are beginning to realize this problem and are comparing interview results with actual performance or other criteria, such as stability of employment. More validation of interviews is needed because they may relate more to personal features of candidates than to the candidates' potential performance. Human rights tribunals also look for explicit links of job descriptions to interview questions when making decisions on discrimination cases.[81]

For example, one study reported that two of the most important variables that influence an interview are fluency of speech and composure.[82] If these findings are applicable to most employment interviews, the results of the interviews may correlate with fluency and composure, instead of potential performance.

Validity coefficients such as 0.24 make interviews a weak predictor of future performance. (A validity coefficient of 0.24 means that less than 6 percent of future performance can be predicted by an interview alone.) This suggests that human resource practitioners should always combine interviews with other predictors while selecting human resources. Carefully structured interviews based on a thorough job analysis may be more useful and valid than unstructured interviews that dwell on applicant opinions about topics not directly related to the job. Also, interviews that probe what the applicant has actually done in the past in situations similar to those described in the job analysis may be better predictors of future performance.

The following pages introduce you to types of interviews and the interview process. After this, the discussion turns to some of the common errors by interviewers and interviewees that you should recognize and avoid during interviews.

Types of Interviews

panel interview
Interview using several interviewers.

Interviews are commonly conducted between the interviewer and the applicant on a one-to-one basis. Panel and group interviews, however, are sometimes used. Variations of group interviews appear in Figure 6-15.

In a **panel interview**, the applicant(s) meet with two or more interviewers. This allows all interviewers to evaluate the individual(s) on the same questions and answers. Since the interviewers are more apt to reach the same conclusion, reliability is improved. A variation is a group interview where two or more applicants are interviewed together by one interviewer. This saves time, especially for busy executives. It also permits the answers of different applicants to be compared immediately.

Whether a one-to-one, panel, or group interview, there are different interview formats that depend on the type of questions that are asked. Questions can be unstructured, structured, mixed, behavioural description, situational, or stress-producing. Figure 6-16 compares these different formats. Although the mixed format is most common in practice, each of the others has an appropriate

| FIGURE 6-15 | Types of Individual and Panel Interviews |

Number of Applicants Interviewed	Number of Interviewers	
	1	2 or More
1	One-to-One Interview	Panel Interview of One Candidate
2	Group Interview	Panel Interview of Group of Candidates

FIGURE 6-16	Different Question Formats in Interviews	
Interview Format	**Types of Questions**	**Useful Applications**
Unstructured	Few if any planned questions. Questions are made up during the interview.	Useful when trying to help interviewees solve personal problems or understand why they are not right for a job.
Structured	A predetermined checklist of questions, usually asked of all applicants.	Useful for valid results, especially when dealing with large numbers of applicants.
Mixed	A combination of structured and unstructured questions, which resembles what is usually done in practice.	Realistic approach that yields comparable answers plus in-depth insights.
Behavioural Description	Questions are limited to actual behaviours. Evaluation is on the solution and the approach of the applicant.	Useful to understand applicant's past work behaviour and abilities under specific work situations.
Stress-Producing	A series of harsh, rapid-fire questions intended to upset the applicant.	Useful for stressful jobs, such as handling complaints.
Situational	Questions focus on important situations likely to arise on the job and what the applicant would do in such situations.	Useful for understanding the applicant's behavioural propensities.

role to play. Figure 6-17 shows the relative popularity of different kinds of interviews in Canadian organizations in the recent past.

Unstructured Interviews

unstructured interviews
Interviews using few if any planned questions to enable the interviewer to pursue, in depth, the applicant's responses.

As the summary in Figure 6-15 indicates, **unstructured interviews** allow human resource specialists to develop questions as the interview proceeds. The interviewer goes into topic areas as they arise, and the end result is more like a friendly conversation. Unfortunately, this unstructured method lacks the reliability of a structured interview because each applicant is asked a different series of questions. Even worse, this approach may overlook key areas of the applicant's skills or background.

Structured Interviews

structured interviews
Interviews wherein a predetermined checklist of questions usually asked of all applicants is used.

Structured interviews rely on a predetermined set of questions. The questions are developed before the interview begins and are asked of every applicant. This approach improves the reliability of the interview process, but it does not allow the interviewer to follow up interesting or unusual responses. Here, the end result is an interview that seems quite mechanical to all concerned. The rigid format may even convey a lack of interest to applicants who are used to more flexible interviews. Situational and behavioural description interviews (discussed below) are two most useful forms of structured interviews.

A survey of 202 Canadian organizations indicates that structured interviews and behavioural description interviews are becoming popular in this country (see Figure 6-18).

Another survey of 592 interviewers from more than 500 Canadian and international organizations showed that trained interviewers are more standardized and formalized in their evaluation processes. They employ more sophisticated questioning strategies and are more consistent in their questioning practices. The study also identified four key factors to a structured interview: evaluation standardization, question consistency, question sophistication, and rapport building.[83]

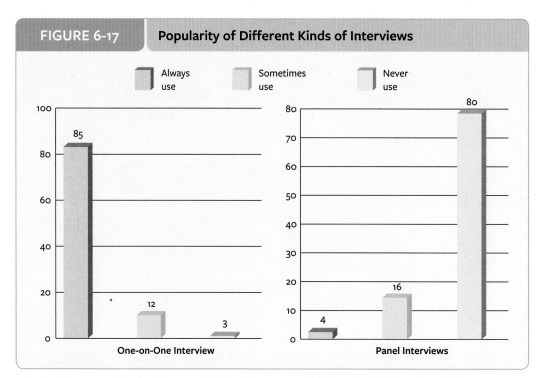

Source: Chart prepared by the authors on the basis of data reported in Murray Axmith & Associates Ltd., *Survey 2000: Canadian Hiring, Retention and Dismissal Practices*, p. 13, Toronto/Courtesy of Right Axsmith, a division of Right Management Consultants.

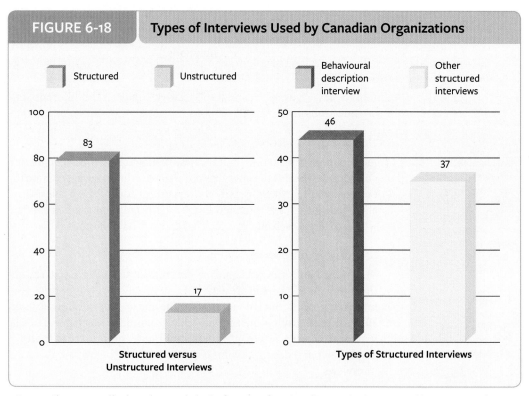

Source: Chart prepared by the authors on the basis of a survey of 202 Canadian organizations reported by Sean Way and James Thacker in "Selection practices: Where Are Canadian Organizations?" *HR Professional*, October/November, 1999, pp. 33–37.

Structured interviews may be behaviourally oriented or not—in other words, the questions may relate to specific behaviours of the job applicant or not. In recent years, there has been an increasing interest in understanding actual job behaviours during interviews, thus making behaviourally oriented interviews more and more popular.

Behaviourally Oriented Interviews. There are two major types of behaviourally oriented interviews: behavioural description interviews and situational interviews.

Behavioural description interviews attempt to find out how job applicants responded to specific work situations in the past. Behavioural description interviews are based on the principle that the best predictor of people's future behaviour is their past behaviour in a similar circumstance. This is especially so if the behaviour being considered occurred most recently and, in addition, is of a long-enduring nature. The question posed to the candidate could be along these lines:

> "Tell me about the most serious disagreement that you have had with a coworker in the past and how you dealt with it."
>
> or
>
> "Tell me about a time in your last job (or in your present job) when you were asked to take on new duties and responsibilities even if they didn't appear in your job description and how you dealt with it."
>
> or
>
> "Tell me about the most unpopular decision you had to make on your last job."

The work situations chosen should be relevant to the job for which the applicant is under consideration. When this is true, questions about a candidate's actual job experiences have high validity in predicting future job behaviour.[84]

> Thus, a job applicant who, in the last job, handled conflict with a coworker by walking away and refusing to discuss the matter and who has had that pattern in all his or her work life is likely to handle conflict in a new job in a similar manner.

To ensure relevancy, "problem situations" selected are common across job families:

> Practically everyone who has worked in retail sales for any considerable length of time has had to deal with an angry customer. Everyone who has worked in an office would have faced a situation where they had to do something outside of their regular job duties.

Choosing *typical* situations such as the above is important when designing behavioural description questions.

Situational interviews attempt to assess a job applicant's likely future response to specific situations, which may or may not have been faced by the applicant in the past. In this type of interview, the interviewer describes situations that are likely to arise on the job and are important for effective job performance and then asks the job applicant what he or she would do in such situations. Here the "behavioural intentions" of the applicant are being assessed (unlike statements of actual behaviour in behavioural description interviews). For the purpose of interview questions, real events that describe either effective or ineffective work behaviour (called "critical incidents") are identified. These are situations faced or actions taken by actual workers on the job and may be gathered from past or present employees themselves, supervisors, clients, and others who come into contact with the persons doing the job. When it is not practical to collect such incidents, the interviewer may do a comparative analysis by considering the most effective and most ineffective employees in the same position. Whatever the approach, the focus is on getting information on relevant job behaviour during the employment interview:

> For example, an organization that attempts to hire managers who must maintain tight cost controls may ask the applicant to describe a past work situation where he or she faced escalating costs. The applicant's behaviour in that situation (e.g., cooperating with others to reduce costs, initiating own action plans to reduce costs, or seeking boss's advice on the matter) is noted during the interview and its appropriateness evaluated.

Behaviourally oriented interviews are claimed to be highly job-related because they reflect behavioural intentions of the job applicant and the critical behaviours needed for successful job performance.[85] Some past research studies have indicated improved reliability and validity for the situational and behavioural description interviews over traditional, unstructured interviews.[86] For example, one study reported interrater reliability estimates ranging from 0.76 to 0.87.[87] A past research study that looked at several situational interview validity coefficients (with a sample

behavioural description interviews Behavioural description interviews attempt to find out how job applicants responded to specific work situations in the past.

situational interviews Situational interviews attempt to assess a job applicant's likely future response to specific situations, which may or may not have been faced by the applicant in the past.

exceeding 900) reported an average validity of 0.50 in predicting later job performance.[88] Some other studies have also produced encouraging validity coefficients in the range of 0.50 to 0.57.[89] In addition to the absolute level of predictive validity, the situational interview has also been shown to be relatively superior to other interview forms. One study that examined 143 validity coefficients found that the average validity for situational interviews was 0.50 and higher than all other job-related interviews (0.39).[90] In the aggregate, the available evidence indicates that this form of interview may currently offer the best hope among interview techniques.

Whether one uses behavioural description or situational interviews, structured questions that are job relevant and assess a job applicant's future behavioural intentions are critical for gaining valid insights. Past studies recommend the following steps to improve the overall validity of an interview method:

1. Conduct a job analysis and develop critical incidents.
2. Select criteria for job success based on the results of the job analysis.
3. Select one or more incidents that indicate a specific performance criterion (for example, cost-consciousness in the previous illustration).
4. Turn each critical incident into a "What did you do when …?" question.
5. Develop a scoring guide to facilitate agreement among interviewers on what constitutes a good, acceptable, or unacceptable response to each question.
6. Evaluate the validity of the instrument and implement.

Mixed Interviews

In **mixed interviews**, interviewers typically use a blend of structured and unstructured questions. The structured questions provide a base of information that allows comparisons between candidates. But the unstructured questions make the interview more conversational and permit greater insights into the unique differences between applicants. Community college and university recruiters, for example, use mixed interviews most of the time.

Stress-Producing Interviews

When the job involves much stress, **stress-producing interviews** attempt to learn how applicants will respond. Originally developed during the Second World War to see how selected recruits might react under stress behind enemy lines, these interviews have useful application in civilian employment.

> For example, applicants for police work are sometimes put through a stress interview to see how they might react to problems they encounter on the job. The interview itself consists of a series of harsh questions asked in rapid succession and in an unfriendly manner.

Since stressful situations are usually only part of the job, this technique should be used in connection with other interview formats. Even then, negative public relations are likely to result among those who are not hired. In Canada, stress interviews are not very popular.

Computer-Assisted Interviewing

Technology is changing how organizations recruit and select in ways that could not have been imagined a few years ago. While automated hiring technologies are still in their infancy, one can envision a future where hiring cycle time is reduced by over 90 percent and recruiters can call up information about a potential hire on their computer screens.

> Nike is one example of a company that has begun to use **computer-assisted interviewing**. When 6,000 persons responded to ads for workers needed to fill 250 positions, Nike used Interactive Voice Response Technology (IVR) to interview the candidates. Applicants responded to eight questions over the telephone; 3,500 applicants were screened out because they were not available when needed or did not have the retail experience. The rest had a computer-assisted interview at the store, followed by a personal interview. Using computer-assisted interviews has helped Nike not only to fill positions quickly but also to reduce turnover in their retail division by 21 percent in two years.[91]

Some controversy surrounds the use of computers in screening new hires. While computer-assisted interviews may make the interviews uniform (thus potentially increasing their reliability),

SPOTLIGHT ON HRM
Long-Distance Interviews

Interviews, while they provide rich, face-to-face information, are expensive to conduct. This is especially so if the interviewer(s) has to travel from one location to the next. Apart from the more obvious travel and lodging costs, there are also other invisible costs such as time lost in travel and lost candidates because of delays in reaching sites (especially in the case of campus-interviews where top graduates are whisked away by early arriving recruiters).

To overcome this, some employers are increasingly resorting to long-distance interviews. Some of the options currently available include audio or videotaping an interview and then having the decision-makers listen to or watch the playback. "Real time" interviews conducted through teleconferencing and videoconferencing represent more innovative approaches. Issues that have contributed to increasing interest in this technology are the expansion of national and international markets, satellite or off-site offices for many organizations, increasing frequency of employees and contractors working from home, and increased competitiveness and reduced budgets.

While most employers still prefer the traditional face-to-face interviews, videoconferencing interviews may be the only option available in some instances (e.g., when several college campuses open their recruiting fairs on the same day). Most employers who have used the technique seem to believe that they are able to gather all relevant information on the basis of videoconference interviews and screen out less qualified candidates. They did not, however, feel ready to make a job offer at the conclusion of the videoconference interview. Both employers and candidates indicate that this enables them to access a wider pool of candidates and prospective employers while reducing the overall time commitment.

Public videoconference room rentals range from about $60 to $200 per hour. The cost of videoconferencing itself is charged on a per minute basis with the costs based on a combination of long-distance telephone rates and the speed of transmission. Currently, three speeds of transmission of images are available: the slower the speed, the cheaper the transmission, but the more blurred the images. One telecommunications company advertises a one-hour videoconferencing between Toronto and Montreal for as little as $272. This compares very favourably to the cost of bringing one or two persons to an interview from Toronto to Montreal plus the time that they would lose from their work.

Long-distance interviews are still very new for most organizations and most managers may not feel comfortable with the process and equipment. Interviewer training is a must if this process is to be effective. Test the equipment and process beforehand; the smoother the technology works, the smoother the interview will go. The limited research evidence available on the process indicates that rating errors (e.g., halo or leniency) and rating patterns (e.g., the spread of ratings) were comparable to traditional interviews. Criterion-related validity studies on long-distance interviews have not emerged to any great extent until now.

Videoconference interviews may become more popular in the future as aggressive marketing and improved technology reduce its costs. At the same time, increasing competition and growing value of managerial time may also raise the demand for this selection tool.

Source: © *Canadian HR Reporter*, October 20, 1997, by permission of Carswell, Toronto, Ontario, 1-800-387-5164, www.hrreporter.com.

a number of human resource managers feel uncomfortable with the in-depth electronic profiling typical of these interviews. Such an approach may exclude persons who do not fall within the desired response range, even though the person might have skills the firm really needs. Thus, human interviewers may pick up valuable information that computers do not and may be able to factor in information the computer does not anticipate. Finally, if profiling selects persons who have the same personality traits, diversity, which can be a company's strength, may be lost.

Video Interviewing

video interview
Interview approach that uses solicited videos of a candidate's answers to provided questions.

More recently, in an effort to cut interview costs, many employers are asking employees to send a copy of a **video interview**, which highlights the candidate's background and experiences. A variety of methods exist: hiring companies produce their own video or CD and send it to employers; streaming video attachments are sent by email; or, third-party hosts of job candidate videos are establishing themselves in the market.

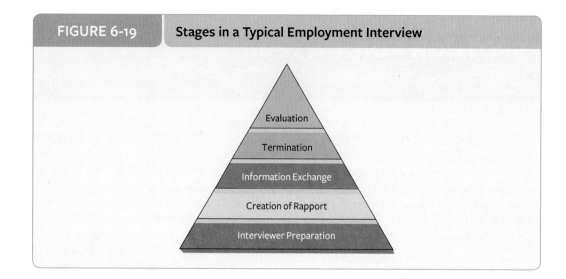

FIGURE 6-19   Stages in a Typical Employment Interview

stages of an interview
Key phases in an employment interview: interview preparation, creation of rapport, information exchange, termination, and evaluation.

Market Yourself Video Résumé hosting company
www.marketyourselfsmarter.com

The Interview Process

The five stages of a typical employment interview are listed in Figure 6-19. These **stages of an interview** are interviewer preparation, creation of rapport, information exchange, termination, and evaluation. Regardless of the type of interview used, each of these steps must occur for a successful interview to result. They are discussed briefly to illustrate how the actual interview process develops.

Stage 1: Interviewer Preparation

Obviously, before the interview begins, the interviewer needs to prepare. This preparation requires that specific questions be developed by the interviewer. It is the answers to these questions that the interviewer will use in deciding the applicant's suitability. At the same time, the interviewer must consider what questions the applicant is likely to ask. Since the interview is used to persuade top applicants to accept subsequent job offers, the interviewer needs to be able to explain job duties, performance standards, pay, benefits, and other areas of interest. A list of typical questions asked by recruiters and other interviewers appears in Figure 6-20. Note that several of these questions, while popular, are of questionable predictive power in assessing the future work performance of the applicant. Further, under the law, questions relating to gender, family status, race, etc., are prohibited. As can be seen from the list, these questions are intended to give the interviewer some insight into the applicant's interests, attitudes, and background. The same figure provides modified versions of the same questions that provide greater insights into an applicant's strengths and attitudes. Specific or technical questions are added to the list according to the type of job opening. Note that in all instances, the questions should not be discriminatory.

Another action the interviewer should undertake before the interview is to review the application form. Research shows that the quality of the interviewer's decision is significantly better when the application form is present.[92] With or without the application form, interviewers seem to take about the same length of time to reach a conclusion—from 4 to 10 minutes.[93] The longer the interview is scheduled to last and the better the quality of the applicants, the longer it takes the interviewers to reach a decision.

With the average cost of hiring new employees often exceeding $5,000 for managerial and professional employees, the interviewer's preparation should be aimed at making the interview process efficient and comfortable for the applicant. Often the interviewer is one of the first representatives of the company with whom the applicant has an opportunity to talk. A strong and lasting impression of the company is likely to be formed at this stage. If the interviewer does not show courtesy to the applicant, that impression is certain to be negative. If the applicant is a promising candidate for the job, he or she likely has other job prospects.

Given the importance of interviewer preparation and skills in determining the overall effectiveness of the interview (as a selection tool), several organizations have begun to train their managers in interview techniques. Large companies often train their interviewers in matters such as human rights legislation and techniques to get more information from job candidates.[94] However, such training

FIGURE 6-20	Popular Employment Interview Questions and Suggested Modifications

Popular Interview Questions	Suggested Modifications
1. Why do you want to work for our organization?	1. How do your skills and career goals match with our organizational activities?
2. What are your hobbies?	2. How do your hobbies/spare-time activities add to your value as an employee in this organization?
3. Describe your last job.	3. What were your duties in the last job? What measures of success or failure were employed? How did you fare on those criteria?
4. Tell me about a project you did recently.	4. Tell me about a project you were involved in the recent past. What was your role in the project? Do you think that it helped you acquire any skills or competencies that can be used in the present position?
5. What was your favourite subject in school/college/university?	5. What was your favourite subject in school/college/university? Can you relate the subject matter to this job or other jobs that you might hold here?
6. Do you have any geographical preferences?	6. This job requires approximately two days of travel each month and periodic (typically, once in three years) relocations. Are there any factors that will prevent you from meeting this requirement?
7. What was your favourite sport at school/college/university?	7. Were you involved in any extracurricular activities at school/college/university? Do you think that the activity provided you with specific competencies that might be relevant for the present job?
8. Have you played any team sports?	8. Your ability to work in a team is critical for success in this position. Can you describe your work in a team that faced a conflict? How was the conflict resolved? What role did you play in the resolution of the conflict?

sessions may not be effective if the interviewers are not made aware of their own stereotypes and biases and behaviours that cause the job candidates discomfort during the interview. Interviewers should also be trained to link interview questions tightly to job analysis results, use a variety of questions, ask the same questions of each candidate, and anchor the rating scales for scoring answers with examples and illustrations.[95]

Stage 2: Creation of Rapport

Once the interview begins, the burden is on the interviewer to establish a relaxed rapport with the recruit. Without a relaxed rapport, the interviewer may not get a clear picture of the applicant's potential. Rapport is aided by beginning the interview on time and starting with nonthreatening questions such as, "Did you have any parking problems?" At the same time, the interviewer may use body language to help relax the applicant. A smile, a handshake, relaxed posture, and moving paperwork aside all communicate without words; such nonverbal communications maintain rapport throughout the interview session. The interviewer has to act the perfect host or hostess, greet the candidate with a warm smile showing him or her into the office, make small talk, and reduce the nervousness of the applicant by friendly conversation. Only in a relationship of mutual trust and comfort will a candidate talk freely. By projecting an image of confidence, competence, and concern, especially in the early stages of the interview, an interviewer can create trust.

**Interview Coach
Preparation for an
interview**
www.interviewcoach.com

Stage 3: Information Exchange

The heart of the interview process is the exchange of information. To help establish rapport, some interviewers may begin by asking the applicant if he or she has any questions. This establishes two-way communication and lets the interviewer begin to judge the recruit by the type of questions asked. Consider the following dialogue. Which response creates the most favourable impression?

Interviewer: Well, let's start with any questions you may have.

Applicant 1: I don't have any questions.

Applicant 2: I have several questions. How much does the job pay? Will I get two weeks' vacation at the end of the first year?

Applicant 3: What will the responsibilities be? I am hoping to find a job that offers me challenges now and career potential down the road.

Each response creates a different impression on the interviewer. But only Applicant 3 appears concerned about the job. The other two applicants appear to be either unconcerned or interested only in what benefits they will receive.

In general, an interviewer will ask questions worded to learn as much as possible. Questions that begin with how, what, why, compare, describe, expand, or "Could you tell me more about ..." are likely to solicit an open response, while questions that can be answered with a simple "yes" or "no" do not give the interviewer much insight.[96] Specific questions and areas of interest to an interviewer are suggested in Figure 6-20.

Besides those questions, the interviewer may want more specific information about the applicant's background, skills, and interests (other popular interview questions relate to expected salary levels, career goals, own strengths and weaknesses, description of ideal boss, and so on). As already noted, asking specific behavioural description questions that assess an applicant's knowledge, skill, ability, and other characteristics (such as work-shift availability, personality characteristics) significantly add to the validity of the information collected. The above four factors, popularly referred to as KSAO, define the essential job requirements.

Selection interviews generally have low validity. Why then have an interview at all?

Skills such as analyzing, problem solving, managing projects, leading work teams, managing a business, making presentations, developing and motivating employees, etc., are some of the most important skills for many supervisory and managerial jobs. This means that the interviewer's focus should be on assessing the candidate's skills in these and related areas. Some interviewers are overly preoccupied with industry experience and give higher weight to applicants who have worked in the same industry before. However, it could be that in several settings, fresh thinking individuals with transferable experience may contribute equally or more. Maintaining an open mind helps the interviewer to assess the key KSAO relevant to the job under consideration.[97]

Stage 4: Termination

As the list of questions dwindles or available time ends, the interviewer must draw the session to a close. Here again, nonverbal communication is useful. Sitting erect, turning toward the door, or glancing at a watch or clock all clue the applicant that the end is near. Some interviewers terminate the interview by asking, "Do you have any final questions?" At this point, the interviewer informs the applicant of the next step in the interview process, which may be to wait for a call or letter.

Stage 5: Evaluation

Immediately after the interview ends, the interviewer should record specific answers and general questions. Figure 6-21 shows a typical checklist used to record these impressions of the interviewee.

FIGURE 6-21	A Post-Interview Checklist

Canadian Home Appliances Limited
Post-interview Checklist

Job Position: Sales Representative   Date Interviewed: _____   Time: _____

Applicant: _____   Interviewer: _____

Selection Criteria	Poor	Fair	Good	Very Good	Excellent	Comments
1. Knowledge of product line	☐	☐	☐	☐	☐	_____
2. Customer service skills	☐	☐	☐	☐	☐	_____
3. Prior selling experience	☐	☐	☐	☐	☐	_____
4. Job-related training/education	☐	☐	☐	☐	☐	_____
5. Interpersonal and persuasion skills	☐	☐	☐	☐	☐	_____
6. Match between candidate's career expectations and company opportunities	☐	☐	☐	☐	☐	_____
7. Potential for future development into supervisory/other positions	☐	☐	☐	☐	☐	_____
8. Availability	☐	☐	☐	☐	☐	_____
9. Knowledge of the firm and industry in general	☐	☐	☐	☐	☐	_____

Follow-up action:

None	☐	_____
Further testing	☐	_____
Further interview	☐	_____
Reject for this job; reconsider for other jobs	☐	_____
Reject—Notify applicant of rejection	☐	_____
Other (specify)	☐	_____

Use of a checklist like the one in the figure can improve the reliability of the interview as a selection technique. As the checklist shows, the interviewer is able to obtain a large amount of information even from a short interview.

Interviewer Errors

Caution must be exercised to avoid some common **interviewer errors**, summarized in Figure 6-22, that decrease the effectiveness of the interview. When the applicant is judged according to the **halo effect** or other personal biases, the results of the interview are misinterpreted. Applicants are accepted or rejected for reasons that may bear no relation to their potential performance. Likewise, leading questions and domination do not allow the interviewer to learn of the applicant's potential either. The evaluation of the applicant then becomes based on a guess, with little or no substantiation. No matter which pitfall is involved, it reduces the validity and reliability of the interview. All the interview does when biases are present is waste organizational

interviewer errors
Mistakes like biases and domination that reduce the validity and usefulness of the job interview.

halo effect
Use of limited information about a candidate to bias the interviewer's evaluation.

FIGURE 6-22	Typical Interviewer Errors

Halo Effect

Interviewers who use limited information about an applicant to bias their evaluation of that person's other characteristics are subject to the halo effect. In other words, some information about the candidate plays a disproportionate part in the final evaluation of the candidate.

Examples:

- *An applicant who has a pleasant smile and firm handshake is considered a leading candidate before the interview begins.*
- *An applicant who wears blue jeans to the interview is rejected mentally.*

Leading Questions

Interviewers who "telegraph" the desired answer by the way they frame their questions are using leading questions.

Examples:

- *"Do you think you'll like this work?"*
- *"Do you agree that profits are necessary?"*

Stereotypes

Interviewers who harbour prejudice against specific groups are exhibiting a personal bias based on stereotypical thinking.

Examples:

- *"I prefer salespersons who are tall."*
- *"Accountants are not outgoing people."*

Interviewer Domination

Interviewers who use the interview to oversell the applicant, brag about their successes, or carry on a social conversation instead of an interview are guilty of interviewer domination.

Examples:

- *Spending the entire interview telling the applicant about the company plans or benefits.*
- *Using the interview to tell the applicant how important the interviewer's job is.*

FIGURE 6-23   Some Dos and Don'ts of Conducting Employment Interviews

Do:

1. Collect only job-related information and not information on general personality traits.
2. Concentrate on securing information about the applicant's past job behaviour.
3. Use several interviewers (to interview each candidate) to increase the reliability of the interview process.
4. Treat all interviewees equally and impartially.
5. Have a checklist of questions to ask each job applicant.
6. Attempt to create a relaxed setting by asking easy, nonthreatening questions first and showing support to the applicant.
7. Provide job-related information to the candidate.
8. Compare your evaluation of each candidate with other interviewers and find out why discrepancies exist.

Do Not:

1. Attempt to predict personality traits from a single interview.
2. Be guided by initial impressions (or nonverbal cues) and generalize them to all relevant work and nonwork behaviour of the applicant.
3. Allow your evaluation of the candidate's job performance to be influenced by a single characteristic (such as how well the applicant dresses).
4. Be tempted to make snap judgments of the candidate early in the interview, thus locking out further information.
5. Ask leading questions that communicate the correct or desired answer to the applicant (e.g., "Do you believe that women workers should be treated equally with males?").
6. Exhibit personal biases ("In my experience, good sales managers are all talkative").
7. Dominate the interview; rather, use the interview to collect relevant information about the candidate.

resources and the applicant's time. Figure 6-23 summarizes some major dos and don'ts in the employment interview.

Interviewee Errors

interviewee errors
Interviewee mistakes such as boasting, not listening, or lack of preparation that reduce the validity and usefulness of an interview.

Interviewees make errors too. Some **interviewee errors** may be to cover job-related weaknesses. Others may emerge from simple nervousness. Although interviewers—especially those in the human resource department—may conduct hundreds of job interviews in a year, most applicants never experience that many in a lifetime. Common interview mistakes made by job candidates:

- playing games
- talking too much
- boasting
- not listening
- being unprepared

Playing games—for example, acting nonchalant—is often taken at face value: the candidate is not interested. The candidate may be excited or nervous and talk too much, especially about irrelevant topics such as sports or the weather. Instead, applicants should stick to the subject at hand.

Likewise, boasting also is a common mistake. Applicants need to "sell themselves," but credential distortion—even if just "embellishment"—about responsibilities and accomplishments or simply bragging too much can turn off the interviewer's interest. Failure to listen may result from anxiety about the interview. Unfortunately, it usually means missing the interviewer's questions and failing to maintain rapport. And, of course, being unprepared means asking poorly thought-out questions and even conveying a lack of interest, neither of which is likely to land the job being sought.

EVALUATING THE SELECTION

How do you know whether the selection procedures in your organization are effective? How can you evaluate whether they achieved your organization's goals? Even if the procedures are effective (namely, they achieve the objective of hiring the right candidates), are they efficient and worth the costs and trouble?

In Chapter 1, it was pointed out that all human resource activities should be cost-effective. The department's contribution in various areas should also be at levels appropriate to an organization's needs. If the selection system is more or less sophisticated than the organization requires, then resources are wasted. This necessitates continuous monitoring of the effectiveness and efficiency of selection procedures.

The final outcome of the selection process is the people who are hired. As one writer pointed out, the goal of HR is "to get more productive workers who show up for work, who use better judgement, who don't harass anyone, who don't cost the company money, and who can inspire people."[98] If the preselection inputs are considered carefully and the major steps of the selection process have been followed correctly, then new employees are likely to be productive. And productive employees are the best evidence of an effective selection process. Some of the questions to ask in this context are as follows:

1. Are the superiors and peers of new hires indicating dissatisfaction with them?
2. Is the selection process too expensive?
3. Are the hiring criteria and practices showing too much variation across even similar jobs and regions?
4. Are the training costs of newer employees increasing?
5. Do managers spend too much time managing new hires?
6. Are the grievances, absenteeism, and turnover inordinately high?[99]

To evaluate both new employees and the selection process requires feedback. Feedback on successful employees is sometimes hard to find for employment managers, since supervisors often claim responsibility for their successes. Feedback on failures is ample. It can include displeased supervisors, growing employee turnover and absenteeism, poor performance, low employee satisfaction, union activity, and legal suits.

More constructive feedback is obtained through specific questions. How well does the new employee adapt to the organization? To the job? To the career of which the job is a part? And lastly, how well does the employee perform? Answers to each of these questions provide feedback about the employee and the selection process.

In the ultimate sense, the utility of a selection procedure is decided by looking at the quality and productivity of the workforce hired and the costs incurred in the process. An elaborate human resource audit is sometimes attempted[100] (see Chapter 15 for more details on auditing). The costs include not only the out-of-pocket costs (such as costs of testing, interviewing, postage, and stationery), but also the costs associated with errors in the decisions made. If the wrong candidate is hired or promoted, the costs are particularly high. However, an exhaustive look at all costs (actual and potential) associated with a selection system may be very difficult in real life. Appendix A to this chapter describes a procedure to assess the utility of the selection system.

SUMMARY

The selection process depends heavily upon inputs such as job analysis, human resource plans, and recruits. These inputs are used within the challenges of the external environment, ethics, and guidelines established by the organization.

With these inputs and challenges, the selection process takes recruits and puts them through a series of steps to evaluate their potential. These steps vary from organization to organization and from one job opening to another. In general, the selection procedure relies on interviews for virtually every opening that is to be filled. References and application blanks are also other steps commonly found in the selection process of most employers. It was pointed out that weighted and biographical application blanks and situational interviews offer great promise as reliable and valid instruments. The increasing popularity of drug tests in several organizations was also noted here. However, the use of any tests that are not empirically justifiable by performance criteria is vulnerable to human rights violation charges.

The supervisor's role should include participation in the selection process, usually through provision of valid job-relevant information and an interview with job candidates. Through participation, the supervisor is more likely to be committed to the new worker's success.

Growing research evidence supports the use of a realistic job preview (RJP). After considerable expense and effort to recruit and select employees, the use of realistic job previews seems well advised as a means of reducing turnover among new employees.

Like all other human resource functions, the costs and benefits of the selection process also have to be compared periodically to evaluate the utility of various predictors. However, this is a very complex activity, often requiring fairly advanced mathematical skills. Notwithstanding, all human resource management systems have to implement evaluation studies to maintain their effectiveness and efficiency.

TERMS FOR REVIEW

application blank p. 219
assessment centre p. 226
attitude tests p. 229
behavioural description
    interviews p. 243
biographical information
    blank (BIB) p. 219
compensatory approach p. 237
computer-assisted interviewing p. 244
computer-interactive performance
    tests p. 227
concurrent validity p. 222
construct validity p. 222
content validity p. 222
differential validity p. 223
drug tests p. 234
employment interview p. 239

employment references p. 229
employment tests p. 220
graphic response test p. 228
halo effect p. 250
integrity tests p. 227
interviewee errors p. 251
interviewer errors p. 250
knowledge tests p. 226
medical evaluation p. 233
mixed interviews p. 244
multiple cutoff approach p. 237
panel interview p. 240
paper-and-pencil integrity
    test p. 228
performance tests p. 226
polygraph p. 228
predictive validity p. 222

psychological tests p. 236
realistic job preview (RJP) p. 233
reference letters p. 230
reliability p. 221
selection process p. 212
selection ratio p. 214
situational interviews p. 243
stages of an interview p. 246
stress-producing interviews p. 244
structured interviews p. 241
subjective approach p. 236
unstructured interviews p. 241
validity p. 222
video interviews p. 245
weighted application
    blank (WAB) p. 219

○ SELF-ASSESSMENT EXERCISE

How Do You Fare as an Interviewee?

This short test helps you assess your behaviours as a job applicant in the context of job interviews. Indicate your behaviours on a scale of "Always," "Often," "Sometimes," and "Never." Do not omit any statements.

Statement	Always	Often	Sometimes	Never
1. Before attending an interview, I gather as much information about the employer as possible by consulting annual reports and newspapers, Internet searching, and/or talking to knowledgeable persons.				
2. During many interviews, I indicate how another employer has expressed interest in hiring me at this time.				
3. I carefully study the job responsibilities involved in the position and link my own competencies and training to each one of them before going for an interview.				
4. During the interview, I make sure that I talk a lot, even if that means I have to use "fillers" such as sports news or jokes.				
5. During the interview, I always maintain my composure and try to project a positive, can-do attitude.				
6. I often "sell" myself to the interviewer by mildly exaggerating my past accomplishments or work responsibilities.				
7. I utilize a part of the interview time to find out more about the job and focus on how I can contribute to its success.				
8. When the interviewer asks me, "Do you have any questions?" my typical response is, "Not really, thank you."				
9. I follow up the interview with a thank-you letter that also highlights my continuing interest in the position.				
10. At times during an interview, I flatter the interviewer and/or the employing organization. After all, is there a person out there who does not like flattery?				

SCORING

For the odd-numbered statements, give yourself a score of 4, 3, 2, and 1 for Always, Often, Sometimes, and Never, respectively. For the even-numbered statements, reverse the scoring. Now add up the scores for all 10 statements.

The total score may range anywhere from 10 to 40. If your score is 34 or above, you are currently doing well and have a general awareness of what is required for a successful interview. Scores below 20 require that you pay serious attention to developing interview skills.

○ REVIEW AND DISCUSSION QUESTIONS

1. What is the strategic importance of the selection function for an organization?

2. List and briefly discuss the various steps in the selection process.

3. What are the five stages of the employment interview? What specific actions should you, as an interviewer, take to conduct a proper interview?

4. What are the different types of validity? If you want to validate a new dexterity test (which measures physical coordination) for workers in an assembly plant, how will you go about it?

5. What attributes of behavioural description and situational interviews make them appear more promising than traditional interview formats?

6. What is a weighted application blank? How is it different from a traditional application form?

⟳ CRITICAL THINKING QUESTIONS

1. Suppose you are an employment specialist. Would you expect to have a large or small selection ratio for each of the following job openings?

  (a) Janitors

  (b) Nuclear engineers with five years' experience designing nuclear reactors

  (c) Pharmacists

  (d) Software programmers

  (e) Elementary-school teachers in the Yukon

  (f) Elementary-school teachers in Ontario

What are the implications for human resource managers?

2. If a human resource manager asked you to streamline the firm's selection process for hourly paid workers, which steps described in this chapter would you eliminate? Why?

3. A Canadian university has been experiencing a high student dropout rate in recent years. One calculation showed that although the first-year enrollment in commerce courses increased from 650 to 980 students in the last four years, the dropout rate for first-year students has worsened from 9 percent to 15 percent. The university has been using uniform admission standards during the years and has not made any significant changes in the grading or instructional procedures. Based on what you've learned in this course until this point, what recommendations would you make to the university to improve its retention rates? Why?

4. If you are hired as a consultant to evaluate the selection process for salespersons in a large car dealership in the Toronto area, what kind of information will you collect?

5. Assume you are hired to improve the interview process employed by a large real estate organization when it hires sales and customer service representatives. When suggesting improvements, what factors will you focus on? What steps will you recommend to check whether your suggestions indeed result in better hires in the future?

6. Suppose you are approached by the human resource department in a large insurance firm that routinely hires dozens of clerical workers. Of the various types of tests discussed in the text, which would you recommend? What are the steps you will suggest to validate the test(s) you recommended?

⟳ ETHICS QUESTION

You are the human resource manager in a large chain of grocery stores about to hire a new IT system programmer. Because of the downturn of the IT sector, you have received a large number of applications for the position. Mike, one of the applicants, is a nephew of your neighbour Mercy, a real estate agent. One day while you were working on your lawn, Mercy approached you and conveyed to you how "nice it would be to see Mike settled in a stable job like the one in your firm." Mercy knows that you are on the lookout for a new, larger house right now. During the conversation, she indicated that she will find one for you without charging you any commission. You looked at Mike's application and found him to have minimum qualifications necessary for the position. However, there are a large number of candidates who have better qualifications and experience. You know that your employer is making some major strategic changes now that will enhance the information needs of the firm significantly.

What considerations will you have in making the decision? What would you do right now?

⟳ WEB RESEARCH EXERCISE

Using the Human Resources and Skills Development Canada Web site and others estimate the demand (and supply where available) of pharmacists, software programmers, accountants, salespersons, and financial analysts in Canada. What selection ratios do they indicate? What are the implications for human resource managers employed in the relevant sectors?

INCIDENT 6-1

A Selection Decision at Empire Inc.

At Empire Inc., the turnover rate is very high among assembly workers. Supervisors in the production department have told the human resource department that they do not have time to conduct a supervisory interview with the large number of applicants who are processed to fill assembly-line openings. As a result, the human resource department's employment specialists make the final hiring decisions. The profiles of three typical applicants are presented below.

	Applicant A	Applicant B	Applicant C
Years of Experience	4	8	1
Education	1 year of university	Finished grade 8	High-school diploma
Age	24	43	32
Test Score	77/100	74/100	82/100
Medical Evaluation	OK	OK	OK
Performance Evaluation	Very good	Excellent	Fair/good (last job)
Work History	Limited data	Stable	Stable
Ranking by: Interviewer 1	1	2	3
Interviewer 2	3	2	1
Apparent Eagerness	Moderate	Strong	Weak
Availability	4 weeks	2 weeks	Immediately

The nature of the assembly jobs is rather simple. Training seldom takes more than an hour or two. Most people master the job and achieve an acceptable level of production during the second full day on the job. The tasks involve very little physical or mental effort. The employment test is valid, but has only a weak relationship between scores and actual performance.

1. What information would you consider irrelevant in the preceding selection profiles?
2. Are there any changes you would recommend in the selection process?
3. Which of the three candidates would you select, given the limited knowledge you possess? Why?

INCIDENT 6-2

National Food Brokers Selection Process

National Food Brokers buys carload orders of nonperishable food products for resale to food wholesalers. Phone-sales personnel take orders from major food wholesalers, write up the orders, and send them to the appropriate food producers. Nearly 90 of National's 130 employees work in the phone-sales department. Since the job requires long hours on the phone to different accounts, the work is not very pleasant and turnover is high.

The manager of the phone-sales department, Carol Decinni, made the following observations in the presence of the human resource manager, Craig Reems:

Most of the people who work in the department fall into two groups. There are those who have been here for two or more years. They seem reasonably content and are the top sellers we have. The other group consists of people who have been here for less than two years. Most of our turnover comes from this group. In fact, we lose one of every three new employees during the first two months. When I talk with the people who are quitting, most of them tell me that they had no idea how much time they had to spend on the phone. I am generally pleased with the quality of recruits the human resource department provides. But we cannot continue with this high turnover. My supervisors are spending most of their time training new workers. Is there anything the human resource department can do to hire more stable workers?

1. Suppose you are asked by the human resource manager to suggest some strategies for improving the selection process in order to hire more stable workers. What suggestions would you make?

2. What role should the supervisory interview play in the selection process? What information conveyed to the applicants can help reduce the future worker turnover rates?

⊘ EXERCISE 6-1

How Do You Select Your Friends?

Consider your closest friend. What are this person's attributes? (List as many items as you can think of including this person's education, age, race, family background, economic situation, interests, behaviours, attitudes, biases, and so on.)

Now consider another close friend you have. Do the same as above for this person.

Consider a person whom you like least at this point in time. Do the same as above in the case of this person.

Choose another person whom you dislike. What are this person's attributes?

Now list the attributes of the persons whom you like and those you dislike. Are they different?

Now rate each attribute on a five-point scale (5 = extremely important from your point of view; 1 = least important).

Do the ratings give you an idea of your own values? Do you think your friends would value the same attributes?

⊘ CASE STUDY 🍁 Maple Leaf Shoes Ltd.

Selection of a Human Resource Manager*

Robert Clark, president and key shareholder of Maple Leaf Shoes, knew that he had a tough situation on his hands. In less than a month, Maple Leaf Shoes will have to negotiate a contract with a newly formed union in its plant, covering approximately 23 percent of the nonmanagerial workforce. A second and a more militant union is due for contract negotiations a few months later. Recently, the firm's human resource manager, John McAllister, left the firm for a better position in Toronto. Despite its best recruitment efforts, Maple Leaf Shoes has not been able to fill the vacancy. The firm ran want ads in the *Globe and Mail, National Post, Vancouver Sun,* and *Halifax Herald.* The ads yielded only 34 potential candidates, out of which a preliminary screening had reduced the number to nine (including a current employee of Maple Leaf Shoes). All nine were interviewed by Clark and five were eliminated from further consideration after this preliminary interview. The remaining four were interviewed a second time by Clark and three senior officers. Summaries of the résumés submitted by the four candidates are given in Exhibits 1 through 4.

Based on their résumés and on his impressions of the interviews with the four candidates, Robert Clark made the following mental evaluations of the applicants: Michael Anderson, Arthur Dougherty, Jane Reynolds, and Steven Robinson. Clark felt that each applicant had several strong points, but also possessed weaknesses.

Michael Anderson: Anderson was the oldest of the lot (observed Clark). A widower with two grown-up children, he had the most diverse background. Anderson impressed Clark as a very interesting, if somewhat reserved, person. He had seven years' experience in the Canadian Armed Forces (with an outstanding record there) and knew several trades ("Jack of all trades"?). During the interview, Anderson came across as a results-oriented individual. As a previous employer noted, Corner Brook Arts and Crafts, where Anderson worked in the past, was about to be declared bankrupt when Anderson entered the company ("for peanuts money") and turned it around to become a successful firm by refining its planning and control systems. In Clark's mind, Anderson was someone who could take charge, but one of the references had warned about Anderson's "need for autonomy in his workplace." Clark felt that personally he would get along better with someone else (for example, Dougherty) than with Anderson. But then, his personal feelings shouldn't play that important a role in the hiring decision. Or should they?

Arthur Dougherty: Dougherty impressed Clark as the most gregarious of the four he interviewed. He was totally at ease with the interviewers and displayed the best interpersonal skills among the four. Not only was he comfortable in the presence of others, but he seemed to have the knack of making others feel comfortable as well. It was true that Dougherty's past experience

EXHIBIT 1	Michael Anderson
Personal:	Age 53 years; widower, two children, Ken (25 years) and Maggie (23 years)
Education:	Grade 12, Belvedere High School, Vancouver
	Two years in B.Com., University of B.C.
	Over 10 Extension courses in Human Resource Management in B.C. and Ontario. Subjects include Negotiation Skills, Human Resource Information Systems, Safety and Health, Employee Involvement and Organizational Change
Experience:	7 years in Canadian Armed Forces; honorary discharge; outstanding record
	4 years, Production Scheduler, Corner Brook Arts & Crafts Ltd., Newfoundland
	6 years, Production Supervisor, Hamilton Steel Limited, Ontario
	12 years, Administrative Manager, De-Brook Safety Glasses Ltd., Mississauga, Ontario
	5 years, Assistant Human Resource Manager, U-Save Groceries Limited, Ontario
Other Activities:	Member, Council for Free Trade, Corner Brook (3 years)
	Initiated Young Entrepreneurs Program in association with a local bank, Mississauga
	Coach for the town soccer team (during the three years he coached, the team won all local games)

EXHIBIT 2	Arthur Dougherty
Personal:	Age 48 years; married for the last 23 years, three children, Jack (22), John (20), and Martha (17)
Education:	Grade 12 from St. John's High School, Mississauga, Ontario
	2 years in Bachelor of Arts Program, University of Toronto
	Dale Carnegie course
	Public Speaking workshop
	4 Human Resource Management courses (non-credit) at McMaster University, Hamilton, Ontario. Topics include Employee Relations, Diversity Management, Safety and Information systems
Experience:	2 years, Clerical (accounting), Great West Insurance Company, Toronto
	4 years, Sales Assistant, Classic Leather Shoes Ltd., Vancouver
	6 years, Sales Supervisor, Metro Auto Lines, Vancouver
	6 years, Senior Sales Supervisor, Fashion Foot Wear Ltd., Ontario
	4 years, Human Resource Supervisor, Ontario EngineeringWorks, Hamilton, Ontario
	4 years, Assistant Human Resource Manager, Madman McIsaac's Carpets and Home Furnishings Ltd., Hamilton, Ontario
Other Activities:	Member, Parish Council Executive (5 years)
	Member, Executive Committee for Trade, Vancouver Chamber of Commerce (3 years)
	Founding member of local animal shelter, Wanderbury, Ontario

EXHIBIT 3	Jane Reynolds

Personal:	Age 36 years; single, one child, John (8 years)
Education:	B.A. Sociology, University of New Brunswick (Dean's Honour List)
	6 Credit courses in Human Resource Management, Saint Mary's University, Halifax, Nova Scotia. The courses were Human Resource Management, Industrial Relations, Wage and Salary Administration, Staffing and Training, Interpersonal Communication, and Organizational Theory and Design
	3 courses (Stress Management, Negotiation Skills and Interpersonal Communication) offered by Ontario Human Resources Association
Experience:	1 year, Employment Recruiter, Atlantic Fishery Products, Saint John
	2 years, Recruiter, Nova Brewery, Halifax
	1 year, Human Resource Assistant, Nova Scotia Power Corporation, Halifax
	3 years, Senior Human Resource Assistant, Ontario Steel Limited, Hamilton
	4 years, Human Resource Supervisor, Maple Leaf Shoes Ltd., Leaf Town
Other Activities:	Volunteer, United Way, Saint John (2 years)
	Leader, Girl Guides, Halifax (4 years)
	Member, Lions Club, Hamilton (3 years) and Leaf Town (2 years)

EXHIBIT 4	Steven Robinson

Personal:	Age 35 years; divorced, one child under Robinson's custody, Melanie (7 years)
Education:	B.A. (Honours) (Political Science), University of Alberta
	Certified Human Resources Professional, Alberta
	Two extension courses on Human Resources Information Systems and the Internet
Experience:	2 years, Correspondent for *The Bugle,* Calgary
	2 Years, Human Resources Assistant, *The Bugle,* Calgary
	4 years, Assistant Human Resource Manager, St. Xavier High School, Calgary
	4 years, Assistant Human Resource Manager, Bedford Town, Nova Scotia
Other Activities:	Member, Basketball Team, University of Alberta
	Organized literacy program for African-Canadians in Edmonton (2 years)
	Founding member and treasurer, African-Canadian Association, Calgary
	Member, Organizational Transitions Committee, Human Resources Association, Nova Scotia

was mostly in sales—he had moved to human resources after more than 15 years of a sales career ("I wanted bigger and more challenging things to do. You can only do so much selling shoes and steel"). He also had a good knowledge of the shoe industry. His references described Dougherty as "a very pleasant person to work with" and "always offering help to anyone who needs him." But Clark wondered whether Dougherty would be able to play the leader and catalyst role in HR at Maple Leaf. In favour of Dougherty was another fact: his children had all grown up, so

he should be able to devote extra time to the new position. This job, with all these union contract negotiations ahead, was going to require a lot of 18-hour workdays!

Jane Reynolds: The fact that struck Clark about Reynolds every time he saw her was the way she dressed. She was so meticulously dressed and had impeccable manners (she reminded him of his German aunt who was very formal and methodical). Reynolds was popular among her colleagues, except for the finance manager, Tim McDonald, who didn't like her at all ("I can't stand that female! She is always asking me do new things and she wants it yesterday!"). Considered a real "mover," Reynolds had been active at Maple Leaf Shoes, always working on some project or other. John McAllister, the previous human resources manager and Reynolds' boss, had, however, mixed evaluations of Reynolds' job performance ("She is very competent, I will say that; but her management style can alienate at least some folks here"). Reynolds was also probably quite junior for the position—after all, she had not held any senior administrative positions until this point. Will she be able to meet the challenges posed by Maple Leaf's growth and change? Clark did not know. Clark also had doubts about the wisdom of hiring a woman for the position. Can Reynolds really face up to Steven Mathews, the new leader of the Leather Workers' Association, who was known for his aggressive bargaining? Mathews had the reputation of being a tough, militant leader who was out to get results for his union. And while Clark didn't consider himself prudish, he still found it hard to accept having a child out of wedlock. Do other managers hold any prejudices against her? Will she fit into the team? The references from Reynolds' previous employers had given her consistently very high to outstanding ratings. There is a rumour that Reynolds has been offered a better position in another local firm and may move out soon. Reynolds impressed Clark as very career-minded.

Steven Robinson: The first thing that struck Clark about Robinson was what hiring him would do to the public's and employees' image of the company. Hiring an African-Canadian is just the thing to do right now—no one could criticize you any more about being insensitive to the multicultural mosaic of Canada. Just by hiring Robinson, he could create the impression of being a "progressive employer." Maple Leaf Shoes Limited has been facing a barrage of criticisms about human rights law violations; now, just by a single act of hiring Robinson, the firm could eliminate all those negative impressions. During the interview, Clark had received good "vibes" from Robinson. Robinson, who is divorced, has a small child. Robinson's mother lives with him to take care of the child. Robinson's referees gave him satisfactory recommendations, although not outstanding. Robinson was the youngest of all the four applicants and seemed full of energy and enthusiasm. Robinson was also the only one with a CHRP certification and extension courses in new information technology and the Internet. If the firm is to embrace new technology soon, Robinson will be the person to hire, Clark concluded.

Clark knew that he had a difficult decision to make. To complicate matters, there was not much agreement among the three managers who interviewed the four job applicants. The rankings given by the finance, marketing, and production managers to the four candidates are shown below (1 = first, 4 = last).

Interviewer	Applicant			
	Anderson	**Dougherty**	**Reynolds**	**Robinson**
Finance manager	2	1	4	3
Marketing manager	3	4	1	2
Production manager	1	3	2	4

Clark realized that he didn't approve of any one of the four applicants completely. Each also had specific strengths that others did not have. He also knew that he urgently needed an energetic, results-oriented person. The person selected should be able to deal with unions, redesign jobs to cut down costs, handle the growing number of employee complaints, and manage the challenges posed by the firm's growth. In the next three years, the firm was planning to expand its operations to other Canadian provinces and two other countries. The firm's management cadre was expected to grow by roughly 3 percent each year for the next four to five years, and the need for management training existed now more than ever. This meant that the new person should be a mover and shaker, but at the same time be able to work with people without offending them.

"A tough problem to resolve," murmured Clark to himself as he sipped the seventh cup of coffee of the day. His doctor had warned him against having too much caffeine in his system due to his heart condition, but this was going to be one of those long, dreary days. In less than an hour, Clark had a meeting with Sam Polanyi, shop steward of the Vinyl and Leather Workers' Union, who wanted to talk about a "serious problem that exists in Plant 1." How much he wished he had a manager who could do all these thankless jobs!

Discussion Questions

1. Based on the information given in the case, what education, experience, job skills, and other competencies would seem to be required for the future human resource manager of Maple Leaf Shoes?

2. How do the various candidates rate on these factors you identified?

3. What is your evaluation of the selection process employed by the firm (especially Robert Clark) in this instance? If you were in charge, would you have done anything differently? How?

4. Among the candidates, who (if any) would seem to be suitable for the position? What are the issues you should consider and tradeoffs you should make when selecting one of these candidates for the position?

CASE STUDY CPIB Canadian Pacific and International Bank

Evaluating a New Selection Test*

CPIB's rapid expansion into foreign markets had necessitated changes in its selection practices. Some of the factors considered by the bank when hiring employees (e.g., behaviour description interviews, assessment centre reports, reference checks over phone, and so on) were either not possible in some of the foreign countries (because of technical and infrastructural difficulties) or not valid due to cultural differences. In one Asian region, this challenge was particularly felt. In this region, in the past only 50 percent of the new hires were considered "satisfactory" by their supervisors. Although the bank expanded its orientation and initial job training program (which now costs the organization approximately $300 per employee), this still has not improved the success rate.

Recently, R. Dennison, CPIB's regional human resource director, attended a HR conference where she came across a selection test that appeared to have considerable promise. The Financial Services Aptitude Test, designed by a large international consulting firm, had a good validation record for job positions similar to those found in the bank. Initial concurrent validation studies at CPIB using two groups of employees also indicated the test's potential usefulness to the organization. The cost of the test per applicant was 30, which included all costs associated with the administration, scoring, and interpretation of test results.

CPIB added the test as an additional predictor in its selection kit. Table 1 shows the scores received by 100 applicants on the test, with a breakdown of number of applicants who were deemed "successful" on the job by their supervisors. The firm will continue to use its orientation and training program for all its selected employees.

Assume that the distribution of the test scores and "success rates" for the next 100 applicants will follow similar patterns as indicated in Table 1. At present, the firm wants to use these test results to fill 40 existing vacancies in the region.

Discussion Questions

1. Calculate the cutoff test score that will minimize the overall cost of testing plus training.

2. To get 40 "successful" employees, how many persons will have to be hired who have:

   (a) a score of 70 or higher on the test?

   (b) a score of 60 or higher on the test?

3. What suggestions will you make to the bank in validating and using the above test?

TABLE 1	Financial Services Aptitude Test: Scores of "Successful" and "Unsuccessful" Candidates (n = 100)		
Score	Number of Persons Who Received This Test score	Number of Persons Deemed "Successful"	Number of Persons Deemed "Unsuccessful"
10	4	—	4
20	5	—	5
30	9	—	9
40	12	2	10
50	14	5	9
60	13	6	7
70	15	9	6
80	13	1	—
90	8	8	—
100	7	7	—
Total	**100**	**50**	**50**

* Case prepared by Professor Hari Das of Department of Management, Saint Mary's University, Halifax. All rights retained by the author © 2000.

⬤ PART-ENDING VIDEOS

Workwell Training: Harassment
Manager's Hot Seat: "Beck 'N Call"
"Scarf Eve"
Source: *The National,* February 9, 2004, running time 9:11.

Go to **www.mcgrawhillconnect.ca** to access the videos.

⬤ ROLE-PLAY 3: Selection Interview

Time required: 40–50 minutes

Objectives of the Role-Play

1. To help the students understand the steps in conducting a behavioural interview
2. To enhance their skills as interviewers
3. To help them prepare for their role as interviewees

Prior Preparation

1. Study Chapter 6 of the text.
2. Read descriptions of Maple Leaf Shoes Ltd. at the ends of Chapters 1, 2, and 6.

Guidelines for Conducting the Role-Play

In this role-play Robert Clark is interviewing Jane Reynolds for the position of Human Resource Manager in the firm.

1. Two students, one for the role of Jane Reynolds and the other for Robert Clark, should be identified.
2. Students should read their own descriptions below along with the company details given at the ends of Chapters 1 and 2.
3. The instructor should signal the beginning and the end of the meeting. The interview will last about 25 minutes.
4. The remainder of the class time is used for discussion of the behaviours during the role-play and outcomes.
5. Observers should be asked to make notes against the questions listed below and discuss their findings at the end of the role-play.
6. Instructor should sum up by highlighting the importance of behaviourally based interviews to improve their reliability.

Instructions for Observers

As you observe the meeting between Jane Reynolds and Robert Clark, make notes against each of the questions below. Pay particular attention to the behaviours and verbal and nonverbal expressions of each person.

1. Were the two of them well prepared for the interview? Why?
2. How did Robert Clark begin the meeting?
3. Was there open communication between the two? Who spoke more? About what?
4. Was the sequence of his questions appropriate? Were the questions behavioural in nature? What could have been done better?
5. Did Jane present herself well during the interview? How? What would you do differently if you were Jane?
6. What is your assessment of the nonverbal behaviours of the interviewer and the interviewee? What changes would you recommend to each?
7. What other improvements to the interview would you recommend?

◆ APPENDIX A

Utility Analysis

The utility of a selection procedure should be assessed only after considering a number of factors. The more important ones among these are (1) the validity of the predictor; (2) the variability in job performance; (3) the selection ratio; (4) the base rate of job success; and (5) selection costs.

1. Validity of the Predictor

Different predictors have differing validity coefficients. One study by Hunter and Hunter[101] showed that predictors such as tests and assessment centres had average validities in the range of 0.43 to 0.54, while others such as reference checks (0.26) and interviews (0.14) were much lower. Of course, when choosing between predictors with equal validity, the cost of the predictor becomes an important consideration; however, as one writer noted, the tradeoff between the cost of a predictor and its validity should almost always be resolved in favour of validity.[102] This is because the potential cost of an error in the course of the test is extremely high.

2. Variability in Job Performance

A useful measure of a job's value to the organization is the variability of job performance for a job expressed in dollar terms. For some jobs, the differences in performance ranges (example: "outstanding" to "totally incompetent") have relatively little effect in terms of dollar value to the organization. For example, the variability of performance of a receptionist or window cleaner is relatively less significant to the organization than that of a production planner or marketing manager. Thus, a "good" receptionist may contribute, say, $6,000 over his or her salary and benefits to the organization, while a "poor" one may cost the firm, say, $2,000 in terms of lost sales because of disgruntled customers who have had bad experiences when paying visits to the organization. In the case of a marketing manager, the effects of outcomes may be far more serious. A good marketing manager may contribute $500,000 above his or her salary and benefits, while a poor one may cost the firm $200,000 in lost sales or decreased market share. The variability in performance in dollar terms for the receptionist is about $8,000; for the marketing manager's position, the corresponding figure may be $700,000. The statistical index used for computing this type of variability is the standard deviation of performance. Hunter and Schmidt's[103] research led them to conclude that a "40 percent rule" prevails for most common job positions—namely, the variability in job performance is typically 40 percent of the average annual salary of a position. Clearly, in the above example, an organization is more likely to spend $5,000 on improving the selection procedures for its marketing manager than for the receptionist.

3. Selection Ratio

As already mentioned in this chapter, a large selection ratio (such as 1:25) means that the firm can afford to be choosy, while a small ratio of 1:2 does not give much freedom to the organization to make selection decisions. On the one hand, a ratio such as 1:25 means that a large number of applicants must be tested and screened (thus adding to the selection costs). On the other hand, it also means that only the "cream" of the applicant group will be selected, thus implying that even a predictor with relatively low validity can be employed.

4. Base Rate of Job Success

The base rate denotes the relative incidence of any given attribute or behaviour in the total population.[104] If 70 percent of the people between 22 and 40 years old are married, then the base rate for marriage for that segment of the society is 70. A low base rate of job success in an organization indicates that few employees reach an acceptable level of job performance. Typically, base rates of success tend to be high for easy and simple jobs. For complex jobs requiring many skills and years of training, the base rates tend to be lower. Generally, the usefulness of a selection procedure increases when it is able to increase the base rate of success for a job. If the base rate is already high at 80 or 90, it is very difficult to find a predictor that will improve on it as the typical validity coefficients for various predictors currently in use range from 0.15 to 0.60.

5. Selection Costs

Selection costs may be actual or potential. Actual costs include costs of administering standardized tests, collecting and processing biographical blanks, conducting employment interviews, and offering money and other benefits to job candidates who are selected. The potential costs include cost of selection errors, as when the wrong person is hired for a job. The benefits of a selection process should also be defined broadly to include not only current benefits but also likely future events (e.g., potential of an employee to hold additional responsibility).

Clearly, a thorough evaluation of all the above variables is a very complex and difficult task. In the past, several writers have offered somewhat different algorithms and formulas to assess the usefulness of the selection procedure.[105] One formula suggested to calculate the utility of the selection procedure is[106]:

$$P = (N) \times (T) \times (C) \times (S) \times (Z) \quad \text{where}$$

P = increase in productivity in dollars

N = number of persons hired

T = average job tenure in years of those hired

C = the correlation between a selection predictor and job performance (or validity coefficient)

S = variability in job performance (measured by standard deviation of job performance in dollars, roughly 40 percent of annual wage)[107]

Z = the average predictor score of those selected (in standard score form)

As an illustration, consider the job position of marketing manager in a consumer goods organization.

Let us assume that the organization used an assessment centre technique (which had an estimated validity of 0.6) to hire 10 managers who are paid a salary of $80,000 each year. Further, let us assume that each manager will stay with the organization for five years. Assuming an average predictor score (standardized) of 1.4, it can be shown that the assessment centre procedure would increase productivity by $1.344 million over five years or an average of $268,800 each year of their tenure.

Utility analysis such as the above has been successfully used in a number of organizations and different work settings.[108] It should be noted that utility analysis does not require reducing all selection-decision outcomes to a dollar figure; indeed, what is more important may be identifying all possible outcomes of a decision and weighing their relative importance systematically.[109] The factors identified earlier in this section (namely, selection ratio, base rate of success, and so on) interact; hence they must be considered together. For example, typically the utility is higher with a low base rate of job success or when the variability in job performance is high. However, given identical base rates of job success, different selection ratios can make a major difference in the context of selection. For example, it can be mathematically shown that with a base rate of 50 percent and a validity coefficient of 0.40, a selection ratio of 70 percent will yield 58 percent successful employees. Keeping the other things the same, if the selection ratio is changed to 40 percent, the proportion of successful employees climbs to 66 percent, while for a 10 percent selection ratio the corresponding figure is a whopping 78 percent.[110] Such interdependence among the relevant selection variables makes utility analysis a very complex procedure indeed. Yet its contribution to an effective human resource management system should not be underestimated.

PART 4

Placing, Developing, and Evaluating Human Resources

New employees need to know what is expected of them and what their responsibilities are, and they have to be trained properly to carry out these responsibilities effectively. A concerned employer will provide a career path for each employee and will provide the opportunities to develop all employees to their fullest potential. Also, employees need feedback on their performance to experience job satisfaction or to find out where they can improve. The next two chapters are about employee development and evaluation. As a student, you need to understand the human resource department's role in these activities. They affect you whether you work in a human resource department or elsewhere in an organization. Knowledge of these activities will assist you to be a better employee or manager.

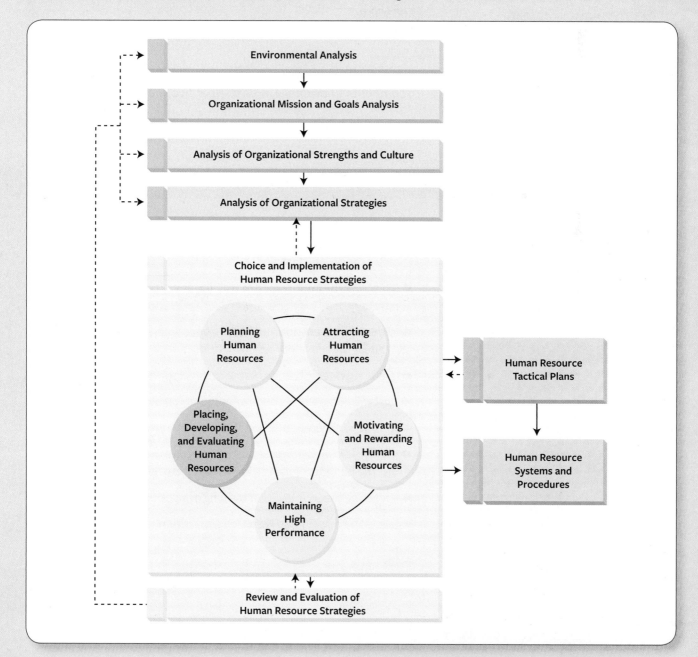

Orientation, Training and Development, and Career Planning

A sound employee orientation program boosts productivity and safety.

Bill Pomfret[1]

In today's marketplace, a well-trained workforce is no longer a competitive advantage, it's a competitive necessity.

John Thomas Howe[2]

CHAPTER OBJECTIVES

After studying this chapter, you should be able to:

➡ *Explain* the impact of a new employee orientation program on turnover and learning.

➡ *Describe* the importance of training as part of the long-range strategy of an organization.

➡ *Explain* different approaches to needs analysis in designing training and development programs.

➡ *Define* strategic human resource development.

➡ *List* the components of developmental strategies.

➡ *Describe* different methods for developing managerial personnel.

➡ *Define* knowledge worker and knowledge management and list the benefits of using a knowledge management system.

➡ *Describe* the four levels of training evaluation.

➡ *Describe* how human resource departments encourage and assist career planning.

CHAPTER 7

The gap between a new employee's expectations and abilities and the job's characteristics and demands may be substantial. That's where the orientation, training, and development functions come in. The hoped-for result is a balance between what the employee can do and what the job demands. Although these efforts are time-consuming and expensive, they reduce employee turnover and help new employees to be productive sooner. This part of the chapter discusses the key steps involved in the orientation process, and the next part discusses the training and development of an organization's workforce.

PURPOSE OF ORIENTATION

Yahoo's Employee Orientation Community Discussions, resources
http://groups.yahoo.com/group/orientation/messages

> **socialization**
> The process by which people adapt to an organization.

Robert Bacal of Bacal & Associates Articles, recommendations
www.articles911.com/Human_Resources/Orientation

Successful organizational entry and maintenance is the objective of employee socialization. Socialization is the continuing process by which an employee begins to understand and accept the values, norms, and beliefs held by others in the organization. New employees need to know, accept, and demonstrate behaviours that the organization views as desirable, in other words "learn the ropes and how to skip them." The overall process involves turning outsiders into insiders.

Socialization

Even before employees join organizations, **socialization** may have taken place: a formal education will prepare, to a degree, a candidate for specific jobs, such as accounting or engineering; a summer job may give a candidate an informal experience relating to a position; even watching a television show or a movie will create certain expectations relating to jobs, such as police officers, paramedics, or archaeologists. The candidate's and the organization's expectations about each other will form a psychological contract. Some of these expectations may be explicitly stated; others may be implicit assumptions about each other. For example, a company policy might state that an employee is expected to follow the company's ethics guidelines; an employee, on the other hand, might assume that he or she will be treated fairly by the supervisor.

The new employee, having some expectations about organizational life, will then encounter the realities of the daily routines and challenges of a job. Formal methods at this stage may include orientation programs, training, and job rotation. Informal approaches may include getting to know and understand the style and personality of one's boss and coworkers. After the day-to-day interactions, with their conditioning and reinforcement properties, recruits will have acquired new values and will solidify new attitudes and behaviours. At this point, the individual has been transformed from an outsider into a full-fledged member of the organization.

Effective orientation should cover such topics as the company's history, policies, rules, and procedures, as well as a tour of the company's facilities. Should orientation also include a discussion of past company failures?

© Fresh Meat Media LLC/Getty Images.

Orientation Programs

Formal **orientation programs** familiarize new employees with their roles, with the organization, and with other employees. Orientation, if properly done, can serve several purposes:

orientation programs
Programs that familiarize new employees with their roles, the organization, its policies, and other employees.

- reduce employee turnover;
- reduce errors and save time;
- develop clear job and organizational expectations;
- improve job performance;
- attain acceptable job performance levels faster;
- increase organizational stability;
- reduce employee anxiety;
- reduce grievances; and
- reduce instances of corrective discipline measures.

Legal Management Resource Center New Employee Orientation Programs
http://thesource.alanet.org/portal/server.pt?open=17&objID=308&DirMode=1&parentname=Dir&parentid=1&mode=2&in_hi_userid=2&cached=true

Reduce Employee Turnover

Employees are more likely to quit during their first few months than at any other time in their employment. The difference between what a person expects to find at the workplace and what one actually finds is referred to as *cognitive dissonance*. If the dissonance is too high, employees take action—which, for new employees, may mean quitting:

> At the Royal Bank of Canada, the annual turnover averages 5 percent of its workforce.* While this at first glance looks reasonable and almost insignificant, the size of the bank's workforce warrants action to reduce it. The bank's annual report shows its workforce to be about 80,000, which means that approximately 4,000 employees leave the bank annually.[3]

As a rule of thumb, turnover costs for nonexempt employees are between 0.25× and 0.5× annual salaries plus benefits, for exempt employees between 1× and 1.5×, and for executives between 3× and 5× plus benefits. For a large firm, a few thousand dollars may seem inconsequential; but if thousands of employees leave every year, the costs can quickly escalate into millions of dollars. Moreover, when experienced, long-service employees quit, the loss may be incalculable because of the training, knowledge, and skills these workers take with them. In general, the human resource department can reduce turnover by meeting the personal objectives of employees. When that happens, both the employee and the organization can benefit.

Two often-quoted studies prove the point. Research at Corning Glass Works revealed that new employees who had gone through a structured orientation program were 69 percent more likely to be with the company three years later than those who had not. Another study at Texas Instruments found that employees who were carefully oriented to the organization and the job reached full productivity two months sooner than those who were not.[4]

Reduce Errors and Save Time

A well-oriented employee knows exactly what is expected of him or her and, hence, is likely to make fewer mistakes. Typically, a new employee is less efficient than an experienced employee.[5] This factor, combined with other additional costs involved in getting a new employee started (e.g., supervisor's time and attention), makes the **startup costs** of new employees very significant.[6]

startup costs
The additional costs associated with a new employee because the new employee is typically less efficient than an experienced worker; the new worker also requires additional supervisory time.

Develop Clear Job and Organizational Expectations

For some jobs, the duties and job expectations are clear. However, for a majority of other jobs, this is simply not the case. There are no clear-cut lists of "desirable" behaviours, outcomes, and job attitudes. Most new employees would like to know "what it takes to survive and get ahead in this organization." In the absence of clear guidelines from their employer, they may have to find answers to their questions informally through the grapevine and by gossiping with others. Unfortunately, in the latter instance, there is no guarantee that they will find the right answers. To tell employees what the organization expects of them and what they can expect in return, effective orientation is absolutely necessary.[7]

---

*This is in contrast to a 8.4 percent turnover rate of the 50 Best Employers in Canada and 12.3 percent of other employers in a 2007 survey done by Hewitt Associates, a major consulting company (www.hrmguide.net/canada/general/50-best-employers.htm).

Improve Job Performance

Employees who establish a good relationship with the organization, their colleagues, and their supervisors tend to be more productive. Establishing that relationship can begin with a good orientation program.

Attain Acceptable Job Performance Levels Faster

Spelling out expected job performance standards at the beginning eliminates uncertainty about what is expected on the job:

> The Queen Elizabeth II Health Sciences Centre in Halifax uses critical incidents as part of its job descriptions to illustrate to new employees effective and ineffective job behaviours. Many new employees comment on how useful such job descriptions are in explaining what is expected of them.

Increase Organizational Stability

Communicating policies and regulations to new employees early on, as in an effective orientation program, clearly reduces undesirable behaviour and friction points.

Reduce Employee Anxiety

New employees will experience less stress if an organization communicates with new employees openly, clarifies their roles, and familiarizes them with organizational objectives.

Reduce Grievances

Grievances often result from ambiguous job expectations and unclear responsibilities. An orientation program specifies both.

Reduce Instances of Corrective Discipline Measures

An effective orientation program clarifies the rights and duties of employees, outlines disciplinary requirements, and spells out the consequences of deviating from the prescribed path.

In summary, the orientation program helps the individual understand the social, technical, and cultural aspects of the workplace. As new employees are accepted, they become part of the social fabric of the organization. Orientation programs help speed up the socialization process and benefit both the employee and the organization.

CONTENT OF ORIENTATION PROGRAMS

employee handbook
A handbook explaining key benefits, policies, and general information about the employer.

buddy systems
Exist when an experienced employee is asked to show a new employee around the job site, conduct introductions, and answer the newcomer's questions.

There are various approaches to orienting new employees. Some are more popular than others. Most organizations conduct orientation on an individual basis, although group orientation programs are also used in large organizations where several employees are hired at the same time.

Most orientation programs introduce new employees to their jobs, colleagues, and the organization's policies. Figure 7-1 lists the topics typically covered during orientation. The program usually explains the organizational issues that new employees need to know. Often a film or computer slide presentation describes the history, products, services, and policies of the organization. Commonly, workers are given an **employee handbook** that explains key benefits, policies, and general information about the company. Human resource experts may also discuss pay rates as part of the program. The human resource department's role in the program often ends when the employees meet their future supervisors or trainers.

Trainers or supervisors continue the orientation program by introducing the new employee to the other trainees and coworkers. Introductions are usually followed by a tour of the facilities and an explanation of the job, its objectives, and related information.

In organizations that hire large numbers of employees, the orientation program may take a half or even a whole day to discuss the topics in Figure 7-1. For employers that hire workers only occasionally and in small numbers, there may be no formal orientation program. Instead, the employee is introduced to a senior worker who shows the new person around. These highly informal **buddy systems** are also used in large companies to help orient the new employee.

FIGURE 7-1	Topics Often Covered in Employee Orientation Programs

Organizational Issues

History of employer	Product line or services provided
Organization of employer	Overview of production process
Names and titles of key executives	Company policies and rules
Employee's title and department	Disciplinary regulations
Layout of physical facilities	Employee handbook
Probationary period	Safety procedures and enforcement

Employee Benefits

Pay scales and paydays	Insurance benefits
Vacations and holidays	Retirement program
Rest breaks	Employer-provided services to employees
Training and education benefits	Rehabilitation programs
Counselling	

Introductions

To supervisor	To coworkers
To trainers	To employee counsellor

Job Duties

Job location	Overview of job
Job tasks	Job objectives
Job safety requirements	Relationship to other jobs

Formal programs explain orientation topics systematically. These programs are also more likely to create a favourable impression on new employees, which may explain why in a U.S. survey 72 percent of firms had formal programs.[8] A Canadian study showed that roughly 10 percent of orientations lasted one hour, but 51 percent took a day or longer. The same study reported that more than two-thirds of the firms conducted the orientation immediately after the employee reported to work.[9] Of course, the experiences of employees during orientation can differ greatly. Here is an example of how an orientation can affect new employees:

Caroline Mathau: I reported to the human resource department 10 minutes early. I was told to have a seat and that someone would "show me around." An hour later I was led to an interview room. After a few minutes, the interviewer realized that I was not an applicant, but a new employee. After apologies, I was taken to meet my supervisor. The supervisor screamed for a claims processor to show me around. While I was being introduced to other people, the claims processor, Irv Porter, complained about what a grouch the supervisor was all the time. At lunch, I asked if I could get a transfer to another claims department. They told me that transfers were not permitted until after the three-month probation period. I am thinking about finding another job.

Harvey Jackson: My orientation was really super! When I arrived, I was shown to the auditorium. After coffee and pastry, we were given an employee handbook that explained most of the company's benefits and policies. We also received some forms to complete and a brief lecture about company policies. The lecture was followed by a really interesting film that explained the company's history, facilities, and how different jobs related to one another. The following hour was spent on questions and answers. We had a tour of the plant and then we were treated to lunch by the company. At lunch, our supervisors joined us to answer questions and tell us about their departments. Afterward, the supervisors introduced us to the people in my department and training began.

If Caroline's experience is a typical one in her company, employees probably begin work with low motivation, poor morale, and a lot of anxiety. The company is "saving" the cost of orientation, but it is paying a high cost in employee attitudes and performance.

Evaluating the Effectiveness of Orientation

That well-prepared orientation programs are effective has been proven in a recent research study. Klein and Weaver examined the impact of attending a new employee orientation program. Results revealed that employees attending the program were significantly more socialized on three of six socialization measures than employees who did not attend the orientation. Employees attending the program also had significantly higher levels of organizational commitment than nonattendees.[10]

How does one evaluate the effectiveness of orientation programs? A few of the approaches are discussed below.

Reactions from New Employees

Probably the single most useful method of evaluating the effectiveness of orientation is getting the reactions of new employees who went through the process. The feedback itself can be obtained through in-depth interviews with randomly selected employees and through questionnaire surveys.

Effects of Socialization on Job Attitudes and Roles

The progress in a person's socialization can be measured attitudinally (e.g., overall satisfaction with the organization and the job, work motivation, and so on) and behaviourally (e.g., labour turnover, ability to carry out roles effectively, spontaneity visible in job performance, and so on). Measures of job satisfaction, work motivation, and job performance may be some useful indications of the effectiveness of the program to achieve this end.

Degree to Which the Program Is Economical

Cost–benefit studies on orientation activities should be carried out continually. The costs of an orientation program typically include cost of materials, salaries of instructors and human resource department staff, rent, lost work time of other employees and supervisors, and the cost of tools such as films, slides, tours, and so on. Benefits emerging from an orientation program include lower labour turnover, shorter time to learn a job, lower scrap rates and wastage, reduced rework, and so on.

Trends in Orientation Programs

Face-to-face meetings for orientation are still the prevailing delivery instrument in organizations, but there is a trend to use the intranet instead because of its greater cost-effectiveness and other advantages. In a survey conducted by Westwood Dynamics, 25 organizations that have implemented online orientation cited the following top four reasons why their organization decided to put orientation online:

- improved consistency of the orientation message (100 percent);
- ability to provide orientation to all employees, regardless of start date (96 percent);
- improved timeliness (96 percent); and
- ability to deliver to a geographically dispersed workforce (75 percent).

Westwood cites the following as additional benefits of online orientation: better employee preparedness, improved connection to the organization, support for the organizational culture, flexibility and convenience, compressed delivery time, ability to test for understanding, reduced workload for trainers, ease of updating and positioning for rapid organizational growth.[11]

EMPLOYEE TRAINING

Purpose of Training

Canadian companies have to compete in a global economy and in a fast-changing business environment. This requires a workforce that has the capability to respond quickly and reliably to new challenges. In turn, this makes training an important part of an organization's long-range strategy.

Examples of the new requirements for survival include the following:

- Competing globally against companies from countries with low wage levels has forced many Canadian companies to flatten their organization and to reduce the number of employees. A flatter organization—with fewer managers and supervisors—needs employees who are able to schedule their work, manage their team, and do their own quality control. Greater flexibility requires multiskilled (or cross-trained) employees who perform diverse tasks.
- Multiskilled employees prefer to be paid according to their competencies, not jobs performed. This requires that a company's compensation and performance appraisal system be changed. Multiskilled employees have to keep up to date on their skills, applying the ability—and motivation—for lifelong learning. The organizational environment must foster and support this new concept.
- Recent changes in immigration policies bring in approximately 200,000 new immigrants to Canada annually, mostly from Asian countries. This makes it essential that Canadian managers learn to work with colleagues who often have very different cultural values. Diversity training helps to alert supervisors and employees against the use of stereotypes and prejudices.
- Changing information technology, recent developments in computer applications, innovative multimedia training methods, pioneering use of the Internet and intranet, and high-tech videoconferencing—these new uses of technology in management and the business environment require fresh skills, necessitating novel training programs and training strategies.

As we discuss in the following paragraphs, training is an investment in human capital, and human capital is really the most important asset a company has, and as such is an essential part of a company's strategy.

Relationship Between Training and Development

Training refers to a planned effort by an organization to make possible the learning of job-related behaviour. The term *behaviour* is used broadly to include any knowledge and skill acquired by an employee through practice. When management wants to prepare employees for future job responsibilities, this activity is called human resource development, which is discussed later in the chapter. This distinction between training and development is primarily one of intent. *Training* prepares people to do their *present* job. *Development* prepares them for *future* jobs. The rest of this chapter explains the major types of training and development programs, along with the underlying learning principles involved, how to evaluate programs, and how career planning fits into development policies.

New employees seldom perform satisfactorily. They must be trained in the duties they are expected to perform. Even experienced employees may need training to reduce poor work habits or to learn new skills that improve their performance. Although *training* seeks to help employees do their present job, the *benefits of training* may extend throughout a person's entire career and help develop that person for future responsibilities. To illustrate the developmental impact of training, consider one human resource director's observations:

> When I was first promoted to head all the job analysts a few years ago, I did not know the first thing about supervising. So I was sent to a training program for new supervisors. In that seminar I learned a lot of things. But the section on delegation really impressed me. I have relied on that knowledge ever since. Probably the reason I head the human resource department today is because that training helped to develop me into a manager.

The Training System

An effective training program benefits employees and the organization. Some of the benefits for the employees are skill improvement, self-development and stronger self-confidence, more effective handling of stress and conflicts, and a sense of growth. For the organization, the benefits may include improved profitability through higher productivity, improved morale, better corporate image, lower costs, and stronger identification with corporate goals.

To develop an effective training program, human resource specialists and managers must assess the needs, objectives, content, and learning principles associated with training.

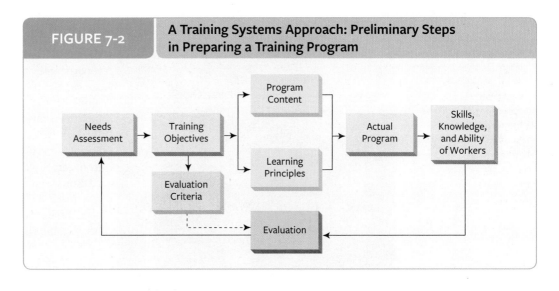

FIGURE 7-2 | **A Training Systems Approach: Preliminary Steps in Preparing a Training Program**

Figure 7-2 shows a training systems approach that describes the sequence of events to be followed before training begins.

Needs Assessment

Although precise figures are not available, it is estimated that the cost of industrial training in Canada is around $4 billion annually, while federal and provincial governments spend over $40 billion on training and education.[12] If organizations are to get maximum benefit from this staggering expenditure, efforts must concentrate on people and situations that can benefit most. **Needs assessment** diagnoses present problems and environmental challenges that can be met through training, or the future challenges to be met through long-term development. For example, changes in the external environment may present an organization with new challenges. The comments of one training director illustrate the impact of the external environment:

> Because of human rights legislation, we have to train every interviewer in the human resource department. This training is needed to ensure that our interviewers are not asking questions that might violate federal or provincial laws. When managers in other departments heard of the training, they, too, wanted to sign up. What was to be a one-time seminar became a monthly session for nearly three years. We evaluated the requests of these other managers and decided that they interviewed recruits and that they should be trained also.

Sometimes, a change in the organization's strategy can create a need for training. For example, new products or services usually require employees to learn new procedures. Sales personnel, programmers, and production workers have to be trained to produce, sell, and service a new product line. Training can also be used when high accident rates, low morale and motivation, or other problems are diagnosed.

Regardless of these challenges, needs assessment must consider each person. Needs may be determined by the human resource department, supervisors, or self-nomination. The human resource department may find weaknesses among those who are hired or promoted. Supervisors are another source of recommendations for training. But their suggestions may be made to banish troublemakers, "hide" surplus employees who are temporarily expendable, or reward good workers. Since these are not valid reasons, the human resource department often reviews supervisory recommendations to verify the need for training. Likewise, the department also reviews self-nominations to determine whether the training is actually needed.

Besides being aware of possible language barriers when training foreign workers, it is important to realize that seemingly equivalent educational levels of employees in industrial and developing nations are not the same. Twelve years of education may have different meanings in different societies.

needs assessment
A diagnosis that presents problems and future challenges that can be met through training or development.

Article on assessment
http://alumnus.caltech.edu/~rouda/T2_NA.html

Soldiers in the armed forces go through intensive and vigorous training exercises with clear training objectives. Should the training be the same for men and women?

CORBIS.

Trainers are alert to other sources of information that may indicate a need for training. Production records, quality control reports, grievances, safety reports, absenteeism and turnover statistics, and exit interviews among departing employees may indicate problems that should be addressed through training and development efforts. Training needs may also become apparent from career planning and development discussions or performance appraisal reviews—discussed in Chapter 8. Regardless of how needs assessment takes place, it is important because the success of the remaining steps in Figure 7-2 depends on an accurate assessment. If the trainer's assessment of needs is not correct, training objectives and program content will be inappropriate.

Training Objectives

An evaluation of training needs results in training objectives. These objectives should state

- the desired behaviour;
- the conditions under which it is to occur; and
- the acceptable performance criteria.

These statements serve as the standard against which individual performance and the program can be measured. For example, the objectives for an airline reservation agent might be stated as follows:

1. Provide flight information to call-in customers within 30 seconds.
2. Complete a one-city, round-trip reservation in 120 seconds after all information is obtained from the customer.

Objectives such as these give the trainer and the trainee specific goals that can be used by both to evaluate their success. If these objectives are not met, failure gives the human resource department feedback on the program and the participants.

Program Content

The program's content is shaped by the needs assessment and the learning objectives. This content may seek to teach specific skills, provide needed knowledge, or try to influence attitudes. Whatever the content, the program must meet the needs of the organization and the participants. If company goals are not furthered, resources are wasted. Similarly, participants must view the content as relevant to their needs, or their motivation to learn may be low.

Learning Principles

Although it is widely studied, little is known about the learning process. Part of the problem is that learning cannot be observed; only its results can be measured. From studies of learning, however, researchers have sketched a broad picture of the learning process and have developed some tentative principles of learning.

learning curve
A visual representation of the rate at which one learns given material.

Perhaps the best way to understand learning is through the use of a **learning curve**, pictured in Figure 7-3. As the curve illustrates, learning takes place in bursts (from points A to B) and in plateaus (from points B to C). Trainers have two goals related to the shape of each employee's curve. *First*, they want it to reach a satisfactory level of performance, shown as a dashed line in the figure. *Second*, they want the curve to get to that level as quickly as possible.

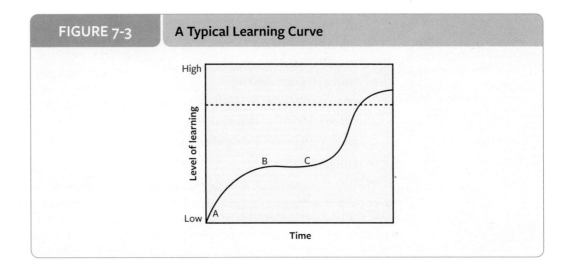

FIGURE 7-3 | **A Typical Learning Curve**

Although the rate at which an individual learns depends upon the person, the use of various learning principles helps speed up the learning process.

Learning principles are guidelines to the ways in which people learn most effectively. The more they are included in training, the more effective training is likely to be. The principles are participation, repetition, relevance, transference, and feedback.

- **Participation.** Learning is usually quicker and more long-lasting when the learner can participate actively. As a result of participation, we learn more quickly and retain that learning longer. For example, once they have learned, most people never forget how to ride a bicycle or drive a car.
- **Repetition**. Although it is seldom fun, repetition apparently etches a pattern into our memory. Studying for an examination, for example, involves memorization of key ideas to be recalled during the test. Likewise, most people learned the alphabet and the multiplication tables by repetition.
- **Relevance**. Learning is helped when the material to be learned is meaningful. For example, trainers usually explain the overall purpose of a job to trainees before explaining specific tasks. This explanation allows the worker to see the relevance of each task and the importance of following the given procedures.
- **Transference**. **Transference** is the application of training to actual job situations. The closer the demands of the training program match the demands of the job, the faster a person learns to master the job. For example, pilots are usually trained in flight simulators, because the simulators very closely resemble the actual cockpit and flight characteristics of the plane. The close match between the simulator and the plane allows the trainee to transfer quickly the learning in the simulator to actual flight conditions.
- **Feedback**. Feedback gives learners information on their progress. With feedback, motivated learners can adjust their behaviour to achieve the quickest possible learning curve. Without feedback, learners cannot gauge their progress and may become discouraged. Test grades are feedback on the study habits of test takers, for example.

learning principles
Guidelines to the ways people learn most effectively.

Recommendations on writing training objectives
http://managementhelp.org/trng_dev/lrn_objs.htm

transference
Applicability of training to job situations; evaluated by how readily the trainee can transfer the learning to his or her job.

TRAINING TECHNIQUES

Before we review the various training techniques, it is important to remember that any method may be applied to both training and development. For example, a class on management techniques may be attended by supervisors and workers who are likely to be promoted to those positions. For supervisors, the class covers how to do their present job better. In the case of workers who have no management responsibilities, the classes are intended to develop them into supervisors. The classroom instruction would be identical for both groups, but it has two different purposes: training for supervisors and development for workers.

In selecting a particular training technique, there are several tradeoffs. That is, no one technique is always best; the best method depends upon the following:

1. cost-effectiveness;
2. desired program content;
3. appropriateness of the facilities;
4. trainee preferences and capabilities;
5. trainer preferences and capabilities; and
6. learning principles.

The importance of these six tradeoffs depends upon the situation. For example, cost-effectiveness may be a minor factor when training an airline pilot in emergency manoeuvres. But whatever method is selected, it has certain learning principles associated with it. Figure 7-4 lists the most common training techniques and the learning principles included in each. As the figure reveals, some techniques make more effective use of learning principles than others. Even those approaches that use few learning principles, such as the lecture, are valuable tools, because they may satisfy one of the other six tradeoffs listed above. For example, lectures may be the best way to communicate some academic content in the most cost-effective manner, especially if the classroom is large and the room does not lend itself to other approaches. Although these six tradeoffs affect the methods used, human resource specialists must be familiar with all the techniques and learning principles found in Figure 7-4.

FIGURE 7-4	Learning Principles in Different Training Techniques				
	Participation	Repetition	Relevance	Transference	Feedback
On-the-Job Techniques					
Job instruction training	Yes	Yes	Yes	Yes	Sometimes
Job rotation	Yes	Sometimes	Yes	Sometimes	No
Apprenticeships	Yes	Sometimes	Yes	Sometimes	Sometimes
Coaching	Yes	Sometimes	Yes	Sometimes	Yes
Off-the-Job Techniques					
Lecture	No	No	No	Sometimes	No
Video presentation	No	No	No	Yes	No
Vestibule training	Yes	Yes	Sometimes	Yes	Sometimes
Role-playing	Yes	Sometimes	Sometimes	No	Sometimes
Case study	Yes	Sometimes	Sometimes	Sometimes	Sometimes
Simulation	Yes	Sometimes	Sometimes	Sometimes	Sometimes
Self-study	Yes	Yes	Sometimes	Sometimes	No
Programmed learning	Yes	Yes	No	Yes	Yes
Laboratory training	Yes	Yes	Sometimes	No	Yes
Computer-based training	Yes	Yes	Sometimes	Yes	Yes
Virtual reality	Yes	Yes	Yes	Yes	Yes

Source: *Training and Industry: The Management of Learning*, 1st edition by Bass/Vaughan © 1968. Reprinted with permission of Wadsworth, a division of Thomson Learning. www.thomsonrights.com. Fax 800-730-2215.

on-the-job training (OJT)
A method in which a person learns a job by actually performing it.

On-the-Job Training

On-the-job training (OJT) is received directly on the job and is used primarily to teach workers how to do their present job. A trainer, supervisor, or coworker serves as the instructor. This method includes each of the five learning principles (participation, repetition, relevance, transference, and feedback) in a series of carefully planned steps.

First, the trainee receives an overview of the job, its purpose, and the desired outcomes, which emphasizes the relevance of the training. *Then* the trainer demonstrates the job to provide the employee with a model to copy. Since the employee is being shown the actions the job actually requires, the training is transferable. *Next*, the employee is allowed to mimic the trainer's example. Demonstrations by the trainer and practice by the trainee are repeated until the job is mastered by the trainee. Repeated demonstrations and practice provide the advantage of repetition and feedback. *Finally*, the employee performs the job without supervision, although the trainer may visit the employee periodically to see if there are any lingering questions.

cross-training
Training employees to perform operations in areas other than their assigned jobs.

apprenticeships
Training programs, generally for tradespeople, in which a new employee learns from a more experienced employee.

coaching
A less formal training experience than an apprenticeship, coaching generally involves a supervisor or manager providing a model for a new employee to observe and emulate.

Job Rotation

To cross-train employees in a variety of jobs, some trainers will move the trainee from job to job. Besides giving workers variety in their jobs, **cross-training** helps the organization when vacations, absences, and resignations occur. Learner participation and high job transferability are the learning advantages to job rotation.

Apprenticeships and Coaching

Apprenticeships involve learning from a more experienced employee or employees. Most tradespeople, such as plumbers and carpenters, are trained through formal apprenticeship programs. Assistantships and internships are similar to apprenticeships. These approaches use high levels of participation by the trainee and have high transferability to the job.

Coaching is similar to apprenticeship in that the coach attempts to provide a model for the trainee to copy. Most companies use some coaching. It tends to be less formal than an apprenticeship program, because there are few formal classroom sessions, and the coaching is provided when needed rather than being part of a carefully planned program. Coaching is almost always handled by the supervisor or manager and not the human resource department. Participation, feedback, and job transference are likely to be high in this form of learning.

An individual who receives coaching by another person to assume that person's specific job is called an *understudy*. A senior executive may designate a replacement well before retirement so that that person can serve as an understudy.

Off-the-Job Training

Lectures and Video Presentations

Lectures and other off-the-job techniques tend to rely more heavily on communications rather than modelling, which is used in on-the-job programs. These approaches are applied in both training and development. Presenting a lecture is a popular approach, because it offers relative economy and a meaningful organization of materials. However, participation, feedback, transference, and repetition are often low. Feedback and participation can be improved when discussion is permitted after the lecture.

Television, films, and slide presentations are comparable to lectures. A meaningful organization of materials and initial audience interest are potential strengths of these approaches.

Vestibule Training

vestibule training
Training opportunities that utilize simulated workstations so that new employees can learn about their job without interfering with activities at the actual workstation.

So that training does not disrupt normal operations, some organizations use **vestibule training**. Separate areas or vestibules are set up with the same kind of equipment that will be used on the job. This arrangement allows transference, repetition, and participation. The meaningful organization of materials and feedback are also possible:

> At the corporate training facilities of Best Western motels and hotels, vestibules exist that duplicate a typical motel room, a typical front desk, and a typical restaurant kitchen. This allows trainees to practise housekeeping, front-desk service, and kitchen skills without disrupting the operations of any one property.

Role-Playing

Role-playing is a method that forces trainees to assume different identities. For example, a male worker and a female supervisor may trade roles. The result? Usually participants exaggerate each other's behaviour. Ideally, they both get to see themselves as others see them. The experience may create greater empathy and tolerance of individual differences. This technique seeks to change attitudes of trainees, such as improving racial understanding. It also helps to develop interpersonal skills. Although participation and feedback are present, the inclusion of other learning principles depends on the situation.

> The RCMP in British Columbia used role-playing exercises to reduce tensions between members of the force who are of Caucasian and Indian (mainly Sikh) origin. Friction between members of the different cultures on the force caused breakdowns in communications.
>
> The role-playing exercises required a small number of members of the two groups to assume the role of the other race. The role-playing leader gave each group an assignment and then directed them to carry it out as they thought members of the other race would do it. Through these exercises and the subsequent discussions, members of the different cultural groups were able to learn how their behaviour and attitudes affected each other. These role-playing exercises were an important step in reducing racial tensions.

Case Study

By studying a case, trainees learn about real or hypothetical circumstances and the actions others took under those circumstances. Besides learning from the content of the case, trainees can develop decision-making skills. When cases are meaningful and similar to work-related situations, there is some transference. There also is the advantage of participation through discussion of the case. Feedback and repetition are usually lacking. This technique is most effective for developing problem-solving skills.

Simulation

Simulation exercises are in two forms. One form involves a mechanical simulator that replicates the major features of the work situation. Driving simulators used in driver's education programs are an example. This training method is similar to vestibule training, except that the simulator more often provides instantaneous feedback on performance.

Self-Study and Programmed Learning

Carefully planned instructional materials can be used to train and develop employees. These are particularly useful when employees are dispersed geographically or when learning requires little interaction. Self-study techniques range from manuals to prerecorded CDs, DVDs, or podcasts. Unfortunately, few learning principles are included in this type of training:

> Pepsi Cola Management Institute is responsible for training bottlers all over the world. To contend with this dispersion, it created a network of videotape recorders and supplied bottlers with videotaped materials. The institute also uses other techniques.

Programmed learning materials are another form of self-study. Commonly, these are printed booklets that contain a series of questions and answers. After a question is read, the answer can be uncovered immediately. If the reader was right, he or she proceeds. If wrong, the reader is directed to review accompanying materials. Of course, computer programs with visual displays may be used instead of printed booklets. Programmed materials do provide learning participation, repetition, relevance, and feedback. The major advantage appears to be the savings in training time.[13]

Laboratory Training

Laboratory training is a form of group training used primarily to enhance interpersonal skills. Participants seek to improve their human relations skills by better understanding themselves and others. It involves sharing their experiences and examining the feelings, behaviour, perceptions, and reactions that result. Usually a trained professional serves as a facilitator. The process relies on participation, feedback, and repetition. One popular form of laboratory training is sensitivity training—also known as T-group, encounter group, or team building—which seeks to improve a person's sensitivity to the feelings of others.

Computer-Based Training

Computer-based training (**CBT**), also known as *computer-assisted learning*, has been gaining prominence in Canada in recent years. CBT offers the student control over the pace of learning and even other training contents in modular-type training programs. It offers the benefits of interactive learning, participation, and positive reinforcement during training.

Current available CBT courses fall into three main categories: off-the-shelf courses on generic topics, support courses with software packages, and custom courseware.

1. **Off-the-Shelf Courses**. Courses available in this category are typically in the areas of personal or professional skills. A number of topics currently exist, ranging from business writing and time management on the one end to complex statistical techniques on the other end.

2. **Support Courses**. Increasingly, courses on a number of topics are making their appearance on CDs and DVDs with supplementary tutorial packages. Many of these courses are on simple skills development (e.g., learning how to use a spreadsheet), but training on more complex skills and management topics can be found in complete tutorial packages (e.g., strategic planning).

3. **Custom Courseware**. Here the focus is on producing customized courses for a particular type of employee or organization. An increasing number of Canadian organizations are using customized CBT techniques for their staffs. One of the most successful CBT programs is used by the Edmonton Police Department. Called DIIT (decentralized, individualized, in-service training), the program uses modern forms of training delivery: a powerful combination of video-based training, for realism and accuracy, plus computer-based training, for efficiency, cost-effectiveness, and record-keeping.

Subcategories of CBT are *computer-assisted instruction (CAI)* and *computer-managed instruction (CMI)*. CAI is an educational medium in which instructional content or activities are delivered by a computer. Students learn by interacting with the computer and are provided with immediate feedback. CMI, on the other hand, uses the computer's branching, storage, and retrieval capabilities to organize instruction and track student records and progress.[14]

Virtual Reality

Virtual reality uses modern computer technology to create a very realistic 3D visual impression of an actual work environment. It allows trainees to respond to job requirements as if they worked on the job, as in a simulation. However, while simulation deals with certain aspects of the job, virtual reality combines all aspects of the job. The trainee works in a three-dimensional space and is able to interact with and manipulate objects in real time.

It allows companies to prepare trainees for job experiences that normally would involve high costs (e.g., flying an airplane); have the risk of costly damage to equipment (e.g., landing a plane on an aircraft carrier); or have the potential for injuries to the trainee (e.g., training in a race car).[15]

Internet or Web-Based Training

The terms *Internet training, Web-based training, virtual education,* and *e-learning* all refer to the same concept: training or education delivered via the Internet. This approach allows very specific training to be delivered at any time and any place in the world. Training via the Internet uses two forms of access: *asynchronous* (accessible anytime), such as email, electronic bulletin boards, and listservs; and *synchronous* (real-time access), such as chat rooms, instant messaging, Web conferencing, whiteboards, wireless technology, and real-time audio and video.

Some of the benefits of these approaches are that they

- provide "just-in-time" training or information;
- allow the learner to learn when it is convenient;
- target the instruction to what the learner needs to know, not what a traditional class must cover; and
- reduce travel and instruction costs.

Internet training is expensive and time-consuming to develop, but the costs are usually recovered quickly through savings in instructor time, travel, less or no time off the job, better retention, and higher general effectiveness.[16]

computer-based training (CBT)
The use of computers to facilitate the training process.

Computer-based training or e-learning
http://en.wikipedia.org/wiki/Electronic_learning

www.personal.psu.edu/bxb11/CBTGuide/CBTGuide.htm

virtual reality
Use of modern computer technology to create a 3D environment.

VR training, explanation, and demonstration
www.virtualrealitytrainingsystem.com/

www.osc.edu/research/video_library/ford.shtml
www.24dash.com/news/Housing/2009-08-04-UKs-first-virtual-reality-construction-training-centre-set-to-open

Trainees using virtual reality equipment train in a three-dimensional environment. Is it sufficiently "real" for all jobs?

© Peter Menzel/Science Photo Library.

Other media used as training tools are blogs, RSS, podcasts, wiki, and Web 2.0.

blog
A Web log—an online journal, diary, or serial published by a person or group of people.

Blogs. An abbreviation of "Web log," a **blog** is a Web site with comments, graphics, and videos, created by an individual or an organization, often interactive, allowing readers to post comments on the material displayed. Some companies use blogs to enhance communication and its corporate culture, others for training and development purposes. The advantage of a blog is that trainees can choose the material they want to study.

RSS (Rich Site Summary). RSS is a format for delivering regularly changing Web content. Many news-related sites, blogs, and other online publishers syndicate their content as an RSS feed to whoever subscribes to it. It saves time by allowing users to retrieve the latest information from several sites without having to visit individual sites or rely on a newsletter.

Podcasts. A derivative of "iPod" and " broadcast," a podcast is an audio or video clip that is automatically delivered to organization members or subscribers. This allows them to handpick the material they want to listen to and have future episodes appear on their computer or mp3 player without taking any further action. The audience will listen from a desktop or take it along in a car, on the plane, or at the gym. Podcasting is becoming increasingly popular in education. It enables students and instructors to share information with anyone at any time. An absent student can download the podcast of the missed lesson. It can be a tool for instructors or administrators to communicate curriculum, assignments, and other information. Instructors can record team discussions and interviews and use it even with embedded slides. Video podcasts can be used in all these ways as well.

wiki
A type of server program that allows multiple users to contribute to a Web site.

Wikis. Hawaiian for "quick," **wiki** is a Web page with information available to everyone that also allows the reader to contribute to or change the information content. The collaborative encyclopedia Wikipedia is one of the best-known wikis. Wikis are used in business to create intranets and knowledge management systems.

Web 2.0. Web 2.0 is not a new type of the World Wide Web (www), but a new use of it. The idea of Web 2.0 is to use the tools available for the Internet to create social networks that can be used internally for information exchange, training and development, enhancing corporate culture, motivating employees, or externally to maintain relationships with customers or the general public, through image cultivation. Well-known public social networks are Facebook, Twitter, Flickr, and MySpace.

Intranet

intranet
An internal computer network that is generally accessible only to individuals within an organization.

Canadian banks use the concept of the **intranet**, an intraorganizational computer network, to deliver their corporate training. The Canadian Imperial Bank of Commerce abolished its $30 million training and development department and delegated the acquisition of relevant professional knowledge to its employees. It uses a competency model as a guide that describes approximately 50 skills that employees need to "provide value to customers." Employees have access to books and software in training rooms, learn from coworkers, and can take courses as needed. They even track their own progress.[17] Similarly, the Royal Bank has put its training programs on its internal "Personal Learning Network." The bank invested $2 million in its PC-based system that uses video, graphics, sound, text, and animation. The award-winning program is now available at more than 1,000 Royal Bank retail and business banking centres.[18]

Videoconferencing

Videoconferencing is widely used for long-distance education. Athabasca University in Alberta specializes in long-distance degree programs up to the Ph.D. level, using the Internet for delivery (it has no in-class programs). Queen's University offers an Executive MBA Program through "multi-point interactive video-conferencing Boardroom Learning Centres" across Canada, allowing students to continue their career while earning a degree; it offers the same degree in a distance-education partnership—named National Electronic Campus—with individual companies, allowing students to earn their degree where they work.

⟳ EMPLOYEE DEVELOPMENT

Government of Canada Training and development options
www.hrsdc.gc.ca/eng.workplaceskills/index.shtml

To be successful, employees must acquire technical, human, and conceptual skills. The objective of employee development activities is to instill a sound analytical and reasoning capability in managers to solve problems and at the same time enhance their ability to acquire, comprehend, interpret, and utilize relevant knowledge. Employee development is more future-oriented and, consequently, is mostly an education process rather than a training process.

As an orientation document for employees, employers, and schools regarding skills required for current jobs, the Conference Board of Canada developed an "Employability Skills Profile," listing critical abilities in three different areas: fundamental skills, personal management skills, and teamwork skills (see Figure 7-5).

It is interesting to note that the Board document puts much emphasis on interpersonal skills, such as communication and working with others, but also on the ability to think and learn, two crucial requirements for the future, more complex jobs Canadians can expect.

As described in Chapters 1 and 4, external and internal pressures have changed the skill and attitude requirements for managers and employees. Economic changes force organizations to do more with less, downsizing requires managers to delegate responsibilities further down the line, and changes in technology demand greater willingness and preparedness of managers and employees to accept change and to learn continuously. Constant change, a contradiction in terms, is an organizational reality. Effective organizations cope with this by including employee development in their strategic human resource development plan.

⟳ STRATEGIC HUMAN RESOURCE DEVELOPMENT

strategic human resource development
The identification of needed skills and active management of employees' learning in relation to corporate strategies.

Strategic human resource development is "the identification of essential job skills and the management of employees' learning for the long-range future in relation to explicit corporate and business strategies." The last part is the most critical in this sentence—namely the linkage between development needs and activities to the organization's mission and strategy:

> In 1979, Xerox Corporation in the United States and its Canadian subsidiary launched a study that compared their manufacturing costs with those of domestic and foreign competitors. The findings revealed that competitors were selling products at a price equal to Xerox's cost of producing them. As a result, the company shifted to adopt externally set benchmark targets to drive its business plans. The results were so dramatic that today benchmarking is a key component in Xerox's human resource strategic development plans.

FIGURE 7-5	Employability Skills Profile: The Critical Skills Required of the Canadian Workforce

Employability Skills 2000+

The skills you need to enter, stay in, and progress in the world of work—whether you work on your own or as a part of a team.
These skills can also be applied and used beyond the workplace in a range of daily activities.

Fundamental Skills	Personal Management Skills	Teamwork Skills
The skills needed as a base for further development	The personal skills, attitudes, and behaviours that drive one's potential for growth	The skills and attributes needed to contribute productively

You will be better prepared to progress in the world of work when you can:

Communicate
- read and understand information presented in a variety of forms (e.g., words, graphs, charts, diagrams)
- write and speak so others pay attention and understand
- listen and ask questions to understand and appreciate the points of view of others
- share information using a range of information and communications technologies (e.g., voice, e-mail, computers)
- use relevant scientific, technological, and mathematical knowledge and skills to explain or clarify ideas

Manage Information
- locate, gather, and organize information using appropriate technology and information systems
- access, analyze, and apply knowledge and skills from various disciplines (e.g., the arts, languages, science, technology, mathematics, social sciences, and the humanities)

Use Numbers
- decide what needs to be measured or calculated
- observe and record data using appropriate methods, tools, and technology
- make estimates and verify calculations

Think & Solve Problems
- assess situations and identify problems
- seek different points of view and evaluate them based on facts
- recognize the human, interpersonal, technical, scientific, and mathematical dimensions of a problem
- identify the root cause of a problem
- be creative and innovative in exploring possible solutions
- readily use science, technology, and mathematics as ways to think, gain, and share knowledge, solve problems, and make decisions
- evaluate solutions to make recommendations or decisions
- implement solutions
- check to see if a solution works, and act on opportunities for improvement

You will be able to offer yourself greater possibilities for achievement when you can:

Demonstrate Positive Attitudes & Behaviours
- feel good about yourself and be confident
- deal with people, problems, and situations with honesty, integrity, and personal ethics
- recognize your own and other people's good efforts
- take care of your personal health
- show interest, initiative, and effort

Be Responsible
- set goals and priorities balancing work and personal life
- plan and manage time, money, and other resources to achieve goals
- assess, weigh, and manage risk
- be accountable for your actions and the actions of your group
- be socially responsible and contribute to your community

Be Adaptable
- work independently or as a part of a team
- carry out multiple tasks or projects
- be innovative and resourceful: identify and suggest alternative ways to achieve goals and get the job done
- be open and respond constructively to change
- learn from your mistakes and accept feedback
- cope with uncertainty

Learn Continuously
- be willing to continuously learn and grow
- assess personal strengths and areas for development
- set your own learning goals
- identify and access learning sources and opportunities
- plan for and achieve your learning goals

Work Safely
- be aware of personal and group health and safety practices and procedures, and act in accordance with these

You will be better prepared to add value to the outcomes of a task, project, or team when you can:

Work with Others
- understand and work within the dynamics of a group
- ensure that a team's purpose and objectives are clear
- be flexible: respect, be open to, and supportive of the thoughts, opinions, and contributions of others in a group
- recognize and respect people's diversity, individual differences, and perspectives
- accept and provide feedback in a constructive and considerate manner
- contribute to a team by sharing information and expertise
- lead or support when appropriate, motivating a group for high performance
- understand the role of conflict in a group to reach solutions
- manage and resolve conflict when appropriate

Participate in Projects & Tasks
- plan, design, or carry out a project or task from start to finish with well-defined objectives and outcomes
- develop a plan, seek feedback, test, revise and implement
- work to agreed quality standards and specifications
- select and use appropriate tools and technology for a task or project
- adapt to changing requirements and information
- continuously monitor the success of a project or task and identify ways to improve

The Conference Board of Canada
Insights You Can Count On

The Conference Board of Canada
255 Smyth Road, Ottawa
ON K1H 8M7 Canada
Tel: (613) 526-3280
Fac (613) 526-4857
Internet: www.conferenceboard.ca/education

Source: *Employability Skills 2000+*, Brochure 2000 E/F (Ottawa: The Conference Board of Canada, 2000). Available at www.conferenceboard.ca/education/learning-tools/pdfs/esp2000.pdf.

benchmarking
Comparing one's own quality and production standards with those of industry leaders.

The idea of comparing one's own quality and production standards with those of industry leaders—**benchmarking**—has become a movement. In 1991, Xerox's success in benchmarking resulted in the creation of the Benchmarking Forum of the American Society for Training and Development, which by 1996 included over 40 of the top U.S. organizations and leaders in training and development. These companies provide data for comparative analyses for training professionals and identify the most successful training and performance improvement practices.[19]

employee development
The process of enhancing an employee's future value to the organization through careful career planning.

Benchmarking Network Information, articles
www.benchmarkingnetwork.com/

1 & 6

Employee development is the process of enhancing an employee's future value to the enterprise through careful career planning. In plain English, it means that human resource management has to plan for the future now. It also means that management has to be willing to commit the financial resources to employee development programs, even if there is no short-term payoff. Employee development is a long-term process that requires the same attention and concern as capital investment, because it is an investment in human capital.

Developmental Strategies

Wexley and Latham propose three basic developmental strategies for organizations:

- **Cognitive:** Being concerned with altering thoughts and ideas (knowledge, new processes).
- **Behavioural:** Attempts to change behaviour (e.g., management style).
- **Environmental:** Strategies to change attitudes and values.[20]

Figure 7-6 describes examples of instruments and programs that are used in the above employee developmental strategies.

The *cognitive component* is part of the ongoing information-sharing process necessary in an "organic" organization, the adaptable type needed in a fast-changing business environment. Cognitive development implies constant learning and upgrading, principles so strongly advocated in the learning organization concept discussed later in this chapter.

The cognitive strategy is probably the least effective in employee development. The methods used are relatively passive: lectures, seminars, and academic education. While this approach tends to increase the knowledge and expertise of individuals, it does little to change a person's behaviour, attitudes, and values—important elements of an employee's career development. This approach fulfills at least part of the definition of employee development: it adds to the value of the person. However, increased knowledge and expertise are necessary, but not sufficient, attributes of an effective employee. Unfortunately, this seems to be the dominant strategy in employee development.

The ideal organizational setting continuously reinforces desirable behaviour, the second of the development strategies. Desirable behaviour includes the appropriate management style (modelled after top management and being part of the corporate culture), proper leadership style (strongly influenced by the CEO), type of communication, conflict resolution, and interaction with customers.

Behavioural strategies aim at making individuals more competent in interacting with their environment—for example, with colleagues, subordinates, or customers. Common instruments or programs used in this strategy are outlined below:

- *Role-playing* is a well-known and effective method to familiarize an employee with how to apply concepts learned in the classroom in a practical setting.
- *Behaviour modelling* teaches a desired behaviour effectively by providing the trainee with a vivid and detailed display of desirable behaviour by a manager (the model), often with strong social reinforcement.[21]
- *The Leadership Grid* (formerly known as the Managerial Grid) approach is an example of attempting to change the dominant management style in an organization—for example, to make managers more person- or task-oriented to increase their effectiveness.[22]

FIGURE 7-6	Training and Development Strategies

Strategies	Instruments/Programs
Cognitive	Articles, lectures, videos, university courses, management seminars
Behavioural	Role-playing, behaviour modelling, Leadership Grid, sensitivity training, outdoors, team building, mentoring
Environmental	Job rotation, organizational development, the learning organization concept, temporary assignments, employee exchange programs, matrix management, project team, internal consulting, cross-cultural management training

SPOTLIGHT ON HRM

Human Capital: Hard to Grow, Vital to Sow

... Although the term *human capital* has come into vogue recently, the concept dates back to work at the University of Chicago around 1957. To date it has been largely developed from an economic perspective, and only recently has the subject been looked at from an organizational perspective.

The fundamental idea is that the long-term success of an organization depends on its ability to attract, retain, enhance, and effectively use the human capital of its employees. Optimizing the competitiveness, growth rate, and cost-effectiveness of any organization depends on its ability to apply its human capital to all aspects of its operations.

Human capital is the most difficult resource for an organization to develop quickly. As organizations become more dependent on highly skilled and knowledgeable employees, enhancing human capital becomes an increasingly critical HR function. A U.S. study by Peter Cappelli, released in 1995, found that increasing the education level of employees by 10 percent generated about three times the return in productivity as a 10 percent investment in capital stock.

Pay versus Investment

In his 1997 book *Intellectual Capital*, Thomas Stewart notes that companies do not manage human capital well because "they have a hard time distinguishing between the cost of paying people and the value of investing in them." It is becoming increasingly important that HR professionals understand the difference.

It is key to note that the human capital of employees is independent of their current job or employer. Rather, it is a reflection of the depth and breadth of their talents, education, experience, knowledge, and skills.

The potential value of a person to an organization depends on the degree of match between the person's human capital and the needs of the organization, as well as the productive value of their capability. The employment cost of a person also depends on the scarcity of his or her human capital and the competition for that person's services from other employers.

Increasing Human Capital—The Personal View

The decision by people to increase their employability depends on their belief that investing in developing their human capital makes sense. The value of human capital to a person depends on the expected increase in their income and employment security throughout their working career.

From an economic perspective, the expected personal gains must be greater than the cost of more education, the foregone income, and the risk that the targeted job opportunities will not exist in the future. (Another interesting implication is that maintaining good health becomes increasingly important in order for people to maximize the return on their investment in developing their human capital.)

Increasing an Organization's Human Capital

Every organization also benefits from investing in developing the human capital of its employees. In today's rapidly changing environment, an organization must invest in developing the specialized knowledge, skills, and experiences that enhance the value of its employees and equip them to be highly productive.

A Long-Term Investment

Governments and employers must view employee training and development as a long-term capital investment, not an operating expense or short-term expedient program. Investing in human capital is a symbiotic relationship; both the employee and employer must contribute in order for both to reap the benefits.

It is ironic that organizational success is increasingly dependent on assets that do not show up on the balance sheet—namely, the human capital of employees. Increasingly, human resource professionals must view themselves as human capital managers. We need to begin to understand how we best invest in and make use of the productive capacity of employees.

We must always remember that employees own the critical productivity capability of our organizations. What we purchase, through our total compensation package, is their time, talents, knowledge, and skills. We need to ask ourselves two questions. What are we doing to enhance the human capital of our organization? And what are we doing to make more productive use of the human capital of our employees?

Source: © *Canadian HR Reporter* (August 11, 1997, p. 9), by permission of Carswell, Toronto, Ontario, 1-800-387-5164, www.hrreporter.com.

- *Sensitivity training* is considered a very effective method for making managers more aware of the impact of their own behaviour on others or to prepare them for more effective interactions with staff in foreign subsidiaries or joint ventures.[23]
- *Outdoors* has become a fashionable development method, involving team-oriented tasks that take place in the wilderness (e.g., mountain climbing, white-water paddling, even surviving in a jungle). The objective is to develop a strong team spirit and to help people learn how to maximize their strengths and stretch their potential.[24]
- *Team building* helps team members to diagnose group processes and to devise solutions to problems.[25]
- *Mentoring* involves establishing a close relationship with a boss or someone more experienced who takes a personal interest in the employee's career and who guides and sponsors it.[26]
- *Coaching* is an ongoing professional relationship between an expert in a chosen field and a trainee. Coaching involves continuous improvement of desired behaviours or skills based on specific expert advice.[27]

The behavioural strategy undoubtedly has a greater impact on the development of employees than the cognitive approach.

The environmental part is concerned with providing the organizational setting in which employees can thrive and develop. Here is an example of how effective it can be:

Jean Crepin, founder and CEO of Norwest Soil Research Ltd. in Edmonton, now Norwest Labs, after experiencing a loss of one-quarter of his sales, decided to get his employees more involved in managing the company. He had read something about "open-book management," which means that management shares financial goals, budgets, income statements, and forecasts with everyone in the organization.

Of course, it means that employees have to learn to read and understand monthly financial reports, so that they can gauge how their own actions affect the bottom line. They also have to learn to use this information to be able to contribute meaningfully to management decisions.

Ms. Diane Smathers, who worked for Norwest for more than eight years, mentioned that most of the staff had never seen a balance sheet and were intimidated. After thorough training, employees became very much interested in the goals and objectives of the company. According to Ms. Smathers, "It gives them a better understanding of where the company comes from. Morale is better. Employees feel they have more input because they have more information."

Many companies are sending their employees on outdoor exercises to build teamwork and trust. How can whitewater rafting or rock-climbing increase trust in a team?

© Stephanie Godin/Getty Images.

Besides becoming "managers" themselves, strong incentives for the employees' involvement were the implementation of a gain-sharing and a stock ownership plan. At Christmas in 1997, Norwest awarded its 140 employees the first gain-sharing payout of $2,000 each. After that, it expects to issue quarterly amounts of $1,000. Mr. Crepin owns about 60 percent. The employees now hold the rest.[28]

The *environmental approach* seems to be the most promising developmental strategy, but, unfortunately, it is also the most difficult to implement. It involves a variety of methods, such as the following:

- *Job rotation* is extremely useful in developing managers with a systems concept in their decision-making style (e.g., the Japanese system of rotating management trainees for two years through all departments of an organization).[29]
- *Organizational development* is a system-wide effort applying behavioural science knowledge to the planned creation and reinforcement of organizational strategies, structures, and processes for improving an organization's effectiveness.[30]
- *The learning organization*, a concept created by Peter Senge, describes an organization in which employees continually strive to expand their horizon and try new ideas, and members of a team support each other in a collective attempt to make the organization more efficient and a better place to work.[31] (This concept is discussed in more detail below.)
- *Temporary assignments* allow management trainees to gain valuable special experiences they could not have had in one job (e.g., a salesperson assigned for a period of time to the engineering department to assist in the development of a saleable product).
- *Employee exchange programs* have been implemented by companies such as Bell Canada, IBM, and Xerox, and the federal government of Canada. Usually, a manager takes a one-year leave (either paid or unpaid, depending on the arrangement with the host organization, with the stipulation that the exchange manager does not lose money) and joins another organization. The manager, the host, and the parent organization all tend to gain from this experience.
- *Matrix management* combines the use of different specialists while maintaining functional units. This approach is best suited for project management with fluctuating workloads. For example, a company might work on several projects. A project manager will "borrow" from different functional units the staff necessary to complete the project. These specialists will report for the duration of the project to the project manager, but will maintain their allegiance to their respective functional departments.[32]
- *Project teams* differ from matrix management in that the functional manager has no involvement with the team for the duration of the project. For example, when IBM developed the personal computer, it put together a project team whose members were independent from their functional units. This strategy allows for a highly concentrated effort.[33]
- *Internal consulting (or troubleshooting assignments)* allows organizational needs and individual development needs to be combined simultaneously. For example, an expert in management information systems may assist the human resource department in developing a human resource information system, not only enhancing the effectiveness of the department but also gaining valuable personal experience.
- *Lateral transfer* is the movement of an employee from one position to another in the same class, but under another supervisor or in another department; or the movement of an employee to a position in a different class that has substantially the same level of duties, responsibility, and salary.
- *Job redefinition/reclassification*—with the consent of the job incumbent—allows management to change an employee's job responsibilities, often to avoid a layoff.
- *Cross-cultural management training* prepares employees to work in a different cultural environment (detailed discussion in Chapter 12).
- *Diversity training* deals specifically with preparing supervisors to manage employees from different cultures. It also sensitizes managers and employees in gender-dominated industries to work with colleagues from the opposite sex, for example in engineering or nursing (diversity management is discussed in Chapter 12).

The Learning Organization

learning organization
An organization that has an enhanced capacity to learn, adapt, and change.

Much has been written lately about the learning organization, a concept put forward first by Chris Argyris, then popularized by Peter Senge. According to Senge, a **learning organization** is where "people continually expand their capacity to create the results they truly desire, where new and expansive patterns of thinking are nurtured, where collective aspiration is set free, and where people are continually learning how to learn together."[34] Senge contrasts what is done in North American organizations with the Japanese approach:

> In North America, the people who spend the most time learning about quality are those on the shop floor. They get the five-day course on statistical process control. Their bosses get the three-day course, and the CEO gets the two-hour briefing. In Japan, by contrast, it is exactly the opposite. This is very significant symbolically. There, the leaders are the learners.[35]

Here is a description of the characteristics of a learning organization:

Treasury Board of Canada Policy for continuous learning
www.tbs-sct.gc.ca/media/nr-cp/2002/0515_e.asp

- *Systems thinking* is the ability to see things as a whole, perceive interrelationships, recognize patterns of change, and infer associations and connections.
- *Personal mastery* is the ability to continually clarify and deepen personal visions, focus energies, and see reality objectively. It combines personal learning and organizational learning.
- *Mental models* are deeply ingrained assumptions, generalizations, or images that influence how we understand the world and how we take action. In organizations, such mental models control what people perceive can or cannot be done. Change rarely takes place until management teams change their shared mental models.
- *Shared vision* binds people together around a common identity and a sense of destiny. A genuine vision causes people to do things because they want to, not because they have to.
- *Team learning* is a tool for raising the collective intelligence of a group above that of anyone in it. It includes talking and thinking together and the ability to recognize and overcome patterns of defensiveness that undermine group learning:

> Molson Breweries seems to be a model of a learning organization. In 1997, it opened the Molson Personal Learning and Development Centre in Etobicoke, Ontario. The objective was to help employees sharpen and broaden the skill sets needed for their jobs and beyond. As Lloyd Livingstone, brewing training specialist and coordinator for the development of the Learning Centre put it, "It really is a fun place; to look around and see these guys excited about learning, it really makes you feel excited too."
>
> Employees are offered a combination of mandatory training and personal career development. Training methods include Personal Learning Maps (a competency-based learning plan for each employee), a database of courses sorted by skills, a platform for launching multimedia training, and an administration program that allows managers to track employee progress and add new skills and courses to the system. The system encourages interaction between employees and managers, and even senior executives participate.[36]

According to Senge, teams are vital, because they, not individuals, are the fundamental learning unit in modern organizations. Unless the team can learn, the organization cannot learn.[37] For human resource managers, this approach means delegating a higher responsibility for acquiring new expertise and skills to the managers and employees and, perhaps, providing guidance and counselling.

Knowledge Management

The term *knowledge worker* was first used by Peter Drucker to describe an employee who "has the ability to use information to solve organizational problems."[38] Knowledge workers are the fastest-growing type of workers in Canada, according to research conducted by Human Resources Development Canada. Over the past 25 years, the number of scientists, engineers, and others involved in the development of ideas increased at an annual average rate of 5.3 percent, about two-and-a-half times the rate of growth of total employment. One in every four workers in Canada is a knowledge worker.[39]

knowledge management
Making use of employees' knowledge.

Knowledge Management Network Articles, information
www.brint.com/km

competencies
Skill, knowledge, and behaviours that distinguish high performance in a broad role, function, or level of the organization.

Athabasca University "Developing a Competency Framework for Career Counsellor Training"
www.contactpoint.ca/natcon-conat/2002/pdf/pdf-02-08.pdf

Today, this concept has been expanded to the idea of **knowledge management**, which can be defined as the ability to utilize people's knowledge,* that is, information stored in employees' heads.[40]

It is a broader concept than *information management*,** which tends to focus on making information available to managers who need it for their decision making. Knowledge management attempts to survey and assess the knowledge and expertise that exists in an organization, to increase it systematically, and to apply it profitably. Not many managers are in a position to do this effectively, and for this reason many companies have created the position of a knowledge manager, whose role has been described by Williams and Bukowitz:

- **Technology expert:** Ensures members of the organization understand the available technology and use it to its fullest potential. A technology trainer and cheerleader.
- **Cataloguer/archivist:** Organizes information to meet the professional needs of the decision makers.
- **Guide:** Directs information users to outside information when appropriate. Maintains high-level information about sources outside the organization.
- **Scout:** Screens information useful to the organization and brings it into the knowledge base.
- **Research librarian:** Prioritizes highly relevant information from a pool of interesting information according to user preferences.
- **Analyst:** Adds value to information by creating a context for understanding.
- **Debriefer:** Elicits understanding so that participants understand what they have learned.[41]

Competency Framework

A *competency framework* is a list of **competencies** (abilities or skills) that provide a competitive advantage to an organization. As one survey indicates, competency-based performance management is becoming the HR model of choice in the Canadian industry. Over 60 percent of all organizations that participated in the 2008 survey reported that they have such a model in place, while others have it under development.[42] A competency approach allows management and employees to pinpoint unique personal and organizational characteristics that make the company successful in its struggle against competitors. As a result, trainers are able to offer training programs that focus on the very specific strengths of employees or, as one author put it, "to invest T & D effort where it increases value for the business and, in the process, to become more strategic."[43] Figure 7-7 illustrates the different meanings of a competency.

One advantage of using the competency framework is the opportunity for employees to manage their own development. The author of another survey, Jean-Pascal Souque, describes it as follows: "As everyone in the organization knows which competencies are needed to get to the next level or to perform in a way that adds value to the business, decision-making relative to training and development can be pushed to lower levels—to the employees themselves."[44]

Company and University/College Partnerships

Four of Canada's retail giants, Hudson's Bay Company, Loblaws Supermarkets, Sears Canada, and Wal-Mart Canada, have put their support behind a $10 million fundraising effort for Ryerson University's School of Retail Management, to make it the premier school for retail education in North America. Each company contributed $1 million to the endowment fund of the school, which offers Canada's only university-level program in retail management.[45]

Such partnerships have several advantages. They offer companies the opportunity to have educational programs tailor-made to their needs; the university benefits financially; the university's

*The University of California at Berkeley is the first university to have established a Chair of Knowledge, sponsored by a US$1 million grant from Xerox Corporation in 1996. Renowned author and Japanese management expert Ikujiro Nonaka was appointed the first Distinguished Professor of Knowledge.
**It may be useful to distinguish between information, data, and knowledge. Information is usually a message that can be stored. Data is a type of information that is structured but has not been interpreted. Knowledge might be described as information that has a use or purpose. Whereas information can be put into a computer, knowledge exists in the heads of people. Knowledge is information to which an intent has been attached.

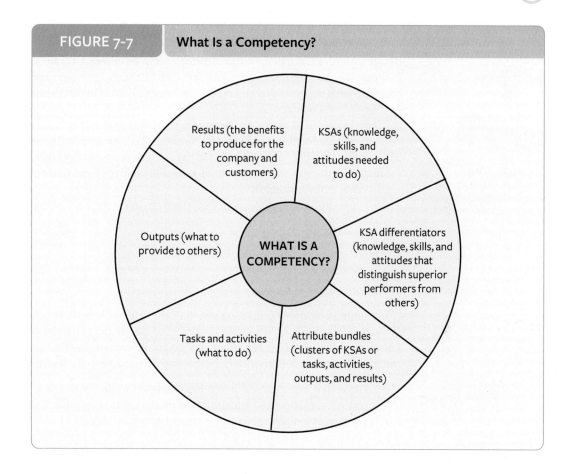

FIGURE 7-7 · What Is a Competency?

- Results (the benefits to produce for the company and customers)
- KSAs (knowledge, skills, and attitudes needed to do)
- WHAT IS A COMPETENCY?
- KSA differentiators (knowledge, skills, and attitudes that distinguish superior performers from others)
- Outputs (what to provide to others)
- Tasks and activities (what to do)
- Attribute bundles (clusters of KSAs or tasks, activities, outputs, and results)

Trends in the use of the Internet for education
http://findarticles.com/p/
articles/mi_moDXK/
is_18_21/ai_n6358702/

faculty gains valuable practical experiences; the students earn a university/college degree; and they are able to use much of their acquired knowledge directly on the job. Of course, the university has to be careful not to relinquish its control over course quality and standards.

Trends Toward the Use of the Internet, Intranet, or Videoconferencing Development Programs

The opportunities to use new technology to deliver development and training programs are growing exponentially. Moore's Law says that the capacity of computers is doubling every 18 months at one-half the price. (Gordon Moore was president and CEO of Intel Corporation. He retired in 1987.) The higher capacity allows new combinations of media to be used in training programs, making them more effective and, undoubtedly, more interesting. The virtual classroom is not a dream anymore.[46]

Outsourcing of the training function is another trend. To keep up to date on the latest training techniques—for example, the use of the Internet and intranet, delivery systems such as Blackboard, or specific applications like embedded information, active control video supplements, blogs, and wikis—can be quite expensive, and many of the new techniques quickly become obsolete. Larger companies might be able to afford to keep their trainers current, but smaller firms may find it cheaper to outsource their training programs.[47]

Top Management Involvement

It is essential that top management take its commitment to human resource development seriously and make it part of the company's strategy. As Hall puts it, "Perhaps the most important factor in ensuring that development is done strategically is the participation of top management in the process. Because top management is the strategic level of the organization, and because top management represents the strategic business planners of the organization, they should also be the human resource planners. Top management should plan and execute employee development activities."[48]

EVALUATION OF TRAINING AND DEVELOPMENT

Articles on training evaluation
http://ezinearticles.com/?Measuring-Training-Evaluation-Effectiveness&id=1075085
http://coe.sdsu.edu/eet/Articles/k4levels/index.htm

Training and development serve as transformation processes. Untrained employees are transformed into capable workers, and present workers may be trained to assume new responsibilities. To verify the program's success, human resource managers increasingly demand that training activities be evaluated systematically.

A lack of evaluation may be the most serious flaw in most training efforts. Simply stated, human resource professionals too seldom ask, "Did the program achieve the objectives established for it?" They often assume it had value because the content seemed important. Or trainers may rely on the evaluation of trainees who comment on how enjoyable the experience was for them, but who cannot yet determine how valuable it is.

Evaluation of training should follow the steps in Figure 7-8. There are four types of criteria:[49]

1. reaction;
2. knowledge;
3. behaviour; and
4. organizational results.

Training objectives determine which of the criteria is the best suited for evaluation purposes. If the objective is to increase the knowledge of the participants, the obvious choice would be the knowledge criterion; if it is behaviour change, the behaviour criterion would be the most appropriate measure. Each criterion has its advantages and disadvantages as described below:

1. **Reaction.** Also known as the happiness or smile sheet, reaction is the most widely used criterion in training evaluation. The usual question asked is, "How satisfied are you with the program?" or "Would you recommend it to a colleague?" This measure evaluates the setup of the program, but not its effectiveness. However, it can provide valuable information for the organizers of programs as to the proper training environment, seating arrangement, satisfaction with training facilities, food, and accommodation.

2. **Knowledge.** Very popular in learning institutions (exams), evaluating on the basis of knowledge is legitimate if an increase in knowledge is the intended objective of a training program (e.g., improved product knowledge). However, it can be reliably assessed only if before and after tests are used. Otherwise, it is uncertain whether a high score means the program was effective or whether the students knew the material beforehand.

3. **Behaviour.** For the measurement of behaviour change, self-reports and observations by others are used (e.g., neutral observers, superiors, peers, subordinates, or customers). Supervisor observation of behaviour change is more effective, but this approach has an inherent weakness. It is usually the supervisor who sent the employee to the training program and, because of this, is less likely to admit that he or she made an error in judgment.

4. **Organizational Results.** Organizational results would be ideal measurements were it not for the difficulty in determining the cause–effect relationship between training programs and organizational results. The time difference between a training program and the availability of reports on organizational results can be many months. Who is then to say whether it was the training program or some other event that caused the results?

Evaluation Methodology

According to *Webster's*, a *method* is an orderly and logical procedure, and *methodology* is the science of method. An example of a nonscientific method to assess the effectiveness of a training program is the popular post-test design: one test is applied at the end of a training program to test its effectiveness.

T   O
(training)   (observation/test)

There are inherent problems with this method. Do we know it was the training that caused a high score? We cannot be sure. Perhaps the participants were already experienced and did not need the training in the first place.

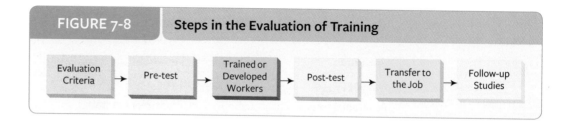

FIGURE 7-8 | **Steps in the Evaluation of Training**

Evaluation Criteria → Pre-test → Trained or Developed Workers → Post-test → Transfer to the Job → Follow-up Studies

A more effective approach is the pre-test post-test design, shown in Figure 7-8, in which the instructor applies tests at the beginning and at the end of the training program to measure first the precondition (baseline characteristic) of the participants and then the outcome:

O   T   O
(observation/test)   (training)   (repeat observation/test)

This allows a more realistic assessment of the outcomes of a training program. Examples of the two approaches are given below:

> One of the authors of this text recently conducted a human resource management seminar in Slovakia. At the end of the 10-day seminar, the organizers used a reaction sheet to assess the outcome of the program. Although it was obvious that participants enjoyed it very much, nobody could say how effective the program really was and whether it had achieved its objectives.
>
> A similar seminar was offered the following year. This time the author suggested to the organizers that a pre-test post-test method be used. At the beginning, a knowledge test and an application test (case) were given to the participants, and equivalent tests were given at the end of the program. The average score at the beginning was 23 out of 100 points; the average score at the end was 66, an almost 300 percent improvement. It was concluded that the training had been effective.

The pre-test post-test design is not a scientific method, since it does not control for other influences on the training outcome, but it should suffice as a practical measurement. If trainers want to test the outcome of training programs scientifically, more appropriate methods can be found in relevant research literature.[50]

RPC 1 & 6

cost–benefit analysis
Analysis undertaken to assess the cost-effectiveness of a project or program.

Cost–Benefit Analysis

A training investment should be treated like any other investment decision. No manager worth his or her salt would invest a significant amount of money without an appropriate **cost–benefit analysis**. Such an analysis assesses the cost-effectiveness of a project or program. It also assists a trainer or human resource manager in demonstrating the contribution the training or human resource management department makes to the organization's profit.

SPOTLIGHT ON ETHICS

Was It Really That Good?

A training officer is asked by his human resource manager to give her an assessment of the effectiveness of the company's training programs for a report to the president, who wants to know "how much bang we get for our training buck." The HR manager was a benefits officer prior to her promotion and knows little about training techniques and evaluation; the president has a sales background. The programs are usually offered in a nearby resort hotel very much liked by the trainees.

So far, the training officer has assessed training outcomes through reaction measurements, because they were cheap and easy to do, and, more importantly, they tended to be very positive. He suspects that the positive results were largely based on the relaxing hotel environment, but he is sure that the HR manager and the president would be quite happy with this kind of feedback.

Please comment.

FIGURE 7-9	Training Costs and Benefits
Activities	**Costs**
Needs analysis	Labour: consultant, clerical staff
Program development	Labour: consultant, clerical staff
	Material: office material; video films
	Equipment rental
	Other potential costs: travel; accommodation; per diem expenses
Course delivery	Equipment
	Room rental
	Food
	Trainers' salaries
	Trainees' salaries
	Lost production
Program evaluation	Evaluator's fee
	Travel and accommodation (assuming external evaluator)
	Overhead costs: staff and clerical support, office
	Benefit examples
	Increased productivity (widgets/hr or $/hr)
	Reduced labour costs ($/hr or per year)
	Reduced error rate ($/hr or per year)
	Reduced accident rate (days lost, reduced absenteeism in $)
	Higher sales ($/year)

Contributions to profit can be made through increasing revenues or by decreasing expenditures according to the formula:

$$\text{Revenue} - \text{Costs} = \text{Profit}$$

Training can contribute to increased revenue by improving the performance of revenue-producing employees, either by increasing output or by reducing production costs, or by both. If training is used to increase productivity, training costs have to be included in the pricing of the product. Figure 7-9 presents factors associated with different training activities. It should be mentioned that companies, depending on industry, spend between 1.7 to 6 percent of their payroll expenditures on training.[51]

TRAINING AND DEVELOPMENT AS STRATEGIC TOOLS

Training and development are investments in human capital.[52] Managers must understand that large investments in physical plant, modern machinery, and new technology cannot be fully realized if there is no equivalent investment in human capital.[53] The acquisition of new skills is not only vital to improving quality and productivity, but also essential if companies want to meet global competition.

Especially for quality-oriented companies, training objectives become part of the overall long-range strategy. A good example of this is offered by Maritime Life Assurance in Halifax, now part of Manulife Financial of Canada, one of the "100 Best Companies to Work for in Canada" and the 2002

Government of Saskatchewan
Example of training strategy
www.sasked.gov.sk.ca/P/
training/contact.html

recipient of the Atlantic Canada Human Resources Award. Bill Black, Maritime's past president and CEO, made it very clear what he thought of training and development:

> Training and development is a crucial part of our company's strategic plan. If we want to reach our company objectives of customer satisfaction, growth, and quality we have to make sure that our human resource system provides us with the effective managers and motivated employees to reach these goals. We can do this by making better hiring decisions, improv[ing] skills, develop[ing] leadership, and fairly reward[ing] superior performance. Training and development is a good investment and for us it pays off in the form of satisfied customers and happy employees. I also believe strongly that the second outcome really causes the first. And happy customers mean higher profits.[54]

CAREER PLANNING

University of Waterloo "Career Development eManual"
www.cdm.uwaterloo.ca/
index2.asp

Inseparably linked with employee development is career planning and career management. Merely planning a career does not guarantee success. Superior performance, experience, education, and some occasional luck play an important part. But when people rely almost wholly on luck, they seldom are prepared for opportunities that arise. To be ready for career opportunities, successful people develop career plans and then take action to achieve their plans. Simply stated, a successful career needs to be managed through careful planning. If it is not, employees are seldom ready for career opportunities, and human resource departments find it extremely difficult to meet their internal staffing needs.[55]

Career Planning and Development Overview

An increasing number of human resource departments see career planning as a way to meet their internal staffing needs.[56] When employers encourage career planning, employees are more likely to set goals. In turn, these goals may motivate employees to pursue further education, training, or other career development activities. These activities then improve the value of employees to the organization and give the human resource department a larger pool of qualified applicants from which to fill internal job openings.

But what do employees want? A study of one group of employees revealed five areas of concern. These include the following:

1. **Career Equity.** Employees want to perceive equity in the organization's performance/promotion system with respect to career advancement opportunities.

2. **Supervisory Concern.** Employees want their supervisors to play an active role in career development and provide timely performance feedback.

3. **Awareness of Opportunities.** Employees want knowledge of the career advancement opportunities that exist in their organization.

4. **Employee Interest.** Employees need different amounts of information and have different degrees of interest in career advancement depending on a variety of factors.

5. **Career Satisfaction.** Employees have different levels of career satisfaction depending on their age and occupation.

Effective career planning and development programs must consider these different perceptions and wants of employees. What employees expect from the career programs developed by the human resource department will vary according to age, sex, occupation, and other variables. In other words, it has to be a flexible approach.

Human Resource Departments and Career Planning

The involvement of human resource managers in career planning has grown during recent years because of its benefits. Here is a partial list of those benefits:

- **Develops Promotable Employees.** Career planning helps to develop internal supplies of promotable talent.
- **Lowers Turnover.** The increased attention to and concern for individual careers generates more organizational loyalty and therefore lower employee turnover.

- **Taps Employee Potential.** Career planning encourages employees to tap more of their potential abilities, because they have specific career goals.
- **Furthers Growth.** Career plans and goals motivate employees to grow and develop.
- **Reduces Hoarding.** Without career planning, it is easier for managers to hoard key subordinates. Career planning causes employees, managers, and the human resource department to become aware of employee qualifications.
- **Satisfies Employee Needs.** With less hoarding and improved growth opportunities for employees, individual needs for recognition and accomplishment are more readily satisfied, and self-esteem is boosted.
- **Assists Employment Equity Plans.** Career planning can help members of protected groups prepare or more important jobs.

Human resource departments encourage career planning in three ways: through career education, planning information, and counselling.

Career Education

Human resource departments can increase employee awareness through a variety of educational techniques. For example, speeches, memoranda, and position papers from senior executives stimulate employee interest at low cost to the employer. If executives communicate their belief in career planning, other managers are likely to do the same.

Workshops and seminars on career planning increase employee interest by pointing out the key concepts associated with career planning. Workshops help the employee set career goals, identify career paths, and uncover specific career development activities. These educational activities may be supplemented by printed or taped information on career planning.

Career Planning Information

Regardless of the educational strategy the human resource department selects, it should provide employees with other information they need to plan their careers. Much of this information is already a part of the human resource department's information system. For example, job descriptions and specifications can be quite valuable to someone who is trying to estimate reasonable career goals. Likewise, human resource departments can identify future job openings through the human resource plan. Human resource specialists can also share their knowledge of potential career paths. For example, they are often keenly aware of the similarities between unrelated jobs. If this information is given to employees, it may reveal previously unseen career paths:

> For example, consider the possible career paths faced by Leslie Stevens, who works at a newspaper. In this type of work, the jobs of advertising assistant, assistant account representative, and account manager call for similar characteristics. But Leslie, an advertising assistant, may not realize that her skills could be applied to a position that may earn her twice as much.

When different jobs require similar skills, they form **job families**. Career paths within a job family demand little additional training, since the skills of each job are closely related. If human resource departments make information about job families available, employees can find feasible career paths. They can then assess these career paths by talking with those who already hold jobs along the path.

job families
Groups of different jobs that require similar skills.

Human Resources and Skills Development Canada
Tools for career planning, self-assessment
www.hrsdc.gc.ca/cgi-bin/search/hrsdc/search-eng.aspx?p7=2&p1=self-assessment&p9=v1&p3=corporate_eng&p8=10&p99=Search

Career Counselling

To help employees establish career goals and find appropriate career paths, some human resource departments offer counselling. The counsellor may simply be someone who has the employee's interests in mind and provides the specific job-related information. Or the counsellor may help employees discover their interests by administering and interpreting aptitude and skill tests. Two tests in particular—the *Kuder Preference Record* and the *Strong Vocational Interest Blank*—are useful for guiding people into occupations likely to be of interest. Other tests are also available to measure individual abilities and interests in specific types of work. But to be truly successful, career counsellors must get employees to assess themselves and their environment.

Employee Self-Assessment. Career counsellors realize that a career is not the entirety of one's life. It may be a large part or even a central part; but career planning is only part of one's life plan—that often ill-defined series of hopes, dreams, and personal goals every person carries through life.

A life plan might consist, for example, of broad objectives to be happy, healthy, and successful combined with specific goals to be a good spouse, parent, student, citizen, neighbour, or manager. Ideally, a career plan is an integral part of it—as opposed to an end (sometimes a dead end!) in itself:

> A husband and wife struggle for decades to achieve a degree of success in their respective careers. When success is within reach, both realize that their personal life-friendships, parental relationships, perhaps even their marriage, is in shambles. It is in this state because career plans were pursued to the exclusion of all else; there were no integral life plans for either one.

To avoid this sense of personal failure, self-assessment coupled with life planning at the beginning of a career and at every major crossroads is important. Self-assessment includes a self-inventory. Components of a self-inventory are listed in Figure 7-10 (more self-assessment instruments are listed in the "Web Research" section at the end of this chapter).

Environmental Assessment.   Regardless of the match between one's skills and the organization's career paths, counsellors need to inform employees of likely changes that will affect their occupational choices. Occupational information is readily available from publications of Human Resources and Skills Development Canada and Statistics Canada. For example, HRSDC periodically publishes information relating to the demand and supply of various jobs in its "Job Futures" section. In another publication, *Canada Occupational Projection System* (COPS), it provides forecasts on the demand for various types of jobs in the country.

FIGURE 7-10	A Self-Inventory for Career Planning

	Low				High
Work Interests and Aptitudes	1	2	3	4	5
Physical work (fixing, building, using hands)	_____	_____	_____	_____	_____
Written work (writing, reading, using words)	_____	_____	_____	_____	_____
Oral work (talking, giving speeches, using words)	_____	_____	_____	_____	_____
Quantitative work (calculating, doing accounting, using numbers)	_____	_____	_____	_____	_____
Visual work (watching, inspecting, using eyes)	_____	_____	_____	_____	_____
Interpersonal work (counselling, interviewing)	_____	_____	_____	_____	_____
Creative work (inventing, designing, ideas)	_____	_____	_____	_____	_____
Analytical work (doing research, solving problems)	_____	_____	_____	_____	_____
Managerial work (initiating, directing, coordinating)	_____	_____	_____	_____	_____
Clerical (keeping records)	_____	_____	_____	_____	_____
Outdoor work (farming, travelling, doing athletics)	_____	_____	_____	_____	_____
Mechanical (repairing, fixing, tinkering)	_____	_____	_____	_____	_____

Work Skills and Abilities

List below specialized skills, unique personal assets, enjoyable experiences, and major accomplishments. Then evaluate.

	Physical	Written	Oral	Quantitative	Visual	Interpersonal	Creative	Analytical	Managerial	Clerical	Outdoor	Mechanical
_____	___	___	___	___	___	___	___	___	___	___	___	___
_____	___	___	___	___	___	___	___	___	___	___	___	___
_____	___	___	___	___	___	___	___	___	___	___	___	___
_____	___	___	___	___	___	___	___	___	___	___	___	___
_____	___	___	___	___	___	___	___	___	___	___	___	___

Dual-Income Couples. According to Statistics Canada, in 7 out of 10 families, both partners work, almost double the number from the 1980s.[57] The combination of each partner pursuing a career and carrying family responsibilities tends to create stress, especially on the woman's side, since she usually has to shoulder a higher burden of the family work, although husbands are increasingly willing to share household chores.[58] Still, for **dual-income couples** a number of questions arise. Is each partner's career of equal importance? What if an advancement opportunity involves a relocation? Who has the stronger career commitment? Who will stay home if a child is sick? Many couples will work out these questions, but for others these issues may create problems or even crises, with potential negative consequences for personal relationships, such as breakup or divorce, or for the organization, such as low morale or even resignations.

A proactive HR department will have career counsellors, internal or outsourced, who are able to deal with the above issues. They will meet with the employees to map out career paths acceptable to both partners and the organization. Being proactive also means offering dual-career couples options that will ease some of their problems, such as flexible work arrangements, telecommuting, or job sharing (discussed in Chapter 2) and child care and/or elder care (discussed in Chapter 10).

Career Plateauing. The term *plateauing* is defined by *Webster's* as "a relative absence of progress," especially in learning (see Figure 7-3). We may also see it in a person's career. **Career plateauing** happens for a number of reasons. Many companies are removing management layers, downsizing, merging, or pushing decisions closer to the actual work. Such measures, besides causing layoffs, sometimes result in lowering the promotion opportunities for employees and middle managers. For ambitious employees, it often means loss of their strongest motivator, the reward for long years of dedicated work. HR managers and career counsellors have to anticipate such consequences and offer solutions. Examples include training for new skills, special assignments, job rotation, lateral moves, sabbaticals, skill-based compensation, or even a career change.

> Hermann Schwind, the first author of this book, is a typical example. At the age of 33, having plateaued in a middle-management position, he realized that his education as a mechanical engineer was not sufficient for him to be promoted into an executive position in his organization. Taking unpaid leave, he earned an MBA and, having become hooked on academia, a Ph.D. His new career as a professor turned out to be an excellent choice, and very rewarding.

Individual Career Development

The starting point for career development is the individual employee. Once a personal commitment has been made, several actions are available:

- **Job Performance.** The most effective action an employee can undertake is good job performance. When performance is substandard, even modest career goals are usually unattainable, because low performers are quickly excluded from promotion considerations.
- **Exposure.** Being known—and held in high regard—by those who decide on promotion and other career opportunities make an employee more likely to be considered for an advancement.[59] Consider how one management trainee gained exposure:

  > Paula Dorsey noticed that two executives worked on Saturday mornings. As one of 12 new management trainees, she decided that coming to work on Saturday mornings would give her additional exposure to these key decision makers. Soon these two executives began greeting her by name whenever they passed in the halls. While still in the training program, she was assigned to the product introduction committee, which planned strategy for new products. At the end of the training program, Paula was made an assistant product manager for a new product line. The other 11 trainees received less important jobs.

- **Resignations.** Some employees—managers and professionals in particular—change employers as part of a conscious career strategy, which is also called leveraging. It usually means a promotion, a pay increase, and a new experience. Astute managers and professionals use this technique sparingly, because too many moves can lead to the label of "job hopper," indicating a lack of commitment.
- **Organizational Loyalty.** Low levels of organizational loyalty are common among recent university graduates (whose high expectations often lead to disappointment with their first employer)

dual-income couple
A couple whose partners both have their own careers.

career plateauing
Reaching a temporary flat point on the advancement continuum during one's career.

and professionals (whose first loyalty is often to their profession).[60] Career-long dedication to the same organization complements the human resource department's objective of reducing employee turnover.

- **Mentors, Sponsors, and Coaches.** A **mentor** is someone who offers informal career advice. If the mentor can nominate the employee for career development activities, such as training programs, transfers, or promotion, the mentor becomes a **sponsor**—someone in the organization who can create career development opportunities for others. *Coaching* was discussed earlier in this chapter in connection with apprenticeship training, but corporate coaching has so far been reserved for executives. However, as *The Globe and Mail* observed, "All kinds of people, from entrepreneurs to new hires to the recently retired, use coaches to move into second careers, to prepare for promotion, to refocus, or to refine communication skills."[61] Some companies even hire professional coaches to assist the human resource department.
- **Growth Opportunities.** Consider this example:

Rachael Holmes was the chief recruiter in the employment department of Brem Paper Products. Her department manager was 60 years old and had indicated that he planned to retire at age 65. At 37, and with three years of experience as a recruiter, Rachael felt she was in a dead-end job. She obtained a transfer to the wage and salary department. Two years later, the company planned a new facility and made Rachael the human resource manager for it. She was selected because of her broad experience in recruiting and compensation—two major concerns in starting the new operation.

Rachael initiated the transfer through self-nomination because she wanted to further her career development. But the real opportunity she obtained from the transfer was a chance to grow—a chance to develop new skills and knowledge.

3 & 6

Human Resource–Supported Career Development

Career development should not rely solely on individual efforts, because they are not always in the organization's best interests. For example, employees may move to another employer or may simply be unaware of opportunities to further their careers and the organization's staffing needs. To guide career development so that it benefits the organization and employees, a human resource department often provides a variety of training and development programs for employees.

Getty Images.

Management Support

Efforts by the human resource department to encourage career development have little impact unless supported by managers. Ideally, this effort is advanced by the practice of evaluating managers on their ability to develop their subordinates:

> The Ford Motor Company has made it part of its performance appraisal for managers that they are assessed on how well they succeeded in developing a successor for themselves. The company is aware of the danger that if the "successors" have to wait too long for a promotion, they will look for opportunities elsewhere. However, the company has the experience that many of those who move return later with significantly more knowledge.[62]

Feedback

Without feedback about their career development progress, employees have difficulties measuring the results of their career efforts. Performance appraisal feedback is an excellent opportunity to discuss career progress.

Succession Planning

It is the responsibility of the human resource department to engage in **succession planning**—that is, to ensure that there are a sufficient number of candidates for key positions ready to take over if an unexpected vacancy occurs, be it because of someone leaving the company, sickness, or death.

> A few years ago, a small plane with seven executives of a Calgary-based oil company on a flight to New York crashed, killing all seven and the crew. It was a catastrophic event for the company, but the company survived because it had a sufficient number of trained managers ready.

As the example shows, having well-trained employees ready to take on critical responsibilities in case of an emergency can be crucial for the survival of a company.

succession planning
The process of making long-range management development plans to fill human resource needs.

Recent Developments

Many organizations now use an intranet for career counselling purposes. The Bank of Montreal's virtual Career Possibilities Centre is a good example of this approach of shifting from employee direct counselling to letting them handle their own career management by providing the necessary tools on the intranet, such as self-testing and workshops on organizational change and how to cope with it. Professional career consultants are still available if employees need special advice.[63]

The Internet may also play a significant role in career planning and career development. Richard Koonce sums it up nicely in a reply to the question: "What is the best way to use the Internet as part of a job search?"

> I don't think of the Internet as just a job search tool. I think of it as a professional development tool for educating yourself on job searches and career transitions, researching prospective employers, tracking trends, making contacts with other people, and identifying and generating professional opportunities.[64]

Now not only are all major newspapers and journals available on the Internet, but also job postings for national and international jobs, discussion groups who share career information, and listservs that provide a rich source of information on developments and trends in specific interest areas, such as training and development, human resource management, industrial relations, and many other relevant topic areas. At the end of this chapter, the "Web Research Exercise" lists Web sites that provide the services mentioned.

The new concept of **360-degree career development,** describing a holistic approach to the various career development functions, includes attracting, finding, evaluating, developing, certifying, and promoting the employees in the organization. There can be little doubt that if these functions are well integrated they will be more efficient and effective.[65]

360-degree career development
A holistic approach to career development that considers all career development functions.

SUMMARY

After workers are selected, they are seldom ready to perform successfully. They must be integrated into the social and work environment of the organization. Orientation programs help a worker begin this socialization process. The organization benefits because training time and costs are lowered, employee satisfaction is higher, and initial turnover is lower.

Training is an essential part of an organization's long-range strategy. If a company wants to survive in a competitive global environment, it requires an efficient and flexible workforce that is adaptable to fast-changing technologies and new approaches to doing business. Canadian managers also have to learn to manage a diverse workforce, made up of new immigrants from very different cultures. Flatter organizations necessitate new skills for employees, who have to shoulder more responsibilities. This, in turn, leads to greater emphasis on employees' competencies, resulting in the need for lifelong learning.

Training begins with an assessment of training needs. Specific training objectives can then be set. These objectives give direction to the training program and serve to evaluate the training program at its completion. The content of the program depends upon the training objectives. The design of the training should consider such learning principles as participation, repetition, relevance, transference, and feedback.

External and internal pressures have changed the skill and attitude requirements for managers. Top management is expected to work with leaner organizations, requiring sharing of power and delegation of authority. This in turn necessitates that lower-level managers must assume greater responsibilities, for which they have to be prepared. It is essential that top management make strategic human resource development a key component in its long-range strategic business plan.

Similarly, if management wants to meet the global challenge and keep the organization competitive, if it wants its managers to be prepared for constant change, new skill requirements, and higher willingness to accept risks, it has to make employee development plans a part of its overall strategic business plan.

Different development strategies may be employed, at the cognitive, behavioural, and environmental levels, with the cognitive method being the least promising and the environmental method the most promising approach.

Once training and development programs are completed, it is essential that they be evaluated. Without evaluation, a company does not know what it gets in return for its training and development investment. Evaluations include a pre-test and a post-test measurement of how well the program content has been transferred to the actual job, and some form of follow-up studies to ensure that the learning has been retained. A cost–benefit analysis should be conducted whenever possible to assess the contribution that any training or development program makes to the profits of the company.

Career planning and development are relatively new concepts to human resource specialists. In recent years, human resource departments have begun to recognize the need for more proactive efforts in this area. As a result, some (mostly large) departments provide career education, information, and counselling. But the primary responsibility for career planning and development rests with the individual employee. The planning process enables employees to identify career goals and the paths to those goals. Then, through developmental activities, the workers seek ways to improve themselves and further their career goals.

Career planning does not guarantee success. But without it, employees are seldom ready for career opportunities that arise. Because of this, their career progress may be slowed and the human resource department may be unable to fill openings internally.

TERMS FOR REVIEW

360-degree career development **p. 298**
apprenticeships **p. 277**
benchmarking **p. 282**
blog **p. 280**
buddy systems **p. 269**
career plateauing **p. 296**
coaching **p. 277**
competencies **p. 288**
computer-based training (CBT) **p. 279**
cost–benefit analysis **p. 291**
cross-training **p. 277**
dual-income couple **p. 296**

employee development **p. 283**
employee handbook **p. 269**
intranet **p. 281**
job families **p. 294**
knowledge management **p. 288**
laboratory training **p. 278**
learning curve **p. 274**
learning organization **p. 287**
learning principles **p. 275**
mentor **p. 297**
needs assessment **p. 273**
on-the-job training (OJT) **p. 277**

orientation programs **p. 268**
role-playing **p. 278**
startup costs **p. 268**
strategic human resource
    development **p. 281**
socialization **p. 267**
sponsor **p. 297**
succession planning **p. 298**
transference **p. 275**
vestibule training **p. 277**
virtual reality **p. 279**
wiki **p. 280**

SELF-ASSESSMENT EXERCISE

Test Your Knowledge of Orientation, Training and Development, and Career Planning

1. Because of the importance of managing a diverse workforce, most Canadian managers have been trained in this type of management.   **T   F**

2. Training programs focus on skill developments.   **T   F**

3. A training needs assessment includes learning principles.   **T   F**

4. Training focuses on management skills; development focuses on interpersonal skills.   **T   F**

5. Strategic human resource development focuses on training future executives.   **T   F**

6. Coaching is mainly used in team building.   **T   F**

7. Virtual reality training uses a real-time approach.   **T   F**

8. A *knowledge worker* is defined as an employee who has scored at least 60 percent on a knowledge test.   **T   F**

9. The fourth level of training evaluation is called "Training & Development Audit."   **T   F**

10. A person's career plan requires an environmental assessment.   **T   F**

SCORING

If you marked statements 2, 3, 7, and 10 as True, give yourself one point for each. The remaining statements are false.

Scores of 8–10: Very good! You seem to have a good understanding of the concepts. Congratulations.

Scores of 5–7: Okay, that keeps you in the running, but you may want to reread the chapter to improve your score.

Scores of less than 5: It may be advisable for you to spend more time studying the concepts and their application.

REVIEW AND DISCUSSION QUESTIONS

1. "If employees are properly selected, there should be no need for an orientation program or training." Do you agree or disagree? Why?

2. What are the employee benefits from orientation programs? The organizational benefits?

3. For each of the following occupations, which training techniques do you recommend? Why?
   (a) a cashier in a grocery store
   (b) a welder
   (c) an assembly-line worker
   (d) an inexperienced supervisor

4. Assume you were hired to manage a research department. After a few weeks, you noticed that some researchers were more effective than others, and that the less effective ones received little recognition from their more productive counterparts. What forms of training would you consider for both groups?

5. What is the purpose of a cost–benefit analysis?

6. Discuss why it is so important that there is a linkage between an organization's human resource development needs and its mission and strategy.

7. Explain the differences between the cognitive, behavioural, and environmental approaches to strategic employee development.

8. In what way does a "learning" organization differ from a "traditional" organization?

9. Why should a human resource department be concerned about career planning, especially since employee plans may conflict with the organization's objectives? What advantages does a human resource department expect to receive from assisting career planning?

10. Suppose you are in a management training position after completing university. Your career goal is not very clear, but you would like to become a top manager in your firm. What type of information would you seek from the human resource department to help you develop your career plan?

11. Why is employee feedback an important element of any organization's attempt to encourage career development?

12. Suppose a hard-working and loyal employee is passed over for promotion. What would you tell this person?

CRITICAL THINKING QUESTIONS

1. Before you entered your college or university, you had certain ideas about what your values and expectations would be as a student. How did the institution's socialization process change those values and expectations?

2. Your company is desperately looking for a systems analyst. You know that your competitor invested heavily in training and has a highly competent systems analyst, who indicated to you privately that she would switch if

you paid her $10,000 more. Your boss thinks that this is a bargain and tells you, "Get her!" It surely would hurt the competitor. What issues does this raise?

3. You are the training and development manager. Your president calls you in and tells you that the employee development budget has to be cut because of the company's financial situation. What arguments can you use to persuade your boss that development money is well spent?

⊙ ETHICS QUESTION

1. **Orientation:** You are about to give an orientation session to new employees and you plan to stress ethical behaviour as outlined in a company brochure. You know that company executives have recently been convicted in a foreign country of bribing government officials. Will you mention this?

2. **Training:** During a training program, which requires taking tests to measure progress, you notice that one of the participants, who struggled in some early tests, suddenly submits tests without mistakes. She is a probationary employee. You notice too that she is dating a staff member in your department, who has access to the test solutions. What do you plan to do?

3. **Development:** Should employees who are to retire soon have access to development programs, if they so desire? Please comment.

4. **Career planning:** You are the HR manager and one of your staff members asks you for career advice on this company. She wants to get ahead and is willing to take courses fitting your company's special needs. You have strongly encouraged such moves in the past. You know that the company is doing badly in its market and has probably less than a year to survive. How will you advise her?

⊙ WEB RESEARCH EXERCISE

Employee Orientation

1. **Robert Bacal of Bacal & Associates**
www.articles911.com/Human_Resources/Orientation

(a) In this quick guide to employee orientation, what does Bacal have to say about the outcomes of an effective orientation program?

(b) What different types of orientation programs does he describe? How do they differ?

Training and Development

1. **Canadian Society for Training and Development**
www.cstd.ca

(a) Give a summary of training publications and resources available from the CSTD. What type of assistance do they offer to trainers? What are they good for?

(b) Discuss the advantages and disadvantages of the designation Certified Training & Development Professional (CTDP) offered by the CSTD. Should all trainers be certified?

2. **Human Resources and Skills Development Canada (HRSDC)**
www.hrsdc.gc.ca/eng/home.shtml

Go to "Individuals" and then to "Training and Learning." Give an overview of what types of training resources are available from the government of Canada. Which ones would be relevant for you? Why?

3. **Service Canada**
www.jobsetc.ca

Go to "Training/Learning," then to "Explore Adult Learning Options," then to "Training and Careers Features"; develop your personal Learning Plan, using the program shown.

4. **Adult/Continuing Education home page**
http://adulted.about.com

Go to "Adult Education." Assume that you have a job a significant distance away from any university, but are determined to earn a degree. What are the different options in distance education? Describe the advantages and disadvantages of these options.

Career

1. **Career Planning**
http://careerplanning.about.com/od/selfassessment/Self_Assessment.htm Go to "Self-Assessment."

(a) Do the self-assessment. Do you agree with the results/recommendations?

(b) Assume that you want to pursue a career in accounting. What steps will you follow?

2. **Other Career Self-Assessment Instruments**
www.keirsey.com/sorter/register.aspx
http://web.mit.edu/is/training/assess/osweb-bas.html;
http://hotjobs.yahoo.com/assessment

CASE STUDY 🍁 Maple Leaf Shoes Ltd.

Developing a Training Program

"How can we develop a training program that will have a significant impact on our manufacturing staff?"

Jane Reynolds, special assistant in the personnel department, faced that challenge from a vice-president of the largest division of Maple Leaf Shoes, manufacturing. Training had never been a high priority at Maple Leaf Shoes, having always been viewed as an expense item, not an investment. If skilled workers were needed, Maple Leaf Shoes preferred to raid other companies to save training costs. If raiding was not successful, a quick on-the-job training was provided by more experienced employees—limited to essential skills, since there was little incentive for the employees to be more involved.

However, when the vice-president attended a convention of shoe manufacturers, he was surprised to learn how cost-efficient some other shoe producers were, especially in Italy and France. Although wages there were similar to the wages paid in Canada, the productivity of the Italian and French workers was significantly higher. The VP found that the Italian and French companies invested heavily in training, allowing them to use cross-trained, flexible staff.

The VP asked Reynolds to develop a training plan, suitable to improve the overall skill level of Maple Leaf Shoes' employees.

Reynolds vaguely remembered something about training from her few courses in human resource management quite some time ago, but she felt that it was not sufficient to develop a training program on her own. Besides, she knew nothing about the skill requirements in the manufacturing division.

She decided to ask Russ Summers, manager of the cutting operation, to chair a committee of first-line supervisors to assist her in the program development.

Discussion Questions

1. You are Russ. Describe the steps you would recommend that Reynolds go through before actually designing the content of the training.

2. What training methods would you suggest be used to train production workers? (First you might ask: What determines the methods?)

3. How would you evaluate the training program to determine how effective it was? (What criteria would you use?)

4. Do you think the first-line supervisors are the appropriate people to design the training program? Whom else would you add, if anyone, to this group?

CASE STUDY CPIB Canadian Pacific and International Bank

Mary Keddy, senior vice-president of human resources, felt somewhat embarrassed. She had just received a call from Michael Bennett, the CEO of the bank. He had asked a blunt question: "Mary, how is our return on investment in training?" At first she had not understood what he meant, but he explained that the board of directors had discussed her proposal to increase the training budget to 4 percent of payroll, and that one board member had asked whether the bank really knew how effective its training programs were and whether the money was well spent. She had to admit that she did not know. Bennett then had asked her to come up with an answer in time for the board meeting next month.

Mary had expected this question to arise sooner or later, but had hoped it would not happen so soon. She had been occupied with breaking the glass ceiling in the bank hierarchy and had been quite successful with it—so much so that even the Canadian Human Rights Commission had praised the bank for its employment equity program, which targeted women and minorities. Training had a high priority in the bank's strategy, as evidenced by its training budget, which exceeded 3 percent of payroll, much more than the average Canadian company and even its bank competitors spent.

The evaluation of its training programs had not been a high priority. So far, training sessions had been assessed mainly by using reaction measurements and the occasional feedback requested from supervisors some time after sessions.

Mary remembered from her HR courses that in order to assess the effectiveness of training programs, somewhat more sophisticated instruments and methods had to be used. Now she had to come up with some good ideas.

Discussion Questions

1. You are Mary Keddy. Develop a proposal that Michael Bennett could present to the board. Consider also the practicality of the plan.

2. As a rule of thumb, 5 to 10 percent of the cost of a training program should be used for the evaluation part of a program, depending on the complexity of the assessment. (The cost is an experience-based figure. The first author of this book worked for five years as the training director for a German company with 2,000 employees, and for 25 years as an instructor, trainer, and consultant for Canadian government and private company programs.) Please develop a "cheap" and an "expensive" proposal. A brief description of your approach and reasons will suffice (e.g., why would one method be cheaper or more expensive than the other?).

Advanced Question, Requiring Extra Readings

3. If you wanted to recommend a "foolproof" evaluation—that is, rule out other causes of success than the training program itself—what approach would you suggest?

Performance Management

Performance management helps an organization define and achieve long-term and short-term goals vital to its success.

Hari Das[1]

CHAPTER OBJECTIVES

After studying this chapter, you should be able to:

➡ *Explain* the purpose of performance management.

➡ *Describe* the characteristics of an effective performance measurement.

➡ *Give examples of* performance objectives.

➡ *Identify* the issues that influence the selection of a performance appraisal system.

➡ *Explain* the uses of performance appraisals.

➡ *Discuss* rater biases in performance appraisals.

➡ *Describe* commonly used appraisal methods.

➡ *Explain* how the results of performance appraisal affect human resource management.

➡ *Rate* the performance appraisal mechanism in your organization.

➡ *Describe* the guidelines for effective performance evaluation interviews.

CHAPTER 8

PERFORMANCE MANAGEMENT

performance management
The use of performance data to effect organizational culture, systems, and processes, set goals, allocate resources, affect policies and programs, and share results.

performance appraisal
The process by which organizations evaluate employee job performance.

Business Performance Management Net
Discussion of challenges and best practices
www.bpmmag.net/magazine/article.html?articleID=14573

For seven editions we titled this chapter "Performance Appraisal," because that was the focal point when the topic of performance in organizations was discussed. Now the focus is shifting from the individual to the organization as a whole. Our new title, "Performance Management," reflects a different orientation: **performance management** encompasses many more variables, of which **performance appraisal** is just one. Other aspects include corporate culture, organizational benchmarks, human capital potential, systems and processes, resources, current policies, program directions, sharing the results with all stakeholders, and asking for stakeholders' input.

Here the human resource function has the potential of creating an enormous influence in how well an organization develops and maintains a sound performance management program. Of course, it requires that human resource professionals have the capacity to be leaders in performance management; that is, they have to develop their competency of thinking strategically and thinking in systems terms, which so far has rarely been their strength.

The ideal performance management system provides incentives for employees to concentrate on improving things that contribute most to value creation, ranging from hiring the right people to producing high-quality goods or services to using the most effective training and development programs. The ideal system also uses measurements that are practical and that provide feedback where needed. Practical means:

- simple to use
- simple to understand
- simple to apply

Simplicity is a necessary but not a sufficient condition, as the following example will illustrate:

The first author of this book remembers his first visit as an engineering student to the famous Hannover Machine Tool Exhibition. There he saw a Russian lathe that was the heaviest in its category, more than double the weight of competing lathes. A discussion with the Russian exhibitors revealed that the manufacturing managers were rewarded by the Russian government for tonnage of production. No wonder that managers concentrated their effort on producing machines as heavy as possible.

This measurement was simple, but hardly appropriate. There is no doubt that a type of quality measurement would have been more effective.

To make performance management work requires several characteristics.

- **Performance Objectives.** This is a critical aspect of a company's strategy which, if not met, may result in lower customer satisfaction and other less desirable organizational results.
- **Performance Goals.** These are achievable and realistic targets to which actual outcomes can be compared.
- **Performance Measurement.** Here we talk about measuring the process of achieving preset goals, including the efficiency of transforming resources into goods and services, their quality, client satisfaction, quality of decision making, and efficiency and effectiveness of management contributions.
- **Output Measures.** Quantity and quality assessments.
- **Outcome Measures.** Results of programs compared to preset targets.

There is an interesting way to illustrate how an ideal performance management system should work. Just imagine the dashboard of a car. It provides instant feedback on speed, engine revolutions, distance travelled, gas consumption, engine temperature, battery charge, time of day, and, depending on the luxury of the car, a host of other information that allows the driver to react instantly to traffic or car conditions that arise. These measurements are direct (real-time), simple, and easy to understand and apply. Today's computer technology makes this type of feedback possible even in organizations. The best business-related example is Wal-Mart:

Explaining the roots of Wal-Mart's phenomenal growth and success, Professor Edna Bonacich put it simply: "The shift in Wal-Mart's power was when it started to develop its control over technology. The key was the power of information hidden in bar codes. It enabled Wal-Mart to track sales on specific items, specific weeks, specific days, specific hours of the day when merchandise sells the most."

Recently Wal-Mart introduced even newer technology for this purpose, the Service Radio Frequency Identification (RFID), chips sending radio signals to an RFID reader somewhere in a warehouse. It gives sales management instant information on the movement of any merchandise through the system. Eventually it will allow supermarket customers to push their cart through a checkout and receive an instantaneous printout of their purchases.[2]

Performance Management System Goals

Organizations concerned with running an efficient and effective performance management system will try to achieve the following objectives:

- Transform organizational objectives into clearly understood, measurable outcomes that define success and are shared with stakeholders in and outside the organization.
- Provide instruments for measuring, managing, and improving the overall health and success of the organization.
- Include measures of quality, cost, speed, customer service, and employee satisfaction, motivation, and skills to provide an in-depth, predictive performance management system.
- Shift from prescriptive, audit- and compliance-based management to an ongoing, forward-looking strategic partnership between top and middle management and employees.

How well do performance management systems work? The data available are not encouraging.

A recent survey of 1,200 U.S. workers found that performance management programs are woefully inadequate. Less than half (44 percent) felt that their company held people accountable for their performance, and slightly more than half (54 percent) believed that a performance management program helped them to improve. More serious was the finding that only 4 out of 10 employees saw the connection between their day-to-day work and their company's goals.[3]

Sound performance management programs make clear the connection between company goals and employee objectives and work plans, as well as criteria for success.

PERFORMANCE MANAGEMENT AS PART OF MANAGERIAL STRATEGY

Zigon Performance Group
Information on performance management and performance appraisal
www.zigonperf.com

The Performance Management & Appraisal Help Center
Articles, books, programs
http://performanceappraisals.org

An important element of any strategic planning is the assessment of the strengths and weaknesses of the human resources in the organization, seen as part of the performance management process. Thorough performance analyses offer management the necessary data to assess the current skill, experience, and performance level of every employee, as well as performance standards critical for future requirements. Such data may have a significant impact on human resource planning, training and development programs, career development, and compensation expense forecasts.

Critical in the performance management process is an effective appraisal system. It makes explicit what constitutes the effective and efficient behaviour on the part of an individual employee that is critical to implementing the strategic plan. Just as the engineering department is concerned with designing equipment, the maintenance department is concerned with running equipment, and manufacturing is concerned with turning out a quality product at minimal cost, the human resource department should be concerned with identifying what the people in engineering, maintenance, and manufacturing must do (*behaviour*) to be proficient in their respective functions. Similarly, they should determine what top management must do to implement the strategic plan once it has been formulated.

The uses of performance appraisals are described in Figure 8-1. Accurate performance evaluations show employees where they are deficient. For the human resource department, appraisals make compensation, placement, training, development, and career guidance decisions more effective. At the same time, the department obtains feedback on its development activities, staffing process, job designs, and external challenges. In short, performance appraisals serve as a quality control check on employee and human resource department performance.

FIGURE 8-1	Uses of Performance Appraisals

- *Performance improvement.* Performance feedback allows the employee, the manager, and human resource specialists to intervene with appropriate actions to improve performance.
- *Compensation adjustments.* Performance evaluations help decision makers determine who should receive pay raises. Many firms grant part or all of their pay increases and bonuses on the basis of merit, which is determined mostly through performance appraisals.
- *Placement decisions.* Promotions, transfers, and demotions are usually based on past or anticipated performance. Often, promotions are a reward for past performance.
- *Training and development needs.* Poor performance may indicate the need for retraining. Likewise, good performance may indicate untapped potential that should be developed.
- *Career planning and development.* Performance feedback guides career decisions about specific career paths one should investigate.
- *Deficiencies in staffing process.* Good or bad performance implies strengths or weaknesses in the human resource department's staffing procedures.
- *Informational inaccuracies.* Poor performance may indicate errors in job analysis information, human resource plans, or other parts of the human resource management information system. Reliance on inaccurate information may have led to inappropriate hiring, training, or counselling decisions.
- *Job design errors.* Poor performance may be a symptom of ill-conceived job designs. Appraisals help diagnose these errors.
- *Avoidance of discrimination.* Accurate performance appraisals that actually measure job-related performance ensure that internal placement decisions are not discriminatory.
- *External challenges.* Sometimes performance is influenced by factors outside the work environment, such as family, finances, health, or other personal matters. If such influences are uncovered through appraisals, the human resource department may be able to provide assistance.

Without an effective appraisal system, promotions, transfers, and other employee-related decisions become subject to trial and error. Career planning and human resource development suffer, because there is no systematic performance feedback. Moreover, the human resource department lacks adequate information to evaluate its performance objectively. This lack of feedback can cause the human resource department to miss its objectives. Sometimes, the consequences of this failure are severe:

> A large agricultural cooperative association in the western provinces rated employees twice a year. But employees were evaluated on personality characteristics, such as attitude, cooperation, and other factors that were only indirectly related to actual performance. Employees who were well liked by their managers received higher ratings. As a result, promotions, pay raises, and other employee-related decisions were biased by personalities. Eventually, several employees filed charges against the cooperative, alleging racial and sexual discrimination. When company lawyers defended past decisions as unbiased, they lost the case, because they could not show how the ratings related to job performance.

As this example emphasizes, an organization cannot have just any appraisal system. It must be effective and accepted. If effective and accepted, it can identify developmental and career planning needs (see Chapter 7). It also can help with replacement summaries (discussed in Chapter 3), along with the other uses illustrated in Figure 8-1.

ELEMENTS OF THE PERFORMANCE APPRAISAL SYSTEM

Figure 8-2 shows the elements of an acceptable appraisal system. The approach must identify performance-related criteria, measure those criteria, and then give feedback to employees and the

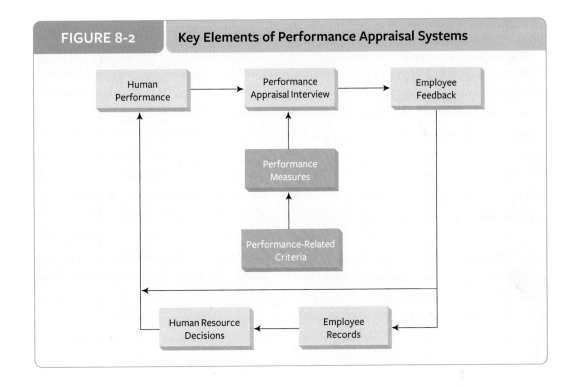

FIGURE 8-2 | Key Elements of Performance Appraisal Systems

human resource department. If performance measures are not job-related, the evaluation can lead to inaccurate or biased results. Not only is performance feedback distorted, but errors in employee records can lead to incorrect human resource decisions, as happened in the above example of the agricultural cooperative.

SPOTLIGHT ON HRM
Performance Appraisal—A Necessary Evil?

Performance appraisal is one of those difficult areas of business that seems to be a necessary evil—all the books say that a company should have a performance appraisal system, employees often express the desire for one, and (if my workload is any indication) businesspeople are keen to find out about them.

Why then is performance appraisal one of the areas of management most commonly complained about by employees and managers alike?

The major mistake made by companies is the failure to recognize what constitutes a performance appraisal system. It certainly is not just about a set of forms that must be completed by various individuals. Nor is it just an opportunity to have an annual chat with the boss to "get it all off your chest."

Seen in isolation, performance appraisal is simply a procedure, which involves the assessment of an individual's performance on a regular basis. That's fine, but it goes

much deeper—performance appraisal lies at the heart of good business practice. A performance appraisal system can only function if the business has a clear idea of where it is heading, and has taken steps to ensure that it is taking the workforce along.

Of course, nothing is that simple. Or is it?

Try this—if you are a businessperson, ask the following questions of your own company. If you are an employee, copy this and give it to your manager, or ask the questions among your peers and pass the results up the chain of command. You never know what might result!

What follows are a series of questions that can be used to rate the performance appraisal mechanisms in organizations. You should be able to answer the questions and get a rating regardless of whether a formal performance appraisal system is in place, and you may be very surprised by the result—there is nothing that says a performance appraisal system must be written down or formalized!

The questions draw on my own experience in line management and consultancy, and from the UK Investors in People Initiative, which provides an excellent framework for business development.

For each of the questions, answer:

- 1=Strongly disagree
- 2=Disagree
- 3=Not sure
- 4=Agree
- 5=Strongly agree

Record your answers and total them up at the end.

1. Management has a clear idea of where they want the company to go.

2. Every employee understands where management is trying to take the company.

3. All departments have clearly defined goals.

4. The department goals fit together to help the company get to where it wants to go.

5. Every employee understands how his or her job contributes to the overall department and company goals.

6. Each employee and their supervisors/managers agree what is expected of the employee.

7. Each employee, together with his/her supervisor/manager, monitors whether he/she is achieving what he/she is expected to.

8. Each employee's training and development needs are reviewed regularly to ensure that they continue to have the skills they need to achieve what is expected of them.

9. Supervisors/managers ensure that employees understand why particular training and development actions are taking place.

10. Supervisors/managers ensure that employees understand what they are expected to do better as a result of particular training and development actions.

11. Employees are happy with the quality and frequency of feedback they receive from their supervisors/managers.

12. Supervisors/managers and employees are trained for their roles in the appraisal process.

How did you score?

- *Under 24*—the company is like a sailing ship without a sail. Lack of a performance appraisal is the least of the worries. Management probably has little idea of where the company is heading, and the workforce almost certainly does not. I would not be surprised if you hit some rocks … soon. Get some help.

- *25 to 40*—the internal systems are poor and may be causing discontent and motivational difficulties in the workforce. It will be possible to improve matters, but firm action is needed. Management must decide on corporate goals, decide what they need to do to achieve them, and then tell the workforce not once, but every day. Communicate, communicate, communicate—that is the key.

- *41 to 50*—I'm impressed. The company has all the basics in place, and they are probably working well. There is obviously room for some improvement in specific areas, and I suggest looking in detail at the areas with the lowest scores.

- *Over 50*—Wow, write a book on how you did it!

Source: Courtesy of Martin Finnigan of Finnigan Consulting.

Key Elements of Performance Appraisal Systems

The human resource department usually develops performance appraisals for employees in all departments. This centralization is meant to ensure uniformity. With uniformity in design and implementation, results are more likely to be comparable among similar groups of employees. Although the human resource department may develop different approaches for managers and workers, uniformity within each group is needed to ensure useful results.

Even though the human resource department usually designs the appraisal system, it seldom does the actual evaluation of performance. Instead, research shows that the employee's immediate supervisor performs the evaluation 95 percent of the time.[4] Although others could rate performance, the immediate supervisor is often in the best position to make the appraisal.

So important is the evaluation of performance that 85 percent of all companies surveyed in one Canadian study used appraisals for their clerical, professional, supervisory, and management employees.[5] To explain the importance of this widely used tool of human resource management, the remainder of this chapter examines the preparation, methods, and implications of performance appraisals.

Performance feedback is crucial for the motivation of employees. The feedback session is also ideal for another motivational tool. Which one? (*Hint:* Setting ...)

© Rob Daly/Getty Images.

Robert Bacal, performance appraisal consultant Free articles
http://performance-appraisals.org/Bacalsappraisalarticles/

performance standards
The benchmarks against which performance is measured.

performance measures
The ratings used to evaluate employee performance.

The appraisal should create an accurate picture of an individual's job performance. To achieve this goal, appraisal systems should be job-related, be practical, have standards, and use dependable measures. *Job-related* means that the system evaluates critical behaviours that constitute job success. If the evaluation is not job-related, it is invalid and probably unreliable. Without validity and reliability, the system may discriminate in violation of antidiscrimination laws. Even when discrimination does not occur, appraisals are inaccurate and useless if they are not job-related, such as if an assessment of a manager's performance is based on a college degree.

However, a job-related approach also must be *practical*. A practical system is one that, first of all, is understood by evaluators and employees; a complicated, impractical approach may cause resentment and nonuse. The confusion can lead to inaccuracies that reduce the effectiveness of the appraisal. An example of a simple and practical approach would be to judge an employee's performance on production—for example, number of widgets.

Performance evaluation requires **performance standards**—benchmarks against which performance is measured. To be effective, they should relate to the desired results of each job; they cannot be set arbitrarily. Knowledge of these standards is collected through job analysis. As discussed in Chapter 2, job analysis uncovers specific performance criteria by analyzing the performance of existing employees.

From the duties and standards listed in the job description, the analyst can decide which behaviours are critical and should be evaluated. If this information is lacking or unclear, standards may be developed from observation of the job or discussion with the immediate supervisor.

Performance evaluation also requires dependable **performance measures**, the ratings used to evaluate performance. To be useful, they must be *easy to use, be reliable*, and *report on the critical behaviours* that determine performance. For example, a telephone company supervisor must observe the following in each operator:

- use of company procedures—staying calm, applying tariff rates for phone calls, and following company rules and regulations
- phone manners—speaking clearly and courteously
- accuracy—placing operator-assisted calls accurately

Such observations can be made either directly or indirectly. *Direct observation* occurs when the rater actually sees the performance. *Indirect observation* occurs when the rater can evaluate only substitutes for actual performance. For example, a supervisor's monitoring of an operator's calls is direct observation; a written test on company procedures for handling emergency calls is indirect observation. <u>Indirect observations are usually less accurate</u>, because they evaluate substitutes for actual performance. Substitutes for actual performance are called *constructs*. Since constructs are not exactly the same as actual performance, they may lead to errors:

> To test how well operators might respond to emergency calls, a provincial telephone company developed a paper-and-pencil test. The test was intended to determine if each operator knew exactly how to proceed when emergency calls were received for such requests as police, ambulance, or fire equipment. After several hundred operators were tested, it was noticed that fast readers scored better. The human resource department decided to scrap the test and use false emergency calls to evaluate the operators.

Another dimension of performance measures is whether they are <u>objective or subjective</u>. *Objective* performance measures are those indications of job performance that are verifiable by others. For example, if two supervisors monitor an operator's calls, they can count the number of misdialled ones. The results are objective and verifiable, because each supervisor gets the same call-placement accuracy percentage. Usually, objective measures are quantitative. They typically include items such as gross units produced, net units approved by quality control, scrap rates, number of computational errors, number of customer complaints, or some other mathematically precise measure of performance.

Subjective performance measures are those ratings that are not verifiable by others. Usually, such measures are the rater's personal opinions. Subjective measures are low in accuracy. When subjective measures are also indirect, accuracy becomes even lower. For example, measurement of an operator's phone manners is done subjectively, since supervisors must use their personal opinions of good or bad manners. Because the evaluation is subjective, accuracy is usually low even if the supervisor directly observes the operator. Accuracy is likely to be even lower when the rater uses an indirect measure, such as an essay test of phone manners. Whenever possible, human resource specialists prefer objective and direct measures of performance.

Rater Biases

The problem with subjective measures is the opportunity for bias. Bias is the (mostly unintentional) distortion of a measurement. Usually it is caused by raters who fail to remain emotionally detached while they evaluate employee performance. The most common rater biases include the following:

- the halo effect
- the error of central tendency
- the leniency and strictness biases
- personal prejudice
- the recency effect

The Halo Effect

halo effect
A bias that occurs when an evaluation allows some information to disproportionately affect the final evaluation.

The **halo effect** (discussed in Chapter 6) occurs when the rater's personal opinion of the employee sways the rater's measurement of performance. For example, if a supervisor likes an employee, that opinion may distort the supervisor's estimate of the employee's performance. The problem is most severe when raters must evaluate their friends:

> Sam was Jim's supervisor. They had been friends in school and had played together in a minor league baseball team for years. Jim was a happy-go-lucky guy and his job performance was so-so, but he was very good with people. When Sam had to write a performance evaluation, he praised Jim for his "excellent social" and "superior communication" skills, but overlooked his shortcomings in productivity aspects. Sam felt that he "could not let down" his friend.

The Error of Central Tendency

error of central tendency
An error in rating employees that consists of evaluating employees as neither good nor poor performers even when some employees perform exceptionally well or poorly.

Some raters do not like to judge employees as "effective" or "ineffective," so they avoid checking extremes—very poor or excellent—and instead place their marks near the centre of the rating sheet so that employees appear to be "average." Thus, the term **error of central tendency** has been applied to this bias. Human resource departments sometimes unintentionally encourage this behaviour by requiring raters to justify extremely high or low ratings.

The first author of this book did his Ph.D. dissertation on performance appraisals in Canadian banks. When he surveyed over 2,000 appraisals, all of which used 7-point scales, he did not find a single evaluation that used the 1 or 7 anchors.[6]

The Leniency and Strictness Biases

The **leniency bias** occurs when raters are too easy in evaluating employee performance. The **strictness bias** is just the opposite; it results from raters being too harsh in their evaluation of performance. Both errors more commonly occur when performance standards are vague. The leniency bias is much more common.

> The "average" performance assessment of officers in the Canadian Armed Forces is about 80 percent.[7]

Personal Prejudice

A rater's dislike for a person or group may distort the ratings. For example, some human resource departments notice that male supervisors give undeservedly low ratings to women who hold "traditionally male jobs." Sometimes, raters are unaware of their prejudice, which makes such biases even more difficult to overcome. Nevertheless, human resource specialists should pay close attention to prejudice in appraisals, since it prevents effective evaluations and violates antidiscrimination laws.

> Ann was the only female welder in a maintenance team, and she was good. She had passed her welder's certification with flying colours and was chosen over a number of male applicants. Tom, the team's foreman, had opposed her hiring, saying that women would not fit into the team, but the HR manager insisted on "hiring the best person." Ann noticed that Tom scrutinized her work much more closely than that of other team members and publicly complained about even her minor mistakes. In her first annual performance assessment she was judged "average, with potential for improvement."

The Recency Effect

When using subjective performance measures, ratings are affected strongly by the employee's most recent actions. Recent actions—good or bad—are more likely to be remembered by the rater. This is known as the **recency effect**.

> John had been an average nurse, paying more attention to his female colleagues than his patients. However, a few weeks ago, by sheer coincidence, he had saved a patient's life. During the recent performance appraisal, Jennifer, the head nurse, concentrated on this one-time event and lavishly praised John's overall job performance.

When subjective measures must be used, human resource specialists can reduce the distortion from biases through training, feedback, and the proper selection of performance appraisal techniques. Training for raters should involve three steps. *First,* biases and their causes should be discussed. *Second,* the role of performance appraisals in employee decisions should be explained to stress the need for impartiality and objectivity. *Third,* raters should be allowed to apply subjective performance measures as part of their training. For example, classroom exercises may require evaluation of the trainer or videos of various workers. Mistakes uncovered during simulated evaluations then can be corrected through additional training or counselling.

➡ CHARACTERISTICS OF AN EFFECTIVE PERFORMANCE APPRAISAL SYSTEM

An appraisal method typically consists of a special scale or a particular process; an appraisal system consists of interlocking, interdependent, and reinforcing methods and processes that make the results synergistic—that is, the system is larger than the sum of its parts. Figure 8-3 shows 12 characteristics of an effective appraisal system, put into question format. These characteristics are outlined below.

1. **Validity.** Validity (relevance) is of utmost importance. Invalid (job-irrelevant) criteria lead to biased assessments. Results are the most valid criteria as they tend to be objective. It would be difficult, for example, to question the relevance of a 10 percent increase in profits for a

leniency bias
A tendency to rate employees higher than their performance justifies.

strictness bias
A tendency to rate employees lower than their performance justifies.

recency effect
A rater bias that occurs when the rater allows recent employee performance to sway unduly the overall evaluation of the employee's performance.

FIGURE 8-3	Characteristics of an Effective Performance Appraisal System

1. Is it valid?
2. Is it reliable?
3. Did employees have input into its development?
4. Are its standards acceptable to employees?
5. Are its goals acceptable to employees?
6. Are its standards under the control of employees?
7. How frequent is the feedback?
8. Have raters been trained?
9. Have ratees been trained?
10. Do employees have input into the appraisal interviews?
11. Do the appraisals have consequences?
12. Are different sources (raters) utilized?

Source: Based on Hermann F. Schwind, "Performance Appraisal: The State of the Art," in Shimon L. Dolan and Randall S. Schuler, eds., *Personnel and Human Resources Management in Canada* (St. Paul, MN: West Publishing, 1987).

performance assessment of a manager in charge of a department. Job-related behaviours are also relevant. However, some still widely used personality traits, such as leadership or intelligence, are of questionable value for performance assessment. They are characteristics the employee brings to the job, not a job outcome. To paraphrase Kane and Lawler: even though traits may relate to performance—an intelligent employee will probably do better than a less intelligent one—this does not justify their use as performance measures any more than the use of intelligence scores as substitutes for school grades.[8]

Valid, or job-related, performance criteria must be based on a thorough job analysis (discussed in Chapter 2) and documented in the job description for each position. Validity is also crucial for the validation of any selection test (discussed in Chapter 6). And finally, validity is essential for any court challenge of performance criteria—for example, in case of a wrongful dismissal suit in which an employee's performance is an issue.

2. **Reliability.** Reliability (consistency), although highly desirable, is difficult to achieve in an organizational setting because of different raters, different instruments, and changing work environments. As a consequence, reliability can be looked at only as a distant aim.[9] However, it is important to know that *valid criteria tend to be reliable, but reliable criteria are not necessarily valid.*

> A good example is the historical practice of craniology (also called "phrenology"), the study of skulls and their relationship to human characteristics. Early craniologists/phrenologists believed that the circumference of the human skull was a measure of intelligence (which is without foundation). It is an example of an absolutely reliable measure (every time one measures the circumference, one gets the same result), but without any validity.

3. **Input into System Development.** Employee participation in the development of performance criteria, appraisal instruments, and the system that manages them increases significantly the probability of acceptance of the system by both supervisors and employees. It gives employees the feeling of ownership. It is true that employees hired after a system has been installed will not have had input into it, but the knowledge that it was developed with the input of those who are rated by it will make it more acceptable.[10]

4. **Acceptable Performance Standards.** How often do supervisors make the mistake of using their own performance standards to assess an employee's performance? The temptation is high, but this approach mostly backfires. Performance standards are derived from a job analysis (discussed in Chapter 2). If standards are set unilaterally by management, they become "management's standards" and get little or no commitment from the employees. This does

A maître-d', a waitress, and a wine steward all do restaurant-related work, but each of their performance evaluations uses different criteria. Or do you recognize some criteria that they may have in common?

Skip Nall/Getty Images.

not mean that employees should set their own performance standards, but rather that the standards should be set with the employees to gain their commitment. It may be necessary for a manager to start out with a lower standard for a new employee until he or she has developed some experience and more self-confidence. Here, the manager's coaching skills become crucial, as do open communication, trust, and support by colleagues.[11]

5. **Acceptable Goals.** Similarly to performance standards, performance goals are often set unilaterally by managers, sometimes too high for an employee. Goals derive from the strategic business plans of the organization, operationalized at the department level by the manager. It is the responsibility of the manager, as coach and counsellor, to set goals seen by the employee as achievable; otherwise, the employee will be discouraged, often resulting in a self-fulfilling prophecy: "That's too high for me, I can't do it." Studies have consistently found that when supervisors set specific goals, performance improves twice as much as when they set general goals.[12]

6. **Control of Standards.** Current performance standards used in appraisals often seem to be based on the assumption that the job in question is independent of other jobs. However, several studies have shown that most jobs are highly interdependent, which means that job incumbents have to rely on the contributions or cooperation of their colleagues. A standard of performance that is not fully under the control of the employee is not valid.[13]

7. **Frequency of Feedback.** Most appraisals take place once a year. Ideally, performance feedback would be given by the supervisor immediately after effective or ineffective job behaviour was observed. However, this is unrealistic in an organizational setting. A compromise may be feedback sessions on a monthly, quarterly, or at least twice-a-year basis. These sessions should be seen by employees as opportunities to receive advice and support from their supervisor, not to be appraised or judged.

8. **Rater Training.** Raters need to be trained in observation techniques and categorization skills (e.g., the use of diaries or critical incidents and how to group job behaviours or apply organizational performance standards). Frame-of-reference training (FORT) aims at improving these skills.[14] Raters also have to be familiar with the many potential rating errors (e.g., the halo effect, leniency) and the ways to minimize them. Research has shown that rater training reduces such errors.[15]

9. **Ratee Training.** If management wants to ensure that a performance appraisal system is well understood and accepted by employees, it should consider training the ratees in addition

to the raters. The ratee training might be part of the process of developing the performance appraisal system, thereby serving two purposes.

10. **Input into Interview Process.** Allowing employees to have a high level of participation in the appraisal interview increases employee satisfaction and morale.[16]

11. **Appraisal Consequences.** Appraisals without consequences lose their effectiveness very quickly. Employees as well as supervisors have to see that appraisal results are taken seriously by management and are followed up on. All too often, evaluation results end up in the personnel file unread, leading to cynical employees and frustrated supervisors.[17] Of course, there is a crucial link to a merit pay system. Especially high-performing employees expect to be rewarded for their effort.[18]

12. **Different Sources (Raters).** Relying on the judgment of one person increases the risk of biases (rating errors). Using different sources either confirms an assessment if all or a majority point in the same direction, or it raises a caution flag if assessments are at variance. Appraisal information can be gathered from the direct supervisor, secondary supervisors, self, peers, subordinates, and clients or customers. Raters from different levels of the organization will have different but valid views of a job and the performance of the incumbent.[19]

A Nurturing Organizational Environment

The social climate in an organization has a significant impact on the effectiveness of a performance appraisal system. A trusting relationship between managers and employees tends to foster two-way communication processes and lead to mutually agreeable performance goals. In organizations with low trust levels, it is questionable whether a performance appraisal should be done at all. One study found that raters with low trust in the appraisal system process rated their subordinates significantly higher (with greater leniency) than raters with high trust in the process.[20]

The development of a performance appraisal system is also seen as an effective tool for organizational change. As one researcher put it: "Designing a successful performance appraisal system for use in an organization is as much an exercise in organizational development as it is a study of performance measurement."[21]

⊙ LEGAL ASPECTS OF PERFORMANCE APPRAISAL

A performance appraisal form is a legal document. The implication is that raters have to be careful to use only performance criteria that are relevant to the job. In a court challenge—for example, where an employee lost a job as a result of inadequate job performance—the human resource manager has to prove that the performance criteria used were *valid* and were used *consistently*. Nonrelevant criteria can be avoided if performance standards are established through a thorough job analysis and recorded in a job description.[22]

It is also a legal requirement that a reasonable time frame be set for performance improvement. The length of time would depend on the job. While it may be reasonable to expect an office clerk to improve his or her performance within a few weeks or months, it might take a manager a year or more to show improvement.

Well-documented performance shortcomings can avoid serious embarrassments in court or with arbitrators.

Performance appraisal systems can use different types of appraisal techniques. For ease of discussion, we have grouped these techniques into those that focus on past performance and those that focus on future performance.

⊙ PAST-ORIENTED APPRAISAL METHODS

The importance of performance evaluations has led academics and practitioners to create many methods to appraise past performance. Most of these techniques are direct attempts to minimize some particular problem found in other approaches. None is perfect; each has advantages and disadvantages.

Past-oriented approaches have the advantage of dealing with performance that has already occurred and, to some degree, can be measured. The obvious disadvantage is that past performance cannot be changed. But by evaluating past performance, employees can get feedback about their efforts. This feedback may then lead to renewed efforts at improved performance. The most widely used appraisal techniques that have a past orientation can be divided into *noncomparative* and *comparative* methods.

Noncomparative Evaluation Methods

Noncomparative evaluation methods, as the name implies, do not compare one employee against another, but use scales or reports with performance criteria developed by supervisors or a committee. Such methods include the following:

- the rating scale
- the critical incident method
- behaviourally anchored rating scales
- performance tests and observations

Rating Scale

Perhaps the oldest and most widely used form of performance appraisal is the **rating scale,** which requires the rater to provide a subjective evaluation of an individual's performance along a scale from low to high. An example appears in Figure 8-4. As the figure indicates, the evaluation is based solely on the opinions of the rater. In many cases, the criteria are not directly related to job performance. Although subordinates or peers may use it, the immediate supervisor usually completes the form.

noncomparative evaluation methods
Appraisal methods that evaluate an employee's performance according to preset data, and not by comparing one person's performance with that of coworkers.

rating scale
A scale that requires the rater to provide a subjective evaluation of an individual's performance.

FIGURE 8-4	A Sample of a Rating Scale for Performance Evaluation

Western Farm Cooperative Association

Instructions: For the following performance factors, please indicate on the basis of the rating scale your evaluation of the named employee.

Employee's Name _____   Department _____

Rater's Name _____   Date _____

Rating Definitions and Score Points

9–10   Outstanding (clearly superior performance)
7–8   Very good (exceeds expectations)
5–6   Good (meets expectations)
3–4   Marginal (needs improvement)
1–2   Poor (unsatisfactory)

Factors	Score	Comments
1. Dependability (reliability of employee)	_____	_____
2. Initiative (willingness to take action)	_____	_____
3. Overall output (productivity of employee)	_____	_____
4. Attendance (overall attendance, punctuality)	_____	_____
⋮ ⋮	⋮ ⋮	⋮
20. Quality of work (accuracy, thoroughness, etc.)	_____	_____
Total	_____	

The form is completed by checking the most appropriate response for each performance factor. Responses may be given numerical values to enable an average score to be computed and compared for each employee. The advantages of this method are that it is inexpensive to develop and administer, raters need little training or time to complete the form, and it can be applied to a large number of employees.

The disadvantages, however, are numerous. A rater's biases are likely to be reflected in a subjective instrument of this type. Specific performance criteria might be omitted to make the form applicable to a variety of jobs. For example, "maintenance of equipment" might be left off because it applies to only a few workers. But for some employees, that item may be the most important part of the job. These omissions tend to limit specific feedback. Also, descriptive evaluations are subject to individual interpretations that vary widely. And when specific performance criteria are hard to identify, the form may rely on irrelevant personality variables that dilute the meaning of the evaluation. The result is a standardized form and procedure that is not always job-related.

Critical Incident Method

The **critical incident method** requires the rater to record statements that describe extremely effective or ineffective employee behaviour related to performance. The statements are called *critical incidents*. These incidents are usually recorded by the supervisor during the evaluation period for each subordinate. Recorded incidents include a brief explanation of what happened. Several typical entries for a laboratory assistant appear in Figure 8-5. As shown in the figure, both positive and negative incidents are recorded. Incidents are classified (either as they occur or later by the human resource department) into categories such as control of safety hazards, control of material scrap, and employee development.

The critical incident method is extremely useful for giving employees job-related feedback. It can also reduce the recency bias. Of course, the practical drawback is the difficulty of getting supervisors to record incidents as they occur. Many supervisors start out recording incidents faithfully, but lose interest. Then, just before the evaluation period ends, they add new entries. When this happens, the recency bias is exaggerated, and employees may feel that supervisors are building a case to support their subjective opinions. Even when the form is filled out over the entire rating period, employees may feel that the supervisor is unwilling to forget negative incidents that occurred months before.

critical incident method The rater records statements that describe extremely effective or ineffective behaviour related to performance.

FIGURE 8-5	Critical Incidents Record for a Lab Assistant

Hartford Chemicals Ltd.
Critical Incidents Worksheet

Instructions: In each category below, record specific incidents of employee behaviour that were either extremely good or extremely poor.

Employee's Name Kay Watts (lab assistant)   Department Chemistry Lab
Rater's Name Nat Cordoba   Rating Period of 10/1 to 12/31

Control of Safety Hazards

Date	Positive Employee Behaviour	Date	Negative Employee Behaviour
10/12	Reported broken rung on utility ladder and flagged ladder as unsafe	11/3	Left hose across storeroom aisle
10/15	Put out small trash fire promptly	11/27	Smoked in chemical storeroom

Control of Material Scrap

Date	Positive Employee Behaviour	Date	Negative Employee Behaviour
10/3	Sorted through damaged shipment of glassware to salvage usable beakers	11/7	Used glass containers for strong bases, ruining glass
		11/19	Repeatedly used glass for storage of lye and other bases. Poured acid into plastic container, ruining countertop

Behaviourally Anchored Rating Scales

behaviourally anchored rating scales (BARS)
Evaluation tools that rate employees along a rating scale by means of specific behaviour examples on the scale.

Behaviourally anchored rating scales (**BARS**) attempt to reduce the subjectivity and biases of subjective performance measures. From descriptions of effective and ineffective performance provided by incumbents, peers, and supervisors, job analysts or knowledgeable employees group these examples into performance-related categories such as employee knowledge, customer relations, and the like. Then specific examples of these behaviours are placed along a scale (usually from 1 to 7).

Actual behaviours for a bank branch manager are illustrated on the rating scale shown in Figure 8-6. Since the positions on the scale are described in terms of job-related behaviour, an objective evaluation along the scale is more likely. The form also cites specific behaviours that can be used to provide performance feedback to employees. The BARS are job-related, practical, and standardized for similar jobs. But the rater's personal biases may still cause ratings to be high or low, although the specific behaviours that "anchor" the scale provide some criteria to guide the sincere rater.[23] If the rater collects specific incidents during the rating period, the evaluation is apt to be more accurate and more legally defensible, besides being a more effective counselling tool. One serious limitation of BARS is that they only look at a limited number of performance categories, such as customer relations or human resource management. Also, each of these categories has only a limited number of specific behaviours. Like the critical incident method, most supervisors are reluctant to maintain records of critical incidents during the rating period, which reduces the effectiveness of this approach when it comes time to counsel the employee.

A slightly different, and less common, method is the *Behaviour Observation Scale* (*BOS*). Like BARS, it uses critical incidents, but instead of making a judgment about whether a specific job behaviour is expected to occur, it measures the frequency of the observed behaviours with scales ranging from high to low.

Performance Tests and Observations

With a limited number of jobs, performance appraisal may be based upon a test of knowledge or skills. The test may be of the paper-and-pencil variety or an actual demonstration of skills. The test must be reliable and valid to be useful. For the method to be job-related, observations should be made under circumstances likely to be encountered. Practicality may suffer when the cost of test development is high:

> Pilots of all major airlines are subject to evaluation by airline raters and Transport Canada. Evaluations of flying ability are usually made both in a flight simulator and while being observed during

FIGURE 8-6	Behaviourally Anchored Rating Scale for Bank Branch Manager

Human Resource Management		Bank of Ontario
Outstanding Performance	— 7 —	Can be expected to praise publicly for tasks completed well, and constructively criticizes in private those individuals who have produced less than adequate results.
Good Performance	— 6 —	Can be expected to show great confidence in subordinates, and openly displays this with the result that they develop to meet expectations.
Fairly Good Performance	— 5 —	Can be expected to ensure that human resource management records are kept right up to date, that reports are written on time, and that salary reviews are not overlooked.
Acceptable Performance	— 4 —	Can be expected to admit a personal mistake, thus showing that he or she is human too.
Fairly Poor Performance	— 3 —	Can be expected to make "surprise" performance appraisals of subordinates.
Poor Performance	— 2 —	Can be expected not to support decisions made by a subordinate (makes exceptions to rules).
Extremely Poor Performance	— 1 —	Can be expected not to accept responsibility for errors and to pass blame to subordinates.

an actual flight. The evaluation is based on how well the pilot follows prescribed flight procedures and safety rules. Although this approach is expensive, public safety makes it practical, as well as job-related and standardized.

Comparative Evaluation Methods

comparative evaluation methods
A collection of different methods that compare one person's performance with that of coworkers.

Comparative evaluation methods are a collection of different methods that compare one person's performance with that of coworkers. Usually, comparative evaluations are conducted by the supervisor. They are useful for deciding merit pay increases, promotions, and organizational rewards because they can result in a ranking of employees from best to worst. The most common forms of comparative evaluations are the ranking method and forced distributions. Although these methods are practical and easily standardized, they too are subject to bias and offer little job-related feedback.

Many large companies use an elaborate group evaluation method. This method reduces biases, because multiple raters are used, and some feedback results when managers and professionals learn how they compared with others on each critical factor. However, these comparative results are often not shared with the employee, since the supervisor and the human resource department want to create an atmosphere of cooperation among employees, and to share comparative rankings might lead to internal competition instead of cooperation. Nevertheless, two arguments in favour of comparative approaches merit mention before discussing specific methods:

> Arguments for a comparative approach are simple and powerful. The simple part of it is that organizations do it anyway, all the time. Whenever human resource decisions are made, the performance of the individuals being considered is ranked and compared. People are not promoted because they achieve their objectives, but rather because they achieve their objectives better than others.
>
> The second reason (the powerful one) for using comparative as opposed to noncomparative methods is that they are far more reliable. This is because reliability is controlled by the rating process itself, not by rules, policies, and other external constraints.[24]

Ranking Method

ranking method
A method of evaluating employees that ranks them from best to worst on some trait.

The **ranking method** has the rater place each employee in order from best to worst. All the human resource department knows is that certain employees are better than others. It does not know by how much. The employee ranked second may be almost as good as the one who was first or considerably worse. This method is subject to the halo and recency effects, although rankings by two or more raters can be averaged to help reduce biases. Its advantages include ease of administration and explanation.

Forced Distributions

forced distributions
A method of evaluating employees that requires raters to categorize employees.

Forced distributions require raters to sort employees into different classifications. Usually a certain proportion must be put in each category. Figure 8-7 shows how a rater may classify 10 subordinates. The classification shown in the figure is overall performance (but this method can be used for other performance classifications such as reliability and controlling costs). As with the ranking method, relative differences among employees are unknown, but this method does overcome the biases of central tendency, leniency, and strictness. Some workers and supervisors strongly dislike this method because employees are often rated lower than they or their supervisor/rater think to be correct. However, the human resource department's forced distribution requires some employees to be rated low. A famous example is the "Vitality Curve" used by GE under its legendary CEO Jack ("Neutron Bomb") Welch:

> Jack Welch insisted that all managers categorize their employees into three types: "Top 20," "The Vital 70," and "Bottom 10" and that the latter be fired every year, regardless of actual performance. It is understandable that many managers strongly resisted this demand, but they had no choice. It should be noted that under Jack Welch's reign, GE had over 400,000 employees.[25]

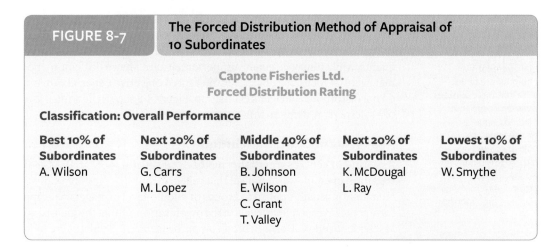

FIGURE 8-7 The Forced Distribution Method of Appraisal of 10 Subordinates

Captone Fisheries Ltd.
Forced Distribution Rating

Classification: Overall Performance

Best 10% of Subordinates	Next 20% of Subordinates	Middle 40% of Subordinates	Next 20% of Subordinates	Lowest 10% of Subordinates
A. Wilson	G. Carrs	B. Johnson	K. McDougal	W. Smythe
	M. Lopez	E. Wilson	L. Ray	
		C. Grant		
		T. Valley		

FUTURE-ORIENTED APPRAISAL METHODS

The use of past-oriented approaches is like driving a car by looking through the rearview mirror: you only know where you have been, not where you are going. Future-oriented appraisals focus on future performance by evaluating employee potential or setting future performance goals. Included here are three techniques used:

1. self-appraisals
2. the management-by-objectives approach
3. the assessment centre technique

Self-Appraisals

Getting employees to conduct a self-appraisal can be a useful evaluation technique if the goal of evaluation is to further self-development. When employees evaluate themselves, defensive behaviour is less likely to occur. Thus, self-improvement is more likely. When self-appraisals are used to determine areas of needed improvement, they can help users set personal goals for future development.

Obviously, self-appraisals can be used with any evaluation approach, past- or future-oriented. But the important dimension of self-appraisals is the employee's involvement and commitment to the improvement process. The process starts with the supervisor telling the employee what is expected. Then the employee gets a worksheet and writes down his or her understanding of the job. Not only does it get the employee involved in forming a self-appraisal of improvement areas, but the completed sheet indicates to the supervisor what he or she needs to do to "eliminate roadblocks to meeting or exceeding job standards."[26]

Management-by-Objectives Approach

management-by-objectives (MBO) approach
Requires an employee and superior to jointly establish performance goals for the future. Employees are subsequently evaluated on how well they have obtained these objectives.

The heart of the **management-by-objectives (MBO) approach** is that each employee and superior jointly establish performance goals for the future.[27] Ideally, these goals are mutually agreed upon and objectively measurable. If both conditions are met, employees are apt to be more motivated to achieve the goal, since they have participated in setting it. Moreover, they can periodically adjust their behaviour to ensure attainment of an objective if they can measure their progress toward the objective. But to adjust their efforts, performance feedback must be available on a regular basis.

When future objectives are set, employees gain the motivational benefit of a specific target to organize and direct their efforts. Objectives also help the employee and supervisor discuss specific developmental needs of the employee. When done correctly, performance discussions focus on the job's objectives and not personality variables. Biases are reduced to the extent that goal attainment can be measured objectively.

Management by objectives articles, information, examples
www.12manage.com/
methods_smart_
management_by_
objectives.html
http://en.wikipedia.org/wiki/
Management_by_objectives
http://managementhelp.org/
plan_dec/mbo/mbo.htm

assessment centres
A standardized form of employee appraisal that relies on several types of evaluation and several raters.

International Congress on Assessment Center Methods Articles, guidelines
www.assessmentcenters.
org/articles.asp

360-degree performance appraisal
Combination of self, peer, supervisor, and subordinate performance evaluation.

In practice, MBO programs have encountered difficulties. Objectives are sometimes too ambitious or too narrow. The result is frustrated employees or overlooked areas of performance. For example, employees may set objectives that are measured by quantity rather than quality, because quality, while it may be equally important, is often more difficult to measure. When employees and managers do focus on subjectively measured objectives, special care is needed to ensure that biases do not distort the manager's evaluation. Figure 8-8 shows the annual assessment of the performance of a salesperson, using an MBO approach.

Assessment Centre Technique

Assessment centres are another method of evaluating potential. Assessment centres are a standardized form of employee appraisal that relies on multiple types of evaluation and multiple raters. The technique is usually applied to groups of middle-level managers who appear to have potential to perform at more responsible levels in the organization. Often, the members of the group first meet at the assessment centre. During a brief stay at the facility, candidates are individually evaluated. The process subjects selected employees to in-depth interviews, psychological tests, personal background histories, peer ratings by other attendees, leaderless group discussions, ratings by psychologists and managers, and simulated work exercises to evaluate potential. The simulated work experiences usually include in-basket exercises, decision-making exercises, computer-based business games, and other job-like opportunities that test the employee in realistic ways.

These activities are usually conducted for a few days at a location physically removed from the job site. During this time, the psychologists and managers who do the rating attempt to estimate the strengths, weaknesses, and potential of each attendee.[28] They then pool their estimates to arrive at some conclusion about each member of the group being assessed.

Some critics question whether the procedures used are objective and job-related, especially as rater biases are possible in forming the subjective opinions of attendees.[29] Nevertheless, assessment centres have gained widespread use, and human resource researchers are finding ways to validate the process.

Interestingly, research indicates that the results of assessment centres are a good prediction of actual on-the-job performance in 75 percent of all cases.[30] Unfortunately, this accurate method is expensive, since it usually requires a separate facility and the time of multiple raters.

Other Developments

The **360-degree performance appraisal**, or "all-around appraisal," is a very popular method of assessment (see Figure 8-3, characteristic 12). There can be little doubt that the combination of self, peer, supervisor, and subordinate evaluation will provide feedback on different aspects of the job, since every contributor probably has a different focus.[31] The trend toward the 360-degree model is also in line with the trend toward a flatter organization, which tends to result in a wider span of control. With fewer managers having to supervise more employees, it becomes more difficult to assess everybody's performance accurately. And there is the trend of today's managers toward teamwork and participative management, which makes the historic approach of one supervisor providing performance feedback look obsolete.[32]

FIGURE 8-8	MBO Evaluation Report for a Salesperson		
Objectives Set	**Period Objective**	**Accomplishments**	**Variance**
1. Number of sales calls	85	98	+15%
2. Number of new customers	10	8	−20%
3. Sales of product xx	2,500	3,100	+24%
4. Sales of product yy	1,500	1,350	−10%
5. Customer complaints	10	22	+120%
6. Number of training courses taken	5	3	−40%
7. Number of monthly reports on time	12	11	−8%

360-degree performance appraisal articles, FAQs
www.360-degreefeedback.com

A caution about 360-degree performance appraisal
www.mansis.com/page1237.htm

Examples of performance appraisal software
www.hr-guide.com/data/209.htm

Example of a competency-based performance appraisals
www.hr.uottawa.ca/appraisal/questions/index.php
www.workitect.com/pdf/PM_Article.pdf
www.umdnj.edu/hrweb/forms/competency_exempt.pdf

Balanced Scorecard
An integrated organizational performance measuring approach, looking at organizational learning and innovation, financial management, internal operations, and customer management.

Balanced Scorecard examples
www.balancedscorecard.org/BSCResources/ExamplesSuccessStories/tabid/57/Default.aspx

Not everybody shares the enthusiasm about the 360-degree approach. It certainly requires a suitable corporate culture.[33]

Performance appraisal software is a new tool many managers probably have been waiting for: developed by experts; adaptable to an organization's needs; easy to use; and with data easily analyzed, stored, and retrieved.[34] Ideally, such a program would be part of an enterprise-wide software system, and even that is already available.[35] It means that all human resource aspects, such as application data, interview guides for selection decisions, computer-based training, performance appraisal, payroll, job evaluation, as well as other organizational functions such as finance, purchasing, distribution, manufacturing, and more, are part of one software package. The development and application of such an integrated software system is often the result of "business process reengineering," a radical rethinking of organizational functions to achieve higher efficiency, quality improvement, and better service.[36]

The advantage of such an integrated system is that everyone in the organization receives the same information. As Turnbull puts it:

> The concept of entering data once, at source, saves time (there is no or very little duplication of data entry) and ensures that data can be treated as a corporate resource, used by any and all who have a need (and have authorized access). Through this horizontal integration of information, issues about whose/which data is correct are avoided, time is saved and the organization as a whole wins.[37]

The disadvantages are that the implementation of such a system is time-consuming, complex, and costly. However, it appears that the savings and higher efficiency make it worthwhile.[38]

Another development is the difficulties associated with the change of paying employees for—and accordingly assessing on—their *competencies* instead of job performance. Historically, it has been the performance standards set in job descriptions that have guided supervisors in their assessment. Now the tendency is to focus more on skill levels than job performance (see discussion on compensation in Chapter 9). As a consequence, employee assessment tends to involve tests rather than supervisor evaluations.

The **Balanced Scorecard** concept has become a very popular performance management approach, combining the performance measures of the total organization instead of relying on independent measures of its parts. The brainchild of Harvard Professor Robert Kaplan and David Norton of Renaissance Solutions (a consulting company), it provides an enterprise view of an organization's overall performance by integrating financial measures with other key performance indicators around customer satisfaction; internal organizational processes; and organizational growth, learning, and innovation.[39] A suitable illustration would be the cockpit of an airplane, with all its instruments and gauges. It would be foolish to rely only on one indicator. The pilot—the CEO—has to take into account all measures to make sure that the plane—the enterprise—gets safely and efficiently to its destination.

Human resources play, of course, a critical part in an organization's performance. HR has direct links to innovation and learning, but it also influences customer satisfaction, quality improvement programs, and other internal processes. One survey found that "people management" made by far the greatest contribution to profitability and productivity compared with "other critical success factors." Factors highly associated with success were employee skills and job design, which promoted autonomy, flexibility, and problem solving.[40] HR will always play a major role in the Balanced Scorecard approach.

Finally, the problem of assessing the performance of contingency employees has to be addressed (for a more detailed discussion on the use of contingency workers, see Chapter 2). Since such employees are hired only for the duration of a project, it makes little sense to sit down with them to develop long-range performance objectives. They also tend to have, by definition, little knowledge of the work culture of the organization, the supervisor's expectations, and their specific job responsibilities and performance standards. It is perhaps easiest to limit their performance assessment to very specific tasks, which have been communicated to them, and to tie rewards to the satisfactory completion of these tasks.

⊙ IMPLICATIONS OF THE APPRAISAL PROCESS

The appraisal system design and its procedures are usually handled by the human resource department. The specific approach is influenced by previous procedures and the purpose of the new appraisal. If the goal is to evaluate past performance to allocate rewards, comparative approaches may be preferred. Similarly, other, past-oriented methods may be best if the appraisal system exists

Critique of the appraisal process
http://performance-
appraisals.org/
Bacalsappraisalarticles/

How to improve the feedback process
http://
performancefeedback.com/
paf.htm

primarily to give employees counselling about their behaviour. Future-oriented appraisals may focus on specific goals, as is the case with MBO techniques. Self-appraisals or assessment centres may seek to uncover a specific weakness or help with internal placement. Regardless of the technique selected by the department, however, the approach must be converted into an ongoing practice among the line managers. Raters are often unfamiliar with the procedures or the forms and have to be taught how to use them properly.

Evaluation systems that involve employees in their design may gain greater acceptance. Human rights legislation supports having employees involved in the design of the appraisal system. Involvement may increase interest and understanding of whatever performance appraisal system the human resource department eventually administers. However, to operate the performance appraisal system may require training for those who serve as raters.

Training Raters

Whether a simple comparative method or a sophisticated assessment centre is used, raters need knowledge of the system and its purpose. Just knowing whether the appraisal is to be used for compensation or placement recommendations may change the rater's evaluation of those being rated.

A major problem is rater understanding and consistency of evaluations. Some human resource departments provide raters with a rater's handbook that describes the employer's approach. Guidelines for conducting the evaluation or for providing ratees with feedback are often included in the handbook. Key terms—such as "shows initiative" or "provides leadership"—may also be defined in the handbook.

Although in the past, rater training has focused on rating errors such as the halo effect, leniency bias, and central tendency, the emphasis has shifted now to the cognitive aspect of the rating process—that is, the ability of raters to make valid judgments on the basis of relatively complex information. One model divides the performance appraisal process into four steps: attention, categorization, recall, and information integration.

Attention

The rater consciously or subconsciously records certain stimuli because they are relevant to a task performed (e.g., the rater is a supervisor and as part of her duty observes an employee performing his job). The more deviant the observed behaviour is from the expected norm, the more strongly the attention-arousing stimuli work. If, for example, the employee does something very wrong, the supervisor is much more likely to pay attention to the observed behaviour than if it were mildly off the mark.

Categorization

This is the process of classifying and storing data. Several studies have shown that human beings have a limited ability to perceive and process information simultaneously, the upper limit being approximately seven items. Categorization helps us to make quick judgments with limited information about something. Stereotyping is one type of categorization that, as we all know, may result in biased conclusions.

Recall

When we have to make a judgment, we try to remember all the relevant information we stored in our memory about the event or person in question. Depending on the strength of an impression we recorded, we will be able to recall some items more easily than others (see the earlier discussion about the recency effect). When supervisors are asked to do a performance appraisal once a year, the probability is low that they recall all the important information about an employee's work. Only if a conscious effort to record such information is made—by writing down critical incidents, for example—will raters be able to do an accurate evaluation.

Information Integration

Once a judgment is called for, such as the annual performance appraisal, the rater tries to recall as much information as possible and to generate an integrated picture of the employee. However, due to the attention-arousing process (only strong stimuli are recorded), the categorization process (limited information is stored), and the recall process (a limited number of events is remembered), the final picture that emerges will be understandably biased.

Several measures can be taken to improve the validity of supervisory ratings:

- use of behaviour-based scales—for example, the use of critical incidents to categorize effective and ineffective job behaviour;
- training in the use of these scales;
- familiarization of raters with performance definitions—for example, what constitutes outstanding performance (with practical examples);
- use of several raters (more eyes see more, and more eyes see different things, resulting in a more balanced judgment);
- use of quantitative criteria whenever possible (measurable results);
- use of job samples for important evaluation decisions—for example, promotions and transfers;
- training of raters to make behaviour sampling a routine part of a supervisor's job to avoid memory-related biases;
- avoidance of trait ratings; and
- creation of positive consequences for both the rater and ratee.

One can easily see that the new focus of rater training makes the job of an instructor in performance appraisal much more difficult. On the other hand, it makes less likely such comments as this, offered by a human resource manager: "Of all the performance appraisal systems I have worked with in 15 years as a supervisor, not one really worked!"[41] Such experiences are as much the result of using invalid criteria as they are the outcome of inadequate rater training.[42]

Once raters are trained, the appraisal process can begin. But the results of the appraisal process do little to improve employee performance unless employees receive feedback on their appraisals. This feedback process is called the *evaluation interview*.

Evaluation Interviews

evaluation interviews
Performance review sessions that give employees feedback about their past performance or future potential.

Evaluation interviews are performance review sessions that give employees feedback about their past performance or future potential. The evaluator may provide this feedback through several approaches: tell and sell, tell and listen, and problem solving. The *tell-and-sell approach* reviews the employee's performance and tries to convince the employee to perform better. It is best used on new employees. The *tell-and-listen* approach allows the employee to explain reasons, excuses, and defensive feelings about performance. It attempts to overcome these reactions by counselling the employee on how to perform better. The *problem-solving approach* identifies problems that are interfering with employee performance. Then through training, coaching, or counselling, efforts are made to remove these deficiencies, often by setting goals for future performance.

Regardless of which approach is used to give employees feedback, the guidelines listed in Figure 8-9 (on page 324) can help make the performance review session more effective. The intent of

SPOTLIGHT ON ETHICS

On Probation

You have recently been hired as a supervisor and accepted a six-month probationary period. You have earned a Certificate in Human Resource Management from a well-known university. Your arrival coincides with performance appraisal time in the company. You quickly realize that the currently used appraisal instrument is of little value, because it consists mainly of subjective measures. The appraisal instrument is the brainchild of the CEO, who is very proud of "his baby," as he explained when he hired you. One of the tasks given to you is the training of supervisors in assessing performance. You know that any training with this instrument is a waste of time, but if you criticize it, there is a danger that you will not survive the probationary period. What will you do?

FIGURE 8-9	Guidelines for Effective Performance Evaluation Interviews

1. *Emphasize* positive aspects of employee performance.

2. *Tell* each employee that the evaluation session is to improve performance, not to discipline.

3. *Conduct* the performance review session in private with minimum interruptions.

4. *Review* performance formally at least annually and more frequently for new employees or those who are performing poorly.

5. *Make* criticisms specific, not general and vague.

6. *Focus* criticisms on performance, not on personality characteristics.

7. *Stay* calm and do not argue with the person being evaluated.

8. *Identify* specific actions the employee can take to improve performance.

9. *Emphasize* the evaluator's willingness to assist the employee's efforts and to improve performance.

10. *End* the evaluation session by stressing the positive aspects of the employee's performance and reviewing plans to improve performance.

these suggestions is to make the interview a positive, performance-improving dialogue. By stressing desirable aspects of employee performance, the evaluator can give the employee renewed confidence in his or her ability to perform satisfactorily. This positive approach also enables the employee to keep desirable and undesirable performance in perspective, because it prevents the individual from feeling that performance review sessions are entirely negative. When negative comments are made, they focus on work performance and not the individual's personality. Specific, rather than general and vague, examples of the employee's shortcomings are used, so that the individual knows exactly what behaviours need to be changed. The review session concludes by focusing on actions that the employee can take to improve areas of poor performance. In that concluding discussion, the evaluator usually offers to provide whatever assistance the employee needs to overcome the deficiencies discussed.

 1, 2, & 3

Human Resource Management Feedback

The performance appraisal process also provides insight into the effectiveness of the human resource management function. If the appraisal process indicates that poor performance is widespread, many employees are excluded from internal placement decisions. They will not be promoted or transferred. In fact, they may be excluded from the organization through termination.

Unacceptably high numbers of poor performers may indicate errors elsewhere in the human resource management function. For example, human resource development may be failing to fulfill career plans because the people who are hired during the selection process are screened poorly. Or the human resource plan may be in error because the job analysis information is wrong or the employment equity plan seeks the wrong objectives. Likewise, the human resource department may be failing to respond to the challenges of the external environment or effective job design. Sometimes, the human resource function is pursuing the wrong objectives. Or the appraisal system itself may be faulty because of management resistance, incorrect performance standards or measures, or a lack of constructive feedback.

Finally, a future-oriented performance appraisal allows the human resource department to provide feedback to employees as to the status of their career progression. If an employee's performance is inadequate, the cause has to be investigated. If it is a lack of skill or experience, the necessary improvements have to be made part of the goals discussed with the employee. Ideally, a step-by-step plan will be the outcome of the interview process.

SUMMARY

Performance management is an ongoing process, which integrates an organization's vision with performance objectives and performance measurements. It requires a well-developed communication system that provides feedback to managers and employees, a training program that corrects deficiencies, and appropriate rewards for motivation purposes (discussed in the following chapter).

Performance appraisal is a critical part of a performance management system. Its goal is to provide an accurate picture of past and/or future employee performance. To do this, performance standards are established. Standards are based on job-related criteria that best determine successful job performance. Where possible, actual performance is then measured directly and objectively. From a wide variety of appraisal techniques, human resource specialists elect those methods that most effectively measure employee performance against the previously set standards. Techniques can be selected both to review past performance and to anticipate performance in the future.

The appraisal process is usually designed by the human resource department, often with little consultation from other parts of the organization. When it is time to implement a new appraisal approach, those who do the rating usually have little idea about the appraisal process or its objectives. To overcome this shortcoming, the department may design and deliver appraisal workshops to train managers.

A necessary requirement of the appraisal process is employee feedback through an evaluation interview. The interviewer tries to balance positive areas of performance and those areas where performance is deficient, so that the employee receives a realistic view of performance. Perhaps the most significant challenge raised by performance appraisals is the feedback they provide about human resource department performance. Human resource specialists need to be keenly aware that poor performance, especially when it is widespread, may reflect problems with previous human resource management activities that are malfunctioning.

TERMS FOR REVIEW

360-degree performance appraisal **p. 320**
assessment centres **p. 320**
Balanced Scorecard **p. 321**
behaviourally anchored rating scales (BARS) **p. 317**
comparative evaluation methods **p. 318**
critical incident method **p. 316**
error of central tendency **p. 310**

evaluation interviews **p. 323**
forced distributions **p. 318**
halo effect **p. 310**
leniency bias **p. 311**
management-by-objectives (MBO) approach **p. 319**
noncomparative evaluation methods **p. 315**
performance appraisal **p. 304**

performance management **p. 304**
performance measures **p. 309**
performance standards **p. 309**
ranking method **p. 318**
rating scale **p. 315**
recency effect **p. 311**
strictness bias **p. 311**

SELF-ASSESSMENT EXERCISE

Performance Appraisal as a Crucial Management Skill

1. Performance appraisal includes assessing managerial attitudes.   **T   F**

2. One application of performance appraisals is to discipline employees   **T   F**

3. One of the key elements of a performance appraisal system is a training needs analysis.   **T   F**

4. Effective performance standards are determined through a survey in ensure employee input.   **T   F**

5. The halo effect occurs when raters are too easy on employees in evaluating their performance.   **T   F**

6. The reliability of a performance appraisal instrument is the most crucial characteristic.   **T   F**

7. Because of potential personal biases, performance appraisal results cannot be used in courts.   **T   F**

8. A weighted checklist weighs the performance evaluation made by a department head higher than that of a direct supervisor.   **T   F**

9. The critical incident method uses employee self-reports of critical events they experience on the job.   **T   F**

10. Self-appraisal is the preferred performance appraisal method for executives.   **T   F**

SCORING

Of course, you realized that all of the above statements are false. If not, it is advisable to reread the sections where the mistake originated.

REVIEW AND DISCUSSION QUESTIONS

1. Discuss the differences between performance management and performance appraisal.

2. Explain why Wal-Mart is a good example of effective performance management. What did management do to make it one of the most efficient and profitable companies in the world?

3. Why is the dashboard example a useful illustration of performance management?

4. What are the uses of performance appraisals?

5. Suppose that a company for which you work uses a rating scale. The items on the scale are generally personality characteristics. What criticisms would you have of this method?

6. If you were asked to recommend a replacement for the rating scale, what actions would you take before selecting another appraisal technique?

7. Why are direct and objective measures of performance usually considered superior to indirect and subjective measures?

8. If your organization were to use subjective measures to evaluate employee performance, what instructions would you give evaluators about the biases they may encounter?

9. Describe how you would conduct a typical performance evaluation interview.

10. How do the results of performance appraisals affect other human resource management activities?

11. Describe the characteristics of a 360-degree performance appraisal.

12. In what ways is the Balanced Scorecard approach a useful performance appraisal instrument?

13. What is the relationship between a performance appraisal system and a selection system?

14. Explain the legal aspect of a performance appraisal system. Under what circumstances could it become a crucial document?

CRITICAL THINKING QUESTIONS

1. If the dean of your faculty asked you to serve on a committee to develop a performance appraisal system for evaluating the faculty, what performance criteria would you identify? Of these criteria, which ones do you think are most likely to determine the faculty members' success at your school? What standards would you recommend to the dean, regardless of the specific evaluation instrument selected?

2. Your organization has dismissed an employee for not performing up to par. She sues the company for unjust dismissal, claiming that the company's performance appraisal instrument is not a valid assessment tool, since no woman had served on the committee responsible for developing it. Are you able to persuade a judge that, despite the fact that no woman served on the committee, your appraisal instrument is a valid one?

3. Can one performance appraisal instrument be used for all levels in an organization—that is, executives, middle managers, and employees? Why or why not?

ETHICS QUESTION

You are a plant manager, and one of your supervisors is a good friend of yours, the friendship going back to your high school years. His normally average performance has been deteriorating over the last two years, mainly because of his sick wife, a situation that causes him to miss many working days. He also has five children. You know that money is a big issue for him, and if you give him above-average performance ratings he would receive significant bonuses.

Discuss the ethical issues involved.

WEB RESEARCH EXERCISE

Help Tips for Performance Appraisal

http://iso9k1.home.att.net/pa/performance_appraisal.html#how

Dexter Hansen describes how traditional performance appraisals can hurt quality and teamwork. What suggestions do you have to avoid this outcome?

360-Degree Performance Appraisal

www.mansis.com/page1237.htm
http://performance-appraisals.org/appraisal-library/360_Degree_Feedback

What are the strengths and weaknesses of a 360-degree performance appraisal? Would you be comfortable using it if you were a manager? Why or why not?

Matthew Effect

www.performance-appraisal.com/bias.htm
What is the Matthew Effect in performance appraisals? Where does the name come from? Can it be avoided? How?

"Ten Stupid Things Managers Do to Screw Up Performance Appraisals"

www.work911.com/performance/particles/stupman.htm
Are the ten "stupid" things some managers do based on research, or do they represent the personal opinion of the author? How valid are they? If they are valid, are there remedies?

"Seven Stupid Things Human Resource Departments Do to Screw Up Performance Appraisals"

www.work911.com/performance/particles/stuphr.htm
In what way are these seven "stupid" things different from the ten "stupid" things managers do (see above)? Who would initiate remedies?

About.com

http://humanresources.about.com/od/performanceman agement
Tips about many topics, one of which is on performance management.

⊙ INCIDENT 8-1

The Malfunctioning Regional Human Resource Department

For one month, the corporate human resource department of Universal Insurance Ltd. had two specialists review the operations of their regional human resource department in Vancouver. The review of the regional office centred on the department's human resource information base. A brief summary of their findings listed the following observations:

- Each employee's performance appraisal showed little change from the previous year. Poor performers rated poor year in and year out.

- Nearly 70 percent of the appraisals were not initialled by the employee even though company policy required employees to do so after they had discussed their review with the rater.

- Of those employees who initialled the evaluations, several commented that the work standards were irrelevant and unfair.

- A survey of past employees conducted by corporate office specialists revealed that 35 percent of them believed performance feedback was too infrequent.

- Another 30 percent complained about the lack of advancement opportunities because most openings were filled from outside, and no one ever told these workers they were unpromotable.

The corporate and regional human resource directors were dismayed by the findings. Each thought the problems facing the regional office were different.

1. What do you think is the major problem with the performance appraisal process in the regional office?

2. What problems do you think exist with the regional office's (a) job analysis information, (b) human resource planning, (c) training and development, and (d) career planning?

⊙ EXERCISE 8-1

Developing a Performance Appraisal System

Time: 1 hour. Form groups of five to six. Assume that your group is the Faculty Evaluation Committee assigned the task to assess the performance of the course instructor.

1. Define at least three performance criteria for the instructor.

2. How would you measure them so that the results would be useful for a tenure and promotion decision?

3. Which type of instrument or method do you suggest? Why?

4. Who should be the appraisers?

5. Time permitting, compare the results in your group with those of another group.

CASE STUDY 🍁 Maple Leaf Shoes Ltd.

Performance Appraisal Issues

Maple Leaf Shoes Ltd. is a medium-sized manufacturer of leather and vinyl shoes located in Wilmington, Ontario. It was started in 1973, and currently employs about 500 persons in its Wilmington plant and some 200 more in offices and warehouses throughout Ontario.

It is time for the annual performance appraisal, the "ritual" as some managers call it. They have received the appraisal forms sent by the personnel department one week prior to the deadline. The current system was developed by John McAllister, the previous personnel manager, who recently left the company for a similar job in Toronto. McAllister believes that performance appraisal forms should be simple to understand and easy to complete, so he has made one up himself (see Table 1).

TABLE 1	Performance Evaluation Form of Maple Leaf Shoes Ltd.

Performance Evaluation

Supervisors: Please complete this form for each of your employees. Evaluate each performance aspect separately. Return this form by September 1.

	5	4	3	2	1	Score
Quantity of work	Excellent	Good	Average	Fair	Poor	
Quality of work	Excellent	Good	Average	Fair	Poor	
Dependability at work	Excellent	Good	Average	Fair	Poor	
Initiative at work	Excellent	Good	Average	Fair	Poor	
Cooperativeness	Excellent	Good	Average	Fair	Poor	
Communication	Excellent	Good	Average	Fair	Poor	
Energy and enthusiasm	Excellent	Good	Average	Fair	Poor	
Getting along with coworkers	Excellent	Good	Average	Fair	Poor	
					Total	_____

Supervisor's signature _____

Employee's name _____

Employee number _____

Supervisors have to assess each employee by August 31. The assessment is supposed to be discussed with the employee and then returned to the personnel department for filing in the employee's personnel records. If promotions come up, the cumulative ratings are to be considered at that time. The ratings are also supposed to be used as a check when raises are given.

Jane Reynolds, special assistant in the personnel department at Maple Leaf Shoes, looks at the pile of completed rating forms in front of her and shakes her head. She dislikes the way performance evaluation in this company is conducted, and would have preferred to come up with a new approach. However, Robert Clark, the company president, has so far resisted any change and she feels hesitant to tell him what she thinks of it.

A month ago, Reynolds conducted an informal survey to find out how managers and employees felt about the current system. The results confirmed her hunch. Over 60 percent of the managers and more than 75 percent of the employees felt either indifferent or negative about the assessment system. Close to 50 percent of the supervisors filled out the forms in three minutes or less and returned the form to personnel without discussing the results with their staff. Another 40 percent spent some time with the employees for feedback, but without much discussion. Only 10 percent tried to do an effective performance feedback job by giving each employee detailed feedback and setting new objectives.

Reynolds knows from her experience at the company that the forms were rarely retrieved for promotion or pay-raise analyses by her previous boss, McAllister. Because of this, most supervisors may feel the evaluation program is a useless ritual.

The company has never offered any training for its supervisors on how to conduct performance reviews.

Then she thinks of Tim Lance, the consultant. Once, Clark had hired Lance to "look into the present and future role of Maple Leaf Shoes personnel department and suggest appropriate action plans to improve its contribution to the organization and help the company meet its future challenges." In his final report, Lance had made a number of recommendations, but Clark had put off any change until a new personnel manager was hired.

Reynolds remembers that, among other items, the consultant recommended a new approach to appraising employee performance. She feels that this gives her a good reason to push for a revision of the current system. Time is a big issue. She has to prepare for contract negotiations with two separate unions next month. Two more are coming up a month later. She is confident that Clark will accept her recommendation to hire Lance again to come up with a new performance appraisal system.

Discussion Questions

1. You are Tim Lance. Write an assessment of Maple Leaf Shoes' performance evaluation system.

2. What changes would you recommend to the company? Why?

● CASE STUDY CPIB Canadian Pacific and International Bank

Part I

The results were in and Mary Keddy, senior vice-president of human resources, was quite pleased. She was looking at the latest employee attitude survey. The vast majority of the bank's employees felt that the CPIB was a good place to work (which, of course, was borne out by a very low turnover rate, 2 percent lower than that of other banks). Satisfaction with supervision, as measured by the JDI,* was also high, a score of 46 out of 54. The last survey two years ago had a score of 38, so this was a significant improvement. She was also intrigued by the results of the measurement on the quality of communication between supervisors and employees, which was seen as close to excellent, 4.6 on a 5-point scale. That was really good news. Perhaps it was time to think of implementing a pet idea of hers: a 360-degree performance appraisal system. She had toyed with it for several years, but she had felt that the time was not right. But the current survey results were very encouraging. She knew that it was a somewhat daring undertaking, given the high risk of failure, but on the other hand, if it worked the positive outcomes would be significant.

She remembered the attempt to introduce an "all round" feedback system by her previous employer, a large steel company in Ontario, an attempt that had failed miserably. It had been the idea of a quite progressive CEO, but only a handful of middle managers had supported the idea, while a majority of the managers feared that the approach would lead to backstabbing and would be seen by many employees as an opportunity to "get back" at their supervisors.

Given that experience, she wanted to make sure her own attempt at the bank would succeed, since she knew a failure would hurt her career. She felt confident that she had the full support of the CEO and her VP colleagues. She was less confident about the willingness of the bank's middle managers to embrace such a new approach. Being evaluated by subordinates, colleagues, and customers—in addition to the direct supervisor, of course—required a strong degree of self-confidence and significant trust in colleagues and subordinates. The result of the employee survey seemed to indicate that the trust was there. How about self-confidence? She was not so sure about that part. She certainly had to take this into account in her plan.

She thought it was interesting that she had greater confidence in the employees' acceptance of the new approach. When she had taken her plan for greater diversity to the employees three years ago, she had been pleasantly surprised about the positive reception the plan had received. Of course, she had carefully planned the introduction through staff meetings and training sessions. She had to come up with something similar now.

Discussion Questions

If you were in Mary Keddy's position, what would you do? Outline a step-by-step plan for the introduction and implementation of a 360-degree performance evaluation system. Include in your plan measures to overcome the anticipated resistance by middle managers.

Part II

There was another issue relating to performance appraisal Mary Keddy had to deal with. In a recent decision, an arbitrator had ruled to reinstate an employee who had been dismissed for inadequate performance. His ruling was somewhat of an embarrassment for the bank, because the arbitrator had argued that the two performance evaluations given the employee over the two years of her employment had rated her performance as below standard, but promising. There was nothing in the written assessment that indicated serious

---

*The Job Descriptive Index (JDI), undoubtedly the best-validated measure of job satisfaction. It includes five measures of satisfaction with nature of work, supervision, peers, advancement opportunities, and pay. It is copyrighted by, and available from, the Psychology Department of Bowling Green University, Bowling Green, OH.

shortcomings. The supervisor had argued she had given the employee several verbal warnings after repeated mistakes, but had not recorded it because she had not wanted to put a blemish on the employee's personnel record. However, after another, more serious mistake, she had decided enough was enough and let the employee go. The union grieved on behalf of the employee, and the case went to arbitration with the above result. Michael Bennett, the CEO, had asked Mary to make sure that such a case did not happen again.

Discussion Questions

How can the bank develop a system that will be legally fool-proof?

⬤ PART ENDING VIDEOS

"Southwest Airlines"

"HotJobs.com"

Go to **www.mcgrawhillconnect.ca** to access the videos.

⬤ ROLE-PLAY 4: Providing Performance Feedback

Time required: 30–40 minutes

Objectives of the Role-Play

1. To give students some experience in providing feedback, which for many supervisors is an unpleasant task. But it can be an effective motivating tool if done properly.

2. To provide an opportunity to improve oral communication skills, since peers and the instructor will give feedback.

Prior Preparation

1. Study Chapter 8.

2. Read role-play instructions.

Guidelines for Conducting the Role-Play

The performance feedback meeting involves Carl Monahan, Production Manager at Maple Leaf Shoes, and Al Sweeny, Supervisor of the Finishing Operation.

1. Two students play the roles of Carl Monahan and Al Sweeny.

2. Each student reads his or her role description.

3. The instructor signals the beginning and end of the meeting. The meeting should last about 30 minutes. It may end earlier.

4. The remainder of the class time is used for discussion of the behaviours during the role-play and outcomes.

5. Observers are asked to make notes against the questions listed below and discuss their findings at the end of the role-play.

6. The instructor discusses the strong and weak points during the interview.

Instructions for Observers

Please read the questions below and write down your observations. Pay particular attention to the verbal and nonverbal communication between Carl and Al.

Observe the manner in which Carl begins the interview.

1. What, if anything, does Carl do to create a cordial atmosphere?

2. Does Carl state the purpose of the interview early in the session?

3. Is the purpose of the interview stated clearly and concisely?

Observe how the interview is conducted.

1. To what extent does Carl learn how Al feels about his job in general?
2. Does Carl use broad, general questions at the outset?
3. Does Carl criticize Al?
4. Does Carl praise Al?
5. Does Carl accept Al's feelings and ideas?
6. Who talked most?

Observe and evaluate the outcome of the interview.

1. To what extent did Carl arrive at a fairer and more accurate evaluation of Al as a result of the interview?
2. What things did Carl do, if any, to motivate Al to improve?
3. Were relations better or worse after the interview? If worse, why?
4. How might Carl have done a better job?

PART 5

Motivating and Rewarding Human Resources

Employees have to be compensated for their performance fairly and equitably. The human resource department assists managers in assessing the value of a job and determining an appropriate salary, and it will administer the proper benefits. It is also one of the responsibilities of a human resource manager to create a motivating job environment.

Each of these topics is discussed in Part 5. They are important management tools for human resource specialists and managers alike. Regardless of your job, you will find that these tools are helpful ways to ensure effective performance.

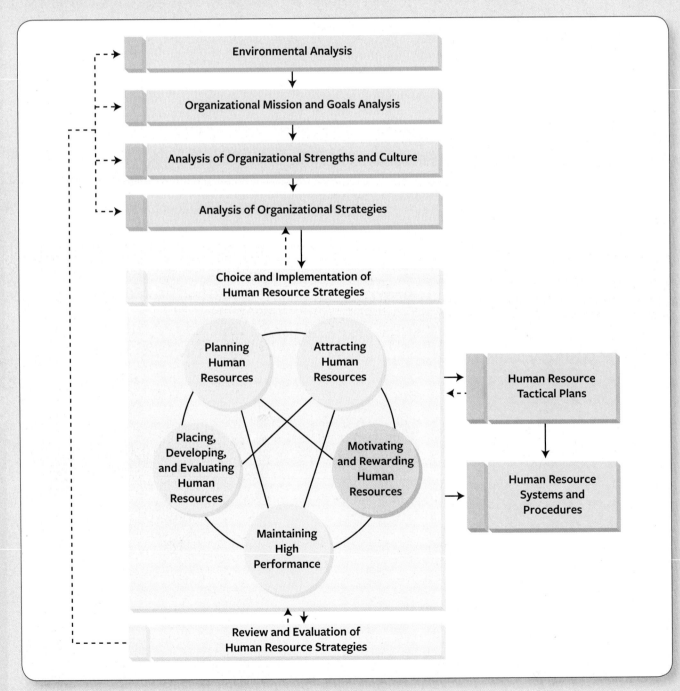

Compensation Management

Management's challenge is to create an environment which stimulates people in their jobs and fosters company growth, and a key aspect of the environment is compensation.

Lance A. Berger and Dorothy R. Berger[1]

Genuine and lasting employee motivation is not something management does, but rather a process that management fosters and allows to happen.

Michael Kavanagh[2]

CHAPTER OBJECTIVES

After studying this chapter, you should be able to:

➡ *Explain* the objectives of effective compensation management.

➡ *Discuss* the consequences of mismanaged compensation programs.

➡ *Describe* how wages and salaries are determined.

➡ *Identify* the major issues that influence compensation management.

➡ *Explain* the differences between "equal pay for equal work" and "equal pay for work of equal value."

➡ *Evaluate* the advantages and disadvantages of incentive systems.

➡ *Explain* the major approaches to group incentive plans.

➡ *Define* total compensation.

➡ *Describe* pay and organizational strategy.

CHAPTER 9

One way the human resource department improves employee performance, motivation, and satisfaction is through the development, implementation, and administration of compensation systems, which tie rewards to the achievement of company objectives. Compensation is the cash and non-cash rewards employees receive in exchange for their work. When the system is properly administered, employees are more likely to be satisfied and motivated to contribute to the achievement of organizational objectives. But when employees perceive their compensation to be inappropriate, performance, motivation, and satisfaction may decline dramatically. The following dialogue is an example of how not to administer pay policy:

> Joan Swensen walked into Al Jorgeson's office, slammed down her clipboard, and said, "I quit!"
>
> "What's the matter, Joan?" Al questioned. "You've been here two years, and I've never seen you so mad."
>
> "That's just the problem. I've been here two years, and this morning I found out that the new man you hired last week, Kurt, is making the same pay that I am," Joan said.
>
> "Well, he does the same work, he works the same hours, and he has the same responsibilities. Would it be fair to pay him less?" Al asked.
>
> "Doesn't experience count for anything around here? When you brought him into the shop, you told me to show him the ropes. So not only did I have more experience, but I am also responsible for training him," Joan responded.
>
> "Okay, okay, I'll talk with Human Resources this afternoon and see if I can get you a raise," Al conceded.
>
> "Don't bother. I'm quitting," Joan asserted, still fuming. "If this company doesn't want to do what is right voluntarily, I'd rather work someplace else."

Compensation programs help to maintain an organization's human resources. When wages and salaries are not administered properly, the firm may lose employees and the money spent to recruit, select, train, and develop them. Even if workers do not quit, as Joan did, they may become dissatisfied with the company.

Dissatisfaction arises because employee needs are affected by *absolute* and *relative* levels of pay. When the total, or absolute, amount of pay is too low, employees cannot meet their physiological or security needs. In industrial societies, the absolute level of pay usually is high enough to meet these basic needs, at least minimally. A more common source of dissatisfaction centres on relative pay, which is an employee's pay compared with that of other workers. For example, Joan's concern was over the relative amount of her salary in comparison with the new, less experienced employee, Kurt. Her additional experience and training responsibilities were not reflected in her pay as compared with Kurt's pay. She felt that her esteem needs were affected, because she did not get the recognition she thought she deserved.

Because compensation affects the organization and its employees, this chapter examines the requirements for an effective compensation system. The chapter also discusses the objectives and procedures used to administer compensation. It concludes with a review of financial incentives.

OBJECTIVES OF COMPENSATION ADMINISTRATION

McGill University, staff handbook
Example of a salary administration policy
www.mcgill.ca/
adminhandbook/
personnel/salary

The administration of compensation must meet numerous objectives. Sometimes, the ones listed in Figure 9-1 conflict with each other and tradeoffs must be made. For example, to retain employees and ensure equity, wage and salary analysts pay similar amounts for jobs of similar value. But a recruiter may want to offer an unusually high salary to attract a qualified recruit. At this point, the hiring manager (the manager of the line department) must make a trade off between the recruiting objectives and the internal equity objectives, with the guidance of the human resource department.

Other objectives of compensation are to reward desired behaviour and to control costs. These objectives can conflict, too. For example, a department manager might want to reward outstanding performance with a raise, but every raise adds to costs. Here again, the human resource manager must decide between two conflicting goals.

Regardless of the tradeoffs, an overriding objective is to maintain legal compliance. For example, the *Canada Labour Code* requires employers to pay minimum wages and time-and-a-half for overtime. Periodically, federal and provincial governments raise minimum wages, and employers must comply regardless of other objectives being sought.

FIGURE 9-1	Objectives Sought Through Effective Compensation Administration

- *Acquire qualified personnel.* Compensation needs to be high enough to attract applicants. Since companies compete in the labour market, pay levels must respond to the supply and demand of workers. But sometimes a premium wage rate is needed to attract applicants who are already employed in other firms.

- *Retain present employees.* When compensation levels are not competitive, some employees quit. To prevent employee turnover, pay must be kept competitive with that of other employers.

- *Ensure equity.* The administration of wages and salaries strives for internal and external equity. Internal equity requires that pay be related to the relative worth of jobs. That is, jobs of similar value get similar pay. External equity involves paying workers at a rate perceived to be fair compared to what the market pays. Internal equity, also called internal consistency, refers to comparisons among jobs or skills levels inside a single organization. The focus is on comparing jobs and skills in terms of their relative contributions to the organization's objectives.

- *Reward desired behaviour.* Pay should reinforce desired behaviours. Good performance, experience, loyalty, new responsibilities, and other behaviours can be rewarded through an effective compensation plan.

- *Control costs.* A rational compensation program helps an organization to obtain and retain its workforce at a reasonable cost. Without a systematic wage and salary structure, the organization might overpay or underpay its employees.

- *Comply with legal regulations.* As with other aspects of human resource management, wage and salary administration faces legal constraints. A sound pay program considers these constraints and ensures compliance with all government regulations that affect employee compensation.

- *Further administrative efficiency.* In pursuing the other objectives of effective compensation management, wage and salary specialists try to design the program so that it can be efficiently administered. Administrative efficiency, however, should be a secondary consideration compared with other objectives.

Examples of job evaluations and forms
www.hr-guide.com/
jobevaluation.htm

Compensation objectives are not rules—they are guidelines. But the less these guidelines are violated, the more effective wage and salary administration can be. To meet these objectives, compensation specialists evaluate every job, conduct wage and salary surveys, and price each job. Through these steps, the appropriate pay level for each job is determined. Figure 9-2 (on page 336) depicts the three major phases of compensation management that take place after the initial job analysis phase. Each phase is discussed in the following sections. Finally, the compensation system has to be part of the overall organizational strategy. The implications are discussed later in this chapter.

JOB EVALUATION

RPC 5

job evaluation
Systematic process of assessing job content and ranking jobs according to a consistent set of job characteristics and worker traits.

Job evaluations are systematic procedures to determine the relative worth or value of jobs. Although evaluations take several different approaches, each one considers the duties, responsibilities, and working conditions of the job. The purpose of job evaluation is to identify which jobs should be paid more than others. Because the process of evaluation is subjective, it is conducted by a group of subject-matter experts. This job evaluation committee is usually made up of compensation specialists and representatives of line management responsible for the job(s) being evaluated.[3] They begin with a review of job analysis information to learn about the duties, responsibilities, and working conditions that shape their evaluation. With this knowledge, the relative worth of jobs is determined by selecting a job evaluation method. Before the enactment of pay equity legislation, there were a number of job evaluation methods, such as job ranking, job grading, and the point system. Now the point system is, by far, the most commonly used evaluation method as it provides, relatively, the best

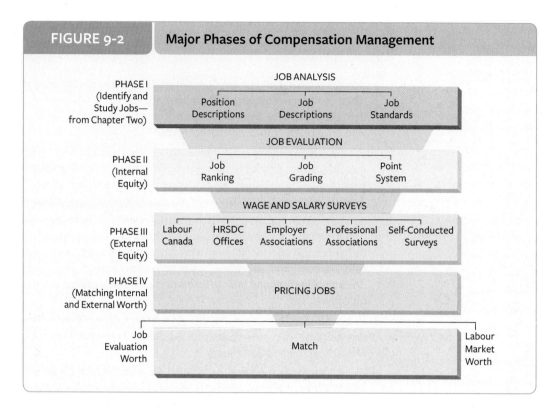

FIGURE 9-2 — Major Phases of Compensation Management

information regarding job values.[4] For comparison purposes, we provide brief descriptions of some of the other evaluation methods, but we focus on the point system.

Job Ranking

job ranking
A form of job evaluation in which jobs are ranked subjectively according to their overall worth to the organization.

The simplest and least precise method of job evaluation is **job ranking**. Specialists review the job analysis information for each job. Then each job is ranked subjectively according to its importance in comparison with other jobs. These are overall rankings, although raters may consider the responsibility, skill, effort, and working conditions of each job. It is quite possible that important elements of some jobs may be overlooked while unimportant items are weighted too heavily. What is even more damaging, these rankings do not differentiate the relative importance of jobs. For example, the job of janitor might be ranked as 1, the secretary's job might get a 2, and the office manager might rank as a 3. But the secretarial position might be three times as important as the janitorial job and half as important as the job of office manager. The job ranking approach does not allow for these relative differences between jobs. Pay scales based on these broad rankings ensure that more important jobs are paid more. But since the rankings lack precision, the resulting pay levels may be inaccurate.

Job Grading

job grading
A form of job evaluation that assigns jobs to predetermined job classifications according to their relative worth to the organization.

Job grading, or job classification, is a slightly more sophisticated method than job ranking, but it too is not very precise. It works by assigning each job a grade, as explained in Figure 9-3. The standard description in the figure that most nearly matches the job description determines the grade of the job. Once again, more important jobs are paid more. But the lack of precision can lead to inaccurate pay levels. The largest user of this approach has been the Canadian Public Service Commission, which is gradually replacing this approach with more sophisticated methods.

Point System

point system
A form of job evaluation that assesses the relative importance of the job's key factors in order to arrive at the relative worth of jobs.

As mentioned before, research shows that the **point system** is used more than any other evaluation method. It evaluates the critical—also called compensable—factors of each job, determines different levels or degrees for each factor, and allocates points to each level. Although it is more difficult to develop initially, it is more precise than other methods because it can handle critical factors in more detail. It is usually done by a job evaluation committee or an individual analyst. In most cases, organizations use a system that has predetermined job factors and assigned points to each factor. This system requires six steps to implement. It is very rare that a company develops a system from scratch.

FIGURE 9-3	A Job Classification Schedule for Use with the Job Grading Method

Empire Machine Shop
Job Classification Schedule

Directions: To determine appropriate job grade, match standard description with job description.

Job Grade	Standard Description
I	Work is simple and highly repetitive, done under close supervision, requiring minimal training and little responsibility or initiative.
	Examples: Janitor, file clerk
II	Work is simple and repetitive, done under close supervision, requiring some training or skill. Employee is expected to assume responsibility or exhibit initiative only rarely.
	Examples: Administrative assistant I, machine cleaner
III	Work is simple, with little variation, done under general supervision. Training or skill required. Employee has minimum responsibilities and must take some initiative to perform satisfactorily.
	Examples: Parts expediter, machine oiler, administrative assistant II
IV	Work is moderately complex, with some variation, done under general supervision. High level of skill required. Employee is responsible for equipment or safety; regularly exhibits initiative.
	Examples: Machine operator I, tool-and-die apprentice
V	Work is complex, varied, done under general supervision. Advanced skill level required. Employee is responsible for equipment and safety; shows high degree of initiative.
	Examples: Machine operator II, tool-and-die specialist

Step 1 : Determine Compensable Factors

Figure 9-4 shows how the factor of responsibility can be broken down into the following components:

- safety of others
- equipment and materials
- assisting trainees
- product/service quality

Step 2 : Determine Levels (or Degrees) of Factors

Because the extent of responsibility, or other factors, may vary from job to job, the point system creates several levels (or degrees) associated with each factor. Figure 9-4 shows four levels, although more or fewer may be used. These levels help analysts to reward different degrees of responsibility, skills, and other critical factors.

Step 3 : Allocate Points to Subfactors

With the factors listed down one side and the levels placed across the top of Figure 9-4, the result is a point system matrix. Points are then assigned to each subfactor to reflect the relative importance of different subfactors. Analysts start with Level IV and weight each subfactor with the number of points they think it deserves. This allocation allows them to give very precise weights to each element of the job. For example, if assisting trainees is twice as important as product/service quality, it is assigned twice as many points, 80 versus 40.

SPOTLIGHT ON HRM

Profit Sharing Plans Help Keep Great Workers

By Larry Ginsberg

Successful entrepreneurs understand that their prosperity depends upon hiring and retaining great employees. One of the key concerns for workers is their compensation package. Compensation will usually include a base salary, commissions (if the position is related to sales or marketing), benefits, employee profit sharing plans, and, if appropriate, stock option plans. To build and keep a winning team, you must determine an appropriate compensation package. Here's what to consider:

Base Salary and Benefits

Your industry association will have information regarding the common base salary and benefits for your business. Confirm this information by talking to your peers. Another significant source is executive search consultants that specialize in your industry. The main advantages of using these consultants from time to time are they are professionally obliged not to steal your employees to fill other positions and they have a great deal of information about your industry.

As a general rule, you should pay somewhere in the third quartile (about 75 percent) of the range for a particular position. For example, if the range is $28,000 to $40,000, your starting salary should be about $37,000. If you pay in the low part of the range, it is easy for new employees to move on to a competitor for much more money—after you have invested the time and effort to train them. Similarly, your benefits package should be at least comparable to the norm for the industry.

If a commission is paid to an employee, as opposed to salary, the employee may be able to claim certain tax-deductible expenses that are allowed as an employee.

Employee Profit Sharing Plans

There are basically two types of employee profit sharing plans. The first is an annual bonus that is generally based upon overall company profit and/or tied to specific items, such as sales, that an employee can influence. A bonus can be set up as a liability in your company books at your fiscal year-end. For the bonus to be tax-deductible to the firm in the fiscal year, Canada Customs and Revenue Agency requires you to pay it within 180 days from your year-end.

The second type of plan is a trust that is set up to allow an employer to share profit from the business with some or all employees. This trust is called an *Employees' Profit Sharing Plan,* or *EPSP*. An EPSP allows an employer to deduct in the current fiscal year all monies paid to the trust within 120 days of the fiscal year-end. Employer contributions are determined using a formula that is tied to the company's profit.

Funds contributed are allocated among employees who are members of the plan. In addition, money earned by the trust and any capital gains or losses of the trust are allocated to the employees, who are taxed on these amounts.

The plan can be established to vest the benefits over time. This helps guarantee employee loyalty, as the funds are not available until they have been vested by the terms of the plan. For example, if the current-year profit allocation is set up to vest 50 percent in the second year and 50 percent in the third year from the date of the contribution, employees who choose to leave after one year receive no money. They only get a credit on their personal tax return for the tax paid on amounts not received. This plan is ideal to help knowledge-based companies retain their vital assets: employees.

The major advantages of an EPSP are that a company receives a current-year deduction but only needs to make the payment within 120 days, that employees who leave voluntarily lose the opportunity to participate in the plan, that funds in the plan are invested by the trustees and earn interest, and that this plan does not affect any other employee compensation or retirement arrangement. But any company should consult with an accountant before setting up a plan.

Smart entrepreneurs are careful to structure their employee compensation packages to ensure they maintain the benefit from the training and experience they give their employees. Hiring a new employee is expensive and the related training is time-consuming; protecting this investment is critical to the long-term success of any venture.

Larry Ginsberg is co-author of *Small Business*, Big Money. He can be reached at ginsberg@ginsorg.com.

FIGURE 9-4	**Point System Matrix**				

Critical Factors	Levels or Degrees				Factor Points
	I	II	III	IV	
1. Responsibility (weight 40%)					**400**
Subfactors:					
a. Safety of others	20	80	140	200	
b. Equipment and materials	10	32	55	80	
c. Assisting trainees	10	32	55	80	
d. Product/service quality	5	17	29	40	
2. Skill (weight 30%)					**300**
Subfactors:					
a. Experience	18	72	126	180	
b. Education/training	12	48	94	120	
3. Effort (weight 20%)					**200**
Subfactors:					
a. Physical	8	32	56	80	
b. Mental	12	48	94	120	
4. Working conditions (weight 10%)					**100**
Subfactors:					
a. Unpleasant conditions	3	12	21	30	
b. Hazards	7	28	49	70	
				Total points	**1,000**

A detailed calculation of the data in Figure 9-4 is provided in Appendix A at the end of this chapter.

Step 4 : Allocate Points to Levels (Degrees)

Once the points for each job element are satisfactory under column IV, analysts allocate points across each row to reflect the importance of the different levels. Usually equal point differences are used, but analysts or job evaluation committees may decide to use variable differences. See Appendix A at the end of this chapter for a calculation of equal differences.

Step 5 : Develop the Point Manual

The point manual contains a written explanation of each job element, as shown in Figure 9-5 for responsibility of equipment and materials. It also defines what is expected for the four levels (degrees) of each subfactor. This information is needed to assign jobs to their appropriate level.

Step 6 : Apply the Point System

When the point matrix and manual are ready, the relative value of each job can be determined. This process is subjective. It requires specialists to compare job descriptions with the point manual for each subfactor. The match between the job description and the point manual statement reveals the level and points for each subfactor of every job. Once completed, the points for each subfactor are added to find the total number of points for the job. An example of this matching process for Machine Operator I appears below:

> The job description of Machine Operator I states: "[O]perator is responsible for performing preventive maintenance (such as cleaning, oiling, and adjusting belts) and repairs." The sample point manual excerpt in Figure 9-5 states: "Level III: ... performs preventive maintenance and repairs. ..." Since the job description and the point manual match at Level III, the points for the equipment subfactor are 55. Repeating this matching process for each subfactor yields the total points for the job of Machine Operator I.

Information about the Hay Chart for job evaluation
http://wiki.answers.com/Q/ The_Hay_Job_Evaluation_ System
http://en.wikipedia.org/wiki/ Hay_Guide_Chart

| FIGURE 9-5 | Point Manual Description of "Responsibility: Equipment and Materials" |

1. Responsibility ...

b. *Equipment and Materials.* Each employee is responsible for conserving the company's equipment and materials. This includes reporting malfunctioning equipment or defective materials, keeping equipment and materials cleaned or in proper order, and maintaining, repairing, or modifying equipment and materials according to individual job duties. The company recognizes that the degree of responsibility for equipment and materials varies widely throughout the organization.

Level I.   Employee reports malfunctioning equipment or defective materials to immediate superior.

Level II.   Employee maintains the appearance of equipment or order of materials and has responsibility for the security of such equipment or materials.

Level III.   Employee performs preventive maintenance and repairs on equipment or corrects defects in materials.

Level IV.   Employee makes replacement and purchasing decisions and is in control of the "equipment and materials" factor.

After the total points for each job are known, the jobs are ranked. As with the job ranking and job grading systems, this relative ranking should be reviewed by department managers to ensure that it is appropriate.

Beyond the three job evaluation methods discussed in this section, many other variations exist. Large organizations often modify standard approaches to create unique in-house variations. The "Hay Plan," for example, is one variation widely used by Canadian and U.S. firms. This proprietary method, marketed by the large consulting firm Hay and Associates, relies on a committee evaluation of critical job factors to determine each job's relative worth. Although other job evaluation approaches exist, all effective job evaluation schemes attempt to determine a job's relative worth to ensure internal equity.

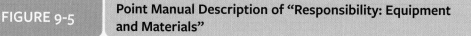

SPOTLIGHT ON ETHICS
Job Evaluation

You are the human resource director of a large grocery chain. As part of a restructuring of its compensation system, and to comply with pay equity legislation, the company has recently switched from the job ranking system to the point system. You are chairing the Job Evaluation Committee, which is ready to allocate points to the cashier job category, the largest category in the company. The discussion so far has focused on how many points to allocate to the responsibility factor, and the committee is essentially split 50–50 on the numbers. As it so happened, there are three women and three men on the committee. The women argue that cashiers have the same responsibility as the accounting clerks, who are all male, in the office. The male members of the committee, on the other hand, disagreed, suggesting that a cashier's responsibility is to balance the cash register,

not accounts, a more difficult task. You seem to have the deciding vote. The dilemma from your point of view is that all the cashiers are women while the three accounting clerks are all male. In your assessment you agree that the accounting clerks carry a higher responsibility and deserve more points. If you support the male members of the committee you are pretty sure that the cashiers will launch a pay equity grievance, usually a costly and time-consuming affair. If you agree with the female members it means cashiers will fall into a higher pay category, increasing payroll expenses significantly. You know very well that the competition in the food market is fierce, with low profit margins (2 to 3 percent). A pay increase would have a direct impact on the bottom line. What do you do?

WAGE AND SALARY SURVEYS

internal equity
Perceived equity of a pay system in an organization.

external equity
Perceived fairness in pay relative to what other employers are paying for the same type of work.

wage and salary survey
A study made of wages and salaries paid by other organizations within the employer's labour market.

All job evaluation techniques result in a ranking of jobs based upon their perceived relative worth. This assures **internal equity**; that is, jobs that are worth more will be paid more. But how much should be paid? What constitutes **external equity**?

To determine a fair rate of compensation, most firms rely on **wage and salary surveys**, which discover what other employers in the same labour market are paying for specific key jobs. The *labour market*—the area from which the employer recruits—is generally the local community; however, firms may have to compete for some workers in a wider market. Consider how the president of one large university viewed the market:

> Our labour market depends on the type of position we are trying to fill. For the hourly paid jobs such as janitor, data entry clerk, and secretary, the labour market is the surrounding metropolitan community. When we hire professors, our labour market is Canada. We have to compete with universities in other provinces to get the type of faculty member we seek. When we have the funds to hire a distinguished professor, our labour market is the whole world.

Sources of Compensation Data

Wage and salary data are benchmarks against which analysts compare compensation levels. Sources for this information include the following:

- Human Resources and Skills Development Canada
- Canadian Human Resource Centres
- Employee associations
- Professional associations
- Private consultants

The major problem with all these published surveys is their varying comparability. Analysts cannot always be sure that their jobs match those reported in the survey. Just matching job titles may be misleading; federal, provincial, and association job descriptions using the same title may be considerably different. Since most government-published surveys rely on the National Occupational Classification (NOC), any job description should be compared with descriptions in the NOC.

At this point, all jobs are ranked according to their relative worth, as a result of the job evaluation process. Through wage and salary surveys, the rate for key jobs in the labour market is also known. This leaves the last phase of wage and salary administration, pricing the jobs.

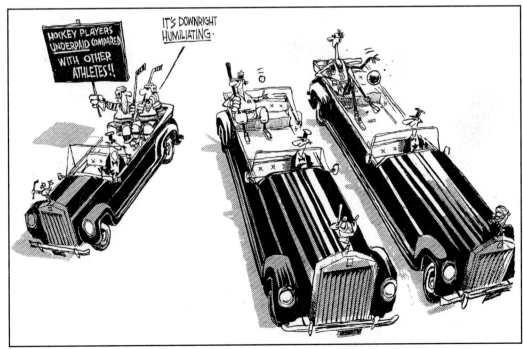

Brian Gable/*The Globe and Mail*. Reprinted with permission from *The Globe and Mail*.

PRICING JOBS

Pricing jobs includes two activities: establishing the appropriate pay level for each job and grouping the different pay levels into a structure that can be managed effectively.

Pay Levels

The appropriate pay level for any job reflects its relative and absolute worth. A job's relative worth is determined by its ranking through the job evaluation process. The absolute worth of a job is influenced by what the labour market pays similar jobs. To set the right pay level means combining the job evaluation rankings and the survey wage rates. Of course, many other considerations will determine the final pay level—for example the organization's pay policy.

This information is combined through the use of a graph called a *scattergram*. As Figure 9-6 illustrates, its vertical axis shows the pay rates. If the point system is used to determine the ranking of jobs, the horizontal axis is in points. The scattergram is created by plotting the total points and wage level for each **key job**. Thus, each dot represents the intersection of the point value and the wage rate for a particular key job. For example, Key Job A in Figure 9-6 is worth 500 points and is paid $16 an hour.

Through the dots that represent key jobs, a *wage-trend line* is drawn as close to as many points as possible. (This line can be done freehand or, more accurately, by a statistical technique called the *least squares method*.[5]) The wage-trend line uses two steps to help determine the wage rates for non-key jobs. *First*, the point value for the nonkey job is located on the horizontal axis. *Second*, a line is traced vertically to the wage-trend line, then horizontally to the dollar scale. The amount on the vertical scale is the appropriate wage rate for the nonkey job. For example, nonkey Job B is worth 700 points. By tracing a vertical line up to the wage-trend line and then horizontally to the vertical (dollar) scale, it can be seen in Figure 9-6 that the appropriate wage rate for Job B is $18 per hour.

The Compensation Structure

A medium-sized organization with 2,000 workers and 325 separately identifiable jobs would present the wage and salary analyst with complex problems. The existence of 325 separate wage rates would be meaningless, because the differences in wages between each job might be no more than a few cents.

Compensation analysts find it more convenient to lump jobs together into job classes. In the job grade approach, jobs are already grouped into predetermined categories. With other methods, the grouping is done by creating job grades based on the previous ranking, pay, or points. In the point system, for example, classifications are based on point ranges: 0 to 100, 101 to 150, 151 to 200, and so forth. This grouping causes the wage-trend line to be replaced with a series of ascending dashes, as shown in Figure 9-7. Thus, all jobs in the same class receive the same wage rate. A job valued at 105 points, for example, is paid the same as a job with 145 points. Having too many grades defeats the

key jobs
Jobs that are similar and common in the organization and its labour market—for example, accountant, tool-and-die maker.

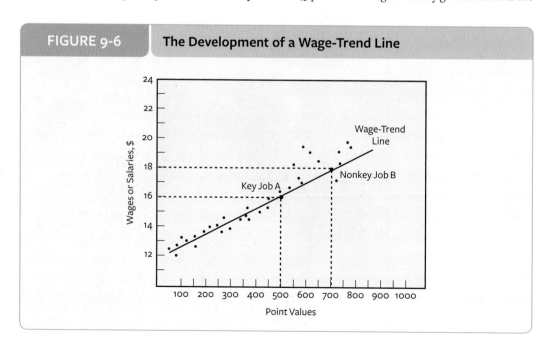

| FIGURE 9-6 | The Development of a Wage-Trend Line |

FIGURE 9-7	The Impact of Job Classes on the Wage-Trend Line

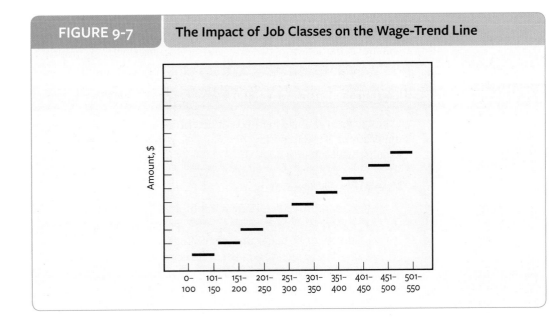

FIGURE 9-8	Varying Wage Ranges for Job Classes

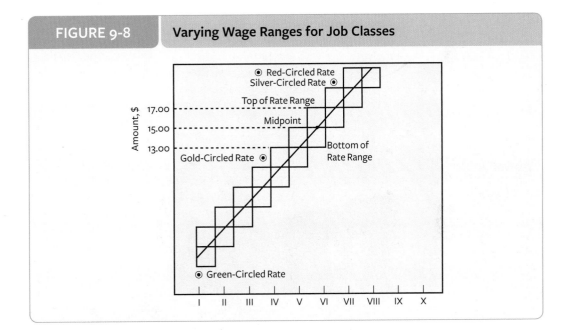

purpose of grouping; having too few groupings results in workers with jobs of widely varying importance receiving the same pay.

The problem with flat rates for each job class is that exceptional performance cannot be rewarded. To give a worker a merit increase requires moving the employee into a higher job class. This upsets the entire balance of internal equity developed through job evaluations. To solve these problems, most firms use rate ranges for each class. A **rate range** is simply a pay range for each job class.

For example, suppose that the wage-trend line indicates $15 is the average hourly rate for a particular job class. Every employee in that class gets $15, if a flat rate is paid. With a rate range of $2 for each class, a marginal performer can be paid $13 at the bottom of the range, as indicated in Figure 9-8. Then an average performer is placed at midpoint in the rate range, or $15. When performance appraisals indicate above-average performance, the employee may be given a **merit raise** of, say, $0.50 per hour for the exceptional performance. If this performance continues, another merit raise of $0.50 can be granted. Once the employee reaches the top of the rate range, no more wage increases will be forthcoming. Either a promotion or a general across-the-board pay raise needs to occur for this worker's wages to exceed $17. An across-the-board increase moves the entire wage-trend line upward.

rate range
A pay range for each job class.

merit raise
A pay increase given to individual workers according to an evaluation of their performance.

As new jobs are created, the wage and salary section performs a job evaluation. From this evaluation, the new job is assigned to an appropriate job class. If the rate ranges are used, the new employee will start at the bottom of the range and receive raises, where appropriate, to the top of the rate range.

CHALLENGES AFFECTING COMPENSATION

2, 4, & 5

Even the most rational methods of determining pay must be tempered by several challenges. The implications of these contingencies may cause wage and salary analysts to make further adjustments to employee compensation.

Prevailing Wage Rates

Some jobs must be paid more than is indicated by their relative worth because of market forces. In the 1990s, there was a scarcity of software specialists. Fitting these jobs onto a wage-trend line often resulted in a wage rate below their prevailing wage rate. Because demand outstripped supply, market forces caused wage rates for these specialists to rise above their relative worth when compared with other jobs. Firms that needed these talents were forced to pay a premium. Diagrammatically, these rates appear on a wage chart as a **red-circled rate**, as seen in Figure 9-8. The term arises from the practice of marking out-of-line rates with a red circle on the chart. In the early 2000s, the shortage of information technology professionals was so serious that firms first offered huge hiring bonuses, but were then eventually forced to raise salaries for these jobs, even at the entry level.[6] Some companies pay more than the maximum salary level to employees with long job tenure. This salary level appears then as *silver-circled*. *Gold-circled* salaries indicate payments beyond the maximum level if an employee receives a special merit pay that does not fit into the established range.

Some jobs may be paid less than the established minimum. This happens when an organization uses salary caps (limits). For example, a company may pay newly hired employees with no experience rates 10 to 20 percent below the pay minimum until they have "learned the ropes." This level is *green-circled*.

red-circled rate
A rate of pay higher than the contractual, or formerly established, rate for the job.

Electricians belong to a dominant union, which is why their wage rates are so high. Is it justified to pay an electrician double—or close to double—what a carpenter makes?

Ryan McVay/Getty Images.

Union Power

When unions represent a portion of the workforce, they may be able to use their power to obtain wage rates out of proportion to their relative worth. For example, wage and salary studies may determine that $16 an hour is appropriate for a truck driver. But if the union insists on $18, the human resource department may believe paying the higher rate is less expensive than a strike. Sometimes the union controls most or all of a particular skill, such as carpentry or plumbing. This enables the union actually to raise the prevailing rate for those jobs.

Productivity

Companies must make a profit to survive. Without profits, the company cannot attract the investors necessary to remain competitive. Therefore, a company cannot pay workers more than they contribute back to the firm through their productivity. When this happens (because of scarcity or union power), companies usually redesign those jobs, train new workers to increase their supply, or automate.

Wage and Salary Policies

Most organizations have policies that cause wages and salaries to be adjusted. One common policy is to give nonunion workers the same raise as that received by unionized workers. Some companies have a policy of paying a premium above the prevailing wages to minimize turnover or to recruit the best workers. Also, some companies have automatic cost-of-living clauses that give employees automatic raises when the Statistics Canada cost-of-living index increases. Raises or policies that increase employee compensation move the wage-trend line upward.

compa-ratio
An index that indicates how an individual's or a group's salary relates to the midpoint of their relevant pay grades.

A useful index for salary administrators is the **compa-ratio**, an indicator of how the salary of an employee relates to the midpoint of the relevant pay grade. A compa-ratio of above or below 1 shows that the individual's salary is above or below the midpoint of the pay grade. The pay-grade midpoint can be viewed as a benchmark for salary decision criteria such as performance, tenure, and experience. The formula for the individual compa-ratio is:

$$\text{Compa-ratio} = \frac{\text{Salary of the employee}}{\text{Midpoint of the pay grade}}$$

Also of interest to salary administrators is the compa-ratio for groups. A ratio above 1 indicates that a large number of employees are bunched at the top of the pay grade (top-heavy). A ratio below 1 may be caused by many new employees or may be an indication of high turnover. The formula for the group compa-ratio is:

$$\text{Compa-ratio} = \frac{\text{Average of salaries paid}}{\text{Midpoint of the pay grade}}$$

Government Constraints

Canada is a nation of wage-earners. What people earn bears a direct relationship to the economy and general welfare of the population. Since the 1930s, the federal government has regulated some aspects of compensation.

Canada Labour Code
Federal law regulating labour relations under federal jurisdiction.

The *Canada Labour Code* in its revised version of 1971 is the most comprehensive law affecting compensation rights for organizations under federal jurisdiction. It sets requirements for minimum wage, overtime pay, equal pay, child labour, and record keeping. The minimum wage (see below) and overtime provisions require employers to pay at least a minimum hourly rate of pay regardless of the worth of the job. (When the minimum is increased by law, it may mean adjusting upward the wages of those who already earn above the minimum. If those just above minimum wage do not also get raises, wage differentials will be squeezed together. This is called *wage compression*.) For every covered job, the organization must pay one-and-a-half times the employee's regular pay rate for all hours over 40 per week. Executive, administrative, professional, and other employees are exempt from the overtime provisions. Laws involving similar regulations have been enacted by each province for organizations under their jurisdiction.

Human Resources and Skills Development Canada Database on Minimum Wages
http://srv116.services.gc.ca/dimt-wid/sm-mw/rpt1.aspx?lang=eng

Minimum Wages

All the provinces have minimum-wage legislation that applies to most classes of workers, other than farm labourers and domestic servants. The legislation provides for a board to set minimum wage rates, and these rates are imposed by means of minimum-wage orders that are periodically issued.[7] Wide discretion is given to all provincial boards for determination of the classes of employees for which minimum wages are to be established. The current minimum-wage rates at the provincial and federal levels can be found on the government homepage shown in the margin. The rates shown are typical for persons 18 years of age and over. For employees under 18, the rates are somewhat lower.

The federal government passed the *Minimum Wages Act* in 1935, in compliance with one of the three conventions adopted by the International Labour Organization. However, under the *Constitution Act, 1867* (formerly the *British North America Act*), minimum-wage legislation comes under provincial jurisdiction. The federal *Minimum Wages Act* currently applies to all government agencies, Crown corporations, and some selected industries as mentioned in Chapter 4.

Contracts with the Government

The *Fair Wages and Hours of Labour Act* applies to contracts made with the Government of Canada for all types of work. It is mandatory on the part of contractors dealing with the Government of Canada to pay fair wages and establish an eight-hour workday during all such work.[8]

Staff Records

The *Canada Labour Code* requires every employer in those industries falling under federal jurisdiction to furnish information relating to wages of employees, their hours of work, general holidays, annual vacation, and conditions of employment whenever the Ministry of Labour demands it. Similar provisions exist in the provincial legislation. Accurate records are also to be kept, for example, on maternity leave and severance pay relating to all affected employees. This is to ensure that all provisions of the legislation relating to such things as minimum wages, maximum weekly hours, and overtime payments are strictly adhered to by each employer.

Criticisms of Minimum-Wage Regulations

It has been pointed out by some that minimum-wage regulations increase the cost of production in Canada. This may eventually work against the workers rather than for them, as Marc Law argues:

> In recent years, minimum wages across Canada have risen more than the average increase in manufacturing wages. And some economists are suggesting ... [that] it could lead to an intolerable increase [in unemployment] and cause the major burdens to fall precisely on the workers it was designed to help.[9]

Increases in minimum wages are usually accompanied by increases in unemployment figures of low-skilled and young persons in the workforce. It is also pointed out by some that continual increases in minimum-wage rates may actually contribute to the inflationary trends in the economy.[10] There is, however, no conclusive evidence on the matter one way or the other at this time.

Study on minimum wages
www.house.gov/jec/
cost-gov/regs/minimum/
50years.htm
www.policyalternatives.
ca/news/1999/09/
pressrelease591/?pa=pa
www.parl.gc.ca/
information/library/
PRBpubs/prb0839-e.htm

PAY EQUITY

equal pay for work of equal value
The principle of equal pay for men and women in jobs with comparable content; based on criteria of skill, effort, responsibility, and working conditions; part of the *Canadian Human Rights Act*.

pay equity
A policy to eliminate the gap between income of men and women, ensuring that salary ranges correspond to value of work performed.

In 1977, the *Canada Labour Code*, Part I, was repealed and replaced by the *Canadian Human Rights Act*. Since this act prohibits, among other things, discrimination because of sex, it is illegal for companies to pay women less than men if their jobs involve equal skills, effort, responsibilities, and conditions. The government enforces these provisions by requiring wrongdoers to equalize pay and make up past discrepancies.

As first mentioned in Chapter 4, an important issue in compensation management and equal opportunity is **equal pay for work of equal value**, the concept that jobs of comparable worth to the organization should be equally paid (referred to as **pay equity**). The idea goes beyond **equal pay for equal work** (referred to as *equal pay*), part of the *Canada Labour Code* since 1971, which requires an employer to pay men and women the same wage or salary when they do the same work. Exceptions to equal pay of both types are allowed when a valid seniority or merit system exists. Employers can pay more for seniority or to workers who perform better and merit higher pay. Exceptions are also allowed when pay is determined by the employee's production, such as sales commissions.

The pay equity concept, however, takes a different perspective. It became law in an amendment to the *Canadian Human Rights Act* in 1978. It makes it illegal to discriminate on the basis of job value (or content). For example, if a nurse and an electrician both received approximately the same number of job evaluation points under the point system, they would have to be paid the same wage or salary, regardless of market conditions. This approach to compensation is sought by governments as a means of eliminating the historical gap between the income of men and women, which results in women in Canada earning about 80 percent as much as men.[11] This gap exists in part because women have traditionally found work in lower-paying occupations, such as teaching, retailing, nursing, and secretarial work, and in such positions as receptionist and telephone operator.

It should be emphasized, however, that the above-mentioned figure of 80 percent as the earning gap between men and women is misleading, although it is widely used by proponents of equal pay to point to the "discrimination" in pay against women. This figure emerges if one compares all men and women wage-earners regardless of job tenure and skill level. But this is not an appropriate comparison. If a woman chooses to leave the labour force to have children and to bring them up and

equal pay for equal work
The principle or policy of equal rates of pay for all employees in an establishment performing the same kind and amount of work, regardless of sex, race, or other characteristics of individual workers not related to ability or performance.

Arguments for and against pay equity
www.cupe1975.ca/bursary/birns.html
www.taxpayer.com/pdf/PayequitystudyNov30-2001.pdf
www.cbc.ca/newsinreview/Dec%2099/Pay%20Equity/wage%20gap.html

For an article by the first author on pay equity see:
http://cid-f5310bad2e82d225.spaces.live.com/default.aspx

then returns to continue her career, she will have missed many training and advancement opportunities in her organization as compared to her male colleague who presumably continued to grow and advance in his career.

By using comparable groups, the pay gap decreases to between 5 to 10 percent, depending on the group studied.[12] For example, the income of single women aged 35 to 44 was 94.5 percent of that earned by men of the same age. (If one looks only at the most educated members of that age group—single females with a university degree—women actually made 6 percent more than their male counterparts.) Taking all of the above factors into account, it still leaves a gap of between 5 and 10 percent that cannot be explained. There is no evidence, however, that there is a conspiracy among entrepreneurs and managers to keep the wages of female-dominated jobs down. (*Note:* A job is gender-dominated if, depending on jurisdiction, 60 to 70 percent of the job occupants are from one sex.)

Then what keeps women's wages below comparable men's wages? Society's expectations about the role of women in our culture have determined, to a large degree, women's job choices. Traditionally, it was the son who, after high school, would go on to study for a profession and pursue a career, while the daughter had to be content to learn household skills, such as cooking and sewing, or, at the most, secretarial skills, such as typing and shorthand. This attitude has changed, as enrollments in our business, engineering, law, and medical schools demonstrate. But even today, a woman's job choice is often influenced by her role as a homemaker and mother, as evidenced in the following study:

> Two researchers were asked to examine a manufacturing company whose management wanted to find out why in some jobs there were so few women despite the company's sincere employment equity program. They found that some of the higher-paying jobs were not attractive to women because of overtime requirements, shift work, and heavy lifting. Women felt that they had a stronger responsibility toward the family and could not afford to work overtime or do shift work. This study—and other studies—shows that some contextual factors such as family considerations, which do not enter the job evaluation process, have a strong impact on job choices.[13]

What makes the issue of equal pay for work of equal value very tricky is the lack of any generally acceptable definition of "equal value" and how it can be measured. The definition offered in the guidelines issued by the Canadian Human Rights Commission is not of much help:

> Value of work is the value which the work performed by an employee in a given establishment represents in relation to the value of work of another employee, or group of employees, the value being determined on the basis of approved criteria, without the wage market or negotiated wage rates being taken into account.[14]

Pay equity ensures equal pay for work of equal value. Why is it then that women workers in Canada make only 80 cents compared to the men's $1?

The approved criteria referred to above are skill, effort, responsibility, and working conditions. These criteria will be considered together; that is, they will form a composite measure. This does not mean that employees must be paid the same salary, even if their jobs are considered equal. The equal wage guidelines define seven "reasonable factors" that can justify differences in wages:

1. different performance ratings (ratings must be based on a formal appraisal system and be brought to the attention of each employee);
2. seniority (based on length of service);
3. red-circling (because of job reevaluation);
4. rehabilitation assignment (e.g., after lengthy absence because of sickness);
5. demotion pay procedures (because of unsatisfactory work performance, or reassignment because of labour force surplus);
6. procedure of phased-in wage reductions; and
7. temporary training positions.[15]

These factors justify a difference in wages only if they are applied consistently and equitably. It must be clearly demonstrable that existing wage differences are not based on sex.

Where does this leave the human resource manager? The *Canadian Human Rights Act* applies only to organizations under federal jurisdiction, such as federal government departments and Crown agencies, the RCMP, the Canadian Armed Forces, banks, airlines, most railway companies, and communication firms. In addition, most provinces have enacted pay equity legislation (Newfoundland and Saskatchewan are exceptions, and Prince Edward Island has such legislation only for the public sector), which means organizations under their jurisdiction have to comply with these laws. Fortunately, these laws are modelled on the federal one, and use similar criteria.

A human resource manager has to make sure that the company's pay system is in line with the province's or the federal government's legislation. The following measures are suggested:

- Review the organization's human resource policies, procedures, and practices with the objective of determining relevance and consistency of application.
- Review recruiting and promotional decisions and track career trends, particularly with respect to compensation levels; examine how the organization has treated employees in the past.
- Review human resource planning techniques and procedures to determine consistency of application throughout the organization.
- Review the underlying philosophy and rationale of the job evaluation plan(s) currently used (e.g., are they appropriate for the organization today; has the evaluation process been as objective as possible; what "groups" fall under which plan, and is this appropriate?).
- By specific position, examine the differential between earnings of men and women in the organization.
- By salary grade, examine the differential between earnings of men and women.
- For groups of positions performing work of "relative importance," examine the differential between earnings of men and women.
- Examine all employee benefits practices across the organization, including those in place for plant and hourly rated employees, to determine if inequalities exist (e.g., to determine if overtime, vacation, and other benefit levels are consistently applied).

Should inequalities be found, it would be advisable to eliminate them; or if the organization is large, it may be useful to implement an employment equity program. Initiation of such a program would not imply any past wrongdoing on the part of the organization, but it is encouraged by federal and provincial human rights commissions.

Provincial Legislation

As mentioned, most provinces have enacted pay equity legislation. Manitoba and Ontario legislators took a new approach to pay equity legislation by creating Pay Equity Bureaus that are responsible for the administration and implementation of the laws. Both also take a proactive approach by requiring employers to evaluate all jobs in an organization under a single, gender-neutral job evaluation scheme, and to apply the scheme to classes of work where one sex predominates. In contrast, the laws of the remaining provinces are reactive, since they deal with inequities only if the latter are brought to the attention of the appropriate human rights commissions.

incentive pay
Compensation
that is directly tied
to an employee's
performance and/or
productivity.

The Pay-for-Performance Model

Incentive systems provide the clearest link between pay and performance or productivity (*performance* is the accomplishment of assigned tasks; *productivity* is the measure of output). **Incentive pay** is directly linked to an employee's performance or productivity. Employees who work under a financial incentive system find that their performance (productivity) determines, in whole or part, their income. A typical example of an incentive pay is a salesperson's commission. The more the salesperson sells, the more he or she earns.

One of the most significant benefits of financial incentives is that better performance is reinforced on a regular basis. Unlike raises and promotions, the reinforcement is generally quick and frequent—usually with each paycheque. Since the worker sees the results of the desired behaviour quickly, that behaviour is more likely to continue. The employer benefits, because wages are given in proportion to performance, not for the indirect measure of time worked. And if employees are motivated by the system to expand their output, recruiting expenses for additional employees and capital outlays for new workstations are minimized. A switch from hourly to direct incentive pay can be quite dramatic as one study shows:

Pay equity legislation in provinces
www.equalpaycoalition.org/
other_prov.php
http://en.wikipedia.org/wiki/
Equal_pay_for_women

> Professor Lazear, Stanford University, followed the changeover from an hourly pay system to piece rate at Safelite Glass Corporation in 1995 and found that productivity increased by 44 percent per worker. He could break down the increase into three components: higher output per worker; (2) lower quitting rates among the highest output workers; and (3) the company's ability to hire more productive workers.[16]

Offsetting these advantages are significant problems. The administration of an incentive system can be complex. As with any control system, standards have to be established and results measured. For many jobs, the standards and measures are too imprecise or too costly to develop. This means that the incentive system may result in inequities. Some incentive systems require less effort than other systems that pay the same. Sometimes, workers make more than their supervisors, who are on salary. Another problem is that the employee may not achieve the standard because of uncontrollable forces, such as work delays or machine breakdowns.

Unions often resist incentive systems, because they fear management will change the standard(s) for the incentive system, and workers will have to work harder for the same pay. This fear of a speedup often leads to peer pressure against anyone who exceeds the group's output norms. The advantages of the incentive system are essentially lost when group pressures restrict output. And incentives tend to focus efforts on only one aspect (output, sales, or stock prices), sometimes to the exclusion of other dimensions (quality, service, and long-term objectives). Some of the more common incentive systems are outlined below.

Individual Incentive Plans

Piecework

piecework
A type of incentive
system that
compensates workers
for each unit of output.

Piecework is an incentive system that compensates the worker for each unit of output. Daily or weekly pay is determined by multiplying the output in units times the piece rate per unit. For example, in agricultural labour, workers are often paid a specific amount per bushel of produce picked. Piecework does not always mean higher productivity, however. Group norms may have a more significant impact if peer pressure works against higher productivity. And in many jobs, it may be difficult to measure the person's productive contribution (e.g., receptionist), or the employee may not be able to control the rate of output (e.g., an assembly-line worker).

Production Bonuses

production bonuses
A type of incentive
system that
provides employees
with additional
compensation when
they surpass stated
production goals.

Production bonuses are incentives paid to workers for exceeding a specified level of output. They are used in conjunction with a base wage rate or salary. Under one approach, the employee receives a predetermined salary or wage. Through extra effort that results in output above the standard, the base compensation is supplemented by a bonus, usually figured at a given rate for each unit of production over the standard. A variation rewards the employee for saving time. For example, if the standard time for replacing an automobile transmission is four hours and the mechanic does it in three, the mechanic may be paid for four hours.

A third method combines production bonuses with piecework by compensating workers on an hourly basis, plus an incentive payment for each unit produced. In some cases, the employee may get

FIGURE 9-9	Examples of Sales Commission and Bonus Plans
Sales Plan Type	**Content**
Base salary only	No other compensation is offered.
Commission only	Total compensation is based on established commission schedule.
Base salary plus commission	The commission is over and above the guaranteed base salary. The salary commission mix varies with the type of product, territory, and sales support.
Base salary plus bonus	The bonus is over and above the guaranteed base salary. The bonus is usually based on task achievement; it is earned only when the established sales quota is met.

Source: J. A. Colleti and D. Cichelly, "Increasing Sales-Force Effectiveness Through the Compensation Plan," in Milton L. Rock and Lance A. Berger, eds., *The Compensation Handbook*, New York, NY: McGraw-Hill, 1991, pp. 290–303. Used with permission.

a higher piece rate once a minimum number of units are produced. For example, the employee may be paid $15 an hour plus $0.30 per unit for the first 30 units each day. Beginning with the 31st unit, the bonus may become $0.40.

Commissions

In sales jobs, the salesperson may be paid a percentage of the selling price or a flat amount for each unit sold. When no base compensation is paid, the salesperson's total earnings come from commissions. Real estate agents and car salespeople are often paid this form of straight commission. Figure 9-9 shows examples of different types of sales commission and bonus plans.

Executive Incentives

Executive incentives vary widely. Young and middle-aged executives are likely to want cash bonuses to meet the needs of a growing or maturing family. As they get older, the need for present income is offset by retirement considerations. Here, bonuses may be deferred until the executive reaches the lower tax rates of retirement.

Executives are sometimes granted *stock options*—that is, the right to purchase the company's stock at a predetermined price. This price may be set at, below, or above the market value of the stock. Thus, the executive has an incentive to improve the company's performance in order to enhance the value of the stock options. Generally, it is considered appropriate to give stock options only to those executives who can have a significant effect on company profits.

Other forms of executive incentives exist, including incentive systems that allow executives to design their own compensation package. The common element in most executive incentive plans, however, is their relation to the performance of the organization. When these systems do not relate the incentive to performance, they are not incentive plans, no matter what they are called. Besides, executive incentives are increasingly being geared to promote long-term performance.[17]

Executive incentives article
http://payroll.naukrihub.
com/compensation/
incentive-management/
executive-incentive/

Executive incentives: International comparison article
http://gsbwww.uchicago.
edu/fac/steven.kaplan/
research/compgov.pdf

Team- (or Group-) Based Pay

When students graduate and join an organization, there is a high probability that they will work as part of a team rather than working alone; their performance will then be measured by how much they contribute to the team results. According to one study, 87 percent of the Fortune 1000 companies have created project teams, and 47 percent have permanent teams.[18] The team concept seems to work best in high-tech companies, where groups of engineers collaborate on solving problems or designing software. A former director of human relations for Coopers & Lybrand (now PricewaterhouseCoopers), has an interesting view: "When I try to build a team environment, I say: individuals win trophies, teams win championships."[19] Figure 9-10 compares characteristics of team-based merit pay and individual merit pay.

FIGURE 9-10	Contrasting Approaches
Team-Based Merit Pay	**Individual Merit Pay**
Rewards teamwork and cooperation	Creates internal competition
Encourages group to improve work systems	Individuals try to improve system—results in failure
Increases flexibility and ability to respond to changing needs	Decreases flexibility
Not incorporated in base pay	Incorporated into base pay
Encourages information sharing and communication	Encourages withholding of information
Focus on wider organization	No focus on wider organization

Source: M. Thompson, "Team Working and Pay," Report 281, Brighton, UK: Institute for Employment Studies, 1995.

There can be a number of advantages in a team-based pay system. For example, in project teams, many jobs are interrelated—that is, they depend on each other for making progress. A team approach tends to foster group cohesion and organizational commitment. Communication in cohesive teams tends to be more open, and decision making can be more effective if a consensus approach is in the team's interest. Team-based pay often includes rewards for developing better interpersonal skills to improve cooperation and incentives for cross-training.

There can be disadvantages to team-based pay systems. If team cohesiveness is not strong, a "freeloader effect" may take place. As in any group, individual contributions to team goals vary. Some put in more effort, others less. If these differences are significant and the high performers do not receive satisfaction for their input, they may cut back their contributions. Usually, however, high-input members get their satisfaction from being recognized as team leaders or higher-status members, for example as experts or specialists. Another potential drawback is social pressure on high performers to lower their input to avoid drawing management's attention to the low performers. This issue will most likely occur in a hostile management–union environment. It is also possible that the team approach is too effective, resulting in competition between teams and undesirable consequences, such as hoarding of resources or withholding of important information.

Team-(or Group-) Based Incentive Plans

Several plans have been developed to provide incentives for teamwork. Most fall into one of the following categories: team results, production incentives, profit sharing, stock ownership, or cost-reduction plans.

Team Results

Under team-based pay plans, employee bonuses and salary increases are based on a team's overall results and are often shared equally. However, a team can also vote shares of a bonus pool to its various members, much like a Stanley Cup or Grey Cup winner votes its members full or partial shares of its championship reward, depending on individual contributions.

Production Incentive Plans

These plans allow groups of workers to receive bonuses for exceeding predetermined levels of output. They tend to be short-range and related to very specific production goals. A work team may be offered a bonus for exceeding predetermined production levels, or may receive a per-unit incentive that results in a group piece rate.

Profit-Sharing Plans

Profit-sharing plans share company profits with the workers. The effectiveness of these plans may suffer, because profitability is not always related to employee performance; a recession or new competitors may have a more significant impact. Even when outside sources do not seriously affect

profit-sharing plan
A system whereby an employer pays compensation or benefits to employees, usually on an annual basis, in addition to their regular wage, on the basis of the profits of the company.

Effectiveness of profit-sharing plans
www.cirano.qc.ca/pdf/publication/2002s-54.pdf

results, it is often difficult for employees to perceive their efforts as making much difference. Some companies further reduce the effectiveness of the incentive by diverting the employees' share of profits into retirement plans. Thus, the immediate reinforcement value of the incentive is reduced, because the incentive is delayed. However, when these plans work well they can have a dramatic impact on the organization, because profit-sharing plans can create a sense of trust and a feeling of common fate among workers and management.

In Canada, the number of profit-sharing plans increased from approximately 2,000 registered plans in the mid-1950s to more than 60,000 by 2000. Since a recent study found that more than 50 percent of all profit-sharing plans are cash plans that do not require registration, the number of profit-sharing plans in Canada is probably well beyond 60,000.

How effective are profit-sharing plans in motivating employees? The evidence is not that clear-cut. Although companies with profit-sharing plans tend to be more profitable, it is by no means certain that the plan is the cause of increased profitability.[20] As usual, many factors play a role.

Studies show that the profitable companies with profit-sharing plans also tend to have open and two-way communication between management and employees. In addition, in these companies, management tends to practise a participative management style, resulting in a supportive and satisfying work environment.[21] In summary, it can be said that profit sharing tends to contribute to higher motivation and productivity, but it does so in conjunction with other factors.[22]

Employee Stock Ownership Plans (ESOPs)

Employee stock ownership plans (ESOPs) have become very popular in North America. One study indicates that over 11,000 of such plans cover almost 9 million employees, who own more than US$200 billion in assets.[23] Because of a lack of tax incentives, only 25 percent of Canadian companies offer an ESOP.[24] Unlike the more traditional profit-sharing plans, ESOPs give employees genuine ownership and voting power when it comes to major decisions relating to the company's future.

> Ten years ago, General Printers was an operation chronically in the red, with absentee owners, employees who didn't care about their work, and the need for round-the-clock supervision.
>
> Today, the value of the Oshawa, Ontario, company has grown by 80 percent, and employees do a first-rate job with no managers on-site for two-thirds of the 24-hour workday. The icing on the cake was being named 1997 Business of the Year by the local chamber of commerce. The latest recognition was the Award of Excellence, earned at the 2005 Ontario Printing and Imaging Competition.
>
> The dramatic turnaround can be traced to one key change: the workers became co-owners of the commercial print shop. An ESOP was established that made them not just workers earning a wage, but investors in the firm with a stake in its success.[25]

ESOPs can be modelled to fit the special needs of a company. This may include the need to do the following:

- attract and retain employees, especially in high-tech, knowledge-based industries;
- motivate employees and improve their productivity;
- rescue a failing firm;
- provide a source of additional financing; or
- create something for firms to offer in lieu of wage and salary increases.

Some recent studies show some very positive results regarding the impact of ESOPs on employee motivation, productivity, and turnover, among other items, and their impact on companies' overall sales, sales per employee, and long-term growth.[26]

As might be expected, events involving companies such as Enron and WorldCom, in which executives received huge stock options that they sold before their companies folded, have had serious repercussions. A number of Canadian companies have given up on the idea of using stock options as an incentive. Among them are Sobeys and its parent company Empire Co., Winpak, St. Lawrence Cement, Calian Technology Ltd., and Leon's Furniture. Instead of ESOPs, these companies rely on cash bonuses or share purchase plans to reward their executives, doing away with any incentive to manipulate the price of their options.[27]

ESOPs: Do they work?
http://esop-canada.com/ ESOPCanada/index.php

Differences between ESOPs and Co-ops
http://web.uvic.ca/bcics/ research/worker/intro.htm

Scanlon Leadership Network
Information on Scanlon plans
www.scanlonleader.org

Scanlon Plan
An incentive plan developed by Joseph Scanlon that has as its general objective the reduction of labour costs through increased efficiency and the sharing of resultant savings among workers.

pay secrecy
A management policy not to discuss or publish individual salaries.

Cost-Reduction Plans

Some critics of group incentive plans argue that profit-sharing schemes do not always reward the employees' efforts if profits fall for reasons beyond the employees' control. For example, the average bonus received by workers at Lincoln Electric, a company with a cost-reduction plan, fell from $22,690 one year to $15,460 the next because of a slowdown in the economy. Although $15,460 is a considerable bonus, the bonus is influenced by forces outside the employees' control.

Another approach is to reward employees for something they can control: labour costs. Most cost-reduction plans seek to tap employee effort and ideas for ways to reduce costs. Often a committee of employees is formed to open new lines of communication that allow employee ideas to be heard, while the plan allows greater psychological and financial participation in the firm's day-to-day operations. Perhaps the best-known of these approaches is the **Scanlon Plan**, which bases bonuses on improvements in labour costs, as compared with historical norms.[28] Under a Scanlon Plan group incentive, employees aim to reduce costs, and then they share in those savings. If, for example, employee productivity increases at the Canadian Valve and Hydrant Manufacturing Company, the ratio of payroll costs to net sales revenue improves. These savings are then shared with employees in the form of a bonus. *Rucker* and *Improshare* plans are similar, but they differ in how bonuses are calculated and in other administrative matters. All three approaches differ from profit sharing in that they focus on something the employee can influence (costs), and not on something that employees may control only indirectly (profitability).

Nonmonetary Rewards

How important is money compared to nonmonetary rewards? A number of studies seem to indicate that money is not as important as, say, a challenging job. One should be cautious about such results, because the answer often depends on how the question is phrased. For example, "high" pay is rated lower than "fair" pay. Of importance is also whether the reward is public—that is, known. Such rewards have much higher status than secret ones. In addition, some people are reluctant to admit that pay is important to them. It seems obvious also that during a recession, job security becomes more important than cash bonuses. It is fair to say that "good old-fashioned cash" is still one of the best incentives.[29]

While monetary rewards are obviously important, research indicates that nonmonetary rewards can be highly motivational, for example praise and recognition. See more on this topic in the section "Tailor-Made Perks" later in this chapter.

Pay Secrecy

Pay secrecy is a touchy topic. Many employers prefer not to publish salary levels to avoid having to defend their pay decisions. If a pay policy is indefensible, disclosure may cause significant dissatisfaction among employees. Research has shown that employees generally prefer secrecy about individual salaries, but favour disclosure of pay ranges and pay policies.[30] Figure 9-11 shows the advantages and disadvantages of insisting on secrecy.

According to Lawler, pay secrecy has two major effects: (1) it lowers the pay satisfaction of employees and (2) it reduces the employees' motivation to perform.[31] It is practically unavoidable that employees will talk about and compare salaries. On the basis of rumours and speculations, employees tend to overestimate the salaries of their colleagues, causing feelings of unfairness,

FIGURE 9-11	Advantages and Disadvantages of Pay Secrecy	
Advantages	**Disadvantages**	
Most employees prefer to have their pay kept secret	May generate distrust in the pay system	
Gives managers greater freedom	Employees may perceive that there is no relationship between pay and performance	
Covers up inequities in the internal pay structure		

inequity, and resentment. Pay secrecy also prevents employees from perceiving the connection between their performance and their pay.

NEW APPROACHES TO PAY

2 & 5

skill- or knowledge-based pay
A pay system based on the skills or knowledge that an employee has (in contrast to the more common job-based pay).

So far, this chapter has dealt with the traditional approach to compensation: paying for the job done. It means that once employees are hired, they are paid for doing what their job descriptions list as job responsibilities or tasks. The amount paid is determined through the process of job evaluation.

A new way of thinking about paying employees is based on the skills or knowledge they have. **Skill- or knowledge-based pay** requires, *first*, the identification of the tasks that have to be performed in the organization. *Second*, the skills required to complete the tasks have to be identified. *Third*, skills have to be priced so that pay rates can be determined. Typically, employees are paid only for those skills they are able to perform, but there is always an incentive to broaden one's skill level:

> NCR Canada's Engineering and Manufacturing Facility in Waterloo, Ontario, employs a staff of 600 to develop and manufacture products and systems for the document processing market. In 1988, management introduced the concept of work teams. Every employee learns all the seven basic functions in the production process. They rotate across the functions every six weeks to first learn and later hone other skills. Wages are based on learning and performing all of the functions in a cell on a regular rotational basis. Individual and team performance is measured and rewarded.[32]

Many companies, especially in the manufacturing industry, provide incentives for the horizontal learning of skills, similar to the job enlargement principle. Workers learn a greater variety of skills so that they are able to perform different jobs. Volvo in Sweden has taken another approach. There, workers are encouraged to learn vertical skills. Volvo gives every member of a work group an increase if the group is able to function without a supervisor, a powerful motivation for the development of **autonomous work groups** (also known as *leaderless work groups*). A similar approach has been taken by Shell Canada in its Brockville, Ontario, plant as described below:

autonomous work groups
Any of a variety of arrangements that allow employees to decide democratically how they will meet their group's work objectives.

> Fewer than 100 people are employed in this ultramodern plant, which produces lubricants. Information technology is the key for the design of this plant, putting a computer at the fingertips of every worker. This has drastically changed the working relationships in this plant. Missing are the traditional foremen and supervisors who tell people what to do and how to do it. Every worker, or team operator, is a supervisor of sorts. Operators must master all the jobs within his or her team, plus at least one skill in two other groups. Pay is based on a number of defined skills. The impact on pay was significant. The average salary increased by 22 percent, and some employees almost doubled their income.[33]

The greatest advantage of skill-based pay is the flexibility of the workforce. This includes filling in after turnovers and covering for absenteeism, for employees who are being trained, and for those who are in meetings. Also, if a company's production or service process is changing frequently, it is very desirable to have a highly trained workforce that can adapt smoothly to changes. This advantage is likely to become increasingly important in the future because of the shorter life cycles of products, the increasing demand for product customization, and the need to respond quickly to market changes.[34] Lawler cites an example in which a highly skilled workforce made a major difference:

Skill-based pay: A Canadian case study
http://irc.queensu.ca/gallery/1/cis-skill-based-pay-in-a-unionized-environment-a-case-study.pdf

> As part of some work I did with Johnson & Johnson, I designed a skill-based pay system for a plant that makes Tylenol. As a result of the Tylenol poisoning tragedy, J&J decided to completely redo its packaging of Tylenol to add greater safety. The skill-based plant quickly installed the new technology needed and got back into production. Not so with its sister plant, which was a traditional, job-based seniority-driven plant. Seniority rights and traditional pay grades got in the way of people's flexibility in adapting to the new technology.[35]

Other advantages come from the fact that skill-based pay may lead to leaner organizations. If multiskilled employees are able to fill in, the organization does not need to have as many extra employees to cover for absenteeism.

Disadvantages lie in the higher pay rates skill-based pay systems tend to generate. This does not mean total wage costs have to be higher; if the organization can make better use of its people, total costs can be significantly lower.[36]

Variable Pay

There is strong evidence that Canadian companies are shifting toward a more performance-linked compensation approach. A survey by Hewitt Associates, a human resource consulting firm, found that of 420 large Canadian companies surveyed in 2008, 86 percent use variable pay as part of their compensation system.[37] Figure 9-12 shows what type of variable pay programs are used by these companies.

The objectives of variable pay are (1) to improve business performance through changed employee behaviour, (2) to keep compensation competitive, and (3) to control labour costs. The advantage of the variable compensation approach is that it is performance-linked. Unlike merit pay, it is able to incorporate the performance of individuals, groups, business units, and corporate financial and stock price performances. The great advantage of a variable pay plan is that the award must be re-earned every year and does not permanently increase base salary.

An earlier Conference Board of Canada survey indicated that compensation systems are undergoing significant changes, as shown in Figure 9-13. The traditional approach, which featured fixed base salaries, required continued upward adjustment to keep pace with the labour market, often with incentive systems restricted to executives, and has given way to a flexible, performance-driven system aimed at all or most levels of employees. Employers can use variable pay to provide incentives to employees to participate in workplace changes. When employees can share the gains from change, the expectation is that they will train and make the effort to adapt to the new workplace. When this increased effort leads to a stronger performance of the organization, employees benefit through increased personal earnings. In linking pay with performance, employers may further benefit by attracting highly productive workers to the company.

FIGURE 9-12	Types of Variable Pay Plans Used by Canadian Companies	
Plan Type	**2002**	**2005**
Business incentive	69%	64%
Special recognition	42%	55%
Individual performance	27%	45%
Cash profit sharing	38%	42%
Stock options	37%	28%
Team/group	12%	15%
Gainsharing	15%	13%

FIGURE 9-13	Characteristics of Changing Compensation Systems	
Traditional		**Modern**
Pay = 100% base salary		Variable component added
Entitlement-base increases		Performance-driven gains
Few incentive/bonus plans, restricted to executives		Many kinds of plans, extended throughout the organization

Source: Patricia L. Booth, "Strategic Rewards Management: The Variable Approach to Pay," Report 52-90; Ottawa: The Conference Board of Canada, 1990, p. 2. The Conference Board of Canada is a membership-based, not-for-profit, independent applied research organization.

FIGURE 9-14	Components of a Total Reward System
1. Compensation	Wages, commissions, and bonuses
2. Benefits	Vacations, health insurance
3. Social interaction	Friendly workplace
4. Security	Stable, consistent position and rewards
5. Status/recognition	Respect, prominence due do work
6. Work variety	Opportunity to experience different things
7. Workload	Right amount of work (not too much, not too little)
8. Work importance	Is work valued by society?
9. Authority/control/autonomy	Ability to influence others; control own destiny
10. Advancement	Chance to get ahead
11. Feedback	Receive information helping to improve performance
12. Work conditions	Hazard free
13. Development opportunity	Formal and informal training to learn new knowledge/skills/abilities

Source: George T. Milkovich, Jerry M. Newman, and Nina Cole, *Compensation*, 1st Canadian ed., Toronto: McGraw-Hill Ryerson, 2005, p. 250. Used with permission.

total reward model
Inclusion of everything employees value in an employment relationship.

broadbanding
Consolidation of a large number of pay grades into a few "broad bands."

Total Reward Model

In the past few years we have seen the increased popularity of a **total reward model** in the compensation field. It is defined as the use as rewards of everything an employee values in an employment relationship. Figure 9-14 lists 13 components of such a system.

The total reward approach requires a reward system tailor-made for the organization, a major undertaking and a reason few organizations have implemented it—though to their great advantage.

Studies have shown that such companies enjoy easier recruitment of high-quality staff, reduced costs because of lower turnover, higher employee performance, and an enhanced reputation as an employer of choice.[38]

Broadbanding

Traditionally, salaries were grouped into a large number of pay grades. It was a system well suited for narrow and specialized jobs. In some organizations, the grade number has become a status symbol. Any additional responsibility usually resulted in a new job evaluation and a move up in the pay grades. With the increased focus on knowledge workers and skill-based pay, **broadbanding** has become a popular alternative. It is defined as a strategy for salary structures that consolidate a large number of pay grades into a few "broad bands." The advantages are several. Broadbanding does the following:

- Assists in flattening large, hierarchical organizations.
- Encourages employees to broaden their skills and abilities.
- Allows for a more flexible workforce and organization.
- Deemphasizes promotion.
- Eases internal transfers.
- Supports a new organizational climate.
- Simplifies paperwork.

Broadbanding is not a cure-all. With its high salary-range maximums, it does not have the salary control features of the traditional salary structure. Maintaining pay equity might also be more difficult. If two employees are in the same broad salary band doing similar work, and one is paid near the bottom of the range—because of lack of broader skills—and the other is paid near the top, how does one justify the salary differential to the employees?[39]

Pros and cons of broadbanding
www.auxillium.com/broadbn2.shtml

Tailor-Made Perks

The latest trend in reward plans is to allow employees to choose their rewards. Nortel Networks came up with the idea to thank employees by allowing supervisors and peers to recommend employees for special points that can be converted into money. The recommendations must be approved by two managers to avoid "back-scratching" between friends. For example, 5,000 points would be a modest thank-you, worth about $100. Points can be cashed in or exchanged for merchandise or saved for higher-value prizes, such as a trip to the National Basketball Association all-star game, valued at 160,000 points.

Martin Cozyn, the compensation vice-president says the beauty of the plan is that the rewards are immediate and concrete. Judy Zwickl, an associate director at the Conference Board of Canada's Centre for Management Effectiveness, says Nortel's reward scheme is in keeping with a general trend by companies to offer employees more choice. Choosing your own rewards, she says, can be viewed as an extension of such developments as flexible work arrangements and benefit plans.[40]

International Pay

"Think globally, act locally!" has become a popular part of business strategies of international companies. For HR managers, this policy has become quite a challenge. Traditionally, when companies went international, they imposed the "home-country system" on their overseas operations. It often led to quite serious discrepancies in HR policies. For example, it was possible that a Canadian middle manager in a Canadian subsidiary in Japan could be earning $150,000 (with generous "overseas benefits") while the Japanese counterpart, having the same job title and responsibilities, may be paid a quarter of the expatriate's salary—surely a cause for frictions.

The next generation of international enterprises were the multinational corporations (MNCs). For most of these, the strategy was to have each country's operation choose HR policies based on local customs and values. However, this approach made it impossible to integrate transnational organizational objectives. An integrated "global" strategy requires a common framework, but not a one-size-fits-all solution, which is quite a challenge when it comes to pay.

A good example is the differences in pay policies in the United States and Japan. U.S. base pay levels and merit increases are highly individualized and based on performance. Contrast this to Japan, where salary differences among those in the same job or level are more reflective of family size (number of dependents), age, and experience (job tenure) than performance differences. Also, in the United States, individual contributions (e.g., as indicated by performance appraisal ratings) tend to play a significant role in an employee's remuneration. In contrast, Japan's semiannual bonuses, measured in months of salary, tend to be far less affected by individual differences.[41]

The third generation of international companies, the truly global enterprises, will preserve national cultural differences while maintaining organizational values that allow the application of a global strategy. For example, these companies hire employees on the basis of their expertise, not nationality. A Japanese employee may work for a Canadian company in Germany. The Japanese employee would be expected to adapt to the German culture, while maintaining his Japanese values. The company, in turn, would have developed a corporate culture, policies, and strategies that would allow it to do business in any country of the world.[42] Pay policies will play a crucial role in the effectiveness of the organization.

The challenge for global HR managers is clear: develop HR policies that take into account global needs, national cultures, and individual differences—a difficult task. There is more discussion on these issues in Chapter 12 on diversity management.

● PAY AND ORGANIZATIONAL STRATEGY

In the past, internal equity has been the major concern of organizations. Because of increased competitiveness, nationally and internationally, the focus is shifting now to maintaining a competitive advantage. The prerequisite for developing a strategic pay plan is a clear corporate strategic agenda.[43] Only then is it possible to identify the behaviours and skills needed for the organization to be successful.

Lawler suggests a concentration on seven areas that affect pay systems:

1. **Motivating Performance.** Money is still a strong motivator. Studies show that effective incentive systems can improve the motivation of individuals to perform by as much as 40 percent.[44] A key determinant of the effectiveness of a pay system is the way performance is measured. Top management has to be able to define the organizational behaviour it wants in accordance with its strategic plan.

2. **Identifying Valued Rewards.** As mentioned, pay is an important motivator, partially because it leads to other rewards, such as status and prestige. Because pay means different things to different people, management has to understand how and why it is important to individuals. Only then is it possible to develop an effective reward system for all employees in the organization.

3. **Relating Rewards to Performance.** It is essential for employees to perceive a connection between their pay and their performance.[45] This relationship is the more effective the closer the tie is between the reward and the performance. The common year-end bonus does little to make individuals aware of any performance–reward connection.

4. **Setting Performance Goals.** Reward systems often fail because the goals are simply set too high. Effective goals have to be acceptable and attainable. Employee participation in setting goals tends to increase goal acceptance and in many cases leads to increased productivity.[46]

5. **Motivation and Punishment.** An individual's motivation to perform is strongly influenced by the consequences of missing set objectives. If the consequences are particularly negative, an individual may not even attempt to succeed. This point is especially relevant in organizations that encourage risk taking in managerial decision making.[47] Organizations have to make sure that their reward system allows for occasional failures. A good example is the 3M Company, which has a reward system that encourages its managers to take risks. They are rewarded on the basis of their long-term track record rather than the immediate success or failure of a venture.

6. **Motivating Skill and Knowledge Development.** A crucial issue for an organization is to develop the right mix of skills for its business objectives. A company in a knowledge work field needs different skills than a company in a service business. The pay system chosen has to reinforce the development of the skills needed, and it has to work for all levels of the organization. The appropriate kinds of skills are determined to a large degree by the management style used in the organization as well as the type of business it is in. An organization managed in a participative way needs very different skills than one managed in a top-down, autocratic way.

7. **Fostering Attraction and Retention.** The pay and reward system of an organization has a major impact on the attraction of individuals to work for it and on the retention of those individuals. Simply stated, companies that offer the most valued rewards tend to have the best attraction and retention rates.[48]

How these broad compensation strategies translate into more specific pay objectives is shown in Figure 9-15. It illustrates the pay philosophy of Honeywell Canada, which consists of four basic pay objectives and four basic pay principles.

FIGURE 9-15	Honeywell Canada's Pay Philosophy

Pay Objectives

- To attract the best person available for each Honeywell job.
- To encourage growth both on an individual basis and as a participant on a work team.
- To recognize the importance of high-quality work performance and to reward it accordingly.
- To encourage a career-long commitment to Honeywell.

Pay Principles

- Pay must be fully competitive in the market, as defined by each business.
- Each individual's pay must be fair in relationship to the pay other employees receive within the same Honeywell business.
- Pay must be communicated. That communication must explain general pay principles, the specific pay system applicable, and the process used to determine individual levels under that system.
- Each Honeywell business has the basic responsibility for establishing and maintaining its own pay system.

Source: Courtesy of Honeywell Canada.

The compensation principles originate from two sources: the overall strategy of the organization and its corporate values. If a company has as part of its strategy a strong emphasis on quality of customer service, the core principles have to focus on rewards that reinforce such behaviour. If, on the other hand, top management wants its managers to behave like entrepreneurs, the reward system has to promote risk-taking behaviour, without punishment for failure.

SUMMARY

Employee compensation, if properly administered, can be an effective tool to improve employee performance, motivation, and satisfaction. Mismanaged pay programs can lead to high turnover and absenteeism, more grievances, poor performance, and job dissatisfaction.

For compensation to be appropriate, it must be internally and externally equitable. Through job evaluation techniques, the relative worth of jobs is determined. This assures internal equity. Wage and salary surveys are used to determine external equity. With knowledge of the relative worth of jobs and external pay levels, each job can be properly priced.

The process of wage and salary administration is affected by several challenges, including union power, the productivity of workers, the company's compensation policies, and government constraints on pay. The *Canada Labour Code* is the major federal law affecting compensation management, regulating minimum wages, overtime, and child labour. The *Canadian Human Rights Act* seeks to eliminate sex-based pay differentials. All provinces have similar laws—labour codes and human rights legislation—for their jurisdictions. (A good example of government constraints on pay is wage and price controls. In 1975, the federal government introduced such a program to fight inflation. Pay and price increases were limited to a certain percentage and were controlled by an anti-inflation board. The program was abolished in 1978.)[49] Pay equity has become a major issue in the past few years. When the *Canadian Human Rights Act* was passed in 1977, it introduced the new concept of "equal pay for work of equal value," which requires employers to compare the content of jobs when determining pay scales and to pay equal wages for jobs of comparable value. The *Canadian Human Rights Commission* specifies four criteria by which jobs can be evaluated: skill, effort, responsibility, and working conditions. Provincial equal pay legislation is usually modelled after the federal law.

Financial incentives are another dimension of compensation management. Individual incentives attempt to relate pay to productivity. Group plans have the same objectives, but the relationship is often not as direct or obvious to workers. Some approaches pay a bonus for reaching a production target, others share the company's profits with workers, and still others share savings in labour costs.

The human resource function is directly and indirectly involved with employee motivation and job satisfaction. Human resource policies and programs have a major effect on organizational motivation.

Compensation consists of more than wages, salaries, and bonuses. Remuneration includes an ever-growing list of fringe benefits and services. Although these benefits are referred to as "noncash compensation," they are a significant part of the total labour cost of most employers. The next chapter describes the range of benefits and services offered by employers.

TERMS FOR REVIEW

autonomous work groups **p. 354**
broadbanding **p. 356**
Canada Labour Code **p. 345**
compa-ratio **p. 345**
equal pay for equal work **p. 347**
equal pay for work of equal value **p. 346**
external equity **p. 341**
incentive pay **p. 349**
internal equity **p. 341**

job evaluation **p. 335**
job grading **p. 336**
job ranking **p. 336**
key jobs **p. 342**
merit raise **p. 343**
pay equity **p. 346**
pay secrecy **p. 353**
piecework **p. 349**
point system **p. 336**

production bonuses **p. 349**
profit-sharing plan **p. 351**
rate range **p. 343**
red-circled rate **p. 344**
Scanlon Plan **p. 353**
skill- or knowledge-based
     pay **p. 354**
total reward model **p. 356**
wage and salary survey **p. 341**

SELF-ASSESSMENT EXERCISE

Examining Compensation Issues

1. One objective of compensation administration is to ensure administrative efficiency. **T F**

2. Job evaluation committees set wage and salary policies. **T F**

3. Job ranking is a superior evaluation method because it compares jobs directly. **T F**

4. The labour market for salary surveys is generally considered to be the local community. **T F**

5. Unions insist that nonunionized employees do not receive the same increases as union members. **T F**

6. Under no circumstances can an employee legally be paid less than minimum wage. **T F**

7. The pay equity concept specifies that women are paid the same as men for the same work. **T F**

8. The wage gap between males and females is between 5 and 10 percent for comparable groups. **T F**

9. Profit-sharing plans are ideal instruments for motivating employees. **T F**

10. The variable pay concept emphasizes a linkage between pay and performance. **T F**

SCORING

If you answered statements 2, 3, 5, 7, 9 as false, you get one point each. All other statements are true, resulting again in one point each.

Scores of 8–10: Very good! Congratulations.
Scores 5–7: You made it, but barely. It is advisable that you go over the chapter text again.

REVIEW AND DISCUSSION QUESTIONS

1. What is the difference between absolute and relative pay?

2. Why is job analysis information, discussed in Chapter 2, necessary before job evaluations can be performed?

3. Suppose that when you interview new employees, you ask them what they think is a fair wage or salary. If you hire them, you pay them that amount as long as it is reasonable and not below minimum wage laws. What problems might you expect?

4. Assume that your company has a properly conducted compensation program. If a group of employees asks you why they receive different hourly pay rates even though they perform the same job, how would you respond?

5. Why is the point system superior to all other systems? Discuss the advantages and disadvantages of the system.

6. If you are told to find out what competitors in your area are paying their employees, how would you get this information without conducting a wage and salary survey?

7. Even after jobs are first priced using a wage-trend line, what other challenges may cause you to adjust some rates upward?

8. Since financial incentives give employees feedback for good performance and they relate pay to performance, why do most companies pay wages and salaries rather than financial incentives?

9. Explain the difference between "equal pay for equal work" and "equal pay for work of equal value," and the implications of the difference for a human resource manager.

10. Under what circumstances are pay differentials justified?

11. Why is it so important to explain to employees the performance–reward relationship?

12. In what ways does the total reward model differ from the regular compensation approach?

CRITICAL THINKING QUESTIONS

1. Suppose that you manage a small business with 30 employees. You discover that some people are much more motivated by money and others are more motivated by security. Is it possible to satisfy the needs of both groups? What difficulties may arise?

2. "Money is a strong motivator" and "In surveys on what employees want from their job, money ranks low." How can you reconcile these two statements?

3. Obviously, profit-sharing plans are not an option as an incentive plan in nonprofit and government organizations. Can you think of incentive plans that will fulfill a similar function?

4. "Minimum wages increase unemployment." Please comment on this statement often made by many economists. Do you agree?

5. How should an HR manager find out what employees value as rewards? Is it acceptable to ask employees directly? Discuss. Are other methods preferable? Which? Why?

⊙ ETHICS QUESTION

The issue of the wage gap between the sexes has been discussed for decades, and pay equity legislation is supposed to take care of it. However, Statistics Canada reports that there is still a gap of about 20 percent in average salaries across jobs and provinces. It has been argued that women will never achieve pay equity, because their role in society often requires them to interrupt a career, have children, and stay home to bring them up. How ethical is it to expect women to make this sacrifice and then pay for it in terms of lower average compensation?

⊙ WEB RESEARCH EXERCISE

1. The National Center for Employee Ownership (U.S.)

   www.nceo.org

   (a) What are the characteristics of an effective employee ownership plan? What steps should be followed in its development?

   (b) Research seems to indicate that employee ownership plans have a different effectiveness depending on the size of the company. Try to determine what the relationship of the effect is to size and why there may be a difference in effectiveness.

2. An interactive program on employee ownership
   www.nceo.org/pages/interactive.cgi?nextpage=1
   Take the demonstration training program.

3. The Conference Board of Canada
   www.conferenceboard.ca
   What different types of information are available to Canadian managers regarding incentive plans?

4. Gainsharing: Different types of plans
   www.hr-guide.com/data/G443.htm
   www.qualitydigest.com/jul/gainshre.html
   Summarize the research studies on the effectiveness of gainsharing programs.

5. Chartered Institute of Personnel and Development
   www.cipd.co.uk/subjects/pay/general/totrewd. htm
   How many other total reward models can you identify? How do they differ?

⊙ INCIDENT 9-1

Compensation Administration at Reynolds Plastic Products

The family-owned Reynolds Plastic Products Co. in London, Ontario, was recently purchased by a much larger company, International Plastics Ltd. When the human resource director of International Plastics, Hans Himmelman, looked at Reynolds Plastic compensation policies, he became concerned that some of them were questionable and in some cases actually seemed to violate the law. When he asked the plant manager, an engineer, who also acted as an HR manager, how he determined pay rates, the manager explained that he would ask applicants what they earned in their previous job and just add 25 or 50 cents to this amount, depending on job experiences they had. To make matters worse, two recently hired female machinists complained that they were paid less for the same work than their male colleagues. The machine shop supervisor disputed their claim, asserting that the male employees had more work experience and deserved higher pay. Himmelman also discovered that productivity in the subsidiary was lower than in other plants of International Plastics.

An HR consultant was hired to assess the compensation system of the Reynolds Plastic subsidiary. The key points of her report are summarized below:

- Executives in the past have received an annual bonus determined by the owner at his discretion.

- Wages for hourly employees ranged from $14.00 for employees during their probationary period to $24.96 per hour for the more skilled or experienced ones.

- The amount of overtime paid by Reynolds was very modest; overtime was paid for all hours over 180 per month.

- The wage rates for different workers varied widely even on the same job; those employees who were heads of households received approximately 18 percent more than those workers who were not. Most heads of households were men.

- Female employees were paid 10 to 20 percent less in all job categories.

- On highly technical jobs, the firm paid a rate of 20 percent above the prevailing wage rate for these jobs. All other jobs were paid an average of 15 percent below the prevailing rate.

- Production workers were eligible for a $100 draw each month if there were no accidents during the month.

- Sales personnel were paid a commission and received a $50 bonus for every new customer.

- Whenever sales went up 10 percent, all the hourly employees got a day off with pay or could work one day at the double-time rate.
- Turnover averaged a modest 12 percent. However, in technical jobs turnover was less than 2 percent; in nontechnical jobs turnover was nearly 20 percent.
- Absenteeism followed the same pattern.

What laws were probably being violated?

What problems do you see with the incentives for (a) executives? (b) production workers? (c) salespeople? (d) hourly employees?

Himmelman read about new approaches to pay policies like broadbanding, variable pay, and profit sharing, and wondered whether either one would be a suitable solution for the subsidiary, especially profit sharing to increase low productivity. How would you advise him?

Develop a step-by-step plan of actions you would take and the order in which you would undertake them if you were made human resource director of the Reynolds subsidiary.

⊙ EXERCISE 9-1

A Realistic Job Evaluation Simulation

Form groups of three to five. (Three students may need approximately 20 minutes, five students about 45 minutes for the exercise.)

Use the following rules:

1. Have each student choose a job he or she is familiar with (ideally, a job description would be available, but is not essential). The jobs should be different, but from a single organization (e.g., hospital, school, manufacturing plant).
2. Use the table below to record numbers.

Critical Factors	Job 1	Job 2	Job 3	Job 4	Job 5

1. Responsibility
   a. Safety of others
   b. Equipment and materials
   c. Assisting trainees
   d. Product/service quality
2. Skill
   a. Experience
   b. Education/training
3. Effort
   a. Physical
   b. Mental
4. Working conditions
   a. Unpleasant conditions
   b. Hazards

3. Using Figure 9-4, find consensus in your group in choosing the most appropriate point level for each job.

Example: For the job of a janitor, what level of responsibility for the safety of others (critical factor) is appropriate? Probably not a high one, so a good choice might be Level I, 25 points. For a bus driver or an emergency room nurse, the appropriate choice might be Level IV, or 100 points.

4. Choose one of the above jobs, called a "key job"—a well-known job, ideally common in many organizations (e.g., secretary, accountant, tool-and-die maker in the manufacturing industry, and so on). Conduct a simulated wage survey. In this exercise it is sufficient to take an educated guess on what the key job is paid in the job market.

It does not matter whether you choose an hourly wage or a monthly or annual salary, but it must be the same for each job.

5. Calculate the pay coefficient by dividing the estimated wage by the point total of the key job, according to the formula:

$$\text{Pay coefficient (pd)} = \frac{\text{Wage of key jobs}}{\text{Point total for key jobs}} = \frac{\$}{\text{Point}}$$

6. Multiply all job point totals by the pay coefficient. The results are the wages/salaries for all the above jobs. (In reality, this procedure would have to be done by the job evaluation committee for all jobs in the organization, often in the hundreds.)

COMMENT

This exercise is a fairly realistic simulation of what is going on in a job evaluation committee. In all probability, the opinions in your group were very diverse when it came to determining the level for each job. The results, of course, are not realistic, since the point table has been created artificially and not by a job evaluation committee and the pay level of the key job has been estimated by you. Nevertheless, this exercise should give

you a good feel for the job evaluation process, using the point method. It also demonstrates the need to choose members of the committee who are knowledgeable about the jobs in the organization and are trained in the application of the point method. One more point: up to the wage survey, money was not part of the discussion, only points.

⊙ CASE STUDY    Maple Leaf Shoes Ltd.

Compensation Policy

Maple Leaf Shoes Ltd. is a medium-sized manufacturer of leather and vinyl shoes located in Wilmington, Ontario. It was started in 1973 and currently employs about 500 persons in its Ontario plant and some 200 more in offices and warehouses throughout Canada.

Recently, the company has been facing a number of issues and challenges that require immediate attention by its management. First, the cost of production at Maple Leaf Shoes has been rising slowly but steadily. Labour costs currently account for over 53 percent of manufacturing costs and have been increasing rapidly. The productivity levels of workers have not shown any increase in the past three years. If the present trend continues, the firm is likely to lose its price advantage over its competitors. Already, in two out of six popular brands sold by Maple Leaf Shoes, the prices for the firm's products are equal to or higher than those of its competition.

Second, over 70 percent of the company's staff are unionized. There are indications that remaining nonmanagerial staff are also about to be unionized. Management believes that this will reduce the already limited autonomy it possesses in hiring, terminating, and managing employees.

Robert Clark, president and majority shareholder of Maple Leaf Shoes, has recently begun reading about profit-sharing (PS) plans. Some time ago, in an airport VIP lounge, he met a CEO of a company that had a PS plan. The CEO marvelled at the productivity of his employees, their commitment, quality-consciousness, concern for customers, low absenteeism, and low turnover. That really got Clark's attention. The more he learned about this incentive system, the more he liked it, and the more he had talked to his managers about it. Since the idea came from him, they tend to support it and even show some enthusiasm. Among themselves, however, most are only lukewarm to the idea of letting workers have part of the company's profits. Managers, yes—they make the company profitable—but blue-collar workers?

So far, Maple Leaf Shoes' workers are paid the straight union wages negotiated two years ago, when the old contract expired. At that time, management tried to introduce a piece-rate incentive system, but no agreement could be reached on how the base rate would be set, something industrial engineers had to do. The unions did not trust Maple Leaf Shoes' engineers, whom they thought to be on management's side.

Recently, Clark asked Jane Reynolds, his special assistant in the Personnel Department, whether she knew much about PS plans. She had taken some human resource management courses and remembered that PS plans had been discussed, but she could not remember whether PS plans were more effective than other incentive plans. Clark then decided to call Tim Lance, the HR consultant, to look into the pros and cons of having a PS plan at Maple Leaf Shoes. He wanted to have the plan ready as soon as possible, since two unions were about to start contract negotiations and he thought it would be a good bargaining tool. He hoped that union representatives would embrace the idea of sharing profit and perhaps moderate their wage demands.

However, he was in for a rude awakening. He once mentioned casually the concept of profit sharing to one of the union presidents, without revealing his ideas of introducing such a plan at Maple Leaf Shoes. He received the following response: "Profit sharing? Forget it. That is a management gimmick. Its only purpose is to make workers work harder and make the company more profitable. And the risk is too great that there are no or low profits. What do we have then? Nothing. We want our negotiated wages and nothing more."

Clark wonders whether it would still be possible to introduce a PS plan. The other CEO has mentioned that his union is a strong supporter of the plan. How can he sell his unions on this concept? Would Tim Lance know a solution?

Discussion Questions

1. You are the consultant. Clark has asked you to submit a proposal for a PS plan for Maple Leaf Shoes. You wonder about the appropriateness of such an incentive system for Maple Leaf Shoes, but you promised to look into it. What will you tell Robert Clark?

2. Do you see a possibility of convincing Maple Leaf Shoes' unions to buy in on a PS plan?

3. What other incentive plans are suitable for Maple Leaf Shoes?

CASE STUDY CPIB Canadian Pacific and International Bank*

Ernie Kemball, an instructor in CPIB's training and development division, specialized in training managers and supervisors in developing human resource skills. One of his favourite topics was "How to motivate employees," an interesting but, as he well knew, difficult topic to teach, because everyone is motivated by different needs.

To get managers involved immediately and to arouse their interest Ernie preferred to use the case-study approach. His opening remark to every motivation seminar was to quote Professor Kavanagh: "Genuine and lasting employee motivation is not something management does, but rather a process that management fosters and allows to happen." He would then proceed to introduce the first case:

"Let's begin by looking at what not to do in terms of creating a motivating work environment. Here is an excellent case and, let me add, a real one. It was written by Dr. Craig Pinder, a professor at the Faculty of Business Administration, University of Victoria. It is based on an interview with 'Pamela Jones,' a bank employee in Vancouver. Use the expectancy model and answer the following questions:

- Did management make the "right" hiring decision?
- How did management fare with respect to providing a motivating work environment?
- To what degree did management fulfill the expectations of Pamela?
- Was the performance–reward connection clear to her?
- What should management have done to create a truly motivating work environment?"

Pamela Jones

Pamela Jones enjoyed banking. She had taken a battery of personal aptitude and interest tests that suggested she might like and do well in either banking or librarianship. She applied for employment with a large chartered bank, the Bank of Winnipeg, and was quickly accepted.

Her early experiences in banking were almost always challenging and rewarding. She was enrolled in the bank's management development program because of her education (a B.A. in languages and some postgraduate training in business administration), her previous job experience, and her obvious intelligence and drive.

During her first year in the training program, Pamela attended classes on banking procedures and policies and worked her way through a series of low-level positions in her branch. She was repeatedly told by her manager that her work was above average. Similarly, the training officer who worked out of the main office and coordinated the development of junior officers in the program frequently told Pamela that she was

"among the best three" of her cohort of 20 trainees. She was proud to be a banker and proud to be a member of the Bank of Winnipeg.

After one year in the management development program, however, Pamela found she was not learning anything new about banking or the bank itself. She was shuffled from one job to another at her own branch, cycling back over many positions several times to help meet temporary problems caused by absences, overloads, and turnover. Turnover—a rampant problem in banking—amazed Pamela. She could not understand for many months why so many people started careers "in the service" of banking, only to leave after one or two years.

After her first year, the repeated promises of moving her into her own position at another branch started to ring hollow. The training officer claimed that there were no openings at other branches suitable for her. On two occasions when openings did occur, the manager of each of the branches in question rejected Pamela, sight unseen, presumably because she had not been in banking long enough.

Pamela was not the only unhappy person at her branch. Her immediate supervisor, George Burns, complained that because of the bank's economy drive, vacated customer service positions were left unfilled. As branch accountant, Burns was responsible for day-to-day customer service. Eventually, George Burns left the bank to work for a trust company, earning $200 a month more for work similar to that he had been performing at the Bank of Winnipeg. This left Pamela in the position of having to supervise the same tellers who had trained her only a few months earlier. Pamela was amazed at all the mistakes the tellers made, but found it difficult to do much to correct their poor work habits. All disciplinary procedures had to be administered with the approval of head office.

After several calls to her training officer, Pamela was finally transferred to her first "real" position in her own branch. Still keen and dedicated, Pamela was soon to lose her enthusiasm.

At her new branch, Pamela was made assistant accountant. Her duties included the supervision of the seven tellers, some customer service, and a great deal of paperwork. The same economy drive that she had witnessed at her training branch resulted in the failure to replace customer service personnel. Pamela was expected to "pick up the slack" at the front desk, neglecting her own work. Her tellers seldom balanced their own cash, so Pamela stayed late almost every night to find their errors. To save on overtime, the manager sent the tellers home while Pamela stayed late, first to correct the tellers' imbalances, and then to finish her own paperwork. He told Pamela that as an officer of the bank, she was expected to stay until the work of her subordinates, and her own work, was satisfactorily completed. Pamela realized that most of her

---

*This case was reproduced, with permission, from C.C. Pinder, *Work Motivation*, Glenview, IL: Scott, Foresman, 1984. All rights reserved by the author.

counterparts in other branches were willing to give this sort of dedication; therefore, so should she. This situation lasted six months, with little sign of change in sight.

One day, Pamela learned from a phone conversation with a friend at another branch that she would be transferred to Hope, British Columbia, to fill an opening that had arisen. Pamela's husband was a professional, employed by a large corporation headquartered in Vancouver. His company did not have an office in Hope; moreover, his training was very specialized so that he could probably find employment only in large cities anyway.

Accepting transfers was expected of junior officers who wanted to get ahead in the bank. Pamela inquired at head office and learned that the rumour was true. Her training officer told her, however, that she could decline the transfer if she wished, but he could not say how soon her next promotion opportunity would come about.

Depressed, annoyed, disappointed, and frustrated, Pamela quit the bank.

➡ APPENDIX A

Calculation of Data in Point System Matrix (Replication of Figure 9-4)

Critical Factors	Levels or Degrees				Factor Points
	I	II	III	IV	
1. Responsibility (weight 40%)					**400**
Subfactors:					
a. Safety of others	20	80	140	200	
b. Equipment and materials	10	32	55	80	
c. Assisting trainees	10	32	55	80	
d. Product/service quality	5	17	29	40	
2. Skill (weight 30%)					**300**
Subfactors:					
a. Experience	18	72	126	180	
b. Education/training	12	48	94	120	
3. Effort (weight 20%)					**200**
Subfactors:					
a. Physical	8	32	56	80	
b. Mental	12	48	94	120	
4. Working conditions (weight 10%)					**100**
Subfactors:					
a. Unpleasant conditions	3	12	21	30	
b. Hazards	7	28	49	70	
Total points					**1,000**

Step 1. Determine Total Point Matrix Number

How many points to be used for allocation purposes is a personal choice. A rule of thumb is the number of compensable factors times 250. Another formula takes the highest-paid job and divides its wage rate by the wage rate of the lowest-paid job times 100. For example, if the president is paid $200,000 and the lowest job $20,000, the result is 10 ($200,000 : $20,000). Multiplying by 100 results in a total of 1000 points for the point system. (For convenience, numbers are rounded.)

Step 2. Determine Individual Factor Weights

This decision is made by the Job Evaluation Committee. In this example the committee decided on the following weight distribution:

Responsibility	40%
Skill	30%
Effort	20%
Working conditions	10%
	100%

Multiplying 1000 points by the weights results in:

Responsibility	400 points
Skill	300
Effort	200
Working conditions	100

Step 3. Determine Subfactor Weights and Allocation of Subfactor Points

Again, the job evaluation committee has to decide the weight of each subfactor.

Responsibility

Safety of others	50%
Equipment and materials	20%
Assisting trainees	20%
Product/service quality	10%

Skill

Experience	60%
Education/training	40%

Effort

Physical	40%
Mental	60%

Working conditions

Unpleasant conditions	30%
Hazards	70%

Now the factor points are multiplied by the subfactor weights. We will use only the first factor, responsibility, for this example.

Safety of others:	400 points × 50% = 200 points
Equipment and materials:	400 points × 20% = 80 points
Assisting trainees:	400 points × 20% = 80 points
Product/service quality:	400 points × 10% = 40 points

The highest subfactor points are always given to the highest level, in this case IV.

The lowest-level point value is calculated by the formula: Subfactor weight × Factor weight.

Safety of others:	50% × 40% = 20 points
Equipment and materials:	50% × 20% = 10 points
Assisting trainees:	50% × 20% = 10 points
Product/service quality:	50% × 10% = 5 points

Step 4. Determine Increments Between Levels

This is calculated by the formula: (Highest-level points – Lowest-level points)/(Number of levels – 1).

For subfactor "Safety of others," this means:

$$\frac{200 - 20}{4 - 1} - \frac{180}{3} = 60 \text{ points}$$

The steps are: 20, 80, 140, 200 (see table at beginning of this Appendix). This assumes equal distance between levels. However, if the job evaluation committee feels that this does not reflect reality, it is free to determine the point differences between levels. *What is important is that employees perceive this judgment to be fair.*

Employee Benefits and Services

In many respects Canada's position in the area of fringe benefits is unique, striking a balance between the situation prevailing in the U.S. and that in Europe.

Bill Megalli[1]

CHAPTER 10

EMPLOYEE BENEFITS

Sources of benefits information
www.hrsdc.gc.ca/eng/
home.shtml
www.benefits.org
www.mercerhr.com
www.watsonwyatt.com
www.hewittassociates.com/
Intl/NA/en-US/Default.aspx
www.ifebp.org

To many people, compensation means pay. Anything else an employer might provide is often considered so minor that it is called a "fringe benefit." The reality is, however, that most employers now make benefits an important part of the total compensation package and use it increasingly as a tool to attract, motivate, and to keep key personnel. Some employers even go so far as to tailor-make benefit packages for individual employees to satisfy their special needs.

"Did you receive another job offer?" Carla asked her brother.

"Yes. I received a letter yesterday from a bank in Vancouver. That's my problem; I don't know which to accept," Ed responded. "The pay, working conditions, and job duties are almost identical. The people I met at both banks seem equally pleasant."

"What about fringe benefits?" Carla asked.

"What about them? They're only the extras. They don't make much difference," Ed answered.

"They don't make much difference? Are you kidding?" Carla questioned. "Some companies spend half as much on benefits as they do on wages."

"Now who's kidding? They're just fringes," Ed asserted.

"I'm not kidding. Let me give you an example. Suppose one bank pays all your supplementary health and life insurance and the other pays half. At a cost of $2,000 a year, you would be $1,200 better off with the bank that pays all of your benefits," Carla said confidently.

Ed interrupted, "You mean $1,000."

"Don't forget taxes," Carla added. "To pay your half of the $2,000 you would have to come up with $1,000, true. But to have $1,000, you would probably have to earn $1,200 before taxes. And that is $100 a month."

"Maybe I should find out more about their benefits before I decide," Ed pondered.

When employees like Ed ignore benefits and services, they exclude from consideration all other forms of compensation except pay. Admittedly, pay is a major concern to employees. But since the typical organization spends a considerable share of its labour costs on benefits and services, ignorance like Ed's raises questions about the role of pay and benefits. Simply put, what is the difference between pay and benefits?

Pay is called *direct compensation* because it is based on critical job factors or performance.

Benefits and services are *indirect compensation*, because they are usually extended as a condition of employment and are not directly related to performance. They include insurance, income security, time off, and scheduling benefits, in addition to educational, financial, and social services.

To explain the broad scope of benefits and services, this chapter discusses the objectives of indirect compensation. We follow this with an examination of legally required benefits. The chapter concludes with a description of voluntary benefit programs.

BENEFITS AND CORPORATE STRATEGY

Benefit programs have become a very significant part of a company's compensation system, slowly approaching the 50 percent mark of annual payroll expenses, as compared to about 15 percent in the early 1950s. This means that when we talk about an employee's annual salary of $50,000 we are really talking about $75,000 in actual payroll expenses for the company. What once were called "fringe benefits" are not "fringe" anymore.

Benefit policies can have a significant impact on the issue of attracting and retaining key and high-performing employees. Benefits will not replace performance incentives as motivators, but especially for older generations health and pension benefits can make a great difference in corporate loyalty.

To make benefits an important part of the company's compensation strategy has paid off tremendously for Husky Injection Molding Systems Ltd. in Bolton, Ontario. The firm spends more than $4 million a year on its 2,800 employees at a time when most companies are considering cutting back. However, Husky managers say that the program more than pays for itself in higher productivity and, ultimately, in lower costs.

Husky's voluntary turnover rate is about 15 percent, or 5 percent below the indu... Absenteeism averages four days a year in contrast with an industry average of 7.3 days. And ... claims are 1.2 for every 200,000 hours worked, as against an industry average of 5.8, according to Dirk Schlimm, Husky's Vice-President of Corporate Affairs.

It is obvious from this example that benefits can play a critical part of a company's staffing strategy.

THE ROLE OF INDIRECT COMPENSATION

Employee benefits and services seek to satisfy several objectives. These include societal, organizational, and employee objectives.

Societal Objectives

Industrial societies have changed from rural nations of independent farmers and small businesses to urban nations of interdependent wage earners. This interdependence was illustrated forcefully by the mass unemployment of the Great Depression of the 1930s. Since that time, industrial societies have sought group solutions to societal problems.

To solve social problems and provide security for interdependent wage earners, governments rely on the support of employers. Through favourable tax treatment, employees can receive most benefits tax-free, while employers can deduct the cost of benefits as a regular business expense. The result has been a rapid growth in indirect compensation since the Second World War.

Today, benefits and services give many employees financial security against illness, disability, and retirement. In fact, the growth of benefits since the Second World War means that the average employer spends more than one-third of its payroll costs on benefits and services. No longer are benefits those "little extras" or "fringes." These outlays are a major and growing cost of doing business. If this trend continues, benefits and services could amount to over one-half of most firms' payroll costs in the near future.

Organizational Objectives

From these large outlays for benefits, what do employers gain? Companies must offer some benefits if they are to be able to recruit successfully in the labour market. If a company did not offer retirement plans and paid vacations, recruits and present employees would work for competitors who did offer these "fringes." Similarly, many employees will stay with a company because they do not want to give up benefits, so employee turnover is lowered. For example, employees may stay to save pension credits or their rights to the extended vacations that typically come with greater seniority.

Vacations, along with holidays and rest breaks, help employees reduce fatigue and may enhance productivity during the hours the employees do work. Similarly, retirement, health care, and disability benefits may allow workers to be more productive by freeing them from concern about medical and retirement costs. Likewise, if these benefits were not available to employees, they might elect to form a union and collectively bargain with the employer. (Although collective action is legal, many nonunion employers prefer to remain nonunion.) Therefore, it is accurate to state that indirect compensation may do the following:

- reduce fatigue
- discourage labour unrest
- satisfy employee objectives
- aid recruitment
- reduce turnover
- minimize overtime costs

Employee Objectives

Employees usually seek employer-provided benefits and services because of lower costs and availability. For example, company insurance benefits are usually less expensive, because the employer may pay some or all of the costs. Even when the workers must pay the entire premium, rates are often lower, because group plans save the insurer the administrative and selling costs of many individual policies. With group plans, the insurer also can reduce the adverse selection of insuring just those who need the insurance. Actuaries—the specialists who compute insurance rates—can pass these savings on to policyholders in the form of lower premiums.

For some employees, the primary objective may be to obtain benefits and services—especially supplementary health and life insurance. Without employer-provided insurance, these policies may not be obtainable if the employee has a preexisting medical condition.

The objectives of society, organizations, and employees have encouraged rapid growth of benefits and services. This growth has affected all areas of benefits and services, including insurance, income security, and time-off benefits.

There are two types of benefits and services: those that are legally required and those that an employer voluntarily gives. This chapter will focus first on the required type.

LEGALLY REQUIRED BENEFITS

Legally required benefits and services are imposed upon organizations by the government. As a result, employers must comply with the law and its procedures. Most of these benefits and services are designed to help employees. In general, government seeks to ensure minimum levels of financial security for the nation's workforce. Figure 10-1 shows that the objective of providing financial security is to ease the monetary burdens of retirement, death, long-term disability, and unemployment. The loss of income from these causes is cushioned by the security provisions. The financial problems of *involuntary unemployment* are lessened by unemployment compensation. And job-related injuries and death are compensated under workers' compensation laws. None of these programs fully reimburses the affected workers; nevertheless, each worker does get a financial base to which additional protection can be added.

Legally required benefits and services are important to the human resource department for two reasons. *First*, top management holds the human resource department responsible for meeting these legal obligations. If the department is to meet this responsibility, it must ensure that the firm is in compliance with the law. *Second*, if the obligations are improperly handled, the result can be severe fines and more taxes. None of these outcomes contributes to the organization's objectives.

FINANCIAL SECURITY

A large majority of Canadians are financially dependent on their monthly paycheques. Only a small percentage of the population is self-employed; most others work for another person or organization. To protect the well-being of society, governmental regulations on retirement plans, employment insurance, disability compensation, and health care are imperative. The major legal provisions concerning the above matters will be discussed below. It should be emphasized that in Canada (unlike in the United States or in some other Western countries), many of these regulations are provincially administered. To suit the specific work environments, many of these statutes and provisions vary from province to province.

The Canada Pension Plan (CPP) and the Quebec Pension Plan (QPP)

The **Canada Pension Plan (CPP)** (Quebec Pension Plan in the province of Quebec), which came into effect on January 1, 1966, is a mandatory plan for all self-employed persons and employees in

Information on Canada Pension Plans
www.hrsdc.gc.ca/eng/isp/cpp/cpptoc.shtml

Canada Pension Plan (CPP)
A mandatory, contributory, and portable pension plan applicable to all employees and self-employed persons in Canada, except those working for the federal government.

FIGURE 10-1	Sources of Financial Protection for Workers	
Protection for Workers	**Sources of Protection**	**Legislating Government**
Fair remuneration	Minimum-wage acts	Federal and provincial
Retirement	Canada Pension Plan	Federal (except in Quebec)
Involuntary unemployment	Employment Insurance	Federal
Industrial accidents	Workers' compensation acts	Federal and provincial
Medical care	Health insurance plans	Provincial
Child sustenance	Family allowances	Federal

contributory plans
Benefits that require the employer to contribute to the cost of the benefit.

portability clauses
Allow accumulated pension rights to be transferred to another employer when an employee changes employers.

Canada. Both CPP and QPP are **contributory plans**—that is, both the employer and the employee pay part of the costs. **Portability clauses** are applicable to the plans in Canada, meaning that pension rights are not affected by changes of job or residence. The plans are also tied to cost-of-living changes.

In May 1999, the Supreme Court of Canada ruled that governments cannot limit benefits by discriminating against same-sex common-law relationships, since it would be contrary to the principles enshrined in the Canadian Charter of Rights and Freedoms as well as the *Canadian Human Rights Act*. Following this ruling the federal government enacted in June 2000 the *Modernization of Benefits and Obligations Act* to ensure that common-law relationships (both opposite- and same-sex) are treated equally under federal law. All other provinces and territories have issued similar laws.

Employment Insurance (EI)

In 1940, Canada started a program called Unemployment Insurance (UI), renamed **Employment Insurance (EI)** in 1995, to help alleviate people's financial problems during the transition from one job to another. The *Unemployment Insurance Act* of 1971 significantly changed and added to the program. Since 1971 there have been several modifications to eligibility criteria and payment schedules. Currently, approximately 11 million Canadians are covered by the scheme. Most salaried and hourly workers who are employed for a minimum number of hours, depending on regional unemployment rates, are covered by EI. The self-employed are not eligible for benefits under the present regulations.

Employment Insurance (EI)
A program to help alleviate the financial problems of workers in Canada during the transition from one job to another.

The *Employment Act* became fully implemented in 2001–2002. It has been fundamentally restructured. Key features include the following:

- benefits based on hours rather than on weeks worked;
- collection of premiums based on first dollar earned;
- reduction in the maximum benefit entitlement period;
- increased eligibility requirements for people entering the labour market;
- reduction in benefit rate based on an individual's claim history;
- a family income supplement top-up for claimants in low-income families; and
- a lower income threshold for the clawback of benefits.

Information on EI
www.hrsdc.gc.ca/eng/corporate/az/index.shtml#e

SPOTLIGHT ON ETHICS

Trust Betrayed

You are the HR manager of a medium-sized, family-owned company. You discovered that a longtime, trusted employee, a purchasing officer, had been embezzling company funds for several years to the tune of close to $20,000. It was found out only because she went on vacation and a replacement had taken over her job for that time. She was known to be hardworking, and it had been the first vacation she had taken in many years. You and all the staff had always admired her dedication and commitment to the company. The company owner did not want to press charges, because of her length of service and because, in his opinion, the loss was not that significant. He also blamed himself for not installing more effective controls. The purchase officer's excuse was that she had had a bad divorce and that her husband did not provide

sufficient support for herself and her children to continue their lifestyle.

When you wanted to dismiss her for cause, she cried and asked you to consider her situation and think of her children. She asked whether you could give as the official reason for her leaving the company a company reorganization and elimination of her job, so that she would be able to draw unemployment benefits and have a better chance to find another job. There has been a precedent for this, when the owner did not press charges against an employee who had stolen company property and who had been officially "laid off for lack of work" and had been receiving unemployment benefits. You feel sorry for her that she has ruined her life and career and you think of her children. What are you going to do?

workers' compensation
Compensation payable by employers collectively for injuries sustained by workers in the course of their employment.

health insurance
Health and medical insurance provided by provincial governments with assistance from the federal government.

Federal and provincial holidays
http://en.wikipedia.org/wiki/
Holidays_in_Canada

Workers' Compensation Acts

All provinces and the territories have some act or other (usually called *Workers' Compensation Act* or *Ordinance*) that entitles workers to **workers' compensation** in the event of personal injury by accident during their regular work (in Ontario, on January 1, 1998, the *Workers' Compensation Act* was replaced by the *Workplace Safety and Insurance Act*, with reductions in benefits and limits to entitlement). The administration is done provincially, and all the provincial acts are of the "collective liability" type: that is, compensation is payable by employers collectively. The industries covered by the act are classified into groups according to their special hazards, and all employers in each group are collectively liable for payment of compensation to all workers employed in that group. The annual contribution rate (a percentage of payroll) is determined on the basis of an employer's total annual payroll figures. However, an employer can also be charged a higher rate of contribution if there are many workers' compensation claims.

Health Insurance Plans

Canada's health and medical insurance, also referred to as simply **health insurance**, is provided by provincial governments with assistance from the federal government. In April 1972, the scope of the *Medical Care Act* of 1966 was widened to include all of Canada. Since then, a major part of the cost of medical care has been paid for by taxes collected at the federal level. Supplementary health plans are discussed below under "Voluntary Benefits."

Holidays and Vacations

Vacations are usually based on the employee's length of service, but federal and provincial laws specify a two-week (in Saskatchewan, three-week) minimum vacation entitlement. In some regions, this increases to three weeks (in Saskatchewan, four) after five, six, or ten years of service. Holidays are also federally and provincially regulated. For a listing of federal and provincial holidays, see the URL in the margin.

Workers' compensation covers a wide variety of benefits, but the law stipulates that workers cannot sue their employers in case of injury. Is this just?

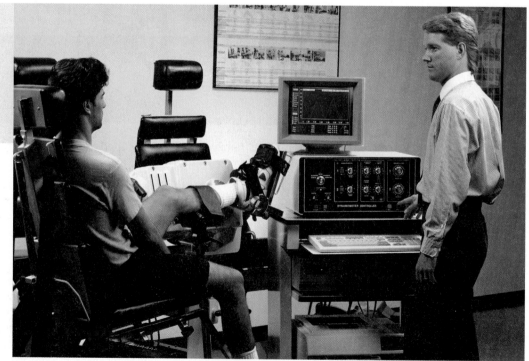

CORBIS.

⊙ VOLUNTARY BENEFITS

Insurance Benefits

Insurance benefits spread the financial risks encountered by employees and their families. These risks are shared by pooling funds in the form of insurance premiums. Then, when an insured risk occurs, the covered employees or their families are compensated.

Life Insurance

Life insurance was the first form of insurance offered to workers by employers. As a result, group life insurance has become a practically universal element in corporate employee benefit programs. Several surveys show that 99 percent of Canadian companies provide a group life insurance program for all of their employees.[2] There are two types of plans. Under the *first*, the deceased's family receives a lump sum payment. Under the *second*, the family receives a generally lower lump sum than in the first case, plus a survivor's pension payable to the deceased's spouse for life. This amount is supplemented by family allowance benefits, CPP benefits, workers' compensation if the death is caused by a work-related accident or illness, and, in certain provinces, automobile insurance act benefits if death is the result of a traffic accident.

Employers generally pay the cost of these life insurance plans. Coverage is commonly based on the employee's pay, often 100 or 200 percent of annual pay. Optional expanded coverage is usually available.

Health-Related Insurance

As mentioned, all Canadian citizens—and landed immigrants—are covered by provincial health care programs. For this reason, employers in Canada offer only supplementary health insurance plans. This is in contrast to the United States, where health insurance is the most common form of coverage.[3]

In addition to the provincial health insurance, group life and disability insurance is widely provided as an employee benefit. Some firms still offer major medical insurance for their employees whenever they travel outside the province or country. Increasingly, many organizations have also been providing dental insurance to their employees. In many cases, the cost of health and dental premiums is shared between the employer and the employee.

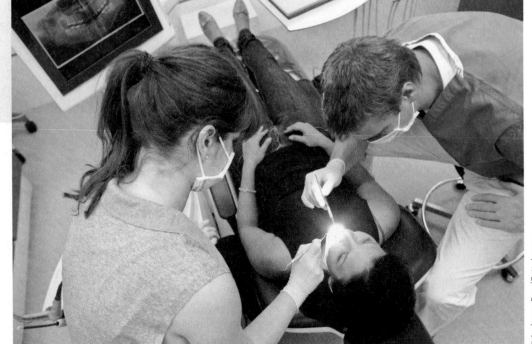

Dental insurance is a common benefit offered by many companies to their employees, but it is a voluntary one. Should it be mandatory?

© Anderson Ross/Getty Images.

Salary Continuation Plans

If an employee misses a few days because of illness, it is usually not crucial from a financial point of view, since most employers grant paid sick leave for a limited time. It becomes more of a problem when an employee becomes disabled for a longer period of time or even permanently. Canadian companies offer short-term and long-term disability plans.

A **short-term disability plan** typically involves crediting or allocating a certain number of days to an employee, to be used as sick leave for nonoccupational accidents or illnesses. Sick leave credits may be cumulative or noncumulative. A plan is cumulative if insured credits earned during one year may be transferred to the following year; it is noncumulative when the employee's entitlement is reviewed on a yearly basis or after each illness.

For workers who are disabled for a prolonged time, employers offer some form of **long-term disability insurance**. Such plans generally have a long waiting period (six months is very common), and they pay the employee a smaller amount (usually 50 or 60 percent) of the employee's working income. Under most plans, these payments, if necessary, are made until the normal retirement age is reached.

short-term disability plan
A benefit plan crediting a number of days to be used as sick leave.

long-term disability insurance
A benefit plan providing the employee with an income in the case of long-term illness or injury.

➤ EMPLOYEE SECURITY BENEFITS

In addition to insurance, there are noninsurance benefits that enhance employee security. These benefits seek to ensure an income before and after retirement.

Employment Income Security

Discharges or layoffs may entail severe economic consequences for an employee; the impact, however, can be cushioned by employer-provided benefits. If employees have not been given at least two weeks' notice, and if the dismissal was not for just cause, according to the *Canada Labour Code* they are entitled to severance pay equal to two weeks' regular wages. For executives, who usually work on a contract basis, **severance pay** can reach six months' or a year's compensation.

Layoffs may be eased by accrued vacation pay. A few companies go so far as to provide a **guaranteed annual wage (GAW)**. These plans assure the worker of receiving some minimum amount of work or pay. For example, employees may be promised a minimum of 1,500 hours of work or pay a year (compare this with the "normal" 52 forty-hour weeks for a total of 2080 hours). Some employers guarantee 30 hours per week. Even on layoff, the employees draw some income.

The auto industry is a leader in another method, **supplemental unemployment benefits (SUB)**. When employees are out of work, employment insurance benefits are supplemented by the employer from monies previously paid to the SUB fund. This assures covered employees an income almost equal to their previous earnings for as long as the SUB fund remains solvent.

severance pay
Payment to a worker upon permanent separation from a company.

guaranteed annual wage (GAW)
A benefits plan by which an employer assures employees that they will receive a minimum annual income regardless of layoffs or a lack of work.

supplemental unemployment benefits (SUB)
Private plans providing compensation for wage loss to laid-off workers.

Retirement Security

Retirement plans were originally designed to reward long-service employees. Through employer generosity and union pressure, retirement plans have grown in scope and coverage, so that in Canada the average firm spends 6.3 percent of its total payroll costs on government and private pension plans alone.[4]

Registered Pension Plans (RPP)

As of January 2006, 38.1 percent of all Canadian employees are covered by RPP, so called because they have to be registered with Revenue Canada for preferential tax considerations.[5] Most employers contribute to such plans. Integrated RPP—which make up approximately two-thirds of all RPP—take into account benefits received from the Canada Pension Plan.[6] (See the discussion in the latter part of this chapter.)

Defined Benefits (DB) Plans. With a **defined benefits (DB) plan**, the employee receives a fixed dollar amount as a pension, depending on age and length of service. Many employees and unions prefer DB plans because of their predictable outcomes. These type of plans are also strictly regulated by the *Employee Retirement Income Security Act*. The advantage for employees is that they know in advance what their retirement benefits will be. For the employer the advantage is that by providing a predictable, guaranteed benefit at retirement that is valued by workers, such a plan can promote worker loyalty and help retain valuable workers.

Information on RPP
www.cra-arc.gc.ca/tx/rgstrd/rpp-rpa/fq-eng.html

defined benefits (DB) plan
A benefits plan whose benefits are defined by a formula based on age and length of service, with the employer assuming responsibility for funding.

Defined Contribution (DC) Plans. When employer and employee contribute to a pension plan, it is called a **defined contribution (DC) plan**; if only the employer makes the contributions, it is called a *noncontributory plan.* In a *contributory plan,* the employee makes a commitment to make regular payments, which are matched by the employer. A typical arrangement would be that the employee allows monthly or weekly deductions from his or her salary, say 5 percent, and the employer either matches this or makes a higher contribution, up to a specific level. These amounts are usually invested in secure funds. After the employee's retirement the money is used to purchase an annuity or may be invested in other approved financial arrangements that pay a regular income to the retiree.

For employees, a DC plan may mean greater benefits, especially if it is started at a younger age (longer investment horizon). This is true even if employees leave the organization, since accumulations continue to participate in the accounts' investment. (In a DB plan, accrued benefits are frozen when the employee leaves. With inflation, benefits can lose much of their value by the time the employee retires.) With a DC plan employees also have more control over their investment, because they own their retirement accounts individually, and it is portable—that is, the investment can be moved to another organization.

Two significant problems have developed in the administration of pension plans. *First,* some employers go out of business, leaving the pension plan unfunded or only partially funded. *Second,* some companies minimize their pension costs by having very long vesting periods. **Vesting** gives the workers the right to pension benefits even if they leave the company. Thus, an employee who quits or is fired before the vesting period has passed often has no pension rights. Since both of these problems may impose hardships on employees and on the nation's welfare programs, Parliament has passed the *Pension Benefits Standards Act.*

Pension Benefits Standards Act

The **Pension Benefits Standards Act** regulates pension plans in industries under the jurisdiction of the Government of Canada, such as banks, railways, shipping companies, and radio and other communications companies. In addition, eight provinces (Alberta, Saskatchewan, Manitoba, New Brunswick, Ontario, Quebec, Nova Scotia, and Newfoundland) have enacted their own pension benefits acts that in content are similar to the federal act. Pension plans in the remaining provinces, to qualify for tax deductions, must conform to certain standards set forth in the federal legislation. The *Pension Benefits Standards Act* requires that pension funds be held in trust for members, and that the funds not be held under the complete custody and control of either the employer or the employees. To accomplish this, the funding of a private pension plan must be carried out by one or more of the following means:

- an insurance contract with a company authorized to conduct a life insurance business in Canada;
- a trust in Canada whose trustees are either a trust company or a group of individuals, at least three of whom live in Canada and one of whom must be independent of the employer and employees;
- a corporate pension society; and
- an arrangement administered by the Government of Canada or a provincial government.

PAID TIME-OFF BENEFITS

Time periods during which the employee is not working, but is getting paid, are the result of time-off benefits. Time-off benefits include legal—such as statutory holidays and vacation—and voluntary benefits such as wash-up time. Although these benefits may seem minor, according to one survey they were the costliest major category, making up 15 percent of gross annual payroll.[7]

On-the-Job Breaks

Some of the most common forms of time-off benefits are those found on the job. Examples include rest breaks, meal breaks, and wash-up time. Through a break in the physical and mental effort of a job, productivity may be increased. The major problem for human resource and line managers is the tendency of employees to stretch these time-off periods:

> When one human resource manager was confronted by a supervisor with the problem of stretched breaks, she suggested a simple solution. Each employee was assigned a specific break time—from 9:15 to 9:30 a.m., or 9:30 to 9:45 a.m., for example—but could not leave for break until the preceding employee returned. Since each clerk was anxious to go on break, the peer group policed the length of breaks and the stretched breaks ended.

defined contribution (DC) plan
A benefits plan based on amounts contributed by the employer and the employee, the final pension depending on amounts contributed, investment income, and economic conditions at retirement.

vesting
A provision in employer-provided retirement plans that gives workers the right to a pension after a specified number of years of service.

Pension Benefits Standards Act
A federal act regulating pension plans in industries under the jurisdiction of the Government of Canada.

David Anderson

Paid Sick Leave

Absences from work are unavoidable. Today, most companies pay workers when they are absent for medical reasons by granting a limited number of days of sick leave per year. Unfortunately, this is one of the most abused benefits; many workers take the attitude that these are simply extra days off. If the human resource policies prohibit employees from crediting unused sick leave to next year's account, absences increase near the end of the year. To minimize abuses, some companies require medical verifications of illness or pay employees for unused sick leave.

A few firms avoid the abuse question by granting "personal leave days." This approach allows an employee to skip work for any reason and get paid, up to a specified number of days per year. Sick leave banks allow employees to "borrow" extra days above the specified number when they use up their individual allocation. Then when they earn additional days, the days are repaid to the sick leave bank.

Holidays and Vacations

As mentioned under federally and provincially regulated holidays and vacation days, most employers grant vacation days beyond the minimum required number, depending on tenure.[8] Like sick leave, however, this benefit is subject to abuse. Employees sometimes try to stretch the holiday by missing the workday before or after the holiday. Policies that require attendance the day before and after a holiday as a condition of holiday pay lessen this problem.

Policies for vacations vary widely. Some companies allow employees to use vacation days a few at a time. Other companies insist that the worker take the vacation all at once. A few employers actually close down during designated periods and require vacations to be taken during this period. Still other companies negate the reason for vacations completely by allowing employees to work and then receive vacation pay as a bonus.

⊙ EMPLOYEE SERVICES

Some companies go beyond pay and traditional benefits. They also provide educational, financial, and social services for their employees.

Educational Assistance

Tuition refund programs are among the more common employer services. These programs partially or completely reimburse employees for furthering their education. They may be limited only to courses that are related to the employee's job, or the employer may reimburse workers for any educational expenditure. In the future, more companies may follow the lead of Kimberly-Clark Corporation in the United States:

> Kimberly-Clark created an educational savings account for employees and their dependants. The company gives employees credits for each year of service. Then when an employee or dependant wants to go to college, he or she can be reimbursed partially from the educational savings account established by the company.

Financial Services

Probably the oldest service is employee discount plans. These programs—common among retail stores and consumer goods manufacturers—allow workers to buy products from the company at a discount.

SPOTLIGHT ON HRM
Women's Work

By Kathryn Dorrell

Juggling the roles of mom, daughter, wife and employee is taking its toll as women's absenteeism outpaces men's. Plan sponsors can implement strategies that acknowledge this reality.

A recent profile of Barbara Stymiest, president and chief executive officer of the Toronto Stock Exchange, in a prominent business magazine discussed the executive's demanding hours in the context of the fact that she has a young daughter. As the mom of an 18-month-old, I was interested in how Stymiest juggled a career and family. But at the same time, I couldn't help bristle at the realization that discussions of businessmen who also happen to be dads seldomly delve into this territory.

Balancing work and family life isn't the juggling act for most working men that it is for women. This seemingly sexist statement is a reality in many organizations, and it's backed up by a new Statistics Canada report, *Women in Canada 2000*.

In 1999, three times as many working women took time off to deal with personal and family issues than men. Female workers missed an average of seven days because of such commitments—up from two days in the mid-'70s—whereas working men missed one day, about the same as two decades ago. Meanwhile, 28% of women worked fewer than 30 hours a week compared to 10% of men, and 20% of these women say they did so because of personal and family responsibilities.

Putting some hard numbers behind the old adage that a woman's work is never done isn't about male bashing or even trying to change what are obviously still ingrained societal trends. (No, I'm not about to suggest that plan sponsors offer lunch-and-learn sessions teaching dads how to take their sick babies to the doctor.) With a growing number of women dominating the workforce—46% in 1999, up from 37% in 1976—and in increasingly senior positions, it simply makes good business sense for plan sponsors to acknowledge and confront this issue.

The Royal Bank has done just that. Three-quarters of its employees are women and it has implemented the kind of progressive benefits strategies that not only keep talented female employees in the working world but help them climb the proverbial ladder, even if it's with a baby or two and an aging parent in tow.

The bank offers leaves, that have ranged from one day to a year and are sometimes paid, for employees to deal with family matters. In addition, 30% of all employees are currently enjoying some sort of flexible working arrangement—be it flex hours or job sharing. And if a supervisor doesn't appear to be supportive of these initiatives, workers can take up the issue using an employee ombudsman phone service.

Norma Tombari, manager of workforce solutions at the Royal Bank, believes that if the company didn't offer these programs it would lose many of its best workers to the competition. "I would love to see more men using these options," she adds. "But right now it's mostly women."

Another beacon of progress is the arrival of Catalyst on the Canadian consulting scene. The New York–based firm, which opened a Toronto office recently and has worked with Bell Canada, specializes in identifying barriers and opportunities for women in the workplace.

However, the best benefit for working women may actually be as simple as creating a work environment and communications strategy that conveys the message that organizations recognize men have personal and family commitments too.

"There is still such a stigma around men taking time off for family matters. It's a huge cultural shift that men are trying to fight. They don't want to say they can't stay for the 5 p.m. meeting because they have to pick up the kids for fear of how they will be viewed," says Judy Hauserman, senior vice-president at Aon Consulting. "If we approach this issue from only a gender perspective, we miss the point."

Kathryn Dorrell is associate editor of *Benefits Canada*. She can be reached at kdorrell@rmpublishing.com.

Source: © 2000 Rogers Media. This article first appeared in the November 2000 edition of *Benefits Canada* magazine.

Credit unions are another well-established employee service. The interest collected by the credit union on loans and investments is distributed to members in the form of dividends. The dividends (interest payments) are allocated in proportion to the amount employees have in their share (savings) account. The lower interest rate on loans, the higher interest on deposits, and payroll deductions for savings or loan repayments are the major employee advantages.

Stock purchase programs are another financial service. These plans enable employees to buy company stock—usually through payroll deductions. In some stock purchase programs, employee outlays may be matched by company contributions.

Social Services

Employers provide a wide range of social services. At one extreme are simple interest groups such as bowling leagues and softball teams; at the other are comprehensive **employee assistance programs** (**EAP**) designed to assist employees with personal problems, e.g., child care, transportation assistance, individual and group counselling, employee quarrels, family disputes, or even assisting managers in dealing with employee complaints.

Employee assistance programs are becoming more common. Human resource managers realize that employee problems affect company performance.[9] Employer services that can lessen these problems offer potential dividends in employee performance, loyalty, and reduced turnover.

One employer service with a growing record of success is alcohol and drug rehabilitation. For example, human resource experts formerly recommended the discharge of alcoholic workers. Over the past 10 years, however, an increasing number of human resource departments have implemented alcohol and drug rehabilitation programs. This service has saved many otherwise good employees in companies such as Canadian National Railways. CN spends over $1 million annually on employee assistance programs, which includes and alcohol and drug rehabilitation programs.[10] When rehabilitation has been effective the company usually gains a hardworking, loyal employee.

Relocation programs are the support in dollars or services a company provides to its transferred or new employees. At minimum, this benefit includes payment for moving expenses. Some employees receive fully paid house-hunting trips with their spouse to the new location before the move, subsidized home mortgages, placement assistance for working spouses, and even family counselling to reduce the stress of the move. A transferred employee also may be able to sell his or her home to the employer for the appraised value to avoid having to sell it on the market.[11]

Employee assistance programs have traditionally involved personal interaction; especially if they were concerned with counselling services, face-to-face communication was important. However, with the advancement of technology, especially the Internet, employers can respond to their employees' needs not only faster, but also more effectively and efficiently. The most prominent of the recent developments in this field is **online service delivery**. The scope of possibilities is vast: opportunities for live chat rooms, one-on-one video counselling, group-help bulletin boards, and online self-help applications are only the tip of the technological iceberg. The goal of online assistance programs is not to replace counselling, but mostly to provide an enhancement to services already offered.[12]

Additional assistance activities are discussed in Chapter 11 in connection with counselling.

employee assistance programs (EAP)
Comprehensive company program that seeks to help employees and their family members overcome personal and work-related problems.

relocation program
A company-sponsored benefit that assists employees who must move in connection with their job.

online service delivery
EAP services available to employees through the Internet and by intranet.

EMERGING SERVICES AND TRENDS

Several studies have attempted to predict the types of benefits that will be in demand over the next 10 years.[13] The more popular options for employees seem to be the following:

- above all, increased medical coverage, dental plans, and optometrist services;
- greater assumption of costs of medical coverage by employers;
- more and longer vacations, coupled with reduced length of service requirements;
- more holidays;
- increased pension coverage, with greater contributions by employers;
- cost-of-living adjustments of pension plans;
- improved portability of pension rights and earlier vesting;
- sabbatical leaves for managers, and paid educational leave for rank-and-file employees;
- child care, with the employer providing either fully or partially subsidized care facilities and staff;

Information on benefit trends

www.towersperrin.com/tp/
thought-leadership-data-
results.jsp?qt=UBTE&cou
ntry=CANE&title=Benefit
s%20Update%20Canada
www.workplace-mag.
com/8-major-trends-
in-pension-employee-
benefits-in-Canada.html

- elder care, offering employees time off to take care of aging and dependent relatives, often coupled with counselling and special assistance;
- all benefits to same-sex couples, in accordance with federal and provincial legislation;
- benefits to part-time employees as well as to retirees; and
- prepaid legal advice.

Some companies will go to extremes when it comes to retaining key employees, offering such nontraditional benefits as free laundry, backup child care, or dog walking services.[14]

> KPMG's 26,000 employees in its 125 U.S. offices were recently given convenience services through LesConcierges. One call to an 800 number and employees may ask for "anything that's legal, ethical, and doesn't harm anyone else," says Kathie Linge, work/life director for KPMG. She used the service to find an electrician on the day after Thanksgiving and to hire an excavator to align the front of her house. She says that studies show that employees who use this program are more productive, more loyal, and more likely to recommend the company to other job applicants.[15]

The recent recessionary economy does not hold promise that these popular wants will in fact be offered. However, current trends indicate that indirect compensation will form a greater proportion of total compensation offered. Perhaps the employer share of contributions to the various current benefit plans will rise without any new types of benefits being added. Employees may also be able to make choices among benefits, and it may well become easier for employees to enroll in benefit plans through liberalized eligibility requirements.

Given the trends outlined above, it will be critical for top management in general and the human resource manager in particular to adopt a total compensation approach when decisions have to be made relating to pay. Organizations cannot afford to treat employee benefits and services independent of direct compensation, especially since they are growing at twice the pace of wages and salaries.

It should also be mentioned that some companies have already taken steps to extend benefits to part-time workers.

Finally, management has to take into account the changes in the labour force that will take place over the next 10 to 20 years. The average age of the labour force will increase, which will result in greater emphasis on pensions as part of the benefit package. More women will be working, and more will do so longer, making their job a career. What impact will this have on benefits and services (paid maternity leave, day care centres, nurseries, etc.)? Part-time work also will become more common, with still unforeseeable consequences, since traditionally part-timers received few or no benefits. There can be little doubt that the issue of employee benefits and services will require more attention and occupy more of management's time than ever before.

Child care, with the employer providing either full or partially subsidized care facilities, and staff, is emerging as an extended benefit for employees. What advantages does this benefit offer to workers?

© IT Stock Free.

Some companies have already taken the first step to extending benefits to part-time workers. In 1996, the Toronto-Dominion Bank included its 1,500 casual part-time workers in its regular benefit plans. Later in the same year the Royal Bank of Canada followed suit, but went even further by making its 7,500 part-time employees eligible for cash performance bonuses normally reserved for full-time staff.[16] This is a significant change in dealing with part-time employees who, for decades, have fought for the right to receive benefits. More recently, in 2000, Air Canada decided to pay all of its part-time employees the same benefits as full-timers. Air Canada uses a large number of part-timers during seasonal peaks such as summer, Christmas, and March breaks, and during the morning and evening rush hours when everybody wants to get to their airplane first. They are paid the same salaries as full-time staff and even get a pension from day one. As Chantal Baril, senior director of airport operations for Air Canada, puts it: "Part-timers used to be treated as second-class. Now it is almost fashionable. We have very low turnover. This is a desirable place to work."[17]

MANAGEMENT OF VOLUNTARY BENEFIT AND SERVICE PROGRAMS

A serious shortcoming of human resource management has been poor management of indirect compensation. Even in otherwise well-managed human resource departments, benefits and services have grown in a haphazard manner. Those costly supplements were introduced in response to social trends, union demands, employee pressures, and management wishes, and so human resource departments seldom established objectives, systematic plans, and standards to determine the appropriateness of benefits and services. This patchwork of benefits and services has caused several problems.

Problems in Administration

The central problem in supplementary compensation is a lack of employee involvement. Once a benefit program is designed by the human resource department and the labour union (if there is one), employees have little discretion. For example, pension and maternity benefits usually are granted to all workers equally. Younger employees see pensions as distant and largely irrelevant; older workers find maternity benefits are not needed. This uniformity fails to recognize individual differences and wishes. Admittedly, uniformity leads to administrative and actuarial economies; but when employees receive benefits they neither want nor need, these economies are questionable.

Because employees have little choice in their individual benefit package, most workers are unaware of all the benefits to which they are entitled:

> Two researchers designed a study to learn how knowledgeable selected workers were about their benefits. In two different plants—one with a union and one without—they asked employees to list all the benefits that they could recall. The average worker could not recall 15 percent of the employer-provided benefits.[18]

Ignorance and the inability to influence the mix of benefits often lead to pressure from employees for more benefits to meet their needs. For example, older workers may request improved retirement plans, while younger workers seek improved insurance coverage of dependants. Often the result is a proliferation of benefits and increased employer costs. These costs, which represented 15.1 percent of an employer's gross annual payroll in 1953, escalated to about 40 percent in 2008.[19] Still, employee ignorance and confusion can lead to complaints and dissatisfaction about their benefit package.

Traditional Remedies

The traditional remedy to benefit problems has been to increase employee awareness, usually through publicizing employee benefits. This publicity starts with orientation sessions that explain the benefit programs and provide employee handbooks. Company newspapers, special mailings, employee meetings, bulletin-board announcements, and responses to employee questions are also used to further publicize the organization's benefit package.

A Proactive Solution: Flexible Benefits

Flexible benefit programs, also known as *cafeteria benefit programs,* allow employees to select benefits and services that match their individual needs. Workers are provided a benefit and services account with a specified number of dollars in the account. Through deductions from this account,

flexible benefit programs
Programs that allow employees to select the mix of benefits and services that will answer their individual needs. Also known as *cafeteria benefit programs*.

employees shop for specific benefits from among those offered by the employer. The types and prices of benefits are provided to each employee in the form of a computer printout. This cost sheet also describes each benefit. Then, as illustrated in Figure 10-2, employees select their package of benefits and services for the coming year.

Figure 10-2 indicates how two different workers might spend the $3,845 the company grants each worker. Workers A and B select two different sets of benefits because their personal situations differ dramatically. Worker A is a young parent who is supporting a family and her husband. A dental plan will assist in defraying the high expenses for dental work, especially if they plan to have another child. Worker B allocated fewer dollars for weekly income benefits. Instead, he put a large portion of his benefit monies into the company pension plan. Although this approach creates additional administrative costs and an obligation for the human resource department to advise employees, there are several advantages. The main advantage is employee participation. Through participation, employees come to understand exactly what benefits the employer is offering, and employees can better match their benefits with their needs.[20]

Flexible benefits, until recently, have offered the usual choices of better long-term disability insurance, dental or vision care, prescription drug coverage, life insurance, group legal services, etc., but it has become now more common that employers offer the opportunity to "purchase" more vacation. Not only this, but it is even possible to sell vacation time.[21] In the past, cafeteria plans often had different choices for single and married employees. The trend now is to offer the choices independent of marital status.

Technology is changing the way companies handle flexible benefits enrollment and communication. In the early days, paper enrollment forms and written communication pieces were the norm. While paper still plays a role in the process in many companies, *interactive voice response systems* (*IVRs*) and Web-based technologies are becoming the norm for the administration of flexible benefit plans, making the communication process more effective.[22]

FIGURE 10-2	Hypothetical Benefit Selection of Two Different Workers	
Worker A		**Worker B**
Age 27, female, married with one child. Husband in graduate school.		Age 56, male, married with two grown and married children. Wife does not work outside the home.

Worker A		Worker B
$ 345	Supplemental dental insurance	$ 0
	Supplemental health insurance:	
245	Maternity	0
935	$100 deductible	0
0	Prescription drug coverage	625
	Life insurance:	
100	$20,000 for worker	100
150	$10,000 for spouse	0
600	Vacations	900
300	Holidays	300
200	Pension plan	1,615
0	Jury duty pay	0
100	Disability insurance	100
870	Weekly income benefit	205
$3,845	Total	$3,845

Canadian Blue Cross now offers Health Spending Account administration services for companies with flexible benefit plans. It saves these companies the headaches of administering the plans and claims to be cheaper than if the company managed the plan on its own.[23]

Implications for Human Resource Management

Change in the field of employee benefits has been dramatic over the last decade. Retirement plans have been and are under constant legal review, tax reforms have added complexity, health care policies have changed and their expenses gone up, all adding to the responsibilities of the human resource professional. Advances in computer hardware technology and the tremendous growth in the range of "friendly" software have resulted in human resource practitioners being able to develop their own applications.

To find the right approach for the administration of benefit plans, a needs analysis is an essential first step. The analysis should deal with five basic questions:

1. What tasks need to be performed, how often, and how quickly?
2. Who currently performs these tasks, and what does it cost now to perform them (including internal as well as external costs)?
3. What alternative ways of performing these tasks are possible and practical?
4. What will each alternative cost, both to install and to maintain?
5. How long will it take to implement each option, and can the implementation ever be truly completed?

The objective of the needs analysis is to identify the best administrative methodology to meet both the short-term and long-term needs of the employer. The result of the analysis should be a report that can be used by decision makers as a reference document against which a detailed implementation process can be tested.

The implications of financial security plans for human resource departments are several. *First,* human resource managers should make sure that the firm adheres to all provisions relating to minimum wages and pension deductions. For example, the *Canada Labour Code* requires every employer to furnish, from time to time, information relating to employee wages, hours of work, general holidays, annual vacations, and conditions of employment. As well, the Canada Labour Standards Regulations require that each employee's social insurance number, sex, and occupational classification be recorded and kept ready for inspection. Accurate records of maternity leave, overtime, and termination should also be maintained.

Second, to avoid duplication, human resource managers need to consider CPP and other benefits available to employees when designing their firm's own benefit and service plans. In many provinces, some of the items included in private group insurance plans are already covered under the workers' compensation and health insurance plans.

Third, human resource specialists also need to be concerned about reducing accidents in order to lower the cost of workers' compensation. These costs are directly related to the claims made against the company by employees. The more that must be paid to these employees, the greater the cost. Yet even aside from cost considerations, many managers feel a moral obligation to provide a safe working environment.

A fourth approach is to challenge all unjustified claims for employment compensation made against employers. Those claims that are successfully challenged may reduce costs in the future:

> Kevin Hirtsman was fired for stealing from the company, since the employee manual stated that stealing was grounds for immediate dismissal. When his claim for employment insurance was sent to the company for its comments, the human resource manager wrote back that Kevin was terminated for cause. Kevin's claim for employment compensation was denied.

To keep ballooning health costs under control, William M. Mercer, a benefit consulting company, recommends that employers take the following measures:

- Instead of having a set employee-paid deductible, ask staff to pay 20 percent of any treatment.
- Stop out-of-country medical coverage for personal travel, or set a 30-day limit or a dollar maximum.
- Remember that many dental plans were designed in pre-fluoride days. Six-month checkups may not be necessary anymore.

- Where they are available, pay only for generic drugs, saving an average of 6 pe
  plans.
- With "maintenance drugs," such as birth control pills, ask employees to get larg
  save on dispensing fees.

An employer who builds a series of these alternatives into its benefit plans could probably save 15 percent of costs.[24]

Retention

The question has been raised earlier what role benefits play in retaining employees. **Retention** of key employees has become a major issue, especially in high-tech companies.[25] Several studies have shown that innovative and flexible benefit plans are very effective tools in attracting and retaining highly skilled staff.[26] "My sense is that benefits become increasingly important as a competitive advantage if you can't negotiate around the total compensation package," said Ann O'Neill, director of the Certified Employee Benefits Specialist program at Dalhousie University in Halifax.[27] This view is confirmed by an opinion survey on 307 CEOs of large Canadian companies.[28]

retention
A company's ability to keep employees.

Benefit Audit

Often, the administration of benefit plans still leaves room for improvement. One approach that readily identifies inefficiencies is a **benefit audit**. It usually consists of two components: a claims audit, which examines claims and claim trends, and an organization audit, which examines the efficiency and effectiveness of handling employee benefits within the employer organization, including dealings with an insurer or third-party administrator.

A benefit audit enables employers to do the following:

benefit audit
A system to control the efficiency of a benefit program.

- identify opportunities for financial and human resource savings;
- ensure that insurers or third-party administrators are doing a good job;
- exert effective control over their benefits area;
- identify who is in control of the benefits budget; and
- check how their employee claiming habits compare against other Canadian employers.

Goods and Services Tax Application to Benefits

Since 1991, the GST applies to some benefits, but not to others. Generally, GST has to be paid on the following benefits:

- company cars (if also used for private purposes)
- car operating costs
- tax return preparation
- short-term residential accommodation
- holiday trips within continental North America
- frequent flyer points
- financial counselling
- parking

Not affected are awards, health benefits, stock options, low-interest or no-interest loans, tuition fees, child care, a Christmas turkey, and gifts under $100.

Benefits and Strategy Implications

As is outlined in Chapter 1, management has to look at the long-term objectives of the organization and match these with organizational conditions to create the necessary environment for reaching the objectives. Specifically, the following steps have to be taken:

- Define the objectives of the organization.
- Link objectives of the human resource department with the objectives of the organization.
- Assess the needs of the employees.
- Assess the legal requirements to ensure that laws are followed.
- Compare the company's benefits with those of the competition.
- Make sure the benefits are valued by the employees.
- Conduct an annual benefit audit.

It is important for human resource managers to integrate benefits into the wage and salary package. This compensation package has to fulfill both short-term and long-term goals. The short-term goals—for example, high motivation and productivity—are usually satisfied with merit pay and incentive systems that reward high performers. A common long-term goal is to retain good employees, an objective that can be achieved by a valued pension or a profit-sharing plan. Another strategy may address the need for downsizing by using an appropriate severance package. These are just a few items of a comprehensive pay strategy.

⬤ SUMMARY

Employee benefits and services are the fastest-growing component of compensation. The Canadian government has instituted compulsory programs that provide citizens with certain benefits and services. Financial security is achieved partially through such benefits as the Canada Pension Plan, employment insurance, and workers' compensation. The Canada Pension Plan provides income at retirement or upon disability. It also provides the family members of a deceased worker with a death benefit and a survivor's annuity, under certain conditions.

Employment insurance pays the worker a modest income to reduce the hardships of losing a job. These payments go to employees who are involuntarily separated from their jobs. Payments last until the worker finds suitable employment or until the worker receives the maximum number of payments permitted by the government.

Workers' compensation pays employees who are injured in the course of their employment. The payments are made to prevent the employee from having to sue to be compensated for injuries. If an employee dies, benefits are paid to the employee's survivors.

Health and medical insurance is provided by provincial governments with assistance from the federal government. In addition to the provincial health insurance, group life and disability insurance is widely provided as an employee benefit. More and more companies are also providing dental insurance for their employees.

Voluntary benefits include insurance, security, and time-off benefits. Employee services encompass educational, financial, and social programs. This diversity contributes to several serious administrative problems. The most significant problem is the orientation of managers and human resource specialists toward cost savings. In pursuit of administrative and actuarial economies, most companies and unions do not allow individualized benefit packages in indirect compensation programs.

A major issue is ballooning health care costs. Management has to pay more attention to the efficient administration of such plans and to the control of their costs. Some studies have shown that savings of up to 15 percent can be achieved if management pays attention to health benefit costs.

A significant development in the field of benefit administration is the benefit audit, consisting of a claims and an organization audit. The audit examines the efficiency and effectiveness of handling employee benefits, including insurers and third-party administrators.

If management wants to be up-to-date in benefits, it has to be aware of the trends in the field. Changing demographics make changing demands on benefit systems: extra medical coverage, company pension plans with better portability and earlier vesting, child care, and elder care are some of the new developments in this field. In all probability, increased part-time work will necessitate offering benefits even to these employees. These developments will make it necessary for top management to adopt a total compensation package as part of a pay strategy.

⬤ TERMS FOR REVIEW

benefit audit **p. 383**
Canada Pension Plan (CPP) **p. 370**
contributory plans **p. 371**
defined benefits (DB) plan **p. 374**
defined contribution (DC) plan **p. 375**
employee assistance programs
    (EAP) **p. 378**
Employment Insurance (EI) **p. 371**

flexible benefit programs **p. 381**
guaranteed annual wage (GAW) **p. 374**
health insurance **p. 372**
long-term disability insurance **p. 374**
online service delivery **p. 378**
Pension Benefits Standards Act **p. 375**
portability clauses **p. 371**
relocation program **p. 378**

retention **p. 383**
severance pay **p. 374**
short-term disability plan **p. 374**
supplemental unemployment benefits
    (SUB) **p. 374**
vesting **p. 375**
workers' compensation **p. 372**

⊙ SELF-ASSESSMENT EXERCISE

Understanding Benefits

Benefits tend to be neglected when it comes to consider-ations of labour costs, but with the average benefit package in Canada now being close to 35 percent of payroll, HR managers are well advised to pay special attention to the management of benefits. Test yourself on your expertise.

1. If the current trend continues, soon benefits will make up over one-half of most firms' payroll. **T   F**

2. Vacations, along with holidays and rest breaks to reduce fatigue and enhance productivity, are part of employees' objectives. **T   F**

3. Salaried, hourly paid, and self-employed persons are eligible for unemployment benefits. **T   F**

4. In Canada, like in the U.S., health insurance is the most common form of insurance coverage. **T   F**

5. Vesting gives workers the right to pension benefits even if they leave the company. **T   F**

6. Meal breaks, rest breaks, wash-up time, sick leave, holidays, and vacations make up the costliest major category of benefits. **T   F**

7. Cafeteria benefits allow employees free meals. **T   F**

8. Benefits play a major role in retaining employees. **T   F**

9. Benefits cannot be taxed. **T   F**

10. Benefits and services are the fastest-growing component of compensation. **T   F**

SCORING

If you marked statements 1, 5, 6, 8, and 10 as true, give yourself one point each. The remaining statements are false.

Scores of 8–10: Very good! Congratulations for your thorough understanding of the content in this chapter.

Scores of 5–7: Well … it's okay, but rereading this chapter could help you do better.

Scores of less than 5: Oops … add this chapter to your reading list again.

⊙ REVIEW AND DISCUSSION QUESTIONS

1. Why has government been interested in providing financial security to workers through laws? What areas do you think are likely to receive government attention in the future to ensure employee financial security?

2. Some people believe that employment insurance has over a period of time worked against workers rather than for them. What is your opinion of employment insurance? Why?

3. Suppose a friend of yours contracted lead poisoning on the job. What sources of income could this person rely on while recovering during the next two months? What if it took two years for your friend to recover? Are other sources of income available?

4. Besides retirement income, what other benefits are provided through the Canada Pension Plan?

5. What changes should be made to the employment insurance system to eliminate its present weaknesses?

6. What factors have contributed to the rapid growth of benefits since the Second World War?

7. Briefly describe the benefits that an organization might give employees to provide them with greater financial security.

8. Why was the Pension Benefits Standards Act needed? What are its major provisions?

9. What are the common problems you would expect to find with the benefits and services program of a large company?

10. If you were asked to increase employee awareness of benefits, what actions would you take without changing the way the company provides benefits? If you could change the entire benefit program, what other methods would you use to increase employee awareness?

CRITICAL THINKING QUESTIONS

1. Suppose you are asked to explain why employees are better off receiving pay and benefits rather than just getting larger paycheques that include the monetary value of benefits. What arguments will you use?

2. For each of the following groups of employees, what types of problems are likely to occur if a company goes from a five-day, 40-hour week to a four-day, 40-hour week: (a) working mothers, (b) labourers, (c) assembly-line workers?

3. Should companies pay educational assistance? Assume that it was for a degree in information technology. What if a competitor offers a higher salary to the successful graduate? How could you make sure the company's investment remains in the organization?

ETHICS QUESTION

It is quite common for fish-processing companies in the Atlantic Provinces to allow employees to work the number of weeks required to qualify for Employment Insurance (EI), then lay them off and hire other family members to let them qualify for EI. Discuss the ethical issues involved.

WEB RESEARCH EXERCISE

1. What are the characteristics of an effective Retirement Savings Program? Look at the following Web site:
www.benefits.org/interface/benefit/retire.htm

2. What are the advantages of a flexible benefit plan? Have a look at:
www.benefits.org/interface/benefit/flex.htm

3. Employee Assistance Programs have become very popular with small and large companies. Give some good reasons for the introduction of an EAP. See (search for "eap"):
www.benefits.org/interface/benefit

4. What are the eligibility criteria for the new Employment Insurance program? Give details.
**www.cbsc.org/servlet/ContentServer?
pagename=CBSC_FE/display&c=Services&cid=
1081944195459&lang=en**
or go to:
http://canadabusiness.gc.ca/gol/cbec/site.nsf/en/index.html
and search for "Employment Insurance." Details are listed in the fourth document.

INCIDENT 10-1

Soap Producers and Distributors Ltd.

Soap Producers and Distributors Ltd. faced a employee turnover problem. The company's annual turnover rate was nearly 20 percent among technical and white-collar workers. Among hourly paid employees, the rate was nearly 30 percent.

Wage and salary surveys repeatedly showed that the company's pay levels were 10 to 11 percent above those of comparable jobs in the labour market. The benefit program was not as impressive, but management thought it was competitive. Employees received supplementary health and life insurance, paid vacations and holidays, and a Christmas bonus of $1,000.

Although some employees complained about the company's benefits, complaints varied widely and no one benefit or lack of benefit seemed to be the key issue.

To make Soap Producers and Distributors' problems worse, they operated in a tight labour market, which meant jobs sometimes took weeks to fill. To hire specialized workers almost always meant recruiting them from other cities and paying their moving expenses.

1. What additions do you think should be made to the company's benefit program? (Hint: what is missing?)

2. What problems in the incident might be solved by a cafeteria approach? Think of specific interest groups.

3. To overcome the company's recruitment problems, what other changes do you suggest? What are the trends in benefit programs?

CASE STUDY Maple Leaf Shoes Ltd.

Flexible Benefit Program

Maple Leaf Shoes Ltd. is a medium-sized manufacturer of leather and vinyl shoes located in Hamilton, Ontario. It was started in 1973 and currently employs about 500 persons in its Hamilton plant and some 200 more in offices and warehouses throughout Canada.

Sam Polanyi, President of Maple Leaf Shoes' Leather Workers Union, was working on a draft of his plan for the upcoming negotiations with management. He knew that he had to be prepared for some tough bargaining, Robert Clark, the company's president and chief negotiator, was no pushover. Almost all negotiations in the past had gone to the wire, sometimes just hours away from a strike, but so far there had always been a last-minute settlement.

Some of Sam's members had approached him to discuss the advantages of a flexible benefit plan. Apparently, some of the

workers' spouses worked in companies that had such a plan, and the workers seemed to like it. It meant they could choose the kind of benefits most useful to them, which was not possible under the rigid "one size fits all" system the company was using now. Could he convince Bob Clark that it would be to the company's advantage? A flexible—or cafeteria—plan would certainly be more expensive, and that was the rub. Sam was willing to compromise on other issues to get the plan, but how could he sell Clark on it?

Discussion Questions

Can you assist Sam Polanyi in his attempt to sell Robert Clark on a flexible benefit plan? What are the advantages and disadvantages of such plans?

CASE STUDY Canadian Pacific and International Bank

Mary Keddy, Senior Vice-President HR, was facing Michael Bennett, the bank's CEO, in his office. He had called her to an urgent meeting regarding the bank's benefit expenses. He showed her some figures he had received from the Internal Auditor. The data indicated that the bank's benefit expenses had reached almost 40 percent of the bank's payroll. He also produced benchmark data from a survey, which showed that the industry average was close to 30 percent. "Why is it our benefit expenses are so much higher than those of our competitors?" he asked.

Mary pointed out that the data had assessed the financial services industry, not just banks, and that the industry included some trust companies with much lower benefit levels than banks—which, by and large, had benefit expenses similar to those of the CPIB—although the CPIB certainly occupied the high end of the scale.

Mr. Bennett wondered whether these expenses were really justified. "Where is the payoff?" he asked. Mary had no problems defending the bank's benefit outlays. She pointed out that the CPIB had the lowest turnover rate among banks, 2 percent lower than any other, and that every employee attitude survey showed that the CPIB staff felt the bank to be a very good place to work and that job satisfaction was high. She also mentioned that the bank had no difficulties attracting top-flight applicants. She was convinced that the bank's generous benefit package contributed significantly to this level of satisfaction. She concluded her explanation by saying: "Mike, look at the level of customer satisfaction. We beat out every other bank on this measure. I am sure the reason is that happy employees mean happy customers. And there is the main payoff."

Bennett appreciated Mary's explanation. He always had been proud when he saw the results of internal surveys. There was

no doubt that people liked to work for the CPIB. "Still," he wondered, "are there ways to cut the expenses without doing too much damage to employee satisfaction?" Mary agreed to look into that matter and to make suggestions regarding more efficient methods of delivering benefit services. She had heard and read about the use of the intranet and the Internet as more effective ways to administer benefit plans, but felt that she did not know enough about it to come up with convincing recommendations. It was obvious that she needed some expert advice.

Additional Information

The last time a benefit audit had been done was seven years ago—a year before Mary joined the bank. Ever since her arrival, Mary had been too busy introducing strategic changes in areas such as selection, diversity management, and training. In the past five years, the bank had also acquired several other financial institutions and expanded into other countries. But the need for a benefit audit had been on her mind for some time.

The bank's flexible benefit package included, besides the usual supplementary health and life insurances, child care, elder care, a drug payment plan, wellness programs (the bank had its own exercise centre), personal counselling service (drugs, alcohol, smoking cessation), educational support, and financial advising. It was also possible to purchase more vacation time. There were three full-time employees responsible for administering the flexible benefit package. The administration expenses, including communication, were close to $300,000 annually. The bank used a quite-effective intranet mainly for training and public announcements.

Discussion Questions

1. Use Web research to find arguments for and against using the Internet and the bank's intranet for the administration and delivery of its benefit services.

2. Is outsourcing benefit administration advisable? Why? What criteria should be used in making the decision?

3. If Mary asks for a benefit audit, what would the auditor look at?

➡ PART ENDING VIDEOS

"21st Century Ventures: Corporate Drumming Up Business"

Source: *Venture*, show number 914, February 15, 2004, running time 3:10. "Finding and Keeping the Best Employees"

Go to **www.mcgrawhillconnect.ca** to access the videos.

➡ ROLE-PLAY 5: Flexible Benefits

Time required: 40–50 minutes

Objectives of the Role-Play

1. To help the students understand the pros and cons of flexible benefits.
2. To enhance their skills to listen and respond to employee concerns.
3. To help them prepare for their role as human resource managers.

Prior Preparation

1. Study Chapter 10 of the text.
2. Read descriptions of Maple Leaf Shoes Ltd. at the end of Chapters 1 and 2.

Guidelines for Conducting the Role-Play

In this role-play, an employee, Megan Litkoff, is meeting with Jane Reynolds to inquire into the possibility of a flexible work hours and benefit plan.

1. Two students, one for the role of Jane Reynolds and the other for Megan Litkoff, should be identified.
2. Students should read their respective descriptions (see the Instructor Resource Manual), along with the company details given at the end of Chapters 1 and 2.
3. The instructor should signal the beginning and end of the meeting. The interview will last about 25 to 30 minutes.
4. The remainder of the class time is used for discussion of the behaviours during the role-play and outcomes.
5. Observers should be asked to make notes against the questions listed below and discuss their findings at the end of the role-play.
6. Instructor should sum up by highlighting the advantages and disadvantages of flexible benefit plans.

Instructions for Observers

As you observe the meeting between Jane Reynolds and Megan Litkoff, make notes regarding each of the questions below. Pay particular attention to the behaviours (both verbal and nonverbal) of each person.

1. How did Jane begin the meeting?
2. Was there open communication between the two? Who spoke more? About what?
3. Was each party listening to the other? Were their concerns realistic? What could have been done better?
4. What is your assessment of the nonverbal expressions of each? What changes would you recommend to each?
5. What other improvements would you recommend?

PART 6

Maintaining High Performance

An organization's culture and working environment has an effect on the motivation and job satisfaction of its employees. To maintain good relationships, an effective communication process is essential. Good interpersonal relations also require appropriate and fair discipline procedures. Workplace safety is also very important. Managing in a union environment requires familiarity with the legal requirements in dealing with unions, the collective bargaining process, and administration of the collective agreement.

The four chapters in Part 6 discuss ways to create a positive work environment, maintain proper discipline, ensure a safe workforce, manage workplace diversity, and deal with union management issues.

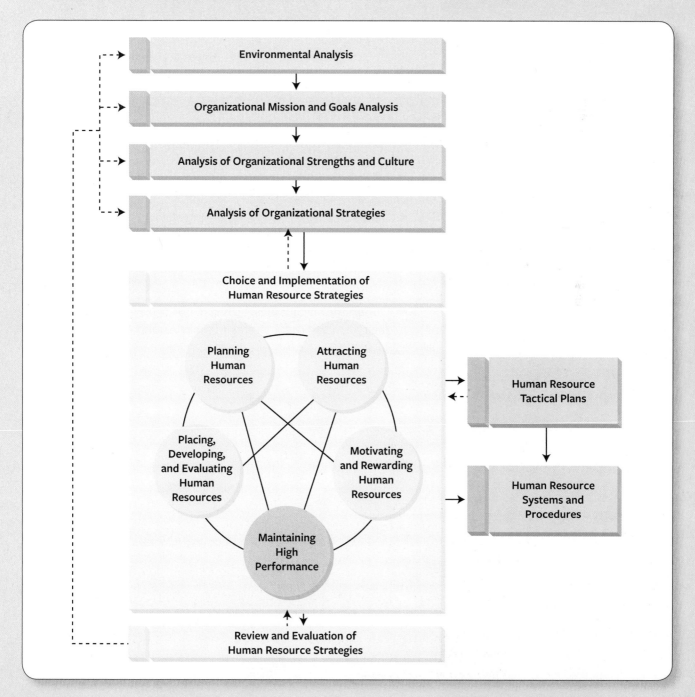

Managing Employee Relations

Although the concept and measurement of high-performance organizations are relatively new to management theory, they have roots that extend at least back to the beginning of the Industrial Revolution.

American Management Association[1]

CHAPTER OBJECTIVES

After studying this chapter, you should be able to:

➡ *Discuss* the importance of downward and upward communication in organizational settings.

➡ *Define* employee counselling and the major types of counselling.

➡ *Describe* how progressive discipline and wrongful dismissal work.

➡ *Explain* the different techniques available to improve quality of work life.

➡ *Outline* the major issues relating to downsizing the workforce and their implications for strategic human resource management.

CHAPTER 11

I n many ways, this entire book is about employee relations. How well the human resource department handles human resource planning, placement, training and development, evaluation, and compensation largely determines the state of employee relations. Even when these activities are performed properly, solid employee relations demand careful attention to organizational communication, employee counselling, discipline, and management of work groups. In addition, a number of organizations are becoming high involvement workplaces that emphasize human resource management.

A number of employees express frustration with their employer. In a recent study of Canadian employees, only 15 percent reported having jobs with both clear feedback and a significant impact (that is, the work is important). Almost 25 percent of employees indicated that their job had both little recognition and low satisfaction. According to study author Paul Fairlie, "Engagement, commitment and performance are important, but these are outputs. They don't happen unless employees view their work as meaningful."[2]

A study by Watson Wyatt Worldwide identified the following seven factors as important in building employee commitment: trust in senior leadership, a chance to use skills on the job, job security, competitiveness of rewards, the quality of the organization's products/services, the absence of work-related stress, and the honesty and integrity of the employer's business conduct.[3]

Although the focus of this chapter is on employee relations, an effective organization also pays considerable attention to relationships among workers. Several human resource initiatives, such as policies on workplace and sexual harassment, conflict resolution procedures, and employee involvement programs, play an important role in enhancing human relations.

STRATEGIC IMPORTANCE OF EMPLOYEE RELATIONS PRACTICES

"Employee relations" is a complex blend of organizational culture, human resource practices, and individual perceptions. Virtually everything the human resource department does affects employee relations, directly or indirectly. But many human resource activities (such as recruitment, selection, and benefits administration) go largely unnoticed by employees. Other important human resource functions affect employees only periodically, as in the case of performance appraisal and salary review sessions. This necessitates ongoing activities to foster good employer–employee relations.

Why are employee relations practices important? At least four major reasons can be offered:

1. *Good employee relations practices improve productivity.* Employee productivity is significantly affected by two factors: ability and attitude. Ability is simply whether the employee is able to perform the job. Ability is influenced by such things as training, education, innate aptitude, tools, and work environments. Attitude, on the other hand, refers to an individual's willingness to perform the job. Attitude is affected by a myriad of factors, such as level of motivation, job satisfaction, and commitment to work. Good employee relations practices help improve both the ability and attitude of the employee. The result is an improvement in employee productivity:

   > A recent University of Melbourne (Australia) study suggests twittering or using Facebook during office hours may actually increase employee productivity. The study indicates that employees who use the Internet for personal reasons while working are about 9 percent more productive than those who do not. According to the study author, Brent Coker, "people need to zone out a bit to get their concentration back. Short and unobtrusive breaks, such as a quick surf of the Internet, enables the mind to rest itself."[4]

2. *Good employee relations ensure implementation of organizational strategies.* In Chapter 1, the importance of the role that human resource activities play in achieving organizational goals was discussed. Unless employees understand their roles and are rewarded for exhibiting desired behaviours, it is unlikely that the organization will be able to generate grassroots support for its plans. Good employee relations practices ensure that organizational goals and strategies are properly communicated to the employees and receive their commitment.

3. *Good employee relations practices reduce employment costs.* When concern for and interest in employees becomes part of the overall organizational culture, significant cost savings in terms of reduced absenteeism and turnover can emerge. Good employee relations practices also

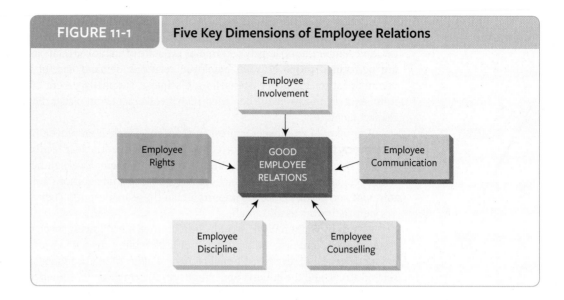

FIGURE 11-1   **Five Key Dimensions of Employee Relations**

give employers a recruiting advantage as most job applicants prefer to work for an organization that treats them fairly and offers them a challenging job with potential for career growth.

4. *Good employee relations help employees grow and develop.* As discussed in Chapter 1, an important goal of human resource departments today is to help employees achieve their personal goals. A keen interest in the employee's work-related and career goals not only brings benefits to the organization (in terms of improved employee morale, loyalty, improved productivity, ready availability of skilled personnel within), but also helps it meet its social objectives.

> What makes a company attractive to employees? According to Martine Bedard, a sales director at Yellow Pages, it is "the dynamism of the company. The company makes a major investment every year in continuous learning and training." Employees are given $2,000 annually to cover the cost of courses at other institutions. Bedard also is impressed with the Yellow Pages sustainability program that focuses on extensive recycling and improving the quality of life. The company's Web site manager, Carlos Caprio, loves the work environment. "People are happy to be here and no one is watching his or her watch. The corporate culture is based on open communication. When you work on projects, everyone, regardless of his title, brings in the same participation."[5]

As Figure 11-1 shows, there are five major components of effective employee relations: communication, counselling, discipline, rights, and involvement. Each of these will be discussed in some detail below. In addition, a section of the chapter will address the issues of employee retention, job security and organizational downsizing.

EFFECTIVE EMPLOYEE COMMUNICATION

Information about the organization, its environment, its products and services, and its people is essential to management and employees. Without information, managers cannot make effective decisions about markets or resources, particularly human resources. Likewise, insufficient information may cause stress and dissatisfaction among employees. Moreover, effective communication is an essential component of learning organizations.

The need for information is met through an organization's communication system. In small or less-sophisticated firms, communication may be informal and subject to infrequent management intervention. In large multibillion-dollar enterprises, specialists may serve as employee communications directors or as chief information officers. The costs of poor employee communication can be substantial:

> Is one of your senior managers a "jerk"? If so, he or she may be costing your company millions of dollars. In today's economy, many people decide life is too short to work for a jerk. Losing top talent can be crushingly expensive. No company can afford to have a jerk as a manager. A lot of companies are beginning to penalize managers based on loss of talent.[6]

Most organizations use a blend of formal, systematically designed communication efforts and informal ad hoc arrangements. For convenience, most of these approaches can be divided into *downward communication systems*, which exist to get information to employees, and *upward communication systems*, which exist to obtain information from employees. Consider the communication challenges one organization faced:

> A large international pharmaceutical company with 70,000 employees in more than 75 countries was introducing a new HR information management model. Challenges facing the organization included communicating in a number of languages, dealing with different cultures, differing technological capabilities, and timing of the communications. To meet these challenges, senior HR executives in the various regions were given the freedom to adjust the model to meet the needs and capabilities of their managers. Contrary to what one might expect, this flexibility allowed for a more consistent message to the various parties.[7]

Downward Communication Systems

downward communication
Information that begins at some point in the organization and feeds down the organization hierarchy to inform or influence others.

Human resource departments operate large communication systems to keep people informed. They try to facilitate an open, two-way flow of information, although often messages are of the top-down variety. **Downward communication** is information that begins at some point in the organization and proceeds down the organizational hierarchy to inform or influence others. Top-down methods are necessary for decision makers to have their decisions carried out. These communications also help give employees knowledge about the organization and feedback on how their efforts are perceived.

Organizations use a variety of downward communication methods because multiple channels are more likely to overcome barriers and reach the intended receivers. For example, limiting messages to an email format will be ineffective in organizations in which few employees use email. Some common examples of downward communication approaches include in-house publications, information booklets, employee bulletins, prerecorded messages, email, and jobholder reports and meetings. Failing to communicate effectively can be very costly:

> According to James Hoggan, a Vancouver public relations expert, "the right communication strategy can help organizations maintain or rebuild corporate credibility that has been hit hard in recent months. Multimillionaire Wall Street CEOs, whose out-of-control mortgage businesses have undermined markets and economies around the world, insisted their companies were healthy only days before their collapse. Whether they were incompetent or dishonest, their actions have shattered public trust in private institutions."[8]

In-House Publications

Many organizations publish internal magazines, newspapers, or bulletins for employees (in both hard copy and electronic formats). Their purpose is to inform employees about current developments and to foster a long-term understanding about objectives and mission. For example, job openings may be posted on bulletin boards and online so that all employees are aware of vacancies within the organization. The growth of desktop publishing and the ability to communicate using the resources of the Internet make the creation and distribution of professional-looking newsletters within the capabilities of both large and small firms:

> At pharmaceutical firm Eli Lilly, good work is recognized almost daily. Employee contributions are written up in the company's newsletter. However, Eli Lilly has taken this further—employees recognized for their work become instant celebrities by appearing on television monitors located throughout the Toronto head office. According to the vice-president of human resources, "our employees really get a kick out of seeing themselves on television."[9]

Information Booklets

Human resource departments often distribute information booklets on various subjects to employees. For instance, an employee handbook is often given to new employees to inform them about regulations and benefits. It is important that the information in employee handbooks is updated regularly and carefully reviewed—in some instances, information contained in employee handbooks has been used by former employees in litigation against the organization.

Other booklets are distributed on specialized subjects relating to human resource activities, such as suggestion programs, employee assistance programs, occupational health and safety, wage incentives, retirement, and fringe benefits. Such information is readily available online in many organizations.

Prerecorded Messages

Some organizations develop their own video programs for later replay to employees. These programs can be viewed in company lunchrooms and other locations or by computer access. Firms with branch operations use this approach to keep their branch employees informed about corporate developments or assist with orientation and training. Firms can also use recorded telephone messages and automated voicemail to present the latest information. A number of employers are also utilizing interactive voice response (IVR) systems as a tool to improving service and allowing HR staff to focus on strategic activities.[10]

> Toronto-based communications company Nortel, which has 26,000 employees in 60 countries, is taking a more strategic approach to employee recognition. Employees historically believed recognition went to few employees on an infrequent basis. The new approach, Excellence@Nortel, has video links and Web casts of employees receiving awards and recipients are interviewed on Nortel's RNN (Recognition News Network). It used to take six weeks for a recipient to receive an award (typically a gift certificate). Now 70 percent of awards are approved and delivered in one day.[11]

Electronic Communication

Using email as a means of communicating with employees is taken for granted in many organizations. One study of email users reported that 70 percent of employees believe email has increased or improved communications with their supervisor.[12] In addition, email can be a vehicle for employee surveys. However, it is important to realize that not everyone in an organization uses email regularly. In addition, email may not be appropriate for all types of communication:

> Esthetician Crystal Bell of Kelowna, BC, checked her Facebook account one morning as she was getting ready for work and discovered that she had been terminated (cybersacked). Bell, who had only been employed for two weeks, showed up for work because she thought her employer was kidding. According to Bell, "it is not the human way to go. I think that using any kind of texting or emailing to let people go is a coward's way out." Ruth Haag, author of *Hiring and Firing*, stated that "doing an email is quickest and easiest but people forget that it is the most public way to communicate because it can be around the world in minutes and you're looking like a jerk for firing someone that way."[13]

intranet
Internal communications system that functions like a smaller version of the World Wide Web.

In addition, more and more employers are using **intranets** (internal communications systems that function like a smaller version of the World Wide Web). One study of small and large Canadian employers indicated that about 11 percent of small firms and 65 percent of large firms have an intranet.[14] The major reasons for firms not having intranets include limited access by employees to computers, HR concerns that employees are not ready for using intranets, and concerns over security.

> Many employees are reluctant to use the company intranet. Workers say that intranets are too hard to use and a number of companies don't bother to update the information. Simple tasks like finding a form or policy manual may take an employee half an hour or more, and there may be utter chaos when employees try to use links to other departments within their organization.[15]

Firms use intranets for a variety of purposes ranging from tracking benefit enrollments to providing copies of employee handbooks, policy manuals, and company newsletters.[16] Human resource departments have found intranet communication to be particularly effective as a means of updating handbooks and manuals and in eliminating some of the administrative burden associated with forms management. Examples of human resource departments using intranets include creating an electronic employee directory, setting up training registration information, using electronic pay stubs, updating of employee accounts, mapping performance achievements, managing succession planning, and creating discussion groups:[17]

> How can HR be made greener? According to Environment Canada, paper still accounts for about one-third of all waste. There are several options available to HR to reduce the use of paper, including online statement delivery (such as payroll information), self-service technology, and electronic solutions (to track HR information such as payroll, time, attendance, and performance management data).[18]

However, with intranet communication, the traditional top-down communication system becomes altered with communication opportunities extended to a much larger group of employees:

> In one manufacturing organization, the human resource management department knew that intranet communication would be meaningless for employees on the shop floor who did not have access to computers. They remedied the situation by installing a number of computer terminals in the lunchroom and at selected work stations.

In addition, the use of technology needs to be carefully managed. One study found that HR technology (including employee self-service) reduced transaction costs for employers by 43 percent. But employee portals regularly fail to meet the goals companies hoped for—almost all employers participating in one study anticipated productivity improvements, but only 54 percent reported some productivity gains and 31 percent of human resource executives indicated that getting employees to use self-service was their most pressing technology-related issue.[19] However, technology can be a very valuable tool:

> Some organizations are also increasing their use of "assistive technology" to help both individuals with disabilities and nondisabled employees. Examples of assistive technology include closed-caption television broadcasting and voice recognition software, and text-to-speech readers that allow blind or low-vision employees to hear their email and read Web pages.[20]

Web sites dedicated to extranets articles, information, discussion
http://technology.inc.com/networking/articles/200610/extranet.html
www.abanet.org/lpm/lpt/articles/tch11042.html

A small number of companies have set up *extranets* (which are really intranets linked with vendors, suppliers or customers). For example, some firms have extranets with benefit providers such as insurance companies and pension managers—this allows employees to contact the benefit provider directly and inquire about the status of benefits or other features of the plan.

As a growing number of employees use the Internet, firms are developing policies on Internet usage. Among the issues to be considered are the restriction of the Internet to business purposes, the right of employers to monitor employee usage of the Internet, and specific prohibitions (relating to such concerns as copyright, distribution of viruses, or the posting or downloading of material that is threatening, abusive, defamatory, or obscene). In addition, firms must be concerned about hackers obtaining confidential company and employee data.

A seven-step plan to protect the organization from the misuse of electronic communications includes (1) developing and implementing a policy addressing electronic communications; (2) being aware of legal issues and limitations associated with monitoring electronic communications; (3) training employees and managers concerning the policy; (4) encouraging prompt reporting of policy violations and immediately addressing all complaints; (5) understanding your system; (6) examining the available tools for controlling Internet access; and (7) developing a policy for telecommuting.[21]

> A survey of more than 10,000 employees indicated that 70 percent found instant messaging distracting and 10 percent had never heard of it. Sixty percent reported that texting was distracting and 16 percent had never sent a text message, and 90 percent found social networking sites a nuisance while 7 percent had not heard about them. It appears that employees are concerned about their jobs and don't want to do anything to jeopardize them.[22]
>
> However, some employers are encouraging the use of electronic communication. Shannon Boudjema, a business manager for marketing communications firm Maritz, posted a message on Twitter asking for help in finding research on young consumers. On returning to work the next day, she had dozens of tweets. Maritz is encouraging employees to find ways to use social networking to help the company. While several Canadian companies block access to IM and social networking sites, other employers believe that using such sites can increase productivity and employee value.[23]

A current issue that has caused some concern for employers revolves around employee blogs (Weblogs). From an organizational perspective, employers are worried about employees (intentionally or unintentionally) leaking confidential information about the company, hurting the organization's reputation, describing the business in a negative way, or exposing the employer to potential liability. Rather than simply trying to ban employees from blogging, some organizations are developing a blogging policy—typical guidelines include writing in the first person (using I) to make it clear that the views are not those of the company, being aware of the responsibilities with respect to corporate information, and adhering to professional standards.[24]

Fredrik Racka outlines four rules: understand that you're personally responsible, abide by existing rules, keep secrets, and use common sense.[25]

Despite developments in *electronic human resources (eHR)*, a number of human resource professionals indicate that technology has failed to meet their expectations. In a study by Towers Perrin, only 5 percent of respondents indicated that their Web service had achieved the goal of lowering HR costs (with an additional 35 percent reporting that they had partially achieved that objective). Similarly, 4 percent responded that the Web service had met the aim of improving overall organizational effectiveness (while 63 percent reported partial attainment of that goal).[26]

Information Sharing and Open-Book Management

Some employers provide reports to employees about the organization's economic performance. The reasoning is that economic information is as important to employees as it is to shareholders. The report is presented in the same style as the annual report, except that it shows how the annual economic results affect workers.

The release of the report may be followed by meetings that are organized and conducted in the same way as shareholder meetings. Top management attends the meetings, and all employees are invited. Management formally presents the report, and employees are invited to question management and make proposals in the same way that owners do in stockholder meetings. These meetings improve communication and give jobholders a stronger feeling of belonging.

> The EDS call centre in Cape Breton is not your typical call centre. Career mobility is frequently communicated to employees and the centre aims to create an environment that will attract and retain workers. According to HR recruiter Jennifer MacDonald, "The environment has a big effect on employees. Employees need to know they are important to the business. We have two quarterly meetings to discuss where the business is going globally and locally."[27]

While many companies believe that the financial performance and budget goals of the firm are not the business of employees, some firms have adopted an approach of sharing such information with employees (for example, a Statistics Canada study indicates that about 49 percent of employers follow a practice of sharing information with workers).[28] Using *open-book management*, some firms are making employees assume more responsibility for the success of the firm. The basic concepts involve educating employees about how the firm earns profits, giving workers a stake in the performance of the business, and providing feedback on how the company is doing.

> Xilinx has a people-centric culture which starts with the CEO who spends up to 20 percent of his time communicating with employees. He moves offices on a regular basis in order to get to know employees better, has monthly meetings with workers, has a Q&A feature on the company's Web site, and encourages storytelling where employees get together and relate stories showing how the company's values affect decision making.[29]

Some things organizations are doing to improve communications internally and to enhance the link between employees and the organization (and its customers or clients) include the following:

- more research/employee surveys to understand employee attitudes toward communication and what is working (and not working)
- "total rewards" communication that addresses the numerous benefits of working for the employer
- performance-oriented communication that outlines performance standards for employees and the effect of employee performance on the organization and its customers
- communications training for managers and employees
- regular review or audit of the communication system[30]

Upward Communication Systems

Perhaps no area of communication is more in need of improvement in most organizations than upward communication. **Upward communication** consists of information initiated by people who seek to inform or influence those higher up in the organization's hierarchy. The cornerstone of all such messages is the employee and the supervisor. When a free flow of information travels between an employee and the supervisor, informal day-to-day communication is often sufficient for most situations. If open communication does not exist, or exists only for a limited range of issues, other approaches are needed.

upward communication
Communication that begins in the organization and proceeds up the hierarchy to inform or influence others.

How do organizations create open, upward communication? No universal formula exists—the type of approach used may vary depending on the situation. However, one common element in many organizations is a genuine concern for employee well-being combined with meaningful opportunities for ideas to flow up the organization's hierarchy. Some of the more common upward communication channels include the grapevine, in-house complaint procedures, manager–employee meetings, suggestion systems, and attitude survey feedback.

Grapevine

grapevine communication
Informal communication within an organization that arises from normal social interaction.

Grapevine communication is an informal system that arises spontaneously from the social interaction of people in the organization. It is the people-to-people system that arises naturally from human desires to make friends and share ideas. For instance, when two employees chat at the water cooler about their problems with a supervisor, that is a grapevine communication.

The grapevine provides a large amount of useful off-the-record feedback from employees. There are many opportunities for feedback because human resource specialists are in regular contact with employees as they discuss benefits, counsel employees, and perform other functions. Employees feel somewhat free to talk with human resource specialists since the occupation of human resource management is oriented toward helping people and human resource specialists do not directly supervise employees in other departments. Some of the types of grapevine feedback that come to the human resource department include information about employee problems, the quality of labour–management relations, important grievance issues, areas of job dissatisfaction, difficulties with supervisors, and acceptance by employees of changes within the organization. In an effort to enhance communications, some organizations use management by walking around (MBWA). MBWA opens up the channels of communication by encouraging daily face-to-face contact by managers with employees. However, the Internet is changing how employees communicate:

Social networking used to involve gossip around the water cooler or lunchroom chats. However, sites like Facebook, YouTube, and Twitter have changed the rules. HR professionals need to be aware of the new social media and the rights of both employers and employees relating to the use of electronic social networking. What an employee posts online could constitute discrimination, bullying, or harassment. In addition, an employee could intentionally or inadvertently divulge private company information. What about employees posting information outside of regular work hours? If the employer can show that its legitimate business interests are affected by the material posted by the employee, the employee may be liable and subject to discipline.[31]

An informal gathering around the water cooler or coffee station is one method by which employees exchange information, but also gossip and rumours. What can management do to keep rumours down?

© Leon/Getty Images.

Electronic Communication

Although the issue of electronic communication has been discussed in detail earlier in the chapter, it is important to recognize that email, intranets, and discussion groups are also very useful in facilitating upward communication. Again, the importance of issues such as security of use, monitoring of employee messages, rules of conduct, and the need for a policy on email and Internet usage needs to be emphasized.

At a lab outside New York, a group of mathematicians spy on IBM's workforce. They are the subject of a book by Stephen Baker called *The Numerati*. Monitoring company email servers allows employers to determine who is networking with whom, who might be meeting with a competitor, and who is checking sports scores or chatting with friends online. Supermarkets are also using data to track customer preferences.[32]

More and more organizations are implementing human resource management systems (HRMS). This is not surprising considering that mastering HR technology has recently been identified as one of the five competency domains for human resource management (along with business knowledge, HR delivery, strategic contribution, and personal credibility).[33] Still, many HRMS are being used for maintaining employee records rather than for strategic human resource issues and communication purposes.[34]

In-House Complaint Procedures

How does an employee solve a problem if the supervisor is not willing to discuss it? In some organizations, the employee has no other option except to talk with the supervisor's superior. Although that may seem reasonable, most people in organizations are very reluctant to do that because they do not want to create negative feelings between themselves and their supervisor. To lessen the burden of "going over the supervisor's head," some organizations have installed **in-house complaint procedures**.

In-house complaint procedures are formal methods through which an employee can register a complaint. Normally these procedures are operated by the human resource department and require the employee to submit the complaint in writing. Then, an employee relations specialist investigates the complaint and advises the employee of the results. In some companies, the employee's name is known only by the employee relations investigator. However, if a supervisor is questioned about the issue, it may be obvious who filed the complaint.

In recent years, there has been growing interest in *alternative dispute resolution* (ADR) programs. The goal of ADR is to resolve disputes in a timely, cost-effective manner. Some types of ADR programs include the following:

1. An **open-door policy** in which an employee is encouraged to meet with his or her supervisor or another member of management to resolve workplace conflict.

2. A *peer review panel* or ombudsperson who hears an employee's presentation of the problem and makes recommendations. While the composition of the peer review panel may vary, a typical structure involves two individuals from a similar job classification as the employee and one management representative. It is estimated that about 90 percent of disputes getting to peer review are settled at this level.

3. *Mediation* in which a neutral third party meets with the parties and tries to resolve the issue. Although the mediator cannot impose a settlement, his or her involvement is often instrumental in resolving the conflict.

4. *Arbitration* in which a neutral third party hears both parties' views of the case and makes a binding decision. While arbitration is common in unionized environments, it is also becoming more popular as a means of resolving disputes in nonunion settings.[35]

The last decade or so has seen considerable growth in the presence of a grievance system for nonunion employees. A nonunion grievance procedure can be defined as one that is in writing, guarantees employees the right to present complaints to management, and is communicated to employees.[36] For example, a study of Canadian firms revealed that about 31 percent had a grievance procedure for nonunion employees, with the typical procedure consisting of a three- or four-step process.[37] In setting up a nonunion grievance procedure, several issues exist. Some questions to consider:

- What subjects may be grieved? For example, can disciplinary actions be grieved?
- Are all nonunion employees eligible to participate in the procedure?
- Are employees protected from retaliation if they use the procedure?
- Must the grievance be filed in writing? Are there time limits for employee filing and management response?
- How many steps will the grievance procedure contain? Can an employee bypass his or her supervisor? What are the specific steps in the procedure?

in-house complaint procedures
Formal methods through which an employee can register a complaint.

open-door policy
A company policy that encourages employees to address their problems to higher levels of management.

Farcus

by David Waisglass
Gordon Coulthart

© 1992 Farcus Cartoons   WAISGLASS/COULTHART   www.farcus.com

**"... and now I'd like to discuss new ways
to fight our absenteeism problem."**

- Does the employee have the right to be present throughout the procedure? Can the employee have someone else (such as another employee, human resource staff member, lawyer) present the case? Can the employee call witnesses?
- What is the final step in the procedure? For instance, who ultimately resolves the issue? Some options include a senior line manager, HR professional, a panel (which can be comprised of just managers, managers and employees, or just employees), or outside arbitration.[38]

Manager–Employee Meetings

Closely related to in-house complaint procedures are meetings between managers and groups of employees to discuss complaints, suggestions, opinions, or questions. These meetings may begin with some information sharing by management to inform the group about developments in the company. However, the primary purpose of these meetings is to encourage upward communication, often with several levels of employees and lower-level management in attendance at the same time. Attendance at such meetings varies according to how the meetings are planned. In small facilities, it may be possible to get all the employees together annually or semiannually; however, this does not reduce the need to keep in touch with employees on a regular basis. In large business units, different formats may be needed:

> One major bank's Open Meeting Program arranges meetings of about a dozen employees at a time. Meetings are held with different groups until at least one in five employees from each department attends. Employees are selected randomly and may decline to participate if they wish. A human resource specialist coordinates each meeting and develops the group report on a newsprint sheet in open discussions with the group. No employee names are used on the report, which becomes the basis of action plans with management. The program is repeated annually, and it has significantly improved upward communication.

Suggestion Systems

suggestion systems
A formal method of generating, evaluating, and implementing employee ideas.

Suggestion systems are a formal method for generating, evaluating, and implementing employee ideas. All three of these elements are crucial to a successful suggestion system.

A successful suggestion system begins with the employee's idea and a discussion with the supervisor. Once the suggestion form is completed, the supervisor reviews and signs the form, indicating awareness of the suggestion, but not necessarily approval. The suggestion system office or committee receives the idea and informs the employee that it has received the suggestion. The idea is then evaluated, and the decision is communicated to the employee. If it is considered a good idea, implementation follows, with the employee receiving recognition and usually some award (often awards are equal to about 10 percent of the first year's savings from the suggestion).

For suggestion systems to work, management must provide prompt and fair assessment of the ideas, supervisors must be trained to encourage employee suggestions, and top management must actively support the program. Unfortunately, this source of upward communication is ineffective in many companies because evaluations often take months or supervisors see suggestions as more work for them with few personal benefits.

Organizations that place a higher focus on teamwork may need to revamp their suggestion system program to reflect a group contribution. Although most suggestion systems pay employees a percentage of the first-year savings, some companies pay a flat dollar amount in order to minimize the need for precision in evaluating the suggestion's exact dollar savings. This approach means that employees receive feedback about their suggestions much faster.

One survey indicated that at least once a month, one-third of employees comes up with a suggestion that they believe will increase organizational performance. However, workers often perceive that they are not rewarded for coming up with suggestions.[39]

HR Solutions, Inc.
Specialists in attitude
surveys
www.hrsolutionsinc.com/

**employee attitude/
opinion survey**
A systematic method
of determining what
employees think of
their organization.

Employee Attitude/Opinion Surveys

What do employees think about the organization? Do they have problems or concerns? Do they understand the human resource department's benefit plan? Compensation program? Career planning efforts? Answers to these and many other questions can make a useful addition to the human resource department's information system.

Employee attitude/opinion surveys are systematic methods of determining what employees think about their organization. While surveys may be conducted through face-to-face interviews, they are usually done through questionnaires that employees complete anonymously. A number of organizations are now using Web technology to conduct employee surveys.

An employee survey typically seeks to learn what employees think about working conditions, supervision, human resource policies, and other organizational issues. New programs or special concerns to management also may be a source of questions. The resulting information can be used to evaluate specific concerns, such as how individual managers are perceived by their employees.

Attitude/opinion surveys can be a frustrating experience for employees if they do not receive any information on the survey results. Without feedback, the survey has little meaning to workers and they may be reluctant to participate in a follow-up survey. Therefore, a summary of the survey results should be provided to employees for their reaction.

> Maple Leaf Automotive Products has for several years relied on employee surveys as a method of facilitating organizational communication. Supervisors in the company are given a workbook to analyze survey results. Trained internal facilitators help the supervisors to interpret the survey results. Then the facilitators conduct a role-playing exercise with the supervisors to prepare them for the questions that employees are likely to ask.
>
> After the role-playing, the supervisor meets with the employees and presents the results. Together, problems are identified and solutions sought. From this meeting a prioritized list of action items emerges with dates for their completion. The result of all these efforts is not only that employees know what others in the organization feel, but it also helps the organization to develop an action plan to resolve its immediate and potential problems.

However, feedback is not enough. Employees need to see that the survey results cause problems to be solved. Feedback of the results and action on the problem areas make survey feedback a powerful communication tool:

> FedEx Canada, along with other FedEx businesses in 210 countries, participates in a global employee satisfaction survey that allows businesses to see how they compare with sister companies. Response rates to the survey are around 98 percent and the survey results are linked to managers' performance appraisals and, in turn, to their base and variable pay. Managers whose scores are low have to submit action plans that are signed off on by their manager, their reports, and an employee relations representative. This is all part of FedEx's People First philosophy. According to the Managing Director of Human Resources, "an engaged employee is an employee who is satisfied, who is committed, and who gives that above-and-beyond discretionary effort."[40]

EMPLOYEE COUNSELLING

counselling
The discussion of
a problem with an
employee, with the
general objective of
helping the worker
resolve the issue or cope
with the situation so that
he or she can become
more effective.

Counselling is the discussion of a problem with an employee, with the general objective of helping the worker resolve the issue or cope with the situation so that the person can become more effective both at work and away from the workplace:

> One company has a program available to employees and their families that covers both personal and work-related problems. The company maintains a 24-hour hotline and uses both company counsellors and community agencies. The service is strictly confidential. An average of 750 employees use the service each month. Many successes have been reported, although the program is unable to solve every employee problem. A study of alcoholic employees reported a remarkable 85 percent reduction in lost work hours, a 47 percent reduction in sick leave, and a 72 percent reduction in sickness and accident benefit payments. In a survey, 93 percent of the employees reported that they believe that counselling is a worthwhile service.

Some firms advise managers to avoid giving personal advice to employees that is not related to the job because the managers are not professionally qualified to do so. There is a chance that they will give inappropriate or wrong advice that aggravates an employee's problem. A growing number of organizations have formal arrangements with outside professional counselling agencies to help their employees.

Employee Assistance Programs

Organizations may establish an employee assistance program (EAP) to assist employees with personal problems (such as family or marital difficulties, substance abuse, or stress) that may be affecting their performance at work.

An interesting development in providing EAP services involves the use of online communications. While online services are not a substitute for face-to-face employee contact, they may supplement existing EAP structures. Use of computer technology in providing EAP services may involve video counselling, chat rooms, bulletin boards, and self-help applications. However, it should be recognized that online services are not appropriate for every case; rather, they represent one of a number of alternative approaches to providing EAP services.[41]

EMPLOYEE DISCIPLINE

Even after counselling, there are instances where an employee's behaviour remains inappropriately disruptive or performance is unacceptable. Under these circumstances, discipline is needed. **Discipline** is management action to encourage compliance with organization standards. It is a type of action that seeks to inform employees about organizational expectations and change worker attitudes and behaviour.

discipline
Management action to encourage compliance with organization standards.

> About 90 percent of the 500 largest employers in the United States have a policy prohibiting employees from downloading child pornography on company computers, and a recent study indicated that 50 percent of the companies applied the policy after finding inappropriate images on at least one of their computers. Of the firms making formal investigations, 44 percent of the employers terminated employees who violated the policy.[42]

There are two types of discipline: preventive and corrective.

Preventive Discipline

Preventive discipline is action prior to an infraction taken to encourage employees to follow standards and rules. The basic objective is to encourage self-discipline among employees. In this way, employees maintain their own discipline, rather than having management impose it.

Management has the responsibility for building a climate of preventive discipline. In doing so, it makes its standards known and understood. If employees do not know what standards are expected, their conduct is likely to be erratic or misdirected. Employees will better support standards that they have helped to create. They will also give more support to standards stated positively instead of negatively, such as "Safety first!" rather than "Don't be careless!"

The human resource department has a major responsibility for preventive discipline. For example, it develops programs to control absenteeism and employee grievances. It communicates standards to employees and encourages employees to follow them. It also provides training programs to explain the reasons behind standards and to build a positive spirit of self-discipline.

preventive discipline
Action taken prior to an infraction to encourage employees to follow standards and rules.

Corrective Discipline

Corrective discipline is an action that follows a rule infraction. It seeks to discourage further infractions so that future acts are in compliance with standards. Typically the corrective action is a penalty of some type and is called a *disciplinary action*. Examples are a warning or suspension without pay. The objectives of disciplinary action are

corrective discipline
Discipline that follows a rule infraction.

- to reform the offender;
- to deter others from similar actions; and
- to maintain consistent, effective group standards.

The objectives of disciplinary action are positive, educational, and corrective. The goal is to improve the future rather than punish past acts. The corrective disciplinary interview often follows a "sandwich model," which means that a corrective comment is sandwiched between two positive

HR information on discipline
www.allbusiness.
com/human-
resources/employee-
development/384684-1.html

comments in order to make the corrective comment more acceptable. An example: "Your attendance is excellent, Jason (a positive comment), but your late return from coffee breaks disrupts our repair operations (negative). Otherwise, your work is among the best in our department (positive)." The supervisor then focuses on ways in which the two of them can work together to correct the problem. However, corrective discipline is frequently not used or not used properly. Many managers receive little or no training addressing employee discipline and the consequences if the disciplinary process is not managed effectively.

Restrictions on Discipline

The ability to discipline may be restricted by union contracts and government legislation. Corrective discipline is an especially sensitive subject with unions who may see it as an area where employees need protection from unreasonable management authority. In addition, the union wants to show employees that the union leadership cares for their interests.

Government legislation makes it illegal for an employer to discipline a worker who is asserting rights protected by law. For example, an employee cannot be disciplined or dismissed for union activities (the right to participate in union activities is protected under labour relations statutes) or for refusing to perform work that is hazardous, unsafe, or unlawful. Other employment restrictions may also apply, depending on the circumstances and the laws of the provinces concerned.

due process
In a disciplinary situation, the following of proper, established rules and procedures, and giving employees the opportunity to respond to allegations.

Due process for discipline may be required of the employer by courts of law, arbitrators, and labour unions. **Due process** means that established rules and procedures for disciplinary action need to be followed and that employees are provided an opportunity to respond to allegations or complaints made against them.[43] It is the human resource department's responsibility to ensure that all parties in a disciplinary action follow the proper rules and procedures so that due process will be used.

If a disciplinary action is challenged, the human resource department must have sufficient documentation to support the action; therefore, human resource policy should require proper documentation for all employer disciplinary actions.

Proper documentation should be specific, beginning with the date, time, and location of an incident. It should also describe the nature of the undesirable performance or behaviour and how it relates to job and organizational performance. Specific rules and regulations that relate to the incident must be identified. Documentation should include what the manager said to the employee and how the employee responded, including specific words and actions. If there were witnesses, they should be identified. All documentation must be recorded promptly, when the incident is still fresh in the memories of the parties. The evidence recorded should be objective, based on observations and not impressions.

hot-stove rule
The principle that disciplinary action should be like what happens when you touch a hot stove: it is with warning, immediate, consistent, and impersonal.

A useful guide for corrective discipline is the **hot-stove rule**. The hot-stove rule states that disciplinary action should have the same characteristics as the penalty a person receives from touching a hot stove. These characteristics are that discipline should be with warning, immediate, consistent, and impersonal.

Progressive Discipline

progressive discipline
The use of stronger and stronger penalties for repeated offences.

Most employers apply a policy of **progressive discipline**, which means that there are stronger penalties for repeated offences. The purpose of this is to give an employee an opportunity to take corrective action before more serious penalties are applied. Progressive discipline also gives management time to work with an employee to help correct infractions:

> When Margaret Stoner had two unauthorized absences, the human resource department provided counselling. It also arranged for her to join a ride pool that allowed her to leave home 30 minutes later than with public transportation. Eventually her unauthorized absences stopped.

A typical progressive discipline system is shown in Figure 11-2. The first infraction leads to a verbal reprimand by the supervisor. The next infraction leads to a written reprimand, with a record placed in the file. Further infractions result in stronger discipline, leading finally to discharge. Usually the human resource department becomes involved at the third step or earlier to ensure that company policy is applied consistently in all departments.

FIGURE 11-2	A Progressive Discipline System

1. Verbal reprimand by supervisor
2. Written reprimand, with a record in file
3. One- to three-day suspension from work
4. Suspension for one week or longer
5. Discharge for cause

It is essential that employers document efforts made to help employees. One possible program involves four steps:

1. Clearly indicate in writing the nature of the problem and the impact of the employee's performance or conduct on the organization.
2. Provide the employee with a clear and unequivocal warning that failure to improve behaviour will result in discipline (up to and including termination).
3. Establish through progressive discipline that the employee's performance was still unacceptable despite repeated warnings.
4. Demonstrate that discipline was applied in a fair and consistent manner.[44]

Some progressive systems allow minor offences to be removed from the employee's record after a period of time (typically between one and five years). However, serious offences, such as fighting or theft, are usually not dealt with by means of progressive discipline. An employee who commits these offences may be discharged on the first offence.

Positive Discipline

Instead of using punishment to discipline employees, some organizations employ an approach called *positive discipline*, which involves an acceptance on the part of the employee that a problem exists, an acknowledgement by the employee that he or she must assume responsibility for the behaviour, and the use of a problem-solving approach to resolving the problem. The key steps in using positive discipline are as follows:

1. Focus on the specific problem rather than the employee's attitude or personality.
2. Gain agreement with the employee that a performance problem exists and that the employee is responsible for changing his or her behaviour.
3. Approach discipline as a problem-solving process.
4. Document suggested changes or commitments by the employee.
5. Follow up to ensure that the employee is living up to his or her commitments and to reduce the likelihood of having to take more severe action.[45]

DISMISSAL

The ultimate disciplinary action is dismissal, which is separation from the employer. Michael Wilson, CEO of Agrium in Calgary is big on collaboration. But he also notes:

> Building a new culture also means you get rid of people who aren't prepared to accept best practices and move towards that. You cannot afford to have a naysayer on the team. If someone's not in support, you have to take them out of the company.[46]

A nonunion employer who does not have just cause for dismissing an employee may be sued for **wrongful dismissal**. Consider the experience of one small business:

> The owner of a small business with 18 employees terminated a manager who had been with the firm for 22 years. Although there was no documented evidence to support his claim, the owner said that the manager's performance had been slipping over the past few years. Shortly after

wrongful dismissal
Terminating an employee without just cause or without giving the employee reasonable notice or compensation in lieu of notice.

being released, the employee contacted an employment lawyer and the parties settled out of court for in excess of $100,000. The business owner had never heard of the law of wrongful dismissal and the settlement put the business in jeopardy.

The law of wrongful dismissal is very complicated and human resource professionals without considerable expertise in this area are advised to seek prudent legal advice. Note that the dismissal of unionized employees (slightly less than 30 percent of the non-agricultural workforce) is governed by the provisions of the collective agreement and the remedy exists with the grievance arbitration process (see Chapter 14). Save for a few exceptions, an employer can terminate a nonunion employee at any time if just cause exists; however, in the absence of just cause, the employer is usually obligated to give the former employee "reasonable notice" or compensation in lieu of notice.

All provinces and the federal jurisdiction have employment standards legislation providing minimum periods of notice for employees terminated without cause. The amount of advance notice an employer is required to give an individual is dependent on the employee's length of service with the employer, and some jurisdictions have specific notice periods that apply if the employer engages in a mass layoff or termination. However, it should be noted that the provisions under employment standards legislation are statutory *minimums* and the amount of reasonable notice awarded by the courts frequently exceeds such provisions.

> One human resource management manager indicated that the company's practice was to provide the minimum notice provisions under employment standards legislation if terminating an employee. The reason for this approach was simply that the manager was uninformed about the law of wrongful dismissal.

Three jurisdictions (federal, Quebec, and Nova Scotia) provide an alternative forum for some wrongfully dismissed employees meeting specified period of service requirements (10 years in Nova Scotia, 5 years in Quebec, and 1 year for the federal jurisdiction). While the provisions of the statutes vary, the thrust of the legislation is to permit employees to bring their cases to an adjudication process in which the adjudicator may order reinstatement and damages if sufficient cause for dismissal does not exist. The specifics of the legislation are quite detailed and legal assistance is advised.

Determining Just Cause

just cause
Legal grounds for termination such as employee misconduct or incompetence.

Cause for dismissal under common law includes any act by the employee that could have serious negative effects on the operation or reputation of the organization. This typically includes incompetence and employee misconduct (such as fraud, drunkenness, dishonesty, insubordination, or refusal to obey reasonable orders). The onus for proving the existence of **just cause** is on the employer.[47] Ideally, there is a carefully planned termination interview to ensure that the separation is as positive and constructive as possible—the Supreme Court of Canada has ruled that an employer must act in a way that demonstrates good faith and fair dealing in the dismissal of employees.[48]

While an employer may terminate an employee at any time if just cause exists, the courts' interpretation of what constitutes just cause for dismissal is often much different from managers' perceptions of cause. Although employers argued just cause for dismissal in 44 percent of wrongful dismissal cases over a 15-year period, the court found that just cause existed in only 37 percent of the decisions—in other words, while employers often believe just cause was present, this belief is frequently not supported by the courts.[49] However, some very recent decisions suggest that the pendulum has swung back toward the employer side.[50] Note that in many instances, cases are settled out of court:

> An executive of the Nova Scotia Liquor Corporation was terminated after eight months of service. The employer asserted that the individual did not fit in and failed to get along with other executives. The former employee was given a severance package that included six months' pay and a bonus (for a total compensation package of $62,000).[51]

Incompetent Work Performance

When considering dismissal on the basis of incompetence, the employment contract contains an implied warranty that the employee is "reasonably competent" and able to perform the work for which the person was hired. If the employee proves to be incompetent, the employer may dismiss the employee on the basis of just cause.

FIGURE 11-3	Requirements in Dismissing an Incompetent Employee

1. Have a reasonable and objective performance standard. It is the employer's responsibility to show that this standard has been effectively communicated to employees and that other employees have achieved the standard.

2. Document employee's performance indicating that he or she has failed to meet the standards (while other employees have been successful).

3. Have evidence of warnings given to the employee.

4. Show that appropriate training, support, time, and feedback has been provided to the employee to enable the employee to learn the tasks.

5. Demonstrate that the employee concerned had reasonable time to improve performance.

Source: © *Canadian Employment Law Today*, June 26, 1991, pp. 685–86, by permission of Carswell, Toronto, Ontario, 1-800-387-5164.

However, employers and the courts often differ in their assessment with respect to cause involving dismissal for incompetence. Employers were able to establish employee incompetence in less than 25 percent of the cases in which they argued just cause for termination on the basis of incompetence—establishing cause on the grounds of incompetence is not easy (see Figure 11-3).

Kathleen Fisher, who had worked at Lakeland Mills Ltd. for 18 years, informed company president Keith Anderson of her intention to stay with the company upon turning 65 years of age. Anderson responded "you can stay with our company for as long as you wish." A year later, the office manager wanted to replace Fisher with someone who was more versatile. In addition to her accounting position, Fisher was asked to back up the shipping clerk—the job required certain computer skills which Fisher did not have but she expressed a desire to acquire the necessary skills. The company then argued that her performance was not up to standards and that they were going to hire someone to take over part of her accounting work unless she retired. Fisher resigned and sued for constructive dismissal. The BC Court agreed that Fisher was wrongfully dismissed and awarded her 10 months' severance with bonus and benefits.[52]

The employer must establish *real* incompetence, an inability to carry out job duties, or substandard work performance that fails to improve even after the employee has been put on notice that his or her performance is not adequate. Performance standards must be nondiscriminatory, reasonable, and applied fairly, while warnings must clearly describe what constitutes acceptable performance and what specific actions the employee should take to improve performance. Merely giving an employee average or substandard ratings is not enough. Also, the employer should make it clear to the employee that his or her job is at risk if performance does not improve. A single incident of incompetence will rarely justify dismissal, especially if the incident is a single blemish on an otherwise clean work record.

Employee Misconduct

The courts have repeatedly found that an allegation of employee misconduct must be decided with reference to the unique factors of each case. Four classes of misconduct identified in the case law include (1) unfaithful service to the employer; (2) misconduct of a general nature; (3) theft, fraud, or dishonesty; and (4) willful disobedience of a reasonable and lawful order.

Acts of unfaithful service, such as conspiracy and competition against the employer or serious conflict of interest, are generally regarded as being in that class of misconduct justifying immediate dismissal. The employer's case is relatively straightforward when there is an intent on the part of the employee to commit an act of unfaithful service and the threat of loss to the employer is real.

What about cases involving drug or alcohol abuse; abuse of coworkers, clients, or customers; or improper activity outside the workplace? In determining whether the misconduct is sufficient to justify dismissal, the courts consider both the nature of the misconduct and the employee's position within the organization. A serious act of misconduct may justify immediate discharge. In addition, employees in senior management or in positions of trust (such as a teacher) may be held to higher standards of conduct regarding misconduct both at and away from the workplace.

Theft, fraud, and dishonesty are among the most serious grounds for dismissal because they call into question the honesty and integrity of the employee. Depending on the circumstances, a single isolated act of theft, dishonesty, or fraud may justify dismissal, but the court carefully reviews any explanation for the employee's behaviour.

> Jatinder Kalsi was a 36-year-old mechanic who had been employed with Canadian Tire in New Westminster, BC, for 19 years. Kalsi, who was on leave after being injured in a car accident, came into the store one day to have a $20 light bulb replaced in his car. Since the mechanic on duty was busy, Kalsi said he would get a replacement light bulb. The clerk in charge of supplies was also busy, so Kalsi was given the keys to the supplies cabinet. Kalsi removed a light bulb, put it in his pocket, and returned the keys to the store manager. He told the manager he was going to check and see if the light bulb was the right one and would return right away if it was not. A security officer observed what was going on, said that Kalsi had committed a theft, and detained him in the lunchroom. A senior advisor met with Kalsi and told him that Kalsi had technically stolen the light bulb but that everything would be fine, so Kalsi admitted taking the bulb. The company immediately fired Kalsi for theft.
>
> The court held that the company's questioning and management's investigation were not up to acceptable standards, and that Kalsi had been wrongfully dismissed. Canadian Tire was ordered to pay Kalsi 16 months' pay in lieu of notice and $6,500 for false imprisonment.[53]

Willful disobedience (which may include absenteeism, tardiness, or a breach of rules or policy) is considered to constitute a repudiation of the employment contract. An employee who refuses to obey the lawful and reasonable order of the employer is in breach of the employment contract. However, disobedience must be seen to be willful or deliberate; petty disagreements and personality conflicts usually do not amount to cause. Furthermore, a reasonable excuse for disobedience will negate the intent required for cause.[54]

Business or Economic Reasons

Contrary to the impressions of many managers, courts have consistently held that terminating an employee because of business or economic factors is not just cause for dismissal because such factors are not related to the employee's behaviour. It is critical that employers seeking to dismiss employees due to declining demand or as a result of an organizational downsizing ensure that terminated employees are provided with reasonable notice or appropriate compensation. It is advisable to seek legal assistance to review the process and compensation or severance package offered to terminated employees.

Constructive Dismissal

Rather than terminate an employee, an employer may decide to change the individual's job in such a way that the employee decides to quit. A major change in the employment terms that results in an employee resigning may be considered as **constructive dismissal**. Some examples of constructive dismissal include a significant change in job function, a demotion, a demand for an employee's resignation, or a forced transfer.[55] The law relating to constructive dismissal is technical in nature and human resource professionals are advised to seek legal advice prior to changing a major term of an employment contract.

constructive dismissal
A major change in the terms of the employment contract that results in an employee resigning.

Reasonable Notice

An employer that does not have just cause for dismissal must provide a dismissed employee with "reasonable notice" or compensation (typically salary, benefits, and reasonable job search expenses) in lieu of notice. While several managers believe that the organization need only provide the minimum notice period outlined under employment standards legislation, it should be emphasized that these provisions are only minimums and courts may (and frequently do) award much greater notice periods.

The major factors used to predict notice include the following:

- *The former employee's age, length of service, salary, and occupational status*—on average, older employees, long-service employees, more highly paid employees, and employees occupying more senior positions in the organization tend to receive higher periods of notice.
- *An attempt to mitigate losses*—employees who are terminated must make reasonable efforts to find similar alternative employment.
- *A less favourable labour market*—when alternative employment opportunities are limited, courts tend to award greater notice periods.

While each case is settled based on its own particular facts, some guidelines relating to wrongful dismissal have been developed. However, it should be underscored that these are only guidelines to provide some guidance to students relating to wrongful dismissal awards. Based on the guidelines, an employee in a clerical/blue-collar position will receive about two weeks' notice (or compensation in lieu of notice) for each year of service, an employee in a supervisory or lower-level management position will receive three weeks' notice (or compensation) for each year of service, and senior management and professional employees will receive one month's notice (or compensation) for each year of service. In the past, it had been rare for notice periods to exceed 24 months.[56]

The Wallace "Effect"

The 1997 decision of the Supreme Court of Canada in *Wallace v. United Grain Growers* has led to the awarding of extended periods of notice in a number of wrongful dismissal cases in which the employer was found to have terminated an employee in bad faith. In the *Wallace* case, the Court ruled that the employer had dismissed Wallace in "bad faith" and thus added an additional 9 months onto a reasonable notice award of 15 months.

In the recent decision in *Honda Canada v. Keays*, the Supreme Court of Canada addressed the issue of *Wallace* damages. As noted by employment lawyer Stuart Rudner:

> The Supreme Court of Canada completely revamped the manner in which bad-faith damages are calculated. The court replaced the notice extension with a compensatory approach that appears to require the employee to prove not only that the employer acted in bad faith but that the employee actually suffered damages as a result. The Court also determined that punitive damages are restricted to advertent wrongful acts that are so malicious and outrageous that they are deserving of punishment on their own.[57]

Managing the Dismissal

There are several guidelines to follow in dismissing an employee:

- Prepare for the interview and conduct a rehearsal.
- Conduct the interview in private.
- Consider the dismissal process from the employee's perspective and ask, "How would I like to be treated in such a situation?"
- Get to the point. Some experts suggest that you convey the message of termination within the first few sentences.
- Select the time and place. Experts often suggest a meeting in the morning and during the middle of the week.
- Have any necessary information ready (such as a severance package and outplacement counselling assistance).
- Notify others in the organization and ensure that the individual's duties are covered.
- In some instances, special security arrangements may be necessary.
- Discuss the process with other colleagues who have had to terminate employees.[58]

⊙ EMPLOYEE RIGHTS

Employee rights refer to those rights desired by employees relating to working conditions and job security. Some of these rights are protected under law, others under the collective agreement with the union (if one exists), and yet others may be listed in the letter of appointment given to the employee at the time of hiring. Regardless of whether these rights are recorded in writing or currently protected by law and agreements, they have a significant impact on the human resource management activities of an organization. Progressive human resource managers recognize this and strive to provide fair and equitable working conditions that help the employee to maintain dignity on the job. Would you be willing to have a computer chip implanted into your body? Consider the following:

> The CEO and two other employees of a surveillance company in Cincinnati, Ohio, had computer chips implanted in their upper arms as a security measure to limit access to a room holding confidential police and government documents. The implanted chip is slightly longer than a grain of rice. Privacy experts in the United States are concerned that if acceptance of the technology grows, there will be pressure on employees to have to accept the chips.[59]

SPOTLIGHT ON HRM
Great Television Doesn't Translate into Great Policy

By Natalie C. MacDonald

"You're fired." Real estate tycoon Donald Trump's catch phrase has captured the attention of the world. Millions of viewers tune in every week to watch *The Apprentice*, a hit reality show where individuals compete for the ultimate prize of being Trump's apprentice.

Contestants are put into teams. Winners get a prize, the losers earn a trip to the boardroom to explain why they lost. Every week, at least one person is "fired."

In Trump's termination process, he and two of his advisors confront the contestants, pummelling each of them with questions about their performance. He sends the contestants out while he deliberates about who shall be terminated. The contestants return to the boardroom where he hands down his decision, listing all of the reasons why he is about to terminate one of them. The drama and the tension build until he makes his final choice.

While this makes for great television, it is not, nor should it inspire, a great way to terminate someone's employment. If employers in Canada were to adopt Trump's method, they would undoubtedly be on the hook for significant damages. Trump's television terminations are insensitive and callous, making the employee's firing much more difficult than it needs to be.

Trump's 10 Biggest Termination Mistakes

In the course of his terminations, Trump commits a number of serious mistakes. Here's a look at 10 of the most serious errors Trump makes that should never be emulated in a Canadian workplace:

- The person being terminated is brought into a boardroom where she is with her peers and is being terminated in front of her peers, not in private just with Trump.

- She is being terminated not only in front of her peers, but also with two of Trump's advisors watching, thereby creating a firing-squad like atmosphere, rather than simply being in front of one advisor and Trump.

- Prior to the termination, all of the team members know that one of the select group being pulled into the boardroom will be terminated, instead of the termination being kept secret amongst only senior management.

- The person being terminated is advised of all the things she did wrong, but is never given a warning and the chance to correct the behaviour before being fired.

- She is terminated for cause where there is likely no legal cause for her termination.

- She is terminated without being provided what she is entitled to under applicable employment standards legislation.

- She is terminated without reasonable notice of the termination or compensation in lieu of notice pursuant to the employer's obligation under the common law.

- She is not provided with a letter of reference, outplacement counselling or anything which will assist her in the transition to new employment.

- She may have been enticed to leave secure employment to be "employed" with Trump, which would increase Trump's liability when firing her.

- An employee terminated in this manner would likely be entitled to significant *Wallace* damages. That's because she was ostracized in front of her peers and Trump's advisors, terminated with cause when there was no cause and made to feel worthless. This is exactly what the Supreme Court of Canada warned against in its decision in *Wallace v. United Grain Growers Ltd.* ...

If any of the contestants on *The Apprentice* had been real employees, and had sued for wrongful dismissal, it is likely that each would be successful in a claim for *Wallace* damages. A court would likely not hesitate in lengthening the notice period because of Trump's actions. In fact, a firing handled like Trump's television ones may even result in a successful claim for mental distress damages.

Steps Employers Should Take

To avoid creating a scenario like Trump's boardroom, it is recommended employers:

- **Keep the termination a secret:** Ensure the termination is only known to those terminating the employee or those involved in the decision.

- **Keep the termination small:** Bring the person being terminated into a room without anyone else except another senior manager as a witness. Never terminate someone in front of her colleagues.

- **Do not allege cause:** If an employer does not have cause, it should not allege it.

- **Do not list:** Don't get into a long list of what the employee has already done wrong.

- **Have a severance package ready:** Have a package ready for the employee, including provision of entitlements pursuant to employment standards legislation and under the common law.

- **Provide transitional assistance:** If the employee is not terminated for cause, consider providing transitional assistance to find another job, including a letter of reference and outplacement counselling.

- **Know the person's employment history:** The employer should have accounted for this person's particular circumstances, especially what happened before she was hired. If the employee was lured away from secure employment, take that into account.

- **Be sensitive:** Being fired is one of the most difficult things for an individual to hear and it is usually a major blow to self-esteem. Those doing the firing should remember the golden rule and treat the worker as they would want to be treated in a similar circumstance.

The Apprentice is only a television show, but if Trump's methods become a reality for employers, it will cause them significant grief. When terminating someone's employment, all the employer has to do is act in good faith and not make the termination more difficult than need be.

Natalie MacDonald is an associate with Grosman, Grosman & Gale, a toronto-based law firm specializing in employment law. She can be reached at 416-364-9599 or nmacdonald@grosman.com.

Source: Natalie C. MacDonald, "Great Television Doesn't translate into Great Policy," *Canadian HR Reporter*, January 31, 2005, pp. R4 and R9.

Right to Privacy

Employer concerns about employee privacy rights mean that many employers are careful to collect only job-related information at the point of hiring. There is an increasing realization among employers that collecting nonwork information is an unnecessary intrusion into the private lives of job applicants. Even when such additional information is not considered illegal, many employers feel that such an action constitutes a moral violation of workers' rights.

Depending on the circumstances, the use of biometrics to track employee work hours may be acceptable. For example, the Empire Ballroom (an Edmonton nightclub) introduced a thumbprint sign-in system to track employee arrivals and departures. One employee expressed concern about how the information would be used and stored. When asked about the company's privacy policy, she was told, "You work for me, I am your privacy policy." The Alberta Information and Privacy Commission found that the use of the data (to track employee shifts) was acceptable but was ordered to notify employees in writing what personal information was being collected by the biometrics procedure, explain how the information would be used, include thumbprint templates in its privacy policy, and provide all employees with a copy of the revised policy.[60]

The *Personal Information Protection and Electronic Documents Act* (PIPEDA) came into force in January 2004 in every province without its own privacy legislation. The aims of the legislation include requiring organizations to hold personal information about individuals in a responsible manner, permitting individuals to access and correct personal information, and allowing individuals control over the handling of information about them (see Figure 11-4).

What is personal information? As defined in PIPEDA, personal information is "factual information, recorded or not, about an individual." Under PIPEDA and provincial privacy legislation, information should only be kept as long as required for the purpose for which it was intended. The main problems with information security often revolve around security expertise and responsibility for security, poor enforcement of policies and procedures, outdated security software, and poor hiring (about 70 percent of identity theft occurs at the workplace).[61] The Privacy Commissioner of Canada is currently reviewing the use of RFID technology (technologies that use data stored on small tags or data chips which can be communicated to a reader using radio transmission).[62]

Two major law firms (one in Toronto and one elsewhere in Ontario) were reprimanded by the Alberta Privacy Commissioner's Office for publishing personal employee information (home addresses and social insurance numbers) of a client involved in a corporate buyout on a public Web site. Although the mistakes appeared to be made inadvertently, the decision suggests that law firms have an onerous task of reviewing every record in a client's records for privacy issues.[63]

| FIGURE 11-4 | The 10 Principles of the *Personal Information Protection and Electronic Documents Act* |

Principle 1: Accountability

An organization is responsible for personal information under its control and shall designate an individual or individuals who are accountable for the organization's compliance with the following principles.

Principle 2: Identifying Purposes

The purposes for which personal information is collected shall be identified by the organization at or before the time the information is collected.

Principle 3: Consent

The knowledge and consent of the individual are required for the collection, use, or disclosure of personal information, except where inappropriate.

Principle 4: Limiting Collection

The collection of personal information shall be limited to that which is necessary for the purposes identified by the organization. Information shall be collected by fair and lawful means.

Principle 5: Limiting Use, Disclosure, and Retention

Personal information shall not be used or disclosed for purposes other than those for which it was collected, except with the consent of the individual or as required by law. Personal information shall be retained only as long as necessary for the fulfilment of those purposes.

Principle 6: Accuracy

Personal information shall be as accurate, complete, and up-to-date as is necessary for the purposes for which it is to be used.

Principle 7: Safeguards

Personal information shall be protected by security safeguards appropriate to the sensitivity of the information.

Principle 8: Openness

An organization shall make readily available to individuals specific information about its policies and practices relating to the management of personal information.

Principle 9: Individual Access

Upon request, an individual shall be informed of the existence, use, and disclosure of his or her personal information and shall be given access to that information. An individual shall be able to challenge the accuracy and completeness of the information and have it amended as appropriate.

Principle 10: Challenging Compliance

An individual shall be able to address a challenge concerning compliance with the above principles to the designated individual or individuals accountable for the organization's compliance.

Source: Adapted from Department of Justice Canada, "Principles Set Out in the National Standard of Canada Entitled *Model Code for the Protection of Personal Information*," CAN/CSA-Q830-96, Schedule 1, Section 5, August 31, 2004. Available Department of Justice Canada site, http://laws.justice.gc.ca/en/p-8.6/93366.html. Retrieved August 27, 2006.

Privacy in the workplace is becoming an extremely sensitive issue and HR professionals must be aware of the legal and ethical challenges surrounding the issue. A 2007 survey by the American Management Association revealed that 24 percent of employers had employee email and instant messages (IM) subpoenaed in the course of a lawsuit or regulatory investigation and 15 percent had a lawsuit (for instance, on the basis of sexual harassment or a hostile work environment allegation) as a result of employee email.[64]

Someone watching you online may well be the same someone paying your salary. Many companies now use compliance systems to monitor the massive amount of Web traffic and email going through their systems. TD Canada Trust is currently investigating whether a group of traders improperly passed on rumours about a stock to clients. Compliance monitoring and email archiving is particularly important because in the case of a lawsuit, previous email messages may be used as evidence. According to one IT specialist, there are also productivity issues. "If an employee spends an hour every day monitoring their auctions on eBay, or reading personal email or chatting on IM, every other employee in the office knows it and resents it. If they are working hard, everyone else should be too."[65]

A 2007 AMA survey on electronic monitoring and surveillance showed that employers are particularly concerned about inappropriate Web surfing, with 66 percent monitoring employee Web site connections. Just under two-thirds of employers have software to block connections to inappropriate Web sites (a 27 percent increase from 2001). Employers blocking Web access are most concerned about employees visiting adult sites with sexual or pornographic content (96 percent), game sites (61 percent), and social networking sites (50 percent). Computer monitoring includes tracking content, key strokes, and time spent at the keyboard (used by 45 percent of employers); storing and reviewing computer files (43 percent); and monitoring the blogosphere (12 percent) to see what is being written about the organization. Most employers (more than 83 percent) inform employees that their activities are being monitored. Approximately 30 percent of the organizations report terminating employees for misuse of the Internet, 28 percent fired employees for email abuse, and 6 percent have dismissed employees for improper use of the telephone. See Figure 11-5 for guidelines for creating an Internet Use Policy.

About 48 percent of the companies participating in the AMA study use video monitoring to reduce or eliminate theft, violence, or sabotage (up from 33 percent in 2001), slightly more than 8 percent use global satellite positioning technology to track employee productivity and movement, and 52 percent use smart card technology to control access to buildings. The use of fingerprint scans (2 percent), facial recognition (0.4 percent), and iris scans (0.4 percent) is quite rare.[66]

Employees tend to be very resistant to computer video monitoring. Some organizations, including Sun Microsystems and Accenture, are trying out awareness monitoring in which a Web cam is placed at each work station and a coworker at a remote location can check out whether a colleague is at his or her work station. Although the stated objective of the monitoring was not to examine employee performance, there was strong concern that it would be used for performance review. As one employee stated: "There was something about seeing the supervisors in there, monitoring away, looking like the police in a van on a drug stakeout that I found absolutely revolting.[67]

Colleen Colwell, a commercial manager with Cornerstone Properties, had been employed with the company for more than seven years when she discovered that a hidden camera had been installed in the ceiling of her office a year earlier. Her boss, VP of Finance Trent Krauel, asserted that the

---

FIGURE 11-5	Creating an Internet Use Policy

To ensure Internet access is not being abused, employers are strongly encouraged to create Internet use policies and monitor use by its employees. In creating such a policy, employers should include the following points:

- the employer owns the computer resources;
- the employer has the ability to monitor, access, and disclose material related to the computer system;
- the purpose for which computer resources are provided;
- employees should not have any expectation of privacy regarding computer resources;
- certain Internet use is acceptable and certain Internet use is unacceptable;
- anything sent by email over the Internet may not be confidential; and
- the consequences for employees who contravene the policy.

The Internet policy should be given to every employee and signed by every employee, acknowledging its contents. It may also be prudent to post such a policy within the high-traffic areas in the workplace. While such a policy may not prohibit situations like those at CIBC* from arising, the policy will help in guiding the employee as to what is acceptable and not acceptable until the issue of whether email is employer property is properly litigated.

---

*This relates to a case before the courts, in which a group of CIBC employees used email to communicate customer-related information to a competitor.

Source: Natalie C. MacDonald, "The BlackBerry Battle," *Canadian HR Reporter*, March 14, 2005, pp. R5 and R8.

camera was used to detect theft by maintenance staff. Colwell sought medical attention because she felt emotionally violated and psychologically distraught. Krauel insisted he had a legal right to install the camera and did not owe Colwell an apology. Ultimately, Colwell resigned and sued for wrongful dismissal. The court concluded that the secret installation of the camera, Krauel's unwillingness to apologize, his assertion of a right to install the camera without advising Colwell, and his preposterous explanation of the reason for installing the camera made it impossible for Colwell to stay in her job. While employers have the right to install cameras in the workplace, the right is limited by the need to exercise it in good faith and fair dealing.[68]

Right to Fair Treatment

Earlier in this book we saw that an individual's age, race, gender, religion, physical disability, and so on should not be considered when hiring unless it is a *bona fide job requirement*. As previously noted, an employer has an obligation to make reasonable accommodation to meet employee needs. The right of employees to fair treatment requires that these principles govern the actual work once the applicants are hired. Thus, employees have the right not to be discriminated against in all employment decisions (such as compensation, training, and promotion issues) as well as the right to work in a safe and harassment-free environment. Proactive employers continuously monitor working conditions through employee surveys, open-door policies, and presence of grievance committees. They also initiate new programs and policies to meet the changing needs of the workforce:

> Today, many organizations emphasize a pollution-free work environment. Employers have banned smoking in any part of the workplace; others have rules governing the use of air sprays and perfumes. Several organizations respect the employees' right to be environmentally conscious by providing recycling bins and helping cut down waste. Other organizations have focused on reducing the noise level at the workplace.

⊙ EMPLOYEE INVOLVEMENT

To increase employee productivity and satisfaction, human resource departments often attempt to improve the satisfaction of employees at the workplace. Most of the approaches to employee involvement focus on the increased participation of workers. The quality of an employee's life while at work is affected by many factors including the quality of supervision, working conditions, pay and benefits, and an interesting and rewarding job:

> A survey conducted during the global financial crisis indicates that 89 percent of employers are introducing strategies to try to improve employee morale. What are companies doing? About 49 percent report increasing the frequency and quality of communication, 28 percent are providing additional professional development opportunities, 25 percent are giving additional financial rewards, 20 percent are enhancing employee recognition programs, and 20 percent are conducting additional team building activities.[69]

A popular method used to improve the quality of work life is employee involvement. *Employee involvement* (EI) consists of a variety of systematic methods that empower employees to participate in the decisions that affect them and their relationship with the organization. Through EI, employees feel a sense of responsibility or even "ownership" of decisions in which they participate. To be successful, however, EI must be more than just a systematic approach; it must become part of the organization's culture and management philosophy.[70] Today, some North American organizations provide employees with considerable involvement in the decision-making process:

> For the second year in a row, EllisDon was first on the Best Employers in Canada list. According to consultant Ted Emond, "A company like EllisDon has so instilled into the DNA of the organization what it is that engages employees. We believe it's going to help them manage the sacrifices and challenges that will be asked of employees on the downsize." At EllisDon, a construction firm with 1100 employees, workers are given access to financial information and the business plan, and have the opportunity to ask questions. Feedback from employees has led to changes in the performance management system.[71]

EI is based on two important principles. *First,* individuals tend to support systems or decisions that they helped to make. For example, if an employee was actively involved in developing a new credit collection procedure, then this individual is more likely to ensure that the new procedure is carried out correctly. *Second,* employees who actually perform a task know more about it than anyone else, including their supervisor. Asking for information from employees who actually perform the job can provide insights not available from their supervisors or outside experts.

While it has been argued that employee loyalty is an outdated concept (and a recent study by Bain and Company revealed that less than half of employees believe that their organization deserves their loyalty), there is evidence that employee loyalty does matter. According to Fred Reichheld, author of *Loyalty Rules*:

> For the average company, loyalty is dying. Of course, this means that the average company is dying. Employees spend half their waking hours working at a company that they don't really believe in. The key to success is building mutually beneficial relationships, a give and take in which employees are offered opportunities to grow, learn and make money—but only if they contribute to custom value creation and the bottom line.[72]

Employee Involvement Interventions

A number of different interventions have been used to increase employee involvement and improve overall employee satisfaction at work.

Self-Directed Work Teams or Groups

self-directed work teams (groups)
Teams of workers without a formal, employer-appointed supervisor who decide among themselves most matters traditionally handled by a supervisor.

A common approach to employee involvement is **self-directed work teams** or **groups**. Self-directed work teams are teams of workers without a formal, company-appointed supervisor who decide among themselves most matters traditionally handled by a supervisor. These groups of workers typically decide daily work assignments, the use of job rotation, orientation for new employees, training, and production schedules. Some groups even handle recruitment, selection, and discipline.

> At Syncrude Canada, all team leaders participate in a one-week leadership workshop every three or four years. According to CEO Eric Newell, "We need employees to redesign how the work is done. Really, what we are trying to do is engage people to get them thinking and acting like owners of the business."[73]

Some observers are critical of the increased focus on innovation and workplace teams. In a number of organizations, managers "stress the system" by speeding up the line, cutting the number of employees or machines, or having workers take on more tasks (at times through "multiskilling"). Under such systems, workers may be required to act like machines. While management by stress may help in raising productivity (at least over the short term), workers often experience considerable personal stress and a sense of being "dehumanized."[74]

High-Involvement Work Practices

high-involvement work practices
A set of human resource practices aimed at increasing employee performance.

There is growing evidence that human resource management practices do matter and are related to organizational performance. In one study, **high-involvement work practices** were related to lower turnover, higher productivity, and improved financial performance.[75] In another study, "low road" practices (such as use of short-term contracts, low levels of training, little commitment to job security, and low levels of HR sophistication) were negatively associated with corporate performance while "high road" practices (characterized by high-commitment human resource management) were strongly related to a high level of organizational performance.[76] The thrust of the work in this area has been away from focusing on any single human resource practice in favour of studying systems or bundles of practices and the strategic impact of human resource management on organizational performance.[77]

> A study by Watson Wyatt found that good human resource management practices can increase market value by as much as 47 percent. Using data from 750 of Europe and North America's biggest companies, the researchers found that human capital practices drive business outcomes to a greater extent than favourable business outcomes result in good human resource practices.[78]

What does this mean for human resource management? The human resource function must focus on business-level outcomes and problems, become a strategic core competency with the ability to understand the human capital dimension of the organization's major business priorities, and develop a systems perspective of human resource management.[79] Seven practices of successful organizations are (1) a focus on employment security, (2) selective hiring, (3) self-managed teams and decentralization of accountability and responsibility as basic elements of organizational design,

Quality circles involve a small group of employee volunteers with a common leader who meet regularly to identify and solve work-related problems. Why the emphasis on volunteers?

© Stuart O'Sullivan/Getty Images.

(4) comparatively high compensation contingent on organizational performance, (5) extensive training, (6) the reduction of status differentials, and (7) the sharing of information with employees.[80]

At HBC, employees used to believe that customers returning merchandise were trying to cheat the store. Despite edicts from the company to treat customers well, secret shoppers would report that they received poor treatment when returning products. Over a period of time HBC met with small groups of employees, helped them realize that quality customer service led to repeat business, and changed the corporate culture.[81]

To what extent are Canadian organizations pursuing high-involvement workplace strategies? The results of a recent study are presented in Figure 11-6. A survey of more than 600 Canadian workplaces found that 50 percent had problem-solving groups, just over one-quarter had a total quality management (or similar) program, and just under 40 percent had training in employee involvement. About 70 percent reported having project teams.

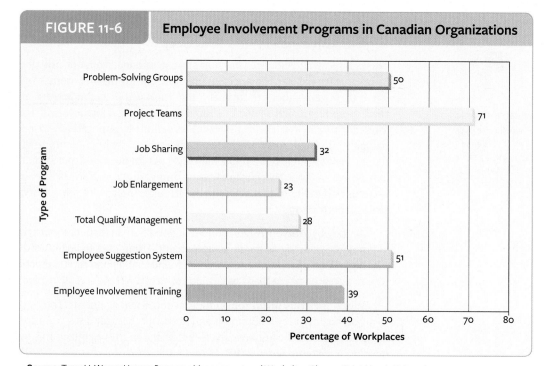

FIGURE 11-6 — **Employee Involvement Programs in Canadian Organizations**

Type of Program	Percentage of Workplaces
Problem-Solving Groups	50
Project Teams	71
Job Sharing	32
Job Enlargement	23
Total Quality Management	28
Employee Suggestion System	51
Employee Involvement Training	39

Source: Terry H. Wagar, *Human Resource Management and Workplace Change,* Saint Mary's University, 2009.

Employee Self-Service

Although employee self-service is a fairly new concept, a growing number of organizations are introducing self-service as a means of reducing the amount of administrative work performed by human resource professionals.

Currently, human resource activities that can be addressed by employee self-service have been divided into two groups:[82]

- **Productivity Applications.** This includes *management of personal data, retirement plans,* and *health and benefits management.* In addition, productivity applications for managers may include the use of management, reports, and approval applications. For example, an employee seeking an approval to participate in a training program could request such an approval electronically and the process could be set up to route the request by email to the appropriate manager.

   At Best Buy, getting payroll stubs to more than 18,000 employees was a very labour-intensive process. Every two weeks, payroll stubs would be printed, placed in an envelope, put into boxes and shipped to one of its 197 stores. Best Buy, working with ePost (Canada Post's electronic delivery service) now provides employees who opt in with the opportunity to get electronic payroll statements (through a password-protected ePost account). About 45 percent of employees immediately signed up for the new service. With noticeably fewer envelopes to stuff, payroll staff have more time to devote to helping employees and other administrative duties.[83]

- **Strategic Applications.** This includes *online recruitment and skills management applications.* By way of example, there are a growing number of programs designed to increase management productivity and free up time for more strategic initiatives.

While employee self-service applications are becoming more common in larger companies, it is expected that their use will increase noticeably in the next five years.

SPOTLIGHT ON ETHICS

The High-Involvement Workplace Dilemma

Consider the following situation and make a note of your answer on a separate sheet of paper.

You are a human resource management associate at a manufacturing company with just under 800 employees. You report to the human resource manager who, in turn, reports to the vice-president of human resource management. Neither you nor the manager is part of the senior executive team. Your most recent project involves an assessment of whether your organization should incorporate a high-involvement workplace strategy.

A few days ago, the following memo appeared (by mistake) in your email inbox:

All members of the senior executive team:

As you are aware, we are carefully considering the implementation of a high-involvement workplace system. The key to making this project succeed is to get employee buy-in. I have had chats with some other friends in our industry, and the gist of what they are saying is that if we sell this right, we can really save ourselves on labour costs. One company set up workplace teams and rewarded employees for coming up with labour-saving ideas—nine months later, the firm was able to cut almost 20 percent of the workforce. I figure we can follow a similar approach and will be able to get rid of between 125 and 150 jobs. Of course, we can't let the employees find out about this.

Maggie Pool (Vice-President of Human Resources)

You are unsure what you should do in this situation. On one hand, it is not illegal for a company to reduce the size of its workforce. On the other hand, both you and the human resource manager believe that the organization is interested in considering a high-involvement strategy as a way of increasing employer performance and employee satisfaction (not as a tool for reducing labour costs and cutting jobs).

JOB SECURITY, DOWNSIZING, AND EMPLOYEE RETENTION

No-Layoff Policies

In the past, loyal, hardworking employees could expect a secure job in return for dedicated work for the organization. However, this is no longer the case and the traditional psychological contract (the unwritten commitments between employers and employees) has been radically rewritten.[84] This new employment relationship has been described as follows:

> You're expendable. We don't want to fire you but we will if we have to. Competition is brutal, so we must redesign the way we work to do more with less. Sorry, that's just the way it is. And one more thing—you're invaluable ... We're depending on you to be innovative, risk-taking, and committed to our goals.[85]

Contrary to the downsizing trend of the 1990s, some organizations are developing no-layoff policies. These firms are using such policies as part of an integrated system of progressive HR practices—the idea is that employees who have job security are more receptive to change, more likely to be innovative and suggest changes that will improve the organization, and are more willing to "go the extra mile."

Organizational Downsizing

In many organizations, lifetime employment has been replaced by job insecurity. The downsizing era of the 1990s was replaced by the "war for talent" until the global financial crisis in 2008. When we talk about downsizing now, we are not dealing with a small number of firms or a small number of employees losing their jobs. Consider, for instance, the following headlines: "350 to Leave as Axe Falls at the CBC" or "Canadian Banks Step Up Job Cuts: Almost 4,000 in Last Quarter" or "700 Face Layoffs; Revenues Up; St. Laurent Complex to Lose Most Jobs."[86]

Major corporations around the world continue to downsize in response to the changing economic conditions:

> For the first time in 18 years, Magna International, the world's third largest auto-parts supplier, is suspending its dividend. In the past six months, Magna has slashed more than 10,000 jobs around the world, shut down or sold several plants, and negotiated wage cuts of up to 20 percent with its European white-collar workforce. For the first quarter of 2009, it reported a loss of $200 million (US) and a 46 percent decrease in sales. According to Magna Chairman Frank Stronach, "The job layoffs are not really the fault of our managers. They are the fault of the lack of government oversight, which allowed our financial system to run out of control. It amazes me that governments are buying up all of the toxic bank liabilities."[87]

Downsizing and layoffs often cause a drop in employee morale and lower productivity. What are the ways to avoid these consequences, or at least to reduce the negative impact?

© Ariel Skelley/Getty Images.

downsizing
Reducing employment to improve efficiency, productivity, and competitiveness.

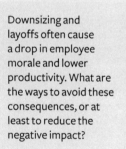

Downsizing may be defined as "a deliberate organizational decision to reduce the workforce that is intended to improve organizational performance."[88] It has also been described as a set of activities undertaken on the part of management and designed to improve organizational efficiency, productivity, and/or competitiveness."[89] It is possible to identify three types of downsizing strategies:

1. **Workforce Reduction.** This is a short-term strategy focused on cutting the number of employees through programs such as attrition, early retirement or voluntary severance incentive packages, or layoffs.

2. **Work Redesign.** This strategy takes somewhat longer to implement and requires that organizations critically examine the work processes and evaluate whether specific functions, products, and/or services should be changed or eliminated.

3. **Systematic Change.** This is a long-term strategy requiring a change in the culture and attitudes and values of employees with the ongoing goal of reducing costs and improving quality. This strategy takes a long time to implement and thus the benefits only accrue over time.[90]

While firms frequently believe that downsizing will enhance organizational performance, study after study shows that "following a downsizing, surviving employees become narrow-minded, self-absorbed, and risk averse. Morale sinks, productivity drops, and survivors distrust management."[91]

There is concern that the economic downturn has led to an increase in workplace violence as workers are becoming fed up with cutbacks. In Reims, France, employees interrupted a management meeting and pelted their bosses with eggs. At a Sony facility in France, a manager was taken hostage by employees. In Scotland, Sir Fred Goodwin, disgraced former head of the Royal Bank of Scotland, had windows in his home and Mercedes smashed by vandals and in New Delhi, an angry mob of factory workers bludgeoned to death the CEO of Italian-owned car parts manufacturer Graziano Transmissioni. In New York, Richard Fuld, then-CEO of Lehman Brothers, was knocked out cold while working out at the company gym.[92]

In addition, there is growing evidence that firms engaging in downsizing do not perform better financially—the bulk of the research indicates that the stock price of downsized firms often declines after a layoff announcement is made.[93]

Downsizing efforts often fail to meet organizational objectives. This is not surprising, considering that many workforce reductions are carried out with little strategic planning or consideration of the costs to the individuals and employer. Frequently, cutting jobs is but a short-term response to a much more serious problem. In several instances, little attention is given to carefully examining and resolving critical human resource issues.

One organization had planned to contract out the maintenance of vehicles to local garages. While huge savings were projected, several of the local garages did not have repair bays big enough to accommodate the vehicles and the hoists were not strong enough to support the trucks.

Still, downsizing may be an appropriate strategic response for some organizations. However, downsizing is not a "quick fix" remedy—before implementing such a program, it is critical to carefully consider the decision, plan the process, and assess the consequences from the perspectives of the organization, the customer, the "survivors" (those employees that remain), and the victims (those that lose their jobs).

Don Walker has more than 33 years in the forest industry. However, in the summer of 2008, he lost his job as a hydraulic log loader when his employer closed down. Walker says he has taken all he can and no longer has the will to pull himself back up after losing his job. He is running out of money and suffering from depression. "I've been beaten down my whole life and pulled myself back up off the ground so many times, but I just don't give a damn anymore. There are zero prospects—I've applied everywhere."[94]

Although most organizations engage in the workforce-reduction stage of downsizing, many ignore the critical elements of redesigning the organization and implementing cultural change.[95] From a best practices perspective, six key principles deserve attention:

1. Change should be initiated from the top but requires hands-on involvement from all employees.

2. Workforce reduction must be selective in application and long-term in emphasis.

3. There is a need to pay special attention both to those who lose their jobs and to the survivors who remain with the organization.

4. It is critical that decision-makers identify precisely where redundancies, excess costs, and inefficiencies exist and attack those specific areas.

5. Downsizing should result in the formation of small semiautonomous organizations within the broader organization.

6. Downsizing must be a proactive strategy focused on increasing performance.[96]

Human resource professionals have an important role to play in downsizing efforts and should be involved in the strategic process. HR people are often in a good position to advise on the impact of restructuring an organization (from a variety of perspectives including work groups, teams, departments, and individuals) to maximize productivity and retain quality performers. Similarly, HR can develop skill inventories and planning charts to evaluate the effects on human resource needs and projected capabilities.

> At the JDS Uniphase plant in Victoria, the firm developed a 112-page directory with biographical sketches of the 180 or more employees who were the victims of a downsizing. The directory was sent to more than 400 employers in Western Canada. According to HR Director Arlene Keis, "The company is determined to treat employees well during good times and bad times." Other assistance to former employees included career transition help, courses for upgrading skills, and a job bulletin board.[97]

Moreover, in light of the compelling evidence that most downsizings have dramatically negative impacts on those who survive, human resource experts can assist in coordinating and communicating the downsizing decision. There is growing evidence that effective communication can reduce some of the negative consequences associated with downsizing.[98] Finally, HR can assist in evaluating the downsizing program. Issues include monitoring who left the organization and who remains, job design and redesign, worker adjustment to change, the need for employee counselling, organizational communication, and a comprehensive review of the appropriateness of existing HRM policies and programs (such as training, compensation and benefits, and orientation of employees into the "new" organization).[99] However, recent research has shown that downsizing employees is professionally demanding and the "downsizers" may experience social and organizational isolation, a decrease in personal well-being, and poorer family functioning.[100]

Retaining Top Performers

While some employers continue to cut back on employees, keeping high-performing employees is often a challenge for both growing and downsized organizations. Many companies lose half of their employees in three to four years and half their customers in five years—keeping employees is as critical as retaining customers because without loyal employees, you won't have loyal customers.[101]

Of course, some organizations may adopt a strategy in which people are not important and easily replaceable and thus be willing to accept high levels of employee turnover.

> One study suggests that the number one reason employees leave their jobs is "shock"—some precipitating event (such as a heated argument with the boss, uncertainty over a corporate merger, or an unexpected and unsolicited job offer) is more likely than job dissatisfaction to cause an employee to leave his or her current job.[102]
>
> Another study of 2,500 Canadian employees suggests that reasons employees quit may be affected by their age. Baby boomers indicated that they would be most likely to leave if asked to do something unethical. For Generation X and Y employees, lack of opportunity for growth was ranked as their top reason for quitting.[103]
>
> A survey by WorldatWork examined what organizations had specifically done to attract and retain employees. The most common responses were making a market adjustment to employee salaries or increasing base salary (60 percent of respondents), improving the work environment (46 percent), and giving a signing bonus (34 percent). About 19 percent of employers indicated that they had given a retention/stay-on bonus while less than 6 percent had a sabbatical program.[104]

What do employees want in a job? A study by Canadian Policy Research Networks and EKOS indicated that the top five factors in terms of importance were being treated with respect, having interesting work, having work that results in a feeling of accomplishment, having good communications among coworkers, and having a balance between work and family issues. Having a job that pays well was rated ninth out of fifteen factors. While the values of younger and older workers did not vary much, women placed more attention on workplace issues such as communication, coworker relations, and work–family balance relative to their male counterparts. In short, female employees were especially concerned about an employee-supportive work climate.

The extent to which some organizations will go to attract and retain talent was revealed in a study of call centres:

> Although call centres are known for high turnover (100 percent a year is not unusual), AnswerPlus in Hamilton, Ontario has focused its attention on an "employer of choice" strategy as a means to reduce turnover (which is now at about 22.5 percent). Employee training, company support, innovative rewards, and promotion from within are all used to help retain employees. According to VP of Operations Barbara Bradbury, "We realized that in order to give our customers the best service they can have, we had to put our employees first. You've got to put some fun into the job. You've got to make every day a bit of an adventure (for employees). Employees are invited to join in any meetings—management meetings, financial meetings, any of the planning meetings that take place. We want people to know what our goals are because they're part of our goals."[105]

Among the factors in retaining key employees are the following:

- Developing a planned approach to employee retention (which examines the usual company benefits, addresses individual needs, focuses on the long term, is part of the vision of the organization, and is based on investment in employees).
- Becoming an employer of choice with a goal of retaining employees from the day they join the organization.
- Communicating the organizational vision and values frequently and in a clear and consistent manner.
- Rewarding supervisors and managers for keeping good people.
- Using exit interviews to obtain information as to why people are leaving the organization.[106]

A number of recent studies have examined whether there is a relationship between the human resource management practices of an organization and employee retention. The findings suggest that employers with high-involvement human resource systems tend to have lower employee turnover.[107]

> A Canada@Work survey revealed that 52 percent of employees surveyed indicated that they would leave their employer for a 20 percent pay raise. According to Eleana Rodriguez, a senior consultant at HayGroup, "If there's uncertainty, top talent are the first people to go and look for other opportunities. Many managers instinctively avoid potentially difficult performance management discussions with employees. Instead, they choose the path of least resistance, spreading pay increases and bonuses out almost evenly."[108]

SUMMARY

The human resource department's role in organizational communication is to create an open two-way flow of information. Part of the foundation of any organizational communication effort is the view held by management of employees. If that view is one that sincerely strives to provide an effective downward and upward flow of information, then the human resource department can help develop and maintain appropriate communication systems.

Downward communication approaches include in-house publications, information booklets, employee bulletins, prerecorded messages, email, jobholder reports, and open-book management. Multiple channels are used to help ensure that each message reaches the intended receivers. Perhaps the greatest difficulty in organizational communication is to provide an effective upward flow of information. In-house complaint procedures, manager–employee meetings, suggestion systems, and attitude survey feedback are commonly used tools.

Counselling is the discussion of a problem with an employee to help the worker cope with the situation. It is performed by human resource department professionals as well as supervisors. Counselling programs provide a support service for both job and personal problems, and there is extensive cooperation with community counselling agencies.

Discipline is management action to enforce organizational standards, and it is both preventive and corrective. The hot-stove rule is a useful general guide for corrective discipline. Most disciplinary action is progressive, with stronger penalties for repeated offences. Some disciplinary programs primarily emphasize a counselling approach.

Employee involvement efforts are systematic attempts by organizations to give workers a greater opportunity to take part in decisions that affect the way they do their job and the contribution they make to their organization's overall effectiveness. They are not a substitute for good, sound human resource practices and policies. However, effective employee involvement efforts can supplement other human resource actions and lead to improved employee motivation, satisfaction, and productivity. Whether that involvement is in solving workplace problems or participating in the design of jobs, employees want to know that their contribution makes a difference.

In this era of downsizing and restructuring, it is important to understand the basic principles relating to wrongful dismissal law. Also, there is evidence that many downsizing efforts fail to meet organizational objectives. Human resource professionals have an important role to play in both growing and downsized workplaces.

TERMS FOR REVIEW

constructive dismissal **p. 406**
corrective discipline **p. 401**
counselling **p. 400**
discipline **p. 401**
downsizing **p. 416**
downward communication **p. 393**
due process **p. 402**

employee attitude/opinion survey **p. 400**
grapevine communication **p. 397**
high-involvement work practices **p. 413**
hot-stove rule **p. 402**
in-house complaint procedures **p. 398**
intranet **p. 394**
just cause **p. 404**

open-door policy **p. 398**
preventive discipline **p. 401**
progressive discipline **p. 402**
self-directed work teams (groups) **p. 413**
suggestion systems **p. 399**
upward communication **p. 396**
wrongful dismissal **p. 403**

SELF-ASSESSMENT EXERCISE

Procedural and Distributive Justice in the Classroom

Consider a grade you obtained in a course. Research suggests that individuals are concerned with not only the outcome—that is, the grade ("distributive justice")—but also the procedures leading to the decision ("procedural justice"). The following self-test gives you a quick assessment of both procedural and distributive justice. Read each statement and give it a score from 1 to 5 (1 indicating that you strongly disagree with the statement and 5 indicating that you strongly agree with the statement).

1. The grading procedures used to arrive at my grade were applied consistently.   _____

2. The grading procedures used to arrive at my grade were free of bias.   _____

3. The grading procedures used to arrive at my grade were based on accurate information.   _____

4. I was able to express my views and feelings during the grading process.   _____

5. The grade I obtained reflected the amount of effort I put into my work.   _____

6. The grade I obtained reflected my contribution in the course.   _____

7. The grade I obtained is appropriate when I consider the amount of work I did in the course.   _____

8. The grade I obtained is fair, given my performance in the course.   _____

SCORING

First add up your scores for statements 1 through 4. These statements address the issue of "procedural justice." A higher score is associated with a stronger perception that the procedures used in grading your work were fair. Then add up your scores for statements 5 through 8. These statements measure "distributive justice." A higher score is associated with a belief that the grade you obtained was appropriate, given your contribution.

Note: This survey is adapted from Jason Colquitt, "On the Dimensionality of Organizational Justice: A Construct Validation of a Measure," *Journal of Applied Psychology*, Vol. 86, 2001, pp. 386–400.

REVIEW AND DISCUSSION QUESTIONS

1. Think of a situation in which you learned some new information from the grapevine and took action on the basis of that information. Discuss.

2. List and describe the different types of programs that can be used by the human resource department to improve communication.

3. Discuss differences between preventive and corrective discipline. What examples of either one were applied to you on the last job you had?

4. What is progressive discipline? How does it work? Is its basic approach realistic in work situations? Explain your answer.

CRITICAL THINKING QUESTIONS

1. Employee involvement has become a popular concept. As a manager, what steps would you take to increase EI in your organization?

2. Suppose you are a plant or division manager and you want to improve the quality of work life in your division. What steps would you take?

3. Think of an organization that you have worked in. What high-involvement work practices could be implemented to improve performance?

4. Assume you have been asked to terminate an employee. How would you conduct the termination interview?

ETHICS QUESTION

You are the human resource manager, and the CEO has just told you that the company is in a financial crisis and has to downsize staff by 500 employees (out of 2,000) to survive. You are asked to prepare for the dismissal and your suggestions as to who should be chosen. It is a family-owned, nonunion firm. There is a precedent: a few years ago, 50 employees had to be let go, and the main criterion was low performance. It seems to be obvious that this time the performance criterion will not be sufficient. Many of the employees have 20 to 30 years of tenure; others have large families, with 6 to 10 children; there are single mothers; and a few have sick spouses or parents to take care of. When you ask some of the supervisors, you are told that they prefer to keep the younger employees who seem to be more productive (and are less expensive to employ). Develop a plan to save the company. What ethical issues are involved?

WEB RESEARCH EXERCISE

1. Visit the Web sites of three employee assistance program (EAP) providers. Compare the programs and approaches of the three providers. What similarities and differences do you observe?

2. Laws relating to dismissal vary among countries. Using the Internet, examine dismissal law Web sites in Canada, the United States, and one other country. Compare the laws regarding dismissal among the three countries.

INCIDENT 11-1

The Machinist's Abusive Comments to the Supervisor

William Lee, a machine operator, worked as a machinist for Horace Gray, a supervisor. Horace told William to pick up some garbage that had fallen from William's work area, and William replied, "I won't do the janitor's work." Horace replied: "When you drop it, you pick it up." William became angry and abusive, calling Horace a number of uncomplimentary names in a loud voice and refusing to pick up the garbage. All employees in the department heard William's comments.

The situation was as follows: Horace had been trying for two weeks to get his employees to pick up garbage in order to have a cleaner workplace and prevent accidents. He talked with all employees in a weekly department meeting and to each employee individually at least once. He stated that he was following the instructions of the superintendent. Only William objected with the comment, "I'm not here to do the janitor's work. I'm a machinist."

William had been in the department for six months and with the company for three years. Horace had spoken to him twice about excessive horseplay, but otherwise his record was good. He was known to have a quick temper.

After William finished his abusive outburst, Horace told him to come to the office and suspended him for one day for insubordination and abusive language to a supervisor. The discipline was within company policy, and similar acts had been disciplined in other departments.

When William walked out of Horace's office, Horace called the human resource director, reported what he had done, and said that he was sending a copy of his action for William's file.

1. As human resource director, what comments would you make?

2. What follow-up actions should the human resource director take or recommend that Horace take? For example, do you recommend counselling for William? Would you reconsider disciplinary procedures and policies?

CASE STUDY 🍁 Maple Leaf Shoes Ltd.

Addressing Employee Relations

As she sat in her office in Winnipeg, Britney MacPherson thumbed through a 1989 textbook on personnel management. As manager of the Winnipeg location of Maple Leaf Shoes, she was responsible for the day-to-day operations of the facility. However, Britney was finding her job particularly challenging—although she had a B.Com., which she received in 1991 from a well-known Ontario university, her training had been focused on accounting and finance and she had had only one course in human resource management (called "personnel management" when Britney completed the course). Things were unravelling in Winnipeg, and Britney knew that she needed help. Unfortunately, her phone calls and emails to head office in Wilmington, Ontario, brought little assistance.

The company policy regarding employee communications was quite simple: "What goes on at the company stays at the company." This policy was communicated regularly to all employees. However, Joan Jorgenson, a clerk in the office, had violated this policy. A couple of weeks ago, Joan had struck up a conversation with a coworker, Natalie King. During their talk, Natalie had mentioned that she had recently moved from Wilmington to Winnipeg, because, according to Natalie, a senior member of management in the Wilmington office had become enraged when Natalie refused his sexual advances. He had threatened Natalie with dismissal, but after a short discussion an agreement was reached that Natalie would move to the Winnipeg location. Joan became enraged when she heard Natalie's story, and immediately notified not only employees of the human rights commission in Ontario but also the media in both Winnipeg and Wilmington. Britney is now trying to decide how she should handle the situation.

Max MacSweeney is a 31-year-old accountant who has been employed by Maple Leaf Shoes for seven years (three years in Wilmington and the last four years in Winnipeg). Although Max is based in Winnipeg, he travels throughout western Canada as part of his job. Max is considered a very good employee. He is well known in the business community, is very involved in the local association of management accountants, and is a highly visible member of a number of charitable organizations in the Winnipeg area. Max is married and has two children.

About three weeks ago, head office started monitoring the Internet usage of employees. Much to their surprise, they found that Max had visited several pornographic Web sites on four different evenings (while on business at the Wilmington office). The records revealed that he had spent an average of about three hours on each of the four evenings visiting such sites. While Max used company property (the computer he accessed the sites from was in an office assigned to him while in Wilmington) when visiting the "undesirable" sites, such visits were made outside of regular working hours. Just over one month ago, the company had begun providing Internet access to employees, but had not developed a policy on Internet usage. Head office personnel in Wilmington have asked Britney to deal with the issue.

As they say, "Problems come in threes." Britney's head was aching as the phone rang. On the line was Rob McEwen from head office in Wilmington. He wanted to find out what Britney was going to do about Paul Bertuzzi. Paul is a 44-year-old warehouse supervisor at the Winnipeg facility. He supervises eight employees, has been with Maple Leaf Shoes for just over 11 years, and earns $46,000 a year. Paul's performance evaluations are among the highest at the Winnipeg office, he attends night school and is two credits away from his B.A., and he is well liked by his coworkers.

One month ago, Paul went to Toronto to attend a two-day training program for warehouse supervisors. After the first day of sessions, Paul and two other warehouse supervisors (from the Montreal and Toronto facilities) went out for dinner. During the meal, the other two supervisors revealed to Paul that they had developed a scheme in which they wrote off a small portion of the shoe inventory as wastage but actually kept the shoes and sold them to a friend at a discount. As one of the individuals said: "We're not talking about big money, Paul. However, I'm sure you could use an extra $100 to $150 a week. After all, we're all underpaid and our salaries are not keeping pace with inflation." In addition, they told Paul of a new moneymaking scheme and asked if he was interested in joining their "team." It appears that a shoe manufacturer overseas was interested in mass-producing Maple Leaf Shoes products—however, the new company needed more information on the latest shoe designs and production techniques. Under the scheme, the warehouse supervisors were going to get information for the overseas company in return for part-ownership in the business.

One week ago, an auditor uncovered the scheme. The two warehouse supervisors from Montreal and Toronto were fired. While the audit confirmed that no other Maple Leaf Shoes employees were involved in the scheme, Paul (and one other Maple Leaf Shoes employee) admitted knowing about the fraud. In discussions with top management, the point was raised of whether Paul had a duty to report the fraud. Again, Britney has been asked to deal with the matter.

Discussion Questions

1. Consider the three issues Britney needs to address. Which one should be addressed first? Last? Explain your reasoning.

2. How should Britney deal with the Joan Jorgenson incident? What suggestions would you make to improve the policy on employee communications?

3. What disciplinary action (if any) would you recommend that Britney take with respect to the case involving Max MacSweeney?

4. Develop a company policy on Internet usage.

5. Do you recommend that Paul Bertuzzi be dismissed? Is there just cause for dismissal?

6. What would be "reasonable notice" in the event that a court ruled that your organization did not have just cause to terminate Paul? Explain your answer.

7. If you were in Paul Bertuzzi's position, would you have reported the scheme to senior management?

CASE STUDY CPIB A Matter of Security at Canadian Pacific and International Bank

Brenda Reid joined Canadian Pacific and International Bank (CPIB) in 1999 and has been employed with CPIB since that time. Brenda, who is 38 years old, is a single mom with two young children (Norris, age seven, and Morris, age five). Brenda graduated from Mount Allison University in 1992 with a B.Com., worked almost five years with another bank (from 1992 to 1997), and returned to school in 1997. She earned a Master of Business Administration from University of Saskatoon in 1999, specializing in finance and information systems. Upon graduation, she joined CPIB as an assistant manager and is now the manager of the main branch in Halifax (a position she assumed three years ago).

Brenda is considered a very strong performer, and senior bank officials believe that she has senior upper-management potential. Brenda has participated in several management training programs and within the next year, the bank had planned to send her to the Advanced Management Seminar provided by the London University Business School. The Advanced Management Seminar is a prestigious program for international bankers with at least 10 years' experience.

Brenda earns just over $100,000 a year, and her performance is very solid (she has consistently ranked within the top 20 percent of bank managers). The only disciplinary incident in her file involved a written warning two years ago for misplacing her security pass card to the main Halifax branch. The card was ultimately found in a CPIB policy and procedures manual that she had borrowed.

On a Friday afternoon three weeks ago, Brenda decided to take home two files, each of which contained detailed financial and corporate information on a major CPIB corporate client in the Atlantic region. Brenda was scheduled to meet with representatives from each of the two companies the following Monday, and removed the files from the bank in order to review them over the weekend. According to Brenda,

taking files home to review was not unusual—several managers did it regularly.

After leaving work on the Friday afternoon, Brenda met a few friends and went out for dinner in downtown Halifax. Later, the group attended a play at Neptune Theatre. When the play was over, Brenda returned to her minivan to find that her briefcase containing the two files had been stolen from the van (which she had locked). Brenda had put the briefcase under the front seat of the van. While Brenda's empty briefcase was found in the parking garage, its contents have not been recovered.

Although CPIB does not have a detailed policy relating to the removal of property from the bank offices, the CPIB handbook contains a provision informing all personnel to exercise extreme caution and care when removing CPIB property from the office. Interviews with loans officers and managers indicate that the typical procedure is to either keep the property on their person or secure the property in the trunk of a vehicle.

Brenda was devastated by the theft and reported it immediately to her supervisor. She broke into tears when discussing the incident with CPIB management, apologized profusely for her mistake, and promised that it would never happen again.

Discussion Questions

1. Would you recommend disciplinary action in this case? Why or why not?

2. Are there long-term implications for the human resource function as a result of this incident?

3. Assume that head office has demanded a new policy addressing the security of bank property. Discuss the merits and drawbacks of having such a policy.

4. Develop a policy for CPIB.

Diversity Management

"While ... diversity brings stimulation, challenge and energy, it does not always lead to harmony. The mix of cultures, genders, life styles, and values often becomes a source of misunderstanding and conflict. Many enlightened managers, from CEOs in the executive suite to supervisors on the shop floor, want to create an environment where differences are valued and where people who look, talk and think differently can work productively together. However, the knowledge and skills to do so are not part of most managers' experience. Like explorers in a new land, they are entering uncharted areas."

Lee Gardenswartz and Anita Rowe[1]

CHAPTER OBJECTIVES

After studying this chapter, you should be able to:

➡ *Define* diversity management.

➡ *Discuss* the strategic importance of diversity management today.

➡ *Discuss* the various steps in managing diversity.

➡ *List* current industry practices in this field.

➡ *Discuss* the special challenges facing global firms in the context of diversity management.

CHAPTER 12

Before he delivers a lecture on gender identity to his philosophy class, Professor Michael Gilbert must decide what to wear. Most likely, he will put on a knee-length skirt, a long-sleeved blouse, and low pumps. Standing before a mirror at home, he'll fix his wig and apply make-up before heading out the door.

Professor Gilbert is a cross-dresser who teaches philosophy at a major Ontario university. He is among a growing cadre of "trans" people on campuses who are going public. Organizations for gay, lesbian, and bisexual students have already begun tacking a "T" on the end of their names to embrace "transgendered" or "transsexual" students. In the recent past, students and professors have also pushed universities to extend protection to transgendered people under policies to prevent discrimination against minorities.[2]

Welcome to the workforce of the new millennium! The emergence of "trans" persons and the demand for recognition of persons with nontraditional sexual orientation is but one dimension of the emerging workforce diversity. Consider some of these statistics indicating major changes in the way we live and work:

- According to the 2006 census, Canada has a total of 45,300 same-sex common-law couples representing 0.6 percent of all couples in the country.[3] The number of same-sex couples surged 32.6 percent between 2001 and 2006, five times the pace of opposite-sex couples (+5.9 percent). The metropolitan areas of Ottawa–Hull and Vancouver had some of the highest proportions of same-sex common-law couples.
- With the legalization of same-sex marriage in July 2005, Canada became the third country in the world to legalize same sex marriage after the Netherlands (2000) and Belgium (2003). (Today, Spain and South Africa also legally recognize same-sex marriage).
- The prevalence of common-law relationships is not only higher in Quebec than in the other Canadian provinces, it is also higher than in many Western European nations and the United States.
- Over 18 percent of Canadians were born outside the country.
- Nearly 5.1 million Canadians or 16.2 percent of the total population (as per 2006 census) were visible minorities such as Chinese, Southeast Asian, black, Latin American, and Japanese. Over 50 percent of residents of major metropolitan areas such as Toronto or Vancouver are not of British, French, or other European origin.
- Today, Canada has over 200 different ethnic origins (in contrast, the 1901 census recorded only about 25 different ethnic groups in Canada). In 2006, 11 ethnic origins had passed the 1 million mark. Among the newer groups reported in the latest census were Montserratan from the Caribbean and Chadian, Gabonese, Gambian, and Zambian from Africa. Over a quarter of Canadians claim to be of more than one ethnic origin.
- In the near future, about 80 percent of women in the age group 18–64 will be in the labour force. But only a tiny proportion of them will be in senior managerial positions or on the board of directors of major organizations. Women still hold very few of the top positions in Canadian and U.S. organizations. A 2008 study found that women hold just 16.9 percent of corporate officer roles in the *Financial Post*'s largest 500 companies although they account for 47.1 percent of the total labour force and 37.2 percent of middle management or supervisory roles.[4]
- Over 6 percent of working Canadians have some disability.
- Canadians of Asian and African origin are more educated when compared to other ethnic groups, yet less than 1 percent of top executives in this country belong to these groups.[5]

A combination of factors including governmental policies, demographic and labour force changes, increasing global operations, technological revolution, and radical changes in social values have fundamentally changed the way Canadian organizations work and whom they employ. The traditional "one size fits all" managerial policies of the past will no longer suffice.[6] A diverse workforce requires managers with new leadership styles who understand their varying needs and creatively respond by offering flexible management policies and practices.

A number of research studies have indicated that men emerge in leadership positions in North America because they are more likely to exhibit traits that are associated with the behaviour of powerful authority figures in the past. These traits include aggressiveness, initiation of

Managing a diverse workforce
www.workforce.com/
section/09/feature/25/55/58/
index.html

more verbal interactions, focus on output issues rather than process issues, and less willingness to reveal information and expose vulnerability.[7]

Many women are also hindered by lack of access to the **old boys' network**, the set of informal relationships that develop among male managers and executives.[8] This results in exclusive fraternizing of men with men that reinforces a "culture" of men without women's perspective and condones behaviour that devalues women. The friendships and contacts built through the network become the basis for assignments and promotions and the network becomes the informal communication link that provides vital information about business from which women are excluded. This means that many women never reach positions of power.

> Women occupy 12 percent of corporate officer jobs in Canada's 560 largest companies. They occupy 6.4 percent of the strategically important line officer positions where their leadership is directly linked to profit and loss. They hold less than 5 percent of top posts in corporate Canada—executive vice-president and above or what are referred to as "clout titles."[9] Only about 7.5 percent of directors at Canada's largest companies are women.[10]

The stereotypes faced by women belonging to specific religious groups prevent them from gaining even lower level jobs:

> Discriminatory hiring practices and workplace racism toward Muslim women are common in Toronto, according to a study by Women Working with Immigrant Women, a nonprofit organization that works with immigrants. Of the 32 Muslim women surveyed, 29 said that employers had commented on their hijab and 13 women reported an employer told them they would have to take the hijab off if they wanted a job. The study also included a field experiment where three teams of applicants—matched in every way except that one wore the hijab and one didn't—visited 16 job sites to apply for a job. At more than half of the sites, the applicant without the hijab was asked to fill out an application or leave a résumé while the applicant with a hijab was not. In two job sites, the woman without the hijab was told there was a job available while the woman with the hijab was told there weren't any jobs.[11]

Even in unconventional work settings, women often find themselves powerless, as in the case of Canadian space researcher Judith Lapierre:

> Judith Lapierre, a Canadian space researcher who spent 110 days with a group of male scientists in an isolation chamber (a replica of a spaceship) in a Russian institute, withdrew from further tests, citing sexual harassment by a Russian crew commander. Dr. Lapierre, a 32-year-old social medical expert from Quebec, complained that she was dragged away from television monitoring cameras in the chamber and kissed aggressively by the commander.[12]

The existing values, norms, and patterns of interactions among managers may also act as a **glass ceiling** that stunts the career growth of women and minority persons beyond a certain level. Promotional opportunities are visible, but invisible obstructions seem to block the way. The perception of the existence of a glass ceiling results in frustration, reduced job and career satisfaction, alienation from the workplace, and ultimately higher employee turnover.

The situation of members of other minorities such as African Canadians and First Nations people is no better.

> As Professor Trigger of McGill University pointed out, until recently, "native people were treated as part of a vanishing past. They were seen as more akin to the forests in which they lived and the animals they hunted ... Canadian historical studies as a whole have suffered from the chronic failure ... to regard native peoples as an integral part of Canadian society."[13]

Despite the transformation of Canadian cities and towns into multicultural mosaics, prejudices against visible minorities continue to exist in the workplace.

This chapter introduces you to the concept of workforce diversity and helps you plan to meet the new workplace challenges. Some of the human resource management strategies and processes that recognize, foster, and capitalize on the diversity will be discussed in the following sections. We will also look at the special challenges facing global organizations where the challenge of diversity is felt to an even greater extent.

MEANING OF DIVERSITY MANAGEMENT

RPC 2 & 3

workplace diversity
Includes important human characteristics that influence employee values, their perceptions of self and others, behaviours, and interpretations of events.

core dimensions of diversity
Age, ethnicity and culture, gender, race, religion, sexual orientation, and capabilities.

secondary dimensions of diversity
Education, status, language, and income levels.

Canada has always been a diverse nation composed of a wide variety of different peoples. Beginning with the 50 distinct Aboriginal nations who originally inhabited this country, Canada later became the home of the French, the English, other Europeans, the Chinese, black Loyalists, the Russians, the Japanese, and the East Indians. In fact, Canada was a racially and ethnically diverse society even by Confederation in 1867.

Like trees in a vast forest, humans come in a variety of sizes, shapes, hues, and life stages. This variety helps to differentiate us. While all of us share the important dimension of humanness, there are biological, cultural, and other environmental differences that separate and distinguish us as individuals and groups.[14] It is these differences that provide the spectrum of human diversity and enrich our lives.

Given such myriad differences among humans, it is very difficult to arrive at a broad and universally acceptable definition of diversity that is inclusive yet does not overwhelm us in the process. Broadly, **workplace diversity** may be defined to include important human characteristics that influence an employee's values, perceptions of self and others, behaviours, and interpretation of events around him or her. Diversity, at a minimum, includes age, ethnicity and culture, gender, race, religion, sexual orientation, and mental and physical capabilities (see Figure 12-1). Several writers consider the above seven areas to be the **core dimensions of diversity** since they exert considerable impact on our early socialization and a powerful, sustained impact throughout our lives.

For example, regardless of whether a particular employee is currently 20, 30, 40, 50, or 60 years old, his or her age has a bearing on how that person is perceived by others as well as the individual's ability to learn, perform (several tasks), and relate to the environment. Age, thus, is a core dimension that affects an individual's workplace perceptions and behaviours.

Several other **secondary dimensions of diversity** such as education, family status, language, and even income levels play important roles in shaping our values, expectations, behaviours, and

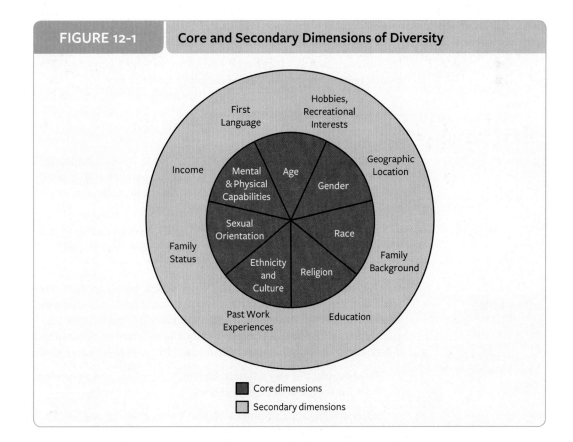

FIGURE 12-1   Core and Secondary Dimensions of Diversity

Canada's cultural mosaic raises several challenges for the manager who must successfully manage a diverse workforce. What advantages and disadvantages would a team made up of members from different cultures have?

© Comstock/Getty Images.

experiences. Hence, their impact on employee behaviours at the workplace should not be underestimated. They are, however, less visible, more mutable, and more variable in their impact on individual behaviours.

managing diversity
Ability to manage individual employees with different cultural values and lead teams made up of diverse employees.

Managing diversity recognizes that an organization is a mosaic where employees with varying beliefs, cultures, values, and behaviour patters come together to create a whole organization and where these differences are acknowledged and accepted. Managing diversity has three major dimensions.[15] First, it assumes that effective management of diversity and differences among employees can add value to an organization; second, diversity includes all types of differences and not simply obvious ones such as gender, race, and so on; and third, organization culture and working environments are key items to focus on in managing diversity.

Another metaphor for diversity is the salad bowl:[16] like a mosaic, each employee makes a unique contribution to the larger bowl (or organization) while maintaining his or her own individuality and cultural or other identity. When diverse backgrounds and talents combine, they make a more effective and creative organization.

Managing diversity requires an organization to treat its employees as individuals rather than as numbers or categories.[17] Most of us tend to group people using dimensions such as race, gender, and age. However, it is important to recognize that the same person may belong to multiple categorical groups:

> Thus, the same individual's identity can be composed of various facets: One can be an African-Canadian (race) woman (gender) who is older (age), married (marital status), and from a low-income family (income status).

stereotyping
The process of using a few observable characteristics to assign someone to a preconceived social category.

This raises the important question: on which one or more of these identities should a human resource manager focus? Grouping people often results in **stereotyping**; yet, a grouping that gives added insights into the person's unique background, capabilities, and individuality is likely to generate better workplace outcomes. Further, the differences between groups need not be intrinsic or innate; they can be differences attributed to history or prevailing culture and subject to change.

> For example, the way a typical Canadian views gay and lesbian couples today is very different from the way he or she did 50 years ago.

Such attributed differences play a key role in human interaction. Cultural conventions and values set "rules" when interacting with others and reduce uncertainty for individuals in a society. These largely unwritten rules themselves have been changing. For some people, many of these "rule changes" are welcome since they reduce inequity and injustice. For others, the pattern and pace of change heightens anxiety and discomfort because longstanding ideals are being eroded. How can we create workplace rules that enhance productivity, growth, and commitment and at the same time minimize anxiety and uncertainty? Herein lies the challenge of managing diversity.

SPOTLIGHT ON HRM
Face of Canada Changes

An examination of Canadian society in 2009 shows a nation that has become increasingly multi-ethnic and multicultural. Immigration to Canada over the past 100 years has shaped Canada, with each new wave of immigrants adding to the nation's ethnic and cultural composition. Less than 50 years ago, most immigrants came from Europe. Now most newcomers are from Asia. The proportion of newcomers who belonged to a visible minority group also increased (see Chart 1), resulting in a new Canadian ethnic image. While English, French, and Scottish ancestry continue to be the most dominant ones, other ethnic groups such as Ukrainian and Dutch now hold very significant positions (see Chart 2).

The snapshot from the latest census tells us that a remarkable experiment is taking place in this country. It is redefining for us our image of who is a Canadian. Canada's quota of immigrants has risen sharply since the 1980s; coupled with a low birth rate in the country, this has resulted in the proportion of Canadians who are foreign born rising to its highest level in more than 50 years.

In recent years, South Asians have become the largest visible minority group, surpassing Chinese for the first time. The populations of both are well over a million now. Chinese persons accounted for 24 percent of the visible minority population while South Asians' corresponding share was 37.7 percent. The number of those who identify themselves as black, the third-largest visible minority group, today account for 15.5 percent of the visible minority population and 3.9 percent of the total population. Other major visible minority groups include Filipinos (8.1 percent of the visible minority population), Latin Americans (6 percent), Arabs (5.2 percent), Southeast Asians (4.7 percent), West Asians (3.1 percent), Koreans (2.8 percent), and Japanese (1.6 percent). Combined, these groups make up over 5 percent of the total Canadian population.

Source: All figures are from Statistics Canada Census 2006 data. The charts are prepared by the authors based on published data.

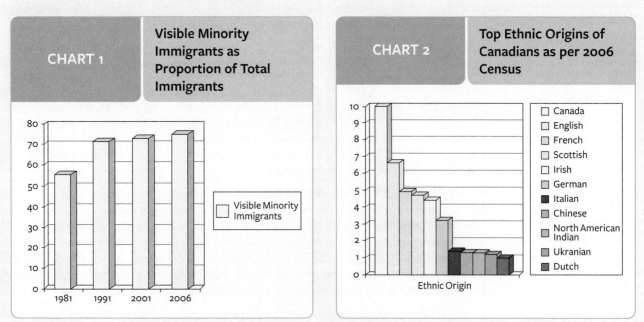

CHART 1 — Visible Minority Immigrants as Proportion of Total Immigrants

CHART 2 — Top Ethnic Origins of Canadians as per 2006 Census

⊙ STRATEGIC IMPORTANCE OF DIVERSITY MANAGEMENT

Several factors make diversity management strategically important.

Changing Workforce

As detailed in Chapters 1 and 3, the Canadian labour market is undergoing rapid and continuous transformation. The average member of the workforce of the past was male, white, approximately 30 years old, and usually held a high school diploma or lower. These men also worked within the region of their birth, were married, and had children. Typically, their wives stayed home to take care of their family. Today's workforce, in contrast, includes women, people of ethnic minorities, native Canadians, people with physical disabilities, and people with alternative lifestyles (for example, people with same-sex partners). If one includes other forms of heterogeneity (such as age and language differences), the workforce diversity is even more striking. Given this state of affairs, diversity management is not merely desirable, but mandatory if an organization is to effectively attract, utilize, and develop human resources.

Importance of Human Capital

Changes in production technology have dramatically increased the importance of human capital. In the past, the entrepreneur raised capital, invested in fixed assets (like a factory), hired others to work, and kept all emerging profits for himself or herself. In today's world of "intellectual capitalism," the situation is quite different. In knowledge-intensive firms, it is not clear who owns the company, its tools, and its products. Often, today's organization may not even have a factory (and may be getting products manufactured by a subcontractor in Taiwan or Mexico). The only tools seen may be computers, cell phones, and fax machines. The knowledge worker may be the key to the success or failure of the firm. Often the departure of even a few workers can spell disaster for the firm. The most valuable parts of the firm's operation may be reflected in human tasks of sensing, judging, and making decisions. In today's information age, no one can afford to use human capital inefficiently.

> As General Electric's past CEO Jack Welch pointed out, with competition fierce, "the only ideas that count are the A ideas. There is no second place. That means that we have to get everybody in the organization involved. If you do that right, the best ideas will rise to the top."[18]

Diversity as a Competitive Advantage

Proactive organizations recognize that competitive strength often lies in focusing on their employees and their clients. In a Canadian survey, 25 percent of senior executives viewed the increasing diversity of the workforce as a competitive opportunity and a sustainable source of competitive advantage.[19] Globalization and changing domestic markets (because of demographic changes, immigration, etc.) mean that a firm's customers are no longer a homogeneous group of persons.

> One writer estimates the spending power of minorities in Canada at about $76 billion. A diverse workforce enables an organization to develop a greater understanding of the needs of diverse customers.[20]

Articles on diverse workforces
www.articlesbase.com/article-tags/workforce-diversity

For Canada, this is particularly important since our biggest trading partner, the United States, itself is undergoing rapid transformation in its population, resulting in greater workforce diversity.

Further, many of the growing export markets for Canadian firms are located in East Asia, South Asia, Latin America, and Africa. It is imperative that we understand the needs of a diverse population and respond effectively and in a timely fashion to maintain our competitive advantage.

> Royal Bank, through its Leveraging Diversity strategy, makes the employee differences increase the competitive advantage of the firm. The bank looks at leveraging diversity as a proactive process to gain a business advantage from the differences and similarities of employees and the marketplace. It recognized that "hammering a wealth of diverse pegs into one-size-fits-all holes can stifle creativity, and give business too narrow a focus." By actively focusing on the needs of women, Aboriginal people, and ethnic, racial, or other employee groups, the bank's Diversity Business Council could recognize definite business advantages. Consider these:
>
> • Women on a product development team give male team members perspective on how female customers may respond to new product ideas.
> • Partnerships with Aboriginal people result in increased economic and business opportunity to the Aboriginal community and improved success for service providers.

- Employees who grew up on the East Coast give the marketing team in central Canada some first-hand insights into regional tastes and expectations.
- Customers in a predominantly Chinese neighbourhood are served by employees who speak the language and relate to the customer needs.
- Older or retired employees of the bank understand and serve the needs of the seniors' market.[21]

Managers learn to achieve productivity gains by leveraging the strengths of all employees. The bank recognizes that there is a world of opportunity to be gained from tapping people's differences and pooling their insights and experiences.[22]

> A study of men and women in first-line sales-management positions at a British firm found that on a wide range of measures, the women in the group consistently showed superior results. The women-led teams showed higher levels of effectiveness in business to business selling, job satisfaction, lower levels of burnout, and less conflict.[23]

Paradigm Shift[24]

There has been a revolutionary change in organizational assumptions about people and their work. A *paradigm* is a shared mindset that reflects a fundamental way of thinking and understanding the world around us. Since our beliefs and understanding direct our behaviour, a **paradigm shift** can have a profound effect on the behaviour of organizations. Figure 12-2 shows the old paradigm and the new paradigm (in the context of diversity) that has replaced it in recent years. Such dramatic changes necessitate fundamental alterations in the way we think, operate, and manage people.

paradigm shift
Fundamental change in a paradigm, e.g., shift from paper filing systems to electronic information storage and retrieval.

Increasing Role of Work Teams

Teams play a dominant role in modern organizations. Work teams are charged with task accomplishment to enable firms to distance themselves from the competitors and ensure survival.[25] While teams always reflected some degree of diversity, today the differences among members are even greater. Race, gender, ethnicity, age, education levels, sexual orientation, and so on are among key factors that separate team members. The differences must be considered as "value added" rather than as "problematic" and the team leader today must have the skills to facilitate and inspire (rather than coach and control as in the past). Assimilation into a homogeneous culture may result in loss of synergy. Valuing differences, on the other hand, can result in improved creativity and innovative problem solving.

FIGURE 12-2	A Comparison of Traditional and New Paradigms

Traditional
- Organizational success is linked to standardization.
- Diversity is a cost.
- Rules and policies are to be shaped by senior executives.
- Emphasis on "masculine" values of competitiveness, aggressiveness, and individuality.
- Change employee behaviours and attitudes to suit the organization's culture.

New
- Success is linked to individual's contribution.
- Diversity is a competitive advantage.
- Rules and policies are to be shaped to satisfy the customer and the employee.
- Recognition that "feminine" values of openness, flexibility, and relationship orientation are equally important for organizational success.
- Modify organizational culture to suit the needs of the employees.

Source: Adapted from Hari Das, *Strategic Organizational Design: For Canadian Firms in a Global Economy*, Scarborough, ON: Prentice-Hall, 1998, p. 16. Reprinted with permission of Pearson Education Canada Inc.; and Marilyn Loden, *Implementing Diversity*, Chicago: Irwin, 1996, p. 35.

Past writings indicate that employee morale and satisfaction are related to the way in which employee and group identities are defined and respected.[26] Indeed, the overall organizational effectiveness measures such as work quality, productivity, absenteeism, and turnover may be significantly influenced by the way individuals and groups are treated. Effective handling of workforce diversity can lead to added creativity, problem solving, and intra-organizational communication.[27]

Organizations that genuinely practise diversity recognize that diversity is more than a human resource management issue and affects all strategies and processes of the organization.[28] Diversity management is tied to the strategic plan, and every employee from senior executives to the lowest-level employee contributes to fostering a diverse workforce.

◯ STEPS IN DIVERSITY MANAGEMENT

Bank of Montreal is a good example of an organization that took the notion of diversity management seriously and altered the internal culture and systems to make it more women friendly.

> Finding that women held 91 percent of the bank's nonmanagement jobs but only 9 percent of the executive positions, the bank made an early attempt to tap the vast potential of its female workforce. The bank established a Task Force on the Advancement of Women to identify the constraints facing women who wanted career progress in the bank. Clear goals and action plans were established to eliminate these hurdles. Surveys, focus groups, intensive interviews, and so on were carried out to find solutions for faster advancement of women to executive careers.
>
> Apart from the financial benefits it received by tapping a hitherto forgotten resource, the bank also received numerous awards for its success in improving the work climates of women, Aboriginal people, and people with disabilities. The Catalyst Award from a New York think tank, the Distinction Award from YWCA, and Catalyst: Mercury Awards from the International Communications Academy of Arts and Sciences in New York are particularly noteworthy in this context.[29]

Transforming an organization's culture is a time-consuming process. Effective, systemwide changes require both attitudinal and behavioural changes. To generate a work climate that respects and builds on human differences may, at times, take several years of commitment. In almost all instances, diversity management efforts require four key steps (see Figure 12-3). These are discussed below.

Today's workforce includes more women participating in careers that were typically exclusive to men. Still, the glass ceiling remains. How can it be cracked?

Brand X/Fotosearch.

Identify Ideal Future State

Implementing a diversity management program begins with an accurate portrayal of its current workforce composition and a forecast of its future workforce.[30] Organizational members have to be identified accurately using demographic categories such as age, gender, ethnicity, education, and disability. Some organizations also expand this to identify the number of employees belonging to other distinct groups on the basis of their language, race, sexual orientation, income level, social class, parental status, and marital status. Practical considerations that vary among firms determine which aspects of diversity can be accommodated. Once the firm has an accurate picture of its workforce composition (and likely future needs), it is critical to assess the values and needs of the workforce. Surveys, focus groups, and interviews with individual employees and work groups are employed to identify present and ideal future states at work.

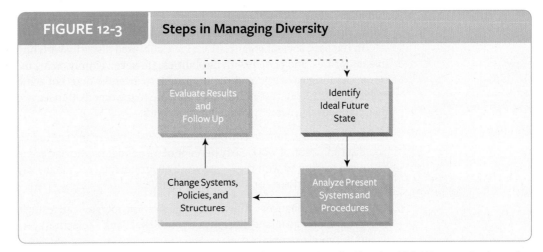

FIGURE 12-3 | **Steps in Managing Diversity**

- Evaluate Results and Follow Up
- Identify Ideal Future State
- Change Systems, Policies, and Structures
- Analyze Present Systems and Procedures

Source: Adapted from Hari Das, *Strategic Organizational Design: For Canadian Firms in a Global Economy*, Scarborough, ON: Prentice Hall, 1998, p. 340. Reprinted with permission by Pearson Education Canada Inc.

For example, through surveys and focus groups, American Express Travel-Related Services found its employees were experiencing significant difficulties in balancing work and family responsibilities. Through follow-up focus groups, the firm identified 14 possible solutions including part-time work, job sharing, child care centres, and compressed workweeks.[31]

Analyze Present Systems and Procedures

The next step is to examine how the present systems are operating. Current policies, systems, practices, rules, and procedures have to be examined for their appropriateness for a diverse workforce. Included here are work assignments, recruitment and hiring, orientation, training, compensation, employee communication, human resource development, and performance appraisal. The validity and fairness of the various systems and rules for different cultures and their compatibility with different **cultural norms** are assessed at this stage.

cultural norms
Values and norms that determine behaviours of individuals and groups in different cultures.

> One major obstacle faced by many immigrants is when employers insist on "Canadian experience" even when equivalent performance experience in other countries is available. In other cases, foreign qualifications are not recognized, forcing hundreds of skilled immigrants to take up low-paying, low-status jobs.[32] In contrast, progressive employers institute new procedures to foster diversity and avoid discrimination. A case in point is Husky Injection Molding of Bolton, Ontario, which employs large numbers of foreign-born people. In the past, when Husky began to benchmark its employees, it realized that not all of its high performers came from traditional sources. Soon, the company put together a matrix of where its employees were coming from. It found that it had not been recognizing the value of schools that had produced star employees. So, Husky sat down with employees and asked them to list the top schools in their countries and it came up with a list of desirable education institutions from which it began to screen in, rather than screen out, applicants. The company is also aggressive in marketing itself to skilled immigrants.[33]

Change Systems, Procedures, and Practices

All existing systems and practices have to be reviewed for their continued relevance to the organizational mission, strategy, and environmental demands. Those that are found lacking should be modified or even discontinued. Five factors are particularly critical in this context: senior management commitment, establishment of a diversity committee, education and retraining, wide communication of changes, and evaluation of results and follow-up.

Senior Management Commitment

In most organizations, changing systems and internal practices is no simple task. Senior management commitment to diversity is one of the most important elements of ensuring the success of diversity efforts; so is whole-hearted support from the unions. While they may be started with considerable enthusiasm, diversity efforts will fail unless all managers and employees see them as an integral part of the firm's business philosophy. This means that particular attention should be paid to communication, hiring, and reward structures to promote diversity.

In the past, several organizations have confused diversity with hiring women, members of visible minorities, and people with disabilities. However, simply hiring more women or other minorities in the absence of a genuine commitment to diversity does not achieve any beneficial outcomes. Indeed, some recent research studies indicate that women often leave organizations and start their own companies to avoid "glass ceilings" at work.

> A study of 650 female entrepreneurs showed that many started their own businesses to avoid discrimination at work. Sixty percent of respondents who had come out of private corporations were frustrated with their past work environments, with many saying their employers did not take them seriously or did not value them.[34]

Sometimes, changes in the way an organization operates can result in simultaneous achievement of organizational goals and diversity targets. Royal Bank's selection system for hiring telephone sales agents is a good example of this:

> When Royal Bank recruited telephone sales agents for its Royal Direct Call Centre in Moncton, applicants competed on a level playing field: the bank used interactive voice response (IVR) and multimedia computers to screen job seekers. All applicants were asked to dial a 1-800 number. An automated voice gathered information about skills such as sales and computer experience. The top candidates progressed to multimedia computer assessments that presented them with confused or irate clients and gave them a chance to respond. Only after the computer screening did the applicants with the highest scores have their first face-to-face interview. The result is that many applicants (and hires) felt that they were being judged on their merits and basic skills without outside factors such as race, gender, or an unconventional employment history biasing the decision. This also helped the bank to attract men to a position that hitherto was concentrated with women. Typically, call centres employ 80 to 90 percent women. The new system resulted in a ratio of 73 percent women and 27 percent men.[35]

Or, consider the efforts of Vancity, a Best Diversity Employer for 2009:

> Vancity pays special attention to recruiting employees from lesbian, gay, bisexual, and transgendered/transsexual (LGBT) persons. It is also a lead sponsor of Vancouver's annual Pride Parade and a sponsor of the Queer Film Festival. A few years ago, it also introduced openly gay images in its advertising. It uses targeted recruitment ads in ethnic community newspapers and has working relationships with a number of community advocacy groups. Today, nearly, two-thirds of its management employees are women, including the board chair and the CEO.[36]

Simply changing a few human resource procedures (such as selection process) without necessary changes in internal culture and processes, however, may not be enough. Consider the experience of Ann States in Western Paper and Pulp Corporation:

> When Ann entered Western Paper and Pulp Corporation as the junior work supervisor, she was the only black woman in her unit. During the job interview, the human resource manager had communicated to Ann the company's strong commitment to diversity management. However, what she experienced at the workplace was very much at odds with the firm's avowed policy. She found that her boss rarely gave her any challenging job assignments; her coworkers often hinted that she would not have been hired but for her skin colour. At some office parties, she was not given a chair at the head table although other supervisors of her rank were seen there. Frustrated and doubting her career growth potential within the firm, Ann left her job after six months.

Figure 12-4 shows the areas where a firm must make changes if diversity initiatives are to succeed. Mere verbal support of system and policy changes is unlikely to produce tangible results. Linking diversity initiatives to business goals and incorporating diversity goals into performance criteria (reflected in salaries) ensures the accountability of managers for diversity.

Establishment of a Diversity Committee

One approach to increase employee involvement is through the establishment of a **diversity committee**. This committee will oversee diversity efforts, implement portions of the process, and serve as a communication link among employees, managers, and union officials. The number of

FIGURE 12-4	Systems and Practices Requiring Modification During a Diversity Effort

- Recruitment and selection processes and criteria
- Orientation
- Work assignments
- Performance management
- Reward systems
- Employee communication systems
- Training
- Career and management development policies and programs
- Employee counselling practices
- Benefits policy
- Group and team practices
- Leadership skills and practices
- Job descriptions and specifications

diversity committee
A committee entrusted to oversee diversity efforts, implement processes, and serve as a communication link.

members in the committee shows variation across organizations. Thus, small organizations may have only two or three members, while larger organizations typically employ six to eight members. What is perhaps even more important than size of the committee is its composition and power. Committee members should not be limited to the traditional "disadvantaged" groups (e.g., women, members of visible minorities), but should represent all employee groups broadly (e.g., occupational groups, geographic location, age groups). The committee should have power not only to identify budgets necessary for diversity efforts but also to hire outside experts, where necessary, to further diversify initiatives and oversee internal communication and education strategies.

Royal Bank has a Diversity Business Council that is entrusted, among other things, with the following responsibilities:

- To identify the opportunity "gaps" and the problems of omission that stand in the way of making the differences work.
- To develop a transition plan to achieve gender gap objectives by a predetermined date.
- To formulate action plans to close the gaps observed.
- To get buy-in, and accountability from, unit heads and all senior management to implement the action plans.
- To build in a process to measure results.[37]

Education and Retraining

Training in the importance of diversity must be provided to all employees, from the CEO to the lowest level employee. Different types of training and training methodologies are used to meet the unique needs of different work group segments.

For example, a training approach to familiarize work supervisors with new appraisal procedures may employ role-plays and case studies. To train the same firm's assembly workers in communication with members of other cultures, these methods are likely to be less successful.

A diverse workforce, while adding to the strategic advantage of the firm, also provides a major managerial challenge. Many Canadians in the workforce today may have origins in cultures or ethnic groups that have vastly different assumptions about work, relationships, and group norms.

Thus, a large number of Asians, Africans, Middle Easterns, Latin Americans, and Canadian Aboriginal persons who originate in rural-based societies have traditional ways of organizing reality and dealing with problems and events.[38] Figure 12-5 shows a comparison of the values and assumptions held by mainstream, urban-industrialized Canadians and persons originating from other cultures. Similar value and behaviour differences can be seen between mainstream employees and other workforce segments as well (e.g., persons of different sexual orientation; persons who belong to different religious groups). Only a deep commitment to understanding the cultural and work-related values held by different work groups will prepare the organization to manage the challenges of diversity.[39]

FIGURE 12-5	A Comparison of Values and Assumptions of Mainstream Canadians and Members of Some Other Cultures	
	Mainstream Canadians	**Members of Some Other Cultures**
1. Assumptions about time	Time is critical; it is scarce and linear in its transition.	Clock time is not important; time is measured by events; time is cyclical.
2. Decision-making practices	Rational procedures are important; logic is the essence of decision making.	Intuitive, holistic problem solving is as (and sometimes even more) important.
3. Focus at work	Achieving organizational outcomes is critical.	Human relations and affiliation with others is as (and sometimes more) important.
4. Verbal communication	"Small talk" is preferable to silence.	Silence during conversation is normal.
	Use "direct" style (e.g., "No" or "I can't do that").	Use "indirect" style (e.g., rather than "No," say, "It might be possible" or "It is interesting in principle").
	"Elaborate" style where quantity of talk is high; description includes great detail and often there is repetition.	"Succinct" style with low quantity of talk; understatements and silence used to convey meaning.
	Communication emphasizes an individual's "personhood."	Communication is related to an individual's role and hence is "contextual."
5. Nonverbal gestures in communication	Eye contact is perceived as a sign of attention or even trustworthiness.	Looking directly into another's eyes signifies disrespect and rudeness.
	A smile usually signifies happiness or pleasure.	A smile may connote embarrassment or discomfort in some instances.
	A "V" with fingers connotes victory.	This gesture has an offensive connotation in some settings.
	An "O" with fingers means Okay in the U.S. and in some parts of Canada.	It means zero or worthless in France.
6. Other general assumptions	Individualism and competition are good; conflicts at work are natural.	The group is the key; cooperation and harmony are critical for success.
7. Values underlying ideal employee behaviours	Individuals can and should display own abilities and achievement in the best possible light; self-selling acceptable; can interrupt, criticize, or confront others and offer unsolicited suggestions. Prefer fight to flight in situations of conflict. Can show anger, frustration, and disappointment.	Individuals should be humble and modest by not presenting themselves too favourably; should downplay own accomplishments; interruptions and questionings are disrespectful to others; avoiding loss of personal or group honour and "face" is a top priority. Prefer flight to fight in situations of conflict. Should exert and expect self-control and restraint in emotional expression.
8. Dress and appearance	"Dress for success" ideal; dress seen as an indication of commitment to the firm and the profession; formal, conforming dress valued.	Dress is often an indication of cultural and religious beliefs, position, and prestige.

Source: Adapted, updated, and summarized from a variety of sources including the following: W.B. Gudykunst and S. Ting-Toomey, *Culture and Interpersonal Communication*, Newbury Park, CA: Sage Publications, 1998; Lee Gardienswartz and Anita Rowe, *Managing Diversity*, New York: Irwin Professional Publishing, 1993, p. 37; G. Hofstede, *Culture's Consequence: International Differences in Work Related Values*, Beverly Hills, CA: Sage Publications, 1980; L.H. Chaney and J.S. Martin, *Communication and Conflict: Readings in Intercultural Relations*, Needham Heights, MA: Ginn Press, 1994.

To sensitize workers to the cultural values and norms held by other groups, a variety of training and employee development techniques may have to be employed. Alternate training approaches, learning principles, and evaluation criteria were discussed in Chapter 7. Transference of learning to the workplace must be given particular importance when evaluating the effectiveness of alternate delivery mechanisms. Giving managers and employees new tools and information without permitting them to put them to use only creates frustration. Hence it is critical that key issues learned during training are incorporated into day-to-day work.

Wide Communication of Changes

Changes in internal systems and procedures must be communicated to all members. Information should be provided on what changes will occur, what the likely results will be, how important these changes are for the success of the organization, accomplishments until this point, and responses to questions related to diversity initiatives. Some of the communication methods in the context of diversity management are listed in Figure 12-6. More on employee communication strategies was discussed in Chapter 11.

> At Warner-Lambert Canada, education and communication of diversity initiatives are ongoing. To ensure inclusion of all employees, early communication focusing on increasing awareness of human rights is attempted.[40]
>
> For a long time, Canada Post had a very stable and homogenous workforce. Over time, the organization attempted to enhance its diversity by recruiting more women, Aboriginal persons, and African-Canadians into its workforce. Today, women account for 48.9 percent of its employees, and fill senior managerial positions. Targeted initiatives such as the Progressive Aboriginal Relations Program helped the organization to attract more Aboriginal persons into its workforce. Members of visible minorities and persons with disabilities account for 10.5 percent of its workforce compared to 13.2 percent in the labour market. To widely communicate its commitment to diversity, Canada Post runs special events such as celebrations around Aboriginal Day or Black History month. Its concerted actions have made Canada Post one of Canada's Best Diversity Employers 2009, a list published by Media Corp Canada that recognizes employers for exceptional workplace diversity and inclusiveness.[41]

Evaluation of Results and Follow-up

Unless the firm monitors the progress of the diversity effort on a systematic basis, corrective actions may not follow. Monitoring will also ensure that quantitative and qualitative indices of change are available to the management, the union, and the workforce. These results should be widely communicated and the gaps between targets and accomplishments publicized along with the proposed corrective actions. The various data collection techniques discussed in Chapter 15 are relevant for this purpose. Indices such as number of hires, promotions, absenteeism, turnover, salary levels, grievances, harassment complaints, and so on are useful for gauging progress, but

FIGURE 12-6	Communication Methods in Diversity Initiatives

- Employee newsletters
- Company magazine
- Electronic mail messages
- Special diversity bulletins, brochures, and pamphlets
- Special promotional events (e.g., "Diversity Awareness Day")
- Material available on company intranets and Web sites
- Diversity information sessions
- "Questions and Answers" booklets
- Notices and memos in employee cafeteria and lounges
- Formation of informal networks or committees representing different groups (e.g., women, physically challenged)
- Posters at workplace

diversity audits
Audits to uncover underlying dimensions, causes, interdependencies, and progress-to-date on diversity management matters.

should not be used in exclusion since qualitative responses from employees may convey other dimensions of work climate and the intensity of employee feelings. More progressive organizations employ **diversity audits** on a regular basis to uncover the underlying dimensions, causes, and progress-to-date on diversity management matters. Prompt follow-up actions to accelerate accomplishments are necessary and should be planned in consultation with the senior managers and the unions to ensure success.

▶ CURRENT INDUSTRY PRACTICES

Articles and discussions on diversity
www.shrm.org/
PUBLICATIONS/pages/
default.aspx

In the previous section, we discussed the need for changing key systems and procedures within organizations to implement diversity management. This section provides an overview of popular industry practices to achieve this objective.

In 2009, nearly two-thirds of Canadian employers surveyed by Catalyst, a New York–based research and advisory organization that promotes women in business, indicated a stated commitment to diversity in their mission or vision statements; however, fewer than half of them had any policies or practices that in fact supported such a vision.[42] Many visible minority managers and professionals report lower satisfaction and more barriers to career advancement than their Caucasian counterparts. However, more progressive employers have adopted a variety of policies and practices to create an inclusive culture that welcomes everyone irrespective of their gender, colour, and religious or other beliefs. As will be seen, the approaches are as varied as organizations. The choice of specific mechanisms should be made after a careful consideration of the unique challenges and constraints facing an organization.

Diversity Training Programs

diversity training programs
Training programs aimed at importing new skills to motivate and manage a diverse workforce.

Managers and lower-level supervisors need to learn new skills that will enable them to manage and motivate a diverse workforce. Often, outside experts are invited to mount **diversity training programs** in organizations. Indeed, in many firms this is one of the first actions taken to implement diversity management. Such training programs help to create awareness of the bottom-line impact of diversity management and the role of managers, supervisors, and coworkers in creating a work climate that is found comfortable by all employees, irrespective of their gender, age, sexual orientation, racial or ethnic identity, and physical or mental capabilities.

> Petro-Canada, DuPont Canada, and Levi Strauss & Co. (Canada) are examples of firms that have pursued diversity training programs in the past.[43] The Toronto Transit Commission has used a four-day, residential simulation of a fictitious transit organization to convey the challenges of bringing an equitable pay system into a firm that employs a diverse workforce.[44]

awareness training
Training employees to develop their understanding of the need to manage and value diversity.

Experts suggest two types of training: awareness training and skill-building training. **Awareness training** focuses on creating an understanding of the need for managing and valuing diversity. It is also meant to increase participants' self-awareness of diversity-related issues such as stereotyping and cross-cultural insensitivity.

skill-building training
Training employees in interpersonal skills to correctly respond to cultural differences at the workplace.

Once individuals develop an awareness, they can then monitor their feelings, reactions, etc., and make conscious decisions about their behaviour, often resulting in improved interpersonal communication. **Skill-building training** educates employees on specific cultural differences and how to respond to differences in the workplace. Often awareness and skill-building training are combined.

Another issue to be resolved by a trainer in managing diversity is content versus process training. *Content training* relates to the question: "Should a training program focus solely on the knowledge and skills related to a single culture?" This would be appropriate for a manager working with a workforce consisting mainly of members of one culture. However, as mentioned before, statistics show that the Canadian workforce is becoming more culturally diverse; therefore, it will become more likely that managers will need to deal effectively with employees from several different cultures in a single organization.

In the long run it is therefore more practical, although more difficult, to focus on *process training*; that is, supervisors and employees have to learn about diversity. Participants in a process-oriented diversity training program develop an understanding of how management style, the interpersonal communication process, teamwork, and other managerial issues are affected by diversity. After such a training program, participants may not have all the answers, but they will have plenty of questions.

Ideally the trainers themselves will reflect diversity. A team of male and female, white and black (or Asian) trainers could work together to cover different topics in a diversity training program. It probably would make participants from different minorities and racial and cultural backgrounds feel more comfortable.

Useful training methods for diversity training are metaphors, stories, and parables. A *metaphor* is a figure of speech that makes an implied comparison between things that are not literally alike. Consider these examples:

> A popular saying among the group-oriented Japanese managers is: "Nails that protrude will be hammered in," implying that a nonconforming group member will be put under pressure to conform.

Parables (or fables) are stories with a moral:

> Two men had a disagreement. To have it resolved they went to a wise man. The first man explained the problem as he saw it. The wise man listened carefully, thought about it for quite some time, and said: "You are right."
>
> Then the second man explained the problem as he saw it. The wise man listened carefully, thought about it for quite some time, and said: "You are right."
>
> A third man, who had listened to the stories, spoke up: "Master," he said, "but both cannot be right." The wise man listened carefully, thought about it for quite some time, and said: "You are right."

The moral of the story is that for all of us perception is reality.

Stories can also be used as tools to get a message across. Here is a story told by a manager with Caterpillar Tractor Company:

> When we opened a joint venture with Mitsubishi Heavy Industries in Japan we had to familiarize our Japanese counterparts with Caterpillar production processes. After having given an explanation we would ask: Everything clear?" and our Japanese colleagues would respond with: "Hai." Since we had learned that "hai" meant "yes," we assumed that everything had been understood, and we would say: "OK, let's do it." We found out too late that to the Japanese "hai" really means "I heard you." As a result of the misinterpretation, we discovered that the Japanese managers had often not understood what we had told them, but they could not admit it because to them that meant losing face. After several such experiences we installed blackboards in each office and established the following rules:
>
> 1. Talk slowly and look for signs of confusion.
> 2. Each explanation has to be repeated by the receiver.
> 3. Oral explanations have to be given also in writing.
> 4. Whenever possible drawings have to be used.
>
> We found that with these rules we dramatically improved communication with our Japanese counterparts.[45]

These tools for diversity training can be used in many different ways. Stories can be told live, on audio or video DVDs and Blu-rays, or be given as handouts. Parables can be shared in a classroom exercise or included as a special feature in an in-house publication, and metaphors can be presented by the trainer or developed by participants. Experienced trainers will have such tools in their own libraries.

Mentoring Programs

Some firms encourage **mentoring programs** where women or members of visible minorities and other disadvantaged groups are encouraged to work with a senior manager who acts like a friend, philosopher, and guide in achieving career success within the firm.

> In the past, Canadian National initiated a program where a woman employee moving toward a managerial position learns the job under a senior manager. At the end of a two-year period, if found effective in carrying out her responsibilities, the woman will be given a permanent job.[46]
>
> To assist with internal and external mentoring and networking, Deloitte & Touche set up a series of Executive Women Breakfast Forums in partnership with AT&T.[47]

mentoring programs
Programs encouraging members of disadvantaged groups (e.g., women) to work with a senior manager who acts like a friend and guide in achieving career success.

Mentors may be identified formally or informally. Organizations can bring greater predictability into diversity outcomes by establishing formal mentoring systems since they result in greater tangible results and accountability on the part of both mentors and protegés.

> One large Canadian bank lists all relevant details of its senior managers on its Web site. All new hires are encouraged to select someone from the list and contact him or her on a regular basis for receiving helpful hints for day-to-day performance and long-term career advice. Both the mentor and the protegé are encouraged to submit reports of their deliberations to the bank.

Mentoring, to be most effective, should be used in conjunction with a complete diversity initiative and not as a stand-alone ritual. Mentors also have to be carefully selected since not everyone can be an effective mentor. Past writings indicate that mentors should hold high rank within the organizational hierarchy, be confident and active, possess counselling skills, understand the power structure within the firm, and be respected by other managers.[48] The results of discussions between the mentor and protegé should be recorded and kept in the files for later use. In some organizations, a manager's performance evaluation reflects the person's contributions as mentor.

Alternate Work Arrangements

alternate work arrangements
Nontraditional work arrangements (e.g., flextime, telecommuting) that provide more flexibility to employees, while meeting organizational goals.

Often, removal of negative factors can enhance employee performance and career growth. This is especially so in the case of women who have multiple and conflicting role demands from work and family or older workers who find the traditional work arrangements difficult. Several **alternate work arrangements** such as flexible work hours, telecommuting, extended leave, job sharing, etc. have been used in the past to accommodate the unique needs of employee groups. These arrangements were discussed in more detail in Chapter 3.

Some of these alternate work arrangements (e.g., extended leave) have been particularly aimed at women who, because of their child-bearing role, face conflicts between work and family demands. These alternate career paths and work patterns (collectively labelled the "mommy track" by some) recognize the fact that men and women face differing challenges in bringing up children. Of late, the term "daddy track" has also been gaining in popularity to recognize the needs of men who opt to spend some time raising children but want to pursue their old career once the children are older.

> To address the balancing of work and family issues, Deloitte & Touche offered adoption assistance, elder care consultation and referral, child care resource and referral, back-up child care, and flexible work arrangements—including reduced work hours, flextime, and parental leave.[49]

Apprenticeships

apprenticeships
A form of on-the-job training in which young people learn a trade from an experienced person.

Apprenticeships are similar to mentoring except that they relate to junior-level or technical jobs and often involve working with prospective employees before they formally join the organization. Such programs are particularly useful to attract members of visible minorities, women, people with disabilities, and other disadvantaged group members to nontraditional jobs within the firm.

> In the past, Warner-Lambert worked with the Scarborough Board of Education to offer training for students with disabilities within the organization. Hewlett-Packard worked with high schools to provide cooperative tracks to employment especially focusing on disadvantaged groups.[50]

Career Development

All progressive employers today offer some form of assistance to employees to reach their career goals. As mentioned in Chapter 1, progressive HR departments pay serious attention to each individual's "employee goal." In several organizations, career development efforts are not restricted to junior or younger workers. Indeed, many progressive employers offer career development for employees heading into their "second middle age." The "second middle age"[51] is a term coined to denote to the 20-year period when an individual is between ages of 60 and 80. Many consider this to be a time of potential and valuable contribution rather than "retirement age" or "old age." Some of the actions taken by progressive employers to tap into the skills of this group include the following:[52]

- Work with employees in their 50s for future roles rather than assuming they will soon retire. Engage in positive career development conversations before frustration sets in.
- People at all levels are rotated through roles to reduce the occurrence of older employees blocking growth of younger workers.

- Rely on experience of older employees to save the organization from repeating past mistakes by engaging them as troubleshooters and internal auditors.
- Offer the opportunity to take sabbaticals to learn new skills.
- Include career development dialogues as integral part of performance assessment sessions.
- Use nonstandard employment options.

Support Groups

support groups
Groups of employees who provide emotional support to a new employee who shares a common attribute with the group (e.g., racial or ethnic membership).

Employees belonging to racial or other groups that are underrepresented in the organization may often feel lonely and uncomfortable at the workplace. Sometimes, this might be simply a feeling of loneliness and distance from mainstream workers. In other instances, the new employee may even face hostility from other members of the work group, especially when others perceive that the employee's minority status resulted in preferential treatment during hiring. Coworker hostility is more likely to happen when a visible minority employee (or woman) is hired for a job that is nontraditional for that group. Often the result is employee alienation, which in turn results in high turnover.

To overcome this problem, one organization formed **support groups** that are designed to provide a nurturing climate for employees who may otherwise feel unwanted or shut out. Socialization in such groups enabled the newcomer not only to share concerns and problems but also to assimilate the organization's culture faster.

Some employers use innovative approaches to make the new minority employee welcome.

ATI, a Toronto based global manufacturer of graphics technology with 3,600 employees worldwide, attempts to create a culture that embraces immigrants. For example, when a woman was hired from Romania for a position, the management sent an email to the employees. The Romanian community within ATI sent her emails welcoming her to the company. The result? The new employee feels welcome and at home even before actually arriving at the workplace.[53]

Communication Standards

communication standards
Formal protocols for internal communications within an organization to eliminate gender, racial, age, or other biases in communications.

Words, language, signs, jokes, and even gestures that may be perceived as neutral or even "fun" to some employees may be offensive to many others. Indeed, the use of some language or words can amount to harassment since they create a "hostile environment" (see Chapter 4). Realizing this factor, several organizations have established **communication standards**—formal protocols for internal messages and communication to avoid offending members of different gender, racial, ethnic, age, or other groups.

The use of "he" when referring to managers in policy manuals has the result of perpetuating the "male" image of a manager. There is no reason why a "chairman" of a meeting is a man; the more progressive organizations recognize this and use the term "chairperson." Similarly, there is no reason why automobiles, yachts, or some other equipment should be referred to as "she" rather than "it."

As the preceding discussion shows, at the present time, there is considerable interest in and focus on diversity management in Canadian industry. However, few organizations are prepared for the resistance that invariably follows the introduction of this concept at the workplace. Resistance to diversity management may emerge from employee groups, unions, work supervisors, and managers. Employee groups and unions fear the emergence of new systems that may bring in hiring quotas, employment and promotion criteria that result in reverse discrimination policies, and lowering of power, status, and rewards. Managers and supervisors share several of the same concerns and may also fear that the new procedures will alter internal systems and performance standards and reduce autonomy. In some instances, the resistance may originate from misperceptions, lack of understanding of the need for change, prevailing stereotypes, and even rumours about negative outcomes associated with diversity implementation elsewhere.

While the reason for resistance may show some variation across employees and groups, its impact is almost always to slow down or stop the change program. To counter resistance, it is very important that the organization anticipates it and uses proactive strategies. The presence of a qualified trainer and consultant who conveys the importance of diversity to the various organizational groups and members is a must for success. Clear articulation of the rationale behind the change and the likely consequences of change (or lack of change now) may result in an attitude shift in the context of diversity management. Involvement of managers, work teams, and other powerful members in the change process and identification of strategies for successful diversity initiatives may reduce their fears about the change.

At Warner-Lambert Canada, a Diversity Task Force was established to increase the success of employee buy-in and to eliminate barriers. The Task Force is composed of people from all functional areas of the organization. To reduce resistance, individuals from the senior levels of the organization provide leadership and are the diversity champions.[54]

SPOTLIGHT ON ETHICS
Should You Pass on That Information?[55]

You work as the director of human resources of a family-owned organization that employs over 400 persons. You report to Mark Strom, the CEO, although you realize that his brother, Peter Strom, financial controller in the firm, is equally, if not more, powerful in the overall setup. Both brothers are extremely conservative in their views and do not hire minorities or persons with different lifestyles into the firm's management group. The result is that, currently, there are no women, minorities, or persons of different religious background or sexual orientation in the management, except for Wendy Chan, whom you hired as human resource manager. The brothers were not very happy with your choice of a person of Chinese descent (and a woman at that), but had finally accommodated your wish on the matter, especially in view of Chan's stellar qualifications. As a human resource professional, you have found the views held by the brothers to be very stifling and uncomfortable, and have often been tempted to leave the firm for other opportunities. After considerable introspection, you have decided that, by staying, you could make a meaningful—albeit very slow—difference to the working conditions and employment policies of the firm. Over the last three years, you have built up a lot of credibility with the two brothers (which helped you to do things such as hiring a person like Chan), and have been successful in bringing about some major improvements in the human resource practices of the firm. You were getting to a point where you were beginning to exert strong influence over the brothers. But, now, you are confronted with a decision where you don't know what your best action should be.

The issue is related to the hiring of a new finance officer who will report directly to Peter, but who also will have to interact, almost on a daily basis with Mark. Mark, Peter, and you interviewed several candidates; two persons, Ron and Chand, were clearly ahead of the rest. Both were put through extensive interviews and reference checks and found to be equally satisfactory. As far as formal qualifications went, Ron was slightly superior, but you liked Chand personally and found him to be better on a couple of criteria, including relevant practical skills. Peter and Mark indicated their clear preference for Ron. Although it was never explicitly pointed

out, you realized that Chand's origin (Indo-Canadian) had something to do with their decision. You feel totally comfortable with Indo-Canadians (your roommate at university was someone from India who became your best friend over time). You feel that such considerations should not bias a hiring decision, but there was really no point in arguing with the brothers. Finally, it was decided to hire Ron, who was currently working in Montreal. He was to join your firm in a month's time.

In connection with some other work, you had to visit Montreal, where you noticed Ron at a restaurant with another man. Although Ron did not see you, from the behaviour of the two, it seemed as if they had a gay relationship. Next day, you "by chance" called on Ron at his office. A look at his office furnishings, including the mantle pictures and magazines, further supported your suspicions about Ron's sexual orientation. You were not totally sure about your conclusions, but feel that your gut feeling on this matter is correct.

You now face a difficult decision: Should you mention your suspicions about Ron to the two brothers? You are almost sure that the new information will result in the withdrawal of the job offer, of course, citing some other reasons. (You remember a past occasion when you accidentally heard a private joke that the brothers were sharing, where you got the tail-end of their conversation, when Peter said, "at least he is not gay," at which both laughed loudly.) On the other hand, if the brothers come to know that you had prior knowledge about Ron and did not confide in them, your own credibility with them may be lost forever. (On arrival, Ron is bound to mention his meeting with you in Montreal.) But you also believe that it is wrong to refuse a person a job because of his or her sexual orientation. How explosive will the situation be if Ron works with these highly conservative individuals? If, for some reason, your conclusions about Ron's sexual orientation are wrong, wouldn't you be harming his career unnecessarily? Would the brothers construe your action as an overt attempt at getting Chand for the position, whom you openly favoured?

What should you do now?

DIVERSITY CHALLENGES FOR GLOBAL FIRMS

The challenge of managing a diverse workforce assumes even greater importance in global firms. The impact on human resource management practices varies depending on the extent of globalization of a firm's operation as well as the strategy it employs to reach foreign markets.

Several firms simply extend their operations into other countries by adapting their products, services, and processes to foreign markets. They are essentially domestic firms that build on their existing capabilities to penetrate international markets.

> Bombardier and Magna are examples of Canadian companies that have adapted their existing capabilities to penetrate European markets. They have not changed much else about their normal operations to expand their operations globally.

On the other end of the spectrum are organizations that provide considerable autonomy to their foreign operations. They use flexible structures and procedures to suit the customs and preferences of people in each country or region where they operate. The foreign operations have a wide latitude to set goals, policies, systems, and procedures that are appropriate to the local conditions.

> Organizations such as Phillips, Unilever, and Shell have given considerable autonomy to their foreign operations to set their own goals and systems and identify practices that fit local operations.

Indeed, as foreign operations grow in size and complexity, most organizations provide greater autonomy and flexibility to their foreign units to respond to local needs and demands. Naturally, the degree of internationalization plays a key role in determining the challenges to human resource managers.

International human resource management requires addition, deletion, and modification of traditional human resource functions. Employee-related activities that need to be added include relocation services, orientation to new cultures and customs, home rental/sale while on foreign assignments, and translation services to help employees communicate and adapt to foreign settings.

Several procedures currently used in the context of benefit planning, tax planning and counselling, investment management, health services, and so on may have to be modified significantly to make them suitable for foreign locations. Several human resource and employee policies related to minimum wages, incentives, employee involvement in decision making, and so on may have to be altogether deleted if they do not match the governmental policies and culture of the host country. Below we discuss five key areas (see Figure 12-7) that require a close look in the context of international human resource management.

expatriates
Home-country nationals sent to foreign locations on temporary or extended stay.

host-country nationals
Local citizens employed by a foreign-owned firm (in the host country).

third-country nationals
Natives of a country other than the home or host country of the firm that has hired them.

Recruitment, Selection, and Termination of Personnel

The employees working in foreign locations of the company may be expatriates, host-country nationals, or third-country nationals. **Expatriates** are home-country nationals who are sent to foreign locations on temporary or extended stay. **Host-country nationals** are local citizens of the host country, while **third-country nationals** are natives of a country other than the home or host countries who

FIGURE 12-7   **Key Focus Areas for Global Firms in the Context of Diversity Management**

| FIGURE 12-8 | Benefits of Various Recruiting Sources for Global Operations |

Expatriates

- Familiarity with company culture and practices.
- Greater control over human resource movements and planning.
- Provide valuable overseas experience to company employees.
- Can become an integral part of career development of employees.
- The firm can reuse newly learned skills and overseas experiences on future occasions.

Host-Country Nationals

- Fluent in local language.
- Knowledge of local customs and culture.
- Typically less expensive than expatriates.
- Host-country governments favour this.
- Avoids problems associated with transfer of company personnel.
- The firm does not have to get work permits or visas for employees, speeding up the hiring process.

Third-Country Nationals

- May know several languages.
- Most likely to have an international outlook.
- Their experience is likely to be broader and may facilitate firm's entry into other foreign locations.

are currently residing in the host country. Each recruiting source has its own unique advantages (see Figure 12-8); however, increasingly, there has been a trend away from use of expatriates to local (or host-country) nationals to minimize culture shock, reduce costs, and meet the demands of local governments. The laws in most countries require the employment of local personnel if adequate numbers of skilled employees are available. This means that expatriates and third-country nationals, in most instances, will require work permits and visas from the local government. This can delay movement of expatriates and third-country nationals into new locations. Hence, planning ahead becomes critical in global operations.

The two sources of potential applicants for openings are present employees and new hires. The reassignment of present employees offers an opportunity for career development of the employee in addition to filling a job opening.

Several large companies, such as Dow Chemicals, Gillette, and Procter & Gamble, move executives around the world.

Although an international assignment often looks attractive to first-time applicants, career, family, language, and cultural considerations may cause more experienced candidates not to apply. Dual-career families, children, and assignments to less developed areas are often significant barriers to recruitment.

It can be tough for Canadian firms to lure foreign executives for a variety of reasons, according to a global executive recruiter.[56] Because of the Canadian tax system, it is very difficult to attract American executives to this country. Many organizations still rely on the "old network" to funnel executives up the ladder,[57] which will not work in today's highly competitive world. Familiarity with someone, or past successes, is no guarantee of their future success in today's global workplace. This means that recruiting and selection procedures have to be adapted to weed out the likely failures.

A lack of knowledge about internal openings can also be a barrier. Some employees are reluctant to apply for international jobs because they fear they will lose touch with developments at headquarters, harming their opportunities for career advancement. As a result, many employees are forced to rely on an informal network when the HR department does not create systematic linkages among people to address these concerns. To overcome these barriers, the organization may consider other sources of recruits as illustrated by Colgate-Palmolive's example:

> In the past, Colgate-Palmolive's senior management noted that the company was having difficulties securing top executive talent for its international operations. Since Colgate's international business is crucial to the company's overall success, management decided to re-examine its recruitment and development practices in this area. As a result, Colgate developed a new strategy: recruiting students from reputed undergraduate and MBA programs whose experience, education, and language skills demonstrated their commitment to an international career.[58]

Several of the recruiting devices discussed in Chapter 5 can, after appropriate modifications, be used for recruiting employees abroad. Naturally, the local cultural values and customs should be borne in mind in all instances. In the case of developing countries, recruiting skilled employees can pose a major challenge because of economic and social conditions.

> The high rate of illiteracy in several less developed countries make print ads irrelevant for several lower-level job positions. In small towns, recruiting may have to be done by word of mouth.

The selection of a person to fill an international opening requires the firm to consider more than just technical or managerial ability. The person's ability to manage a diverse workforce and adapt to the company and country culture are also critical here. This means that the person selected should be mature and emotionally stable while possessing all relevant managerial and technical competencies. Some past writings indicate that one in four (and in some instances, one in two) expatriate managers fail in their new job assignments costing their employers anywhere from US$40,000 to $250,000.[59] The manager's inability to adapt to new settings, the spouse's inability to adapt to the new surroundings, family-related problems, and mismatch between manager personality and new work culture, etc. have been found to be key factors causing expatriate manager failure.[60]

For women managers, working in some foreign settings that have given historically low status to women may pose special problems although host country nationals often view women first as foreigners and only secondly as women. This means that cultural barriers that typically constrain women in male-dominated societies may not totally apply in the case of female expatriates. Indeed, the success rate for female expatriates has been estimated to be about 97 percent—a rate far superior to that of men.[61] Part of this may be attributable to the fact that many firms do not send women abroad unless they are the very best in their group. The increased visibility of women expatriates and the novelty factor (since senior women managers are rare in several foreign settings) may also account for their higher success rate.[62] Some of the characteristics associated with expatriate manager success are listed in Figure 12-9.

transnational teams
Teams composed of members of multiple nationalities working on projects that span several countries.

Increasingly, many firms use **transnational teams** composed of members from multiple nationalities working on projects that span several countries. Such teams are vital for carrying out assignments that no single manager may be able to do alone. They are also very important when the firm is not yet fully organized (with a clear organizational structure, systems, and processes) to meet the unknown challenges facing it in foreign locations. These teams of experts can transcend existing organizational structure, transfer technology and other resources from one region or country to another, respond to new challenges, and make faster decisions. When forming such teams care should be taken to represent all critical functions and skills and include persons who also have the interpersonal skills to work as a team.

> When one large European beer manufacturer formed a transnational team to consolidate production facilities abroad, it made sure that team members were drawn from all major regions in Europe. The team members were also selected on the basis of their unique expertise in an area like marketing, finance, or production management.

Whether selecting managers or teams, firms can adapt and use the various methods discussed in Chapter 6. Many firms use interviews, tests, and assessment centres for selecting managers for foreign locations. Tests measuring attitudes and characteristics necessary for working in foreign settings and ability to learn foreign languages are currently available. Prior track record within the firm and the industry and prior experience in foreign settings is usually given considerable weight by many employers when selecting personnel for foreign locations. Some firms focus not only on a person's ability to work in a foreign culture but also on the spouse's adjustment to the new setting.

FIGURE 12-9 Core Competencies of an Expatriate Manager

Past writings indicate that successful expatriate managers possess several core competencies. Here are the key ones:

Multidimensional Perspective

Ability to consider multiple dimensions of a problem and their interrelationships and ability to integrate them. Ability to conceptualize and resolve a problem at multifunctional, multi-product, multi-industry, and multi-country levels.

Cultural Adaptability

Ability to understand and adapt to local cultural norms and practices without losing track of one's objectives.

Decision-Making Ability

Strategic-thinking ability, ability to process information and identify creative alternatives to problems, evaluate and test alternatives for their feasibility, and ability to modify own decision process to suit the needs of the situation.

Team-Building and Leadership Ability

Ability to understand the motivations of a culturally diverse workforce, bring them together as a high-performing team to accomplish organizational objectives.

Resourcefulness

Ability to adapt own actions and practices to the needs of the situation. Ability to accurately gauge the various political, cultural, technological, and other constraints surrounding own firm and find creative solutions to meet them.

Negotiation Skills

Ability to conduct successful strategic business negotiations in a multicultural and political environment. An understanding of the motivations of the "other side" at the bargaining table and ability to identify solutions that result in win-win solutions.

Change-Agent Skills

Ability to bring about changes in a foreign setting and influence others into newer ways of thinking and acting. Ability to understand the cultural parameters surrounding oneself and adapt one's change strategy to meet these cultural requirements.

Source: Reprinted with the permission of *HR Magazine* published by the Society for Human Resource Management, Alexandria, VA. © January 1990, Vol. 44, No. 1; *Training and Development*, American Society of Training & Development. Reprinted with permission. All rights reserved; Allan Bird and Roger Dunbar, "Getting the Job Done over There: Improving Expatriate Productivity," *National Productivity Review*, Vol. 10, No. 2, Spring, 1991, pp. 145–56. © 1991. Reprinted by permission of John Wiley & Sons, Inc.; reprinted from Rosalie Tung, "Selection and Training of Personnel for Overseas Assignments," *Columbia Journal of World Business*, Vol. 16, No. 1, Spring, 1981, pp. 68–78. With permission of Elsevier Science.

While most firms interview only the candidate, there are firms that interview both the candidate and the spouse. This is a recognition of the importance of spousal adjustment to foreign locations. However, this also raises questions of validity and fairness in selection procedures and may be valid grounds for discrimination complaints by rejected candidates.

Just as recruitment and selection practices in different regions show considerable variations, termination of employees also requires an understanding of the different practices that exist in each country. In some regions, the employees have some procedural rights before a termination can become effective.

For example, in Germany, the basic notice period before terminating an employee is four weeks. It increases with years of service over two years. Pay in lieu of notice is not possible because tax laws prevent this. Although not legally required, it is customary to pay one month's salary for each year of service as severance pay. Employers should also notify the local employment office if more than 5 employees in a unit of 20 to 60 workers are terminated. The termination must also occur within a period of 30 days and cannot become effective earlier than 1 month after the information is filed with the employment office.

In contrast, in the U.K., notice requirements are based on years of service with a low of 1 week and a high of 12 weeks. These notice requirements can be converted to pay in lieu of notice. A termination indemnity is also payable when an employee has more than two years of service.[63]

Orientation, Training, and Development

Global managers have to be more versatile, aware of global issues, sensitive to challenges provided by cultural diversity, capable of managing decentralized operations, and making in-roads into the new social milieu.[64] Some of the qualities of successful expatriates include the following:[65]

- cultural self-awareness
- curiosity about differences between people
- tolerance for ambiguous situations
- acceptance of differences in cultural values
- ability to understand and value differences
- ability to develop relationships with people
- willingness to expand definition of success

Many of the above qualities and skills can be acquired through training, coaching, and development. Recognizing this, many firms focus on providing additional orientation, training, and development activities for their international staff.

The orientation should touch on the policies, place, procedures, and people whom the new job incumbent will encounter in the near future. Unlike new employee orientations, which in many firms may last only a few hours, international orientations may begin weeks or even months before and last for weeks after an assignment is made. Although pre-departure orientation is common and important, an onsite orientation after arrival in an international post is often necessary to help the new job incumbent to settle well into the role. Details of culture, language, local customs, social attitudes toward time and punctuality, power, teamwork, use of titles, social taboos, and degree of formality in interaction with the local population, etc. are integral components of such an orientation. The employee's spouse may also be invited to participate in such an orientation.

> One large firm with global operations invites the spouse of the newly hired employee to all orientation events. An integral part of the orientation in this firm is a two-week language and culture orientation course, which both the husband and wife attend. The orientation often includes a visit from an employer or spouse who has served in the location. Apart from the personal touch, repatriated families are likely to have keen insights about a particular locale.[66]

Departing employees need to be trained in the local language, cultural norms of the host country, and managing personal and family life in the new location.[67]

Language

While English is almost universally accepted as the primary language for international business, Canadian managers will significantly enhance communication by being familiar with other foreign languages. Many Canadian managers are also already familiar with French, which should facilitate international travel and communication. However, English and French usage abroad may show systemic variations.

> In England, to "table" a topic at a meeting means to discuss it now; in Canada, it means to postpone discussion of a subject. The "elevator" is a "lift" in several countries, just as "gum" is "glue." The trunk of a car is a "dickey" in India, a word that denotes the male sex organ in New Zealand.

Cultural Norms

Learning the language is only one part of communicating with another culture. The expatriate employee must also learn about how the locals think and behave in a specific setting.

Different societies show consistent and marked differences on several cultural dimensions. For example, countries like Canada and the U.S. score high on *individualism*, or preference for a social framework in which individuals are supposed to take care of themselves and their immediate families only. In contrast to this, many Asian and South American countries value *collectivism*, or a preference for a tightly knit social framework in which individuals can expect their relatives, clan, or other ingroup to look after them in exchange for unquestioning loyalty. Canadians and Americans score high on *masculinity*, or a preference for achievement, heroism, assertiveness, and material success;

while Nordic countries such as Sweden or Finland value *femininity* or a preference for relationships, modesty, caring for the weak, and quality of life.

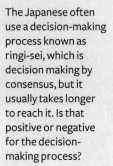

ringi-sei
A type of decision making by consensus often used by the Japanese; literally, "bottom-up decision making."

In Japan, the decision-making process most frequently used in organizations is *ringi-sei*, decision making by consensus. Most widely used by lower- and middle-level managers, *ringi-sei* requires the circulation of documents to organizational members to gain their approval before implementation. This enables the subordinates to voice their views and influence the final decision.

This means that when dealing with members of other cultures, Canadian managers need to make a basic attitudinal shift away from monocultural assumptions that value conformity to organizational rules. Such a shift necessitates different behaviours even in casual meetings. The basic nuts and bolts of social interaction vary widely and need to be learned for each specific culture.

Managing Personal and Family Life

culture shock
Cultural disorientation causing stress and the inability to respond appropriately.

Culture shock, a cultural disorientation that causes physical and emotional stress and inability to respond to situations appropriately, is experienced by many expatriates. Hundreds of day-to-day events and factors are involved—such as inability to communicate to local citizens (because of language differences), differences in technology that have an impact on everyday events (e.g., making telephone calls, cooking, shopping), and a myriad of other everyday matters. This means that a firm's pre-departure training should prepare the expatriate employee for all major aspects of life abroad. Even minor frustrations can, if unanticipated and unprepared for, become catastrophic events that drain the new employee emotionally and physically.

The Japanese often use a decision-making process known as ringi-sei, which is decision making by consensus, but it usually takes longer to reach it. Is that positive or negative for the decision-making process?

Cross-Cultural Training Methods

A number of training methods aimed at preparing employees for a foreign work environment have been tried. Some of the more promising approaches are described below.

Sensitivity Training

This has been successfully used by several organizations to prepare managers for overseas assignments. The objective of sensitivity training is to increase self-awareness and the ability to assess the impact of one's own behaviour on others. (This method was discussed in Chapter 7.)

Culture Assimilators

These consist of a series of episodes dealing with interpersonal issues in a cross-cultural situation. By responding to individual episodes and referring to explanations describing why their responses were appropriate or not, trainees have an opportunity to test their cross-cultural effectiveness and to learn about the appropriate responses in a specific culture. Studies have shown that assimilator-trained subjects performed better in another culture than subjects who did not receive such training. The following is an example of a culture assimilator episode:

> You offer a Japanese manager a generous gift if he would be helpful in getting your sales bid accepted by his boss. He reacts by sucking air through his teeth. Do you assume that:
>
> a) he is pleasantly surprised;
>
> b) he is deeply embarrassed;
>
> c) he is unsure how to respond and would prefer more information and clarification; or
>
> d) it is a sign that the value of the proposed gift is insufficient to obtain his support.
>
> The correct answer is (b). Japanese respond to embarrassing situations by sucking air through their clenched teeth. This reaction is often accompanied by the comment: "That will be difficult," which to the Japan expert means, "No, don't bother."

Critical Incidents

These are brief descriptions of effective or ineffective behaviours that illustrate problems an expatriate employee may encounter in an organization abroad. Below are examples of an effective and an ineffective behaviour:

> When a newly appointed Canadian manager began his job in Mexico, he was complimented by his employees for his mastery of the Spanish language. He explained that he had studied the language for six months intensively before coming to Mexico.
>
> The Japanese employees of an international company suggested to the foreign chief executive officer that a new company building should be dedicated on *taian*, a day of good luck. The CEO rejected the idea because it would have meant waiting another three weeks.

Cases

Cases are more detailed and complex than critical incidents. They illustrate a variety of cross-cultural problems in management within a single setting. The Maple Leaf Shoes Ltd case at the end of this chapter provides a good example of the challenges of working in a multinational, multiracial team.

Role-Play

Role-play is a semistructured activity. Participants are given a description of a situation with specific role instructions, but no script, forcing the participants to improvise their reactions to the setting. The results usually reveal personal values and biases that can be analyzed and discussed. A significant learning experience can be achieved if participants are asked to advocate a position that is contrary to their own beliefs. Studies indicate that this method is relatively effective in changing a person's attitudes.[68]

Simulation

Simulation is a common cross-cultural training method.

> A popular simulation game is *Ba Fa' Ba Fa'*.[69] Participants are divided into two cultures: Alpha and Beta. After learning the "rules" of their own culture, participants have to interact with

members of the other culture. Since the interaction rules for each culture are different, confusion and frustration, even hostility, result. These experiences are then discussed at a debriefing session.

It is unlikely that any single method will be sufficient to prepare an employee for the complex experiences that lie ahead when going abroad.[70] More likely, a combination of the methods described will be most effective, as people react differently to different methods. Whatever the method(s) chosen, effective diversity training aims to develop a **global mindset** for managers. Mindsets can be defined as the differing ways the subject at hand is perceived, understood, reasoned about, and acted upon by individuals. Persons with a global mindset are able to do the following:

- look at events in the context of the bigger, broader picture;
- recognize the diversity and inherent contradictory forces that exist in any situation;
- appreciate and even welcome ambiguity and surprises; and
- understand the need for change and establish processes that facilitate change.

A global mindset thus indicates the capacity to scan the world with a broad view—always looking for unexpected trends and opportunities to achieve the firm's and the individual manager's objectives.[71] In today's global marketplace, this is perhaps what distinguishes a leader from other organizations.

global mindset
The capacity to scan the world with a broad view, to value diversity, and to appreciate change.

Performance Appraisal

Employees in international operations need to be evaluated and require assistance in career planning. Performance appraisal is particularly difficult in **home-country evaluations** because the evaluator may be thousands of kilometres away and may not fully understand the challenges faced by the person being evaluated.[72] Geographical and cultural distance pose severe communication problems for expatriates and home-country managers. While improvements in information technology have significantly reduced the distance and time barriers, this has not always facilitated communication between an individual and his or her superior in the home office. A conscious effort to overcome this communication problem is often required as in the case of Dow Chemicals:

home-country evaluations
Performance appraisals carried out by an expatriate's home office.

> At Dow Chemicals, a senior manager in the same function is assigned to the role of godfather to an employee. The employee and his mentor (or "godfather") are expected to keep each other informed about performance and other matters that affect the person's career. The godfather then becomes involved with pay raises and locating a job in the home country when the employee is repatriated.[73]

When **host-country evaluations** take place, the evaluator has a better awareness of the constraints under which an expatriate works. However, even here problems exist. Local cultural values may bias one's perception of the manager's effectiveness.

host-country evaluations
Performance appraisals carried out by an expatriate's local (or host) office.

> For example, a manager who uses a participative or consultative style of leadership may be considered as "weak" or ineffective by members of a culture that in the past have been under autocratic leaders and expect their leader to make all important decisions.

Further, local evaluators may not possess adequate information about the larger organizational priorities. Even actions that are not appropriate from the point of view of local operations may be desirable for the long-term growth and success of the parent organization in the region.

Given this, the appraisals should attempt to balance the two sources of appraisal information.[74] While the host-country managers are in a good position to observe day-to-day behaviours of the employee concerned, the individual is still formally tied to the parent organization for his or her pay, career development, and other decisions. This factor should be kept in mind when designing an appraisal system.

Compensation Decisions

International compensation and protection go beyond pay and benefits. Pay is expanded to compensate for additional taxes, living expenses, and personal costs. Incentives may be added, especially for assignments to less desirable locations. Supplements may be given to cover extra costs of

TABLE 2	Profile of Senior-Middle-Level Managers at HBI					
	Experience (months)		Leadership Rating		% with Univ. Education	
Division	Male	Female	Male	Female	Male	Female
Administration	46.0	60.5	7.0	8.5	60	100
Marketing	43.7	44.5	7.7	8.0	50	100
Operations	45.5	11.0	7.2	9.0	92	100

had remained with the firm. This was slightly higher than the proportion for male management trainees. While some of these women had made it into junior and middle management, most of the women at these levels had over 15 years' experience. It had also begun recruiting males at entry level (nonmanagement cadre) before any other major financial institution. Several of these men had made it into supervisory and even junior management in the past few years.

Dickoff knew that she had to look into the numbers of other protected group members at HBI. HBI had hired some members of the other protected groups in the past six years, but only one—a visible minority person—had stayed with the firm. Mr. Johnson, in Marketing, had been with HBI for over

five years and had a BA in Psychology. There were no other protected group members at HBI.

Dickoff looked at the memo again. "Two weeks ... that's not a long time. I have to get cracking ..." she said to herself.

Discussion Questions

1. From the data provided, what conclusions can you form about the status of male and female employees (managerial and other) at HBI?

2. What suggestions do you have for Dickoff to diversify the workforce (managerial and other) at HBI?

Ensuring Health and Safety at the Workplace

Those who suffer (from work-related injuries) include not only the injured worker but his or her family and friends as well. Also, the impact of work injuries on human productivity reaches well beyond the workplace and includes a worker's ability to contribute to family and community.

Julian Barling and Michael Frone[1]

CHAPTER OBJECTIVES

After studying this chapter, you should be able to:

➡ *Describe* the major Canadian laws relating to occupational health and safety.

➡ *Assess* the traditional thinking with respect to occupational health and safety issues.

➡ *Explain* the new thinking with respect to employee rights relating to occupational health and safety issues.

➡ *Outline* the safety and health responsibilities of employers and employees.

➡ *Discuss* the impact of stress on employees and the workplace.

➡ *Summarize* the relationship between health and safety issues and human resource management.

CHAPTER 13

Even today, too many employees are injured at the workplace. Employers, supervisors, and employees must work together to reduce on-the-job injuries and illness. At the turn of the twentieth century, the thinking and attitudes of employers and employees toward accident prevention were quite different from today. Comments made during this period by employers illustrate this:

- "I don't have money for frills like safety."
- "Some people are just accident prone, and no matter what you do they'll hurt themselves some way."
- "Ninety percent of all accidents are caused by just plain carelessness."
- "We are not in business for safety."[2]

assumption of risk
The worker accepting all the customary risks associated with his or her occupation.

During this period, the courts used a legal expression, **assumption of risk**, meaning that the worker accepted all the customary risks associated with the occupation he or she worked in. Workers were instructed to protect themselves from special hazards such as extreme heat or molten and sharp metal. Furthermore, the attitudes of employees paralleled those of the employers. Scars and stumps on fingers and hands were often proudly referred to as badges of honour. The thought that safety was a matter of "luck" was frequently reflected in such statements as "I never thought he'd get it; he was always one of the lucky ones," or "When your number's up, there's not much you can do."

Over a four-year period in the early 1900s, records of one steel company show that 1,600 of its 2,200 employees lost time from work because of injury. In other words, 75 percent of this plant's entire workforce lost time from work because of accidents on the job.[3]

careless worker model
The early approach to safety in the workplace, which assumed that most accidents were due to workers' failure to be careful or to protect themselves.

shared responsibility model
A newer approach to safety in the workplace that assumes the best method to reduce accident rates relies on the cooperation of the employer and the employees (who may be represented by a union).

The early approach to safety at work used the **careless worker model**. It assumed that most accidents were due to workers' failure to be careful or to protect themselves. Even if training was provided to make workers more aware of the dangers in the workplace, this approach still assumed that it was mainly the worker's fault if an accident happened. A new approach, the **shared responsibility model**, assumes that the best method to reduce accident rates relies on the cooperation of the two main partners: the employer and the employees (who may be represented by a union).[4] Accident rates are reduced when the following occurs:

- management is committed to safety in the workplace;
- employees are informed about accident prevention;
- consultation between the employer and employees takes place on a regular basis (for example, the creation of a health and safety committee);
- there is a trusting relationship between the employer and staff; and
- employees have actual input into the decision-making process.

Over the last 25 years, there has been a growing emphasis on health and safety in the workplace. Strong union pressure, together with an increased public interest in greater corporate responsibility, has resulted in better and more comprehensive federal and provincial legislation and health and safety measures. Still, a survey of HRM professionals indicated that only 30 percent ranked health and safety as very important to HR strategy and only 16 percent rated wellness as very important. Furthermore, just 11 percent believed that wellness and disability management were very important to senior management.[5]

In Chapter 10, one of the topics was workers' compensation, which has as its aim the compensation of an employee for injuries suffered on the job. These programs have a serious defect: they are after-the-fact efforts. They attempt to compensate employees for accidents and illnesses that have already occurred. Many early supporters of these laws had hoped that costs would force employees to become more safety-conscious. Yet even with greater efforts by employers, accident rates continue to remain high. In addition, toxins and unhealthy work environments continue to create new health hazards.

A home building company and contractor were charged in Alberta after a workplace accident left a father of two paralyzed from the waist down. The employee severed his spinal cord after falling 6 metres through an open stairwell at a construction site. According to a spokesperson for Occupational Health (Alberta), "The prime employer is always on the hook. If there's another company directing work, they can also be accountable." The contractor who hired the employee (a personal friend for several years) said that the charges were an insult. "It was a tragic accident. If it could have been avoided, it would have been. That is why they're called accidents."[6]

A 19-year-old Ontario man who was distributing pay slips died at a Kanata construction site when he was crushed between a backhoe and a large excavator. The employee was new on the job but had worked for the employer the previous summer. The company president stated that they had been in business for 36 years and "this is the first time anything like this has happened. We've got a great safety record and we train our employees well. This is a family company. We really care for our employees."[7]

⊙ WORKPLACE INJURIES AND HEALTH HAZARDS

Injury Cost Calculator
www2.worksafebc.com/sc/
calculator/default.htm

Human Resources and Skills Development Canada estimates that about 4 Canadian workers die every working day from an occupational injury or disease and 1 in 48 workers is injured severely enough to miss at least one day of work a year (that is, there is a compensated time-lost injury every 21 seconds worked). Every minute worked costs the Canadian economy about $60,000 in compensation payments to injured workers. Workplace accidents and occupation-related illnesses cost about $7 billion annually in compensation payments alone. The total cost is more than $13.5 billion a year when indirect expenses are taken into account, and this does not include the incalculable social toll associated with workplace-related accidents.[8]

In Alberta, a farm group is arguing that the province needs to strengthen safety training and education in the province's second largest industry. The province, which has only four employees dedicated to farm safety, is reviewing a proposal to include paid farm workers under the Occupational Health and Safety Act. Since 2000, there have been more than 160 farm-related deaths in Alberta. Lorna Chandler, whose husband was killed in a farming accident, was shocked to learn that farm workers are not eligible for injury or death benefits. "I have to work full-time to support my children and myself. He wasn't covered by WCB."[9]

Accidents at work are caused by a complex combination of unsafe employee behaviour and unsafe working conditions. Several factors contribute to the complexity of managing safety in the workplace: the effects of some industrial diseases do not show up for years; employers may "clean up" a health or safety problem before an inspector arrives; companies may fail to monitor or disclose health risks; or employees may fail to follow safe practices at the workplace or engage in dangerous behaviour (such as drinking alcohol or taking drugs while on the job). Consider what happened at a City of Winnipeg facility:

Over 25 years ago, the City of Winnipeg sprayed the ceiling of a pool with asbestos to reduce noise. Over time, the ceiling tiles began to fall off and a construction company was hired to repair the ceiling. However, the city failed to warn the construction firm employees about the asbestos, which wasn't detected until construction was completed and one of the workers sent in a piece of the tile for testing. An earlier memo in the aquatic supervisor's files warned about the presence of asbestos but this information was either forgotten about or not read. The City of Winnipeg was fined $90,000 (at the time, the largest penalty ever imposed in Manitoba for a safety violation). While none of the construction workers have had medical problems to date, lung damage or cancer resulting from asbestos may not show up for years.[10]

It is also critical that organizations consider the safety of members of the public who enter onto company property.

**Association of Workers'
Compensation Boards of
Canada
Statistics on work-related
injuries**
www.awcbc.org/en/
statistics.asp

In November 2000, two 14-year-old children were killed during the Take Our Kids to Work Day at the John Deere plant in Welland, Ontario. The fatal accident occurred when they crashed the small vehicle they were driving. An inquest into the accident resulted in several recommendations including the use of an informed consent form containing health and safety messages and requiring the signature of both the student and a parent or guardian, a requirement that children are under adult supervision at all times, refusing to allow a student to operate a motorized vehicle, and a mandatory orientation program for student participants which addresses health and safety issues.[11]

Workplace Injuries

Data from the Association of Workers' Compensation Boards of Canada provide some perspective on the extent of workplace injury and illness in Canada. While the number of workplace injuries has levelled off in recent years, the direct cost of injuries (such as lost wages, first aid and medical

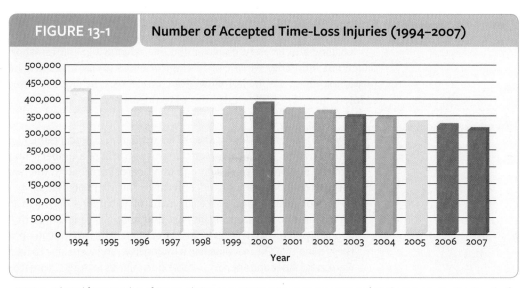

FIGURE 13-1 — **Number of Accepted Time-Loss Injuries (1994–2007)**

Source: Adapted from *Number of Accepted Time-Loss Injuries 1982–2007*: Association of Workers' Compensation Boards of Canada, "National Work Injuries Statistics program," http://awcbc.org/common/assets/nwisptables/lti_summary_jurisdiction.pdf

treatment, rehabilitation, and disability compensation) has not. Moreover, workplace injuries result in several indirect costs (including lost production, recruiting, selecting and training of new employees, damage to facilities and equipment) that are incurred by the employer.

Research on the number of time-loss injuries is provided in Figure 13-1 and information on the number of workplace fatalities is contained in Figure 13-2. There are approximately 1 million occupational injury claims each year and about 37 percent of these claims are accepted time-loss injuries warranting compensation. In 2007, 1,055 workers died as a result of a workplace injury (an average of about three workers each day of the year). April 28 is the National Day of Mourning to commemorate employees killed or injured on the job.

When considering the injury incidence, there are about 5.5 injuries for each 100 workers. When considering the gender of the worker, men were more than twice as likely as women to have a time-loss injury; when measured per 100 workers, 3.43 men and 1.55 women suffered a workplace injury. With reference to age, younger workers were most likely to be injured; the time-loss injury incidence

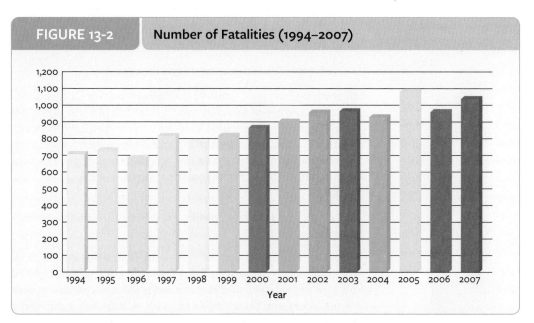

FIGURE 13-2 — **Number of Fatalities (1994–2007)**

Source: Adapted from *Number of Fatalities 1993–2007*: Association of Workers' Compensation Boards of Canada, "National Work Injuries Statistics Program," http://awcbc.org/common/assets/nwisptables/fat_summary_jurisdiction.pdf

rate per 100 workers was 2.93 for employees age 15 to 24, 2.59 for employees from age 25 to 54, and 1.91 for workers age 55 and over.[12]

Logging and forestry, construction, manufacturing, and transportation are among the most dangerous industries when considering time-loss injury rates. The most common type of injury involves strains and sprains, followed by contusions, crushing, or bruises. An employee is most likely to injure his or her back, while injuries to fingers and legs are the second and third most common body parts injured.[13]

> Reynold Hert, now head of the BC Forest Safety Council, remembers being a sawmill manager almost two decades ago and watching an operator of a lumber-trimming machine stick his hands into the equipment to straighten out a board. Fortunately, the man was not injured but could easily have lost fingers, a hand, or an arm. The man said that taking risks was necessary to avoid costly work disruptions. Hert told him to follow safety procedures and the man had to shut down his machine 90 times during his next shift to straighten out boards, reducing his productivity by about 33 percent. When Hert asked an engineer and maintenance employee to examine the issue, they found that the machine had a timing flaw, and were able to fix the problem. Last year, there were 21 fatalities and approximately 7,000 injuries in the B.C. forest industry. Hert recognizes that some of the 4,000 employers the industry may cut corners in order to keep bids as low as possible. According to Hert, investing in safety training may increase short-term costs but the contractors that don't pay attention to safety will find it hard to get work. "When you are staring at the spot where a person died, you realize it is preventable."[14]

Health Hazards

It is possible to combine the various health hazards into four categories:[15]

1. **Physical Agents.** Exposure to physical elements such as noise, temperature, lighting, vibrations, and radiation.

2. **Biological Agents/Biohazards.** Exposure to such natural organisms as parasites, bacteria, insects, viruses, and so on.

3. **Chemical Agents.** Exposure to chemical compounds or other harmful toxic substances.

4. **Ergonomically Related Injuries.** Caused by the work environment and including repetitive strain, stress, over-exertion/fatigue, and back injuries. In simple terms, *ergonomics* involves the "study of the relationship between people and their jobs." More specifically, ergonomics uses scientific principles to examine the nature of the task that the employee is doing, the equipment or machinery needed to carry out the task, and the environment in which the task is carried out. Some ways in which ergonomics has been applied include preventing back injuries, developing proper work positions, organizing the work space, and managing the light at work.[16]

Awareness of health hazards is very important:

> In 2007, the average Canada Post employee was off sick for almost 15 days (compared to the Canadian average of about 10 days). Letter carriers walk about 8 to 10 kilometres a day carrying a bag that weighs about 16 kilograms. Not surprisingly, this leads to hip, back, knee, and neck injuries. Fluctuations in weather, attacks by dogs, wasp attacks, and faulty stairs are some of the hazards confronting carriers. In Toronto, carriers were given ice cleats, which reduced the absenteeism rate by 18 percent. Still, about 17 percent of the Canada Post workforce was on modified duties.[17]

Moreover, a number of employers have given little (if any) thought to preparing for emerging health hazards:

> With the confirmation of the H1N1 virus (swine flu) in Mexico in early 2009, it is important for organizations to have a pandemic plan in place and policies relating to sick leave and time-off. Health Canada estimates that a major influenza pandemic would result in up to 35 percent of the workforce being unable to work at least half a day and absenteeism rates of up to 60 percent for a period of up to four weeks with people too sick to work or staying at home to care for family members. Many small and medium-sized firms have not considered the implications of a pandemic and their obligations to take reasonable steps to protect employees.

Even some large companies are unprepared for emergencies—a December 2008 survey revealed that half of Canadian companies with 500 or more employees do not have a pandemic plan and among those with a plan, only 1 percent have the 15 key components identified by experts.[18]

Younger Workers and Workplace Safety

Canadian Centre for Occupational Health and Safety
www.ccohs.ca/youngworkers/employers/

Across the country, there is growing emphasis on the health and safety of young workers. About one in seven young workers is injured on the job and approximately one-fourth of all workplace injuries involve employees in the 15 to 29 age group. The most common injuries affecting young workers include electrocution and machine injuries. According to the Canadian Centre for Occupational Health and Safety, a number of younger workers are not aware of their health and safety rights and responsibilities at the workplace.

Across the country, governments are trying to make young workers aware of workplace safety. For instance, Alberta has followed the lead of other provinces and introduced the Work Safe Alberta Video Contest in which high school students submit videos addressing issues relating to safe work. Each video must be less than five minutes long and the winner gets $1,000.[19]

Many employees fail to appreciate the wide range of health and safety hazards while performing a job. Consider, for example, a student working part-time as a cook at a small restaurant or fast food outlet. Potential hazards include exposure to biological and chemical elements, ergonomic issues, and a wide variety of safety risks including electrical shock, cuts, burns, collisions with coworkers, getting a limb or hair caught in a piece of equipment, and so on. The Canadian Centre for Occupational Health and Safety documents the risks associated with several jobs often performed by younger workers.

A 16-year-old Grade 10 student got his first summer job at Rona. On his second shift as a foot soldier in the lumberyard, he hopped on a forklift driven by a friend and coworker. The 2,300 kilogram forklift was not meant to carry passengers and consequently tipped over and crushed him. He died before paramedics could help him. An online safety campaign (www.bloodylucky.ca) focuses on young workers and the importance of safety at work.[20]

➤ FEDERAL AND PROVINCIAL SAFETY REGULATIONS

Each province and the federal jurisdiction have detailed legislation addressing health and safety, and most employers and employees are governed by provincial legislation. Although this chapter examines safety legislation at the federal level, students interested in learning about the specific legislation in their province can obtain such information by contacting the relevant provincial government department. Provincial government Web sites typically contain both the legislative provisions and detailed guides to understanding health and safety law.

At the federal level, the *Canada Labour Code* (Part II) details the elements of an industrial safety program and provides for regulations to deal with various types of occupational safety problems. All provinces and the territories have similar legislation. Part II of the *Code* establishes three fundamental employee rights:

1. The right to know about hazards in the workplace.
2. The right to participate in correcting those hazards.
3. The right to refuse dangerous work.

A key element of health and safety laws is the joint occupational **health and safety committee**, which is usually required in every workplace with 20 or more employees. These committees have a broad range of responsibilities, such as those described here for committees under federal jurisdiction:

- To meet at least once a month.
- To ensure adequate records are kept regarding accidents and health hazards.
- To investigate and resolve complaints by employees.
- To participate in investigations of health and safety-related injuries.
- To regularly monitor health and safety programs.
- To monitor records of injuries and illnesses.

health and safety committee
A group consisting of representatives of the employer and employees that meets regularly in order to reduce accident rates.

Health Canada Information about WHMIS
www.hc-sc.gc.ca/ewh-semt/ occup-travail/whmis-simdut/ index-eng.php

- To cooperate with safety officers investigating a complaint or accident.
- To develop, establish, and promote health and safety programs and procedures.
- To obtain information from the employer and government agencies concerning existing or potential hazards in the workplace.[21]

Some other relevant federal laws are the *Hazardous Products Act*, the *Transportation of Dangerous Goods Act*, and the *Canadian Centre for Occupational Health and Safety Act*.

The *Hazardous Products Act*, which already had a broad industrial application, was substantially amended in 1985. Its primary objective was the protection of consumers by regulating the sale of dangerous products. It is now an important part of the **Workplace Hazardous Material Information System** (**WHMIS**), which became law in 1988. It requires that suppliers label all hazardous products and provide a Material Safety Data Sheet (MSDS) on each one (see Figure 13-3 for class and division hazard symbols). In 1991, a WHMIS Enforcement Issues Subcommittee was formed to ensure that WHMIS is applied in all Canadian jurisdictions and there are ongoing discussions with other countries with the goal of having WHMIS become an international standard.[22]

FIGURE 13-3   WHMIS Class and Division Hazard Symbols

Class A—Compressed Gas

Class B—Flammable and Combustible Material
1 Flammable Gas   4 Flammable Solid
2 Flammable Liquid   5 Flammable Aerosol
3 Combustible Liquid   6 Reactive Flammable Material

Class C—Oxidizing Material

Class D—Poisonous and Infectious Material

1 Materials Causing Immediate and Serious Toxic Effects

2 Materials Causing Other Toxic Effects
3 Biohazardous Infectious Material

Class E—Corrosive Material

Class F—Dangerously Reactive Material

Source: *Hazardous Products Act*, June 1987. Reproduced with the permission of the Minister of Public Works and Government Services Canada, 2001.

The *Hazardous Products Act* also requires that an employer provide training to enable employees to recognize the WHMIS hazard symbols and understand the information in the MSDS. In addition to the symbol on it, the MSDS contains information on the properties and composition of the product or substance in question, the nature of the potential hazard that may result from misuse of the product (e.g., "Toxic Material—eye and skin irritant"), and suggested emergency treatment procedures.[23] Employees interested in learning more about particular hazards can obtain a great deal of information from the Internet.[24] Moreover, training will allow employees to take the necessary precautions to protect themselves:

> Employees of Citizenship and Immigration Canada in Sydney, Nova Scotia, refused to return to work after a mailroom supervisor died shortly after opening a package containing a brown, sandy material. The workers thought that the substance may have been anthrax and exercised their right to refuse to carry out dangerous work. Subsequent testing of the material indicated that it was just dirt and an autopsy revealed that the supervisor had died of natural causes.[25]

The *Transportation of Dangerous Goods Act* makes Transport Canada, a federal government agency, responsible for handling and transporting dangerous materials by federally regulated shipping and transportation companies. It requires that such goods are identified, that a carrier is informed of them, and that they are classified according to a coding system.

In the *Canadian Centre for Occupational Health and Safety Act*, the Parliament of Canada established a public corporation with the following objectives:

(a) to promote health and safety in the workplace in Canada and the physical and mental health of working people in Canada;
(b) to facilitate
    (i) consultation and cooperation among federal, provincial, and territorial jurisdictions, and
    (ii) participation by labour and management in the establishment and maintenance of high standards of occupational health and safety appropriate to the Canadian situation;
(c) to assist in the development and maintenance of policies and programs aimed at the reduction or elimination of occupational hazards; and
(d) to serve as a national centre for statistics and other information relating to occupational health and safety.[26]

The centre is supervised by a board of governors made up of representatives of the federal government, labour, and employers. Several hundred organizations are now connected electronically with the centre and have access to information relating to health and safety generally and to hazardous materials specifically.

The administration of safety programs comes mainly under provincial jurisdiction. Each province has legislated specific programs for the various industries and occupations within it. Across the country, provinces are following a trend of consolidating health and safety legislation and streamlining the enforcement of the relevant statutes by combining different agencies into one body.[27]

Safety Enforcement

In the federal jurisdiction, all industrial units are inspected at least once a year to confirm their safe operation. Depending on the unit's accident record and its size, the safety inspectors may visit more or less frequently. For the purposes of such inspection, a safety officer may at any reasonable time enter any property or place used in connection with the operation of any business or undertaking. To carry out their duties effectively, safety inspectors are given a wide range of powers. Section 141 of the *Canada Labour Code* (Part II) details these powers:

1. A safety officer may, in the performance of the officer's duties and at any reasonable time, enter any work place controlled by an employer and, in respect of any work place, may:
    (a) conduct examinations, tests, inquiries, investigations and inspections or direct the employer to conduct them;
    (b) take or remove for analysis, samples of any material or substance or any biological, chemical or physical agent;
    (c) be accompanied or assisted by any person and bring any equipment that the officer deems necessary to carry out the officer's duties;
    (d) take or remove, for testing, material or equipment if there is no reasonable alternative to doing so;

(e) take photographs and make sketches;

(f) direct the employer to ensure that any place or thing specified by the officer not be disturbed for a reasonable period of time pending an examination, test, inquiry, investigation or inspection in relation to the place or thing;

(g) direct any person not to disturb any place or thing specified by the officer for a reasonable period pending an examination, test, inquiry, investigation, or inspection in relation to the place or thing;

(h) direct the employer to produce documents and information relating to the health and safety of the employer's employees or the safety of the workplace and to permit the officer to examine and make copies or take extracts from those documents and that information;

(i) direct the employer or an employee to make or provide statements, in the form and manner that the officer may specify, respecting working conditions and material and equipment that affect the health or safety of employees;

(j) direct the employer or an employee or a person designated by either of them to accompany the officer while the officer is in the workplace; and

(k) meet with any person in private or, at the request of the person, in the presence of the person's legal counsel or union representative.[28]

Provincial laws provide similar powers to the safety officers under their jurisdiction.

In 2008, WorkSafeBC conducted more than 30,000 inspections and issued more than 60,000 orders. One company, EnCana Corp., was fined $150,000 (the highest ever assessed by WorkSafeBC), for failure to coordinate activities resulting in "a lack of first aid services and a lack of evacuation procedures that may have prevented the worker's death following the incident" in which a faller died after being struck by two hung-up trees. The second highest fine ($93,387) was to Delta Pacific Seafoods for repeated failures to ensure that employees operating forklifts wore seatbelts, highly visible clothing, and have lights on the forklifts.[29]

RESPONSIBILITY FOR HEALTH AND SAFETY

So far the focus in this chapter has been on the legal requirements for maintaining a safe and healthy work environment. It should be emphasized, however, that these must be seen as the minimum requirements for employers. A major purpose of occupational health and safety laws is to prevent injuries from happening.

An electrician working on a switchboard in a sewage treatment facility in Dartmouth, Nova Scotia, was badly burned due to electrical arcing resulting from the build-up of silver fines. The electrician successfully sued the Halifax Regional Municipality and was awarded a settlement of $90,000 for extreme pain and loss of his profession, $68,119 for lost income, and $1,713 in special damages. In finding the City liable, Nova Scotia Supreme Court Justice Gerald Moir stated that "the content of the duty of care to the employee included reasonably regular inspection and cleaning of the motor control centres. The failure to inspect or clean for years, if not decades, caused the silver fines to go undetected."[30]

Historically, it was believed that the responsibility for health and safety rested primarily with the employer. However, this view is changing. A number of jurisdictions have legislation requiring the establishment of joint health and safety committees or health and safety representatives. The requirement of establishing a joint committee varies among the provinces; for example, a committee may be required if a workplace has a minimum number of employees (typically 10 or 20 workers). The relevant legislation will outline the duties of the committee (such as maintaining records, conducting meetings, inspecting the workplace, and so on) and the makeup of the committee (number of members, employee representation on the committee, and so on).

There is also a focus on educating young employees about workplace safety. Several programs exist to make young workers aware of safety issues, to educate them about safety, and to provide information on rights and obligations under safety legislation.[31]

No law, by itself, can make a workplace safe. It is far more effective—and less costly in the long run—if the responsibility for safety becomes a concern for everyone: top management, supervisors, and employees.

A bus driver was attacked from behind and punched in the face and shoulder by an intoxicated female passenger while driving down a Winnipeg street. The union representing transit drivers has argued for the provision of face shields to drivers and training in self-defence. Winnipeg Transit has installed onbus video- and audio-recording devices and is revising employee training to include basic self-defence skills. While the use of face shields is being studied, there are concerns that they may impact on the ability of the drivers to operate buses and provide quality customer service.[32]

Many organizations neglect safety issues when designing orientation programs. A comprehensive safety orientation program will address several issues such as fire safety, smoking at the workplace, accident procedures, personal clothing, protective equipment, material and chemical hazards, waste disposal, safety representatives and the safety committee, occupational health, and the safety policy or policies in existence. It is important that employees understand the various issues and know how to respond in a crisis situation.[33]

Similarly, employers often fail to consider the safety issues related with shift work. According to the Institute for Work and Health, about 30 percent of Canadians work shift work (17 percent) or on call (13 percent). Shift workers may experience higher stress and may be prone to an increase in accidents and mistakes due to such factors as sleepiness and fatigue. In addition, shift workers may not eat properly and those on longer shifts may be at a greater risk resulting from exposure to health hazards. Of particular note is that shift workers are most at risk when they are driving home from work.[34]

Top Management. Top management must set policies and make concern for health and safety part of the organization's culture and strategy. This ensures that health and safety aspects will be considered whenever business decisions are made and training programs developed. A failure on the part of managers to pay attention to health and safety issues is being considered seriously by the courts in Canada. Consider the following cases:

Petro-Canada was fined $150,000 after a worker at a refinery was severely burned when steam and scalding water poured out of a tank. Shaw Cable Systems was fined $75,000 when an employee was severely burned after making contact with an unguarded and uninsulated powerline. The company failed to appoint a safety watcher and failed to provide safety equipment where there was a high-voltage hazard. TDL Spring and Suspension Specialists were fined $120,000 for violating safety regulations after an employee died when a sidebin on a recycling truck he was working on fell and crushed the worker. The sidebin had blocking pins to prevent the bin from falling but they were not used and the employer failed to provide proper tools to prevent the bin from falling.[35]

Some organizations, recognizing that they lack the internal expertise to address safety issues, are now outsourcing some health and safety needs. Options for such firms include hiring a health and safety expert on a part-time or contract basis or seeking the assistance of a firm that specializes in health and safety. While the cost of a health and safety consultant generally ranges from about $50 to $100 per hour, companies often save three to five times the cost of the consulting bill from lower experience ratings alone. According to safety consultant Geoff Wright:

We get invited to a workplace that has just bought all new work stations and ergonomic chairs. And they would have ended up saving all that money, and prevented musculoskeletal injuries, if they had just asked for advice beforehand. The earlier an ergonomist is brought in, the cheaper it is. For every dollar you spend at the design stage, it will cost you a hundred times more to fix it at the implementation stage.[36]

Do members of the public believe that senior management should be held more responsible for safety in the workplace? A poll of Canadians indicated that 85 percent would like to see corporate executives made criminally responsible for avoidable accidents that occur in the workplace.[37] In addition, the Bill C-45 amendments to the *Criminal Code* imposed a new duty on individuals and organizations. Section 217.1 of the *Criminal Code* states:

Everyone who undertakes, or has the authority, to direct how another person does or performs work or performs a task is under a legal duty to take reasonable steps to prevent bodily harm to that person, or any other person, arising from that work or task.

Safety gear, such as that worn by construction workers, is essential to reducing work injuries. Should penalties be imposed for not wearing it?

© Photodisc/Getty Images.

The first Bill C-45 conviction involved the death of an employee in Quebec:

> Transpave, a stone-paving manufacturer, was fined $110,000 for criminal negligence causing death after a 23-year-old employee was crushed by a machine being used with an unplugged safety device. The employee's mother was disappointed with the amount of the fine, saying that she expected a fine to be millions of dollars.[38]

Other countries are also developing legislation making safety violations a criminal offence:

> A British firm is the first company to be charged with corporate manslaughter under the United Kingdom's 2007 Corporate Manslaughter Act. A 27-year-old geologist was killed when the pit he was working near collapsed. Cotswold Geotechnical Holdings director Peter Eaton is charged with gross negligence manslaughter and could face a life sentence if convicted while the company could be fined an unlimited amount. An organization is guilty of corporate manslaughter if "the way senior management organizes or manages the business activities causes a person's death and amounts to a gross breach of the firm's duty of care owed to the person who died."[39]

Supervisors. As part of their management training, supervisors must become proficient in managing safety, which means knowing about health and safety laws, safety regulations, training in observing safety violations, and learning communication skills to convey the necessary information to their employees.

> A roofing company in Dartmouth, Nova Scotia, was fined $25,000 and a victim surcharge of $3,750 and a supervisor was fined $8,000 and a surcharge of $1,200 after they pleaded guilty to failing to reasonably ensure the health and safety of an employee who died after falling through a hole in the roof of a school. Plywood originally covering a skylight opening had been taken away and the employee fell through the foam insulation covering the hole. The company admitted that the accident could possibly have been avoided if more stringent safety procedures were in place. The accident was particularly hard on the employee's supervisor, who was a friend of the employee and got him employment with the company while they were working at the school.[40]

The ingredients of an effective safety training program include the following:

- accident investigation and analysis;
- communication skills and report writing;
- overview of legislative requirements;
- meeting with management and objective setting;
- organization and responsibility of joint health and safety committee;
- team problem-solving/problem-solving techniques;
- audits and inspections;
- principles of occupational health and safety; and
- ergonomics.

An issue that supervisors may have to deal with but feel uncomfortable about involves an employee's right to refuse unsafe work. It is important that the supervisor know the provincial legislation relating to work refusals and recognize the importance of taking every work refusal seriously (even if the supervisor believes that the work is safe).

> David Law, a lawyer specializing in health and safety believes that "whenever employees feel so concerned about their health risks that they would resort to such a drastic measure as refusing to work, the first thing you do is shut up and listen. To dismiss out of hand would be disrespectful about an issue that, in the employee's perception, could have serious, harmful consequences. People are often very poor judges of risk, but if we don't listen to them, what can they conclude except that we don't care."[41]

Employees. While employers are responsible for providing a safe work environment, and supervisors are responsible for the safety of their people in the workplace, employees are responsible for working safely. Employees must be trained to understand safety rules and how to operate equipment safely.

> Teenager Sarah Wheelan began working part-time at a deli counter of a supermarket. Standard practice was to clean the machines between each use. Rather than taking the machine apart and washing the blade, the practice was to hold one's hand to a spinning blade and clean the blade. While Wheelan did not lose any fingers or suffer any injuries, it took her about two months to get up the courage to confront her supervisor, concerned that she would look stupid or unable to handle the pressure and responsibility of the job. Her supervisor, a butcher, told her that new butchers would frequently nick themselves or lose a finger—that was just the nature of the job. One week later, Wheelan quit.[42]

It is also important that a system of enforcement is in place, understood, and followed. If necessary, progressive discipline has to be applied for violation of safety rules in the same way as for other rule violations.

A poll of 651 Canadian workers revealed that 32 percent had an accident requiring medical attention and 30 percent responded that they are afraid to report workplace accidents. In addition, 29 percent indicated that they know someone who has reported false claims and 27 percent stated that they know their employers are not reporting accidents.[43]

Good safety performance should be recognized and rewarded by managers. On the other side, unsatisfactory practices should be documented and corrected. Rewarding good performance is preferable. The objective of safety incentives should be to promote safety awareness and should therefore benefit as many workers as possible. Group awards may help to reinforce safety-consciousness through peer pressure.

In addition, the importance of safety training cannot be overemphasized:

> Thirty-two miners in Esterhazy, Saskatchewan, were trapped 1 kilometre below ground while a fire burned at the Mosaic potash mine. The miners stayed in "refuge stations" (chambers that can be sealed off and are equipped with food, water, and beds) and waited to be rescued. The situation ended with the rescue of the miners, and it was acknowledged that their safety training was invaluable. As one miner said, "Follow every rule you were taught, even if they don't make sense, and it all works out in the end."[44]

Implications for Human Resource Management

Human resource professionals should ensure consistent enforcement of all safety and health rules. If one worker is allowed to violate safety rules, other workers may follow—and if an accident results, the employer may be subject to penalties.

> In the United States, Wal-Mart was fined $2 million after a temporary maintenance employee was trampled to death by bargain-hungry shoppers. Although the company was not charged criminally, it will implement a new crowd-management plan.[45]

Health and safety law permits an employee to refuse to work when working conditions are perceived to be unsafe. In such instances, the employee should report the circumstances of the matter to his or her supervisor or to the supervisor's manager and to the safety committee in the firm. In most

Industrial Accident Prevention Association Information on accident prevention
www.iapa.on.ca

Young Worker Awareness Program An Ontario program on health and safety issues
www.youngworkers.ca

National Institute of Disability Management and Research Provides training and cortication for professional designation
www.nidmar.ca

jurisdictions, an employee with reasonable cause to believe that the work is unsafe will not receive any loss in pay for refusing to work.

When charged with a health and safety offence, a company's best defence is "due diligence," which means that the company took all reasonable steps to avoid the particular event. In examining the organization's behaviour, the court considers several factors including the magnitude of the risks involved and the nature of the potential harm, with a focus on the part of the safety program designed to prevent the accident in question. An effective safety program only helps establish due diligence—preparing a defence based on due diligence begins well before an accident ever happens.[46]

Health and Safety Audit

With increased attention on health and safety, more and more organizations are having a health and safety audit conducted. Some of these audits are voluntary and others are as a result of being targeted by government health and safety officials. While health and safety audits vary, they may include a review of the employer's occupational health and safety documentation (such as training records, manuals, etc.), a tour of the workplace, and interviews (and/or surveys) of front-line employees, supervisors, and senior management.

Of course, some employers may decide to take the risk and not comply with health and safety standards. As one lawyer stated:

> I think that there has always been a lack of enforcement and that has been well known and for many employers that is all they need to know. No matter how good the laws are, they know that they will not be enforced.[47]

However, a growing number of employers are being more proactive and rather than waiting for a provincial audit, they are either conducting internal audits or hiring consultants to assess the health and safety system. A number of provinces, such as Nova Scotia, provide detailed information on how to establish and evaluate a health and safety system.[48]

Safety Climate

> According to Dennis Locking, an HR manager for a Calgary road-building company, "Safety is all about the way you run your business. Wherever you see poor safety there is always a poor-run company. The unfortunate aspect is that the ownership isn't even aware that it is poorly run. If a company has a poor attitude toward safety, it makes us wonder if that attitude is indicative of other aspects of their business."[49]

Why should employers and human resource professionals be concerned with safety climate? There is growing evidence that safety climate is an important factor affecting safety knowledge and motivation. Neal and Griffin have developed a framework for conceptualizing safety climate (perceptions about the value of safety in an organization) and safety behaviour.[50] They assert that safety climate is an important factor affecting safety knowledge and motivation, which in turn impacts on safety behaviour (see Figure 13-4).

> Faced with one of the worst injury rates in the country, Saskatchewan has introduced a new educational campaign called "Mission Zero" in an effort to reduce workplace deaths and injuries. David Eberle, chair of the province's Workers Compensation Board, notes that safety requires that employers and employees work together with the same goal of a safe work environment. He believes that safety is "an attitude thing" with a culture where safety is out front.[51]

Neal and Griffin outline eight dimensions of safety climate. Organizational level dimensions include the following:

- management commitment to safety (Does management place a high priority on safety and communicate and act on safety issues effectively?)
- human resource management practices (To what extent are the HRM practices of the organization perceived to enhance safety?)
- safety systems (To what extent are hazard management systems, incident investigation and safety policies and procedures perceived to be effective and of high quality?)

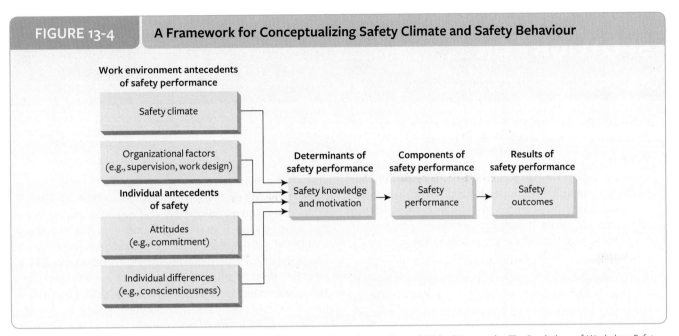

| FIGURE 13-4 | A Framework for Conceptualizing Safety Climate and Safety Behaviour |

Source: Andrew Neal and Mark Griffin, "Safety Climate and Safety at Work," in Julian Barling and Michael Frone, eds., *The Psychology of Workplace Safety,* Washington, DC: American Psychological Association, 2004, p. 17.

Local work group dimensions include the following:

- supervisor support for safety (including placing a high priority on safety and responding to safety issues)
- internal group processes (communication and support for safety issues within the group)
- boundary management (quality of communication between the group and other stakeholders)
- risk (are the work tasks perceived to be hazardous, dangerous, or unsafe?)
- work pressure (is workload perceived to exceed the employee's capacity of perform the work safely?)

The importance of top management commitment is critical:

A recent report to the House of Commons describes the "culture of fear" at Canadian National Railways. CN received a score of 1 out of 5 when evaluated on its efforts to implementing the safety management standards introduced as an update to the Railway Safety Act. Railway workers described how difficult it was to develop a safety culture when they were working in a culture of fear in which they feared reprisals and disciplinary action if they voiced concerns relating to safety. There was evidence that safety management systems were getting little more than lip service, thus increasing the risk of train derailments and other accidents.[52]

Downsizing and Safety

Another issue that is beginning to attract attention is the relationship between downsizing and employee safety. This is particularly relevant in light of the global financial crisis that began in 2008. The research evidence suggests that downsizing creates job insecurity which is strongly associated with low levels of job satisfaction. Low job satisfaction, in turn, is related to *safety motivation* (the motivation to perform a job in a safe manner) and *safety knowledge* (an understanding of safe operating procedures). When safety motivation is low, employees are less likely to comply with safety procedures and carry out their work in a safe manner (what is known as *safety compliance*). Finally, lower levels of safety compliance are associated with more workplace accidents. It is suggested that during a downsizing, employees concerned with keeping their jobs view productivity as more important than safety. However, in downsizings in which employees perceived that the safety climate was positive and the organization viewed safety as very important, the negative outcomes associated with job insecurity were not seen.[53]

SPOTLIGHT ON ETHICS
A Question of Safety

Consider the following situation and make a note of your answer on a separate sheet of paper.

You are a supervisor at a local dairy. Your job involves supervising employees who work in the dairy while another individual is responsible for supervising the employees who deliver milk to various stores. In the past six months, the labour market has been fairly tight and your company has been having problems attracting and retaining good delivery people.

Two weeks ago, the human resource management department hired a new milk delivery employee named Lucy Lynn. Lucy's job involves driving a milk van and making deliveries to grocery stores. By all accounts, Lucy is a very competent and reliable employee, and the human resource professional who hired her did so without any hesitation. Lucy is also the mother of one of your best friends. Lucy, who is 54 years of age, was recently downsized from her job as a delivery person at a large courier company.

Two days ago, you were invited to dinner at Lucy's house. Lucy commented on how much she was enjoying her new job

and how grateful she was to obtain employment so quickly. Lucy had recently gone through a messy divorce, and you were aware that she was having some financial problems.

Just after dinner, you went out to the kitchen and found Lucy sitting on a chair with her head resting on the kitchen table. When you asked whether she was okay, she replied that "Everything is fine. It's just that over the last few months, I have been getting really bad headaches and have had three or four dizzy spells. When my head starts whirling, I just need to sit down and put my head between my knees. it's no big deal—the dizziness passes in a few minutes. I'm telling you this in confidence. Please don't tell anyone at work. I can't afford to lose my job."

What are you going to do? Complicating the decision is that you know the company asks individuals who will be driving company vehicles to provide a detailed medical history. The questions include whether the individual has experienced dizzy spells and severe headaches. After completing the form, individuals are required to sign that they have answered the questions honestly and to the best of their ability.

WORKPLACE STRESS

American Institute of Stress
All you want to know about stress
www.stress.org

The term *stress management* is now part of the regular vocabulary of managers and employees, but what is "workplace stress"? *Workplace stress* is "the harmful physical and emotional responses that can happen when there is a conflict between job demands of the employee and the amount of control the employee has over meeting those demands."[54] Although high levels of stress are usually associated with poorer job performance, it should be emphasized that not all stress is harmful. Moderate levels of stress may actually increase workplace performance.

A recent National Health Survey revealed that 80 percent of Canadians went to work while sick or exhausted during the past year, with a number of participants indicating that they were concerned that missing work would be viewed negatively or they were unable to afford a day without getting paid. About 90 percent of respondents believed that stress-related mental health problems (such as burnout, depression, and anxiety) are increasing. It is estimated that mental health issues cost the Canadian economy about $30 billion annually.[55]

Health Canada has developed a self-assessment tool for measuring the costs of workplace stress. In a pretest of the instrument using an employer with 4,000 employees, the results indicated direct and indirect costs of stress to be $1,950,000. About 80 percent of this amount is associated with absenteeism and 20 percent with presenteeism. The total direct and indirect costs amount to 11,880 days lost.[56]

Senior management officials are also recognizing the importance of health issues on employee performance. A survey of more than 100 CEOs revealed that 66 percent placed burnout, stress, and other mental and physical health issues as the most important factor affecting workforce productivity.[57] It has been estimated that more than 50 percent of employee absences from work are stress-related, and the average duration of leave due to stress is four times greater than the amount of leave due to occupational injuries and industrial disease.[58]

The actual experience or the perceived threat of a corporate takeover, merger, downsizing, or plant closing, all of which could put large numbers of employees out of jobs, can lead to a variety of symptoms

Too much stress on the job can lead to employee burnout. What measures can an employer take to reduce stress? Can stress be avoided?

Dynamic Graphics/JupiterImages.

of stress that can harm employees' job performance. These symptoms involve both mental health and physical health. Persons who are stressed may become nervous, easily provoked to anger, and chronically worried about things.

There is a growing body of research indicating that stress may be associated with cardiovascular disease (in particular, among employees in psychologically demanding jobs that allow workers little control over the work process), musculoskeletal disorders (such as back injuries), psychological disorders (for example, depression and burnout), workplace injuries, suicide, cancer, ulcers, and impaired immune functions.[59] In addition, employer immunity from lawsuits as a result of contributing to the workers' compensation system is being eroded as more courts allow employees to sue their employers for stress resulting from a poisoned work environment.

Causes of Stress at Work

A model of job stress has been developed by the National Institute for Occupational Safety and Health.[60] According to the model, exposure to stressful working conditions (called "job stressors") can directly influence the health and safety of employees. However, the model also recognizes that individual and situational factors can intervene to strengthen or weaken the relationship between stressful job conditions and the risk of injury or illness. Examples of individual and situational factors include one's outlook or attitude, the presence of a support network of coworkers or friends, and the balance between work and family life. Although major distress can occur from only one stressor, usually **stressors** combine to affect an employee in a variety of ways until distress develops.

While almost any job condition may cause stress (depending upon an employee's reaction to it), there are, however, a number of job conditions that frequently cause stress for employees. Some of the major causes of workplace stress are outlined in Figure 13-5.

7

stressors
Stressful working conditions that can directly influence the health and safety of employees.

FIGURE 13-5	**Major Causes of Workplace Stress**

Factors Unique to the Job
- Workload
- Work pace/variety/meaningfulness of work
- Autonomy
- Hours of work/shift work
- Physical environment (noise, air quality, etc.)
- Isolation (physical or emotional)

Role in the Organization
- Role conflict/role ambiguity
- Level of responsibility

Relationships at Work
- Supervisors/coworkers/subordinates
- Threat of violence, harassment, and so on

Organizational Climate
- Participation (or nonparticipation) in decision making
- Management style
- Communication patterns

Career Development
- Under- or overpromotion
- Job security
- Career development opportunities
- Overall job satisfaction

Source: Based on "Major Causes of Workplace Stress." Adapted from L.R. Murphy, "Occupational Stress Management: Current Status and Future Direction," *Trends in Organizational Behavior*, 1995, pp. 1–14.

It is also possible to distinguish between *acute stressors*, which occur infrequently but are extremely stressful events (such as a major organizational change), and *chronic stressors*, which are the ongoing, daily problems and hassles that occur at work. While many wellness programs are aimed at chronic stress, organizations regularly ignore the impacts on employees associated with major organizational changes.

> With many employers cutting back on staff due to the global economic recession, employees are being told to work smarter, but there is evidence that many are not able to face the added pressure. One study found that as people work longer hours, their risk of injury and illness goes up. This includes workplace accidents, depression, hypertension, stress, cardiovascular disease, and chronic infections.[61]

Psychological stress tends to be highest in jobs where employees have high demands but little latitude in making decisions, with 40 percent of employees in such jobs scoring high on measures of psychological distress. In high-demand jobs that permitted greater employee involvement in decision making, 27 percent of employees scored high on psychological-distress measures. Work-stress scores were highest in blue-collar and service occupations and lowest among employees in professional and administrative positions.[62]

Poor supervision can cause stress. For example, the following stressful conditions are mostly created by poor supervision: an insecure workplace climate, lack of performance feedback, and inadequate authority to match one's responsibilities. Workers frequently complain in private about "bad bosses."

> A study of workers in Finland revealed that a bad boss may be hazardous to employee health. Employees who perceived that they were being treated fairly at work by their supervisors had a 30 percent lower risk of coronary heart disease compared with coworkers who did not believe that their supervisors treated them fairly.[63]

A general and widely recognized cause of stress is *change of any type*, because it requires adaptation by employees. Change tends to be especially stressful when it is major, unusual, or frequent. One particular type of change that dominated the 1990s and is making a comeback with the global recession is *organizational* downsizing. In many organizations, the "survivors" of workplace change are being asked to work longer hours and do more with limited resources. Working in such an environment may increase both employee stress and the probability of having an accident. As well, downsizing may have an impact on an employee's family. Research suggests that the job loss of a parent affects their children. Perceptions of the job insecurity of a parent were associated with negative attitudes toward work and lower grades on exams.[64]

One study of stress in the Canadian workplace indicated that about 47 percent of Canadian workers experience a great deal of stress at work and 41 percent believe that their company does not do enough to help manage workplace stress. About 64 percent of workers reported feeling anxious or irritable, 42 percent experienced insomnia, and 11 percent reported booking off sick more often as a result of stress. When asked to indicate the most common factors contributing to stress, participants indicated that workload (43 percent of respondents), personal financial responsibilities (35 percent), work–life balance (32 percent), the work environment (26 percent), and job security (23 percent) were the major contributors.[65] Consider the impact of stress on Canadian call centres:

> A study of call centre employees revealed that employees in the industry suffer higher rates of stress and emotional difficulty than workers in other industries. The call centre industry currently employs about half a million Canadians. It is estimated that among 100 recent hires at a call centre, 14 percent may experience high levels of stress and 10 percent may experience high levels of depression. Each day about 10 percent of employees call in sick, turnover may run as high as 50 percent or more a year, and the cost of training a replacement employee is more than $6,000. As observed by Karen Seward, senior vice-president at Shepell-fgi, "It doesn't take long to do the math to figure out the impact of this on a company's profits."[66]

In a study on stress and productivity, 90 percent of employers indicated that their employees are experiencing greater workloads. The results showed that 68 percent of employers reported increased absenteeism, 64 percent indicated that "emotional tension is prevalent among employees," and 61 percent stated that productivity is declining. However, most employers have no plans to deal with mental health concerns—less than 10 percent of organizations have managers with training to identify and address mental health issues despite a clear link between work overload, absenteeism, and productivity.[67]

Burnout

burnout
A condition of mental, emotional, and sometimes physical exhaustion that results from substantial and prolonged stress.

Burnout is a condition of mental, emotional, and sometimes physical exhaustion that results from substantial and prolonged stress. It can occur for any type of employee, whether one is a professional employee, secretary, or labourer. There is growing concern over what has become known as *presenteeism* which describes an employee who is able to come to work but is inhibited from achieving optimal levels of productivity due to ongoing health issues.[68] One employee described a burned-out associate in the following way: "His body is here today, but his mind stayed home." Employers cannot merely ignore requests by an employee for help:

> Suzanne Zorn-Smith, a 21-year employee of a Canadian bank, suffered from burnout due to the heavy workload placed on her. She sought EAP counselling and then applied for short-term disability, citing exhaustion, inability to focus, and feeling overwhelmed. The bank took the position that the injury was not totally disabling and demanded that she return to work on a specified date or they would assume that the employment relationship was over. Zorn-Smith did not return to work by the specified date and sued the bank for wrongful dismissal. The court found that she was entitled to a 16-month notice period (or compensation in lieu of notice) and also awarded $15,000 for intentional infliction of mental suffering. The court noted that the bank was aware of the staffing shortage, knew about Zorn-Smith's burnout and requests for relief, and chose to do nothing about the situation.[69]

With respect to burnout, the human resource department's role is a proactive one to help employees prevent burnout before it occurs. For example, the human resource department can train supervisors to recognize stress and rearrange work assignments to reduce it. Jobs may be redesigned, staff conflicts resolved, counselling provided, and temporary leaves arranged. Weeks or months of rest, reassignment, and/or treatment may be required before recovery occurs. Some emotional or health damage can be permanent. Preventive strategies can yield impressive results:

> One large paper and forest products firm was faced with problems of employee absenteeism, a large number of accidents, and poor employee morale. After trying other methods that did not yield any great success, the company decided to make a counselling program available to all its employees. Most counselling problems related to the job, alcohol and drug abuse, marital relations, family problems, and personal finances. One year after the counselling program was started, there was a 43 percent reduction in absences and a 70 percent reduction in the number of accidents.

Stress and Job Performance

Stress can be either helpful or harmful to job performance. When there is no stress, job challenges are absent and performance tends to be low. As stress increases, performance tends to increase, because stress helps a person call up resources to meet job requirements. It is a healthy stimulus to encourage employees to respond to challenges. Eventually it reaches a plateau that represents approximately a person's top day-to-day performance capability. At this point, additional stress tends to produce no more improvement. Finally, if stress becomes too great, performance begins to decline, because stress interferes with it. An employee loses the ability to cope, becomes unable to make decisions, and is erratic in behaviour.

SPOTLIGHT ON HRM

Parents' Job Anxiety Wreaks Havoc on Children

A Queen's university researcher has documented a relationship that HR specialists have long recognized—children absorb the job anxieties of their parents. Business professor Dr. Julian Barling surveyed 154 commerce undergraduates and their parents and found that children's perceptions of their parents' job insecurities affect their attitudes about work and jobs and, indirectly, their grades.

Barling, an expert in work and family relationships at the Kingston, Ontario, university, said that he undertook the study because "we need to be aware of how the next generation is being affected by current insecurity in the workplace." In his study, he found a close correlation between students' perceptions and their midterm grades. Barling considers school performance to be a matter of great concern because "how children perform at school affects their self-esteem and how they are perceived by peers, teachers and families. And, in the long term, grades obtained will influence the educational and occupational opportunities open to them."

In a companion study ... in the *Journal of Applied Psychology*, Barling writes that children's perceptions of their parents' job insecurity also affect their beliefs and attitudes toward work. He notes that the waves of layoffs in both the public and private sectors in the last decade may produce "a generation of young people with pre-existing negative work beliefs and attitudes which may not be amenable to change."

Parents Anxious over More Than Security

Barling is not alone in his observations. "Professor Barling has quantified something I have been observing for well over a decade—children are sponges and readily absorb their parents' anxiety and ambivalence about work," said Barbara Moses, president of BBM Human Resource Consultants, Inc., and author of *Career Intelligence*. She added that parental anxieties extend beyond job insecurity to include dissatisfaction with promotions, wages, workload, and perquisites.

"Is it any wonder that children are ambivalent? They see their parents tired and complaining, or more likely, they rarely see their parents. They grow to feel their parents are abused by work, and work denies them access to their parents. They see their parents as victims of their jobs and careers. And, despite these sacrifices, their employers treat them badly and let them go."

HR's Role Goes Beyond EAPs

Moses said HR professionals have a role to play in reducing employee anxiety and the communication of this anxiety to sons and daughters. "At a minimum, HR should ensure that corporate communications do not unnecessarily incite job anxiety among employees," she said. "In addition, HR can promote career management among employees. Career support services reassure employees that they will be okay even if they lose their jobs. Encourage them to talk the language of employability rather than job security."

The assistance can be provided through support groups and Employee Assistance Programs, although Moses and others say EAPs are insufficient because they are reactive rather than proactive, and fail to address the needs of employees who do not identify themselves as anxious.

Sam Klarreich, president of the Berkeley Centre for Wellness, described the success of a support group he was involved with a few years ago at Imperial Oil. "We set up a group to help employees deal with on-the-job stress. We brought guest speakers, reprinted and shared articles on stress, held group discussions, published a newsletter. By working together the group members learned better ways to cope with stress. The program was such a success the group grew from an initial membership of 20 to over 200."

There are several solutions to the problem of workplace stress. Curative solutions try to correct the outcome of stress, while preventive solutions attempt to change the cause of stress:

Some employers, such as the Canadian Imperial Bank of Commerce, are setting up back-up child care centres to help employees when an emergency arises and the regular child care provider cannot care for the children. Benefits include increased employee commitment, lower absenteeism, increased productivity, and a recognition by all employees that workers with children are not going to be stressed because of an emergency child care issue.[70]

In terms of *curative measures*, some employers give employees the opportunity to relax through such activities as aerobic exercises, yoga, and meditation. Some companies have

FIGURE 13-6	Actions to Reduce Stress

- Ensure that an employee's workload is compatible with the individual's capabilities and resources.
- Design jobs to provide meaningful opportunities for employees to use their skills.
- Clearly define employee roles and responsibilities.
- Provide workers with the opportunity to participate in decision making.
- Improve the communications process.
- Increase opportunities for social interaction among employees.
- Develop appropriate work schedules.
- Train managers and employees to be sensitive to the symptoms of stress.
- Establish a stress management policy.

Source: National Institute for Occupational Health and Safety, *Stress at Work.*

counselling professionals on staff or employ an external consulting service that provides assistance in diagnosing the causes of stress and developing ways to cope with it.

With regard to *preventive measures,* there are different approaches to dealing with stress at the workplace. First, organizations can establish stress management training sessions and EAP assistance to help workers deal with stress. Second, some organizations are looking at improving working conditions in order to reduce stress at work—the employer needs to identify stressful situations and design strategies to reduce or eliminate the stressors. In managing stress, it may be necessary to bring in outside experts.[71]

Management should look at the structure of the organization and the design of jobs. Several Canadian organizations have developed programs that provide workers with more diversified tasks, greater control over decisions that affect their work, and a chance for wider participation in the overall production process. Figure 13-6 shows some of the specific actions that the human resource department should take to reduce employee stress and burnout.

The Stress Audit

Human resource managers must be sensitive to the many possible sources and causes of stress at the workplace. It is possible to evaluate the extent of dysfunctional stress by performing a stress audit, which assists in identifying the causes of stress.[72] The stress audit asks the following questions:

- Do any individuals demonstrate physiological symptoms?
- Is job satisfaction low, or are job tension, turnover, absenteeism, strikes, or accident proneness high?
- Does the organization's design contribute to the symptoms described?
- Do interpersonal relations contribute to the symptoms described?
- Do career-development variables contribute to the symptoms described?
- What effects do personality, sociocultural influences, and the nonwork environment have on the relationship between the stressors—individual careers, interpersonal relations, and organizational design—and stress?

Fitness and Employee Wellness Programs

Fitness programs, also called "wellness" or "lifestyle programs," have become quite popular in organizations and have been shown to have a positive impact on reducing stress and absenteeism and increasing productivity. Many employees want access to health promotion programs in the workplace and the National Wellness Survey Report indicates that about 90 percent of Canadian organizations offer some type of wellness initiative (up from 44 percent in 1996). However, only 15 percent of employers have an operating plan for wellness programs, less than 30 percent evaluate their wellness initiatives, and less than 50 percent of initiatives have senior level management support. Moreover, many organizations lack a comprehensive wellness program (as opposed to single-issue initiatives like smoking cessation).[73]

A study on smoking at work indicated that while many smokers don't think having a cigarette at work bothers many people, about 52 percent of employees who work with smokers do not like it. In addition, smokers take an average of three breaks a day, compared with about two breaks for nonsmokers. In addition, a new Statistics Canada report indicates that obesity is associated with increased absenteeism, lower productivity at work, higher job stress, and a perception of receiving less support from coworkers and supervisors.[74]

How effective are fitness programs? While most evaluations have come from large American corporations with comprehensive programs, the evidence indicates that such programs:

- improve employee health
- decrease health care costs
- improve employee satisfaction
- decrease absenteeism and turnover
- improve corporate image

A review of 73 published studies revealed an average of $3.50 to $1.00 savings-to-cost ratio in reduced absenteeism and health care costs. A meta-analysis of 43 studies indicated an average reduction of 28 percent in sick leave absenteeism and a 30 percent reduction in workers' compensation and disability management claims associated with health promotion.[75] Specific programs also show significant benefits:

A study of eight organizations in Halifax demonstrated the benefits of wellness programs. A survey of 2,700 employees from the 8 participating employers showed that 61 percent of the respondents had at least two modifiable cardiovascular risk factors such as high blood pressure, obesity, smoking, or lack of physical activity. For every dollar spent on wellness, an employer saved $1.64. For employees with three to five risk factors, the saving is $2.04, and for smokers, the saving is $3.35. Returns are greater for a workforce made up primarily of blue-collar workers.[76]

More and more companies are promoting health by providing health programs. Would the money be better spent by paying bonuses that serve to motivate employees?

JupiterImages.

In evaluating the success of wellness programs, employers are focusing on positive feedback from participants (86 percent of employers), good participation (64 percent), improved employee morale (61 percent), and reduced absenteeism (45 percent). Only 19 percent of organizations were using a positive return on investment as a measure of success. When asked to identify health risk concerns, the three biggest issues included poor stress management skills (69 percent), lack of exercise by employees (65 percent), and an inability to balance work and family issues (59 percent).[77] Consider the extensive program at Vancouver International Airport Authority (a 2007 Psychologically Healthy Workplace Award Winner):

At the Vancouver International Airport Authority, the employee Fitness and Balance Wellness Program has a 50 percent participation rate (up from 17 percent in 2001). Employees can participate in "lunch and learn" sessions dealing with such topics as nutrition and stress, health assessments, and dental checkups. The organization has an Employee Assistance Program and parents can take up to two years' leave in addition to maternity or paternal leave to care for children. Although the number of employees has increased since 1999, the number of days lost due to injury has declined from 222 to 32, the average attendance rate is 97 percent, and the turnover rate is less than 6 percent.[78]

Although labour unions have been strong supporters of health and safety initiatives, organized labour has not always been an advocate of wellness programs: unions are often skeptical about employer motivations behind wellness programs and there is a concern that employee information may be collected and tracked to be used in attendance management. However, a study by the *Canadian Labour and Business Centre* revealed that union respondents were more likely to perceive that employee stress, work/family pressures, and workplace violence were more of a problem today compared with two years ago. The number of wellness and healthy workplace initiatives was noticeably higher when the labour–management relationship was better:[79]

> According to Lydia Makrides of the Atlantic Canada Health and Wellness Institute, "what happens is when we [wellness providers] approach the employer, the union is often ignored. The union finds out about the initiative after the fact, and therefore there's no buy-in."[80]

OTHER CONTEMPORARY SAFETY ISSUES

Workplace Security

The events of September 11, 2001, have increased employer and employee awareness of workplace security issues. This has led to a reassessment of security policies used to make workplaces safe. In addition to terror concerns, other issues include preparations for a disaster (such as an earthquake or flood) and access to workplace property.

> In high-risk workplaces such as airports, employers are considering using retina scanners as a means of identification because the scanners are both fast and reliable. Other organizations rely heavily on swipe cards, the use of video cameras, and a sign-in procedure for any visitors entering the workplace.[81]

A number of organizations have developed emergency plans (such as evacuation of buildings), implemented training programs associated with security issues, assessed the work site for hazards and security shortcomings, and established safety competencies for managers and supervisors.[82] However, not all employees feel secure at work:

> Incensed by the scandals in the banking industry and huge government bailouts, customers in Ireland have spat at and threatened bank employees with physical violence. The union representing the employees reports that bank workers are facing growing abuse and are reluctant to go out at night or identify themselves as bank workers.[83]

Sick Building Syndrome (SBS)

Sick building syndrome is used to describe situations in which employees experience acute health and comfort effects that appear to be linked to the length of time spent in a building but no specific illness or cause can be identified. However, the term *building-related illness* is used when symptoms of diagnosable illness are identified and are attributable directly to airborne contaminants in a building.[84]

People spend up to 90 percent of their lives indoors and a growing number report becoming sick while working in a particular building. Symptoms range from headaches to dizziness to nausea to eye, ear, and/or throat irritation, to allergic reactions. Sick building syndrome may be caused by major combustion pollutants (caused, for instance, by malfunctioning heating systems), biological air pollutants (such as mites, mould, and dander), volatile organic compounds (including pesticides, solvents, and cleaners), and heavy metals (such as lead). Human resource professionals should take proactive steps to prevent sick building syndrome—it is estimated that SBS will cost about $1 billion annually in health costs and considerably more in lost productivity and employee stress.[85] The impact of sick building syndrome on an employee's life can be devastating:

> Jim Crane was the general manager of a well-known hotel chain. One day, he received a call about a leak in one of the hotel rooms. He and the hotel's engineer started ripping out the wall and discovered that the Aspergillus strain of mould was growing in a number of other rooms and had made its way into the ventilation and vending-machine areas. For a year, Crane worked on

removing the mould, unaware that he was inhaling the mould's toxic fungal spores. He developed chronic inflammation of his lungs and now must take 17 drugs every day.[86]

Workplace Violence

One area of safety management that has been neglected to some extent concerns workplace violence. However, a scan of newspapers and television reports indicates that workplace violence is not a rare event. In this era of restructuring and productivity improvement, there have been a number of accounts of terminated employees returning to the workplace and injuring or killing other employees. A study by the International Labour Organization ranked Canada fourth in terms of workplace aggression (with Argentina first followed by France and England/Wales).[87] Several provinces have introduced or are in the process of introducing legislation addressing workplace violence.[88]

> A study of on-the-job abuse by patients revealed that 46 percent of male nurses and 33 percent of female nurses reported being physically assaulted by a patient in the previous year. In addition, 55 percent of male nurses and 46 percent of female nurses had been emotionally abused.[89]
>
> At the Toronto East General Hospital, there are about two "code whites" a week, indicating a violent situation within the hospital. Six months ago, the hospital introduced a zero-tolerance approach to workplace violence and has reduced the average security response time from 2.5 minutes to 59 seconds. What is making the difference is a small wireless device that can be clipped on a shirt or worn on a lanyard. A double-click of the device opens up a two-way communication between the employee and every security officer in the building. It saves the employee from having to find a phone, make a call, and explain what is happening and where the incident is occurring.[90]

Evidence from the United States indicates that violence is the third-highest cause of all workplace deaths and the leading cause of workplace death for women. In terms of deaths per 100,000 workers, U.S. evidence indicates that the highest-risk jobs (in order of risk) include taxi drivers, law enforcement officers, hotel clerks, gas station attendants and security guards, liquor store workers, detective or protective service workers, and jewellery store workers. The jobs with the greatest risk of workplace violence are police officers, security guards, taxi drivers, prison guards, bartenders, mental health professionals, gas station attendants, and convenience or liquor store clerks.[91] Measures aimed at preventing or reducing the incidence of workplace violence include an anti-violence/zero-tolerance policy, self-defence training, and safety and security measures. Some employers are developing extensive programs to address safety concerns and workplace violence:

> At McDonald's Restaurants of Canada, personal safety is a major part of the management and staff training program, with the use of role-plays so that employees can anticipate and respond to potentially dangerous situations. In addition, the layout of restaurants and unobstructed and well-lit parking lots also contribute to increasing safety.[92]

Research suggests that workplace conflict is increasing, with employees dealing with the public (such as sales clerks and teachers) at greatest risk. In addition, many managers have less time to meet with employees and observe warning signs that the employee is having difficulty coping.[93]

What are the most common incidents of violence at the workplace? Research from the United States indicates that verbal threats are most common (accounting for 41 percent of the incidents), followed by pushing or shoving (19 percent), robbery (9 percent), fist-fighting (9 percent), and stalking (9 percent).[94] Moreover, about 29 percent of organizations report having a policy/prevention program on workplace violence and 21 percent report doing some training relating to workplace violence.[95]

A recent study entitled *Violence and Aggression in the Workplace* involved a survey of Canadian CEOs. The results indicated that the three most common incidents of workplace violence were loud screaming or yelling, destruction of employer property during a fit of anger, and throwing a telephone, pen, or some other office object in anger. There was a slight increase in workplace violence when comparing the 2004 and 2007 results. Based on CEO perceptions, the top three contributors to workplace violence were consumption of drugs and alcohol, lack of management authority, and poor morale.[96]

With the growth of the Internet, one of the most recent threats at the workplace involves "cyberstalking," which is the use of electronic communications to harass or threaten another individual.

Some organizations now use software that is designed to assist in "profiling" potentially violent employees or potential new hires, but opinion is divided as to the effectiveness of this technique:[97]

> Although one might expect that careful selection of new hires may be an important step in reducing workplace violence, a recent study places more attention on situational factors and poor management. According to Julian Barling, co-author of a recent study entitled *Supervisor-Targeted Aggression*, "in trying to understand why people behave aggressively in the workplace, we should give primary responsibility to situational rather than personal considerations." Barling believes that in creating a healthy work environment where workers are treated fairly, quality supervision is important to reducing workplace violence. Moreover, when an act of workplace violence does occur, he suggests looking inside the workplace for a potential cause rather than assuming that the worker has a psychological problem.[98]

In workplace violence lawsuits, courts in the United States are placing a much heavier onus on employers to take reasonable care in making sure that the workplace is safe. Factors considered by the courts include the crime rate in the neighbourhood, the security measures in place at the business, the lighting of the buildings and grounds, the architectural design of the buildings, and recommendations from security consultants:

> A store manager at a shopping centre in the United States was robbed, beaten, and suffered permanent brain damage. In a lawsuit by the victim's family against the shopping centre, it was shown that a security consultant recommended a 24-hour foot patrol of the property because of the difficulty in controlling access to the various stores. The shopping centre owner decided to have a guard patrol the mall on a part-time basis using an automobile. The lawsuit was settled out of court for $9.25 million.[99]

It is estimated that workplace violence costs more than $8 billion a year, with costs including medical care, disability and worker's compensation, higher insurance rates, negative public relations and company image, consulting fees, greater security measures, and lower morale and productivity. Experts point out that under Bill C-45, employers and executives may be criminally liable for failing to take reasonable steps to prevent workplace violence and accidents. Proactive suggestions include careful employee selection, development of a comprehensive policy on workplace violence, employee training, assessment of the likelihood of workplace violence, and rigorous security standards.[100]

> In September 2005, an Ottawa teenager was killed shortly after midnight while walking home after her shift had ended at a Wendy's restaurant. Emile Therien, President of the Canada Safety Council, stated that getting workers home safely should be an employer responsibility. "You are asking very young kids—most of them under 19—to leave these places at very late hours when there's no public transportation. There's no assurance that they'll get home safely." While some organizations are reviewing their policies, McDonald's already has a program to ensure that an employee has a pre-arranged ride home or door-to-door transportation with a manager, coworker, or parent. If this is not possible, transportation by taxi will be arranged and paid for by McDonald's.[101]

Ergonomics

An area of health and safety that is attracting more attention is **ergonomics** (also known as *human factors engineering*). Ergonomics focuses on the interaction between employees and their total working environment.[102] An ergonomics program seeks to ensure that the physical and behavioural characteristics of the employee are compatible with the work system (including methods of work, machines and equipment, the work environment, and the workplace or work station layout).[103]

ergonomics
The study of relationships between physical attributes of workers and their work environment to reduce physical and mental strain and increase productivity and quality of work life.

While a number of organizations wait until employees complain about the work system or sustain an injury, proactive employers aim to ensure that the work system is compatible with employees; recent research indicates that about 33 percent of employers provide some type of wellness initiative associated with ergonomics.[104] Consultants specializing in ergonomics can assist organizations in the design and implementation of the work system.

> New software called Ergowatch evaluates the risk of repetitive-stress injuries in workers' hands and arms. The software can evaluate the load or impact of a task and estimate the potential

International Ergonomics Association All you want to know about ergonomics
www.iea.cc

physical demands as well as the risk of injury. In addition, the software examines risk factors over the whole day because the probability of injury is also related to fatigue.[105]

Two common types of injuries that may be reduced by the application of ergonomic principles are (1) overexertion and lower back injury and (2) repetitive-strain injuries (RSI), which may include cumulative trauma disorder (CTD), overuse syndrome (OS), and musculoskeletal injury (MSI). Repetitive strain injuries are caused by repeated actions resulting in muscle or skeletal strain.

Research suggests that the most rapidly growing category of workplace illnesses involves ergonomic disorders. In 1981, when the IBM PC was introduced, 18 percent of all illnesses reported to the Occupational Health and Safety Administration in the United States involved repetitive-strain injuries. Three years later, that figure had grown to 28 percent, and to 52 percent by 1992. Now it is estimated that about 70 percent of all occupational illnesses will be repetitive-strain injuries and $1 of every $3 spent on compensation costs is associated with improper ergonomics.[106]

The treatment of repetitive-strain injuries is complex and varied. Some of the approaches used include physical treatments (such as physiotherapy or chiropractic treatments), postural treatments (often aimed at correcting bad habits relating to posture), relaxation (such as meditation), exercise and stretching, acupuncture, and cognitive behavioural therapy (with a focus on coping with pain).[107]

A properly designed work station can play a major role in reducing workplace injuries. The key factors in designing an ergonomically sound work station relate to the layout of the work station, the characteristics of control and display panels, seating arrangements at the work station, and lighting quality and quantity.[108] While a number of organizations have moved to an open-office concept, workers complain about such things as reduced privacy and noise spillover:

> One woman at a public relations firm could not concentrate while a coworker in an adjoining cubicle completed the ritual of clipping his nails. Another employee complained about the lack of privacy when she spoke on the phone to a former boyfriend, while a different employee lamented hearing a coworker blurt out a crude phrase to tell a client he had to use the washroom.[109]

One group of employees often overlooked in terms of ergonomics is teleworkers. It is estimated that almost 1.5 million Canadians are involved in telework, but many employers do not have policies, procedures, and training for employees working from their homes. As a consequence, teleworkers may suffer from repetitive stress, eye strain, and back injuries. Employers should be aware of their obligation to provide a safe work environment and balance the requirement of due diligence with employee privacy concerns.[110]

AIDS

RPC 3 & 7

Canadian AIDS Society Information on AIDS
www.cdnaids.ca

A chapter on occupational health and safety would be incomplete if no reference were made to the *Acquired Immune Deficiency Syndrome* (AIDS) or the *Human Immunodeficiency Virus* (HIV) that causes AIDS. By 2007, an estimated 73,000 individuals in Canada were living with AIDS.[111] Both HIV and AIDS have a potentially immense impact on the human resource function.[112]

AIDS and Human Resource Management

Consider the following case that occurred more than two decades ago:

> Ron Lentz was hired January 4, 1988, by the Toronto Western Hospital as a nurse and fired on January 23. He complained to the Ontario Human Rights Commission that he was discriminated against because he was HIV-positive. The commission agreed and negotiated with the hospital a settlement that included reinstatement, about $14,000 in back pay, $1,400 in benefits, $5,000 in legal fees, restoration of seniority, and a clean employment record.[113]

This case points to challenges that human resource managers have to face if one of their employees is HIV-positive, develops AIDS, or if a job applicant happens to mention that he or she has an HIV-related infection. It is a breach of human rights laws to discriminate against that person.

But what if colleagues refuse to work with that person? What if a supervisor expressed concern about the employee's contact with customers? To be prepared for such questions, each employer should establish a policy and have an action plan in place before a case arises among employees or their dependants. Some recommendations on how to set up a successful AIDS program are outlined below.

1. A *policy* regarding HIV-infected employees should

    - protect an employee's right to privacy;
    - guarantee the employee will not be isolated from other workers; and
    - keep those diagnosed with AIDS productive as long as they are able.

2. *Mandatory training* for managers, supervisors, and union leaders should

    - present facts on HIV;
    - address personal concerns about AIDS in the workplace;
    - reiterate the company's policy;
    - help with job restructuring; and
    - discuss how to manage coworker concerns.

3. *Education programs* for all employees should

    - explain policy;
    - present facts on transmission and prevention;
    - encourage empathy for those with AIDS; and
    - provide workshops or forums for frank, open discussion.

4. *Counselling and support* should be provided to

    - help employees with AIDS cope with their disease;
    - assist others in coming to terms with an HIV-infected coworker; and
    - explore with supervisors the issues involved in managing AIDS.[114]

Despite the considerable amount of information on HIV and AIDS, many individuals are still not well informed about the disease. One of the problems human resource managers must deal with is the lack of knowledge on the part of employees. There are still questions asked such as "Can I get AIDS from germs in the air? From touching an infected worker? From a toilet seat? From infected water in a swimming pool? From insect bites?" It has been found that a comprehensive education program for coworkers can halt the hysteria that often results when a colleague is diagnosed with HIV or AIDS.[115]

OCCUPATIONAL HEALTH AND SAFETY STRATEGY

It must be continually stressed that top management's involvement in setting health and safety policies is essential. If it does not assume a leadership role, it sets an example by its inaction, and middle managers, first-line supervisors, and employees will behave accordingly. Part of an effective occupational health and safety strategy is to clearly assign responsibilities for plant safety and health programs to ensure that the company's policies are carried out. An occupational health and safety committee with enforcement authority is a very helpful tool to implement health and safety policies. Such a committee should be made up of representatives of management and employees, ideally with balanced representation. This increases the probability that the committee's decisions are accepted as fair by the employees.

It is important to have a control process in place. Causes of accidents should be identified and either eliminated or controlled to prevent recurrence. The human resource department should use its information system to monitor for patterns of accidents or health problems that may be otherwise overlooked. An effective training program is another critical part of a good occupational health and safety program. Moreover, a number of organizations are hiring occupational health and safety specialists to design and administer comprehensive workplace health and safety programs. Finally, management should continually encourage safety awareness on the part of supervisors and employees.

SUMMARY

Occupational health and safety has become an important aspect in organizations and will have an even higher priority for human resource managers in the future. The federal and provincial governments have created a variety of laws that require the attention of human resource professionals. Most occupational health and safety acts now require the establishment of safety committees in companies with 20 or more employees.

The Workplace Hazardous Materials Information System (WHMIS) is a law that requires suppliers to provide detailed information on any danger their material may pose, but it also asks the user to make sure that the information is available and that employees are trained to understand it.

Accident prevention is a major concern, but human resource managers should not forget to look at the psychological aspect of the work environment. Stress-related losses—absenteeism, turnover, low productivity, accidents—cost Canada billions of dollars. Preventive programs such as employee assistance programs, professional counselling, time management, and fitness programs can go a long way to reduce stress-related costs.

AIDS and the workplace is an important issue facing human resource managers. Some organizations will experience individual cases of AIDS or HIV that, given present experiences, can lead to severe friction among work groups and irrational actions from some frightened employees. Human resource managers should be prepared for this by appropriate training and communication programs.

TERMS FOR REVIEW

assumption of risk **p. 461**
burnout **p. 477**
careless worker model **p. 461**
ergonomics **p. 483**

Hazardous Products Act **p. 466**
health and safety committee **p. 465**
shared responsibility model **p. 461**
stressors **p. 475**

Workplace Hazardous Materials
Information System
(WHMIS) **p. 466**

SELF-ASSESSMENT EXERCISE

Stress EQ Test

Complete this short "Stress EQ Self-Test," which measures one aspect of emotional intelligence or EQ (emotional quotient)—how well you deal with stressful situations. There are no right or wrong answers. The scoring key follows the test.

Item	Question	Yes (X)	No (X)
1	Do you handle adverse events well?		
2	Do you manage frustration effectively?		
3	Do you live life so as not to create a feeling of "overload"?		
4	Do you cope well in new situations, with significant unknown factors?		
5	Do you usually minimize anxiety to avoid feeling stuck?		
6	Do you generally get a good night's sleep?		
7	Are you able to hold back comments in a disagreement even though you would like to "blast" the person?		
8	Can you say that "road rage" for you personally is under control?		
9	Do you cope well with daily events that can sometimes be frustrating?		
10	Do you avoid losing control so as not to hurt people physically, verbally, or emotionally?		
11	Would associates say you manage your anger well?		
12	Do you deal well with disappointment?		
Total			

How did you do?

High EQ types will consistently score between 10–12 yes answers almost every time.

A more formal term for what I have called *the manageable you* is what the EQ-i (or Emotional Quotient—Inventory) calls the "Stress Management EQ Scale."

People who score high on the *stress management scale* are people who for the most part handle what life throws at them. They can "roll with the punches," so to speak. They do not get out of control. And yet, with life's stressful events, they do not fall apart either.

Let's look at the 12 items again that make up the stress management EQ scale. There are 2 sub-components to the interpersonal scale. They are listed below.

- **Items 1–6: Stress Tolerance.** This EQ core competency allows individuals to withstand adverse events and stressful situations without "falling apart." In addition, these individuals positively manage the stress. They are resourceful in coming up with methods, techniques to diffuse the stress and to remain effective, on the job and at home. Sometimes psychologists have referred to this competency as "ego strength." High scorers on this EQ factor face difficulties head on, and don't get carried away by strong emotions. "Even keel" is a good expression to describe them. We even hear about this type of person: "She just doesn't get flustered!"

Workplace application. Obviously in today's workplaces, being able to "juggle a lot of balls" seems to be a prerequisite. Some can do it well, others can't. If employees feel overwhelmed with stress-related assignments or a culture that is not healthy, the business is simply asking for trouble: legal, psychological, and financial. You will know if this is occurring because there will be an inordinate number of mistakes made by employees. We can always say that making mistakes is part of learning; but we should not make repetitive or ongoing dangerous mistakes. These mistakes, of course, will show up through poor concentration, difficulties in making decisions, and inappropriate or inadequate ways of handling difficulties.

Recommendation. We cannot change the macro dynamics that are coursing through our world today. But knowing that change for most people creates, or, at least, invites, a bout of anxiety, managers must do their best to keep open the channels of communication, treat employees with extra care, and be genuine in their relationships. Companies must continually be on the lookout for symptoms and signs of burnout: ongoing employee frustration, absenteeism, tardiness, sleep deprivation, shortness of temper, glassy eyes, cynicism, etc. As we saw in the opening vignette, the use of power and force only exacerbates the problem. Build a work culture that minimizes helplessness and hopelessness.

- **Items 7–12. Impulse Control.** This EQ core competency allows individuals to cope with delayed gratification. They don't have to have everything "right now!" In an age when children have been raised with instant gratification, through technology and the fast pace of living, we are often reaping the negative results of wanting things now. In schools, on the streets, in malls, people seem less friendly, most pushy, showing greater disrespect and belligerence. Parking lots and crowded highways all too often show evidence of low EQ types and their lack of impulse control. To use a gun to settle your anger makes the result permanent when the other person dies.

Workplace application. Violence in the workplace is today's number one killer of employees, especially in the United States. The 1998 summer release by the Geneva-based International Labour Organization of its "Violence at Work" report showed shocking statistics. It is worth quoting key items:

1. In the U.S., 1,000 people are killed in job settings each year. Homicide is the leading cause of death on the job for women and the second-leading cause for men.

2. In European Union countries, 4 percent of employees have experienced physical violence and 8 percent have faced bullying. Figures are higher for employees in the public sector, at 8 and 13 percent respectively.

3. Workers who are at high risk of experiencing violence are the ones who handle valuables, provide health care or social services, or do jobs that involve inspection and enforcement. Transit workers are also at risk.

4. Immigrant workers and members of minority ethnic groups experience a disproportionate amount of violence. This includes homicide at work among immigrants to the U.S. and abuse and sexual harassment among Filipino domestic workers overseas.

5. When sexual harassment is included, Canada comes in fourth behind France, Argentina, and Romania, with almost 10 percent of women reporting harassment.

6. The *ILO Report* described a 1994 survey by the Canadian Union of Public Employees in which nearly 70 percent of the respondents claimed "verbal aggression" was the leading form of violence against employees.

Recommendation: We are at a stage now, I believe, in our workplaces where tensions can boil over more than ever. Corporate downsizings have been one major stressor, for sure. But what about outrageous executive compensation packages that are handed out even when a company loses money! On a personal basis, if you find that you are acting out your frustrations and anger, you need to seek professional help or, at least, talk to a good friend who will give you sound feedback.

Transactional Analysts of the "I'm OK, You're OK" school of psychology will say that about 97% of all anger is "racket." By "racket" they mean that it is not authentic. Authentic anger is indignation, outrage over an actual injustice, e.g., a child murdered. If 97% of all anger is masquerading for other buried feelings, then we need to uncover these feelings, release them appropriately which, in turn, frees up tremendous positive energy so that an individual can get on with life. On-the-job abusiveness, explosive and unpredictable behaviour are clear signs of low impulse control. If you manage someone like this, get help for them. If you are like that, get help for yourself. It is not only a psychological requirement; it is an ethical one as well.

Source: Michael E. Rock, "Stress EQ and Unstress You! EQ and the new Workplace," *CanadaOne Magazine* (online), www.canadaone.com/ magazine/eq100198.html. Retrieved August 30, 2006.

REVIEW AND DISCUSSION QUESTIONS

1. Explain the legal term *assumption of risk*.
2. What factors affect occupational accidents?
3. What responsibilities do joint occupational health and safety committees have?
4. Explain the requirements of the Workplace Hazardous Materials Information System (WHMIS).

CRITICAL THINKING QUESTIONS

1. Develop a strategy and identify the implementation steps you would follow to lower the incidence of workplace accidents in your organization.
2. Think about a time when you felt under considerable stress. What were the causes of that stress? What efforts (by you and/or others) were or could have been taken to reduce the stress?
3. What can be done to prepare an organization for an AIDS case?
4. Consider an organization that you have worked in. Critically review its safety procedures and training. Evaluate the organization in terms of the presence of physical, biological, and chemical hazards. Also be sure to address issues relating to ergonomics.

ETHICS QUESTION

You are a maintenance worker in a refinery where smoking is strictly prohibited and any violation is punished by immediate dismissal. The refinery has had several accidents based on secret—and careless—smoking, resulting in injury and even death. Just now, when you go to a machine room to do some repairs, you surprise two of your colleagues who are smoking. Both are long-time employees, and you have known them well for many years. You even belong to the same bowling club, and your family socializes with theirs. When you challenge them, they respond, "Don't worry. This is a safe room, nothing flammable is stored here. You won't report us, will you?" If you report them, they will be dismissed. Both have families with children. If you do not report them, you are sure that they will continue to violate the no-smoking policy and thus endanger the lives of others. What do you do?

WEB RESEARCH EXERCISE

1. Visit the Human Resources and Skills Development Canada Web site (**www.hrsdc.gc.ca**) and examine the relevant sections of the *Canada Labour Code* that deal with occupational health and safety. Also, explore other Web sites that address health and safety law within your province.
2. Go to the Web site of the American Institute of Stress (**www.stress.org**). Check out three other Web sites that also have information on workplace stress. Compare the information from the various sites.

◐ INCIDENT 13-1

Safety at Canada Chemicals Ltd.

Canada Chemicals Ltd. is a large wholesaler of industrial chemicals in Ontario. It handles swimming pool supplies, industrial solvents, fertilizers, and special lubricants. The sales and clerical operations caused few safety worries, but the warehouse facilities caused Sam Peterson sleepless nights. Sam's title was manager of safety and security. He had worked in the human resource department since his job was created in 1992.

His biggest problem was the warehouse manager, Garfield McKenney. Gar simply did not appreciate safety. Nearly every action Sam took to improve safety resulted in objections from Gar, especially if it meant warehouse workers were to be slowed or delayed in their jobs. Most of the workers liked Sam, but they paid more attention to Gar. The only time employees wore their safety goggles, shoes, and acid-resistant gloves was when Sam was around. They knew Gar did not care and would not discipline good workers for safety violations unless company property was damaged.

One day a case of sulphuric acid was dropped, badly burning a new employee. The employee recovered after four weeks and two plastic surgery operations. Immediately after the accident, Sam requested a meeting with Gar, the human resource manager, and the general manager.

1. If you were the general manager, what would you do to gain greater cooperation on safety from (a) Gar and (b) the workers under him?

2. Should Sam be given authority to discipline those who violate safety rules?

◐ CASE STUDY 🍁 Maple Leaf Shoes Ltd.

Safety at the Workplace

As he sat in his cubicle (what some would call an office) sipping what remained of a cold cup of coffee, Jon Atherton thought about his family back home in Vancouver. He missed his wife and two young daughters, and at times, he longed for his old job and his life back in British Columbia. On the other hand, his family would be joining him in Wilmington in a couple of months, and the job that he had left six weeks ago in Vancouver had ceased to provide much challenge. Although his job as a supervisor on the shop floor of a small manufacturing firm gave him some experience in the area of health and safety, his new position in Wilmington was that of safety coordinator. Deep down, he knew that he loved the work—it was just that upon his arrival in Wilmington, everything seemed to be in turmoil. As soon as he solved one problem, another one would pop up.

THE FIRST ISSUE

A week ago, Jon met with Sam Johnson, a 42-year-old man who has been with Maple Leaf Shoes for eight years. Sam is one of two nonunion employees working at the snack bar—his job requires that he serve customers and prepare "snack" foods (such as toast, muffins, and cold sandwiches) for employees. The snack bar is located in the employee lounge, a common hangout for employees on break or having lunch. Fellow employees get along well with Sam—he is always cheerful and his laugh can be heard throughout the lounge on a regular basis. As well, Sam's supervisor says that Sam is a solid performer. Jon also recalled that Sam is taking computer courses on a part-time basis at a nearby community college.

Jon thought back to his talk with Sam a week ago. Sam appeared to be uneasy and reserved when he entered Jon's office and told Jon he had something very important to tell him. Jon recalled how they struggled to get through the conversation— ultimately, Sam revealed to Jon that he had become infected with the AIDS virus and asked Jon for advice. Jon and Sam had arranged to meet in a week's time.

Catherine Reading, who is 56 years of age and has been with Maple Leaf Shoes for 12 years, is the other employee who works with Sam at the snack bar. Catherine is a dependable worker, and while she and Sam are not close friends, they get along well at work. Aside from getting a warning for being 14 minutes late a few years ago, Catherine has a clean work record. Shortly after meeting with Jon, Sam told Catherine that he had been infected with the AIDS virus (saying "Since you work with me, I felt I had to tell you"). Catherine was very troubled by this information. The next day, she reported for work but refused to work with Sam. Her supervisor asked Catherine if she was refusing to obey his orders. Catherine replied "Yes, I am. I am scared, and I'll never work with someone who has AIDS." The supervisor told Catherine that refusing to carry out his request amounted to insubordination. He sent Catherine home and went to see Jon for advice.

Discussion Questions

1. Does Maple Leaf Shoes have just cause to dismiss Sam? Catherine?

2. What should Jon do in this case?

3. Develop a policy on AIDS and describe how you would administer this new policy.

THE SECOND ISSUE

Alexandra (Alex) Dixon, a 26-year-old employee at Maple Leaf Shoes, has been employed in her current secretarial position for almost two years. Prior to receiving the promotion to this position, Alex worked with Maple Leaf for six years as an office assistant. She is a single mother with a five-year-old daughter. Note that the secretarial staff is unionized.

Alex's performance evaluations have been slightly above average. However, her personnel file indicates that 18 months ago she received a three-day suspension because she and another employee were caught drinking on the job during regular working hours ("just a couple of drinks on a boring Friday afternoon," according to Alex).

Over the past few years, Maple Leaf Shoes has had some problems with substance abuse at work (although the problems have been confined almost entirely to employees in the production and warehouse facilities). In one case, a forklift operator under the influence of cocaine dropped a wooden pallet loaded with shoes from about 15 feet in the air—luckily, no one was seriously hurt. Six months ago, Alex's supervisor called in all of her staff to let them know that the company was concerned about safety and would not tolerate the use of drugs at work. There had not been problems of drug use among the office staff, and the topic of drug use was not mentioned again.

Two weeks ago, Alex's supervisor thought that she saw Alex take a puff on a marijuana cigarette on company property (actually on the far side of the company parking lot) at the end of the day. The next day, the supervisor confronted Alex at her workstation and accused her of taking drugs while at work. This meeting was witnessed by six other office employees. Alex admitted smoking the cigarette (saying that she only had about three puffs while on company property), made it clear that she was on her own time ("It was well past quitting time"), said that she was very sorry, and promised never to do it again. However, the supervisor told Alex that the company was clamping down on drug use and terminated her.

The union is filing a grievance about Alex's discharge. The collective agreement gives Maple Leaf Shoes the right to discipline or discharge an employee for "just cause."

Discussion Questions

1. Does Maple Leaf Shoes have just cause to terminate Alex?

2. In discharge cases, the grievance procedure at Maple Leaf Shoes goes directly to the third step, a meeting between senior union and management representatives. The management side is looking to Jon for advice on how to proceed. Help Jon formulate an appropriate strategy.

⊙ CASE STUDY   CPIB   Canadian Pacific and International Bank

Stressful Times at a CPIB Branch

The downtown branch of the Canadian Pacific and International Bank in Brandon, Manitoba, is known for its friendly service and high levels of employee morale. Although the branch gets very busy at times, the employees regard it as a good place to work. There is a spirit of cooperation among the employees, and the bank manager, Marsha Cobourg, is well liked by the staff.

Roselynn Barkhouse, a 26-year-old customer service representative, has been employed at the Brandon branch for just over nine months. In general, co-workers describe Roselynn as a good, solid worker, but most also agree that she is somewhat shy.

Three weeks ago, Roselynn was working at the counter when Roy Romanowski came in to deposit money into his business account. Roy has operated his small convenience store, which is located about three blocks from the bank, for 31 years. He is a loyal CPIB client and visits the bank at least once a day. Everyone in the area knows Roy—while he is a very hard worker, he is also an impatient man and not overly friendly. Some area residents refuse to buy anything from Roy's store because, in the words of one woman who lives near the store, "He is just so unfriendly, cold, and abrupt, I will never support his store." However, Roy's wife and children, who also work in the family store, are well liked in the community.

Roy approached Roselynn's counter and gave her his deposit bag. A careful count of the money revealed that Roy had $2,314 to deposit. Roselynn filled out the deposit slip for Roy, had him initial it, and went to the computer to enter the transaction. However, Roselynn mistakenly pressed the withdrawal button (instead of the deposit button), so when Roy looked at his passbook, it showed a withdrawal from his account of $2,314. He noticed the error immediately because he always keeps a close eye on his account.

Upon seeing the error, Roy started to scream at Roselynn. The following conversation ensued:

> **Roy:** "What are you doing? Are you stupid or something? You trying to steal my money? I work real hard for my money."
>
> **Roselynn:** "I am very sorry, Mr. Romanowski. I will fix up the mistake right away."
>
> **Roy:** "How can I trust you? I have always gone to this bank, and they always treated me right. Now, this happens. How many mistakes have you made before? I want to see the manager. I want to get you fired. There is no room in the bank for stupid people."

At this point, two other employees and the manager, Marsha Cobourg, arrived at Roselynn's counter. Roselynn was in tears, and once again apologized to Roy. Within seconds, the error was corrected, and Cobourg also offered her apologies to Roy and walked him to the door.

Since the incident, however, Roy has continued to come into the bank at least daily (and more often when his store is busier). Whenever he enters the store, he makes a rude comment to Roselynn if she is working. Often, his comments are overheard by other customers. At times, he also tells other people to avoid going to Roselynn's counter. Both Marsha Cobourg and Roselynn's co-workers have reassured her that her work is fine and have advised her just to ignore Roy.

Two days ago, Roy entered the bank and, as luck would have it, Roselynn was the next available representative. Roy, however, refused to go to her workstation and made this known to all the customers around him. The bank was very busy at the time, and Roselynn burst into tears, left her counter, and went home. The next day, she called Cobourg and told Marsha: "I am totally stressed out and just can't take it anymore. I'm quitting and am going to look for work somewhere else. The job is just not worth it." Marsha tried to comfort Roselynn and after much discussion, was able to get Roselynn to come in for a meeting the next day.

Discussion Questions

1. The day of the meeting between Roselynn and Marsha has arrived. Was arranging such a meeting a good idea?

2. What should Marsha try and achieve during the meeting? Were there any steps that could have been taken to prevent this incident from occurring?

The meeting with Roselynn ended at 11 a.m., and Marsha Cobourg went back to her office. Forty minutes later, as she glanced out her office door, she saw a man wearing dark glasses and a baseball hat burst into the bank. At the time, there were six bank employees and seven customers in the bank.

The man was waving a shotgun and yelling, "Everyone on the floor. Don't look up and don't try and stop me. No one will get hurt." He swore several times and ran to the cash station. "Open the drawer and give me the money." The bank representative at the cash station complied with his request, and in a matter of seconds the bank robber had run out the door.

Within a few minutes, the police arrived, as Marsha had pressed the silent alarm in her office. Everyone was told to remain calm, and the bank doors were locked. No new customers were allowed into the bank, and everyone present when the robbery occurred had to remain inside. Each customer was interviewed by the police. Marsha also asked each customer how they were. Three of the customers were very upset—one woman who was in the bank with her one-year-old son was particularly distraught.

A number of the bank employees were also visibly upset. Others seemed to take a deep breath and appeared ready to deal with the business at hand.

One customer commented on how the atmosphere in the branch had changed so rapidly. Prior to the robbery, everyone was relaxed and people were chatting.

During the robbery, there was extreme tension. Then, the aftermath of the robbery was very different—some people were in shock, some seemed emotionally drained, and others were trying to think through what had occurred. The customer also noted that while a number of the bank employees were terribly upset, they seemed in total control during the robbery: "It was like they knew what to do. I only caught a glimpse of what happened but there was no show of fear or panic on the employees' faces. It was almost like they were doing a drill, but in real life."

After about 45 minutes, the customers were permitted to leave the bank. As Marsha returned to her office, she received a phone call from the police notifying her that they had just arrested a suspect as he was preparing to rob another bank.

Discussion Questions

1. Develop a safety training program for bank employees. What are the basic components of the program? What requirements would you build into such a program?

2. As a result of the robbery, a number of employees and customers may feel traumatized. What should the bank do in such a situation? Be sure to consider both short- and long-term suggestions.

The Union–Management Framework

HRM focuses on the shared interests of workers and managers in the success of their enterprise. Conflict is de-emphasized in favour of "win-win" scenarios where problems are solved or put aside to fulfil organizational objectives. By contrast, industrial relations assumes conflict is inherent in the employment relationship.

Daphne Gottlieb Taras, Allen Ponak, and Morley Gunderson[1]

CHAPTER OBJECTIVES

After studying this chapter, you should be able to:

➡ *Describe* the structure of Canadian unions.

➡ *Discuss* the major reasons why workers join unions.

➡ *Identify* conditions that indicate unionization may occur.

➡ *Explain* how a union organizing campaign is carried out.

➡ *Summarize* the core legal principles relating to collective bargaining.

➡ *Outline* the key steps in negotiating a union contract.

➡ *List* common techniques to resolve disputes.

➡ *Describe* how unions affect the human resource management environment.

➡ *Suggest* ways to build union–management cooperation.

CHAPTER 14

Workers may join together and form a union. A *union* is an organization with the legal authority to represent workers, negotiate the terms and conditions of employment with the employer, and administer the collective agreement.

Many successful companies have one or more unions among their employees. While unionized organizations are often lumped together, there is growing evidence that the quality of the relationship between an employer and union is a major factor in predicting firm performance. Still, the presence of a union places limits on the role of human resource management and many managers find these new limitations hard to accept:

> CUPE Local 118 in Saint John, New Brunswick, has a clause in its contract with the city that guarantees a minimum of 293 full-time outside employees. The clause, which was introduced in the early 1980s, has been renewed several times to avoid damaging union–management relations and labour unrest. Terry Totten, who has been City Manager for more than 15 years, believes that the clause is fundamentally wrong and impairs the ability of the city to save money by contracting out services. Totten believes that the clause will only be removed when the economic climate is right and council have the political will to remove the clause. Union officials report that the clause was introduced to stop corruption, poor quality work, and kickback schemes with outside contractors, and believe that the clause has benefited both employees and taxpayers.[2]

As shown in Figure 14-1, the industrial relations and human resource perspectives on workplace conflict are somewhat different.

WHY EMPLOYEES SEEK UNION REPRESENTATION

Unions do not just happen. They are frequently caused by some management action or inaction that workers perceive as unfair. Once a union is organized, it becomes the employees' bargaining agent and the employer is legally obligated to meet with the union and bargain a labour contract called a **collective agreement**. The collective agreement, which is known as the "rule book" by some managers and union officials, addresses a variety of issues such as wages and benefits, hours of work, working conditions, and related issues such as grievance procedures, safety standards, probationary periods, and work assignments. The collective agreement is usually negotiated between the local union's bargaining committee and the human resource or industrial relations department.

FIGURE 14-1	Industrial Relations and Human Resource Perspectives on Workplace Conflict

Industrial Relations Perspective

1. Conflict stems from an employer–employee power imbalance.

2. Conflict between labour and management is enduring.

3. Correcting the power imbalance between labour and management often requires institutional intervention in the forms of union representation and legislation.

4. Conflict can be constructive even when the conflict is addressed in an adversarial, non-problem-solving fashion.

Human Resource Perspective

1. Conflict stems from poor management.

2. Conflict can be partially reduced by organizational and workplace innovations that build an employer–employee unity of interests.

3. Conflict can further be reduced by cooperative, mutual gains-oriented problem-solving techniques.

4. As a result of improved management, conflict will fade from the employment relationship.

Source: Adapted from D. Lewin, "IR and HR Perspectives on Workplace Conflict: What Can Each Learn from the Other?", *Human Resource Management Review,* (2001), Vol. 11, pp. 453–485.

The collective agreement places restrictions on management's rights in managing the workplace. When a new collective agreement is negotiated, it is important that supervisors and managers dealing with unionized employees are made aware of the terms of the agreement and provided with training regarding the interpretation and application of the new agreement. All too often, a union grievance arises because the supervisor did not understand the terms of the collective agreement:

> Shane Warren was a supervisor for a local municipality. Under the terms of the collective agreement, the employer was required to provide overtime opportunities on the basis of seniority. One evening, Warren needed an employee to work overtime doing snow removal. Rather than take the time to contact employees based on their seniority, he asked an employee in the shop who agreed to the overtime assignment. The union was successful in their grievance because Warren had failed to follow the collective agreement.

Causes of Unions

Why do employees join unions? The reasons for joining a union vary from person to person and there is no single force that motivates people to join unions. Instead, perceptions are shaped by a variety of reasons. The *union push explanation* asserts that some employees are pushed or forced into joining a union because of employer treatment of the workforce, peer pressure by coworkers to join a union, or collective agreement provisions requiring an employee to join if he or she wants the job in question. The *union pull explanation* states that employees are pulled into the union because of the benefits of union representation (such as higher wages, greater benefits, job security, and grievance representation).

When considering union joining, it is important to distinguish between the desire for union representation and the opportunity to do so.[3] Three factors—job dissatisfaction, individual attitudes toward unions in general, and perceived union instrumentality (beliefs about what unions can do for an employee)—appear to be most important in the decision of an individual to join a union.[4]

Reasons for not joining a union are equally diverse. Workers who want to become managers may believe union membership damages their chances for promotion. Other employees view unions as "just another boss" that leads to extra costs, such as union dues or lost wages from strikes. Likewise, past experiences or isolated stories of union wrongdoing may cause some people to form a negative opinion of collective action. Also, employer policies and supervisory treatment may be fair and consequently, employees are not motivated to join a union.

As the following example shows, people within a community may have vastly differing views concerning unionization:

> In the small town of Brooks, Alberta, a strike shut down the Lakeside Packers slaughterhouse. Management was determined to open the plant (which employs about one-quarter of the town's population) during the dispute, which has divided the town. While some citizens strongly support the employees and their union (the United Food and

CP/Fred Lunn.

Commercial Workers), others are concerned that the strike will hurt other businesses in the community and leave lasting divisions among the town's residents. Striking workers are very upset—despite an Alberta Labour Relations Board order that banned strikers from doing more than delaying vehicles seeking to enter the plant, workers are committed to restricting access to the facility. As one worker stated, "If they kill us, they can go in. This is modern slavery for me."[5]

Canadians' Views Toward Unions

A recent (2008) survey by Nanos Research polled 1,000 Canadian adults concerning their attitudes toward unions. While the survey provides important information, it should be emphasized that the results are aggregated and important differences may exist among workers based on demographic characteristics. Some of the major findings with regard to attitudes toward work and employers are reported below:

- Among Canadians who are not unionized, 20 percent reported that they were very or somewhat interested in being unionized, 3 percent don't know or refused to respond, and 77 percent do not want to be unionized.
- Among unionized employees, 77 percent perceived that the presence of a union was very important or somewhat important for receiving fair treatment from their employer.
- Among current union members, 70 percent would choose to remain unionized if given the choice between remaining unionized and not being a member of a union.
- Among Canadians, 92 percent indicated that they were satisfied with their job and 88 percent were satisfied with management at work, with current union members expressing slightly lower levels of satisfaction.
- Among respondents, 82 percent perceived that the presence of a union had a positive impact on employee job security, with 94 percent of current union members supporting that statement (and 79 percent of employees who have never been unionized).
- Among union respondents, 67 percent indicated that the presence of a union had a positive impact on the promotion of an innovative working atmosphere (compared with only 46 percent for employees who have never been unionized).
- Also, 67 percent of union respondents believed that unions are still relevant today (compared with only 38 percent of employees who had never been unionized).[6]

LABOUR UNIONS: GOALS AND STRUCTURE

Labour unions alter the work environment. Their presence changes the relationship between employees and the organization, especially the role between supervisors and the human resource department. As seen through the eyes of one veteran supervisor, the human resource department's involvement in union-related issues is not always well received by lower levels of management:

> When I started working here more than 25 years ago, supervisors had it made. We handled our own discipline, hiring, and firing. We had clout around here. Then we got a union. Immediately, the human resource department grew and got involved in everything we did. We had training in how to deal with the union, training in the labour laws, training in what the contract meant, and training in all the new rules we had to follow.
>
> Even worse, the human resource department started to have a bigger part in hiring, firing, and discipline. At the same time, I had to deal with the union representative. Of course, my manager still expected me to meet my department's objectives and its budget. Supervising sure is less satisfying than it used to be before the union and the human resource department made all these changes.

As this supervisor's comments indicate, unions have a major effect on the work environment, but in many other ways the environment remains unchanged. Supervisors and managers retain their primary responsibility for employee performance. Profit objectives and budgetary goals are often not shared with the union (although this is changing in some organizations). Nor do unions reduce the need for effective human resource policies and procedures. In short, management must still manage, and the union does not assume the responsibilities of the human resource department. To understand how and why unions influence human resource management, it is necessary to examine their goals and structure.

Union Goals and Philosophy

A union's objectives are influenced internally by the wishes of their members, the aspirations of their leaders, and the financial and membership strength of the union. Like other organizations, unions are open social systems that are affected by their external environment: the financial condition of the employer, the gains of other unions, the inflation and unemployment rates, and government policies influence the union's objectives.

Yet among all these internal and external considerations, there exists a common core of widely agreed-upon objectives. Writing more than 90 years ago, one prominent labour leader stated that the mission for the labour movement was to protect workers, increase their pay, improve their working conditions, and help workers in general.[7] This approach has become known as **business unionism**, primarily because it recognizes that a union can survive only if it delivers a needed service to its members in a businesslike manner. But some unions have chosen to address broader social issues of politics and economics when such concerns are in the best interest of their members. This second kind of union, engaged in what is called **social (or reform) unionism**, tries to influence the economic and social policies of government at all levels—municipal, provincial, and federal.[8] In practice, union leaders pursue the objectives of social unionism by speaking out for or against government programs. For example, many union leaders rejected wage restraint legislation introduced by several governments in the 1990s because such controls removed the right of the union to engage in free collective bargaining with management over a variety of compensation issues.

Human resource management is influenced by both business and social unionism goals. The growth of benefits discussed in Chapter 10 has resulted partly from union pressure. Even non-unionized employers have added many benefits in order to remain competitive in the labour market or to forestall unionization among their employees. Consider how one human resource department responded to the business and social goals of unions:

> Michelin Tire (Canada) Ltd. has three plants in Nova Scotia and is a major employer in the province. To prevent the employees from seeking unionization, management pays wages significantly above those provided by unionized companies in the region. In addition, the company provides several other benefits such as free dental insurance. To date, several attempts over the past 25 years have failed—due, at least in part, to the human resource management practices of the company.

Union Structure and Functions

It has been argued that employees lost direct contact with the owners as organizations grew larger, so unions emerged to help workers influence workplace decisions.[9] Through unions, workers were able to exert control over their jobs and their work environment.[10] Then when attempts were made by employers to cut wages or employment, the employees relied on unions to resist these actions.[11] The most important levels of union structure are local unions, national and international unions, and labour congresses.

Local Unions

For most union members and industrial relations practitioners, the **local unions** are the most important part of the union structure. They provide the members, the revenue, and the power of the entire union movement. Historically, the two major types of local unions were craft and industrial unions. **Craft unions** are composed of workers who possess the same skills or trades; these include, for example, all the carpenters who work in the same geographical area. **Industrial unions** include the unskilled and semiskilled workers at a particular location. When an employer has several locations that are unionized, employees at each location are usually represented by a different local union. Members of the Canadian Auto Workers are an example.

Figure 14-2 shows the structure of a typical local. The union steward is usually elected by the workers and helps them present their problems to management. If the steward of an industrial or

business unionism
Unionism whose mission is to protect workers, increase their pay, improve their working conditions, and help workers in general. Recognizes that a union can survive only if it delivers a needed service to its members in a businesslike manner.

social (reform) unionism
A type of unionism that tries to influence the economic and social policies of government at all levels. In practice, union leaders pursue such objectives by speaking out for or against government programs.

local union
A union that provides the members, the revenue, and the power of the union movement.

craft union
A type of local union composed of workers who possess the same skills or trades.

industrial union
A type of local union that includes the unskilled and semiskilled works at a particular location.

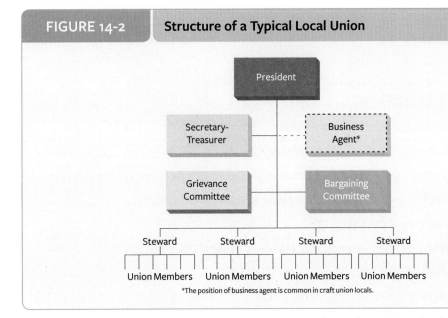

FIGURE 14-2 | Structure of a Typical Local Union

*The position of business agent is common in craft union locals.

Source: Human Resources and Social Development Canada, "Structure of a Typical Union." Reproduced with the permission of the Minister of Public Works and Government Services Canada, 2003.

mixed local cannot help the employee, the problem is given to the grievance committee, which takes the issue to higher levels of management or to the human resource department. In craft unions, the steward, who is also called the representative, usually takes the issue directly to the business agent, who is often a full-time employee of the union.

National and International Unions

Links to Canadian unions
www.canadianlabour.ca

Canadian Auto Workers
www.caw.ca

International Labour Organization
www.ilo.org

Many local unions are part of a larger union—which may be a *national union* (such as the Canadian Auto Workers or the Canadian Union of Public Employees) or an *international union* (such as the United Steelworkers of America or the International Brotherhood of Teamsters). National unions are based in Canada, while international unions have their headquarters outside of the country (typically in the United States).

National and international unions exist to organize and help local unions. They also pursue social objectives of interest to their members and frequently maintain a staff that assists the local unions with negotiations, grievance handling, and expert advice. Some national and international unions leave many key decisions (including bargaining a collective agreement) with their local unions. In other relationships, the national or international union plays a very active role in local union affairs. Figure 14-3 (on page 498) shows the membership of the largest unions in Canada. Note that the two largest unions represent public sector employees.

Canadian Labour Congress

Canadian Labour Congress (CLC)
An organization, with a membership of more than 3 million, that represents many unions in Canada.

The **Canadian Labour Congress** (**CLC**) represents many unions in Canada, and has more than 3 million members. The President, Ken Georgetti, was elected in 2000. The CLC has five main functions: (1) representing Canada at the International Labour Organization, (2) influencing public policy at the federal level, (3) enforcing the code of ethics set out in its constitution, (4) providing services (such as research and education) for its member unions, and (5) resolving jurisdictional disputes among its member unions.

While the Canadian Labour Congress is the largest labour federation, it is not the only one. In addition to other federations at the national level, there are also federations operating at the provincial and municipal or regional level (for instance, the Quebec Federation of Labour and the Ottawa and District Labour Council).

Secession

Canadian Labour Congress
www.canadianlabour.ca

In 1960, about two-thirds of union members belonged to an international union. Over the past half-century, that percentage has declined noticeably so that now only about 28 percent of union

FIGURE 14-3	Membership in Canada's Largest Unions (2008)	
Union		**Membership (000s)**
Canadian Union of Public Employees (CLC)		570
National Union of Public and General Employees (CLC)		340
United Steelworkers of America (AFL-CIO/CLC)		280
National Automobile, Aerospace, Transportation and General Workers Union of Canada (CLC)		255
United Food and Commercial Workers International Union (AFL-CIO/CLC)		245
Public Service Alliance of Canada (CLC)		173
Communications, Energy and Paperworkers Union of Canada (CLC)		143
Social Affairs Federation (CSN)		117
Teamsters Canada		109
Service Employees International Union		93

Source: Strategic Policy, Analysis, and Workplace Information Directorate, Labour Program, HRSDC.

members belong to international unions.[12] This trend, referred to as *secession*, has been motivated, in part, by a desire for more autonomy on the part of Canadian locals and the development of policies aimed at specifically addressing the needs of Canadian workers. The most dramatic breakaway occurred in 1985 when the Canadian Auto Workers union, led by former president Bob White, severed ties with the United Auto Workers and held its founding convention in Toronto. Canadian members of international unions have often complained that they receive a disproportionately small share of union benefits.

TRENDS IN UNION MEMBERSHIP

Union Growth and Decline

In 2008, about 4.6 million workers belonged to unions (about 30.5 percent of the non-agricultural paid workforce). In terms of industry sector, education and public administration were the most highly unionized at 68 percent, followed closely by utilities (67 percent). The lowest rates of unionization were in the agricultural (4 percent), wholesale trade (7 percent), and food and beverage (8 percent) sectors.[13] Although these sectors have been hard for unions to organize, there have been some successful union drives:

> In Gatineau, Quebec, eight employees at a Wal-Mart Tire and Lube Express (TLE) Centre had their first collective agreement following three years of negotiations and litigation between Wal-Mart and the United Food and Commercial Workers. The agreement was the first for Wal-Mart in North America and a company spokesperson stated that the company was disappointed and the agreement would have a significant impact on the company's business model. The TLE was subsequently closed by Wal-Mart, but 180 Wal-Mart employees in St. Hyacinthe, Quebec, recently gained a union contract. According to National UFCW president Wayne Hanley, "Because of their [employees'] determination, the workers have made history, but it was hard won."[14]

In recent years, the number of women members in Canadian unions has been increasing rapidly. In 1967, women made up only 20 percent of total union membership; now, more than 50 percent of union members are female—the unionization rate for women surpassed that of men for the first time in 2004. While about one in six female employees belonged to a union in 1967, that ratio has doubled over 35 years and now about 1 in 3 women are union members. Thirty years ago, 4 out of 10 male employees were union members; today that proportion has fallen to 3 in 10.

Historically, unions have been strong in the manufacturing and not-for-profit sectors. Smaller firms and employers in the service sector have been resilient to unionization. However, unions are placing greater emphasis on organizing service employers:

> The United Food and Commercial Workers union, which represents most of the employees at Loblaws (Canada's largest food retailer), has turned its organizing efforts to organizing the second-largest food retailer (Sobeys). Sobeys has sent a letter to employees indicating that the union merely wants their dues money and emphasized the good and open relationship the company has with employees. Loblaws executives indicate that they would welcome the move to remove the competitive disadvantage of paying 35 percent higher wage payments to employees.[15]

In comparing unionization across provinces, Newfoundland had the highest rate (37 percent), followed closely by Quebec and Manitoba (36 percent) while the lowest union density was in Alberta (22 percent). Also of note is the lower probability that a part-time worker will be unionized (the union density rate for full-time workers is 31.2 percent compared with 22.9 percent for their part-time counterparts). In addition, larger workplaces are more likely to be unionized—about 13 percent of employees in firms with less than 20 employees were unionized, 30 percent in firms with 20 to 99 employees, 41 percent in firms with 100 to 500 employees, and 51 percent in firms with more than 500 employees.[16]

On the global scene, a number of countries have experienced a decline in union density (that is, union members as a percentage of the paid non-agricultural workforce). Explanations for the decline in union representation include (1) the decline in the manufacturing sector, (2) the constraints that globalization of financial markets have put on macroeconomic policies, and (3) competition from developing countries with low labour costs, resulting in the loss of low-skilled labour-intensive jobs in high-wage countries.[17]

THE IMPACT OF UNION REPRESENTATION

Strikes

Members of the public frequently associate unions with strikes. However, the reality is that most collective agreements are settled without the union resorting to strike action or the employer locking out the workers. Still, there are exceptions:

> In April 2009, approximately 1,800 City of Windsor (Ontario) inside and outside workers went on strike. By the six-week mark of the strike, frustration was setting in. A bar owner reported that her employees were harassed by city workers for removing the bar's garbage during the strike and a newspaper columnist said his car was vandalized after he wrote an article about taking garbage to a private firm. There have been allegations of individuals putting clothes hangers in tall grass to prevent it from being mowed and spreading nails on the road leading to a private waste disposal site. The local CUPE president insists that there are no reports of union picketers doing anything. Rather, one CUPE member stated that he suffered a broken ankle and cuts to his face after a confrontation with a private contractor cutting grass and other picketers revealed that they had been nudged by people seeking to drive past the picket line. One picketer was the victim of a hit-and-run and another was put in a headlock by an irate driver.[18]

In studying why strikes occur, it is possible to classify strikes into one of two categories:

1. **Strikes as Mistakes/Misjudgment.** At least some strikes occur because the parties have uncertain and imperfect information when trying to negotiate an agreement or because one or both negotiation teams are inexperienced negotiators. For example, some negotiators become frustrated easily when bargaining and make their "final offer" too early or without carefully considering the implications of shutting down bargaining.

2. **Strikes as Collective Voice.** In a number of instances, the decision to go out on strike is not because of a mistake or misjudgment but because of a perception on the part of workers that they are not being treated fairly. A strike is considered a mechanism by which to voice discontent to management:[19]

> A prolonged strike in 2009 between the City of Ottawa and OC Transpo shows how adversarial a dispute can become and its impact on labour–management relations. The city wants more

control over route assignments and scheduling in an effort to improve the quality of the transit service but the union is strongly opposed. As one union member stated, "This offer is going to destroy my family life. I won't be home for my family." The scheduling issue has the most impact on senior drivers with more seniority and some of the other employees are anxious to return to work. According to one attendant, "In this economy, I don't think anybody wants to be out of work for a long period of time.[20]

In a strike environment, there are several issues to consider:

An extended strike puts considerable financial pressure on employees. As well, the family is at risk for more than just financial reasons and normal family patterns and routines are seriously disrupted. Physical and emotional harm may also be an issue. Once the dispute is settled, employees have to return to a workplace and work teams that just a few days before were divided by a fundamental conflict. While companies need to get on with business, the human issues do not go away by themselves. It can take four to six weeks to return to normal working conditions, and some workplaces are never really the same.[21]

What factors distinguish firms with lower strike activity? Strikes were less common in smaller firms and in organizations where

- workers had more autonomy in the workplace;
- the employer introduced progressive human resource management practices;
- the union was in a strategically weak position; and
- employers have a large share of the market.[22]

How common are strikes? The number of workdays lost due to strikes and lockouts decreased marginally in the mid-1990s (see Figure 14-4). However, the number of strikes increased during the 1998–2001 period, but declined somewhat in the years since 2002; there was some variation over this time frame when considering the number of workers involved and the number of person days not

FIGURE 14-4	Strikes and Lockouts in Canada		
Year	Number of Strikes and Lockouts	Workers Involved (000)	Person-days Not Worked (000)
1995	328	149	1,583
1996	330	276	3,269
1997	284	258	3,607
1998	381	244	2,440
1999	413	160	2,441
2000	378	143	1,644
2001	381	221	2,203
2002	294	166	2,986
2003	266	79	1,730
2004	297	259	3,185
2005	260	199	4,148
2006	151	42	793
2007	206	66	1,771
2008	187	41	876

Source: Strategic Policy, Analysis, and Workplace Information Directorate, Labour Program, HRSDC.

worked. Obviously, a small number of large strikes in a given year can markedly affect these results. In addition, the cost of a strike can be substantial:

> A bitter three-week strike between the *Toronto Star* and its 2,000 newspaper carriers was estimated to cost the newspaper more than $30 million. The company was able to proceed with the outsourcing of home-delivery service after agreeing to guarantee jobs to carriers with the distributors for six months at their current wage rate. Union leader John Deverell estimated the costs to the paper to include about $19 million for buyouts, $3 million for strike replacement workers, $6 million for advertising discounts, and $3 million for half-price subscriptions to home delivery subscribers. Outsourcing newspaper delivery is estimated to save the *Toronto Star* $6 million annually.[23]

One issue that frequently comes up after a strike is settled concerns rebuilding the labour–management relationship. A strike changes the relationship, often leads to workplace conflict, and typically destroys the trust between the parties:

> When a seven-week strike at CBC ended, management announced plans to hire consultants to "reintegrate" the workers with their managers. The reaction from most employees was "they've got to be [expletive] kidding." According to one consultant, "there is always a dramatic erosion in trust of management after a strike, which creates lingering resentment and lack of productivity unless it is addressed properly." While each strike is different, some companies have outside consultants with expertise in psychology and social work conduct confidential debriefing sessions for employees. As well, some organizations have "return to work" training programs (again run by consultants) for managers; the programs focus on role plays, dealing with employees, and getting the team back and running. In addition, employees should be made aware of the EAP program and other assistance available to them.[24]

Wages and Benefits

What are the effects of unions on wages and benefits? The average hourly wage for full-time unionized employees in 2006 was $23.34 an hour (compared with $19.84 for nonunion workers). This difference was more dramatic when comparing part-time workers—$19.36 for unionized employees and $12.00 for nonunion workers.[25] Moreover, as indicated in Figure 14-5, unionized employees tend to have more comprehensive benefit plan coverage.

Unions and Productivity

One major issue of interest for human resource management and industrial relations practitioners is the relationship between unionization and productivity. On one hand, it can be argued that unions have a "monopoly" face that creates economic inefficiency by introducing restrictive and inflexible

FIGURE 14-5	Union Status and Work Conditions	
Work Condition	**Union Employees**	**Nonunion Employees**
% of employees with pension coverage	82.8	32.9
% of employees with supplemental health plan coverage	83.7	44.4
% of employees with dental plan coverage	77.0	41.9
% of employees with paid sick leave	77.2	44.7
% of employees with paid vacation leave	84.1	65.3
% of employees with flextime option	16.7	27.1
% of employees in job sharing arrangement	12.1	6.8
Average annual paid vacation leave (days)	20.9	15.1

Source: "Strikes and Lockouts in Canada," adapted from the Statistics Canada publication "Perspectives on Labour and Income," Catalogue No. 75-001, Autumn 2000.

SPOTLIGHT ON HRM
Making Peace at Work

Communication is vital to rebuilding a workplace after a labour dispute, the experts say. Here are tips from Steve Kennedy, Ottawa-based mental-health practitioner for employee assistance provider FGIworld:

- Before employees return, managers should discuss how the new agreement changes the workplace and how they will welcome back the staff.

- Employees and managers may need counselling to help them recover if they experienced conflicts at the picket line. "It's important from the get-go to acknowledge that both sides have a legal right to do what they did," Mr. Kennedy says.

- As soon as possible after employees return, managers should acknowledge that the strike caused stresses and that efforts will be made to relieve them. A full-scale staff meeting is best.

- Attendance at the meeting should be mandatory. "The message is not 'Come if you want to,'" Mr. Kennedy says. Employees usually are anxious to participate.

- To help employees refocus, managers should state goals clearly and express optimism. They should also commit to supporting employees and trying to better resolve issues in the future.

- Allow ample time for employee questions and discussions.

- Managers should set up processes to discuss and resolve any outstanding issues among teams or individuals.

- Employees should be encouraged to take stock of their role and consider what they can do to create a better work environment. They should also remember that managers are human, too.

Source: Wallace Immen, "How to Heal a Bruised Workplace," *Globe and Mail*, October 5, 2005, pp. C1, C2.

work rules, withdrawing labour in the form of a strike if an employer fails to meet union demands, and increasing compensation costs. On the other hand, it can also be asserted that unions have a "voice" face that increases productivity by reducing turnover, enhancing employee morale, improving communications with workers, and "shocking" management into employing more efficient workplace practices.[26] Studies have shown that unions

- reduce employee turnover (fewer quits);
- increase tenure with the firm; and
- raise productivity or output per worker.[27]

However, the relationship between unionization and productivity is open to considerable debate and has not been universally agreed upon. In fact, management perceptions are opposite to some of the empirical work—while managers from both the union and nonunion sectors tend to believe that unions lower productivity, some studies indicate that in a number of industries, productivity is actually higher in unionized firms. There is also evidence that unions recognize the importance of increasing productivity:

The International Boilermakers Union believed that union members who were shutting down work sites illegally, sleeping on the job and being disrespectful were giving the union a bad name. As a result, the union got tough and decided to adopt a zero-tolerance policy for poor worker behaviour. As one senior union official stated, "a majority of our members are honest, hard-working, skilled trades people. Unfortunately, a small group are destroying other members' careers with their personal agenda of bad attitudes, late starts, early quits, poor productivity, absenteeism and job disruptions." The union implemented a new policy with strict guidelines addressing union member behaviour.[28]

One issue that comes up during a strike is whether the employer should use replacement workers:

The PotashCorp Allan mine chose to operate using nonunion labour during a recent strike. Director of Communications, Bill Johnson, indicated that while management is running the mine, there were some jobs (such as operating machinery at the hoist and steam plant) that management is not trained to run. A representative from the United Steel Workers union expressed concerns about the safety of the managers working, noting that people have been injured when managers have been operating equipment during other labour disputes.[29]

In most jurisdictions, employers have the right to operate during a strike but some choose not to:

According to one labour relations expert: "The employer has to calculate very carefully if bringing in replacement workers is going to exacerbate the bitterness of the dispute. After a strike it takes a while to put the relationship back together. There's a lot of bitterness left over. The employer takes some chance of exacerbating that when they bring in replacement workers—at a substantial cost to the labour–management relationship over the long term."[30]

THE LEGAL ENVIRONMENT

Government shapes the union management framework through both the enactment of laws and in their role as employer. Unlike the United States, where employers and unions across the country are regulated by the *National Labour Relations Act*, the federal government and each province has its own labour legislation. This division of responsibilities for trade union law is a result of the *British North America Act* (now the *Constitution Act, 1867*), which specifies the powers of the federal government and the provinces.

The issue of jurisdiction over labour relations is quite significant for human resource practitioners. The Canadian Parliament is restricted in its jurisdiction over labour relations matters to organizations involved in interprovincial trade and commerce (e.g., banks, airlines, railways, and federal government agencies). All other organizations fall under the jurisdiction of the provinces. It has been estimated that only about 10 percent of the Canadian labour force comes under federal jurisdiction. Consequently, it is important that human resource practitioners are aware of the appropriate legislation.

The Common Core of Canadian Labour Legislation

The fact that each province and the federal jurisdiction all have their own labour relations statutes makes dealing with unions somewhat more difficult, particularly for employers operating in more than one province. Some of the key aspects of Canadian labour law (which will be discussed in more detail later) include the following:

- **Right to Join a Union.** Employees have the right to join a trade union of their choice and participate in the union's activities.
- **Good Faith Bargaining.** In attempting to negotiate a collective agreement, both labour and management have a duty to "bargain in good faith."
- **No Strikes or Lockouts During the Life of the Collective Agreement.** It is illegal for a union to strike or an employer to lock out employees during the life of the contract.
- **Prohibition on Unfair Labour Practices.** All jurisdictions have legislation prohibiting unfair labour practices by employers and unions.
- **Conciliation.** The right of a union to strike or an employer to lock out employees is (in most provinces) delayed until the conciliation process has been exhausted.

While each province and the federal jurisdiction have some unique features in their labour law, there is a "common core" of provisions contained in the various labour relations acts (refer to Figure 14-6).[31]

FIGURE 14-6	Common Characteristics of Federal and Provincial Labour Legislation

1. All jurisdictions create labour relations boards to decide who has the right to participate in collective bargaining and what bargaining unit should be permitted to represent those who are organized.
2. Most jurisdictions prohibit strikes during the life of an agreement.
3. Most jurisdictions contain regulations that delay strike action until a conciliation effort has been made and has failed.
4. All jurisdictions require that a collective agreement be in force for at least one year.
5. All jurisdictions specify and prohibit certain "unfair labour practices" by management and unions.

Labour Relations Boards

To enforce labour legislation, the federal and all provincial governments have created **labour relations boards** (LRB). These agencies investigate violations of the law and have the power to determine: (1) whether a person is an employee for the purposes of the law; (2) whether an employee is a member of a trade union; (3) whether an organization is an appropriate bargaining agent for bargaining purposes; (4) whether a collective agreement is in force; and (5) whether any given party is bound by it. The enforcement procedures of an LRB relating to unfair labour practice allegations are summarized in Figure 14-7.

In comparison to traditional courts of law, LRBs are more flexible in their procedures for resolving a conflict. They may rely on expert evidence instead of adhering to precedents, suggest a compromise, or even impose a solution upon the parties. In all jurisdictions, the boards' decisions are final and binding and cannot be appealed except on procedural matters.

When charges have been filed against an employer, the human resource department usually assists the organization's lawyer in preparing the case. For example, the HR department may be involved in compiling job descriptions, performance appraisals, attendance records, and other documents that help the company prove its case.

> **labour relations boards (LRBs)**
> Board set up in the federal and provincial jurisdictions to administer labour relations legislation.

FIGURE 14-7	LRB Procedures for Redressing Unfair Labour Practices

1. The aggrieved individual or organization contacts the appropriate LRB office (federal or provincial) and explains the alleged violation.

2. If the case appears to have merit, the LRB informs the other party of the complaint and asks for a response.

3. The LRB gives the parties involved the opportunity to present evidence and to make representations. If the complaint cannot be solved informally, the LRB conducts an official hearing with the interested parties present and usually represented by legal counsel.

4. On the basis of the evidence, the board will either dismiss the case or, if one party is found guilty of a violation, issue a cease-and-desist order. In the event of noncompliance, this order is enforceable in a court of law.

5. It is up to the courts to decide whether a verdict can be appealed or not. In any case, an appeal can be made in matters of jurisdiction, failure to pursue legitimate complaints, and procedural irregularities.

⊙ THE COLLECTIVE BARGAINING PROCESS

Union Organizing

It is worth remembering that a union exists only when workers create it. While unions may use professional organizers, the outcome of the organizing drive depends primarily upon the employees. As George Meany, the first president of the AFL-CIO in the United States, once commented:

> Despite the well-worn trade union phrase, an organizer does not organize a plant. Now, as in the beginning, the workers must organize themselves. The organizer can serve only as an educator; what he or she organizes is the thinking of the workers.[32]

In addition to professional organizers, employees interested in unionization often play an important role in convincing coworkers to join the union. During regular working hours, employees are not allowed to discuss unionization with coworkers. However, several other techniques are used to encourage workers to sign **authorization cards**—including handbills, speeches, conversations, and even home visits. Depending on the jurisdiction, a union is typically certified either on the basis of card signatures or as a result of an election. Some unions are particularly creative in the organizing process:

> The United Food and Commercial Workers (UFCW) have developed a Youth Internship Program which involves about 12 to 16 youth activists who are given the opportunity to work with union

> **authorization cards**
> Cards signed by workers to join a union. Depending on the jurisdiction, a union may be certified either on the basis of card signatures or as a result of an election.

representatives to learn negotiating skills and experience hands-on union organizing campaigns. The UFCW also have an outreach program—Talking Union—in Ontario and Saskatchewan high schools where representatives talk to students about what unions do and explain student rights at the workplace.[33]

Union organizers educate the workers by explaining how the union can help employees and reduce mistreatment of workers. However, professionals only assist workers; they do not cause workers to join a union. Even experienced organizers find it difficult to organize a well-managed and growing company with proactive human resource practices.[34] Still, some unions are using new technology to help organize workers:

> Some union activists are advocating using the Internet to build support through virtual organizing and virtual picketing. Derek Blackadder, a CUPE organizer, tried to organize a group of workers using Facebook but was banned from the network for having too many friends. However, an email campaign by a colleague was used to have Facebook administrators restore his privileges. Some experts believe social networks are particularly appropriate for union organizing as unions are very committed to increasing membership of young people (who are primary users of social networks).[35]

Prior to many union organizing campaigns, there are signs of employee interest in union representation. Of particular importance is the work environment. For example, are the turnover and absenteeism rates higher than the norms for the industry and community? Is morale poor? Are pay and benefits below average for the industry? Does the employer have a procedure for resolving employee complaints or issues and if so, is the process used by workers? Changes in employee behaviour may also suggest that a union drive is under way (see Figure 14-8). It is important to remember that these are only indications of a possible union drive.

> One manager who observed some suspicious activities notified the human resource department. A few days later she was "pleasantly" surprised when the employees presented her with a gift certificate and a card as a Christmas present. What this manager saw was a group of employees passing around a card and collecting contributions for a gift. She thought they were signing up to join a union.

Once a union drive begins, management's choice of responses becomes limited in several important ways. A labour relations board (LRB) will protect workers from management reprisals. For example, the discipline of union supporters is illegal, unless the employer can prove the basis for punishment was not involvement in a union but improper behaviour.

When unions are organizing, labour relations boards pay particularly close attention to the actions of employers. Unlike the United States, Canadian labour law provides employers with relatively little freedom to counter a union organizing drive.[36] Both the context and content of statements about unionization are carefully examined by labour relations boards. Consequently, employers are well advised to obtain prudent legal advice in the wake of a union organizing campaign.

FIGURE 14-8	Employee Behaviour That Suggests Union Activity

- Groups of employees in huddled conversations that end when a manager walks by
- More time in washrooms (where union cards are frequently signed)
- Problems being created or magnified by a few workers
- More militant employee behaviour
- An increase in questions about company policies and benefits
- Sudden disappearance of sources of gossip and information

Source: Adapted from Howard Levitt, "Keep in Touch If You Want to Keep the Union at Bay," *Financial Post,* September 13, 1999, p. C11.

SPOTLIGHT ON ETHICS
Hiring a Union Supporter?

Consider the following situation and make a note of your answer on a separate sheet of paper.

You are a recent university graduate and three months ago started working for a small manufacturing firm. The company currently has 17 employees, including 10 labourers who are responsible for product assembly. Although wage levels in the firm are slightly above average when compared to the competition in the immediate area, the business owner is known as a tough manager who isn't exactly a "people person."

While your official title is assistant manager of operations, your job involves some aspects of production as well as marketing. Although the hours are long, you have found the job to be quite rewarding and have enjoyed the exposure to the "real world of business." Four days ago, the owner of the business came to you and asked you to also assume responsibility for human resources, saying, "I'm not into all that people management stuff but we are expanding and I know we've got to have somebody do it. You can pretty much do what you want when it comes to hiring—the only thing that's important to me is that we don't ever get a union around here."

Yesterday, the owner dropped by your office to tell you that the company was going to need to hire two labourers.

He said, "Here's a chance for you to use some of that stuff you learned in university. I've been doing most of the hiring around here but I'm just getting too busy. As I mentioned the other day, the only thing I want is to be sure that we don't get a union around here. Oh, also, the people you hire better be good! I'll let you in on a little secret—when you bring someone in for an interview, ask them the usual stuff about qualifications and so on. Then, carefully bring the conversation around to unions. But you've got to be careful—I don't want the labour board down here bothering us. I usually bring up some labour dispute—the NHL collective bargaining situation, a strike by the post office or nurses, or some other union issue. If you are careful, you can find out what the person really thinks about unions. And, obviously, if you think that they are sympathetic to unions, don't hire them. It's worked for me for more than 25 years. Whatever you do, don't mess this up!"

On one hand, you know the views of the business owner concerning unions. On the other hand, you are fully aware that under Canadian labour law, employees have the right to join a union and participate in its activities and that it is illegal to discriminate against an employee or job candidate because they are interested in union representation. What are you going to do in this situation?

Canadian labour relations boards are quite vigilant in enforcing unfair labour relations practices. Human resource administrators should stress to every member of management, from supervisor to chief executive officer, the following two cautions:

1. Can management actions be judged as unfair labour practices by the LRB?
2. Will management actions provide fuel for the organization drive?

In Prince Edward Island, two fish processing plants were closed down upon the arrival of union organizers. The P.E.I. Labour Relations Board ordered the employer (Polar Foods) to compensate 150 workers for lost wages (a total settlement of almost $500,000) following evidence at an unfair labour practices hearing that Polar Foods closed the plants to avoid unionization.[37]

When an unfair labour practice is committed by any member of management, it can lead to expensive, time-consuming lawsuits and (in some instances) automatic certification of the union. Moreover, union supporters can point to management violations as further justification for a union.

unfair labour practices
Practices by management such as interfering with or discriminating against employees who undertake collective action. Unions may also commit unfair labour practices.

Unfair Labour Practices

To prevent employers from interfering with employee rights, the law prohibits specific **unfair labour practices** by management. These legal prohibitions are summarized in Figure 14-9. They require that management neither interfere with nor discriminate against employees who undertake collective action.

Labour legislation also makes company-dominated unions illegal. In the past, some employers believed that if they could not prevent their employees from organizing, the next best thing would be

FIGURE 14-9	Unfair Labour Practices by Management

Every jurisdiction in Canada has specific provisions dealing with unfair labour practices by management. Some of the most common provisions addressing unfair labour practices are provided below. Activities that management may not engage in include:

1. Interfering in the formation of a union or contributing to it financially (although there have been allowances for the providing of an office for the union to conduct business and for paid leave for union officials conducting union business)

2. Discriminating against an employee because the individual is or is not a member of a trade union

3. Discriminating against an employee because that individual chooses to exercise rights granted by labour relations statutes

4. Intimidating or coercing an employee to become or not become a member of a union

to encourage a union they could dominate. Through threats, bribes, or infiltration, some companies tried to control union activities. For example:

> Robin Hood Multi-Foods Inc. in Ontario arranged for an employee to infiltrate the Service Employees International Union, take part in its deliberations, and report back to general management about its activities. The Ontario Labour Relations Board issued a "cease and desist" order and required the company to post a notice in the plant explaining the board's order and making it clear that the company would not engage in any of a long, specified list of unfair labour practices.[38]

Unfair labour practices by unions are also prohibited. A summary of such practices is provided in Figure 14-10.

Obtaining Bargaining Rights

Legal recognition or bargaining rights may be obtained in three ways: (1) voluntary recognition, (2) through certification by a labour relations board, and (3) a prehearing vote or automatic certification resulting from unfair labour practice.

1. **Voluntary recognition** occurs if a union has organized a majority of employees and the employer is satisfied that the union did not apply undue pressure in the organization process. The employer then accepts the union as the legal bargaining agent without any involvement of a third party.

2. **Regular certification** may take different forms (depending on the jurisdiction):
   - In some provinces, if a substantial number of employees (usually between 50 and 60 percent, depending on jurisdiction) sign union cards, the labour relations board may

FIGURE 14-10	Unfair Labour Practices by Unions

While every jurisdiction has laws regulating trade union conduct, some of the most important unfair labour practice provisions are presented below. Activities that a union is not permitted to engage in include:

1. Seeking to compel an employer to bargain collectively with the union if the union is not the certified bargaining agent

2. Attempting, at the workplace and during working hours, to persuade an employee to become or not become a union member

3. Intimidating, coercing, or penalizing an individual because he or she has filed a complaint or testified in any proceedings pursuant to the relevant labour relations statute

4. Engaging in, encouraging, or threatening illegal strikes

5. Failing to represent employees fairly

certify the unit without an election. If the union is unable to get enough employees to sign cards to qualify for automatic certification but still gets a significant number of card signatures (typically between 35 and 45 percent of bargaining-unit members, again depending on the jurisdiction), an election is mandatory. A secret ballot is taken under the supervision of the labour relations board at the employer's place of business. If the union loses, another election among the same employees cannot be held for one year. If the union wins (that is, the majority of eligible employees who vote cast ballots in favour of the union), then the employer must prepare to negotiate with the union and attempt to reach a collective agreement.

- Five provinces—Alberta, British Columbia, Newfoundland, Nova Scotia, and Ontario—do not automatically certify unions based on card signatures. Rather, an election is held if there is sufficient support for the union in the form of signed cards. Again, the union is certified if the majority of the ballots cast are in favour of the union. While employers generally favour a mandatory secret ballot vote for certification, the legislative change away from certification on the basis of card signatures was strongly opposed by unions.

3. **Prehearing votes** are taken in cases when there are significant indications that an employer has committed unfair labour practices to prevent unionization. In such a case a union can ask an LRB to conduct a prehearing vote. In addition, most jurisdictions provide for automatic certification if employer actions (in the form of unfair labour practices) are such that the true wishes of employees may not be known.[39]

⊙ NEGOTIATING A COLLECTIVE AGREEMENT

Postal strikes tend to have a serious impact on customers, especially small businesses. Should postal strikes be prohibited? Could such prohibitions be done legally?

RPC 4

CP/Sean Kilpatrick.

Once a union is certified, the various labour relations statutes require both the union and management to bargain in good faith. This means that both sides are required to make a reasonable effort to negotiate a collective agreement. The failure of either party to do so can lead to unfair labour practice charges.

The collective bargaining process has three overlapping phases. Preparation for negotiations is the first and often the most critical stage. The success of the second stage, face-to-face negotiations, largely depends on how well each side has prepared, the skill of the management and union negotiators, and the bargaining power of each side. The third phase involves the follow-up activities of contract administration. An organization may establish an industrial relations department or create a labour relations specialist position within the human resources department to administer the collective agreement and coordinate contract negotiations.

Preparing for Negotiations

The purpose of negotiations is to achieve a *collective agreement*. The agreement specifies the rights and responsibilities of management and the union. Detailed preparations are required if each party is to achieve its objectives.[40]

Labour relations specialists need to monitor the environment to obtain information about likely union demands. A number of strategies can be employed. The labour relations department must be sensitive to the rate of inflation and the settlements made by other unions.

One set of bargaining issues revolves around **management rights**. These rights provide management with the freedom to operate the business subject to any terms in the collective agreement.[41] They often include the right to reassign employees to different jobs, to make hiring decisions, and to decide other matters important to management.

Under what is known as the *residual rights theory* of management, employers argue that they have the authority over all issues not contained in the collective agreement. On the other hand, union leaders assert that residual rights do not exist and that they are free to bargain over any issue affecting workers. Most collective agreements have a *management rights clause*. A typical clause might be:

> Nothing in this agreement shall be deemed to restrict management in any way in the performance of all functions of management except those specifically abridged or modified by this agreement.[42]

In negotiating a collective agreement, management may want to include contract language that increases their flexibility at the workplace. For example, supervisors may want all job descriptions to include the phrase "and other duties assigned by management." This clause prevents workers from refusing work because it is not in their job description. The clause also gives supervisors greater freedom in assigning employees. Labour relations specialists in the human resource department may use a variety of sources (such as surveys, discussions, focus groups, provisions in other collective agreements, and information from grievance claims) to discover which rights are important.

> In an effort to cut costs, at least six hospitals in Ontario have contracted out cleaning jobs to the lowest bidder. There are concerns that hiring cheap labour means less-trained staff, and hospitals in Scotland recently brought cleaning services back in-house. According to CUPE Local 786 president, Mike Tracey, "contracting out is a dangerous practice."[43]

management rights
Rights that provide management with the freedom to operate the business subject to any terms in the collective agreement.

Negotiating with the Union

After preparing for bargaining, the second phase of negotiations is face-to-face bargaining with the union. Discussions often start as much as 60 to 90 days before the end of the present contract. If the negotiations are for a first contract, they begin after the union is recognized by the employer or wins a certification election.

Negotiations cover a variety of issues relating to terms and conditions of employment including wages, hours of work, and working conditions. These areas are interpreted broadly. *Wages* means all forms of compensation such as pay, insurance plans, retirement programs, and other benefits and services. *Hours of work* include the length of the workday, breaks, holidays, vacations, and any other component of the work schedule. *Working conditions* involve such issues as safety, supervisory treatment, and other elements of the work environment.

Successful bargaining usually begins with easy issues in order to build a pattern of give-and-take. Negotiations almost always take place in private, permitting more open discussion of the issues. When deadlocks occur, several tactics can keep negotiations moving toward a peaceful settlement. By settling easy issues first, bargainers often point to this progress and say, "We've come too far to give up on this impasse. Surely, we can find a solution." This sense of past progress may increase the resolve of both sides to find a compromise.

> Richard Dixon, vice-president of human resources for NAV-Canada, states: "In any unionized environment, if you're sitting at the collective bargaining table, you're sitting across from individuals who know the business very well. When trying to introduce a new business process or negotiate a more streamlined way of doing things, the HR professionals who don't know the business as well as the people on the other side of the table could have their pockets picked."[44]

Compromises may be achieved by offering counterproposals that take into account the needs of the other party. Sometimes progress is made by simply dropping the issue temporarily and moving on

Union leaders, like politicians, are elected. Are there other similarities?

CP/Deborah Baic.

to other items. Further progress on other issues may lead to compromises regarding earlier impasses. If no progress results, bargainers may request the assistance of federal or provincial mediators or conciliators.

Many management teams will exclude top executives. They are kept out of negotiations because top managers are often not experienced in collective bargaining. Also, their exclusion gives management bargainers a reason to ask for a temporary adjournment when the union introduces demands that require a careful review. Rather than refusing the union's suggestion, management bargainers may ask for a recess to confer with top management (using the old adage "my hands are tied").

Experienced bargainers realize that the other side must achieve some of its objectives. If the employer is powerful enough to force an unacceptable contract on the union negotiating team, the union membership may refuse to ratify the contract or union officials and members may refuse to cooperate with management once the collective agreement goes into effect. In addition, if management does not bargain in good faith, the union may file unfair labour practice charges:

> During a bitter labour dispute between Telus and the Telecommunications Workers Union, the employer sent an email to each employee describing the company's offer and customizing the message so that each individual would know how much they would get in terms of annual raises and variable pay. The union filed unfair labour practice charges—the Canadian Labour Relations Board had previously ordered Telus to stop communicating with bargaining unit employees on matters relating to employment and collective interest.[45]

Mutual Gains Bargaining

Rather than use the traditional adversarial approach to negotiating a collective agreement, some unions and employers are employing *mutual gains bargaining*. This approach moves away from the us-versus-them or win-lose attitude in favour of a win-win approach in which both parties work together to solve common problems. There is a feeling among some labour relations experts that the parties need to work together to compete and survive in the competitive economy of today.[46] However, labour unions are often skeptical about win-win bargaining. According to one senior union official:

> It has been our experience that most employers only become "less adversarial" and talk about cooperation when they want something that will benefit them. Many employers have approached unions wanting to extract concessions, normally accompanied by promises of future employer cooperation. It is also usually followed by an acute case of amnesia on the part of the company. Any level of cooperation between the union and company must be accompanied by a commitment

that front-line supervisors are prepared to treat our members with dignity and respect on the shop floor. Without that commitment, cooperation between the union and company is meaningless.[47]

However, mutual gains bargaining does not mean "soft" bargaining or one side giving in. Rather, both parties sit down at the bargaining table as equals and engage in joint problem-solving activities. The process is usually preceded by training in conflict resolution for both employer and union representatives. In addition, mutual gains bargaining requires substantial commitment, trust, and respect, and a long-term focus on the part of both labour and management. Consider, for example, the experience at NorskeCanada's Powell River Plant:

> In the 1990s, the British Columbia pulp and paper industry was characterized by some of the most bitter labour–management relations in the country. At Powell River, the relationship between union and management was extremely confrontational and third-party assistance was needed to resolve almost all disputes. When Norwegian company Norske Skog became owners of the plant, they encouraged a cooperative relationship with employees and the union.
>
> During negotiations in 2003, the company informed the union that some customers had indicated that they would not renew contracts with the company because of a threat of a strike. After a series of customer visits to the mill, the parties decided to engage in early negotiations rather than pattern bargaining that was common in the industry. Company and union leaders met jointly and with their own teams to finalize the agenda for bargaining. When they got to the bargaining table, they reached an agreement in nine days. Both parties understood their interdependence in attaining the goals of a profitable plant and keeping employee jobs. In moving to being a high-involvement organization, the company now has regular meetings attended by managers, supervisors, union officials, and employees to discuss plant operations and ideas for improvement.[48]

What does a mutual gains enterprise need to succeed? At the workplace level, it is important to have high standards of employee selection, broad design of tasks and a focus on teamwork, employee involvement in problem solving, and a climate based on cooperation and trust. At the human resource policy level, key elements include a commitment to employment stabilization, investment in training and development, and a contingent compensation strategy that emphasizes participation, cooperation, and contribution. Finally, at the strategic level, there must be a strong commitment from top management to the mutual gains concept, business strategies that support and are aligned with the mutual gains model, and an effective voice for human resource management in strategy making.[49] Research by the Conference Board of Canada revealed that 36 percent of employers and 42 percent of unions have attempted interest-based or mutual gains bargaining techniques.[50]

Still, many labour relations experts are somewhat skeptical about interest-based bargaining. According to labour lawyer Michael Ford:

> If you ask seasoned negotiators (about interest-based bargaining), they'll give you the look of death and say, "Are you crazy?" Mutual gains bargaining requires both sides to invest so much time and energy in being trained in things like "What do you need?" "What are our needs?" "How do we negotiate in a collaborative fashion?" But to go from traditional bargaining into mutual interest takes a diametric mind-shift. You need to invest the resources and the relationship has to be mature enough.[51]

Labour Management Partnership program Federal Mediation and Conciliation Service
www.hrsdc.gc.ca/eng/labour/labour_relations/partner_program.shtml

Approving the Proposed Agreement

The bargaining stage of negotiations is completed when the agreement has been approved. Often final approval for the employer rests with top management. Negotiations are not complete until the union also approves the proposed agreement. Typically, the union bargaining team submits the proposal to the membership for ratification. If a majority of the members vote for the proposal, it replaces the previous collective agreement. If members reject it, union and management bargainers reopen negotiations. Administration of the collective agreement begins when both sides sign it.

Conciliation and Mediation

What happens in the event that negotiations between labour and management break down? In their legislation, all jurisdictions provide for **conciliation** and mediation services. Actually, in most provinces, no strike action is permitted before a conciliation effort has been made and has failed.[52] A 10-year review of conciliation cases in Nova Scotia revealed that conciliation officers settled more

conciliation
Use of a government-appointed third party to explore solutions to a labour–management dispute.

mediation
Use of a neutral third party to help settle a labour–management dispute.

than 90 percent of the cases.[53] However, the results vary among provinces and some jurisdictions have not come close to matching the 90 percent figure.

Conciliators are appointed by the federal or provincial minister of labour, at the request of either one or both of the parties involved or at the discretion of the ministers. A conciliator is requested to submit a report to the minister within a specified time period. If conciliation fails, strikes or lockouts can legally commence, usually two weeks after the submission of the conciliator's report. Although labour relations legislation may include an option to have a conciliation board meet with the parties, this is used infrequently.

With reference to **mediation**, often a mediator will meet separately with each bargaining team, especially when the negotiations take place in a hostile atmosphere. Effective mediation requires a high degree of sensitivity, patience, and expertise in the psychology of negotiation.

ADMINISTERING THE COLLECTIVE AGREEMENT

grievance procedure
A formalized procedure for resolving disputes if the parties have a disagreement regarding the interpretation of a term of the collective agreement.

Upon ratification by union members and approval by management, the parties begin living with the collective agreement. What happens if the parties have a disagreement regarding the interpretation of a term of the agreement? As discussed below, alleged violations of the agreement typically go through the **grievance procedure**. A *grievance* is defined as a complaint by an employee or employer that alleges that some aspect of a collective agreement has been violated. Almost every collective agreement in Canada contains some type of formalized procedure for resolving disputes. Furthermore, labour legislation typically requires that a grievance that cannot be resolved between the parties be submitted to an arbitrator or arbitration board whose decision is final and binding. To give an example, consider the following case:

> Robert MacDonald, a cable repair person with 17 years of work experience at Aliant Telecom, was picketing the employer. He threatened to kill a tow truck driver if the driver crossed the picket line. When the driver was leaving the parking lot, he bumped into MacDonald. Shortly after, MacDonald showed up at the driver's workplace and hit the driver with a hammer he had concealed up his sleeve. Fortunately, the driver survived the attack. However, Aliant decided to fire MacDonald and the union grieved the dismissal. Noting MacDonald's good relationship with coworkers and his supervisor, his clean work record and that the actions were out of character, Arbitrator Innis Christie ruled that discharge was inappropriate and replaced it with a suspension for time served (about 15 months).[54]

Grievance Procedures

While either management or the union may file a grievance when the collective agreement is violated, most workplace decisions are made by management. Consequently, most grievances are filed by the union. The grievance procedure consists of an ordered series of steps. Figure 14-11 describes

FIGURE 14-11	Typical Steps in a Union–Management Grievance Procedure

- *Preliminary discussion.* The aggrieved employee discusses the complaint with the immediate supervisor with or without a union representative. At this stage, or at any other step in the process, management may resolve the grievance to the satisfaction of the union or the union may decide to drop the grievance. Otherwise, the grievance proceeds to the next step in the process.
- *Step 1.* The complaint is put in writing and formally presented by the shop steward to the first-level supervisor. Normally, the supervisor must respond in writing within a contractually specified time period, usually two to five days.
- *Step 2.* The chief steward takes the complaint to the department superintendent. A written response is required, usually within a week.
- *Step 3.* The complaint is submitted to the plant manager/chief administrative officer by the union plant or grievance committee. Again, a written response is typically required.
- *Step 4.* If Step 3 does not solve the dispute, arrangements are made for an arbitrator or an arbitration board to settle the matter.

the steps through which an employee's grievance typically passes. An example further demonstrates how a grievance may proceed:

> One winter day, a bus driver for the Hamilton Street Railway Company was following closely another bus as they were to begin their routes. The road conditions were poor and when the bus in front stopped, the bus driver slid her bus into it. Both drivers were injured and both buses were damaged. The collective agreement listed several infractions that would "conclusively be deemed to be sufficient cause for dismissal." One such infraction was for accidents due to "carelessness, negligence or disregard to normal safety precautions." The driver had been involved in two other accidents over the past four months so the company decided to terminate her. The union grieved the dismissal and an arbitrator overturned the termination. The company appealed the decision and the Ontario Superior Court of Justice held that termination was appropriate because the collective agreement clearly spelled out dismissal as the specific penalty for carelessness or negligence. Consequently, the arbitrator lacked jurisdiction to substitute a lesser penalty.[55]

The number of steps in the grievance procedure and the staff involved at each step will vary from organization to organization, but most grievance procedures have between three and five steps. The purpose of a multistep grievance procedure is to allow higher-level managers and union representatives to look at the issue from different perspectives and to assess the consequences of pursing the matter further. This approach increases the chance that the dispute gets resolved without going to arbitration.

Handling Grievances

Once a grievance has been filed, management should seek to resolve it fairly and quickly. Failure to do so can be seen as a disregard for employee needs and is not conducive to building and maintaining effective labour relations. However, in resolving grievances, management should consider several issues. Most important, grievances should be settled on their merits. Complaints need to be carefully investigated and decided on the facts. Second, the cause of each grievance should be recorded. A large number of grievances coming from one or two departments may indicate poor supervision or a lack of understanding of the contract. Third, the final solution to the grievance needs to be explained to those affected.

Arbitration

All jurisdictions require that collective agreements include a provision for final settlement by **arbitration**, without stoppage of work, of all differences concerning the interpretation or administration of a contract. This means that as long as a collective agreement is in force, any strike or lockout is illegal. An arbitrator may be selected from a list provided by the appropriate ministry of labour or the parties may agree to the selection of an arbitrator. The arbitrator's decision is final and cannot be changed or revised, except in rare instances (such as corruption, fraud, or a breach of natural justice).[56] There is growing concern that the arbitration process is becoming too costly, too slow (some cases take two years or more to be resolved), and too legalistic.[57]

Arbitration holds two potential problems for labour relations practitioners: costs and unacceptable solutions. An arbitration case can cost both the union and employer several thousand dollars. There are also time commitment costs in terms of preparing for arbitration, attending the actual hearings, and case follow-up. From the perspective of management, a potential problem occurs when an arbitrator renders a decision that is against management's best interest. Since the ruling is binding, it may alter drastically management's rights and set a precedent for future cases. For example, if an arbitrator accepts the union's argument of extenuating circumstances in a disciplinary case, those extenuating circumstances may be cited in future cases. Consider what happened in a chain of convenience markets:

> The Quick Foods Market had a policy that stealing from the company was grounds for immediate discharge. Brandon Brown, a new employee, took a sandwich from the cooler and ate it without paying. He was discharged when caught by the store manager. The union argued that Brandon should get a second chance since he was a new employee. The arbitrator ruled in favour of management but added that discharge for such a minor theft might be too harsh a penalty if Brandon had not been a probationary employee.

arbitration
The settling of a dispute between labour and management by a third party.

This decision suggests that the ruling may have been different had a senior employee been caught stealing. The union may use this argument to argue that discharge is an inappropriate penalty and there exists the possibility that an arbitrator may agree with the union position. Consequently, it is important that an employee grievance is treated seriously by management representatives and that the organization attempts to resolve grievances with the union in a fair and timely matter. However, there may be some instances where arbitration is unavoidable.

Contract Provisions

Every collective agreement contains specific terms and provisions. A number of the most common ones are listed in Figure 14-12. These clauses are important because they define the rights and obligations of the employer and the union. For instance, union security is a very important issue from the union's perspective. In addition, some of the most frequent disputes concern seniority and discipline.

FIGURE 14-12	Common Provisions in Union–Management Agreements

- *Union recognition.* Normally near the beginning of a contract, this clause states management's acceptance of the union as the sole representative of designated employees.

- *Union security.* To ensure that the union maintains members as new employees are hired and present employees quit, a union security clause is commonly demanded by the union. Common forms of union security are:
  a. *Union shop.* All new workers must join the union shortly after being hired.
  b. *Agency shop/Dues check-off.* All new workers must pay to the union an amount equal to dues, but are not required to join the union.
  c. *Check-off.* Upon authorization, management agrees to deduct the union dues from each union member's paycheque and transfer the monies to the union.

- *Wage rates.* The amount of wages to be paid to workers (or classes of workers) is specified in the wage clause.

- *Cost of living.* Unions may negotiate automatic wage increases for workers when price levels go up. For example, one approach is for wages to go up in response to an increase in the consumer price index above some specified amount.

- *Insurance benefits.* This section specifies which insurance benefits the employer provides and how much the employer contributes toward these benefits. Frequently included benefits are life and supplemental hospitalization insurance and dental plans.

- *Pension benefits.* The amount of retirement income, years of service required, penalties for early retirement, employer and employee contributions, and vesting provisions are described in this section if a pension plan exists.

- *Income maintenance.* To provide workers with economic security, some contracts give guarantees of minimum income or minimum work. Other income maintenance provisions include severance pay and supplements to employment insurance.

- *Time-off benefits.* Vacations, holidays, rest breaks, washup periods, and leave-of-absence provisions typically are specified in this clause.

- *Seniority clause.* Unions seek contract terms that require human resource decisions to be made on the basis of seniority. Often, senior workers are given preferential treatment in job assignments, promotions, layoffs, vacation scheduling, overtime, and shift preferences.

- *Management rights.* Management must retain certain rights to do an effective job. These may include the ability to require overtime work, decide on promotions, design jobs, and select employees. This clause reserves to management the right to make decisions that management thinks are necessary for the organization's success.

- *Discipline.* Prohibited employee actions, penalties, and disciplinary procedures are either stated in the contract or included in the agreement by reference to those documents that contain the information.

- *Dispute resolution.* Disagreements between the union and management are resolved through procedures specified in the contract.

- *Duration of agreement.* Union and management agree on a time period during which the collective agreement is in force.

Union Security

Can an employee be required to join a union as a condition of employment? An employer and union can negotiate clauses dealing with union security and, in some jurisdictions, compulsory dues check-off is required.

The highest form of union security is the *closed shop* (found in about 8 percent of agreements), which requires an employee to be a union member prior to obtaining employment. The closed shop, which is frequently operated through a hiring hall, is common in construction and longshore industries.

Under a **union shop** security arrangement, the employer is free to hire an individual but as a condition of employment the new hire must join the union within a specified period of time after being hired. If the individual refuses to join the union, the employer is required to terminate the worker's employment. About 40 percent of agreements have a union shop provision.[58]

Dues checkoff, which is a very common provision in collective agreements, requires an employer to deduct union dues at source from the wages of an employee and remit the funds to the union. However, the employee is not required to join the union. In some jurisdictions, dues checkoff clauses must be negotiated; in other jurisdictions, compulsory dues checkoff is enshrined in law.

While the amount of dues varies, it is typically in the range of about 1 percent of an employee's earnings. Most workers covered by a collective agreement are subject to a dues checkoff requirement.[59] Some jurisdictions allow workers who object to joining a union on the basis of religious grounds to pay the equivalent amount to a registered charity.

In an *open shop*, an individual does not have to join the union and is not required to pay dues.

union shop
A union security provision in which employers may hire anyone they want, but all new employees must join the union within a specified period.

Seniority

Unions typically prefer to have employee-related decisions determined by the length of the worker's employment, called **seniority**. Seniority assures that promotions, overtime, layoffs, and other employee concerns are handled without favouritism. As well, the influence of seniority is not restricted to the union environment; several nonunion organizations also place considerable weight on seniority in making human resource decisions.

Seniority is often very important in deciding layoff rights. For example, when a company plans a layoff, the most recently hired workers are typically the first to go. The remaining employees probably receive higher wages if there is a premium for service with the organization. Thus, the higher-paid employees are retained, even though the layoff may have been implemented as a cost-reduction measure. Moreover, layoffs may undermine a company's employment equity plan, since employees hired through the employment equity program may have low seniority.

seniority
Length of the worker's employment, which may be used for determining order of promotion, layoffs, vacation, etc.

Discipline

Unions often challenge the discipline of a union member. Due to the difficulty of trying to list employee behaviours that may warrant discipline, many collective agreements provide the employer with the right to discipline or discharge if "just cause" exists. In any disciplinary action, management must abide by the terms of the collective agreement. Arbitration cases are frequently lost because management failed to establish grounds for disciplinary action, neglected to document past disciplinary procedures, and failed to adhere to the provisions of the collective agreement.

In deciding discipline and discharge cases, the starting point is the collective agreement. However, many collective agreements have a provision indicating that the employer must have "just cause" to discipline or discharge an employee. In determining just cause, a number of factors may be important:

- nature and seriousness of the offence
- due process and procedure
- past record of the grievor
- seniority and age of the grievor
- knowledge of rules
- previous warnings from management
- lax enforcement/condonation by management in the past
- unequal treatment of employees
- provocation by management

- isolated incident
- sincere apology/remorse on the part of the grievor[60]

Although an employer may believe that clear grounds for discipline or dismissal exist, arbitrators consider a number of issues in making their decisions:

> A Brewers Retail employee in Ontario took a Toronto Maple Leafs shirt from a case of beer being returned by a customer. Cases of beer containing Maple Leaf shirts were part of a special promotion and the employee's daughter was a big Leafs fan. The employee put the shirt in his coat pocket (with part of it hanging out) and went to serve a customer. The employer terminated the employee as part of its zero-tolerance theft policy while the employee argued that he had intended to ask his supervisor whether he could keep the shirt. An arbitrator ruled that the employee, who had 23 years of service with the employer, had not intended to steal the shirt and replaced the termination with a three-day suspension.[61]

Past Practice

precedent
A new standard that arises from the past practices of either the company or the union.

The actions of managers and union officials sometimes change the meaning of the agreement. A **precedent** is a new standard that arises from the past practices of either party. Once a precedent results from unequal enforcement of disciplinary rules, the new standard may affect similar cases in the future.

The fear of past practices usually causes two changes in human resource policies and procedures. First, employee-related decisions are often centralized in the human resource department. Supervisors are stripped of their authority to make decisions on layoffs, discipline, and other employee matters. Instead, supervisors are required to make recommendations to the human resource department to ensure uniformity and consistency of application and to prevent precedents.

The second change is to increase the training of supervisors in the administration of the contract. Training is needed to ensure that supervisors administer the collective agreement in a consistent manner. For example, if each supervisor applies a different standard to tardiness, some employees may be disciplined while others with more lenient supervisors may not receive any penalty. In time, the union might argue that unequal treatment makes it unfair to discipline those who are late. Through centralization and training, human resource departments create a more uniform enforcement of the contract.

PUBLIC SECTOR BARGAINING

Public Service Staff Relations Act (PSSRA)
Provides federal public servants with the right o either opt for compulsory arbitration or strike.

When Parliament passed the *Public Service Staff Relations Act (PSSRA)* in 1967, it essentially gave federal civil servants bargaining rights similar to those granted workers in the private sector—usually the right to bargain for wages, hours, and certain working conditions. More important, it also gave them the right to strike. This is in contrast to civil servants in the United States, who since 1962 have had the right to bargain collectively, but not to withhold their services. Under the PSSRA, the methods of conflict resolution are different from those in the private sector. Before a bargaining agent can give notice that it wishes to bargain, a decision must be made as to whether a conciliation-strike procedure or a binding-arbitration procedure will be used should a deadlock occur. The union has the right to choose different procedures for each subsequent collective agreement. If the strike route has been chosen, conciliation procedures must be followed before a strike can begin.

Another difference from the private sector is that the law allows the employer to designate certain employees as performing essential services, thus divesting them of the right to strike. The union, however, may challenge the list of "designated employees," in which case the Public Service Staff Relations Board makes the final decision.

A comparison of the federal and provincial legislation for government employees reveals little uniformity across Canada. While municipal government employees generally fall under the same legislation as private sector workers, the legislation applicable to provincial civil servants varies markedly. For instance, Saskatchewan government employees come under the same legislation as private sector employees; in some provinces, there is specific legislation applicable only to provincial government employees; and in other jurisdictions, there may be two or more statutes applicable to government employees. In addition, some provinces markedly restrict or prohibit strikes by public sector workers.[62]

HUMAN RESOURCE PRACTICES IN THE UNION ENVIRONMENT

While there is a significant and growing body of information about human resource management from the perspective of the employer, less attention has been paid to examining what human resource management practices are found within unionized workgroups.

A key issue for human resource management practitioners involves obtaining union involvement in managing change. Bob White, former president of the Canadian Labour Congress, had this to say about unions and change:

> For workers, change will be judged to be positive if higher productivity is shared in the form of better wages and benefits; if change results in more rather than less security of employment; if change gives workers access to new skills and opportunities; and if change improves the overall quality of working life in terms of the ability of workers to make a productive contribution.[63]

A survey of Canadian union officials examined a number of human resource issues in the unionized environment. Concerning human resource management policies, union officials were asked to indicate whether a number of specific HRM programs or practices applied to bargaining unit employees. As revealed in Figure 14-13 (on page 518), more than 95 percent of units had a policy addressing sexual harassment, 86 percent had an orientation program for new hires, 86 percent had an employee assistance plan (EAP), and 66 percent had some type of formal performance appraisal system. About 51 percent of respondents reported that the employer shared business information with union members.

Union officials were also asked to indicate whether bargaining unit employees were involved in a number of specific team-based and incentive programs (Figure 14-13). As the figure reveals, 28 percent of the union locals reported having work teams, 22 percent had quality circles and 40 percent had problem-solving groups. Unions have generally stayed away from contingency compensation plans such as profit sharing, productivity sharing, and employee stock ownership plans; overall, less than 20 percent of respondents reported having such plans.

IMPLICATIONS OF UNION AVOIDANCE APPROACHES

In nonunion facilities, an implicit objective of many employers is to remain nonunion. Employers frequently adopt either a *union suppression* or a *union substitution* approach in order to avoid unionization. The union suppression approach involves fighting union representation. An employer may try to intimidate workers, threaten closing or moving the plant or facility, or discriminate against union supporters.

> An employer in the food services industry heard that four of the workers were discussing unionization as a means of improving wages and working conditions. Senior management learned about the issue and decided to terminate six employees—the four union activists and two other employees who were considered poor performers. The termination notices were issued under the guise of incompetent work performance.

The union substitution approach examines what unions bring to the employment relationship and then tries to introduce such features into the nonunion workplace. This approach requires that human resource specialists do the following:

- Design jobs that are personally satisfying to workers.
- Develop plans that maximize individual opportunities while minimizing the possibility of layoffs.
- Select workers who are well qualified.
- Establish fair, meaningful, and objective standards of individual performance.
- Train workers and managers to enable them to achieve expected levels of performance.
- Evaluate and reward behaviour on the basis of actual performance.
- Provide employees with a "voice" in the workplace.
- Implement a compensation plan in which wages/salary and benefits parallel those available in the union sector.

FIGURE 14-13	HRM Practices/Programs Among Canadian Unions

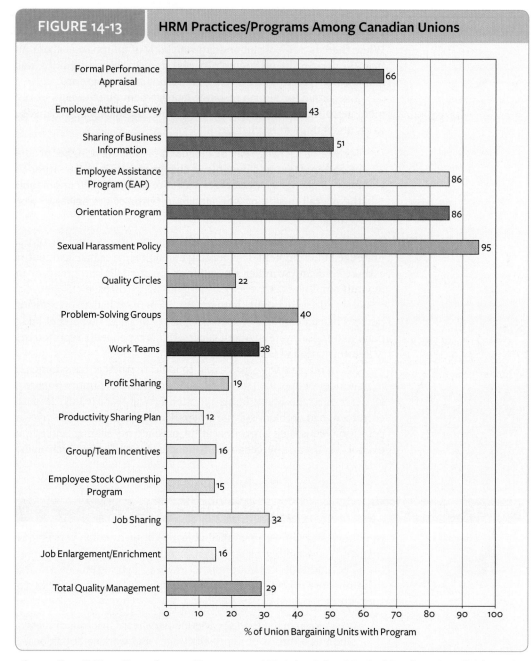

Source: Terry H. Wagar, *Human Resource Management and Workplace Safety: A Study of Canadian Union Officials,* unpublished report, Saint Mary's University, 2009.

The union substitution approach is advocated by many HR practitioners, consultants, and labour lawyers. According to employer lawyer Jamie Knight:

> Nonunion companies that want to remain nonunion should steal some of their best features from their competitors' collective agreements. Often a collective agreement will contain provisions that do not contradict an efficient and effective operation. Employers should have a nonunion dispute resolution process. Dealing with complaints is the biggest challenge in a nonunion workplace.[64]

On the other hand, Canadian labour relations legislation requires that workers need to take the initiative in establishing collective bargaining relationships knowing that many employers are opposed to unions. Consequently, the beginning of the new union–management relationship is already characterized by conflict and adversarialism.[65] Roy Adams argues that the practice of union avoidance sabotages the right to bargain collectively and contravenes the International Labour

Organization's Declaration of Fundamental Principles and Rights at Work which includes the effective recognition of the right to bargain collectively. In North America, this right is generally not available until workers go though an arduous certification procedure which results in an adversarial relationship.[66]

MANAGING IN A UNION ENVIRONMENT

When unions are present, the human resource function is changed. In many organizations, the human resource department is expanded by the addition of specialists in labour relations who deal with such critical areas as negotiations and contract administration, while human resource professionals attend to their more traditional roles. Although some organizations establish separate industrial relations departments to deal with labour relations issues, industrial relations is often considered a subset of human resource management.

Unionization may be associated with greater centralization of employee record-keeping and discipline to ensure uniformity of application. This change can mean that line managers lose some of their authority to the human resource department. They may also find their jobs more difficult because of the new rules imposed by the contract—while management has the right to act, the union may have the right, under the contract, to react to management's actions.

Line managers may become dissatisfied because their authority diminishes while their responsibility increases. These added responsibilities are likely to result from requests of human resource professionals, who may need to monitor the work environment more closely and need more information from the line managers. For example, the line manager may have to compile new reports on such issues as absenteeism, lateness, productivity, and employee grievances (a growing number of organizations are using computer technology to collect such information). Such demands on supervisors may create friction between line managers and human resource staff members.

The presence of a union means that management has less freedom to make unilateral changes. No longer can an employer simply decide what changes to implement. Instead, collective agreement provisions and labour laws must also be considered.

Labour–Management Cooperation

Some unions and employers are moving toward greater cooperation and there is increasing acceptance that labour and management must cooperate and work together if they are to survive and prosper in the highly competitive global economy.[67]

> As noted by the Conference Board of Canada, "There is a high degree of maturity within Canadian labour relations; both parties now openly acknowledge that their individual interests are inextricably linked. Management is making more of an effort to provide unions with high-level information and generally making more of an effort to involve the unions with the business. Similarly, unions have a better sense of business realities and no longer make the 'knee-jerk' reactions they once did."[68]

There is growing evidence that organizational performance is enhanced when labour and management cooperate. For example, research using data from both employers and unions indicated that a more positive labour climate was associated with perceptions of higher productivity, enhanced product or service quality, and greater customer or client satisfaction.[69] However, cooperation is a very challenging process:

> Industrial relations experts assert that a 51-day strike at OC Transpo will lead to even lower levels of morale unless both union and management work on improving their relationship. As Professor Laurel Sefton MacDowell noted, "If relations aren't good, it will start to show itself with an increased number of grievances, which are both expensive and time consuming." Professor Gene Swimmer observed, "It's not clear to me that there will be a lot of antagonism between front-line supervisors and union members because both sides will just be happy to be back at work. But a better relationship is needed at the top level."[70]

Obstacles to Cooperation

Industrial relations specialists often seek union cooperation to improve the organization's effectiveness. However, cooperation may not be politically attractive to union leaders who see little gain in cooperating with management. In fact, if leaders do cooperate, they may be accused by workers of forgetting the union's interests. These accusations can mean defeat by political opponents within the union. Thus, cooperation may not be in the union leader's best interest.

In addition to political obstacles, union leaders may mistrust management. For example, bitter remarks during the organizing drive or arbitration case may convince union officials that human resource specialists are anti-union. Within this climate, cooperative gestures are often seen as tricks or gimmicks aimed at hurting the union. If cooperative proposals threaten the members or leaders, mistrust increases and cooperation usually fails.

While employers often have good reasons for seeking more cooperation with their unionized workforce, a number of cooperative programs have the underlying goal of increasing managerial domination in the workplace. As well, some employers use cooperation to "stress the system" by reducing employees or resources, giving workers more tasks, or speeding up the assembly line; such practices may dramatically increase the stress level of workers and dehumanize the workplace.[71]

In an effort to manage costs, a number of employers are looking to more variable pay programs. However, many unions have been unwilling to cooperate with management on this issue. According to Peggy Bell of the Canadian Auto Workers Union:

> Our job as a union is to fight as hard as we can to protect the jobs of our members. There is no point in tying workers' salaries to something that workers have little if any ability to influence. We don't have any control over those productivity increases. I'm not saying workers don't have any input into productivity, but the big gains in productivity are in the way the work is organized and that is in the control of engineers and supervisors. Labour flexibility is often a code word for no union or a very meek union.[72]

Support for Cooperative Programs

In one study, employer and union participants were asked to indicate their perceptions of the degree of support for cooperative programs (using a six-point scale where 1 = no support and 6 = strong support for cooperative programs) for the five groups referred to in Figure 14-14. Although there was modest support for cooperative programs, one interesting finding was that employers perceived that the greatest opposition to cooperative programs came from national and international union leaders while union officials reported that management (supervisors and upper management) were most opposed to cooperative efforts.

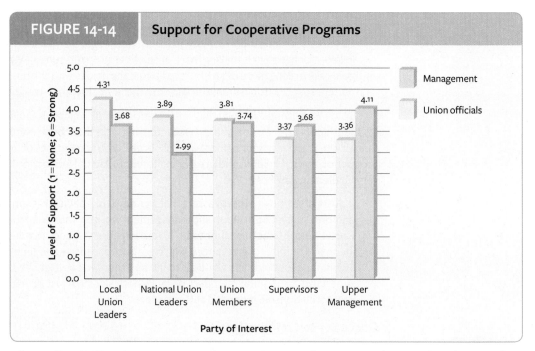

FIGURE 14-14   Support for Cooperative Programs

Level of Support (1 = None; 6 = Strong)

Party of Interest	Management	Union officials
Local Union Leaders	4.31	3.68
National Union Leaders	3.89	2.99
Union Members	3.81	3.74
Supervisors	3.37	3.68
Upper Management	3.36	4.11

Source: Terry H. Wagar, *Human Resource Management, Strategy and Organization Change: Evidence from Canadian Employers*, unpublished report, Saint Mary's University, 2003; Terry H. Wagar, *Examining Labour Relations in Canada: Evidence from Union Officials*, unpublished report, Saint Mary's University, 2003.

FIGURE 14-15	Methods of Building Labour–Management Cooperation

Managers and human resource specialists can build cooperation between the employer and the union through:

- *Prior consultation* with union leaders to defuse problems before they become formal grievances
- *Sincere concern* for employee problems and welfare even when management is not obligated to do so by the collective agreement
- *Training programs* that objectively communicate the intent of union and management bargainers and reduce biases and misunderstandings
- *Joint study committees* that allow management and union officials to find solutions to common problems
- *Third parties* who can provide guidance and programs that bring union leaders and managers closer together to pursue common objectives

An employer and union interested in greater labour–management cooperation have several options to consider. Some of the most common cooperative efforts are summarized in Figure 14-15.[73] One of the most basic actions is prior consultation with the union. While not every management decision must be approved by the union, actions that affect unionized employees may result in grievance filing unless explained in advance to the union.

> In one manufacturing organization, the employer introduced radically new production technology. However, before doing so, the employer met with the union, explained the reason for the change being made, indicated that the change would not result in the loss of any union jobs, and set up a joint committee to study how best to implement the new technology.

Human resource specialists can also build cooperation through a sincere concern for employees. This concern may be shown through the prompt settlement of grievances. As well, employers can establish programs (such as employee assistance programs and job counselling) that assist employees who are experiencing personal difficulties.

Training programs are another way to build cooperation. After a new contract is signed, the human resource department often trains just managers. The union does the same for its leaders. The result is that both sides continue their biases and misunderstandings. If human resource management sponsors training for both the union and management, a common understanding of the contract is more likely to be brought about. The training can be as simple as taking turns paraphrasing the contract or outside neutrals can be hired to do the training. Either way, supervisors and union officials end the training with a common understanding of the contract and a new basis for cooperation.

When a complex problem confronts the union and employer, *joint study committees* are sometimes formed. For example, one organization recently set up a joint committee with its union to establish a policy on sexual harassment. Other employers use joint study committees to address such issues as workplace rules, quality of work life, technological change, budget reduction strategies, and safety. However, union participation and support is absolutely essential:

> At Toronto Hydro, the company implemented a recognition program in which employees who demonstrated certain behaviours that reduced costs, improved productivity, or surpassed performance standards would receive a nonmonetary reward of up to $300. The union strongly opposed the program on the grounds that it pitted workers against each other and violated the union's right to be the exclusive bargaining agent for the employees, refused management's offer to develop the program, and filed a grievance. The arbitrator found in favour of the union. HR Consultant Eric Cousineau commented, "What Toronto Hydro should have done right from the start is to do it with the union, not to the union."[74]

A final method of building cooperation is through the use of third parties, such as consultants or government agencies, who may act as change agents or catalysts to cooperation. For example, in

Nova Scotia, the provincial government has established and delivers a variety of joint union–management programs (including grievance mediation, joint supervisor–steward training, and labour–management committees) with the goal of increasing cooperation in the workplace.

There is no single best approach to building cooperation. Since each relationship is unique, the methods used will depend upon the situation. Improving union management relations is an important function that can be addressed by human resource professionals in unionized organizations.

○ SUMMARY

The labour management framework consists of unions, government, and management. Although each union is unique, unions share the common objectives of protecting and improving their members' wages, hours, and working conditions. To further these objectives, the union movement has created local, national, and international structures, plus federations at the provincial and federal levels.

In Canada, the federal government has jurisdiction in labour relations matters over Crown corporations, airlines, most railways, communication companies, and federal government agencies—or approximately 10 percent of the labour force. All other organizations fall under the jurisdiction of the provinces, which have enacted separate but similar legislation.

Unionization often occurs when workers perceive the need for a union as a response to unsatisfactory treatment by management. During the organizing process, management's response is limited by laws and employee reactions. The employer's primary defence is sound policies implemented by competent supervisors before unionization begins.

If workers form a union, federal or provincial law requires management and the union to bargain in good faith.

The success of the employer at the bargaining table is affected by its actions before negotiations begin. Negotiations with the union usually result in a "collective agreement" that must be approved by union members and top management. Once negotiated, the collective agreement is administered by the union and management.

In administering the agreement, human resource specialists face several challenges. For example, contract clauses place limits on management, day-to-day administration of the contract can lead to precedents, and limitations often result from the resolution of disputes through the grievance procedure or arbitration.

Although unions may represent the employees, management remains ultimately responsible for organizational performance and effectively utilizing the human resources. Through prior consultation, sincere concern for employees, training programs, joint study committees, or third parties, human resource specialists can lay the foundations of a cooperative union–management relationship.

○ TERMS FOR REVIEW

arbitration **p. 513**
authorization cards **p. 504**
business unionism **p. 496**
Canadian Labour Congress (CLC)
    p. 497
collective agreement **p. 494**
conciliation **p. 512**

craft union **p. 496**
grievance procedure **p. 512**
industrial union **p. 496**
labour relations boards (LRBs) **p. 504**
local union **p. 496**
management rights **p. 509**
mediation **p. 512**

precedent **p. 516**
Public Service Staff Relations Act
    (PSSRA) **p. 516**
seniority **p. 515**
social (reform) unionism **p. 496**
unfair labour practices **p. 506**
union shop **p. 515**

○ SELF-ASSESSMENT EXERCISE

What Are Your Views Toward Unions?

The following self-test gives you a quick assessment of your attitudes toward unions. Read each statement and give it a score from 1 to 5 (with 1 indicating that you strongly disagree with the statement and 5 indicating that you strongly agree with the statement).

SCORE

1. Unions give members their money's worth.   _____

2. Unions improve job security for their members.   _____

3. Unions protect workers against unfair actions by the employer.   _____

4. Unions represent the wishes of their members.   _____

5. Unions are a positive force in our society.   _____

6. Unions are still needed today.   _____

7. Unions need more power.   _____

8. Laws should be changed to make it easier to get a union at the workplace   _____

9. I would prefer to work in a unionized job.   _____

10. If a union was organizing my workplace, I would vote for the union.   _____

Add up your score for each of the statements. A higher score is associated with a more positive view of unions.

REVIEW AND DISCUSSION QUESTIONS

1. In your own words, summarize the primary objectives of unions.

2. What distinguishes craft and industrial unions from each other?

3. What roles does the Labour Relations Board serve in labour management relations?

4. In preparing to negotiate an agreement with a union, what types of information would you gather before arriving at the bargaining table?

5. If you were asked to explain why various types of people are on the employer's bargaining team, what reasons would you give for (a) the company lawyer, (b) the director of industrial relations, (c) a wage and salary specialist, (d) a benefit specialist, and (e) the assistant plant manager?

6. Since grievance procedures are found in most contracts, both managers and unions must want them. Explain why both managers and unions want grievance procedures.

CRITICAL THINKING QUESTIONS

1. "Unions do not happen, they are caused by management." Do you agree or disagree with this statement? Why?

2. If you had to advise the manager of a small chain of bakeries how to prepare for a possible strike, what would you suggest?

3. Suppose an employee in your department is an active member of the union, but is performing improperly. After several sessions with the employee, performance is still unacceptable. What type of support would you want to gather before you terminated that employee? What legal complications might result from your action?

4. If you worked in the human resource department of a small company that is suddenly unionized, what changes would you expect to occur in the human resource department?

5. What role do you think federal and provincial governments will play in future labour management relations? What actions can unions and management take to reduce the probability of future government involvement?

6. Obtain a copy of two different collective agreements. Compare and contrast the contract items and the grievance procedure.

ETHICS QUESTION

You are the HR manager in a small, private specialty-steel mill that is nonunionized. Over the years, the company has been quite profitable and has shared profits with its employees through a profit sharing plan. Last year, however, due to global economic conditions, the company incurred its first loss in a decade, so there were no profits to share. The United Steelworkers Union (USU), a union with a reputation for militancy, saw this as a great opportunity to try to organize your company again—its fifth attempt. In the past, their attempts have been abysmal failures, but they keep trying. This time, however, because of the discontent of the employees about the missing bonus, you perceive that the union might have a real chance to win enough votes for certification. You know who the union activist is: a loudmouthed individual who has been disciplined several times for abusive behaviour and foul language directed at supervisors. You know too that it would be easy to provoke him to be abusive again, giving you an excuse for his dismissal; the last time he had had an encounter with his supervisor, he had been warned in writing that one more provocation would result in dismissal. The supervisor even volunteers to find an excuse for an encounter. If the union lost its internal organizer, there is a very good chance that the certification drive would fail again. Temptation is great. What do you do?

○ WEB RESEARCH EXERCISE

1. Visit the Web site of the International Labour Organization (www.ilo.org). What are the major objectives of the ILO? What are some of the major issues affecting workers around the world?

2. Go to the Web site for the Canadian Labour Congress (www.canadianlabour.ca). Also visit the Web site for a provincial federation of labour (for instance, the Nova Scotia Federation of Labour). Compare and contrast the functions of the two federations. What similarities and differences exist? What assistance do the federations provide to organized labour?

○ INCIDENT 14-1

A Routine Discharge at ITC

Four months ago, Pete Ross was discharged from ITC. The supervisor requested that the human resource department discharge Pete because he was caught drinking alcohol in the employee locker room. Drinking on company property was prohibited, as it had been since publication of the ITC Employees' Handbook in 1980.

All employees of ITC were given a copy, and whenever new employees joined, as had Pete in 1993, they too were given one as part of the orientation program. The handbook stated in part: "The consumption of alcoholic beverages on company premises is grounds for immediate termination."

The discharge appeared rather routine to the human resource manager and to the plant manager. Although drinking violations were uncommon, the plant manager believed clear-cut violations of company policy should be punished. Besides, he was frequently heard to say, "We must support our first-line managers."

Pete's fellow machinists did not see it as a "routine discharge." John Briggs, a fellow machinist, summed up the group's feelings: "Pete was a darn good machinist. He was seldom tardy, never absent, and always did a first-class job. If Pete did it, it was done right! That bugged George [the supervisor] because George would pressure Pete to get out the work and say, 'Don't worry about the quality; they only measure quantity.' But Pete wasn't slow. He'd turn out a quality product as fast as some people turned out junk. I don't think George liked Pete. I don't know if Pete took a drink before leaving the plant Wednesday evening, but I think George just wanted to can Pete."

The following Monday, John Briggs spent his rest breaks and lunch hour talking with the other machinists, telling them that "If we don't want to end up like Pete, we'd better get a union." He even had authorization cards from the International Association of Machinists Union. By Monday evening, Briggs had 32 signed cards. There were 39 machinists in the shop.

On Tuesday morning, John Briggs was called into the supervisor's office. The plant manager and the supervisor grilled him. They asked him if he had been distributing authorization cards, who had signed them, and how many he had obtained. Briggs simply replied by saying, "That is none of your business." The plant manager adjourned the meeting without saying a word.

On Thursday (payday at ITC), Briggs received a termination notice with his paycheque. The notice was effective immediately. The notice said termination was for low productivity and excessive absences during the previous 12 months.

1. What unfair labour practices may have occurred?

2. Should management offer reinstatement to Pete Ross or John Briggs?

3. Was Briggs correct when he answered, "That is none of your business," to the questions about the authorization cards?

○ CASE STUDY   Maple Leaf Shoes Ltd.

Absenteeism at Maple Leaf Shoes

Another busy day for Jane Reynolds, special assistant to the human resource manager. Pat Lim, the general manager of marketing (who has also assumed responsibility for the human resource function), had sent yet another memo to Jane (see top of next page).

First things first. Jane decided that resolving the Feltham grievance was her first priority. While she recognized the importance of developing a good attendance policy, that would take some time. At 11 a.m., Jane met with the employee, Glenda Feltham, and her union steward, Shaun Robberman. The facts of the Feltham grievance are reported below.

THE FELTHAM GRIEVANCE

Ms. Glenda Feltham, 32 years of age, has worked at Maple Leaf Shoes for six years. During the past year, as a result of family and health problems, she was absent or late on a number of

---

Memorandum—Maple Leaf Shoes

To: Jane Reynolds

From: Pat Lim

Re: Absenteeism Case/Absenteeism Policy

Dear Jane:

As you are aware, we're having trouble with absenteeism at the plant. Could you look into the following grievance involving Glenda Feltham, discuss it with the union, and see if we can resolve it?

Also, the problem is much deeper than simply a single grievance. Please review the relevant part of the collective agreement and the absenteeism policy that we developed some years ago with the union. Meet with the union and see if we can put together a more proactive policy.

Don't hesitate to contact me if you need my assistance.

Regards,

Pat

---

occasions. The collective agreement between Maple Leaf Shoes and the union does not specifically address the issue of absence from work; it merely states that "no employee may be given a written reprimand or written warning, or be suspended, demoted, or dismissed unless the employer has just cause."

The absenteeism policy at Maple Leaf Shoes, which was developed several years ago as a joint effort between union and management, requires the application of progressive discipline for offences involving tardiness or absenteeism. The policy also provides for "wiping the slate clean" if an employee's attendance is satisfactory for a one-year period. Both union and management acknowledge that, at times over the years, the policy has not been strictly enforced. However, four months ago, Maple Leaf management notified the union that it would strictly enforce the policy.

A review of Glenda Feltham's file showed that she has received the following disciplinary penalties:

- Fourteen months ago—oral warning for being 22 minutes late.
- Nine months ago—written warning for being absent for two days. Glenda failed to call in sick or provide any explanation for her absence upon returning to work.
- Seven months ago—one-day suspension for being 1 hour and 14 minutes late.
- Six months ago—five-day suspension for being absent for one day. Again, Glenda failed to call in sick or explain the reason for her absence.

It appeared that the five-day suspension had alerted Glenda to the fact that unexplained absenteeism and lateness are not acceptable behaviours at Maple Leaf Shoes. After this suspension, Glenda was not late or absent for almost six months. However, one week ago, Glenda failed to show up at work or call in sick. When her supervisor called Glenda's home, no one answered. The next day, Glenda called in sick, but was

reportedly seen that afternoon entering a local fitness club. The following day, Glenda showed up for work, met with her supervisor, and explained that her absence was due to the fact that her boyfriend of six years had told her he was moving out of their apartment and ending their relationship. She said that she was so upset she couldn't face coming to work or trying to explain her absence over the telephone.

Instructions

Assume the role of management representatives (Jane Reynolds' perspective) or union representatives (Shaun Robberman's perspective). The first objective of this case is to ask the parties to meet and try to negotiate a resolution to the Glenda Feltham grievance.

THE POLICY ON ABSENTEEISM

Prior to meeting with the union to address the development of a new policy on absenteeism, Jane reviewed the absence records for the plant. She found that, on average, employees missed about 7.9 days a year. A recent consulting report for the industry indicated that the absence rate for the industry as a whole was 6.7 days a year. Jane realized that the number of absences varied among individuals, but still she was troubled by the high absenteeism rate at the Maple Leaf plant. A review of the absenteeism policy indicated that the policy was very short and had not been updated in several years. The policy read as follows:

1. The need for managing absenteeism is recognized by both the employer and union. While some absence from work is unavoidable, management is concerned that an employee absence creates more work for other employees. Management also believes that it is important to acknowledge both healthy and sick employees.

2. In instances of absenteeism or lateness, the employer will apply principles of progressive discipline. If an employee is able to maintain a satisfactory attendance

record for one year, all previous disciplinary infractions relating to attendance issues will be removed from the employee's file.

3. Management has the right to discipline employees for "excessive absenteeism." In the event that an employee will be late for work or absent from work, the employee is required to make a reasonable effort to contact the employer and indicate that he or she will be late or not present at work. Upon returning to work, the employee is required to provide an explanation for his or her lateness or absence. Depending on the circumstances, the employee may be asked to provide a doctor's note in support of the explanation.

Instructions

The second objective of the case involves the joint meeting of union and management representatives in order to develop a new policy on absenteeism. Work in two groups—management and union—and develop a new policy on absenteeism. Several sources on the Internet are extremely helpful in developing an absenteeism policy.

● CASE STUDY CPIB Canadian Pacific and International Bank

Labour–Management Relations: CPIB and the Maple Leaf Trust Acquisition

The acquisition of Maple Leaf Trust has given Mary Keddy, Senior Vice-President of Human Resources, some cause for concern. She has assigned two senior human resource management employees to review labour relations at Maple Leaf, with a particular focus on the Credit Card Centre, located in Mississauga, Ontario. The Credit Card Centre, which has been unionized for about four years, has had some labour turmoil since the certification of the Canadian Union of Bank Employees (CUBE). Negotiations for a first contract were very difficult, but Maple Leaf Trust and CUBE were able to reach a two-year agreement without resorting to strike action. About 18 months ago, the parties negotiated a second contract (also two years in duration) that was settled after a short (two-day) strike. Approximately 285 unionized workers are employed at the Credit Card Centre, performing a variety of clerical and administrative tasks. Keddy believes that successful integration of the Credit Card Centre employees is very important, but that it represents a major challenge to the human resources department.

A few weeks ago, Keddy met with Pat Jameson, the human resource manager responsible for labour relations issues at the Credit Card Centre. In addition to discussing the adversarial relationship between labour and management, Keddy was able to obtain some data addressing labour relations issues at the Credit Card Centre. This information is summarized below.

Over the four years that the Credit Card Centre has been unionized, employee grievances have increased by about 12 percent a year. Jameson echoed the concern of the company with respect to the amount of time being spent by company officials, union representatives, and employees in contract negotiations and administering the collective agreement. According to Jameson, "During contract negotiations, we met with the union bargaining team on a weekly basis. Each meeting was a good six or seven hours, and it took us almost four months to ultimately hammer out a contract. Things were further complicated by the strike, and we also spent three days in conciliation. Furthermore, we seem to be spending way too much time dealing with grievances. While our wages are competitive, the morale at the Credit Card Centre is low and turnover is clearly a problem."

A review of company records revealed the following grievance pattern:

Total grievances filed	398
Number settled at:	
Step 1—First-level supervisor stage	55
Step 2—Second-level supervisor stage	232
Step 3—Senior HR manager stage	104
Arbitration	7

While some of the grievances involved more than one issue, most of them were single-issue matters. The breakdown of grievances based on the type of issue was also available:

Grievance issues:	
Lateness or absenteeism	154
Overtime allocation	88
Other discipline or discharge	34
Job scheduling	67
Job posting	22
Multiple-issue disputes	33

Jameson also provided Keddy with the results of a recent survey of managers and employees at the Credit Card Centre. All of the managers and 266 of the 285 unionized employees completed the survey. The survey was conducted by a Toronto consultant and was supported by both the company and union (with the understanding that the completed survey forms would go directly to the consultant and the survey results would be provided in summary form to both the company and union). As Jameson noted, "We didn't think the union would cooperate, and we needed them on board in order to survey the unionized workers. I'm getting a sense that both management and the union are getting concerned about the impact of the negative labour relations climate on our ability to compete. And this is even more of an issue since we are now a part of CPIB." Some of the initial findings from the survey are provided below.

1. Assume that you are one of the two senior HRM employees assigned to examining labour relations at the Credit Card Centre. Review the material for Mary Keddy and briefly summarize your major findings.

2. What specific recommendations would you give Mary? Are there any programs or initiatives that you would suggest?

Initial Results from the Labour–Management Survey

PART A:

Workplace Performance Measures	Average Management Response	Average Union Response
Workplace productivity	3.66	3.54
Service quality	3.78	3.45
Union member morale	3.64	2.43
Union member job satisfaction	3.75	2.38
Quality of union member/supervisor relations	3.98	2.93

Note: Each of these questions uses a 5-point scale (1=Very low; 5=Very high).

PART B:

Labour Climate Measures	Average Management Response	Average Union Response
Grievances are settled promptly	4.01	2.87
The working conditions are fair	4.22	3.21
The parties cooperate to solve problems	3.88	2.63
The parties share information	3.66	2.44
The relationship is adversarial	2.94	4.09

Note: Each of these questions uses a 5-point scale (1=Strongly disagree; 5=Strongly agree).

⬢ PART ENDING VIDEOS

"Made in Canada"
Source: *The National*, January 16, 2004, running time 19:11.

"Food and Obesity"
Source: *The National*, January 16, 2004, running time 15:47.

"Union Battles Walmart Effect: No WalMart Wages"
Source: *Venture*, Show Number: 911, January 25, 2004, running time: 10:00.

Go to www.mcgrawhillconnect.ca to access the videos.

Workwell Training: Conflict Violence Communication Skills

⬢ ROLE-PLAY 6: Employee Dismissal Interview

Time required: 30–45 minutes

Objectives of the Role-Play

1. To help the students understand the steps in conducting a dismissal interview.
2. To enhance their skills as interviewers.
3. To help them understand the challenges involved in dismissing an employee.

Prior Preparation

1. Study Chapter 11 of the text.
2. Read descriptions of Maple Leaf Shoes Ltd. at the ends of Chapters 1, 2, and 6.

Guidelines for Conducting the Role-Play

In this role-play, a sales manager (Matt Duritzski) is being terminated from his employment at Maple Leaf Shoes. Note that Matt Duritzski is a nonunion employee. Jane Reynolds will be responsible for conducting the dismissal interview.

1. Two students, one for the role of Jane Reynolds and the other for Matt Duritzski, should be identified.
2. Students should read their own role description in the Instructor Resource Manual along with the company details given at the end of Chapters 1 and 2.
3. The instructor should signal the beginning and the end of the meeting. The length of the interview will vary depending on the approaches taken by Jane Reynolds and Matt Duritzski.
4. The remainder of the class time is used for discussion of what happened during the interview and for reviewing the proper procedure for conducting a dismissal interview.
5. Observers should be asked to make notes against the questions listed below and discuss their findings at the end of the role-play.
6. The instructor should sum up by highlighting the important issues relating to employee dismissal. In addition to reviewing how to conduct a dismissal interview, the instructor should also discuss the concepts of "just cause" and "reasonable notice."

Instructions for Observers

As you observe the meeting between Jane Reynolds and Matt Duritzski, make notes against each of the questions below. Pay particular attention to the behaviours (verbal and nonverbal) of each person.

1. Were the two participants well prepared for the interview? Why?
2. How did Jane Reynolds begin the meeting?
3. Was there open communication between Reynolds and Duritzski? Who spoke more? About what? Did one party control the interview?
4. Was the sequence of his questions appropriate? Was the interview too short or too long? Did Reynolds give Duritzski the opportunity to argue that he should not have been terminated? What could have been done better?
5. Did Jane Reynolds present herself well during the interview? How? What would you do differently if you were Jane? What would you do differently if you were Matt Duritzski?
6. What other improvements to the interview would you recommend?

PART 7

Strategy Evaluation

A human resource department must not become content with its performance. It must proactively search for new ways to help the organization and its people. One way is through an audit of its activities. The research findings from an audit point to opportunities for improvement and prepare for future challenges. Thus, an audit provides feedback on how HR departments perform now and how they should in the future.

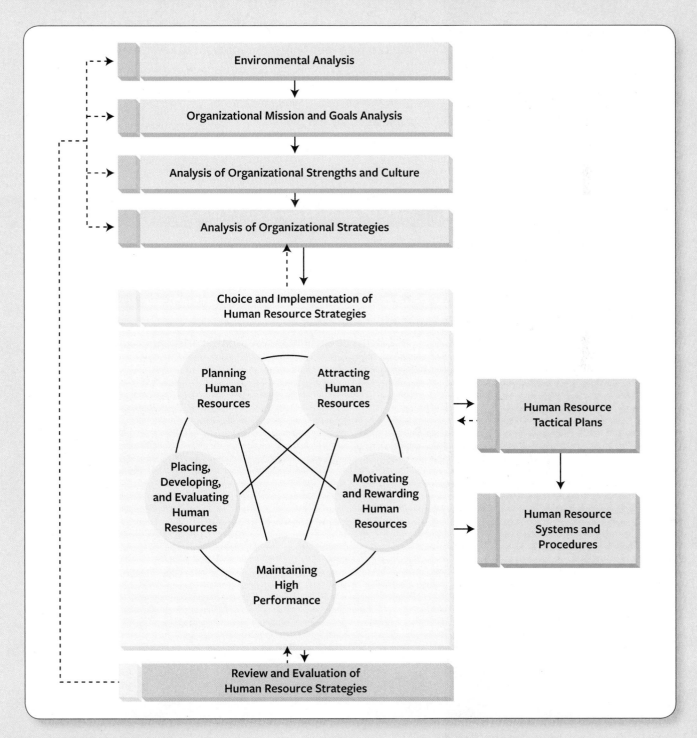

Human Resource Auditing

There is a new phenomenon sweeping the globe—a battle for the best in business talent. While some see it as a fight to attract high performers to their firms, the street smart know it is something entirely different: having the ability to hold onto the people you want to keep (and only those you want to keep) for longer than your competitors. To paraphrase Rudyard Kipling, 'If you can keep your heads when all around are losing theirs, then you are a manager, my son'.

Mike Johnson[1]

CHAPTER OBJECTIVES

After studying this chapter, you should be able to:

➡ *Discuss* the strategic importance of a human resource audit.

➡ *Describe* the steps and research tools used in a human resource audit.

➡ *Discuss* how a human resource department should prepare for the future.

C onsider the following conversation between the manager of an underwriting department in an insurance company and the firm's human resource manager:

Linda Desmarais: I know that auditing is important for a department like ours since we deal in large claims. We do try our best to avoid errors, but errors still do occur. Fortunately, most errors are caught and corrected before major damage is done. But sometimes outside auditors catch our mistakes for us. But why audit human resource practices?

Fred Nolin: We realized that there is room for improvement. We would also like to know from managers like yourself about your needs so that we can improve our service.

Linda Desmarais: What do you hope to discover?

Fred Nolin: First, we want to see if our present procedures are being followed. We need uniformity in our selection, career planning, compensation, and other activities. If there is a lack of consistency, we want to find out why. Maybe people don't understand our procedures. Or maybe our methods aren't practical and should be changed. Second, we are checking to ensure compliance with employee relations laws such as human rights, safety, and others. This audit is not a "witch hunt." We are simply trying to improve our performance.

STRATEGIC IMPORTANCE OF HUMAN RESOURCE AUDITS

human resource audit
An examination of the human resource policies, practices, and systems of a firm (or division) to eliminate deficiencies and improve ways to achieve goals.

A **human resource audit** evaluates the human resource activities used in an organization. The audit may include one division or an entire company.

The benefits from a human resource audit are many and include the following:

- It helps align the human resource department's goals with larger organizational strategies.
- It almost invariably uncovers better ways for the department to contribute to societal, organizational, and employee objectives. This, in turn, clarifies the human resource department's duties and responsibilities.
- It ensures timely compliance with legal requirements.
- It discloses how well managers are meeting their human resource duties.
- It uncovers critical human resource problems and possible solutions.
- It reduces human resource costs through more effective procedures.
- It provides specific, verifiable data on the human resource department's contributions.
- It stimulates uniformity of human resource policies and practices.
- It helps review and improve the human resource department's information system.
- It enhances the professional image of the department among various stakeholders.

Human resource research grows more important with each passing year. Several reasons account for this. First, human resource work carries with it many legal implications for the employer. Failure to comply with equal employment or safety laws, for example, subjects the organization to lawsuits. Second, "people costs" are significant. Pay and benefits often are a major operating expense for most employers. Improper compensation plans can be costly, even fatal, to the company's survival. Third, the department's activities help shape an organization's productivity and its employees' quality of work life. Fourth, the critical resource in many organizations today is not capital, but rather, information, knowledge, and expertise.[2] This means that an audit of the calibre of a critical resource—namely, human resources—is necessary for the success of the organization. Finally, the growing complexity of human resource work makes research necessary. Today, more than ever before, human resource activities aimed at productivity improvement, succession planning, and organization's cultural change are critical to competitive survival. More and more executives expect the department to make strategic contributions and place the function at a higher level in the organizational hierarchy.

Information on HR developments
www.shrm.org

Over 50 percent of 520 Canadian organizations surveyed in one study were found to have a vice-president in charge of human resources. Over 78 percent of these organizations employed at least one trained professional to deal with human resource matters.[3]

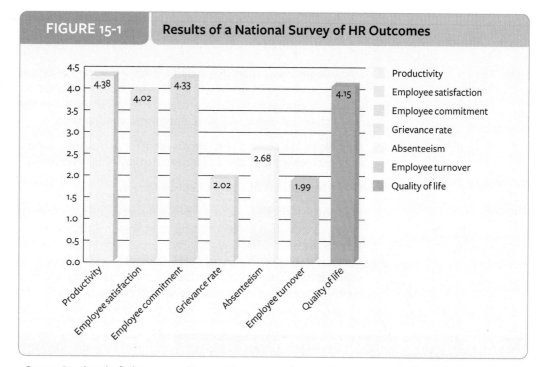

FIGURE 15-1   Results of a National Survey of HR Outcomes

Source: Based on the findings reported in terry Wagar, *Human Resource Management and Labour Relations: A Study of Canadian Organizations*, department of Management, unpublished report, Saint Mary's university, halifax, October 1993, pp. 11–13.

How effective are human resource departments in achieving various organizational and employee objectives discussed in Chapter 1? One study of 650 Canadian organizations[4] found that on criteria such as employee satisfaction and commitment, most Canadian organizations receive a satisfactory, though not exemplary, ratings (see Figure 15-1). Data such as these provide approximate benchmarks for individual firms to compare their own performance. Indices such as these also result in the initiation of new programs such as literacy training and better responses to employees with disabilities (see Spotlight on HRM later in this chapter), which can significantly improve employee productivity and morale.

STEPS IN CONDUCTING HUMAN RESOURCE AUDITS

Human resource auditing involves four major steps:

1. Define the scope of the audit.
2. Choose the research approach.
3. Select the research design and data collection method.
4. Analyze the data, evaluate it, and prepare the report containing findings and recommendations.

Figure 15-2 shows these steps, which are discussed in detail below.

The Scope of Human Resource Audits

The scope of an audit extends beyond just the human resource department's actions. The department does not operate in isolation. Its success depends on how well it performs and how well its programs are carried out by others in the organization. Consider how supervisors in a firm reduced the effectiveness of the performance appraisal process:

> To appraise performance, Kanata Electronics used a critical-incident procedure, which means supervisors had to record both positive and negative incidents as they occurred. To become a

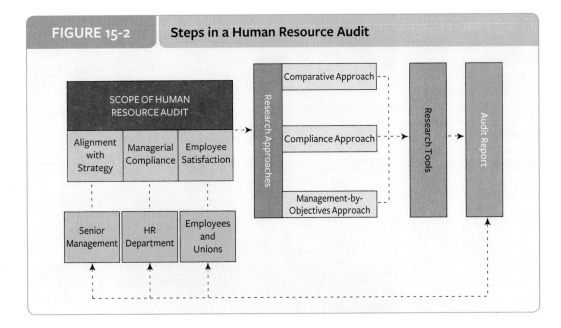

FIGURE 15-2 **Steps in a Human Resource Audit**

section supervisor, an employee needed three years of good or superior performance evaluations. However, in practice, supervisors stressed employee mistakes when they recorded incidents; as a result, few employees received the three years of good ratings needed to qualify for a promotion. Many of them blamed the human resource department's appraisal process for their lack of promotions.

An audit uncovered this misuse of the program and led to additional training for supervisors in the use of the critical-incident method. If the audit had not uncovered this problem, employee dissatisfaction might have worsened.

As the above example illustrates, "people problems" are seldom confined to just the human resource department. Indeed, in recent years, human resource professionals have found that the scope of the audit must transcend even the concerns of the department and operating managers. In practice, human resource audits, typically, focus on alignment of HR strategy with overall corporate strategy, managerial compliance, and employee satisfaction.

Audit of Alignment with Corporate Strategy

Human resource professionals significantly influence the strategic success of an organization. Whether the company stresses superior marketing (McCain Foods), service (IBM), innovation (Nortel), low-cost operations (Canadian Tire), or some other approach, human resource management plays a key role in making the strategy successful. As pointed out in Chapter 1, the human resource strategy and systems must be not only consistent with an organization's present strategy but continually examined for their appropriateness in the light of the outcomes. Consider this case:

Historically, a large accounting firm used to hire a large number of junior accountants at low wages to conduct routine accounting and audit. It was the firm's strategy to keep its overall costs low by keeping its labour costs lower than competitors. Although this strategy resulted in higher-than-average turnover among the new hires, the firm continued the practice until a human resource audit showed considerable dissatisfaction among new hires. Armed with the evidence, the human resource manager was able to influence the corporate strategy and change it. Although labour costs increased in the short run, overall operational costs did not increase substantially because of the reduced turnover that resulted and the decrease in training costs. The improved employee morale had a welcome effect: it enabled the firm to expand own operations in the longer term.

© Nathan Denette/The Canadian Press.

With 450 stores, 45,000 employees, and revenues of over $4 billion, Canadian Tire is one of the country's largest retailers. In such a huge enterprise, is an HR audit more or less useful than in a smaller company?

audit team
Team responsible for assessing the effectiveness of the human resource function.

audit of managerial compliance
An audit to review how well managers comply with HR policies and procedures and labour laws.

Audits should logically begin with a review of the human resource department's work. Figure 15-3 lists the major areas they cover. As shown in the figure, an audit should focus on the human resource management information system, staffing and development, and organizational control and evaluation.

For each item chosen for audit, an **audit team** of human resource specialists should do the following:

- Identify who is responsible for each activity.
- Evaluate how objectives associated with each activity support organizational strategies.
- Review the policies and procedures used to achieve these objectives.
- Examine whether policies and procedures are being following correctly.
- Develop a plan of action to make improvements and report them to all concerned.
- Follow up on the plan of action to ensure continued compliance.

Audit of Managerial Compliance

An **audit of managerial compliance** reviews how well managers comply with human resource policies and procedures. If managers ignore these policies or violate employee relations laws, the audit should uncover these errors so that timely corrective action can be taken.

> The manager of a fast-food restaurant in British Columbia hired two high-school students to do janitorial work on a part-time basis. The two boys were glad to earn $5 an hour. But one boy's father complained to the government that the restaurant was paying below minimum wage. Not only was the parent company found guilty of violating the minimum wage laws, but the complaint triggered an investigation of the pay and overtime practices of the firm's other restaurants. Had this company used an internal human resource audit, the error could have been corrected before formal government action was taken.

Besides assuring compliance, the audit can improve the human resource department's image and contribution to the company. Operating managers may gain a higher respect for the department when an audit seeks their views. If the comments of managers are acted upon, the department will be seen as more responsive to their needs, and effective in achieving organizational objectives.

When internal audits are not routinely carried out, this can increase the probability of an employer violating laws even if unintentionally.

> Between 2005 and 2007, 73 employers were convicted of offences under the *Occupational Health and Safety Act* or *Workplace Safety and Insurance Act*. While this represents a small proportion of total employers, it still underscores the likelihood of employers being caught for legal violations if routine internal audits of legal compliance are not carried out.[5]

audit of employee satisfaction
Assessment of employee satisfaction with a variety of work-related matters and the implications for HR practices and systems.

Audit of Employee Satisfaction

As mentioned in Chapter 1, effective human resource departments are also employee champions and should attempt to meet their objectives where feasible. When employee needs are not met, high employee turnover and absenteeism, and adversarial union–management relations are more likely to emerge. To learn how well employee needs are met, the audit team gathers data from workers.[6] Information that the team collects from an **audit of employee satisfaction** includes details of

FIGURE 15-3	Major Areas Covered in a Human Resource Audit

Human Resource Management Information System

Human rights legislation
- Information on compliance

Human resource plans
- Supply and demand estimates
- Skills inventories
- Replacement charts and summaries

Job analysis information
- Job standards
- Job descriptions
- Job specifications

Compensation administration
- Wage and salary levels
- Benefit package
- Employer-provided services

Staffing and Development

Recruiting
- Source of recruits
- Availability of recruits
- Employment applications

Selection
- Selection ratios
- Selection procedures
- Human rights legislation compliance

Training and orientation
- Orientation program
- Training objectives and procedures
- Learning rate

Career development
- Internal placement success
- Career planning program
- Human resource development effort

Organization Control and Evaluation

Performance appraisals
- Standards and measures of performance
- Performance appraisal techniques
- Evaluation interviews

Labour–management relations
- Legal compliance
- Management rights
- Dispute resolution problems

Human resource controls
- Employee communications
- Discipline procedures
- Change and development procedures

Human resource audits
- Human resource function
- Operating managers
- Employee feedback on human resource department

wages, benefits, supervisory practices, career planning assistance, and the feedback employees receive about their performance:

> The audit team of an automobile parts distributor received one common complaint from employees: they felt isolated because they worked in retail stores or warehouses located all over Canada. They had little sense of belonging to the large company of which they were a part. To bolster sagging morale and to help employees feel that they were members of a fast-growing and dynamic company, the human resource department started a biweekly "Employee Newsletter." The two-page letter was stuffed in every pay envelope each payday. It gave tips on new developments at headquarters and different field locations. The firm also hired a consultant to explore the introduction of a corporate intranet to which all employees could sign in for the latest developments in the company. In this way, the department used the audit to make the firm more responsive to its employees' needs.

Many progressive organizations conduct employee attitude surveys regularly. This enables the organization to solve problems before they evolve into larger and more complex challenges.

SPOTLIGHT ON ETHICS
How to Ensure Ethical Compliance?

You are the director of human resources in a medium-sized organization which has a 20-member senior management team. You report to the vice-president, administration. You have reason to believe that four or five members of the senior management team (as well as a number of persons at the lower levels) have been making decisions you consider unethical. Your organization has a code of ethics, but it does not seem to be well-enforced by the management, including the CEO. Indeed, you believe that the problems start from the top. A number of employees own the company's stock in their retirement savings plans. You believe that the decisions taken by the management (some of which you consider to be financially reckless as well) may reduce the value of the company stock and hence hurt the employees. You realize that you don't have enough power to make significant changes. In any case, your actions may alienate a number of influential members of management who can determine your career advancement and success in this organization.

What actions will you take? How will you ensure ethical compliance by all concerned?

Research Approaches to Audits

Human resource audits may be done using a variety of research approaches. The three most popular approaches are the comparative approach, compliance approach, and management by objectives approach. These are discussed in some detail below.

Comparative Approach

comparative approach
HR audit approach comparing one firm's (or division's) HR practices with another firm (or division) to uncover areas of poor performance.

benchmarking
A strategy to improve a firm's HR practices or systems by identifying the best possible ways to carry out various activities.

Perhaps the simplest form of research is the **comparative approach**. Most typically, it uses another division or company as a model. Alternatively, the benchmarks offered by an outside expert or general industry standards may be used as indices against which the department's or firm's performance is measured and compared.

Benchmarking aims to improve the firm's human resource practices or systems by identifying the best possible ways of carrying out the various activities. Some of the questions asked during benchmarking exercise are as follows:

- How do our HR outcome measures (e.g., absenteeism, employee turnover) compare with that of the best in the industry and elsewhere?
- How safe are our practices and work premises compared to the best workplaces in our industry?
- How do our overall productivity levels and labour costs compare to the industry averages? Compared to those of our key competitors (where figures are available)?
- How involved and satisfied are our employees compared to others in the industry?
- What are the HR practices of best employers in the country? In the world? How do our own practices measure up to these?

As may be seen from the above, the focus is on identifying the best practices and emulating or exceeding them. Consequently, benchmarking is a continuous exercise and not to be thought of as a one-time event. Benchmarking is particularly helpful when a new procedure is being tried for the first time.

When B.C. Lumber installed an alcohol rehabilitation program, it copied salient features of a long-running similar program at another local firm. Later the results of the two programs were compared, which helped B.C. Lumber to remove "bugs" in its program.

Sometimes, an organization's own internal benchmarks (e.g., past records or accomplishments) are used for benchmarks. For example, research into the company's records reveals its absenteeism and turnover rates. The trends in these indices over time can help the human resource department and operating managers to take appropriate control actions. This is usually supplemented with comparisons against external information, which may be gathered from other firms and often expressed as ratios:

> Metro Groceries, which has a workforce of approximately 200 employees, had 32 quit during a year. In the previous year, 28 employees had left the firm. The firm recognized that its turnover rate had increased from 14 to 16 percent. What was even worse, the rate was significantly higher than the industry standard of 10 percent. Metro Groceries decided to look into the problem in greater detail.

Compliance Approach

compliance approach
Review of past human resource practices to determine if they conform to formally stated policies and legally defensible standards.

The **compliance approach** is another human resource audit strategy. This method reviews past practices to determine if they followed company policies and procedures. Often the audit team reviews a sample of employment, compensation, discipline, and employee appraisal forms. The purpose of the review is to ensure that field offices and operating managers comply with internal rules and legal regulations:

> An internal audit of the selection process used at Bio-Genetics Ltd. revealed that the employment manager followed the correct procedures. But the audit team noticed that many applications had comments written in the margins. These comments were added by operating managers who also interviewed applicants. Most of their notes referred to personal data that were not asked on the form, such as sex, age, marital status, ages of dependants, and race. Managers did this to help them remember individual candidates. But in the case of an applicant who was not hired, these comments could lead to charges of discrimination on the basis of age, sex, or race.

For global organizations, the existence of uniform human resource policies and practices throughout their world operations may be desirable, but hard to achieve. Different countries and cultures value different rewards; geographical and cultural distance pose severe communication problems for expatriate managers in performance appraisal, job design, and employee relations; and the legal frameworks across various countries show marked differences making the same practice acceptable and unacceptable in different cultural settings. Given these differences, how does a HR department ensure common global standards? Yet, to ensure equity and improve predictability, some degree of uniformity in HR practices may be necessary. Compliance audits may provide an important tool in the context of the philosophy that counsels to "Think globally, act locally."

Management-by-Objectives Approach

management-by-objectives (MBO) approach
Assessment of HR functions and systems by comparing actual results with stated HR objectives.

The **management-by-objectives** (**MBO**) **approach** creates specific objectives against which the performance of individual managers and the human resource department can be assessed on various dimensions critical for successful people management.[7] The audit team researches actual performance and compares it with the previously set objectives.

> For example, operating managers may set a goal for employee turnover or absenteeism. The actual turnover or absenteeism is then compared to these objectives and progress assessed. The audit may also uncover ways of improving performance in various areas.

Almost all modern organizations have multiple goals. These goals need not be necessarily converging or complementary to each other.

> For example, an organization that wants to achieve a short-term labour cost reduction may downsize its workforce to achieve that objective. However, this may result in the lowering of employee satisfaction, another important goal of many organizations. In the same manner, an increase in profitability may be accompanied by increased environmental pollution.

balanced scorecard
An approach that includes financial, customer-related, employee-related, and internal system–oriented goals of a firm, along with a set of measures of for assessing their accomplishment.

More recently, several organizations have introduced a balanced scorecard to reflect the multiple stakeholders in the firm. A **balanced scorecard** includes financial, customer-related, employee-related, and internal system–oriented goals of a firm, along with a set of measures for assessing their accomplishment. The balanced scorecard approach allows managers to look at a business from multiple perspectives, thus minimizing the risk of overlooking important stakeholders or activity.

No single audit approach works for all situations. More commonly, audit teams use several of the strategies, depending on the specific human resource activities under evaluation. Whatever the approach used, it is desirable to involve managers in developing relevant criteria for evaluating the HR function. An Australian company's past experience provides a good example of how HR performance measurement indicators can be developed in a manner that enhances overall utility of the audit exercise:

> The HR staff at Australian Global Insurance (AGI), as part of its audit process, interviewed senior managers to identify appropriate HR performance indicators useful for strategic decision making. Fifty-two indicators were identified and were grouped into seven categories: organizational effectiveness, compensation, absenteeism and turnover, staffing, training and development, occupational health and safety, and other miscellaneous areas. Managers were also asked to rank the measures in order of importance for strategic decision making. HR performance indicators for each category and various items were next identified. (For example, a measure of internal recruitment was the time taken to fill vacancies from internal sources.) Such indicators allowed the HR function not only to indicate its contribution to bottom-line performance but also to benchmark practices of highly successful firms. The active involvement of senior management in determining these performance indicators also enhanced the overall usefulness of the audit.[8]

Research Design and Data Collection Method

Regardless of the audit team's approach, it must collect data about the organization's human resource activities. In practice, this is a very difficult task. Part of the reason lies in the fact that it is very difficult to define its effectiveness. Many of the indices available are subjective in nature and organization-dependent. Further, human resource management effectiveness at the organizational level may be quite different from the effectiveness and efficiency of the human resource department itself. In addition, one must also consider issues related to research efficiency. Most research requires a considerable investment in time and resources, and some designs are more expensive than others.[9]

Typically, a number of tools may be needed to gauge human resource management effectiveness even approximately. Each research tool provides partial insights into the firm's human resource activities. If these tools are used skillfully, the team can weave these insights into a clear picture of the organization's human resource activities. These tools include interviews, surveys, records analysis, and experiments. These are briefly discussed below.

Interviews

Interviews with employees and managers are one source of information about human resource activities. Their comments help the audit team identify areas that need improvement. Criticisms by employees may pinpoint those actions that the department should take to meet their needs. Likewise, suggestions by managers may reveal ways to provide them with better service. When their criticisms are valid, changes should be made. But when it is the human resource department who is right, it may have to educate others in the firm by explaining the procedures being questioned:

> Bob Gordon served as a member of the audit team at Canadian Furniture Company. He interviewed various managers, who complained that the frequent transfer of managerial staff was a problem. Bob understood their concerns. He explained that the unique type of furniture the company dealt with led to too many fluctuations in market demand for the company's products. Unless senior managers were frequently transferred to faraway branches, the sales of these branches could not be pulled up. Although many managers still disliked the situation, the audit interview helped them understand the need for the frequent transfers of managers.

Another useful source of information is the exit interview.[10] **Exit interviews** are conducted with departing employees to learn their views of the organization. Figure 15-4 shows the typical questions asked during the interview. It is done separately from the human resource audit, and employee comments are recorded. Then during the audit, these answers are reviewed to find the causes of employee dissatisfaction and other human resource management problems.

Surveys

Many human resource departments supplement interviews with questionnaires and **surveys**. These tools are used because interviews are time-consuming, costly, and usually limited to only a few people. Through surveys of employees, a more accurate picture of employee treatment can be developed. Also, questionnaires may lead to more candid answers than face-to-face interviews.

FIGURE 15-4	An Exit Interview Form

Saskatoon Kitchen Appliances Ltd.
Exit Interview Form

Employee's name _____   Date hired _____
Interviewed by _____   Interviewed on _____
Supervisor's name _____   Department _____

1. Were your job duties and responsibilities what you expected?

   If not, why? _____

2. What is your frank and honest opinion of:
   a. Your job? _____
   b. Your working conditions? _____
   c. Your orientation to your job? _____
   d. Your training provided by the company? _____
   e. Your pay? _____
   f. Your company-provided benefits and services? _____
   g. Your treatment by your manager? _____

3. What is your major reason for leaving the company? _____

4. What could we have done to keep you from leaving? _____

5. What could be done to make Saskatoon Kitchen appliances a better place to work? _____
   _____
   _____

attitude survey
Systematic assessment of employees' opinions about various work-related factors, typically using a questionnaire.

One popular approach is an employee **attitude survey**. These multipage paper-and-pencil tests are used to learn how employees view their manager, their job, and the human resource department. Sometimes several hundred questions are asked. These questions seek answers to the critical issues listed in Figure 15-5 (on page 540). Then the answers are grouped into areas of analysis to find out where employee attitudes are high and where low. The survey results may also be compared across departments, to other similar firms, to past survey findings, or to corporate objectives. Further analysis may identify problems with specific supervisors, employee subgroups, jobs, or benefits:

Attitude surveys give valuable feedback about required changes in jobs or supervision. The human resource department learns how its efforts are viewed by employees. Of particular importance are trends revealed through repeated, periodic administration of questionnaires. The discovery of research-based trends suggests whether specific challenges are becoming more or less important to those surveyed.

For example, in one food processing facility, during an employee survey, many women employees complained about poor supervisory practices. The first-line supervisors were reported to be insensitive to the needs of women employees and often openly ignoring them. The supervisors were provided with summary feedback and suggestions for improvement. When the next year's survey results showed little improvement in supervisory ratings on this dimension, the human resource department decided to introduce an intensive diversity management training for all first-line supervisors. In the following year's survey, the number of complaints was reduced by over 40 percent.

record analysis
Review of past company records as part of an HR audit.

safety and health records
An audit of safety and health records can find past or potential violations and suggest ways to eliminate them.

Records Analysis

Sometimes problems can be found only by studying records. **Record analysis** is particularly important when investigating compliance with company procedures and laws that may not be truly measured either through interviews or surveys. The records normally reviewed by an audit team are listed in Figure 15-6 (on page 541) and discussed in the following paragraphs.

Safety and Health Records. An analysis of **safety and health records** may reveal violations of provisions of the *Canada Labour Code* or other provincial safety and health regulations. Under the record-keeping requirements of the *Canada Labour Code*, Part IV, accurate records of all matters coming under the jurisdiction of the safety and health committee should be kept by every organization.

FIGURE 15-5	Critical Concerns to Be Answered by Attitude Surveys

Employee attitudes about supervisors

- Are employees working in specific departments or under specific supervisors exceptionally satisfied or dissatisfied?
- Do specific supervisors need training in supervisory and human relations skills?
- Have attitudes improved since the last survey?

Employee attitudes about their Jobs

- What are common elements of jobs that cause negative attitudes? Positive attitudes?
- Can jobs that cause poor attitudes be redesigned to improve satisfaction?
- Can jobs that cause poor attitudes be given alternative work schedules (such as shorter work weeks or flextime)?

Perceived effectiveness of the human resource department

- Do employees think they work for a good or bad employer?
- Do employees think they have a career or merely a job?
- Do employees feel they have some place to turn in order to solve their problems, besides to their immediate supervisor?
- Do employees feel informed about company developments?
- Do employees know what is expected of them in their jobs?
- Are employees satisfied by the amount and type of feedback they get about their performance?
- Are employees satisfied with their pay? Benefits?

A human resource audit can help to document the firm's compliance with safety and health requirements in each province. Number of employees who have made claims on workers' compensation plans classified by job, employee category and time periods, number of safety violations observed, and number of complaints from employees about workplace safety are among popular indices looked at in this context.[11]

productivity records
An analysis of records on production, absenteeism, wastage, and labour costs can identify and improve productivity levels.

grievance records
An audit of these can detect patterns in employee grievances.

Productivity Records. An analysis of **productivity records**, absenteeism patterns, scrap rates and wastage, and so on provides clues to the human resource department about prevailing productivity levels and trends. Statistics on absenteeism patterns and turnover figures may provide the human resource department with important clues about underlying, more serious problems.[12]

Grievance Records. The audit team may also be able to uncover a pattern in employee **grievance records**. Patterns may emerge by jobs, supervisors, union representatives, age groups, or contract provisions. If patterns are detected, human resource specialists seek out the underlying causes and take corrective action to reduce the causes of these complaints. Interviews with supervisors and union officials may reveal the underlying causes of grievances. And if union officials participate in finding patterns of grievances, they may support management's suggested changes:

> A grievance audit at the Kelowna Logging Company indicated that supervisors and managers were spending too much of their time dealing with grievances. In fact, the lost production time by workers and costs of arbitration were seriously reducing the company's profitability. Low profitability meant that the union had to accept the smallest wage increases in the area. The audit team asked the two top union officials to help review the causes of grievances. The union leaders thought the problem was a poor understanding of the contract by both supervisors and union representatives. The audit team's analysis matched the union leaders' comments. As a result, the company asked the town's part-time mayor to help train both sides. The training led to a noticeable drop in grievances.

FIGURE 15-6	Records Commonly Reviewed as Part of a Human Resource Audit

Safety and Health Records
- Statistics on accidents before and after safety training programs
- Number of employees who have made claims on workers' compensation plans classified by job, employee category, and time period
- Number of safety violations observed in past audits
- Number of complaints from employees about working conditions and workplace safety

Productivity Records
- Cost of production of different components and products
- Wastage, scrap rates (especially focusing on impact of training, bonuses, or other human resource programs on wastage)
- Absenteeism records
- Employee turnover records

Grievance Records
- Patterns in grievances (e.g., arising from specific contract clauses or supervisors)
- Clarity of clauses in union–management agreements

Compensation Records
- Statistics examining external and internal wage equity
- Statistics on benefits offered along with trends in the firm; comparisons with industry data on file

Human Rights Compliance Records
- Firm's compliance with all human rights laws as evidenced by its application form, job specifications, and so on
- Number and patterns of sexual or other harassment charges
- Workforce statistics on concentration, underutilization, and so on
- Employment equity goals of the firm versus actual achievements

Human Resource Implementation Records
- Comparisons of targets and achievements of HR department in various areas
- Number of employee complaints on various HR-related matters
- Past feedback from managers on file on HR department's effectiveness or needed improvements

Employee Files and Records
- Turnover and absenteeism records classified by age, gender, department, and so on
- Comparison of the above across time, departments, and industry data on file
- Performance of employees before and after specific training programs
- Career progression patterns of specific groups of employees (e.g., visible minorities, women)
- Accuracy, completeness, and currency of information contained in random inspections
- Number, type, and patterns in disciplinary and interpersonal problems

Special Programming Reports
- Results (planned versus actual) of special programs

Job Placement/Selection Records
- Percentage of jobs filled internally
- Performance evaluation of internally promoted candidates by their supervisors
- Usefulness of existing replacement charts/summaries
- Performance of recruits classified by source of recruits
- Recruitment and selection costs (actual against plans and those of other firms)

Safety audits at Ontario Power Generation stations continuously monitor safety at the workplace. An ongoing safety audit not only reduces costs but also saves lives. Can you name examples?

compensation records
A study of wages, benefits, and services can show whether they are fair and competitive.

External compensation information
www.highbeam.com/doc/1G1-7291146.html

human rights compliance audits
Audits of hiring, placement, and compensation practices, to ensure compliance with human rights legislation.

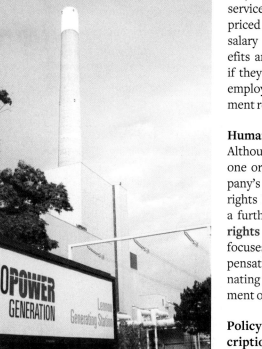

CP/Richard Buchan.

Compensation Records. Audit teams carefully review the human resource department's **compensation records**. Primarily, they study the level of wages, benefits, and services that are provided. If jobs have been priced properly through job evaluations and salary surveys, pay levels will be fair. Benefits and services are also studied to learn if they are competitive with those of other employers and in compliance with government regulations.

Human Rights Compliance Records. Although several large companies employ one or more persons to monitor the company's compliance with Canadian human rights legislation, the audit team serves as a further check on compliance. In **human rights compliance audits**, the team usually focuses on the hiring, placement, and compensation of all minority groups; if discriminating practices exist, it informs management of the need for corrective action.

Policy Documents and Procedural Descriptions. Inspecting other records relating to an organization's general HR policy and procedures may also bring valuable insights and uncover areas requiring improvement. Consider this example:

Two years after Seafood Canners Ltd. adopted a "promotion from within" policy, most supervisors were still recruited from outside the firm. Few workers applied for supervisory openings, even though these jobs were posted throughout the plant and employees were encouraged to apply. The audit team learned that during peak seasons, production workers earned more money than supervisors because of overtime pay and the incentive system. Many employees viewed supervisory jobs as entailing more responsibility and less pay. To remedy the problem, supervisors were given a percentage of their department's production bonus. A year later, 90 percent of the supervisory openings were being filled internally.

As the Seafood Canners example illustrates, policies ("promotion from within") may conflict with other programs (the incentive system). And legal requirements (overtime pay) may conflict with the department's goals. Virtually every human resource policy and program affects at least one other. Thus, a thorough audit needs to include all the major human resource policies and programs and how they relate to each other.

Figure 15-6 also identifies other typical records reviewed by audit teams. These records are evaluated to find areas of poor performance and conflicts between policies, programs, and laws governing employee relations.

Human Resource Experiments

Research experiments are yet another powerful tool available to an audit team. The ideal research design is a **human resource experiment** that allows the HR department to compare an experimental and a control group under realistic conditions.

human resource experiment
Comparison of impact of a treatment on experimental and control groups in real-life settings, while controlling for effects of extraneous factors.

For example, the human resource department may implement a safety training program for half of the department supervisors. This half is the experimental group. The control group is the other half of the department supervisors who are not given training. Then the subsequent safety records of both groups are compared several months after the training is completed. If the experimental group has significantly lower accident rates, this is evidence that the safety training program was effective.

Experimentation does have some drawbacks. Many managers are reluctant to experiment with only some workers because of morale problems and potential dissatisfaction among those who were not selected. Those involved may feel manipulated. And the experiment may be confounded by changes in the work environment or simply by the two groups talking with each other about the experiment. Several of these problems are lessened by using a research design that involves two organizations, as did one school board:

> The human resource department of a rural school district gave all the elementary school teachers of one school a special two-day training program. The teachers at another school located 30 kilometres away did not receive the training. At the end of the year, the school board's audit team compared the teacher evaluations and pupil scores on provincewide tests to assess the success of the development program.

This design reduced the likelihood that the experimental and control groups would discuss the training with each other. For the school principals, it also prevented the problem of having half of their faculty in each group. Of course, the difficulty with this design is that it assumes the two organizations, their teachers, and their students were comparable before the experiment began.

The Audit Report

audit report
A comprehensive description of HR activities, containing commendation for effective practices and recommendations for improving ineffective practices.

For making the audit information useful and directive, it is compiled into an audit report. The **audit report** is a comprehensive description of human resource activities, which includes both recommendations for effective practices and recommendations for improving practices that are ineffective. A report's recognition of both good and bad practices is evidence of a more balanced approach and encourages acceptance of the report.

Audit reports often contain several sections. One section is for line managers, another is for managers of specific human resource functions, and the final section is for the human resource manager. For line managers, the report summarizes their human resource objectives, responsibilities, and duties.

> A line manager's duties include interviewing applicants, training employees, evaluating performance, motivating workers, and satisfying employee needs. The report also identifies "people problems." Violations of policies and employee relations laws are highlighted. Poor management practices are revealed in the report along with recommendations.

Those specialists who handle employment, training, compensation, and other human resource activities also need feedback. The audit report they receive isolates specific areas of good and poor performance.

> For example, one audit team observed that many job incumbents lacked qualified replacements. This information was given to the manager of training and development along with the recommendation for more programs to develop promising supervisors and managers.

The human resource manager's report contains all the information given to line managers and specialists within the human resource department. In addition, the human resource manager gets feedback about the following:

- attitudes of operating managers and employees toward the human resource department services;
- a review of the department's objectives and its organization to achieve them;
- human resource problems and their implications; and
- recommendations for needed changes, which may be stated in priority as determined by the audit team.

With the information contained in the audit report, the human resource manager can take a broad view of the human resource function. Instead of solving problems in a random manner, the manager now can focus on those areas that have the greatest potential for improving the department's contribution to the firm. Emerging trends can be studied and corrective action taken while the problems are still minor. Prompt response to the problems of operating managers may earn added support among them.

Perhaps most important, the audit serves as a map for future efforts and a reference point for future audits. With knowledge of the department's present performance, the manager can make long-range plans to upgrade crucial activities. These plans identify new goals for the department.[13]

And these goals serve as standards—standards that future audit teams will use to evaluate the firm's human resource management activities.

PREPARING FOR THE FUTURE

Audits are necessary, but they are backward-looking. They uncover only the results of past decisions. Although past performance should be evaluated, human resource departments also should look to the future in order to be more proactive. A proactive approach requires human resource managers and their staff to develop a future orientation. They must constantly scan their professional and social environment for clues about the future. New developments may mean new challenges.

For example, high divorce rates may lead to more employer-provided child care facilities and flexible work schedules so that working parents can fulfill their parental duties.

What will the world of work look like in the next decade?

PricewaterhouseCoopers (PwC) in the United Kingdom examined what the world of work will look like in year 2020. It came out with three (or possibly four) alternate scenarios. A "blue world" characterized by large corporations that often resemble mini states and exert considerable influence on the larger society; an "orange world" where focus is on specialization and the rise of collaborative networks of employees; or a "green world" where the environmental agenda drives the business strategy. It is also conceivable that a fourth scenario emerges where all the above three co-exist. Needless to point out, HR's role in each case will be significantly different. This means that the HR function, today, should prepare itself for vastly different future roles.[14]

Without a future orientation, the human resource department becomes reactive, not proactive. And reactive approaches allow minor problems to become major ones. The area of planning provides an appropriate example:

Several top managers of West Coast Paper Products Ltd. seldom took more than a one-week vacation. They felt that no one else was qualified to take their place for longer than a week. When one mill manager quit, the replacement problem became a crisis for several weeks until a new manager was found. Even then, the mill had problems for months until the new manager had learned the company's policies.

Had the human resource office used human resource planning, replacement procedures could have been developed ahead of time. Even without human resource planning, a future-oriented human resource manager would have questioned the lack of replacements.

Major environmental, governmental, technological, and professional challenges facing human resource departments were discussed in Chapters 1 and 4. Key challenges facing the human resource function are summarized in Figure 15-7.

Labour market and economic information
www.statcan.gc.ca/start-debut-eng.html
www.hrsdc.gc.ca/eng/home.shtml

An audit can reveal that a certain segment of the population, such as retirees, is looking for part-time work. Why would that be an advantage to the organization? Focus on retirees.

© Will McIntyre/Getty Images.

This entire text has emphasized a strategic approach to human resource management. This is because, increasingly, human resource managers are expected to contribute to the organization's strategic thinking. Marketing, production, and financial strategies depend upon the abilities of the firm's human resources to execute these plans. To assist with the "people side" of implementation, human resource directors will be forced to uncover, through audits and research, the causes of and solutions to

| **FIGURE 15-7** | **Selected Challenges Facing Human Resource Managers in the Immediate Future** |

- **Productivity improvement**—This will continue to be the main thrust of the near future. To maintain our competitive position in the international market, HR will have to ensure that the workforce is competent, committed, and creative.

- **Encouraging innovation**—Tied closely with the above is the importance of encouraging innovation. If Canada is to maintain its competitiveness in the new global world, our industries have to come out with continuous innovations in products and processes. Unfortunately, our track record in this regard so far has not been very impressive. HR managers have to work closely with line managers to create a work setting that facilitates continuous innovation and entrepreneurship.

- **Integrating immigrants into the organization**—More immigration of skilled employees is an almost certainty; however, because of their different social and cultural backgrounds, the effective integration of new immigrants into the workforce will be a challenge for human resource specialists. Human resource managers will need to have better training to evaluate foreign qualifications and integrate immigrants into the workforce.

- **Preparing for a greying workforce**—The decline in birth rate coupled with longevity means that the average age of Canadian population and the workforce is rising. Employee productivity may go up as workers gain experience. But those same people are likely to seek more job security and improved pensions, affecting compensation costs. Ergonomic considerations may assume greater importance to account for the emerging needs of an older workforce.

- **Changing values**—The values held by gen X-ers are qualitatively different from those of the boomers, affecting workforce attitudes toward work, retirement, loyalty, attendance, and tardiness, and shape the demands placed on human resource management.

- **Innovation**—To cope and survive in the new economy, human resource specialists will require continued innovation in own practices and facilitate organizational change and innovation.

- **Portable pensions**—Increased mobility of Canadian workers is likely to make it necessary to offer portable pension plans, which in turn necessitate changes in HR systems.

- **Technological changes**—Revolutionary changes in technology necessitate fundamental changes in how, where, and when work is done, which in turn require more frequent job redesign and improved systems for human resource planning, selection, and training.

- **Employee rewards**—When the recession is over and the economy returns to a steady state, a strong demand for skilled workers and tradespersons may cause "wage compression" and offer of noncash compensation to attract scarce talents.

- **Women and minority workers**—The higher participation rates of women and members of visible minorities will require better diversity management tools on the part of work supervisors and managers.

- **Dual-career families**—With the emergence of more dual-career families, child care, elder care, spousal transfer, and so on will demand much greater attention from HR practitioners. The day care plans under two major federal parties are qualitatively different; this means that depending on which is the governing party, the employer's involvement in arranging day care facilities may be vastly different.

- **Protecting employee privacy**—With the growth of computerized information systems, companies maintain ever-growing databanks on employees. The need to ensure privacy to employees against abuse of this information may cause greater attention to be paid to the privacy of employee records.

people-related problems. Their diagnostic abilities to assess present and potential human resource issues will be needed as they and their staff increasingly serve as internal consultants to others who are facing human resource–related challenges.[15] They then will be called on to facilitate changes in the organization that maximize the human contribution. In short, the traditional administrative skills associated with human resource management must grow to accommodate diagnostic, assessment, consulting, and facilitative skills.

SPOTLIGHT ON HRM
Conducting a Disability Audit

As a manager of consulting services at the Saskatchewan Association of Health Organizations, Leanne Hamm has long been training health administrators across the province on such issues as return to work, disability management and case management.

Now, she hopes to be able to provide another service: a disability management audit that would help organizations identify what they're good at and what they need to work on. The association provides its 160 members, including regional health authorities, hospitals and special care homes, with a range of support services in payroll, collective bargaining, benefit programs, professional development and health and safety.

The audit tool Hamm will be using is the Consensus Based Disability Management Audit, developed by the National Institute of Disability Management and Research (NIDMAR), a Victoria-based non-profit education, training and research organization. To conduct a disability audit, Hamm would typically spend five days poring through policies and procedures, committee minutes and individual case files, both open and closed, to find out how they were handled. She would then sit down with representatives of both management and employees to determine a score for each of the audit's 84 questions. Both parties will have to agree on the score for each question. If they don't, it's the lower score that's registered.

Then she would verify those scores against employee perception by conducting a survey of the general employee population. She would select a random sample representing five or 10 per cent of the workforce, depending on the size of the organization. Whereas the employee representative helping her score the questions would be well-versed in how the program works, the workers participating in this part of the audit will help give her a sense of what the employee population at large knows of the program.

If she's auditing a regional health authority, her work would take her to each of the authority's major facilities to get a good understanding of how things work at each site.

"It's a lot of work, but it will be worth it," said Hamm, who works out of the association's workplace health, safety and education services department in Regina. "I don't know of any other audit that's that complete, where you're looking at evidence and surveying employees and bringing together all the parties to answer the questions."

Hamm said the cost of doing such an audit typically runs $8,500 to $10,000, but the association has yet to determine a price structure for the member organizations.

The audit tool has come a long way since it was created by NIDMAR in 1996 and is gaining acceptance around the world. Late last year, the United Kingdom subsidiary of UnumProvident, one of the largest disability insurance providers in the country, adopted the tool. It began training nine of its vocational rehabilitation employees to be certified to carry out the audit.

Joy Redmund, head of vocational rehabilitation services for UnumProvident in the U.K., said she sees it as another service the insurer can provide to its larger client companies.

"We see the NIDMAR assessment as having great potential to assist employers in this area by giving them a standardized benchmark. This will help them see how they compare with their industry competitors; a starting point, so that they can see how they change over time; a confirmation that they are employing best practices in this area; and an analysis not only of their strengths but also their weaknesses, with recommendations for how they can improve," said Redmund.

In Australia, the audit tool is being licensed by Employers Mutual, a workers' compensation insurance provider in the states of New South Wales, South Australia and Victoria. A not-for-profit organization for workers with disabilities in Ireland is also using the audit tool to help employers improve their return to work and disability management programs.

For Wolfgang Zimmerman, executive director of NIDMAR, the biggest accolades came when the audit tool, the curriculum and the professional designations of certified disability management professional and certified return to work co-ordinator were adopted by the German Federation of Institutions for Statutory Accident Insurance and Prevention (HVBG), the umbrella group representing all 35 of Germany's insurance providers for workplace accidents and injuries.

Noting that Germany is the country where the workers' compensation board (WCB) system was created, Zimmerman said he once asked Joachim Breuer, the director general of the federation, why "the oldest and largest WCB in the world" would use a Canadian protocol as a standard for its 3,500 return-to-work and case management professionals.

"The answer he gave was, 'We never had these standards,' and 'What I'm doing is no different than what leading organizations do,' which is to continuously scour the world for innovative products," said Zimmerman.

Part of the appeal of the audit tool is its grounding in research. Zimmerman said the tool draws on the key principles identified in a 1998 research project by the

International Labour Organization, a United Nations agency.

The *International Research Project on Job Retention and Return to Work Strategies for Disabled Workers* examined and evaluated return-to-work policies in eight countries and found a number of universal success factors. These include a safety program, a health promotion program, transitional work options and early intervention as part of a formal return-to-work program. Key factors also include policies and procedures that are jointly endorsed by labour and management, strong internal and external communications systems and a supportive enterprise culture. And, not least, successful disability management programs are those run or co-ordinated by someone who's well-versed in return to work and accommodation.

It's with the goal of setting professional standards in this line of work that NIDMAR has made it mandatory that anyone using the tool be certified as an auditor. Last month, Zimmerman came to Toronto to take part in the launch of a new organization, the Canadian Society of Professionals in Disability Management, which has 100 members. An international association of these professionals is being launched March 22 in Berlin.

"If I get injured at work, it's the skill set of the person co-ordinating the return to work that is pivotal to whether or not I'll have an income and a future, or just join the ranks of those sitting at home," said Zimmerman.

Source: Uyen Vu, "Conducting a Disability Audit: Made-in-Canada Tool Gains Worldwide Acceptance," *Canadian HR Reporter* (March 13, 2006), www.hrreporter.com/loginarea/members/viewing.asp?ArticleNo=4311, retrieved March 27, 2006.

SUMMARY

A human resource audit evaluates the human resource activities used in an organization. Its purpose is to ensure that operating managers and human resource specialists are following human resource policies and maintaining an effective workforce.

The scope of the audit involves human resource specialists, operating managers, employees, and the external environment. Inputs are sought from all four sources because each has a unique perspective. To be truly effective, human resource activities cannot meet just the wishes of experts in the field. They must also meet the needs of employees and operating managers and the challenges from the environment.

The audit team uses a variety of research approaches and tools to evaluate human resource activities. Data are gathered through interviews, questionnaire surveys, internal records, and experimentation. Through these tools, the audit team is able to compile an audit report. The audit report provides feedback to top management, operating managers, human resource specialists, and the human resource manager. Armed with this information, the human resource manager then can develop plans to ensure that human resource activities better contribute to the objectives of the organization.

If human resource management is to be responsible, it must review its past performance through audits and research. At the same time, it needs a future orientation to anticipate upcoming challenges. Finally, a proactive view encourages human resource management to contribute to both people and company goals. To be proactive requires modern information systems, increased professionalism, and a future orientation to meet the major environmental, governmental, and technological challenges facing human resource departments. These evolving challenges will necessitate human resource managers to identify new approaches.

With all the challenges facing human resource management, its role is sure to grow in scope and importance. The key to this growth is unlocking the contribution that people make to organizations. It is through this contribution that organizations prosper. In turn, it is through our life-sustaining organizations that we prosper as individuals and as a society.

TERMS FOR REVIEW

⊙ SELF-ASSESSMENT EXERCISE

An Audit of This Course

This audit of human resource management course which you have just completed has three parts. Do not omit any questions. Circle the appropriate number (or indicate your responses on a separate paper) against each item and compute the average score for each part.

1. If you are part of a team in this course, how does your score compare against the team's average score?
2. Are the scores you received on the three parts consistent? In other words, did you receive high or low scores on all the three parts or some high and low scores?

PART 1: OBJECTIVES

To what extent where the following course objectives met?

	Completely	To a Great Extent	To a Limited Extent	Not at All
1. I now have an overall awareness of key human resource functions and activities.	4	3	2	1
2. I have an awareness of the legal responsibilities of managers and organizations as they relate to managing employees.	4	3	2	1
3. I understand the strategic role human resource management plays in modern organizations.	4	3	2	1
4. I have knowledge of specific HR techniques or tools to conduct job analysis, human resource planning, hiring, training, appraisal, and compensation.	4	3	2	1

Scoring: Add up the scores on all four items and divide the sum by 4. This is your average score on this part.

PART 2: MASTERY GAINED

To what extent did you gain mastery over the following topics? (Note: If a particular topic is not covered in your course, check "Not Applicable")

	Very Much	Moderate	Very Little	Not Applicable
Role of human resource manager	3	2	1	
Challenges facing human resource managers	3	2	1	
Job analysis	3	2	1	
Human resource planning	3	2	1	
Legal challenges and human rights laws	3	2	1	
Employee recruitment	3	2	1	
Selection	3	2	1	
Orientation and training	3	2	1	
Performance appraisal	3	2	1	
Compensation	3	2	1	
Employee relations	3	2	1	
Managing diversity	3	2	1	
Occupational safety and health	3	2	1	
Union–management relations	3	2	1	
Human resource audit	3	2	1	

Scoring: Add up all scores and divide by the number of items you rated. Do not include any item that you checked "Not Applicable." This is your average score on this part.

PART 3: TEACHING AIDS OR PROCEDURES

	Excellent	Very Good	Good	Fair	Poor	Not Applicable
Lectures by instructor	5	4	3	2	1	
Guest lectures	5	4	3	2	1	
Films and audiovisual aids	5	4	3	2	1	
Field trips	5	4	3	2	1	
Class discussions	5	4	3	2	1	
Case discussions	5	4	3	2	1	
Class exercises and role-plays	5	4	3	2	1	
Quality of cases used in this course	5	4	3	2	1	
Quality of the textbook used	5	4	3	2	1	
Quality of the readings used	5	4	3	2	1	
Overall classroom climate	5	4	3	2	1	
Overall quality of this course	5	4	3	2	1	

Scoring: Add all the numbers you circled and divide the total by the number of statements you rated (ranging from 1 to 12). This is your average score on this part.

⟹ REVIEW AND DISCUSSION QUESTIONS

1. What are the benefits of a human resource audit to an organization? To the human resource department?

2. If you were asked to conduct an audit of selection function, what steps would you follow?

3. If you had to conduct an audit of employee job satisfaction, what tools would you use?

4. What are the areas where a HR department should focus now to be proactive?

⟹ CRITICAL THINKING QUESTIONS

1. What research approach would you follow to audit the following: (a) evaluation of a new company-sponsored drug rehabilitation program, (b) an analysis of employee tardiness patterns, (c) the appropriateness of present recruiting costs?

2. Today, in cities such as Toronto and Vancouver, about a third of the citizens are members of visible minorities. What impact will such a heterogeneous workforce have on organizations? What changes in human resource practices may be necessary to meet this new reality?

3. Today, there is less and less government involvement in several sectors. Many former public sectors have been privatised; a "pay-as-you-go" mentality has become popular in several other sectors. What impact does this shift have for human resource practices, especially in the areas of employee training, compensation, and development?

4. In the last two decades, many cultural values have changed—some rather drastically. Briefly describe two major changes you have noticed and their implications for human resource managers.

⟹ ETHICS QUESTION

Your organization has a Code of Ethics. However, you believe that it is incomplete in a number of respects. As a human resource manager, you believe that you have to take the initiative to update the ethics code. How will you go about it? What areas will your Code of Ethics now cover?

WEB RESEARCH EXERCISE

Conduct a Web search to find out major environmental trends that have implications for the human resource function. Write a brief report about the emerging trends and present your recommendations on what HR departments should do to respond to these.

INCIDENT 15-1

Maritime Coal Industries Ltd.

Maritime Coal Industries ran two underground coal mines and a coke oven for converting coal into industrial coke. The locations were about 60 kilometres apart, and so each operation had a branch human resource office. The branch offices did their own hiring, administration of employee benefits, safety programs, and labour relations with the local union. After reading an article about the merits of a human resource management audit, the human resource director at Maritime, Gabe Robertson, discussed the need for an audit with the three branch human resource officers. Their individual reactions are summarized below:

Tony Masone: We don't need an audit. It will take weeks to conduct, and it won't change a thing. Each of us branch human resource managers does the best job we know how. Besides, most of our actions are audited daily by the union. If we make a mistake in employee treatment, pay, benefits, safety, or most of the traditional audit areas, the union lets us know promptly. When you have a union, an audit is not needed.

Joyce McDonald: I disagree with Tony. The union would complain if we made an error against their members. But if our errors were detrimental to the best interests of Maritime, I doubt the union would say anything. Besides, in the matter of recruiting, selection, orientation, and training, the union has little say or interest. An audit might even reveal areas where each branch might improve. I for one welcome an audit and a chance to see how my office compares with the other two.

Sylvie Gagnon: Joyce makes a good case for an audit, but if we were having problems in training, selection, or the other areas she mentions, we'd know it. We have gotten along for years without an audit; I see no need to put in a lot of overtime and disrupt everything else just to compile a report that will tell us what we already know.

1. Assuming you agree with Joyce, what other arguments would you add to justify the overtime and disruption that worry Sylvie?

2. Even though the union contract specifies many areas in detail, briefly describe the possible benefits from an audit of Maritime's (a) compensation program, (b) safety program, (c) grievance process, and (d) labour relations training for supervisors.

3. Do you think Tony and Sylvie would have a different attitude if they and Joyce were assigned to the audit team? Why?

INCIDENT 15-2

Employee Attitudes at Anko Ltd.

Anko Ltd. rents sports equipment. Its main business is renting out ski equipment and snowmobiles. During the winter, the number of employees ranges between 50 and 60 at five locations in various winter resort areas. Al Anko, the owner, hired a management consultant to evaluate employee satisfaction and attitudes. After interviewing nearly 20 employees and supervisors, the consultant developed an attitude survey that was mailed to all employees. From the interviews and attitude surveys, the consultant made the following observations:

- Nearly two-thirds of the employees felt little loyalty to the firm because they considered their jobs temporary.

- Many employees applied to work at Anko because they were interested in skiing.

- Although the firm gave few benefits, many employees commented about the reduced rental rates on equipment as an important "extra" of their jobs.

- Every supervisor mentioned that the most important selection criterion was whether an applicant knows how to fit and adjust ski bindings.

- Over half of the employees worked split shifts from 7 to 10 a.m. and from 4 to 7 p.m., which were the hours most skis were rented and returned. Some employees liked those hours because they could ski during the day. However, employees who lived in the resort area all year long generally disliked the hours.

- Employee turnover was very low. But many employees indicated that they would quit if they could find a better-paying job.

- Several employees who had worked for Anko in previous years thought it was unfair that they received the same hourly wage as new employees.

1. If you were the consultant, what recommendations would you make to the owner about (a) the use of split shifts, (b) the types of people recruited, and (c) the treatment of employees who have worked for Anko more than one season?

2. Should Anko treat employees who permanently live in the resort areas differently from those who move there just for the ski season? If so, what differences in treatment would you recommend?

➡ CASE STUDY 🍁 Maple Leaf Shoes Ltd.

*An Exercise in Human Resource Audit**

Jane Reynolds, senior assistant in the human resource department in Maple Leaf Shoes, was bewildered by the findings of the employee survey she had just completed. True, she had expected the results to show some of these trends; however, their magnitude and underlying patterns were quite puzzling.

Reynolds keyed a set of new codes into the computer. The screen flickered momentarily and a new set of figures and tables appeared on her computer screen. "This is going to be a very long day," she murmured to herself as she looked at the data on the screen.

She got up from her chair, stretched, and walked to the coffee machine to pour herself her seventh cup of coffee.

As she sat down at her desk, Reynolds took a sip of the warm coffee. Then she patiently began to key more numbers into the computer.

Maple Leaf Shoes Ltd., a medium-sized manufacturer of leather and vinyl shoes located in Ontario, has been going through some challenging times (see the end of Chapter 1 for more details of the company and its operations). On the instruction of Robert Clark, Jane Reynolds had conducted an employee survey. She had wanted to survey the entire workforce, but this would have been too time-consuming. Instead, she selected the Lady's Shoes Division as the candidate for her survey. This was one of the larger divisions of the company and employed 202 persons. (Exhibit 1 shows the number of employees in the division and the profile of survey respondents.)

Reynolds had developed a short questionnaire in consultation with her friend (a business student in a local university). Reynolds wanted the questionnaire to be a short and easy one to understand and respond to. Her final questionnaire had 15 items anchored on a five-point scale (see Exhibit 2).

Reynolds received 80 responses to the survey, but did not expect to receive any more. She had reminded the staff twice about the importance of the survey and the need for getting their input to help make changes. But, by and large, she had received a lukewarm response to her requests, especially from plant employees. Three or four employees openly confronted her, asking, "Why should we waste our time, when nothing will change anyway?" One male plant employee, muttering curses, had thrown the questionnaire into a nearby garbage can in her presence.

Exhibit 3 shows the results Reynolds received from her preliminary analysis of the data. She is aware of the need for further analysis of the data for each subgroup and each category.

Discussion Questions

1. What is your evaluation of the various steps taken by Reynolds to collect information from employees?

2. Based on the survey results, what conclusions would you form?

3. What actions would you recommend that the company take now? In the long term?

EXHIBIT 1	Profiles of Survey respondents							
	Managerial		**Supervisory**		**Clerical**		**Manufacturing**	
	Male	**Female**	**Male**	**Female**	**Male**	**Female**	**Male**	**Female**
Number of employees	5	0	15	2	8	22	95	55
Number who responded to the survey	2	0	2	1	3	12	20	40

---

*Case written by Professor Hari Das of Department of Management, Saint Mary's University, Halifax, N.S. All rights retained by the author. Das © 2002.

EXHIBIT 2	A Sample of Questionnaire Used

Maple Leaf Shoes
Employee Opinion Survey

Please take a few minutes to complete this brief questionnaire. The information you supply will help us make changes in the company in the near future. You can check (or circle) any number corresponding to an item. You don't have to disclose your name or employee number anywhere on this form. Return all completed forms to Jane Reynolds in the Human Resource Department (Office 102A). Call local 5678 if you need clarification on any item below or have a question.

A. Work

1. Satisfying	5	4	3	2	1	Frustrating
2. Challenging	5	4	3	2	1	Boring
3. Non-routine	5	4	3	2	1	Routine
4. Has lot of potential for career growth	5	4	3	2	1	Has no potential for career growth

B. Pay

5. Fair	5	4	3	2	1	Unfair
6. Equitable	5	4	3	2	1	Not equitable
7. Competitive with other firms	5	4	3	2	1	Not competitive with other firms

C. Supervisor

8. Very professional in approach	5	4	3	2	1	Not at all professional in approach
9. Has high leadership skills	5	4	3	2	1	Has no leadership skills
10. Caring	5	4	3	2	1	Uncaring
11. Controlling	5	4	3	2	1	Delegating

D. Working Conditions

12. Safe	5	4	3	2	1	Unsafe
13. Pleasant	5	4	3	2	1	Unpleasant
14. Helpful coworkers	5	4	3	2	1	Unhelpful coworkers
15. Receive all instructions on time	5	4	3	2	1	Do not receive most instructions on time

E. Information about you

Male _____   Female _____

Managerial _____   Supervisory _____   Clerical _____   Manufacturing _____

Age: 20–29 _____   30–39 _____   40–49 _____   50+ _____

Thank you for participating in the survey.

EXHIBIT 3	Preliminary Results Emerging from the Survey

Average scores for the various items in the survey are shown below.

	Managerial		Supervisory		Clerical		Manufacturing	
	Male	Female	Male	Female	Male	Female	Male	Female
A. Work								
1. Satisfying	3.8		3.6	3.2	3.5	3.6	3.1	3.0
2. Challenging	4.1		3.9	3.8	3.3	3.2	3.0	3.1
3. Non-routine	3.9		2.8	2.9	3.1	3.2	2.9	3.0
4. Has potential for career growth	3.6		3.1	2.8	3.8	2.9	3.0	3.0
B. Pay								
5. Fair	4.0		3.9	3.6	3.6	3.4	3.6	3.1
6. Equitable	4.2		4.2	3.4	3.9	3.3	3.8	3.0
7. Competitive	3.9		3.8	3.6	3.7	3.5	3.6	3.4
C. Supervisor								
8. Professional	3.5		3.7	3.5	3.9	3.4	3.7	3.3
9. Has leadership skills	3.6		3.8	3.2	3.9	3.2	3.7	2.9
10. Caring	4.3		3.8	3.5	3.6	3.3	3.6	3.3
11. Controlling	3.7		4.0	4.3	4.1	4.3	4.2	4.4
D. Working Conditions								
12. Safe	4.4		3.9	3.7	4.2	3.8	3.6	3.2
13. Pleasant	4.2		4.0	3.8	4.0	3.9	3.5	3.1
14. Helpful coworkers	4.4		4.3	3.7	4.1	3.8	4.0	3.4
15. Timely receipt of instructions	4.3		3.6	3.6	4.0	3.9	3.4	3.3

CASE STUDY CPIB Canadian Pacific and International Bank

Preparing for the Future*

Canadian Pacific and International Bank (CPIB) is one of Canada's premier financial institutions, with assets over $150 billion. CPIB, which began as a "western" bank in the early 1950s in British Columbia, today employs over 25,000 persons and provides personal, commercial, corporate and investment banking services to individuals and businesses in 33 countries. More details of the bank are given at the end of Chapter 1.

Mary Keddy, senior vice-president, human resources, is currently looking at the bank's plans for the immediate future and identifying their human resource implications. She identified the following as some of the more immediate challenges facing the human resource function:

1. Globally, CPIB serves more than six million customers in three key areas: personal and commercial banking, wealth management, and wholesale and corporate banking. This figure is expected to reach ten million in the next three years. Most of the growth will come through foreign expansion and achieving a higher percentage of the wealth management market. With an aging North American and

*Case written by Professor Hari Das of Department of Management, Saint Mary's University, Halifax, Canada. All rights retained by the author. Das © 2002.

European market, this market is likely to grow much faster than commercial or wholesale banking.

2. Most of the routine banking will be done in the future through automated tellers and Internet banking. Compared to the 22 percent of customers who use Web-based brokerage, CPIB expects over 65 percent to be using this technology within five years.

3. CPIB primarily used a growth through acquisition strategy. In the last three years, it acquired three major investment brokerages and trusts. In the next five years, this number is likely to become even greater. While all the acquisitions have proved to be economically viable, they had also provided some challenges. The organizational culture of the brokerages and trust companies differed from that at CPIB, presenting a host of difficulties during the transition period.

4. As CPIB extends its operations to foreign countries, it has become increasingly difficult to institute similar HR practices across all its world branches. The compensation and performance appraisal systems must recognize cultural and economic differences across countries; yet, some degree of uniformity across all its operations is necessary to facilitate planning and human resource transfer and development. How to achieve uniformity without losing flexibility? There seems to be no simple answer. Also what is considered as unethical in Canada may be very acceptable in some of the Asian or African countries. For example, several manufacturers in developing economies employ seven-to-eight-year-old children and pay low wages. These manufacturers are important customers of the bank—often accounting for 25 percent or more of its loans in some regions. How can the bank be ethical without placing too many constraints on the managers in foreign branches?

5. While the bank has been a progressive employer, the number of female senior managers in its ranks continues to be low. At the junior levels of management, the ratio between male and female managers is currently 65 to 35; however, as one goes up the hierarchy, the ratio changes drastically in favour of the males. Further, even at the supervisory and junior managerial level, the percentage of visible minorities has been insignificant (often amounting to less than one-tenth of 1 percent). The bank would like to encourage more women, minorities, and people with physical disabilities to reach middle and senior managerial levels.

6. The failure of large organizations such as Enron and WorldCom, mainly attributable to the fraudulent and reckless activities of its senior management, has been a wakeup call to all financial institutions about the high risk of corporate lending. CPIB has been no exception to this. Over time, CPIB would like to develop a code of ethical and sound business practices that will be used in assessing corporate clients. For the immediate future, traditional financial figures and indexes will continue to be used, but incorporating such "soft" information into the decision model has become more imperative with the passage of time.

Discussion Questions

Assume Keddy has decided to conduct an audit of the human resource function of CPIB. How should she proceed further on the matter? What research approach should she take? What tools of research should she use? What additional external information should she collect?

➡ PART ENDING VIDEOS

"Westray Mine"

Source: *The National*, July 3, 1998, running time 3:08.

Go to **www.mcgrawhillconnect.ca** to access the videos.

➡ ROLE-PLAY 7: HR System Evaluation at The Exit Interview

Time required: 40–50 minutes

Objectives of the Role-Play

1. To help the students understand the steps in conducting an exit interview.
2. To enhance their skills in assessing HR system effectiveness.

Prior Preparation

1. Study Chapter 15 of the text.
2. Read description of Maple Leaf Shoes Ltd. at the end of Chapter 1.

Guidelines for Conducting the Role-Play

The role-play enacts an exit interview between Jane Reynolds and Jaswant Singh, an employee in the Shaping Section of Maple Leaf Shoes Ltd. Mr. Singh, who had consistently received superior performance ratings, suddenly quit last week and is rumoured to be joining a competing firm. Ms. Reynolds is about to meet with him to find out more about his decision and, if possible, persuade him to remain with the company.

1. Two students, one for the role of Jane Reynolds and the other for Jaswant Singh, should be identified.

2. Students should read their own role descriptions in the Instructor Resource Manual along with the company details given at the end of Chapter 1.

3. The instructor should signal the beginning and the end of the meeting. The interview will last about 25 minutes.

4. The remainder of the class time is used for discussion of the behaviours during the role-play and outcomes.

5. Observers should be asked to make notes against the questions listed below and discuss their findings at the end of the role-play.

6. Instructor should sum up by highlighting the importance of diversity management, employee relations, and continuous human resource audit to enhance HR effectiveness.

Instructions for Observers

As you observe the meeting between Jane Reynolds and Jaswant Singh, make notes against each of the questions below.

1. How did Jane begin the meeting? Would it have been better to begin it in some other manner?

2. What was Singh's response? Did he provide true reasons for his departure?

3. Did Jane make an attempt to get at the true reasons for Singh's departure?

4. What in your opinion, did Jane learn from this interview? What actions should she take?

5. What did you learn from this exercise?

References

Chapter 1

1. Subhir Chowdhury, *Management 21C*, London: Pearson Education Limited, 2000, p. 12.

2. "The New Age of Discovery," *Time* (special issue), Winter 1997–98, pp. 11–66.

3. Robert Granford Wright, "Managing Management Resources Through Corporate Constitutionalism," *Human Resource Management*, Summer 1973, p. 15.

4. Sarah Boesveld, "Trust Fall," *The Globe and Mail*, April 13, 2009, pp. L1–L2.

5. Statistics Canada, www.40.statcan.ca/101/cst01/gblec04.htm; downloaded on August 3, 2009.

6. Andrew Purvis, "Super Exporter," *Time*, April 28, 1997, p. 37.

7. David Brown, "HR Issues Top of Mind for Execs Worldwide: Study," *Canadian HR Reporter*, May 5, 2003, p. 1.

8. Bruce Little, "We're Less Dependent But More Entangled," *The Globe and Mail*, May 15, 2000, p. A2.

9. *World Competitiveness Year Book 2008*, Lausanne, Switzerland: IMD International, see www02.imd.ch.

10. John McCallum, "Will Canada Matter in 2020?" *Royal Bank Current Analysis*, Royal Bank of Canada Economics Department, May 2000, p. 5.

11. "Innovation in Industry," *The Economist*, February 20, 1999, pp. 5–28.

12. Statistics Canada, *Long Term Productivity Growth in Canada and the United States 1961 to 2006*. Catalogue No. 15-206-XIE, No. 013, ISSN: 1710-5269, August 2007.

13. "Canada's Ranking Slips in Ability to Innovate," *The Globe and Mail*, March 12, 1999, p. B3.

14. Elizabeth Church, "Canada's Progress in Science, Innovation Mediocre, Study Finds." *The Globe and Mail*, May 6, 2009, A6.

15. Conference Board of Canada, "Innovation: Share of World Patents," October 2008, www.conferenceboard.ca/hcp/details/innovation/share-of-world-patents.aspx, downloaded October 1, 2009.

16. CBC Television, *Venture*, undated.

17. Randall Litchfield, "The Sunrise Economy," *Canadian Business*, June 1992, pp. 85–86.

18. AdvantEdge site, www.hradvantedge.com/Outsourcing%20Human%20Resources.pdf, downloaded September 2003.

19. Ibid., pp. 48–49.

20. Internet World Stats, "Canada Internet Usage, Broadband and Telecommunication Reports," www.internetworldstats.com/am/ca.htm, downloaded on April 15, 2009. See also Simon Tuck, "Internet Milestone Set as 50% Connected in Canada," *The Globe and Mail*, May 1, 1999, p. B1.

21. "Working from Home Cuts Employee Stress, Study Finds," *The Globe and Mail*, November 16, 1994, p. B19.

22. Shari Caudron, "Working at Home Pays Off," *Personnel Journal*, Vol. 71, No. 11, November 1992, pp. 40–49.

23. See Lynne McGee, "Setting Up Work at Home," *Personnel Administrator*, Vol. 33, No. 12, December 1988, pp. 58–62.

24. "5 Telework Pitfalls to Avoid," *Canadian HR Reporter*, October 20, 2008, p. 2.

25. "McCarthy's Reinvents the Practice," *The Globe and Mail*, December 6, 1999, p. M1.

26. Sandra Mingail, "Technology No Longer the Driver," *Canadian HR Reporter*, April 11, 2005, p. 11.

27. Statistics Canada, www.12.statcan.ca/English/census01/Products/Analytic/companion/paid/Canada.efm.

28. Ross Laver, "Kids, Bosses and Work," *Maclean's*, February 24, 1997, p. 38.

29. Human Resources Development Canada (Applied Research), *Quarterly Labour Market and Income Review*, Vol. 3, No.1, Summer 2002, pp.14–15.

30. Statistics Canada, www.12.statcan.ca/English/census01/Products/Analytic/companion/paid/Canada.efm.

31. "The Path to Unlocking Employee Knowledge," *The Globe and Mail*, October 25, 1999, p. M1.

32. "Employment Trends in the Information Economy," *Applied Research Bulletin*, Vol. 3, No. 2, 1997; HRDC site, www.hrdc-drhc.gc.ca.

33. "The Industries That Will Define the Decade," *The Globe and Mail*, April 21, 1997, p. A6.

34. *Quarterly Labour Market and Income Review*, Human Resources Development Canada, Vol. 3, No. 1, Summer 2002, p. 13.

35. Ibid., pp. 16–17.

36. Results of International Adult Literacy Survey reported on the National Adult Literacy Survey Database site, www.nald.ca/nts/ials/ialsreps/high2.htm, February 10, 1998. See also Morton Ritts, "What If Johnny Still Can't Read," *Canadian Business*, May 1986, pp. 54–57, 124.

37. Human Resources Development Canada, *Quarterly Labour Market and Income Review*, Vol. 3, No. 1, Summer 2002, p. 18.

38. Statistics Canada, op. cit.

39. Corporate Council on Education, "Employability Skills Profile," a program of the National Business and Education Centre, Ottawa: The Conference Board of Canada, undated.

40. Workplace Education—PEI, "Creating Partnerships with Business and Industry," Charlottetown: April 2000.

41. "Our Coming Old Age Crisis," *Maclean's*, January 17, 1983, p. 24.

42. Statistics Canada, www.12.statcan.ca/English/census01/Products/Analytic/companion/paid/Canada.efm.

43. Ibid.

44. Susan Singh, "Globalization Puts Focus on HR," *Canadian HR Reporter*, June 6, 2005, pp. 1, 15.

45. Statistics Canada, "Latest Release from Labour Force Survey," *The Daily*, March 10, 2006.

46. John Kettle, "Casual Work Get Serious," *The Globe and Mail*, November 20, 1997, p. B4.

47. "Part-Timers Being Shut Out, Study Says," *The Globe and Mail*, November 17, 1997, p. A3.

48. Paul Nyhof, "Managing Generation X: The Millennial Challenge," *Canadian HR Reporter* Vol. 13, No. 10, May 22, 2000, pp. 7–8.

49. For a good exposition of the difference between two age groups, see, Claire Raine and Jim Hunt, *The X-ers and the Boomers*, Berkely, CA: Crisp Publications, 2000, pp. 32–39.

50. Barbara Kofman and Kaitlin Eckler, "They Are Your Future: Attracting and Retaining Generation Y," *Canadian HR Reporter*, April 25, 2005, pp. 7, 10.

51. KPMG's *Ethics Survey 2000-*, Managing for Ethical Practice, cited in Leslie Young, "Companies Not Doing Right by Their Ethics Codes," *Canadian HR Reporter*, Vol. 13, No 7, April 10, 2000, p. 17.

52. Ibid.

53. L. Kohlberg, "Moral Stages and Moralization: The Cognitive-Development Approach." In T. Lickona, ed., Moral Developmental and Behavior: Theory, Research, and Social Issues (New York: Holt, Rinehart and Winston, 1976, pp. 31–35)

54. 2003 Business Ethics Survey conducted by the Society for Human Resource Management, reported in Canadian HR Reporter, May 19, 2003, p. 1.

55. John Porter, *The Vertical Mosaic: An Analysis of Social Class and Power in Canada*, Toronto: University of Toronto Press, 1965. See also V.V. Murray, "Canadian Cultural Values and Personnel Administration," in Harish Jain, ed., *Contemporary Issues in Canadian Personnel Administration*, Scarborough, ON: Prentice-Hall, 1974.

56. "No Longer a Two-Language Nation," *The Mail Star*, December 3, 1997, p. A19.

57. Rae Corelli, "How Very Different We Are," *Maclean's*, November 4, 1996, pp. 36–39.

58. Professor Richard Woodward of University of Calgary quoted by McMurdy, "Falling Expectations," *Maclean's*, January 4, 1993, p. 36.

59. Frank Vallee and Donald Whyte, "Canadian Society: Trends and Perspectives," in Harish Jain, ed., *Contemporary Issues in Canadian Personnel Administration*, p. 31.

60. Ibid., pp. 29–42.

61. Joe Chidley and Andrew Wahl, "The New Worker's Paradise," *Canadian Business*, March 12, 1999, pp. 37–38.

62. Sarah Dobson, "It Pays to Be Green" *Canadian HR Reporter*, April 20, 2009, page 15.

63. Andrew Campbell, "Turning Workers into Risk Takers," *Canadian Business*, February 1985, p. 109.

64. Hari Das, *Strategic Organizational Design*, Scarborough, ON: Prentice-Hall, 1998, pp. 324–329.

65. Ibid., p. 204.

66. Adapted and summarized from Randall Schuler and Susan Jackson, "Linking Competitive Strategies with Human Resource Management Practices," *Academy of Management Executive*, Vol. 1, No. 3, 1987, pp. 207–19; see also Susan Jackson and Randall Schuler, "Understanding Human Resource Management in the Context of Organizations and Their Environments," *Annual Review of Psychology*, Vol. 46, 1995, pp. 237–64; Randall Schuler, Steven Galante, and Susan Jackson, "Matching Effective HR Practices with Competitive Strategy," *Personnel*, September 1987.

67. Uyen Vu, "'Strategic' Overused in HR," *Canadian HR Reporter*, July 14, 2008, p. 8.

68. Uyen Vu, "Performance Management Tool Makes Company More Strategic," *Canadian HR Reporter*, February 27, 2006, p. 3.

69. Uyen Vu, "Standing up to the Bad Boss," *Canadian HR Reporter*, February 13, 2006, p. 5.

70. Gordon Sova, "What Do the Stats Tell Us?" *Canadian HR Reporter*, February 27, 2006, p. 9.

71. D.P. Lepak and S.A. Snell, "The Strategic Management of Human Capital: Determinants and Implications of Different Relationships," *Academy of Management Review*, Vol. 24, No. 1,1999, pp. 1–18.

72. Peter Bamberger and Ilan Meshoulam, *Human Resource Strategy*, Thousand Oaks, CA: Sage Publications, 2000, p. 57.

73. For example, see Lepak and Snell, op. cit.; D. Organ, *Organizational Citizenship Behaviour*, Lexington, MA: D.C. Heath, 1988; Bamberger and Meshoulam, op. cit.; L. Dyer and G.W. Holder, "A Strategic Perspective of Human Resources Management," in L. Dyer and G.W. Holder, eds., *Human Resources Management: Evolving Roles and Responsibilities*, Washington, DC: American Society for Personnel Administration, 1988, pp. 1–45; P. Osterman, "Choice of Employment Systems in Internal Labour Markets," *Industrial Relations*, Vol. 26, No. 1, 1987, pp. 48–63; P. Osterman, "Work/Family Programs and the Employment Relationship," *Administrative Science Quarterly*, 40, 1995, pp. 681–700; P.M. Swiercz, "Research Update: Strategic HRM," *Human Resource Planning*, Vol. 18, No. 3, 1995, pp. 53–62.

74. J. Arthur, "Effects of Human Resource Systems on Manufacturing Performance and Turnover," *Academy of Management Journal*, 37, 1994, pp. 670–87.

75. P. Osterman, "Choice of Employment Systems in Internal Labour Markets," op. cit.; P. Osterman, "Work/Family Programs and the Employment Relationship," op. cit.; Bamberger and Meshoulam, op. cit., p. 61.

76. P. Osterman, "Choice of Employment Systems in Internal Labour Markets," op. cit.; P. Osterman, "Work/Family Programs and the Employment Relationship," op. cit.

77. Bamberger and Meshoulam, op. cit., p. 61.

78. David Brown, "Innovative HR Ineffective in Manufacturing Firms," *Canadian HR Reporter*, April 7, 2003, p. 1.

79. John Gibbons and Christopher Woock, "Evidence-Based HR in Action," *Canadian HR Reporter*, March 23, 2009, pp. 16, 20.

80. "HRM Measurement Projects Issues First Report," *Resource*, December 1985, p. 2.

81. R.E. Miles and C.C. Snow, "Designing Strategic Human Resource Systems," *Organizational Dynamics*, Vol. 13, No. 1, 1984, pp. 36–52.

82. Ibid.

83. Kevin Schwenker, Hari Das, Laird Mealiea, Hermann Schwind, Allister Thorne, and Gerald Walsh, *CCHRA National Standards Project—Phase III, The Nova Scotia Pilot Assessment Project*, National Capabilities Committee, Canadian Council of Human Resource Associations, December 1999.

84. Deloitte & Touche Human Resource Consulting Services, *The State of the Human Resources Management Function in Canada*, 1994, p. ii.

85. Arthur Young, Wayne Brockbank, and Dave Ulrich, "Lower Cost, Higher Value: Human Resource Function in Transformation," *Human Resource Planning*, Vol. 17, No. 3, 1994, pp. 10–12.

86. Shannon Klie, "Do You Have What It Takes?" *Canadian HR Reporter*, November 17, 2008, p. 17.

87. Ibid.

88. Kevin Schwenker, et al., 1999, op. cit., p. 44.

89. Peter Drucker, "The Coming of the New Organization," *Harvard Business Review*, January–February 1988, p. 45.

90. Peter Drucker, "The End of Money?" *The Globe and Mail*, May 13, 2000, p. A16.

91. "'Love Bug' Hits World's E-mail," *The Globe and Mail*, May 5, 2000, p. A1.

92. Richard Blackwell, "Banks Give Shareholders a Voice," *The Globe and Mail*, March 3, 2000, p. B10.

93. "Finance Minister to Have Wide Bank Powers," *The Globe and Mail*, June 1, 2000, p. B1.

94. Mary Janigan, "Feud without End," *Maclean's*, April 24, 2000, p. 60.

95. "Scotiabank Warns of 'Intrusive' Consumer Regulation," *The Globe and Mail*, March 1, 2000, p. B3.

96. Keith McArthur and Dawn Walton, "Protecting What Is Right," *The Globe and Mail*, February 15, 2000, p. B16.

Chapter 2

1. Philip C. Grant, "What Use Is a Job Description?" *Personnel Journal*, Vol. 67, No. 2, February 1988, p. 50.

2. Steven F. Cronshaw. "Job Analysis: Changing Nature of Work," *Canadian Psychology*, February–May 1998; see also "Job Analysis: Overview," 2001. Available at HR Internet Guide Web site, www.hr-guide.com/data/G000.htm; downloaded July 21, 2006.

3. William Wooten, "Using Knowledge, Skill and Ability (KSA) Data to Identify Career Planning Opportunities: An Application of Job Analysis to Internal Manpower Planning," *Public Personnel Administrator*, Vol. 22, No. 4, 1993, pp. 551–63.

4. *Canadian Human Rights Reporter*, Vol. 6, 1985, p. 6.

5. Sidney A. Fine and Steven F. Cronshaw, *Functional Job Analysis: A Foundation for Human Resource Management*, Mahwah, NJ: L. Erlbaum Associates, 1999.

6. N.G. Peterson, M.D. Mumford, W.C. Borman, P.R. Jeanneret, and E.A. Fleishman, eds., *An Occupational Information System for the 21st Century: The Development of O*NET*, Washington, DC: American Psychological Association, 1999.

7. Michael T. Brannick and Edward L. Levine, *Job Analysis: Methods, Research, and Applications for Human Resource Management in the New Millennium*, London, UK: Sage Publications, Inc., 2002.

8. Purdue Research Foundation, *Position Analysis Questionnaire*, West Lafayette, IN: 1989; see also R.A. Ash, "Review of the Position Analysis Questionnaire," in J.C. Conoley and J.C. Impara, eds., *The Twelfth Mental Measurements Yearbook*, Lincoln, NE: The Buros Institute of Mental Measurements, 1995, pp. 787–89.

9. Wayne Cascio, *Managing Human Resources*, 7th ed., New York: McGraw-Hill Irwin, 2006, p. 165.

10. See Brannick and Levine, op. cit.; Luis R. Gomez-Mejia, Ronald C. Page, and Walter W. Tormow, "A Comparison of the Practical Utility of Traditional, Statistical and Hybrid Job Evaluation Approaches," *Academy of Management Journal*, Vol. 25, No. 4, 1982, pp. 790–809; Ronald A. Ash and Edward Levine, "A Framework for Evaluating Job Analysis Methods," *Personnel*, November/December 1980, pp. 53–59.

11. E.L. Levine, R.A. Ash, and N. Bennett, "Explorative Comparative Study of Four Job Analysis Methods," *Journal of Applied Psychology*, Vol. 65, 1980, pp. 524–35; and E.L. Levine, R.A. Ash, H. Hall, and F. Sistrunk, "Evaluation of Job Analysis Methods by Experienced Job Analysts," *Academy of Management Journal*, Vol. 26, No. 2, 1983, pp. 339–48.

12. Human Resources and Skills Development Canada, National Occupational Classification, 1991, www23.hrdc-drhc.gc.ca/2001/e/generic/welcome.shtml.

13. Brian Orr, "Position Management Has Its Rewards," *Canadian HR Reporter*, March 24, 1997, p. 15; see also Erisa Ojimba, "Job Salary Negotiation Tips & Advice," 2004, available at Salary.com Web site, www.salary.com/advice/layoutscripts/advl_display.asp?tab=adv&cat=Cat14&ser=Ser65&part=Par144; downloaded July 21, 2006.

14. Hari Das, Peter J. Frost, and J. Thad Barnowe, "Behaviourally Anchored Scales for Assessing Behavioural Science Teaching," *Canadian Journal of Behavioural Science*, Vol. 11, No. 1, January 1979, pp. 79–88; Tom Janz, "Estimating the Standard Deviation of Job Performance: A Behavioural Approach," *Administrative Sciences Association of Canada (Organizational Behaviour Division) Meeting Proceedings*, Vol. 2, Part 5, 1981, pp. 70–78.

15. Richard Mirabile, "Everything You Wanted to Know About Competency Modeling," *Training and Development*, August 1997, pp. 73–77; Kenneth Carlton Cooper, *Effective Competency Modeling & Reporting*, New York: AMACOM, AMA Publications, 2000.

16. Patricia A. McLagan, "Competencies: The Next Generation," *Training and Development*, May 1997, p. 41.

17. Jean-Pascal Souque, *Focus on Competencies*, Report No. 177-96, Ottawa: The Conference Board of Canada, 1996, p. 18.

18. Brian Orr, "The Challenge of Benchmarking HR Performance," *Canadian HR Reporter*, April 21, 1997, p. 6.

19. William H. Glick, G. Douglas Jenkins, Jr., and Nina Gupta, "Method Versus Substance: How Strong Are Underlying Relationships Between Job Characteristics and Attitudinal Outcomes?" *Academy of Management Journal*, Vol. 29, No. 3, 1985, pp. 441–64. See also Daniel A. Ondrack and Martin Evans, "Job Enrichment and Job Satisfaction of Quality of Working Life and Nonquality of Working Life Work Sites," *Human Relations*, Vol. 39, No. 9, 1986, pp. 871–89; D.R. Ilgen and J.R. Hollenbeck, "The Structure of Work: Job Design and Roles," in M.D. Dunnette and L.M. Hough, eds., *Handbook of Industrial and Organizational Psychology*, Vol. 2, Palo Alto: Consulting Psychologists Press, 1991, pp. 165–207.

20. Michael Losey, "HR Comes of Age," *HR Magazine*, 50th Anniversary Issue, 1998, pp. 40–53.

21. Robert Inman, "Workflow," *Transactions*, Vol. 28, No. 7, July 1996, pp. 555–56.

22. E. Joy Mighty and Judy Ann Roy, "Re-designing Job Design," *Global Business Trends: Contemporary Readings*, Cumberland, MD: Academy of Business Administration, 1997, pp. 261–69.

23. E. Grandjean, *Fitting the Task to the Man*, 4th ed., Bristol, PA: Taylor and Francis, 1990; see also Chris Knight, "Office Workers Frustrated with Their Workspace," *Canadian HR Reporter*, December 1, 1997, p. 21.

24. Monica Belcourt, Arthur Sherman, George Bohlander, and Scott Snell, *Managing Human Resources*, 2nd ed., Toronto: Nelson Canada, 1999, pp. 112–13.

25. Glenn Harrington, "Ergonomics Preaches Prevention as Alternative to High Cost Injuries," *Canadian HR Reporter*, September 9, 1996, p. 22.

26. Glenn Harrington, "Older Workers Need Ergonomic Aid," *Canadian HR Reporter*, November 17, 1997, p. 20.

27. Adapted from Hari Das, *Your Motivation at Work,* © Hari Das, 2001; reprinted by permission of the author.

28. Patricia Chisholm, "Redesigning Work," *Maclean's,* March 5, 2001, p. 36.

29. Frederick Herzberg, Bernard Mausner, and Barbara Snyderman, *The Motivation to Work,* New York: Wiley, 1959; J.R. Hackman and G. Oldham, *Work Redesign,* Reading, MA: Addison-Wesley, 1980; Paul Sparrow, "New Employee Behaviours, Work Designs and Forms of Work Organization: What Is in Store for Future of Work?" *Journal of Managerial Psychology,* Vol. 15, No. 3, 2000, pp. 202–18.

30. Ian Gellatly and Gregory Irving, "The Moderating Role of Perceived Autonomy on Personality–Performance Relations Within a Public Sector Organization," *ASAC 1999 Proceedings (Human Resources),* Vol. 20, No. 9, 1999, Saint John, NB: University of New Brunswick.

31. Richard W. Woodward and John J. Sherwood, "A Comprehensive Look at Job Design," *Personnel Journal,* August 1977, p. 386.

32. Mohr, Robert D., and Cindy Zoghi, "Is Job Enrichment Really Enriching?" (a study of Canadian workers), research report, University of Chicago, May 2005. http://gsbwww.uchicago.edu/labor/MohrZoghi.pdf.

33. P. Booth, *Challenge and Change: Embracing the Team Concept,* Ottawa: Conference Board of Canada, 1994.

34. For example, see Donna Deeprose, *The Team Coach: Vital New Skills for Supervisors and Managers in a Team Environment,* New York: American Management Association, 1995.

35. Ageeth Balkema and Eric Molleman, "Barriers to the Development of Self-Organizing Teams," *Journal of Managerial Psychology,* Vol. 14, No. 2, 1999, pp. 134–50.

36. For instance, see Paul Sparrow, loc. cit.

37. William Bridges, "The End of the Job," *Fortune,* September 19, 1994, p. 64.

38. Peter Coy, "The 21st Century Organization," *Business Week,* August 28, 2000.

39. Karen May, "Work in the 21st Century: Implications for Job Analysis," *The Industrial-Organizational Psychologist,* The Society for Industrial and Organizational Psychology, December 18, 2000, www.siop.org.

Chapter 3

1. Abdul Rahman bin Idris and Derek Eldridge, "Reconceptualising Human Resource Planning in Response to Institutional Change," *International Journal of Manpower,* Vol. 19, No. 5, 1998, p. 346.

2. Matt Hennecke, "The 'People' Side of Strategic Planning," *Training,* November 1984, pp. 25–32; Anil Gupta, "Matching Managers to Strategies: Points and Counterpoints," *Human Resource Management,* Vol. 25, No. 2, Summer 1986, pp. 215–34.

3. "Minority Lawyers Get Boost," *The Mail Star,* September 7, 2000, p. A1.

4. For an example, see, Judith Cooksey, "Workforce Challenges for Dentists and Pharmacists," www.hrsa.dhhs.gov/newsroom/features/workforcechallenges.htm, January 2000.

5. "Good Jobs, No Jobs," *The Globe and Mail,* January 15, 1997, p. B3.

6. News from Canada Newswire quoted by www.globeinvestor.com, June 29, 2000.

7. Sarah Dobson, "Labour Shortage Still to Come," *Canadian HR Reporter,* March 23, 2009, pp. 1, 9.

8. A.L. Delbecq, A.H. Van de Ven, and D.H. Gustafson, *Group Techniques for Progress Planning: A Guide to Nominal and Delphi Process,* Glenview, IL: Scott, Foresman, 1975; J.M. Bartwrek and J.K. Muringhan, "The Nominal Group Technique: Expanding the Basic Procedure and Underlying Assumptions," *Group and Organizational Studies,* Vol. 9, 1984, pp. 417–32.

9. James W. Walker, "Human Resource Planning: Managerial Concerns and Practices," *Business Horizons,* June 1976, pp. 56–57. See also George S. Odiorne, "The Crystal Ball of HR Strategy," *Personnel Administrator,* December 1986, pp. 103–6; John A. Byrne and Alison L. Cowan, "Should Companies Groom New Leaders or Buy Them?" *Business Week,* September 22, 1986, pp. 94–96.

10. John Hooper and R.F. Catalanello, "Markov Analysis Applied to Forecasting Technical Personnel," *Human Resource Planning,* Vol. 4, 1981, pp. 41–47.

11. Richard J. Niehaus, "Human Resource Planning Flow Models," *Human Resource Planning,* Vol. 3, 1980, pp. 177–87.

12. P.F. Buller and W.R. Maki, "A Case History of a Manpower Planning Model," *Human Resource Planning,* Vol. 4, No. 3, 1981, pp. 129–37.

13. Brian Parker and David Caine, "Holonic Modelling: Human Resource Planning and the Two Faces of Janus," *International Journal of Manpower,* Vol. 17, No. 8, 1996, pp. 30–45.

14. Statistics Canada, "Labour Force Survey," *The Daily,* March 10, 2006, www.statcan.ca/Daily/English/060310/d060310a.htm, downloaded September 4, 2006.

15. Statistics Canada, "Labour Force Survey," *The Daily,* April 9, 2009, www.statcan.gc.ca/subjects-sujets/labour-travail/lfs-epa/lfs-epa-eng.htm, downloaded on April 20, 2009.

16. Wayne Roth, "COPS: A Presentation of Results Using a Revised Framework." Research Paper Series T-95-3, 1995, HRDC site, www.hrdc-drhc.gc.ca.

17. Human Resources and Skills Development Canada, "New COPS Occupational Projection Methodology—October 1999," September 8, 2006, www.hrsdc.gc.ca/eng/cs/sp/hrsd/prc/publications/research/1999-000135/page05.shtml, downloaded October 1, 2009.

18. See www.aved.gov.bc.ca/labourmarketinfo/chgngskills/content/append1.htm

19. Louis-Philippe Bergeron, Kevin Dunn, Mario Lapointe, Wayne Roth, and Nicolas Tremblay-Cote, *Looking Ahead: A Ten Year Outlook for the Canadian Labour Market, 2004–2013,* Report number SP-615-10-04E, October 2004, Human Resources & Social Development, Government of Canada.

20. "Notions and Numbers—The Canadian Occupational Projection System," Ottawa: Employment and Immigration Canada, WH-3-418 undated. See also these publications by Employment and Immigration Canada: "The Canadian Occupational Projection System—Supply Issues and Approaches," WH-3-335E, January 1983, and "Demand Methodology," WH-3-341, January 1983.

21. Service Canada, JobFutures.ca site, www.jobfutures.ca/en/home.shtml, downloaded September 4, 2006.

22. Service Canada, "Financial Auditors and Accountants (NOC 1111)," Jobfutures.ca site, www.jobfutures.ca/noc/1111p3.shtml, downloaded September 4, 2006.

23. R.J.Q. Castley, "The Sectoral Approach to the Assessment of Skill Needs and Training Requirements," *International Journal of Manpower,* Vol. 17, No. 1, 1996, pp. 56–68.

24. "Tools for Identifying Skill Shortages: A Cross-Country Comparison," Research Paper Series No. T-96-3E, 1996, HRDC site, www.hrdc-drhc.gc.ca.

25. Survey by Watson Wyatt Consultants, "Employers Turn to Phased Retirement as Workers Age and Labor Shortages Increase," September 8, 1999.

26. McGill University site, www.mcgill.ca/academic/5_1.htm.

27. Mercer Communiqué, June 6, 1997.

28. Kulig, "Flextime Increasing in Popularity with Employers," See also Rosemary Collins, "Flex Appeal," *Canadian Banker,* May/June 1997, pp. 12–16; Larry MacDougal, "Work-Sharing Programs on the Rise," *The Globe and Mail,* December 28, 2001, pp. B1, B5.

29. MacDougal, op. cit.

30. Clare Brennan, "What Is Job-Sharing?" www.ivillage.co.uk/workcareer/worklife/flexwork/articles/0,9545,202_156231-2,00.html, downloaded October 2002.

31. Oliver Bertin, "Part-Time Work: Boon or Bust?" *The Globe and Mail,* November 6, 2002, p. C3; also see, Statistics Canada, *The Daily,* March 10, 2006.

32. Pat Booth, "Contingent Work: Trends, Issues and Challenges for Employers," The Conference Board of Canada, 1997.

33. Bettina Lankard Brown, "Part-Time Work and Other Flexible Options," ERIC Digest #192, 1998.

34. Ibid.

35. Grant Schellenberg, "The Changing Nature of Part-Time Work," The Canadian Council on Social Development, November 17, 1997.

36. Bertin, op. cit.

37. Shannon Klie, "Part-Timers Could Go Full Time at Grocery Giant," *Canadian HR Reporter,* March 23, 2009, p. 1.

38. Peggy Stuart, "New Internal Jobs Found for Displaced Employees," *Personnel Journal,* Vol. 71, No. 8, August 1992, pp. 50–56.

39. Jennifer Fantini and Lisa de Piante, "Temporary Lay-offs Risk Dismissal Claims," *Canadian HR Reporter,* March 23, 2009, p. 5.

40. Valerie Frazee, "Share Thy Neighbor's Workers," *Personnel Journal,* June 1996, pp. 81–84. See also Robina A. Gangemi, "The Problems Many Companies Face Hiring and Training Seasonal Workers Can Be Solved by Sharing Workers," *INC magazine,* December 1, 1995, http://inc.com/incmagazine.

41. "Silver Parachute Protects Work Force," *Resource,* January 1987, p. 3. Later figures received through personal communication with the HR office of the company.

42. Ibid., p. 8.

43. "Benefits for Part-Time Employees," *Rights & Responsibilities Guide,* Saskatchewan Labour site, www.labour.gov.sk.ca/standards/guide/benefits.htm, downloaded on June 19, 2006.

44. David Nye, "Not Made in Heaven," *Across the Board,* October 1996, Vol. 33, No. 9, pp. 41–46. See also Anthony V. Martin, "Outsourcing: Is Contingent HR For You?" *HR Focus,* November 1997, Vol. 74, No. 11, pp. 13–14.

45. Carolyn Hirschman, "All Aboard," *HRMagazine,* September 1997, pp. 80–85. See also "Benefits of Employee Leasing," www.solutions.on.ca/solutions_html's/employeeleasing.htm, downloaded November 2002.

46. Craig C. Pinder and Hari Das, "The Hidden Costs and Benefits of Employee Transfers," *Human*

Resource Planning, Vol. 2, No. 3, 1979. See also Craig C. Pinder, "Employee Transfer Studies—Summary," Vancouver: Faculty of Commerce and Business Administration, University of British Columbia, November 1985; Jeanne M. Brett, "Job Transfer and Well Being," *Journal of Applied Psychology,* Vol. 67, No. 4, 1982, pp. 450–63; Jeanne M. Brett and James Werbel, *The Effect of Job Transfer on Employees and Their Families,* Washington, DC: Employer Relocation Council, 1980.

47. Simmons da Silva, & Sinton, "Employee or Independent Contractor?" www.lawcan.com/articles/business/art-biz-employee_ind_part1.html, downloaded November 2002. See also Selene McLeod, "Consulting and Independent Contractors, " *The Quill,* publication of the Southwestern Ontario Chapter of the Society for Technical Communication, April 2002, www.stc.waterloo.on.ca/publications/april02quill.pdf, downloaded September 4, 2006.

48. Susan N. Houseman, "Flexible Staffing Arrangements: A Report on Temporary Help, On-Call, Direct-Hire Temporary, Leased, Contract Company, and Independent Contractor Employment in the United States," Center for Urban Economic Development at the University of Illinois at Chicago, August 1999, available www.uic.edu/cuppa/uicued/tempwork/RESEARCH/LitReviews/Houseman-Futurework.pdf#search=%22Houseman%2C%20%2Flexible%20Staffing%20Arrangements%2C%22%22, downloaded September 4, 2006.

49. Sharon Lebrun, "Growing Contract Workforce Hindered by Lack of Rules," *Canadian HR Reporter,* May 1997, pp. 1–2; Chris Night, "Contractors Become Fixture in Workplace," *Canadian HR Reporter,* October 21, 1996, pp. 14–15.

50. Tim Cestnick, "How to Check If You're Really Self-employed," *The Globe and Mail,* October 7, 2000, p. N5. See also Daphne Kelgard, "Beware of the Legal Pitfalls of Contract Workers," *Canadian HR Reporter,* September 8, 1997, pp. 18–19. A more comprehensive discussion of the legal and tax issues involved can be found in Joanne Magee, "Whose Business Is It? Employees Versus Independent Contractors," *Canadian Tax Journal,* 1997, Vol. 45, No. 3.

51. Ronald W. Clement, George E. Stevens, and Daniel Brenenstuhl, "Promotion Practices in American Business Colleges: A Comprehensive Investigation," *Manhattan College Journal of Business,* Spring 1986, pp. 9–15.

52. Laurence J. Peter and Raymond Hull, *The Peter Principle,* New York: William Morrow, 1969.

53. Leslie A. Perlow, "Finding Time: How Corporations, Individuals, and Families Can Benefit from New Work Practices," Ithaca, NY: Industrial Labor Relations Press, Cornell University, 1997.

54. Sharon Lebrun, "New Work Styles Gain Converts," *Canadian HR Reporter,* June 2, 1997, p. 16.

55. Bredan Lipsett and Mark Reesor, "Flexible Work Arrangements," *Applied Research Bulletin,* Human Resource Development Canada, 1997; Conference Board of Canada, "Work–Life Balance: Are Employers Listening?" June 27, 2000.

56. Ibid.

57. HOP Associates, "Is Time on Your Side? An Overview of Flexible Time Work Options," www.flexibility.co.uk/flexwork/time/time-options.htm, downloaded November 2002.

58. Ibid.

59. Ibid.

60. *Canadian HR Reporter,* "A First Look at Long-Term Effects of Flex Time," August 14, 2000.

61. David Quigley, "Plugged in! Computers Let Millions of Canadians Punch a Clock at Home," *Edmonton Sun,* December 12, 1999. See also Sharon Abreu, "How to Manage Telecommuters," *NetworkWorld,* June 19, 2000, www.cnn.com/2000/TECH/computing/06/19/telecommuting.idg/index.html, downloaded September 4, 2006.

62. Catherine Roseberry, "Telework Centres & Flexible Options," http://telecommuting.about.com/library/weekly/aa082799.htm, downloaded November 2002.

63. Garner Dataquest, "Employed Telworker Forecast," quoted in "Canadian Studies on Telework," www.ivc.ca/studies/canadianstudies.htm, downloaded September 14, 2006.

64. Colleen Emerick, "Take a Shortcut to Work: The Telecommuting Alternative," http://members.tripod.com/-emerick/telecommuting_term_paper.htm, downloaded October 2002. See also Ipsos-Reid, survey conducted for the Royal Bank of Canada, "Canadian Families and the Internet," October 2001, www.ivc.ca/studies/20020123CanFam_Full_Report-E.pdf, downloaded September 5, 2006.

65. Joseph A. Gibbons, "Telecommuting—The Experiment that Works," *Canadian HR Reporter,* September 9, 1996, pp. 16–17.

66. Work/Life's ROI, IndustryWeek.com, April 19, 1999, www.industryweek.com/CurrentArticles/asp/articles.asp?ArticleID=522, downloaded September 5, 2006.

67. "CTA (Canadian Telework Association) Members Tell Their Stories," www.ivc.ca/stories/judith, downloaded November 2002. Check out her website: www.geocities.com/judith_mathison/.

68. "Telecommuting Causing Work Condition Worries," *The Globe and Mail,* January 7, 2000, p. B8.

69. Joyce Everhart, "Telecommuting: A Business Solution That Is Here to Stay," www.publicworks.com, downloaded November 21, 2000.

70. "50 Best Companies to Work for in Canada," Report on Business, *The Globe and Mail,* December 28, 2001.

71. David North, "Is Your Head Office a Useless Frill?" *Canadian Business,* November 14, 1997, pp. 78–80. See also Sacha Cohen, "On Becoming Virtual," *Training & Development,* May 1997, pp. 30–38; Sandra O'Connell, "The Virtual Workplace Moves at Warp Speed," *HRMagazine,* March 1996, pp. 51–57; "50 Best Companies to Work for in Canada," op. cit.

72. David Ulrich and Richard W. Beaty, "The Role of the HR Professional in the Virtual Organization," unpublished paper, University of Michigan, www.daveulrich.com/pdf/papers/roleofHR professional.pdf, downloaded November 2002. For more examples, see William Landay, "Extended Enterprises Spell Success," Reengineering Resource Center, May 1996, www.reengineering.com/articles/may96/extenter.htm.

73. Michelle Conlin, "And Now, the Just-in-Time Employee," *Business Week,* August 28, 2000, pp. 169–70.

74. Jay F. Straight, Jr., "Introducing CHRIS: Chevron's Human Resource Information System," *Personnel Administrator,* May 1987, pp. 24–28.

75. For assessing HRIS needs, see, Gijs Houtzagers, "The Implementation of a Human Resource Management Information System (HRMIS)," available Gijs Houtzagers site, http://web.inter.nl.net/users/houtzagers/paginas/Engelseversie/papersgb/hrmisimplementation.htm, downloaded September 5, 2006.

76. Sandra E. O'Connell, "System Redesign Makes FedEx a Technology Leader," *HRMagazine,* April, 1994, pp. 33–37.

77. "What VIP Means," Human Resources Information System, University of Manitoba site, http://umanitoba.ca/computing/projects/hris/vipmean.html, downloaded September 5, 2006.

78. Ibid.

79. "What VIP Means," Human Resources Information System, University of Manitoba site, http://umanitoba.ca/computing/projects/hris/vipmean.html, downloaded September 5, 2006.

80. Ibid.

81. Sharon Lebrun, "Wired Workers Threaten Data," *Canadian HR Reporter,* January 27, 1997, pp. 1–2.

82. Wayne Blackburn, a senior white-collar crime investigator quoted in Lebrun, 1997, p. 2.

83. Robert Bickel, "Building Intranets," *Internet World,* March 1996, www.internetworld.com.

84. Guy Huntington, "Intranet Benefits," *Canadian HR Reporter,* September 9, 1996, p. 6.

85. Gijs Houtzagers, "Electronic Services for HR," http://web.inter.nl.net/users/houtzagers/paginas/Engelseversie/papersgb/Eservices.htm, downloaded September 5, 2006.

86. "HRIS 2000: Internet and Enterprise-wide Systems Seen as the Next Big Things in HRIS," Guide to HR Technology, *Canadian HR Reporter,* April 7, 1997, p. G-3.

87. Bo Lykkegaard, "How Zeiss Used SAP NetWeaver to Improve Time-to-Market," 2003, SAP.com site, www.sap.com/solutions/netweaver/pdf/Misc_ROI_Carl_Zeiss.pdf, downloaded September 5, 2006.

88. Hari Das and Mallika Das, "One More Time: How Do We Place a Value Tag on Our Employees? Some Issues in Human Resource Accounting," *Human Resource Planning,* Vol. 2, No. 2, 1979, pp. 91–101.

89. See ibid. for a discussion of the various models.

Chapter 4

1. Canadian Charter of Rights and Freedoms, as part of the *Constitution Act of 1982.*

2. Ibid.

3. H.W. Arthurs, "The Right to Golf: Reflection on the Future of Workers, Unions, and the Rest of Us Under the Charter," paper presented at the Conference on Labour Law Under the Charter, Industrial Relations Centre, Queen's University, September 1987. For a more detailed discussion of the impact of the Charter on Canadian labour relations, see S.D. Carter, "Canadian Labour Relations Under the Charter," *Relations Industrielles,* Vol. 43, No. 2, 1988, pp. 305–21.

4. "Human Rights and the Canadian Human Rights Commission," brochure, Catalogue Number H21-35/1999, Canadian Human Rights Commission; see also Canadian Human Rights Commission, *Annual Report 2004,* www.chrc-ccdp.ca/pdf/AR_2004_RA_en.pdf, downloaded September 5, 2006.

5. *Canadian Human Rights Act,* Paragraph 2, Subsection (a).

6. Doreen Pitkeathly, "Phoenix Rising," *Human Resource Professional,* February 1990, pp. 16–18.

7. Canadian Human Rights Commission, *Annual Report 1991,* p. 59, www.chrc-ccdp.ca/publications/2001_ar/default-en.asp, downloaded September 5, 2006; see also "A Place for All: A Guide to Creating an Inclusive Workplace," Catalogue No. HR21-55/2001, Ottawa: Minister of Public Works and

Government Services, 2001, www.chrc-ccdp.ca/pdf/chrc_place_for_all.pdf, downloaded September 5, 2006.

8. This case and the following cases have been taken from either Canadian Human Rights Commission, *Legal Reports*, Ottawa: Government of Canada, 1979 to present, or the annual reports of the Canadian Human Rights Commission, Ottawa: Government of Canada, 1980 to 2004. As of September 5, 2006, many of these reports are available at www.chrc-ccdp.ca/publications/reports_archive_rapports-en.asp.

9. "Accommodating Employees' Religious Beliefs," *The Worklife Report*, Vol. 7, No. 5, p. 8, Kingston, ON: IR Research Services, 1990; for more examples, see annual report of the Canadian Human Rights Commission, 2004, www.chrc-ccdp.ca/publications/reports_archive_rapports-en.asp, downloaded September 5, 2006.

10. CHRC, *Annual Report 1999*, pp. 6–7, www.chrc-ccdp.ca/publications/reports_archive_rapports-en.asp, downloaded September 5, 2006.

11. Kevin Bourassa and Joe Varnell "It's a Quiet Thing: Equal Marriage Is Law," Equal Marriage for Same-Sex Couples site, July 21, 2005, www.samesexmarriage.ca/legal/qui210705.htm, downloaded September 5, 2006.

12. CHRC, *Annual Report 1996*, p. 85, www.chrc-ccdp.ca/publications/reports_archive_rapports-en.asp, downloaded September 5, 2006. See also CHRC, "Drug Testing Policy Review," *Annual Report 2001*, p. 14.

13. Ibid., p. 86.

14. CHRC, *Annual Report 1991*, p. 31. See also *Annual Report 2001*, pp. 15–16.

15. CHRC, *Annual Report 2001*, p. 12, available www.chrc-ccdp.ca/publications/reports_archive_rapports-en.asp, downloaded September 5, 2006. See also "Submission of the Ontario Human Rights Commission Concerning Barrier-Free Access Requirements in the Ontario Building Code: March 1, 2002," 2002, Ontario Human Rights Commission site, www.ohrc.on.ca/english/publications/building-code-submission.shtml, downloaded September 5, 2006.

16. "Correctional Service Agrees to Hire Ex-convict," news release, a publication of the Canadian Human Rights Commission, Ottawa: Government of Canada, undated.

17. CHRC, "Harassment and the *Canadian Human Rights Act*," 2005, Canadian Human Rights Commission site, www.chrc-ccdp.ca/pdf/publications/har-chra.pdf, downloaded September 5, 2006.

18. *Canadian Human Rights Act*, Paragraph 46, Section 2(a), (b).

19. Indigenous Blacks & Mi'kmaq (IB&M) Initiative site, Dalhousie Law School, http://ibandm.law.dal.ca, downloaded September 5, 2006.

Chapter 5

1. Dave Ulrich, *Human Resource Champions*, Boston, MA: Harvard Business School Press, 1997, p. 13.

2. Todd Humber (2005) "Recruitment Isn't Getting Any Easier: Report on Recruitment and Staffing," Special supplement to *Canadian HR Reporter*, May 23, 2005, p. R2.

3. Tom Long, Toronto-based partner of executive recruiter Egon Zehnder International Inc. quoted by Wallace Immen, "Going Abroad to Get Ahead," *The Globe and Mail*, February 22, 2006, page C1.

4. Results of surveys by Global Recruitment Consultancy Robert Walters, Korn/Ferry International, 2005 Survey of Executives Worldwide reported in Wallace Immen, "Going Abroad to Get Ahead," *The Globe and Mail*, February 22, 2006, page C1.

5. For example, see J.A. Bellizzi and R.W. Hasty, "The Effects of Hiring Decisions on the Level of Discipline Used in Response to Poor Performance," *Management Decision*, Vol. 38, No. 3, 2000, pp. 154–59.

6. Lisa Butler, "Corporate Culture Can Be Your Key to Success on the Hiring Front," *Canadian HR Reporter*, May 3, 1999, p. 22.

7. Lesley Young, "Canadian Workers Want to be Loyal," *Canadian HR Reporter*, June 14, 1999, p. 1.

8. "Disabled at Pizza Hut," *Business Month*, September 1989, p. 16.

9. Virginia Galt , "Better Shifts, Better Training, Better Pay," *The Globe and Mail*, February 24, 2006, page C1.

10. Human Resources and Skills Development Canada, "Estimating and Forecasting Aggregate Retirement Flows in the Canadian Labour Market," March 2005, www.hrsdc.gc.ca/eng/publications_resources/research/categories/labour_market_e/sp_785_12_05_e/page00.shtml, downloaded October 1, 2009.

11. Rod Nutt, "There's a War on for Talent Out There," *The Globe and Mail*, May 12, 2001, page D3.

12. C.S. Manegold, Bill Powell, and Yuriko Hoshiai, "Hanging the Help-Wanted Sign," *Newsweek*, July 16, 1990, p. 39.

13. "What Benefits Are Companies Offering Now?" *HR Focus*, Vol. 77, No. 6, June 2000, p. 5.

14. Shannon Klie, "Diversity Makes Employers More Attractive to Candidates," *Canadian HR Reporter*, April 20, 2009, page 20.

15. "Discussion Paper No. 156," Ottawa: Economic Council of Canada, 1980.

16. "E-mail Is Now the Preferred Way to Receive Resumes," *HR Focus*, Vol. 77, Issue 7, July 2000, p. 8.

17. Larry Stevens, "Resume Scanning Simplifies Tracking," *Personnel Journal*, Vol. 72, No. 4, April 1993, pp. 77–79.

18. Alan Halcrow, "Employees Are Your Best Recruiters," *Personnel Journal*, November 1988, pp. 42–48.

19. S.L. Bem, *Bem Sex Role Inventory: Professional Manual*, Palo Alto, CA: Consulting Psychologists Press, 1981.

20. James Breaugh, *Recruitment: Science and Practice*, Boston: PWS-Kent Publishing Company, 1992, p. 294.

21. Bem, op. cit.

22. James Breaugh, op. cit., p. 294.

23. "Government of Canada Services for You," Catalogue No. PF4-2/2000, Minister of Public Works and Government Services, 2000.

24. Al Doran, "Popularity of Recruiting on the Internet Up," *Canadian HR Reporter*, January 13, 1997, p. 8.

25. Ben V. Luden, "HR vs. Executive Search," *Personnel Journal*, May 1992, pp. 104–10.

26. Al Doran, op. cit.

27. John J. Wypich, "The Head Hunters Are Coming," *Canada Commerce*, Fall 1986, pp. 27–28.

28. Pamela d'Eon Scott and Hari Das, "Searching for a Search Firm," *Journal of Academy of Business Administration*, July 2000, pp. 25–31.

29. V. Catano, S. Cronshaw, W. Wiesner, R. Hackett, and L. Methot, *Recruitment and Selection in Canada*, Toronto: ITP Nelson, 1997, p. 263.

30. Shannon Klie, "Mining for New Graduate Hires," *Canadian HR Reporter*, November 17, 2008, p. 1.

31. Madalyn Freund and Patricia Somers, "Ethics in College Recruiting: Views from the Front Lines," *Personnel Administrator*, April 1979, pp. 30–33; Joe Thomas, "College Recruitment: How to Use Student Perceptions of Business," *Personnel Journal*, January 1980, pp. 44–46; Donald P. Rogers and Michael Z. Sincoff, "Favorable Impression Characteristics of the Recruitment Interviewer," *Personnel Psychology*, Autumn 1978, pp. 495–504.

32. Stephen Jackson, "Performance Based Selection Nets Top Performers," *Canadian HR Reporter*, January 25, 1999, p. 6.

33. Nathan Laurie and Mark Laurie, "No Holds Barred in Fight for Students to Fill Internship Programs," *Canadian HR Reporter*, January 17, 2000, p.15.

34. S. Drake, "Temporaries Are Here to Stay," *Human Resource Executive*, 1992, Vol. 6, No. 2, pp. 27–30.

35. Ann Kerr, "Accounting Firm Makes Sure to Stay in Touch with Past Staff," *The Globe and Mail*, June 30, 2004, p. C1.

36. Joey Goodings, "Job Fairs: It's a Jungle Out There," *Canadian HR Reporter*, February 22, 1999, p. G11.

37. "Giving Job Fairs a Fair Shot," *Canadian HR Reporter*, November 17, 2008, p. 21.

38. Al Doran, op. cit.

39. "Half of Resumes coming by Email," *Canadian HR Reporter*, February 23, 2004, p. 2.

40. Sherwood Ross, "Job Hunt Moves on Line," *The Globe and Mail*, March 27, 2001, p. B16.

41. Ross, op. cit.

42. Shannon Klie, "Lights, Camera and Recruitment," *Canadian HR Reporter*, December 19, 2005, p. 1.

43. Society for Human Resource Management site, www.shrm.org.

44. Yves Lermusiaux, "Recruiting Effectively Over the Internet," *Canadian HR Reporter*, April 5, 1999, p. 2.

45. Mark Swartz, "Jobs Are Online: What About Job Seekers?" *Canadian HR Reporter*, June 2, 1997, p. 21.

46. Anne Freedman, "The Web Worldwide," *Human Resource Executive*, March 6, 2002, pp. 44–48.

47. Al Doran, "The Site Is Up: Now How Do You Attract Job Seekers?" *Canadian HR Reporter*, September 8, 1997, p. 9.

48. Ibid.

49. Richard Nelson Bolles, *Job-Hunting on the Internet*, Berkeley, CA: Ten Speed Press, 1997.

50. Gabriel Bouchard, "A Panoply of Web Recruiting Ideas," *Canadian HR Reporter*, January 12, 1998, p. 4.

51. Debbie McGrath, "Is Your Internet Recruiting Strategy Sending Qualified Candidates to Your Competitors?" *Canadian HR Reporter*, Guide to HR Technology, October 6, 1997, pp. G22–G23.

52. Al Doran, "Paper Resumes Out, Electronic Resume Creation In," *Canadian HR Reporter*, February 8, 1999, p. 9.

53. Peg Anthony, "Track Applicants, Track Costs," *Personnel Journal*, April 1990, pp. 75–81. Also see William C. Delone, "Telephone Job Posting Cuts Costs," *Personnel Journal*, Vol. 72, No. 4, April 1993, pp. 115–18.

54. J. Ross, "Effective Ways to Hire Contingent Personnel," *HR Magazine*, February 1991, pp. 52–54.

55. Chris Knight, "Contractors Become Fixture in Workplace," *Canadian HR Reporter*, October 21, 1996, p. 14.

56. Roger Smithies and Leslie Steeves, "Define Contractor Relationships with Care," *Canadian HR Reporter*, January 12, 1998, p. 12.

57. T. Lee, "Alumni Go Back to Schools to Hunt Jobs," *Wall Street Journal,* June 11, 1991, p. B1.

58. Alar Prost, "Successful Recruiting from an Untapped Resource," *Canadian HR Reporter,* January 16, 2006, p. 11.

59. C.D. Fyock, "Ways to Recruit Top Talent," *HR Magazine,* 1991, Vol. 36, No. 7, pp. 33–35.

60. Seyed-Mahmoud Aghazadeh, "Human Resource Management: Issues and Challenges in the New Millennium," *Management Research News,* 1999, Vol. 22, No.12, pp.19–32.

61. Ian Clark, "Corporate Human Resources and 'Bottom-line' Financial Performance," *Personnel Review,* 1999, Vol. 28, No. 4, pp. 290–306.

62. Robert Sibson, "The High Cost of Hiring," *Nation's Business,* February 14, 1975, pp. 85–88; Magnus, "Is Your Recruitment All It Can Be?" pp. 54–63; J. Scott Lord, "How Recruitment Efforts Can Elevate Credibility," *Personnel Journal,* Vol. 66, No. 4, April 1987.

Chapter 6

1. Jeffrey Pfeffer, *Human Equation,* Boston: Harvard Business School Press, 1998, pp. 70–71.

2. Lawrence Rout, "Going for Broker: Our Man Takes Part in Stock-Selling Test," *The Wall Street Journal,* April 4, 1979, p. 1.

3. Merrill Lynch Web site, February 8, 2003, www.ml.com.

4. Ben Lupton, "Pouring the Coffee at Interviews?" *Personnel Review,* Vol. 29, No.1, 2000, pp. 48–68.

5. James Braham, "Hiring Mr. Wrong," *Industry Week,* March 7, 1988, pp. 31–34.

6. P.V. LeBlanc, J.P. Gonzalez, and J.A. Oxman, "Maximise Your Compensation ROI with High Yield Investments in Human Capital," *Compensation and Benefits Review,* Vol. 30, March–April 1998, pp. 59–68.

7. Michael Valpy, "Human-Rights Victory Brings Little Relief," *The Globe and Mail,* February 27, 2006, p. A6.

8. Stephen Jackson, "All of HR Reaps Benefits from Performance-Based Job Descriptions," *Canadian HR Reporter,* September 7, 1998, p. 12.

9. Sharon Lebrun, "Retailers Lose $3 Million a Day to Employees," *Canadian HR Reporter,* May 5, 1997, pp. 1–2.

10. J.W. Thacker and R.J. Cattaneo, "Survey of Personnel Practices in Canadian Organizations," Working Paper No. W-87-03, University of Windsor, Faculty of Business Administration, April 1987.

11. H.C. Jain, "Human Rights: Issues in Employment," in H.C. Jain and P.C. Wright, eds., *Trends and Challenges in Human Resource Management,* Scarborough, ON: Nelson, 1994, p. 69.

12. Stephen Jackson, "Resumes: The Good, The Bad and The Maybe," *Canadian HR Reporter,* January 27, 1997, p. 9.

13. G.W. England, *Development and Use of Weighted Application Blanks,* Minneapolis: University of Minnesota Industrial Relations Center, 1971.

14. See for example, W.A. Sands, "A Method for Evaluating Alternative Recruiting-Selection Strategies: The CAPER Model," *Journal of Applied Psychology,* 1973, Vol. 57, pp. 222–27; W.A. Owens, "Background Data" in M.D. Dunnette, ed., *Handbook of Industrial and Organizational Psychology,* Chicago, IL: Rand McNally, 1976.

15. R.R. Reilly and G.T. Chao, "Validity and Fairness of Some Alternative Employee Selection Procedures," *Personnel Psychology,* 1982, Vol. 35, pp. 1–62.

16. J.E. Hunter and R.F. Hunter, "Validity and Utility of Alternative Predictors of Job Performance," *Psychological Bulletin,* Vol. 96, 1984, pp. 72–98.

17. Al Doran, "Paper Resumes Out, Electronic Resume Creation In," *Canadian HR Reporter,* February 8, 1999, p. 9.

18. David Brown, "Waterloo Forced to Fire Top Bureaucrat Weeks After Hiring," *Canadian HR Reporter,* October 11, 2004, p. 3.

19. Thacker and Cattaneo, op cit.

20. Norman Trainor, "Using Measurement to Predict Performance," *Canadian HR Reporter,* November 16, 1998, p. 7.

21. Martin Dewey, "Employers Take a Hard Look at the Validity and Value of Psychological Screening," *The Globe and Mail,* February 7, 1981, p. B1.

22. James Leduinka and Lyle F. Schoenfeldt, "Legal Development in Employment Testing: Albermarle and Beyond," *Personnel Psychology,* Spring 1978, pp. 1–13.

23. For an example of this, see, William G. Doerner and Terry Nowell, "The Reliability of the Behavioural-personnel Assessment Device (B-PAD) in Selecting Police Recruits," *Policing: An International Journal of Police Strategies and Management,* Vol. 22, No. 3, 1999, pp. 343–52.

24. Julie McCarthy and Richard Goffin, "Test Taking Anxiety in a Selection Context: The Moderating Role of Applicant Gender," Joanne D. Leck, ed., *ASAC-IFSAM 2000 conference Human Resource Division Proceedings,* Vol. 21, No. 9, 2000, pp. 69–77.

25. P.T. Costa, Jr., "Work and Personality: Using the NEO-PI-R in Industrial/Organizational Psychology" *Applied Psychology: An International Review,* Vol. 45, 1996, pp. 225–41.

26. L. Smith, "Stamina: Who Has It, Why You Need It and How You Can Get It," *Fortune,* November 28, 1994, p. 31.

27. Ian Gellatly and P. Gregory Irving, "The Moderating Role of Perceived Autonomy on Personality-Performance Relations within a Public Sector Organization," in Gerard Seijts, ed., *ASAC 1999 (Human Resource Division) Proceedings,* Vol. 20, No. 9, 1999, pp. 49–58.

28. For example, see, S. Adler, "Personality and Work Behaviour: Exploring the Linkages," *Applied Psychology: An International Review,* 1996, pp. 207–24.

29. Simon Taggar, "Personality, Cognitive Ability and Behaviour: The Antecedents of Effective Autonomous Work Teams," in Joanne Dick, ed., *ASAC-IFSAM 2000 Conference Human Resource Division Proceedings,* Vol. 21, No. 9, 2000, pp. 59–66.

30. Robert Wood and Tim Payne, *Competency Based Recruitment and Selection,* Chichester, U.K.: Wiley, 1998, pp.153–69.

31. S. Sillup, "Applicant Screening Cuts Turnover Costs," *Personnel Journal,* May 1992, pp. 115–16.

32. Electronic Selection Systems Corporation, *AccuVision: Assessment Technology for Today, Tomorrow and Beyond,* Maitland, FL: Electronic Selection Systems, Inc., 1992.

33. For example, see, R.C. Overton, H.J. Harms, L.R. Taylor, and M.J. Zickar, "Adapting to Adaptive Testing," *Personnel Psychology,* Vol. 50, 1997, pp. 171–85.

34. Jeff Weekley and Casey Jones, "Video-Based Situational Testing," *Personnel Psychology,* Vol. 50, 1997, pp. 25–49.

35. "Should You Tell All?" *Parade Magazine,* May 27, 1990, p. 5.

36. D.T. Lykken, "The Case Against the Polygraph in Employment Screening," *Personnel Administrator,* September 1985, pp. 59–65.

37. "Workplace Privacy," Ontario Commissioner's Report, *Worklife Report,* Vol. 9, No. 3, 1994, pp. 8–9.

38. Bison Security Group site, December 25, 2000, www.bsgcorp.com/journal/journal.html.

39. P.R. Sackett and M.M. Harris, "Honesty Testing for Personnel Selection: A Review and a Critique," *Personnel Psychology,* 1984, Vol. 37, pp. 221–45.

40. D.S. Ones, C. Visweswaran, and F.L. Schmidt, "Comprehensive Meta Analysis of Integrity Test Validities: Findings and Implications for Personnel Selection and Theories of Job Performance," *Journal of Applied Psychology,* Vol. 78, August 1993, pp. 679–703; see also P.R. Sackett, L.R. Burris, and C. Callahan, "Integrity Testing for Personal Selection: An Update," *Personnel Psychology,* Vol. 42, Autumn 1989, pp. 491–529.

41. Dennis S. Joy, "Basic Psychometric Properties of a Pre-employment Honesty Test: Reliability, Validity and Fairness," in John W. Jones, ed., *Pre-employment Honesty Testing,* New York: Quorum Books, 1991, pp. 65–88.

42. E. Bean, "More Firms Use 'Attitude Tests' to Keep Thieves Off the Payroll" *Wall Street Journal,* Vol. 219, 1987, p. 41; see also Robert M. Madigan, K. Dow Scott, Diana L. Deadrick, and J.A. Stoddard, "Employment Testing: The U.S. Job Service Is Spearheading a Revolution," *Personnel Administrator,* September 1986, pp. 102–12.

43. Adelheid Nicol and Sampo Paunonen, "Workplace Honesty: The Development of a New Measure," in Caroline Weber, ed., *ASAC 1998 (Human Resources Divison) Proceedings,* Vol. 19, No. 9, 1998, pp. 31–42.

44. Charles D. Johnson, Lawrence A. Messe, and William D. Crano, "Predicting Job Performance of Low Income Workers: The Work Opinion Questionnaire," *Personnel Psychology,* Summer 1984, Vol. 37, No. 2, pp. 291–99.

45. Lesley Young, "Reference Checking Skills Sorely Lacking," *Canadian HR Reporter,* January 25, 1999, p. 1.

46. Hari Das and Mallika Das, "But He Had Excellent References: Refining the Reference Letter," *The Human Resource,* June–July 1988, pp. 15–16.

47. Stephen Jackson, "Objective Descriptions—Not Opinions—Should Be Aim of Reference Checks," *Canadian HR Reporter,* April 21, 1997, p. 10.

48. Bob Smith, "The Evolution of Pinkerton," *Management Review,* Vol. 82, September 1993, p. 56.

49. L. Shiffman, "Employers Use Facebook Information When Hiring," *North by Northwestern,* November 12, 2007, www.northbynorthwestern. com/2007/11/5072/employers-use-facebook-information-when-hiring/, downloaded October 1, 2009.

50. Anthony Moffatt, "The Danger of Digging Too Deep," *Canadian HR Reporter,* August 11, 2008, p. 5.

51. Stephen Jackson, "Give Job Applicants the Whole Truth," *Canadian HR Reporter,* March 24, 1997, p. 9.

52. Paula Popovich and John P. Wanous, "The Realistic Job Preview as a Persuasive Communication," *Academy of Management Review,* October 1982, p. 571.

53. *Kearsley v. City of St. Catherines,* Board of Inquiry decision on April 2, 2002, Ontario Human Rights Commission, www.ohrc.on.ca/English/cases/summary-2002.shtml, downloaded September 5, 2006.

54. Ontario Human Rights Commission, "Human Rights at Work," approved by Commission on September 22, 1999, pp.58–60. See also www.obrc.on.ca.

55. Jane Easter Bahls, "Drugs in the Workplace," *HR Magazine,* February 1998, www.shrm.org/hrmagazine/articles/0298cov.asp, downloaded September 5, 2006.

56. Ted Thaler, "Substance Abuse Costing Employers Estimated $2.6-B," *Canadian HR Reporter,* October 24, 1990, p. 1.

57. B.L. Thompson, "A Surprising Ally in the Drug Wars," *Training,* November 1990.

58. C. Languedoc, "Battle Lines Forming Over Worker Drug Test," *The Financial Post,* April 13, 1987, pp. 1, 4.

59. "Imperial Oil to Test Staff for Drugs," *The Globe and Mail,* October 5, 1991, p. B1. See also "Mandatory Drug Testing Attracts Controversy," *Canadian Employment Law Today,* April 9, 1991, pp. 635–46.

60. Jeffrey Miller, "Drug Testing Dealt a Blow by Federal Court," *Canadian HR Reporter,* September 21, 1998, p. 5.

61. Virginia Galt, "Total Ban Sought on Drug Testing by Employers," *The Globe and Mail,* February 22, 1992.

62. Canadian Human Rights Commission, *Annual Report 1993,* Ottawa: Minister of Supply and Services Canada, 1994, pp. 35–36.

63. "The Case Against Drug Testing," editorial, *The Globe and Mail,* August 19, 1994, p. A18.

64. Miller, op. cit., p. 5.

65. Ontario Human Rights Commission, op. cit.

66. Janice Rubin and Sharaf Sultan, "Drug and Alcohol Testing: Where Are We Now?" *Canadian HR Reporter,* March 9, 2009, p. 15.

67. Ibid.

68. "Catch-22: Under Imperial Oil's Revamped Drug Policy," *Journal of the Addiction Research Foundation,* Vol. 22, No. 6, November–December 1994, p. 12.

69. Adapted from Hari Das, *Recruitment, Selection and Deployment,* Toronto: Pearson Education, 2006, p. 320.

70. Cynthia D. Fisher, Lyle F. Schoenfeldt, and James B. Shaw, *Human Resource Management,* Boston: Houghton Mifflin, 1990, p. 231.

71. Hari Das, op. cit.

72. Milton L. Blum and James C. Naylor, *Industrial Psychology: Its Theoretical and Social Foundations,* New York: Harper & Row, 1969, pp. 67–70.

73. B. Kleinmutz, "Why We Still Use Our Heads Instead of Formulas: Toward an Integrative Approach," *Psychological Bulletin,* Vol. 107, 1990, pp. 296–310.

74. R. R. Reilly and W.R. Manese. "The Validation of a Minicourse for Telephone Company Switching Technicians," *Personnel Psychology,* Vol. 32, 1979, pp. 83–90.

75. Hari Das, *Recruitment, Selection and Deployment,* Toronto: Pearson Education, 2006, p. 318.

76. Dale E.Yeatts, M. Hipskind, and D. Barnes, "Lessons Learned from Self-Managed Work Teams," *Business Horizon,* July/August, 1994, pp. 11–18.

77. "How to Form Hiring Teams," *Personnel Journal,* August 1994, pp. 14–17.

78. David Whitten, "Steering Clear of Contract Landmines," *Canadian HR Reporter,* June 20, 2005, p. 5.

79. Marc Belaiche, "Put Your Company's Best Foot Forward with New Hires," *Canadian HR Reporter,* September 21, 1998, p. 66.

80. See Hermann F. Schwind, "How Well Do Interviews Predict Future Performance?" *The Human Resource,* June–July 1987, pp. 19–20; G.P. Latham, L.M. Saari, E.D. Pursell, and M.A. Champion, "The Situational Interview," *Journal of Applied Psychology,* Vol. 65, No. 4, 1989, pp. 422–27.

81. Helen Gardiner and Rick Hackett, "Employment Interviewing: A Review and Analysis of Canadian Human Rights Cases," Jacques Barrette, ed., *ASAC 1997 (Human Resource Division) Proceedings,* Vol. 18, No. 9, 1997, pp. 46–55.

82. James G. Hollandsworth, Jr., et al., "Relative Contributions of Verbal Articulative and Nonverbal Communication to Employment Decisions in the Job Interview Setting," *Personnel Psychology,* Summer 1979, pp. 359–67. See also Angelo Kimicki and Chris A. Lockwood, "The Interview Process: An Examination of Factors Recruiters Use in Evaluating Job Applicants," *Journal of Vocational Behaviour,* Vol. 26, 1985, p. 117.

83. Survey by Professors David Zweig and Derek Chapman quoted by Shannon Klie, "'Armchair Psychology' Doesn't Make for Good Hiring Choices," *Canadian HR Reporter,* December 19, 2005, Page 3.

84. M.A. Campion, J.E. Campion, and J.P. Hudson, "Structured Interviewing: A Note on Incremental Validity and Alternative Question Types," *Journal of Applied Psychology,* Vol. 79, 1994, pp. 998–1002; E.D. Pulakos and N. Schmitt, "Experience and Situational Based Interview Questions: Studies of Validity," *Personnel Psychology,* Vol. 48, 1995, pp. 289–308.

85. Stephen Maurer, "The Potential of Situational Interview: Existing Research and Unresolved Issues," *Human Resource Management Review,* Vol. 7, No. 2, 1997, pp. 185–201.

86. Tom Janz, "The Patterned Behavioural Description Interview: The Best Prophet of the Future is the Past," in Eder and Ferris, *The Employment Interview,* pp. 158–68; Janz, "The Selection Interview," p. 160; C. Orpen, "Patterned Behavioural Description Interview Versus Unstructured Interviews: A Comparative Validity Study," *Journal of Applied Psychology,* Vol. 70, 1985, pp. 774–76; J. Tom Janz, "Comparing the Use and Validity of Opinions Versus Behavioural Descriptions in the Employment Interview," unpublished manuscript, University of Calgary, 1988; Latham, "The Reliability, Validity and Practicality of Selection Interviews."

87. Michael Harris, "Reconsidering the Employment Interview: A Review of Recent Literature and Suggestions for Future Research," *Personnel Psychology,* 1989, Vol. 42, pp. 691–726.

88. M.A. McDaniel, D.L. Whetzel, F.L. Schmidt, and S.D. Maurer, "The Validity of Employment Interviews: A Comprehensive Review and Meta Analysis," *Journal of Applied Psychology,* Vol. 79, 1994, pp. 599–616.

89. Ibid., A.I. Huffcutt and W. Arthur, Jr., "Hunter and Hunter Revisited: Interview Validity for Entry Level Jobs," *Journal of Applied Psychology,* Vol. 22, 1994, pp. 184–90.

90. Huffcutt and Arthur, op. cit.

91. Linda Thornburg, "Computer Assisted Interviewing Shortens Hiring Cycle," *HR Magazine,* February 1998, pp. 1–5.

92. William L. Tullar, Terry W. Mullins, and Sharon A. Caldwell, "Effects on Interview Length and Applicant Quality on Interview Decision Time," *Journal of Applied Psychology,* Vol. 64, No. 6, 1979, pp. 669–74.

93. D.H. Tucker and P.M. Rowe, "Consulting the Application Form Prior to the Interview: An Essential Step in the Selection Process," *Journal of Applied Psychology,* Vol. 62, 1977.

94. Stephen Jackson, "Interviewers Need to Be Taught, Not Told, How to Hire the Best," *Canadian HR Reporter,* June 16, 1997, p. 8.

95. Wayne Cascio, *Applied Psychology in Human Resource Management,* 5th ed., Upper Saddle River, NJ: Prentice-Hall, 1998, p. 199.

96. Michael H. Frisch, *Coaching and Counselling Handbook,* New York: Resource Dynamics, 1981.

97. James Parr, "Do Experience and Skills Transfer Across Sectors?" *Canadian HR Reporter,* November 21, 2005, p. 9.

98. Anthropologist Jennifer James quoted by Bob Rosner, "Coming of Age in HR," *Workforce,* August 2000, p. 61.

99. Stephen Jackson, "If Low Performers Outnumber High Performers, It's Time to Review Your Selection Process," *Canadian HR Reporter,* March 8, 1999, p. 8.

100. Sharon Ifill and Neil Moreland, "Auditing Recruitment and Selection Using Generic Benchmarking: A Case Study," *The TQM Magazine,* Vol. 11, No. 5, 1999, pp. 333–40.

101. Hunter and Hunter, op. cit., pp. 72–98; see also Schwind, op. cit.

102. Wayne Cascio, *Managing Human Resources,* 7th ed., New York: McGraw-Hill Irwin, 2006, p. 199.

103. J.E. Hunter and F.L. Schmidt, "Quantifying the Effects of Psychological Interventions on Employee Job Performance and Work Force Productivity," *American Psychologist,* 38, 1983, pp. 473–78; see also J.E. Hunter and F.L. Schmidt, "Fitting People to Jobs: The Impact of Personnel Selection on National Productivity," in Marvin D. Dunnette and E.A. Fleishman, eds., *Human Capability Assessment,* Hillsdale, NJ: Lawrence Erlbaum Associates, 1982.

104. Marvin D. Dunnette, "Personnel Selection and Placement," *Personnel Selection and Placement,* Belmont, CA: Wadsworth, 1966.

105. Hunter and Schmidt, "Fitting People to Jobs"; F.L. Schmidt, J.E. Hunter, R.C. McKenzie, and T.W. Muldrow, "Impact of Valid Selection Procedures on Work Force Productivity," *Journal of Applied Psychology,* Vol. 64, 1979, pp. 609–26; Ralph B. Alexander and Murray R. Barrick, "Estimating the Standard Error of Projected Dollar Gains in Utility Analysis," *Journal of Applied Psychology,* Vol. 72, 1987, pp. 463–74; J.E. Hunter, *The Economic Benefits of Personnel Selection Using Ability Tests: A State of the Art Review Including a Detailed Analysis of the Dollar Benefit of U.S. Employment Service Placement and a Critique of the Low Cutoff Method of Test Use,* Washington, DC: U.S. Employment Service, U.S. Department of Labor, January 15, 1981; F.L. Schmidt, J.E. Hunter, and K. Pearlman, "Assessing the Economic Impact of Personnel Programs on Work Force Productivity," *Personnel Psychology,* Vol. 35, No. 3, 1982, pp. 333–43; Wayne F. Cascio, *Costing Human Resources: The Financial Impact of Behaviour in Organizations,* Boston: Kent Publishing, 1982; W.F. Cascio and V. Silbey, "Utility of the Assessment Centre as a Selection Device," *Journal of Applied Psychology,* Vol. 64, pp. 107–18;

W.F. Cascio and N.F. Philips, "Performance Testing: A Rose Among Thorns? *Personnel Psychology,* Vol. 32, pp. 751–66.

106. Adapted from Cascio, *Managing Human Resources,* op. cit., p. 199.

107. See Hunter and Schmidt, "Quantifying the Effects of Psychological Interventions," op. cit., pp. 474–77.

108. See, for example, Hunter and Schmidt, "Fitting People to Jobs"; Schmidt, Hunter, McKenzie, and Muldrow, "Impact of Valid Selection Procedures on Work Force Productivity"; Cascio, *Managing Human Resources*; Schmidt, Hunter, and Pearlman, "Assessing the Economic Impact of Personnel Programs on Work Force Productivity." See also Steven F. Cranshaw, "The Utility of Employment Testing for Clerical/Administrative Trades in the Canadian Military," *Canadian Journal of Administrative Sciences,* Vol. 3, No. 2, 1986, pp. 376–85; Steven F. Cranshaw, Ralph A. Alexander, Willi H. Weisner, and Murray R. Barrick, "Incorporating Risk into Selection Utility: Two Models of Sensitivity Analysis and Risk Simulation," *Organizational Behaviour and Decision Processes,* Vol. 40, 987, pp. 270–86.

109. Dunnette, op. cit., p. 174.

110. H.C. Taylor and J.T. Russell, "The Relationship of Validity Coefficients to the Practical Effectiveness of Tests in Selection: Discussion and Tables," *Journal of Applied Psychology,* 23, 1939, pp. 565–78.

Chapter 7

1. Bill Pomfret, "Sound Employee Orientation Program Boosts Productivity and Safety," *Canadian HR Reporter,* January 25, 1999, p. 17.

2. John Thomas Howe, "What's Right for You?" *Canadian HR Reporter,* May 17, 1999, p. G3, G6.

3. Royal Bank of Canada, *Annual Report 2008,* www.rbc.com/investorrelations/pdf/ar_2008_e.pdf, downloaded January 2009.

4. Rebecca Ganzel, "Putting Out the Welcome Mat," *Training Magazine,* March 1998 (citing research at Corning Glass Works [1981] and Texas Instruments [1981]).

5. Edward Lowe, "Understanding the Costs of Employee Turnover," Edward Lowe Foundation site, http://edwardlowe.org/index.peer?page=main&storyid=0010, downloaded September 5, 2006.

6. Howe, op. cit.

7. Herbert G. Heneman and Timothy A. Judge, *Staffing Organizations,* 5th ed., New York: McGraw-Hill/Irwin, 2006, pp. 598–602.

8. "Industry Report," *Training,* Vol. 36, No. 11, October 1999, p. 58. For more recent survey results, see www.westwood-dynamics.com/all_about_orientation/surveys_north_american.htm, downloaded September 5, 2006.

9. Steven L. McShane and Trudy Baal, "Employee Socialization Practices on Canada's West Coast: A Management Report," *Faculty Research,* Burnaby, BC: Faculty of Business Administration, Simon Fraser University, December 1984.

10. Howard J. Klein and Natasha A. Weaver, "The Effectiveness of an Organizational-Level Orientation Training Program in the Socialization of New Hires," *Personnel Psychology,* Vol. 53, No. 1, Spring 2000, pp. 44–62.

11. Roberta L. Westwood, "Orientation: Taking It Online and the Trend to Blend," www.westwood-dynamics.com/all_about_orientation/article_taking_it_online.htm, downloaded September 5, 2006.

12. Owen Parker, "The Real Bottom Line on Training: It's How, Not How Much," Ottawa: The Conference Board of Canada, www.conferenceboard.ca/humanresource/training-inside.htm, downloaded September 5, 2006.

13. Irwin Goldstein and Kevin Ford, *Training in Organizations: Needs Assessment, Development, Evaluation,* 4th ed., Belmont, CA: Thomson-Wadsworth Publishing, 2002, p. 272.

14. P. Wright, M. Belcourt, and Alan Saks, *Managing Performance Through Training & Development,* Scarborough, ON: Nelson, 2000, pp. 138–40.

15. T. Middleton, "The Potential of Virtual Reality Technology for Training," *The Journal of Interactive Instructional Development,* Spring 1992, pp. 8–12. See also Ken Mark, "Virtual Training—At Your Pace, in Your Space," *Human Resource Professional,* February/March 1998, pp. 15–17. See also Defence Research and Development Canada, "DRDC Develops Virtual Reality Simulator for Use in Helicopter Deck-Landing Training," July 2002, www.drdc-rddc.gc.ca/newsevents/newstand/release/020701farn_e.asp, downloaded September 5, 2006.

16. Jacques Surveyer, "Net-Based Learning Goes Mainstream," *The Computer Paper,* Eastern ed., July 2000, p. 68; Eugene Sadler-Smith, Simon Down, and Jonathan Lean, "Modern Learning Methods: Rhetoric and Reality," *Personnel Review,* April 29, 2000, pp. 474–90; "What Is Web-Based Training?" *Web-Based Training,* July 27, 2000, Web-Based Training Information Center site, www.wbtic.com/home.aspx.

17. Verna Allee, "Principles of Knowledge Management," American Society for Training and Development, ehrCentral site, www.providersedge.com/docs/km_articles/12_Principles_of_Knowledge_Management.pdf, downloaded September 5, 2006.

18. The Personal Learning Network, Royal Bank of Canada, described in www.ii3.com/case_studies/pln.html, and in Treasury Board of Canada, "Career Development in the Federal Public Service: Building a World-Class Workforce," www.tbs-sct.gc.ca/Pubs_pol/partners/workreport8_e.asp, downloaded September 5, 2006.

19. Robert C. Camp, "Xerox Benchmarks the Spot," *Journal of Business Strategy,* 1992. See also Laurie J. Bassi and Scott Cheney, "Changes in Benchmarked Training," *Training and Development,* December 1996, pp. 29–30; "What Is Benchmarking?" http://management.about.com/cs/benchmarking/a/Benchmarking.htm, downloaded September 5, 2006.

20. Kenneth N. Wexley and Gary P. Latham, *Developing and Training Human Resources in Organizations,* 3rd ed., New York: Prentice Hall, 2001.

21. A. Pescuric and W.C. Byham, "The New Look of Behavior Modeling," *Training & Development,* July 1996, pp. 24–30; see also M.M. Najjar and J.W. Boudreau, "The Effect of Behavior Modelling Training," paper provided by Center for Advanced Human Resource Studies, Cornell University, 1996.

22. R.R. Blake and A.A. McCanse, *Leadership Dilemmas—Grid Solutions,* Houston: Gulf Publishing Co., 1991; Robert R. Blake and Rachel Kelly McKee, *Solution Selling: The GridScience Approach,* Houston: Gulf Publishing Company, 1994.

23. Keystone Basanti Majumdar and Lori A Cuttress, "Cultural Sensitivity Training Among Foreign Medical Graduates," *Medical Education,* Vol. 33, No. 3, March 1999, p. 177.

24. Gary Kroehnert, *Games Trainers Play Outdoors,* McGraw-Hill Education, 2002.

25. Diana Whitney, Amanda Trosten, Jay Cherney, and Ron Frey, "Appreciative Team Building: Positive Questions to Bring Out the Best of Your Team," *jUniverse, Inc.,* Lincoln, NB: 2004.

26. Suzan Butyn, "Mentoring Your Way to Improved Retention," *Canadian HR Reporter,* January 27, 2003, pp. 13–15.

27. Susan M. Heathfield, "Tips for Effective Coaching," http://humanresources.about.com/od/coachingmentoring/a/coaching.htm, downloaded September 5, 2006.

28. Gayle MacDonald, "An Open-Book Approach to Motivation," *The Globe and Mail,* March 31, 1997, p. B9; see also www.norwestlabs.com.

29. Dan MacLeod and Eric Kennedy, "Job Rotation System," a consulting report, 1993, Dan MacLeod's Ergo Web site, www.danmacleod.com/Articles/job%20rotation.htm, downloaded September 5, 2006.

30. Thomas G. Cummings and Christopher G. Worley, *Organization Development and Change,* 8th ed., Mason, OH: South-Western, Thompson Publishing, 2005.

31. Peter M. Senge, *The Fifth Discipline: The Art and Practices of the Learning Organization,* New York: Doubleday/Currency, 1990.

32. Steven L. McShane, *Canadian Organizational Behaviour,* 5th ed., Toronto: McGraw-Hill Ryerson, 2004, pp. 439–41.

33. Russ Finney, "Winning Project Teams," white paper, itmWEB, www.itmweb.com/essay003.htm, downloaded September 5, 2006.

34. Senge, op. cit.

35. Patricia A. Galagan, "Interview with Peter Senge," *Training and Development Journal,* October 1991, pp. 37–44.

36. Jamie Harrison, "Molson Opens Learning Centre," *Canadian HR Reporter,* January 26, 1998, pp. 1–2. See also Norman L. Trainor, "Defining the Learning Organization," in the same issue, p. 9. For more details see www.nald.ca/molson/molsonindex.html, downloaded September 5, 2006.

37. Senge, op. cit.; see also David A. Ganin, *Learning in Action: A Guide to Putting the Learning Organization to Work,* Cambridge: Harvard University Press, 2000; a review of Senge's work is available at www.rtis.com/nat/user/jfullerton/review/learning.htm, downloaded September 5, 2006.

38. Peter F. Drucker, *Innovation and Entrepreneurship,* New York: Harper and Row, 1985.

39. Uyen Vu, "Knowledge Workers Now Account for One-Quarter of Workforce," *HR Reporter,* December 1, 2003, p. 2.

40. Knowledge Management Network, www.brint.com/km, downloaded September 5, 2006. See also "Managing Knowledge Workers: Brain Teasing," *The Economist,* October 13, 2005, available www.economist.com/business/globalexecutive/reading/displayStory.cfm?story_id=5016986, downloaded September 5, 2006.

41. R.L. Williams and W.R. Bukowitz, "Knowledge Managers Guide Information Seekers," *HR Magazine,* January 1997, pp. 77–81.

42. Jean-Pascal Souque, "Focus on Competencies: Training and Development Practices, Expenditures and Trends," Report 177-96, Ottawa: Conference Board of Canada, 1996. See also Richard J. Mirabile, "Everything You Wanted to Know About Competency Modeling," *Training & Development,* August 1997, pp. 73–77; Patricia A. McLegan, "Competencies: The Next Generation," *Training & Development,* May 1997, pp. 40–47.

43. McLegan, op. cit, pp. 40–47.

44. Ibid.

45. "Retail Giants Support Ryerson," *Campus News,* Summer 2000, available www.ryerson.ca/news/2000/20000622.html, downloaded September 5, 2006.

46. Jen Ross, "Virtual University Education," *The Gazette,* student newspaper at Dalhousie University, December 3, 1997, p. 16.

47. Dan Miller, "The Advantages of Outsourcing Training," General Physics Corporation site, www.gpworldwide.com/pdf/bpo/TBPOWhitePaper.pdf, downloaded September 5, 2006.

48. Douglas T. Hall, "Human Resource Development and Organizational Effectiveness," in Charles Fombrun, Noel M. Tichy, and Mary A. Devanna, eds., *Strategic Human Resource Management,* New York: John Wiley, 1984, pp. 159–81.

49. Donald L. Kirkpatrick, "Techniques for Evaluating Training Programs," *Journal of the American Society of Training Directors,* Vol. 13, 1959, pp. 3–9, 21–26; Vol. 14, 1960, pp. 13–18, 28–32.

50. D.T. Campbell and J.C. Stanley, *Experimental and Quasi-Experimental Design,* Chicago: Rand McNally, 1963.

51. Shaun Killian, "What Percentage of Salary Should Go to Training?" January 2, 2009; http://hrthought leaders.org/2009/01/02/what-percentage-of-salary-should-go-to-training/, downloaded October 1, 2009.

52. Thomas A. Stewart, *Intellectual Capital: The New Wealth of Organizations,* New York: Currency Doubleday, 1997. See also Gordon Pitts, "The Next Hot Market Commodity? Human Capital," *The Globe and Mail,* June 20, 2000; Lester Thurow, "Cheque-mate!," *The Globe and Mail,* June 5, 2000.

53. Carol Kinsey Goman, *The Human Side of High-Tech: Lessons from the Technology Frontier,* New York: John Wiley & Sons, Inc., 2000.

54. "CEOs Talk," *Canadian HR Reporter,* October 7, 2002, pp. 17–18.

55. Barbara Moses, "Career Planning Mirrors Social Change," *Canadian HR Reporter,* May 17, 1999, p. G10.

56. Douglas T. Hall, "Managing Yourself: Building a Career," in A.R. Cohen, ed., *The Portable MBA in Management,* New York: Wiley, 1993, pp. 190–206.

57. Statistics Canada, "Income Trends in Canada," 2002, available www.statcan.ca/bsolc/english/bsolc?catno=13F0022XIE, downloaded September 5, 2006.

58. Suzanne Spiker-Miller and Nathalie Kees, "Making Career Development a Reality for Dual-Career Couples," *Journal of Employment Counseling,* March 1, 1995. See also Lori Block, "Making It Work When Both of You Work," *womentodaymagazine,* www.womentodaymagazine.com/career/dualwork.html, downloaded September 5, 2006. See also Nicole Seymour, "Copreneurs," www.celcee.edu/publications/digest/Dig02-03.html, downloaded September 5, 2006.

59. James Hunt and Joseph R Weintraub, *The Coaching Manager: Developing Top Talent in Business,* Sage Publications Inc., 2002.

60. Carole Kanchier, "Loyal Workers Reward Companies," *National Post,* December 3, 2005.

61. Celene Adams, "Coaches Offer More Than Game Plan," *The Globe and Mail,* July 8, 2002, p. 1.

62. Personal communication by the first author with a Ford HR executive at the Cologne plant in Germany.

63. Chartered Institute of Personnel and Development, annual survey report 2005 on Training and Development, www.cipd.co.uk/NR/rdonlyres/271CD424-507C-4E4A-99B6-1FAD80573E4A/0/traindevtsurvrept05.pdf, downloaded October 1, 2009.

64. Barbara Moses, "What Do You Really Want to Be?" *The Globe and Mail,* April 30, 2003, pp. C1, 6.

65. Nikola Menalo, "The 360 Degrees of Career Development," *ComputerWorld Canada,* July 28, 2000, p. 37. See also Susan M. Heathfield, "360 Degree Feedback: The Good, the Bad, and the Ugly," http://humanresources.about.com/od/360feedback/l/aa_360_good2.htm, downloaded September 5, 2006.

Chapter 8

1. Hari Das, *Performance Management,* Toronto: Prentice Hall, 2003.

2. Beth Lewallen, "Wal-Mart & the Bar Code," *Frontline,* November 16, 2004, Public Broadcasting Service, www.pbs.org/wgbh/pages/frontline/shows/walmart/secrets/barcode.html, downloaded September 5, 2006.

3. Karyn Siobhan Robinson, "Workers Give Performance Management Programs a Failing Grade," *HR News,* Society for Human Resource Management, www.shrm.org/hrnews_published/archives/CMS_008228.asp, downloaded March 2006.

4. Richard C. Grote, "Performance Appraisal Reappraised," *Harvard Business Review,* January 1, 2000.

5. Terry H. Wagar, "Union Status, Organization Size and Progressive Decision-Making Ideology as Predictors of Human Resource Management Practices," *International Journal of Employment Studies,* April 1996, pp. 79–93.

6. Hermann F. Schwind, "Developing and Evaluating a New Performance Appraisal and Training Evaluation Instrument: The Behaviour Description Index," unpublished Ph.D. dissertation, University of British Columbia, 1978.

7. Testimony from several members of the Canadian Armed Forces, all officers, in classes of the first author.

8. J.S. Kane and E.E. Lawler, "Performance Appraisal Effectiveness: Its Assessment and Determinants," *Research in Organizational Behavior,* Vol. 1, 1980, pp. 425–78.

9. Kane and Lawler, op. cit.

10. G.R. Ferris, T.A. Judge, K.M. Rowland, and D.E. Fitzgibbons, "Subordinate Influence and the Performance Evaluation Process: Test of a Model," *Organizational Behavior and Human Decision Process,* Vol. 58, 1995, pp. 223–38.

11. Hermann F. Schwind, "Performance Appraisal: The State of the Art," in S.L. Dolan and R.S. Schuler, eds., *Personnel and Human Resources Management in Canada,* Minneapolis/St. Paul: West Publishing, 1987, pp. 197–210.

12. L.A. Wilk and W.K. Redmon, "The Effects of Feedback and Goal Setting on the Productivity and Satisfaction of University Admissions Staff," *Journal of Organizational Behavior Management,* Vol. 18, 1998, pp. 45–68. See also E.A. Locke and G.P. Latham, *A Theory of Goal Setting and Task Performance,* Englewood Cliffs, NJ: Prentice-Hall, 1990.

13. Andrew E. Schwartz and Deborah Zemke, "Performance Management," *Barron's Educations Series,* October 1999. See also A.M. Mohrman, S.M. Resnick-West, and E.E. Lawler, *Designing Performance Appraisal Systems,* San Francisco: Jossey-Bass, 1989.

14. Lorne M. Sulsky and David V. Day, "Frame-of-Reference Training and Cognitive Categorization: An Empirical Investigation of Rater Memory Issues," *Journal of Applied Psychology,* Vol. 77, No. 4, 1992, pp. 501–10. See also Sylvia G. Roch and Brian J. O'Sullivan, "Frame of Reference Rater Training Issues: Recall, Time and Behavior Observation Training," *International Journal of Training and Development,* Vol. 7, June 2003, pp. 93–1007.

15. R.L. Cary, and T.J. Keefe, "Observational Purpose and Valuative Articulation in Frame-of-Reference Training: The Effects of Alternative Processing Models on Rating Accuracy," *Organizational Behavior and Human Decision Processes,* Vol. 57, 1994, pp. 338–57. See also D.J. Schleicher and D.V. Day, "A Cognitive Evaluation of Frame-of-Reference Rater Training: Content and Process Issues," *Organizational Behavior and Human Decision Processes,* Vol. 73, No. 1, January 1998, pp. 76–101.

16. Daniel R. Ilgen, Janet L. Barnes-Farrell, David B. McKellin, "Performance Appraisal Process Research in the 1980s: What Has It Contributed to Appraisals in Use?" *Organizational Behavior and Human Decision Processes,* Vol. 54, No. 3, April 1993, pp. 321–68.

17. Gary P. Latham and Kenneth N. Wexley, *Increasing Productivity Through Performance Appraisal,* 2nd ed., Reading, MA: Addison-Wesley, January 1994.

18. George T. Milkovich, ed., *Pay for Performance: Evaluating Performance Appraisal and Merit Pay,* Washington, DC: National Academies Press, January, 1991.

19. J.F. Hazucha, S.A. Gentile, and R.J. Schneider, "The Impact of 360-Degree Feedback on Management Skills Development," *Human Resource Management Review,* Vol. 3, No. 2, 1993, pp. 32–45.

20. Nat J. Salvemini, Richard R. Reilly, James W. Smither, "The Influence of Rater Motivation on Assimilation Effects and Accuracy in Performance Ratings," *Organizational Behavior and Human Decision Processes,* Vol. 55, No. 1, June 1993, pp. 41–60.

21. D.L. DeVries, "Viewing Performance Appraisal with a Wide-Angle Lens," *Issues and Observation,* 1984, pp. 6–9.

22. James D. Grant and Terry H. Wagar, "Dismissal for Incompetence: An Analysis of the Factors Used by Canadian Courts in Determining Just Cause of Termination," in Natalie Lam, ed., *Proceedings of the Administrative Science Association of Canada, Personnel and Human Resource Division,* 1991, pp. 1–10.

23. K.R. Murphy and J.I. Constans, "Behavioral Anchors as a Source of Bias in Rating," *Journal of Applied Psychology,* Vol. 72, November 1987, pp. 573–86.

24. J. Peter Graves, "Let's Put Appraisal Back in Performance Appraisal: II," *Personnel Journal,* December 1982, p. 918.

25. Jack Welch, *Straight from the Gut,* New York: Warner Business Books, 2001.

26. Jeanne D. Makiney and Paul E. Levy, "The Influence of Self-Ratings Versus Peer Ratings on Supervisors' Performance Judgments," *Organizational Behavior and Human Decision Processes,* Vol. 74, No. 3, June 1998, pp. 212–28.

27. R. Rodgers and J.E. Hunter, "Impact of Management by Objectives on Organizational Productivity," *Journal of Applied Psychology,* Vol. 77, No. 2, 1991, pp. 322–36.

28. Richard. J. Campbell, "Use of an Assessment Center as an Aid in Management Selection," *Personnel Psychology,* Vol. 46, 1993, pp. 691–99; see also: J.R. Kauffman, S.M. Jex, K.G. Love, and T.M. Libkuman, "The Construct Validity of Assessment Centre Performance Dimensions,"

International Journal of Selection and Assessment, Vol. 1, 1993, pp. 213–23; Lisa Donohue, Donna Denning, Richard J. Klimoski, Kenneth N. Wexley, and Deborah L. Whetzel, "Chipping Away at the Monument: A Critical Look at the Assessment Center Method," Symposium Presented at the 2000 IPMAAC Conference 2000, Arlington, Virginia, June 3–7, 2000, IPMA-HR Assessment Council site, www.ipmaac.org/confoo/acpanel.pdf, downloaded September 5, 2006.

29. G.C. Thornton, *Assessment Centers in Human Resource Management*, Reading, MA: Addison-Wesley, 1992; S.B. Parry, "How to Validate an Assessment Tool," *Training*, April 1993, pp. 37–42.

30. Gail J. Gunderson, Bill R. Haynes, "Assessment Technology: Its Use in Improving Leadership and Management Performance," *Journal of Extension*, Vol. 38, No. 6, December 2000.

31. J.F. Hazucha, S.A. Gentile, and R.J. Schneider, "The Impact of 360-Degree Feedback on Management Skills Development," *Human Resource Management Review*, Vol. 3, No. 2, 1993, pp. 32–45.

32. R.J. Klimoski and R.G. Jones, "Staffing for Effective Group Decision Making: Key Issues in Matching People and Teams," in Klimoski and Jones, eds., *Team Effectiveness and Decision Making in Organizations*, San Francisco: Jossey-Bass, 1995.

33. Mehrdad Derayeh and Stephane Brutus, "Learning from Others' 360-Degree Experiences," *Canadian HR Reporter*, February 10, 2003, pp. 18, 23.

34. Bob Nelson and Peter Economy, "Can Software Improve Performance Appraisals?" *HR Reporter*, June 16, 1997, pp. 21–22.

35. Ian Turnbull, "Enterprise-wide Software Gaining Popularity," *Canadian HR Reporter*, June 16, 1997, pp. 10–11. See also special supplement to the *Canadian HR Reporter*, March 10, 2003, "Guide to HR Technology."

36. Michael Hammer and James Champy, *Reengineering the Corporation: A Manifesto for Business Revolution*, New York: HarperCollins, 1993.

37. See Turnbull, op.cit.

38. Ibid.

39. Robert S. Kaplan and David P. Norton, *The Balanced Scorecard: Translating Strategy into Action*, Boston, MA: Harvard Business School Press, 1992; Robert S. Kaplan and David P. Norton, *The Strategy-Focused Organization: How Balanced Scorecard Companies Thrive in the New Business Environment*, Boston, MA: Harvard Business School Press, 2000.

40. Richard H. Hopf et al., "Guide to a Balanced Scorecard: Performance Management Methodology," U.S. Department of Commerce, 1999, Acquisition Community Connection site, https://acc.dau.mil/GetAttachment.aspx?id=46158&pname=file&aid=13701, downloaded September 5, 2006.

41. Comment made by a human resource manager during a guest lecture in one of the first author's classes. He had worked for 15 years with a number of U.S. and Canadian department stores.

42. Schwind, "Performance Appraisal: The State of the Art," op. cit.

Chapter 9

1. Lance A. Berger and Dorothy R. Berger, eds., *Handbook of Wage and Salary Administration*, 4th ed., New York: McGraw-Hill, 2000, p. xiii.

2. Michael Kavanagh, "In Search of Motivation," in T.T. Herbert, *Organizational Behavior: Readings and Cases*, New York: Macmillan, 1976.

3. James F. Reda, *Compensation Committee Handbook*, Mississauga, ON: John Wiley and Sons Canada, Ltd., December 2001. See also Rabindra Kanungo and Manuel Mendonca, *Compensation—Effective Reward Management*, Mississauga, ON: John Wiley and Sons Canada, Ltd., 1997, pp. 264–65.

4. Kanungo and Mendonca, op. cit., p. 257.

5. The least squares method is explained in any introductory statistics book.

6. "Odd Perks Becoming the Norm," *The Globe and Mail*, June 22, 2000, p. B13. See also Barbara Moses, "Employers: Dangle the Right Carrots to Entice Workers," *The Globe and Mail*, February 17, 2006, p. C1.

7. Human Resources and Social Development Canada, "Minimum Wage Data Base," www110.hrdc-drhc.gc.ca/psait_spila/lmnec_eslc/eslc/salaire_minwage/index.cfm/doc/english, downloaded September 5, 2006.

8. Human Resources and Social Development Canada, "Contracting with the Government of Canada: Construction—Labour Conditions," www.sdc.gc.ca/en/gateways/topics/cgp-rsr.shtml, downloaded September 5, 2006.

9. Marc Law, "The Economics of Minimum Wage Laws," Vancouver: The Fraser Institute, February 9, 1999. See also Jason Clemens, "Hike in the Minimum Wage Hurts the Poor," news release, Vancouver: The Fraser Institute, August 29, 2000, www.fraserinstitute.ca/shared/readmore.asp?sNav=nr&id=309, downloaded September 5, 2006.

10. Clemens, op. cit. See also Michael Goldberg and David Green, "Raising the Floor: The Economic and Social Benefits of Minimum Wages in Canada," Canadian Centre for Policy Alternatives, September 2, 1999, www.policyalternatives.ca/index.cfm?act=news&call=244&do=article&pA=BB736455, downloaded September 5, 2006; Errol Black and Jim Silver, "Manitoba's Minimum Wage? Be Realistic!" *Fastfacts*, August 5, 2005, www.policyalternatives.ca/documents/Manitoba_Pubs/2005/FastFacts_Aug4_05.pdf, downloaded September 5, 2006; Sylvia LeRoy, "Minimum Wage Hike May Have Perverse Result: Poverty and Low Income Are Not the Same," *Calgary Herald*, October 11, 2005, www.fraserinstitute.ca/shared/readmore1.asp?sNav=ed&id=382, downloaded September 5, 2006.

11. Statistics Canada, "Survey of Labour and Income Dynamics: The Wage Gap Between Men and Women," *The Daily*, December 20, 1999, www.statcan.ca/Daily/English/991220/d991220a.htm; Marie Drolet, "The Male–Female Wage Gap," *Highlights*, Vol. 2, No. 12, December 2001, www.statcan.ca/english/studies/75-001/01201/hi-fs_200112_01_a.html; Luiza Chwialkowska, "StatsCan Study Casts Doubt on Male–Female Wage Gap," *National Post*, December 21, 1999, www.tom.quack.net/wagegap.html. All downloaded September 5, 2006.

12. "The Male–Female Wage Gap ... Again," *CANSTATS Bulletins*, www.canstats.org/readdetail.asp?id=359, July 20, 2002, downloaded September 5, 2006. See also "Fact & Fallacy: AFL-CIO Study's Estimates of Losses from 'Unequal Pay' Are Meaningless," *Employment Policy Foundation*, newsletter, June 1999.

13. C.C. Hoffmann and K.P. Hoffmann, "Does Comparable Worth Obscure the Real Issues?" *Personnel Journal*, Vol. 66, No. 1, January 1987, pp. 82–95.

14. "Equal Pay for Male and Female Employees Who Are Performing Work of Equal Value,"

interpretation guide for Section 11 of the *Canadian Human Rights Act*, Ottawa: Canadian Human Rights Commission, undated.

15. Ibid.

16. Lester Thurow, "Productivity Pay," *Newsweek*, May 3, 1982, p. 69.

17. David Brown, "Pay for Performance Better for Executives, Companies," *Canadian HR Reporter*, March 25, 2002. See also Ray Murrill, "Stock Options Still the Preferred Incentive," *Canadian HR Reporter*, June 21, 2005.

18. Edward E. Lawler, *Rewarding Excellence: Pay Strategies for the New Economy*, San Francisco: Jossey-Bass, December 1999.

19. Steve Ginsberg, "Team Pay Rewards the Players Behind the Superstars," *San Francisco Business Times*, August 15, 1997.

20. David E. Tyson, *Profit Sharing in Canada*, Toronto: John Wiley and Sons, 1996. See also H.F. Schwind, S. Pendse, and A. Mukhopadhyay, "Characteristics of Profit Sharing Plans in Canada," *Journal of Small Business and Entrepreneurship*, Spring 1987, pp. 32–37; Richard J. Long, "Consequences and Moderators of Employee Profit Sharing: An Empirical Study," *Proceedings of the Administrative Science Association (Human Resource Division)*, May 30–June 2, 1998, pp. 10–22.

21. Douglas L. Kruse, *Profit Sharing: Does It Make a Difference?* Washington, DC: W.E. Upjohn Institute for Employment Research, 1996, http://ss519.logika.net/cgi-bin/ss_query?keys=Kruse&ct=10&sitenbr=33596283, downloaded September 5, 2006. See also Hermann F. Schwind, "Do Profit Sharing Plans Motivate Employees?" in *Profit sharing in Canada* (Toronto: Tyson & Associates Ltd.), Vol. 1, No. 1, Autumn 1996, pp. 6–7; Richard J. Long, "Motives for Profit Sharing: A Study of Canadian Chief Executive Officers," *Proceedings of the Annual Meeting of the Administrative Science Association HR Division*, Vol. 17, No. 9, 1996, pp. 12–22.

22. Schwind, "Do Profit Sharing Plans Motivate Employees?" op. cit. See also Michel Magnan and Sylvie St-Onge, "The Impact of Profit-Sharing on the Performance of Financial Services Firms," accepted for publication in *Journal of Management Studies*; Michel Magnan, Sylvie St-Onge, and Denis Cormier, "The Adoption and Success of Profit-Sharing Plans in Strategic Business Units: Opportunism or Contingency?" *International Journal of Productivity and Performance Management*, Vol. 54, No. 5/6, 2005, pp. 355–69.

23. Frank A. Amato, "Employee Stock Ownership: Gaining a Foothold Worldwide," *American Compensation Association Journal*, Vol. 43, No. 2, February 2000, pp. 34–36. See also Margot Gibb-Clark, "Share Plans Can Benefit More than Employees," *The Globe and Mail*, February 14, 2000, p. B6.

24. Sharon Lebrun, "ESOP Saves the Day," *Canadian HR Reporter*, November 1997, pp. 1–2.

25. ESOP Builders Inc., "An Information Circular on a Workplace Option for the New Economy—Employee Share Ownership Plans," 2001, www.esopbuilders.com/media.html, downloaded September 5, 2006.

26. The National Center for Employee Ownership, "Employee Ownership and Corporate Performance," *Research Report*, April 2006, www.nceo.org/library/corpperf.html, downloaded September 5, 2006. See also Sylvie St-Onge, Michel Magnan, Sophie Raymond, and Linda Thorne, "The Effectiveness of Stock Option Plans: A Field Investigation of Senior Executives,"

Journal of Management Inquiry, Vol. 10, No. 3, 2001, pp. 250–66; Stephane Renaud, Sylvie St-Onge, and Michel Magnan, "The Impact of Stock Purchase Plan Participation on Workers' Individual Cash Compensation," *Industrial Relations (Berkeley)*, Vol. 43, No. 1, 2004, pp. 120–47.

27. Janet McFarland, "How to Build a Better Option Plan," *The Globe and Mail*, November 20, 2002, p. B2. See also Gordon Pitts, "Calian Head Keen on Good Governance," *The Globe and Mail*, November 18, 2002, p. B3; Ray Murrill, "Stock Options Still the Preferred Incentive," *Canadian HR Reporter*, June 20, 2005, pp. 12–13.

28. Carl F. Frost, John H. Wakeley, and Robert A. Ruh, *The Scanlon Plan for Organizational Development*, Ann Arbor, MI: University of Michigan Press, 2000. For more information about Scanlon plans, see www.scanlonleader.org.

29. Sherry Ryan, "Rewards and Recognition," Allison Rossett home page, EdWeb, http://edweb. sdsu.edu/people/ARossett/pie/Interventions/ incentivesrewards_2.htm, downloaded April 2006.

30. "Tossing the Coin—Pay Secrecy," The ManageMentor site, www.themanagementor. com/enlightenmentorareas/hr/rr/tossingthecoin. htm, downloaded September 5, 2006. See also David Cameron, "Challenge the Culture of Secrecy About Pay," A2Mediagroup.com, March 13, 2006, http://www.a2mediagroup.com/?c=133&a=3942, downloaded September 5, 2006.

31. Lawler, op. cit.

32. NCR home page, www.ncr.com; November 2002. See also "NCR Canada Recognized for Workplace Health," *The Mississauga News*, September 22, 2002.

33. Bruce Little, "How to Make a Small, Smart Factory," *The Globe and Mail*, February 2, 1993, p. B24. See also "Shell Canada's Brockville Lubricants Plant Is Growing," March 17, 2006, www.brockville. com/newsdetails.cfm?IDln=417, downloaded September 5, 2006.

34. See Lawler, op. cit.

35. Ibid.

36. Ibid.

37. Hewitt Associates, "Effective Compensation Programs Involve More than Base Salary, According to Hewitt Survey," September 24, 2008, Hewitt Associates, www.hewittassociates. com/Intl/NA/en-CA/AboutHewitt/Newsroom/ PressReleaseDetail.aspx?cid=5606, downloaded October 1, 2009.

38. Paul Thompson, "Total Rewards," London, UK: Chartered Institute of Personnel and Development, October 2002, www.cipd.co.uk/ subjects/pay/general/totrewd.htm, downloaded April 2006.

39. Barbara Paus, "Broadbanding Highly Effective, Survey Shows," *ACA News*, July/August 1998, pp. 40–42.

40. Elizabeth Church, "Nortel Workers Pick Tailor-Made Perks," *The Globe and Mail*, December 8, 2000, p. B11.

41. Hideo Inohara, *Human Resource Development in Japanese Companies*, 2nd ed., Tokyo: Asian Productivity Organization, 1998.

42. Nancy Adler, *International Dimensions of Organizational Behavior*, 4th ed., Cincinnati, OH: South-Western College Publishing, 2002.

43. Chris Ashton, "Strategic Compensation: How to Align Performance, Pay and Rewards to Support Corporate Transformation," London, UK: Business Intelligence Ltd., April 2002, http://shopping.sify.com/shopping/book_detail.

php?prodid=14944127&cid=2, downloaded September 5, 2006.

44. Alan S. Binder, *Paying for Productivity: A Look at the Evidence*, Washington, DC: Brookings Institution, 1998.

45. David Hume, *Reward Management: Employee Performance, Motivation and Pay*, Oxford: Blackwell Publishers, November 1995.

46. Ibid.

47. Lawler, op. cit.

48. Ibid.

49. Allan M. Maslow and Gene Swimmer, *Wage Controls in Canada, 1975–78: A Study of Public Decision Making*, Toronto: Institute for Research on Public Policy, 1982.

Chapter 10

1. Bill Megalli, "The Fringe Benefit Debate," *The Labour Gazette*, July 1978, p. 313.

2. William M. Mercer, "2005/2006—Canada—Corporate Boards 2005/2006: Insights into Director Compensation," www.mercerhr.com/ summary.jhtml?idContent=1210475&originUrl=/ home.jhtml, downloaded April 2006.

3. Kaiser Family Foundation, "Survey Shows Private Health Insurance Premiums Rose 11.2% in 2004," www.kff.org/insurance/chcm090904nr.cfm, downloaded September 5, 2006.

4. "36th Annual Canadian Salary Survey," Toronto: Watson Wyatt Consulting, 2005. www.watsonwyatt. com/canada-english/research/anss36/default.asp, downloaded September 5, 2006.

5. Statistics Canada, "Proportion of Labour Force and Paid Workers Covered by a Registered Pension Plan," www.statcan.ca/english/Pgdb/labor26a.htm, downloaded September 5, 2006.

6. Mercer, op. cit.

7. William M. Mercer, "Reducing Costs, Improving Productivity," www.mercerhr.com/summary. jhtml?idContent=1089885.

8. Human Resources and Social Development Canada, "Vacations and Statutory Holidays," April 2006, www.sdc.gc.ca/en/lp/spila/wlb/wfp/18Vacations_ and_Statutory_Holidays.shtml; Canadian Heritage, "Public Holidays and Other Important Dates," www.pch.gc.ca/progs/cpsc-ccsp/jfa-ha/index_e.cfm. All downloaded September 5, 2006.

9. Barb Jaworski, "Employee Assistance: I'll Have My People Call Your People ... ," *Canadian HR Reporter*, March 27, 2006, p. 13. See also Susan Pinker, "SOS? Call your EAP," *The Globe and Mail*, December 11, 2002.

10. Personal communication with Shiela Sheila Hagen-Bloxham, Western Regional Coordinator of CN EAPs.

11. Runzheimer International, Family Assistance Programs for Transferees, "Runzheimer Reports on Relocation," Vol. 23, No. 1, June 2004, www. runzheimer.com/web/publications/RRR/ RRR-2004-06.pdf, downloaded September 6, 2006.

12. Scott Ion, "Are You Ready for Online EAP Services?" *Canadian HR Reporter*, May 3, 1999, pp. 17–19. See also Ceridian Corporation, "First-Ever Study Finds Employees Highly Motivated to Use Online EAP and Work-Life Services," press release, March 7, 2002, www.ceridian.com/corp/printer/ friendly/1,2878,10963-52769,00.html, downloaded September 6, 2006.

13. Jon J. Meyer, "The Future of Flexible Benefit Plans," *Employee Benefits Journal*, June 2000, pp. 3–7. See also Gaelyn Mitchell, "E-Benefits: Taking It Online," *Employee Benefits Journal*,

June 2000, pp. 42–44; "What's in the Future for Employee Benefits?" *Workforce*, May 2000, downloaded September 6, 2006, www.findarticles. com/p/articles/mi_m0FXS/is_5_79/ai_62792459; Manulife of Canada, "Predicting the Future of Your Benefits Plan," http://groupbenefits.manulife.com/ canada/GB_V2.nsf/LookupFiles/EBNQ106Predic tingthefuture/$File/predictingfuture_Q106.htm, downloaded April 2006; Jaworski, loc. cit.

14. Jill Elswick, "Never Enough Fluff," *Employee Benefit News*, May 2000, www.benefitnews.com/ subscriber/00_05/feature2.html, downloaded September 6, 2006. See also her article "Green Without Envy," *Employee Benefit News*, June 15, 2002, www.benefitnews.com/subscriber/Article. cfm?id=37880708, downloaded September 6, 2006.

15. Elswick, loc. cit.

16. "Royal Bank Gives Benefits to Part-Timers," *The Globe and Mail*, September 4, 1996.

17. Oliver Bertin, "Part-Time Work: Boon or Bust?" Workopolis.com, November 6, 2002, http://globeandmail.workopolis.com/servlet/ Content/qprinter/20021106/CANJOBS, downloaded September 6, 2006.

18. William H. Holley, Jr. and Earl Ingram II, "Communicating Fringe Benefits," *Personnel Administrator*, March/April 1973, pp. 21–22. See also "3rd Annual Communications Awards," *Benefits Canada Magazine*, June 2000; Charles Benayon, "Lack of EAP Awareness—What's It Costing You?" *Canadian HR Reporter*, December 14, 1998, pp. 25–27; Jim Browning, "The EAP Conundrum: It Doesn't Pay to Cut Costs in Employee Communication," *Canadian HR Reporter*, May 3, 1999, pp. 18–19; Canada's DC Forum, "Employee Communication Linked to Financial Performance," *Benefits Canada*, March 2006, p. 5.

19. Watson Wyatt Consulting, 34th Annual Canadian Salary Survey.

20. "Flexible Benefit Plans Continue to Gain Momentum in Canada, Says Hewitt Associates," July 6, 2005, http://was4.hewitt.com/ hewitt/ resource/newsroom/pressrel/2005/07-06-05eng. htm, downloaded April 2006.

21. Meyer, op. cit.

22. Ibid.

23. Blue Cross Canada, www.bluecross.ca.

24. Mercer, "2005/2006—Canada—Corporate Boards 2005/2006: Insights into Director Compensation," op. cit.

25. Don Faller, "Sink-or-Swim Benefits Packages Offer Lifeline in Tight Labor Market," *Employee Benefit News*, September 15, 2000, www.benefitnews.com/ subscriber/00_09_15/feature4.html, downloaded September 6, 2006.

26. Craig Gunsauley, "Benefits Are Key to Successful Retention Strategies," *Employee Benefit News*, August 2000, www.benefitnews.com/ subscriber/00_08/quality1.html, downloaded September 6, 2006.

27. Ann O'Neill, "Benefits of Compensation," *Employee Benefit News Canada*, June 2004, www.findarticles. com/p/articles/mi_km2923/is_200406/ai_n14719347, downloaded September 6, 2006.

28. Dorenda McNeil, "Mercer Canada Resource Centre," *Beyond the Bottom Line—What CEOs Are Thinking*, news release, February 26, 1999.

Chapter 11

1. American Management Association, "How to Build a High-Performance Organization," AMA, 1997, p. 1. AMA site, www.amanet.org.

2. Paul Fairlie, "Five Must-Haves of Meaningful Work," *Canadian HR Reporter*, June 15, 2009.

3. "What Drives Employee Commitment (and the Higher Productivity That Follows)," *HRFocus*, April 2000, p. 9.

4. "Internet Use Boosts Productivity, Study Finds," *Times-Colonist* (Victoria), April 10, 2009, p. C12.

5. Stephanie Whittaker, "Employees Feel Like They Make an Important Contribution," *Montreal Gazette*, October 18, 2008, p. G6.

6. "Companies Are Waking Up to the Huge Costs of Harbouring a Jerk in Their Ranks," *Financial Post*, January 15, 2000, p. D6.

7. Mart Teplisky, "Mixed Messages," *Canadian HR Reporter*, April 19, 2004, pp. 12, 13.

8. "10 Tips for Communicating in Tough Times," *Canadian HR Reporter*, November 13, 2008.

9. Laura Cassiani, "Being a Best Employer Means Being Serious About Recognition," *Canadian HR Reporter*, March 12, 2001, pp. 7, 10.

10. "The Truth About Leveraging HR Information Services," *HRFocus*, June 2000, pp. 11–12.

11. Derek Irvine, "Bring Back That Lovin' Feeling," *Canadian HR Reporter*, November 3, 2008.

12. "How E-mail Has Become Integral to the Workplace," *HRFocus*, July 2000, p. 8. More details of the survey can be found at www.vault.com.

13. Janice Tibbetts, "Fired on Facebook, Spa Worker Cries Foul as Controversy Rages," *Edmonton Journal*, January 5, 2009, p. A5.

14. Mark Uhrbach and Bryan von Tol, "Information And Communication Technology Use: Are Small Firms Catching Up?" Statistics Canada, February 2004, Catalogue No. 11-621-MIE2004009, www.statcan.ca/english/research/11-621-MIE/2004009/issue.htm, downloaded September 6, 2006.

15. Showwei Chu, "Intranets Become Intramess," *The Globe and Mail*, March 7, 2002, p. B17.

16. Martha I. Finney, "Harness the Power Within," *HR Magazine*, January 1997, pp. 66–74.

17. Samuel Greengard, "12 Ways to Use an Intranet," *Workforce*, March 1997, p. 94.

18. Janice MacLellan, "Electronic Solutions a Greener Option," *Canadian HR Reporter*, April 20, 2009.

19. Andrew McIlvaine, "Encouraging Repeat Self-Service Use," August 2004, www.workindex.com.

20. Frank Jossi, "High Tech Enables Employees," HR Magazine, Vol. 51, No. 2, February 1, 2006, Society for Human Resource Management Online www.dors.state.md.us/NR/rdonlyres/96523EAE-E2F6-466C-B938-8DF2FE8400BA/0/HRM Magazine.pdf, downloaded September 6, 2006.

21. "How to Protect Your Company from Misuse of Electronic Communications," *HRFocus*, April 2000, p.7.

22. "Fear of Losing Jobs Has Workers Avoiding Facebook, IM and Texting at Work," *National Post*, May 27, 2009, p. FP12.

23. Wallace Immen, "Tweet at Work, Your Boss May Thank You," *The Globe and Mail*, June 3, 2009, p. B14.

24. Annie Massey, "Blogging Phobia Hits Employers," *Canadian HR Reporter*, September 26, 2005, pp. 15, 17.

25. See www.corporateblogging.info.

26. David Brown, "e HR—Victim of Unrealistic Expectations," *Canadian HR Reporter*, March 11, 2002. See also "Three New Surveys Track the Growth of e-HR," *HR Focus*, April 2002, pp. 4–6.

27. Asha Tomlinson, "Call Centres Work to Shed Negative Image," *Canadian HR Reporter*, August 12, 2002, p. 25.

28. Statistics Canada, *Workplace and Employee Survey Compendium*, Ottawa: Statistics Canada, 2002.

29. Graham Lowe, "Want to Reach Staff?: Tell Them a Story," *Canadian HR Reporter*, September 12, 2005, pp. 16, 20.

30. See Claudine Kapel and Maggie Thompson, "Effective Communications Link Employees to Business and Customers," *Canadian HR Reporter*, January 17, 2005, p. 12.

31. Vita Lobo, "Dealing with the Social Media Monster," *Canadian HR Reporter*, June 6, 2009.

32. Eddie Evans, "New Age Makes Serfs of Us All: Numerati Track Our Every Move," *Windsor Star*, September 15, 2008, p. B6.

33. Wayne Brookbank and David Ulrich, *Competencies for the New HR*, Ann Arbor, MI: University of Michigan Business School, 2003.

34. A detailed examination of the use of HR technology is found in "Guide to HR Technology," supplement to *Canadian HR Reporter*, October 22, 2001.

35. Shari Caudron, "Blow the Whistle on Employment Disputes," *Workforce*, May 1997, pp. 50–57.

36. See Peter Feuille and Denise R. Chachere, "Looking Fair or Being Fair: Remedial Voice Procedures in Nonunion Workplaces," *Journal of Management*, Vol. 21, 1995, pp. 27–42; and Rosemary Batt, Alexander Colvin, and Jeffrey Keefe, "Employee Voice, Human Resource Practices and Quit Rates: Evidence from the Telecommunications Industry," *Industrial and Labor Relations Review*, Vol. 55, 2002, pp. 573–94.

37. Terry H. Wagar, "Grievance Procedures in the Non-Union Environment," *Labour Arbitration Yearbook*, 2001, pp. 127–36. See also Alexander J.S. Colvin, "The Relationship Between Employee Involvement and Workplace Dispute Resolution," *Relations Industrielles*, Vol. 59, 2004, pp. 681–702.

38. These are just some of the issues discussed in Feuille and Chachere, op. cit.

39. Survey by Angus Reid Group completed for the Royal Bank. See *Canadian HR Reporter*, November 3, 1997, pp. 1, 3.

40. See "Employee Engagement," *Canadian HR Reporter*, September 12, 2005, pp. 7–8.

41. Scott Ion, "Are You Ready for Online EAP Services?" *Canadian HR Reporter*, May 3, 1999, pp. 17, 19.

42. "Downloading of Child Porn Still a Workplace Problem," *The Globe and Mail*, July 22, 2005, p. C1.

43. Howard A. Levitt, *The Law of Dismissal in Canada*, 3rd ed., Aurora, ON: Canada Law Book, 2009.

44. Paul Falcone, "The Fundamentals of Progressive Discipline," *HR Magazine*, February 1997, pp. 90–94.

45. This material is based largely on the video *Discipline without Punishment (Revised)*, which was released in 1996 by Owen Stewart Performance Resources.

46. "CEOs Talk," *Canadian HR Reporter*, December 6, 2004, p. 10.

47. Levitt, op. cit.

48. *Wallace v. United Grain Growers Ltd.*, Supreme Court of Canada, October 30, 1997.

49. Terry H. Wagar, "Wrongful Dismissal: Perception vs. Reality," *Human Resources Professional*, June 1996, pp. 8, 10.

50. See Stuart Rudner, "Just Cause—Back From the Dead," *Canadian HR Reporter*, September 22, 2008, and Natalie MacDonald, "Progressing Toward Just Cause," *Canadian HR Reporter*, September 22, 2008.

51. David Jackson, "6 Months Severance for 8 Months Work," *Chronicle Herald* (Halifax), March 15, 2006, pp. 1, 2.

52. Howard Levitt, "Promise of Job for Life Proves Costly for Employer," *Times-Colonist* (Victoria), March 18, 2009, p. B7.

53. Jeffrey Smith, "19-Year Employee Fired Over $20 Light Bulb," *Canadian HR Reporter*, April 27, 2009.

54. For more information on just cause see Randall Scott and Matthew L.O. Certosimo, *Just Cause: The Law of Summary Dismissal in Canada*, Aurora, ON: Canada Law Book, 2002; and Levitt, op. cit.

55. Levitt, op. cit.

56. An excellent source of information on reasonable notice awards is John Sproat, *Wrongful Dismissal Handbook*, 2nd ed., Toronto: Carswell, 2002. See also Howard Levitt, "Four Factors Drive Severance Packages," *Telegraph-Journal* (Saint John), March 7, 2009, p. E7.

57. Rudner, op. cit.

58. More detail on these points is provided in Jeffrey Connor, "Disarming Terminated Employees," *HR Magazine*, January 2000, pp. 113–16. See also David Bell, "No Easy Way to Say You're Fired," *Canadian HR Reporter*, June 15, 2009; and Donna Nebenzahl, "Ethics of Dismissal: Boss Must Do It in Person and with Privacy," *The Province* (Vancouver), May 31, 2009, p. A39.

59. Estanislao Oziewicz, "Would Chip Implant Get Under Your Skin?" *The Globe and Mail*, February 14, 2006, p. A14.

60. Jeffrey Smith, "Biometrics Given Cautious Approval in Alberta," *Canadian HR Reporter*, September 29, 2008.

61. See Ian Turnbull, "Technology Hurts and Helps Privacy Management," *Canadian HR Reporter*, May 9, 2005, p.11.

62. "Privacy Commissioner Looking at RFID Technology," *Canadian HR Reporter*, March 11, 2008.

63. Beppi Crosariol, "Firms Get Wrists Slapped Over Privacy Breach," *The Globe and Mail*, July 20, 2005, p. B7.

64. See American Management Association, "2007 Electronic Monitoring and Surveillance Survey," 2008, AMA site, www.amanet.org.

65. Omar El Akkad, "When Using a Corporate Computer, Don't Assume Privacy," *The Globe and Mail*, June 4, 2009, p. L1.

66. See American Management Association, "2007 Electronic Monitoring and Surveillance Survey," op. cit.

67. Uyen Vu, "Employees Resistant to Any Form of Computer Video Monitoring, Study Says," *Canadian HR Reporter*, March 8, 2004, p. 2.

68. Howard Levitt, "Spy without Cause—and Pay Price," *Vancouver Sun*, January 24, 2009, p. H5.

69. "Employers Boost Morale," *Canadian HR Reporter*, February 24, 2009.

70. Brian E. Becker, Mark A. Huselid, Peter S. Pickus, and Michael F. Spratt, "HR as a Source of Shareholder Value: Research and Recommendations," *Human Resource Management*, Spring 1997, pp. 39–47.

71. Sarah Dobson, "Engagement Drives Top Employers," *Canadian HR Reporter*, January 26, 2009.

72. Asha Tomlinson, "Loyalty Isn't Dead But It Does Need Some Critical Care," *Canadian HR Reporter*, November 5, 2001, p. 3. For more information on Fred Reichheld's work on loyalty, see www.loyaltyeffect.com.

73. "CEOs Talk," *Canadian HR Reporter*, October 8, 2001, pp. 15–16.

74. A good review of this perspective is presented in Mike Parker and Jane Slaughter, "Management by Stress," *Technology Review*, October 1988, pp. 37–44. See also D. Mehri, "The Darker Side of Lean: An Insider's Perspective on the Realities of the Toyota Production System," *Academy of Management Perspectives*, Vol. 20, 2006, pp. 21–42.

75. Mark Huselid, "The Impact of Human Resource Management Practices on Turnover, Productivity, and Corporate Financial Performance," *Academy of Management Journal*, June 1995, pp. 635–72. See also Jeffrey Pfeffer, "Producing Sustainable Competitive Advantage Through the Effective Management of People," *Academy of Management Executive*, Vol. 19, 2005, pp. 95–108.

76. Jonathan Michie and Maura Sheehan-Quinn, "Labour Market Flexibility, Human Resource Management and Corporate Performance," *British Journal of Management*, 2001, Vol. 12, pp. 2187–306. See also Jonathan Michie and Maura Sheehan, "Business Strategy, Human Resources, Labour Market Flexibility, and Competitive Advantage," *International Journal of Human Resource Management*, 2005, Vol. 16, pp. 445–64.

77. For an extensive review of the current literature, see Brian Becker and Mark Huselid, "Strategic Human Resources Management: Where Do We Go From Here?" *Journal of Management*, Vol. 32, 2006, pp. 898–925.

78. David Brown, "Profit Driven by Good HR, Study Finds," *Canadian HR Reporter*, November 19, 2001, p. 3.

79. Becker, Huselid, Pickus, and Spratt, op. cit.

80. Jeffrey Pfeffer and John Veiga, "Putting People First for Organizational Success," *Academy of Management Executive*, May 1999, p. 43.

81. Shannon Klie, "Culture Guides Behaviour at Work," *Canadian HR Reporter*, August 11, 2008.

82. David Link, "HR Self Service Applications Grow in Number and Depth," *Canadian HR Reporter*, August 11, 2003, pp. 9, 11.

83. Jeffrey Smith, "Online Pay System Best Practice for Best Buy," *Canadian HR Reporter*, February 19, 2009.

84. Denise Rousseau, "Changing the Deal While Keeping the People," *Academy of Management Executive*, Vol. 10, 1996, pp. 50–59.

85. B. O'Reilly, "The New Deal: What Companies and Employees Owe One Another," *Fortune*, June 13, 1994, p. 44.

86. The sources of these headlines are Greg Quill, "350 to Leave as Axe Falls on CBC," *Toronto Star*, May 28, 2009, p. E1; Doug Alexander and Sean Pasternak, "Canadian Banks Step Up Job Cuts: Almost 4,000 in Last Quarter," *Montreal Gazette*, June 11, 2009, p. B1; and Francois Shalom, "700 Face Layoffs; Revenues Up; St. Laurent Complex to Lose Most Jobs," *Montreal Gazette*, May 15, 2009, p. B1.

87. Nicolas Van Praet, "Meltdown Forces Magna Cutbacks; Suspends Dividend," *National Post*, May 7, 2009, p. FP1.

88. Steve W.J. Kozlowski, Georgia T. Chao, Eleanor M. Smith, and Jennifer Hedlund, "Organizational Downsizing: Strategies, Interventions, and Research Implications," in C.L. Cooper and I.T. Robertson, eds., *International Review of Industrial and Organizational Psychology*, Vol. 8, 1993, pp. 263–332.

89. Kim Cameron, "Strategies for Successful Organizational Downsizing," *Human Resource Management*, Summer 1994, p. 192.

90. Ibid.

91. Wayne Cascio, *Responsible Restructuring: Creative and Responsible Alternatives to Layoffs*, San Francisco: Berrett-Koehler, 2002.

92. Jessica Leeder, "Economic Uncertainty Boils Over in Workplace," *The Globe and Mail*, March 26, 2009, p. B1.

93. See, for instance, Robert D. Nixon, Michael A. Hitt, Ho-Uk Lee, and Eui Jeong, "Market Reactions to Announcements of Corporate Downsizing Actions and Implementation Strategies," *Strategic Management Journal*, Vol. 25, 2004, pp. 1121–29; E. Love and N. Nohria, "Reducing Slack: The Performance Consequences of Downsizing by Large Industrial Firms," *Strategic Management Journal*, Vol. 26, 2005, pp. 1087–108.

94. Andrew Duffy, "Forest Workers Lose Hope as Downturn Deepens; Log Loader No Longer Gives a Damn," *Times-Colonist* (Victoria), March 14, 2009, p. B1.

95. Cameron, op. cit.

96. Kim Cameron, Sarah Freeman, and Anil Mishra, "Best Practices in White Collar Downsizing: Managing Contradictions," *Academy of Management Executive*, Vol. 5, 1991, pp. 57–73.

97. David Brown, "Take My Workers—Please," *Canadian HR Reporter*, February 11, 2002, p. 3.

98. See, for instance, Terry H. Wagar, "What Do We Know About Downsizing?" *Benefits and Pensions Monitor*, June 1996, pp. 19–20, 69.

99. These issues are discussed in more detail in Mark Mone, "Relationships Between Self-Concepts, Aspirations, Emotional Responses, and Intent to Leave a Downsizing Organization," *Human Resource Management*, Summer 1994, pp. 281–98.

100. Barry Wright and Julian Barling, "The Executioners' Song: Listening to Downsizers Reflect on their Experiences," *Canadian Journal of Administrative Sciences*, December 1998, pp. 339–55. See also J. Clair and R. Dufresne, "Playing the Grim Reaper: How Employees Experience Carrying Out a Downsizing," *Human Relations*, Vol. 57, 2004, pp. 1597–625.

101. This is discussed in more detail in Frederick F. Reichheld, *The Loyalty Effect*, Boston: Harvard Business School Press, 1996.

102. Virginia Galt, "Shock: The Number 1 Reason People Leave Their Jobs," *The Globe and Mail*, September 10, 2005, p. B10.

103. Danielle Harder, "Why Employees Leave," *Canadian HR Reporter*, November 19, 2007.

104. For more details, see *Canadian HR Reporter*, September 10, 2001, p. 2.

105. Uyen Vu, "Answering Call Centre Turnover," *Canadian HR Reporter*, August 15, 2005, p. 13.

106. Charlene M. Solomon, "Keep Them! Don't Let Your Best People Get Away," *Workforce*, August 1997, pp. 46–51.

107. See, for example, Rosemary Batt, "Managing Customer Services: Human Resource Practices, Quit Rates, and Sales Growth," *Academy of Management Journal*, Vol. 45, 2002, pp. 587–97; Lisa Hughes, "The Effects of Human Resource Management and Union Member Status on Employees' Intentions to Quit," Queen's University Industrial Relations Centre Research Program, January 2006.

108. Asha Tomlinson, "Top Talent a Flight Risk in Tough Times," *Canadian HR Reporter*, February 25, 2002, pp. 1, 11.

Chapter 12

1. Lee Gardenswartz and Anita Rowe, *Managing Diversity: A Complete Desk Reference and Planning Guide*, Burr Ridge, Illinois: Irwin Professional Publishing Co., 1993, p. 4.

2. Robin Wilson, "To Sir—uh, Madam—With Love," *The Globe and Mail*, February 21, 1998, p. D9.

3. 2006 Census figures reported by Statistics Canada, www12.statcan.ca/census-recensement/2006/as-sa/97-553/p4-english.

4. 2008 Catalyst Census of Women Corporate Officers and Top Earners of the FP500 cited by Shannon Klie, "Women Make Small Gains," *Canadian HR Reporter*, April 6, 2009, p. 1.

5. Mallika Das, "Workforce 2000: Diversity in the Workplace," in *Managing Diversity: Gender and Other Issues*, 3rd. ed., Halifax: Mount Saint Vincent University, 1997, p. 4. See also A.V. Subbarao, "Managing Workforce Diversity in Canada: Problems and Prospects," Working Paper 94-25, Ottawa: University of Ottawa, 1994.

6. Mallika Das, op. cit.

7. J.E. Baird Jr. and P.H. Bradley, "Styles of Management and Communications: A Comparative Study of Men and Women," *Communication Monographs*, Vol. 46, June 1979, pp. 101–110; Susan LeBlanc, "The Feminine Factor: Do Women Do Business Differently than Men?" *The Mail Star*, September 26, 1995, p. C1; S.H Applebaum and B.T. Shapiro, "Why Can't Men Lead Like Women?" *Leadership and Organization Development Journal*, Vol.14, 1993, pp. 28–34; J.B. Rosener, "Ways Women Lead," *Harvard Business Review*, Vol. 68, Nov.–Dec. 1990, pp. 119–25.

8. A. DePalma, "Women Can Be Hindered by Lack of 'Boys' Network." *Boulder Daily Camera*, November 12, 1991, p. B9.

9. Elizabeth Church, "Women Still Shut Out of Many Top Posts," *The Globe and Mail*, February 10, 2000, p. B15.

10. Keith McArthur, "Group Calls for Equal Numbers on Boards," *The Globe and Mail*, January 20, 2000, p. B15.

11. Shannon Klie, "Muslims Face Discrimination in Workplace," *Canadian HR Reporter*, February 27, 2006, pp. 1, 16.

12. Geogrey York, "Space Researcher Quits Over Sexual Harassment," *The Globe and Mail*, March 27, 2000, pp. A1, A8.

13. Bruce G. Trigger, *Natives and Newcomers*, Montreal: McGill University Press, 1985, pp. 3–4.

14. Marilyn Loden, *Implementing Diversity*, Chicago, IL: Irwin, 1996, p. 14.

15. R. Kandola, "Managing Diversity: New Broom or Old Hat?" *International Review of Industrial and Organizational Psychology*, Vol. 10, 1995, pp. 131–67.

16. Anne Marie Francesco and Barry Allen Gold, *International Organizational Behaviour*, New Jersey: Prentice Hall, 1998, p. 225.

17. Mallika Das, op. cit., p. 13.

18. GE's Chairman, Jack Welch, quoted by Thomas Stewart, *Intellectual Capital: The New Wealth of Organizations*, New York: Currency Doubleday, 1997, p. 106

19. Christine Taylor, "Building a Business Case for Diversity," *Canadian Business Review*, Spring, 1995, pp.12–14; see also Christine Taylor, *Building a Business Case for Valuing Ethnocultural Diversity*, Ottawa: The Conference Board of Canada, 1995.

20. Professor Belcourt quoted by Cleta Moyer in "Diversity Management: The Bottom Line Impact of an Equitable Employment System," *Human Resources Professional*, 1995, pp. 21–22.

21. "Making the Differences Work," a progress report on closing the gender gap and leveraging diversity at Royal Bank Financial Group, October, 1996, p. 1.

22. Ibid.

23. Elizabeth Church, "Female Led Sales Teams Have Superior Morale, Performance, Study Finds," *The Globe and Mail*, February 17, 2000, p. B14.

24. The term "paradigm shift" was coined by Thomas Kuhn in his book, *The Structure of Scientific Revolutions*, Chicago: University of Chicago Press, 1962.

25. Lee Gardenswartz and Anita Rowe, *Diverse Teams at Work*, Chicago, IL: Irwin, 1994, p. 17.

26. Taylor Cox, Jr. and Ruby Beale, *Developing Competency to Manage Diversity*, San Francisco, CA: Berrett-Koehler Publishers Inc, 1997, p. 31.

27. Cox and Beale, op. cit., p. 32.

28. Phebe-Jane Poole, *Diversity: A Business Advantage*, Ajax, ON: Poole Publishing Company, 1997, pp. 21–25.

29. Michelle Martinez, "Equality Effort Sharpens Bank's Edge," *HR Magazine*, January 1995, pp. 38–43.

30. Hari Das, *Strategic Organization Design: For Canadian Firms in a Global Economy*, Scarborough, Ontario: Prentice-Hall, 1998, p. 340.

31. Susan Jackson and Associates, *Diversity in the Workplace*, New York: Guildford Press, 1992, pp. 203–26.

32. David Brown, "Ottawa Asks Why Skilled Immigrants Drive Cabs," *Canadian HR Reporter*, January 31, 2005, p. 1.

33. Todd Humber, "Making Immigrants Feel at Home," in Report on Recruitment and Staffing, *Canadian HR Reporter*, December 5, 2005, page R3.

34. "Women Flee Jobs to Start Firms: Study," *The Globe and Mail*, February 26, 1998, p. B17.

35. "Making the Differences Work," op. cit., p. 4.

36. Sarah Dobson, "Employers Rewarded for Diversity," *Canadian HR Reporter*, March 9, 2009, p. 6.

37. "Making the Differences Work," op. cit., p. 6.

38. "Managing Diversity: A Guide to Effective Staff Management," *The McDonald Series,* Winnipeg: Cross Cultural Communications International Inc., undated, p. 24.

39. Lee Gardenswartz and Anita Rowe, *Managing Diversity*, New York: Irwin Professional Publishing, 1993, p. 37.

40. Christine Taylor, *Building a Business Case for Valuing Ethnocultural Diversity*, Ottawa: The Conference Board of Canada, 1995.

41. Dobson, op. cit., p. 3.

42. Catalyst study quoted by Shannon Klie, "Firms Short on Diversity Practices: Report," *Canadian HR Reporter*, March 23, 2009; see also *Career Advancements in Corporate Canada: A Focus on Visible Minorities*, a report from Catalyst, New York, 2008.

43. C. Moyer, "Diversity Management: The Bottom-Line Impact of an Equitable Employment System," *Human Resources Professional*, November 1995, pp. 21–22.

44. D. Davies, "Equity Equations: Scrapping Equity Programs When Profits Are Down Does Not Add Up," *Human Resources Professional*, April 1993, p. 15.

45. Personal communication by the first author with a U.S. Caterpillar-Mitsubishi executive in the CM joint venture plant in Sagamihara, Japan, 1991.

46. Davies, op. cit.

47. Gillian Flynn, "Deloitte & Touche Changes Women's Minds. Cultural Audit Boosts Retention," *Personnel Journal*, April 1996, pp. 56–68.

48. For example, see Susan Vinnicombe and Nina Colwill, *The Essence of Women in Management*, London: Prentice-Hall, 1995.

49. Flynn, op. cit.

50. Davies, op. cit., p. 17.

51. See, Helen Harkness, *Don't Stop the Career Clock*, Palo Alto, CA: Davies Black Publishing, 1999.

52. Marge Watters, "Career Development for Employees Heading into Their 'Second Middle Age,'" *Canadian HR Reporter*, February 13, 2006, p. 13.

53. Humber, op. cit.

54. Taylor, 1995, op. cit.

55. From unpublished manuscript by Hari Das, Department of Management, Saint Mary's University, H. Das © 2002. Reprinted by permission of the author.

56. Shawn Cooper, Managing director of Russell Reynold Associates, Toronto, quoted by Todd Humber in "Is Your Exec Hire Working Overseas?" in Report on Recruitment and Staffing, *Canadian HR Reporter*, May 23, 2005, page R11.

57. Susannah Kelly of Boyden Global Executive Search quoted by Todd Humber in "Is Your Exec Hire Working Overseas?" in Report on Recruitment and Staffing, *Canadian HR Reporter*, May 23, 2005, page R11.

58. Paul Brocklyn, "Developing the International Executive," *Personnel*, March 1989, p. 44.

59. For example, see Gary Hogan and Jane Goodson, "The Key to Expatriate Success," *Training and Development Journal*, January 1990, Vol. 44, No.1, pp. 50–52; Raymond Stone, "Expatriate Selection and Failure," *Human Resource Planning*, Vol.14, No.1, 1991, pp. 9–18; Allan Bird and Roger Dunbar, "Getting the Job Done Over There: Improving Expatriate Productivity," *National Productivity Review*, Spring 1991, Vol.10, No. 2, pp.145–56.

60. Stone, op. cit.; Rosalie Tung, "Selection and Training of Personnel for Overseas Assignments," *Columbia Journal of World Business*, Vol.16, No.1, Spring 1981, pp. 68–78.

61. C.G. Howard, "Profile of the 21st-Century Expatriate Manager," *HR Magazine*, June 1992, pp. 93–100.

62. Nancy Adler, "Women Managers in a Global Economy," *HR Magazine*, 1993, Vol. 38, No. 9, September, pp. 52–55; Hilary Harris, "Women in International Management: Opportunity or Threat?" *Women in Management Review*, Vol. 8, No. 5, 1993, pp. 9–14.

63. George Avraam, Adrian Ishak, and Trish Appleyard, "Terminating Employees Around the World," *Canadian HR Reporter*, April 6, 2009, p. 12.

64. Peter Blunt, "Recent Developments in Human Resource Management: The Good, the Bad and the Ugly," *International Journal of Human Resource Management*, June 1990, pp. 45–59; Sheila Rothwell, "Leadership Development and International HRM," *Manager Update*, No. 4, Summer 1993, pp. 20–32.

65. Linda Grobovksy, "Relocating Employees in a Global Workforce," *Canadian HR Reporter*, November 16, 1998, pp.16–17.

66. See Brocklyn, op. cit., p.46; see also Nancy Napier and Richard Peterson, "Expatriate Re-entry: What do Repatriates Have to Say?" *Human Resource Planning*, March 1991, pp. 19–28.

67. Edward Dunbar and Allan Katcher, "Preparing Managers for Foreign Assignments," *Training and Development Journal*, Vol. 44, No. 9, September 1990, pp. 45–47; Paul Sullivan, "Training's Role in Global Business," *Executive Excellence*, No. 9, September 1991, pp. 9–10.

68. B.T. King and I.L. Janis, "Comparison of the Effectiveness of Improvised versus Non-Improvised Role-Playing in Producing Opinion Change," *Human Relations,* May 1956, pp. 177–86; see also W.A. Scott, "Attitude Change Through Reward of Verbal Behaviour," *Journal of Abnormal and Social Psychology*, Vol. 55, July 1957, pp. 72–75.

69. R.G. Shirts, *Ba Fa' Ba Fa', A Cross-Cultural Simulation*, Del Mar, CA: Sirrile, 1977.

70. H.F. Schwind, "The State of the Art in Cross-Cultural Management Training," *International HRD Annual*, Vol. 1 (R. Doktor, ed., American Society for Training and Development, Washington, DC, 1985).

71. Stephen Rhinesmith, "Global Mindsets for Global Managers," *Training and Development*, October 1992, pp. 63–68.

72. R.S. Schuler, J.R. Fulkerson and P.J. Bowling, "Strategic Performance Measurement and Management in Multinational Corporations," *Human Resource Management*, Vol. 30, No. 3, Fall 1991, pp. 365–92.

73. See Brocklyn, op. cit.; see also Werther and Davis, op. cit., p. 79.

74. Stewart Black and Hal Gregersen, "Serving Two Masters: Managing the Dual Allegiance of Expatriate Employees," *Sloan Management Review*, Vol. 33, No. 4, Summer 1992, pp. 61–71.

75. Ellen Brandt, "Global HR," *Personnel Journal*, March 1991, p. 41.

76. L. Gomez-Mejia and T. Welbourne, "Compensation Strategies in a Global Context," *Human Resources Planning*, Vol. 14, No. 1, 1991, pp. 29–41; Richard Hodgetts and Fred Luthans, "U.S. Multinationals' Compensation Strategies for Local Management: Cross Cultural Implications," *Compensation and Benefits Review*, March–April 1993, Vol. 25, No. 2, pp. 42–48.

77. Douglas Carey and Paul Hows, "Developing a Global Pay Program," *Journal of International Compensation and Benefits*, July–August 1992, pp. 26–33; Mariah De Forest, "Thinking of a Plant in Mexico?" *Academy of Management Executive*, February 1994, pp. 33–40.

78. Wayne Cascio and Manuel Serapio, Jr., "Human Resource Systems in an International Alliance: The Undoing of a Done Deal?" *Organizational Dynamics*, Winter 1991, pp. 63–74.

Chapter 13

1. Julian Barling and Michael Frone, eds., *The Psychology of Workplace Safety*, Washington: APA, 2004, p. 4.

2. F.E. Bird, Jr., *Management Guide to Loss Control*, Atlanta, GA: Institute Press, 1974.

3. Ibid.

4. E. Kevin Kelloway, Lori Francis, and James Montgomery, *Management of Occupational Health and Safety*, 3rd ed., Toronto: Nelson, 2006.

5. Canadian HR Reporter's 2001 Strategic HR Survey.

6. "Charges Laid in Workplace Accident," *Calgary Herald*, November 13, 2008, p. B5.

7. "Worker, 19, Dies in Accident at Kanata Construction Site," *Ottawa Citizen*, March 19, 2009, p. C2.

8. Human Resources and Social Development Canada, *Occupational Injuries and Diseases in Canada: 1996–2005*, Ottawa, ON: Government of Canada, 2007.

9. Renata D'Aliesio, "Farm Safety Training Lacking, Say Producers; Workers Need Coverage, Says Widow," *Calgary Herald,* March 10, 2009, p. A4.

10. "Record Manitoba Workplace Safety Fine," *Canadian HR Reporter,* August 15, 2001.

11. Joyce Grant, "Inquest Reports on Kids At Work Tragedy," *Canadian HR Reporter,* June 18, 2001, p. 13.

12. Human Resources and Development Canada, *Work Safely for a Healthy Future.*

13. See Association of Workers' Compensation Boards of Canada site, www.awcbc.org.

14. Paul Luke, "Safety Yields Bigger Returns," *The Province* (Vancouver), March 15, 2009, p. A28.

15. This information is taken from Dilys Robertson, "The Scope of Occupational Health and Safety in Canada," *HRM in Canada,* Scarborough, ON: Carswell, 1996.

16. Also see James Montgomery and Kevin Kelloway, *Management of Occupational Health and Safety,* Toronto: Nelson Canada, 2000.

17. Francine Kopun, "Neither Rain Nor Sleet ... Maybe Snow: Treacherous Footing Blamed for Surge in Injuries Among Mail Carriers in Winter," *Toronto Star,* March 11, 2009, p. A3.

18. See Jim Middlemiss, "Don't Panic, Prepare; Employers Have Obligation to Protect Workers," *National Post,* May 19, 2009, p. FP7; and Sarah Dobson, "Employers Prepare for Worst," *Canadian HR Reporter,* May 18, 2009.

19. "Students Pick Up Cameras to Tackle Workplace Health and Safety," *Calgary Herald,* May 3, 2009, p. N3.

20. Jamie Hall, "Keeping Teenagers on the Job; Provincial Ad Campaign Emphasizes Workplace Safety," *Edmonton Journal,* November 1, 2008, p. A1.

21. Part II of the *Canada Labour Code* was recently amended. For more information, see Human Resources and Social Development Canada, "An Overview to Part II of the *Canada Labour Code,*" which is available at the HRSDC Web site, www.hrsdc.gc.ca/asp/gateway.asp?hr=/en/lp/lo/ohs/publications/overview.shtml&hs=oxs, downloaded September 6, 2006.

22. Kelloway, Francis, and Montgomery, op. cit.

23. Commerce Clearing House, *Canadian Master Labour Guide,* North York, ON: CCH, 2002.

24. The Health Canada Web site is particularly informative. See www.hc-sc.gc.ca/ewh-semt/occup-travail/whmis-simdut/application/msds-fiches_signaletiques_e.html, downloaded September 6, 2006.

25. "Anthrax Scare Prompts Work Refusal," *Canadian HR Reporter,* December 3, 2001.

26. More information on the Canadian Centre for Occupational Health and Safety is available from the Centre's Web site, www.ccohs.ca, and from their annual reports.

27. The Web sites for the various provincial governments are very informative.

28. For a full copy of the *Canada Labour Code,* see http://laws.justice.gc.ca.

29. Marke Andrews, "Safety Agency Fines EnCana $150,000 Over Death; Penalty the Highest Assessed by WorkSafeBC," *Vancouver Sun,* February 6, 2009, p. D3.

30. Sherri Borden Colley, "HRM Must Pay Badly Burned Worker," *Chronicle Herald* (Halifax), June 21, 2005, p. B1.

31. See, for example, Ontario's Young Worker Awareness Program. More information about the program is available at www.yworker.com. In addition, the CANOSH Web site has links for all of the jurisdictions in Canada at www.canoshweb.org/en/young_workers.html.

32. Gabrielle Giroday, "Face Shields for Bus Drivers Sought," *Winnipeg Free Press,* May 6, 2009, p. B1.

33. Bill Pomfret, "Sound Employee Orientation Program Boosts Productivity and Safety," *Canadian HR Reporter,* January 25, 1999, pp. 17, 19.

34. See Institute for Work and Health site, www.iwh.on.ca.

35. See "Petro-Canada Fined After Worker Burned," *Times-Colonist* (Victoria), December 11, 2008, p. A7; Daryl Slade, "Shaw Fined $75K After Employee Burned," *Calgary Herald,* March 21, 2009, p. B2; "Truck Repair Firm Fined $120K After Worker Killed on Job," *Ottawa Citizen,* May 13, 2009, p. D4.

36. Lesley Young, "Are You Sure You've Got Health and Safety Covered?" *Canadian HR Reporter,* May 17, 1999, pp.18–19.

37. Mark MacKinnon, "Canadians Want Executives to Pay for Fatal Mistakes in Workplace," *The Globe and Mail,* June 6, 2000, p. A2.

38. "First Bill C-45 Conviction and Fine," *Daily Commercial News,* April 30, 2008.

39. "British Firm First to Be Charged with Corporate Manslaughter," *Canadian HR Reporter,* April 23, 2009.

40. Ian Fairclough, "Firm Fined for Death," *Chronicle Herald* (Halifax), April 13, 2005, p. B5.

41. Uyen Vu, "Right to Refuse Dangerous Work Expands," *Canadian HR Reporter,* August 9, 2004, pp. 1, 2.

42. Todd Humber, "Target: Zero Fatalities," *Canadian HR Reporter,* October 20, 2008.

43. Ipsos-Reid 2003 Survey reported in *Canadian HR Reporter,* April 19, 2004, p. 17.

44. Tim Cook, "Miners' Safety Training Paid Off," *Chronicle Herald* (Halifax), January 31, 2006, p. A3.

45. "Walmart to Pay $2 Million After Employee Trampled to Death," *Canadian HR Reporter,* May 14, 2009.

46. Daniel Black, "Due Diligence: Your Company's Best Defence Against an Occupational Health and Safety Offence," *Canadian HR Reporter,* May 31, 1999, pp. 17, 19.

47. Joyce Grant and David Brown, "The Inspector Commeth," *Canadian HR Reporter,* January 31, 2005, pp. 13, 17.

48. "Occupational Health and Safety: Policy and Program Guide," Workers' Compensation Board of Nova Scotia, www.wcb.ns.ca/prevention_news/ohspolicy.pdf, downloaded September 6, 2006.

49. Rob Stewart, "The Challenge of Creating a Culture of Safety," *Canadian HR Reporter,* March 28, 2005, p. 11.

50. Andrew Neal and Mark Griffin, "Safety Climate and Safety at Work," in Julian Barling and Michael Frone, eds., *The Psychology of Workplace Safety,* Washington: APA, 2004, pp. 15–34.

51. Will Chabun, "Safety a State of Mind," *Leader Post* (Regina), May 11, 2009, p. D1.

52. Scott Simpson, "Report Attacks CN's Approach to Safety," *Vancouver Sun,* May 31, 2008, p. A3.

53. For an interesting review of the safety–job insecurity issue, see T. Probst, "Job Insecurity: Exploring a New Threat to Employee Safety," in Julian Barling and Michael Frone, eds., *The Psychology of Workplace Safety,* Washington: APA, 2004, pp. 63–80.

54. Canadian Centre for Occupational Health and Safety, "Workplace Stress," April 28, 2000, www.ccohs.ca/oshanswers/psychosocial/stress.html, downloaded September 6, 2006.

55. Carla Wilson, "Mental-health Issues Cost Economy $30 Billion per Year," *Times-Colonist* (Victoria), May 2, 2008, p. B1.

56. See Health Canada, "Assessing the Costs of Workplace Health," Research Report, 2006.

57. Uyen Vu, "CEOs Rank Health Issues as Major Concern: Survey," *Canadian HR Reporter,* July 18, 2005, pp. 1, 3.

58. "How Stress Is Shown," *Chair in Occupational Health and Safety Management,* Université Laval, 2005, p. 5.

59. International Labour Organization, *Encyclopaedia of Occupational Health and Safety,* 4th ed., Waldorf, MA: ILO. This volume can be accessed at www.ilo.org/encyclopaedia/.

60. National Institute for Occupational Safety and Health, *Stress at Work,* Washington, DC: U.S. Department of Health and Human Services, 1999. This publication can be accessed at www.cdc.gov/niosh/stresswk.html.

61. Sarah Boesveld, "Exhaustion, Longer Hours, Heavier Workload, Greater Responsibility, Unbearable Stress Juggling," *The Globe and Mail,* March 2, 2009, p. L1.

62. Statistics Canada, *Work Stress and Health,* 1999.

63. "Bad Bosses May Affect Health of Workers," *The Globe and Mail,* October 28, 2005, p. C2.

64. Doug Burn, "Parents' Job Anxiety Wreaks Havoc on Children," *Canadian HR Reporter,* December 29, 1997, pp. 16, 20.

65. Krista Foss, "The Truth About Sex, Work and Stress," *The Globe and Mail,* May 17, 2000, pp. A1, A6. See also "What Causes the Problem: The Sources of Workplace Stress," *Chair in Occupational Health and Safety Management,* Université Laval, 2005, pp. 1–20.

66. Helen Morris, "Study Finds High Levels of Stress at Call Centres," *Ottawa Citizen,* September 2, 2008, p. D8.

67. Virginia Galt, "Rising Workloads, Stress Seen Taking Toll on Productivity," *The Globe and Mail,* July 29, 2004, p. B6.

68. "Employers Feeling the Pain of Poor Worker Health, But Concern Not Translating Into Action," news release, 2005 Watson Wyatt Staying@Work Survey, September 29, 2005, www.watsonwyatt.com/canada-english/news/press.asp?ID=15216, downloaded September 6, 2006.

69. Natalie C. MacDonald, "Paying for Pain," *Canadian HR Reporter,* April 19, 2004, pp. 17, 20.

70. Kira Vermond, "Backup Child Care a Winner at Work," *The Globe and Mail,* March 29, 2002, p. B21.

71. National Institute for Occupational Health and Safety, op. cit.

72. Ibid.

73. Buffet Taylor, *National Wellness Survey Report 2006,* Ottawa, Health Canada.

74. See "Smoking at Work Makes an Impact," *Canadian HR Reporter,* August 8, 2008; and Shannon Proudfoot and Claire Biddiscombe, "Obesity Linked to Work Absences, Study Indicates," *Leader Post* (Regina), February 21, 2009, p. E7.

75. Creative Wellness Solutions, "Building the Business Case for Workplace Health,"

http://www.wellnesssolutions.ca/index.
php?id=66&spage=234, downloaded October 1,
2009.

76. David Brown, "Wellness Programs Bring
Healthy Bottom Line," *Canadian HR Reporter,*
December 17, 2001, pp. 1, 14.

77. See *Canadian HR Reporter,* April 11, 2005, p. 20. See
also www.worksmartlivesmart.com.

78. Lesley Young, "Healthy Workplace Keeps in
Touch with Employees," *Canadian HR Reporter,*
February 28, 2000, p. 9. Information about the
National Quality Institute's Healthy Workplace
awards and additional resources is available at
www.nqi.ca.

79. Jennifer Newman and Darryl Grigg, "Psychologically
Healthy Workplace Award Winners," see
Psychologically Healthy Workplace Collaborative
site, www.phwc.ca.

80. Uyen Vu, "Unions, Management See Wellness
Through Different Prisms," *Canadian HR
Reporter,* May 9, 2005, pp. 7, 10.

81. Asha Tomlinson, "Re-evaluating Your Workplace:
Is It Safe and Secure," *Canadian HR Reporter,*
February 25, 2002, pp. 3, 12.

82. "Safety Strategies for a Post-Sept. 11 World,"
HRFocus, October 2002, pp. 3–5.

83. "Angry Clients Spit at Irish Bank Workers,"
Calgary Herald, February 20, 2009, p. C1.

84. This material is taken from the U.S.
Environmental Protection Agency, see
www.epa.gov/iaq/pubs/sbs.html.

85. This information is based on an article by Kat
Morgan, "Sick Building Syndrome," *Human
Resources Professional,* February–March 1998,
pp. 39–40.

86. Michelle Conlin, "Is Your Office Killing You?"
Business Week, June 5, 2000, pp. 114–130.

87. See International Labour Organization site,
www.ilo.org.

88. Shannon Klie, "Ontario to Protect Workers from
Violence," *Canadian HR Reporter,* May 18, 2009.

89. Tiffany Crawford, "Male Nurses Take Brunt of
Patient Abuse," *Calgary Herald,* April 16, 2009,
p. A12.

90. Theresa Boyle, "Toronto East General Goes High-
Tech to Fight Violence," *Toronto Star,* February 17,
2009, p. GT1.

91. See www.vault.com and http://crimeprevention.
rutgers.edu/crime/violence/workplace/riskyjobs.
htm (this site has some excellent resource
material pertaining to workplace violence),
downloaded September 6, 2006.

92. Doug Burn, "Preventing Violence in the
Workplace," *Human Resources Professional,*
October–November 1998, pp. 15–20.

93. Dana Flavelle, "Rising Stress Blamed for Workplace
Rage," *Halifax Mail Star,* April 11, 2000, p. C3.

94. Society for Human Resource Management, *1999
Workplace Violence Survey,* Alexandria, VI: SHRM,
1999.

95. American Society of Safety Engineers, *2004
Workplace Violence Survey and White Paper,*
www.asse.org/press394_survey.pdf, downloaded
September 6, 2006. See also Bureau of Labor
Statistics, *Survey of Workplace Violence Preventions,*
2005.

96. COMPAS, "Violence and Aggression in the
Workplace," www.compas.ca/pages/FrameMain.
html, downloaded September 6, 2006.

97. "Two Prescriptions for Preventing Violence,"
HRFocus, April 2000, pp. S2, S3.

98. Shannon Klie, "Screening New Hires Won't End
Workplace Violence, Study Says," *Canadian HR
Reporter,* November 21, 2005, pp. 1, 3.

99. Milo Geyelin, "Firms Often Blamed for Violence at
Work," *The Globe and Mail,* March 18, 2002, p. C2.

100. Paul Viollis and Chris Mathers, "Companies Need
to Re-engineer Their Cultural Thinking About
Workplace Violence," *Canadian HR Reporter,*
March 14, 2005, p. 19.

101. Uyen Vu, "Teen's Death Prompts Calls for Late-
shift Policies," *Canadian HR Reporter,* October 10,
2005, pp. 1, 2.

102. Kelloway, Francis, and Montgomery, op. cit.

103. P. Laing, *Accident Prevention Manual for Business
and Industry: Engineering and Technology,*
Washington, DC: National Safety Council, 1992.

104. See Health Canada and Buffett Taylor Consultants,
Canadian HR Reporter, June 3, 2002, p. 7.

105. Mike Moralis, "Ergowatch Gives Canadian
Software a Lift," *Canadian HR Reporter,* April 22,
2002.

106. See "Repetitive Strain Injuries—The Hidden
Cost of Computing," WebReference.com,
www.webreference.com/rsi.html, downloaded
October 1, 2009.

107. For further information, see http://home.clara.
net/ruegg/info.html.

108. Ergonomic issues are discussed in much more
detail in Kelloway, Francis, and Montgomery, op. cit.

109. Nancy Stuart, "Open Offices Drive Workers up
the Wall," *The Globe and Mail,* October 6, 2000,
p. B11.

110. Bob Fortier, "Ergonomics for Teleworkers Often
Overlooked," *Canadian HR Reporter,* June 6, 2005,
pp. 18, 21.

111. Data on Canada and other countries around
the world are available from the UNAIDS: The
Joint United Nations Programme on HIV/AIDS
at www.unaids.org. Detailed Canadian statistics
are available from the Public Health Agency of
Canada's report "HIV and AIDS in Canada 2005,"
see www.phac-aspc.gc.ca.

112. Information on AIDS can be obtained from the
Canadian AIDS Society's various publications
available at www.cdnaids.ca.

113. J.J. Breckenridge, "Nurse with AIDS Gets
Job Back, But Row Over Dismissal Goes On,"
The Globe and Mail, June 29, 1988, p. A10.

114. *Business Week,* February 1, 1993, p. 53. Also see
"The National Aids Fund Toolkit," SHRM Online,
www.shrm.org/diversity/aidsguide/default.asp,
downloaded September 6, 2006.

115. The Canadian Human Rights Commission has
considerable information about AIDS on its Web
site, www.chrc-ccdp.ca. Similarly, information
is readily available from provincial human rights
commissions. For example, see the Ontario
Human Rights Commission's "Policy on HIV/
Aids-Related Discrimination" at www.ohrc.
on.ca/english/publications/hiv-aids-polcy.shtml,
downloaded September 6, 2006.

Chapter 14

1. Morley Gunderson, Allen Ponak, and Daphne
Gottlieb Taras, *Union–Management Relations in
Canada,* 4th ed., Toronto: Pearson, 2005, p. 10.

2. John Chilibeck, "Clause That Clogs the Wheel,"
Telegraph Journal, December 23, 2008, p. C1.

3. Gregor Murray, "Unions: Membership, Structure
and Actions," in Morley Gunderson and Allen
Ponak, eds., *Union–Management Relations in
Canada,* 3rd ed., Don Mills, ON: Addison-Wesley,
1995.

4. Julian Barling, Clive Fullagar, and Kevin Kelloway,
The Union and Its Members: A Psychological Approach,
New York: Oxford University Press, 1992.

5. Patrick Brethour, "Bitter Strike Divides Alberta
Town," *The Globe and Mail,* October 17, 2005,
pp. 1, 7.

6. Nanos Research, *Labour Watch Survey of Employed
Canadians,* August 2008.

7. Samuel Gompers, *Labor and the Common Welfare,*
Freeport, NY: Books for Libraries Press, 1919, p. 20.

8. An editorial in *Canadian Labour,* June 1968, p. 5.

9. Frank Tannenbaum, *The Labour Movement, Its
Conservative Functions and Consequences,* New York:
Alfred A. Knopf, 1921.

10. Selig Perlman, *A Theory of the Labour Movement,*
New York: Macmillan, 1928.

11. Charles Lipton, *The Trade Union Movement in
Canada, 1827–1959,* Montreal, QC: Canadian Social
Publications, 1967, p. 4.

12. "Union Membership in Canada—January 2008,"
Strategic Policy, Analysis, and Workplace
Information Directorate, Human Resources and
Skills Development Canada.

13. "Unionization," *Perspectives on Labour and Income,*
August 2007, pp. 1–8.

14. See Lorna Harris, "Wal-Mart Workers in Quebec
have Collective Agreement," *Canadian HR Reporter,*
August 19, 2008, and "Union Contract at Wal-Mart,"
Canadian HR Reporter, May 4, 2009.

15. Gordon Sova, "Union Targeting Second-Largest
Food Retailer," *Canadian HR Reporter,* January 15,
2009.

16. "Unionization," *Perspectives on Labour and Income,*
August 2007, pp. 1–8.

17. More information on international union density
trends is available in International Labour
Organization, *World Labour Report: Industrial
Relations, Democracy and Social Stability (1997–98),*
Geneva: ILO, 1997. Also see Jelle Visser, "Union
Membership Statistics in 24 Countries," *Monthly
Labor Review,* January 2006, pp. 38–49.

18. Trevor Wilhelm, "Tension Rising on the Line: City
Strike Turns Ugly," *Windsor Star,* May 22, 2009, p. A1.

19. John Godard, "Strikes as Collective Voice: A
Behavioral Analysis of Strike Activity," *Industrial
and Labor Relations Review,* October 1992,
pp. 161–75.

20. Mohammed Adam and Bruce Deachman, "Transit
Workers Vow to Strike as Long as it Takes," *Ottawa
Citizen,* January 6, 2009, p. A1.

21. Don Herald, "Back to Work Doesn't Mean Back
to Normal," *Canadian HR Reporter,* September 9,
2002, pp. 8, 11.

22. Ibid.

23. Oliver Bertin, "Star Ends Bitter Three-week Carrier
Strike," *The Globe and Mail,* April 16, 2001, p. B3.

24. Wallace Immen, "How to Heal a Bruised
Workplace," *The Globe and Mail,* October 5, 2005,
pp. C1, C2.

25. "Unionization," *Perspectives on Labour and Income,*
August 2007, pp. 1–8.

26. Richard B. Freeman and James L. Medoff, *What Do
Unions Do?* New York: Basic Books, 1984.

27. Morley Gunderson and Douglas Hyatt, "Union
Impact on Compensation, Productivity, and
Management of the Organization," in Morley
Gunderson and Daphne Gottlieb Taras, eds.,
Canadian Labour and Employment Relations, 6th ed.,
Toronto: Pearson, 2009.

28. Asha Tomlinson, "Union Cracks Down on Workers with Bad Habits," *Canadian HR Reporter,* August 12, 2002, pp. 1, 11.

29. Ashleigh Mattern, "Allan Mine Hires Non-Union Workers," *Leader Post,* August 28, 2008, p. D1.

30. Shannon Klie, "Replacement Workers Put Pressure on the Union ... But at What Cost?" *Canadian HR Professional,* October 24, 2005, pp. 11, 12.

31. George W. Adams, *Canadian Labour Law,* 2nd ed., Aurora, ON: Canada Law Book, 2006.

32. Ibid.

33. Lorna Harris, "Youthful Propositions for Unions," *Canadian HR Reporter,* October 20, 2008.

34. For an interesting view of union organizing in the United States, see William E. Fulmer, "Step by Step Through an Organizing Campaign," *Harvard Business Review,* 1991, Vol. 59, pp. 94–102.

35. Lorna Harris, "Technology Providing Organizing Options," *Canadian HR Reporter,* June 25, 2008.

36. Adams, op. cit.

37. "Fish Processor Pays for Union-Busting Closures," *Canadian HR Reporter,* December 5, 2005, p. 2.

38. Wilfred List, "Food Processing Firm Used Employee as Spy, Board Certifies Union," *The Globe and Mail,* July 30, 1981, p. 2.

39. Adams, op. cit.

40. Richard E. Walton, Joel E. Cutcher-Gershenfeld, and Robert B. McKersie, *Strategic Negotiations: A Theory of Change in Labor–Management Relations,* Boston: Harvard Business School Press, 1994.

41. Jon Peirce, *Canadian Industrial Relations* 2nd ed., Scarborough: Prentice Hall, 2003.

42. Ibid.

43. Tanya Talaga, "Contracting Cleaning in Hospitals Decried," *Toronto Star,* October 22, 2008, p. A23.

44. "Developing HR's Business Skills," *Canadian HR Reporter,* September 13, 2004, p. 9.

45. Uyen Vu, "Telus E-Mails Staff, Union Cries Foul," *Canadian HR Reporter,* May 23, 2005, pp. 1, 10.

46. Dan Cameron, "The Interest Based Approach to Union–Management Negotiation," *Human Resources Professional,* February–March 1999, pp. 37–39.

47. Michael J. Fraser, "Labour Skeptical About Win-Win," *Canadian HR Reporter,* September 10, 2001, pp. 11, 12.

48. Claudine Kapel, "The Feeling's Mutual," *Human Resources Professional,* April 1995, pp. 9–13.

49. Thomas A. Kochan and Paul Osterman, *The Mutual Gains Enterprise,* Boston, MA: Harvard Business School Press, 1994.

50. Judy Lendvay-Zwickl, *The Canadian Industrial Relations System: Current Challenges and Future Options,* Ottawa: Conference Board of Canada, 2005.

51. Uyen Vu, "Interest Wanes on Interest-Based?" *Canadian HR Reporter,* February 28, 2005, pp. 6, 9.

52. Each jurisdiction has defined procedures relating to conciliation and mediation. As well, the distinction between these terms has been blurred. Consequently, human resource professionals need to consult the relevant legislation for their jurisdiction.

53. See the Nova Scotia Department of Labour Annual Reports for the 1992 to 2001 period.

54. Lorna Harris, "Picket-Line Dispute Ends in Hammer Attack," *Canadian HR Reporter,* December 5, 2005, p. 5.

55. Jeffrey Smith, "Collective Agreement Gave Transit Company Discretion to Fire Driver After Accident," *Canadian HR Reporter,* December 16, 2008.

56. The judicial review of labour board and arbitration decisions is a very technical area of labour law. For an in-depth treatment, see Richard L. Charney and Thomas E.F. Brady, *Judicial Review in Labour Law,* Aurora, ON: Canada Law Book, 2005.

57. These issues are discussed in more detail in Terry H. Wagar, "The Arbitration Process: Employer and Union Views," in W. Kaplan, J. Sack, and M. Gunderson, eds., *Labour Arbitration Yearbook 1996–1997,* Toronto: Lancaster House, pp. 3–11.

58. Anthony Giles and Akivah Starkman, "The Collective Agreement," in Morley Gunderson, Allen Ponak, and Daphne Gottlieb Taras, *Union–Management Relations in Canada,* 5th ed., Toronto: Pearson Addison Wesley, 2005, p. 306.

59. Ibid.

60. For a comprehensive review of the arbitration process, see Donald J.M Brown and David M. Beatty, *Canadian Labour Arbitration,* 3rd. ed., Aurora, ON: Canada Law Book, 2006.

61. Lorna Harris, "Promotional T-shirt Runs Afoul of Zero Tolerance," *Canadian HR Reporter,* November 8, 2004, p. 5.

62. An excellent summary of the legislative requirements applicable to public sector workers is found in Adams, op. cit.

63. This quote is taken from Human Resources Development Canada and the Organisation for Economic Co-operation and Development, *Changing Workplace Strategies: Achieving Better Outcomes for Enterprises, Workers and Society,* Hull: HRDC, 1997.

64. Virginia Galt, "Benefits Seen in Union-like Workplace," *The Globe and Mail,* February 18, 2002, p. C1.

65. Roy Adams, "Canadian Industrial Relations at the Dawn of the 21st Century—Prospects for Reform," *Workplace Gazette,* Vol. 3, 2000, pp. 109–15.

66. Roy Adams, *Labour Left Out: Canada's Failure to Protect and Promote Collective Bargaining as a Human Right,* Ottawa: Canadian Centre for Policy Alternatives, 2006.

67. See, for instance, William N. Cooke, *Labor–Management Cooperation,* Kalamazoo, MI: W.E. Upjohn Institute, 1990; Kochan and Osterman, op. cit.

68. "Industrial Relations Outlook," Ottawa: Conference Board of Canada, 2002.

69. See, for instance, Terry H. Wagar, "Is Labor–Management Climate Important? Some Canadian Evidence," *Journal of Labor Research,* Winter 1997, pp. 101–12; and Ali Dastmalchian, "Industrial Relations Climate," in Paul Blyton, Nicolas Bacon, Jack Fiorito, and Edmund Heery, eds., *The Sage Handbook of Industrial Relations,* London: Sage, 2008, pp. 548–68.

70. Chris Cobb, "Workers, City Must Mend Morale Together," *Ottawa Citizen,* February 1, 2009, p. A4.

71. Guillermo Grenier and Raymond Hogler, "Labor Law and Managerial Ideology: Employee Participation as a Social Control System," *Work and Occupations,* August 1991, pp. 313–33. For an excellent discussion of management by stress, see Mike Parker and Jane Slaughter, "Management by Stress," *Technology Review,* October 1988, pp. 37–44.

72. David Brown, "Management Holds Upper Hand in Labour Negotiations," *Canadian HR Reporter,* March 8, 2004, pp. 1, 17.

73. For a review of the U.S. approach, see Warner Woodward and Christopher Meek, *Creating Labor–Management Partnerships,* Lebanon, IN: Addison-Wesley, 1995.

74. David Brown, "Union Says Recognition Divides Workers," *Canadian HR Reporter,* March 11, 2002, pp. 1, 13.

Chapter 15

1. Mike Johnson, *Winning the People Wars,* London: Pearson Education Limited, 2000, p. xv.

2. Christopher Bartlett, "Companies Must Gear Up for a Management Revolution," *The Globe and Mail,* January 16, 1998, p. B23.

3. James W. Thacker and R. Julian Cattaneo, *Survey of Personnel Practices in Canadian Organizations,* unpublished manuscript, University of Windsor, Faculty of Business Administration, March 1993.

4. Terry Wagar, *Human Resource Management and Labour Relations: A Study of Canadian Organizations,* Halifax: Department of Management, Saint Mary's University, October 1993, pp. 11–13.

5. Shannon Klie, "Fixes Needed for WSIB Rebate Program: Report," *Canadian HR Reporter,* April 6, 2009, pp. 1, 6.

6. Chisholm, Patricia, "Re-designing Work," *Maclean's,* March 5, 2001, pp. 34–38.

7. George Odiorne, "Evaluating the Personnel Program," in Joseph Famularo, ed., *Handbook of Modern Personnel Administration,* New York: McGraw-Hill, 1972, chapter 8. See also Mahler, "Auditing PAIR," in D. Yoder and H. Heneman, eds., *ASPA Handbook of Personnel and Industrial Relations,* Washington, DC: Bureau of National Affairs, Inc., 1979, pp. 2–103; Vytenis P. Kuraitis, "The Personnel Audit," *Personnel Administrator,* November 1981, pp. 29–34.

8. Peter Howes and Pat Foley, "Strategic Human Resource Management: An Australian Case Study," *Human Resource Planning,* Vol. 16, No. 3, 1993, p. 64.

9. Alan Saks, Neal Schmitt, and Richard Klimoski, *Research, Measurement, and Evaluation of Human Resources,* Scarborough, ON: ITP Nelson, 2000, pp. 38–39.

10. Robert Wolfe, "Most Employers Offer Exit Interviews," *HR News,* June 1991, p. A2.

11. For example, see Russ Kisby, "The ROI of Healthy Workplaces," *Canadian HR Reporter,* October 20, 1997, p. 31.

12. Nora Spinks, "The Absence of Absence in the Changing Workplace," *Canadian HR Reporter,* March 24, 1997, pp. 19–20.

13. For example, see Linda Alker and David McHugh, "Human Resource Maintenance?" *Journal of Managerial Psychology,* Vol. 15, No. 4, 2000, pp. 303–23.

14. *Managing Tomorrow's People: The Future of Work in 2020,* report by PricewaterhouseCoopers, UK, cited by Shannon Klie, "What Will Working World Look Like in 2020?" *Canadian HR Reporter,* September 22, 2008, pp. 1, 8.

15. For a good discussion on HR's emerging role, see Seyed-Mahmoud Aghazadeh, "Human Resource Management: Issues and Challenges in the New Millennium" *Management Research News,* Vol. 22, No. 12, 1999, pp. 19–32.

Glossary

360-degree career development A holistic approach to career development that considers all career development functions.

360-degree performance appraisal Combination of self, peer, supervisor, and subordinate performance evaluation.

alternate work arrangements Nontraditional work arrangements (e.g., flextime, telecommuting) that provide more flexibility to employees, while meeting organizational goals.

alumni associations Associations of alumni of schools, colleges, or other training facilities.

applicant tracking systems Databases of potential candidates that enable a good match between job requirements and applicant characteristics and also enlarge the recruitment pool.

application blank A job application form.

apprenticeships A form of on-the-job training in which young people learn a trade from an experienced person.

arbitration The settling of a dispute between labour and management by a third party. An arbitrator may be selected from a list provided by the appropriate ministry of labour, or the parties may agree to the selection of an arbitrator. The arbitrator's decision is final and cannot be changed or revised, except in such cases as corruption, fraud, or a breach of natural justice.

assessment centre A standardized form of employee appraisal that relies on several types of evaluation and multiple assessors.

assumption of risk The worker accepting all the customary risks associated with his or her occupation. For example, workers may be instructed to protect themselves from special hazards such as heat extremes or molten and sharp metal.

attitude survey Systematic assessment of employees' opinions about various work-related factors, typically using a questionnaire.

attitude tests Tests that seek to learn the attitudes of job applicants and employees about job-related subjects.

attitudes toward government Basic assumptions about the role of government in business and society, including desirability of a welfare state with a key interventionist role for the government.

attitudes toward work Variety of work-related assumptions and values including the role of work in a person's life and the role of women and diverse groups in organizations.

attrition Loss of employees due to their voluntary departures from the firm through resignation, retirement, or death.

audit of employee satisfaction Assessment of employee satisfaction with a variety of work-related matters and the implications for HR practices and systems.

audit of managerial compliance An audit to review how well managers comply with HR policies and procedures and labour laws.

audit report A comprehensive description of HR activities, containing commendation for effective practices and recommendations for improving ineffective practices.

audit team Team responsible for assessing the effectiveness of the human resource function.

authorization cards Cards signed by workers to join a union. Depending on the jurisdiction, a union may be certified either on the basis of card signatures or as a result of an election.

automation The automatically controlled operation of a process, system, or equipment by mechanical or electronic devices.

autonomous work groups Any of a variety of arrangements that allow employees to decide democratically how they will meet their group's work objectives.

autonomy In a job context, independence—having control over one's work and one's response to the work environment.

awareness training Training employees to develop their understanding of the need to manage and value diversity.

balanced scorecard An integrated organizational performance measuring approach, looking at organizational learning and innovation, financial management, internal operations, and customer management.

behavioural description interviews Behavioural description interviews attempt to find out how job applicants responded to specific work situations in the past.

behaviourally anchored rating scales (BARS) Evaluation tools that rate employees along a rating scale by means of specific behaviour examples on the scale.

benchmarking Comparing one's own quality and production standards with those of industry leaders.

benefit audit A system to control the efficiency of a benefit program.

biographical information blank A type of application blank that uses a multiple-choice format to measure a job candidate's education, experiences, opinions, attitudes, and interests.

blind ads Want ads that do not identify the employer.

blog A Weblog—an online journal, diary, or serial published by a person or group of people.

bona fide occupational qualification (BFOQ) A justified business reason for discriminating against a member of a protected class.

broadbanding Consolidation of a large number of pay grades into a few "broad bands."

buddy systems Exist when an experienced employee is asked to show a new employee around the job site, conduct introductions, and answer the newcomer's questions.

burnout A condition of mental, emotional, and sometimes physical exhaustion that results from substantial and prolonged stress.

business unionism Unionism whose mission is to protect workers, increase their pay, improve their working conditions, and help workers in general. Recognizes that a union can survive only if it delivers a needed service to its members in a businesslike manner.

buy-back A method of convincing an employee who is about to resign to stay in the employ of the organization, typically by offering an increased wage or salary.

Canada Labour Code Federal law regulating labour relations under federal jurisdiction.

Canada Pension Plan (CPP) A mandatory, contributory, and portable pension plan applicable to all employees and self-employed persons in Canada, except those working for the federal government.

Canadian Charter of Rights and Freedoms Federal law enacted in 1982, guaranteeing individuals equal rights before the law.

Canadian Human Rights Act A federal law prohibiting discrimination.

Canadian Human Rights Commission (CHRC) Supervises the implementation and adjudication of the *Canadian Human Rights Act.*

Canadian Labour Congress (CLC) An organization, with a membership of more than 3 million, that represents many unions in Canada. It has five main functions: (1) representing Canada at the International Labour Organization, (2) influencing public policy at the federal level, (3) enforcing the code of ethics set out in its constitution, (4) providing services (such as research and education) for its member unions, and (5) resolving jurisdictional disputes among its member unions.

Canadian Occupational Projection System (COPS) Provides up to 10-year projection of Canadian economy and human resource needs.

career plateauing Reaching a temporary flat point on the advancement continuum during one's career.

careless worker model The early approach to safety in the workplace, which assumed that most accidents were due to workers' failure to be careful or to protect themselves. Even if training was provided to make workers more aware of the dangers in the workplace, this approach still assumed accidents to be mainly the worker's fault.

coaching A less formal training experience than an apprenticeship, coaching generally involves a supervisor or manager providing a model for a new employee to observe and emulate.

collaborative strategy An organizational strategy that relies on highly skilled contract labour to supply the needed specialized by hiring them on an "as-needed" basis or retaining them on an "on-call" basis.

collective agreement A labour contract that addresses a variety of issues such as wages and benefits, hours of work, working conditions, grievance procedures, safety standards, probationary periods, and work assignments. Usually negotiated between the local union's bargaining committee and the human resource or industrial relations department.

combination Concurrent use of two or more job analysis techniques (e.g., interviews and observation).

commitment strategy An organizational strategy that attempts to forge a commonality of interest between the organization (often symbolized by the management) and its employees.

communication standards Formal protocols for internal communications within an organization to eliminate gender, racial, age, or other biases in communications.

compa-ratio An index that indicates how an individual's or a group's salary relates to the midpoint of their relevant pay grades.

comparative approach HR audit approach comparing one firm's (or division's) HR practices with another firm (or division) to uncover areas of poor performance.

comparative evaluation methods A collection of different methods that compare one person's performance with that of coworkers.

compensation records A study of wages, benefits, and services can show whether they are fair and competitive.

compensatory approach In a compensatory approach, a higher score on a predictor may compensate a low score on another.

competencies Skill, knowledge, and behaviours that distinguish high performance in a broad role, function, or level of the organization.

competency A knowledge, skill, ability, or characteristic associated with superior job performance.

competency model (competency framework) A list of competencies required in a particular job.

competitive advantage Creating an environment in which people are open to new ideas, responsive to change, and eager to develop new skills and capabilities.

compliance approach Review of past human resource practices to determine if they conform to formally stated policies and legally defensible standards.

compliance strategy An organizational strategy whose focus is on achieving labour efficiencies through control over labour costs, use of temporary or contingent workforce, and maximum control over processes and using it as a key competitive weapon.

computer-assisted interviews Use of computers to electronically profile job candidates and screen new hires.

computer-based training (CBT) The use of computers to facilitate the training process.

computer-interactive performance tests Performance tests using computer simulations that can measure skills, comprehension, spatial visualization, judgment, etc.

computerization A major technological change allowing the processing of vast amounts of data at great speeds, enabling organizations to improve efficiency, responsiveness, and flexibility in operations.

concentration A condition that exists when a department or employer has a greater proportion of members of a protected class than are found in the employer's labour market.

conciliation Use of a government-appointed third party to explore solutions to a labour–management dispute. Less formal than mediation. In most provinces, no strike action is permitted before a conciliation effort has been made. Conciliators are appointed by the federal or provincial minister of labour, at the request of either one or both of the parties involved, or at the discretion of the ministers. A conciliator is requested to submit a report to the minister within a specified time period. If conciliation fails, strikes or lockouts can legally commence.

concurrent validity An empirical approach to validation that measures the predictor and criterion scores concurrently.

construct validity A rational approach to validation that seeks to establish a relationship to a construct, attribute, or quality related to job performance.

constructive dismissal A major change in the terms of the employment contract that results in an employee resigning.

content validity A rational approach to validation that examines the extent to which the selection device includes elements of the job domain.

contingent/contract workers Freelancers (self-employed, temporary, or leased employees) who are not part of the regular workforce and are paid on a project completion basis.

contributory plans Benefits that require the employer to contribute to the cost of the benefit.

core dimensions of diversity Age, ethnicity and culture, gender, race, religion, sexual orientation, and capabilities.

corrective discipline Discipline that follows a rule infraction.

cost–benefit analysis Analysis undertaken to assess the cost-effectiveness of a project or program.

cost leadership strategy Strategy to gain competitive advantage through lower costs of operations and lower prices for products.

costs Expenses related to attracting recruits.

counselling The discussion of a problem with an employee, with the general objective of helping the worker resolve the issue or cope with the situation so that he or she can become more effective.

craft union A type of local union composed of workers who possess the same skills or trades. Craft unions are composed of workers who possess the same skills or trades; these include, for example, all the carpenters who work in the same geographical area.

critical incident method The rater records statements that describe extremely effective or ineffective behaviour related to performance.

cross-training Training employees to perform operations in areas other than their assigned jobs.

cultural challenges Challenges facing a firm's decision makers because of cultural differences among employees or changes in core cultural or social values occurring at larger societal level.

cultural mosaic Canadian ideal of encouraging each ethnic, racial, and social group to maintain own cultural heritage, forming a national mosaic of different cultures.

cultural norms Values and norms that determine behaviours of individuals and groups in different cultures.

culture shock Cultural disorientation causing stress and the inability to respond appropriately.

defined benefits (DB) plan A benefits plan whose benefits are defined by a formula based on age and length of service, with the employer assuming responsibility for funding.

defined contribution (DC) plan A benefits plan based on amounts contributed by the employer and the employee, the final pension depending on amounts contributed, investment income, and economic conditions at retirement.

Delphi technique The soliciting of predictions about specified future events from a panel of experts, using repeated surveys until convergence in opinions occurs.

demographic changes Changes in the demographics of the labour force (e.g., education levels, age levels, participation rates) that occur slowly and are usually known in advance.

differential validity Test validation process aimed at discovering the validity of a test for various subgroups, e.g., females and members of visible minorities.

differentiation strategy Strategy to gain competitive advantage by creating a distinct product or offering a unique service.

direct mail recruiting Recruitment targeted at specified population segments or regions using a variety of means.

discipline Management action to encourage compliance with organization standards.

diversity audits Audits to uncover underlying dimensions, causes, interdependencies, and progress-to-date on diversity management matters.

diversity committee A committee entrusted to oversee diversity efforts, implement processes, and serve as a communication link.

diversity management Recognition of differences among employees belonging to heterogeneous groups and creating a work environment in which members of diverse groups feel comfortable.

diversity training programs Training programs aimed at importing new skills to motivate and manage a diverse workforce.

downsizing Reducing employment to improve efficiency, productivity, and competitiveness.

downward communication Information that begins at some point in the organization and feeds down the organization hierarchy to inform or influence others.

drug tests Tests that include whether a job applicant uses marijuana, cocaine, or other drugs. A growing number of employers have instituted drug testing as part of the selection process. Substance abuse in the workplace costs employers billions of dollars each year.

dual-income couple A couple whose partners both have their own careers.

due process In a disciplinary situation, the following of proper, established rules and procedures, and giving employees the opportunity to respond to allegations.

duty to accommodate Requirement that an employer must accommodate the employee to the point of "undue hardship."

economic challenges Economic factors facing Canadian business today, including global trade challenges and the challenge to increase one's own competitiveness and productivity levels.

educational attainment The highest educational level attained by an individual worker, employee group, or population.

educational institutions High schools, technical schools, community colleges, and universities where applicants for job positions are sought.

efficiency Achieving maximal output with minimal input.

employee assistance programs (EAP) Comprehensive company program that seeks to help employees and their family members overcome personal and work-related problems.

employee attitude/opinion survey A systematic method of determining what employees think of their organization.

employee development The process of enhancing an employee's future value to the organization through careful career planning.

employee handbook A handbook explaining key benefits, policies, and general information about the employer.

employee leasing The practice of outsourcing job functions, such as payroll, to organizations specializing in the field.

employee log Approach to collecting job- and performance-related information by asking the jobholder to summarize tasks, activities, and challenges in a diary format.

employee objectives Goals set by HR department to assist employees to achieve personal goals that will enhance their contribution to the organization.

employee referrals Recommendations by present employees to the recruiter about possible job applications for a position.

Employment Equity Act Federal law to remove employment barriers and to promote equality.

employment equity programs Developed by employers to undo past employment discrimination or to ensure equal employment opportunity in the future. Called *affirmative action programs* in the United States.

Employment Insurance (EI) A program to help alleviate the monetary problems of workers in Canada during the transition from one job to another.

employment interview A face-to-face meeting for evaluating a job applicant.

employment references Evaluations of an employee's past work performance and job-relevant behaviours provided by past employers.

employment tests Devices that assess the probable match between applicants and job requirements.

environmental considerations The influence of the external environment on job design. Includes employee ability, availability, and social expectations.

equal pay for equal work The principle or policy of equal rates of pay for all employees in an establishment performing the same kind and amount of work, regardless of sex, race, or other characteristics of individual workers not related to ability or performance.

equal pay for work of equal value The principle of equal pay for men and women in jobs with comparable content; based on criteria of skill, effort, responsibility, and working conditions; part of the *Canadian Human Rights Act.*

ergonomics The study of relationships between physical attributes of workers and their work environment to reduce physical and mental strain and increase productivity and quality of work life.

error of central tendency An error in rating employees that consists of evaluating employees as neither good nor poor performers even when some employees perform exceptionally well or poorly.

evaluation interviews Performance review sessions that give employees feedback about their past performance or future potential.

exit interviews Interviews with departing employees to gauge their impressions of a firm's strengths and weaknesses, especially relating to HR systems and policies.

expatriates Home-country nationals sent to foreign locations on temporary or extended stay.

external equity Perceived fairness in pay relative to what other employers are paying for the same type of work.

extrapolation Extending past rates of change into the future.

feedback Information that helps evaluate the success or failure of an action or system.

flexible benefit programs Programs that allow employees to select the mix of benefits and services that will answer their individual needs. Also known as *cafeteria benefit programs.*

flexiplace A flexible work arrangement in which employees are allowed or encouraged to work at home or in a satellite office closer to home.

flextime A scheduling innovation that abolishes rigid starting and ending times for each day's work.

focus strategy Strategy to gain a competitive advantage by focusing on needs of a specific segment(s) of the total market.

forced distributions A method of evaluating employees that requires raters to categorize employees.

forecasts Estimates of future resource needs and changes.

functional authority Authority that allows staff experts to make decisions and take actions normally reserved for line managers.

glass ceiling Invisible, but real obstructions to career advancement of women and people of visible minorities, resulting in frustration, career dissatisfaction, and increased turnover.

global mindset The capacity to scan the world with a broad view, to value diversity, and to appreciate change.

grapevine communication Informal communication within an organization that arise from normal social interaction.

graphic response tests Tests that attempt to measure an applicant's honesty by measuring body responses.

grievance procedure A formalized procedure for resolving disputes if the parties have a disagreement regarding the interpretation of a term of the collective agreement. A *grievance* is a complaint by an employee or employer that alleges that some aspect of a collective agreement has been violated. Labour legislation typically requires that a grievance that cannot be resolved between the parties be submitted to an arbitrator or arbitration board whose decision is final and binding.

grievance records An audit of these can detect patterns in employee grievances.

guaranteed annual wage (GAW) A benefits plan by which an employer assures employees that they will receive a minimum annual income regardless of layoffs or a lack of work.

halo effect A bias that occurs when an evaluation allows some information to disproportionately affect the final evaluation.

harassment Occurs when a member of an organization treats an employee in a disparate manner because of that person's sex, race, religion, age, or other protective classification.

Hazardous Products Act An act whose primary objective is the protection of consumers by regulating the sale of dangerous products.

health and safety committee A group consisting of representatives of the employer and employees that meets regularly in order to reduce accident rates.

health insurance Health and medical insurance provided by provincial governments with assistance from the federal government.

high-involvement work practices A set of human resource practices aimed at increasing employee performance.

home-country evaluations Performance appraisals carried out by an expatriate's home office.

host-country evaluations Performance appraisals carried out by an expatriate's local (or host) office.

host-country nationals Local citizens employed by a foreign-owned firm (in the host country).

hot-stove rule The principle that disciplinary action should be like what happens when you touch a hot stove: it is with warning, immediate, consistent, and impersonal.

human resource accounting A process to measure the present cost and value of human resources as well as their future worth to the organization.

human resource audit An examination of the human resource policies, practices, and systems of a firm (or division) to eliminate deficiencies and improve ways to achieve goals.

human resource experiment Comparison of impact of a treatment on experimental and control groups in real-life settings, while controlling for effects of extraneous factors.

human resource information system Gathers, analyzes, summarizes, and reports important data for formulating and implementing strategies by HR specialists and line managers.

human resource plan A firm's overall plan to fill existing and future vacancies, including decisions on whether to fill internally or by recruiting from outside.

Human Resources and Skills Development Canada Federal agency that provides programs and services for employers and present and potential employees.

human rights compliance audits Audits of hiring, placement, and compensation practices, to ensure compliance with human rights legislation.

incentive pay Compensation that is directly tied to an employee's performance and/or productivity.

indexation A method of estimating future employment needs by matching employment growth with some index, such as the ratio of production employees to sales.

inducements Monetary, nonmonetary, or even intangible incentives used by a firm to attract recruits.

industrial union A type of local union that includes the unskilled and semiskilled works at a particular location.

in-house complaint procedures Formal methods through which an employee can register a complaint.

integrity tests Employment tests that measure an applicant's honesty and trustworthiness.

internal equity Perceived equity of a pay system in an organization.

Internet recruiting Job recruitment using the Internet.

interview Approach to collecting job- and performance-related information by a face-to-face meeting with jobholder, typically using a standardized questionnaire.

interviewee errors Interviewee mistakes such as boasting, not listening, or lack of preparation that reduce the validity and usefulness of an interview.

interviewer errors Mistakes like biases and domination that reduce the validity and usefulness of the job interview.

intranet An internal computer network that is generally accessible only to individuals within an organization.

job Group of related activities and duties.

job analysis Systematic study of a job to discover its specifications, skill requirements, and so on, for wage-setting, recruitment, training, or job-simplification purposes.

job analysis schedules Checklists that seek to collect information about jobs in a uniform manner.

job code A code that uses numbers, letters, or both to provide a quick summary of the job and its content.

job description A recognized list of functions, tasks, accountabilities, working conditions, and competencies for a particular occupation or job.

job design Identification of job duties, characteristics, competencies, and sequences taking into consideration technology, workforce, organization character, and environment.

job enlargement Adding more tasks to a job to increase the job cycle and draw on a wider range of employee skills.

job enrichment Adding more responsibilities and autonomy to a job, giving the worker greater powers to plan, do, and evaluate job performance.

job evaluation Systematic process of assessing job content and ranking jobs according to a consistent set of job characteristics and worker traits.

job families Groups of different jobs that are closely related by similar duties, responsibilities, skills, or job elements.

job grading A form of job evaluation that assigns jobs to predetermined job classifications according to their relative worth to the organization.

job identity Key part of a job description, including job title, location, and status.

job performance standards The work performance expected from an employee on a particular job.

job ranking A form of job evaluation in which jobs are ranked subjectively according to their overall worth to the organization.

job rotation Moving employees from one job to another to allow them more variety and to learn new skills.

job sharing A plan whereby available work is spread among all workers in a group to reduce the extent of layoffs when production requirements cause substantial decline in available work.

job specification A written statement that explains what a job demands of jobholders and the human skills and factors required.

just cause Legal grounds for termination such as employee misconduct or incompetence.

key jobs Jobs that are similar and common in the organization and its labour market—for example, accountant, tool-and-die maker.

knowledge management Making use of employees' knowledge.

knowledge tests Tests that measure a person's information or knowledge.

knowledge workers Members of occupations generating, processing, analyzing, or synthesizing ideas and information (such as scientists and management consultants).

laboratory training A form of group training primarily used to enhance interpersonal skills.

labour market analysis The study of a firm's labour market to evaluate the present or future availability of different types of workers.

labour relations boards (**LRBs**) Board set up in the federal and provincial jurisdictions to administer labour relations legislation. They have the power to determine: (1) whether a person is an employee for the purposes of the law; (2) whether an employee is a member of a trade union; (3) whether an organization is an appropriate bargaining agent for bargaining purposes; (4) whether a collective agreement is in force; and (5) whether any given party is bound by it.

learning curve A visual representation of the rate at which one learns given material.

learning organization An organization that has an enhanced capacity to learn, adapt, and change.

learning principles Guidelines to the ways people learn most effectively.

leniency bias A tendency to rate employees higher than their performance justifies.

line authority Authority to make decisions about production, performance, and people.

local union A union that provides the members, the revenue, and the power of the union movement. For most union members and industrial relations practitioners, the most important part of the union structure. Historically, the two major types of local unions were craft and industrial unions.

long-term disability insurance A benefit plan providing the employee with an income in the case of long-term illness or injury.

mailed questionnaires Surveying employees using standardized questionnaires to collect information about jobs, working conditions, and other performance-related information.

management inventories Comprehensive reports of available management capabilities in the organization.

management rights Rights that provide management with the freedom to operate the business subject to any terms in the collective agreement. They often include the right to reassign employees to different jobs, to make hiring decisions, and to decide other matters important to management.

management-by-objectives (**MBO**) **approach** Assessment of HR functions and systems by comparing actual results with stated HR objectives; requires an employee and superior to jointly establish performance goals for the future. Employees are subsequently evaluated on how well they have obtained these objectives.

managing diversity Ability to manage individual employees with different cultural values and lead teams made up of diverse employees.

Markov analysis Forecast of a firm's future human resource supplies, using transitional probability matrices reflecting historical or expected movements of employees across jobs.

mediation Use of a neutral third party to help settle a labour–management dispute. Often a mediator will meet separately with each bargaining team, especially when the negotiations take place in a hostile atmosphere.

medical evaluation Assessment of health and accident information of a job applicant through self-reports or physical exam by company medical personnel.

mentor Someone who offers informed career guidance and support on a regular basis.

mentoring programs Programs encouraging members of disadvantaged groups (e.g., women) to work with a senior manager who acts like a friend and guide in achieving career success.

merit raise A pay increase given to individual workers according to an evaluation of their performance.

mission statement Statement outlining the purpose, long-term objectives, and activities the organization will pursue and the course for the future.

mixed interviews Mixed interviews are a combination of structured and unstructured interviews.

multiple cutoff approach In a multiple cutoff approach, scores are set for each predictor and each applicant evaluated on a pass–fail basis.

National Occupational Classification (**NOC**) An occupational classification created by federal government, using skill level and skill types of jobs.

natural justice Minimum standards of fair decision making imposed on persons or bodies acting in a judicial capacity.

needs assessment A diagnosis that presents problems and future challenges that can be met through training or development.

nominal group technique Structured meeting that identifies and ranks problems or issues affecting a group.

noncomparative evaluation methods Appraisal methods that evaluate an employee's performance according to preset data, and not by comparing one person's performance with that of coworkers.

observation An approach to collecting job- and performance-related information by direct observation of jobholder by a specialist.

old age crisis Refers to the social (health care) and organizational (new workplace ergonomics) challenges caused by aging of population.

old boys' network Set of informal relationships among male managers providing increased career advancement opportunities for men and reinforcing a male culture.

online service delivery EAP services available to employees through the Internet and by intranet.

on-the-job training (**OJT**) A method in which a person learns a job by actually performing it.

open-door policy A company policy that encourages employees to address their problems to higher levels of management.

organization character The product of all the organization's features—people, objectives, technology, size, age, unions, policies, successes, and failures.

organizational culture The core beliefs and assumptions that are widely shared by all organizational members.

organizational objectives An organization's short- and long-term goals that the HR department aims to achieve.

organizational policies Internal policies that affect recruitment, such as "promote-from-within" policies.

orientation programs Programs that familiarize new employees with their roles, the organization, its policies, and other employees.

outplacement Assisting employees to find jobs with other employers.

outsourcing Contracting tasks to outside agencies or persons.

panel interview Interview using several interviewers.

paper-and-pencil integrity tests Measures of honesty that rely on written responses rather than observations.

paradigm shift Fundamental change in a paradigm, e.g., shift from paper filing systems to electronic information storage and retrieval.

part-time workers Persons working fewer than required hours for categorization as full-time workers and who are ineligible for many supplementary benefits offered by employers.

paternalistic human resource strategy An organizational strategy in which some minimal degree of training and competency-building through training, job rotation, etc. is done with the objective of achieving flexibility of staffing and task assignments and maintain workforce stability.

pay equity A policy to eliminate the gap between income of men and women, ensuring salary ranges correspond to value of work performed.

pay secrecy A management policy not to discuss or publish individual salaries.

Pension Benefits Standards Act A federal act regulating pension plans in industries under the jurisdiction of the Government of Canada.

performance appraisal The process by which organizations evaluate employee job performance.

performance management The use of performance data to effect organizational culture, systems, and processes, set goals, allocate resources, affect policies and programs, and share results.

performance measures The ratings used to evaluate employee performance.

performance standards The benchmarks against which performance is measured.

performance tests Test that measure ability of job applicants to perform the job for which they are to be hired.

phased retirement Gradual phase into retirement with loss or reduction of pension benefits.

piecework A type of incentive system that compensates workers for each unit of output.

point system A form of job evaluation that assesses the relative importance of the job's key factors in order to arrive at the relative worth of jobs.

polygraph Machine that attempts to measure a person's honesty by assessing body reactions. Often called a lie detector.

portability clauses Allow accumulated pension rights to be transferred to another employer when an employee changes employers.

position Collection of tasks and responsibilities performed by an individual.

precedent A new standard that arises from the past practices of either the company or the union. Once a precedent results from unequal enforcement of disciplinary rules, the new standard may affect similar cases in the future.

predictive validity An empirical approach to validation that correlates predictor and criterion scores.

preventive discipline Action taken prior to an infraction to encourage employees to follow standards and rules.

proactive A management approach wherein decision makers anticipate problems and likely challenges and take action before a problem occurs.

production bonuses A type of incentive system that provides employees with additional compensation when they surpass stated production goals.

productivity The ratio of a firm's outputs (goods and services) divided by its inputs (people, capital, materials, energy).

productivity records An analysis of records on production, absenteeism, wastage, and labour costs can identify and improve productivity levels.

professional search firms Agencies that, for a fee, recruit specialized personnel by telephone and, at times, recruit from a computer.

profit-sharing plan A system whereby an employer pays compensation or benefits to employees, usually on an annual basis, in addition to their regular wage, on the basis of the profits of the company.

progressive discipline The use of stronger and stronger penalties for repeated offences.

provincial human rights laws All provinces and two territories have their own human rights laws and human rights commissions, with discrimination criteria, regulations, and procedures.

psychological tests Tests that measure a person's personality or temperament.

Public Service Staff Relations Act (PSSRA) Provides federal public servants with the right to either opt for compulsory arbitration or strike.

ranking method A method of evaluating employees that ranks them from best to worst on some trait.

rate range A pay range for each job class.

rating scale A scale that requires the rater to provide a subjective evaluation of an individual's performance.

reactive A management approach wherein decision makers respond to problems rather than anticipate them.

realistic job preview Involves showing the candidate the type of work, equipment, and working conditions involved in the job before the hiring decision is final.

reasonable accommodation Voluntary adjustments to work or workplace that allow employees with special needs to perform their job effectively.

recency effect A rater bias that occurs when the rater allows recent employee performance to sway unduly the overall evaluation of the employee's performance.

record analysis Review of past company records as part of an HR audit.

recruiter habits The propensity of a recruiter to rely on methods, systems, or behaviours that led to past recruitment success.

recruitment The process of finding and attracting capable applicants to apply for employment.

red-circled rate A rate of pay higher than the contractual, or formerly established, rate for the job.

reference letters Written evaluations of a person's job-relevant skills, past experience, and work-relevant attitudes.

regulations Legally enforceable rules developed by governmental agencies to ensure compliance with laws that the agency administers.

reliability A selection device's ability to yield consistent results over repeated measures. Also, internal consistency of a device of measure.

relocation assistance Financial or other assistance to help expatriates move to the new work destination.

relocation program A company-sponsored benefit that assists employees who must move in connection with their job.

replacement charts Visual representations of who will replace whom when a job opening occurs.

replacement summaries Lists of likely replacements for each job and their relative strengths and weaknesses.

résumé A brief listing of an applicant's work experience, education, personal data, and other information relevant for the job.

Retention A company's ability to keep employees.

ringisei A type of decision making by consensus often used by the Japanese; literally, "bottom-up decision making."

role-playing A training technique that requires trainees to assume different identities in order to learn how others feel under different circumstances.

safety and health records An audit of safety and health records can find past or potential violations and suggest ways to eliminate them.

Scanlon Plan An incentive plan developed by Joseph Scanlon that has as its general objective the reduction of labour costs through increased efficiency and the sharing of resultant savings among workers.

secondary dimensions of diversity Education, status, language, and income levels.

selection The identification of candidates from a pool of recruits who best meet job requirements using tools such as application blanks, test, and interviews.

selection process A series of specific steps used by an employer to decide which recruits should be hired.

selection ratio The ratio of the number of applicants hired to the total number of applicants.

self-directed work teams (groups) Teams of workers without a formal, employer-appointed supervisor who decide among themselves most matters traditionally handled by a supervisor.

seniority Length of the worker's employment, which may be used for determining order of promotion, layoffs, vacation, etc.

severance pay Payment to a worker upon permanent separation from a company.

sexual harassment Unsolicited or unwelcome sex- or gender-based conduct that has adverse employment consequences for the complainant.

shared responsibility model A newer approach to safety in the workplace that assumes the best method to reduce accident rates relies on the cooperation of the employer and the employees (who may be represented by a union).

shorter workweek Employee scheduling variations that allow full-time employees to complete a week's work in less than the traditional five days.

short-term disability plan A benefit plan crediting a number of days to be used as sick leave.

situational interviews Situational interviews attempt to assess a job applicant's likely future response to specific situations, which may or may not have been faced by the applicant in the past. In this type of interview, the interviewer describes situations likely to arise on the job and important for effective job performance, and then asks the applicant what he or she would do in such situations.

skill- or knowledge-based pay A pay system based on the skills or knowledge that an employee has (in contrast to the more common job-based pay).

skill-building training Training employees in interpersonal skills to correctly respond to cultural differences at the workplace.

skills inventories Summaries of each nonmanagerial worker's skills and abilities.

social (reform) unionism A type of unionism that tries to influence the economic and social policies of government at all levels. In practice, union leaders pursue such objectives by speaking out for or against government programs.

social expectations The larger society's expectations from employees regarding job challenge, working conditions, and quality of work life.

socialization The process by which people adapt to an organization.

societal objectives Societal priorities (e.g., lower pollution levels) that HR department targets while setting own objectives and strategies.

sponsor A person in an organization who can create career development opportunities for others.

staff authority Authority to advise, but not to direct, others.

staffing table A lost of anticipated employment openings for each type of job.

stages of an interview Key phases in an employment interview: interview preparation, creation of rapport, information exchange, termination, and evaluation.

startup costs The additional costs associated with a new employee because the new employee is typically less efficient than an experienced worker; the new worker also requires additional supervisory time.

stereotyping The process of using a few observable characteristics to assign someone to a preconceived social category.

strategic human resource development The identification of needed skills and active management of employees' learning in relation to corporate strategies.

strategic human resource management Integrating human resource management strategies and systems to achieve overall mission, strategies, and success of the firm while meeting needs of employees and other stakeholders.

strategic plan An identification of a firm's mission and objectives and its proposals for achieving those objectives.

stressors Stressful working conditions that can directly influence the health and safety of employees.

stress-producing interviews Job interviews that use a series of harsh, rapid-fire questions to upset the applicant and learn how he or she handles stress.

strictness bias A tendency to rate employees lower than their performance justifies.

structured interviews Interviews wherein a predetermined checklist of questions usually asked of all applicants is used.

subjective approach In a subjective approach, the decision maker looks at the scores received by the various applicants on predictors and subjectively evaluates all of the information and comes to an overall judgment.

succession planning The process of making long-range management development plans to fill human resource needs.

suggestion systems A formal method of generating, evaluating, and implementing employee ideas.

supplemental unemployment benefits (SUB) Private plans providing compensation for wage loss to laid-off workers.

support groups Groups of employees who provide emotional support to a new employee who shares a common attribute with the group (e.g., racial or ethnic membership).

surveys Use of preprinted questionnaires (or email) to gauge employee attitudes on a variety of work and company-related matters.

systemic discrimination Any company policy, practice, or action that is not openly or intentionally discriminatory, but has an indirect discriminatory impact or effect.

task identity The feeling of responsibility of pride that results from doing an entire piece of work, not just a small part of it.

task significance Knowing that the work one does is important to others in the organization or to outsiders.

telecommuting Paid labour performed at the employee's home, full-time or part-time, with assistance of PCs, modems, fax machines, etc.

temporary-help agencies Agencies that provide supplemental workers for temporary vacancies caused by employee leave, sickness, etc.

third-country nationals Natives of a country other than the home or host country of the firm that has hired them.

total reward model Inclusion of everything employees value in an employment relationship.

transfer Movement of an employee from one job to another that is relatively equal in pay, responsibility, and organizational level.

transference Applicability of training to job situations; evaluated by how readily the trainee can transfer the learning to his or her job.

transition matrices Describe the probabilities of how quickly a job position turns over and what an incumbent employee may do, over a forecast period of time, from that job situation, such as stay in the current position, move to another position within the firm, or accept another job in another organization.

transnational teams Teams composed of members of multiple nationalities working on projects that span several countries.

underutilization A condition that exists when a department or employer has a lesser proportion of members of a protected class than are found in the employer's labour market.

unfair labour practices Practices by management such as interfering with or discriminating against employees who undertake collective action. Unions may also commit unfair labour practices.

union shop A union security provision in which employers may hire anyone they want, but all new employees must join the union within a specified period.

unstructured interviews Interviews using few if any planned questions to enable the interviewer to pursue, in depth, the applicant's responses.

upward communication Communication that begins in the organization and proceeds up the hierarchy to inform or influence others.

validity A key attribute of a selection device that indicates its accuracy and relationship to job-relevant criteria.

variety An attribute of jobs wherein the worker has the opportunity to use different skills and abilities, or perform different activities.

vestibule training Training opportunities that utilize simulated workstations so that new employees can learn about their job without interfering with activities at the actual workstation.

vesting A provision in employer-provided retirement plans that gives workers the right to a pension after a specified number of years of service.

video interview Interview approach that uses solicited videos of a candidate's answers to provided questions.

virtual organization An operational domain of any organization whose workforce includes a significant portion of remote workers.

virtual reality Use of modern computer technology to create a 3D environment.

wage and salary survey A study made of wages and salaries paid by other organizations within the employer's labour market.

walk-ins/write-ins Job seekers who arrive at or write to the human resource department in search of a job without prior referrals and not in response to a specific ad.

want ads Advertisements in a newspaper, magazine, etc. that solicit job applicants for a position.

weighted application blank A job application form in which various items are given differential weights to reflect their relationship to criterion measure.

wiki A type of server program that allows multiple users to contribute to a Web site.

work flow The sequence of and balance between jobs in an organization needed to produce the firm's goods or services.

work options Various and flexible alternatives to the traditional workplace or the traditional 40-hour work week.

work practices The set ways of performing work in an organization.

workers' compensation Compensation payable by employers collectively for injuries sustained by workers in the course of their employment.

working conditions Facts about the situation in which the worker acts. Includes physical environment, hours, hazards, travel requirements, and so on, associated with a job.

workplace diversity Includes important human characteristics that influence employee values, their perceptions of self and others, behaviours, and interpretations of events.

Workplace Hazardous Materials Information System (WHMIS) Legislation that requires suppliers to label all hazardous products and provide a Material Safety Data Sheet (MSDS) on each.

wrongful dismissal Terminating an employee without just cause or without giving the employee reasonable notice or compensation in lieu of notice.

Index